PERSONAL FINANCIAL PLANNING

Ninth Edition

PERSONAL FINANCIAL PLANNING

Ninth Edition

Lawrence J. Gitman
San Diego State University

Michael D. Joehnk
Arizona State University

End-of-chapter feature, *Money Online,* prepared by Marilynn E. Hood,
Texas A&M University

SOUTH-WESTERN
™
THOMSON LEARNING

Australia • Canada • Mexico • Singapore • Spain
United Kingdom • United States

SOUTH-WESTERN

™

THOMSON LEARNING

Editor: Mike Reynolds
Development Editor: Elizabeth Thomson
Editorial Assistant: Lauren Feldman
Marketing Manager: Charlie Stutesman
Project Manager, Editorial Production: Elaine Hellmund
Print/Media Buyer: Lisa Kelley
Permissions Editor: Linda Blundell
Production Service: Graphic World

Text Designer: Rokusek Design
Copy Editor: Steve Henne
Cover Designer: Rokusek Design
Cover Image: Rokusek Design
Cover Printer: Lehigh Press, Inc.
Compositor: Graphic World
Printer: R.R. Donnelley

Printed in the United States of America
1 2 3 4 5 6 7 05 04 03 02 01

For more information about our products,
contact us at:
**Thomson Learning Academic
Resource Center
1-800-423-0563**

For permission to use material from this text,
contact us by:
Phone: 1-800-730-2214
Fax: 1-800-730-2215
Web: http://www.thomsonrights.com

Library of Congress Catalog Card Number: 2001095654
ISBN: 0-03-033001-7

Asia
Thomson Learning
60 Albert Street, #15-01
Albert Complex
Singapore 189969

Australia
Nelson Thomson Learning
102 Dodds Street
South Melbourne, Victoria 3205
Australia

Canada
Nelson Thomson Learning
1120 Birchmount Road
Toronto, Ontario M1K 5G4
Canada

Europe/Middle East/Africa
Thomson Learning
Berkshire House
168-173 High Holborn
London WC1 V7AA
United Kingdom

Latin America
Thomson Learning
Seneca, 53
Colonia Polanco
11560 Mexico D.F.
Mexico

Spain
Paraninfo Thomson Learning
Calle/Magallanes, 25
28015 Madrid, Spain

To our colleagues for
their work in improving personal
financial literacy by conveying
important financial concepts, tools,
and techniques to their students.

"Consumer Prices Continue Their Slow Growth"
"Major Tax Overhaul Becomes Law"
"Short-Term Interest Rates Drop"
"Mortgage Rates Hit New Low"
"Major Insurers Cut Rates in Price War"
"The Dow and Nasdaq Continue to Struggle"
"Congress Proposes Cutting Estate Taxes"

During recent years we have seen numerous headlines similar to these. Continuous changes in the financial environment, along with changes in our own lives—family, health, job—make personal financial planning both necessary and challenging. This book *Personal Financial Planning, Ninth Edition,* provides the framework and tools for preparing personal financial plans that serve as road maps for goal achievement. *Personal Financial Planning* emphasizes the dynamics of the personal financial planning process by considering the impact of life changes—birth, marriage, divorce, job and career, and death.

The book serves individuals who are, or will be, actively developing their own personal financial plans. It meets the needs of instructors and students in the first course in personal financial planning (often called "personal finance") offered at colleges and universities, junior and community colleges, professional certification programs, and continuing education courses. The experiences of individuals and families are used to demonstrate successes and failures in various aspects of personal financial planning. A conversational style and liberal use of examples and worksheets guide students through the material and emphasize important points. Clearly the benefits of the book's readability accrue not only to students but also to their instructors.

Major Changes in the Ninth Edition

The ninth edition has been thoroughly updated to reflect the cutting edge of contemporary personal financial planning. It reflects feedback from past users as well as nonusers, practicing financial planners, students, and our own research. It provides helpful new approaches, expanded coverage in certain areas, streamlined coverage in others, and enhanced pedagogy anchored by a state-of-the-art integrated learning system. The basic organizational structure, topical coverage, superior readability, and useful instructional aids that marked the success of the first eight editions have been retained. The new engaging chapter opening scenarios describe a "financial shock," experienced by a person or family, that relates to the chapter content. These openers replace the more general financial planning scenarios included in the eighth edition to better emphasize the dynamic and often challenging nature of personal financial planning. Important changes in this edition will be described first as general changes and then as specific chapter-by-chapter changes.

GENERAL CHANGES

- The *book has been totally redesigned and printed in a four-color format* to allow improved presentation of each of the text's numerous pedagogical features. Additionally, the new four-color design is expected to increase the interest of readers, most of whom are a product of today's colorful visual media environment.

- This edition *places more emphasis on the use of the Internet.* A number of features that either link students to relevant Internet sites or describe how the Internet can be incorporated into the personal financial planning process are included in the ninth edition. The Internet feature introduced in the last edition, *Money Online,* has been refined, revised, and included at the end of each chapter of this edition. Each of these elements has two parts. The first part includes eight to ten Web addresses, each followed by a brief paragraph that in an interesting fashion challenges the reader to go to the site and either research for specific information or merely review the resources that are available there. All of the Web topics presented within the chapter are intended to reinforce as well as expand the reader's practical grasp of the key concepts, tools, and technique presented in the chapter. The second part of *Money Online,* titled "Just for Fun!", includes one to three Web addresses followed by brief paragraphs that direct the reader to interesting sites to obtain information, perform an activity, or answer specific questions. These sites, while expanding the reader's knowledge, tend to entertain a bit more than do the sites in the first part. Each chapter also includes a number of *Smart Sites,* brief boxes within the chapter that direct the reader to specific sites closely related to the topics under discussion. This element helps keep the reader in touch with the Web while reading and studying the chapter. In addition, some Web addresses are embedded in the text. These Web links are included when referencing a specific company, information provider, or organization and provides the reader with a convenient way to learn more about the topic, obtain information, or make inquiries or transactions. Another source of additional Internet insights are the *Money in Action* boxes (described in detail below); some of these boxes are focused on technology and include descriptions and links to useful sites on the Internet. In summary, this edition's emphasis on the Internet is significant, and widely present both in the chapter and in the end-of-chapter materials.

- The *text organization has been refined* in this edition. The basic part and chapter organization has been retained, but certain chapters have been reorganized based on feedback from users and reviewers. The most notable changes were in Chapter 5 and Part 5 (Chapters 11 and 12). Chapter 5, *Making Automobile and Housing Decisions,* has been reorganized so that autos are covered before rather than after housing. In addition, discussion of auto financing is now included as part of the automobile purchase decision. In Part 5, *Managing Investments,* Chapters 11 and 12 have been reorganized. Chapter 11, *Investment Planning,* focuses on the securities markets, transactions, and investment information, including online trading and day trading. Chapter 12, *Investing in Stocks and Bonds,* focuses on risk and return and the merits, features, and performance of common stocks, bonds, preferred stocks, and convertible securities. These organizational improvements are believed to result in a more logical sequence of topics that will improve learning.

- The *focus of the text has been improved* by eliminating certain noncritical discussions and elements, tightening and streamlining wherever possible, and moving material to the text's Web site. Clearer focus on the dynamics of the personal financial planning process and the concepts, tools, and techniques used to implement this process are embodied in the ninth edition. Specific changes include new opening scenarios that focus on a short "financial shock"; the inclusion of a marginal, rather than end-of-chapter, glossary; more concise *Money in Action* boxes; elimination of the critical thinking statements; moving the continuous case to both the text's Web site and the *Instructor's Manual;* and refining certain discussions by tightening the writing. In addition, some of the more esoteric discussions have been eliminated on the basis of user and reviewer suggestions. Some of the discussions have been restructured to eliminate the need to reintroduce topics that were presented in previous chapters. All of these changes are believed to clarify and enhance reader understanding and comprehension of the text's content.

- Step-by-step *use of a financial calculator* to make time value of money calculations is integrated into relevant discussions in this edition. The basics of using a financial calculator are introduced in Chapter 2 and then reinforced in later chapters where time value techniques are applied. For example, the use of a calculator to find the future value of a deposit given various compounding periods is shown in Chapter 4, *Managing Your Cash and Savings,* and in Chapter 5, *Making Automobile and Housing Decisions,* the use of a calculator to find mortgage payments is explained. The inclusion of calculator keystrokes should help the reader learn how to more effectively develop financial plans using an important tool of the trade.

- This edition includes 2 *Money in Action* boxes in each chapter. Most of these boxes are new to this edition; some have been revised and updated from the eighth edition. The use of a broad descriptor for all boxes allows us to better link the interesting and informative sidebar material contained in each box to the text discussions. These boxes address a variety of informative topics that help to ground many of the text discussions to actual financial planning ideas, experiences, practices, and events—all intended to fully engage readers in the personal financial planning process. Examples of the *Money in Action* boxes include those on financial portal Web sites (Chapter 1, page 5), buying a car online (Chapter 5, page 181), how to choose a managed care plan (Chapter 9, page 396), and choosing between individual securities and mutual funds (Chapter 13, page 580). The 30 boxes included in the text are drawn from recent articles in the popular press, thereby providing both relevant and timely information.

- The *integrated learning system* has been refined in this edition to help students better anchor their study to a set of chapter learning goals. Each chapter begins with a list of six numbered learning goals, LG1 through LG6. The learning goal numbers are tied to first-level chapter headings and restated and reviewed point by point in the end-of-chapter summary. Another element of this system is the *Concept Check* questions that appear at the end of each section of the chapter (located ahead of the next first-level heading). As students read through the chapters, they can test their understanding of the material in each section. The most effective advanced pedagogical features from the eighth edition—glossary (now marginal rather than chapter end), exhibit and worksheet captions, and end-of-chapter questions, problems, and cases have also been retained and improved as part of the integrated learning system. Also included at the end of each chapter is a new element— *Applying Personal Finance*—that involves a challenging outside exercise dealing with the main topic(s) presented in the chapter.

- *Each chapter now opens with an engaging financial shock* experienced by an individual or family. Each shock is related to an important financial planning issue tied to the chapter content. The financial shocks replace the more general financial planning scenarios included in the eighth edition, because they better emphasize the dynamic and often challenging nature of personal financial planning. The shocks involve both traditional and nontraditional family situations and focus attention on the text's "change" theme by describing how families and individuals adapt to change. In addition, these chapter openers are expected to pique the reader's interest and cause her or him to think critically about the issue and appreciate the importance of the chapter content.

- The highly regarded *Worksheets* continue to be included with this edition. The expanded and revised worksheets are separately labeled and numbered as "Worksheet X.Y." The labels make text references to the worksheets much clearer. All end-of-chapter problems that can be solved using a given worksheet provide the worksheet reference which directs the student to its application.
- In addition to the worksheets, *Financial Planning Software (FPS),* a software program developed by Kathryn E. Coates and David Geis of KDC Software Solutions accompanies each new text. Students will find that the chapter concepts, worksheets, problems, and cases that are accompanied by this symbol can be solved with the use of FPS. We feel that students using FPS will be more inclined to begin and continue their own financial planning given the ease of using this software program.
- The *continuous case, The Lee Case, has been revised, updated, and moved to the text's Web site and Instructor's Manual.* The case provides personal and financial information about a real-life young couple and challenges students with the task of developing a specific comprehensive financial plan. The Lee case begins with Megan and Kevin Lee, a newlywed couple who subsequently have relevant life experiences and a number of other financial "shocks" as their story unfolds and the textual material progresses. This case, therefore, is consistent with the theme of change that is integrated throughout the text. The case was moved out of the text in order to include it as an enrichment opportunity rather than what may be perceived as obligatory material. The widespread access to and use of the Internet by instructors and students justifies locating this feature on the Web to achieve our goal of focusing the text on the material considered of greatest importance by the vast majority of users and reviewers. Its inclusion in the *Instructor's Manual* is intended to meet the needs of those who prefer hard copy.

SPECIFIC CHAPTER-BY-CHAPTER CHANGES

Because users often like to know where new material appears, the significant but less sweeping changes that have been made in the ninth edition are summarized below, on a chapter-by-chapter basis.

Chapter 1 on understanding the financial planning process has been revised and restructured to provide readers with earlier exposure to the financial planning process and to enhance readability. The steps in the financial planning process now appear in Chapter 1 (rather than Chapter 2) and a new exhibit depicting these steps accompanies this section. The material on financial goals that formerly appeared in several chapters is now consolidated in this chapter, along with a new worksheet that groups financial goals by time frame (short-, intermediate-, and long-term goals). New *Money in Action* boxes discuss how Americans feel about money and using financial portals to tap the wealth of personal finance material on the Internet. We begin our emphasis on practical information with advice on how to assess your current wealth and monitor it in the future and tips to avoid common online job search mistakes.

Chapter 2 on your financial statements and plans is more streamlined and cohesive. The content of a number of exhibits is now integrated into the text discussions. Explanations of how to prepare personal financial statements are easier to follow. The section on budget preparation is simplified and now uses just one consolidated worksheet plus the budget control worksheet. We continue to include business calculator keystrokes. On the practical side, we discuss new Web sites that offer online financial planning, show how even the smallest expenses can lead to big savings, and provide tips to tame the paper tiger and get started with budgeting.

Chapter 3 on managing your taxes has been completely updated to reflect the tax laws, rates, procedures, and forms in effect at the time we revised the chapter. However, Congress passed a new tax bill in early June 2001, and complete details and new forms will not be available until late in the year. Although we explain the key aspects of the 2001 Tax Act, we use material from the year 2000 to present a complete picture of the tax preparation process. In addition, new exhibits show the sources of federal income and outlays and the process used to calculate taxable income. The chapter also gives readers advice on using the most popular tax preparation software, reducing taxes, and avoiding common filing errors.

Chapter 4 on managing your cash and savings has been reorganized to include all banking products in one section. The discussion of electronic banking has been expanded and updated. The chapter includes the latest return and institutional data to accurately reflect current market rates and structure. A number of background discussions have been condensed in order to maintain better focus on the future. A new exhibit demonstrates how to use financial calculators to find interest compounded daily.

Chapter 5 on making automobile and housing decisions now begins with a discussion of how to buy an automobile, given that this is the first big purchase students typically make. The sections on buying a home follow. The chapter has been streamlined as well; the mortgage sections have been reorganized to improve the flow of material. New exhibits include the 10 steps to buying a car, using a financial calculator to find an auto loan amount, a comparison of types of used cars, and how to road test a car. Readers also will find helpful hints on the essential numbers to know before leasing a car, how to decide whether they are ready to buy a home, and more information on wise use of the Internet to research and buy a car and a home.

Chapter 6 on borrowing on open account has been updated to reflect current developments in the consumer credit field, including the growing role that the Internet plays in the selection and management of credit card debt. We also expanded the coverage of credit scoring and the major components that go into a FICO credit score; in addition, a *Money in Action* box about credit cards and college students has been added, and the discussion of bankruptcy laws has been expanded to include potential changes to these laws now under consideration in Washington, D.C.

Chapter 7 on using consumer loans continues to emphasize the positive aspects of what it takes to build a strong credit history; in addition, we've updated the discussion on where to obtain consumer loans by showing, among other things, how it's becoming easier than ever to obtain consumer loans online. We also added financial calculator elements that show the keystrokes used to find the monthly payment and annual percentage rate (APR) on an installment loan.

Chapter 8 on insuring your life has been streamlined and reorganized for greater clarity. The discussion of the benefits of life insurance now occurs early in the chapter. We've also updated social security benefits and included a new exhibit that lets readers compare total premiums on the three types of term life and variable life premiums. A new *Money in Action* box provides practical advice about filing a life insurance claim. We continue to provide valuable Internet resources and advice on buying life insurance online.

Chapter 9 on insuring your health includes the latest industry and policy data and new exhibits to show industry trends. We've tightened the content and improved the flow of topics, moving the discussion of group versus individual policies earlier in the chapter. A new Worksheet 9.2, Health Care Plan Checklist, assists students in comparing costs and features of health insurance plans. The chapter also includes tips on choosing both health and long-term care policies and Web links to additional health insurance resources.

Chapter 10 on protecting your property has been revised to improve clarity, simplify the chapter structure, and refine and update topic coverage. The introductory section on Basic Property Insurance Principles has been condensed, and the section on Other Property and Liability Coverages now groups all property coverages together. We continue to emphasize practical advice that readers can use to reduce premiums, file claims, and employ the Internet to select and buy the right property insurance.

Chapter 11 on investment planning has been totally restructured and, in fact, represents a brand new chapter. Beginning with the role that investing plays in the financial planning process, this new chapter deals with all the market infrastructure issues that are so important to becoming a knowledgeable investor. Included in this chapter is discussion of different types of securities markets (primary vs. secondary, listed vs. OTC), as well as the institutions, mechanisms, and procedures involved in making security transactions (types of brokers, sources and types of investment information, and ways to manage your investment holdings—i.e., portfolio management). There's also a section devoted to online investing that covers everything from online investor services, such as investment research and screening or portfolio tracking, to day trading.

Chapter 12 on investing in stocks and bonds has been streamlined and now concentrates on investing in common stocks, bonds, preferred stocks, and convertible securities (coverage of making security transactions and other preliminary investment matters has been moved to Chapter 11). Starting with the risks and rewards of investing, this chapter now deals with measures of return, basic valuation concepts, and the basic principles of investing in stocks and bonds. We've also added coverage of tech stocks and the comparative returns between stocks and bonds.

Chapter 13 on investing in mutual funds has been thoroughly revised and updated to reflect the continuing growth in this form of investing. We've also added a whole new section on exchange traded funds (or ETF's, as they're more commonly known) that covers basic institutional descriptions as well as how they can be used by investors. Also included in this chapter is expanded discussion of the various ways that the Internet can be used in managing mutual fund investments.

Chapter 14 on meeting retirement goals has gone through some extensive last minute revisions, in keeping with passage of the $1.3 trillion Economic Growth and Tax Relief Reconciliation Act of 2001—especially with regard to annual contribution limitations to IRA and other defined-contribution retirement programs. Other parts of the chapter have also been updated to reflect the latest legislation as it pertains to everything from Social Security to variable annuities; and of course, we provide ample coverage of the growing role of the Internet in retirement planning.

Chapter 15 on preserving your estate has been updated to reflect the changes to estate tax laws passed by Congress in mid-2001. The chapter has also been streamlined and revised to make this often-technical subject more reader-friendly. We added an exhibit that summarizes the steps in estate planning and two new *Money in Action* boxes—one discussing how to talk to parents about estate planning and the other explaining how to be sure that IRAs receive proper attention during the estate planning process. We provide readers with useful tips to help them choose a guardian for their children and use trusts effectively, as well as links to Web sites with a checklist on what to do when a loved one dies, and additional information on wills, living wills, trusts, and estate tax planning.

■ Organization of the Book

Personal Financial Planning addresses all of the major personal financial planning problems that individuals and families encounter. It is built around a model that links together all of the major elements of effective money management. All of the latest financial planning tools and techniques are discussed. Most of the chapter opening scenarios and widely used examples involve relatively young people so that the student reader may more easily identify with each situation.

This comprehensive text is written in a low-key, personal style and uses state-of-the-art pedagogy to present the key concepts and procedures used in sound personal financial planning and effective money management. The roles of various financial decisions in the overall personal financial planning process are clearly delineated.

The book is divided into six parts. Part One presents the foundations of personal financial planning, beginning with the financial planning process and then covering financial statements and plans, and taxes. Part Two concerns the management of basic assets, including cash and savings instruments, automobiles and housing. Part Three covers credit management, including the various types of open account borrowing and consumer loans. Part Four deals with managing insurance needs, and considers life insurance, health care insurance, and property insurance. Part Five concerns investments, including stocks, bonds, and mutual funds, and how to make transactions in securities markets. Part Six is devoted to retirement and estate planning. A continuous case for the Lee family, available on our Web site at **http://finance.swcollege.com**, is available to tie all of these parts together. It includes segments to be covered beginning at the end of Chapter 1 with an extensive inventory of financial data with additional elements tied to the ends at Parts One through Five, and Chapters 14 and 15 so that the students can deal with the unfolding elements of a complete personal financial plan.

■ Pedagogy

Each chapter opens with a brief "financial shock" that describes some sort of financial planning situation being faced by a person or family, and which relates to the key issues being discussed in the chapter. Along with the opening financial shock are six learning goals that link the material covered to specific learning outcomes and, as noted earlier, anchor the text's *integrated learning system*. Then, at the end of each of the major sections are *Concept Check* questions that allow readers to confirm their understanding of the material before moving on to the next section.

Each chapter contains two *Money in Action* boxes set off from the text material and containing brief discussions of relevant personal financial planning material that serve to enrich the topical coverage. Also found in each chapter are 2 or 3 *Financial Road Signs,* a new element to this edition of the book. Set off from the text at various points throughout the chapter, each of these financial road signs provides some important hints or suggestions to consider when implementing certain parts of a financial plan, such as "Picking an IRA That's Right for You," or "Some Things to Keep in Mind about Student Loans." *Worksheets,* which are typically filled out and discussed, are included to simplify demonstration of various calculations and procedures and to provide students with helpful materials they can use in managing their own personal finances. The worksheets are numbered to provide convenient reference to them in the end-of-chapter problems, and they include descriptive captions. Numerous exhibits, each containing descriptive captions, are used throughout to more fully illustrate key points in the text. Also included in each chapter is a *running glossary* that appears in the margin and which provides brief definitions of all highlighted terms that appear in the accompanying text.

Most chapters contain discussions and illustrations of how both the Internet and the personal computer can be used in various phases of personal financial planning. In addition, each chapter contains as many as 6 or 8 Smart Sites, each of which directs the reader to specific Internet sites that deal with the topic(s) being discussed at that point, and which enable the reader to broaden his or her understanding of key financial planning concepts. End-of-chapter material includes a Summary that restates each learning goal and follows it with a summary of the material related to it. The next element is Questions and Problems that students can use to test their grasp of the material. And that's followed by *Applying Personal Finance,* which generally involves some type of outside project or exercise. Two *Contemporary Case Applications* highlighting the important analytical topics and concepts are also supplied. Following the cases is the new and improved *Money Online* element that includes helpful Web addresses, homepage descriptions, and a series of Web-related interactive exercises. And of course, as noted previously, each part of the book ends with the *Lee Continuous Case,* available on our Web page (**http://finance.swcollege.com**) for instructors who wish to use it.

▇ Supplementary Materials

Recognizing the importance of outstanding support materials to the instructor and the student, we have continued to improve and expand our supplement package.

WORKSHEETS

A packet containing *blank worksheets* identical to those presented and used in the text is included free of charge with each new copy of the book. Each worksheet provides a logical format for dealing with some aspect of personal financial planning such as preparation of a cash budget, home affordability analysis, or automobile lease versus purchase analysis.

INSTRUCTOR'S MANUAL AND TEST BANK

A comprehensive *Instructor's Manual,* compiled by Marilynn E. Hood of Texas A&M University, has been prepared to assist the teacher. For each chapter, the manual includes

- An outline
- Discussion of major topics
- A list of key concepts
- Solutions to all Concept Check questions, end-of-chapter discussion questions and problems, and cases
- Solutions to all Lee continuous case questions
- Two additional integrative cases, each with a detailed solution. One of the cases deals with a young couple, and the other addresses the financial concerns faced by single parents.

The *Test Bank* has been revised, updated, and expanded by Vickie L. Hampton of Texas Tech University. It includes true-false and multiple-choice questions, as well as four to six short problems for nearly every chapter.

COMPUTERIZED TEST BANK

A computerized version of the printed test bank is available in Windows, Microsoft Word, or Macintosh featuring Thomson Learning's computerized test bank program EXAMaster+. EXAMaster+ has many features that allow the instructor to modify test questions, select items by key words, scramble tests for multiple class sections, and test completely online.

WORKBOOK

Vickie L. Hampton of Texas Tech University has updated the *Workbook* to assist students in mastering the information and techniques presented in the text, and to serve as a resource manual as they develop personal financial plans. Specific components for each chapter include

- A thorough outline of concepts discussed
- Completion exercises that stress vocabulary
- Comprehensive case problems (with solutions) that demonstrate the application of chapter concepts and use the worksheets

Most chapters include both problem-solving exercises (with solutions) and comprehensive cases.

PERSONAL FINANCIAL PLANNING SOFTWARE

The Windows problem-solver—Financial Planning Software—was revised and updated for this edition of the book by KDC Software Solutions. The disk performs like any of the widely used commercially available software packages and is completely interactive; best of all, being user-friendly, it streamlines the recordkeeping and problem-solving activities presented in the text. A computer logo [] is used in the margin to identify sections of the book to which the disk is applicable. End-of-chapter problems and cases that can be solved with the disk are keyed with the same logo. Most of the worksheets used in the text are formatted on the disk to provide assistance in applying some of the more complex procedures, ranging from financial statement and budget preparation to investment management and retirement planning. In addition to various interactive calculations performed by the software, two new elements have been added to this edition of the book. The first is new and extensive *graphing capabilities* (with several of the time-value and asset valuation computations) that allow the user to immediately see the impact of changes to the input variables. The second is a *Calculator Keystroke Tutorial,* which provides basic user instructions and illustrations for several of the more popular financial calculators, including the HP12C and the TI-BAII-Plus. Of course, the software has been extensively tested to ensure its accuracy and ease of use.

PRESENTATION SOFTWARE

For instructors who enjoy working with computerized presentations, we have a complete lecture presentation in PowerPoint, which has been revised by Marilynn E. Hood of Texas A&M University. Each chapter's file includes an outline, appropriate numerical concepts, and key topics. Instructors can easily modify the presentations using PowerPoint's many features.

WEB PAGE

In order to provide the most current information and resources available related to financial planning we have developed a Web page. Instructors and students can access up-to-date teaching and learning aids through **http://finance.swcollege.com**.

Acknowledgments

In addition to the many individuals who made significant contributions to this book by their expertise, classroom experience, guidance, general advice, and reassurance, we also appreciate the students and faculty who used the book and provided valuable feedback on it, confirming our conviction that a truly teachable personal financial planning text could be developed.

Of course, we are indebted to all the academicians and practitioners who have created the body of knowledge contained in this text. We particularly wish to thank several people who gave the most significant help in developing and revising it. They include Marilynn E. Hood of Texas A&M University for writing *Money Online* and the IM, and developing the PowerPoint lecture presentation software as well as reviewing the manuscript. In addition, we want to thank Vickie L. Hampton of Texas Tech University for her intensive review of the entire manuscript and for her work on the continuous cases, Test Bank, and Workbook. Also, we want to thank KDS Software Solutions for developing the state-of-the-art software. Thanks is also due attorney Robert J. Wright of Wright & Wright, CPAs, for his assistance in the chapter on taxes; and John C. Bost Esq., of San Diego State University, for his help in revising and updating the estate planning chapter.

Thomson Learning shared our objective of producing a truly teachable text and relied on the experience and advice of numerous excellent reviewers for the ninth edition: Harold David Barr, Blinn College; Stephen Ferris, University of Missouri; Joseph D. Greene, Augusta State University; Marilynn E. Hood, Texas A&M University; Judy Kamm; and Rosemary Walker, Michigan State University.

We also appreciate the many suggestions from previous reviewers, all of whom have had a significant impact on the earlier editions of this book. Our thanks go to the following: Linda Afdahl, Micheal J. Ahern III, Robert J. Angell, H. Kent Baker, Catherine L. Bertelson, Steve Blank, Kathleen K. Bromley, D. Gary Carman, Dan Casey, P.R. Chandy, Tony Cherin, Larry A. Cox, Maurice L. Crawford, Carlene Creviston, Rosa Lea Danielson, William B. Dillon, David Durst, Jeanette A. Eberle, Mary Ellen Edmundson, Ronald Ehresman, Jim Farris, Sharon Hatten Garrison, Alan Goldfarb, Carol Zirnheld Green, C.R. Griffen, John L. Grimm, Chris Hajdas, James Haltman, Vickie L. Hampton, Forest Harlow, Kendall B. Hill, Darrell D. Hilliker, Arlene Holyoak, Marilynn E. Hood, Frank Inciardi, Kenneth Jacques, Dixie Porter Johnson, Ted Jones, William W. Jones, Peggy Keck, Gary L. Killion, Earnest W. King, Karol Kitt, George Klander, Xymena S. Kulsrud, Carole J. Makela, David Manifold, Charles E. Maxwell, Charles W. McKinney, Robert W. McLeod, George Muscal, Robert Nash, Charles O'Conner, Albert Pender, Franklin Potts, Fred Power, Alan Raedels, Charles F. Richardson, Arnold M. Rieger, Vivian Rippentrop, Gayle M. Ross, Kenneth H. St. Clair, Brent T. Sjaardema, Rosemary Walker, Tom Warschauer, Gary Watts, Grant J. Wells, Betty Wright, and R.R. Zilkowski.

Because of the wide variety of topics covered in this book, we called on many experts for whose insight on recent developments we are deeply grateful. We would like to thank them and their firms for allowing us to draw on their knowledge and resources, particularly Mark D. Erwin, Northwestern Mutual Financial Network; Paul Fairweather, Northern Trust Bank of California; Robin Gitman, Willis M. Allen Co. Realtors; John Markese, President of the American Association of Individual Investors; Mark Nussbaum, UBS Paine Webber, Inc.; Patt Rupp, CFP, IDS, Inc.; Sherri Tobin, Farmers Insurance Group; Fred Weaver, Washington Mutual; Karen Weston, Coldwell Banker Realtors; Keith Wibel, CFA, Foothills Asset Management; and Lynn Yturri, CFA, Bank One Investment Management.

We would like to thank our colleagues at San Diego State University and Arizona State University for their expertise, encouragement, and support. Also, we want to thank Drew Fones, of American Express, for his invaluable help in preparing the credit chapters, and Marlene G. Bellamy of Writeline Associates, La Jolla, California for revising the chapter opening scenarios and preparing the boxes and *Smart Sites,* and her outstanding assistance in research and writing. Thanks is also due Marilynn Hood for preparing the Instructor's

Manual. We would also like to express our appreciation to Vickie L. Hampton for revising the *Test Bank* and *Workbook.*

The editorial staff of Thomson Learning has been most cooperative. We wish to thank Elaine Hellmund, project manager; Linda Blundell, picture and rights editor; and Lauren Feldman, editorial assistant. Special thanks go to Mike Reynolds, executive editor, and Elizabeth Thomson, developmental editor, without whose support this revision would not have been as lively and contemporary in approach as we believe it is and whose expert management of the writing and reviewing of the text proved invaluable. We are also grateful to Keith Roberts and Bruce Siebert of Graphic World Publishing Services, who ably assured the book's timely and accurate production.

Finally, our wives, Robin and Charlene, have provided needed support and understanding during the writing of this book. We are forever grateful to them.

Lawrence J. Gitman
La Jolla, California

Michael D. Joehnk
Flagstaff, Arizona

July 2001

About the Authors

Lawrence J. Gitman is a professor of finance at San Diego State University. He received his bachelor's degree from Purdue University, his M.B.A. from the University of Dayton, and his Ph.D. from the University of Cincinnati. Professor Gitman is a prolific textbook author and has more than 45 articles appearing in *Financial Management*, the *Financial Review*, the *Journal of Financial Planning*, the *Journal of Risk and Insurance*, the *Journal of Financial Research*, *Financial Practice and Education*, the *Journal of Financial Education*, and other scholarly publications. He currently serves as an associate editor of *Financial Practice and Education*.

His major textbooks include *Introduction to Finance*, which is coauthored with Jeff Madura; *Principles of Managerial Finance*, Second Brief Edition; *Principles of Managerial Finance*, Ninth Edition; *Foundations of Managerial Finance*, Fourth Edition; *The Future of Business*, Interactive Edition, which is coauthored with Carl McDaniel; and *Fundamentals of Investing*, Eighth Edition, which is coauthored with Michael D. Joehnk. Gitman and Joehnk also wrote *Investment Fundamentals: A Guide to Becoming a Knowledgeable Investor*, which was selected as one of 1988's ten best personal finance books by *Money* magazine.

An active member of numerous professional organizations, Professor Gitman is past president of the Academy of Financial Services, the San Diego Chapter of the Financial Executives Institute, the Midwest Finance Association, and the FMA National Honor Society. In addition, he is a Certified Financial Planner (CFP). Gitman recently served as a Director on the CFP Board of Governors, as vice-president—Financial Education for the Financial Management Association, and as director of the San Diego MIT Enterprise Forum. He lives with his wife and two children in La Jolla, California, where he is an avid bicyclist.

Michael D. Joehnk is an emeritus professor at Arizona State University. In addition to his academic appointments at A.S.U., Professor Joehnk spent a year (1999) as a visiting professor of finance at the University of Otago in New Zealand. He received his bachelor's and Ph.D. degrees from the University of Arizona and his M.B.A. from Arizona State University. A Chartered Financial Analyst (CFA), he has served as a member of the Candidate Curriculum Committee and of the Council of Examiners of the Institute of Chartered Financial Analysts—now the Association for Investment Management and Research (AIMR). He has also served as a director of the Phoenix Society of Financial Analysts, secretary-treasurer of the Western Finance Association, and was elected to two terms as a vice-president of the Financial Management Association.

Professor Joehnk is the author or coauthor of some 50 articles, five books, and numerous monographs. His articles have appeared in *Financial Management*, the *Journal of Finance*, the *Journal of Bank Research*, the *Journal of Portfolio Management*, the *Journal of Consumer Affairs*, the *Journal of Financial and Quantitative Analysis*, the *AAII Journal*, the *Journal of Financial Research*, the *Bell Journal of Economics*, the *Daily Bond Buyer*, *Financial Planner*, and other publications.

In addition to coauthoring several books with Lawrence J. Gitman, Professor Joehnk is the author of a highly successful paperback trade book, *Investing for Safety's Sake*. In addition, Dr. Joehnk was the editor of *Institutional Asset Allocation*, which was sponsored by the Institute of Chartered Financial Analysts and published by Dow Jones-Irwin. He also was a contributor to the Handbook for *Fixed Income Securities*, and *Investing and Risk Management*—Vol. 1 of the Library of Investment Banking. In addition, he served a 6-year term as executive co-editor of the *Journal of Financial Research*. He and his wife live in Flagstaff, Arizona, where they enjoy hiking and other activities in the nearby mountains and canyons.

Brief Contents

Preface vii

PART I   **Foundations in Financial Planning**   1
Chapter 1   Understanding the Financial Planning Process   2
Chapter 2   Your Financial Statements and Plans   38
Chapter 3   Managing Your Taxes   86

PART II   **Managing Basic Assets**   133
Chapter 4   Managing Your Cash and Savings   134
Chapter 5   Making Automobile and Housing Decisions   172

PART III   **Managing Credit**   223
Chapter 6   Borrowing on Open Account   224
Chapter 7   Using Consumer Loans   272

PART IV   **Managing Insurance Needs**   313
Chapter 8   Insuring Your Life   314
Chapter 9   Insuring Your Health   360
Chapter 10   Protecting Your Property   404

PART V   **Managing Investments**   443
Chapter 11   Investment Planning   444
Chapter 12   Investing in Stocks and Bonds   504
Chapter 13   Investing in Mutual Funds   556

PART VI   **Retirement and Estate Planning**   599
Chapter 14   Planning for Retirement   600
Chapter 15   Preserving Your Estate   648

Appendix A   Table of Future Value Factors   690
Appendix B   Table of Future Value of Annuity Factors   691
Appendix C   Table of Present Value Factors   692
Appendix D   Table of Present Value of Annuity Factors   693

Index   694
Credits   709

Contents

Preface   vii

■ **PART 1   Foundations in Financial Planning   1**

Chapter 1   UNDERSTANDING THE FINANCIAL PLANNING PROCESS   2
The Rewards of Sound Financial Planning   3
The Personal Financial Planning Process   6
WORKSHEET 1.1   *Summary of Personal Financial Goals*   13
From Goals to Plans: A Lifetime of Planning   14
The Planning Environment   21
What Determines Your Personal Income?   26
An Overview of the Text   31
Money Online   35

Chapter 2   YOUR FINANCIAL STATEMENTS AND PLANS   38
Mapping Out Your Financial Future   39
WORKSHEET 2.1   *Analyzing the Benefit of a Second Income*   42
The Time Value of Money: Putting a Dollar Value on Financial Goals   48
The Balance Sheet: A Statement of Your Financial Condition   53
WORKSHEET 2.2   *Balance Sheet*   58
The Income and Expense Statement: Measuring Your Financial Performance   60
WORKSHEET 2.3   *Income and Expense Statement*   62
Using Your Personal Financial Statements   65
Setting Up a Cash Budget   69
WORKSHEET 2.4   *Annual Cash Budget by Month*   71
WORKSHEET 2.5   *Budget Control Schedule for January, February, and March 2002*   75
Money Online   84

Chapter 3   MANAGING YOUR TAXES   86
Principles of Federal Income Taxes   87
It's Taxable Income That Matters   94
Calculating and Filing Your Taxes   102
WORKSHEET 3.1   *2000 Tax Return (Form 1040EZ)*   107
WORKSHEET 3.2   *2000 Tax Return (Form 1040)*   110
Other Filing Considerations   113
Effective Tax Planning   119
Other Forms of Personal Taxes   123
Money Online   131

■ PART II Managing Basic Assets 133

Chapter 4 MANAGING YOUR CASH AND SAVINGS 134

The Role of Cash Management in Personal Financial Planning 135
Today's Financial Services Marketplace 137
The Growing Menu of Cash Management Products 141
Establishing a Savings Program 150
Maintaining a Checking Account 157
WORKSHEET 4.1 *An Account Reconciliation Form Statement* 164
Money Online 170

Chapter 5 MAKING AUTOMOBILE AND HOUSING DECISIONS 172

Buying or Leasing an Automobile 173
WORKSHEET 5.1 *Comparing Automobile Lease versus Purchase Costs* 184
Meeting Housing Needs 186
How Much Housing Can You Afford? 189
WORKSHEET 5.2 *Home Affordability Analysis* 197
The Rental Option 199
WORKSHEET 5.3 *Rent-or-Buy Cost Comparison* 201
The Home-Buying Process 202
Financing the Transaction 207
WORKSHEET 5.4 *Mortgage Refinancing Analysis* 215
Money Online 221

■ PART III MANAGING CREDIT 223

Chapter 6 BORROWING ON OPEN ACCOUNT 224

The Basic Concepts of Credit 225
Types of Open Account Credit 232
Obtaining and Managing Open Account Credit 246
Using Credit Wisely 256
Money Online 270

Chapter 7 USING CONSUMER LOANS 272

Basic Features of Consumer Loans 273
Managing Your Credit 286
Single-Payment Loans 289
WORKSHEET 7.1 *Tracking Your Consumer Debt* 290
Installment Loans 296
WORKSHEET 7.2 *To Borrow or Not To Borrow* 305
Money Online 311

■ **PART IV   MANAGING INSURANCE NEEDS   313**

Chapter 8   INSURING YOUR LIFE   314
Basic Insurance Concepts   315
How Much Life Insurance Is Right for You?   319
WORKSHEET 8.1   *Determining the Need for Life Insurance*   325
What Kind of Policy Is Right for You?   328
Key Features of Life Insurance Policies   342
Buying Life Insurance   349
Money Online   358

Chapter 9   INSURING YOUR HEALTH   360
The Need for Health Care Insurance Coverage   361
Types and Sources of Health Care Plans   364
Medical Expense Coverage and Policy Provisions   373
Long-Term Care Insurance   380
Disability Income Insurance   385
WORKSHEET 9.1   *Estimating Disability Income Insurance Needs*   387
A Guide to Buying Health Care Insurance   390
WORKSHEET 9.2   *Health Care Plan Checklist*   395
Money Online   401

Chapter 10   PROTECTING YOUR PROPERTY   404
Some Basic Principles of Property Insurance   405
Homeowner's Insurance   410
Automobile Insurance   420
Other Property and Liability Insurance   431
Buying Insurance and Settling Claims   432
Money Online   440

■ **PART V   MANAGING INVESTMENTS   443**

Chapter 11   INVESTMENT PLANNING   444
The Objectives and Rewards of Investing   445
WORKSHEET 11.1   *Finding the Amount of Investment Capital*   449
Securities Markets   454
Making Transactions in the Securities Markets   461
Becoming an Informed Investor   470
Online Investing   482
Managing Your Investment Holdings   489
WORKSHEET 11.2   *Keeping Tabs on Your Investment Holdings*   496
Money Online   502

Chapter 12   INVESTING IN STOCKS AND BONDS   504
The Risks and Rewards of Investing   505
Investing in Common Stock   513
Investing in Bonds   530
Preferreds and Convertibles   545
Money Online   554

Chapter 13   INVESTING IN MUTUAL FUNDS   558
Mutual Funds: Some Basics   557
Types of Funds and Fund Services   573
Making Mutual Fund Investments   584
Money Online   597

PART VI   RETIREMENT AND ESTATE PLANNING   599

Chapter 14   PLANNING FOR RETIREMENT   600
An Overview of Retirement Planning   601
WORKSHEET 14.1   *Estimating Future Retirement Needs*   606
Social Security   610
Pension Plans and Retirement Programs   619
Annuities   632
Money Online   646

Chapter 15   PRESERVING YOUR ESTATE   648
Principles of Estate Planning   649
Wills   656
WORKSHEET 15.1   *A Checklist of Items to Keep in a Safe-deposit Box*   663
Trusts   667
Gift Taxes   671
Estate Taxes and Planning   674
WORKSHEET 15.2   *Computing Federal Estate Tax Due*   676
Money Online   686

Appendix A   Table of Future Value Factors   690

Appendix B   Table of Future Value of Annuity Factors   691

Appendix C   Table of Present Value Factors   692

Appendix D   Table of Present Value of Annuity Factors   693

Index   694
Credits   709

PART I

Foundations of
Financial Planning

CHAPTER 1
Understanding the
Financial Planning
Process

CHAPTER 2
Your Financial
Statements and Plans

CHAPTER 3
Managing Your Taxes

Chapter 1

Understanding the Financial Planning Process

LEARNING GOALS

LG1.   Identify the benefits of using personal financial planning techniques to manage your finances.

LG2.   Describe the personal financial planning process and define your major financial goals.

LG3.   Explain why personal financial plans must change according to your life situation.

LG4.   Describe how government, business, and consumer actions and changing economic conditions affect personal financial plans.

LG5.   Evaluate the impact of age, marital status, education, geographic location, and career choice on personal income.

LG6.   Recognize the importance of career planning and its relationship to personal financial planning.

Down but Not Out

Brian Scott worked for a software company that was the dominant employer in his rural town. Unfortunately, Brian's big plans for the future were put on hold when his employer was acquired by a large Internet company. The new owner closed the local offices and laid off about half the employees, including the 24-year-old software developer. Although national demand was high for workers with Brian's technical skills, he would have to relocate to get an equivalent job. Another option was starting his own software consulting business. But was this the right time to do it? He still had $16,000 in outstanding education loans, a $7,000 car loan, and $3,000 in credit card debt.

Because he had wisely funded an emergency savings account with 3 months' living expenses and received several months' severance pay, Brian could cover his basic living expenses while he sorted out his options. He researched job opportunities in several cities that he liked and also contacted local businesses to see if there was enough demand for his consulting services to justify taking the risk of going out on his own. Another factor to consider was employee benefits; he wouldn't have any if he became self-employed!

Brian quickly realized the value of the personal financial planning course he had taken in college. He now had the tools to prepare a new set of personal financial plans to help him make an informed career choice and plan for his future.

The Rewards of Sound Financial Planning [LG1]

What does it take to live "the good life?" Is it owning a house in a certain part of town, starting your own company, being debt-free, driving a particular type of car, taking luxury vacations, or having a large investment portfolio? Your needs may be more modest, but no matter how you define "the good life," you need to develop plans to reach your goals.

In today's complex, fast-paced world, we are faced with a bewildering array of choices—where to live, what career to follow, what car to buy, when to change jobs, how much to save or invest. Add this to the rapidly changing social, economic, political, and technological environments and we may find it increasingly difficult to develop personal financial strategies to improve our lifestyles. Many of the financial goals our parents took for granted—home ownership, a college education, job security, being able to retire at age 65—are becoming harder to obtain. A couple may need two incomes to maintain an acceptable standard of living, or we may have to wait longer to buy a home.

Even if we're managing our personal finances pretty well today, we worry about the future. We want to maintain and improve our current lifestyle and also prepare for the future so we can send our children to college and have funds to retire comfortably. The estimated cost to raise a child born in 2000 to age 18 is more than $300,000. Add to that four years of college, at an estimated cost of $113,000 for public and $245,000 for private universities, and the need to plan ahead becomes very clear.

The best way to achieve these and other financial objectives is through *personal financial planning*. It helps us define our financial goals and develop appropriate financial strategies to reach them.

However, many people find the financial environment and volatile economy intimidating. We can no longer depend on employee or government benefits like steady salary increases or enough funding from employer-paid pensions or social security to retire comfortably. We must plan our own financial security—a daunting task, indeed!—but may not know where to start. We have direct access to financial tools and research once reserved for stockbrokers, but do we know how to best use them? The goal of this book is to take the mystery out of the personal financial planning process and provide the tools you need to take charge of your personal finances.

Because needs and goals change as personal circumstances change, personal financial planning is a lifelong activity. As you will learn, creating flexible plans and revising them on a regular basis is the key to building a sound financial future. Among the rewards of financial planning are an improved standard of living, wise spending patterns, and increased wealth. Of course, planning alone does not guarantee success, but if used effectively and consistently, it can help you control your life and use your resources wisely.

IMPROVING YOUR STANDARD OF LIVING

Through personal financial planning we learn to acquire, use, and control our financial resources more efficiently. In essence, it allows us to gain more enjoyment from our income and thus improve our **standard of living**—the necessities, comforts, and luxuries we have or desire.

standard of living
The necessities, comforts, and luxuries enjoyed or aspired to by an individual or group.

The quality of our lives is, for most of us, closely tied to our standard of living. The presence or absence of certain material items—such as a nice house, car, and clothing—is commonly associated with quality of life. Having money for health, education, art, music, travel, and entertainment also contributes to the quality of life. Although many other factors—geographic location, public facilities, local cost of living, pollution, traffic, and population density—also affect the quality of an individual's life, wealth is commonly viewed as its primary determinant. Of course, many so-called wealthy people live "plain" lives, choosing to save or invest their money rather than spend it on luxuries and frills. Even so, their quality of life is probably no lower than that of a more flamboyant consumer. The *Money in Action* box on page 5 reveals some of our attitudes toward getting and keeping wealth.

One trend that has had a profound effect on our standard of living is the *two-income family*. What was relatively rare in the early 1970s has become commonplace today, and the incomes of millions of families have risen sharply. Granted, two incomes increase the things we can afford to buy, but they also require greater responsibility for managing money wisely and coordinating the partners' financial and career goals and plans.

SPENDING MONEY WISELY

Using money more wisely is another payoff of financial planning. Whatever your income, you can either spend it now or save a portion of it for future needs. Determining both your current and future spending patterns is an important part of personal money management. The goal, of course, is to plan how to spend your money to get the most satisfaction from your income dollar.

MONEY IN ACTION

How Americans Feel about Money

As the twenty-first century began, Americans were in the midst of an era of unprecedented prosperity. Yet despite the economic boom, people still had financial concerns. According to *Money* magazine's 13th annual survey on "Americans and their Money," our top three financial worries were having enough money for retirement, medical costs, and education/college costs. And 56 percent of those surveyed said that they often worried about money. These and other poll findings provide an interesting look at our attitudes toward money matters.

For the most part, we are confident about our financial future. About two-thirds of survey respondents believe they are better off financially than 4 years ago and are satisfied with their current financial situation. Even more—80 percent—expect their standard of living to rise in the future. We aren't taking this for granted, however, as the percentage of those saving for retirement jumped from 44 percent in 1997 to 60 percent.

How much does it take for us to feel rich? About 35 percent felt that $1 million was enough, while 17 percent needed $3 million and 18 percent, $5 million. As for the best way to get rich, it's not through salary increases, as most respondents ranked low raises as their number one job concern. The top three ways to increase wealth were to invest in real estate, start a business, and invest in stocks.

Gender differences also emerged from the survey. Women tend to be more conservative and less confident than male investors, but more married men (59 percent) trust their wives with managing money than women trust their husbands (41 percent). Women worry more about money, 64 percent compared to 51 percent of men.

Sources: "Gender Gaps," *Money.com*, downloaded from **cgi.money. com/cgibin/money/polls/womenpoll/womenpoll.plx;** Suzanne Woolley, "Americans & Their Money," *Money*, December 1999, pp. 143–156; and Suzanne Woolley, "Beating the Gender Rap," *Money For Women* (Special Bonus Issue), May–June 2000, downloaded from **www.money.com**.

CURRENT NEEDS. Your current spending level is based on the necessities of life and your average propensity to consume. A minimum level of spending would allow you to obtain only the **necessities of life:** food, clothing, and shelter. Although the quantity and types of food, clothing, and shelter purchased may differ among individuals depending on their wealth, we all need some amount of these items to survive.

> **necessities of life**
> Items that are needed for survival—food, clothing, and shelter.

Average propensity to consume refers to the percentage of each dollar of income, on average, that is spent for current needs rather than being saved. Some people with high average propensities to consume earn low incomes, and must spend a large portion just for basic necessities. On the other hand, many "ultra consumers" choose to splurge on a few items and scrimp elsewhere. These people also exhibit high average propensities to consume. Conversely, individuals earning large amounts quite often have low average propensities to consume, because the cost of necessities represents only a small proportion of their income.

> **average propensity to consume**
> The percentage of each dollar of income, on average, that a person spends for current consumption.

Still, it is not unusual to find two people with significantly different incomes but the same average propensity to consume due to differences in standard of living. The person making more money may believe it is essential to buy better-quality items or more items, and will thus, on average, spend the same percentage of each dollar of income as the person making far less.

FUTURE NEEDS. In any carefully developed financial plan, you should set aside a portion of current income for deferred, or future, spending. Placing these funds in various savings and investment vehicles allows you to generate a return on your funds until you need them. For example, you may want to build up a retirement fund to maintain a desirable standard of living in your later years. Instead of spending the money now, you defer actual spending until the future, when you retire. Other examples of deferred spending include saving for a child's education, a primary residence or vacation home, a major acquisition (like a car or home entertainment center), or even a vacation.

The portion of current income we commit to future needs is a function of how much we earn and our level of current spending. The more we earn and the less we devote to current spending, the more we can commit to meeting future needs. In any case, some portion of current income should be set aside regularly for future use. This practice creates good saving habits.

ACCUMULATING WEALTH

In addition to using current income for everyday expenses of living, we also spend it to acquire assets, such as cars, a home, or stocks and bonds. For the most part, our assets determine how wealthy we are. Personal financial planning plays a critical role in the accumulation of wealth by helping to direct our financial resources to the most productive areas.

wealth
The total value of all items owned by an individual, such as savings accounts, stocks, bonds, home, and automobiles.

As a rule, a person's **wealth** at any point in time is a function of the total value of all the items he or she owns. Wealth consists of financial and tangible assets. **Financial assets** are intangible, paper assets, such as savings accounts and securities (stocks, bonds, mutual funds, and so forth). They are *earning* assets that are held for the returns they promise. **Tangible assets,** in contrast, are physical assets, such as real estate, that can be held for either consumption (like your home, car, artwork, or jewelry) or investment purposes (like the duplex you bought for rental purposes). In general, the goal of most people is to accumulate as much wealth as possible while maintaining current consumption at a level that provides a desired standard of living. To see how you compare with the typical American in financial terms, check out the statistics in Exhibit 1.1.

financial assets
Intangible assets, such as savings accounts and securities, that are acquired for some promised future return.

tangible assets
Physical assets, such as real estate and automobiles, that can be held for either consumption or investment purposes.

CONCEPT CHECK

1-1.   What is a *standard of living?* What factors affect the quality of life?
1-2.   Are consumption patterns related to quality of life? Explain.
1-3.   What is *average propensity to consume?* Is it possible for two people with very different incomes to have the same average propensity to consume? Why?
1-4.   Discuss the various forms in which wealth can be accumulated.

■ The Personal Financial Planning Process [LG2]

Many people erroneously assume that personal financial planning is only for the wealthy. Nothing could be farther from the truth! Whether you have a lot of money or too little, you still need personal financial planning. If you have enough money, planning can help you spend and invest it wisely. If your income seems inadequate, taking steps to control

EXHIBIT 1.1

THE AVERAGE AMERICAN, FINANCIALLY SPEAKING

This financial snapshot of the "Average American" in the year 2000 gives you an idea of where you stand in terms of income, net worth, and other measures. This should help you set some goals for the future.

INCOME AND ASSETS
What Do We Earn? *(average)*

All households	$ 53,100
Self-employed	109,000
Retired	32,900

What are We Worth? *(median)*

All households	$ 71,600
Self-employed	248,100
Retired	113,000

Home and Hearth *(median)*

Value of primary residence	$100,000
Equity in home	38,000
Monthy mortgage payment	720

HOW MUCH DO WE SAVE? *(average)*

Mutual Funds	$25,000
Individual stocks	17,500
Bank accounts	18,100
Retirement accounts	24,000
401K balance	39,970

Source: Adapted from Melynda Dovel Wilcox, "Are You Above Average?" *Kiplinger's Personal Finance,* January 2001, pp. 86–87.

$ Financial Road Sign

Evaluate Your Personal Wealth

Use the following seven steps to assess your current wealth and monitor it in the future. Find statistics for comparison online and in *Money* and other personal finance magazines.

1. Calculate your net worth (see Chapter 2).
2. Compare your net worth with others in your age and income bracket.
3. Compare your earnings with others in your field.
4. Compare your investment assets.
5. Examine your spending habits.
6. Total up your debt.
7. Review your results and adjust your financial plan accordingly.

Source: Adapted from Walter Updegrave, "How Are You Doing?" *Money,* July 1999, pp. 63–73.

your financial situation will lead to an improved lifestyle. This is what **personal financial planning** is all about: taking conscientious and systematic steps toward fulfilling your financial goals.

No one is exempt from the need to develop personal financial plans, whether you are a recent college graduate, single professional, young married couple, single parent, mid-career married breadwinner, or senior corporate executive. Knowing what you hope to accomplish financially and how you intend to do it gives you an edge over someone who merely reacts to financial events as they unfold.

For example, purchasing a new car immediately after graduation may be an important goal for you. Evaluating and possibly arranging financing before your shopping trip, as opposed to simply accepting the financing arrangement offered by an auto dealer, might save you a considerable amount of money. Moreover, because some dealers advertise low-interest loans but then charge higher prices for their cars, knowing all your costs in advance can help you identify the best deal. For most people, buying a car is a major expenditure involving a substantial up-front cash outlay. It also usually results in additional consumer debt to repay over time. Therefore it warrants careful planning. Likewise, using personal financial planning concepts to reach other goals will bring similar positive benefits.

personal financial planning Planning that covers the important elements of an individual's financial affairs and is aimed at fulfilling his or her financial goals.

STEPS IN THE FINANCIAL PLANNING PROCESS

Take a closer look at financial planning and you will see that the process translates personal financial goals into specific financial plans, and then implements the plans through financial strategies. The financial planning process generally involves the six steps, shown in sequence in Exhibit 1.2.

In effect, the financial planning process runs full circle. You start with financial goals, formulate and implement financial plans and strategies to reach them, monitor and control progress toward goals through budgets, and evaluate plan and budget results. This leads you back to redefining your goals to better meet your current needs and revising your financial plans accordingly.

Let's now look at how goal setting fits into the planning process. In Chapters 2 and 3 we will provide other tools essential to creating your financial plans: a basic understanding of personal financial statements, budgets, and taxes.

DEFINING YOUR FINANCIAL GOALS

financial goals
Short-, intermediate-, and long-term results that an individual wants to attain, such as controlling living expenses, managing one's tax burden, establishing savings and investment programs, and meeting retirement needs.

What are your **financial goals**? Have you spelled them out, at least over the short run? The fact is, without financial goals it is difficult, if not impossible, to effectively manage your financial resources. We all need to know where we are going, in a financial sense, to direct the major financial events in our lives. Perhaps achieving financial independence at a relatively early age is important to you. If so, then activities like saving, investing, and retirement planning will become an important part of your life. Whatever your financial goals or preferences, they must be stated in monetary terms, because money, and the *utility* (defined later) it buys, is an integral part of financial planning.

 EXHIBIT 1.2

THE SIX-STEP FINANCIAL PLANNING PROCESS

The financial planning process translates personal financial goals into specific financial plans, and then implements those plans through financial strategies. This process typically involves the six steps shown in sequence here.

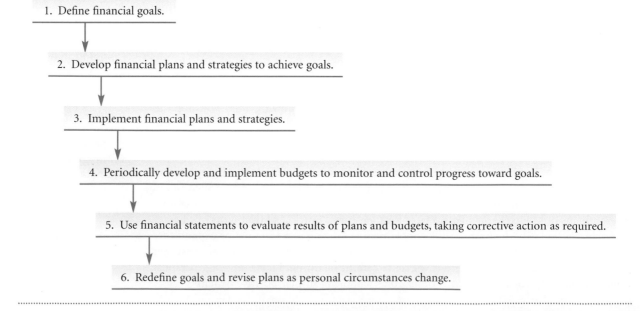

1. Define financial goals.

2. Develop financial plans and strategies to achieve goals.

3. Implement financial plans and strategies.

4. Periodically develop and implement budgets to monitor and control progress toward goals.

5. Use financial statements to evaluate results of plans and budgets, taking corrective action as required.

6. Redefine goals and revise plans as personal circumstances change.

THE ROLE OF MONEY. **Money** is the common denominator by which all financial transactions are gauged. It is the medium of exchange used as a measure of value in financial transactions. Without the standard unit of exchange provided by the dollar, it would be difficult to set specific personal financial goals and measure progress toward achieving them. Money, as we know it today, is the key consideration in establishing financial goals. Yet it is not money as such that most people want.

Rather, we want the **utility,** the amount of satisfaction a person receives from purchasing certain types or quantities of goods and services, that money makes possible. Often the utility or satisfaction provided, rather than the cost, is the overriding factor in the choice between two items of differing price. People may choose one item over another because of a special feature that provides additional utility. For example, many people pay more to buy a car with a CD player rather than buy one with a "standard" cassette player. The added utility may result from the actual usefulness of the special feature, from the "status" it is expected to provide, or both. Regardless, different people receive varying levels of satisfaction from similar items that are not necessarily related to the cost of the items. When evaluating alternative qualities of life, spending patterns, and forms of wealth accumulation, we need to consider utility along with cost.

THE PSYCHOLOGY OF MONEY. Money and its utility are not only economic concepts. They are also closely linked to the psychological concepts of values, emotion, and personality. Your personal value system—the ideals and beliefs you hold important and use to guide your life—will also shape your attitudes toward money and wealth accumulation. If status and image are important to you, you may spend a high proportion of your current income to acquire luxuries. If you place a high value on family life, you may choose a career that offers regular hours and less stress or an employer who offers "flextime" rather than a higher-paying position requiring travel and lots of overtime. You may have plenty of money but choose to live a frugal lifestyle and do things yourself rather than hire someone to do them for you. Clearly, your financial goals and decisions should be consistent with your personal values. Identifying your values allows you to formulate financial plans that provide greater personal satisfaction and quality of life.

 Is getting the lowest price important to you? Web sites like **www.pricescan.com** and **www.shoppinglist.com** search for the best prices, both online and off.

People react differently to similar situations involving money. Depending on timing and circumstances, emotional responses to money may be positive—such as love, happiness, and security—or negative—such as fear, greed, and insecurity. For example, some people, on receipt of a paycheck, feel satisfaction in their work. Others feel relief in knowing that they can pay past-due bills. Still others worry over what to do with the money. Most Americans know they must prepare for their financial futures. However, a recent survey about financial planning and security conducted by Prudential Insurance Company found that we are very unsure of how to make informed decisions about financial planning.

Money is a primary motivator of personal behavior. It has a strong effect on one's self-image. Therefore each individual's unique personality and emotional makeup determine the importance and role of money in her or his life. You should become aware of your own attitudes toward money because they are the basis of your "money personality" and management style.

Some questions to ask yourself are: How important is money to you? Why? What types of spending give you satisfaction? Are you a risk taker? Do you need large financial reserves to feel secure? Knowing the answers to these questions is a prerequisite to developing realistic

money
The medium of exchange used as a measure of value in financial transactions.

utility
The amount of satisfaction an individual receives from purchasing certain types or quantities of goods and services.

and effective financial goals and plans. For example, if you prefer immediate satisfaction, you will find it more difficult to achieve long-term net worth or savings goals than if you are highly disciplined and primarily concerned with achieving a comfortable retirement at an early age. Clearly, tradeoffs between current and future benefits are strongly affected by values, emotion, and personality.

While this book emphasizes a rational, unemotional approach to personal financial planning, we also recognize that universally applicable financial plans do not exist. In all cases, a key to effective personal financial planning is a realistic understanding of the role of money and its utility in the individual's life. Effective financial plans are both economically and psychologically sound. They must not only consider the individual's wants, needs, and financial resources, but must also realistically reflect his or her personality and emotional reactions to money.

You must resolve conflicts between personality, goals, and values early in the planning process. If you like to spend most of what you earn, you will find it hard to stick to a plan requiring high levels of annual savings to achieve future goals. You'll have to moderate your goals to achieve an acceptable balance between current and future needs.

MONEY AND RELATIONSHIPS. Money is one of the most emotional issues in any relationship, whether it be with a partner or with your parents or children. Most people are uncomfortable talking about money matters and avoid such discussions, even with their partners. However, differing opinions of how to spend a family's money may threaten the stability of a marriage or cause arguments between parents and children. Learning to communicate about money with your partner is a critical step in developing effective financial plans.

Your parents also play an important role in your financial planning. As they age, we tend to assume a greater responsibility for their care. Do you know what financial and health care planning steps they have taken? For example, where do they keep important financial and legal documents? What preferences do they have for health care should they become incapacitated? Asking these questions may be difficult, but having the answers will save you many headaches in event of an emergency involving them.

As we noted earlier, there are many distinct money personality types. One person may be analytical and see money as a means of control, another may view it as a way to express affection, and yet another may use it to boost his or her self-esteem. When couples have very different attitudes toward money—for example, if one person likes to prepare detailed budgets but the other is an impulse shopper—conflicts are bound to arise.

The best way to resolve money disputes is to be aware of your partner's financial style, keep the lines of communication open, and be willing to compromise. It's highly unlikely that you can change your partner's style—or your own, for that matter—but you can work out your differences. Financial planning is an especially important part of the conflict resolution process. You will gain a better understanding of your differences by working together to establish a set of financial goals that takes into account each person's needs and values. For instance, you may be a risk taker who likes to speculate in the stock market, while your cautious partner wants to put all your money into a savings account in case one of you loses your job. If you can agree on the amount of money you should have readily available in low-risk investments and savings accounts, you can then allocate a specific portion of your funds to riskier investments.

TYPES OF FINANCIAL GOALS

Financial goals cover a wide range of financial desires—from controlling living expenses to meeting retirement needs, from setting up a savings and investment program to minimizing the amount of taxes you pay. Some of the most-often cited financial goals include having enough money to live as well as possible now, being financially independent, sending children to college, and providing for retirement.

You should define your financial goals as specifically as possible and focus them on the results you want to attain. Simply saying you want to save money next year is not a specific goal. How much do you want to save, and for what purpose? A goal such as "save 10 percent of my take-home pay each month to start an investment program" clearly states what you want to do and why.

Equally important, as mentioned earlier, your goals should be realistically attainable, because they form the basis for your financial plans. If you set your savings goals too high—for example, 25 percent of your take-home pay when your basic living expenses already account for 85 percent of your take-home pay—the goal becomes unattainable. If set too low, you may not accumulate enough funds for a meaningful investment program. Clearly, if your goals are little more than "pipe dreams," the integrity of your financial plans may be suspect as well (not to mention a possible source of frustration).

Goal-setting is a process that should involve your immediate family. Having each family member effectively "buy into" these goals eliminates potential future conflicts and improves the family's chances of achieving them. Once you define and approve your goals, you can prepare appropriate cash budgets. Finally, you should assign priorities and a definite time frame to financial goals. Are they short-term goals for the next year, or intermediate- or long-term goals, not to be realized for many more years? For example, saving for a vacation might be a medium-priority short-term goal, whereas buying a larger home may be a high-priority intermediate-term goal, and purchasing a vacation home a low-priority long-term goal. Normally, long-term financial goals are set first, followed by a series of corresponding short- and intermediate-term goals. In addition, your goals will change as your life situation changes, as Exhibit 1.3 demonstrates.

PUTTING TARGET DATES ON FINANCIAL GOALS

Financial goals are most effective when set in reference to certain goal dates. Goal dates are target points in the future when you expect to achieve or complete certain financial activities. They may serve as progress checkpoints toward some financial goals or as deadlines for others. One goal may be to purchase a boat in 2006 (the goal date), and another to accumulate a net worth of $200,000 by 2020, with goal dates of 2007 and 2012 set as checkpoints for the attainment of net worth of $10,000 and $110,000, respectively. It is usually helpful to set goal dates at intervals of 2 to 5 years for the first 10 years or so and at 5- to 10-year intervals thereafter.

LONG-TERM GOALS. Long-term financial goals should indicate the individual's or family's wants and desires for a time period covering about 6 years out to the next 30 or 40 years. Although it's difficult to pinpoint exactly what you will want 30 years from now, you should establish some tentative long-term financial goals. Recognize, though, that many long-term goals will change over time and you'll need to revise them accordingly. If the goals appear to be too high, you'll want to make them more realistic. If they are too low, you'll want to adjust them to a level that will encourage you to make financially responsible decisions rather than squandering surplus funds. An individual might set a goal of retiring at age 55 with a net worth of $500,000. At age 50, this same person might decide to purchase a condominium in Florida. Note, however, that the short-term goals will remain pretty much the same: to make substantial, regular contributions to savings or investments to accumulate the desired net worth.

 EXHIBIT 1.3

HOW FINANCIAL GOALS CHANGE DURING A PERSON'S LIFE CYCLE

Financial goals are not static, but change continually over a lifetime. Here are some typical long-, intermediate-, and short-term goals for a number of different personal situations.

Personal Situation	Long-Term Goals (6+ years)	Intermediate-Term Goals (2–5 years)	Short-Term Goals (1 year)
College senior	Begin an investment program	Repay college loans	Find a job
	Buy a condominium	Trade in car and upgrade to nicer model	Rent an apartment
	Earn a master's degree	Buy new furniture	Get a bank credit card
			Buy new stereo
Single, mid-20s	Begin law school	Begin regular savings program	Prepare a budget
	Build an investment portfolio	Take a Caribbean vacation	Buy a new television and VCR
	Save enough for down payment on a home	Buy life insurance	Get additional job training
		Start a retirement fund	Build an emergency fund
			Reduce expenses 10%
Married couple with children, late 30s	Diversify investment portfolio	Buy a second car	Repaint house
	Buy a larger home	Increase college fund contributions	Get braces for children
		Increase second income: from part-time to full-time	Review life and disability insurance
Married couple with grown children, mid-50s	Decide whether to relocate when retired	Take cruise vacation	Buy new furniture
	Retire at age 62	Shift investment portfolio into income-producing securities	Review skills for possible career change
	Travel to Europe and the Orient	Sell house and buy smaller residence	

SHORT- AND INTERMEDIATE-TERM GOALS. Short-term financial goals are set each year and cover a 12-month period. Intermediate-term goals bridge the gap between short- and long-term goals (about 2 to 5 years). Both should be consistent with established long-term goals. Short-term goals become the key input for the cash budget, a tool used to plan for short-term income and expenses. To define your short-term goals, you should consider your immediate goals, expected income for the year, and long-term goals. Short-term planning should also include establishing an emergency fund with 3 to 6 months' worth of income. This special savings account serves as a safety valve in case of financial emergencies such as a temporary loss of income.

Unless you attain your short-term goals, you probably won't achieve your intermediate- and long-term goals, either. It's tempting to let our desire to spend now take priority over the need to save for future goals. However, by making some short-term sacrifices now we are more likely to have a comfortable future. If you don't realize this for another 10 or 20 years, you may discover that some of your most important financial goals are unattainable.

Worksheet 1.1 provides a convenient way to summarize your own financial goals. It groups them by time frame (short-term, intermediate-term, or long-term) and lists for each goal its priority (high/medium/low), a target date to reach the goal, and estimated cost.

We have filled out the form showing the goals Tim and Andrea Shepard set in December 2001. The Shepards were married in 1998, own a condominium in a midwestern suburb, and have no children. Because Tim and Andrea are 28 and 26 years old,

WORKSHEET 1.1

SUMMARY OF PERSONAL FINANCIAL GOALS

Set financial goals carefully and realistically, as they form the basis for your personal financial plans. They should be defined in measurable, specific terms and have a priority and time frame.

Personal Financial Goals

Name(s) _Tim and Andrea Shepard_ _____ Date _December 27, 2001_

Short-Term Goals (1 year or less)

Goal	Priority	Target Date	Cost Estimate
Buy new tires and brakes for Ford Escort	High	Feb. 2002	$ 500
Buy career clothes for Andrea	High	May 2002	1,200
Take Colorado ski trip	Medium	Mar. 2002	1,800
Replace stereo components	Low	Sept. 2002	1,100
Buy new work clothes for Tim	Medium	June 2002	750

Intermediate-Term Goals (2 to 5 years)

Goal	Priority	Target Date	Cost Estimate
Start family	High	2004	−
Repay all loans except mortgage	High	2005	c. $ 7,500
Trade Escort and buy larger car	High	2005	c. 10,000
Buy new bedroom furniture	Low	2006	c. 4,000
Take 2-week Hawaiian vacation	Medium	2003/4	c. 5,000
Review insurance needs	High	2004	−
Accumulate $100,000 net worth	High	2006	−

Long-Term Goals (6+ years)

Goal	Priority	Target Date	Cost Estimate
Begin college fund	High	2007	?/year
Diversify/increase investment portfolio	High	2008	Varies
Buy larger home	High	2010	$250,000
Take European vacation	Low	2009	$ 10,000
Retire from jobs	High	2034	?
Increase college fund contributions	High	2009	−

respectively, they have set their longest-term financial goal 33 years from now, when they want to retire. Tim has just completed his fifth year as a marketing representative for a large auto products manufacturer. Andrea, a former elementary school teacher, finished her MBA in May 2001 and began working at a local advertising agency. Tim and Andrea love to travel and ski. They plan to have children in a few years, but for now they want to develop some degree of financial stability and independence. Their goals include different financial planning areas, such as purchasing assets (clothes, stereo, furniture, car), reducing debt, reviewing insurance, increasing savings, and planning for retirement.

Your goals may be very different, depending on your personal situation. As you go through life, some financial goals will become more important than others. You will want a set of personal financial goals that is meaningful to you at this particular stage of your life.

CONCEPT CHECK

1-5. What is the role of money in setting financial goals? What is the relationship of money to utility?

1-6. Explain why financial plans must be psychologically as well as economically sound. What is the best way to resolve money disputes in a relationship?

1-7. Identify three financial goals that are important to you now. Why is it important to set realistically attainable financial goals? Explain using examples of realistic and unrealistic personal financial goals. Select one of your personal financial goals and develop a brief financial plan to reach it.

1-8. Distinguish between long-term, intermediate-term, and short-term financial goals. Give examples of each.

From Goals to Plans: A Lifetime of Planning [LG3]

How will you achieve the financial goals you set for yourself? The answer, of course, lies in the financial plans you establish. Financial plans provide the direction necessary to reach your goals. The six-step planning process results in a set of different yet interrelated plans that cover the most important financial dimensions of your life.

Some deal with the more immediate aspects of money management, such as preparing budgets to help manage spending. Others focus on acquiring major assets, such as a car or home. Liability plans control borrowing; insurance plans reduce financial risks; savings and investment plans provide emergency funds and future wealth accumulation. An employee benefit plan will help you take advantage of and manage your employer-sponsored benefits and coordinate them with your other financial plans. You also need retirement plans to provide financial security when you stop working and estate plans to ensure the orderly and cost-effective transfer of assets to your heirs. In the following sections we'll take a closer look at six specific types of financial plans that form a comprehensive personal financial plan.

As noted earlier, discussing your personal financial goals and attitudes toward money with your partner is important to successful personal financial planning. You also must allocate responsibility for money management tasks and decisions. Many couples divide routine financial decision making on the basis of expertise and interest and make major decisions jointly.

Giving children an allowance is a good way to start teaching them to budget and save. Allowing them to participate in the personal financial planning process, whether at regular "financial meetings" or on a less formal basis, shows them where the household's money goes. By setting their own financial goals and taking steps to reach them, they will develop their own good money management skills.

THE LIFE CYCLE OF FINANCIAL PLANS

Financial planning is a dynamic process. As you move through different stages of your life, your needs and goals will change. Certain financial goals are important regardless of age. Having extra resources to fall back on in an economic downturn or period of unemployment should be a priority whether you are 25, 45, or 65. Some changes—a new job, marriage, children, moving to a new area—may be part of your original plan.

However, more often than not, you will face unexpected "financial shocks" during your life: loss of a job, a car accident, divorce or death of a spouse, a long illness, or the need to support adult children or aging parents. With careful planning you can get through tough times and prosper in good times. To cope with life's financial shocks, you need to plan ahead and take steps—for example, setting up an emergency fund or reducing monthly expenses—that will protect you and your family financially if a setback occurs.

As we move from childhood to retirement age, we traditionally go through different life stages. Exhibit 1.4 illustrates the various components of a typical *financial planning life cycle* as it compares with these different life stages. As we pass from one state of maturation to the next, our patterns of income change simultaneously. From early childhood, when we relied on our parents for support, to early adulthood, when we started our families and, very likely, held our first "real" jobs, we can see a noticeable change in income pattern.

EXHIBIT 1.4

THE TRADITIONAL PERSONAL FINANCIAL PLANNING LIFE CYCLE

As you move through life and your income patterns change, you'll typically have to pursue a variety of financial plans. For instance, when you graduate from college, you'll be focused on buying a car and a house, and you'll be concerned about health and automobile insurance to protect against loss.

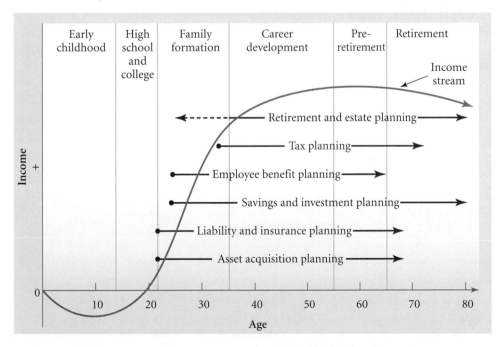

First, we replace negative income—in the form of reliance on our parents for money—with a rapidly increasing positive stream of earnings as we embark on our chosen careers. Then, as we move from career development to pre-retirement years, our income becomes more stable. Finally, our income begins to trail off (ideally, only a bit) as we enter our retirement years. Thus, as our emphasis in life changes, so do the kinds of financial plans we pursue.

Obviously, not everyone follows these typical patterns, and each life situation needs its own financial goals and plans. Today, many people in their 20s are waiting to marry and have children, focusing first on their careers and building a financial base. Controlling expenses, managing credit, and saving for a new car may be goals when you are 25 and single. They may also be important goals for people in their 40s and 50s who lose their jobs due to corporate downsizing or early retirement and must cope with reduced income.

New career strategies—planned and unplanned job changes, several different careers over a lifetime, for example—are common and may require revising financial plans. Families of women who interrupt their careers to stay home with their children, whether for six months or six years, need to plan for periods of reduced income. A divorce, the death of a spouse, and remarriage can drastically change one's financial circumstances. Many people in their 30s, 40s, and 50s find themselves in the "sandwich generation," supporting their elderly parents while they are still raising their children and paying for college. We'll look at these and other special planning concerns in Chapter 2.

Exhibit 1.5 summarizes data that demonstrate life cycle differences in the finances of various age groups. Income tends to increase, then decline over the life cycle; home ownership and other assets tend to increase; debts tend to increase and then decline. Note that those in the 45–64 age range tend to have more income than those less than age 45, and those age 65–74 tend to have more non-mortgage debt than persons in other age groups.

 EXHIBIT 1.5

LIFE CYCLE FINANCIAL DATA

The finances of those in different stages of the life cycle vary. Income tends to increase and then decline over the life cycle, while home ownership and other assets tend to increase. Debts tend to increase and then taper off over the life cycle.

Age of Family Head	Average Household Income	Percent Who Own Home	Median Equity in Home	Median Value of Nonfinancial Assets[1]	Median Value of Financial Assets[2]	Median Non-Mortgage Debt Level[3]
Under 35	$36,100	38.9%	$13,000	$115,400	$ 49,600	$68,300
35–44	60,000	67.1	31,000	146,900	149,800	56,100
45–54	69,700	74.4	51,200	245,800	192,000	59,800
55–64	71,700	80.3	60,600	228,000	332,900	61,200
65–74	46,600	81.5	66,000	201,900	283,400	68,100
75 and over	29,200	77.0	63,800	214,000	242,100	41,100

[1]Includes personal assets other than primary residence, such as cars, business ownership, and investment real estate.

[2]Includes bank accounts, CDs, savings bonds, investment portfolios, life insurance, and other managed assets.

[3]Excluding mortgage debt on principal residence.

Source: Arthur B. Kennickell, Martha Starr-McCluer, and Brian J. Surette, "Recent Changes in U.S. Family Finances: Results from the 1998 Survey of Consumer Finances," *Federal Reserve Bulletin,* Board of Governors of the Federal Reserve System, Washington, D.C., January 2000, pp. 5, 11, 17, and 21.

PLANS TO ACHIEVE YOUR FINANCIAL GOALS

As discussed earlier, financial goals can range from short-term goals like saving for a new stereo to long-term goals, such as saving enough to start your own business. Reaching your particular goals requires different types of financial plans. Let's take a brief look at what each major plan category includes.

ASSET ACQUISITION PLANNING. One of the first categories of financial planning we typically encounter is asset acquisition. We accumulate *assets*—things we own—throughout our lives. These include *liquid assets* (cash, savings accounts, and money market funds) used for everyday expenses, *investments* (assets such as stocks, bonds, and mutual funds acquired to earn a return), *personal property* (movable property such as automobiles, household furnishings, appliances, clothing, jewelry, home electronics, and similar items), and *real property* (immovable property; land and anything fixed to it, such as a house). Chapters 4 and 5 focus on important considerations with regard to acquiring liquid assets and major assets such as automobiles and housing.

LIABILITY AND INSURANCE PLANNING. Another category of financial planning is liability planning. A *liability* is something we owe and is represented by the amount of debt we incur. We create liabilities by borrowing money. By the time most of us graduate from college, we have debts of some sort: education loans, car loans, credit card balances, and so on. Our borrowing needs typically increase as we acquire other assets, such as a home, furnishings, and appliances. Regardless of the source of credit, such transactions have one thing in common: *The debt must be repaid at some future time.* The way we manage our debt burden is just as important as how we manage our assets. Using credit effectively requires careful planning and is the topic of Chapters 6 and 7.

Obtaining adequate *insurance coverage* is also essential. Like borrowing money, it is generally something that is introduced at a relatively early point in our life cycle (usually early in the family formation stage). Insurance is a means of reducing financial risk and protecting both income (life, health, and disability insurance) and assets (property and liability insurance). Most consumers regard insurance as absolutely essential, and for good reason. One serious illness or accident can wipe out everything that one has accumulated over years of hard work. However, having the wrong amount of insurance can be costly, too. We'll examine the appropriate types and amounts of insurance coverage in Chapters 8, 9, and 10.

SAVINGS AND INVESTMENT PLANNING. As your income begins to increase, so does the importance of savings and investment planning. People save initially to establish an emergency fund for meeting unexpected expenses. Eventually, however, they devote greater attention to investing excess income as a means of accumulating wealth, either for major expenditures, such as a child's college education, or for retirement. They acquire wealth through savings and subsequent investing of funds in various investment vehicles—common or preferred stocks, government or corporate bonds, mutual funds, real estate, and so on. The higher the returns on investments of excess funds, the greater the wealth they accumulate.

The impact of alternative rates of return on accumulated wealth is illustrated in Exhibit 1.6. It shows that if you had $1,000 today and could keep it invested at 8 percent, you would accumulate a considerable sum of money over time. For example, at the end of 40 years you would have $21,725 from your original $1,000. Earning a higher rate of return has even greater rewards. Some might assume that earning, say, 2 percentage points more—that is, 10 rather than 8 percent—would not matter a great deal. But it certainly would!

EXHIBIT 1.6

HOW A $1,000 INVESTMENT CAN GROW OVER TIME

Eight percent, ten percent. What's the big deal? The deal is more than twice the money over a 40-year period! Because of the power of compound interest, a higher return means dramatically more money as time goes on.

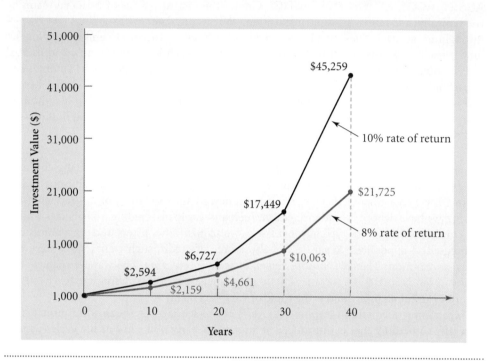

Note that if you could earn 10 percent over the 40 years, you would accumulate $45,259, or more than twice as much as what you would accumulate at 8 percent.

How long you invest is just as important as how much you earn on your investments. With either rate of return, you can accumulate more than twice as much capital by investing for 40 rather than 30 years. This is the magic of compound interest, which explains why it's so important to create strong savings and investment habits early in life. We will more fully examine compounding in Chapter 2, savings in Chapter 4, and investments in Chapters 11, 12, and 13.

EMPLOYEE BENEFIT PLANNING. Your employer may offer a wide variety of employee benefit plans, especially if you work for a large firm. These could include life, health, and disability insurance; tuition reimbursement programs for continuing education; pension and profit-sharing plans and 401(k) retirement plans; flexible spending accounts for child care and health care expenses; stock options; sick leave, personal time, and vacation days; and miscellaneous benefits, such as employee discounts and subsidized meals or parking. Many of these plans will be more fully described in later chapters.

Managing employee benefit plans and coordinating them with your other plans is an important part of the overall financial planning process. For example, such benefits as tax-deferred retirement plans and flexible spending accounts offer tax advantages. Some retirement plans allow you to borrow against them. Employer-sponsored insurance programs may need to be supplemented with personal policies. In addition, in today's volatile labor market, you can no longer assume that you will be working at the same company for many years. If you change jobs, your new company may not offer the same benefits. Your personal financial plans should include contingency plans to replace employer-provided benefits as required. We will discuss employee benefits in greater detail in Chapters 2 (planning); 3 (taxes); 8, 9, and 10 (insurance); and 14 (retirement).

TAX PLANNING. In spite of all the talk about tax reform, our tax code remains highly complex. Income can be taxed as active (ordinary), portfolio (investment), passive, tax-free, or tax-deferred income. Then there are tax shelters, which use various aspects of the tax code (such as depreciation expenses) to legitimately reduce an investor's tax liability. Tax planning considers all these dimensions and more. It involves looking at an individual's current and projected earnings and developing strategies that will defer and minimize taxes. Tax plans are closely tied to investment plans and will often specify certain investment strategies. Although the use of tax planning is most common among individuals with high incomes, sizable savings can also result for people with lower levels of income. We will examine taxes and tax planning in Chapter 3.

RETIREMENT AND ESTATE PLANNING. While you are still working, you should be managing your finances to attain those goals you feel are important after you retire. These might include maintaining your standard of living, extensive travel, plans for visiting children, dining out frequently at better restaurants, and perhaps a vacation home or boat. Retirement planning actually begins long before you retire. As a rule, most people do not start thinking about retirement until well into their 40s or 50s. This is unfortunate, because it usually results in a substantially reduced level of retirement income. The sooner you start, the better off you will be. Take, for instance, the IRA (individual retirement arrangement), in which certain wage earners are allowed to invest up to $2,000 per year. If you start investing for retirement at age 40, put $2,000 per year in an IRA for 25 years, and earn 10 percent, your account will grow to $196,694. However, if you start your retirement program 10 years earlier (at age 30), your IRA will grow to a whopping $542,049. Although you are investing a total of only $20,000 more ($2,000 per year for an extra 10 years), your IRA will nearly triple in size. We will look at IRAs and other aspects of retirement planning in Chapter 14.

Accumulating assets to enjoy in retirement is only part of the long-term planning process. As people grow older, they also must consider how they can most effectively pass on their wealth to heirs, an activity called *estate planning*. We will examine this complex subject, which includes such topics as wills, trusts, and the effects of gift, estate, and inheritance taxes, in Chapter 15.

TECHNOLOGY IN FINANCIAL PLANNING

As they have in so many other aspects of our lives, the personal computer (PC) and the Internet have found their way into financial planning. Indeed, financial planning is a natural application of the PC. What better way is there to handle all the number crunching involved in budgeting, tax planning, and investment management? There are many reasonably priced, "user-friendly" programs available for personal financial planning and money management, including the popular *Quicken* and *Microsoft Money* packages.

The Internet puts a wealth of financial information literally at your fingertips. To help you find useful online resources, every chapter includes numerous *Smart.Sites* to relevant financial planning Web sites. The *Money Online* feature at the end of each chapter describes related Web sites and includes companion exercises to help you effectively use the Web in financial planning. By bookmarking (saving) these sites, you will build up a valuable library of personal financial Web sites.

Where applicable, we will point out ways to use the computer and Internet to simplify and reduce the time required to manage your personal finances. As a start, check out the general personal finance sites described in the *Money in Action* box below. We also include a simple, menu-driven computer program to use with many of the analytical and computational procedures addressed in the text. This Financial Planning System (FPS) runs on IBM and IBM-compatible computers. Keyed to various sections of this book, it offers short programs that perform many of the routine financial calculations and procedures used in the text. FPS also automates the completion of the majority of the chapter worksheets. The following symbol identifies the major text headings and end-of-chapter problems that use FPS routines:

MONEY IN ACTION

Financial Portals Open the Door to Online Information

With thousands of personal financial Web sites crowding the Internet, the overabundance of online information can be intimidating. Don't let that stop you, however, as no matter how much you know—or don't know—about personal finance and investing, the Web is an educational resource without equal. Not to mention that many worthwhile sites are free.

Of the many sites trying to be your Web gateway to the Internet's financial riches, financial portals are an ideal starting place for the beginner. They are jam-packed with financial information, from personal-finance tasks like paying bills online, shopping for a mortgage, or estimating taxes, to investment essentials like stock quotes, online portfolio tracking, investment research, and news. Some also provide the weather, a personal calendar, and an address book.

Several comprehensive sites that consistently get rave reviews are Yahoo! Finance (**finance.yahoo.com**), Microsoft's MSN MoneyCentral (**investor.msn.com**), and Intuit's Quicken.com (**www.quicken.com**). Each has a slightly different look, emphasis, and organization scheme. A visit to discover their special features will help you find the one that suits your needs.

YAHOO! FINANCE: No-frills design and fast access to financial data such as stock quotes, company profiles, and breaking news stories from the opening screen. Most customizable home page allows you to delete any content you don't want; other sites aren't as flexible. Among the options available for viewing the home page is one that calls up recent headlines for each of your stock holdings. Extensive message boards are available for investor discussions.

MSN MONEYCENTRAL: More emphasis on articles, tools, and step-by-step guides for investor education. Wide range of sophisticated interactive tools like stock screening and charting capabilities plus investment research. Access to online brokers. Research Wizard provides data and explains why it's important.

QUICKEN.COM: Excels at broad coverage and consistency of personal finance topics, not just investments. Each area—investments, home and mortgage, small business, banking and borrowing, and retirement—has its own bulletin boards, reference materials, and advice.

Sources: "How to Plumb the Investing Secrets of the Internet," *The Wall Street Journal*, May 25, 2000, pp. C1, C12; Sarah Rose, "The 50 Best Financial Websites," *Money*, December 1999, pp. 179–181; Matthew Schifrin, "Best of the Web: Investing—Financial Portals," *Forbes Best of the Web* (special issue), February 28, 2000, pp. 36–37.

CONCEPT CHECK

1-9. What types of financial planning concerns does a complete set of financial plans cover?

1-10. Discuss the relationship of life-cycle considerations to personal financial planning. What are some factors to consider when revising financial plans to reflect changes in a person's life cycle?

1-11. Mark Potter's investments over the past several years have not lived up to his full return expectations. He is not particularly concerned, however, because his return is only about 2 percentage points below his expectations. Do you have any advice for Mark?

1-12. Describe employee benefit planning and tax planning. How do they fit into the financial planning framework?

1-13. There's no sense in worrying about retirement until you reach "middle age." Discuss this point of view.

1-14. What role do the personal computer and Internet play in personal financial planning?

◼ The Planning Environment [LG4]

Financial planning is not carried out in isolation, but in an economic environment created by the actions of business, government, and consumers. Your purchase, saving, investment, and retirement plans and decisions are influenced by both the present and future state of the economy. Understanding the economic environment will allow you to make better financial plans and decisions.

For example, a strong economy can lead to big profits in the stock market, which can positively affect your investment and retirement programs. The economy can also affect the interest rates you pay on your mortgage and credit cards and those you earn on savings accounts and bonds. Periods of high inflation can lead to price increases that come so fast it is hard to make ends meet. This section briefly looks at two important aspects of the planning environment: the major financial planning players and the economy.

THE PLAYERS

The financial planning environment contains various interrelated groups of players, each attempting to fulfill certain goals. Although their objectives are not necessarily incompatible, they do impose some constraints on one another. There are three vital groups: government, business, and consumers. Exhibit 1.7 depicts the relationship among these groups.

GOVERNMENT. The federal, state, and local governments provide us with many essential public goods and services, such as police and fire protection, national defense, highways, public education, and health care. The federal government also plays a major role in regulating the level of economic activity. Government is also a customer of business and an employer of consumers. As a result, it is a source of revenue for business and wages for consumers. The two principal constraints from the perspective of personal financial planning are taxes and government regulations.

Taxation. The federal government levies taxes on income, state governments levy taxes on sales and income, and local governments levy taxes primarily on real estate and personal

EXHIBIT 1.7

THE FINANCIAL PLANNING ENVIRONMENT

Government, business, and consumers are the major participants in our economic system. They all interact with one another to produce the environment in which we carry out our financial plans.

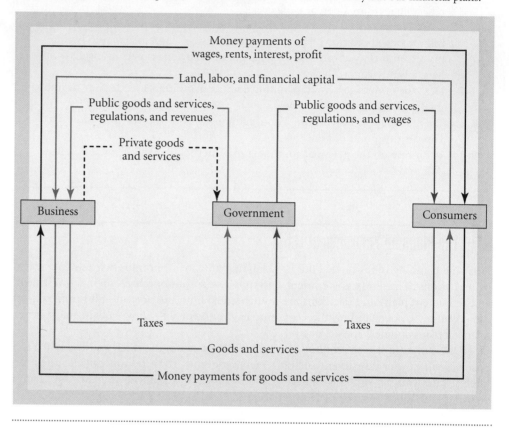

property. The largest tax bite for consumers is federal income taxes, which in 2000 could take as much as 39.6 percent of earnings. (*Note:* The tax-cut package passed by Congress in mid-2001 will slowly reduce tax rates through 2006, when the top bracket will be 35.0 percent.) These taxes are somewhat progressive, because (up to a point) the greater the taxable income, the higher the tax rate. Because changes in tax rates and procedures will increase or decrease the amount of income consumers have to spend, you should factor the effects of taxes into your personal money management activities. Due to the constraints of the tax structure and the potential magnitude of taxes, financial decisions should be evaluated on an "after-tax" basis. (Taxes are discussed in Chapter 3.)

Regulation. Federal, state, and local governments place many regulations on activities that affect consumers and businesses. Aimed at protecting the consumer from fraudulent and undesirable actions by sellers and lenders, these regulations require certain types of businesses to have licenses, maintain certain hygienic standards, adequately disclose financial charges, and warrant their goods and services. Other laws protect sellers from adverse activities by consumers—for example, shoplifting and nonpayment for services rendered. Certainly, any decisions relating to achieving personal financial goals should take into consideration the legal requirements that protect consumers and those that constrain their activities.

BUSINESS. As shown in Exhibit 1.7, business provides consumers with goods and services and in return receives payment in the form of money. To produce these goods and services, firms must hire labor and use land and capital (what economists refer to as *factors of production*). In return, firms pay out wages, rents, interest, and profits to the various factors of production. Thus businesses are an important part of the circular flow of income that sustains our free enterprise system. In general, their presence creates a competitive environment in which consumers may select from an array of goods and services. There are, of course, certain industries, such as public utilities, in which the degree of competition or choice offered the consumer is limited for economic reasons by various regulatory bodies. As indicated in the preceding section, all businesses are limited in some way by federal, state, or local laws.

CONSUMERS. The consumer is the central player in the financial planning environment. Consumer choices ultimately determine the kinds of goods and services businesses will provide. In addition, the consumer's choice of whether to spend or save has a direct impact on the present and future circular flows of income. A cutback in spending is usually associated with a decline in economic activity, while an increase helps the economy recover. Consumers are often thought to have free choices in the marketplace, but they must operate within an environment that interacts with government and business. Although they can affect these parties through their elected officials and by their purchase actions, lobbyists and consumer groups are necessary for any real impact. The individual consumer should not expect to change government or business independently. As an individual consumer, you are best off accepting the existing environment and planning your transactions within it.

THE ECONOMY

Our economy is the result of interaction among government, business, and consumers, as well as economic conditions in other nations. The government's goal is to regulate the economy and provide economic stability and high levels of employment through specific policy decisions. These government decisions have a major impact on the economic and financial planning environment. The federal government's *monetary policy*, programs for controlling the amount of money in circulation (the money supply), is used to stimulate or contract economic growth. For example, increases in the money supply tend to lower interest rates. This typically leads to a higher level of consumer and business borrowing and spending that increases overall economic activity. The reverse is also true. Reducing the money supply raises interest rates, reducing consumer and business borrowing and spending and slowing economic activity.

The government's other principal tool for managing the economy is *fiscal policy*, its programs of spending and taxation. Increased spending for social services, education, defense, and other programs stimulates the economy, while decreased spending slows economic activity. Increasing taxes, on the other hand, gives businesses and individuals less to spend and, as a result, negatively affects economic activity. Conversely, decreasing taxes stimulates the economy.

ECONOMIC CYCLES. Although the government uses monetary and fiscal policy to regulate the economy and provide economic stability, the level of economic activity changes constantly. The upward and downward movement creates *economic cycles* (also

expansion
The phase of the economic cycle during which the level of employment and growth of economic activity are both high; generally accompanied by rising prices for goods and services.

recession
The phase of the economic cycle during which the level of employment falls and growth of economic activity slows.

depression
The phase of the economic cycle during which the employment level is low and economic growth is at a virtual standstill.

recovery
The phase of the economic cycle during which the employment level is improving and the economy is experiencing increased activity and growth.

gross domestic product (GDP)
The total of all goods and services produced by workers located within a country; used to monitor economic growth.

called *business cycles*). These cycles vary in length and in how high or low the economy moves. An economic cycle typically contains four stages: *expansion, recession, depression,* and *recovery*.

Exhibit 1.8 shows how each of these stages relates to employment and production levels, two important indicators of economic activity. The stronger the economy, the higher the levels of employment and production. Eventually a period of economic **expansion** will peak and begin to move downward, becoming a **recession** when the decline lasts more than six months. A **depression** occurs when a recession worsens to the point where economic growth is almost at a standstill. The **recovery** phase, with increasing levels of employment and production, follows either a recession or a depression. For about 70 years, the government has been reasonably successful in keeping the economy out of a depression, although we have experienced periods of rapid expansion and high inflation followed by periods of deep recession.

After the recession of the early 1990s, the economy went through a very long and drawn out expansion phase. Inflation and interest rates remained generally low, while the stock market soared to record levels. In early 2001, the stock market experienced some significant declines.

Economic growth is measured by changes in the **gross domestic product (GDP),** the total of all goods and services produced by workers located within the country. The broadest measure of economic activity, GDP is reported quarterly and is used to compare trends in national output. A rising GDP means the economy is growing. The *rate* of GDP growth

 EXHIBIT 1.8

THE ECONOMIC CYCLE

The economy goes through various stages over time, although real depressions are extremely rare. These stages tend to be cyclical and directly affect the levels of employment and production.

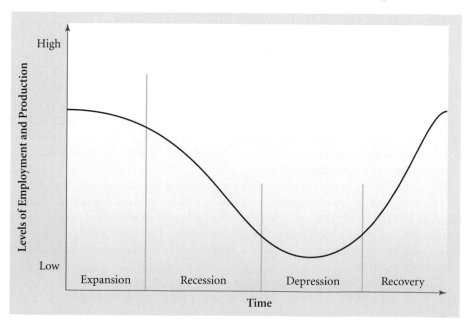

is also important. For example, although actual GDP rose year after year for much of the 1990s, the annual rate of GDP growth varied widely.

Another important yardstick of economic health is the *unemployment rate*. The swings in unemployment from one phase of the cycle to the next can be substantial. For example, during the Great Depression of the 1930s, U.S. unemployment reached a staggering 25 percent of the workforce. In contrast, during the expansion in 1968, unemployment dropped to slightly less than 4 percent. During the 1981-1982 recession, unemployment rose to over 10 percent. During the expansion that followed and lasted until late 1990, unemployment fell to 5.3 percent before rising to about 7.4 percent during the recessionary period of the early 1990s. By mid-2000, unemployment had dropped to 4.0 percent.

Unemployment, inflation, interest rates, bank failures, corporate profits, taxes, and government deficits can have a direct and profound impact on our financial well-being; these factors affect the very heart of our financial plans—our level of income, investment returns, interest earned and paid, taxes paid, and, in general, prices paid for goods and services consumed.

 How is the U.S. Economy doing this month? Check out the Bureau of Labor Statistics "Economy at a Glance" page, **www.bls.gov/eag/eag.us.htm**.

INFLATION, PRICES, AND PLANNING. As we have discussed, our economy is based on the exchange of goods and services between businesses and their customers—consumers, government, and other businesses—for a medium of exchange called money. The mechanism that facilitates this exchange is a system of *prices*. Technically speaking, the price of something is *the amount of money the seller is willing to accept in exchange for a given quantity of some good or service*—for instance, $3 for a pound of meat or $10 for an hour of work. When the general level of prices *increases* over time, the economy is said to be experiencing a period of **inflation.** The most common measure of inflation is the **consumer price index (CPI)**, which is based on the changes in the cost of a market basket of consumer goods and services. At times the rate of inflation has been substantial. In 1980, for instance, prices went up by 13.5 percent. Fortunately, inflation has dropped dramatically in this country and the annual rate of inflation has remained below 5 percent in every year since 1983, except 1990, when it was 5.4 percent. Recently inflation has been in the 2.4 to 4 percent range.

Inflation is of vital concern to financial planning. It affects not only what we pay for the various goods and services we consume, but also what we earn in our jobs. Inflation tends to give an illusion of something that does not exist. That is, while we seem to be making more money, we really aren't. As prices rise, we need more income because our **purchasing power**—the amount of goods and services we can buy with our dollars—declines. For example, assume that you earned $30,000 in 2000 and received annual raises so that your salary was $34,000 by 2003. That represents an annual growth rate of 4.3 percent. If inflation averaged 5 percent per year, however, your purchasing power would have decreased, even though your income rose. You would require $34,729 just to keep pace with inflation. So be sure to look at what you can earn in terms of its purchasing power, not just in absolute dollars.

Inflation also directly affects interest rates. High rates of inflation drive up the cost of borrowing money as lenders demand compensation for their eroding purchasing power. Higher interest rates mean higher mortgage payments, higher monthly car payments, and so on. High inflation rates also have a detrimental effect on stock and bond prices. Finally, sustained high rates of inflation can have devastating effects on retirement plans and other long-term financial goals. Indeed, for many people it can put such goals out of reach.

inflation
A state of the economy in which the general price level is rising due to excessive demand or rapidly rising production costs; usually occurs during the recovery and expansion phases of the economic cycle.

consumer price index (CPI)
A measure of the cost of living and inflation based on changes in the cost of a market basket of consumer goods and services.

purchasing power
The amount of goods and services each dollar buys at a given point in time.

Clearly, low inflation is good for the economy, for interest rates and stock and bond prices, and, in general, for financial planning.

CONCEPT CHECK

> 1-15. Discuss the following statement: "It is the interaction among government, business, and consumers that determines the environment in which personal financial plans must be made."
>
> 1-16. What are the stages of an economic cycle? Explain their significance for your personal finances.
>
> 1-17. What is *inflation*, and why should it be a concern in financial planning?

◼ What Determines Your Personal Income? [LG5, LG6]

An obvious and important factor in determining how well we live is the amount of income we earn. In the absence of any inheritance or similar financial windfall, your income will depend in large part on such factors as your age, marital status, education, geographic location, and choice of a career. Making a lot of money is not easy, but it can be done! A high level of income—whether derived from your job, your own business, or your investments—is within your reach if you are willing to provide the necessary dedication and hard work, along with a well-thought-out set of financial plans. According to data from the U.S. Bureau of the Census, shown in Exhibit 1.9, the closer you are to middle age, the more education you have, and the more professionally or managerially oriented your career, the greater your income will be.

YOUR AGE AND MARITAL STATUS

Typically, people with low incomes fall into the very young or very old age groups, whereas the period of highest earnings generally occurs between the ages of 35 and 55. This distribution results because those below age 35 are just developing their trades or beginning to move up in their jobs, and many over 55 are working only part-time or are completely retired. In the 25–34 age group, the median income of the heads of household is about $40,000; this jumps to about $54,000 for those in the 45–54 age group, and then falls sharply in the 65-and-over age group to about $22,000. Your own income will vary over time, too, so you need to incorporate these expected changes in earnings in your financial planning.

Unfortunately, gender and race have historically affected earning potential. Although the gap between the earnings of men and women has been narrowing, women still earn, on average, only about 74 percent as much as men. On average, African Americans earn only about 64 percent as much as caucasian workers, and Hispanics about 68 percent. With the elimination of many barriers that prevented these groups from acquiring the education and skills necessary for higher-paying careers, pay differences continue to decrease. Women and minorities are now better represented in managerial, high technology, and professional positions.

Your family income also depends on whether you are married or single. The median income of married couples is currently about $52,000, compared with only $19,000 for single people. Although many singles may be supporting only themselves, others have children or other dependents to support.

EXHIBIT 1.9

HOW AGE, EDUCATION, GENDER, AND CAREER AFFECT ANNUAL INCOME

The amount of money you earn is closely tied to your age, education, gender, and career. Generally, the closer you are to middle age (35-55), the more education you have, and the more professionally or managerially oriented your career, the greater your income will be.

Annual Income (Head of Household)

AGE	Under $25,000	$25,000–$34,999	$35,000–$49,999	$50,000–$74,999	Over $75,000	Median Income
			Percent in Each Income Bracket by Age			
15–24	53.2%	16.4%	16.2%	9.5%	4.7%	$23,564
25–34	27.7	15.6	18.6	22.3	15.8	40,069
35–44	21.1	12.3	18.3	23.1	25.2	48,451
45–54	19.4	10.5	15.5	22.9	31.7	54,148
55–64	29.2	12.4	15.4	18.4	24.7	43,167
65 and over	56.4	14.2	12.2	8.7	8.4	21,729

EDUCATION (HIGHEST LEVEL)	Under $25,000	$25,000–$34,999	$35,000–$49,999	$50,000–$74,999	Over $75,000	Median Income
			Percent in Each Income Bracket by Education			
Elementary:						
Less than 9th grade	77.5%	13.0%	9.5%	5.7%	3.0%	$16,154
High School						
1–3 years	58.1	13.9	13.7	9.5	4.9	20,724
Graduate	35.0	15.8	18.1	18.7	12.4	34,373
College						
Some college, no degree	26.3	14.5	18.7	21.6	19.0	41,658
Associate degree	20.8	12.3	18.4	25.1	23.4	48,604
Bachelor's degree or more	11.8	8.6	13.7	23.2	42.7	66,474

CAREER (FULL-TIME)	Women	Men
	Median Income by Gender	
Executive, administrators, and managerial	$34,755	$51,351
Professional specialty	36,261	51,654
Technical and related support	27,849	40,546
Sales	23,197	37,248
Administrative support (incl. clerical)	23,835	31,153
Precision production, craft, and repair (incl. construction)	23,907	31,631
Machine operators, assemblers, and inspectors	19,015	27,890
Transportation and material moving	21,449	30,422
Handlers, equipment cleaners, helpers, and laborers	16,550	21,871
Service workers	15,647	22,515
Farming, forestry, and fishing	15,865	18,855

Source: Based on data from U.S. Department of Commerce, Bureau of the Census, *Statistical Abstract of the United States, 2000,* 120th edition, Washington, D.C., 2000, Table No. 697 (page 438) and No. 738 (page 467).

YOUR EDUCATION

Your level of formal education is a controllable factor that has a considerable effect on your income. As Exhibit 1.9 illustrates, heads of household who have more formal education earn higher annual incomes than those with lesser degrees. According to recent census bureau data, the median salary of a high school graduate is about $34,400, compared with $66,500 for someone with a bachelor's degree. Add a PhD or other professional degrees and the earnings of a college graduate rise substantially. Over a lifetime, these differences really add up! Although education alone cannot guarantee a high income, these statistics suggest that a good formal education greatly enhances your earning potential.

WHERE YOU LIVE

Geographic factors also affect your earning power. Salaries vary regionally and tend to be higher in the Northeast and West than in the South. Typically, your salary will be higher if you live in a large metropolitan area rather than in a smaller one or in a rural area. Such factors as economic conditions, labor supply, and industrial base also affect salary levels in different areas. In addition, living costs vary considerably throughout the country. You would earn more in Los Angeles than Boise, Idaho, but your salary would probably not go as far due to the higher cost of living. However, you may decide that lifestyle considerations take priority over earning potential. Your local chamber of commerce can provide an inter-city cost of living index (see Exhibit 1.10) that compares living costs in major cities and serves as a useful resource for comparing jobs in different areas. The overall index is developed by tracking costs in six major categories: groceries, housing, utilities, transportation, health care, and miscellaneous goods and services.

 EXHIBIT 1.10

COST OF LIVING INDEX—SELECTED METROPOLITAN AREAS (FOURTH QUARTER 1999)

A comparison of the cost of living indexes (index of 100 equals the average for the more than 200 cities surveyed) shows that living costs are typically higher in large metropolitan areas than in smaller rural areas.

City	All Items	City	All Items	City	All Items
Albuquerque, NM	105.0	Denver, CO	110.3	New York, NY	240.1
Atlanta, GA	104.3	Des Moines, IA	95.4	Oklahoma City, OK	92.8
Baltimore, MD	96.0	Fairbanks, AK	123.4	Omaha, NE	94.3
Baton Rouge, LA	102.9	Fargo, ND	96.7	Orlando, FL	98.9
Billings, MT	101.7	Houston, TX	95.1	Philadelphia, PA	116.2
Birmingham, AL	97.7	Indianapolis, IN	96.6	Phoenix, AZ	102.4
Boise, ID	96.7	Jackson, MS	92.0	Portland, OR	111.7
Boston, MA	136.9	Lansing, MI	103.3	Richmond, VA	104.8
Buffalo, NY	99.8	Las Vegas, NV	106.4	St. Louis, MO-IL	97.5
Burlington, VT	115.1	Lawrence, KS	99.5	Salt Lake City, UT	106.5
Charleston, SC	103.8	Little Rock, AR	98.2	San Antonio, TX	90.6
Charlotte, NC	100.6	Los Angeles, CA	123.0	Sioux Falls, IA	97.3
Cheyenne, WY	99.1	Louisville, KY	97.5	Spokane, WA	104.0
Chicago, IL	117.9	Memphis, TN	92.5	Washington, DC	108.3
Cleveland, OH	110.3	Minneapolis-St. Paul, MN	106.3	Wilmington, DE	109.7
Dallas, TX	100.3	Mobile, AL	93.4		

Source: U.S. Department of Commerce, Bureau of the Census, *Statistical Abstract of the United States, 2000* (120th edition), (Washington, D.C., 2000), Table No. 771 (pages 490–492).

YOUR CAREER

How much you earn over your lifetime also depends on your career. The career you choose is closely related to your level of education and your particular skills, interests, lifestyle preferences, and personal values. Social, demographic, economic, and technological trends also affect your decision as to what fields offer the best opportunities for the future. Although not a prerequisite for many types of careers, such as sales, service, and certain types of manufacturing and clerical work, formal education generally leads to greater decision-making responsibilities—and increased income potential—within a career. Exhibit 1.11 presents an alphabetical list of median salaries from entry-level, mid-level, and managerial positions for a variety of careers, compiled from the 2000-2001 Edition of the *Occupational Outlook Handbook*. As shown in Exhibits 1.9 and 1.11, professional and managerial workers, who typically have a college degree, tend to earn the highest salaries.

PLANNING YOUR CAREER

Career planning and personal financial planning are closely related activities, and the decisions you make in one area affect the other. Like financial planning, career planning is a lifelong process that includes short- and long-term goals. You can no longer expect to stay in one field or remain with one company your whole life, and your career goals are likely to change several times.

EXHIBIT 1.11

MEDIAN SALARIES FOR SELECTED PROFESSIONS

Professional and managerial workers, who typically have a college degree, tend to earn the highest salaries.

	Salary		
Profession	**Entry-Level**	**Mid-Level**	**Managerial**
Accountant, public	$31,125	$55,125	$73,625
Architect	35,200	47,900	132,500
Computer programmer	27,670	47,550	88,730
Dentist	n/a	110,600	n/a
Electrical engineer	45,200	63,500	91,500
Engineering technician	21,710	35,970	62,540
Family practice medical doctor	n/a	132,000	n/a
Financial manager	27,680	55,070	118,950
Human resources manager	25,750	49,010	91,040
Industrial designer (avg.)	31,000	51,000	100,000
Lawyer	45,000	78,170	114,520
Paralegal	21,770	34,000	50,290
Pharmacist	n/a	59,700	n/a
Police patrol officer	22,270	37,710	63,530
Psychologist	37,900	48,050	88,280
Registered nurse	29,480	40,690	69,300
Teacher, K-12	25,700	39,300	61,000
Systems analyst	32,470	52,180	87,810

Source: *Occupational Outlook Handbook*, 2000–2001 Edition, U.S. Department of Labor, downloaded from **stats.bls.gov/ocohome.htm**.

You might graduate with a computer science degree and accept a job with a software company. Your financial plan might include furnishing your apartment, saving for a vacation or new car, and starting an investment program. If 5 years later you decide to go to law school, your revised financial plan will have strategies to cover living expenses and finance your tuition. You may decide that you need to go to school at night while you earn a living during the day.

The average American starting his or her career today can expect to have at least 10 jobs with five or more employers, and many of us will have three, four, or even more careers during our lifetimes. Some of these changes will be based on personal decisions; others may result from layoffs due to corporate downsizing. For example, a branch manager for a regional bank who feels that bank mergers have reduced her prospects for another banking job may buy a quick-print franchise and become her own boss. Job security is practically a thing of the past, and corporate loyalty has given way to a more self-centered career approach requiring new career strategies.

Through career planning, you can improve your work situation to gain greater personal and professional satisfaction. Some of the steps are similar to the financial planning process described earlier:

- Identify your interests, skills, needs, and values.
- Set specific long- and short-term career goals.
- Develop and implement an action plan to achieve your goals.
- Review and revise career plans as your situation changes.

Your action plan will depend on your job situation. For example, if you are unemployed, it will focus on your job search. If you have a job but want to change careers, it might include researching career options, networking to develop a broad base of contacts, listing companies to contact for information, and getting special training to prepare for your chosen career.

 One of the first steps in the job-search process is to assess your personality. Use this link to take the Keirsey Temperament Sorter as a starting point: **www.keirsey.com/cgi-bin/newkts.cgi**.

A personal portfolio of skills, both general and technical, will protect your earning power during economic downturns and advance it during prosperous times. Employers need flexible, adaptable workers as companies restructure and pare down their operations. Continually upgrade your skills through on-the-job training programs and continuing education courses, and add new skills such as computer and language skills to keep up with changing technology and workplace requirements. Keep up with marketplace changes. Broaden your contacts within your industry and among your professional colleagues, know which industries have potential and which are in trouble, and know what skills are in demand in your field.

Good job-hunting skills will serve you well throughout your career. Learn how to research new career opportunities and investigate potential job opportunities, taking advantage of online resources as well as traditional ones. Develop a broad base of career resources, starting with your college placement office, public library, and personal contacts such as family and friends. Know how to market your qualifications to your advantage in your résumé and cover letters, on the phone, and in person during a job interview.

 The *U.S. News & World Report* Career Center has material on a variety of career topics, from internships and resumes to the hottest careers and benefits: **www.usnews.com/usnews/edu/careers/cchome.htm**.

CONCEPT CHECK

1-18. "All people having equivalent formal education earn similar incomes." Do you agree or disagree with this statement? Explain your position.

1-19. Discuss the need for career planning throughout the life cycle and its relationship to financial planning. What are some of your personal career goals?

■ An Overview of the Text

This text is divided into six parts, each devoted to the explanation of a different aspect of personal financial planning.

Part 1: Foundations of Financial Planning
Part 2: Managing Basic Assets
Part 3: Managing Credit
Part 4: Managing Insurance Needs
Part 5: Managing Investments
Part 6: Retirement and Estate Planning

The book is developed around the organizational model shown in Exhibit 1.12.

Our organizational scheme revolves around financial decision making that is firmly established on an operational set of financial plans. We believe that through sound financial plans, individuals can make financial decisions that will lead to desired financial results. Therefore, starting with Part 1, where we look at personal financial statements, plans, and taxes, we move successively through the various types of decisions individuals make when implementing their financial plans.

To allow you to gain some hands-on financial planning experience, we include continuous case components for the ends of various chapters and parts of the text in both the instructor's manual and on the Web site for *Personal Financial Planning, Ninth Edition,* at **http://finance.swcollege.com**. The first case component ties to the end of this chapter with an inventory of personal and financial data for Megan and Kevin Lee. Using this data, you will be able to develop various parts of the Lees' financial plan using the components for

 EXHIBIT 1.12

ORGANIZATIONAL PLANNING MODEL

This text emphasizes making financial decisions regarding assets, credit, insurance, investments, and retirement and estates.

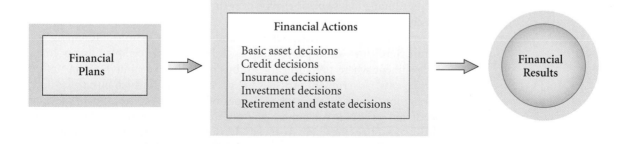

Financial Plans → Financial Actions: Basic asset decisions, Credit decisions, Insurance decisions, Investment decisions, Retirement and estate decisions → Financial Results

the end of Parts 1 through 5 and Chapters 14 and 15. In each component, we provide additional data, if needed, along with statements and questions to help you prepare the part of the Lees' financial plan related to that part or chapter. When you finish these components, you will have a comprehensive financial plan for the Lees. (Depending on course objectives and time constraints, the preparation of the Lees' financial plan may or may not be required by your instructor, which is why the Lees' case is in the instructor's manual and on our Web site.)

SUMMARY

LG1. Identify the benefits of using personal financial planning techniques to manage your finances. Personal financial planning helps you marshal and control your financial resources. It should allow you to improve your standard of living, get more enjoyment from your money by spending it wisely, and accumulate wealth. By setting short- and long-term financial goals, you will enhance your quality of life both now and in the future. The ultimate result will be an increase in wealth.

LG2. Describe the personal financial planning process and define your major financial goals. Personal financial planning is a six-step process that helps you achieve your financial goals. The six steps in the financial planning process are: (1) define financial goals; (2) develop financial plans and strategies to achieve goals; (3) implement financial plans and strategies; (4) periodically develop and implement budgets to monitor and control progress toward goals; (5) use financial statements to evaluate results of plans and budgets, taking corrective action as required; and (6) redefine goals and revise plans as personal circumstances change. Before you can manage your financial resources, you must realistically spell out your short-, intermediate-, and long-term financial goals. Goals, which are essential to sound financial planning, reflect your values and circumstances; they may change as personal circumstances dictate. They should also be specifically stated in terms of the desired results. Once you define your goals, you can develop and implement an appropriate personal financial plan. A complete set of financial plans covers asset acquisition planning, liability and insurance planning, savings and investment planning, employee benefit planning, tax planning, and retirement and estate planning. These plans should be reviewed regularly and revised as required.

LG3. Explain why personal financial plans must change according to your life situation. As you move through various life-cycle stages, you must revise your financial plans to include goals and strategies appropriate to each stage. Income and expense patterns change with age. Changes in your life due to marriage, children, divorce, remarriage, and job status also require adapting financial plans to meet current needs. Although these plans change over time, they provide the direction necessary to achieve your financial goals.

LG4. Describe how government, business, and consumer actions and changing economic conditions affect personal financial plans. Financial planning occurs in an environment where the government, business, and consumers are all influential participants. Government provides the structure within which businesses and consumers function, as well as certain types of essential services. Businesses provide goods and services to consumers, whose choices influence the products and services businesses offer. Personal financial decisions are affected by economic cycles (expansion, recession, depression, and recovery) and the impact of inflation on prices, and, therefore, purchasing power and personal income.

LG5. **Evaluate the impact of age, marital status, education, geographic location, and career choice on personal income.** Demographics, education, and career are all important factors that affect your income level. As a rule, people age 35 to 55 tend to earn more than others, as do those who are married. Equally important, statistics show a direct correlation between level of education and income. Where you live is another consideration; salaries and living costs are higher in some areas than in others. Career choice also affects the level of income; those in professional and managerial positions tend to earn the highest salaries.

LG6. **Recognize the importance of career planning and its relationship to personal financial planning.** Career planning is a lifetime process that involves goal setting and career development strategies. A career plan should be flexible and able to adapt to new workplace requirements, using continuing education and job training, and to facilitate making changes in job, employer, and even career. When making career plans, you should identify your interests, skills, needs, and values; set specific long- and short-term career goals; develop and implement an action plan to achieve your goals; and review and revise career plans as your situation changes. Many career decisions have monetary implications; you should therefore coordinate your career plans with your personal financial plans.

QUESTIONS AND PROBLEMS

1. How can using personal financial planning tools help you improve your financial situation? Describe changes you can make in at least three areas.
2. *Use Worksheet 1.1.* Describe your current status based on the personal financial planning life cycle shown in Exhibit 1.4. Fill out Worksheet 1.1, *Summary of Personal Financial Goals,* with goals that reflect your current situation, and your expected life situation in 5 and 10 years. Discuss the reasons for the changes in your goals and how you will need to adapt your financial plans as a result. Which types of financial plans do you need for your current situation, and why?
3. Recommend three financial goals and related activities for someone in the following circumstances:
   a. Junior in college
   b. 25-year-old computer programmer who wants to get a master's degree in Business Administration
   c. Couple in their 30s with two children, ages 3 and 6
   d. Divorced 45-year-old man with 15-year-old child and a 75-year-old father who is ill
4. Summarize the current and projected trends in the economy with regard to GDP growth, unemployment, and inflation. How should you use this information to make personal financial and career planning decisions?
5. Assume you graduated from college with a major in marketing and took a job with a large consumer-products company. After 3 years, you are laid off when the company downsizes. Describe the steps you'd take to "repackage" yourself for another field.

APPLYING PERSONAL FINANCE

How Do I Feel About Money?

Everyone has opinions about money and the accumulation of wealth; such opinions can have a profound impact on one's personal financial plans. This exercise will help you explore your feelings about money and wealth.

Based on the discussion in the text and what you know about yourself, respond to the following questions:

1. Am I a saver, or do I spend almost all the money I receive?
2. Is it important for me to have new clothes, a new car, frequent vacations, etc., or am I willing to get along with the same old things?
3. Do I enjoy spending money on myself and others?
4. Where do I want to be professionally and financially in five years? Ten years?
5. If I dropped out of school today or lost my job, what would I do?
6. How financially independent am I?

These questions are really just icebreakers. Your responses will help you think about and formulate realistic goals and plans.

CONTEMPORARY CASE APPLICATIONS

1.1   Neil's Need to Know: Personal Finance or Tennis?

During the Christmas break of his final year at Mountain View College, Neil Strong planned to put together his résumé so that he could seek full-time employment as a medical technician during the spring semester. To help Neil prepare for the job interview process, his older brother arranged for him to meet with a friend, Marilyn Nolan, who has been a practicing medical technician since her graduation from Mountain View 2 years earlier. Neil and Marilyn met for lunch, and Marilyn provided him with numerous pointers on résumé preparation, the interview process, job opportunities, and so on.

After answering Neil's many questions, Marilyn asked Neil to bring her up-to-date on a variety of topics related to Mountain View College. Of special interest to Marilyn were the many changes that had taken place in the faculty and curriculum of the medical technology department since her graduation. As they discussed courses, Marilyn indicated that of all the electives she had taken, she had found the course in personal financial planning most useful. Neil said that he still had one elective to take and had been giving some thought to personal financial planning, although he was currently leaning toward a beginning tennis course. Neil felt that because a number of his friends would be taking tennis, it would be a lot of fun. He pointed out that he never expected to get rich and already knew how to balance his checkbook, so the personal financial planning course did not seem well suited to his needs. Marilyn said that there is certainly much more to personal financial planning than balancing a checkbook and that the course was highly relevant regardless of income level. She strongly believed that the personal financial planning course would be more beneficial to Neil than beginning tennis—a course that she also had taken while at Mountain View College.

Questions

1. Describe to Neil the goals and rewards of the personal financial planning process.
2. Explain to Neil what is meant by financial planning and why it is important regardless of income.
3. Describe the financial planning environment to Neil. Explain the role of the consumer in this environment, and the impact of economic conditions on financial planning.
4. What arguments would you present to convince Neil that the personal financial planning course would be more beneficial for him than beginning tennis?

1.2   Sid's Dilemma: Finding a New Job

Sid Como, a 47-year-old retail store manager earning $65,000 a year, had worked for the same company during his entire 28-year career. Then came a major recession that resulted in massive layoffs throughout the retail industry. He was among the unlucky people who lost their jobs. Now, 10 months later, he is still unemployed. Sid's 10 months' severance pay and 6 months' unemployment compensation have run out. However, when he first became a store manager he had taken a personal financial planning course offered at the local university. Because he then adopted careful financial planning practices, he now has sufficient savings and investments to carry him through several more months of unemployment. Currently, his greatest financial need is to find a job.

Sid has actively sought work, but finds himself overqualified for the lower-paying jobs that are available and underqualified for higher-paying, more desirable positions. There have been no new openings for positions equivalent to the manager's job he lost. Although Sid attended college for 2 years after high school, he did not earn a degree. Sid is divorced and close to his two grown children, who live in the same city.

The options facing Sid are:

- Wait out the recession until another, equivalent, retail store manager position opens up.
- Move to another area of the country where store manager positions are still available.
- Accept a lower-paying job for 2 or 3 years and go back to school evenings to finish his college degree and qualify for a better position.
- Consider other types of jobs that could benefit from his managerial skills.

Questions

1. What important career factors should Sid consider when evaluating his options?
2. What important personal factors should Sid consider when deciding among his career options?
3. What recommendations would you give Sid in light of both the career and personal dimensions of his options noted in Questions 1 and 2?
4. What career strategies should today's workers employ in order to avoid Sid's dilemma?

MONEY ONLINE

CAREERS!

Note: Web addresses change frequently, so you may need to determine the home page and do a site search to find the page or topic that's referenced.

1. **www.jobreviews.com**
   What's it *really* like to work in various job positions? Find out from the professionals at the JobReview Web site. Browse the Job Position reviews for various positions and industries, read accounts of fellow job hunters' interviewing experiences, and find advice on writing cover letters and negotiating your salary at the site where job hunters help each other.

2. **stats.bls.gov/cghome.htm**
   Examine the employment outlook for the career you've chosen in the *Career Guide to Industries*, published by the Bureau of Labor Statistics. Research other topics as well, such as the nature of a given industry, working conditions, and training and advancement.

3. **www.jobstar.org/hidden**
   Tap into the hidden job market! An estimated 80 percent of all positions are filled *without* employer advertising. Find out why and what you can do about it at JobStar's Web site. Also from this site, tap into the resources of *Careerjournal.com*, a site prepared by *The Wall Street Journal* where you can browse their library of career and job search information, or use their Futurestep recruiting service.

4. **www.coolworks.com**
   Vacation every day! Find a job at a resort, ski area, national park, ranch, or camp. Or find a job on the water—perhaps river rafting or working aboard a yacht or cruise ship. Let the Cool Works Web site help you find a job at one of these great places so you can live and work where others only visit.

5. **monster.com**
   Visit this site to search for a job, post your resume, find out who's hiring, or get tips on how to create either a traditional or scannable resume. Research companies and find out more about today's top employers. Explore Monster's global network or let them e-mail you when suitable job openings come to their attention.

6. **www.cfp-board.org/cert_career.html**
   What about a career in financial planning? Find out about the financial planning industry and what a financial planner does at the Web site of the Certified Financial Planner Board of Standards. Click on "Guide to CFP Certification" to download their *General Information Booklet* which outlines the requirements for becoming licensed as a Certified Financial Planner.

7. **kiplinger.com/tools**
   Have you received job offers from all around the country? Use Kiplinger's tool, "Cost of Living Comparison Calculator," to help you determine how far your paycheck will stretch. Compare where you live now with New York, Atlanta, Chicago, or Bowling Green.

Just for Fun!

8. **woodrow.mpls.frb.fed.us/economy/calc/cpihome.html**

   What's a dollar worth? Use this inflation calculator at Woodrow, the Web site of the Federal Reserve Bank of Minneapolis, to determine today's equivalent of:

   > a meal purchased in 1930 for $1
   > a home purchased in 1970 for $40,000
   > a car purchased in 1985 for $10,000

   While you're there, compare the change in inflation from one decade to the next from 1950 to the present. Which decade saw the greatest amount of change?

9. **www.westegg.com/inflation**

   Calculate the impact of inflation all the way back to 1800, and see the effects of inflation both backwards and forwards in time! For example, type in 1812 and 1999 to see that something which cost $1 in 1812 would cost $9.70 in 1999. Conversely, a item purchased for $1 in 1999 would have cost only $.10 in 1812. Compare the present with the years 1836, 1865, 1900, 1929, 1942, 1951, 1974, 1987, and 1990.

Chapter 2

Your Financial Statements and Plans

LEARNING GOALS

LG1.   Describe the role of financial statements, professional financial planners, and special planning concerns in the personal financial planning process.

LG2.   Put a monetary value on financial goals using *time value of money* concepts.

LG3.   Prepare a personal balance sheet.

LG4.   Generate a personal income and expense statement.

LG5.   Develop a good record-keeping system and use ratios to interpret personal financial statements.

LG6.   Construct a cash budget and use it to monitor and control spending.

Singing the Budgeting Blues

"Where does all the money go?" Tom and Mary Gibson wonder. "We can't seem to balance our budget, no matter how hard we try." In their early thirties with two daughters ages 5 and 3, the Southern California couple struggles to live on Tom's $70,000 salary as a corporate accountant, plus any extra from his seasonal tax-return business. Because most of Mary's salary would go for day care, they agreed she would stay home with the girls for now. Compounding the problem, Mary's mother died suddenly. She had been taking care of Mary's father, who has Parkinson's Disease, and now Mary must find either in-home care or a nursing home—both of which are expensive.

The Gibsons bought a home in the early 1990s and also own 30 percent of a rental property that is just starting to earn a profit. However, they are heavily in debt—$20,000 in car loans and credit card spending—and they have only about $2,200 in cash to cover living expenses and emergencies. They want to save but never seem to have extra money at the month's end to put toward their financial goals, such as buying a second car, establishing a savings/emergency fund, and paying for the girls' college. Tom would also like to earn a graduate degree.

Although Tom and Mary track their expenses with a personal finance program on their computer, they have not used the information to become more disciplined when it comes to spending and saving. By learning how to prepare and use budgets, they can take the first step toward controlling their personal finances. Chapter 2 shows how personal financial statements and budgets can help them reach their goals.

■ Mapping Out Your Financial Future [LG1]

On your journey to financial security, you need navigational tools to guide you to your destination: the fulfillment of your financial goals. Financial plans, financial statements, and budgets provide direction by helping you work toward specific financial goals. *Financial plans* are the road maps that show you the way, whereas *personal financial statements* let you know where you stand financially. *Budgets,* detailed short-term financial forecasts that compare estimated income with estimated expenses, allow you to monitor and control expenses and purchases consistent with your financial plans. All three are essential to sound personal financial management and achievement of goals. They provide control by bringing the various dimensions of your personal financial affairs into focus.

As we learned in Chapter 1, the financial planning process includes six steps that translate personal financial goals into specific financial plans and the strategies to achieve these goals. We discussed the importance of clearly defining your financial goals in measurable terms. Another important aspect of financial planning is putting target dates and a monetary value on your short-, intermediate-, and long-term goals. In the first part of this chapter, we will discuss briefly some special planning concerns and the use of professional financial planners. Next, we will learn how to use time value of money concepts to calculate the value of a financial goal that occurs several years in the future. In the remainder of the chapter we explain how to prepare and use your own personal financial statements and budgets.

THE ROLE OF FINANCIAL STATEMENTS IN FINANCIAL PLANNING

Before you can set realistic goals, develop your financial plans, and effectively manage your money, you must know your current financial situation. You also need tools to monitor your progress. Personal financial statements are planning tools that provide an up-to-date evaluation of your financial well-being, help you identify potential financial problems, and, in general, help you make better-informed financial decisions. They measure your financial condition so you can establish realistic financial goals and evaluate your progress toward those goals. Knowing how to prepare and interpret personal financial statements is therefore a cornerstone of personal financial planning.

Two types of personal financial statements—the *balance sheet* and *income and expense statement*—are essential to developing and monitoring personal financial plans. They show your financial position as it *actually* exists and report on financial transactions that have *really* occurred.

The **balance sheet** describes your financial position—the assets you hold, less the debts you owe, equal your net worth (general level of wealth)—at a *given point* in time. It helps you track the progress you're making in building up your assets and reducing your debt.

In contrast, the **income and expense statement** measures financial performance *over* time. It tracks income earned, as well as expenses made, during a given period (usually a month or a year). You use it to compare your actual expenses and purchases with the amounts budgeted and then make the necessary changes to correct discrepancies between the actual and budgeted amounts. This information helps you control your future expenses and purchases so you'll have the funds needed to carry out your financial plans.

Budgets, another type of financial report, are *forward* looking. Because they are based on expected income and expenses, budgets allow you to monitor and control spending.

Exhibit 2.1 summarizes the various financial statements and reports and their relationship to each other in the personal financial planning process. Note that *financial plans* provide direction to annual budgets. Budgets directly affect your balance sheet and income and expense statement. As you move from plans to budgets to actual statements, you can compare your actual results with your plans. This will show you how well you are meeting your financial goals and staying within your budget. Subsequent sections of this chapter take a detailed look at preparing and evaluating basic personal financial statements.

SPECIAL PLANNING CONCERNS

Throughout your life, you will face changes in your personal circumstances that call for special attention during the personal financial planning process. Changing job status, relocating to a new state, getting married, having children, being in a serious car accident, getting a chronic illness, losing a spouse through divorce or death, retiring, taking responsibility for dependent parents—these and other stressful events are "financial shocks" that require reevaluation of your financial goals and plans.

However, don't rush to make major financial decisions at these times, when you are most vulnerable. Postpone any action until you have had time to recover from the event and evaluate all your options carefully. This can be difficult, because some financial salespeople will rush to contact you in these circumstances. For example, when you have a child, insurance agents, financial planners, and stockbrokers actively encourage you to buy insurance and start investing in a college fund. Although these are valid objectives, don't be pushed

---

balance sheet
An important financial statement that describes a person's financial position—the assets held, less the debts owed, equal the net worth (general level of wealth)—at a *given point* in time.

income and expense statement
An important financial statement that measures financial performance over time by presenting income earned and expenses made during a given period.

budget
A detailed financial report looking *forward*, based on expected income and expenses, used to monitor and control spending.

EXHIBIT 2.1

THE INTERLOCKING NETWORK OF FINANCIAL PLANS AND STATEMENTS

Personal financial planning involves a whole network of financial reports that link future goals and plans with actual results. Such a network provides direction, control, and feedback.

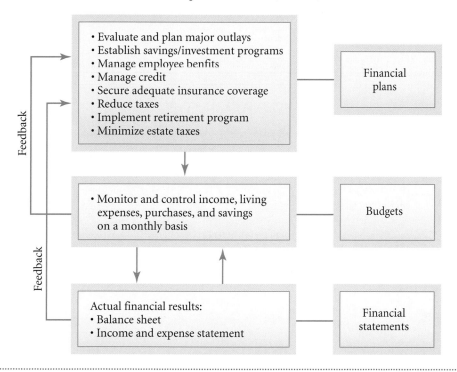

into any expensive decisions. People who get large sums of money—from severance packages, retirement benefits, or insurance policies when a loved one dies—are also likely to hear from financial salespeople eager to help them invest the funds. This is another time to wait. These brokers may have a greater interest in selling their own products than advising you on the best strategy for your needs.

 The GE Center for Financial Learning offers lots of advice on planning for changing life situations: **www.financiallearning.com**.

MANAGING TWO INCOMES. Today, dual-income couples account for the majority of U.S. households. Many depend on the second income to make ends meet, whereas for others it provides financial security and a way to afford "extras." Often, however, a second income does not add as much as expected to the bottom line. With it may come higher expenses—such as child care, taxes, clothing, dry cleaning, transportation, and lunches—that consume a large portion of the second paycheck.

Worksheet 2.1 allows you to assess the net monthly income of a second paycheck, both with and without the impact of employer-paid benefits. Be sure to include only those expenses that *directly relate to the second job*; some personal expenses would exist even without the second job. In addition, couples should coordinate their employee benefits to obtain the needed coverage at a minimum cost.

WORKSHEET 2.1

ANALYZING THE BENEFIT OF A SECOND INCOME

Use this worksheet to estimate the contribution of a second paycheck. Without the employer-paid benefits of $1,632 (line 2) the Diazes would realize a net monthly income of $1,808 (line 1–line 3), and with them their net monthly income would be $3,440 (line 4).

Second Income Analysis

Name(s) _Ariana and Marcos Diaz_ _____ Dated _December 31, 2001_

MONTHLY CASH INCOME

Gross pay	$5,000
Pretax contributions (401(k) plans, dependent-care-reimbursement accounts)	400
Additional job-related income (bonuses, overtime, commissions)	0
(1) Total Cash Income	$5,400

EMPLOYER-PAID BENEFITS

Health insurance	$550
Life insurance	100
Pension contributions	600
Thrift-plan contributions	0
Social security	382
Profit sharing	0
Other deferred compensation	0
(2) Total Benefits	$1,632

MONTHLY JOB-RELATED EXPENSES

Federal income tax	$1,500
Social security tax	382
State income tax	250
Child care	640
Clothing; personal care; dry cleaning	400
Meals away from home	200
Public transportation	0
Auto-related expenses (gas, parking, maintenance)	220
Other	0
(3) Total Expenses	$3,592
(4) Net Income (Deficit) [(1) + (2) − (3)]	$3,440

Source: Adapted from Kevin McManus, "How to Get the Most from Two Incomes," *Changing Times,* July 1989, p. 24.

Analyzing a second income requires us to examine not just the higher total income and out-of-pocket costs, but also the intangible costs (additional demands on your life, less time with family, and higher stress) and benefits (career development, job satisfaction, and sense of worth). Taking a part-time job while the children are young may not add much to household income, but it could keep the spouse on a career track and ease the transition to full-time work later.

Financial plans should spell out how the couple intends to use the second income: to meet basic expenses, afford a more luxurious lifestyle, save for a special vacation, or invest in retirement accounts. The plans should also take into account the possible loss of one income for any reason, including a spouse's staying at home with young children, going back to school, or losing a job. Analyzing past income and expense statements will reveal spending patterns and identify areas for expense reductions that could be incorporated into the budgeting process (described later in this chapter).

The dual-income situation often complicates the establishment of a money management system. Spouses need to decide how to allocate income to household expenses, family financial goals, and personal spending goals. Some couples place all income into a single joint account. Others have each spouse contribute *equal* amounts into a joint account, which is used to pay expenses consistent with achieving shared goals, but retain individual discretion over remaining income. Still others contribute a *proportional* share of each income to finance joint expenses and goals. Couples may experiment with different strategies until they find one that works best for them. Consideration, of course, must be given to the amount each spouse earns and various emotional and behavioral factors in their relationship. Regardless of the money management system, both spouses should have money of their own that they can spend without accountability.

MANAGING EMPLOYEE BENEFITS. As discussed in Chapter 1, if you hold a full-time job, your employer probably provides a variety of employee benefits, ranging from health and life insurance to pension plans. Most people rely on their employee benefit plans for a large part of their financial security. For example, the majority of American families depend solely on employer-sponsored group plans for their health insurance coverage and a big piece of their life insurance coverage and retirement needs.

Today's well-defined employee benefits packages cover a full spectrum of benefits that may include:

- Health and life insurance
- Disability insurance
- Long-term care insurance
- Pension and profit-sharing plans
- Supplemental retirement programs, such as 401(k) plans
- Dental and vision care
- Child care, elder care, and educational assistance programs
- Subsidized employee food services

Each company's benefit package is different. Some companies and industries are known for generous benefit plans, whereas others offer far less attractive packages. In general, large firms can afford more benefits than small ones. Because employee benefits can increase your total compensation by 30 percent or more, you should thoroughly investigate your employee benefits to choose those appropriate for your personal situation. Companies change their benefit packages often and today are shifting more costs to employees. While an employer may pay for some benefits in full, typically employees pay for a portion of the cost of group health insurance, supplemental life insurance, long-term care insurance, and participation in voluntary retirement programs.

Two-income couples should avoid paying for overlapping benefits from two employers. For example, if both spouses pay extra for family health insurance policies from their employers, they won't get double the coverage. Instead, one policy will govern, and the other policy might pick up only a fraction of what it was intended to cover had it been the primary coverage.

Because of the prevalence of two-income families and an increasingly diverse work force, many employers today are replacing traditional programs, where the company sets the type and amount of benefits, with **flexible-benefit (cafeteria) plans**. In flexible-benefit programs, the employer allocates a certain amount of money to each employee and then lets the employee "spend" that money for benefits that suit his or her age, marital status, number of dependent children, level of income, and so forth. These plans usually cover everything from child care to retirement benefits, offer several levels of health and life insurance coverage, and have some limits on the minimum and maximum amount of coverage. Within these constraints, you can select the benefits that do you the most good. In some plans, you can even take a portion of the benefits in the form of more take-home pay or extra vacation time!

Along with greater choice comes the responsibility to manage your benefits carefully. You should periodically assess the benefits package you have at work relative to your own individual/family needs. Make sure you have the coverage or protection you need and supplement any shortfall in company benefits with personal coverage. Except perhaps for group medical coverage, don't rely on your employer as the sole source of financial security. Your coverage may disappear if you change jobs or become unemployed, and, especially with life insurance and retirement plans, most employee benefits fall short of your total financial needs.

flexible-benefit (cafeteria) plan
A type of employee benefit plan wherein the employer allocates a certain amount of money, and the employee "spends" that money for benefits selected from a menu covering everything from child care to health and life insurance to retirement benefits.

ADAPTING TO OTHER MAJOR LIFE CHANGES. Other situations that require special consideration include changes in marital status and the need to support grown children or elderly relatives. Marriage, divorce, or death of a spouse result in the need to revise financial plans and money management strategies.

As mentioned earlier, couples should discuss their money attitudes and financial goals and decide how to manage joint financial affairs before they get married. Take an inventory of your financial assets and liabilities, including savings and checking accounts; credit card accounts and outstanding bills; auto, health, and life insurance policies; and investment portfolios. You may want to eliminate some credit cards if there is overlap. Too many cards can hurt your credit rating, and most people need only one or two. Each partner should have a card in his or her name to establish a credit record. Compare employee benefit plans to figure out the lowest-cost source of health insurance coverage and coordinate other benefits. Change the beneficiary on your life insurance policies. Adjust withholding amounts as necessary based on your new filing category.

In event of divorce, income may decrease because alimony and child support payments cause one salary to be divided between two households. Single parents may have to stretch limited financial resources farther to meet added expenses such as child care. Remarriage brings additional financial considerations, including decisions involving children from prior marriages and managing the assets that each spouse brings to the marriage. Some couples develop a prenuptial contract that outlines their agreement on financial matters, such as the control of assets, their disposition in event of death or divorce, and other important money issues.

Death of a spouse is another change that greatly affects financial planning. The surviving spouse is typically faced with decisions on how to receive and invest life insurance proceeds and manage other assets. In families where the deceased made most of the financial decisions with little or no involvement of the surviving spouse, the survivor may be overwhelmed by the need to take on financial responsibilities. Advance planning can minimize many of these problems.

Couples should regularly review all aspects of their finances. Each spouse should understand what is owned and owed, participate in formulating financial goals and investment strategies, and fully understand estate plans (covered in detail in Chapter 15).

USING PERSONAL FINANCIAL PLANNERS

Today, more people than ever recognize the importance of managing and controlling their personal finances. They get planning help from personal finance magazines like *Money, Kiplinger's Personal Finance, Smart Money,* and *Worth,* and from personal finance software. With the increased variety and complexity of financial products offered, many people turn to **professional financial planners** for help in developing and carrying out personal financial plans. This field has experienced tremendous growth, and there are now more than 250,000 financial planners in the United States.

Financial planners provide a wide range of services, including preparing comprehensive financial plans that evaluate a client's total personal financial situation or abbreviated plans focusing on a specific concern, such as managing clients' assets and investments and retirement planning. Where once only the very wealthy used professional planners, now financial firms such as H&R Block's Financial Centers and American Express Financial Advisors compete for the business of middle-income people as well.

professional financial planner An individual or firm that helps clients establish long- and short-term financial goals and develop and implement financial plans to achieve those goals.

 smart.sites To find a financial planner in your area, use the Financial Planning Association's search feature, **www.fpanet.org/plannersearch/index.cfm**.

TYPES OF PLANNERS. Most financial planners fall into one of two categories based on how they get paid: commissions or fees. Commission-based planners earn commissions on the financial products they sell, whereas fee-only planners charge fees based on the complexity of the plan they prepare. Many financial planners take a hybrid approach and charge fees and collect commissions on products they sell, offering lower fees if you make product transactions through them.

Insurance salespeople and securities brokers who continue to sell the same financial products (life insurance, stocks, bonds, mutual funds, and annuities) often now call themselves "financial planners." Other planners work for large, established financial institutions that recognize the enormous potential in the field and train their planners to compete with the best financial planners. Still others work in small firms, promising high-quality advice for a flat fee or an hourly rate. Regardless of their affiliation, full-service financial planners help their clients articulate their long- and short-term financial goals, systematically plan for their financial needs, and help implement various aspects of the plans.

In addition to one-on-one financial planning services, some institutions offer computerized financial plans. Merrill Lynch, IDS/American Express, T. Rowe Price, and other major investment firms provide these computerized plans on the Internet to help clients develop plans to save for college or retirement, reduce taxes, or restructure investment portfolios. You can even turn to the Internet for financial planning help, as the *Money in Action* box on page 46 explains.

Personal finance programs such as Quicken and Microsoft Money also have a financial planning component that can help you set a path to your goals and do tax and retirement planning. As we'll see in later chapters, some Web sites provide planning advice on one topic, such as taxes, insurance, or estate planning. Although these plans are relatively

MONEY IN ACTION

Planning on Online Financial Advice

Financial planning was once considered a luxury item, for those wealthy enough to pay high fees for personal advice from a financial professional. Today financial advice is just a click away for most Americans, courtesy of specialized Web sites that provide tools and advice ranging from retirement planning tools to advice on how to diversify your assets. Many sites have automated financial advisers. Some are limited to one area, such as the T. Rowe Price college planning advisor (**www.troweprice.com/college**). Many other mutual fund Web sites have online financial advisers; Vanguard Total Planning and American Century Fund Advisor are two. You'll find broader planning capabilities at several independent advice sites, including Financial Engines, AdviceAmerica.com, and DirectAdvice.com. Although only 1 million people currently use the online financial advisory sites, U.S. Bancorp Piper Jaffray Equity Research predicts that these sites could increase in popularity and help about 35 million people by 2005.

Let's see how one of these sites approaches the financial planning process. Financial Engines (**www.financialengines.com**) is one of the most sophisticated online advisors, specializing in tax-deferred investment planning for retirement. It offers a free forecast based on your financial profile—demographic information, current income, investments in your portfolio, savings rate, risk tolerance, retirement age, tax status, retirement income goal,

etc. Rather than asking you to make estimates about future inflation rates, interest rates, or investment returns, the planning model runs thousands of possible economic scenarios to simulate many different future financial climates. After taking into account your personal variables like savings rate, retirement age, and tax status, it charts the probability that you will achieve your goals.

The financial profile forecast is free; for $55 a year ($150 for multiple accounts) you can experiment with your forecast and make changes to your portfolio or goals by adjusting portfolio risk, projected retirement age, ideal retirement income, or your annual contribution to a tax-deferred account. Financial Engines provides portfolio suggestions based on these variables. It's easy to run "what if" scenarios with different assumptions to quickly see a new portfolio with recommended changes. It also shows the trade-offs between risk and reward.

Other independent advice sites that offer broad planning capabilities worth checking out include AdviceAmerica.com (**www.adviceamerica.com**) and DirectAdvice.com (**www.directadvice.com**). Because the planning sites take different approaches, explore several to find one with the features you need.

Sources: Wayne Harris, "Plan on the Web," *Mutual Funds* (September 2000), pp. 60-63; Philip J. Longman, "Fiscal Therapy Online Is Right at Your Fingertips," *U.S. News & World Report* (August 7, 2000), pp. 66–67.

inexpensive or even free, they tend to be somewhat impersonal. However, they are a good solution for those who need help getting started and for do-it-yourself planners who want some help.

 How effective is an online financial plan? Try "Roadmap to the Future" at the American Express site, **finance.americanexpress.com**.

The cost of financial planning services depends on the type of planner, the complexity of your financial situation, and the services you want. The cost may be well worth the benefits, especially for people who have neither the time, inclination, discipline, nor expertise to plan on their own. Remember, however, that the best advice is worthless if you are not willing to change your financial habits.

EXHIBIT 2.2

FINDING AND USING A FINANCIAL PLANNER

The following suggestions from the Certified Financial Planner Board of Standards will help you choose and work with a competent personal financial planner.

1. *Know what you want:* Determine your general financial goals and specific needs (insurance policy analysis, estate planning, investment advice, college tuition financing, etc.) to better focus your search for a suitable financial planner.
2. *Be prepared:* Read personal finance publications (*Worth, Money, Smart Money, Kiplinger's Personal Finance,* etc.) to maximize your familiarity with financial planning strategies and terminology.
3. *Talk to others:* Get referrals from advisors you trust, and from business associates and friends. Or contact one of the financial planning membership organizations for a referral to a financial planner in your area.
4. *Look for competence:* A number of specialty designations exist in the financial planning and services professions. Choose a financial planning professional with the designation that indicates that he or she is ethical and has met standards of financial planning competency, the Certified Financial Planner (CFP) designation.
5. *Interview more than one planner:* Ask the planners to describe their educational backgrounds, experience, specialties, the size and duration of their practice, how often they communicate with clients, and whether an assistant handles client matters. Make sure you feel comfortable discussing your finances with the planner you select. Then review a sample financial plan and contact several client references to evaluate the quality and completeness of the advice.
6. *Check the planner's background:* Depending on the financial planner's area of expertise, call the securities or insurance departments in your state regarding each planner's complaint record. Call the CFP Board toll-free at 888-CFP-MARK to determine if a planner is currently licensed to use the CFP marks or has ever been publicly disciplined by the CFP Board.
7. *Know what to expect:* Ask for a registration or disclosure statement (such as an ADV Form) detailing the planner's compensation methods, conflicts of interest, business affiliations, and personal qualifications.
8. *Get it in writing:* Request a written advisory contract or engagement letter to document the nature and scope of services the planner will provide. You should also understand whether compensation will be fee- or commission-based, or a combination of both.
9. *Re-assess the relationship regularly:* Financial planning engagements are often long-term relationships. Review your professional relationship on a regular basis and ensure that your financial planner understands your goals and needs as they develop and change over time. If the advisor purchases insurance or securities for you, make sure you receive regular statements from the insurance company or investment broker as well as from the planner. Question anything you don't understand until you are satisfied with the response. If you have questions regarding the conduct of your CFP certificant, call the CFP Board toll-free at 888-CFP-MARK and ask for a Complaint Package.

Source: "Tips on Choosing a Financial Planner," **www.cfp-board.org/cons_tips.html.**

CHOOSING A FINANCIAL PLANNER. Planners who have completed the required course of study and earned the Certified Financial Planner (CFP) or Chartered Financial Consultant (ChFC) designation are often a better choice than the many self-proclaimed financial planners. Of course, CPAs, attorneys, investment managers, and other professionals without such certifications in many instances do provide sound financial planning advice. Unlike accounting and law, the field is still largely unregulated, and almost anyone can call himself or herself a financial planner. Most financial planners are honest and reputable, but there have been cases of fraudulent practice. It is therefore critical to thoroughly check out a potential financial advisor—and preferably interview two or three—using the tips in Exhibit 2.2 and the checklist you'll find at the CFP Board Web site.

 For "10 Questions to Ask When Choosing a Financial Planner" and an interview checklist, see the Certified Financial Planner Board Web site, **www.cfpboard.org/cons_10qs.html.**

The way a planner is paid—fees, commissions, or both—should be one of your major concerns. Obviously, you need to be aware of potential conflicts of interest when using a planner with ties to a brokerage firm, insurance company, or bank. Many planners now provide clients with disclosure forms outlining fees and commissions for various transactions. In addition to asking questions of the planner, you should also check with your state securities department and the Securities and Exchange Commission (for planners registered to sell securities). Ask if the planner has any pending lawsuits, complaints by state or federal regulators, personal bankruptcies, or convictions for investment-related crimes. However, even these agencies may not have accurate or current information; simply being properly registered and without a record of disciplinary actions provides no guarantee that the planner's track record is good. You may also want to research the planner's reputation within the local financial community. Clearly, you should do your homework before engaging the services of a professional financial planner.

CONCEPT CHECK

2-1. How do financial statements fit into the personal financial planning process?

2-2. What is the difference between a *budget* and a *financial plan?* Does a budget play any role in a financial plan?

2-3. Discuss briefly how the following situations affect personal financial planning:
    a. Being part of a dual-income couple
    b. Major life changes, such as marriage or divorce
    c. Death of a spouse

2-4. What is a *professional financial planner?* Does it make any difference whether the financial planner earns money from commissions made on products sold as opposed to the fees he or she charges?

The Time Value of Money: Putting a Dollar Value on Financial Goals [LG2]

Some financial goals can be defined in rather general terms. Others should be defined more precisely, perhaps with fairly specific dollar values. Consider, for example, the goal of buying your first home in 6 years. The first question is how much to spend. Let's say you have done some "window shopping" and feel that, taking future inflation into consideration, you will have to spend about $150,000 to get the kind of house you like. Of course, you will not need the full amount, but given a 20 percent down payment ($150,000 × .20 = $30,000) plus closing costs, you estimate that you will need around $35,000. You now have a fairly well-defined long-term financial goal: *to accumulate $35,000 in 6 years to buy a home costing about $150,000.*

The next question is how to get all that money. You will probably accumulate it by saving or investing a set amount each month or year. You can easily estimate how much to save or invest each year if you know your goal and what you expect to earn on your savings or investments. In this case, if you have to start from scratch (that is, have nothing saved today) and estimate that you can earn about 10 percent on your money, you will have to save or invest about $4,550 per year for each of the next 6 years to accumulate $35,000 over that time period. Now you have another vital piece of information: *You know what you must do over the next 6 years to reach your financial goal.*

How did we arrive at the $4,550 figure? We used a concept called the **time value of money**, the idea that a dollar today is worth more than a dollar received in the future. With time value concepts, we can correctly compare dollar values occurring at different points in time. As long as you can earn a positive rate of return (interest rate) on your investments (ignoring taxes and other behavioral factors), in a strict financial sense you should always prefer to receive equal amounts of money sooner rather than later. The two key time value concepts, future value and present value, are discussed separately below. (*Note:* The following time value discussions and demonstrations initially rely on the use of financial tables; a later section summarizes the use of financial calculators, which have tables built into them, to conveniently make time value calculations.)

time value of money
The concept that a dollar today is worth more than a dollar received in the future; this is true as long as one can earn a positive rate of return (interest rate) on investments.

FUTURE VALUE

Future value is the value to which an amount today will grow if it earns a specific rate of interest over a given period. Assume, for example, that you make annual deposits of $2,000 into a savings account that pays 5 percent interest per year. At the end of 20 years, your deposits would total $40,000 (20 × $2,000). If you made no withdrawals, your account balance would have increased to $66,132! This growth in value occurs not only as a result of earning interest, but because of **compounding**—the interest earned each year is left in the account and becomes part of the balance (or principal) on which interest is earned in subsequent years.

To demonstrate future value, let's return to the goal of accumulating $35,000 for a down payment to buy a home in 6 years. You might be tempted to solve this problem by simply dividing the $35,000 goal by the 6-year period: $35,000/6 = $5,833. Unfortunately, this procedure would be incorrect, because it would fail to take into account *the time value of money*. The correct way to approach this problem is to use the *future value* concept. For instance, if you can invest $100 today at 10 percent, you will have $110 in a year: You will earn $10 on your investment ($100 × .10 = $10), plus get your original $100 back. Once you know the length of time and rate of return involved, you can find the future value of any investment by using the following simple formula:

future value
The value to which an amount today will grow if it earns a specific rate of interest over a given period. It can be used to find the yearly savings needed to accumulate a given future amount of money.

compounding
When interest earned each year is left in the account and becomes part of the balance (or principal) on which interest is earned in subsequent years.

Future value = Amount invested × Future value factor

Tables of future value factors simplify the computations in this formula (see Appendix A). The table is very easy to use; simply find the factor that corresponds to a given year and interest rate. Referring to Appendix A, you will find the future value factor for a 6-year investment earning 10 percent is 1.772 (the factor that lies at the intersection of 6 years and 10 percent).

Returning to the problem at hand, let's say you already have accumulated $5,000 toward the purchase of a new home. To find the future value of that investment in 6 years earning 10 percent, you can use the above formula as follows:

Future value = $5,000 × 1.772 = <u>$8,860</u>

The $8,860 is how much you will have in 6 years if you invest the $5,000 at 10 percent. Because you feel you are going to need $35,000, you are still $26,140 short of your goal. How are you going to accumulate an additional $26,140?

Again you can use the future value concept, but this time you will employ an *annuity factor*. An **annuity** is a fixed sum of money that occurs annually; for example, $1,000 per year for each of the next 5 years with payment to be made at the end of each year. To find out how much you have to save each year to accumulate a given amount, use the following equation:

annuity
A fixed sum of money that occurs annually.

$$\text{Yearly savings} = \frac{\text{Amount of money desired}}{\text{Future value annuity factor}}$$

When dealing with an annuity you have to use a different table of factors, such as that in Appendix B. Note that it is very much like the table of future value factors and, in fact, is used in exactly the same way: The proper future value annuity factor is the one that corresponds to a given year *and* interest rate. For example, you'll find in Appendix B that the future value annuity factor for 6 years and 10 percent is 7.716. Using this factor in the above equation, you can find out how much to save each year to accumulate $26,140 in 6 years, given a 10 percent rate of return, as follows:

$$\text{Yearly savings} = \frac{\$26,140}{7.716} = \underline{\underline{\$3,387.77}}$$

You will have to save about $3,390 a year to reach your goal. Note in the example that you must add $3,390 each year to the $5,000 you already have to build up a pool of $35,000 in 6 years. At a 10 percent rate of return, the $3,390 per year will grow to $26,140 and the $5,000 will grow to $8,860, so in 6 years you will have $26,140 + $8,860 = $35,000.

How much, you may ask, would you have to save each year if you did not have the $5,000 to start with? In this case, your goal would still be the same (to accumulate $35,000 in 6 years), but because you would be starting from scratch, the full $35,000 would have to come from yearly savings. Assuming you can still earn 10 percent over the 6-year period, you can use the same future value annuity factor (7.716) and compute the amount of yearly savings as follows:

$$\text{Yearly savings} = \frac{\$35,000}{7.716} = \underline{\underline{\$4,536.03}}$$

or approximately $4,550. Note that this amount corresponds to the $4,550 figure cited earlier.

Using the future value concept, you can readily find either the future value to which an investment will grow over time or the amount that you must save each year to accumulate a given amount of money by a specified future date. In either case, the procedures allow you to put monetary values on long-term financial goals.

 Still confused about time value concepts? Get another lesson at www.teachmefinance.com/timevalueofmoney.html.

THE RULE OF 72

rule of 72
A useful approximation for estimating how long it will take to double a sum at a given interest rate. Dividing 72 by the annual compound interest rate results in a good estimate of the number of years it will take to double your money.

Suppose you don't have access to a time value of money tables or financial calculator, but want to know how long it takes for your money to double. There is an easy way to approximate this using the **rule of 72**. Simply divide the number 72 by the percentage rate you are earning on your investment:

$$\text{Number of years to double money} = \frac{72}{\text{Annual compound interest rate}}$$

For example, assume that you recently opened a savings account with $1,000 that earns an annual compound rate of interest of 4.5 percent. Your money will double in 16 years (72 ÷ 4.5 = 16). If you can find a $1,000 investment that earns 6.25 percent, you will have $2,000 in about 11.5 years (72 ÷ 6.25 = 11.5).

The rule of 72 also applies to debts. Your debts can double very quickly with high interest rates, such as those charged on most credit card accounts. So keep the rule of 72 in mind whether you invest or borrow!

PRESENT VALUE

Present value is the value today of an amount to be received in the future. It is the amount you would have to invest today at a given interest rate over the specified time period to accumulate the future amount. The process of finding present value is called **discounting**, which is the inverse of *compounding* to find future value. For instance, assume that you are 35 years old and wish to accumulate a retirement fund of $300,000 by the time you are age 60 (25 years from now). You estimate that you can earn 7 percent annually on your investments during the next 25 years. Assuming you wish to create the retirement fund (future value) by making a single lump-sum deposit today, you can use the following formula to find the amount you need to deposit:

$$\text{Present value} = \text{Future value} \times \text{Present value factor}$$

Tables of present value factors make this calculation easy (see Appendix C). First, find the present value factor for a 25-year investment at a 7 percent discount rate (the factor that lies at the intersection of 25 years and 7 percent) in Appendix C; it is .184. Then, substitute the future value of $300,000 and the present value factor of .184 into the formula as follows:

$$\text{Present value} = \$300,000 \times .184 = \underline{\underline{\$55,200}}$$

The $55,200 represents the amount you would have to deposit today into an account paying 7 percent annual interest to accumulate $300,000 at the end of 25 years.

Present value techniques can also be used to determine how much you can withdraw from your retirement fund each year over a specified time horizon. Assume that at age 55 you wish to begin making equal annual withdrawals over the next 30 years from your $300,000 retirement fund. At first, you might think you could withdraw $10,000 per year ($300,000/30 years). However, the funds still on deposit would continue to earn 7 percent annual interest. To find the amount of the equal annual withdrawal, you again need to consider the time value of money. Specifically, you would use the following formula:

$$\text{Annual withdrawal} = \frac{\text{Initial deposit}}{\text{Present value annuity factor}}$$

The present value annuity factors for various numbers of years and rates are given in Appendix D at the end of this text. To find the annual withdrawal (or payment), which is an annuity, substitute the $300,000 initial deposit and the present value annuity factor for 30 years and 7 percent of 12.409 (from Appendix D) into the equation above to get:

$$\text{Annual withdrawal} = \frac{\$300,000}{12.409} = \underline{\underline{\$24,176}}$$

You can withdraw $24,176 each year for 30 years. This value is clearly much larger than the $10,000 annual withdrawal mentioned earlier.

Furthermore, present value techniques can be used to analyze investments. Suppose you have an opportunity to purchase an annuity investment that promises to pay you $700 per year for 5 years. You know that you will receive a total of $3,500 ($700 × 5 years) over the 5-year period. However, you wish to earn a minimum annual return of 8 percent on your investments. What is the most you should pay for this annuity today? You can answer this question by rearranging the terms in the equation above to get:

$$\text{Initial deposit} = \text{Annual withdrawal} \times \text{Present value annuity factor}$$

Adapting the equation to this situation, "initial deposit" represents the maximum price to pay for the annuity, and "annual withdrawal" represents the annual annuity payment of

---

present value
The value today of an amount to be received in the future; it is the amount that would have to be invested today at a given interest rate over a specified time period to accumulate the future amount.

discounting
The process of finding present value; the inverse of *compounding* to find future value.

EXHIBIT 2.3

IMPORTANT FINANCIAL KEYS ON THE TYPICAL FINANCIAL CALCULATOR

The important financial keys on a typical financial calculator are depicted and defined below. On some calculators the keys may be labeled using lowercase characters for "N" and "I".

CPT – Compute Key; Used to initiate financial calculation once all values are input
N – Number of Periods
I – Interest Rate per Period
PV – Present Value
PMT – Amount of Payment; Used only for annuities
FV – Future Value

$700. The present value annuity factor for 5 years and 8 percent (found in Appendix D) is 3.993. Substituting this into the equation, we get:

$$\text{Initial deposit} = \$700 \times 3.993 = \underline{\$2{,}795.10}$$

The most you should pay for the $700, 5-year annuity, given your 8 percent annual return, is $2,795.10. At this price, you would earn exactly 8 percent on the investment.

Using the present value concept, you can easily determine the present value of a sum to be received in the future, equal annual future withdrawals available from an initial deposit, and the initial deposit that would generate a given stream of equal annual withdrawals. These procedures, like future value concepts, allow you to place monetary values on long-term financial goals.

USING A FINANCIAL CALCULATOR

The handheld financial calculator makes it easy to calculate time value. Once you have mastered the time value of money concepts using tables, we suggest you use such a calculator. For one thing, it becomes very cumbersome to use tables when calculating anything other than annual compounding. For another, calculators rather than tables are used almost exclusively in the business of personal financial planning.

You don't want to become overly dependent on calculators, however, because you may not be able to recognize a nonsensical answer in the event that you accidentally push the wrong button. The important calculator keys are shown and labeled in Exhibit 2.3. Before using your calculator to make the financial computations described in this text, be aware of the following points.

1. The keystrokes on some of the more sophisticated and expensive calculators are menu-driven: after you select the appropriate routine, the calculator prompts you to input each value; a compute key (**CPT**) is not needed to obtain a solution.
2. Many calculators allow the user to set the number of payments per year. Most of these calculators are preset for monthly payments—12 payments per year. Because we work primarily with annual payments—one payment per year—it is important to *make sure that your calculator is set for one payment per year*. Although most calculators are pre-

set to recognize that all payments occur at the end of the period, it is important to *make sure your calculator is in the END mode.* Consult the reference guide that accompanies your calculator for instructions for setting this value.

3. To avoid including previous data in current calculations, *always clear all registers of your calculator before inputting values and making each computation.*
4. The known values *can be punched into the calculator in any order;* the order specified in this and other calculator use demonstrations included in this text results merely from convenience and personal preference.

Let's go back to the future value calculation on page 49, in which we're trying to calculate the future value of $5,000 at the end of 6 years invested at 10 percent. Here are the steps to solve the problem with a calculator:

1. Punch in 5000 and press **PV**.
2. Punch in 6 and press **N**.
3. Punch in 10 and press **I**.
4. To calculate the future value, press **CPT** and then **FV**. The future value of 8,857.81 should appear on the calculator display.

On many calculators, this value will be preceded by a minus sign, which is a way of differentiating cash inflows from outflows. *For our purposes, this sign can be ignored.*

To calculate the yearly savings (the amount of an annuity), let's continue with the example on page 49. This time, you're given the interest rate of 10 percent, the number of periods is 6, and the future value is $26,140. Your job is to solve the equation for the annuity. The steps using the calculator are:

1. Punch in 6 and press **N**.
2. Punch in 10 and press **I**.
3. Punch in 26140 and press **FV**.
4. To calculate the yearly payment or annuity, press **CPT** and then **PMT**.

The annuity of 3,387.94 should appear on the calculator display. Again, *a negative sign can be ignored.*

A similar procedure is used to find present value of a future sum or an annuity, except you would input the **FV** or **PMT** and press **CPT** and then **PV** to calculate the desired result. To find the equal annual future withdrawals from an initial deposit, the **PV** would be input and you would solve for the **PMT** by pressing **CPT** and then **PMT**.

CONCEPT CHECK

2-5. Why is it important to use time value of money concepts in setting personal financial goals?

2-6. What is *compounding?* Explain the *rule of 72.*

2-7. When might you use future value? Present value? Give specific examples.

The Balance Sheet: A Statement of Your Financial Condition [LG3]

The *balance sheet, or statement of financial position,* summarizes a person's (or family's) financial condition at a certain point in time. Think of a balance sheet as a snapshot taken of a person's financial position on one day out of the year. A balance sheet represents a summary of what you own—your *assets*—balanced against what you owe—your *liabilities*, or debts—and what you are worth—your *net worth*. The accounting relationship among these three categories is called the *balance sheet equation* and is expressed as follows:

$$\text{Total assets} = \text{Total liabilities} + \text{Net worth}$$

or

$$\text{Net worth} = \text{Total assets} - \text{Total liabilities}$$

ASSETS: THE THINGS YOU OWN

assets
Items that one owns.

Assets are the items you own. An item is classified as an asset regardless of whether it was purchased for cash or financed with debt. In other words, even if you haven't fully paid for an asset, you should list it on the balance sheet. An item that is leased, in contrast, is not shown as an asset, because someone else actually owns it.

A useful way to group assets is on the basis of their underlying characteristics and uses. This results in four broad categories: liquid assets, investments, real property, and personal property. About a third of the average household's assets consists of *financial assets* (liquid assets and investments); nearly half is real property (including housing); and the rest is other nonfinancial assets. Worksheet 2.2 lists the typical assets you'd find on a personal balance sheet.

fair market value
The actual value of an asset, or the price that it can reasonably be expected to sell for in the open market.

All assets, regardless of category, are recorded on the balance sheet at their current **fair market value**, which may differ considerably from their original purchase price. Fair market value is either the actual value of the asset (such as money in a checking account) or the price that the asset can reasonably be expected to sell for in the open market (like a used car or a home).

Those of you who have taken accounting will notice a difference between the way assets are recorded on a personal balance sheet. Under Generally Accepted Accounting Principles, the accounting profession's guiding rules, assets appear on a company's balance sheet at *cost*, not *fair market value*. One reason for the disparity is that in business, an asset's value is often subject to debate and uncertainty. The user of the statements may be an investor, and accountants like to be conservative in their measurement. For purposes of personal financial planning, the user and the preparer of the statement are one and the same. Besides, most personal assets have market values that can be easily estimated.

liquid assets
Assets that are held in the form of cash or can be readily converted to cash with little or no loss in value. They help to meet everyday needs of life and provide for emergencies and unexpected opportunities.

LIQUID ASSETS. **Liquid assets** are low-risk financial assets held in the form of cash or instruments that can readily be converted to cash with little or no loss in value. They help us meet the everyday needs of life and provide for emergencies and unexpected opportunities. We can hold cash as either *cash on hand* or in a *demand deposit* (checking account). Savings are also part of one's liquid assets, and include such financial instruments as *time deposits* (savings accounts), money market deposit accounts, money market mutual funds, or certificates of deposit that mature within 1 year.

investments
Assets such as stocks, bonds, mutual funds, and real estate that are acquired for the purpose of earning a return rather than providing a service.

INVESTMENTS. **Investments** are assets acquired to earn a return rather than provide a service. These assets, which typically consist largely of intangible *financial assets* (stocks, bonds, and other types of securities), tend to be held for the anticipated future benefit they offer. Popular investment assets include common and preferred stocks and corporate, government, and municipal bonds. Certificates of deposit with maturities of greater than 1 year, shares of mutual funds, and real estate are also popular investments. Business ownership, the cash value of life insurance and pensions, retirement funds such as IRAs and 401(k) plans, and other investment vehicles such as commodities, financial futures, and options represent still other forms of investment assets. (With regard to retirement fund accounts, *only those balances that are eligible to be withdrawn should be shown as an asset on the balance sheet.*) Investment assets are typically acquired to achieve long-run personal financial goals. They vary in marketability (the ability to sell quickly) from high (stocks and bonds) to low (real estate and business ownership investments).

REAL AND PERSONAL PROPERTY. Real and personal property are categories of tangible assets that we use in our everyday lives to provide support for our activities. **Real property** refers to immovable property: land and anything fixed to it, such as a house. Real property generally has a relatively long life and high cost, and it may *appreciate*, or increase in value. **Personal property** is movable property, such as automobiles, recreational equipment, household furnishings and appliances, clothing, jewelry, home electronics, and similar items. Except for some kinds of older collectible cars, and perhaps jewelry and artwork, most types of personal property *depreciate*, or decline in value, shortly after being put into use. In fact, the resale value of clothing and furniture quickly drops to a fraction of their original cost.

LIABILITIES: THE MONEY YOU OWE

Liabilities represent an individual's or family's debts. They could result from department store charges, bank credit card charges, installment loans, or mortgages on housing and other real estate. A given liability, regardless of its source, is something you owe and must repay in the future.

Liabilities are generally classified as either current or long term. A **current**, or **short-term**, **liability** is any debt due within 1 year of the date of the balance sheet. A **long-term liability** is a debt due 1 year or more from the date of the balance sheet. Lenders evaluate a prospective borrower's liabilities carefully. Very high levels of debt and overdue debts are both viewed with a great deal of disfavor. On Worksheet 2.2, you'll find the most common categories of liabilities.

CURRENT LIABILITIES. One type of current liability arises from charges for the purchase of consumable goods and services. Utility bills, rent, insurance premiums, taxes, medical bills, repair bills, and all similar debts fall into this category. Typically, you must pay these bills in full upon receipt or by a specified date, usually within one month of the billing date. Include these bills as liabilities only if you owe the funds now (an unpaid bill). Do not include something you may owe in the future, such as next month's utility bill.

A second type of current liability is **open account credit obligations**—the balances outstanding against established credit lines, with which you purchase various types of goods and services. For most people, such credit means the use of "plastic"—that is, a credit card. The balances on some credit cards (like bank and department store credit cards) can be paid off over time with small "minimum payments"; others, however, like gas or most travel and entertainment cards (American Express, for example), require payment in full upon receipt of the monthly statement.

Another type of open account credit is the *line of credit* offered by most banking institutions, which provides an authorized amount of credit. Rather than use a credit card, you access the line of credit by writing a check against either your regular checking account or a special credit line set up at your bank or financial institution. The amount of the liability on open account credit obligations is the *total balance outstanding*, not the monthly payment; the outstanding balance will be printed on your monthly statement.

LONG-TERM LIABILITIES. Debt obligations with final repayment dates more than 1 year from the date of the balance sheet are classified as *long-term liabilities*. They typically

real property
Tangible assets that are immovable, such as land and anything fixed to it, such as a house. It generally has a relatively long life and high cost.

personal property
Tangible assets that are movable and used to provide the general comforts of life; includes automobiles, household furnishings, and jewelry.

liabilities
Debts, such as credit card charges, installment loans, and real estate mortgages.

current (short-term) liability
Any debt due within 1 year of the date of the balance sheet.

long-term liability
Any debt due 1 year or more from the date of the balance sheet.

open account credit obligations
Current liabilities that represent the balances outstanding against established credit lines, which are used to purchase various types of goods and services.

include real estate mortgages, most consumer installment loans, education loans, and margin loans used to purchase securities.

Real estate mortgages are loans associated with housing and other real estate purchases; they normally have lives of 15 years or more. They most commonly result from the purchase of a home, but sometimes arise from real estate investments such as apartments or office buildings. Real estate mortgages are normally paid on an installment basis.

Consumer installment loans include all debts (other than mortgages) for which a series of payments is required over a specified period. Installment loans generally finance such purchases as automobiles, appliances, furniture, and boats. Other types of long-term liabilities include single-payment bank loans, education loans, and margin loans on securities.

You must show all types of loans on your balance sheet. Although most loans will fall into the category of long-term liabilities, *any loans that come due within a year should be shown as current liabilities.* Examples of such short-term loans include a 6-month, single-payment bank loan and a 9-month consumer installment loan for a refrigerator.

Regardless of the type of loan, *only the latest outstanding loan balance should be shown as a liability on the balance sheet,* because at any given point in time it is the balance still due—not the initial loan balance—that matters. Another important and closely related point is that *only the principal portion of a loan or mortgage should be listed as a liability on the balance sheet.* In other words, you should not include the interest portion of your payments as part of your balance sheet debt. The principal actually defines the amount of debt you owe at a given point in time and does not include any future interest payments.

NET WORTH: A MEASURE OF YOUR FINANCIAL WORTH

Net worth is the amount of actual wealth or **equity** an individual or family has in owned assets. It is the amount of money that would remain after selling all owned assets at their estimated fair market values and paying off all liabilities (assuming there are no transaction costs). As noted earlier, every balance sheet must "balance" so that total assets equal total liabilities plus net worth. Rearranging this equation, we see that net worth equals total assets minus total liabilities. Once you establish the fair market value of assets and the level of liabilities, you can easily calculate net worth by subtracting total liabilities from total assets. If net worth is less than zero, the family is *technically insolvent.* Although this form of **insolvency** does not mean that the family will end up in bankruptcy proceedings, it does reflect the absence of adequate financial planning.

Net worth typically increases over the life cycle of an individual or family, as Exhibit 2.4 illustrates. For example, the balance sheet of a college student will probably be fairly simple. Assets would include modest liquid assets (cash, checking and savings accounts) and personal property, which may include a car. Liabilities might include utility bills, perhaps some open account credit obligations, and automobile and education loans. At this point in life, net worth would typically be very low, because assets are small in comparison with liabilities. A 29-year-old, single school teacher would have more liquid assets and personal property, may have started an investment program, and may have purchased a condominium. Net worth would be rising but may still be low due to the increased liabilities associated with real and personal property purchases. The higher net worth of a two-career couple in their late 30s with children would reflect a greater proportion of assets relative to liabilities as they save for college expenses and retirement.

In the long-term financial planning process, the level of net worth is important. Once you have established a goal of accumulating a certain level or type of wealth, you can track progress toward that goal by monitoring net worth.

real estate mortgages
Loans associated with housing and other real estate purchases; they normally have lives of 15 years or more.

consumer installment loans
Loans (other than mortgages) for which a series of payments is required over a specified period.

net worth
An individual's or family's actual wealth; determined by subtracting total liabilities from total assets.

equity
The actual ownership interest in a specific asset or group of assets.

insolvency
The financial state in which net worth is less than zero.

EXHIBIT 2.4

MEDIAN NET WORTH AND INCOME BY AGE

While net income peaks in the 35–54 age brackets, net worth continues to climb until age 65 and beyond.

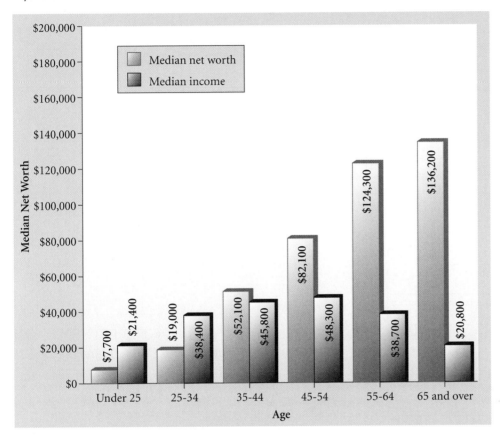

Source: Walter Updegrave, "How Are You Doing?" *Money*, July 1999, p. 66.

BALANCE SHEET FORMAT AND PREPARATION

Worksheet 2.2 presents a hypothetical balance sheet prepared for Tim and Andrea Shepard, the young couple we met in Chapter 1, on December 31, 2001. Assets are listed on the left side, the most liquid first, and liabilities on the right, starting with the most recent. The net worth entry is shown on the right side of the statement just below the liabilities. The statement should *balance*: Total assets equal the sum of total liabilities and net worth, as shown in the balance sheet equation.

You should prepare your personal balance sheet at least once a year, preferably every 3 to 6 months. Begin by listing your assets at their fair market value as of the date you are preparing the balance sheet, using the categories in Worksheet 2.2 as a guide. To determine the fair market value of liquid and financial assets, use checking and savings account records and investment account statements. The values of homes and cars are easier to estimate using published sources of information, such as advertisements for comparable homes and the *Kelley Blue Book* for used car values. Certain items—for example, homes, jewelry, and

WORKSHEET 2.2

BALANCE SHEET FOR TIM AND ANDREA SHEPARD

A balance sheet is set up to show what you owe on one side (your assets) and how you paid for them on the other (debt or net worth). As you can see, the Shepards have more assets than liabilities.

BALANCE SHEET

Name(s) ___Tim and Andrea Shepard___ Dated ___December 31, 2001___

ASSETS			LIABILITIES AND NET WORTH		
Liquid Assets			**Current Liabilities**		
Cash on hand	$	90	Utilities	$	120
In checking		575	Rent		
Savings accounts		760	Insurance premiums		
Money market funds and deposits		800	Taxes		
Certificates of deposit (<1 yr. to maturity)			Medical/dental bills		75
			Repair bills		
			Bank credit card balances		395
Total Liquid Assets	$	2,225	Dept. store credit card balances		145
			Travel and entertainment card balances		125
Investments			Gas and other credit card balances		
Stocks	$	1,250	Bank line of credit balances		
Bonds Corp.		1,000	Other current liabilities		45
Certificates of deposit (>1 yr. to maturity)			**Total Current Liabilities**	$	905
Mutual funds		1,500	**Long-Term Liabilities**		
Real estate			Primary residence mortgage	$	92,000
Retirement funds, IRA		2,000	Second home mortgage		
Other			Real estate investment mortgage		
Total Investments	$	5,750	Auto loans		4,250
			Appliance/furniture loans		800
Real Property			Home improvement loans		
Primary residence	$	120,000	Single-payment loans		
Second home			Education loans		3,800
Other			Margin loans used to purchase securities		
Total Real Property	$	120,000	Other long-term loans (from parents)		4,000
Personal Property			**Total Long-Term Liabilities**	$	104,850
Auto(s): '99 Toyota Corolla	$	9,500			
Auto(s): '96 Ford Escort		4,500	**(II) Total Liabilities**	$	105,755
Recreational vehicles					
Household furnishing		3,700			
Jewelry and artwork		1,500	**Net Worth [(I) - (II)]**	$	41,420
Other					
Other					
Total Personal Property	$	19,200			
(I)Total Assets	$	147,175	**Total Liabilities and Net Worth**	$	147,175

artwork—may appreciate, or increase in value, over time. The values of other assets, like cars and most other types of personal property, depreciate, or decrease in value, over time.

 What's the fair market value of your car? The silver tea set you inherited from your grandmother? Find out at www.bluebook.com.

Next, list all current and long-term liabilities, using the categories in Worksheet 2.2 as a starting point. Show all outstanding charges, *even if you have not received the bill,* as current liabilities on the balance sheet. For example, assume that on June 23 you used your Visa card to charge $240 for a set of tires. You typically receive your Visa bill around the tenth of the following month. If you were preparing a balance sheet dated June 30, you should include the $240 as a current liability, even though the bill won't arrive until July 10. Remember to list only the principal balance of any loan obligation.

The final step in preparing your balance sheet is to calculate net worth: Subtract your total liabilities from your total assets. This is your net worth, which reflects the equity you have in your assets.

A BALANCE SHEET FOR TIM AND ANDREA SHEPARD

The relationship between assets, liabilities, and net worth and the general format of the balance sheet is perhaps best illustrated with an example. Toward that end, let's examine Tim and Andrea Shepard's balance sheet as of December 31, 2001, shown in Worksheet 2.2.

Given their ages, the Shepards' asset position looks quite good. Their dominant asset is their condo. They also have $5,750 in investments and retirement funds and appear to have adequate liquid assets to meet their bill payments and cover small, unexpected expenses. But we can't accurately measure their financial position without examining their debts.

The Shepards' primary liability is the $92,000 mortgage on their condo. Their equity, or actual ownership interest, in the condo is approximately $28,000 ($120,000 market value minus $92,000 outstanding mortgage loan). Their current liabilities, most of which must be paid over the next month, total $905. Other debts total $12,850 and include auto, furniture, and education loans, plus a personal loan from their parents that was used as part of the down payment on their home. Comparing the Shepards' total liabilities of $105,755 to their total assets of $147,175 provides a more realistic view of their current wealth position.

The Shepards' net worth (from Worksheet 2.2) is $41,420—a respectable figure considering their ages. By calculating their net worth at specified points in time, they can measure how their financial plans and decisions affect their wealth position. As you'd expect, a large or increasing wealth position is preferable to a low or declining one.

CONCEPT CHECK

2-8. Describe the balance sheet, its components, and how you would use it in personal financial planning. Differentiate between investments and real and personal property.

2-9. What is the balance sheet equation? Explain when a family may be viewed as technically insolvent.

2-10. Explain two ways in which net worth could increase (or decrease) from one period to the next.

The Income and Expense Statement: Measuring Your Financial Performance [LG4]

Whereas the balance sheet describes a person's or family's financial position at a given point in time, the *income and expense statement* captures the various financial activities that have occurred over time—normally over the course of a year, although it technically can cover any time period (monthly, quarterly, and so on). Think of this statement as a motion picture that not only shows actual results over time but allows for their comparison with budgeted financial goals as well. Equally important, the statement evaluates the amount of saving and investing that has taken place during the period covered.

The income and expense statement has three major parts: *income*, *expenses*, and *cash surplus* (or *deficit*). A cash surplus (or deficit) is merely the difference between income and expenses. The statement is prepared on a **cash basis**, which means that *only transactions involving actual cash receipts or actual cash outlays are recorded*. The term *cash* is used in this case to include not only coin and currency but also checks drawn against demand deposits and certain types of savings accounts.

Income and expense patterns change depending on where an individual or a family is in its life cycle. Income and spending levels rise steadily to a peak in the 45–54 age bracket. On average, persons in this age group, whose children are typically in college or no longer at home, generally have the highest level of income. They also spend more than other age groups on entertainment, dining out, transportation, education, insurance, and charitable contributions. Families in the 35–44 age bracket have slightly lower average levels of income and expenses but very different spending patterns. Because they tend to have school-age children, they spend more on groceries, housing, clothing, and other personal needs. The average percentage of income spent, however, is about the same: 85 to 87 percent for all age brackets through age 55, when it drops slightly to 82 percent. It rises sharply to 98 percent, however, for persons age 65 and over.

INCOME: CASH IN

Common sources of **income** include earnings received as wages, salaries, self-employment income, bonuses, and commissions; interest and dividends received from savings and investments; and proceeds from the sale of assets, such as stocks and bonds or an auto. Other income items include pension or annuity income; rent received from leased assets; alimony and child support; scholarships, grants, and social security received; tax refunds; and miscellaneous types of income. Worksheet 2.3 has general categories to record your income.

Note also that the proper figure to use is *gross* wages, salaries, and commissions, which constitute the amount of income you receive from your employer *before* taxes and other payroll deductions. The gross value is used because the taxes and payroll deductions will be itemized and deducted as expenses later in the income and expense statements. Therefore, you should not use *take-home* pay, because it will understate your income by the amount of these deductions.

EXPENSES: CASH OUT

Expenses represent money used for outlays. Because there are many different kinds of expenses, it is perhaps easiest to categorize them by the types of benefits they provide, as shown in Worksheet 2.3: (1) living expenses (such as housing, utilities, food, transportation, medical, and insurance); (2) asset purchases (like autos, stereos, furniture, appliances,

---

cash basis
A method of preparing financial statements in which only cash income and cash expenses are recorded.

income
Earnings received as wages, salaries, self-employment income, bonuses, and commissions; interest and dividends received from savings and investments; and proceeds from the sale of assets.

expenses
Money spent on living expenses and to purchase assets, pay taxes, or repay debt.

EXHIBIT 2.5

HOW WE SPEND OUR INCOME

Just three categories account for almost two-thirds of spent after-tax income: food, housing, and transportation.

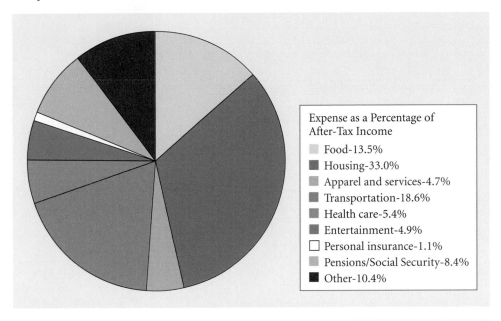

Expense as a Percentage of After-Tax Income

- Food-13.5%
- Housing-33.0%
- Apparel and services-4.7%
- Transportation-18.6%
- Health care-5.4%
- Entertainment-4.9%
- Personal insurance-1.1%
- Pensions/Social Security-8.4%
- Other-10.4%

Source: "Consumer Expenditures in 1998," Washington D.C.: U.S. Department of Labor, Bureau of Labor Statistics Report 940, February 2000, p. 4.

and clothing); (3) tax payments; and (4) debt payments (on mortgages, installment loans, credit cards, and so on). Some are **fixed expenses**, which are usually contractual, predetermined, and involve equal payments each period (typically each month). Examples include mortgage and installment loan payments, insurance premiums, professional or union dues, club dues, monthly savings or investment programs, and cable television fees. Others (such as food, clothing, utilities, entertainment, and medical expenses) are **variable expenses**, because their amounts vary from period to period.

Exhibit 2.5 shows the average annual expenses by major category as a percentage of after-tax income. It provides a useful benchmark to see how you compare with national averages. However, your own expenses will vary according to your age, lifestyle, and where you live. For example, it costs considerably more to buy a home in San Diego than in Indianapolis. If you live in the suburbs, your commuting expenses will be higher than for city dwellers.

Just as you show only the amounts of cash actually received as income, record only the amounts of money you actually pay out in cash as expenses. If you borrow to acquire an item, particularly an asset, you include only the *actual cash payment—purchase price minus amount borrowed*—as an expense, as well as *payments on the loan* in the period you actually make them. You show credit purchases of this type as an asset and corresponding liability *on the balance sheet*. Record only the cash payments on loans, not the actual amounts of the loans themselves, on the income and expense statement.

fixed expenses
Expenses involving equal payments each period (typically each month).

variable expenses
Expenses that involve payments of varying amounts from one time period to the next.

INCOME AND EXPENSE STATEMENT FOR TIM AND ANDREA SHEPARD

The income and expense statement essentially shows what you earned, how you spent your money, and how much you were left with (or, if you spent more than you took in, how much you went "in the hole").

INCOME AND EXPENSE STATEMENT

Name(s) _Tim and Andrea Shepard_

For the _Year_ Ending _December 31, 2001_

INCOME

Wages and salaries	Name: Tim Shepard	$	55,000
	Name: Andrea Shepard		15,450
	Name:		
Self-employment income			
Bonuses and commissions	Tim-sales commissions		2,275
Pensions and annuities			
Investment income	Interest received		195
	Dividends received		120
	Rents received		
	Sale of securities		
	Other		
Other income			
	(I) Total Income	$	73,040

EXPENSES

Housing	Rent/mortgage payment (include insurance and taxes, if applicable)	$	16,864
	Repairs, maintenance, improvements		1,050
Utilities	Gas, electric, water		1,750
	Phone		480
	Cable TV and other		240
Food	Groceries		2,425
	Dining out		3,400
Transportation	Auto loan payments		2,520
	License plates, fees, etc.		250
	Gas, oil, repairs, tires, maintenance		2,015
Medical	Health, major medical, disability insurance (payroll deductions or not provided by employer)		1,200
	Doctor, dentist, hospital, medicines		305
Clothing	Clothes, shoes, and accessories		1,700
Insurance	Homeowner's (if not covered by mortgage payment)		425
	Life (not provided by employer)		260
	Auto		695
Taxes	Income and social security		15,430
	Property (if not included in mortgage)		1,000
Appliances, furniture, and other major purchases	Loan payments		800
	Purchases and repairs		450
Personal care	Laundry, cosmetics, hair care		700
Recreation and entertainment	Vacations		2,000
	Other recreation and entertainment		2,630
Other items	Tuition and books: Andrea		1,400
	Gifts		215
	Loan payments: Education loans		900
	Loan payments: Parents		600
	(II) Total Expenses	$	61,704
	CASH SURPLUS (OR DEFICIT) [(I)-(II)]	$	11,336

For example, assume you purchase a new car for $15,000 in September. You make a down payment of $3,000 and finance the remaining $12,000 with a 4-year, 10.5 percent installment loan. Your September 30 income statement would show a cash expenditure of $3,000, and each subsequent monthly income statement would include your monthly loan payment of $307. Your September 30 balance sheet would show the car as an asset valued at $15,000 and the loan balance as a $12,000 long-term liability. The market value of the car and the loan balance would be adjusted on future balance sheets.

Finally, when developing your list of expenses for the year, remember to include the amount of income tax and social security taxes withheld from your paycheck, and any other payroll deductions, such as health insurance, savings plans, retirement and pension contributions, and professional/union dues. These deductions (from gross wages, salaries, bonuses, and commissions) represent personal expenses, even if they do not involve the direct payment of cash.

You might be shocked when you make a list of what is taken out of your paycheck. Even if you're in a fairly low federal income tax bracket, your paycheck could easily be reduced by more than 40 percent for taxes alone. Your federal tax could be withheld at 28 percent, your state income tax could be withheld at 9 percent, and your social security tax could be withheld at 7 percent. That doesn't even count health and disability income insurance.

CASH SURPLUS (OR DEFICIT)

The third component of the income and expense statement shows the net result of the period's financial activities. Subtracting total expenses from total income gives you the cash surplus (or deficit) for the period. At a glance, you can see how you did financially over the period. A positive figure indicates that expenses were less than income, resulting in a **cash surplus**. A value of zero indicates that expenses were exactly equal to income for the period, while a negative value means that your expenses exceeded income and you have a **cash deficit**.

cash surplus
An excess amount of income over expenses that can be used for savings or investments, to acquire assets, or to reduce debt. Results in increased net worth.

You can use a cash surplus for savings or investment purposes, to acquire assets, or to reduce debt. Adding to savings or investments should increase your future income and net worth, and making payments on debt affects cash flow favorably by reducing future expenses. In contrast, when a cash deficit occurs, you must cover the shortfall from your savings or investments, reduce assets, or borrow. All of these strategies will have undesirable effects on your financial future.

One final point: a cash surplus does not necessarily mean that funds are simply lying around waiting to be used. Because the income and expense statement reflects what has actually occurred, the disposition of the surplus (or deficit) is reflected in the asset, liability, and net worth accounts on the balance sheet. For example, if you used the surplus to make investments, this would increase the appropriate asset account. If it were used to pay off a loan, the payment would reduce that liability account. Of course, if you used the surplus to increase cash balances, you'd have the funds to use. In each case, your net worth *increases*. Whereas surpluses *add* to net worth, deficits *reduce* it, whether the shortfall is financed by reducing an asset (for example, drawing down a savings account) or by borrowing.

cash deficit
An excess amount of expenses over income resulting in insufficient funds that must be made up by drawing down savings or investments, reducing assets, or borrowing. Results in decreased net worth.

PREPARING THE INCOME AND EXPENSE STATEMENT

As shown in Worksheet 2.3, the income and expense statement is dated to define the period covered. The first step in preparing the statement is to determine your income from all sources for the chosen period. Although you probably have a very good idea of your salary, you can look at your check stubs to verify your gross pay for the period. Do not overlook bonuses, commission checks, and overtime pay. Check your bank and investment account statements for information on interest earned, securities bought and sold, interest and dividends received, and other investment matters. You should also keep a running list of other income sources, such as rents, tax refunds, and asset sales.

Next, establish meaningful expenses categories, such as those shown on Worksheet 2.3, breaking down fixed and variable expenses. Information on monthly house (or rent) payments, loan payments, and other fixed payments (such as insurance premiums and cable TV), is readily available from either the payment book or your checkbook (or, in the case of payroll deductions, your check stubs). (*Note:* Be careful with so-called *adjustable-rate loans,* because the amount of monthly loan payments will change when the interest rate changes.) You will probably pay for most major variable expenses by check, debit card, or credit card, so it's easy to keep track of them.

It's more difficult to keep tabs on all the items in a month that you pay with cash, like parking, lunches, movies, and incidentals. Most of us don't care to write down every little expense to the penny. You might try counting the cash in your wallet at the beginning of the month, then count again after a week goes by to see how much money is missing. Try to reconstruct in your mind what you spent during the week, and write it down on your calendar to the nearest $5. If you can't remember, then try the exercise over shorter and shorter periods until you can.

The final step is to subtract total expenses from total income to get the cash surplus (a positive number) or deficit (a negative number). This "bottom line" summarizes the *net cash flow* resulting from your financial activities during the designated period.

Preparing income and expense statements can involve a lot of number crunching. Fortunately, a number of good computer software packages, such as *Quicken* and *Microsoft Money*, can simplify the job of preparing personal financial statements and doing other personal financial planning tasks.

AN INCOME AND EXPENSE STATEMENT FOR TIM AND ANDREA SHEPARD

Tim and Andrea Shepard's income and expense statement for the year ended December 31, 2001, provided in Worksheet 2.3, illustrates the relationship among total income, total expenses, and cash surplus (or deficit). This statement was prepared using the background material presented earlier, along with the Shepards' balance sheet (Worksheet 2.2).

Tim's wages clearly represent the family's chief source of income, although Andrea has finished her MBA and will now be making a major contribution. Other sources of income include $195 in interest on their savings accounts and bond investments and $120 in dividends from their common stock holdings. The Shepards' total income for the year ended December 31, 2001, amounts to $73,040.

The Shepards' major expenses are their home mortgage, food, auto loan, clothing, and income and social security taxes. Other sizable expenses during the year include home repairs and additions, gas and electricity, auto license and operating expenses, insurance, tuition, and education loan payments. Total expenses for the year were $61,704.

The Shepards end the year with a cash surplus of $11,336 (total income of $73,040 minus total expenses of $61,704). This surplus could be used to increase savings, invest in stocks, bonds, or other vehicles, or make payments on some outstanding debts. The best strategy depends on their financial goals. If they had a cash deficit, the Shepards would have to withdraw savings, liquidate investments, or borrow an amount equal to the deficit to meet their financial commitments (that is, "make ends meet"). With their surplus of $11,336, the Shepards have made a positive contribution to their net worth.

CONCEPT CHECK

> 2-11. What is an *income and expense statement?* What role does it serve in personal financial planning? Name its three components, some major sources of income, and the four basic types of expenses.
>
> 2-12. Explain what *cash basis* means in the following statement: "An income and expense statement should be prepared on a cash basis." How and where are credit purchases shown when statements are prepared on a cash basis?
>
> 2-13. Distinguish between fixed and variable expenses, and give examples of each.
>
> 2-14. Is it possible to have a cash deficit on an income and expense statement? If so, how?

■ Using Your Personal Financial Statements [LG5]

Your balance sheet and income and expense statement provide the information you need to examine your financial position, monitor your financial activities, and track the progress you're making toward achieving your financial goals. Very likely, your financial statements are like those of most other people—not a lot of substance, perhaps, but certainly no shortage of potential. Regardless of the particulars surrounding your situation, having a thorough understanding of your current financial status will enable you to better direct your financial plans and activities toward reaching your personal financial goals.

KEEPING GOOD RECORDS

Although record keeping doesn't rank high on most "to do" lists, a good record-keeping system helps you manage and control your personal financial affairs. With organized, up-to-date financial records, you'll prepare more accurate personal financial statements and budgets, pay less to your tax preparer, not miss any tax deductions, and save taxes when you sell a house or securities or withdraw retirement funds. Also, good records make it easier for a spouse or relative to manage your financial affairs in an emergency. To that end, you should prepare a comprehensive list of these records, their locations, and your key advisors (financial planner, banker, accountant, attorney, doctors) for family members.

Prepare your personal financial statements at least once each year, ideally when you draw up your budget. Many people update their financial statements every 3 or 6 months. You may want to keep a *ledger*, or financial record book, to summarize all your financial transactions. The ledger has sections for assets, liabilities, sources of income, and expenses; these sections contain separate accounts for each item. Whenever any accounts change, make an appropriate ledger entry. For example, if you buy a DVD player for $300 cash, you'd show the DVD player on your balance sheet as an asset (at its fair market value) and as a $300 expenditure on your income and expense statement. If you borrowed to pay for the DVD player, the loan amount would be a liability on the balance sheet and any loan payments made during the period would be shown on the income and expense statement. You'd keep similar records for asset sales, loan repayments, income sources, and so on.

ORGANIZING YOUR RECORDS. Your system doesn't have to be fancy to be effective. You'll need a bank safe-deposit box, the ledger book described earlier, and a set of files with general categories, such as banking and credit cards, taxes, home, insurance, investments, and retirement accounts. An expandable file, with a dozen or so compartments for incoming bills, receipts, pay stubs, or anything you might need later, works well.

Start by taking an inventory. Make a list of everything you own and owe. Check it at least once a year to make sure it's up to date and to review your financial progress. Then record transactions manually in your ledger or with financial planning software.

Tax planning records for income (paycheck stubs, interest on savings accounts, and so on) and deductions need separate files, as do individual mutual fund and brokerage account records. Hard-to-replace records go in the safe-deposit box, with photocopies and a list of what's in the box at home. These include securities certificates; home deed and purchase and sale documents on all homes owned; birth, adoption, and marriage certificates; divorce, alimony, and custody records; military service records; and powers of attorney. Written inventories, appraisals, and photos or videos of your home and its contents also belong in your safe-deposit box, to verify their existence and condition in event of damage. Once you set up your files, be sure to go through them at least once a year and throw out unnecessary items.

TYPES OF RECORDS TO KEEP. Here are some guidelines for the types of records to keep, and how long to retain them.

Banking and Credit Cards. Keep a list of bank accounts and 1 year's account statements, and a list of credit card numbers in case your cards are lost or stolen. Credit card statements help track expenses, but toss them after a year unless you need them for tax purposes. Retain any loan agreements, purchase slips, and billing statements until the debts are paid off. Save checks written for major purchases, disputed transactions, and those relating to legal matters indefinitely.

Taxes. The better your income and deduction files, the easier it is to prepare your tax returns. Save time each month by filing checks and receipts that relate to tax deductions or major purchases in appropriate folders, like charitable contributions, medical expenses, or home improvements. Keep returns with supporting documentation for the current year plus the past 6 years, the maximum time for IRS audits unless fraud is suspected. After 6 years, it's generally safe to discard tax-supporting documents. Some financial planners suggest keeping old returns (without backup records) as reminders of past financial actions.

Home. In addition to deeds and purchase and sale documents on all homes you've owned, document major home improvement expenses. These expenses increase the cost of your home for tax purposes and reduce the gain on its sale, particularly if the gain is in excess of the allowable exemption (described in Chapter 3). Keep home-related documents at least 3 years after the due date of the tax return in which you report the sale, the period the IRS has to challenge your return.

Insurance. Keep current policies and discard expired ones unless you think there may be a claim later. Put a list of policies and insurance agents in your safe-deposit box.

Investment and Retirement Accounts. Designate a folder for each mutual fund, partnership investment, or brokerage account. Keep security purchase and sale confirmations, dividend reinvestment notices, and records of stock splits for at least 3 years after you sell a security; these records will document the information you provided on tax forms. Toss monthly mutual fund and brokerage statements if your year-end statements are cumulative. Keep retirement fund records (pension plans, IRAs, and so on) indefinitely to know which portions of them are tax-deferred and therefore not subject to tax until funds are withdrawn.

Trusts and Wills. Trust agreements and wills should not go in your safe-deposit box because it may be sealed at death, making the information unavailable to your heirs. Keep copies at home and give the original to your attorney. Destroy prior wills; they may cause later confusion and disputes.

Other Records. Keep product warranties until they expire. In case of emergency, you should have photos and fingerprints of your children. Medical records are also good to keep.

TRACKING FINANCIAL PROGRESS: RATIO ANALYSIS

Each time you prepare your financial statements, you should analyze them to see how well you are doing in light of your financial goals. For example, with an income and expense statement, you can compare actual financial results with budgeted figures to make sure your spending is under control. Likewise, comparing a set of financial plans with a balance sheet will reveal whether you are meeting your savings and investment goals, reducing your debt, or building up a retirement reserve. You can compare current performance with historical performance to find out if your financial situation is improving or getting worse.

Calculating certain financial ratios can help you evaluate your financial performance over time. Moreover, if you apply for a loan, the lender probably will look at these ratios to judge your ability to carry additional debt. Four important money management ratios are the (1) solvency ratio, (2) liquidity ratio, (3) savings ratio, and (4) debt service ratio. The first two are associated primarily with the balance sheet, while the last two relate primarily to the income and expense statement.

BALANCE SHEET RATIOS.

When evaluating your balance sheet, you should be most concerned with your net worth at a given point in time. As explained earlier in this chapter, you are *technically insolvent* when your total liabilities exceed your total assets—that is, when you have a negative net worth. The **solvency ratio** shows, as a percentage, your degree of exposure to insolvency, or how much "cushion" you have as a protection against insolvency. It is calculated as follows:

solvency ratio
Total net worth divided by total assets; measures the degree of exposure to insolvency.

$$\text{Solvency ratio} = \frac{\text{Total net worth}}{\text{Total assets}}$$

Using data from Worksheet 2.2, the Shepards' solvency ratio in 2001 is:

$$\frac{\$41,420}{\$147,175} = 0.28, \text{ or } 28 \text{ percent}$$

This tells us that Tim and Andrea could withstand only about a 27 percent decline in the market value of their assets before they would be insolvent. The low value for this ratio suggests they should consider improving it in the future.

Although the solvency ratio gives an indication of the potential to withstand financial problems, it does not deal directly with the ability to pay current debts. This issue is addressed with the **liquidity ratio**, which shows how long you could continue to pay current debts with existing liquid assets in event of income loss. It is calculated by dividing liquid assets by total current debts; "current" in this case means any bills or charges that must be paid *within 1 year*. The ratio is computed as follows:

liquidity ratio
Liquid assets divided by total current debts; measures ability to pay current debts.

$$\text{Liquidity ratio} = \frac{\text{Liquid assets}}{\text{Total current debts}}$$

The Shepards' liquid assets (see Worksheet 2.2) total $2,225. Their current liabilities of bills and open account credit balances total $905. The portions of their loan payments due within 1 year total $21,684 ($16,864 in mortgage payments + $2,520 in auto loan payments + $800 in furniture loan payments + $900 in education loan payments + $600 in loan payments to parents)—all found on the income and expense statement in Worksheet 2.3. Adding their total current liabilities ($905) to the current portion of their loans ($21,684) yields total current debts of $22,589. Thus, in 2001 the Shepards have a liquidity ratio of:

$$\frac{\$2,225}{\$22,589} = 0.10, \text{ or } 10 \text{ percent}$$

This ratio indicates that the Shepards can cover only about 10 percent of their existing 1-year debt obligations with their current liquid assets. In other words, they have slightly over 1 month (1 month is $\frac{1}{12}$, or 8.3 percent) of coverage. If an unexpected event curtailed their income, their liquid reserves would be exhausted very quickly. Although there is no hard and fast rule as to what this ratio should be, it seems low for the Shepards. They should consider strengthening it along with their solvency ratio. They should be able to add to their cash surpluses now that Andrea is working full-time.

The amount of liquid reserves will vary with your personal circumstances and "comfort level." Another useful liquidity guideline is to have a reserve fund equal to 3 to 6 months of after-tax income available to cover living expenses. The Shepards' after-tax income for 2001 was $4,801 per month ([$73,040 total income − $15,430 income and social security taxes] ÷ 12). Therefore, this guideline suggests they should have between $14,403 and $28,806 in liquid assets—considerably more than the $2,225 on their latest balance sheet. If you feel your job is secure or you have other potential sources of income, you may be comfortable with 3 or 4 months in reserve. If you tend to be very cautious financially, you may want to build a larger fund. In troubled economic times, you may want to keep 6 months or more of income in this fund as protection should you lose your job.

INCOME AND EXPENSE STATEMENT RATIOS. When evaluating your income and expense statement, you should be concerned with the bottom line, which shows the cash surplus (or deficit) resulting from the period's activities. You can relate it to income by calculating a **savings ratio**, which is done most effectively with after-tax income, as follows:

savings ratio
Cash surplus divided by after-tax income; indicates relative amount of cash surplus achieved during a given period.

$$\text{Savings ratio} = \frac{\text{Cash surplus}}{\text{Income after taxes}}$$

Using data from Worksheet 2.3, the Shepards savings ratio in 2001 is

$$\frac{\$11,336}{\$73,040 - \$15,430} = \frac{\$11,336}{\$57,610} = 0.197, \text{ or } 19.7 \text{ percent}$$

Tim and Andrea saved about 20 percent of their after-tax income, which is on the high side (American families, on average, normally save about 5 to 8 percent). How much to save is a personal choice. Some families would plan much higher levels, particularly if they are saving to achieve an important goal, such as buying a home.

While maintaining an adequate level of savings is obviously important to personal financial planning, so is the ability to pay debts promptly. In fact, debt payments have a higher priority. The **debt service ratio** allows you to make sure you can comfortably meet your debt obligations. It is calculated as follows:

debt service ratio
Total monthly loan payments divided by monthly gross (before-tax) income; provides a measure of ability to meet monthly debt obligations in a prompt and timely fashion.

$$\text{Debt service ratio} = \frac{\text{Total monthly loan payments}}{\text{Monthly gross (before-tax) income}}$$

This ratio excludes current liabilities and considers only mortgage, installment, and personal loan obligations. On an *annual* basis, the Shepards' obligations total $21,684 ($16,864 in mortgage payments, $2,520 in auto loan payments, $800 in furniture loan payments, $900 in education loan payments, and $600 in loan payments to parents, from Worksheet 2.3). The Shepards' total *monthly* loan payments are about $1,807 ($21,684 ÷ 12 months). Dividing the Shepards' *annual* gross income, also found in Worksheet 2.3, of $73,040 by 12 equals $6,087 monthly ($73,040 ÷ 12). The Shepards' debt service ratio in 2001 is calculated as follows:

$$\frac{\$1,807}{\$6,087} = 0.30, \text{ or 30 percent}$$

Monthly loan payments account for about 30 percent of Tim and Andrea's gross income. This relatively low debt service ratio indicates that the Shepards should have little difficulty in meeting their monthly loan payments. From a financial planning perspective, you should try to keep your debt service ratio somewhere under 35 percent or so, because that's generally viewed as a manageable level of debt—and, of course, the lower the debt service ratio, the easier it is to meet loan payments as they come due.

CONCEPT CHECK

2-15. How can accurate records and control procedures be used to ensure the effectiveness of the personal financial planning process?

2-16. Describe some of the areas or items you would consider when evaluating your balance sheet and income and expense statement. Cite several ratios that could help in this effort.

◼ Setting Up a Cash Budget [LG6]

Once you define your short-term financial goals, you can prepare a cash budget for the coming year. Recall that a *budget* is a short-term financial planning report that helps you achieve your short-term financial goals. By taking the time to evaluate your current financial situation, spending patterns, and goals, you can develop a realistic budget consistent with your personal lifestyle, family situation, and values. A cash budget is a valuable money-management tool that helps you:

1. Maintain the necessary information to monitor and control your finances
2. Decide how to allocate your income to reach your financial objectives
3. Implement a system of disciplined spending—as opposed to just existing from one paycheck to the next
4. Reduce needless spending so you can increase the funds allocated to savings and investments
5. Achieve your long-term financial goals

Just as your goals change over your lifetime, so will your budget. As you move through the life cycle, your financial situation will become increasingly more complex. Typically, the number of income and expense categories increases as you accumulate more assets and debts, and you have more family responsibilities. For example, the budget of a college student should be quite simple, with limited income from part-time jobs, parental

cash budget
A budget that takes into account estimated monthly cash receipts and cash expenses for the coming year.

contributions, and scholarships and grants. Expenses might include room and board, clothes, books, auto expenses, and entertainment. Once a student graduates and goes to work full time, his or her budget will cover additional expenses, such as rent, insurance, work clothes, and commuting costs. Not until retirement can you expect this process to perhaps begin to simplify.

THE BUDGETING PROCESS

Like the income and expense statement, *a budget should be prepared on a cash basis*; thus, we call this document a *cash budget*. A **cash budget** deals with cash receipts and cash expenses that are expected to occur in the coming year. It contains annual estimates of income and expenses, including savings and investments. It is usually divided into monthly intervals, although in some cases other time intervals may be more convenient.

The cash budget preparation process has three stages: estimating income, estimating expenses, and finalizing the cash budget. When estimating income and expenses, you should take into account any anticipated changes in the cost of living and their impact on your budget components. If your income is fixed—not expected to change over the budgetary period—increases in various items of expense will probably cause the purchasing power of your income to deteriorate. Worksheet 2.4, Annual Cash Budget by Month, has separate sections to record your income and expenses and lists the most common categories for each.

ESTIMATING INCOME. The first step in the cash budget preparation process is to estimate your income for the coming year. Because you receive and pay most bills monthly, it is best to estimate income as well as expenses on a monthly basis. The income forecast takes into consideration all income expected for the year: the take-home pay of both spouses, expected bonuses or commissions, pension or annuity income, and investment income—interest, dividend, rental, and asset (particularly security) sale income.

When estimating income, keep in mind that *any item you receive for which repayment is required is not considered income*. For instance, loan proceeds are treated not as a source of income but as a *liability* for which scheduled repayments are required.

Note also that, unlike the income and expense statement, *take-home pay* (rather than gross income) should generally be used in the cash budget. In a cash budget you want to direct your attention to those areas over which you have control—and most people effectively have limited control over things like taxes withheld, contributions to company insurance and pension plans, and the like. In effect, take-home pay represents the amount of *disposable income* you receive from your employer.

ESTIMATING EXPENSES. The second step in the cash budgeting process is by far the most difficult: preparing a schedule of estimated expenses for the coming year. This is usually done using actual expenses from previous years (as found on income and expense statements and in supporting information for those periods), along with predetermined short-term financial goals. Good financial records, as discussed earlier, make it easier to develop realistic expense estimates. If you do not have past expense data, you could re-examine old checkbook registers and credit card statements to approximate expenses, or take a "needs approach" and attach dollar values to projected expenses. Pay close attention to expenses associated with medical disabilities, divorce and child support, and similar special circumstances.

Regardless of whether you have historical information, you should *become aware of your expenditure patterns and how you spend money*. After tracking your expenses over

$ Financial Road Sign

Budget Basics
No one likes making a budget, so here are some helpful hints to get you going:
1. Use built-in budget-making tools in personal finance software like Quicken or Microsoft Money.
2. Don't get bogged down by details. Concentrate on categories where you can cut spending.
3. Watch for cash leakage. Keep records of what happens to ATM withdrawals.
4. If you spend more than you make, you're probably buying luxuries that you consider a need.
5. Spend no more than 90 percent of your income and save the rest.
6. Don't count on windfalls.
7. Beware of spending creep as your annual income climbs.

Source: adapted from "Money 101: Making a Budget: Top 10 Things to Know," *Money.com*, downloaded from **www.money.com**.

WORKSHEET 2.4

THE SHEPARDS' ANNUAL CASH BUDGET BY MONTH

The Shepards' cash budget summary shows several months in which substantial cash deficits are expected to occur; they can use this information to develop plans for covering these monthly shortfalls.

ANNUAL CASH BUDGET BY MONTH

Name(s) **Tim and Andrea Shepard**

For the **Year** Ending **December 31, 2002**

INCOME	Jan.	Feb.	Mar.	April	May	June	July	Aug.	Sep.	Oct.	Nov.	Dec.	Total for the Year
Take-home pay	$ 4,775	$ 4,775	$ 4,775	$ 4,965	$ 4,965	$ 5,140	$ 5,140	$ 5,140	$ 5,140	$ 5,140	$ 5,140	$ 5,140	$ 60,235
Bonuses and commissions						1,350						1,300	2,650
Pensions and annuities													
Investment income			90			90			90			90	360
Other income													
(I) Total Income	$ 4,775	$ 4,775	$ 4,865	$ 4,965	$ 4,965	$ 6,580	$ 5,140	$ 5,140	$ 5,230	$ 5,140	$ 5,140	$ 6,530	$ 63,245
EXPENSES													
Housing (rent/mtge, repairs)	$ 1,506	$ 1,856	$ 1,506	$ 1,506	$ 1,505	$ 1,505	$ 1,505	$ 1,505	$ 1,505	$ 1,505	$ 1,505	$ 1,505	$ 18,414
Utilities (phone, elec., gas, water)	245	245	245	175	180	205	230	245	205	195	230	250	2,650
Food (home and away)	575	575	575	575	575	575	575	575	575	575	575	575	6,900
Transportation (auto/public)	370	620	370	540	370	370	575	370	370	450	370	370	5,145
Medical/dental, incl. insurance	30	30	30	30	30	45	30	30	30	30	30	30	375
Clothing	150	150	500	400	200	200	300	500	200	300	300	300	3,500
Insurance (life, auto, home)				225	370		300			225	370		1,490
Taxes (property)		550						550					1,100
Appliances, furniture, and other (purchases/loans)	60	60	30			750			300	300	300		1,800
Personal care	100	100	100	100	100	100	100	100	100	100	100	100	1,200
Recreation and entertainment	250	250	3,200	200	200	300	300	200	200	200	200	2,050	7,550
Savings and investments	375	375	375	375	375	375	375	375	375	375	375	375	4,500
Other expenses	135	250	235	135	610	180	135	285	245	135	605	385	3,335
Fun money	230	230	230	230	230	230	230	230	230	230	230	230	2,760
(II) Total Expenses	$ 4,026	$ 5,291	$ 7,396	$ 4,491	$ 4,745	$ 4,835	$ 4,655	$ 4,965	$ 4,335	$ 4,620	$ 5,190	$ 6,170	$ 60,719
CASH SURPLUS (OR DEFICIT) [(I)-(II)]	$ 749	$ (516)	$ (2,531)	$ 474	$ 220	$ 1,745	$ 485	$ 175	$ 895	$ 520	$ (50)	$ 360	$ 2,526
CUMULATIVE CASH SURPLUS (OR DEFICIT)	$ 749	$ 233	$ (2,298)	$ (1,824)	$ (1,604)	$ 141	$ 626	$ 801	$ 1,696	$ 2,216	$ 2,166	$ 2,526	$ 2,526

several months, you can study your spending habits to see if you are doing things that should be eliminated (like going to the ATM too often or using credit cards too freely).

You will probably find it easier to budget expenses if you group them into several general categories, rather than trying to estimate each item. Worksheet 2.4 provides an example of one such grouping scheme, patterned after the categories used in the income and expense statement. You may also want to refer back to the average expense percentages given in Exhibit 2.5.

Initially, your expense estimates should include the transactions necessary to achieve your short-term goals. You should also quantify any current or short-term contributions toward your long-term goals and schedule them into the budget. Equally important are scheduled additions to savings and investments, because planned savings should be high on everyone's list of goals. If your budget doesn't balance with all these items, you will have to make some adjustments in the final budget.

Base estimated expenses on current price levels and then increase them by a percentage that reflects the anticipated rate of inflation. For example, if you estimate the monthly food bill at $350 and expect 4 percent inflation, you should budget your monthly food expenditure at $364, or $350 + $14 ($350 × 4 percent).

Don't forget an allowance for "fun money," which family members spend as they wish. This gives each person a degree of financial independence and helps provide a healthy family budget relationship.

FINALIZING THE CASH BUDGET. After you estimate income and expenses, finalize your budget by comparing projected income to projected expenses. Show the difference in the third section as a surplus or deficit. In a *balanced budget*, the total income for the year equals or exceeds total expenses. If you find that you have a deficit at year-end, you will have to go back and adjust your expenses accordingly. If you have several months of large surpluses, you should be able to cover any shortfall in a later month, as explained below. Budget preparation is complete once all monthly deficits are resolved and the total annual budget balances.

Admittedly, there is a lot of "number crunching" in personal cash budgeting. As discussed earlier, personal financial planning software can greatly streamline the budget preparation process.

DEALING WITH DEFICITS

Even if the annual budget balances, in certain months expenses may exceed income, causing a monthly budget deficit. Likewise, a budget surplus occurs when income in some months exceeds expenses. Two remedies exist:

- Shift expenses from months with budget deficits to months with surpluses (or, conversely, transfer income, if possible, from months with surpluses to those with deficits).
- Use savings, investments, or borrowing to cover temporary deficits.

Because the budget balances for the year, the need for funds to cover shortages is only temporary. In months with budget surpluses, you should return funds taken from savings or investments or repay loans. Either remedy is feasible for curing a monthly budget deficit in a balanced annual budget, although the second is probably more practical.

Three approaches exist to resolve the more difficult problem of an annual budget deficit. The first is to either *liquidate enough savings and investments* or *borrow enough to meet the total budget shortfall for the year*. Obviously, this action is not recommended, because it violates the objective of budgeting: To set expenses at a level that allows you to enjoy a reasonable standard of living *and* progress toward achieving your long-term goals. Reducing savings and investments or increasing debt to balance the budget reduces net worth. People who use this approach are *not* living within their means.

 Find links to a variety of money saving resources at About.com's Frugal Living site, **frugalliving.about.com/parenting/frugalliving/mbody.htm**.

A second, and preferred, approach is to *cut low-priority expenses from the budget*. This method balances the budget without using external funding sources. Low-priority items are those associated with your least important short-term goals. They are flexible, or discretionary, expenses for nonessential items (such as recreation, entertainment, and some clothing) that can be reduced or cut to balance the budget. The *Money in Action* box on page 73 can help you find easy ways to spend less.

MONEY IN ACTION

Small Savings Mean Big Bucks!

It should be obvious: Spend less than you earn so you'll have money to invest. Yet so many people don't recognize this simple fact. They run up large credit card bills and take out loans instead of building up a nest egg for the future.

Where to start? How about with the little stuff? You'd be amazed at how reducing even your smallest expenses can lead to big savings! Here are some examples of how reducing your discretionary spending now will yield big payoffs later.

• Instead of buying 40 $5 lottery tickets a year, invest the $200 at the end of each year at 8 percent. If you start at age 18, you'd have $106,068—about twice the median household's net worth—by the time you reach age 67!

• Buy a used car instead of a new one and invest the amount you saved at 8 percent for 40 years. If you saved $9,000 buying a used car, you'd have more than $195,000 available for your retirement fund!

• Avoid the vending machines and coffee carts at work to save $1.50 a day. Assuming 240 work days, you can invest $360 at the end of each year at 8 percent for 40 years and accumulate more than $93,000!

• Buy a regular cup of coffee rather than a latte or espresso and take a brown-bag lunch to work several days a week. If you save $15 a week for 50 weeks a year at 8 percent for 40 years, your savings will grow by more than $194,000!

You'll soon find many other ways to "save small," such as taking public transportation, comparing prices before you buy, reading books and magazines from the library instead of buying them, and using coupons to buy groceries.

Then make saving a given, not something you do when you have money left over. Pay yourself first. Have your employer deposit the maximum amount in your 401(k) plan each pay period. It will grow even faster if your employer matches your contributions. You can also authorize withdrawals from your checking account to an investment account or to a mutual fund.

Sources: Scott Burns, "The Seven Laws of Personal Finance," *Dallas Morning News*, January 5, 1997, downloaded from **www.scott burns.com**; Scott Burns, "You Have A Fortune, You Just Have to Find It," *Dallas Morning News*, January 3, 1999, downloaded from **www.scottburns.com**.

The third approach is to *increase income* by finding a higher-paying job or perhaps a second, part-time job. This is obviously the most difficult technique and may result in a significant reduction in leisure activities and bring unwanted lifestyle changes. However, individuals who have no savings or investments to liquidate, cannot borrow funds, and cannot cover necessary expenses may have to choose this route to balance their budgets.

A CASH BUDGET FOR TIM AND ANDREA SHEPARD

Using their short-term financial goals (Worksheet 1.1 in Chapter 1) and past financial statements (Worksheets 2.2 and 2.3), Tim and Andrea Shepard have prepared their cash budget for the 2002 calendar year. Worksheet 2.4 shows the Shepards' estimated total 2002 annual income and expenses by month, as well as the monthly and annual cash surplus or deficit.

The Shepards list their total 2002 income of $63,245 by source for each month. By using take-home pay, they eliminate the need to show income-based taxes, social security payments, and other payroll deductions as expenses. The take-home pay increases in April and June reflect Tim's and Andrea's expected salary increases, respectively.

In estimating annual expenses for 2002, the Shepards anticipate a small amount of inflation and have factored some price increases into their expense projections. They have also allocated $4,500 to savings and investments, a wise budgeting strategy, and included an amount for fun money, divided between them.

During their budgeting session, Tim and Andrea discovered that their first estimate resulted in expenses of $63,459, compared with their estimated income of $63,245. To eliminate the $214 deficit to balance their budget and allow for unexpected expenses, Tim and Andrea identified several areas to make cuts: omit some low-priority goals, reschedule some loan payments, or reduce their fun money. After discussing their options, they decided to spend less on stereo equipment, shorten the Hawaii vacation they planned for 2002 (instead of the Colorado ski trip shown in Worksheet 1.1), reschedule $200 of loan repayment to parents, and reduce fun money. These reductions of $2,740 lower their total scheduled expenses to $60,719, giving them a surplus of $2,526 ($63,245 − $60,719) and more than balancing the budget on an annual basis. Of course, the Shepards may decide they want to reduce other discretionary expenses as well to further increase the budget surplus and have a cushion for unexpected expenses.

The Shepards' final step is to analyze monthly surpluses and deficits and determine whether to use savings, investments, or borrowing to cover monthly shortfalls. The bottom line of their annual cash budget lists the cumulative, or running, totals of monthly cash surpluses and deficits. Despite their $2,526 year-end cumulative cash surplus, they have cumulative deficits for the months of March through May, primarily because of their March Hawaii vacation. To cover these deficits, Tim and Andrea have arranged an interest-free loan from their parents. If they had dipped into savings to finance the deficits, they would have lost some interest earnings, included as income. They could delay clothing and entertainment expenses until later in the year to reduce the deficits more quickly. If they were unable to obtain funds to cover the deficits, they would have to reduce expenses further or increase income. At year end, they should use their surplus to increase savings or investments or repay part of a loan.

COMPARING ACTUAL RESULTS WITH BUDGETED FIGURES

In the final analysis, a cash budget has value only if (1) you use it and (2) you keep careful records of actual income and expenses. These records show whether you are staying within budget limits. Record this information in a budget record book often enough so you don't overlook anything of significance, yet not so often that it becomes a nuisance. A loose-leaf binder with separate pages for each income and expense category works quite well. Rounding entries to the nearest dollar simplifies the arithmetic.

At the beginning of each month, record the budgeted amount for each category and enter income received and money spent on the appropriate pages. At month-end, total each account and calculate the surplus or deficit. With the exception of certain income accounts (like salary) and fixed expense accounts like mortgage or loan payments, most categories will end the month with a positive or negative variance, indicating a cash surplus or deficit.

This monthly comparison makes it easy to identify major budget categories where income falls far short or spending far exceeds desired levels (variances of 5 to 10 percent or more). Once you pinpoint these areas, you can take corrective action to keep your budget on course. Don't just look at the size of the variances. Analyze them, particularly the larger ones, to discover *why* they occurred. An account deficit that occurs in only one period is obviously less of a problem than one that occurs in several periods. If recurring deficits indicate that an account was underbudgeted, you may need to adjust the budget to cover the outlays, reducing overbudgeted or nonessential accounts. Only in

WORKSHEET 2.5

THE SHEPARDS' BUDGET CONTROL SCHEDULE FOR JANUARY, FEBRUARY, AND MARCH 2002

The budget control schedule provides important feedback on how the actual cash flow is stacking up relative to the forecasted cash budget. If the variances are significant enough and/or continue month after month, the Shepards should consider altering either their spending habits or their cash budget.

BUDGET CONTROL SCHEDULE

Name(s) _Tim and Andrea Shepard_

For the _3_ _____ Months Ending _March 31, 2002_

	Month: January				Month: February				Month: March			
INCOME	Budgeted Amount (1)	Actual (2)	Monthly Variance (3)	Year-to-Date Variance (4)	Budgeted Amount (5)	Actual (6)	Monthly Variance (7)	Year-to-Date Variance (8)	Budgeted Amount (9)	Actual (10)	Monthly Variance (11)	Year-to-Date Variance (12)
Take-home pay	$ 4,775	$ 4,792	$ 17	$ 17	$ 4,775	$ 4,792	$ 17	$ 34	$ 4,775	$ 4,792	$ 17	$ 51
Bonuses and commissions												
Pensions and annuities												
Investment income									90	86	(4)	(4)
Other income												
(I) Total Income	$ 4,775	$ 4,792	$ 17	$ 17	$ 4,775	$ 4,792	$ 17	$ 34	$ 4,865	$ 4,878	$ 13	$ 47
EXPENSES												
Housing (rent/mtge, repairs)	$ 1,506	$ 1,506	$ 0	$ 0	$ 1,856	$ 1,856	$ 0	$ 0	$ 1,506	$ 1,506	$ 0	$ 0
Utilities (phone, elec., gas, water)	245	237	(8)	(8)	245	252	7	(1)	245	228	(17)	(18)
Food (home and away)	575	559	(16)	(16)	575	548	(27)	(43)	575	450	(125)	(168)
Transportation (auto/public)	370	385	15	15	620	601	(19)	(4)	370	310	(60)	(64)
Medical/dental, incl. insurance	30	0	(30)	(30)	30	45	15	(15)	30	0	(30)	(45)
Clothing	150	190	40	40	150	135	(15)	25	500	475	(25)	0
Insurance (life, auto, home)												
Taxes (property)					550	550	0	0				0
Appliances, furniture, and other (purchases/loans)	60	60	0	0	60	60	0	0	30	30	0	0
Personal care	100	85	(15)	(15)	100	120	20	5	100	75	(25)	(20)
Recreation and entertainment	250	210	(40)	(40)	250	240	(10)	(50)	3,200	3,285	85	35
Savings and investments	375	375	0	0	375	375	0	0	375	375	0	0
Other expenses	135	118	(17)	(17)	250	245	(5)	(22)	235	200	(35)	(57)
Fun money	230	200	(30)	(30)	230	225	(5)	(35)	230	230	0	(35)
(II) Total Expenses	$ 4,026	$ 3,925	$ (101)	$ (101)	$ 5,291	$ 5,252	$ (39)	$ (140)	$ 7,396	$ 7,164	$ (232)	(372)
CASH SURPLUS (OR DEFICIT) [(I)-(II)]	$ 749	$ 867	$ 118	$ 118	$ (516)	$ (460)	$ 56	$ 174	$ (2,531)	$ (2,286)	$ 245	$ 419
CUMULATIVE CASH SURPLUS (OR DEFICIT)	$ 749	$ 867	$	$	$ 233	$ 407	$	$	$ (2,298)	$ (1,879)	$	$

Key: Col. (3) = Col. (2) - Col. (1); Col. (7) = Col. (6) - Col. (5); Col. (11) = Col. (10) - Col. (9); Col. (4) = Col. (3); Col. (8) = Col. (4) + Col. (7); Col. (12) = Col. (8) + Col. (11).

exceptional situations should you finance budget adjustments with savings and investments or borrowing.

Control is important not only in individual categories but also in the total monthly budget. By examining month-end totals for all accounts, you can discover whether you have a net budget surplus or deficit and take appropriate action to maintain a balanced budget for the rest of the year.

The Shepards' **budget control schedule** for January through March 2002 (Worksheet 2.5) compares their actual income and expenses with the various budget categories and shows the variances. Looking at this feedback on a regular basis helps the couple make sure that their actual income and expenses stay within the budgeted amounts. They can quickly identify problems and take steps to bring individual accounts and the whole budget into balance.

budget control schedule
A summary that shows how actual income and expenses compare with the various budget categories and where surpluses or deficits exist.

Looking at the Shepards' budget, we see that actual income and expense levels are reasonably close to their targets and have a positive variance for the months shown (their surpluses exceed the budgeted surplus amounts). The biggest variances were in food and transportation expenses, but neither was far off the mark. Thus, for the first 3 months of the year, the Shepards seem to be doing a good job of controlling their income and expenses. They have, in fact, achieved a cumulative cash deficit $419 smaller than the budgeted deficit (actual of −$1,879 versus budget of −$2,298) by cutting discretionary spending.

CONCEPT CHECK

2-17. Describe the *cash budget* and its three parts. How does a budget deficit differ from a budget surplus?

2-18. The Smith family has prepared their annual cash budget for 2002. They have divided it into 12 monthly budgets. Although only one monthly budget balances, they have managed to balance the overall budget for the year. What remedies are available to the Smith family for meeting the monthly budget deficits?

2-19. Why is it important to analyze actual budget surpluses or deficits at the end of each month?

SUMMARY

LG1.   Describe the role of financial statements, professional financial planners, and special planning concerns in the personal financial planning process. Preparing and using personal financial statements is important to personal financial planning, because they allow you to keep track of your current financial position and monitor your progress toward achieving your financial goals. Situations that require special attention include the timing of financial decisions (especially during periods of personal stress or major life changes), managing two incomes, and adapting to changes in your personal situation, such as marital status or taking responsibility for elderly relatives' care. Professional financial planners can help you with the planning process. Investigate a prospective financial planner's background carefully and understand how he or she is paid (fees, commissions, or both).

LG2.   Put a monetary value on financial goals using *time value of money* concepts. When putting a dollar value on your financial goals, be sure to consider the time value of money and, if appropriate, use the notion of future value or present value when preparing your estimates. These techniques explicitly recognize that a dollar today is worth more than a dollar in the future.

LG3.   Prepare a personal balance sheet. A balance sheet reports on your financial position at a given point in time. It provides a summary of the things you own (assets), the money you owe (liabilities), and your financial worth (net worth). Assets include liquid assets, investments, and real and personal property. Liabilities include current liabilities that are due in less than 1 year (unpaid bills, open account credit obligations), and long-term liabilities (real estate mortgages, consumer installment loans, education loans). Net worth represents your actual wealth and is the difference between your total assets and total liabilities.

LG4. **Generate a personal income and expense statement.** The income and expense statement summarizes the income you received and the money you spent over a given time period. It is prepared on a cash basis and, as such, reflects your actual cash flow. Expenses consist of cash outflows to (1) meet living expenses, (2) purchase various kinds of assets, (3) pay taxes, and (4) reduce debts. A cash surplus (or deficit) is the difference between income and expenses. A cash surplus can be used to increase assets or reduce debts, and therefore has a positive effect on the balance sheet's net worth account. A cash deficit, in contrast, reduces assets or increases debts, acting to reduce net worth.

LG5. **Develop a good record-keeping system and use ratios to interpret personal financial statements.** Good records facilitate the preparation of accurate personal financial statements. Organized records also simplify tax return preparation and provide the necessary documentation for tax deductions. Ratio analysis allows you to interpret your personal financial statements to assess how well you are doing relative to your past performance. Four important financial ratios are the solvency, liquidity, savings, and debt service ratios.

LG6. **Construct a cash budget and use it to monitor and control spending.** A cash budget will help you implement a system of disciplined spending. By curbing needless spending, it can increase the amount of funds allocated to savings and investments. Household budgets identify planned monthly cash income and cash expenses for the coming year. The objective is to take in more money than you spend so you'll save money and add to your net worth over time. The final step in the budgeting process is to compare actual income and expenses with budgeted figures to learn whether, in fact, you are living within your budget and, if not, to take appropriate corrective actions.

QUESTIONS AND PROBLEMS

1. Chris Jones is preparing his balance sheet and income and expense statement for the year ending June 30, 2001. He is having difficulty classifying six items and asks for your help. Which, if any, of the following transactions are assets, liabilities, income, or expense items?
   a. He rents a house for $950 a month.
   b. On June 21, 2001, he bought diamond earrings for his wife and charged it using his Visa card. The earrings cost $600, but he has not yet received the bill.
   c. He borrowed $2,000 from his parents last fall but so far has made no payments to them.
   d. He makes monthly payments of $120 on an installment loan, about half of which is interest and the balance is repayment of principal. He has 20 payments left totaling $2,400.
   e. He paid $2,800 in taxes during the year and is due a tax refund of $450, which he has not yet received.
   f. He invested $1,800 in some common stock.
2. Put yourself 10 years into the future. Construct a fairly detailed and realistic balance sheet and income and expense statement reflecting what you would like to achieve by that time.
3. *Use Worksheet 2.2.* Elizabeth Walker has been asked by her banker to submit a personal balance sheet as of June 30, 2001, in support of an application for a $3,000 home improvement loan. She has come to you for help in preparing it. So far, she has prepared the list of her assets and liabilities at June 30, 2001, as shown in the following.

Cash on hand		$ 70
Balance in checking account		180
Balance in money market deposit account with Mid-American Savings		650
Bills outstanding:		
Telephone	$ 20	
Electricity	70	
Charge account balance	190	
Visa	180	
MasterCard	220	
Taxes	400	
Insurance	220	1,300
Home and property		68,000
Home mortgage loan		52,000
Automobile: 1997 Honda Accord		10,000
Installment loan balances:		
Auto loans	$3,000	
Furniture loan	500	3,500
Personal property:		
Furniture	$1,050	
Clothing	900	1,950
Investments:		
U.S. government savings bonds	$ 500	
Stock of WIMCO Corporation	3,000	3,500

From the data given, prepare Elizabeth Walker's balance sheet, dated June 30, 2001 (follow the balance sheet form shown in Worksheet 2.2). Then evaluate her balance sheet relative to the following factors: (a) solvency, (b) liquidity, and (c) equity in her dominant asset.

4. *Use Worksheet 2.3.* Chuck and Judy Schwartz are about to construct their income and expense statement for the year ending December 31, 2001. They have put together the following income and expense information for 2001:

Judy's salary	$37,000
Reimbursement for travel expenses	1,950
Interest on:	
Savings account	110
Bonds of Alpha Corporation	70
Groceries	4,150
Rent	9,600
Utilities	960
Gas and auto expenses	650
Chuck's tuition, books, and supplies	3,300
Books, magazines, and periodicals	280
Clothing and other miscellaneous expenses	2,700
Cost of photographic equipment purchased with charge card	2,200
Amount paid to date on photographic equipment	1,600
Judy's travel expenses	1,950
Purchase of a new car (cost)	9,750
Outstanding loan balance on car	7,300
Purchase of bonds in Alpha Corporation	4,900

Using the information provided, prepare an income and expense statement for the Schwartzes for the year ending December 31, 2001 (follow the form shown in Worksheet 2.3).

5. Over the past several years, Helen Chang has been able to save regularly. As a result, today she has $14,188 in savings and investments. She wants to establish her own business in 5 years and feels she will need $50,000 to do so.

   a. If she can earn 12 percent on her money, how much will her $14,188 savings/investments be worth in 5 years? Will Helen have the $50,000 she needs? If not, how much more money will she need?

   b. Given your answer to part **a**, how much will Helen have to save *each year* over the next 5 years to accumulate the additional money, assuming she can earn interest at a rate of 12 percent?

   c. If Helen can afford to save only $2,000 a year, given your answer to part **a**, will she have the $50,000 she needs to start her own business in 5 years?

6. Bill Shaffer wishes to have $200,000 in a retirement fund 20 years from now. He can create the retirement fund by making a single lump-sum deposit today.

   a. If he can earn 10 percent on his investments, how much must Bill deposit today to create the retirement fund? If he can earn only 8 percent on his investments? Compare and discuss the results of your calculations.

   b. If upon retirement in 20 years Bill plans to invest the $200,000 in a fund that earns 11 percent, what is the maximum annual withdrawal he can make over the following 15 years?

   c. How much would Bill need to have on deposit at retirement to annually withdraw $35,000 over the 15 years if the retirement fund earns 11 percent?

   d. To achieve his annual withdrawal goal of $35,000 calculated in part **c**, how much more than the amount calculated in part **a** must Bill deposit today in an investment earning 10 percent annual interest?

7. Use future or present value techniques to solve the following problems:

   a. Starting with $10,000, how much will you have in 10 years if you can earn 15 percent on your money? If you can earn only 8 percent?

   b. If you inherited $25,000 today and invested all of it in a security that paid a 10 percent rate of return, how much would you have in 25 years?

   c. If the average new home costs $125,000 today, how much will it cost in 10 years if the price increases by 5 percent each year?

   d. You feel that in 15 years it will cost $75,000 to give your child a college education. Will you have enough if you take $25,000 *today* and invest it for the next 15 years at 8 percent? If you start *from scratch,* how much will you have to save *each year* to have $75,000 in 15 years if you can earn an 8 percent rate of return on your investments?

   e. If you can earn 12 percent, how much will you have to save *each year* if you want to retire in 35 years with $1 million?

   f. You plan to have $750,000 in savings and investments when you retire at age 60. Assuming you earn an average of 9 percent on this portfolio, what is the maximum annual withdrawal you can make over a 25-year period?

8. Dave and Betty Williamson are preparing their 2002 budget. Help the Williamsons reconcile the following differences, giving reasons to support your answers:

   a. Their only source of income is Dave's salary, which amounts to $3,000 a month before taxes. Betty wants to show the $3,000 as their monthly income, whereas Dave argues that his take-home pay of $2,350 is the correct value to show.

   b. Betty wants to make a provision for *fun money,* an idea that Dave cannot understand. He asks, "Why do we need fun money when everything is provided for in the budget?"

9. Below is a portion of Jeffrey Cook's budget record for April 2002. Fill in the blanks in columns 6 and 7.

Item Number (1)	Item (2)	Amount Budgeted (3)	Amount Expended (4)	Beginning Balance (5)	Monthly Surplus (Deficit) (6)	Cumulative Surplus (Deficit) (7)
1	Rent	$350	$360	$20	$_____	$_____
2	Utilities	150	145	15	_____	_____
3	Food	310	275	−15	_____	_____
4	Auto	25	38	−5	_____	_____
5	Recreation and entertainment	50	60	−50	_____	_____

10. *Use Worksheet 2.4.* Prepare a record of your income and expenses for the last 30 days; then prepare a personal budget for the next 3 months. (Use the format in Worksheet 2.4 but fill out only 3 months and the total column.) Use the budget to control and regulate your expenses during the next month. Discuss the impact of the budget on your spending behavior, as well as any differences between your expected and actual spending patterns.

APPLYING PERSONAL FINANCE

Where Am I Financially?

This chapter is designed to help you begin thinking about your financial situation by learning how to prepare your balance sheet and income and expense statement. The approach given in Worksheets 2.2 and 2.3 should be quite helpful in this regard. However, many people do not wish to share their personal financial statements with others. Prepare and analyze your personal financial statements using this exercise and use them as a basis for a general discussion of your financial condition.

It isn't easy to prepare personal financial statements for the first time. If you have ever applied for a loan, you already recognize the importance of good, current financial information. If you have trouble preparing your statements, use what is discussed in class as an aid. In the process consider the following questions:

1. Have you included all your assets at fair market value on your balance sheet?
2. Have you included all your debt balances as liabilities on your balance sheet?
3. Have you included all items of income on your income and expense statement?
4. Have you included all debt payments as expenses on your income and expense statement?
5. Are there occasional expenses that you've forgotten about or hidden expenses like entertainment that you have overlooked?

Once the statements are completed, calculate the solvency, liquidity, savings, and debt service ratios. Assess where you are financially and indicate if you are in good financial shape. If not, suggest corrective actions.

CONTEMPORARY CASE APPLICATIONS

2.1   The Sullivans' Version of Financial Planning

John and Irene Sullivan are a married couple in their mid-20s. John is a financial analyst and Irene works as a sales representative. Since their marriage 4 years ago, John and Irene have been living comfortably. Their income has exceeded their expenses, and they have accumulated a net worth of nearly $45,000—$36,000 from equity in their home, cars, furniture, and other personal belongings, and $10,000 from savings accounts and common stock investments. Because their income has always been more than adequate to allow them to live in the fashion they desire, the Sullivans have done no financial planning.

Irene has just learned that she is 2 months pregnant and is concerned about how they will make ends meet if she quits work after their child is born. Each time she and John discuss the matter, John tells her not to worry because "we have always managed to pay our bills on time." Irene cannot understand this, as her income will be completely eliminated. To convince Irene there is no need for concern, John points out that their expenses for necessities last year were $24,885, which just about equaled his take-home pay of $26,480. With an anticipated promotion to a managerial position and an expected 10 percent pay raise, his income next year should exceed this amount. John also points out that they can reduce luxuries (trips, recreation, and entertainment) and can always draw down their savings or sell some of their stock if they get in a bind. When asked about the long-run implications of their finances, John replies that there will be "no problems" because his boss has assured him of a bright future with the company. John also emphasizes that Irene can go back to work in a few years, if necessary.

In spite of John's somewhat convincing arguments, Irene still feels uncomfortable with their rather matter-of-fact approach to financial planning. She knows there has to be a better way and has gathered the following financial information for the year ending December 31, 2001:

Salaries	Take-home	Gross Salary
John	$26,480	$38,350
Irene	18,090	26,000

Item	Amount
Food	$ 4,200
Clothing	2,300
Mortgage payments, including property taxes ($1,400)	9,400
Travel and entertainment card balances	2,000
Gas, electric, water expenses	1,990
Household furnishings	4,500
Telephone	640
Auto loan balance	2,650
Common stock investments	7,500
Bank credit card balances	675
Income taxes	16,940
Credit card loan payments	2,210
Cash on hand	85
1997 Nissan Sentra	7,000
Medical expenses (nonreimbursed)	600
Homeowner's insurance premiums paid	400
Checking account balance	485
Auto insurance premiums paid	800

Transportation	2,800
Cable television	480
Estimated value of home	85,000
Trip to Europe	5,000
Recreation and entertainment	4,000
Auto loan payments	2,150
Money market account balance	2,500
Purchase of common stock	7,500
Addition to money market account	500
Mortgage on home	70,000

Questions

1. Using this information and Worksheets 2.2 and 2.3, construct the Sullivans' December 31, 2001, balance sheet and income and expense statement for the year ending December 31, 2001.

2. Comment on the Sullivans' financial condition with respect to (a) solvency, (b) liquidity, (c) savings, and (d) ability to pay debts promptly. If the Sullivans continue to manage their finances as described, what do you expect the long-run consequences to be? Discuss.

3. Critically evaluate the Sullivans' approach to financial planning. Point out any fallacies in John's arguments, and be sure to mention (a) implications for the long term, (b) the potential impact of inflation, and (c) the impact on their net worth. What procedures should they use to get their financial house in order? Be sure to discuss the role that long- and short-term financial plans and budgets might play.

 2.2   Joe Garcia Learns to Budget

Joe Garcia graduated from college in 2000 and moved to Atlanta to take a job as a market research analyst. He was pleased to be financially independent and was sure that, with his $35,000 salary, he could cover his living expenses and also have plenty of money left over to furnish his studio apartment and enjoy the wide variety of social and recreational activities available in Atlanta. He opened several department store charge accounts and also obtained a bank credit card.

For a while Joe managed pretty well on his monthly take-home pay of $2,250, but by the end of 2001 he was having trouble fully paying all his credit card charges each month. Concerned that his spending had gotten out of control and that he was barely making it from paycheck to paycheck, he decided to compile a list of his expenses for the past calendar year and develop a budget. He hoped not only to reduce his credit card debt but also to begin a regular savings program.

He prepared the following summary of expenses for 2001:

Item	Annual Expenditure
Rent	$9,600
Auto insurance	520
Auto loan payments	3,340
Clothing	2,200
Installment loan for stereo	540
Personal care	240
Phone	600
Cable TV	240
Gas and electricity	960

Medical care	120
Dentist	70
Groceries	2,500
Dining out	2,000
Car expenses (gas, repairs, fees, and so on)	1,560
Furniture purchases	900
Recreation and entertainment	1,900
Other expenses	600

After reviewing his 2001 expenses, Joe made the following assumptions about his expenses for 2002:

1. All expenses remain at the same levels, with the following exceptions:
   a. Auto insurance, auto expenses, gas and electricity, and groceries will increase 5 percent.
   b. Clothing purchases will decrease to $1,850.
   c. Phone and cable TV will increase $5 per month.
   d. Furniture purchases will decrease to $660, most of which is for a new television.
   e. He will take a 1-week vacation to Lake Tahoe in July at a cost of $1,100.
2. All expenses will be budgeted in equal monthly installments except for the vacation and the following:
   a. Auto insurance is paid in two installments due in June and December.
   b. He plans to replace the brakes on his car in February at a cost of $120.
   c. Visits to the dentist will be made in March and September.
3. He will eliminate his bank credit card balance by making extra monthly payments of $75 during each of the first 6 months.

With regard to his income, he has just received a small raise, so his take-home pay will be $2,375 per month.

Questions
1. a. Prepare a preliminary cash budget for Joe for the year ending December 31, 2002, using the format shown in Worksheet 2.4.
   b. Compare Joe's estimated expenses with his expected income and make recommendations that will help him balance his budget.
2. Make any necessary adjustments to Joe's estimated monthly expenses and revise his annual cash budget for the year ending December 31, 2002, using Worksheet 2.4.
3. Analyze the budget and advise Joe on his financial situation. Suggest some long-, intermediate-, and short-term financial goals for Joe and discuss some steps he can take to reach them.

MONEY ONLINE

YOUR PERSONAL FINANCES!

Note: Web addresses change frequently, so you may need to determine the home page and do a site search to find the page or topic that's referenced.

1. **www.familymoney.com**
   Great articles, great tools, and great tips are all assembled for you at Family Money's Web site. Under "Managing," click on "Budgeting" for help with Sticking to a Budget and Record Keeping. Under "Tools," plug in your numbers to use their various Budgeting, Savings, and Investing worksheets.

2. **metlife.com**
   Big events in your life present special needs. At Met Life's "Life Advice Center" select "Family" to find coverage on topics such as marriage, remarriage, becoming a parent, choosing child care, divorce, loss of a loved one, and leaving the military.

3. **metlife.com**
   Walk through the steps in the financial planning process. Select "Money" at Met Life's "Life Advice Center," and scroll down to "Planning Financial Security" to begin this rewarding journey. Other topics in this section can assist you in finding financial freedom, choosing a financial advisor, creating a budget, investing for the first time, and helping your child understand money.

4. **financenter.com/calculate/planning/paycheck.fcs**
   How much of your paycheck will you get to bring home? Pull up the FinanCenter's Paycheck Planning Calculators and click on "How much of my paycheck do I take home as a salaried employee?" Select your state and determine the take-home pay of a single person who makes $50,000 annually and is paid monthly.

5. **www.healthy.net/library/articles/cash/assessment/assessment.htm**
   Your spending personality could be costing you big bucks every year! Take the Spending Personality Assessment Test to determine your dominant spending personality and obtain information on how best to deal with it. Explore other articles at the HealthyCash Web site **www.healthy.net/library/articles/cash** to help you develop a healthy attitude toward money and to learn to make better financial decisions.

6. **kiplinger.com/tools/budget.html**
   Project your expenditures and then compare those projections with what you actually spend using Kiplinger's tool, "A Budget for Today and Tomorrow." Start now and get a handle on your expenditures. Other useful tools on the page, **kiplinger.com/tools**, include "My Cash Flow for the Past Year," "What's My Net Worth," and "How Much am I Spending."

7. **cbs.marketwatch.com**
   Keep up to date with the latest news and developments in the personal finance arena at the CBS MarketWatch Web site. Click on "Personal Finance" and then on "Life & Money," "Retirement," or "Mutual Funds" to sample their many offerings.

8. **moneycentral.msn.com**
   Find articles and information on almost any personal finance topic imaginable at MoneyCentral. For starters, click on "Saving & Spending" or "Family & College." Then scroll down to "Search MoneyCentral" to search on topics such as budget, goals, or debt.

Just for Fun!

9. **www.financenter.com**

   Want to become a millionaire? Once you get that million, what will it be worth in today's dollars? Find the answers to both these questions by clicking on "Planning" and then "Calculate." Scroll down to "Savings Calculators" to find "What will it take to become a millionaire?" Try the following scenarios:

   Give yourself a 10-year time frame, no current savings, and invest $200/month at 10%. Give yourself a 30-year time frame, $20,000 in current savings, and invest $500/month at 10%.

10. **www.consumerworld.org**

    Compare online buying services, find product reviews, or plug into a wealth of consumer resources, guides, and information at Consumer World.

Chapter 3

Managing Your Taxes

LEARNING GOALS

LG1.   Discuss the basic principles of income taxes and determine your filing status.

LG2.   Classify the various types of gross income, differentiate between itemized and standard deductions and exemptions, and calculate taxable income.

LG3.   Prepare a basic tax return using the appropriate tax forms and rate schedules.

LG4.   Explain who needs to pay estimated taxes, when to file your return, how to handle an audit, where to get help with your taxes, and computer-based tax returns.

LG5.   Implement a tax planning strategy.

LG6.   Describe the other major forms of personal taxes.

Audit Alert Taxes the Ashers

David Asher viewed the ominous looking envelope from the Internal Revenue Service (IRS) with concern. He and his wife Mary had filed their taxes on time and had been careful to check Form 1040 and the supporting schedules carefully before sending them to the IRS. When he opened the letter, his worst fear was confirmed: the IRS was auditing the Ashers' tax return from last year.

After a momentary panic, David realized that in all probability the IRS was questioning some of their deductions. As a self-employed psychologist, he knew that small business owners and self-employed professionals were more likely to be audited. The potential to cross the line between what defines business and personal expenses was much greater, for one thing. He also had a home office for which he claimed certain deductions—a red flag for the IRS. Unfortunately, the rate of audits for returns with home office deductions is about six times higher than the national average.

Over dinner that night, the Ashers discussed the best way to prepare for the upcoming audit. Mary pointed out that they were in very good shape because they had detailed records for every deduction they claimed. This would help them document the legitimacy of any questioned items.

What could have been a financial disaster turned out to be only a minor problem, thanks to the Ashers' well-organized money management system and understanding of income tax basics. They were able to answer the IRS examiner's questions and avoid any tax penalties. After reading the material presented in Chapter 3, you will also be familiar with procedures to manage your income taxes.

■ Principles of Federal Income Taxes [LG1]

A typical American family currently pays *about one-third of its gross income in taxes:* federal income and social security taxes and numerous state and local income, sales, and property taxes. It is, therefore, no surprise that tax planning is an important aspect of personal financial planning. Although you may think of tax planning as an activity to do between January, when tax forms arrive in the mail, and April 15, the filing deadline, tax planning is actually a year-round activity. You should always consider tax consequences when making major financial decisions and developing and revising your financial plans.

The overriding objective of tax planning is very simple: to maximize the amount of money you keep by minimizing the amount of taxes you pay. As long as it is done honestly and within the tax codes, there is nothing immoral, illegal, or unethical about trying to minimize your tax bill. Most tax planning centers on ways to minimize income and estate (see Chapter 15) taxes. This chapter concentrates on income taxes paid by individuals, particularly the federal income tax, the largest and most important tax for most taxpayers.

Taxes are dues we pay for membership in our society; they are the cost of living in this country. Federal, state, and local tax receipts fund government activities and a wide variety of public services, from national defense to local libraries. We cannot directly control the tax laws because they are established by the legislators we elect. However, with good tax planning, especially with regard to federal income taxes, you will have more money to spend and invest.

 How long does the average American have to work this year to pay federal, state, and local taxes? Get the answer at the Tax Foundation Web site, **www.taxfoundation.org**. You'll also find information about tax policy, tax rates, tax collections, and the economics of taxation.

The *Internal Revenue Code of 1939* outlined the federal income tax law. The code's various sections and amendments deal with the tax effects of practically all personal and business transactions. In 1954 this code was revised to further clarify and more precisely state its provisions. Since then, Congress has added a number of amendments to the code that attempt to simplify it, eliminate rarely used provisions, and repeal and modify other provisions. The IRS, which is part of the U.S. Department of the Treasury, is responsible for administering and enforcing federal tax laws and making sure that people pay their taxes as required by the various tax codes.

Without a doubt, the biggest and perhaps most controversial piece of tax legislation to come out of Congress in the last 50 years was the *Tax Reform Act of 1986*. (The *Technical and Miscellaneous Revenue Act of 1988* later refined and clarified a number of the 1986 act's provisions.) The purpose of this act was threefold: (1) to simplify the tax code for individual taxpayers; (2) to reduce taxpayer abuses by closing many existing loopholes; and (3) to shift a significant amount of the tax burden from individuals to corporations. The net result of this legislation was far reaching. It removed millions of low-income families from the tax rolls, reduced the number of tax brackets from fifteen to just three, eliminated some popular tax deductions, did away with the preferential treatment of capital gains (which was reinstated in the *Taxpayer Relief Act of 1997*), and sharply curbed the ability of individual taxpayers to generate tax-sheltered income. In both 1993 and 1994, an additional tax bracket was added, for a total of five. The *Economic Growth and Tax Relief Reconciliation Act of 2001*, passed in mid-2001 and retroactive to January 1, 2001, added a new 10-percent tax bracket and reduced the tax rates in all of the existing tax brackets. Among its many provisions it also provided for phasing in more tax brackets through 2006.

The Taxpayer Relief Act of 1997 brought other changes to the tax code, especially for taxpayers falling within specific income categories. These include the Roth Individual Retirement Arrangement (IRA), which allows money to accumulate tax-free (see Chapter 14); educational credits; a deduction for student loan payments; and the option to withdraw IRA funds before age $59\frac{1}{2}$ for educational expenses, or up to $10,000 for first-time home buyers. Although taxpayers do not owe any penalty for these early withdrawals, they still must pay income taxes on the funds; IRAs defer taxes, but don't eliminate them. Despite the many amendments to the original 1939 tax act, the U.S. tax code remains so complex that taxpayers who itemize their deductions often require costly professional help just to file a return.

The provisions of the tax code may change annually with regard to tax rates, amounts and types of deductions and personal exemptions, and similar items. Often these changes are not finalized until late in the year. Although some of the provisions of the tax-cut package passed by Congress in mid-2001 will be noted, the tax tables, calculations, and sample tax returns presented in this chapter are based on the tax laws applicable to the calendar year 2000—those in effect at the time this book was being revised. *Although tax rates and other provisions will change, the basic procedures will remain the same.* Before preparing your tax returns, be sure to review the current regulations; IRS publications and other tax preparation guides should be helpful in this regard.

EXHIBIT 3.1

MAJOR CATEGORIES OF FEDERAL INCOME AND OUTLAYS FOR FISCAL YEAR 1999

These pie charts show the relative sizes of the major categories of Federal income and outlays for fiscal year 1999.

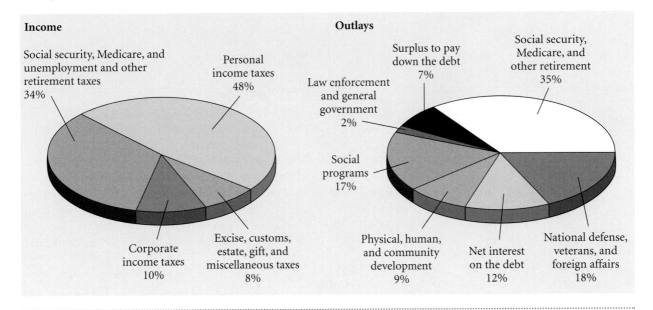

Source: Based on data from U.S. Office of Management and Budget, cited in *2000 Form 1040A Instructions*, Washington, DC: Internal Revenue Service, 2000, p. 62.

THE ECONOMICS OF INCOME TAXES

It should come as little surprise to learn that most people simply do not like to pay taxes. Some of this feeling undoubtedly stems from the widely held perception that a lot of government spending amounts to little more than bureaucratic waste. But a good deal of this feeling is probably also due to the fact that taxpayers get nothing tangible in return for their money. After all, paying taxes is not like spending $7,000 on furniture, a boat, or a European vacation. The fact is, we too often tend to overlook or take for granted the many services that are provided by the taxes we pay—public schools and state colleges, roads and highways, and parks and recreational facilities, not to mention police and fire protection, retirement benefits, and many other health and social services. In Exhibit 3.1 we can see where the government gets its tax dollars and how it uses them.

Income taxes provide the major source of revenue for the federal government. Personal income taxes are scaled on progressive rates. To illustrate how this **progressive tax structure** works, we will use the following data for single taxpayers filing 2000 returns:

income taxes
A type of tax levied on taxable income by the federal government and many state and local governments.

progressive tax structure
A tax structure in which the larger the amount of taxable income, the higher the rate at which it is taxed.

Taxable Income	Tax Rate
$0 to $26,250	15%
$$26,251 to $63,550	28%
$63,551 to $132,500	31%
$132,501 to $288,350	36%
Over $288,350	39.6%

Now let's use these rates to calculate the tax liability on three possible taxable incomes: (1) $20,000, (2) $40,000, and (3) $80,000:

Taxable Income	Tax Calculation	Tax Liability
(1) $20,000	$20,000 × .15	$ 3,000.00
(2) $40,000	[($40,000 − $26,250) × .28] + [$26,250 × .15]	$ 7,787.50
(3) $80,000	[($80,000 − $63,550) × .31] + [($63,550 − $26,250) × .28] + [$26,250 × .15]	$19,481.00

Notice that as income moves from a lower to a higher bracket, the higher rate applies *only to the additional income in that bracket* and not to the entire income. For example, you pay the 28 percent rate only on that portion of the $40,000 in income that exceeds $26,250. As a result of this kind of progressive scale, the more money you make, the progressively more you pay in taxes. According to the IRS and the Tax Foundation, the top 50 percent of taxpayers in terms of income paid 96 percent of the total income taxes; the top 5 percent accounted for 32 percent of total individual income and 52 percent of taxes. Note also that the progressive tax structure actually results in total taxes that are lower than implied by the stated tax rates. When you relate the amount of taxes paid to the level of income earned, the tax rate drops considerably. Returning to the three income levels illustrated above, we can see what happens to the **average tax rate,** which is calculated by dividing the tax liability by taxable income:

average tax rate
The rate at which each dollar of taxable income is taxed on average; calculated by dividing the tax liability by taxable income.

Taxable Income	Tax Liability	Stated Tax Rate	Average Tax Rate
(1) $20,000	$ 3,000.00	15%	15.0% ($3,000/$20,000)
(2) $40,000	$ 7,787.50	28%	19.5% ($7,787.50/$40,000)
(3) $80,000	$19,481.00	31%	24.4% ($19,481/$80,000)

Clearly, taxes are still progressive, but the size of the bite is not as bad as the stated tax rate might suggest.

The *Economic Recovery Tax Act (ERTA) of 1981* attempted to mitigate the impact of inflation on our income taxes, often referred to as *bracket creep*. **Bracket creep** occurs when rising income moves you into the next higher tax bracket, even though your real income—adjusted for inflation—may be stagnant. If this occurs, the growth in your after-tax income will fall short of the inflation rate. The progressive nature of taxes is at the core of bracket creep and, when combined with inflation, can have a cruel effect on family income.

bracket creep
A situation in which increases in income lead to higher tax rates, causing the growth in after-tax income to fall short of the inflation rate.

In an attempt to keep bracket creep in check, one of the provisions of ERTA was to *index* to the consumer price index the tax brackets, standard deductions, and personal exemptions. In this way, as inflation increased, so, too, would the income-level steps in each tax bracket and the personal exemption amounts. The Tax Reform Act of 1986 further curtailed the effects of bracket creep by *reducing* the number of tax brackets and *widening* the income levels within each bracket. Thus, a jump to a higher tax bracket occurs less often today than it did in the past, and it takes a much larger increase in income to trigger a jump to a new bracket. The 2001 Tax Act, which will add one or more new brackets through 2006, is expected to continue to minimize bracket creep by further widening income levels within brackets and reducing the size of the rate changes between brackets.

YOUR FILING STATUS

The taxes you pay depend in part on your *filing status*, which is based on your marital status and family situation. Filing status is an important factor in determining whether you are required to file an income tax return, the amount of your standard deduction, and your tax rate. Your filing status is based on your status on the last day of your tax year (usually December 31). If you have a choice of filing status, you should calculate taxes both ways and choose the status that results in the lower tax liability. There are five different filing status categories:

- *Single* taxpayers—unmarried or legally separated from their spouses by either a separation or final divorce decree.
- *Married filing jointly*—married couples who combine their income and allowable deductions and file one tax return.
- *Married filing separately*—each spouse files his or her own return, reporting only his or her income, deductions, and exemptions.
- *Head of household*—a taxpayer who is unmarried or considered unmarried and pays more than half of the cost of keeping up a home for himself or herself and an eligible dependent child or relative.
- *Qualifying widow or widower with dependent child*—persons whose spouses died within 2 years of the tax year (for example, in 1998 or 1999 for the 2000 tax year) and who support a dependent child. They may use joint return tax rates and are eligible for the highest standard deduction. (After the 2-year period, they may file under the head of household status if they qualify.)

In general, married taxpayers who file jointly have a lower tax liability than if they file separately. However, sometimes these married couples pay more in total taxes than if they were single taxpayers. Combining the two incomes results in *bracket creep*—it pushes the couple into a higher tax bracket resulting in a "marriage tax." In an attempt to eliminate the marriage tax, the 2001 Tax Act lowered taxes for married couples by making the standard deduction and the 15-percent bracket twice as large for couples compared with singles.

Through 2000, the amount of the marriage tax depends on the level of each spouse's earnings and usually occurs when the smaller of the two partners' taxable income is equal to at least 30 percent of the couple's total taxable income. For example, compare the taxes (calculated using the 2000 Tax Rate Schedule, Exhibit 3.7 on page 102) owed by a married couple *filing jointly* with total taxable income of $110,000 to those owed by *two single taxpayers* with taxable incomes of $55,000 each:

Filing Status	Total Tax Due
Married couple filing jointly	$25,221
Two single taxpayers: taxes of $11,987.50 each	−23,975
"Marriage tax"	$ 1,246

Combining their incomes pushes the married couple into the 31 percent tax bracket and results in a tax liability $1,246 higher than the amount paid by the two *single* taxpayers, who fall into the 28 percent tax bracket. It is illegal for married individuals to use the single filing status. But a couple planning a December wedding may reap considerable tax savings by postponing their wedding until January.

The tax brackets (rates) and payments for married couples filing separately are typically higher than for joint filers because the spouses rarely account for equal amounts of taxable income. In some cases, however, it may be advantageous for spouses to file separate returns. For instance, if one spouse has a moderate income and substantial medical expenses and the other has a low income and no medical expenses, filing separately may provide a tax savings. It's worth your time to calculate your taxes under both scenarios to see which results in lower taxes. Of course, much of the disparity in rates between married couples filing jointly and separately is expected to be eliminated by the 2001 Tax Act.

Every individual or married couple who earns a specified level of income is required to file a tax return. Exhibit 3.2 provides a list of some of the more common filing requirements

EXHIBIT 3.2

INCOME TAX FILING REQUIREMENTS (2000)

Individuals and married couples are required to file tax returns only if their incomes meet or exceed minimum levels. These minimums vary depending upon the taxpayer's filing status.

Filing Status	Minimum Income
Single individual, under 65	$ 7,200*
Single individual, 65 or older	8,300
Married couple, joint return, both under 65	12,950
Married couple, joint return, one spouse 65 or older	13,800
Married couple, joint return, both 65 or older	14,650
Married couple, separate return, any age	2,800
Head of household, under 65	9,250
Head of household, 65 or older	10,350
Qualifying widow(er) with dependent child, under 65	10,150
Qualifying widow(er) with dependent child, 65 or older	11,000

*Anyone who is claimed as a dependent on someone else's tax return (such as a student or elderly parent) must file a return if his or her *gross* income or *unearned* income (such as interest and dividends) exceeds $700, or if his or her *earned* income (such as wages and salary) exceeds $4,400.

that existed in 2000. Like the personal tax rates, these minimums are adjusted annually based on the annual rate of inflation. Note that if your income falls below the prevailing minimum levels, you are not required to file a tax return. However, if you had any tax withheld during the year, you must file a tax return—even if your income falls *below* minimum filing amounts—in order to receive a refund of these taxes.

YOUR TAKE-HOME PAY

pay-as-you-go basis A method of paying income taxes in which the employer (or self-employed person) withholds (deducts) a portion of income every pay period (or quarter) and sends it to the IRS.

Although many of us don't give much thought to taxes until April 15 approaches, we actually pay taxes as we earn income throughout the year. Income taxes are usually collected on a **pay-as-you-go basis**: your employer withholds (deducts) a portion of your income every pay period and periodically sends it to the IRS. Self-employed persons must likewise deduct and forward a portion of their income to the IRS each quarter. The amounts withheld are based on a taxpayer's estimated tax liability. After the close of the taxable year, you calculate the actual taxes you owe and file your tax return. When you file, you receive full credit for the amount of taxes withheld from your income during the year. You will either (1) receive a refund from the IRS (if too much tax was withheld from your paycheck), or (2) have to pay additional taxes (when the amount withheld was not enough to cover your tax liability). Your employer normally withholds funds not only for federal income taxes, but also for FICA (or social security) taxes and, if applicable, state and local income taxes. In addition to taxes, you may have other deductions for items such as life and health insurance, savings plans, retirement programs, professional or union dues, or charitable contributions—all of which lower your take-home pay. Your *take-home pay* is what you are left with after subtracting the amount withheld from your *gross earnings*.

federal withholding taxes Taxes—based on the level of earnings and the number of withholding allowances claimed—that are deducted by an employer from the employee's gross earnings each pay period.

FEDERAL WITHHOLDING TAXES. The amount of **federal withholding taxes** deducted from your gross earnings each pay period depends on both the level of your earnings and the number of withholding allowances you have claimed on a form called a *W-4*, which you must complete for your employer. Obviously, given the progressive nature of federal income taxes, the more money you make, the more you can expect to have withheld from your paycheck. Withholding allowances, which are based for the most part on the number of people your income supports, act to reduce the amount of taxes withheld from your income. A taxpayer is entitled to one allowance for himself or herself, one for the spouse (if filing jointly), and one for each dependent claimed.

In addition, a *special allowance* can be taken by those (1) who are single and have one job; (2) who are married, have only one job, and have a nonworking spouse; or (3) whose wages from a second job or whose spouse's wages (or the total of both) are $1,000 or less. *Additional withholding allowances* can be claimed by (1) heads of households, (2) those with at least $1,500 of child or dependent care expenses for which they plan to claim a credit, and (3) those with an unusually large amount of deductions. Of course, you can elect to have your employer withhold amounts greater than those prescribed by the withholding tables.

If you know you will work less than 8 months during a year—as you would if you are a college graduate starting your first job in the summer—you can ask your employer to calculate withholding using the part-year method. This method calculates withholding on what you actually earn in the tax year, rather than your annual salary. Under the part-year plan, if you began a $30,000 per year job in September your withholding would be based not on the entire year's salary but rather on the $10,000 you'd earn during that calendar year. This results in substantially lower withholding.

FICA AND OTHER WITHHOLDING TAXES. In addition to withholding on earnings, all employed workers (except certain federal employees) have to pay a combined old-age, survivor's, disability, and hospital insurance tax under provisions of the **Federal Insurance Contributions Act (FICA)**. Known more commonly as the **social security tax**, it is applied to a stipulated amount of every employee's wages as mandated by Congress. This tax is paid equally by employer and employee. In 2000, the total social security tax rate was 15.3 percent (allocated 12.4 percent for social security and 2.9 percent for Medicare), and was levied against the first $76,200 of an employee's earnings. Therefore, in 2000, 7.65 percent would have been deducted from your paycheck (6.2 percent for social security and 1.45 percent for

Federal Insurance Contributions Act (FICA); social security tax
The law establishing the combined old-age, survivor's, disability, and hospital insurance tax levied on both employer and employee; also called the *social security tax*.

CONCEPT CHECK

3-1. Discuss the following items and explain their significance with respect to personal taxes: (a) Internal Revenue Code of 1939, (b) the IRS, (c) federal withholding taxes, and (d) FICA. What was the purpose of the Tax Reform Act of 1986?

3-2. What is a *progressive tax structure?* What is the economic rationale underlying the notion of progressive income taxes? What impact will the 2001 Tax Act have on federal income tax brackets?

3-3. Mo Huang has an opportunity to earn $2,000 working overtime during the Christmas season. He thinks he will turn it down, however, because the extra income would put him in a higher tax bracket and the government would probably get most of it. Discuss Mo's reasoning.

3-4. Briefly define the five filing categories available to taxpayers. When might married taxpayers choose to file separately?

3-5. Distinguish between gross earnings and take-home pay. What does the employer do with the difference?

3-6. What two factors determine the amount of federal withholding taxes that will be deducted from gross earnings each pay period? Explain.

Medicare) until your year-to-date earnings reached $76,200. You would continue to pay the 1.45 percent Medicare surcharge on amounts in excess of $76,200. Self-employed persons pay the full tax—15.3 percent in 2000—and can deduct 50 percent of it on their tax returns.

Most states have their own income taxes, which differ from state to state. If levied, these taxes are generally tied to the individual's level of earnings. Some cities assess income taxes as well. These state and local income taxes will also be withheld from earnings. They are deductible on federal returns, but deductibility of federal taxes on the state or local return depends on state and local laws.

We'll discuss social security and other income taxes in more detail later in the chapter.

■ It's Taxable Income That Matters [LG2]

taxable income
The amount of income that is subject to taxes; calculated by subtracting adjustments, the larger of itemized or standard deductions, and exemptions from gross income.

To pay your income taxes, you must first calculate your **taxable income**. This requires you to make adjustments to *gross income* and then subtract the deductions and exemptions to which you are entitled. This is not as easy as it sounds, however. Various sections of the Internal Revenue Code place numerous conditions and exceptions on the tax treatment and deductibility of certain income and expense items and define certain types of income as tax-exempt. The actual amount of taxable income is often difficult to determine. Exhibit 3.3 depicts the procedure for and components of computing your taxable income and subsequent tax liability.

The procedure given in Exhibit 3.3 looks simple enough—just subtract certain adjustments, deductions, and exemptions from your gross income, and you will get taxable income. As we will see, however, there are a number of problems that arise in defining what may be subtracted.

GROSS INCOME

gross income
The total of all of a taxpayer's income (before any adjustments, deductions, or exemptions) subject to federal taxes; it includes active, portfolio, and passive income.

Basically, **gross income** includes any and all income subject to federal taxes. Some of the more common forms of gross income include:

- Wages and salaries
- Bonuses, commissions, and tips
- Interest and dividends received
- Alimony received
- Business and farm income
- Gains from the sale of assets
- Income from pensions and annuities
- Income from rents and partnerships
- Prizes, lottery, and gambling winnings

In addition to these sources of income, some types are considered *tax exempt* and as such are excluded—totally or partially—from gross income. Tax-exempt income does not even have to be listed on the tax return. A partial list of different types of tax-exempt income is shown in Exhibit 3.4.

THREE KINDS OF INCOME. One of the major provisions of the Tax Reform Act of 1986 was the creation of three basic categories of income, devised as a way to limit write-offs from tax-sheltered investments. Active (ordinary "earned") income is the broadest category, whereas portfolio (investment) and passive income are more specialized:

- *Active income*—income *earned* on the job such as wages and salaries, bonuses and tips; most other forms of *noninvestment* income, including pension income and alimony.

EXHIBIT 3.3

CALCULATING TAXABLE INCOME

To find taxable income you must first subtract all adjustments to gross income and then subtract deductions and personal exemptions.

Step A: Determine Adjusted Gross Income	**Gross income** [all income subject to income taxes]
	Less ↓
	Adjustments to (gross) income [tax-deductible expenses and retirement plan contributions]
	Equals ↓
	Adjusted Gross Income (AGI)
	Less ↓
Step B: Calculate Taxable Income	Larger of itemized deductions or the standard deduction
	Less ↓
	Total personal exemptions
	Equals ↓
	TAXABLE INCOME

EXHIBIT 3.4

COMMON TYPES OF TAX-EXEMPT INCOME

On some forms of income you do not have to pay any taxes at all because they can be totally or partially excluded from gross income. Some common types of tax-exempt income are listed here.

Child support payments	Military allowances
Compensation from accident, health, and life insurance policies	Return of original investment capital
Disability payments (limited in some cases)	Scholarships and fellowships (limited as to amount and time)
Employee fringe benefits (limited to certain items)	Social security benefits (amount exempted depends on total income)
Federal income tax refunds	Stock rights and stock dividends
Gifts	Veterans' benefits
Inheritances	Welfare and other public assistance benefits
Interest on state or local government obligations	Workers' compensation payments

- *Portfolio income*—earnings (interest, dividends, and capital gains [profits on the sale of investments]) generated from most types of investment holdings; includes savings accounts, stocks, bonds, mutual funds, options, and futures.
- *Passive income*—a special category of income that includes income derived from real estate, limited partnerships, and other forms of tax shelters.

These categories limit the amount of deductions and write-offs that taxpayers can take, particularly with regard to portfolio and passive income. Specifically, the amount of allowable, deductible expenses associated with portfolio and passive income *is limited to the amount of income derived from these two sources.* For example, if you had a total of $380 in portfolio income for the year, you could write off no more than $380 in portfolio-related interest expense. Note, however, that if you have more portfolio expenses than income, you can "accumulate" the difference and write it off in later years (when you have sufficient portfolio income) or when you finally sell the investment. Likewise, the same rules generally apply to passive income and related expenses (with a few notable exceptions, which will be discussed later in this chapter). Thus, if you own limited partnerships that generate no income, you cannot write off the losses from those partnerships in the year in which they occur; as with portfolio expenses, however, you can accumulate these losses and write them off later when you have sufficient passive income or when you sell the investment.

It is important to understand that for deduction purposes, portfolio and passive income cannot be mixed or combined with each other or with active income. *Investment-related expenses can be used only with portfolio income*, and with a few exceptions, *passive investment expenses can be used only to offset the income from passive investments.* All the other allowances and deductions we'll describe below are written off against the total amount of *active* income the taxpayer generates. In essence, the taxpayer adds up all income from wages, salaries, bonuses, tips, pensions, alimony, and so on and then subtracts the various deductions from this amount to arrive at *adjusted gross income* and, ultimately, the amount of taxable income.

CAPITAL GAINS. Technically, a *capital gain* occurs whenever an asset (such as a stock, a bond, or real estate) is sold for more than its original cost. Thus, if you purchased stock for $50 per share and sold it for $60, you'd have a capital gain of $10 per share.

As of 2001, capital gains are taxed at four different rates depending on the holding period. Exhibit 3.5 shows the different holding periods and applicable tax rates based on

EXHIBIT 3.5

CAPITAL GAINS TAX CATEGORIES AS OF 2001 (USING YEAR 2000 RATES)

Captial gains tax rates have fallen recently to 8 or 18 percent, depending on the tax bracket (year 2000). The lowest rates went into effect on January 1, 2001.

Holding Period	Tax Bracket (2000)	Tax on Capital Gains
Less than 12 months	All [15%, 28%, 31%, 36%, 39.6%]	Same as ordinary income
Over 12 months but		
less than 5 years	15%	10%
	28%, 31%, 36%, 39.6%	20%
Over 5 years	15%	8%
	28%, 31%, 36%, 39.6%	18%*

*Applies only to assets purchased after January 1, 2001.

the year 2000 schedule. As a rule, taxpayers include most capital gains as part of *portfolio income*. They will add any capital gains to the amount of dividends, interest, and rents they generate to arrive at total investment income.

Although there are no limits on the amount of capital gains taxpayers can generate, the IRS imposes some restrictions on the amount of capital losses taxpayers can take in a given year. Specifically, a taxpayer can write off capital losses, dollar for dollar, against any capital gains. For example, a taxpayer with $10,000 in capital gains can write off up to $10,000 in capital losses. After that, he or she can write off a maximum of $3,000 in additional capital losses against other (active, earned) income. Thus, if the taxpayer in our example had $18,000 in capital losses in 2000, only $13,000 could be written off on 2000 taxes: $10,000 against the capital gains generated in 2000 and another $3,000 against active income. The remainder—$5,000 in this case—will have to be written off in later years, in the same order as indicated above: first against any capital gains and then up to $3,000 against active income. (*Note:* To qualify as a deductible item, the capital loss *must result from the sale of some income-producing asset*, such as stocks and bonds. The capital loss on a non–income producing asset, such as a car or TV set, does *not* qualify for tax relief.)

 The Guide to Capital Gains and Losses, **www.fairmark.com/ buystock/index.htm**, can help you understand the tax treatment of securities sales. It's just one of many tax guides you'll find at the site's Tax Guide for Investors.

Selling Your Home: A Special Case. Homeowners, for a variety of reasons, receive special treatment in the tax codes, including the taxation of capital gains on the sale of a home. The Taxpayer Relief Act of 1997 made most home sales tax free. Under the new law, single taxpayers may exclude from income the first $250,000 of gain on the sale of a principal residence. Married taxpayers may exclude the first $500,000. To get this favorable tax treatment, the taxpayer must own and occupy the residence as a principal residence for at least 2 of the 5 years prior to the sale. For example, the Greenmans (married taxpayers) just sold their principal residence for $475,000. They had purchased their home 4 years earlier for $325,000. They may exclude their $150,000 gain ($475,000 − $325,000) from their income because they occupied the residence for more than 2 years, and the gain is less than $500,000.

This exclusion is available on only one sale every 2 years. A loss on the sale of a principal residence is not deductible. Generally speaking, this law is quite favorable to homeowners.

ADJUSTMENTS TO (GROSS) INCOME

adjustments to (gross) income
Allowable deductions from gross income; includes certain employee, personal retirement, insurance, and support expenses.

Now that you have totaled up your gross income, you deduct your **adjustments to (gross) income**. These are allowable deductions from gross income, including certain employee, personal retirement, insurance, and support expenses. Most of these deductions are nonbusiness in nature. The following list, though not exhaustive, includes items that can be treated as adjustments to income:

- IRA contributions (limited)
- Self-employment taxes paid (limited to 50 percent of amount paid)
- Self-employed health insurance payments (limited to 25 percent of amount paid)
- Keogh retirement plan and self-employed SEP contributions (limited)
- Penalty on early withdrawal of savings
- Alimony paid
- Moving expenses (some limits)

(*Note*: The limitations on deductions for self-directed retirement plans, such as IRAs and Keoghs, are discussed in Chapter 14.)

adjusted gross income (AGI)
The amount of income remaining after subtracting all available adjustments to income from gross income.

When the total of all allowable adjustments to income is subtracted from gross income, you are left with **adjusted gross income** (**AGI**). AGI is in itself an important value, because AGI is used to determine limits to certain itemized deductions.

DEDUCTIONS: ITEMIZED OR STANDARD?

As we see from Exhibit 3.3, the next step in calculating your taxes is to subtract allowable deductions from your AGI to determine taxable income. This is perhaps the most complex part of the tax preparation process. You have two options: list your *itemized deductions* (specified tax-deductible personal expenses) or take the *standard deduction*, a blanket deduction that depends on your filing status. Obviously, you should use the method that results in larger allowable deductions.

itemized deductions
Personal expenditures that can be deducted from AGI when determining taxable income.

ITEMIZED DEDUCTIONS. **Itemized deductions** allow taxpayers to reduce their AGI by the amount of their allowable personal expenditures. The Internal Revenue Code defines the types of nonbusiness items that can be deducted from AGI. Some of the more common ones follow:

- Medical and dental expenses (in excess of 7.5 percent of AGI)
- State, local, and foreign income and property taxes; and state and local personal property taxes
- Residential mortgage interest and investment interest (limited)
- Charitable contributions (limited to 50 percent, 30 percent, or 20 percent of AGI depending on certain factors)
- Casualty and theft losses (in excess of 10 percent of AGI; reduced by $100 per loss)
- Job and other expenses (in excess of 2 percent of AGI)
- Moving expenses (some restrictions; also deductible for those who don't itemize)

We'll describe medical and dental, mortgage, job and other expenses in greater detail later in this chapter.

Beginning in 1991, taxpayers with AGI over a specified amount lost part of their itemized deductions. The amount is adjusted upward annually; in 2000 the level of AGI at which the phase-out began was $128,950 (or $64,475 for married persons filing separately). This limitation applies to certain categories of deductions, including other types of taxes, home mortgage interest, charitable contributions, unreimbursed employee expenses, moving expenses, and other miscellaneous deductions subject to the 2 percent limit. Medical expenses, casualty and theft losses, and investment interest are exempt from this limit on deductions, and the amount of the total reduction in itemized deductions cannot be more than 80 percent of the total deductions to which the limitation applies. These total itemized deductions are reduced by the smaller of 3 percent of AGI over $128,950 (or $64,475 for married taxpayers filing separately) or 80 percent of the deductions to which the limitation applies.

For example, assume your AGI is $150,000, deductions (in excess of any specified percentages of AGI) affected by the income limitation total $45,000, and other deductions total $10,000. You must reduce deductions by $631.50 [($150,000 AGI − $128,950) × .03 = $631.50]. Therefore, you would subtract $631.50 from your $55,000 total itemized deductions, for an allowed deduction of $54,368.50. This loss of itemized deductions has the effect of raising the tax rate applied to your top bracket (in this case) from 31 percent to 31.93 percent [31.00% + (3% × 31%)]. Married taxpayers with combined income over the AGI deduction threshold and high itemized deductions that can be allocated to one spouse (such as medical expenses) may find that filing separately will allow them to avoid this limit on deductions. Note that the 2001 Tax Act provides for repeal of the provisions requiring reduction in itemized deductions for taxpayers with high levels of AGI. This repeal will be phased in during 2006 to 2010.

Taxpayers may deduct medical and dental expenses they pay during the taxable year. However, this deduction is limited to the amount by which such expenditures *exceed*, not equal, 7.5 percent of AGI. You may include as medical and dental expenses medical insurance premiums and any expenses incurred in the diagnosis, cure, mitigation, and treatment of disease and injury or in the prevention of disease. Some qualifying expenses include costs related to doctors, dentists, hospitals, corrective devices such as eyeglasses, transportation, medicine and drugs, and education for the physically or mentally handicapped. You may not deduct surgery for purely cosmetic reasons. Of course, you cannot deduct any item for which you are reimbursed by medical insurance.

Another deduction is permitted for interest paid on first and second mortgages. These mortgages must be on the taxpayer's principal residence, or on a second home such as a summer cabin or vacation condominium. In most cases, you can deduct all your home mortgage interest. There are some limitations, however, depending on the date of the mortgage, the amount of the mortgage, and how you used the proceeds. Interest on mortgages of any amount acquired before October 13, 1987, was fully deductible. After October 13, 1987, mortgages taken out to buy, build, or improve your home are fully deductible if these mortgages, together with any mortgages taken out before October 13, 1987, total $1 million or less.

Interest on mortgages taken out for uses other than to buy, build, or improve your home (called *home equity loans* and described more fully in Chapter 6) is deductible on loans up to $100,000. If a home equity loan exceeds $100,000, interest on the portion used for home improvements or for educational or medical purposes is tax deductible up to the $1 million total mortgage interest limit.

As explained in the preceding discussion of *gross income*, interest may also be deductible when incurred for investment purposes as long as such interest expense does not exceed the amount of *portfolio income* reported by the taxpayer. The deduction for interest paid on consumer loans, allowed for decades, was eliminated in 1991.

Another category of allowable deductions is for job and other expenses. This catchall category includes everything from unreimbursed employee expenses, such as job travel, union and professional association dues, and job-related subscriptions to professional

EXHIBIT 3.6

CALCULATING STANDARD DEDUCTION AMOUNTS UNDER VARIOUS FILING ALTERNATIVES (2000)

The standard deduction for taxpayers depends on filing status, age, and vision. The following IRS form can be used to estimate your allowable standard deduction.

STEP 1. Check the correct number of boxes below.

You	65 or older ❏	Blind ❏
Your spouse	65 or older ❏	Blind ❏

Total number of boxes you checked   _____

STEP 2. Find your standard deduction.

If Your Filing Status is:	And Number of Boxes Checked in Step 1 Above Are:	Your Standard Deduction is:
Single	0	$ 4,400
	1	5,500
	2	6,600
Married filing jointly or Qualifying widow(er) with dependent child	0	$ 7,350
	1	8,200
	2	9,050
	3	9,900
	4	10,750
Married, filing separately*	0	$ 3,675
	1	4,525
	2	5,375
	3	6,225
	4	7,075
Head of household	0	$ 6,450
	1	7,550
	2	8,650

* If your spouse itemizes deductions on a separate return, you must also itemize deductions rather than take the standard deduction.

journals, to safe-deposit box rental and tax preparation fees. (The amount of allowable deductions for business-related meals and entertainment is limited to 50 percent of the amount actually spent on them.) The total of all these job and other expenses is deductible *only to the extent that it exceeds 2 percent of adjusted gross income.* Thus, if you have an AGI of $25,000, your total job and other expense deductions would have to exceed $500 (which is 2 percent of the AGI, or .02 × $25,000 = $500). If expenses amounted to $800, for instance, you would write off $300 in these deductions: $800 − $500 = $300.

standard deduction
A blanket deduction that depends on the taxpayer's filing status, age, and vision and can be taken by a taxpayer who doesn't have sufficient itemized deductions.

STANDARD DEDUCTION. Instead of itemizing personal deductions, a taxpayer can take the **standard deduction**, which is a type of blanket deduction meant to capture the various deductible expenses that taxpayers normally incur. People who don't have sufficient itemized deductions take the stipulated standard deduction, which varies depending on the taxpayer's filing status (single, married filing jointly, and so on), age (65 or older), and vision (blind). In 2000 the standard deduction varied from $4,400 to $10,750. Exhibit 3.6 includes the 2000 table that can be used to calculate your standard deduction. Each year the standard deduction amounts are adjusted in response to changes in the cost of living.

Note that the 2001 Tax Act will (over 2005 to 2009) make the standard deduction twice as great for married couples as for singles.

CHOOSING THE BEST OPTION. Your decision to itemize deductions or take the standard deduction may change from year to year, or even in the same year. Taxpayers who find they have chosen the wrong option and paid too much may recalculate their tax using the other method and claim a refund for the difference. For example, suppose you computed and paid your taxes, which amounted to $2,450, using the standard deduction. A few months later you find that had you itemized your deductions, your taxes would have been only $1,950. Using the appropriate forms, you can file an *amended return (Form 1040X)* showing a $500 refund ($2,450 − $1,950). To avoid having to file an amended return as a result of using the wrong deduction technique, you should estimate your deductions using both the itemized and standard deduction amounts and then choose the alternative that results in lower taxes. Interestingly, most taxpayers use the standard deduction; generally homeowners who pay home mortgage interest and property taxes itemize because those expenses alone typically exceed the allowable standard deduction.

EXEMPTIONS

Deductions from AGI based on the number of persons supported by the taxpayer's income are called **exemptions**. A taxpayer can claim an exemption for himself or herself, his or her spouse, and any *dependents*—which include children or other relatives earning less than a stipulated level of income ($2,800 in 2000) and for whom the taxpayer provides more than half of their total support. This income limitation is waived for children under the age of 24 (at the end of the calendar year) who are full-time students. Therefore, a college student, for example, could earn $8,000 and still be claimed as an exemption by his or her parents as long as all other dependency requirements are met. In 2000, each exemption claimed was worth $2,800. The personal exemption amount is tied to the cost of living and changes annually in line with the prevailing rates on inflation.

Exemptions are phased out and eliminated altogether for taxpayers with high levels of AGI. The phase-out provision was introduced in 1991. After adjustment for inflation, it applies to single taxpayers with 2000 AGI over $128,950 and married couples filing jointly with 2000 AGI over $193,400. This phase-out, together with the itemized deduction phase-out, raises the effective tax rate for a single taxpayer with AGI over $128,950 and one exemption to about 33

exemptions
Deductions from AGI based on the number of persons supported by the taxpayer's income.

CONCEPT CHECK

3-7. Define and differentiate between *gross income* and *AGI*. Name several types of tax-exempt income. What is *passive income*?

3-8. Define what is meant by a *capital gain*. What is the tax treatment of capital gains?

3-9. If you itemize your deductions, certain expenses may be included as part of your itemized deductions. Discuss five types of itemized deductions and the general rules that apply to them.

3-10. Larry Tolle was married on January 15, 2001. His wife, Rebecca, is a full-time student at the university and earns $125 a month working in the library. How many personal exemptions will Larry and Rebecca be able to claim on their joint return? Would it make any difference if Rebecca's parents paid for more than 50 percent of her support? Explain.

percent, and for a married couple with two children to more than 34 percent. Note that the 2001 Tax Act provides for repeal (phased in over 2006 to 2010) of the provisions requiring reduction in personal exemptions for taxpayers with hight levels of AGI.

Moreover, a personal exemption can be claimed only once. If a child is *eligible* to be claimed as an exemption by his or her parents, then the child does not have the choice of using a personal exemption on his or her own tax return regardless of whether the parents use the child's exemption.

In 2000, a family of four could take total exemptions of $11,200—that is, 4 × $2,800. Subtracting the amount claimed for itemized deductions (or the standard deduction) and exemptions from AGI results in the amount of your *taxable income*, which is the basis on which your taxes are figured. A taxpayer who makes $40,000 a year may have only, say, $25,000 in taxable income after adjustments, deductions, and exemptions. It is the *lower*, taxable income figure that determines how much tax an individual must pay.

 ## ◼ Calculating and Filing Your Taxes [LG3]

Now that we have reviewed the general principles of federal income taxes and the components of taxable income, we can direct our attention to calculating the amount of income tax due. To do this, we need to address several key aspects of measuring taxable income and taxes: (1) the tax rates applicable to various types of personal income, (2) tax credits, (3) the basic tax forms and schedules, and (4) the procedures for determining tax liability.

TAX RATES

As we saw earlier in this chapter, to find the amount of *taxable income* we subtract itemized deductions (or the standard deduction for nonitemizers) *and* personal exemptions from AGI. *Both itemizers and nonitemizers* use this procedure, which is a key calculation in determining your tax liability. It is *reported taxable income* that determines the amount of income subject to federal income taxes. Once you know the amount of your taxable income, you can refer to *tax rate tables* to find the amount of taxes you owe. (When actually filing a tax return, taxpayers with taxable income of more than $100,000 must use the tax rate schedules.)

Tax rates vary not only with the amount of reported taxable income, but also with filing status. Thus different tax rate schedules apply to each filing category, as shown in Exhibit 3.7. The vast majority of taxpayers—perhaps 90 percent or more—fall into the first two brackets and are subject to tax rates of either 15 or 28 percent. As noted previously, the 2001 Tax Act provides for reduction in rates and the addition of brackets over the period of 2001 to 2006.

To see how the tax rates in Exhibit 3.7 work, consider two single taxpayers: one has taxable income of $12,500, the other of $29,600. We would calculate their respective tax liabilities as follows:

- For taxable income of $12,500: $12,500 × .15 = $1,875
- For taxable income of $29,600: $3,937.50 + [($29,600 − $26,250) × .28] = $3,937.50 + $938 = $4,875.50

The income of $12,500 is taxed at the 15 percent tax rate, and the $29,600 is partially taxed at 15 percent and the remainder at 28 percent. Keep in mind that taxpayers use the same procedures at this point whether they itemize or not. To show how the amount of tax liability will vary with the level of taxable income, Exhibit 3.8 lists the taxes due on a range of taxable incomes, from $500 to $200,000, for individual and joint returns.

Recall from our earlier discussions that the *average tax rate* is found by dividing your tax liability by the amount of reported taxable income. Returning to our example involving the taxpayer with an income of $29,600, we see that this individual had an average tax

EXHIBIT 3.7

TAX RATE SCHEDULES (2000)

Tax rates levied on personal income vary with the amount of reported taxable income and the taxpayer's filing status.

Single

Taxable Income	Tax Rate	Taxes Due
$0 to $26,250	15%	15% of reported taxable income
$26,251 to $63,550	28%	$3,937.50 plus 28% of the amount over $26,250
$63,551 to $132,600	31%	$14,381.50 plus 31% of the amount over $63,550
$132,601 to $288,350	36%	$35,787.00 plus 36% of the amount over $132,600
Over $288,350	39.6%	$91,857.00 plus 39.6% of the amount over $288,350

Married Filing Jointly or Qualifying Widow(er)

Taxable Income	Tax Rate	Taxes Due
$0 to $43,850	15%	15% of reported taxable income
$43,851 to $105,950	28%	$6,577.50 plus 28% of the amount over $43,850
$105,951 to $161,450	31%	$23,965.50 plus 31% of the amount over $105,950
$161,451 to $288,350	36%	$41,170.50 plus 36% of the amount over $161,450
Over $288,350	39.6%	$86,854.50 plus 39.6% of the amount over $288,350

Married Filing Separately

Taxable Income	Tax Rate	Taxes Due
$0 to $21,925	15%	15% of reported taxable income
$21,926 to $52,975	28%	$3,288.75 plus 28% of the amount over $21,925
$52,976 to $80,725	31%	$11,982.75 plus 31% of the amount over $52,975
$80,726 to $144,175	36%	$20,585.25 plus 36% of the amount over $80,725
Over $144,175	39.6%	$43.427.25 plus 39.6% of the amount over $144,175

Head of Household

Taxable Income	Tax Rate	Taxes Due
$0 to $35,150	15%	15% of reported taxable income
$35,151 to $90,800	28%	$5,272.50 plus 28% of the amount over $35,150
$90,801 to $147,050	31%	$20,854.50 plus 31% of the amount over $90,800
$147,051 to $288,350	36%	$38,292.00 plus 36% of the amount over $147,050
Over $288,350	39.6%	$89,160.00 plus 39.6% of the amount over $288,350

rate of 16.5 percent ($4,875.50 ÷ $29,600), which is considerably *less* than the stated tax rate of 28 percent. Actually, the 28 percent represents the taxpayer's **marginal tax rate**—the rate at which the next dollar of taxable income is taxed. Notice in our calculations that the 28 percent tax rate applies only to that portion of the single person's income that exceeds $26,250. Thus the first $26,250 in income is taxed at 15 percent—only the balance ($29,600 − $26,250 = $3,350) is subject to the marginal tax rate of 28 percent.

Some taxpayers are subject to the *alternative minimum tax (AMT)*, currently 26 percent of the first $175,000 and 28 percent of the excess. A taxpayer's tax liability is the higher of the AMT or the regular tax. The AMT was originally designed to ensure that high-income taxpayers with many deductions and tax shelter investments that provide attractive tax write-offs pay their fair share of taxes. The AMT includes in taxable income certain types of deductions otherwise allowed, such as state and local income and property taxes, miscellaneous itemized deductions, unreimbursed medical expenses, and depreciation. Therefore, taxpayers with moderate levels of taxable income, including those living in states with high tax rates and self-employed persons with depreciation deductions, may be subject to the AMT.

marginal tax rate
The rate at which the next dollar of taxable income is taxed.

EXHIBIT 3.8

TAXABLE INCOME AND THE AMOUNT OF INCOME TAXES DUE (2000)

Given the progressive tax structure that exists in this country, it follows that the larger your income, the more you can expect to pay in taxes.

| | Taxes Due | |
Taxable Income	Individual Returns	Joint Returns
$ 500	$ 75.00*	$ 75.00*
1,000	150.00	150.00
5,000	750.00	750.00
10,000	1,500.00	1,500.00
20,000	3,000.00	3,000.00
30,000	4,987.50**	4,500.00
50,000	10,587.50	8,299.50**
75,000	17,931.00***	15,299.50
120,000	30,187.50	28,321.00***
150,000	42,051.00****	37,621.00
200,000	60,051.00	55,048.50****

*Income is taxed at 15%.

**28% tax rate now applies.

***31% tax rate now applies.

****36% tax rate now applies.

TAX CREDITS

tax credits
Deductions from a taxpayer's tax liability that directly reduce his or her *taxes due* rather than *taxable income*.

Once you have determined your taxable income and calculated the *tax liability*, or amount of taxes you owe, you have one final step to determine the amount of taxes due. Some taxpayers are allowed to take certain deductions, known as **tax credits**, directly from their tax liability.

A tax credit is much more valuable than a deduction or an exemption, because it directly reduces, dollar for dollar, the amount of *taxes due*, whereas a deduction or an exemption merely reduces the amount of *taxable income*. For example, assume that a single taxpayer with $38,000 of gross income and $6,000 of other deductions/exemptions (in the 28 percent tax bracket) has $1,000 in deductions, and another single taxpayer with the same gross income and other deductions/exemptions has a $1,000 tax credit. Look at what happens to the amount of taxes paid:

		$1,000 Deduction	$1,000 Tax Credit
	Gross income	$38,000.00	$38,000.00
Less:	Other deductions/ exemptions	6,000.00	6,000.00
Less:	$1,000 deduction	1,000.00	—
	Taxable income	$31,000.00	$32,000.00
	Tax liability*	$ 5,267.50	$ 5,547.50
Less:	$1,000 tax credit	—	1,000.00
	Taxes paid	$ 5,267.50	$ 4,547.50

*The tax liability is figured as follows: the first $26,250 of taxable income is taxed at 15%, the balance at 28%.

In effect, the tax credit in this example has reduced taxes (and therefore *increased* after-tax income) by over $700.

An often-used tax credit is for child and dependent care expenses. This credit is based on the amount spent for dependent care while a taxpayer (and spouse, if married) works or goes to school. The qualifying dependent must be less than 13 years old, except in the case of a disabled dependent or spouse. The base amount of the credit is limited to $2,400 for one dependent and $4,800 for two or more dependents. The actual amount of the credit is a percentage of the amount spent or of the limit, whichever is less. The percentages range from 20 to 30 percent, depending on the taxpayer's AGI. For example, a couple with AGI of $30,000 who spent $3,000 on child care expenses for their two young children would receive a dependent care credit of $600 (.20 × $3,000). The 2001 Tax Act provided for an increase in the dependant-care credit in 2001 to 2003.

An important credit for lower-income workers is the *earned income credit.* In 2000, this credit is worth up to $2,353 for taxpayers with one qualifying child living with them in their home in the United States. The credit is worth $3,888 with two qualifying children, and $353 for taxpayers between 25 and 65 years old with no qualifying children. The credit is gradually phased out for taxpayers with earned income (from wages) and AGI in excess of $12,700 ($5,800 if there is no qualifying child). It is phased out completely when earned income or AGI reaches $27,413 for one qualifying child, $31,152 for two or more qualifying children, or $10,380 for no children.

Beginning in 1997, an *adoption tax credit* of up to $5,000 is available for the qualifying costs of adopting a child under age 18. The credit is $6,000 for adoption of a child with special needs. The adoption tax credit is phased out for those with AGI between $75,000 and $115,000. The 2001 Tax Act provided for an increase in the adoption credit during 2002 to 2003.

Beginning in 1998, taxpayers with dependent children under age 17 became entitled to a child tax credit which in 2000 was $500 per qualifying child. The credit is phased out for married couples with AGI above $110,000, $75,000 for single filers, and $55,000 for married persons filing separately. The 2001 Tax Act provided for doubling the $500 per child tax credit and making it refundable for taxpayers with earned income of more than $10,000. These provisions are scheduled to phase in 2001 through 2010. Other common tax credits include:

- Credit for the elderly or the disabled
- Foreign tax credit
- Credit for prior year minimum tax
- Mortgage interest credit
- Credit for qualified electric vehicle

To receive one of these credits, the taxpayer must file a return, along with a separate schedule in support of the tax credit claimed.

TAX FORMS AND SCHEDULES

The IRS requires taxpayers to file their returns using certain specified tax forms. As noted earlier, these forms and a variety of instruction booklets on how to prepare them are available to taxpayers free of charge. Generally, all persons who filed tax returns in the previous year are automatically sent a booklet containing tax forms and instructions for preparing returns for the current year. Inside the booklet is a form that can be used to obtain additional tax forms for filing various tax-related returns and information. Exhibit 3.9 provides a list of some of the more commonly used tax forms.

 Need a tax form or instructions on how to fill it out? Head for the IRS Digital Daily, **www.irs.gov**, where you will find tax forms, instructions, IRS publications, and regulations. You can also use the W-4 calculator to make sure you aren't having too much or too little withheld from your paycheck.

EXHIBIT 3.9

COMMONLY USED TAX FORMS

A number of types of 1040 tax return forms are available. If the standard Form 1040 is used, one or more forms (listed below the 1040s) may be included with the tax return, depending on the amount and types of deductions claimed.

1040	Standard tax return, used with itemized deductions
1040A	Short-form tax return
1040EZ	Short-form tax return for single persons with no dependents
1040X	Amended U.S. individual tax return
1040-ES	Estimated tax for individuals
2106	Employee business expenses
2119	Sale of your home
2441	Child and dependent care expenses
3903	Moving expenses
4562	Depreciation and amortization
4684	Casualties and thefts
4868	Application for automatic extension of time to file U.S. individual tax return
8829	Expenses for business use of your home

VARIATIONS OF FORM 1040. All individuals use some variation of Form 1040 to file their tax returns. *Form 1040EZ* is a simple, one-page form. You qualify to use this form if you are single or married filing a joint return; under age 65 (both if filing jointly); not blind; do not claim any dependents; have taxable income of less than $50,000 from only wages, salaries, tips, or taxable scholarships or grants; have interest income of less than $400; and do not itemize deductions or claim any tax credits. Worksheet 3.1 shows the Form 1040EZ filed in 2000 by Yoshio Ohno, a full-time graduate student at Anystate University. His sources of income include a $6,000 scholarship, of which $1,200 was used for room and board, $6,500 earned from part-time and summer jobs, and $50 interest earned on a savings account deposit. Because scholarships used for tuition and fees are not taxed, he must include as income only the portion used for room and board. He had a total of $250 withheld for federal income taxes during the year.

To use *Form 1040A*, a two-page form, your income must be less than $50,000 and derived only from specified sources. Using this form you may deduct certain IRA contributions and claim certain tax credits, but you cannot itemize your deductions. If your income is over $50,000 or you itemize deductions, you must use the standard Form 1040 along with appropriate schedules, briefly described as follows:

Schedule	Description
A	For itemized deductions
B	For interest and ordinary dividend income of more than $400 each
C	For profit (or loss) from a personally owned business
D	For capital gains and losses
E	For supplemental income and losses from rents, royalties, partnerships, estates, trusts, etc.
F	For profit and loss from farming
R	For credit for the elderly or disabled
SE	For reporting social security self-employment tax

The use of these schedules, which provide detailed guidelines for calculating certain entries on the first two pages of *Form 1040*, varies among taxpayers depending on the relevance

2000 TAX RETURN (FORM 1040EZ) FOR YOSHIO OHNO

Form 1040EZ is very easy to use, and most of the instructions are printed right on the form itself. Yoshio Ohno qualifies to use it because he is single, under age 65, not blind, and meets its income and deduction restrictions.

Department of the Treasury—Internal Revenue Service

Form 1040EZ

Income Tax Return for Single and Joint Filers With No Dependents **2000** OMB No. 1545-0675

Use the IRS label here

Your first name and initial: Yoshio   Last name: Ohno

If a joint return, spouse's first name and initial   Last name

Home address (number and street). If you have a P.O. box, see page 12. 1000 State University Drive   Apt. no. 14A

City, town or post office, state, and ZIP code. If you have a foreign address, see page 12. Anytown, Anystate 10100

Your social security number 978 56 1432

Spouse's social security number

Presidential Campaign (p. 12) **Note.** Checking "Yes" will not change your tax or reduce your refund. Do you, or spouse if a joint return, want $3 to go to this fund? ▶

You: ☒ Yes ☐ No   Spouse: ☐ Yes ☐ No

	Dollars	Cents

Income

Attach Form(s) W-2 here. Enclose, but do not attach, any payment.

1 Total wages, salaries, and tips. This should be shown in box 1 of your W-2 form(s). Attach your W-2 form(s). ..... 1 — 7,700.00

2 Taxable interest. If the total is over $400, you cannot use Form 1040EZ. ..... 2 — 50.00

3 Unemployment compensation, qualified state tuition program earnings, and Alaska Permanent Fund dividends (see page 14). 3

4 Add lines 1, 2, and 3. This is your **adjusted gross income.** ..... 4 — 7,750.00

Note. You **must** check Yes or No.

5 Can your parents (or someone else) claim you on their return?
Yes. Enter amount from worksheet on back. ☐
No. If **single**, enter 7,200.00 If **married**, enter 12,950.00 See back for explanation. ☒ ..... 5 — 7,200.00

6 Subtract line 5 from line 4. If line 5 is larger than line 4, enter 0. This is your **taxable income.** ▶ 6 — 550.00

Payments and tax

7 Enter your Federal income tax withheld from box 2 of your W-2 form(s). ..... 7 — 250.00

8a **Earned income credit (EIC).** See page 15.
b Nontaxable earned income: enter type and amount below.
Type ___ $ ___ 8a

9 Add lines 7 and 8a. These are your **total payments.** ..... 9 — 250.00

10 **Tax.** Use the amount on **line 6 above** to find your tax in the tax table on pages 24–28 of the booklet. Then, enter the tax from the table on this line. ..... 10 — 84.00

Refund

Have it directly deposited! See page 20 and fill in 11b, 11c, and 11d.

11a If line 9 is larger than line 10, subtract line 10 from line 9. This is your **refund.** ..... 11a — 166.00

b Routing number ___
c Type: ☐ Checking ☐ Savings   d Account number ___

Amount you owe

12 If line 10 is larger than line 9, subtract line 9 from line 10. This is the **amount you owe.** See page 21 for details on how to pay. 12

I have read this return. Under penalties of perjury, I declare that to the best of my knowledge and belief, the return is true, correct, and accurately lists all amounts and sources of income I received during the tax year.

Sign here
Keep copy for your records.

Your signature: Yoshio Ohno
Date: 3/12/2000   Your occupation: Student

Spouse's signature if joint return. See page 11.
Date   Spouse's occupation

For Official Use Only 1 2 3 4 5 / 6 7 8 9 10

May the IRS discuss this return with the preparer shown on back (see page 21)? ☐ Yes ☐ No

For Disclosure, Privacy Act, and Paperwork Reduction Act Notice, see page 23.   Cat. No. 11329W   2000 Form 1040EZ

Financial Road Sign

Avoiding Common Tax Form Errors
Careful planning can save you from these common but unnecessary tax mistakes.

Identification mistakes: Omitting or providing incorrect names, social security numbers, or tax-identification numbers for taxpayers or dependents.

Refund/amount due errors: Calculating the refund or amount due incorrectly.

Tax amount: Choosing the wrong tax amount from the tax tables.

Capital gains tax: Miscalculating or incorrectly recording this tax.

Deductions and exemptions: Miscalculating or incorrectly recording the standard deduction and personal exemptions.

Earned-income credit: Omitting nontaxable earned income from W-2 form; miscalculating or incorrectly entering amounts used in calculations.

Source: Internal Revenue Service, cited in Dinah Wisenberg Brin, "Oops!" *Wall Street Journal*, February 28, 2000, p. R8.

of these entries to their situations. Pages 1 and 2 of Form 1040, which summarize all items of income and deductions detailed on the accompanying schedules, are used to determine and report the taxable income and associated tax liability.

Despite detailed instructions that accompany the tax forms, taxpayers make many blunders when filling them out. Common errors include missing information and arithmetic errors. So check and recheck your forms before submitting them to the IRS.

THE 2000 TAX RETURN OF TERRY AND EVELYN BECKER

Let's now put all the pieces of the tax preparation puzzle together to see how Terry and Evelyn Becker calculate and file their income taxes. The Beckers own their own home and are both 35 years old. Married for 11 years, they have three children—Tom (age 9), Dick (age 7), and Harriet (age 3). Terry is an accounting clerk for a major oil company headquartered in their hometown of Anytown, Anystate. Evelyn has 1½ years of college and works part-time as a sales clerk in a major department store. During 2000, Terry's salary totaled $30,415 while Evelyn earned $3,750. Terry's employer withheld taxes of $3,560, and Evelyn's, $550. During the year, the Beckers earned $500 interest on their joint savings account, received $750 in cash dividends on stock they owned jointly, and realized $850 in capital gains on the sale of securities they had owned for 11 months. In addition, Terry kept the books for his brother's car dealership, from which he netted $3,600 during the year. Because no taxes were withheld from any of their outside income, during the year they made estimated tax payments totaling $500. The Beckers' records indicate they had $8,613 of itemized deductions during the year. Finally, Terry Becker plans to contribute $2,000 to his traditional IRA account, something he's been doing for the past 6 years. He does this each year without fail, and, beginning in 2001, he plans to switch to a Roth IRA (see Chapter 14).

FINDING THE BECKERS' TAX LIABILITY: FORM 1040. An examination of the Beckers' 2000 tax return (Worksheet 3.2) will show the basic calculations required in preparing Form 1040. Although we don't include the supporting schedules here, we illustrate the basic calculations they require. The Beckers have detailed records of their income and expenses, which they use not only for tax purposes but as an important input into their budgeting process. Using this information, the Beckers intend to prepare their 2000 tax return in a fashion that will allow them to reduce their tax liability as much as possible. Like most married couples, the Beckers file a *joint return*.

Gross Income. The Beckers' gross income in 2000 amounted to $39,865—the amount shown as "Total Income" on line 22 of their tax return. They have both active income and portfolio income, as follows:

Active Income		
Terry's earnings	$30,415	
Evelyn's earnings	3,750	
Terry's business income (net)	3,600	
Total active income		$37,765
Portfolio Income		
Interest from savings account	$ 500	
Cash dividends on stock	750	
Capital gains realized*	850	
Total portfolio income		2,100
Total income		$39,865

*Because this gain was realized on stock held for less than 12 months, the full amount is taxable as ordinary income.

They have no investment expenses to offset their portfolio income, so they'll be liable for taxes on the full amount of portfolio income. Because they have portfolio income, the Beckers must file Schedule B (for their interest and dividend income—each of which is in excess of $400) with the Form 1040. In addition, Terry will have to file Schedule C, detailing the income earned and expenses incurred in his bookkeeping business, and Schedule D to report capital gains income.

Adjustments to Gross Income. The Beckers have only two adjustments to income: Terry's IRA contribution and 50 percent of the self-employment tax on Terry's net business income. Because the Beckers fall below the $40,000 income ceiling (just barely), they can deduct their entire $2,000 contribution to an IRA account even if Terry and/or Evelyn are already covered by a company-sponsored retirement program (see Chapter 14). Even though they could put more money into the IRA, they have chosen to stick with Terry's $2,000 contribution (see line 23). Terry's self-employment tax will be 15.3 percent of his $3,600 net business income, and he will be able to deduct one-half that amount—$275 [(.153 × $3,600)/2]—on line 27.

Adjusted Gross Income. After deducting the $2,000 IRA contribution and the $275 self-employment tax from their gross income, the Beckers are left with an AGI of $37,590, as reported on lines 33 and 34.

Itemized Deductions or Standard Deduction? The Beckers are filing a joint return and neither is over age 65 or blind, so according to Exhibit 3.6 (married filing jointly with zero boxes checked), they are entitled to a standard deduction of $7,350. However, they want to evaluate their itemized deductions before deciding which type of deduction to take— obviously they'll take the highest deduction, because it will result in the lowest amount of taxable income and keep their tax liability to a minimum. Their preliminary paperwork resulted in the following deductions:

Medical and dental expenses	$ 723
State income and property taxes paid	1,060
Mortgage interest	5,893
Charitable contributions	475
Job and other expenses	1,262
Total	$9,413

The taxes, mortgage interest, and charitable contributions are deductible in full; so at the minimum, the Beckers will have itemized deductions that amount to $7,428 ($1,060 + $5,893 + $475). However, to be deductible, the medical and dental expenses and job and other expenses must exceed stipulated minimum levels of AGI—only that portion which exceeds the specified minimum levels of AGI can be included as part of their itemized deductions. For medical and dental expenses, the minimum is 7.5 percent of AGI and for job and other expenses it is 2 percent of AGI. Because 7.5 percent of the Beckers' AGI is $2,819 (.075 × $37,590), they cannot deduct any medical and dental expenses—they fall short of the minimum. In contrast, because 2 percent of the Beckers' AGI is $752 (.02 × $37,590), they can deduct any job and other expenses that exceed that amount, or $1,262 − $752 = $510. Adding the amount of their allowable job and other expenses ($510) to their other allowable deductions ($7,428) results in total itemized deductions of $7,938. This amount exceeds the standard deduction of $7,350 by a slight margin, so the Beckers itemize their deductions. They would provide the details of these deductions on Schedule A and attach it to their Form 1040. (The total amount of the Beckers' itemized deductions is listed on line 36 of Form 1040.)

2000 TAX RETURN (FORM 1040) FOR THE BECKERS

Because they itemize deductions, the Beckers use standard Form 1040 to file their tax return. When filed with the IRS, their return will include not only Form 1040, but also other schedules and forms that provide details on many of the expenses and deductions

---

Form 1040

Department of the Treasury—Internal Revenue Service

U.S. Individual Income Tax Return **2000** (99) IRS Use Only—Do not write or staple in this space.

For the year Jan. 1–Dec. 31, 2000, or other tax year beginning _____, 2000, ending _____, 20 _____ OMB No. 1545-0074

Label (See instructions on page 19.)

Use the IRS label. Otherwise, please print or type.

LABEL HERE

Your first name and initial: *Terry B.*   Last name: *Becker*   Your social security number: 123 45 6789

If a joint return, spouse's first name and initial: *Evelyn A.*   Last name: *Becker*   Spouse's social security number: 987 65 4321

Home address (number and street). If you have a P.O. box, see page 19.: *125 Laughing Lane*   Apt. no.

City, town or post office, state, and ZIP code. If you have a foreign address, see page 19.: *Anytown, Anystate 10010*

▲ **Important!** ▲
You **must** enter your SSN(s) above.

Presidential Election Campaign (See page 19.)

Note. Checking "Yes" will not change your tax or reduce your refund.
Do you, or your spouse if filing a joint return, want $3 to go to this fund? ▶

You: ☑ Yes ☐ No   Spouse: ☑ Yes ☐ No

Filing Status

Check only one box.

1 ☐ Single
2 ☑ Married filing joint return (even if only one had income)
3 ☐ Married filing separate return. Enter spouse's social security no. above and full name here. ▶ _____
4 ☐ Head of household (with qualifying person). (See page 19.) If the qualifying person is a child but not your dependent, enter this child's name here. ▶ _____
5 ☐ Qualifying widow(er) with dependent child (year spouse died ▶ _____). (See page 19.)

Exemptions

If more than six dependents, see page 20.

6a ☑ **Yourself.** If your parent (or someone else) can claim you as a dependent on his or her tax return, **do not** check box 6a
b ☑ **Spouse**
c **Dependents:**

(1) First name Last name	(2) Dependent's social security number	(3) Dependent's relationship to you	(4) ☑ if qualifying child for child tax credit (see page 20)
Thomas T. Becker	465 01 2347	son	☑
Richard L. Becker	012 34 5678	son	☑
Harriet M. Becker	234 56 7890	daughter	☑
			☐
			☐
			☐

No. of boxes checked on 6a and 6b: **2**

No. of your children on 6c who:
• lived with you: **3**
• did not live with you due to divorce or separation (see page 20)

Dependents on 6c not entered above

d Total number of exemptions claimed

Add numbers entered on lines above ▶ **5**

Income

Attach Forms W-2 and W-2G here. Also attach Form(s) 1099-R if tax was withheld.

If you did not get a W-2, see page 21.

Enclose, but do not attach, any payment. Also, please use Form 1040-V.

7	Wages, salaries, tips, etc. Attach Form(s) W-2	7	34,165 —
8a	**Taxable** interest. Attach Schedule B if required	8a	500 —
b	**Tax-exempt** interest. **Do not** include on line 8a ... 8b		
9	Ordinary dividends. Attach Schedule B if required	9	750 —
10	Taxable refunds, credits, or offsets of state and local income taxes (see page 22)	10	
11	Alimony received	11	
12	Business income or (loss). Attach Schedule C or C-EZ	12	3,600 —
13	Capital gain or (loss). Attach Schedule D if required. If not required, check here ▶ ☐	13	850 —
14	Other gains or (losses). Attach Form 4797	14	
15a	Total IRA distributions . 15a ___ b Taxable amount (see page 23)	15b	
16a	Total pensions and annuities 16a ___ b Taxable amount (see page 23)	16b	
17	Rental real estate, royalties, partnerships, S corporations, trusts, etc. Attach Schedule E	17	
18	Farm income or (loss). Attach Schedule F	18	
19	Unemployment compensation	19	
20a	Social security benefits . 20a ___ b Taxable amount (see page 25)	20b	
21	Other income. List type and amount (see page 25) _____	21	
22	Add the amounts in the far right column for lines 7 through 21. This is your **total income** ▶	22	39,865 —

Adjusted Gross Income

23	IRA deduction (see page 27)	23	2,000 —	
24	Student loan interest deduction (see page 27)	24		
25	Medical savings account deduction. Attach Form 8853	25		
26	Moving expenses. Attach Form 3903	26		
27	One-half of self-employment tax. Attach Schedule SE	27	275 —	
28	Self-employed health insurance deduction (see page 29)	28		
29	Self-employed SEP, SIMPLE, and qualified plans	29		
30	Penalty on early withdrawal of savings	30		
31a	Alimony paid b Recipient's SSN ▶ _____	31a		
32	Add lines 23 through 31a		32	2,275 —
33	Subtract line 32 from line 22. This is your **adjusted gross income** ▶		33	37,590 —

For Disclosure, Privacy Act, and Paperwork Reduction Act Notice, see page 56.   Cat. No. 11320B   Form **1040** (2000)

claimed by the Beckers. The Form 1040 depicted here is the one used in 2000; it is expected that there will be modifications in this form in subsequent years.

Form 1040 (2000)   Page **2**

Tax and Credits	34	Amount from line 33 (adjusted gross income)	34	37,590	—
	35a	Check if: ☐ **You** were 65 or older, ☐ Blind; ☐ **Spouse** was 65 or older, ☐ Blind. Add the number of boxes checked above and enter the total here . . . ▶ 35a			
	b	If you are married filing separately and your spouse itemizes deductions, or you were a dual-status alien, see page 31 and check here . . . . . . ▶ 35b ☐			
Standard Deduction for Most People	36	Enter your **itemized deductions** from Schedule A, line 28, **or standard deduction** shown on the left. **But** see page 31 to find your standard deduction if you checked any box on line 35a or 35b **or** if someone can claim you as a dependent	36	7,938	—
Single: $4,400	37	Subtract line 36 from line 34	37	29,652	—
Head of household: $6,450	38	If line 34 is $96,700 or less, multiply $2,800 by the total number of exemptions claimed on line 6d. If line 34 is over $96,700, see the worksheet on page 32 for the amount to enter .	38	14,000	—
Married filing jointly or Qualifying widow(er): $7,350	39	**Taxable income.** Subtract line 38 from line 37. If line 38 is more than line 37, enter -0- .	39	15,652	—
	40	**Tax** (see page 32). Check if any tax is from a ☐ Form(s) 8814 b ☐ Form 4972 . . .	40	2,347	80
Married filing separately: $3,675	41	Alternative minimum tax. Attach Form 6251	41	—	
	42	Add lines 40 and 41 . . . . ▶	42	2,347	80
	43	Foreign tax credit. Attach Form 1116 if required	43		
	44	Credit for child and dependent care expenses. Attach Form 2441	44		
	45	Credit for the elderly or the disabled. Attach Schedule R . .	45		
	46	Education credits. Attach Form 8863	46		
	47	Child tax credit (see page 36)	47	1,500 00	
	48	Adoption credit. Attach Form 8839	48		
	49	Other. Check if from a ☐ Form 3800 b ☐ Form 8396 c ☐ Form 8801 d ☐ Form (specify) _____	49		
	50	Add lines 43 through 49. These are your **total credits**	50	1,500	00
	51	Subtract line 50 from line 42. If line 50 is more than line 42, enter -0-. . . . . . ▶	51	847	80
Other Taxes	52	Self-employment tax. Attach Schedule SE	52	551	00
	53	Social security and Medicare tax on tip income not reported to employer. Attach Form 4137	53		
	54	Tax on IRAs, other retirement plans, and MSAs. Attach Form 5329 if required	54		
	55	Advance earned income credit payments from Form(s) W-2	55		
	56	Household employment taxes. Attach Schedule H	56		
	57	Add lines 51 through 56. This is your **total tax** . . . . ▶	57	1,398	80
Payments	58	Federal income tax withheld from Forms W-2 and 1099 . .	58	4,110 00	
	59	2000 estimated tax payments and amount applied from 1999 return	59	500 00	
If you have a qualifying child, attach Schedule EIC.	60a	**Earned income credit (EIC)**	60a		
	b	Nontaxable earned income: amount . . ▶ [ ] and type ▶ ----------			
	61	Excess social security and RRTA tax withheld (see page 50)	61		
	62	Additional child tax credit. Attach Form 8812	62		
	63	Amount paid with request for extension to file (see page 50)	63		
	64	Other payments. Check if from a ☐ Form 2439 b ☐ Form 4136	64		
	65	Add lines 58, 59, 60a, and 61 through 64. These are your **total payments** . . . . ▶	65	4,610	00
Refund	66	If line 65 is more than line 57, subtract line 57 from line 65. This is the amount you **overpaid**	66	3,211	20
	67a	Amount of line 66 you want **refunded to you** . . . . ▶	67a	3,211	20
Have it directly deposited! See page 50 and fill in 67b, 67c, and 67d.	b	Routing number [ ] ▶ c Type: ☐ Checking ☐ Savings			
	d	Account number [ ]			
	68	Amount of line 66 you want **applied to your 2001 estimated tax** ▶ 68			
Amount You Owe	69	If line 57 is more than line 65, subtract line 65 from line 57. This is the **amount you owe**. For details on how to pay, see page 51 . . . . ▶	69		
	70	Estimated tax penalty. Also include on line 69 70			

Sign Here

Joint return? See page 19.

Keep a copy for your records.

Under penalties of perjury, I declare that I have examined this return and accompanying schedules and statements, and to the best of my knowledge and belief, they are true, correct, and complete. Declaration of preparer (other than taxpayer) is based on all information of which preparer has any knowledge.

Your signature	Date	Your occupation	Daytime phone number
Terry B. Becker	4-1-2001	Acctg. Clerk	(555) 555-5555
Spouse's signature. If a joint return, **both** must sign.	Date	Spouse's occupation	May the IRS discuss this return with the preparer shown below (see page 52)? ☐ Yes ☐ No
Evelyn A. Becker	4-1-2001	Sales Clerk	

Paid Preparer's Use Only

Preparer's signature ▶		Date	Check if self-employed ☐	Preparer's SSN or PTIN
Firm's name (or yours if self-employed), address, and ZIP code ▶			EIN	
			Phone no. ( )	

Form **1040** (2000)

Personal Exemptions. The Beckers are entitled to claim two exemptions for themselves and another three exemptions for their three dependent children, for a total of five (see line 6d). Because each exemption is worth $2,800, they receive a total personal exemption of $14,000 (5 × $2,800), which is the amount listed on line 38 of their Form 1040.

The Beckers' Taxable Income and Tax Liability. Taxable income is found by subtracting itemized deductions and personal exemptions from AGI. Thus, in the Beckers' case, taxable income amounts to $37,590 − $7,938 − $14,000 = $15,652. This is the amount shown on line 39. Given this information, the Beckers can now refer to the tax rate schedule (like the one in Exhibit 3.7) to find their appropriate tax rate and, ultimately, the amount of taxes they'll have to pay. (Because the Beckers' taxable income is less than $100,000, they could use the *tax tables* [not shown] to find their tax. For clarity and convenience, we use the schedules here.) As we can see, the Beckers' $15,652 in taxable income places them in the lowest (15 percent) tax bracket. Note in the tax rate schedule (in Exhibit 3.7) that joint returns with taxable incomes of up to $43,850 fall into the 15 percent tax bracket. At this point, all the Beckers have to do is multiply their taxable income by 15 percent to find their tax liability: $15,652 × .15 = $2,347.80. They enter this amount on line 40. (Note: Had the tax tables been used, the tax would have been $2,351.)

The Beckers also qualify for the child tax credit: $500 for each child under age 17. They enter $1,500 on lines 47 and 50 and subtract that amount from the tax on line 42, entering $847.80 on line 51. In addition, the Beckers owe self-employment (social security) tax on Terry's $3,600 net business income. This will increase their tax liability by $551 (.153 × $3,600) and would be reported on Schedule SE and entered on line 52 of Form 1040. (Remember, the Beckers deducted 50 percent of this amount—$275—on line 27 as an adjustment to income.) The Beckers enter their total tax liability on line 57: $1,398.80 ($847.80 + $551).

Do They Get a Tax Refund? Because the total amount of taxes withheld of $4,110 ($3,560 from Terry's salary and $550 from Evelyn's wages) shown on line 58 plus estimated tax payments of $500 shown on line 59 total $4,610, the Beckers' total tax payments exceed their tax liability, and, as a result, they are entitled to a refund. (About 65 percent of all taxpayers receive refunds each year.) The amount of the refund is found by subtracting the tax liability from the total tax payments: $4,610.00 − $1,398.80 = $3,211.20 in tax refund, shown on lines 66 and 67a. Instead of paying the IRS, they'll be getting money back. (Generally, it takes 1 to 2 months after a tax return has been filed to receive a refund check.)

All the Beckers have to do now is sign and date their completed Form 1040 and send it, along with any supporting forms and schedules, to the nearest IRS district office on or before April 15, 2001.

One reason the Beckers' refund was so large was the child tax credit. With such a sizable refund, the Beckers may want to stop making estimated tax payments because their combined withholding more than covers the amount of taxes they owe. Another option is to change their withholding to reduce the amount withheld.

CONCEPT CHECK

3-11. Define and differentiate between the *average tax rate* and the *marginal tax rate*. How does a tax credit differ from an itemized deduction?

3-12. Explain how the following are used in filing a tax return: (a) Form 1040, (b) various schedules that accompany Form 1040, and (c) tax rate schedules.

Note that if total tax payments had been less than the Beckers' tax liability, they would have owed the IRS money—the amount owed is found by subtracting total tax payments made from the tax liability. If they owed money, they would include a check in the amount due with Form 1040 when they filed their tax return.

Other Filing Considerations [LG4]

The preparation and filing of tax returns does not merely involve filling out and filing a tax return on or before April 15. Other related considerations include the need to pay estimated taxes, file for extensions, or amend the return; the possibility of a tax audit; and whether to use a tax preparation service or computer software to assist in preparing your return. Here we give attention to each of these filing considerations.

ESTIMATES, EXTENSIONS, AND AMENDMENTS

Like Terry Becker, who provided accounting services to his brother's business, you may have income that is not subject to withholding. You may need to file a declaration of estimated taxes with your return and to pay taxes on a quarterly basis. Or perhaps you are unable to meet the normal April 15 filing deadline or need to correct a previously filed return. Let's look at the procedures for handling these situations.

ESTIMATED TAXES. Because federal withholding taxes are regularly taken only from employment income, such as that paid in the form of wages or salaries, the IRS requires certain people to pay **estimated taxes** on income earned from other sources. This requirement allows the principle of "pay as you go" to be applied not only to employment income subject to withholding but also to other sources of income. The quarterly payment of estimated taxes is most commonly required of investors, consultants, lawyers, business owners, and various other professionals who are likely to receive income in a form that is not subject to withholding. Generally, if all your income is subject to withholding, you probably do not need to make estimated tax payments.

If you meet certain IRS requirements with regard to your tax liability and withholding you must file a declaration of estimated taxes (Form 1040-ES) and make estimated tax payments. When the total of tax withheld and estimated payments does not meet IRS guidelines, you must pay estimated taxes consistent with the actual income earned in the immediately preceding quarter to avoid penalties. Each estimated tax payment equals the tax payable on income earned in the preceding quarter, or one-fourth of the total amount paid in taxes during the immediately preceding year, less the amount of tax withheld during the preceding quarter.

The declaration of estimated taxes is normally filed with the tax return. Estimated taxes must be paid in four quarterly installments on April 15, June 15, and September 15 of the current year, and January 15 of the following year. Failure to estimate and pay these taxes in accordance with IRS guidelines can result in a penalty levied by the IRS.

APRIL 15: FILING DEADLINE. As we've seen from the Becker family example, at the end of each tax year those taxpayers required to file a return must determine the amount of their tax *liability*—the amount of taxes that they owe as a result of the past year's activities. The tax year corresponds to the calendar year and covers the period January 1 through December 31. Taxpayers may file their returns any time after the end of the tax year and *must* file no later than April 15 of the year immediately following the tax year (or by the first business day after that date if it falls on a weekend or federal holiday). Taxpayers who

---

$ **Financial Road Sign**

Time for Taxes
To minimize tax hassles, follow these tips:
1. File on time, even if you can't pay what you owe.
2. Don't overlook tax-free income, such as an inheritance, tuition, scholarships, and gifts of money (limited to $10,000 per year from any one person).
3. Don't forget to sign your return, even if you file online.
4. Use Direct Deposit to get your refund faster.
5. Pay in installments if you can't pay your whole tax bill (file Form 9465).
6. Pay what you think you will owe even if you get an extension.
7. Include receipts for all noncash charitable gifts valued at more than $500 with Form 8383.

Source: Tax Tips 2001, *Money.com*, downloaded from **www.money.com/ money/depts/taxes/ taxtips/archive.html**.

estimated taxes Quarterly tax payments required on income not subject to withholding.

file Form 1040EZ can file their returns by touch-tone phone using *TeleFile*. (Qualifying taxpayers receive special TeleFile tax packages.) If you have a computer, a modem, and tax preparation software, you can use the IRS's *e-file* to file your return electronically. This is often done for a fee through an "Authorized *e-file* Provider." (We'll discuss computer-based tax returns in greater detail later.)

Depending on whether the total of taxes withheld and any estimated tax payments is greater or less than the computed tax liability, the taxpayer either receives a refund or has to pay additional taxes. For example, assume that you had $2,000 withheld and paid estimated taxes of $1,200 during the year. After filling out the appropriate tax forms, you find your tax liability is only $2,800. In this case, you have overpaid your taxes by $400 ($2,000 + $1,200 − $2,800) and will receive a $400 refund from the IRS. On the other hand, if your tax liability had amounted to $4,000, you would owe the IRS an additional $800 ($4,000 − $2,000 − $1,200). Starting in 2000, taxpayers can pay their taxes using a credit card. However, because the IRS cannot pay credit card companies an issuing fee, taxpayers must pay a fee of about 2.5 percent of the amount and call a special number to arrange for the payment.

FILING EXTENSIONS AND AMENDED RETURNS. It is possible to receive an extension of time for filing your federal tax return. You can apply for an automatic 4-month **filing extension**, which makes the due date August 15, simply by submitting Form 4868. In filing for an extension, however, the taxpayer must estimate the taxes due and remit that amount with the application. The extension does *not* give taxpayers more time to pay their taxes. Taxpayers can also request additional extensions beyond the 4-month automatic extension, but the IRS will review reasons for the request to decide whether to grant the extensions.

After filing a return, you may discover that you overlooked some income or a major deduction or made a mistake, and, as a result, paid too little or too much in taxes. You can easily correct this by filing an **amended return** (Form 1040X) that shows the corrected amount of income or deductions and the amount of taxes you should have paid, along with the amount of any tax refund or additional taxes owed. You generally have 3 years from the date you file your original return or 2 years from the date you paid the taxes, whichever is later, to file an amended return. If you prepare and file your amended return properly and it reflects nothing out of the ordinary, it generally will not trigger an audit. By all means, do not "correct" an oversight in 1 year by "adjusting" next year's tax return—the IRS frowns on that.

AUDITED RETURNS

Because taxpayers themselves provide the key information and fill out the necessary tax forms, the IRS has no proof that taxes have been correctly calculated. Therefore, it more or less randomly selects some returns for a **tax audit**—an examination to validate the return's accuracy. The odds of being audited are actually quite low; the IRS audits fewer than 1 percent of returns. However, higher-income earners tend to have a greater chance of audit. For example, those with incomes between $25,000 and $50,000 have less than a 1 percent chance of being audited, but the chance of audit jumps to nearly 5 percent for those with incomes over $100,000. The outcome of an audit is not always additional tax owed to the IRS. In fact, about 5 percent of all audits result in a refund to the taxpayer, and in 15 percent of all audits the IRS finds that returns are correctly prepared.

IRS audits attempt to confirm the validity of filed returns by carefully examining the data reported in them. In the course of an audit, the IRS may arrange a meeting at which

filing extension
An extension of time beyond the April 15 deadline during which taxpayers, with the approval of the IRS, can file their returns without incurring penalties.

amended return
A tax return filed to correct errors or adjust for information received after the filing date of the taxpayer's original return.

tax audit
An examination by the IRS to validate the accuracy of a given tax return.

the IRS examiner asks the taxpayer to explain and document some of the deductions taken. Even with documentation, the examiner may still question the legitimacy of the deductions. If the taxpayer and the IRS examiner cannot informally agree on the disputed items, the taxpayer can meet with the examiner's supervisor to discuss the case further. If there is still disagreement, the taxpayer can appeal through the IRS Appeals Office. Finally, if the Appeals Office hearing does not resolve the issue to the taxpayer's satisfaction, the taxpayer can bring the case before the U.S. Tax Court, the U.S. Claims Court, or a U.S. District Court.

You can see why it is particularly important to keep satisfactory and thorough tax records, because some day you may be audited by the IRS. Although the IRS does not specify any type of record-keeping system, you should keep track of the source or use of all cash receipts and cash payments. Notations with respect to the purpose of the expenses are important, as well as proof that you actually made the expenses for which you have claimed deductions. Typically, audits question both (1) whether all income received has been properly reported and (2) if the deductions claimed are legitimate and the correct amount. The IRS can take as many as 3 years from the date of filing to audit your return—and in some cases an unlimited period of time—so you should retain records and receipts used in preparing returns for several years. Severe financial penalties—even prison sentences—can result from violating tax laws.

In sum, while you should take advantage of all legitimate deductions to minimize your tax liability, you must also be sure to properly report all items of income and expense as required by the Internal Revenue Code.

TAX PREPARATION SERVICES: GETTING HELP ON YOUR RETURNS

Many people prepare their own tax returns. These "do-it-yourselfers" typically have fairly simple returns that can be prepared without a great deal of difficulty. Of course, some taxpayers with quite complicated financial affairs may also invest their time in preparing their own returns. The IRS offers many informational publications to help you prepare your tax return. You can order them directly from the IRS by mail, from the IRS Web site, or by calling the IRS's toll-free number (1-800-829-3676 or special local numbers in some areas). You can also download most of them from the IRS Web site (**www.irs.gov**). An excellent (and free) comprehensive tax preparation reference book is IRS *Publication 17, Your Federal Income Tax*. Other publications cover special topics, such as the earned income credit, self-employment taxes, and business use of your home. Each form and schedule comes with detailed instructions to guide you, step by step, in completing the form accurately. Another IRS information service is *TeleTax*, which provides recorded phone messages on selected tax topics. The toll-free telephone number for this service is 1-800-829-4477, and some areas have special local TeleTax phone numbers.

HELP FROM THE IRS. The IRS, in addition to issuing various publications for use in preparing tax returns, also provides direct assistance to taxpayers. The IRS will compute taxes for those whose AGI is not more than $100,000 and who do not itemize deductions. Persons who use this IRS service must fill in certain data, sign and date the return, and send it to the IRS on or before April 15 of the year immediately following the tax year. The IRS attempts to calculate taxes to result in the "smallest" tax bite. It then sends taxpayers a refund, if their withholding exceeds their tax liability, or a bill, if their tax liability is greater than the amount of withholding. People who either fail to qualify for or do not want to use this total tax preparation service can still obtain IRS assistance in preparing their returns from a toll-free service. Consult your telephone directory for the toll-free number of the IRS office closest to you.

Even the IRS sometimes makes mistakes, however. It may not always correctly answer your tax questions. To increase your chances of getting correct information, use Publication 17 and other resources to research your question before calling. State your question as clearly as you can, and make sure that the IRS representative fully understands your question. Remember: *You are liable for any underpayment of taxes, including interest and penalties, that results from incorrect information provided by the IRS over the phone.* As an alternative, you may put the question in writing and receive a written response from the IRS. If the written answer is incorrect, and as a result you underpay your taxes, you will have to pay the additional taxes and interest due, but no penalties.

PRIVATE TAX PREPARERS. More than half of all taxpayers prefer to use professional *tax preparation services* because (1) they are concerned about accuracy and minimizing their tax liability as much as possible, and (2) they believe the complexity of the tax forms makes preparation too difficult and time consuming. The fees charged by professional tax preparers range from about $50 for very simple returns to $1,000 or more for complicated returns that include many itemized deductions, partnership income or losses, or self-employment income. The average preparation fee at H&R Block in a recent year was $84. You can select from several different types of tax preparation services:

- *National and local tax services:* These include national services like H&R Block or independent local firms. These are best for taxpayers with relatively common types of income and expenditures.
- *Enrolled Agents (EAs):* Federally licensed individual tax practitioners who have passed a difficult, 2-day, IRS-administered exam. They are fully qualified to handle tax preparation at various levels of complexity.
- *Certified Public Accountants (CPAs):* Tax professionals who prepare returns and can advise taxpayers on planning.
- *Tax attorneys:* Lawyers who specialize in tax planning.

Because the services provided by EAs, CPAs, and tax attorneys can be expensive, they are usually best used only by those taxpayers with relatively complicated financial situations.

 Use the tax section of H&R Block's Web site, **www.hrblock.com/ tax_center/index.html**, to locate an H&R Block office near you and to check the glossary of tax terms.

As with any financial planning professional, choose your tax preparer carefully. Bad or fraudulent advice can cost plenty. Although attorneys and CPAs are state-licensed and EAs have federal licenses, no license or certification is required to call oneself a tax preparer. Before hiring a tax professional, ask about the preparer's qualifications, what fields he or she specializes in (divorce, complex investments, and so on), and how you will be charged. He or she should carry malpractice insurance and pay for penalties and interest resulting from an accounting error. Make sure the advisor can give you the level of advice you need—someone who is basically a return preparer is not the best person to help you do complex tax planning—and that you get impartial advice. A tax advisor should make recommendations but not earn fees or commissions from tax-sheltered investments you buy. You must also be comfortable with the advisor's suggestions, especially with regard to strategies that involve gray areas of the tax law.

Taxpayers should check their own completed returns carefully before signing them. Remember that *taxpayers themselves must accept primary responsibility for the accuracy of their returns.* The IRS requires professional tax preparers to sign each return as the preparer, enter their own social security number and address, and provide the taxpayer with a copy of the return being filed. Tax preparers with the necessary hardware and software can electronically file their clients' tax returns, thereby permitting eligible taxpayers to more quickly receive refunds.

There is no guarantee that your professional tax preparer will correctly determine your tax liability. Even the best preparers may not have all the answers at their fingertips. In a recent *Money* magazine annual tax return test, none of the 45 experienced tax preparers they contacted prepared the tax return for a fictional family correctly, and only 24 percent of them calculated a tax liability that was within $1,000 of the correct amount of $42,336. To reduce the chance of error, you should become familiar ith the basic tax principles and regulations, check all documents (such as W-2s and 1099s) for accuracy, maintain good communication with your tax preparer, and request an explanation of any entries on your tax return that you do not understand.

COMPUTER-BASED TAX RETURNS

Many people use their personal computers to help with tax planning and tax return preparation. Several good tax software packages will save hours of figuring out the forms and schedules involved in filing tax returns. They often identify tax-saving opportunities you might otherwise miss. These computer programs are not for everyone, however. Very simple returns do not require them (although there are now Web sites like Online 1040EZ by H&R Block where you can prepare and file your return on paper or electronically free of charge). And for very complex returns, there is no substitute for the skill and expertise of a tax accountant or attorney. Tax preparation software will be most helpful for taxpayers who itemize deductions but do not need tax advice.

Basically there are two kinds of software: tax planning and tax preparation. Planning programs like *Quicken* let you experiment with different strategies to see their effects on the amount of taxes you must pay. The other category of tax software focuses on return preparation. As we discuss in the *Money in Action* box on page 118, there are a number of excellent software programs on the market to help you complete and file your tax return.

In certain situations, you should probably let a professional rather than a PC prepare your return. These include major life changes such as marriage, divorce, remarriage, and inheritance. The tax treatment of stock options, an increasingly common employee benefit, is tricky to figure out. Self-employed persons may want the advice of a tax professional when it comes to deciding where to draw the line between business and personal expenses.

 Which version of TaxCut software is best for you? Find out at **www.taxcut.com**, where you will also find tax tips, a tax-withholding calculator, and more.

The IRS recently introduced "fill-in forms" that allow you to enter information while the form is displayed on your computer by Adobe Acrobat Reader version 3.0 or later.(Acrobat Reader is free software readily available on the Web.) After entering the requested information, you can print out the completed form. Fill-in forms give you a cleaner, crisper printout for your records and for filing with the IRS. Unlike tax preparation software, these fill-in-forms have no computational capabilities, so you must do all your cal-

MONEY IN ACTION

On April 15 Your Computer Is Your Friend

Not many people look forward to preparing their taxes. It takes hours, it's tedious, and the punch line—how much is due—is often bad news. But just as the computer has made other dreary tasks easier, it has also made this annual ritual almost fun. You can choose a CD-ROM package, download software from a Web site, or use an online version of some tax software.

Tax software is appropriate for people who need to file the long Form 1040 and some supporting forms. Anyone who invests in the stock market, owns real estate, or has foreign income or a home-based business can probably benefit. Instead of taking a week or more with pencil and paper, the computer will allow you to shrink the time down to a few hours. It will be even easier if you have used a personal finance program to keep tabs on your income and expenses, because the software will read personal finance files and extract the appropriate data. This saves even more time, and reduces potential data entry errors.

The best thing about using tax software is that it can turn that shoe box full of receipts and check stubs into a neat, arithmetically correct tax return. The programs know that X percent of the amount you entered on Line Z has to be transferred to Line Q, saving you the agony of remembering to do it yourself. The programs know all about the hundreds of changes in tax laws, so you don't need the Internal Revenue Code on your desk. Another advantage is that the programs feed data to state tax returns, so you only have to enter them once.

The two major software players are Intuit's TurboTax (for Windows)/MacInTax (for Macintosh) or Block Financial Software's TaxCut (for Windows and Macintosh). TaxChecker Individual, by Tax Defenders, Inc., is an add-on to either TurboTax or TaxCut, and it simulates an IRS audit of your return.

Both programs feature a clean interface and guide you through the steps in preparing your return. In addition to the primary tax-form preparation section, they include extensive resources, video clips to make tricky concepts easier to understand, tax planning questionnaires, deduction finders, and more. Included in the software's price is one electronically filed federal return. State tax return packages cost more, and filing an electronic state return costs about $4.95.

The programs guide you through the tax-preparation process by asking you the right questions. For example, if you claim a home office, TurboTax prompts you for expenses, such as your mortgage interest, that apply to the business use of the home. It automatically transfers the amount that doesn't qualify for the deduction to Schedule A, where you list itemized deductions. TaxCut will warn you that a number you've typed looks out of line. Both TurboTax and TaxCut guarantee their calculations and will pay any penalties you incur because of program errors. The cost for the programs is under $50 for the CD-ROM versions. Both programs make extensive references to Internet Web sites that can help you with your tax preparation.

Using a computer also makes it easier to file electronically instead of mailing your return to the IRS. Before you push the "submit" button, however, you might want to run the completed tax return by a friendly CPA. The cost to review a return is a fraction of the cost to prepare it.

Sources: Brian Clark, "This Year's Best Tax Software," *Money*, January 2000, pp. 112-113; Patrick J. Lyons, "Computing Returns the Feel-Good Way," *New York Times*, March 1, sec. 3; 1998, p. 16; "Tax Preparation Made Simple," *Money Matters*, March 1998, p. 3.

culations before you start. In addition, you should be ready to enter all the data at once, because with just Acrobat Reader you can't save your completed forms. (If you purchase the complete Acrobat suite, you can save your forms to disk.) To find out more, check out **www.irs.gov/forms_pubs/fillin.html**.

CONCEPT CHECK

3-13. Define *estimated taxes,* and explain under what conditions such tax payments are required.

3-14. What is the purpose of a tax audit? Describe some things you can do to be prepared if your return is audited.

3-15. Briefly discuss the tax preparation services available from (a) the IRS, (b) national or local tax preparation services, (c) an EA, (d) CPAs and tax attorneys, and (e) tax preparation computer software. Discuss the relative costs of each. When is each of these preferred, and how should you choose a tax preparer?

Effective Tax Planning [LG5]

A key ingredient of personal financial planning is *tax planning.* The overriding objective of effective tax planning is to maximize total after-tax income by reducing, shifting, or deferring taxes to as low a level as legally possible.

Keep in mind that *avoiding taxes* is one thing, but *evading* them is another matter altogether. By all means, don't confuse tax avoidance with tax evasion, which includes such illegal activities as omitting income or overstating deductions. **Tax evasion**, in effect, involves a failure to fairly and accurately report income or deductions, and, in extreme cases, a failure to pay taxes altogether. Persons found guilty of tax evasion are subject to severe financial penalties and even prison terms. **Tax avoidance**, in contrast, is concerned with reducing taxes in ways that are legal and compatible with the intent of Congress.

tax evasion
The illegal act of failing to accurately report income or deductions, and, in extreme cases, failing to pay taxes altogether.

tax avoidance
The act of reducing taxes in ways that are legal and compatible with the intent of Congress.

FUNDAMENTAL OBJECTIVES OF TAX PLANNING

Tax planning basically involves the use of various investment vehicles, retirement programs, and estate distribution procedures to (1) reduce, (2) shift, or (3) defer taxes. You can *reduce* taxes, for instance, by using techniques that create tax deductions or credits, or that receive preferential tax treatment—such as investments that produce depreciation (like real estate) or that generate tax-free income (like municipal bonds). You can *shift* taxes by using gifts or trusts to shift some of your income to other family members who are in lower tax brackets and to whom you intend to provide some level of support anyway, such as a retired, elderly parent.

The idea behind *deferring* taxes is to reduce or eliminate your taxes today by postponing them to some time in the future when you may be in a lower tax bracket. Perhaps more important, *deferring taxes gives you use of the money that would otherwise go to taxes*—which you can invest to make even more money. Deferring taxes is usually done through various types of retirement plans, such as IRAs, or by investing in certain types of annuities, variable life insurance policies, or even Series EE bonds (U.S. savings bonds).

The fundamentals of tax planning include making sure you take all the deductions to which you are entitled and taking full advantage of the various tax provisions that will minimize your tax liability. Thus comprehensive tax planning is an ongoing activity with both an immediate and long-term perspective. *It plays a key role in personal financial planning*—in fact, one of the major components of a comprehensive personal financial plan is a summary of the potential tax impacts of various recommended financial strategies. Tax planning is closely interrelated with many financial planning activities, including investment, retirement, and estate planning.

MONEY IN ACTION

Tax Planning Pays Off

Do you think that only the very rich can benefit from tax avoidance strategies? In fact, almost all taxpayers can avoid problems with the IRS and save money with the following tips for filing and year-round tax planning.

1. **File accurate and complete returns.** Although this may seem obvious, check your completed return carefully—names, social security numbers, filing status, arithmetic—before submitting it to the IRS. Errors can delay refunds and result in fines or penalties plus interest (compounded *daily*) for underpayment of taxes. Take all allowed exemptions. Put schedules and forms in the designated order (by sequence number, *not* form number, for numbered forms, alphabetically for schedules).

2. **Keep good records.** "The main reason people miss deductions is because they are poor record keepers," says Ed Slott, a New York accountant. A good filing system for receipts of tax-deductible items will save you many headaches at tax time.

3. **Defer income until next year.** If you are self-employed, receive bonuses, or have income outside of a regular job (such as consulting), deferring income into the next tax year may keep you under the level where deduction and exemption phase-outs begin or prevent you from moving into a higher tax bracket. The amount you save depends on your current and anticipated income and tax bracket.

4. **Calculate tax credits carefully.** IRS rules for earned income and child tax credits are complicated, and it can be tricky to determine whether you qualify. It's important to take the time to calculate these correctly, because these credits can add up to substantial tax savings—in the case of the earned income credit, thousands of dollars in refunds even if a family doesn't have to pay any taxes. If you are in qualifying tax brackets, don't forget two recently added credits: the Hope credit for college costs and the lifetime learning credit for college tuition.

5. **Look at the tax implications of investment decisions.** Keep tax consequences in mind whenever you sell securities—but *never allow tax considerations to dictate investment decisions.* Consider waiting to sell a stock until it either qualifies for long-term capital gains treatment or you can use it to offset gains or losses. If you have securities in a company whose prospects aren't good, you may want to sell them to offset other gains or losses. Report any changes in your mutual fund holdings, even if you just switch from one fund to another within the same fund family, because you incur a capital gain or loss. Failure to report such transfers and the resulting capital gains or losses could trigger an IRS audit.

6. **File electronically, if possible.** The error rate for electronically filed returns is under 1 percent, compared with 2 to 18 percent for paper returns. Using tax preparation software eliminates many common errors such as mathematical mistakes. An added benefit: if you are due a refund, you'll get it much sooner.

Sources: Lynn Asinof, "Subtractions that Add Up," *Wall Street Journal*, February 28, 2000, p. R8; Dinah Wisenberg Brin, "Oops!" *Wall Street Journal*, February 28, 2000, p. R8.

SOME POPULAR TAX STRATEGIES

Managing your taxes is a year-round activity. Because Congress considers tax law changes throughout the year, you may not know all the applicable regulations until the middle of the year or later. Like other financial goals, tax strategies require review and adjustment when regulations and personal circumstances change.

Tax planning can become very complex at times and may involve rather sophisticated investment strategies. In such cases, especially those involving large amounts of money, you should seek professional help. Many tax strategies are fairly simple and straightforward and can be used by the average middle-income taxpayer. You certainly don't have to be in the top income bracket to enjoy the benefits of many tax-saving ideas and procedures. For example, the interest income on Series EE bonds is free from state income tax, and the holder can elect to delay payment of federal taxes until the earlier of the year the bonds are redeemed for cash or the year in which they finally mature. This feature makes Series EE bonds an excellent vehicle for earning tax-deferred income. Some other popular (and fairly simple) tax strategies follow. The *Money in Action* box on this page provides additional tips to help you reduce your tax liability.

There are other strategies that can cut your tax bill. Accelerating or bunching deductions into a single year may permit itemizing deductions. Shifting income from one year to another is one way to cut your tax liability. If you expect to be in the same or a higher income tax bracket this year than you do next year, defer income until next year and shift expenses to this year so you can accelerate your deductions to reduce taxes this year.

MAXIMIZING DEDUCTIONS. Review a comprehensive list of possible deductions for ideas, because even small deductions can add up to big tax savings. Accelerate or bunch deductions into one tax year if it will allow you to itemize rather than take the standard deduction. For example, make your fourth quarter estimated state tax payment before December 31 rather than on January 15 to deduct it in the current taxable year. Group miscellaneous expenses and schedule nonreimbursed elective medical procedures to fall into one tax year to exceed the required "floor" for deductions (2 percent of AGI for miscellaneous expenses; 7.5 percent for medical expenses). Increase discretionary deductions like charitable contributions.

INCOME SHIFTING. One way of reducing income taxes is to use a technique known as **income shifting**. Here the taxpayer shifts a portion of his or her income—and thus taxes—to relatives in lower tax brackets. This can be done by creating trusts or custodial accounts or by making outright gifts of income-producing property to family members. For instance, parents with $125,000 of taxable income (31 percent marginal tax rate) and $18,000 in corporate bonds paying $2,000 in annual interest might give the bonds to their 15-year-old child—with the understanding that such income is to be used ultimately for the child's college education. The $2,000 would then belong to the child, who would probably have to pay approximately $195 (0.15 × [$2,000 − $700 minimum standard deduction for a dependent]) in taxes on this income, and the parents' taxable income would be reduced by $2,000, reducing their taxes by $620.

income shifting
A technique used to reduce taxes in which a taxpayer shifts a portion of income to relatives in lower tax brackets.

Unfortunately, this strategy is not as simple as it might at first appear. The Tax Reform Act of 1986 specifies that the investment income of a minor (under the age of 14) is taxed at the same rate as the parents *to the extent that it exceeds $1,300*. For example, if a 5-year-old girl received $2,500 from a trust set up for her by her parents, the first $1,300 of that income (subject to a minimum $700 standard deduction) would be taxed at the child's rate and the remaining $1,200 would be subject to the parents' (higher) tax rate. These restrictions do not apply to children 14 and over, so it is possible to employ such techniques with older children (and presumably, with other older relatives, like elderly parents).

Parents need to be aware that shifting assets into a child's name to save taxes could affect the amount of college financial aid for which the child qualifies. Most financial aid formulas expect students to spend 35 percent of assets held in their own name, compared with only 5.6 percent of the parents' nonretirement assets.

Income shifting is allowed because there is a positive side to the practice. Not only does income shifting reduce taxes, but it also allows parents to build savings to meet some specific future outlay such as a child's college education. According to what is known as the "fruit-of-the-tree" doctrine, individuals cannot give away or place in trust income (fruit) alone. Instead, they must also give away the income-producing property (fruit-bearing tree) as well. Additional tax implications of gifts to dependents are discussed in Chapter 15.

tax shelters
Certain types of investments, such as real estate and natural resources, that provide *noncash tax write-offs* in the form of *depreciation, amortization*, or *depletion*.

TAX SHELTERS. **Tax shelters** are forms of investments that take advantage of certain *tax write-offs*. Some real estate (*income-generating* property) and natural resource investments (oil and gas drilling) provide these desirable deductions.

The favorable write-offs come from deductions from gross income permitted by the IRS; they do not involve an actual outlay of cash by the investor. In accounting terminology, these write-offs are called *depreciation, amortization*, or *depletion*. The presence of these noncash expenditures can lower the amount of taxes paid by taxpayers in certain income brackets. Tax-sheltered investments are generally considered *passive* investments; the amount of write-offs that can be taken is limited to the amount of income generated. There are a few exceptions, however. This rule does not apply to income-property investments of taxpayers (married, filing jointly) with AGI under $100,000 and to certain oil and gas investments. Thus, if your income is under $100,000 a year and you own some rental property in which you actively participate, or you invest in an oil or a gas drilling partnership, you may be able to benefit from all or most of the associated tax write-offs. Specifically, if your write-offs from these investments exceed the income they generate, you can use the excess write-offs *to shelter your other income*—the net result will be to reduce your taxable income and, therefore, the amount of taxes you have to pay. For example, you could invest in an apartment project that provided both an actual cash return of $5,000 and a depreciation deduction (from gross income) of $9,000. The net result of this investment would be to completely shelter the $5,000 cash income from taxes; even better, if you met the income limitations, you would have an additional $4,000 write-off ($9,000 − $5,000) that would reduce both your taxable income and tax liability.

With the exceptions noted above, the Tax Reform Act of 1986 has almost eliminated tax-sheltered investments that rely heavily on tax write-offs as the major (or only) source of income. Today these investments must stand on their *investment*, not tax-shelter, merit. Two other noteworthy provisions relate to rental real estate. First, the passive investment limits do not apply if the taxpayer spends over half of his or her time materially participating in real estate rental activities and the amount of time spent totals at least 750 hours per year. Also, the law provides that as much as $25,000 in write-offs from rental real estate could be used each year (to offset income from other sources) by people who "actively participate in the rental activity" and whose AGI is less than $100,000. This provision is phased out completely for AGIs of $150,000 or more.

tax deferred
Income that is not subject to taxes immediately but which will be subject to taxes at a later date.

TAX-FREE INCOME OR TAX-DEFERRED? There are some investments that provide tax-free income; in most cases, however, the tax on the income is only deferred (or delayed) to a later day. Although there aren't many forms of tax-free investments left today, probably the best example would be the *interest* income earned on *municipal bonds*. Such income is free from federal income tax. No matter how much municipal bond interest income you make, you don't have to pay any taxes on it. (Tax-free municipal bonds are discussed in Chapter 12.) Income that is **tax deferred**, in contrast, only delays the payment of taxes to a future date. Until that time arrives, however, tax-deferred investment vehicles allow you to *accumulate earnings* in a tax-free fashion. A good example of tax-deferred income would be income earned in a *traditional IRA*. See Chapter 14 for a detailed discussion of this and other similar arrangements.

Basically, any wage earner can open an IRA and contribute up to $2,000 a year to the account. (Note: The 2001 Tax Act provides for an increase in the maximum IRA contribution to $5,000 over the period of 2002 to 2008.) Of course, as noted earlier in this chapter, although any employed person can contribute to an IRA, only those people meeting certain pension and/or income constraints can deduct the annual contributions from their tax returns. If you fail to meet these restrictions, you can still have an IRA but you can't deduct the $2,000 annual contribution from your income. So why have an IRA? *Because all the income you earn in your IRA accumulates tax-free.* This is a *tax-deferred* investment, so you'll eventually have to pay taxes on these earnings, but not until you start drawing down your account. Thus, if you were in, say, the 31 percent tax bracket and could not write off your annual IRA deduction, you'd still be well advised to put $2,000 a year into an IRA to obtain the tax-deferred income feature. That is, if you could earn 12 percent before taxes on your investments, you could put $2,000 a year into fully taxable investments and end up with about $152,000 in 25 years. Or you could put the $2,000 each year into a tax-deferred IRA account and (given the same 12 percent rate of return) end up with approximately *$267,000* at the end of 25 years. You'll eventually have to pay taxes on your earnings when you start drawing down your IRA account, but you can't overlook the fact that the tax-deferred IRA investments result in fully *75 percent more income* (that is, $267,000 with the IRA versus $152,000 without). In addition to IRAs, tax-deferred income can also be obtained from other types of pension and retirement plans and annuities. See Chapter 14 for more information on these financial products and strategies.

 For still more tips and long-term tax planning strategies, head to **www.money.com/money/depts/taxes**. This well-organized site also features a mini-course on tax basics and articles on a variety of tax topics.

CONCEPT CHECK

3-16. Differentiate between *tax evasion* and *tax avoidance*.

3-17. Explain each of the following strategies for reducing current taxes: (a) maximizing deductions, (b) income shifting, (c) tax shelters, (d) tax-free income, and (e) tax-deferred income.

3-18. Identify and briefly discuss at least six specific tax strategies that can be used by individuals to reduce their current taxes.

Other Forms of Personal Taxes [LG6]

Although the largest tax a person will normally pay is federal income tax, there are other forms of taxes to contend with. For example, additional federal taxes may be levied on income and on certain types of transactions. At the state and local levels, sales transactions, income, property ownership, and licenses may be taxed. Because most individuals have to pay many of these other types of taxes, their impact on one's financial condition must be understood. Thus, a person saving to purchase a new automobile costing $18,000 should realize that the state and local sales taxes, as well as the cost of license plates and registration, may add another $1,500 or so to the total cost of the car.

OTHER FEDERAL TAXES

Although income taxes are the single most important source of revenue, the federal government also raises funds through social security, excise, and gift and estate taxes. Next to income taxes, the most common form of tax is social security, which is paid by just about every gainfully employed individual except certain federal employees and some state and local government employees. None of the federal taxes described in the following sections, including social security, can be claimed as a deduction for federal income tax purposes.

SOCIAL SECURITY TAXES. People probably pay more in social security taxes than in any other form of federal tax except income tax. In fact, many families (especially those with incomes of less than $15,000 to $20,000 a year) actually pay more in social security taxes than they do in federal income taxes. As noted earlier in this chapter, social security taxes are paid at a uniform, stipulated rate on a specified maximum amount of income earned from such sources as wages, salaries, bonuses, and commissions. The basis for determining the amount of social security taxes due is the total amount of gross earnings before any adjustments, deductions, or exemptions. In essence, *social security taxes are taken out of the first dollar you earn* and continue to be withdrawn up to a specified maximum amount of taxable income. Once you hit that maximum, your social security taxes stop for the year and begin again on January 1.

In 2000, with a social security tax rate of 7.65 percent and maximum taxable earnings of $76,200, the maximum tax was $5,829.30 (7.65% × $76,200). The 1.45 percent Medicare tax (part of the 7.65 percent social security tax) continues to be charged on income over $76,200. The maximum wages to which the social security and Medicare tax apply are adjusted each year in response to changes in the cost of living. Note that an amount equal to the employee's contribution is also paid by the taxpayer's employer. In other words, the total amount of social security taxes paid for every wage earner amounts to twice the amount the employee pays (employers are subject to the same tax rates and taxable maximums as employees). Of course, if you earn less than the maximum taxable income, your social security benefits will also be less than the maximum. The social security tax rate, however, remains the same no matter how much or how little you earn. For example, if you earned only $20,000 in 2000, you would have paid social security taxes of only $1,530 (7.65% × $20,000). Keep in mind that the full amount of social security taxes is paid by each wage earner, regardless of what the spouse or any other household member pays.

On the other hand, if an individual works for more than one employer during the year and earns more than the wage base ($76,200 in 2000), he or she is entitled to a tax credit for the amount of overpayment. This credit can be claimed on your federal income tax return (see line 61 of the 2000 Form 1040).

excise taxes
Taxes paid at the time of purchase on certain items and services, such as automobiles, gasoline, telephone services, tobacco products, and liquor.

EXCISE, GIFT, ESTATE, AND OTHER TAXES. In addition to income and social security taxes, the federal government receives revenue from the following types of taxes:

- *Excise taxes:* **Excise taxes** are added to the purchase price of certain items and services, such as automobiles, gasoline, telephone services, tobacco products, and liquor, and paid at the time of purchase.
- *Gift and estate taxes:* Both federal and state governments levy *gift taxes,* based on the value of the gift, that must be paid by the giver. *Estate taxes,* also levied at the federal and state levels, are based on the estate's value upon the death of its

owner, and may reduce the amount of inheritance passed on to the heirs. Chapter 15 on estate planning discusses these taxes in greater detail.

- *Other taxes:* Duties on imports, entrance fees to federal properties, such as parks and museums, and taxes on special types of transactions are still other types of federal taxation.

STATE TAXES

To raise revenue to finance their operations, state governments levy a variety of taxes. Probably the largest source of state revenue is the sales tax; other sources are income taxes, property taxes, and licensing fees.

- *State sales tax:* All but a few states levy statewide **sales taxes** at the point of sale on most consumer purchases, though some may exempt food, prescription medications, or services. Although sales tax rates vary from state to state, most are in the 4 to 7 percent range. Because sales taxes are tied to purchases, there is really no practical way to avoid them. When making or budgeting for large purchases, you should recognize that sales taxes will add to their cost.

- *State income taxes:* Most states have personal income taxes ranging from about 3 to 10 percent of reported taxable income. These taxes are either graduated tax rates that increase with taxable income or fixed rates that apply to all levels of income. Nearly all states follow the federal law in defining taxable income, though many provide for different exclusions and adjustments. Some states, however, tax only certain types of income, such as interest, dividends, and capital gains. The calculation of state taxes is generally similar to that for federal income taxes, so that filing state tax returns is relatively easy. Like the federal government, most states withhold a portion of income from each paycheck. Many allow taxpayers to deduct federal taxes from taxable income before calculating their state tax liability. (For federal tax purposes, persons who itemize can deduct the state income taxes they paid.)

- *State property taxes, licensing fees, and other taxes:* Although most states obtain the vast majority of their revenues from sales and income taxes, some also tax various forms of property, particularly automobiles and other motor vehicles. However, as a principal source of revenue, property taxes are levied primarily by local governments. State governments also obtain revenues from the sale of automobile licenses and by licensing certain professions. In addition, most states have excise taxes on gasoline, tobacco, and liquor, and gift and estate taxes similar to those levied by the federal government (see Chapter 15). Of these miscellaneous types of state taxes, only property taxes are deductible for federal income tax purposes.

LOCAL TAXES

Local governments, which include everything from cities and counties to school districts and stadium authorities, levy taxes to fund a variety of public services. Although the majority of local revenues come from property taxes, local governments often use income taxes, sales taxes, and licensing fees to add to their coffers.

- *Local property taxes:* **Property taxes** on real estate and other personal property, such as automobiles and boats, are primary sources of revenue to cities, counties, school districts, and other municipalities. Because for most people the home is the largest form of property ownership, real estate taxes are the dominant form of property

sales taxes
Taxes levied at the point of sale by state and local governments on most consumer purchases, though food, prescription medications, or services may be exempt.

property taxes
Taxes typically levied by local governmental units on the value of real estate and certain personal property to finance their operations.

taxes. Property taxes are typically collected by the county and then distributed among other governmental units—the city and school district, for example. The governmental unit to which taxes are paid determines the value of the taxed property. In general, the more expensive the home, the higher the real estate tax. If deductions are itemized, these taxes can be deducted when calculating federal income taxes. Further discussion of these taxes is included in the discussion of housing in Chapter 5.

- *Local income taxes:* Local governments—particularly larger cities in the eastern part of the United States—sometimes levy income taxes on all those employed within their boundaries. These taxes are similar to federal and state income taxes, but the rates are lower—usually about 1 to 2 percent but sometimes as high as 4 to 5 percent of taxable income (an exception is the District of Columbia, where the income tax rate is above 10 percent). Most cities withhold income taxes, with final settlement made at the end of the year. These taxes are a deductible itemized expense for federal income tax purposes.

- *Local sales taxes and licensing fees:* Many cities have sales taxes. Licensing fees, such as building permits, provide local governments with added revenue. In some states, a portion of the fees collected for automobile and other licenses represents a local licensing fee or property tax.

CONCEPT CHECK

3-19. Explain how the federal government raises funds through social security, excise, and gift and estate taxes.

3-20. Briefly discuss the various types of taxes levied by state and local governments.

SUMMARY

LG1. **Discuss the basic principles of income taxes and determine your filing status.** Because taxes impact most individuals and families, understanding them is essential for effective personal financial planning and intelligent money management. The dominant tax in our country today is the federal income tax, a levy that provides the government with most of the funds it needs to cover its operating costs. The administration and enforcement of federal tax laws is the responsibility of the IRS, a part of the U.S. Department of the Treasury. Because the government operates on a pay-as-you-go basis, employers are required to withhold taxes from their employees' paychecks. The amount of taxes you owe depends on your filing status—single, married filing jointly, married filing separately, head of household, or qualifying widow(er) with dependent child—and the amount of taxable income you report.

LG2. **Classify the various types of gross income, differentiate between itemized and standard deductions and exemptions, and calculate taxable income.** Gross income includes active income (such as wages, bonuses, pensions, alimony), portfolio income (dividends, interest, and capital gains), and passive income (income derived from real estate, limited partnerships, and other tax shelters). You must decide whether to itemize your various deductions or take the standard deduction. Some allowable deductions for those who itemize include mortgage interest, medical expenses over 7.5 percent of AGI, and certain job-related expenses. To calculate taxable income, deduct allowable adjustments, such as IRA contributions and alimony paid, from gross income to get AGI, and subtract from AGI the amount of deductions and personal exemptions claimed.

LG3. **Prepare a basic tax return using the appropriate tax forms and rate schedules.** Once you determine your taxable income, you can find the amount of taxes owed using either the tax rate tables or, if your taxable income is over $100,000, the tax rate schedules. Tax rates vary with level of reported income and filing status. Personal tax returns are filed using one of the following forms: 1040EZ, 1040A, or 1040.

LG4. **Explain who needs to pay estimated taxes, when to file your return, how to handle an audit, where to get help with your taxes, and computer-based tax returns.** Persons with income not subject to withholding may need to file a declaration of estimated taxes and make estimated quarterly tax payments. Annual returns must be filed on or before April 15, unless the taxpayer requests an automatic 4-month filing extension. The IRS audits selected returns to confirm their validity by carefully examining the data reported in them. Assistance in preparing returns is available from the IRS, private tax preparers, and computer programs that can be used both for tax planning and tax preparation.

LG5. **Implement a tax planning strategy.** Effective tax planning is closely tied to other areas of personal financial planning. The objectives of tax planning are to reduce, shift, or defer taxes so the taxpayer gets maximum use of and benefits from the money he or she earns. Some of the more popular tax strategies include maximizing deductions, shifting income to relatives in lower tax brackets, investing in real estate and other types of tax shelters, investing in tax-exempt municipal bonds, setting up IRAs, and using other types of pension and retirement plans and annuities to generate tax-deferred income.

LG6. **Describe the other major forms of personal taxes.** In addition to income taxes, the federal government also levies social security taxes, excise taxes, and gift and estate taxes. Individuals also pay state and local taxes, including income taxes, sales taxes, property taxes, and various licensing fees.

QUESTIONS AND PROBLEMS

1. Mary Parker is 24 years old, single, lives in an apartment, and has no dependents. Last year she earned $21,600 as a sales assistant for Texas Instruments; $1,800 of her wages were withheld for federal income taxes. In addition, she had interest income of $142. Estimate her taxable income, tax liability, and tax refund or tax owed.

2. Tina Marcelle received the following items and amounts of income during 2001. Help her calculate (a) her gross income and (b) that portion (dollar amount) of her income that is tax exempt.

Salary	$19,500
Dividends	800
Gift from mother	500
Child support from ex-husband	2,400
Interest on savings account	250
Rent	900
Loan from bank	2,000
Interest on state government bonds	300

3. If Jenny Perez is in the 31 percent tax bracket, calculate the tax associated with each of the following transactions using the tax schedules in Exhibit 3.7 and the IRS regulations for capital gains in effect in 2000:
    a. She sold stock for $1,200 that she purchased for $1,000 five months earlier.
    b. She sold bonds for $4,000 that she purchased for $3,000 three years earlier.
    c. She sold stock for $1,000 that she purchased for $1,500 fifteen months earlier.

4. Demonstrate the differences resulting from a $1,000 tax credit versus a $1,000 deduction for a single taxpayer in the 28 percent tax bracket with $35,000 of pre-tax income.

5. ***Use Worksheets 3.1 and 3.2.*** John Otsubo graduated from college in 2000 and began work as a systems analyst in July 2000. He is preparing to file his income tax return for 2000 and has collected the following financial information for calendar year 2000:

Tuition scholarships and grants	$ 4,750
Scholarship, room, and board	1,850
Salary	13,850
Interest income	185
Deductible expenses, total	3,000
Income taxes withheld	1,600

    a. Prepare John's 2000 tax return, using the standard deduction amount given in Exhibit 3.6, a personal exemption of $2,800, and the tax rates given in Exhibit 3.7. Which tax form should John use, and why?
    b. Prepare John's 2000 tax return using the data in part **a** along with the following information:

IRA contribution	$1,000
Cash dividends received	150

    Which tax form should he use in this case? Why?

6. Ron Ballard is married and has one child. He is putting together some figures so he can prepare their joint 2000 tax return. He can claim three personal exemptions (including himself). So far, he's been able to determine the following with regard to income and possible deductions:

Total unreimbursed medical expenses incurred	$ 1,155
Gross wages and commissions earned	38,820
IRA contribution	2,250
Mortgage interest paid	5,200
Capital gains realized on assets held less than 12 months	1,450
Income from limited partnership	200
Job expenses and other allowable deductions	875
Interest paid on credit cards	380
Dividend and interest income earned	610
Sales taxes paid	2,470
Charitable contributions made	1,200
Capital losses realized	3,475
Interest paid on a car loan	570
Alimony paid by Ron to first wife	6,000
Social security taxes paid	2,750
Property taxes paid	700
State income taxes paid	1,700

Given the above information, how much taxable income will the Ballards have in 2000? (*Note*: Assume Ron is covered by a pension plan where he works, the standard deduction amounts in Exhibit 3.6 are applicable, and each exemption claimed is worth $2,800.)

7. Maureen and Bob O'Flaherty have been notified that they are being audited. What should they do to prepare for the audit, and what steps can they take if they do not agree with the outcome of the audit?

APPLYING PERSONAL FINANCE

Tax Shelters: Are They Alive and Well?

Although tax shelter opportunities have been greatly reduced with the passage of the Tax Reform Act of 1986, some opportunities still exist to shelter income from the heavy tax burden. Your job is to check various sources to learn about any available tax shelters.

Where can you go to find tax shelter opportunities? First, try the financial section of your newspaper. There may be advertisements or articles on tax shelters such as tax-free bond funds. A bank is another source. Simply ask at "new accounts" if they can give you any tax shelter information. Another major source of new tax shelters are brokerage houses which sell stocks, bonds, and other securities to the investing public. If you have access to a brokerage house, ask them for tax shelter information. You may be surprised to learn about the wide variety of tax shelters still available.

CONTEMPORARY CASE APPLICATIONS

3.1   The Aggarwals Tackle Their Tax Return

Sabash and Sue Aggarwal are a married couple in their early 20s living in Dallas. Sabash earned $30,600 in 2000 from his job as a sales manager with Carson Corporation. During the year, his employer withheld $2,900 for income tax purposes. In addition, the Aggarwals received interest of $350 on a joint savings account, $750 interest on tax-exempt municipal bonds, and a dividend of $400 on jointly owned stocks. At the end of 2000, the Aggarwals sold two stocks, A and B. Stock A was sold for $700 and had been purchased 4 months earlier for $800. Stock B was sold for $1,500 and had been purchased 3 years earlier for $1,100. Their only child, Rohn, age 2, received (as his sole source of income) dividends of $200 on stock of Kraft, Inc.

Although Sabash was covered by the Carson Corporation's pension plan, he planned to contribute $2,000 to an IRA for 2000. Following are the amounts of money paid out during the year by the Aggarwals:

Medical and dental expenses (unreimbursed)	$ 200
State and local property taxes	831
Interest paid on home mortgage	4,148
Charitable contributions	1,360
Total	$6,539

In addition, Sabash incurred some travel costs (not reimbursed) for an out-of-town business trip as follows:

Airline ticket	$250
Taxis	20
Lodging	60
Meals (as adjusted to 50% of cost)	36
Total	$366

Questions

1. Using the above information, prepare a joint tax return for Sabash and Sue Aggarwal for the year ended December 31, 2000, to give them the smallest tax liability—that is, either itemize their deductions or take the standard deduction. (*Note:* Use Worksheet 3.2, Form 1040, and the tax rate schedule in Exhibit 3.7 to determine the Aggarwals' taxes. Assume the standard deductions in Exhibit 3.6 are applicable and each exemption claimed is worth $2,800.)
2. How much have you saved the Aggarwals as a result of your treatment of their deductions?
3. Discuss whether the Aggarwals need to file a tax return for their son.
4. Suggest some tax strategies the Aggarwals might use to reduce their tax liability for next year.

3.2   Joan Cavander: Bartender or Tax Expert?

Joan Cavander, who is single, goes to graduate school part-time and works as a bartender at the Twin Towers Supper Club in Atlanta. During the past year (2000), her gross income was $18,450 in wages and tips. She has decided to prepare her own tax return because she cannot afford the services of a tax expert. After preparing her return, she has come to you for advice. The following is a summary of the figures she has prepared thus far:

Gross income:	
Wages	$10,250
Tips	8,200
Adjusted gross income (AGI)	$18,450
Less: Itemized deductions	2,300
	$16,150
Less: Standard deduction	4,150
Taxable income	$12,000

Joan believes that if an individual's income falls below $20,350, the federal government considers him or her "poor" and allows both itemized deductions and a standard deduction.

Questions

1. Calculate Joan Cavander's taxable income, being sure to consider her exemption. (Assume the standard deductions in Exhibit 3.6 are applicable and each exemption claimed is worth $2,800.)
2. Discuss with Joan her errors in interpreting the tax laws, and explain the difference between itemized deductions and the standard deduction.
3. Joan has been dating Sam Haley for nearly 4 years, and they are seriously thinking about getting married. Sam has income and itemized deductions identical to Joan's. How much tax would they pay as a married couple (filing a joint return) versus the total amount the two paid as single persons (filing separate individual returns)? Strictly from a tax perspective, does it make any difference whether Joan and Sam stay single or get married? Explain.

MONEY ONLINE

TAXES, TAXES, AND MORE TAXES!

Note: Web addresses change frequently, so you may need to determine the home page and do a site search to find the page or topic that's referenced.

1. **metlife.com**
   How does a tax audit sound? Find information and advice on "Surviving an IRS Audit" when you search on "Money" at MetLife's "Life Advice Center." Learn what an audit is and what to expect during an audit.

2. **ftp.fedworld.gov/pub/irs-pdf/p1.pdf**
   What are your rights as a taxpayer? Pull up Publication 1 from the IRS Web site to find out that among other rights, you are entitled to privacy and confidentiality, professional and courteous service, and representation.

3. **www.irs.gov/ind_info/appeals/index.html**
   What if you disagree with the IRS's findings in your case? Refer to this page for information on how to appeal an IRS decision, the review process, and alternative dispute resolution if you have trouble resolving your appeals case.

4. **www.irs.gov/bus_info/tax_pro/rep-client.html**
   Become an enrolled agent and earn the privilege of representing taxpayers before the IRS. Consult the IRS Web site for the forms, fees, and information concerning these tax professionals.

5. **www.nolo.com**
   Find legal self help on taxing issues at Nolo's Web site. Search on "taxes" and discover hundreds of books and articles packed with legal information and resources.

6. **financenter.com**
   Need tax preparation software? Click on "Planning" and "Compare" at the FinanCenter to find a comparison chart of "Tax Preparation Software." Then click on "Online Preparation" to find a list of tax preparation sites.

7. **www.familymoney.com**
   Attend "Income Tax 101" or learn tax-lowering strategies at FamilyMoney's Web site. Under "Managing," click on "Taxes" to find numerous tax information offerings.

8. **quicken.com/taxes**
   Quicken has it all. Consult their "Deduction Center," find the tax rates and rules that affect you, get help preparing and filing your taxes or learn tax planning strategies. Whether you need information on individual or small business taxes, *Quicken* has articles and calculators to suit your needs.

9. **www.dtonline.com**
   Estimate your taxes using Deloitte and Touche's Tax Forecasting Worksheet. Click "Personal Finance Advisor" to browse interesting publications and click on "Tax Planning Guide" to find the Planning Worksheet and other tax tools. Also look through their "Tips and Strategies" for everyone.

10. **taxes.yahoo.com**
    What do beginning investors need to know about taxes? Consult Yahoo's "Beginner's Guide" for help with managing the tax liability on investments, planning for capital gains, and purchasing and selling investments. While you're there, check out Yahoo's "Tools and Resources."

11. **www.taxadmin.org**
    Federal income taxes are only part of your total tax burden. Click on "Tax Rates/Surveys" at the Web site of the Federation of Tax Administrators to find information on state income taxes, state taxation of Social Security and pension benefits, state sales taxes, and state excise taxes.

Just for Fun!
12. **cbs.marketwatch.com**
    Keep up with the latest news on taxes at the CBS MarketWatch Web site. Click on "Personal Finance" and then on "Taxes" to find recent articles in their "Tax Library." Also check out the features "Taxing Times" and "Ask the Taxman."

PART II

Managing Basic Assets

CHAPTER 4
Managing Your Cash and Savings

CHAPTER 5
Making Automobile and Housing Decisions

Chapter 4

Managing Your Cash and Savings

LEARNING GOALS

LG1.   Understand the role of good cash management in the personal financial planning process.

LG2.   Describe today's financial services marketplace: traditional and nondepository financial institutions and deposit safety.

LG3.   Select the checking and savings products, electronic banking services, and other bank services that meet your needs.

LG4.   Find the interest earned on your money using compound interest and future value techniques.

LG5.   Develop a savings strategy that incorporates a variety of savings plans.

LG6.   Open and use a checking account.

Breaking the Bank (Account)

Jennifer Samuels tossed her monthly bank statement on her desk, amidst a pile of bills and prior months' bank statements. Because she had her employer directly deposit her biweekly salary checks into her checking account, she knew there was enough money in her account to cover her needs.

About a week later, however, an envelope marked "urgent" arrived from the bank. When she opened it, Jennifer discovered she had overdrawn her account, bouncing two checks. She immediately pulled out the bank statements for the past 4 months and began to review them. Although she did record each check she wrote, she discovered she had not been as diligent about purchases made with her debit card and about withdrawals from automated teller machines (ATMs). Nor did she keep a running balance in her checkbook, but rather "eyeballed" the checks she wrote and estimated the current balance based on the last balance she'd entered.

Compounding the problem were the bank's additional service charges. Jennifer had a free account—as long as she kept a minimum daily balance of $1,000. If she dipped below that amount in any month, the bank charged her a service fee of $7.50 plus a per-check charge of 25 cents. During several months these charges added up! Jennifer was even more upset when she realized that she in fact had plenty of money in a savings account at the same bank. It would have been a simple matter to transfer funds to cover any shortfalls.

Jennifer vowed to pay closer attention to cash management in the future. She called her bank and found out she could link her accounts to combine balances and use online banking to check balances frequently and quickly transfer funds. With a better handle on her bank balances, she could also shift more to accounts that earned higher interest rates.

Like Jennifer, you may need to get a better handle on your cash management practices. In Chapter 4 you'll learn how to start.

The Role of Cash Management in Personal Financial Planning [LG1]

As Jennifer Samuels learned, establishing good financial habits applies to managing cash and other areas of personal finance. In this chapter we'll focus on **cash management**—an activity that deals with the routine, day-to-day administration of cash and near-cash resources by an individual or family. We identified these resources in Chapter 2 as liquid assets. They are considered liquid because they are either held in cash or can be readily converted to cash with little or no loss in value.

In addition to cash, there are several other kinds of liquid assets, including checking accounts, savings accounts, money market deposit accounts, money market mutual funds, and other short-term investment vehicles. Exhibit 4.1 briefly describes the more popular types of liquid assets and the representative rates of return they earned in early 2001. As a rule, near-term needs are met using cash on hand, and unplanned or future needs are met using some type of savings or short-term investment vehicle.

cash management The routine, day-to-day administration of cash and near-cash resources by an individual or family.

 **EXHIBIT 4.1**

POPULAR LIQUID ASSETS

The wide variety of savings vehicles available makes it possible to meet just about any savings or short-term investment need. Rates vary considerably, so shop around to get the best interest rate.

Type	Representative Rates of Return (Early 2001)	Description
Cash	0%	Pocket money; the coin and currency in one's possession.
Checking account	0–2.0%	A substitute for cash. Offered by commercial banks and other financial institutions such as savings and loans and credit unions.
Savings account	2.0–4.0%	Money is available at any time but cannot be withdrawn by check. Offered by banks and other financial institutions.
Money market deposit account (MMDA)	6.0–6.5%	Primarily a savings vehicle that pays market rates of interest. Offers limited check-writing privileges and requires a fairly large (typically $1,000 or more) minimum deposit.
Money market mutual fund (MMMF)	6.00–6.75%	Savings vehicle that is actually a mutual fund (not offered by banks, S&Ls, and other depository institutions). Like an MMDA, it also offers check-writing privileges.
Certificate of deposit (CD)	5.0–7.5%	A savings instrument where funds are left on deposit for a stipulated period (1 week to 1 year or more); imposes a penalty for withdrawing funds early. Market yields vary by size and maturity; no check-writing privileges.
U.S. Treasury bill (T-bill)	4.8–5.6%	Short-term, highly marketable security issued by the U.S. Treasury (originally issued with maturities of 13 and 26 weeks); smallest denomination is $1,000.
U.S. savings bond (EE)	4.5–5.5%	Issued by U.S. Treasury; rate of interest is tied to U.S. Treasury securities. Long a popular savings vehicle (widely used with payroll deduction plans). Mature in approximately 5 years; sold in denominations of $50 and more.

In personal financial planning, cash management is the way you make sure adequate funds are available for household outlays and an effective savings program. The success of your financial plans depends on your faithfulness to established cash budgets.

An effective way to keep your spending in line is to make all household transactions (even the allocation of fun money or weekly cash allowances) using a tightly controlled *checking account.* In effect, you should write checks only at certain times of the week or month and, more important, you should avoid carrying your checkbook with you when you might be tempted to write checks for unplanned purchases. If you are going shopping, establish a maximum spending limit beforehand—ideally, an amount consistent with your cash budget. Such a system not only helps you avoid frivolous, impulsive expenditures but also documents how and where you spend your money. Then, if your financial outcomes are not consistent with your plans, you can better identify causes and initiate appropriate corrective actions.

Another aspect of cash management, establishing an ongoing savings program, is an important part of personal financial planning. Savings are not only a cushion against financial emergencies but also a way to accumulate funds to meet future financial goals. You may want to put money aside so you can go back to school in a few years to earn a graduate degree, buy a new home, or perhaps take a luxury vacation. These specific financial objectives can be met through savings.

CONCEPT CHECK

4-1. What is *cash management?* What are its major functions?

4-2. Give two broad reasons for holding liquid assets. Identify and briefly describe the popular types of liquid assets.

■ Today's Financial Services Marketplace [LG 2]

Thanks to advanced technology and less restrictive regulations, the pace of change in the financial services industry is accelerating. With the click of a mouse you can check your bank account balances, pay your bills, open a checking account, and search online for the best rates on savings instruments. You can even get money from your local bank at a Paris ATM! Consumers can choose services from the many financial institutions competing for their business. No longer must we go to one place for our checking accounts, another for credit cards or loans, and yet another for stock brokerage services. You can choose "one-stop shopping" or have accounts at a variety of financial services providers, depending on what's best for your needs.

Before 1980 very little competition existed in the financial marketplace. The distinctions among various kinds of financial institutions were clear. Commercial banks offered checking accounts and short-term loans. Savings and loans offered savings accounts and real estate mortgage loans. Brokerage firms assisted in trading securities, and insurance companies offered life, disability, health, auto, and homeowner's insurance. This segmented marketplace changed in the early 1980s with passage of the *Depository Institutions Deregulation and Monetary Control Act of 1980.* This important law, together with additional legislation passed in 1982, removed many restrictions on banks and savings institutions and allowed them to compete with each other and with nonbank financial institutions.

As a result of deregulation, the differences among financial institutions have blurred considerably. Savings and loan institutions and commercial banks now offer many of the same financial products and services. In addition, at many banks you can make securities transactions and buy mutual funds and insurance, while stockbrokers offer check-writing services, credit cards, loans, and access to ATMs. To compete with nonfinancial institutions, many banks and savings and loans now offer help with personal financial planning, take deposits across state lines, sell insurance, and offer securities brokerage services.

Thus the *financial services industry* as we know it today embraces all institutions that market various kinds of *financial products* (such as checking and savings accounts, credit cards, loans and mortgages, insurance, and mutual funds) and *financial services* (such as financial planning, taxes, securities brokerage, real estate, trusts, retirement, and estate planning). In effect, what used to be several distinct (though somewhat related) industries is now, in essence, one industry whose firms are differentiated more by organizational structure than by name or product offerings.

TYPES OF FINANCIAL INSTITUTIONS

In spite of the growing number of firms entering the financial services field, individuals and families continue to make the vast majority of their financial transactions at traditional financial institutions: commercial banks, savings and loan associations, savings banks, and credit unions. Although these are organized and regulated by different agencies, they commonly are referred to as "banks" because of their similar products and services. Unlike their nonbanking counterparts, such as stock brokerages and mutual funds, they accept deposits. Probably the two biggest advantages of these depository institutions are that they are familiar and convenient. Further, although most people have checking and savings accounts, a much smaller number own stocks, bonds, or mutual funds. As a result, many people are not accustomed to dealing with brokerage firms and other types of financial service companies.

commercial bank
A financial institution that offers checking and savings accounts and a full range of financial products and services, including several types of consumer loans. It's the only institution that can offer *non–interest-paying checking accounts (demand deposits)*.

COMMERCIAL BANKS. To millions of Americans, banking means doing business with a **commercial bank.** Of the four types of traditional financial institutions, commercial banks are by far the largest. In addition to checking and savings accounts, commercial banks offer a full range of financial products and services, including a variety of savings vehicles, credit cards, several types of consumer loans, trust services, and such items as safe-deposit boxes, traveler's checks, and check-cashing privileges. It is little wonder that they are commonly called *full-service banks.*

Commercial banks are the only financial institutions that can offer *non–interest-paying checking accounts (demand deposits)*—a feature that in today's deregulated financial market provides little competitive advantage. Therefore commercial banks also offer a variety of checking accounts that combine check-writing privileges with features of savings accounts and several types of pure savings accounts. Most prevalent among these is the *regular savings account,* a basic savings account paying a minimum rate of interest. There is no limit on how much interest a bank can pay on regular savings accounts. However, most of these accounts still pay low (2 to 4 percent) interest rates, so it clearly pays to shop around. Whereas to many savers, regular savings accounts are simply a convenient way of accumulating money, for many others, they are the only savings or investment vehicle.

Commercial banks typically differentiate between their *special savings accounts* on the basis of deposit minimums. For higher minimum balances, they offer a slightly higher rate of interest (.25 to .5 percent more) than on accounts requiring lower or no minimum balance. If the account balance falls below the required minimum balance, the interest rate drops to the rate on no-minimum-balance accounts.

savings and loan association (S&L)
A financial institution that channels the savings of its depositors primarily into mortgage loans for purchasing and improving homes. Due to deregulation, however, S&Ls now offer a competitive range of financial products and services.

SAVINGS AND LOAN ASSOCIATIONS. **Savings and loan associations (S&Ls)** are found in most parts of the country. One type of S&L is a *mutual association,* in which the depositors actually own the institution. (In finance the word *mutual* indicates a type of cooperative ownership arrangement.) Although the returns they receive technically are called *dividends,* they are treated as *interest* for all practical purposes. The other type of S&L is *stockholder owned;* depositors receive interest on their deposits instead of dividends.

Regardless of their organizational structure, savings and loans are important because they channel depositors' savings into mortgage loans for purchasing and improving homes. Since deregulation, S&Ls have greatly expanded their product and service offerings. Although they still cannot offer non–interest-paying checking accounts (demand deposits), they do offer many of the same checking, savings, and lending products and services as commercial banks—in fact, it is difficult to differentiate between the two institutions. Typically, savings deposits at S&Ls earn about .25 to .5 percent more than those at commercial banks. The availability of products and services at numerous branch offices and their attractive rates of interest contribute to the popularity of savings and loan associations.

SAVINGS BANKS. **Savings banks** are a special type of financial institution, similar to savings and loan associations and located primarily in the New England states. In addition to offering a number of different interest-paying checking accounts, they accept a variety of savings deposits on which they pay interest at a rate on par with that paid by savings and loans. Because most savings banks are *mutuals,* depositors are their actual owners. The savings bank accepts deposits and, after deducting the expenses of doing business from its revenues, distributes the profits to the owners in the form of dividend payments, which are technically equivalent to interest payments. However, instead of distributing all profits, the mutual savings bank typically distributes only enough to provide depositors with a stated return of, say, 3.5 percent. It then reinvests any remaining profits in order to provide greater protection for depositors.

CREDIT UNIONS. A **credit union** is a special type of mutual association that provides financial products and services to specific groups of people who belong to a common occupation, religious or fraternal order, or residential area. Credit unions are owned (and, in some cases, operated) by their members. Although credit unions are used by more than 75 million people, they are quite small when compared with commercial banks or S&Ls. A person who qualifies for membership in a credit union may buy a share by making a minimum deposit— often $5 to $10. One *must* be a member—that is, have money on deposit—to borrow from a credit union. Because the credit union is run to benefit its members, the rate of interest it pays on savings is normally .5 to 1.5 percent above that paid by other savings institutions. Like other mutual associations, credit unions technically pay dividends rather than interest on savings.

smart.sites To learn more about credit unions and to find one in your area, visit the Credit Union National Association Web site, **www.cuna.org**.

Most credit unions, in addition to offering different types of interest-paying checking accounts—called **share draft accounts**—offer a variety of savings accounts to their members. Savers often do not know the dividend rate until the end of the savings period because the dividends paid in each period depend on the credit union's earnings for that period. Because credit unions pay a favorable return on savings deposits and also allow members to borrow money at advantageous rates, they are attractive to many people.

NONDEPOSITORY FINANCIAL INSTITUTIONS. With deregulation, other types of financial institutions began offering what we consider banking services. Because they do not accept deposits like traditional banks, they are considered "nondepository" institutions. Today you might hold a credit card issued by a stock brokerage firm or have an account through a mutual fund that allows you to write a limited number of checks. Other non-depository financial institutions include life insurance and finance companies.

- *Stock brokerage firms* offer several cash management options, including *money market mutual funds* that invest in short-term securities and earn a higher rate of interest than bank accounts, special "wrap" accounts, and credit cards.
- *Mutual funds,* discussed in detail in Chapter 13, provide yet another alternative to bank savings accounts. Like stockbrokers, they offer money market mutual funds.

HOW SAFE IS YOUR MONEY?

The 1980s and early 1990s were tumultuous times in the banking industry. The large number of failures in the commercial banking and savings and loan industries raised concern about the strength of the deposit insurance system, and many banks merged. As a result,

savings bank
A type of financial institution, similar to an S&L and located primarily in the New England states, that is most often a mutual association owned by its depositors.

credit union
A depositor-owned mutual association that offers different types of interest-paying checking (share draft) accounts, savings accounts, and loans to its members.

share draft account
An account offered by credit unions that is similar to interest-paying checking accounts offered by other financial institutions.

EXHIBIT 4.2

FEDERAL DEPOSIT INSURANCE PROGRAMS

If you have your checking and savings accounts at a federally insured institution, you are covered up to $100,000.

Savings Institution	Insuring Agency	Amount of Insurance
Commercial bank	Federal Deposit Insurance Corporation (FDIC)	$100,000/depositor through the Bank Insurance Fund (BIF)
Savings and loan association	Federal Deposit Insurance Corporation (FDIC)	$100,000/depositor through the Savings Association Insurance Fund (SAIF)
Savings bank	Federal Deposit Insurance Corporation (FDIC)	$100,000/depositor through the Bank Insurance Fund (BIF)
Credit union	National Credit Union Administration (NCUA)	$100,000/depositor through the National Credit Union Share Insurance Fund (NCUSIF)

many depositors were concerned about the safety of their deposits. Fortunately, the booming economy of the 1990s has made the U.S. banking industry very healthy. Today, the main reason that a bank goes out of business is its purchase by another bank.

Almost all commercial banks, S&Ls, savings banks, and credit unions are *federally insured* by U.S. government agencies. The few that are not are usually insured through either a state-chartered or private insurance agency. Most experts believe that these so-called *privately insured* institutions have less protection against loss than do the federally insured ones. Exhibit 4.2 lists the insuring agencies and maximum insurance amounts provided under the various federal deposit insurance programs.

deposit insurance
A type of insurance that protects funds on deposit against failure of the institution. Insuring agencies include the Federal Deposit Insurance Corporation (FDIC) and the National Credit Union Administration (NCUA).

Deposit insurance protects the funds you have on deposit at banks and other depository institutions against institutional failure. In effect, the insuring agency stands behind the financial institution and guarantees the safety of your deposits up to a specified maximum amount ($100,000 per depositor in the case of federal insurance).

 Look up your bank's financial profile and deposit insurance status at the Federal Deposit Insurance Corp. Web site, **www.fdic.gov**.

Note that deposit insurance is provided to each *depositor* and *not* on the *deposit account*. Thus the checking *and* the savings accounts of each depositor are insured and, *as long as the maximum insurable amount is not exceeded,* the depositor can have any number of accounts and still be fully protected. This is an important feature to keep in mind because many people mistakenly believe that the maximum insurance applies to *each* of their accounts. Not so. For instance, a negotiable order of withdrawal (see explanation in next section) account with a $15,000 balance at a branch office of a given bank, a MMDA with a $60,000 balance at the bank's main office, and a $50,000 certificate of deposit (CD) issued by the same bank is covered entirely by only $100,000 of deposit insurance. Of course, if either the MMDA or CD were transferred to another bank or financial institution, it would be insured for up to $100,000 and the total amount in all the accounts would then be fully protected.

Now that banks are offering a greater variety of products, including mutual funds, it is very important to remember that *only deposit accounts, including certificates of deposit, are covered by deposit insurance. Securities purchased through your bank are not subject to any form of deposit insurance.*

Although $100,000 in deposit insurance is quite a bit, it is possible to increase the amount of coverage if the need arises. Depositors can increase their coverage by opening accounts in multiple depositor names at the same institution. A married couple, for example, can obtain $500,000 in coverage by setting up *individual* accounts in the name of each spouse (good for $200,000 in coverage), a *joint* account in both names (good for another $100,000), and *separate trust or self-directed retirement (IRA, Keogh, etc.)* accounts in the name of each spouse (good for an additional $200,000). Note that in this case each depositor is treated as a separate legal entity and as such receives full insurance coverage—the husband alone is considered one legal entity, the wife another, and the man and wife as a couple a third. The trust and self-directed retirement accounts also are viewed as legal entities.

 At Veribanc (**www.veribanc.com**) learn about how this bank rating service ranks financial institutions on their safety and soundness.

CONCEPT CHECK

4-3. Discuss the effect that deregulation has had on institutions.

4-4. Briefly describe the basic operations and products and services offered by each of the following financial institutions: (a) commercial bank; (b) savings and loan association; (c) savings bank; (d) credit union; (e) stock brokerage firm; and (f) mutual fund.

4-5. What role does the FDIC play in insuring financial institutions? What other federal insurance program exists? Explain.

4-6. Would it be possible for an *individual* to have, say, six or seven checking and savings accounts at the same bank and still be fully protected under federal deposit insurance? Explain. Describe how it would be possible for a *married couple* to obtain as much as $500,000 in federal deposit insurance coverage at a single bank.

The Growing Menu of Cash Management Products [LG3]

Now that you are familiar with the different types of financial institutions, let's look at the various cash management products they offer. In addition to checking and savings accounts, they offer customers a variety of convenient services. Many of these services, such as ATMs and online banking, rely on the use of current technology to transfer funds electronically.

CHECKING AND SAVINGS ACCOUNTS

People hold cash and other forms of liquid assets, like checking and savings accounts, for the convenience they offer in (1) making purchase transactions; (2) meeting normal, recurring living expense and purchase requirements; and (3) providing a safety net (or cushion) to meet unexpected expenses or to take advantage of unanticipated opportunities. As mentioned before, deregulation has resulted in greater competition among financial institutions, which now offer a wide array of products to meet every liquid-asset need.

The federal *Truth-in-Savings Act of 1993* helps consumers evaluate the terms and costs of banking products. Commercial banks, savings institutions, and credit unions must fully and clearly disclose fees, interest rates, and terms of both checking and savings accounts. The act places strict controls on bank advertising and what constitutes a "free" account. For example, banks cannot advertise free checking if there are minimum balance requirements or per-check charges. Banks must use a standard *annual percentage yield (APY)* formula that takes compounding (discussed later) into account when stating the interest paid on accounts. This makes it easier for consumers to compare each bank's offerings. The law also requires banks to pay interest on a customer's full daily or monthly average deposit balance. No longer can banks pay interest only on the lowest daily balance or avoid paying any interest if the account balance falls below the minimum balance for 1 day. In addition, banks must notify customers 30 days before lowering rates on deposit accounts or certificates of deposit.

CHECKING ACCOUNTS. A checking account held at a financial institution is a **demand deposit,** meaning that the withdrawal of these funds must be permitted whenever demanded by the account holder. You put money into your checking account by *depositing* funds; you withdraw it by *writing checks* or *making cash withdrawals.* As long as you have sufficient funds in your account, the bank, when presented with a valid check, must immediately pay the amount indicated by charging your account for the amount of the check. Money held in checking accounts is liquid and therefore can easily be used to pay bills and make purchases.

Regular checking is the most common type of checking account. It pays no interest, and any service charges that exist can be waived if you maintain a minimum balance (usually about $750 to $1,500). Technically, non–interest-paying regular checking accounts can be offered only by commercial banks. S&Ls, savings banks, and credit unions also offer checking accounts; these accounts, which must pay interest, are called *NOW (negotiable order of withdrawal) accounts* or, in the case of credit unions, *share draft accounts.* Because checks are generally accepted in paying bills and purchasing goods and services, demand deposit balances are considered a common and important type of cash balance. An important benefit of demand deposits is that using checks to pay bills provides a convenient payment record.

SAVINGS ACCOUNTS. A savings account is another type of liquid asset that may be kept in commercial banks, savings and loan associations, credit unions, and many other types of financial institutions. Savings deposits are referred to as **time deposits** because they are expected to remain on deposit for a longer period than demand deposits. Because generally higher interest rates apply to savings deposits, savings accounts are typically preferable to checking accounts when the depositor's purpose is to accumulate money for a future expenditure or maintain balances for meeting unexpected expenditures. Most banks pay higher interest rates on larger savings account balances. For example, a bank might pay 3.50 percent on balances up to $2,500, 3.75 percent on balances between $2,500 and $10,000, and 4.00 percent on balances of more than $10,000.

Although financial institutions generally retain the right to require a savings account holder to wait a certain number of days before receiving payment of a withdrawal, most are willing to pay withdrawals immediately. In addition to withdrawal policies and deposit insurance, the stated interest rate and method of calculating interest paid on savings accounts are important considerations in choosing the financial institution in which to place savings.

INTEREST-PAYING CHECKING ACCOUNTS. As a result of changes that took place in the late 1970s and early 1980s, financial institutions introduced a variety of new

demand deposit
An account held at a financial institution from which funds can be withdrawn (by check or in cash) on demand by the account holder; same as a *checking account.*

time deposit
A savings deposit at a financial institution; so-called because it is expected to remain on deposit for a longer period than a demand deposit.

interest-bearing financial products. Depositors can now choose from money market deposit accounts, NOW accounts, and money market mutual funds.

Money Market Deposit Accounts. **Money market deposit accounts (MMDAs),** a popular offering at banks and other depository institutions, compete for deposits with money market mutual funds. MMDAs are popular with some savers and investors due to their convenience and safety because deposits in MMDAs, unlike those in money funds, are *federally insured.* Most banks require a minimum MMDA balance of $1,000 or more.

Depositors can use check-writing privileges or ATMs to access MMDA accounts. They receive a limited number of checks and transfers—usually six—without charge each month, but pay a fee on additional withdrawals or transfers. Although this feature obviously reduces the flexibility of these accounts, most depositors consider MMDAs to be savings rather than convenience accounts and do not consider it a serious obstacle. Moreover, MMDAs pay the highest interest rate of any bank account on which checks can be written.

> **money market deposit account (MMDA)**
> A federally insured savings account, offered by banks and other depository institutions, that is meant to be competitive with a MMMF.

NOW Accounts. **Negotiable order of withdrawal (NOW) accounts** are checking accounts on which the financial institution can pay interest. Since the deregulation of interest rates in January 1986, the NOW account has become widely accepted as an "interest-paying checking account." There is no legal minimum balance for a NOW, but many institutions impose their own requirement, often between $500 and $1,000. Some have no minimum, paying interest on any balance in the account. Many institutions pay interest at a higher rate for all balances more than a specified amount such as $2,500.

The higher rates of interest, however, can be misleading. As we will see later in this chapter, one of the major problems in the growth of these interest-paying checking accounts has been a rise in monthly bank charges, which can easily amount to more than the interest earned on all but the highest account balances. Consumers should view NOW accounts primarily as checking accounts that can also serve as potentially attractive savings vehicles, earning interest on balances that must be kept for transaction purposes anyway and would otherwise lie idle.

> **negotiable order of withdrawal (NOW) account**
> A checking account on which the financial institution can pay whatever rate of interest it deems appropriate.

Money Market Mutual Funds. Starting from zero in the mid-1970s, money market mutual funds have become the most successful type of mutual fund ever offered. (Mutual funds are discussed in greater detail in Chapter 13.) A **money market mutual fund (MMMF)** pools the funds of many small investors and purchases high-return short-term marketable securities offered by the U.S. Treasury, major corporations, large commercial banks, and various government organizations.

The portfolio of a typical MMMF contains specialized short-term securities that mature in as little as 1 day to as long as 1 year. The securities are all highly liquid and marketable forms of debt sold in denominations of at least $10,000 (except for U.S. Treasury bills, which are described later) and often as much as $250,000 or more. Because of their lofty minimum denominations, few individuals are able to afford these securities directly. However, they can do so indirectly through the purchase of MMMFs, many of which require low minimum deposits of as little as $500 to $1,000. The MMMF interest rate depends on returns earned on its investments, which fluctuate with general interest rate movements in the economy.

MMMFs generally pay interest at rates 3 to 5 percent above those paid on regular savings accounts; however, when short-term interest rates are low, the gap between them narrows to 1 to 2 percent. Moreover, investors have instant access to their funds through check-writing privileges although the checks often must be written for a stipulated minimum amount (usually $500). These checks look and are treated like any other check drawn on a demand deposit account, and, as with all interest-bearing checking accounts, you continue to earn interest on your money while the checks make their way through the banking system.

> **money market mutual fund (MMMF)**
> A mutual fund that pools the funds of many small investors and purchases high-return short-term marketable securities offered by the U.S. Treasury, major corporations, large commercial banks, and various government organizations.

ASSET MANAGEMENT ACCOUNTS.

asset management account (AMA)
A comprehensive deposit account, offered primarily by brokerage houses and mutual funds, that combines checking, investing, and borrowing activities and automatically sweeps excess funds into short-term investments and provides loans when shortages exist.

electronic funds transfer systems (EFTS)
Systems that use the latest telecommunications and computer technology to electronically transfer funds into and out of customers' accounts.

debit cards
Specially coded plastic cards used to transfer funds from a customer's bank account to the recipient's account to pay for goods or services. An ATM card is a debit card that also provides access to a variety of banking transactions through an ATM.

automated teller machine (ATM)
A type of remote computer terminal at which customers of a bank or other depository institution can make basic transactions 24 hours a day, 7 days a week.

ASSET MANAGEMENT ACCOUNTS. Perhaps the best example of a banking service offered by a nondepository financial institution is the **asset management account (AMA),** or *central asset account.* First introduced in 1977 by the Wall Street brokerage firm Merrill Lynch, the AMA is a comprehensive deposit account that combines checking, investing, and borrowing activities. These accounts are offered primarily by brokerage houses and mutual funds. AMAs appeal to many investors because they can consolidate most of their financial transactions at one institution and on one account statement.

The typical AMA account includes a MMDA with unlimited free checking, a Visa or MasterCard debit card, use of ATMs, and loan and brokerage accounts. Annual fees and account charges (such as a per-transaction charge for ATM withdrawals) vary, so it pays to shop around. AMAs pay higher interest rates on checking account deposits than banks, and they have increased in popularity as more institutions have lowered minimum balance requirements to $5,000. Their distinguishing feature is that they automatically "sweep" excess balances—for example, those more than $500—into a higher-return MMMF daily or weekly. When the account holder needs funds to purchase securities or cover checks written on the MMDA, the funds are transferred back to the MMDA. If the amount of securities purchased or checks presented for payment exceeds the account balance, the needed funds are supplied automatically through a loan.

Although AMAs are an attractive alternative to a traditional bank account, they have some drawbacks. Compared with a bank, there are fewer "branch" locations. (However, AMAs are affiliated with ATM networks, making it easy to withdraw funds.) ATM transactions are more costly, checks can take longer to clear, and you may not be able to get some bank services such as traveler's and certified checks. AMAs are not covered by deposit insurance although these deposits are protected by the Securities Investor Protection Corporation (explained in Chapter 11) and the firm's private insurance.

ELECTRONIC BANKING SERVICES

The fastest changing area in cash management today is electronic banking services. Whether using an ATM or checking your account balance online, electronic banking services make managing your money much easier and more convenient. No longer are you restricted to the hours that your bank is open. Electronic funds transfer systems allow you to conduct many types of banking business any hour of the day or night.

ELECTRONIC FUNDS TRANSFER SYSTEMS. Electronic funds transfer systems (EFTSs) use the latest telecommunications and computer technology to electronically transfer funds into and out of your account. For example, your employer may use an EFTS to electronically transfer your pay from its bank account directly into your personal bank account at the same or another bank. This eliminates the employer's need to prepare and process checks and the employee's need to deposit them. Electronic transfers make possible such services as debit cards and ATMs, pre-authorized deposits and payments, bank-by-phone accounts, and online banking.

Debit Cards and Automated Teller Machines. This form of EFTS uses specially coded plastic cards, called **debit cards,** to transfer funds from the customer's bank account (a debit) to the recipient's account. A debit card may be used to make purchases at any place of business set up with the point-of-sale terminals required to accept debit card payments. The personal identification number (PIN) issued with your debit card verifies that you are authorized to access the account.

Visa and MasterCard issue debit cards linked to your checking account, and an **automated teller machine (ATM)** card is another type of debit card that gives even more flexibility. In addition to using the card to purchase goods and services, it can be used at ATMs, which have become a popular way to make banking transactions. ATMs are actually remote computer terminals that allow customers of a bank or other depository institution to make deposits, withdrawals, and other transactions such as loan payments or transfers between accounts, 24 hours a day, 7 days a week. Suppose you need cash at 1:30 A.M. Although no bank is open, you can go to an ATM machine and use your card to withdraw funds from your account. Many people who were previously reluctant to use these cards now find them more convenient than cash and checks.

Most banks have ATMs outside their offices, and some locate freestanding ATMs in shopping malls, airports, grocery stores, at colleges and universities, and other high-traffic areas to enhance their competitive position. If your bank belongs to an EFTS network, such as Cirrus, Star, or Interlink, you can get cash from the ATM of any bank in the United States or overseas that is a member of that network. (In fact, the easiest way to get foreign currency when you travel overseas is through an ATM on your bank's network! It also gives you the best exchange rate for your dollars.) Most banks charge a per-transaction fee of $1 to $4 for using the ATM of another bank, and some also charge when you use your ATM card to pay certain merchants.

Debit card use is increasing because these cards are convenient both for retailers, who don't have to worry about bounced checks, and for consumers, who don't have to write checks and can often get cash back when they make a purchase. First accepted by supermarkets, gas stations, and convenience stores, ATM and other debit cards can now be used at many retail stores, doctors' offices, fast-food outlets, dry cleaners, and hair salons. Because most card issuers belong to regional or national networks, the cards are accepted in many states. Debit cards now account for about one-third of all debit and credit card transactions, excluding those made at ATMs, and are expected to increase to 50 percent by 2005.

The convenience of debit cards may, in fact, be their biggest drawback: It can be easy to overspend. To avoid problems, make sure to record all debit card purchases immediately in your checkbook ledger and deduct them from your balance. Also, if there is a problem with a purchase, you can't stop payment—an action you could take if you had instead paid by check or credit card.

Pre-Authorized Deposits and Payments. Two related EFTS services are *pre-authorized deposits and payments.* They allow you to receive automatic deposits or make payments that occur on a regular basis. For example, you can arrange to have your paycheck or monthly pension or social security benefits deposited directly into your account. Regular, fixed-amount payments, such as mortgage and consumer loan payments or monthly retirement fund contributions, can be pre-authorized to be made automatically from your account. You can also pre-authorize regular payments of varying amounts such as monthly utility bills. In this case each month you would specify by phone the amount to be paid.

Charges for pre-authorized payments may vary from bank to bank. Typically, customers must maintain a specified minimum deposit balance and pay fees averaging 25 to 50 cents per transaction. Not only does this system better allow the customer to earn interest on deposits used to pay bills, but it is a convenient payment mechanism that eliminates postage costs.

Bank-by-Phone Accounts. Bank customers can initiate a variety of banking transactions by telephone, either by calling a customer service operator who handles the transaction or by using the keypad on a touch-tone telephone to instruct the bank's computer. After the customer provides a secret code to access his or her accounts, the system then provides the appropriate codes to perform various transactions such as learning an account balance,

MONEY IN ACTION

The Check's in the (E-)Mail

Do you hate writing checks, so that you put off bill-paying until the very last minute, run out of stamps, and have to dash to the post office? Online bill payment may be the solution to your cash management problems. Just turn on your computer, check your bank balance to make sure sufficient money is in your account, and send bill payments on their ways. It's fast and convenient, and you can schedule bills for later payment as soon as they arrive.

Online bill paying comes in two forms. In the more traditional service you continue to receive your bills by mail and authorize a third party—this can be your bank or a company like Bills.com (**www.bills.com**) or the U.S. Postal Service (**www.usps.gov**)—to access your bank account to pay them. The initial set up, where you provide names, addresses, phone numbers, and account numbers for your payee list, may be a bit time consuming. But once you've entered the information, all you have to do is select the recipient, fill in the amount, and click the "pay" button.

With the second type, *electronic bill presentment and payment (EBPP)*, the EBPP company offers a complete online bill management service, allowing you to avoid the clutter of paper entirely. It acts as a virtual mailbox, receiving your bills and notifying you via email that a bill has arrived. Then you go to the Web site to review it and arrange payment from any account with check-writing privileges. EBPP services will also confirm that the payment has been made, remind you that an unpaid bill is due, and let you view and print a report of bill payments by date or expense category. Companies that offer EBPP include CyberBill's StatusFactory (**www.statusfactory.com**), Bills.com (**www.bills.com**), and Paytrust (**www.paytrust.com**).

"Although online bill paying certainly seems convenient, there are certain issues people need to seriously consider—privacy, security, and what happens when things go wrong," cautions Frank Torres of Consumers Union, publisher of *Consumer Reports*. Among the advantages:

- **Convenience:** You can pay all your bills at once from one Web site, without writing checks or buying stamps. If you travel a lot, you can access your bill-paying site while you are on the road or schedule payments up to 1 year ahead. Some services will even pay people who don't normally send you bills, like your baby-sitter!

- **Organization:** EBPP services remind you if a payment due date is approaching and you haven't paid your bill. With credit card

continued

finding out what checks have cleared, transferring funds to other accounts, and dispatching payments to participating merchants. To encourage banking by telephone, many banks today charge no fee on basic account transactions or allow a limited number of free transactions per month.

ONLINE BANKING AND BILL PAYMENT SERVICES. About 6 million households now use some form of *online banking* services, and that number is growing steadily as people become more comfortable using the Internet for financial transactions and banks make online services easier to use. Many just check their balances, but more than half use the Internet to transfer funds as well. Thanks to improved Internet security procedures, most online bank services are delivered through the Internet although some may use direct dial-up connections with the customer's bank. Today about 800 banks compete for your online banking business. It's in their best interests to do so, for one recent study showed that the cost of a full-service teller transaction was $1.07; an ATM transaction, 27 cents; and an Internet transaction, just 1 cent.

An online banking service lets you access your bank's online banking Web site from your computer at any time. After logging on with your personal identification codes, you can see a current account statement to check your balance and review recent transactions.

MONEY IN ACTION

The Check's in the (E-)Mail *(continued)*

companies assessing $30 late-payment-fees, this feature alone can save you a lot of money!

- **Record keeping:** Many services save your payments so you can retrieve and print a record for the year (some go back several years). This is especially helpful at tax time.
- **Customization:** You can arrange automatic payment for bills whose amounts do not change, such as mortgage or car loan payments, or if the amount is below a certain amount. With manual payments, you decide how much to pay and when.
- **Round the clock help:** E-mail help lines are available at any time, or you can call for help during normal business hours.

On the downside:

- **Start-up confusion:** With EBPP, there will be a lag time of several billing cycles while you change the address on all your bills to that of the service. This makes it difficult to just try the service first, and you will still have to pay some bills by hand.
- **Monthly fees:** Convenience isn't free. Most services charge $4 to $10 to pay from 10 to 30 bills per month, with a per-bill fee of up to 50 cents for additional bills.

- **Computer literacy:** If you are not comfortable using the Internet, wait until you master the basics and make a few online purchases.
- **Float:** Most bill-paying services immediately withdraw funds from your account when you hit the pay button, so you lose "float," the period between when you write a check and when the recipient cashes it, typically 3 to 10 days. Be sure the money is already in your account!
- **Privacy and security:** These are always a concern when you give a third party such valuable information as your social security number and bank and credit card numbers.

Still interested in trying e-bill payment? Use the checklist in Exhibit 4.3 to choose an online bill payment service wisely.

Sources: Christine Dugas, "Virtual Banks Get Real, Offer Deals To Woo Customers," *USA Today*, April 13, 2000, p. 12B; Hank Ezell, "Online Banking Growing Rapidly," *The Atlanta Journal and Constitution*, August 13, 2000, p. G3; R. J. Ignelzi, "Online Bill Paying: Does It Make Good Cents for You?" *San Diego Union-Tribune ComputerLink*, October 17, 2000, pp. 6–8; Karen Thomas, Millions Turn PCs into Personal Tellers, *USA Today*, October 3, 2000, p. 3D; "Weighing the Pros and Cons of Online Bill Paying," *San Diego Union-Tribune ComputerLink*, October 17, 2000, pp. 7–8.

Then you can transfer funds electronically from one account to another or pay bills electronically. You can also download account information to money management software such as *Quicken* or *Microsoft Money.*

Although a computer-based bank-at-home system doesn't replace the use of an ATM to obtain cash or deposit money, it can save both the time and the postage involved in paying bills. Other benefits include convenience and the potential to earn higher interest rates and pay lower fees. Customers like the ability to check their account balances any time of the day or night, not just when the printed statement comes once a month. Online banking does not always live up to its promises, however. You can't make cash deposits, checks may get lost in the mail, and you don't know when the funds will reach your account.

Most online banking services charge about $4 to $10 per month, which typically includes some bill payments. Some banks do not charge for merely viewing your accounts and transferring funds. The *Money in Action* box above and Exhibit 4.3 provide more information to help you decide if online bill paying is right for you.

Your current "traditional" bank probably offers online banking services. Most consumers prefer the security of a bank with a physical presence and a variety of other banking options like branches, ATMs, and phone services. Another option is to open an account at a *virtual bank* that exists only online and has few or no physical locations. Because they

HOW TO CHOOSE AN ONLINE BILL PAYING SERVICE

To get the features and security you need from your e-bill service, use the following checklist.

1. *Does the service have a written privacy policy stating it will not share your personal information with anyone at any time?* If not, look elsewhere.
2. *What is the company's reputation?* Check the Better Business Bureau and your state attorney general's office to see if others have registered complaints.
3. *What happens if there is a mistake?* Know in advance the service's policies for handling bills that don't get paid due to its error. It may take more than making up the money or paying a late fee. Will they help clear up any blots on your credit record?
4. *How does the service ensure security?* According to Consumer Action, a nonprofit group, to ensure technological security the service should have 128-bit encryption—the industry standard—for data transmittal and a firewall to protect data from hackers. It should provide a written guarantee to protect you from losses due to fraud and perform background checks on its employees.

Source: "Some Tips for Choosing an Online Bill-Paying Service," *San Diego Union-Tribune ComputerLink,* October 17, 2000, p. 8.

don't incur branch costs, Internet-only banks can offer high interest rates on checking and savings accounts and CDs, attractive loan rates, and low fees and charges. However, only 2 percent of all households that bank online choose these banks. Customers are concerned that virtual banks are less secure and find it inconvenient to have to deposit checks by mail. To counter these concerns, many Internet-only banks are moving to a "clicks-and-bricks" strategy, adding a physical presence such as ATM networks and staffed mini-branches with ATMs and videoconferencing stations.

 Is an EBPP Service for you? Look into Paytrust's site, **www.paytrust.com**, to decide for yourself.

 Gomez.com ranks online banks quarterly on such attributes as ease of use, customer confidence, on-site resources, relationship services, and overall cost. To see how your bank compares, go to **www.gomez.com** and click on "Banks."

REGULATION OF EFTS SERVICES

The federal *Electronic Fund Transfer Act of 1978* delineates your rights and responsibilities as an EFTS user. Under this law, you cannot stop payment on a defective or questionable purchase (however, individual banks and state laws have more-lenient provisions). In the case of an error you must notify the bank within 60 days of its occurrence on your periodic statement or terminal receipt. The bank must investigate and tell you the results within 10 days. The bank can then take up to 45 additional days to investigate the error but must return the disputed money to your account until the issue is resolved. If you fail to notify the bank within 60 days of the error, the bank has no obligation under federal law to conduct an investigation or return your money. In addition, it is very important that you notify the bank immediately about the theft, loss, or unauthorized use of your EFTS card. Notification within 2 business days after you discover the card missing limits your loss to $50. After 2 business days, you may lose up to $500 (but never more than the amount that was actually withdrawn by the thief). In addition, if you do not report the loss within 60 days after your periodic statement was mailed, you can lose all the money in your account.

When reporting errors or unauthorized transactions, it is best to notify your bank by telephone and follow up with a letter. Keep a copy of the letter in your file.

Many state regulations offer additional consumer protection regarding your use of EFTS. However, your best protection is to carefully guard the PIN used to access your accounts by EFTS. Do not write the PIN on your EFTS card, or on anything else for that matter. And be sure to check your periodic statements for possible errors or unauthorized transactions.

OTHER BANK SERVICES

In addition to the numerous services described earlier in this chapter, banks offer several other types of money management services: safe-deposit boxes, trust services, and mutual-fund sales.

- **Safe-deposit boxes.** A *safe-deposit box* is a rented drawer in a bank's vault. The annual rental fee depends on the box size. Small boxes can be rented for about $25 per year, while large ones may cost hundreds of dollars per year. When you rent a box, you receive one key to it, and the bank retains another key. The box can be opened only when both keys are used. This arrangement protects items in the box from theft and serves as an excellent storage place for jewelry, contracts, stock certificates, titles, and other special documents.
- **Trust services.** Bank trust departments provide investment and estate planning advice. They manage and administer the investments in a trust account or from an estate.
- **Mutual-fund sales.** Most major commercial banks now offer mutual funds to their customers. Some of these mutual funds are from major mutual fund companies, whereas others are bank-sponsored funds. (Detailed discussion of mutual funds is the focus of Chapter 13.) Often bank representatives will suggest mutual funds to customers as an alternative to CDs. However convenient it may be to purchase these securities through your bank, be sure to evaluate these funds carefully. Investigate the fund's performance and all fees and sales expenses, and compare these with other mutual funds before committing yourself. Many bank mutual fund customers are novice investors who are not aware that, unlike CDs, the return on these investments is not guaranteed. Remember, too, that mutual funds are not deposits and are therefore not covered by federal deposit insurance.

CONCEPT CHECK

4-7. Distinguish between a checking account and a savings account.

4-8. Define and discuss (a) *demand deposits*; (b) *time deposits*; (c) *interest-paying checking accounts*.

4-9. Briefly describe the key characteristics of each of the following forms of interest-paying checking accounts: (a) money market deposit account (MMDA); (b) NOW account; and (c) money market mutual fund (MMMF).

4-10. Describe the features of an asset management account (AMA), its advantages, and its disadvantages.

4-11. Briefly describe (a) debit cards; (b) banking at ATMs; (c) pre-authorized deposits and payments; (d) bank-by-phone accounts; and (e) online banking and bill payment services.

4-12. What are your legal rights and responsibilities when using EFTS?

4-13. Describe briefly the following additional services that banks provide: (a) safe-deposit boxes, (b) trust services, and (c) mutual-fund sales.

Establishing a Savings Program [LG4, LG5]

The good news: An estimated 75 percent of American households have some money put away in savings. Clearly, saving money is considered an important activity by many individuals and families. The bad news: the personal savings rate in the U.S. is dropping. It even dipped into negative numbers in mid-2000, reaching a record low of –0.8 percent in October as consumers spent more than they earned.

Although the personal savings rate is down, most of us understand the value of saving for the future. The act of saving is a deliberate, well-thought-out activity designed to preserve the value of money, ensure liquidity, and earn a competitive rate of return. Almost by definition, *smart savers are smart investors.* They regard saving as more than putting loose change into a piggy bank; rather, they recognize the importance of saving and know that savings must be managed as astutely as any security. After all, what we normally think of as "savings" is really a form of investment—a short-term, highly liquid investment that is subject to minimum risk. Establishing and maintaining an ongoing savings program is a vital element of personal financial planning. To get the most from your savings, however, you must understand your savings options and how different savings vehicles pay interest.

STARTING YOUR SAVINGS PROGRAM

Careful financial planning dictates that you hold a portion of your assets to meet liquidity needs and accumulate wealth. Although opinions differ as to how much you should keep as liquid reserves, the consensus is that most families should have an amount equal to 3 to 6 months of after-tax income. Therefore, if you take home $2,000 a month, you should have between $6,000 and $12,000 in liquid reserves. If your employer has a strong salary continuation program covering extended periods of illness, or if you have a sizable line of credit available, the lower figure is probably suitable. If you lack one or both of these, however, the larger amount is probably more appropriate.

You should develop a specific savings plan to accumulate funds. Make saving a priority item in your budget, not an event that occurs only when income happens to exceed expenditures. Some people do this by arranging to withhold savings directly from their paychecks. You can transfer funds regularly to other financial institutions such as commercial banks, savings and loans, savings banks, credit unions, and even mutual funds. Not only do direct deposit arrangements help your savings effort, they also enable your funds to earn interest sooner. The key to success is to establish a *regular* pattern of saving.

You should make it a practice to set aside an amount you can comfortably afford *each month,* even if it is only $50 to $100. (Keep in mind that $100 monthly deposits earning 4 percent interest will grow to more than $36,500 in 20 years.) Exhibit 4.4 lists 10 strategies you can use to increase your savings and build a nest egg.

You must also decide which savings products best meet your needs. Many savers prefer to keep their emergency funds in a regular savings or money market deposit account at an institution with federal deposit insurance. Although these accounts are safe, convenient, and highly liquid, they tend to pay relatively low rates of interest. Other important considerations include your risk preference, the length of time you can leave your money on deposit, and the level of current and expected interest rates.

Suppose 1 year from now you plan to use $5,000 of your savings to make the down payment on a new car, and you expect interest rates to drop during that period. You should lock in today's higher rate by purchasing a 1-year certificate of deposit (CD). On the other hand, if you are unsure about when you will actually need the funds or believe interest rates will rise, you are better off with an MMDA or MMMF because their rates change with market conditions and you can access your funds at any time without penalty.

EXHIBIT 4.4

TEN STRATEGIES TO BUILD YOUR NEST EGG

Having trouble getting your savings program started? Here are 10 strategies you can use to begin to build a nest egg:

1. **Make saving a priority.** Each month when you pay your bills, write a check to yourself and deposit it in a savings account as if it were another invoice.
2. **Take a hard look at your spending habits.** Surely you can find places to cut back. Bring your lunch to work or school. Comparison shop. Carpool. Cut back on your trips to the ATM.
3. **Set up payroll deductions.** Ask your employer to deduct some money from your paycheck and have it deposited directly into your savings. It's painless because you never see the money in your checking account.
4. **Bank your raises.** Great, your boss thinks you deserve a raise. Keep your lifestyle where it is and put the difference in your savings account.
5. **Work a little harder.** Are you wasting time watching too much TV like most Americans? Spend another 5 hours a week working and deposit the cash into your savings.
6. **Keep making those loan payments.** Once you get used to paying a mortgage or car payments, you feel rich when those obligations finally end. Why not keep writing the checks—only now it's for your savings account.
7. **Keep an eye on your returns.** What kind of return are you getting on your savings account? If your bank is only paying you 3 percent or 4 percent, you might be able to add another percentage point or two by moving your money to an asset management account at a brokerage firm.
8. **Reinvest interest and dividends.** If you have a savings account, make sure the interest is reinvested rather than paid into your non–interest-bearing checking account. If you own stocks or mutual funds, virtually all offer dividend reinvestment plans. You won't miss the money, and your account will grow faster.
9. **Set up a retirement plan.** Make sure you contribute to your company's retirement plan. Your contributions are tax deductible, and many employers match your contributions. Check out the new individual retirement account options that were created by the Taxpayer Relief Act of 1997 and improved by the 2001 Tax Act (Chapter 14).
10. **Splurge once in a while.** All work and no play makes for a dull life. Once you've reached a savings goal, take some money and enjoy yourself. The boost you get will make saving money a little easier.

Short-term interest rates generally fluctuate more than long-term rates, so it pays to monitor interest rate movements, shop around for the best rates, and place your funds in savings vehicles consistent with your needs. When short-term interest rates drop sharply, as they did in the early 1990s, you won't be able to reinvest the proceeds from maturing CDs at comparable rates. You will need to reevaluate your savings plans and may choose to move funds into other savings vehicles that pay higher rates of interest but may be more risky.

Many financial planning experts recommend keeping a minimum of 10 to 25 percent of your investment portfolio in savings-type instruments in addition to the 3 to 6 months of liquid reserves noted earlier. Thus someone with $50,000 in investments should probably have a minimum of $5,000 to $10,000—and possibly more—in such short-term vehicles as MMDAs, MMMFs, or CDs. At times the amount invested in short-term vehicles could far exceed the recommended minimum and approach 50 percent or more of the portfolio. This generally depends on expected interest rate movements. If interest rates are relatively high and you expect them to fall, you would invest in long-term vehicles in order to lock in the attractive interest rates. On the other hand, if rates are relatively low and you expect them to rise, you might invest in short-term vehicles so you can more quickly reinvest them when interest rates rise. Clearly, the amount held in savings accounts and short-term vehicles—both for maintaining liquid reserves and as a part of an investment portfolio—can be substantial.

FINDING INTEREST EARNED ON YOUR MONEY

Interest earned is the reward for putting your money in a savings account or short-term investment vehicle. Because there is no other source of return with such accounts or securities, it is important for you to understand how interest is earned. Unfortunately, even in the relatively simple world of savings, all interest rates are not created equal.

THE MATTER OF COMPOUNDING. Basically, interest can be earned in one of two ways. First, some short-term investments are sold on a *discount basis*. This means that the security is sold for a price that is lower than its redemption value; the difference being the amount of interest earned. Treasury bills, for instance, are issued on a discount basis. Another way to earn interest on short-term investments is by *direct payment*, which occurs when interest is applied to a regular savings account. Although this is a simple process, determining the actual rate of return can involve several complications.

compound interest
When interest earned in each subsequent period is determined by applying the nominal (stated) rate of interest to the sum of the initial deposit and the interest earned in each prior period.

The first complication relates to the method used to arrive at the amount and rate of **compound interest** earned annually: You have probably read or seen advertisements by banks or other depository institutions touting the fact that they pay daily, rather than annual, interest. To understand what this means, consider the following example. Assume you invest $1,000 in a savings account advertised as paying annual **simple interest** at a rate of 5 percent. With simple interest, the interest is paid only on the initial amount of the deposit. This means that if you leave the $1,000 on deposit for 1 year, you will earn $50 in interest, and the account balance will total $1,050 at year-end. Note that in this case the **nominal (stated) rate of interest,** which is the promised rate of interest paid on a savings deposit or charged on a loan, is 5 percent.

simple interest
Interest that is paid only on the initial amount of the deposit.

In contrast, the **effective rate of interest** is the annual rate of return that is *actually earned* (or *charged*) during the period funds are held (or borrowed). You can calculate it with the following formula:

$$\text{Effective rate of interest} = \frac{\text{Amount of interest earned during the year}}{\text{Amount of money invested or deposited}}$$

nominal (stated) rate of interest
The promised rate of interest paid on a savings deposit or charged on a loan.

In our example, because $50 was earned during the year on an investment of $1,000, the effective rate is $50/$1,000 or 5 percent, which is the same as the nominal rate of interest. (Note that in the above formula it is interest earned during the *year* that matters; if you wanted to calculate the effective rate of interest on an account held for 6 months, you would double the amount of interest earned.)

effective rate of interest
The annual rate of return that is *actually earned* (or *charged*) during the period funds are held (or borrowed).

But suppose you can invest your funds elsewhere at a 5 percent rate, *compounded semiannually*. Because interest is applied to your account at midyear, you will earn *interest on interest* for the last 6 months of the year, thereby increasing the total interest earned for the year. The actual dollar earnings are determined as follows:

First 6 months' interest $= \$1,000 \times 0.05 \times 6/12 = \$25.00$
Second 6 months' interest $= \$1,025 \times 0.05 \times 6/12 = \underline{25.63}$
Total interest $= \underline{\underline{\$50.63}}$

Interest is generated on a larger investment in the second half of the year because the amount of money on deposit has increased by the amount of interest earned in the first half year ($25). Although the nominal rate on this account is still 5 percent, the effective rate is 5.06 percent ($50.63/$1,000). As you may have guessed, *the more frequently interest is compounded, the greater the effective rate for any given nominal rate*. These relationships

EXHIBIT 4.5

NOMINAL AND EFFECTIVE RATES OF INTEREST WITH DIFFERENT COMPOUNDING PERIODS

The effective rate of interest you earn on a savings account will exceed the nominal (stated) rate of interest if interest is compounded more than once a year (as are most savings and interest-paying accounts).

Nominal Rate	Effective Rate				
	Annually	Semiannually	Quarterly	Monthly	Daily
3%	3.00%	3.02%	3.03%	3.04%	3.05%
4	4.00	4.04	4.06	4.07	4.08
5	5.00	5.06	5.09	5.12	5.13
6	6.00	6.09	6.14	6.17	6.18
7	7.00	7.12	7.19	7.23	7.25
8	8.00	8.16	8.24	8.30	8.33
9	9.00	9.20	9.31	9.38	9.42
10	10.00	10.25	10.38	10.47	10.52
11	11.00	11.30	11.46	11.57	11.62
12	12.00	12.36	12.55	12.68	12.74

are shown for a sample of interest rates and compounding periods in Exhibit 4.5. Note, for example, that with a 7 percent nominal rate, daily compounding adds one-fourth of a percent to the total return—not a trivial amount.

You can calculate the interest compounded daily by using a financial calculator similar to that described in Chapter 2. Let's assume you want to invest $1,000 at 7 percent interest compounded daily. How much money will you have in the account at the end of the year? Exhibit 4.6 shows the steps to follow.

COMPOUND INTEREST EQUALS FUTURE VALUE. Compound interest is the same as the *future value* concept introduced in Chapter 2. You can use the procedures described there to find out how much an investment or deposit will grow over time at a compounded rate of interest. For example, using the future value formula and the future

EXHIBIT 4.6

USING A FINANCIAL CALCULATOR TO FIND INTEREST COMPOUNDED DAILY

How much will you have at the end of 1 year if you invest $1,000 at 7 percent, compounded daily?

Step 1: Enter 1000 and press **PV**.
Step 2: Enter the number of compounding periods, 365, and press **N**.
Step 3: Convert annual interest to a daily rate: press 7 divided by 365; then press **I** for the interest rate.
Step 4: Calculate the account value in 1 year: press **CPT** and then **FV**.

The result should be 1072.50 (i.e., $1,072.50). This is clearly greater than the $1,070 that annual compounding would return. The effective interest rate would have been 7.25 percent ($72.50 interest earned/$1,000 initially invested), as noted in Exhibit 4.5.

value factor from Appendix A (see Chapter 2), you can determine how much $1,000 will be worth in 4 years if it is deposited into a savings account that pays 5 percent interest per year compounded annually like this:

$$\text{Future value} = \text{Amount deposited} \times \text{Future value factor}$$
$$= \$1,000 \times 1.216$$
$$= \underline{\$1,216}$$

You can use the same basic procedure to find the future value of an *annuity,* except you would use the future value annuity factor from Appendix B (see Chapter 2). For instance, if you put $1,000 a year into a savings account that pays 5 percent per year compounded annually, in 4 years you will have:

$$\text{Future value} = \text{Amount deposited yearly} \times \text{Future value annuity factor}$$
$$= \$1,000 \times 4.310$$
$$= \$4,310$$

HOW MUCH INTEREST WILL YOU EARN? Before you open a deposit account, you should investigate several factors that determine the amount of interest you earn on your savings or interest-bearing checking account:

- **Frequency of compounding.** The more often interest is compounded, the higher your return.
- **Balance on which interest is paid.** With regard to balances that qualify to earn interest, most banks now use the *actual balance,* or *day of deposit to day of withdrawal,* method. The actual balance method is the most accurate and fairest because it pays depositors interest on all funds on deposit for the actual amount of time they remain there.
- **Interest rate paid.** As mentioned earlier, the Truth-in-Savings Act standardized the way banks calculate the rate of interest they pay on deposit accounts. This makes it easy to compare each bank's *annual percentage yield (APY)* and to choose the bank offering the highest APY.

A VARIETY OF WAYS TO SAVE

During the past decade or so there has been a tremendous proliferation of savings and short-term investment vehicles, particularly for the individual of modest means. As the *Money in Action* box on page 155 shows, there will always be a place in your portfolio for cash savings.

Today, investors can choose from savings accounts, money market deposit accounts, money market mutual funds, NOW accounts, certificates of deposit, U.S. Treasury bills, Series EE bonds, and asset management accounts. We examined several of these savings vehicles earlier in this chapter, including savings accounts, MMDAs, MMMFs, NOW accounts, and asset management accounts. Let's now look at the three remaining types of deposits and securities.

certificate of deposit (CD)
A type of savings instrument issued by certain financial institutions in exchange for a deposit; typically requires a minimum deposit and has a maturity ranging from 7 days to as long as 7 or more years.

CERTIFICATES OF DEPOSIT. **Certificates of deposit (CDs)** differ from the savings instruments discussed earlier in this chapter in that CD funds (except for CDs purchased through brokerage firms) must remain on deposit for a specified period, which can range from 7 days to as long as 7 or more years. Although it is possible to withdraw funds prior to maturity, an interest penalty usually makes withdrawal somewhat costly. Although the bank or other depository institution is free to charge whatever penalty it likes, most result in forfeiture of some interest. Since October of 1983, banks, S&Ls, and other depository institutions have been free to offer any rate and maturity CD they wish. As a result, today a wide variety of CDs are offered by most banks, depository institutions, and other financial institutions such

MONEY IN ACTION

There's Always a Place for Cash in Your Portfolio

If you're a college student just starting to build your savings, then you're most likely going to keep your money in a bank, perhaps the one with a branch on campus. Maybe it's with the financial institution that provided you with a student loan. Right now, the choices for these savings may seem limited.

In a few short years, however, you may suddenly find yourself with a home, cars, paid-off student loans, and an investment portfolio of stocks, bonds, and mutual funds. Will there still be a place for cash savings? The answer is yes, but the purpose will probably be different.

You should, of course, continue to allocate 3 to 6 months' income to an "emergency fund" that you can access immediately. However, rather than putting *all* your savings into a short-term certificate of deposit or a money market mutual fund, you'll increasingly allocate your money into investments with long-term growth potential such as stocks and mutual funds. During a 20-year period the stock market provides a much higher return than anything you could get in the bank. Remember, however, that stocks are volatile and investment professionals recommend that money you invest in the stock market should stay there for many years.

If you need money for short-term needs, such as buying a house or car or paying for education, the money should be taken out of the stock market gradually and put into short-term savings. After all, you want to be sure the money will be there when you need it. Short-term savings, whether in the form of certificates of deposit, U.S. Treasury bills, or money market mutual funds, have a big advantage: They don't go down in value.

True, you won't make a fortune, but there are more options for short-term investments today. Take

CDs, for instance. Chances are you can find better rates than are offered by your local bank. Because each percentage point means $100 a year on a $10,000 investment, do some research, but don't spend too much time searching for that extra fraction of a percent.

A good place to shop for CDs is the *Bank Rate Monitor*, which tracks bank rates. Go to its Web site at **www.bankrate.com** for the latest in national CD rates. Don't worry if the bank you choose is across the country, as long as it is federally insured. Keep in mind that if you're buying a CD so you can access your money in a matter of months, it doesn't make sense to sign up for one with a 5-year maturity; 6 months is a better choice. In addition, you can buy CDs through most big brokerage firms; unlike CDs sold through banks, they are negotiable so you can cash them in early without penalty. Because they originate at banks, they are insured. You can also buy CDs online through BankDirect.com (**www.bankdirect.com**) and eBank (**www.ebank.com**), which offer both CDs and money market accounts.

As your net worth grows, a smaller and smaller percentage of your assets will be in cash. The reason not to keep a big percentage of your net worth in cash savings is that you risk being left in the dust by inflation and taxes. Even if you can get 5 percent in a cash savings account, you'll lose up to 2 percent to taxes and the rest to inflation.

Sources: Ken Brown, "The Best Short-Term Investments," *Smart Money,* August 1997, p. 79; Jonathan Burton, "Cash Ain't Trash," *Bloomberg Personal,* May/June 1997, p. 106; Kevin Demarrais, "T-Bills, CDs Are Wise Short-Term Investments," *The Record* (Bergen County, NJ), June 18, 2000, p. B1.

as brokerage firms. As a rule, most pay higher rates for larger deposits and longer periods of time. CDs are convenient to buy and hold because they offer attractive and highly competitive yields plus federal deposit insurance protection.

 If you are not satisfied with the CD rate at your local bank, go to Bankrate.com (**www.bankrate.com**). You will find not only the highest rates on CDs and savings accounts nationwide but also the checking account and ATM fees at banks in your city.

**U.S. Treasury bill
(T-bill)**
A short-term
(3-month or 6-month
maturity) debt
instrument issued by
the U.S. Treasury in
the ongoing process
of funding the
national debt.

U.S. TREASURY BILLS. The **U.S. Treasury bill (T-bill)** is considered the ultimate safe haven for savings and investments. T-bills are obligations of the U.S. Treasury issued as part of its ongoing process of funding the national debt. They are sold on a discount basis in minimum denominations of $1,000 and are issued with 3-month (13-week) or 6-month (26-week) maturities. The bills are auctioned off every Monday. Backed by the full faith and credit of the U.S. government, T-bills pay an attractive and safe return that is free from state and local income taxes.

T-bills are almost as liquid as cash because they can be sold at any time (in a very active secondary market) without any interest penalty. However, should you have to sell before maturity, you may lose some money on your investment if interest rates have risen, and you will have to pay a broker's fee as well. Treasury bills pay interest on a *discount basis* and as such are different from other savings or short-term investment vehicles—that is, their interest is equal to the difference between the purchase price paid and their stated value at maturity. For example, if you paid $980 for a bill that will be worth $1,000 at maturity, you will earn $20 in interest ($1,000–$980).

An individual investor may purchase T-bills directly by participating in the weekly Treasury auctions or indirectly through a commercial bank or a security dealer who buys bills for investors on a commission basis. A very recent change allows direct T-bill purchases over the Internet or by using a touch-tone phone (call 800-722-2678 and follow the interactive menu to complete transactions).

 At the T-bill page of the Bureau of the Public Debt Online, **www.publicdebt.treas.gov/sec/sec.htm**, you can learn about T-bills and then buy them online.

Outstanding Treasury bills can also be purchased in the secondary market through banks or dealers. This approach gives the investor a much wider selection of maturities from which to choose, ranging from less than a week to as long as 6 months.

To buy T-bills directly in the weekly auction, simply submit a "tender" to the nearest Federal Reserve Bank or branch specifying both the amount and maturity desired (tender forms are easy to fill out and readily available from commercial banks). The Treasury tries to accommodate individual investors through its noncompetitive bidding system. In essence, all noncompetitive tender offers are awarded T-bills at a price equal to the average of all the accepted competitive bids. Similar results can be obtained using the Internet or touch-tone phone to purchase T-bills (access the Treasury Web site or 800 number to learn about these new methods of T-bill purchase). On the downside, T-bills purchased using any of these direct methods are meant to be held to maturity and therefore lack the liquidity of bills that are acquired competitively.

Series EE bond
A savings bond
issued in various
denominations by
the U.S. Treasury.

SERIES EE BONDS. **Series EE bonds** are the well-known savings bonds that were first issued in 1941 and formerly called Series E bonds. Although issued by the U.S. Treasury on a discount basis and free of state and local income taxes, they are quite different from T-bills. Savings bonds are *accrual-type securities,* which means that interest is paid when they are cashed on or before maturity, rather than periodically during their lives. The government does make Series HH bonds available through the exchange of Series E or Series EE bonds; they have a 10-year maturity and are available in denominations of $500 to $10,000. Unlike EE bonds, HH bonds are issued at their full face value and pay interest semiannually at the current fixed rate of 4 percent.

Series EE bonds are backed by the full faith and credit of the U.S. government and can be replaced without charge in case of loss, theft, or destruction. You can purchase them at banks or other depository institutions, or through payroll deduction plans. Issued in denominations from $50 through $10,000, their purchase price is a uniform 50 percent of the face amount (thus a $100 bond will cost $50 and be worth $100 at maturity).

 Everything you always wanted to know about U.S. Savings Bonds—from how to buy them, current rates, and a pricing calculator for bonds you own—is at www.savingsbonds.gov.

The actual maturity date on EE bonds is unspecified because the issues pay a variable rate of interest. The higher the rate of interest being paid, the shorter the time it takes for the bond to accrue from its discounted purchase price to its maturity value. As of May 1, 1997, the rate of interest paid on EE bonds is 90 percent of the average 5-year Treasury security market yields for the preceding 6 months. Bonds can be redeemed any time after the first 6 months although redeeming EE bonds in less than 5 years results in a penalty of the last 3 months of interest earned. Interest rates are calculated every 6 months (in May and November) and change with prevailing Treasury security market yields. To obtain current rates on Series EE bonds, call your bank, call 800-487-2663, or use the Web link for the savings bond site. (For bonds purchased after May 1, 1997, the rate for the 6-month period ending October 31, 2001, was 4.50 percent.) Interest is credited every 6 months and compounds semiannually.

In addition to being exempt from state and local taxes, Series EE bonds provide their holders with an appealing tax twist: *Savers need not report interest earned on their federal tax returns until the bonds are redeemed.* Although interest can be reported annually (for example, when the bonds are held in the name of a child who has limited interest income), most investors choose to defer it.

A second attractive tax feature allows partial or complete tax avoidance of EE bond earnings when proceeds are used to pay education expenses, such as college tuition, for the bond purchaser, a spouse, or other IRS-defined dependent. To qualify, the purchaser must be age 24 or older and, as of 2000, have adjusted gross income below $69,100 for single filers and $111,100 for married couples. (These maximum income levels are adjusted annually.)

CONCEPT CHECK

4-14. In general, how much of your annual income should you save in the form of liquid reserves? What portion of your investment portfolio should you keep in savings and other short-term investment vehicles? Explain.

4-15. Define and distinguish between the *nominal rate of interest* and the *effective rate of interest*. Explain why a savings and loan association that pays a nominal rate of 4.5 percent interest, compounded daily, on its savings accounts actually pays an effective rate of 4.6 percent.

4-16. What factors determine the amount of interest you will earn on a deposit account? Which combination provides the best return?

4-17. Briefly describe the basic features of each of the following savings vehicles: (a) certificates of deposit; (b) U.S. Treasury bills; and (c) Series EE bonds.

Maintaining a Checking Account [LG6]

A checking account is one of the most useful cash management tools you can have. Checking accounts not only provide a safe and convenient way to hold money, but they also streamline point-of-sale purchases, debt payments, and other basic transactions. In one

form or another (regular or interest-paying checking accounts) you can have these accounts at commercial banks, S&Ls, savings banks, credit unions, and even at brokerage houses through asset management accounts. For convenience, we will focus our attention on commercial bank checking accounts, although our discussion applies to checking accounts maintained at other types of financial institutions as well.

OPENING AND USING YOUR CHECKING ACCOUNT

The factors that typically influence the choice of where to maintain a checking account are convenience, services, and cost. Many people choose a bank solely on the basis of convenience factors: business hours, location, number of drive-in windows, and number and location of branch offices and ATMs. Ease of access is obviously an important consideration because most people prefer to bank near home or work. Services differ from bank to bank, although today most banks offer several types of accounts; debit, ATM, and credit cards; and loans. Depending on their size, banks may also offer online and telephone banking and bill-paying services, rent safe-deposit boxes, provide for direct deposits and withdrawals, and offer mutual-fund sales.

Once you determine the banking services you need, you should evaluate the offerings of conveniently located, federally insured financial institutions. In addition to convenience and safety, consider interest rates, types of accounts (including special accounts that combine such features as credit cards, free checks, and reduced fees), structure and level of fees and charges, and quality of customer service.

THE COST OF A CHECKING ACCOUNT. One of the byproducts of deregulation and the growth of interest-paying checking accounts has been a sharp increase in bank service charges. Today few, if any, banks and other depository institutions let you write as many checks as you wish free of charge. The rest levy monthly and per-check fees when your balance drops below a stipulated minimum, and some charge you for checking no matter how large a balance you carry in your account.

Usually you must maintain a minimum balance of $500 to $1,000 or more in order to avoid a service charge. Although some banks use the *average monthly* balance in an account to determine whether to levy a service charge, the vast majority use the *daily* balance procedure. This means that if your account should happen to fall just $1 below the minimum balance *just once* during the month, you will be hit with the full service charge—even if you keep an average balance that is three times the minimum requirement. Further, you'll pay substantial service charges, in two forms: (1) a base service charge of, say, $7.50 a month, and (2) additional charges of, say, 25 cents for each check you write and 10 cents for each ATM or bank-by-phone transaction. Using these fees as an illustration, assume you write 20 checks and make seven ATM transactions in a given month. If your balance falls below the minimum, you will have to pay a service charge of $7.50 + (20 × $.25) + (7 × $.10) = $13.20.

In addition to the service charges levied on checking accounts, banks have increased most other check-related charges and raised the minimum balances required for free checking and waivers of specified fees. The charge on a returned check can be as high as $15 to $20, and stop payment orders typically cost $10 to $25. Some banks charge fees for more than a specified number of ATM or bank-by-phone transactions. Most also charge for using the ATM of another bank that is a member of the same network. It is not surprising, therefore, that many smart consumers today are using cost as the single most important variable in choosing where to set up a checking account.

INDIVIDUAL OR JOINT ACCOUNT. Two people wishing to open a checking account may do so in one of three ways: (1) They can each open individual checking accounts (on which the other cannot write checks); (2) they can open a joint account that requires both signatures on all checks; or (3) they can open a joint account that allows either one to write checks (the most common type of joint account).

One advantage of the joint account over two individual accounts is that it lowers the service charges. In addition, the account has rights of survivorship, which, in the case of a married couple, means that if one spouse dies, the surviving spouse, after fulfilling a specified legal requirement, can draw checks on the account. (If account owners are treated as tenants in common rather than having rights of survivorship, the survivor gets only his or her share of the account. Thus, when opening a joint account, it is important to specify the rights preferred.) It is impossible to say what type of arrangement will be successful for a given couple. One financial expert recommends that couples experiment with different arrangements until they find the one most comfortable for them.

GENERAL CHECKING ACCOUNT PROCEDURES. After you select the bank that meets your needs and the type of account you want, it's a simple matter to actually open the account. The application form is straightforward, asking for basic personal information like name, date of birth, social security number, address, phone, and place of employment. You will also have to provide identification, sign signature cards, and make an initial deposit. The bank will give you a supply of checks to use until your personalized checks arrive.

Once you open a checking account, you should follow certain basic procedures. Always write checks in ink and include the name of the person being paid, the date, and the amount of the check—written in both numerals and words for accuracy. If these amounts don't agree, the written amount rather than the numbers is considered legally correct. The check should be signed the same as the signature card you filled out when you opened the account; otherwise, the bank may not accept it. It is also a good idea to note the check's purpose directly on the check—usually on the line provided in the lower left corner. This information is very helpful for both budgeting and tax purposes.

Make sure to enter all checking account transactions—checks written, deposits, point-of-sale debit purchases, ATM transactions, and pre-authorized automatic payments and deposits—in the **checkbook ledger** provided with your supply of checks. Then subtract the amount of each check, debit card purchase, ATM cash withdrawal, or payment, and add the amount of each deposit to the previous balance to keep track of your current account balance. Good transaction records and an accurate balance prevent overdrawing the account.

Include with each deposit a deposit slip (generally included with your checks and also available at your bank) listing the currency, coins, and checks being deposited. List checks by the *transit I.D. number* printed on the check, usually at the top right. You should also properly endorse all checks that you are going to deposit. Federal regulations require your endorsement to be made in black or blue ink, within $1\frac{1}{2}$ inches of the check's trailing edge (left end of the check when viewed from the front) so as not to interfere with bank endorsements. (If you don't comply, you'll still get your money, but it may take longer.)

To protect against possible loss of endorsed checks, it is common practice to use a special endorsement, such as "Pay to the order of XYZ Bank," or a restrictive endorsement, such as "For deposit only." If the way your name is written on the check differs from the way you signed the signature card, you should sign your correct signature below your endorsement. To further ensure that the deposit is properly entered into your account, write your account number below your endorsement.

You can make deposits in several ways: at the bank during normal banking hours; at a remote banking facility such as a drive-in window; at an ATM; in the bank's night depository, a protected type of mail slot on the exterior of the bank, using the special envelopes banks usually provide for after-hours deposits; or by mail, using the self-addressed, sometimes postage-paid deposit envelopes often provided for this purpose. The use of ATMs, night

checkbook ledger
A ledger, provided with a supply of checks, used to maintain accurate records of all checking account transactions.

depositories, and banking by mail is not advised when cash is being deposited because of the risk of an unaccountable loss.

When you deposit checks, you may encounter a delay in funds availability due to the time required for them to clear. To avoid overdrawing your account, you should know your bank's "hold" policy on deposits. In 1988 the government established maximum funds-availability delays on deposits. It generally takes between 1 and 5 business days for funds to become available. For example, on a check drawn on another local bank, funds must be made available no later than the second business day after deposit. An out-of-town check, however, may take up to 5 business days to clear. Longer holds—up to 9 business days—can be applied by banks under special circumstances such as when more than $5,000 is deposited into a given account in 1 day or when the depositor has repeatedly overdrawn his or her account within the immediately preceding 6 months.

OVERDRAFTS. When a check is written for an amount greater than the current account balance, the result is an **overdraft.** Poor bookkeeping on the part of the account holder or a delay in the bank's receipt of a deposit can be the cause. If the overdraft is proven intentional, the bank can initiate legal proceedings against the account holder. The action taken by a bank on an overdraft depends on the amount involved and the strength of its relationship with the account holder. In many cases the bank stamps the overdrawn check with the words "insufficient balance (or funds)" and returns it to the party to whom it was written. This is often called a "bounced check." The account holder is notified of this action, and the holder's bank deducts a penalty fee of as much as $15 to $20 or more from his or her checking account. In addition, the depositor of a "bad check" may be charged as much as $10 to $15 by his or her bank, which explains why merchants typically charge customers who give them bad checks $10 to $20 or more and often refuse to accept future checks from such customers.

When you have a strong relationship with your bank or arrange **overdraft protection,** the bank will pay a check that overdraws the account. In cases where overdraft protection has not been prearranged but the bank pays the check, the account holder is usually notified by the bank and charged a penalty fee for the inconvenience. However, the check does not bounce, and the check writer's creditworthiness is not damaged.

There are several ways to arrange overdraft protection. Many banks offer an overdraft line of credit, which automatically extends a loan to cover the amount of overdrafts. In most cases, however, the loans are made only in specified increments, such as $50 or $100, and interest (or a fee) is levied against the loan amount, not the actual amount of the overdraft. This can be an expensive form of protection, particularly if you do not promptly repay such a loan.

For example, if you had a $110 overdraft and the bank made overdraft loans in $100 increments, it would automatically deposit $200 in your account. If the bank charged 12 percent annually (or 1 percent per month) and you repaid the loan within a month, you would incur total interest of $2 ([$200 × 12 percent]/12). But remember, you paid interest on $90 ($200–$110) you didn't need, and the annualized rate of interest on this overdraft loan is *21.8 percent* ([$2/$110] × 12)!

Another way to cover overdrafts is with an *automatic transfer program,* which automatically transfers funds from your savings account to your checking account in the event of an overdraft. Under this program, some banks charge both an annual fee and a fee on each transfer. Of course, the best form of overdraft protection is to employ good cash management techniques and regularly balance your checking account.

STOPPING PAYMENT. Occasionally it is necessary to **stop payment** on a check that has been issued because (1) checks or a checkbook are either lost or stolen; (2) a good or service paid for by check is found to be faulty (some states prohibit you from stopping payment on faulty goods or services); or (3) a check is issued as part of a contract that is not carried out.

overdraft
The result of writing a check for an amount greater than the current account balance.

overdraft protection
An arrangement between the account holder and the depository institution wherein the institution automatically pays a check that overdraws the account.

stop payment
An order made by an account holder asking the depository institution to refuse payment on an already issued check.

(Note that if you lose your checkbook for any reason, you are probably better off closing the account and opening another rather than stopping payment on a large number of checks.)

To stop payment on a check, you must notify the bank. Normally the account holder fills out a form indicating the check number and date, amount, and the name of the person to whom it was written. Sometimes you can initiate stop-payment orders by telephone, in which case a written follow-up is normally required. Telephone-initiated stop payments generally remain in effect for 14 days and written ones for 6 months.

Once you place a stop-payment order, the bank refuses payment on the affected check. At the same time, the bank places stop-payment information in its information system so that the check will be rejected if another bank presents it in the check-clearing process. Most banks require account holders who wish to stop payment to sign a statement relieving the bank of any liability if payment is erroneously made on the check in question. Banks typically charge a fee ranging from $10 to $25 to stop payment on a check.

MONTHLY STATEMENTS

Once each month, your bank will provide a statement that contains an itemized listing of all transactions (checks written, ATM transactions, debit purchases, automatic payments, and deposits made) within your checking account; also included are any service charges levied and interest earned (see James C. Morrison's May 2001 bank statement shown in Exhibit 4.7). Some banks include canceled checks with the bank statement although most are moving away from this practice. Banks that do not return canceled checks will provide photocopies of them on request, generally for a fee. You can use your monthly statement to verify the accuracy of your account records and to reconcile differences between the statement balance and the balance shown in your checkbook ledger. The monthly statement is also an important source of information for your tax records.

ACCOUNT RECONCILIATION. You should reconcile your bank account as soon as possible after you receive your monthly statement. The **account reconciliation** process (or *balancing the checkbook,* as the process is also known) can uncover errors in recording checks or deposits, in addition or subtraction, and, occasionally, in the bank's processing of the checks. It can also help you avoid overdrafts because it forces you to periodically verify your account balance. Discrepancies between the account balance reflected in your checkbook ledger and that shown in the bank statement can be attributed to one of four basic factors, assuming neither you nor the bank has made any errors:

1. Checks that you have written, ATM withdrawals, debit purchases, or other automatic payments subtracted from your checkbook balance have not yet been received and deducted by your bank and therefore remain outstanding.
2. Deposits that you have made and added to your checkbook balance have not yet been credited to your account.
3. Any service (activity) charges levied on your account by the bank have not yet been deducted from your checkbook balance.
4. Interest earned on your account (if it is an MMDA or a NOW account) has not yet been added to your checkbook balance.

Take the following steps to reconcile your account:

1. On receipt of your bank statement, arrange all canceled checks in ascending numerical order based on their sequence numbers or issuance dates. (Skip this step if your bank does not return canceled checks.)
2. Compare each check with the corresponding entry in your checkbook ledger to make sure no recording errors exist. (If your bank does not return canceled checks, compare

account reconciliation The process of verifying the accuracy of one's checking account records in light of the bank's records as reflected in the monthly statement, which contains an itemized listing of all transactions within the checking account.

EXHIBIT 4.7

A CHECKING ACCOUNT STATEMENT

Each month you receive a statement from your bank or depository financial institution that summarizes the month's transactions and shows your latest account balance. This sample statement for May 2001 for James C. Morrison not only shows the checks that have been paid but also lists all ATM transactions, point-of-sale transactions using the ATM card (the Interlink payments at Lucky Stores), and direct payroll deposits.

```
YOUR BANK                          #240
P.O. BOX 516  ANY CITY, USA    90000-0000

     JAMES C. MORRISON
     1765 SHERIDAN DRIVE            N          CALL (800) 222-0000
     YOUR CITY, STATE 12091         21         24 HOURS/DAY, 7 DAYS/WEEK
                                               FOR ASSISTANCE WITH
                                               YOUR ACCOUNT.

PAGE 1 OF 1      THIS STATEMENT COVERS: 4/30/01 THROUGH 5/29/01
```

	SUMMARY			
PREMIUM ACCOUNT				
	PREVIOUS BALANCE	473.68	MINIMUM BALANCE	21.78
0123-45678	DEPOSITS	1,302.83+		
	WITHDRAWALS	1,689.02-		
	SERVICE CHARGES	7.50-		
	DIRECT DEPOSIT DISCOUNT	1.00+		
	NEW BALANCE	80.99		

CHECKS AND WITHDRAWALS	CHECK	DATE PAID	AMOUNT	CHECK	DATE PAID	AMOUNT
	203	5/01	10.00	213	5/08	40.00
	204	4/30	15.00	214	5/09	9.58
	205	5/10	635.00	215	5/20	66.18
	206	5/08	25.00	216	5/20	64.92
	207	5/07	19.00	217	5/21	25.03
	208	5/07	50.00	218	5/21	37.98
	209	5/08	15.00	219	5/22	35.00
	210	5/10	83.00	220	5/22	105.00
	211	5/10	10.00	222*	5/22	100.00
	212	5/08	70.00	223	5/21	40.00
				224	5/29	40.82

ATM TRANSACTIONS			
	PREMIUM ACCOUNT FEE LESS $1.00 DISCOUNT	4/30	6.50
	INTERLINK PURCHASE #572921 ON 04/30 AT LUCKY STORE NO 043	5/01	50.00
	WITHDRAWAL #08108 AT 00165A ON 05/04	5/06	20.00
	INTERLINK PURCHASE #807409 ON 05/11 AT LUCKY STORE NO 056	5/13	12.51
	WITHDRAWAL #01015 AT 00240C ON 05/17	5/17	20.00
	WITHDRAWAL #04792 AT 00167C ON 05/20	5/20	20.00
	WITHDRAWAL #04386 AT 00240D ON 05/21	5/21	40.00
	INTERLINK PURCHASE #880318 ON 05/28 AT LUCKY STORE #043	5/29	30.00

DEPOSITS		DATE POSTED	AMOUNT
	AVS RNT CAR SYST PAYROLL G2 000000035382	5/03	618.69
	AVS RNT CAR SYST PAYROLL G2 000000035382	5/17	83.39
	AVS RNT CAR SYST PAYROLL G2 000000035382	5/17	600.75

ATM LOCATIONS USED	
	00165A: 249 PRIMROSE RD, ANY CITY, USA
	00240C: 490 BROADWAY, ANY CITY, USA
	00167C: 1145 BROADWAY, ANY CITY, USA
	00240D: 490 BROADWAY, ANY CITY, USA

the bank statement information for each check with the corresponding entry in your checkbook ledger.) Place a check mark in your ledger alongside each entry compared. Also, check off any other withdrawals such as from ATMs, point-of-sale debit transactions, or automatic payments.

3. List the checks and other deductions (ATM withdrawals or debit purchases) still *outstanding*—that is, those deducted in your checkbook but not returned with your bank statement (see step 2). Total their amount.

4. Compare the deposits indicated on the statement with deposits shown in your checkbook ledger. Total the amount of deposits still outstanding—that is, those shown in your checkbook ledger but not yet received by the bank. Be sure to include all automatic deposits and deposits made at ATMs in your calculations.

5. *Subtract* the total amount of checks outstanding (from step 3) from your bank statement balance, and *add* to this balance the amount of outstanding deposits (from step 4). The resulting amount is your *adjusted bank balance*.

6. Deduct the amount of any bank service charges from your checkbook ledger balance, and add any interest earned to that balance. Make sure you include all service charges for the period, including those for any returned checks, stop payments, or new checks ordered. The resulting amount is your *new checkbook balance.* This amount should equal your adjusted bank balance (from step 5). If it does not, you should check all addition and subtraction in your checkbook ledger because you have probably made an error.

The reverse side of your bank statement usually provides a form for reconciling your account along with step-by-step instructions. Worksheet 4.1 includes an account reconciliation form that James Morrison completed for the month of May 2001 following the reconciliation procedures we have described. You can use the form to reconcile either regular or interest-paying checking accounts (like MMDAs or NOWs).

TAX RECORDS. Your monthly bank statement, along with your checkbook ledger, is an important tax record that helps evaluate past income and expenses. Although you may maintain accurate records of these items as part of your budgeting process, the statement can be used to provide proof of payment, which you might need if the Internal Revenue Service decides to audit your tax return. When you write a check, indicate its purpose both in the checkbook ledger and on the front of the check. Retain your bank statements for at least 5 years because an audit can still be conducted several years after a tax return has been filed.

SPECIAL TYPES OF CHECKS

In some circumstances sellers of goods or services may not be willing to accept a personal check because they can't be absolutely sure that a check is good. This is common for large purchases or when the buyer's bank is not located in the area in which the purchase is being made. They will instead request a form of check that guarantees payment: cashier's checks, traveler's checks, or certified checks.

CASHIER'S CHECK. Anyone can buy a **cashier's check** from a bank. These checks are often used by people who do not have checking accounts. They can be purchased for about $5 and are occasionally issued at no charge to bank customers. In exchange for the amount of the check plus a service charge, the bank issues a check drawn on itself. In this way the bank is now writing the check, not you—which is about the best assurance you can give that the check is good.

TRAVELER'S CHECK. A number of large financial organizations—such as Citibank, American Express, MasterCard, Visa, and Bank of America—issue **traveler's checks,** which

cashier's check
A check payable to a third party that is drawn by a bank on itself in exchange for the amount specified plus, in most cases, a service fee (of about $5).

traveler's check
A check sold (for a fee of about 1.5 percent) by many large financial institutions, in denominations ranging from $20 to $100, that can be used for making purchases and exchanged for local currencies in most parts of the world.

WORKSHEET 4.1

AN ACCOUNT RECONCILIATION FORM— JAMES MORRISON'S MAY 2001 STATEMENT

James Morrison used this form to reconcile his checking account for the month of May 2001. Because line A equals line B, he has fully reconciled the difference between the $80.99 bank statement balance and his $339.44 checkbook balance. Accounts should be reconciled each month—as soon as possible after receipt of the bank statement.

CHECKING ACCOUNT RECONCILIATION

For the Month of___May___ , 20_01_

Accountholder Name(s) __James Morrison__

Type of Account __Regular Checking__

---

1. Ending balance shown on bank statement _____ $ 80.99

Add up checks and withdrawals still outstanding:

Check Number or Date	Amount	Check Number or Date	Amount
221	$ 81.55		$
225	196.50		
Lucky—5/28	25.00		
ATM—5/29	40.00		
TOTAL	$ 343.05		

2. Deduct total checks/withdrawals still outstanding from bank balance _____ – $ 343.05

Add up deposits still outstanding:

Date	Amount	Date	Amount
5/29	595.00		
TOTAL	$ 595.00		

3. *Add* total deposits still outstanding to bank balance _____ + $ 595.00

A Adjusted Bank Balance (1 – 2 + 3) _____ $ 332.94

4. Ending balance shown in checkbook _____ $ 339.44

5. Deduct any bank service charges for the period (–$7.50 + $1.00) _____ – $ 6.50

6. Add interest earned for the period _____ + $ 0

B New Checkbook Balance (4 – 5 + 6) _____ $ 332.94

Note: Your account is reconciled when line A equals line B.

can be purchased at commercial banks and most other financial institutions in denominations ranging from $20 to $100. A fee of about 1.5 percent is charged on their purchase. If properly endorsed, traveler's checks are accepted by most U.S. businesses and can be exchanged for local currencies in most parts of the world. These checks are not valid unless properly countersigned by the purchaser, and because they are insured against loss or theft by the issuing agency, they provide a safe, convenient, and popular form of money for travel.

CERTIFIED CHECK. A **certified check** is a personal check that the bank certifies, to indicate that the funds are available. The bank immediately deducts the amount of the check from your account and then stamps the check to indicate its certification. There is normally a charge of $10 to $15 or more for this service. In effect, the bank has guaranteed that because the funds are there to cover the check, the check is good. Because the bank has become the guarantor, it usually will not return the canceled check to you but will keep it for its own records.

certified check
A personal check that is guaranteed (for a fee of $10 to $15 or more) by the bank on which it is drawn.

CONCEPT CHECK

4-18. What are the key factors to consider when opening a checking account? Discuss the advantages and disadvantages of individual versus joint accounts.

4-19. Is it possible to bounce a check due to insufficient funds when the checkbook ledger shows a balance available to cover it? Explain what happens when a check bounces. Is it possible to obtain protection against overdrafts?

4-20. Describe the procedure used to stop payment on a check. Why might one wish to initiate this process?

4-21. What type of information is found in the monthly bank statement, and how is it used? Explain the basic steps involved in the account reconciliation process.

4-22. Briefly define and differentiate between each of the following special types of checks:
   a. Cashier's check
   b. Traveler's check
   c. Certified check

SUMMARY

LG1. Understand the role of good cash management in the personal financial planning process. Cash management plays a vital role in personal financial planning. It involves the administration and control of liquid assets—cash, checking accounts, savings, and other short-term investment vehicles. With good cash management practices, you will have the necessary funds to cover your expenses and to establish a regular savings program.

LG2. Describe today's financial services marketplace: traditional and nondepository financial institutions and deposit safety. Financial deregulation has changed the financial marketplace by increasing the number and types of firms providing financial services. Individuals and families continue to rely heavily on traditional depository financial institutions—commercial banks, S&Ls, savings banks, and credit unions—for most of their financial services needs. Nondepository financial institutions also offer some banking services such as credit cards and money market fund accounts with check-writing privileges. You should make sure your bank has federal deposit insurance and is financially sound. Most traditional depository institutions are federally insured for up to $100,000 per depositor name.

LG3. **Select the checking and savings products, electronic banking services, and other bank services that meet your needs.** Financial institutions provide a variety of accounts to help you manage your cash: regular checking accounts, savings accounts, interest-paying checking accounts, money market deposit accounts, NOW accounts, and money market mutual funds. Asset management accounts offered by brokerage firms and mutual funds combine checking, investment, and borrowing activities and pay higher interest on deposits than other types of checking accounts. Financial institutions also provide other money management services. Electronic funds transfer systems (EFTSs) use telecommunications technology to electronically transfer funds. Popular EFTS services include ATMs, debit cards, pre-authorized deposits and payments, bank-by-phone accounts, and online banking. Safe-deposit boxes safely store valuables and important documents. Today many banks also provide trust services and mutual-fund sales.

LG4. **Find the interest earned on your money using compound interest and future value techniques.** Once you know the interest rate, frequency of compounding, and how the bank determines the balance on which interest is paid, you can calculate how much interest you will earn on your money. Compound interest is the same as future value. Future value and future value of an annuity formulas can be used to find out to what levels your savings will grow. The more frequently interest is compounded, the greater the effective rate for a given nominal rate of interest. Most banks now use the actual balance method to determine which balances qualify to earn interest; this is the most accurate and fairest method for depositors.

LG5. **Develop a savings strategy that incorporates a variety of savings plans.** Your savings strategy should include establishing a regular pattern of saving and having liquid reserves of about 3 to 6 months of after-tax income. The choice of savings products depends on your needs, your risk preference, the length of time you can leave money on deposit, and current and expected interest rate levels. You may wish to put some of your savings into vehicles that pay a higher rate of interest than savings or NOW accounts such as certificates of deposit, U.S. Treasury bills, and Series EE bonds.

LG6. **Open and use a checking account.** A checking account provides a convenient way to hold cash and pay for goods and services. The sharp increase in bank service charges makes it important to evaluate different types of checking accounts and their service charges, minimum balance requirements, and other fees. You should understand how to write and endorse checks, make deposits, keep good checking account records, prevent overdrafts, and stop payment on a check. The account reconciliation, or balancing the checkbook, process confirms the accuracy of your account records and the monthly bank statement. Other special types of checks you may use occasionally include cashier's, traveler's, and certified checks.

QUESTIONS AND PROBLEMS

1. What type of bank serves your needs best? Visit the Web sites of the following institutions and prepare a chart comparing the services offered such as traditional and online banking, investment services, and personal financial advice. Which one you would choose to patronize, and why?

   a. Bank of America (**www.bankofamerica.com**)—a nationwide full-service bank

   b. A leading local commercial bank in your area

   c. A local savings institution

   d. A local credit union

2. Suppose someone stole your ATM card and withdrew $650 from your checking account. How much money could you lose, according to federal legislation, if you reported the stolen card to the bank: (a) the day the card was stolen; (b) 6 days after the theft; and (c) 65 days after receiving your periodic statement?

3. If you put $5,000 in a savings account that pays interest at the rate of 4 percent, compounded annually, how much will you have in 5 years? (*Hint:* Use the *future value* formula.) How much will you earn in interest during the 5 years? If you put $5,000 *each* year into a savings account that pays interest at the rate of 4 percent a year, how much would you have after 5 years?

4. Bill and Betty Jacobs together earn approximately $42,000 a year after taxes. Through an inheritance and some wise investing, they also have an investment portfolio with a value of almost $90,000.

   a. How much of their annual income do you recommend they hold in some form of savings as liquid reserves? Explain.

   b. How much of their investment portfolio do you recommend they hold in savings and other short-term investment vehicles? Explain.

   c. How much, in total, should they hold in short-term liquid assets?

5. You are getting married and are unhappy with your present bank. Discuss your strategy for choosing a new bank and opening an account, including the factors that are important to you in selecting a bank such as the type and ownership of new accounts and bank fees and charges.

6. Determine the annual net cost of the following checking accounts:

   a. Monthly fee $5, per check processing fee of 25 cents, average of 19 checks written per month

   b. Annual interest of 2.5 percent paid if balance exceeds $750, $8 monthly fee if account falls below minimum balance, average monthly balance $815, account falls below $750 during 4 months

7. *Use Worksheet 4.1.* Javier Rodriguez has a NOW account at the Third State Bank. His checkbook ledger lists the following checks:

Check Number	Amount
654	$206.05
658	55.22
662	103.00
668	99.00
670	6.10
671	50.25
672	24.90
673	32.45
674	44.50
675	30.00
676	30.00
677	111.23
678	38.04
679	97.99
680	486.70
681	43.50
682	75.00
683	98.50

In addition, he made the following withdrawals and deposits at an ATM near his home (shown at the top of page 168):

Date	Amount	
11/1	$ 50.00	(withdrawal)
11/2	525.60	(deposit)
11/6	100.00	(deposit
11/14	75.00	(withdrawal)
11/21	525.60	(deposit)
11/24	150.00	(withdrawal)
11/27	225.00	(withdrawal)
11/30	400.00	(deposit)

Javier's checkbook ledger shows an ending balance of $286.54. He has just received his bank statement for the month of November. It shows an ending balance of $622.44; it also shows that he had interest earned for November of $3.28, had a check service charge of $8 for the month, and had another $12 charge for a returned check. His bank statement indicates the following checks have cleared: 654, 662, 672, 674, 675, 676, 677, 678, 679, and 681. ATM withdrawals on 11/1 and 11/14 and deposits on 11/2 and 11/6 have cleared; no other checks or ATM activities are listed on his statement, so anything remaining should be treated as outstanding. Use a checking account reconciliation form like the one in Worksheet 4.1 to reconcile Javier's checking account.

APPLYING PERSONAL FINANCE

Which Financial Service Provider Should You Choose?

With the increased competition among financial service providers, you can find the services you need at one of several financial institutions. The purpose of this project is to help you evaluate the different options available to you so you can select the one best suited to your needs.

As noted above, there are probably many companies offering financial services in your community. Survey your community via the phone book, interviews with finance professionals, and other methods in order to identify the various financial institutions in your area. Consider, for example: What additional services do local banks offer besides checking, savings, and loans? Can you get banking services from other institutions, like stock brokerage firms? Compare the services, products, and fees charged. Decide where you wold do business and why. Bring your findings to class, compare them with your classmates, and discuss your findings with them.

CONTEMPORARY CASE APPLICATIONS

4.1   Susan Chan's Savings and Banking Plans

Susan Chan, a registered nurse earning $2,250 per month after taxes, has been reviewing her savings strategies and current banking arrangements to determine if she should make any changes. She has a regular checking account using the flat fee plan (described following), writes an average of 18 checks a month, and carries an average balance of $795 (although it has fallen below $750 during 3 months of the past year). Her only other account is a money market deposit account with a balance of $4,250. She tries to make regular monthly deposits of $50 to $100 but has only done so about every other month.

Of the many checking accounts Susan's bank offers, the three that best suit her needs are:

Regular Checking, per item plan: $3 per month service charge plus 35 cents per check.
Regular Checking, flat fee plan: Monthly fee of $7 regardless of the number of checks written. With either of these accounts, she can avoid any charges by keeping a minimum *daily* balance of $750.
Interest Checking: Monthly service charge of $7; interest of 3 percent, compounded daily (refer to Exhibit 4.5). With a minimum balance of $1,500, the monthly charge is waived.

Her bank also offers certificates of deposit for a minimum deposit of $500; the current interest rates are 3.5 percent for 6 months, 3.75 percent for 1 year, and 4 percent for 2 years.

Questions
1. Calculate the annual cost of each of the three accounts, assuming that Susan's banking habits remain the same. Which plan would you recommend, and why?
2. Should Susan consider opening the interest checking account and increasing her minimum balance to at least $1,500 to avoid service charges? Explain your answer.
3. What other advice would you give Susan about her overall saving strategy?

4.2. Reconciling the Pattersons' Checking Account

Nick and Rosalyn Patterson opened their first checking account at The American Bank on September 14, 2001. They have just received their first bank statement for the period ending October 5, 2001. The statement and checkbook ledger are shown in the following table.

Bank Statement

NICK & ROSALYN PATTERSON 2128 E. 51ST ST. DETROIT, MICHIGAN			THE AMERICAN BANK 800-000-0000 STATEMENT PERIOD SEPT. 6 TO OCT. 5, 2001	
	Opening Balance	Total Deposits for Period	Total Checks/Withdrawals for Period	Ending Balance
	$0	$569.25	$473.86	$95.39
Date	Withdrawals (Debits)		Deposits (Credits)	Balance
Sept. 14			$360.00	$360.00
Sept. 23			97.00	457.00
Sept. 25	$ 45.20		9.25	421.05
Oct. 1			103.00	524.05
Oct. 1	3.00 BC			521.05
Oct. 2	65.90	$49.76	$45.00	360.39
Oct. 5	265.00			95.39

RT = Returned Check   DM = Debit Memo   BC = Bank Charges
FC = Finance Charges   CM = Credit Memo

Checkbook Ledger

Check Number	Date 2001	Details	Check Amount	Deposit Amount	Account Balance
—	Sept. 14	Cash-gift from wedding		$360.00	$360.00
—	Sept. 24	Nick's wages from library		97.00	457.00
101	Sept. 24	Kroger-groceries	$ 45.20		411.80
102	Sept. 27	Michigan Bell Telephone bill	28.40		383.40
—	Oct. 1	Nick's wages for library work		103.00	486.40
103	Oct. 1	Univ. bookstore-college books	65.90		420.50
104	Oct. 1	Kmart-sewing material	16.75		403.75
105	Oct. 1	G. Heller-apartment rent	265.00		138.75
106	Oct. 2	Blue Cross-health insurance	17.25		121.50
107	Oct. 3	Kroger-groceries	49.76		71.74
108	Oct. 4	Cash, gas, entertainment, laundry	45.00		26.74
—	Oct. 5	Rosalyn's salary-Universal Corp.		450.00	476.74

Questions

1. From this information, prepare a bank reconciliation for the Pattersons as of October 5, 2001, using a form like the one in Worksheet 4.1.
2. Given your answer to Question 1, what, if any, adjustments will the Pattersons need to make in their checkbook ledger? Comment on the procedures used to reconcile their checking account and their findings.
3. If the Pattersons earned interest on their idle balances as a result of the account being a NOW account, what impact would this have on the reconciliation process? Explain.

MONEY ONLINE

STASH YOUR CASH!

Note: Web addresses change frequently, so you may need to determine the home page and do a site search to find the page or topic that's referenced.

1. **www.fdic.gov/bank/individual/online/index.html**
   Do you want to bank online? Find out from the FDIC if your online bank has a legitimate charter and FDIC insurance. Also, learn how to protect your privacy, keep your transactions secure, and report Internet sites which may be misrepresenting themselves.
2. **www.financenter.com**
   Find an online bank. At the FinanCenter, click on "Banking" and "Compare" to pull up a comparison chart of online banking institutions. Then click on "Learn" to find information on the pros and cons of online banking, choosing an online bank, and comparing online banks.
3. **www.bankrate.com/brm/safesound/ss_home.asp**
   How financially sound is your bank? Research your bank, savings and loan, savings bank, or credit union using Bankrate's Safe and Sound rating system to obtain and evaluation of your institution.

4. **www.bankrate.com**

   What are the best rates in your area? Select your state at Bankrate's Web site to find the rate offerings on auto loans, home equity loans, home mortgages, personal loans, and savings and CDs. While you're at their site, look in Bankrate's "How to" section to find information on banking terminology, learn the basics of various financial products, and get advice.

5. **www.imoneynet.com**

   Do you need to find a money fund? Consult iMoneyNet, Inc., the leading provider of money market mutual fund data. Find what money funds are averaging, the top-yielding money fund, or click on their "Money Fund Selector" for help in choosing the fund that meets your needs.

6. **www.ny.frb.org/links.html**

   Where is your Federal Reserve District Bank located? Find your state on this map of the Federal Reserve System, and then click on the link to your district bank. Learn more about our nation's central banking system and its main functions.

7. **smartmoney.com/bonds**

   What shape is the yield curve today? Under Bond Tools, click on SmartMoney's "Living Yield Curve" to play the "Charting the Curve" graph of interest rates both backwards and forwards in time. Learn the different shapes of the yield curve and what they tell us about the future of our economy.

8. **www.quicken.com/saving/checkup**

   Are you financially fit? Use Quicken's "Financial Health Checkup" to help you evaluate your financial soundness. When you've completed the exercise, you'll get a summary based on your personal financial objectives and a detailed set of tips that you can act on now!

9. **moneyadvisor.com**

   Do you need help with your money questions? The MoneyAdvisor provides tools for consumers to use in making their financial decisions. Try their free calculators, or link to online government agencies and financial institutions.

Just for Fun!

10. **www.ny.frb.org/pihome/addpub/goldvaul.pdf**

    See the gold! Discover the unique role of the Federal Reserve Bank of New York in storing and safeguarding the world's largest accumulation of gold! Their colorful brochure, *The Key to the Gold Vault,* outlines the history of gold, explores its financial significance, and shows where it is stored.

11. **www.xe.com/ucc**

    Convert your currency! Pull up the Universal Currency Converter and plug in any amount of money to find the current conversion value from one country's currency to another. Convert one U.S. dollar into euros, Canadian dollars, Deutsche Marks, French francs, and Japanese yen. Then convert one unit of each of these currencies into U.S. dollars.

Chapter 5

Making Automobile and Housing Decisions

LEARNING GOALS

LG1.   Implement a plan to choose and buy or lease an automobile.

LG2.   Identify housing alternatives that meet your needs.

LG3.   Evaluate the benefits and costs of home ownership and estimate how much you can pay for a home.

LG4.   Assess the rental option and perform a rent-or-buy analysis.

LG5.   Describe the home-buying process.

LG6.   Choose mortgage financing that meets your needs.

Losing the Lease

Sean Weston got a new car every 2 or 3 years. With so many great leasing deals available, buying didn't seem to make sense. Three years ago he leased a Jeep Cherokee for $325 per month and just $1,500 in drive-off costs. With plenty of deals to choose from offering $200 to $300 a month with nothing down, most of his friends leased as well.

But this time around he found good lease deals scarce. Getting a new Cherokee with a similar monthly payment would take $3,500 in drive-off costs. Any deals he found were for cars that weren't selling well—and of no interest to him. After doing a lease-versus-purchase analysis, he decided to buy his next car.

Like Sean, many car buyers now face tougher decisions on whether to lease or buy their next car. Car manufacturers who offered big lease subsidies to boost auto sales overestimated resale values. These deals disappeared when many posted big losses on sales of previously leased vehicles. With fewer attractive lease deals, Sean had his work cut out for him. He researched new cars online to learn dealer costs and find financing offers he could compare with bank loans. Armed with this information and several price quotes from online car dealers, he was able to negotiate a great price just over dealer cost on a new Ford Explorer, along with a good interest rate for a loan. This chapter provides information and advice to help you have a positive experience like Sean's when you purchase a car or a home.

Sources: Adapted from Karen Lundegaard and Sholnn Freeman, "Auto Lease Bargains Dry Up, Victims of a Used-Car Glut and Bad Bets," *The Wall Street Journal*, January 5, 2001, pp. B1, B4; and Susan Tompor, "Lost Luster," *San Diego Union-Tribune*, February 4, 2001, pp. H3, H7.

■ Buying or Leasing an Automobile [LG1]

Buying a car is probably the first major expenditure you will make. Most people purchase an automobile every 2 to 5 years, paying anywhere from $3,000 to $30,000 (or more) for it, depending on its make, model, and age. The automobile purchase is second only to housing in terms of amount of money spent by the typical consumer. Because you probably will buy an automobile many times during your life, a systematic approach to selecting and financing a vehicle can help you realize significant savings. (In the material that follows we use the terms *automobile* or *car* to describe all types of passenger vehicles.)

Before you make any major purchase, whether a car, house, or large appliance, you should follow some basic rules for wise purchasing decisions:

- *Research* your purchase thoroughly, considering not only the market but also your personal needs.
- *Select* the best item for your needs.

EXHIBIT 5.1

10 STEPS TO BUYING A CAR

These 10 steps summarize the car-buying process discussed in this chapter.

1. Analyze how much car can you afford.
2. Choose the best way to pay for your new car—cash, finance, or lease.
3. Select the right car for you in terms of size, performance, safety, and styling. Choose at least three "target cars" to consider buying.
4. Set your price based on dealer's cost for the car and options, less rebates and incentives, plus a markup for the dealer's profit.
5. Test drive the car at least once. For used cars, get an independent inspection.
6. Decide whether to trade in your used car or sell it yourself.
7. Begin negotiations. Visit three or more dealers.
8. Close the deal, holding firm on your target price and going to other dealers as necessary.
9. Review and sign contracts with the dealer's finance manager, avoiding pressure to buy unnecessary extras.
10. Consider alternate buying strategies such as Internet buying services or faxing your offer to local dealerships for competitive bids.

Source: Adapted from Phil Read, "10 Steps To Buying A New Car: What Everyone Should Know," Edmunds.com, **www.edmunds.com/edweb/advice**.

- *Buy* the item after negotiating the best price and arranging financing on favorable terms. Be sure you understand all the terms of the sale before you sign any contracts.
- *Maintain* your purchase and make necessary repairs promptly.

Exhibit 5.1 summarizes the steps in the car buying process.

CHOOSING A CAR

Sport utility vehicle (SUV) or pickup truck? Sedan, convertible, or coupe? Car buyers today have more categories from which to choose than ever before, and more than one type of vehicle may interest you. A good way to start your research is by tapping into the many available sources of information about cars, their prices, features, and reliability. Industry resources include manufacturers' brochures and dealer personnel. Car magazines, such as *Car and Driver, Motor Trend,* and *Road and Track,* and consumer magazines, such as *Consumer Reports* and *Consumers Digest,* regularly compare and rate cars. In addition, both consumer magazines and *Kiplinger's Personal Finance Magazine* publish annual buying guides that include comparative statistics and ratings on most domestic and foreign autos. *Consumer Reports* includes information on used cars in its guide, and it offers a fee-based service, called *Consumer Reports* Auto Price Service, that provides the list price and dealer's cost of a new car and the available options.

The Internet has made it especially easy to do your homework before ever setting foot in a dealer's showroom. In addition to finding online versions of automotive magazines, you can visit one of the many comprehensive Web sites for car shoppers that offers pricing and model information and links to other useful sites. Don't forget the Web sites of the automobile companies themselves; for example, General Motors is online at **gm.com**, and so on. Once you've done the research, you will be in a better position to negotiate with the dealer. The *Money in Action* box on page 181 explores the online world of car buying.

EXHIBIT 5.2

USING A FINANCIAL CALCULATOR TO FIND AN AUTO LOAN AMOUNT

How large a loan can you pay off in 3 years with a $450 monthly payment?

Step 1: Multiply years by 12 to find total number of payments: $3 \times 12 = 36$.
Press **N** to enter 36 as the number of payment periods.

Step 2: Divide annual interest by 12 to get monthly rate: 9 percent/12 $=$ .75 monthly rate.
Press **I** to enter the monthly rate.

Step 3: Enter the monthly payment, $450, and press **PMT**.

Step 4: Press **CPT** then **PV** to find the beginning loan amount: $14,151.

Although the primary motivation for automobile ownership is to provide transportation, automobiles are sometimes viewed as status symbols or purchased as part of a hobby or as an investment. Regardless of your motive, it's important to evaluate all of the following areas before buying a car. Knowing what you want and can afford before purchasing either a new or used car will prevent a slick auto salesperson from talking you into buying a car you do not need.

AFFORDABILITY. Before you shop for a car, you should determine how much you can afford to spend. Unless you can pay cash for the entire amount of the car, you will need to calculate two numbers. First, how much of a down payment can you make? This money will come from savings, so be sure not to deplete your emergency fund. Then figure out the amount you can pay on a monthly basis for a loan or lease payment, after analyzing your available resources in view of other necessary expenses (including housing) and your transportation requirements. Don't forget to include insurance. You should keep your monthly car payment to no more than 20 percent of your monthly net income.

You can also use the down payment and monthly amount to back into the total amount you can afford for a car. For example, suppose you have $2,500 for a down payment, can pay $450 a month, and your bank is offering 3-year car loans at 9 percent annual interest. How much of a loan can you afford? Using a financial calculator and the steps shown in Exhibit 5.2, you will discover that you can pay off a loan of about $14,150. Add that to the $2,500 down payment, and you'll be able to afford a car costing $16,650. If you paid off the loan over 48 months, you could borrow $18,100. It pays to shop around for loans because the rates can vary as much as 2 percent!

 With Bankrate.com's (**www.bankrate.com**) Auto Loan calculators, you can evaluate auto financing options, then go to the rate page to find the lowest auto loan rates in your area.

OPERATING COSTS. The out-of-pocket cost of operating an automobile consists of not only car payments, but also insurance, license, fuel, oil, tires, and other operating and maintenance outlays. Certain of these costs are *fixed* and remain so regardless of how much you drive; others are *variable* with the number of miles you drive. The biggest fixed cost is likely to be the *installment payments* associated with the loan or lease used to acquire the car; the biggest variable cost will probably be fuel.

Another purchase cost is **depreciation,** which is the loss in value that occurs from driving the vehicle. In effect, depreciation is the difference between the price you paid for the

depreciation
The loss in the value of an asset such as an automobile that occurs over its period of use; calculated as the difference between the price initially paid and the subsequent sale price.

car and what you can get for it when you sell it. If you paid $15,000 for an automobile that can be sold 3 years later for $9,000, the car will cost you $6,000 in depreciation. Although depreciation cost may not be a recurring out-of-pocket cost, it is nonetheless an important operating expense that should not be overlooked.

NEW, USED, OR "NEARLY NEW"? One decision you must make is whether to buy a new, used, or "nearly new" car. If you cannot afford to buy a new car, the decision is made for you. Some people always buy used cars, even though they can afford to buy a new car, because they would rather have a better model—a used luxury car like a BMW, Lexus, or Mercedes—than a new car of a less-expensive brand such as a Chevrolet.

 Looking for a 1998 Toyota Camry? At Internet classified service AutoTrader.com, **www.autotrader.com**, you can see ads from local sellers, some with pictures. The rest is up to you! Checking the ads is also a good way to learn the value of a car you want to trade.

The advantages of buying a used car are: (1) it is less expensive than a comparable new car; (2) it will not depreciate in value as quickly as a new car; and (3) because it is less expensive, the purchaser does not have to put down as much money as is required on a new car. For example, the average retail selling price of a used car at a new car dealer in 1999 was $12,500. Moreover, purchasing a used car less than 18 months old often means saving the 20 to 25 percent depreciation in value typically experienced during the first 12 to 18 months of a car's life. The recent popularity of short-term car leases has increased the availability of late-model, attractively priced used cars. Today's cars are more reliable, too. Auto industry analysts J.D. Power and Associates report that the quality and durability of well-maintained 2- to 4-year-old cars makes them more reliable and less expensive to maintain than new cars of 10 years ago.

The main disadvantage of buying a used car is uncertainty regarding its mechanical condition. Although it might look good and have low mileage, it could still have some mechanical problems requiring maintenance and repair expenditures in the near future. Although a salesperson says the car "has been driven only to and from church by a little old lady," you should have it checked by a reputable mechanic or independent inspection service. The money spent on a thorough examination prior to purchase could save hundreds of dollars and much aggravation later.

Purchasers of used cars have another means of protecting their investments: the *federal odometer disclosure law.* The penalties for violation of this law, which requires sellers to give buyers a signed statement attesting to the fact that the mileage shown on the odometer of their used cars is correct, are quite stringent. A seller of a used car should always be asked to provide such a statement.

With the increasing popularity of used cars, car dealers are trying to dispel the bad image associated with buying a used, or "preowned," car. You'll find used cars advertised in local or nearby city newspapers, publications like *AutoTrader,* and their Web sites. These provide an excellent source of information on used cars for sale. Exhibit 5.3 compares several types of used cars you're likely to encounter. Once you know what you want, shop at the following places:

- **Franchise dealerships:** Offer the latest model used cars, financing, and will negotiate on price. Be sure to research values before shopping.
- **Superstores:** AutoNation USA, CarMax, and similar dealers offer no-haggle pricing and a large selection. They certify cars and may offer limited short-term warranty. May cost slightly more than a dealer who will negotiate.

EXHIBIT 5.3

WHICH TYPE OF USED CAR SHOULD YOU BUY?

In addition to trade-ins and privately sold vehicles, you should also check out these types of used cars.

Type	Pros	Cons
Certified used car	"Near-new" cars; dealer inspects and reconditions car; generally includes warranty.	Cars cost $500 to $1,500 more; may be able to have own mechanic inspect for less.
Off-lease cars	Single driver; usually fully equipped; inspected on return	Lessee may not do scheduled maintenance
Rental cars ("program cars")	Price; may still be under factory warranty or have limited warranty	Fewer features, multiple drivers; heavy mileage
Corporate fleet cars	Well maintained	High mileage—60,000+ miles in 2 or 3 years

Source: Adapted from Linda Kulman, "Why Buy New?" *U.S. News & World Report,* November 22, 1999, pp. 68–72; and Mark Maynard, "Used Cars," *San Diego Union-Tribune,* June 3, 2000, pp. Wheels-1, 2.

- **Independent used car lots:** Usually offer older (4 to 6 years) cars and have lower overhead than franchise dealers. No industry standards, so check Better Business Bureau before buying.
- **Private individuals:** Generally cost less because there is no dealer overhead; may have maintenance records. Be sure seller has title to car.

 Which auto dealers have the best used car certification programs? IntelliChoice (**www.intellichoice.com**) rates the programs of 23 dealers according to their inspection lists, warranties, roadside assistance benefits, and return and exchange policies.

SIZE, BODY STYLE, AND FEATURES. When considering size, body style, and features, give some thought to not only your likes and dislikes, but also their cost. Also take into account performance, handling, appearance, fuel economy, reliability, repair problems, and the resale value of the car.

There is a great variety of sizes and body styles from which to choose. A two-passenger compact car may not be appropriate if you need the car for business or if you have children. What type of car do you need? This should be your first consideration; don't try to adapt your needs to fit the car you want. In most instances there is a direct relationship between size and cost: the larger the car, the more expensive it will be to purchase and to operate. More than one style category may work for you. For example, a family of five can buy a mid-size or full-size sedan, station wagon, minivan, or compact or full-size SUV.

You can also select certain optional features providing a broad range of conveniences and luxuries—for a price. Most cars have at least some options. On new cars a window sticker details each option and its price, but on a used car only close observation serves to determine the options. Window stickers quite often list standard features that might be considered optional on some other models, and vice versa. When shopping for a new car, make certain you are comparing comparably equipped models.

By listing all options you want before shopping for a new car, you can avoid paying for features you really do not need. There are literally hundreds of options available ranging in price from a few dollars up to $1,500 or more, including automatic transmission, a bigger engine, air conditioning, high-performance brakes, CD player, clock, power windows, power seats, electric door locks, leather seats, navigation systems, rear window defroster, and special suspension. Other appearance-related options are two-tone or metallic paint, electric sunroof, whitewall tires, sport wheels, and various interior and exterior trim packages.

RELIABILITY AND WARRANTIES. The *reliability* of a car can be assessed by talking with friends owning similar cars and through objective assessments published in various consumer magazines and buying guides such as *Consumer Reports.* Study the *warranty* offered by new car manufacturers, comparing those for cars that interest you. Significant differences may exist. Be sure to read the warranty booklet included with a new car and to understand the terms of the warranty. Most warranties are void if the owner has not performed routine maintenance or has somehow abused the car.

On all new cars, the manufacturer in effect guarantees the general reliability and quality of construction for a specified period in a written warranty that obligates it to repair or replace, at little or no cost to the owner, any defective parts and flaws in workmanship. Today, most new car warranties cover a minimum of the first 3 years of ownership or 36,000 miles, whichever comes first, and some provide coverage for as long as 7 years or 70,000 miles. However, most warranties have limitations; for example, longer warranty periods may apply to only the engine and drive train. Auto manufacturers and private insurers also sell extended warranties and service contracts, sometimes called "buyer protection plans." Most experts consider these unnecessary and not worth their price, given the relatively long initial warranty periods now being offered by most manufacturers.

OLD CAR: TRADE-IN OR SELL? When buying a new or used car from a dealer to replace an old car, the question of a trade-in arises. Although trading-in is convenient, you are generally better off financially selling your old car outright. If you are willing to take the time, you can usually sell your car above the wholesale price typically offered by a dealer on a trade-in.

OTHER CONSIDERATIONS. You should carefully consider fuel economy. The *Environmental Protection Agency (EPA) mileage ratings* are especially useful on new vehicles, which carry a sticker indicating the number of miles per gallon each model is expected to get (as determined through EPA tests) for both city and highway driving. *Safety features* built into the car are also important. These features are likely to be similar in new cars as a result of government regulations, but older used cars may not have some features such as airbags. Don't forget to include *auto insurance costs,* which vary depending on make, model, safety features, and other factors (and are discussed in detail in Chapter 10), when considering automobile purchase alternatives.

THE PURCHASE TRANSACTION

Once you have determined the amount you can afford to spend and the features you desire, you are ready to begin shopping for a car. If you plan to purchase a new car, visit all dealers who have cars meeting your requirements. Look the cars over and ask questions—but don't make any offers until you have isolated two or three cars with the desired features that are priced within your budget. Also, if you can be flexible about the model and options you want, you can sometimes negotiate a better deal than if you have your heart set on a

 **EXHIBIT 5.4**

TESTING 1, 2, 3

Start your examination of a car you like with an inspection of key points. Don't overlook the obvious:

- *How easy is it to get people and things into and out of the car?*
  Do the doors open easily?
  How big is the trunk?
  Does the car offer a pass-through or fold-down rear seat for larger items?

- *Comfort and visibility.*
  Are the seats comfortable?
  Can you adjust the driver's seat properly?
  What are the car's blind spots for a person of your height?
  Can you see all the gauges clearly?
  Can you reach the controls for the radio, CD player, heater, air conditioner, and other features easily while driving?

Then take the car for a test drive.

- Allow about 20 minutes and include highway and local roads.
- Merge into traffic getting onto the highway. Does it have enough acceleration to safely merge with freeway traffic or to pass another car?
- If possible, drive to your house and make sure the car fits into your garage. This can be an important factor for the larger SUVs!
- For a used car, turn off the air conditioner and listen for any unusual engine noises. Test the heater as well.
- Check out overall handling by parallel parking, making a U-turn, braking hard, etc. Pay attention to where the gears shift. If testing a standard transmission, try to determine if the clutch is engaging too high or too low, which might indicate excessive wear or a problem.

As soon as you return to the car lot, take notes on how well the car handled and how comfortable you felt driving it. This is especially important if you are testing several cars.

Source: Bob Storck, "Check it Out," *San Diego Union-Tribune,* June 3, 2000, p. Wheels-3; and Bob Storck, "Exam Time," *San Diego Union-Tribune,* June 3, 2000, p. Wheels-3.

particular model and options. Make an appointment to test-drive the cars you are interested in. Drive—then leave! You need time to evaluate the car yourself, without pressure to buy from the salesperson.

Comparison shopping is essential because one dealer selling the same brand as another may give you a better deal. Watch out for the sales technique called *low-balling* where the salesperson quotes a low price for the car to get you to make an offer and then negotiates the price upward prior to your signing the sales contract. Exhibit 5.4 lists some other factors to consider once you get to the dealer and begin looking at cars.

Because low-balling, price haggling, and other high-pressure sales tactics often make car buying an unpleasant experience, many dealers during recent years have refocused their sales practices to emphasize customer satisfaction. Some manufacturers are offering firm prices, so if you buy today, you can be sure that no one will get a better deal tomorrow. Saturn dealers use this strategy, and other manufacturers offer "value pricing" on certain models equipped with popular options. More individual car dealers also are offering a one-price, no-haggling policy. However, you should still research prices, as described in the next section, because a set selling price does not guarantee the lowest cost.

NEGOTIATING PRICE. The price you pay for a car, whether new or used, can vary widely. Choosing among various makes, models, and options can make comparisons difficult. The more you can narrow your choices to a particular car, the better off you will be. Then you can get price quotes from several dealers and make an "apples to apples" comparison.

The "sticker price" posted on a new car represents the manufacturer's *suggested retail price* for that particular car with the listed options. This price really means very little. The key to negotiating a good price is knowing the *dealer's cost* for the car. The easiest and quickest way to find the dealer's invoice cost is going to the Edmunds and Kelley Blue Book Web sites mentioned earlier or checking car-buying guides available at your library or bookstore.

Before making an offer, prepare a worksheet with the cost versus the list price for the exact car you want. This will help you avoid high-pressure salesmanship and being pushed to pay for options you don't want or need. Try to negotiate the lowest acceptable markup (3 to 4 percent for cars priced under $20,000; 6 to 7 percent for higher-priced models), push for a firm quote, and make it clear that you are comparison shopping. Don't let the salesperson pressure you into signing a sales contract or leaving a deposit until you are sure that you have negotiated the best deal. Good cost information will improve your bargaining position and possibly allow you to negotiate a price that is only several hundred dollars above the dealer's cost.

To research used car prices, you can check one of the popular price guides—the National Automobile Dealers Association (NADA) *Official Used Car Guide,* the *Kelley Blue Book,* or *Edmund's Used Car Prices*—available on the Internet or at your library or bank, and the classified ads in your local newspaper.

If you want to avoid negotiating entirely, you can buy your car through a buying service, either by phone or over the Internet. These include independent companies, such as AutoVantage and Nationwide Auto Brokers, and services offered through credit unions, motor clubs, and discount warehouses like Costco. Buying services can work in a variety of ways. They may have an arrangement with a network of dealers to sell cars at a predetermined price above invoice, provide you with competitive bids from several local dealers, find the car you want and negotiate the price with the dealer, or place an order with the factory for a made-to-order car. The price for these services ranges from about $35 for a Costco membership to as much as $600, and results vary. You will get a good price through a service—although you can't assume that it will be the best price. The *Money in Action* box on page 181 tells you how to use the Internet to your advantage when buying a car.

It is best not to discuss your plan to finance the purchase or the value of your trade-in until you have settled the question of price. These should be separate issues. Salespeople will typically want to find out how much you can afford monthly and then offer financing deals with payments close to that amount. In the case of trade-ins, the dealer might offer you a good price for your old car and raise the price of the new car to compensate. The dealer may offer financing terms that sound attractive, but be sure to compare them with the cost of bank loans. Sometimes dealers increase the price of the car to make up for a low interest rate, or the attractive financing may apply only to certain models. If you are interested in dealer financing, make sure the monthly payment quoted by the dealer's finance manager is just for the loan. Learn and compare the annual percentage rate (APR) with the rate quoted on a bank loan. Often the financing charges include unneeded extras such as credit life insurance, accident insurance, an extended warranty, or a service package.

Manufacturers and dealers often offer buyers special incentives, such as rebates and cut-rate financing, particularly when car sales are slow. (Rebates should be deducted from the dealer's cost when you are negotiating the price.) You may have a choice between a rebate and low-cost financing. To determine which is the better deal, calculate the difference between the monthly payments on a market-rate bank loan and the special dealer loan

MONEY IN ACTION

Clicking the Tires

Getting a new car is exciting—once you have finished with the hassles of the car-buying process. It can be fun to research different car makes and test drive the ones you like. Deciding how much you can afford to pay and how to finance the car and negotiating the interest rate may be more of a hassle. But now you can do much of your searching online and perhaps even buy the car from an online dealer.

Online research is popular with car buyers today; over 40 percent shop the Internet first. Unsure which car is for you? Netscape's Auto Decision Guide (**home. netscape.com/decisionguides**; click on "Car Match") asks your preferences on model type, price, and important features, then provides a list of cars that match your specifications. If you already know the cars you like, you can run comparisons. Or going through the quiz may turn up models you wouldn't have considered. Comprehensive sites like Edmunds (**www. edmunds.com**), Kelley Blue Book (**www.kbb.com**), and AutoSite (**www.autosite.com**) provide comparative new and used car prices, reviews, incentives and rebates, and advice on buying and selling, financing, and insurance. If safety is a priority, you'll find government crash-test ratings at the National Highway Traffic Safety Association site (**www.nhtsa.gov**) and real-world accident and injury statistics at **www.carsafety .com**. After you've chosen several models, leave your computer to visit a dealer and test drive the cars. Then head back to the Internet to compare prices. Only about 3 percent of car buyers actually buy online, however, because many car-buying services don't deliver on their promises. You may not get a quote, and the price may change when you go to the dealer to finalize the transaction. Although it may be easy to contact various online dealers to get price quotes, there is no guarantee you will get the lowest price. One study showed that people buying their vehicle online actually paid 6.5 percent more than those negotiating in person.

Not all car-buying sites operate in the same manner. Autobytel (**www.autobytel.com**), Autoweb (**www.autoweb.com**), and CarPoint (**www.carpoint .com**) are referral services that connect customers to dealers in their geographical area—who pay for the leads. AutoNationDirect (**autonationdirect.com**) actually owns dealerships and sells vehicles from its own inventory. CarOrder (**www.carorder.com**) and CarsDirect (**www.carsdirect.com**) have agreements with dealers for guaranteed price quotes. Getting the best deal means visiting as many Web sites as you can to gather information. In a test by *Kiplinger's Personal Finance* magazine to find the best deal on a Toyota Land Cruiser, price quotes varied by as much as $3,000.

You shouldn't overlook your local dealers, however. In today's competitive market they often match Internet offers. But you'll never know unless you get and Internet offer first!

Source: Jerry Edgerton, "Driving a Deal Online," *Money*, September 1999, pp. 177–179; and Ed Henry, "Hitting the Web," *Kiplinger's Personal Finance*, July 2000, pp. 112–115.

for the same term. Multiply the payment difference by the loan maturity, in months, and compare it with the rebate. For example, assume the dealer offers either a $1,000 rebate or a 5 percent interest rate on a $10,000, 4-year loan. Your payments would be $230 with dealer financing and $254 on a 10 percent bank loan with similar terms. The payment savings over the life of the loan are $1,152 ($24 per month × 48 months), which is greater than the $1,000 rebate. In this case you would be better off with the 5 percent loan.

CLOSING THE DEAL. Whether you are buying a new or a used car, to make a legally binding offer you must sign a **sales contract** that specifies the offering price and all the conditions of your offer. The sales contract will also specify whether the offer includes a trade-in; when it does, the offering price will represent the amount in addition to the trade-in you are willing to pay. Because this agreement contractually binds you to purchase the

sales contract
An agreement to purchase an automobile that states the offering price and all conditions of the offer; when signed by the buyer and seller, the contract legally binds them to its terms.

car at the offering price, you should be certain that you want and can afford the car prior to signing such an agreement. To show that you are making an offer in good faith, you may be required to include a deposit of $100 or more with the contract.

Once the dealer accepts your offer, you complete the purchase transaction and take delivery of the car. If you are not paying cash for the car, you can arrange financing through the dealer, at your bank, credit union, or a consumer finance company. The key aspects of these types of installment loans, which can be quickly negotiated if your credit is good, are discussed in Chapter 7. Prior to delivery, the dealer is responsible for cleaning the car and installing any optional equipment. It is a good idea to make sure that all equipment you are paying for has been installed and the car is ready for use before paying the dealer. When you pay, you should receive a title or appropriate documents that evidence your ownership of the car.

LEASING YOUR CAR

A new car every 2 or 3 years. No need to worry about temperamental engines or transmissions. Just drive it off the lot today and return it for another new model. Nothing down. Easy payments—usually lower than getting a loan to buy a car. No wonder leasing is popular! It accounts for about 25 percent of all vehicles sold today.

When you **lease,** you (the lessee) receive the use of a car in exchange for making monthly lease payments over a specified period, usually 2 to 5 years. Leasing appeals to a wide range of car buyers, due in large part to rising new car prices and the nondeductibility of consumer loan interest. However, in most cases the total cost of leasing is generally more expensive than buying a car with a loan. And at the end of the lease, you have nothing. The car—and the money you paid to rent it—is gone. So why do so many buyers lease their cars? Reasons include the lower monthly payments, getting a more expensive car for the same monthly payment, and minimizing the down payment to preserve cash.

With all the advertisements promising low monthly lease payments, it's easy to focus on only the payment. But with a lease you're not paying for the whole car, you're only paying for its use during a specified period. Leasing is a more complex arrangement than borrowing to buy a car, and until you understand how leasing works and compare the lease terms with bank financing, you won't know if leasing makes sense for you.

THE LEASING PROCESS. The initial step is the same for leasing and purchasing: Research car types and brands, comparison shop at several dealers, and find the desired car at the best price. Don't ask the dealer about leasing or any financing incentives until *after* you've negotiated the best price. Also, compare the terms offered by at least one independent leasing firm. Just as with a purchase, try to negotiate lower lease payments; a payment reduction of $20 a month saves nearly $1,000 on a 4-year lease. And don't reveal what you can afford to pay per month; such a disclosure can lead you to a poor lease deal. Once you agree on leasing terms, be sure to get everything in writing.

Nearly 80 percent of all customers choose the **closed-end lease,** often called the *walk-away lease,* because at the end of its term you simply turn in the car, assuming you have neither exceeded the preset mileage limit nor abused the car. Under the less popular **open-end lease,** the estimated **residual value**—the remaining value of the car at the end of the lease term—is used to determine lease payments; if the car is actually worth less than this value at the end of the lease, you have to pay the difference.

One of the commonly cited benefits of leasing is the absence of a down payment. However, today most leases ask for a "capital cost reduction," which is nothing more than a down payment that lowers the potential depreciation and therefore your monthly lease payments. You may be able to negotiate a lower capital cost reduction or find a lease that doesn't require one.

lease
An arrangement in which the lessee receives the use of a car (or other asset) in exchange for making monthly lease payments for a specified period.

closed-end lease
The most popular form of automobile lease, often called a *walk-away lease* because at the end of its term the lessee simply turns in the car, assuming the preset mileage limit has not been exceeded and the car hasn't been abused.

open-end lease
An automobile lease under which the estimated *residual value* of the car is used to determine lease payments; if the car is actually worth less than this value at the end of the lease, the lessee must pay the difference.

residual value
The remaining value of a leased car at the end of the lease term.

The lease payment calculation is based on four variables: (1) the **capitalized cost** of the car, the price of the car you are leasing; (2) the forecast *residual value* of the car at the end of the lease; (3) the **money factor,** or financing rate on the lease, which is similar to the interest rate on a loan; and (4) the lease term. The *depreciation* during the lease term (which is what you are financing) is the capitalized cost minus the residual value. Dividing the sum of the depreciation and the sales tax (on the financed portion only) by the number of months in the lease term and adding the lessor's required monthly return (at the money factor) results in the monthly payment. (To convert the money factor to an annual percentage rate, multiply it by 2400. For example, a money factor of .00450 is the equivalent of paying interest at 10.8 percent on a loan.) The lower the cost and higher the residual value, the lower your payment. Residual values quoted by different dealers often vary, so check several sources to find the highest residual value so you can minimize depreciation.

Lease terms typically run 2 to 5 years. Terminating a lease early is often difficult—and costly—so be reasonably certain that you can keep the car for the full lease term. The lease contract should outline all costs and additional fees associated with early termination. Early termination clauses also apply to cars that are stolen or totaled in an accident; some leases require "gap insurance" to cover the lost lease payments that would result from early termination caused by one of these events.

Under most leases, you are responsible for insuring and maintaining the car. At the end of the lease, you are obligated to pay for any "unreasonable wear and tear." A good lease contract should clearly define what is considered unreasonable. In addition, most leases require the lessee to pay a disposition fee of about $150 to $250 when the car is returned.

Most auto leases include a **purchase option** (e.g., a fixed price, the market price at the end of the lease term, or the residual value of the car) that specifies the price at which the lessee can buy the car at the end of the lease term. A lower residual results in a lower purchase price but raises monthly payments. Experts recommend negotiating a fixed-price purchase option, if possible.

The annual mileage allowance—typically, about 10,000 to 15,000 miles per year for the lease term—is another important lease consideration. Usually the lessee must pay between 8 and 15 cents per mile for additional miles. If you expect to exceed the allowable mileage, you can negotiate a more favorable rate for extra miles before signing the lease contract.

THE LEASE VERSUS PURCHASE ANALYSIS. To decide whether it is less costly to lease rather than purchase a car, you need to perform a *lease versus purchase analysis* to determine the total cost of leasing and the total cost of purchasing (using an installment loan) a car over equal periods to choose the least costly alternative. Generally in this analysis the purchase is assumed to be financed with an installment loan with the same term as the lease.

For example, assume Mary Dixon is considering either leasing or purchasing a new Ford Focus sedan costing $15,000 with the options she wants. The 3-year, closed-end lease she is considering requires a $1,500 down payment (capital cost reduction), a $300 security deposit, and monthly payments of $300, including sales tax. If she purchases the car, she will make a $2,500 down payment and finance the balance with a 3-year, 8 percent loan requiring monthly payments of $392. In addition, she will have to pay 5 percent sales tax ($750) on the purchase, and she expects the car to have a residual value of $8,000 at the end of 3 years. Mary can earn 4 percent interest on her savings with short-term CDs. After filling in Worksheet 5.1, Mary concludes that purchasing is better because its *total cost* of $9,662 is $2,854 less than the $12,516 total cost of leasing—even though the monthly lease payment is $92 lower. Clearly, all else being equal, the least costly alternative is preferred.

Some Web sites can help you with your analysis. Intellichoice's lease area, **www.intelli choice.com,** has descriptions of current manufacturer lease deals. For example, in January

Financial Road Sign

Auto Leasing Prerequisites
Smart leasing customers should insist on knowing the following eight figures before negotiating a lease:
1. The list price for the car and options
2. The *capitalized cost,* or the value on which the monthly payments are based
3. The *money factor,* or interest rate assumption
4. The total interest paid
5. The total sales tax
6. The residual value for which the car can be purchased at the lease's end
7. The *depreciation,* which equals the capitalized cost minus residual value
8. The lease term

capitalized cost
The price of a car that is being leased.

money factor
The financing rate on a lease; similar to the interest rate on a loan.

purchase option
A price specified in a lease at which the lessee can buy the car at the end of the lease term.

WORKSHEET 5.1

COMPARING MARY DIXON'S AUTOMOBILE LEASE VERSUS PURCHASE COSTS

This worksheet illustrates Mary Dixon's lease versus purchase analysis for a new car costing $15,000. The three-year closed-end lease requires an initial payment of $1,800 ($1,500 down payment + $300 security deposit) and monthly payments of $300. Purchasing requires a $2,500 down payment, sales tax of 5 percent ($750), and 36 monthly payments of $392. *Because the total cost of leasing of $12,516 is greater than the $9,662 total cost of purchasing, Mary should purchase rather than lease the car.*

AUTOMOBILE LEASE VERSUS PURCHASE ANALYSIS*

Name _Mary Dixon_ Dated _March 4, 2002_

Item	Description		Amount
LEASE			
1	Initial payment:		
	a. Down payment (capital cost reduction):	$ 1,500	
	b. Security deposit:	300	$ 1,800
2	Term of lease and loan (years)*		3
3	Term of lease and loan (months) (Item 2 × 12)		36
4	Monthly lease payment		$ 300
5	Total payments over term of lease (Item 3 × Item 4)		$ 10,800
6	Interest rate earned on savings (in decimal form)		.04
7	Opportunity cost of initial payment (Item 1 × Item 2 × Item 6)		$ 216
8	Payment/refund for market value adjustment at end of lease ($0 for closed-end leases) and/or estimated end-of-term charges		$ 0
9	**Total cost of leasing (Item 1a + Item 5 + Item 7 + Item 8)**		$ 12,516
PURCHASE			
10	Purchase price		$ 15,000
11	Down payment		$ 2,500
12	Sales tax rate (in decimal form)		.05
13	Sales tax (Item 10 × Item 12)		$ 750
14	Monthly loan payment (Terms: _12,500_, _36_ months, _8_ %)		$ 392
15	Total payments over term of loan (Item 3 × Item 14)		$ 14,112
16	Opportunity cost of down payment (Item 2 × Item 6 × Item 11)		$ 300
17	Estimated value of car at end of loan		$ 8,000
18	**Total cost of purchasing (Item 11 + Item 13 + Item 15 + Item 16 − Item 17)**		$ 9,662

DECISION

If the value of Item 9 is less than the value of Item 18, leasing is preferred; otherwise the purchase alternative is preferred.

---

*Note: This form is based on assumed equal terms for the lease and the installment loan, which is assumed to be used to finance the purchase.

2001 you could lease a 2001 Honda Accord LX for $239 per month for 39 months with a capital cost reduction of about $1,500. The net interest rate on this lease is 8.32 percent. You can compare this number with interest rates for other types of financing. If it is less than a bank loan, leasing would cost less. Click on the "calculate" page of FinanCenter, **www. financenter.com**, and go to the auto section for several calculators to analyze a car purchase, including lease versus purchase. You can quickly run several "what if" scenarios to compare costs. The average cost per year of either owning or leasing is the highest in the first 2 years. Note also that the average cost of ownership is usually much lower if you own a vehicle for 4 years or more.

If you are fortunate enough to be able to pay all cash to buy your car, you may still want to investigate leasing. Sometimes dealers offer such advantageous lease terms that you can come out ahead by investing the money you would pay for the car. To compare the total cost of a cash purchase, simply take the cost of the car, including sales tax, add to it the opportunity cost of using all cash, and deduct the car's value at the end of the lease or loan term. At 4 percent per year on her savings, Mary's total cost of the car is as follows: $15,750 cost + $1,890 lost interest (3 × .04 × $15,750) − $8,000 residual value = $9,640. In this case the cost of purchasing the car for cash is about the same as its purchase cost with financing, so Mary could do either.

WHEN THE LEASE ENDS. At the expiration of the lease, you will be faced with a major decision. Should you return the car and walk away, or should you buy the car? If you turn in the car and move on to a new model, you may be hit with "excess wear and damage" and "excess mileage" charges and disposition fees. To minimize these, replace worn tires, get repairs done yourself, and document the car's condition before returning it. You may be able to negotiate a lower disposition fee. If you can't return the car without high repair charges or greatly exceeded mileage allowances, you may come out ahead by buying the car.

Whether exercising the purchase option makes sense depends on the residual value. Sometimes, with popular cars, the residual value in your lease agreement is below the car's market value. Buying the car makes sense; even if you want a different car, you exercise the purchase option and then sell the car on the open market and net $1,000 or more. If the reverse is true, and the residual is higher than the price of a comparable used car, just let the lease expire. Find your car's market value by looking in used-car price guides and newspaper ads and compare it with the residual value.

CONCEPT CHECK

5-1. Briefly discuss how each of the following purchase considerations would affect your choice of a car:
   a. Affordability
   b. Operating costs
   c. New, used, or "nearly new" car
   d. Model and feature selection
   e. Reliability and warranty protection

5-2. Describe the purchase transaction process, including shopping, price negotiation, and closing the deal on a car.

5-3. What are the advantages and disadvantages of leasing a car? Given your personal financial circumstances, if you were buying a car today, would you probably pay cash, lease, or finance it, and why?

▪ Meeting Housing Needs [LG2]

Everybody's housing needs differ. Some people prefer quiet and privacy; others like the hustle and bustle of big-city life. Some demand to live within walking distance of work, shopping, and restaurants; others do not mind a 45-minute commute. Because you have your own unique set of likes and dislikes, the best way to start your search for housing is to list your preferences and then classify them according to whether their satisfaction is essential, desirable, or merely a "plus." This exercise is important for three reasons. First, it serves to screen out housing that will not meet your minimum requirements. Second, it helps you recognize that you may have to make tradeoffs because you will seldom find any single home that meets all your needs. Third, it can help you focus on those needs for which you are willing and able to pay.

Because there are so many different types of residences, it is difficult to describe a "typical" home. Housing in America is diverse, including single-family homes, townhouses, condominiums, cooperative apartments, and numerous types of rental units. We do know a few things, however, about what the "average" American home is like. Today's new home typically has at least three bedrooms and probably more than one bathroom, at least a one-car garage or carport, a fireplace, and central heating and air conditioning. We also know something about home prices. For example, in early 2001, the median price for existing homes nationally was about $140,000. However, as shown in Exhibit 5.5, prices varied widely from one part of the country to another.

SINGLE-FAMILY HOMES. The single-family, detached home remains the first choice in housing. Basically, such homes stand alone on their own legally defined lots. Sometimes homes are built side by side and share common side walls; these are known as *row houses* or *townhouses.* As a rule, single-family homes offer their buyers privacy, prestige, pride of ownership, and maximum property control. In recent years, however, the cost of single-family residences—and especially residential lots—has increased dramatically. At the same time, the size of the average U.S. household has drastically decreased. These factors have led to a trend toward building smaller homes. To compensate for their smaller size, new homes often offer luxurious amenities and features. Higher costs and changing lifestyles also have led to alternative types of housing; thus, although the single-family, detached home is still the most popular type of residence, its dominant position is declining.

condominium (condo)
A form of direct ownership of an individual unit in a multi-unit project in which lobbies, swimming pools, and other common areas and facilities are jointly owned by all property owners in the project.

cooperative apartment (co-op)
An apartment in a building in which each tenant owns a share of the corporation that owns the building.

CONDOMINIUMS. The term **condominium** or **condo** describes a form of ownership rather than a type of building. Condominiums can be apartments, townhouses, or cluster housing. The condominium buyer receives title to an individual unit and joint ownership in any common areas and facilities such as lobbies, swimming pools, lakes, and tennis courts. Because buyers own their units, they arrange their own mortgages, pay their own taxes, and pay for maintenance and building services. They typically are assessed on a monthly basis with a *homeowner's fee* to cover their proportionate share of common facility costs. Condominium owners belong to a *homeowners' association* that elects a board of managers to supervise the project's buildings and grounds. Condominiums generally cost less than single-family, detached homes because they are designed for more efficient land use and lower construction costs. Many home buyers are attracted to condominiums because they do not want the responsibilities of maintaining and caring for their property. Exhibit 5.6 lists some of the key things to check before buying a condominium.

COOPERATIVE APARTMENTS. An apartment in a building in which each tenant owns a share of the corporation that owns the building is known as a **cooperative apartment**

EXHIBIT 5.5

PRICES FOR EXISTING SINGLE-FAMILY HOMES IN SELECTED CITIES (2000)

The price of housing varies widely from one part of the country to another. For example, the median price of an existing home is $80,000 in Buffalo, New York, whereas in Miami it is $144,000, and in San Diego it is $269,000.

Location	Median Price	Location	Median Price
Albuquerque, NM	$130,000	Louisville, KY	$129,000
Atlanta, GA	137,000	Miami, FL	144,000
Austin, TX	137,000	Minneapolis-St. Paul, MN	151,000
Baltimore, MD	152,000	New Orleans, LA	112,000
Baton Rouge, LA	109,000	New York, NY	231,000
Birmingham, AL	124,000	Oklahoma City, OK	86,000
Boston, MA	318,000	Orlando, FL	112,000
Buffalo, NY	80,000	Philadelphia, PA	137,000
Charlotte, NC	138,000	Phoenix, AZ	134,000
Chicago, IL	172,000	Portland, OR	170,000
Cincinnati, OH	129,000	Raleigh/Durham, NC	156,000
Columbia, SC	112,000	Richmond, VA	130,000
Columbus, OH	125,000	Saint Louis, MO	126,000
Dallas, TX	102,000	Salt Lake City, UT	142,000
Denver, CO	197,000	San Antonio, TX	96,000
Des Moines, IA	116,000	San Diego, CA	269,000
Hartford, CT	160,000	San Francisco, CA	417,000
Honolulu, HI	295,000	Seattle, WA	220,000
Houston, TX	116,000	Springfield, IL	85,000
Indianapolis, IN	112,000	Syracuse, NY	81,000
Jacksonville, FL	100,000	Tallahassee, FL	123,000
Kansas City, MO/KS	126,000	Toledo, OH	104,000
Las Vegas, NV	137,000	Washington, DC	187,000
Los Angeles, CA	216,000		

Source: National Association of REALTORS®.

or **co-op.** Residents lease their units from the corporation and are assessed monthly in proportion to their ownership shares, which are based on the amount of space they occupy. The assessments cover the cost of service, maintenance, taxes, and the mortgage on the entire building. These are subject to change depending on the actual costs of operating the building and the actions of the board of directors, which determines the corporation's policies. Cooperative owners may find that the value of their ownership interest increases over time as a result of increases in the market value of the property and a reduction in the outstanding loan balance. Because cooperative apartments are not profit-motivated, monthly assessments are likely to be lower than the rent on similar accommodations in a rental unit. Furthermore, the cooperative owner receives the tax benefits resulting from interest and property taxes attributable to his or her proportionate ownership interest.

However, there are also some drawbacks of co-op ownership. First, it may be more difficult to obtain a mortgage because many financial institutions are not satisfied to use

EXHIBIT 5.6

THINGS TO CHECK BEFORE BUYING A CONDO

In the long run, it pays to carefully check out the various operating and occupancy features of a condo before you buy.

- Thoroughly investigate the reputation of the developer—through local real estate brokers, banks, or the Better Business Bureau—whether the building is brand new, under construction, or being converted.
- Read the rules of the organization.
- Investigate the condo homeowners' association, the restrictions on condo owners, and the quality of the property management.
- Check the construction of the building and its physical condition. If the building is being converted to condos, ask to see an independent inspection firm's report on the building's condition.
- Insist that any planned changes in the property be detailed in writing.
- Talk to the occupants to see if they are satisfied with the living conditions.
- Determine how many units are rented; generally, owner-occupied units are better maintained.
- Determine if there is sufficient parking space.
- Watch for unusually low maintenance fees that will probably have to be increased soon.
- Consider the resale value.
- For new developments, compare the projected monthly homeowner's fees with those of similar buildings already in operation.

---

shares of a corporation rather than property as collateral. Second, co-op owners must agree to abide by the decisions of the co-op board of directors when they authorize capital improvements such as roof and plumbing repairs. Such decisions usually involve expense assessments in addition to the normal monthly assessments.

RENTAL UNITS. The forms of housing discussed above represent different ways of achieving home ownership. However, for one reason or another, a large number of individuals and families choose to *rent* or *lease* their place of residence rather than own it. They live in apartments and other types of rental units ranging from duplexes, four-plexes, and even single-family homes to large, high-rise apartment complexes containing several hundred units. These types of housing are popular and widely available. The cost and availability of rental units vary from one geographic area to another.

People choose to rent for a variety of reasons. They may be just starting out and have limited funds for housing, or they may be uncertain where they want to live. Perhaps they like the short-term commitment and limited maintenance. Apartment life does come with restrictions, however. You may not be allowed to have a pet or to make changes to the unit's appearance.

CONCEPT CHECK

> 5-4. In addition to single-family homes, what other forms of housing are available in the United States? Briefly describe the advantages and disadvantages of each.
>
> 5-5. Differentiate between a *condominium* and a *cooperative apartment*.

■ How Much Housing Can You Afford? [LG 3]

Spending many thousands of dollars to buy a home obviously involves a good deal of careful planning and analysis. Not only must you decide on the kind of home you want (its location, number of bedrooms, and so on), you must also consider its cost, what kind of mortgage to get, how large a monthly payment you can afford, what kind of homeowner's insurance coverage to have, and so forth.

Buying a home (or any other major, big-ticket item) touches on many of the elements of personal financial planning. The money you use for a down payment will likely be drawn from your *savings program;* the homeowner's policy you choose is a part of your *insurance planning;* and your monthly mortgage payments undoubtedly will have an enormous impact on your *cash budget* and *tax plans.*

Sound financial planning dictates caution when buying a home or any other major item. Spending too much for a home or automobile can have a detrimental effect not only on your budget and lifestyle, but also on your savings and investment plans, and possibly even your retirement plans. Knowing how much housing you can afford will go a long way toward helping you achieve your financial goals.

MOTIVES FOR OWNING A HOME

Whether it is a detached home or a condominium, home ownership is important to most people. It is preferred over renting for several reasons, the most important of which is probably the basic security and peace of mind derived from living in one's own home—pride of ownership, a feeling of permanence, and a sense of stability. This so-called "psychic reward" is the only reason that many people need to own a home. However, there's also a financial payoff from home ownership.

THE HOME AS A TAX SHELTER. Perhaps the biggest financial payoff from owning a home is the tax shelter it offers. You get a tax break from owning a home because you can deduct both mortgage interest and property taxes when calculating your federal and, in most states, state income taxes. As explained in Chapter 3, mortgage interest (on mortgage loans up to a total of $1,000,000 taken out to buy, build, or improve a principal residence and second home, such as a vacation home, if any) and property taxes can be treated as a tax deduction. Such write-offs reduce your taxable income and thus the amount of taxes you pay. The only requirement is that you itemize your deductions. This tax break is so good that people who have never itemized usually begin doing so after they buy their first house. Also, keep in mind that for the first 15 to 20 years of ownership (assuming a 30-year mortgage), most of your monthly mortgage payment is made up of interest and property taxes—in fact, during the first 5 to 10 years or so, these could well account for *85 to 90 percent of your total payment.* This means you are allowed to write off nearly all of your monthly mortgage payment.

Here is how it works. Suppose you make mortgage payments of $1,000 a month, of which $850 is interest and property taxes. That is $10,200 a year in tax deductions. Assuming you are single with no other itemized deductions, that $10,200 will reduce your taxable income by an additional $5,800 ($10,200 minus your $4,400 standard deduction in 2000). If you are in the 28 percent tax bracket, such a tax deduction will reduce the amount of taxes you pay by an additional $1,624 ($5,800 × .28).

THE HOME AS AN INFLATION HEDGE. Another financial payoff is the *inflation hedge* usually provided by home ownership. An inflation hedge is an investment or asset that appreciates in value at a rate equal to or greater than the rate of inflation. In the mid-to-late 1980s few inflation hedges could match the performance of home ownership. In fact, a home became one of the best investments you could make because it generated a far better return than stocks, bonds, or mutual funds. Many people bought homes simply for their investment value. The rampant inflation and appreciation in home prices came to a halt in the early 1980s and again in the early 1990s. Although many real estate markets were strong in the late 1980s, housing values fell sharply during the recession of the early 1990s. In many areas of the country sellers who had owned their homes for a short time were unable to sell them at a profit.

Today, housing prices in most parts of the country are increasing at a rate about equal to or slightly above the rate of inflation. Because of this and the fact that the inflation rate has declined dramatically, housing prices in most areas are rising at a much slower pace than in the past. Whether a real estate market is "hot" or "cold" is literally a matter of supply and demand. For example, in the Pacific Northwest cities of Portland and Seattle, home prices during the late 1990s escalated sharply as the regional economy boomed and people moved there in increasing numbers. In California home prices sagged in the early 1990s during a prolonged recession, but roared back in the late 1990s with the boom in high technology, entertainment, and other industries replacing the withering defense industry. On the West Coast, the demand for housing exceeded the supply for much of the 1990s.

THE COST OF HOME OWNERSHIP

Although there definitely are some strong emotional and financial reasons for owning a home, there's still the question of whether you can afford to own one. There are two important aspects to the consideration of affordability: You must come up with the down payment and other closing costs and also be able to meet the recurring cash-flow requirements associated with monthly mortgage payments and other home maintenance expenses. In particular, there are five items you should consider when evaluating the cost of home ownership and determining how much home you can afford: (1) the down payment, (2) points and closing costs, (3) mortgage payments, (4) property taxes and insurance, and (5) maintenance and operating expenses.

down payment
A portion of the full purchase price provided by the purchaser when a house or other major asset is purchased; often called *equity*.

loan-to-value ratio
The maximum percentage of the value of a property that the lender is willing to loan.

THE DOWN PAYMENT. The first hurdle is the **down payment.** Most buyers finance a major part of the purchase price of the home, but they also are required by lenders to invest money of their own, called *equity.* The actual amount of down payment required varies among lenders, mortgage types, and properties. To determine the amount of down payment that will be required in specific instances, lenders use the **loan-to-value ratio,** which specifies the maximum percentage of the value of a property that the lender is willing to loan. For example, if the loan-to-value ratio is 80 percent, the buyer will have to come up with a down payment equal to the remaining 20 percent.

A property financed with a high loan-to-value ratio involves only a small percentage of borrower equity. For example, a mortgage that equals 90 to 95 percent of a property's purchase price is a high-ratio loan. It involves only 5 to 10 percent equity dollars; thus, if you buy a $100,000 home with a 95 percent loan-to-value ratio, you need to put down only $5,000 and can finance the other $95,000 through a mortgage.

Generally, first-time home buyers must spend a number of years accumulating enough money to afford the down payment and other costs associated with the home purchase transaction. You can best accumulate these funds if you plan ahead, using future value techniques (presented in Chapters 2, 4, 11, and 14) to determine the monthly or annual savings necessary to have a stated amount by a specified future date. A detailed demonstration of this process is included in Chapter 11 (see Worksheet 11.1B). A disciplined savings program is the best way to obtain the funds to purchase a home or any other big-ticket item requiring a sizable down payment or purchase outlay.

If you do not have enough savings to cover the down payment and closing costs, you can consider several other sources. You may be able to obtain some funds by withdrawing (subject to legal limitations) your contributions from your company's profit-sharing or thrift plan. Your IRA is another option. The *Taxpayer Relief Act of 1997* permits first-time home buyers to withdraw $10,000 without penalty before age $59\frac{1}{2}$. However, using retirement money should be a last resort because you must still pay income tax on retirement distributions. Thus, if you're in the 28 percent income-tax bracket, your $10,000 IRA withdrawal would net you only $7,200 ($10,000 − $2,800) for your down payment.

The Federal National Mortgage Association (known as "Fannie Mae") has several programs to help buyers who have limited cash for the down payment and closing costs. The "Fannie 3/2" program is available from local lenders. Borrowers who meet certain income criteria may qualify for a 95 percent loan-to-value mortgage, and may obtain up to 2 percent of their 5 percent down payment from a public or nonprofit agency or relative. "Fannie 97" helps the home buyer who can handle monthly mortgage payments but doesn't have cash for the down payment. It requires only a 3 percent down payment from the borrower's own funds, and the borrower needs to have only 1 month's mortgage payment in cash savings, or reserves, after closing.

As a rule, when the down payment is less than 20 percent, the lender will require the buyer to obtain **private mortgage insurance (PMI),** which protects the lender from loss if the borrower defaults on the loan. Usually PMI covers the lender's risk above 80 percent of the price of the house. Thus, with a 10 percent down payment, the mortgage will be a 90 percent loan, and mortgage insurance will cover 10 percent of the home's price. The cost of mortgage insurance varies from about 0.5 percent to 1.0 percent of the loan balance each year, depending on the size of your down payment. It can be included in your monthly payment, and the average cost ranges from about $40 to $70 per month. You should contact your lender to cancel the mortgage insurance once the equity in your home reaches 20 to 25 percent. Under federal law, private mortgage insurance on most loans made on or after July 29, 1999, ends automatically once the mortgage is paid down to 78 percent of the original value of the house.

private mortgage insurance (PMI) An insurance policy that protects the mortgage lender from loss in the event the borrower defaults on the loan; typically required by lenders when the down payment is less than 20 percent.

 To find out how much more house you could afford with private mortgage insurance, visit the Mortgage Insurance Companies of America site on this subject: **www.privatemi.com**.

POINTS AND CLOSING COSTS. A second hurdle to home ownership relates to mortgage points and closing costs. **Mortgage points** are fees charged by lenders at the time they grant a mortgage loan. In appearance, points are like interest in that they are a charge for borrowing money. They are related to the lender's supply of loanable funds and the demand for mortgages; the greater the demand relative to the supply, the more points you can expect to pay. One point equals 1 percent of the amount borrowed. If you borrow $100,000, and loan fees equal 3 points, the amount of money you will pay in points will be $100,000 × .03 = $3,000.

mortgage points Fees (one point equals 1 percent of the amount borrowed) charged by lenders at the time they grant a mortgage loan; they are related to the lender's supply of loanable funds and the demand for mortgages.

Lenders typically use points as a way of charging interest on their loans. They can vary the interest rate along with the number of points they charge to create loans with comparable effective rates. For example, a lender might be willing to give you a 7 percent rather than an 8 percent mortgage if you are willing to pay more points; that is, you choose between an 8 percent mortgage rate with 1 point or a 7 percent mortgage with 3 points. If you choose the 7 percent loan, you will end up paying a lot more *at closing* (although the amount of interest paid *over the life of the mortgage* may be considerably less).

Points increase the *effective rate of interest* on a mortgage. The amount you pay in points and the length of time you hold a mortgage determine the increase in the effective interest rate. For example, on an 8 percent, 30-year, fixed-rate mortgage, each point increases the annual percentage rate by about .11 percent if the loan is held for 30 years, .17 percent if held for 15 years, .32 percent if held 7 years, and .70 percent if held 3 years. You pay the same amount in points regardless of how long you keep your home. Therefore the longer you hold the mortgage, the longer the period over which you amortize the points and the smaller the effect of the points on the effective annual interest rate.

According to recent IRS rulings, the points paid on a mortgage at the time a home is originally purchased are usually considered immediately tax deductible. The same points are *not* considered immediately tax deductible if they are incurred when *refinancing* a mortgage; rather, the amount paid in points must be written off (*amortized*) over the life of the new mortgage loan.

closing costs
All expenses (including mortgage points) that borrowers ordinarily pay at the time a mortgage loan is closed and title to the purchased property is conveyed to them.

Closing costs are all expenses that borrowers ordinarily pay at the time a mortgage loan is closed and title to the purchased property is conveyed to them. Closing costs are like down payments: They represent money you must come up with *at the time you buy the house*. Closing costs are made up of such items as (1) loan application fees, (2) loan origination fees, (3) mortgage points (if any), (4) title search and insurance fees, (5) attorneys' fees, (6) appraisal fees, and (7) other miscellaneous fees for things like mortgage taxes, filing fees, inspections, credit reports, and so on.

The loan application and loan origination fees are charges the lender makes for doing all the paperwork; the other charges are associated primarily with fulfilling the legal and credit requirements necessary to complete the home-purchase transaction. As Exhibit 5.7

 EXHIBIT 5.7

THE HIDDEN COSTS OF BUYING A HOME: CLOSING COSTS

The closing costs on a home mortgage loan can be substantial—as much as 5 to 7 percent of the price of the home. Except for the real estate commission (which is generally paid by the seller), the buyer incurs the biggest share of the closing costs and must pay them—in addition to the down payment—at the time the loan is closed and title to the property is conveyed.

	Size of Down Payment	
Item	20%	10%
Loan application fee	$ 200	$ 200
Loan origination fee	800	900
Points	1,600	2,700
Mortgage insurance	—	675
Title search and insurance	500	550
Attorneys' fees	400	400
Appraisal fees	150	150
Home inspection	250	250
Mortgage tax	575	650
Filing fees	25	25
Credit reports	25	25
Miscellaneous	100	100
Total closing costs	$4,625	$6,625

Note: Typical closing costs for a $100,000 home—2 points charged with 20 percent down, 3 points with 10 percent down. Actual amounts will vary by lender and location.

shows, these costs can amount to 50 percent or more of the down payment. For example, with a 10 percent down payment on a $100,000 home, the closing costs, as shown in Exhibit 5.7, are nearly 70 percent of the down payment, or $6,625. A little simple arithmetic also indicates that this buyer will need nearly $17,000 to buy the house (the $10,000 down payment plus another $6,625 in closing costs).

Many first-time home buyers are shocked to find out how much they must pay in closing costs. In many instances *sellers,* by custom or contract, will assume responsibility for some of a buyer's mortgage points and other closing costs. Seldom, however, can a buyer escape all—or even most—of the expenses. At best, the seller will probably pick up just a small percentage (perhaps 10 to 15 percent) of the total amount of the closing costs, leaving the buyer to pay the rest.

MORTGAGE PAYMENTS. The monthly mortgage payment is determined using a fairly complex formula. Each monthly mortgage payment is made up partly of principal repayment on the loan and partly of interest charges. However, as Exhibit 5.8 shows, for most of the life of the mortgage the vast majority of each monthly payment goes to *interest.* The loan illustrated in the exhibit is an $80,000, 30-year, 9 percent mortgage with monthly payments of $643.76. Note that it is not until after the 22nd year of this 30-year mortgage that the principal portion of the loan payment exceeds the amount that goes to interest.

 ## EXHIBIT 5.8

TYPICAL PRINCIPAL AND INTEREST PAYMENT PATTERNS ON A MORTGAGE LOAN

For most of the life of a mortgage loan, the vast majority of each monthly payment goes to interest and only a small portion goes toward principal repayment. Over the 30-year life of the 9 percent, $80,000 mortgage illustrated here, the homeowner will pay more than $150,000 in interest.

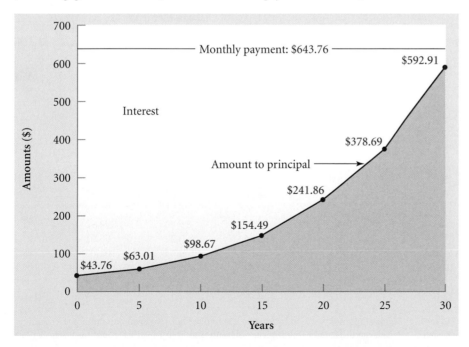

Note: Dollar amounts noted on graph represent the principal amount in the first scheduled payment of the given year.

In practice, mortgage lenders and realtors use *comprehensive mortgage payment tables* to find monthly payments. These tables contain monthly payments for virtually every combination of loan size, interest rate, and maturity. Exhibit 5.9 provides an excerpt from one such comprehensive mortgage payment table (with values rounded to the nearest cent). It lists the *monthly payments* associated with a $10,000, fixed-rate loan for selected maturities of 10 to 30 years and various interest rates ranging from 5 to 13 percent. This table can be used to find the monthly payment for any size loan. Alternatively, you can purchase a relatively inexpensive business calculator for about $30 and quickly and precisely calculate monthly mortgage payments.

Suppose you wish to use the mortgage payment tables to find the monthly loan payment on an $80,000, 9 percent, 30-year mortgage. To do this, simply divide the amount of the loan ($80,000) by $10,000 and then multiply this factor (8.0) by the payment amount shown in Exhibit 5.9 for a 9 percent, 30-year loan ($80.47):

$$\$80,000/\$10,000 = 8.0 \times \$80.47 = \$643.76$$

The resulting monthly mortgage payment would be $643.76.

Using Your Calculator. You can use a handheld business calculator to easily calculate mortgage payments. Before using your calculator, be sure that you've reviewed the instructions given in Chapter 2 on pages 52–53.

 EXHIBIT 5.9

A TABLE OF MONTHLY MORTGAGE PAYMENTS (MONTHLY PAYMENTS NECESSARY TO REPAY A $10,000 LOAN)

The monthly loan payments on a mortgage vary not only by the amount of the loan, but also by the rate of interest and loan maturity.

Rate of Interest	Loan Maturity				
	10 Years	15 Years	20 Years	25 Years	30 Years
5.0%	$106.07	$ 79.08	$ 66.00	$ 58.46	$ 53.68
5.5	108.53	81.71	68.79	61.41	56.79
6.0	111.02	84.39	71.64	64.43	59.96
6.5	113.55	87.11	74.56	67.52	63.21
7.0	116.11	89.88	77.53	70.68	66.53
7.5	118.71	92.71	80.56	73.90	69.93
8.0	121.33	95.57	83.65	77.19	73.38
8.5	123.99	98.48	86.79	80.53	76.90
9.0	126.68	101.43	89.98	83.92	80.47
9.5	129.40	104.43	93.22	87.37	84.09
10.0	132.16	107.47	96.51	90.88	87.76
10.5	134.94	110.54	99.84	94.42	91.48
11.0	137.76	113.66	103.22	98.02	95.24
11.5	140.60	116.82	106.65	101.65	99.03
12.0	143.48	120.02	110.11	105.33	102.86
12.5	146.38	123.26	113.62	109.04	106.73
13.0	149.32	126.53	117.16	112.79	110.62

Note: **To use:** (1) Divide amount of the loan by $10,000, (2) find the loan payment amount in table for the specific interest rate and maturity, and (3) multiply the amount from step 1 by the amount from step 2.

Example: The monthly payment for a $98,000, 9.5 percent, 30-year loan would be (1) $98,000/$10,000 = 9.8; (2) the payment associated with a 9.5 percent, 30-year loan, from table, is *$84.09*; (3) monthly payment required to repay a $98,000, 9.5 percent, 30-year loan is 9.8 × $84.09 = $824.08.

To find the mortgage payment on the $80,000, 9 percent, 30-year mortgage, we must first convert the number of years to months and the annual interest rate to a monthly rate, as follows:

$$\text{Number of months} = 12 \times \text{Number of years} = 12 \times 30 = 360$$
$$\text{Monthly interest rate} = \text{Annual interest rate}/12 = 9\%/12 = .75\%$$

Having made these transformations, we can input the values into our calculator. We use the following steps:

1. Punch in 360 and press **N**.
2. Punch in .75 and press **I**.
3. Punch in 80000 and press **PV**.
4. To calculate the monthly mortgage payment, press **CPT** and then **PMT**. The payment value of 643.70 should appear on the calculator display.

(As noted in Chapter 2, the negative sign can be ignored.) The slightly more precise value of $643.70 agrees with the value calculated earlier using the table of monthly mortgage payments.

Affordability Ratios.   Obviously, the key issue with respect to mortgage payments is *affordability*. To ensure that the financing expenses associated with the purchase of a home are within your budget, you must determine the monthly mortgage payment you can afford. This, in turn, will determine how much you can borrow to finance the purchase of a home.

To obtain a mortgage, a potential borrower must be "qualified"—that is, demonstrate that he or she has an acceptable credit record and adequate income to comfortably make scheduled loan payments. Various federal and private mortgage insurers and institutional mortgage investors have certain standards they expect borrowers to meet to reduce the risk of default. Because of the influence these insurers and investors have on the mortgage market, their guidelines tend to be widely followed.

Probably the most important affordability guideline relates *monthly payments to borrower income.* This is done by comparing (1) the size of the monthly mortgage payment and (2) the borrower's total monthly installment loan payments (which would include payments on automobile loans, furniture loans, and any other consumer installment loan in addition to the mortgage) to monthly income. In this regard the most widely followed ratios for a *conventional mortgage* stipulate that (1) monthly mortgage payments cannot exceed 25 to 30 percent of the borrower's monthly *gross* (before-tax) income, and (2) the borrower's total monthly installment loan payments cannot exceed 33 to 38 percent of monthly gross income. Because both conditions stipulate a range, the lender has some leeway in deciding on the most appropriate ratio for a particular loan applicant.

Here is how these affordability ratios work. Assume your monthly gross income is $4,500. Using the lower end of the ranges (that is, 25 percent and 33 percent) for illustrative purposes, we see that this income level supports mortgage payments of $1,125 a month *so long as total monthly installment obligations do not exceed $1,500.* (These values were found as follows: $4,500 × .25 = $1,125 and $4,500 × .33 = $1,500.) Note that if your other monthly installment loan payments exceeded $375 (the difference between $1,500 and $1,125), your mortgage payment would have to be reduced accordingly. For instance, if you had $500 in other installment payments, your maximum monthly mortgage payment would be $1,500 − $500 = $1,000.

Determining the largest mortgage for which you qualify is just the first step, however. You also need to consider your lifestyle. Will taking on the responsibility of a mortgage require you to perhaps forgo some luxuries or radically change your spending habits? To see how buying a house affects your cash flow, you should revise your personal budget to include the costs of buying a home—monthly mortgage payments, utilities, maintenance, insurance, and so on. Only you can decide how much of your income you are willing to allocate to a mortgage. You may have to make some tradeoffs and may choose a lower-priced house with a smaller mortgage to maintain greater financial flexibility.

PROPERTY TAXES AND INSURANCE. Aside from loan costs, mortgage payments often include property tax and insurance payments. When this occurs, the monthly mortgage payment is made up of four parts, which (1) reduce the *principal* amount of the loan, (2) pay the *interest* on the loan, (3) pay property *taxes,* and (4) pay homeowner's *insurance.* The mortgage payment therefore consists of *p*rincipal, *i*nterest, *t*axes, and *i*nsurance (or **PITI** for short). Actually, that portion of the loan payment that goes for taxes and insurance is paid into an *escrow account,* where it accumulates over time. Then, once or twice a year, the lender draws funds from this account to pay required property taxes and homeowner's insurance premiums. Increases in tax rates or insurance premiums are passed on to the home buyer in the form of higher monthly loan payments.

Interestingly, some but not all lenders pay interest—typically at no higher than the regular savings rate—on escrow account balances. Generally, though, it is advisable for disciplined borrowers to negotiate with the lender to avoid paying into an escrow account. Such a strategy, if successful, gives you greater flexibility and an opportunity to earn a higher return on the funds that would otherwise be held in an escrow account.

Because they are local taxes levied to fund schools, law enforcement, and other local services, the level of **property taxes** differs from one community to another. Within a given community, individual property taxes will vary with the *assessed value* of the real estate—generally, the more expensive the home, the higher the property taxes, and vice versa. As a rule, annual property taxes vary from less than .5 percent to more than 2 percent of a home's approximate market value. Thus the property taxes on a $100,000 home could vary from about $500 to more than $2,000 a year, depending on location and geographic area.

The other component of the monthly mortgage payment is **homeowner's insurance.** Its cost varies with such factors as the age of the house, location, materials used in construction, and geographic area. Homeowner's insurance is carried only on the replacement value of the home and its contents and not on the land. Annual insurance costs usually amount to approximately .25 to .5 percent of the home's market value or from $250 to $500 for a $100,000 house. The types, characteristics, and features of homeowner's insurance policies are discussed in Chapter 10.

MAINTENANCE AND OPERATING EXPENSES. In addition to the monthly mortgage payments, home buyers incur maintenance and operating expenses. Maintenance costs should be anticipated even on new homes. Painting, mechanical and plumbing repairs, and lawn maintenance, for example, are inescapable facts of home ownership. Such costs are likely to be greater, though, for larger, older homes. Thus, although a large, established home may have an attractive purchase price, a new, smaller home may be the better buy in view of its lower maintenance and operating costs.

Another point to consider in the selection process is the cost of operating the home, specifically the cost of utilities such as electricity, gas, water, and sewage. These costs have skyrocketed in the past 10 to 15 years and today represent a sizable component of home ownership costs. Because they are unavoidable and vary with geographic location, type of heating and air conditioning, size of home, amount of insulation, and other factors, you should get operating cost estimates when evaluating a particular home for purchase.

PERFORMING A HOME AFFORDABILITY ANALYSIS

To estimate the amount you can afford for a home, use Worksheet 5.2. This analysis determines the maximum home-purchase price using your monthly income and down payment amount after meeting estimated closing costs.

PITI
Notation used to refer to a mortgage payment that includes stipulated portions of *p*rincipal, *i*nterest, property *t*axes, and homeowner's *i*nsurance.

property taxes
Taxes levied by local governments on the *assessed value* of real estate for the purpose of funding schools, law enforcement, and other local services.

homeowner's insurance
Insurance (required by mortgage lenders) that typically covers the replacement value of a home and its contents.

WORKSHEET 5.2

HOME AFFORDABILITY ANALYSIS FOR THE RENÉE AND PIERRE GOULET FAMILY

By using the following variables in the home affordability analysis form, the Goulets' estimate a maximum home purchase price of about $137,000: their combined annual income of $48,400; the $22,500 available for a down payment and paying all closing costs; estimated monthly taxes and homeowner's insurance of $150; the lender's 28 percent monthly affordability ratio; an average interest rate of 9 percent and expected loan maturity of 30 years; and a minimum down payment of 10 percent.

HOME AFFORDABILITY ANALYSIS*

Name _Renée and Pierre Goulet_ _____ Dated _December 12, 2001_

Item	Description	Amount
1	Amount of annual income	$ 48,400
2	Monthly income (Item 1 ÷ 12)	$ 4,033
3	Lender's affordability ratio (in decimal form)	.28
4	Maximum monthly mortgage payment (PITI) (Item 2 × Item 3)	$ 1,130
5	Estimated monthly tax and homeowner's insurance payment	$ 150
6	Maximum monthly loan payment (Item 4 − Item 5)	$ 980
7	Approximate average interest rate on loan	9%
8	Planned loan maturity (years)	30
9	Mortgage payment per $10,000 (using Item 7 and Item 8 and Table of Monthly Mortgage Payments in Exhibit 5.9)	$ 80.47
10	Maximum loan based on monthly income ($10,000 × Item 6 ÷ Item 9)	$ 121,785
11	Funds available for making a down payment and paying closing costs	$ 22,500
12	Funds available for making a down payment (Item 11 × .67)	$ 15,000
13	Maximum purchase price based on available monthly income (Item 10 + Item 12)	$ 136,785
14	Minimum acceptable down payment (in decimal form)	.10
15	Maximum purchase price based on down payment (Item 12 ÷ Item 14)	$150,000
16	Maximum home purchase price (lower of Item 13 and Item 15)	$ 136,785

*Note: This analysis assumes that $\frac{1}{3}$ of the funds available for making the downpayment and paying closing costs are used to meet closing costs while the remaining $\frac{2}{3}$ are available for a down payment. This assumption means that closing costs will represent an amount equal to 50 percent of the down payment.

Financial Road Sign

Are You Ready to Buy a Home?
If you can answer yes to the following questions, you are probably ready for home ownership:

1. Do you demonstrate a steady level of income and job history (working consistently for at least the last 2 years)? If not, can you explain any gaps?

2. Have you established a favorable credit profile, with a track record of debts owed and repaid on time?

3. Have you saved the money for a cash down payment and closing costs?

4. Are the monthly mortgage payments for the house you want within the lender's limits for both your gross monthly income and your total monthly debt?

Source: "Are You Ready to Buy a Home?" Realtor.com, **www.realtor.com**.

In our example the Renée and Pierre Goulet family had combined annual income of $48,400, and $22,500 available for a down payment and closing costs. They estimated monthly taxes and homeowner's insurance of $150 and expected the mortgage lender to use a 28 percent monthly mortgage-payment affordability ratio, to lend at an average interest rate of 9 percent on a 30-year mortgage, and to require a 10 percent minimum down payment. The Goulets' analysis showed they can afford to purchase a home costing about $137,000.

Let's take a closer look at how the Goulet family came to this conclusion by walking through Worksheet 5.2. The first thing they did was write down their annual income of $48,400 and divide it by 12 to arrive at a monthly income of $4,033 in Item 2. The lender would only consider a mortgage that totaled 28 percent of $4,033, or $1,130 in Item 4. Of the $1,130, $150 are taxes and insurance, leaving a true mortgage of $980 in Item 6. Using Exhibit 5.9, a $10,000 loan for 30 years at 9 percent would result in a monthly payment of $80.47, as indicated in Item 9. How much of a loan would a payment of $980 support? Take $10,000 and multiply by $980/$80.47 to arrive at $121,785 in Item 10. With a down payment of $15,000,

EXHIBIT 5.10

HOW MUCH MORTGAGE WILL YOUR PAYMENT BUY?

This table provides a quick way to estimate the size of the mortgage you can afford based on the monthly mortgage payment and mortgage interest rate. It assumes a 30-year, fixed-rate loan. Remember that this amount is only for mortgage principal and interest; you must have funds available for paying taxes and insurance as well.

Monthly Mortgage Payment	Mortgage Interest Rate							
	6%	7%	8%	9%	10%	11%	12%	13%
$ 500	$ 83,396	$ 75,154	$ 68,142	$ 62,141	$ 56,975	$ 52,503	$ 48,609	$ 45,200
600	100,075	90,185	81,770	74,569	68,370	63,004	58,331	54,240
700	116,754	105,215	95,398	86,997	79,766	73,504	68,053	63,280
800	133,433	120,246	109,027	99,425	91,161	84,005	77,775	72,320
900	150,112	135,277	122,655	111,854	102,556	94,506	87,497	81,360
1,000	166,792	150,308	136,283	124,282	113,951	105,006	97,218	90,400
1,100	183,471	165,338	149,912	136,710	125,346	115,507	106,940	99,440
1,200	200,150	180,369	163,540	149,138	136,741	126,008	116,662	108,480
1,300	216,829	195,400	177,169	161,566	148,136	136,508	126,384	117,520
1,400	233,508	210,431	190,797	173,995	159,531	147,009	136,106	126,560
1,500	250,187	225,461	204,425	186,423	170,926	157,510	145,828	135,599

Note: **To use:** (1) Find the amount of monthly mortgage payment you can afford, to the nearest $100. Then find the current mortgage interest rate to the nearest percent. The approximate mortgage amount will be at the intersection of the two columns. (2) To estimate the mortgage size if the interest rate ends in .5 percent, add the mortgage amounts for the lower and higher mortgage interest rates and divide by 2. (3) To estimate the mortgage size for a payment ending in 50, add the mortgage amounts for the lower and higher monthly mortgage payments and divide by 2.

Examples: (1) The estimated mortgage size if you have a monthly mortgage payment of $900 on a 30-year, 10 percent loan is $102,556. (2) To find the estimated mortgage size if you have a monthly mortgage payment of $900 and the mortgage interest rate is 9.5 percent, add the mortgage sizes for $900 at 9 percent and at 10 percent and divide by 2: ($111,854 + $102,556) ÷ 2 = $214,410 ÷ 2 = $107,205. (3) To find the estimated mortgage size if you have a monthly mortgage payment of $950 and the mortgage interest rate is 9 percent, add the mortgage sizes for $900 and $1,000 at 9 percent and divide by 2: ($111,854 + $124,282) ÷ 2 = $236,136 ÷ 2 = $118,068.

the Goulet family can afford a home costing $136,785 (Item 13). Although the $15,000 down payment would allow purchase of a $150,000 home using a 10 percent down payment as shown in Item 15, the Goulets' maximum home purchase price is limited to $136,785 (Item 16) by their ability to make the monthly payments (Item 13).

Exhibit 5.10 provides a quick way to estimate the size of the mortgage you can afford, based on different monthly mortgage payment and mortgage interest rate assumptions. First, determine the maximum monthly mortgage payment you can handle. Follow that line across to find the approximate size of the mortgage your payment will buy at each mortgage interest rate. (This figure assumes a 30-year, fixed-rate loan and does *not* include taxes and insurance.) For example, if you estimate that you have $1,000 available per month and the prevailing mortgage interest rate is 8 percent, you can afford a mortgage of about $136,000. Of course, the price of the home you can afford to buy also depends on the amount of cash available for making the down payment and paying closing costs.

CONCEPT CHECK

5-6. Briefly describe the various motives for owning a home. Which one is most important to you? Which is least important?

5-7. What does the *loan-to-value ratio* on a home represent? Is the down payment on a home related to its loan-to-value ratio? Explain.

5-8. What are *mortgage points*? How much would a home buyer have to pay if the lender wanted to charge 2.5 points on an $85,000 mortgage? When would this amount have to be paid? What effect do points have on the mortgage's rate of interest?

5-9. What are *closing costs,* and what items do they include? Who pays these costs, and when?

5-10. What are the most common guidelines used to determine the monthly mortgage payment one can afford?

5-11. Why is it advisable for the prospective buyer to investigate property taxes, insurance, maintenance, and operating expenses when shopping for a home? Explain.

■ The Rental Option [LG4]

Many people choose to rent rather than buy their home. For example, young adults usually rent for one or more of the following reasons: (1) They do not have the funds for a down payment and closing costs; (2) they are unsettled in their jobs and family status; (3) they do not want the additional responsibilities associated with home ownership; or (4) they may be able to afford a nicer home later by renting now because housing market conditions or mortgage rates are currently unattractive. A big drawback of renting is that the payments are *not* tax deductible.

THE RENTAL CONTRACT

When you rent an apartment, duplex, house, or any other type of unit, you normally will be required to sign a **rental contract,** or **lease agreement.** Although oral agreements are generally binding, a written contract is a legal instrument that better protects both the *lessor* (the person who owns the property) and the *lessee* (the person who leases the property).

rental contract (lease agreement) A legal instrument that protects both the lessor and the lessee from an adverse action by the other party; it specifies the *amount* of the monthly payment, the payment *date, penalties* for late payment, the *length* of the lease agreement, *deposit* requirements, the distribution of *expenses, renewal* options, and any *restrictions,* for example, on children, pets, subleasing to another tenant, or the use of facilities.

Because the rental contract binds you—the lessee—to various actions, you should make certain that you fully understand it before signing it.

As a rule, the contract specifies the *amount* of the monthly payment, the payment *date*, *penalties* for late payment, the *length* of the lease agreement, *deposit* requirements, the distribution of *expenses, renewal* options, and any *restrictions,* for example, on children, pets, subleasing to another tenant, or the use of facilities.

Most leases have a minimum term of either 6 months or 1 year and require payments at the beginning of each month. They initially require a deposit or payment of the last month's rent as security against damages and violation of the lease agreement. In the absence of any serious damage, most of the deposit should be refunded to the lessee shortly after the lease expires; a portion of the deposit is sometimes retained by the lessor to cover the cost of cleaning and minor repairs, regardless of how clean and well kept the unit is left. Because the landlord has control over the deposit, a written statement describing any damage in evidence *prior* to occupancy may help the lessee avoid losing the entire deposit. Renters should also clarify who bears expenses such as utilities and trash collection and exactly what, if any, restrictions are placed on the use of the property. It's also a good idea for renters to check the various renter-landlord laws in their state to fully understand their *rights* and responsibilities.

THE RENT-OR-BUY DECISION

Today, about 34 percent of all U.S. families live in rented housing and about 66 percent own their own home. The economics of renting or buying a place to live depends, in large part, on three factors: (1) housing prices and mortgage interest rates, (2) tax write-offs for homeowners, and (3) the increase or decrease in home values over time.

To choose the lowest-cost alternative, compare the cost of renting with the cost of buying, as illustrated by the rent-or-buy analysis in Worksheet 5.3. Note that because the interest deduction nearly always exceeds the amount of the standard deduction ($4,400 for single and $7,350 for married filing jointly in 2000), the form assumes the taxpayer will itemize deductions.

Assume that you must decide between renting an apartment for $700 a month or buying a similar-sized, $100,000 condominium. Purchasing the condo involves a $15,000 down payment, an $85,000, 9-percent, 30-year mortgage with monthly mortgage payments of $684 (from Exhibit 5.9, $80.47 × $85,000/$10,000), $4,500 in closing costs, and property taxes, insurance, and maintenance. With renting, the only costs would be the $700 monthly rental payment, an annual renter's insurance premium of $300, and the opportunity cost of interest lost on the security deposit. Assume you will itemize deductions if you purchase the home and that you are in the 28 percent ordinary income tax bracket. Substituting the appropriate values into Worksheet 5.3 and making the required calculations results in the total cost of each alternative.

The cost of renting in part A of Worksheet 5.3 is simply the annual rent (monthly rent multiplied by 12) plus the annual renter's insurance premium of $300 plus the opportunity cost of interest lost on the security deposit. This results in a total annual cost of $8,732. The annual cost of buying in part B includes: mortgage payments, property taxes, homeowner's insurance, annual maintenance, lost interest on the down payment, and closing costs to arrive at $12,386.

Then, subtract the portion of the mortgage payment going to pay off the loan balance because it is not part of the interest cost. Subtract the tax benefits derived from interest and property taxes to arrive at Item 11, the out-of-pocket, after-tax cost of home ownership, $9,126. If you stop there, it looks like renting is the way to go.

But as a homeowner, you enjoy the benefits of appreciation. Assuming a modest 3 percent inflation in the value of the home reduces the annual cost to $6,126. Buying appears

WORKSHEET 5.3

RENT-OR-BUY COST COMPARISON

Using this procedure to make the rent-or-buy decision, you should *rent* if the total cost of renting is less than the total cost of buying, and *buy* if the total cost of renting is more than the total cost of buying. In this illustration, the rental option requires monthly payments of $700. The purchase option is a $100,000 condo, financed with a $15,000 down payment and an $85,000, 9-percent, 30-year mortgage, with additional closing costs of $4,500.

RENT-OR-BUY ANALYSIS

A. COST OF RENTING

1. Annual rental costs
   (12 × monthly rental rate of $ _700_) $ 8,400

2. Renter's insurance   300

3. Opportunity cost of security deposit: $ _700_ × after-tax savings rate _.045_   32

       Total cost of renting (line A.1 + line A.2 + line A.3) $ 8,732

B. COST OF BUYING

1. Annual mortgage payments (Terms: $ _85,000_ , _360_ months, _9_ %) $ 8,208
   (12 × monthly mortgage payment of $ _684_)

2. Property taxes   2,000
   (_2_ % of price of home)

3. Homeowner's insurance   500
   (_.5_ % of price of home)

4. Maintenance   800
   (_.8_ % of price of home)

5. After-tax cost of interest on down payment and closing costs   878
   ($ _19,500_ × _4.5_ % after-tax rate of return)

6. Total costs (sum of lines B.1 through B.5) $ 12,386

Less:

7. Principal reduction in loan balance (see note below) $ 558

8. Tax savings due to interest deductions*   2,142
   (Interest portion of mortgage payments $ _7,650_ × tax rate of _28_ %)

9. Tax savings due to property tax deductions*   560
   (line B.2 × tax rate of _28_ %)

10. Total deductions (sum of lines B.7 through B.9)   3,260

11. Annual after-tax cost of home ownership $ 9,126
    (line B.6 − line B.10)

12. Estimated annual appreciation in value of home   3,000
    (_3_ % of price of home)

       Total cost of buying (line B.11 − line B.12) $ 6,126

Note: Find monthly mortgage payments from Exhibit 5.9. An easy way to approximate the portion of the *annual* loan payment that goes to interest (line B.8) is to multiply the interest rate by the size of the loan (in this case, $85,000 × .09 = $7,650). To find the principal reduction in the loan balance (line B.7), simply subtract the amount that goes to interest from total annual mortgage payments ($8,208 − $7,650 = $558).

*Tax-shelter items.

better than renting because the total cost of renting is $2,606 ($8,732 − $6,126) a year more than the total cost of buying.

However, you should not make the rent-or-buy decision solely on the basis of numbers. Your personal situation and needs and the general condition of the housing market are important considerations. If you think you may want to move to a different city in a few years or you are worried about job security, renting may make sense, even if the numbers favor buying. For some people, factors such as the need for privacy, the desire to personalize one's home, and the psychic satisfaction gained from home ownership outweigh the financial considerations. In some housing markets a relative surplus of rental properties causes the cost of renting to be lower than the cost of owning a comparable house or condominium. It is a good idea to look at the rent-or-buy decision over a time horizon of several years, using different assumptions regarding rent increases, mortgage rates, home appreciation rates in the area, and the rate of return you can earn on the funds you can invest (if you rent) rather than use them for a down payment (if you buy).

CONCEPT CHECK

> 5-12. Why is it important to have a written lease? What should a rental contract include?
>
> 5-13. Discuss the relative advantages and disadvantages of renting a home. Does a homeowner have any advantage over a renter with respect to taxes? Explain.

■ The Home-Buying Process [LG5]

Buying a home usually requires a good deal of time, effort, and money. Learning about the available properties and their prices requires a systematic search and careful property analysis. Also, a buyer should have a basic understanding of the mortgage application process, real estate sales contracts, and other documents required to close a deal.

SHOP THE MARKET FIRST

Most people who shop the housing market rely on real estate agents for information, access to properties, and advice. Other sources of information, such as newspaper ads, also are used widely to identify available properties. Occasionally a person seeking to buy or rent property will advertise his or her needs and wait for sellers to initiate contact. Today the Internet is another valuable resource for home buyers. You may be able to access an online real estate database. By specifying certain preferences—for example, location, price, size—buyers can get lists of properties that meet their needs. Other systems allow buyers to use a touch-tone phone to get a recorded description of homes listed by a particular agency or an electronic kiosk to see and print descriptions and color pictures of homes for sale.

 A great place to begin your home search is at Realtor.com, **www.realtor.com**. From a Real Estate 101 course to lists of local realtors, homes for sale in a particular area, and financing information, this site has it all!

Buying a home involves many factors, both emotional and financial. The emotional factors often carry the greatest weight. As noted earlier, you must begin by figuring out what *you* require for your particular lifestyle in terms of living space, style, and special features. The location, neighborhood, and school district are usually important considerations as well. You should divide your list into *necessary* features, such as the number of bedrooms and baths, and *optional*—but desirable—features. And of course, affordability analysis is a critical component of your housing search.

However, once you start looking, you may find that you like a different house than you thought you originally wanted. For example, you may begin your search by looking for a one-story, contemporary ranch house with a pool, but fall in love with a two-story colonial with wonderful landscaping, no pool, and all the other features you want. It is a good idea to be flexible at first and look at a variety of homes in your price range; this can really help you define your wants and needs more clearly.

If you already own a house but want or need a larger or different type of home, you can either trade up or remodel. You may choose to remodel if you like your neighborhood and can make the desired changes to your current home. In some cases the cost to remodel will be less than the transaction costs of buying another house. The best remodeling projects are those whose costs you can recover when you sell the house. Kitchen improvements, additional bathrooms, and family rooms tend to best enhance a home's market value. Although a swimming pool may give you pleasure, you may not recover its cost when you sell the house.

You are unlikely to find the "perfect" home at the "perfect" price. You will have to make some compromises, and the greater your research and advance preparation, the better off you will be. This approach should help reduce the *buyer's remorse* that often accompanies a major purchase. Soon after signing the sales contract, home buyers often question whether they did the right thing: Did I pay too much? Should I have negotiated harder? Is the location as good as I thought? Can I really afford the monthly payments? Can I manage without a pool, playroom, or workshop? These feelings are normal and usually decrease once you move in. One way to reduce buyer's remorse is to shorten, if possible, the time that elapses between signing the sales contract and closing the deal. Exhibit 5.11 contains 10 tips on how to avoid some common mistakes in the home-buying process.

USING AN AGENT. Most home buyers rely on real estate agents because they are in daily contact with the housing market. Once you describe your needs to an agent, he or she can begin to search for appropriate properties. The agent also will help you negotiate with the seller, obtain satisfactory financing, and, although not empowered to give explicit legal advice, prepare a real estate sales contract.

Most real estate firms belong to the local **Multiple Listing Service (MLS).** Basically, MLS compiles a list of properties for sale from information provided by the member firms in a given community or metropolitan area. A brief description of each property and its asking price are included, and the list is updated daily. As a rule, it is best to deal with a realtor who works for an MLS member firm; otherwise, you might lack access to a large part of the market.

Buyers should remember that *agents typically are employed by the sellers.* Unless you have agreed to pay a fee to the sales agent you are working with, that agent's primary responsibility, by law, is to sell listed properties at the highest possible prices. Further, because agents are paid only if they make a sale, some might pressure you to "sign now or miss the chance of a lifetime." You should avoid that type of agent. Select someone who will listen to your wants and then work to match you with the right property under terms that will benefit both the seller and you. Good agents recognize that their best interests are served when all parties to a transaction are satisfied.

Depending on the geographic location, real estate commissions range from 5 to 6 percent for new homes and 6 to 7 percent for previously occupied homes. It is sometimes possible to negotiate a lower commission with your agent, or to find a discount broker or one

Multiple Listing Service (MLS)
An organization of real estate companies that compiles and updates daily a list and brief description, including asking price, of all properties for sale by the member firms in a given community or metropolitan area.

who charges a flat fee. However, such commissions are paid only by the seller; the buyer pays the real estate agent nothing. Of course, because the price of a home is likely to be affected by the size of the real estate commission—indeed, many builders are believed to factor commission costs into the prices of their new homes—the buyer probably absorbs some or even all of the commission paid by the seller.

 EXHIBIT 5.11

TIPS ON HOW TO AVOID SOME COMMON HOME-BUYING MISTAKES

Buying a home can be an enjoyable and exciting experience. Because it is also the largest single purchase you'll ever make, it can be an intimidating—and even scary—process as well. The following 10 tips will help you feel more confident about embarking on your home-buying adventure.

1. *Think beyond your present needs.* Many first-time buyers, especially those who are single and in their late 20s and early 30s, buy one-bedroom condominiums without considering that they are likely to marry and have families and will therefore require more space.

2. *Choose a reputable agent* who knows the neighborhood where you're looking for a home. If you decide to look in a different area, ask to be referred to a new agent.

3. *Don't look at homes you can't afford;* you will gain nothing, except feeling disappointed by the homes in your price range. When considering what's affordable, don't forget to factor in your debts, property taxes, insurance premiums, private mortgage insurance, the down payment, and maintenance and upkeep costs.

4. *Avoid jumping at the first home you see.* When you begin your search, look at 5, 10, or even 20 houses. You will then have a more seasoned eye, and perhaps your priorities will have changed. Revisit your top three or four choices; you'll be better able to evaluate them and choose with confidence.

5. *Spend some time in the neighborhood* before buying that house you love, to make sure that it's appropriate for you. Are the neighbors your age? Do many have children? Is it a transient neighborhood, or do families tend to stay for a long time? Are schools and shopping nearby? Is there a lot of traffic? Are the streets clean and the walls graffiti-free? Is there a high crime rate?

6. *Try to evaluate how easy it would be for you to resell the house.* If you don't mind living in the evening flight path of the local airport, ask yourself if most potential buyers would. And even if you don't plan to have children, check out the quality of the local schools; that's often a key concern of home buyers.

7. *Have the house thoroughly inspected before you buy.* Don't rely on a realtor's estimate of repair costs. Get a licensed contractor's estimate, then add at least 10 percent to that figure. Most structural problems can be fixed, but major repairs of termite damage, the foundation, or the roof can be quite costly. Don't forget to evaluate the land on which the house is built.

8. *Don't say no to a house that needs some cosmetic repairs.* In fact, such a "fixer-upper" can be a good investment. It will be more reasonably priced than a home in mint condition, and, by completing the work it needs (such as painting, carpeting, or landscaping), you will increase its value.

9. *Avoid a bidding war.* If another buyer makes a bid on the house you want, wait to see what happens, rather than creating a competition that allows the seller to drive up the price.

10. *Read everything,* including the seller's disclosure statement, reports on the property, and especially the sales contract—*before* you sign it! Ask your real estate agent to explain anything you don't understand, and get copies of everything you sign.

Sources: Adapted from Ilyce R. Glink, "Avoid Common Mistakes Made by Many First-Time Home Buyers," *San Diego Union-Tribune,* April 24, 1994, pp. H-7, 12; Dian Hymer, "Ten Common Pitfalls to Avoid When Buying a House," *San Diego Union-Tribune,* April 25, 1993, p. H-3; Dian Hymer, "Perseverance Is Needed in Negotiating a Home Purchase," *San Diego Union-Tribune,* April 24, 1994, pp. H-6, 12.

Two other types of agents can help you buy a house. A *buyer's broker,* as the term implies, is hired by the buyer to negotiate on his or her behalf, whereas the traditional agent represents the seller's interests. The commission to the buyer's broker is typically negotiated and may ultimately be paid by the seller. The *facilitator,* on the other hand, represents neither the buyer nor seller but is paid, typically by both parties, to serve as a neutral intermediary between them.

PREQUALIFYING AND APPLYING FOR A MORTGAGE

Before beginning your home search, it may be helpful to meet with one or more mortgage lenders and prearrange a mortgage loan. **Prequalification,** as it is called, can work to your advantage. You will know ahead of time that you qualify for a specific mortgage amount (subject, of course, to changes in rates and other terms) and can therefore focus your search on homes within an affordable price range. Prequalification also provides estimates of the required down payment and closing costs for different types of mortgages. It identifies in advance of purchase any problems, such as credit report errors, that might arise as a result of your application, and allows you more time to correct them. Finally, prequalification enhances your bargaining power with the seller of a house you want by letting her or him know that the deal won't fall through because you can't afford the property or obtain suitable financing, and that the time required to close the sale should be relatively short.

There are many sources of mortgage loans, and you should begin investigating them while you are looking for your house. When you actually apply for a mortgage loan on a particular home, you will need to give the lender information on your income, assets, and outstanding debts. Documents the lender may request include proof of your monthly income (paycheck stubs, W-2 forms, and so on); statements showing all debt balances (credit cards, car and education loans, bank lines of credit, and so on); lists of financial assets such as savings accounts and securities; several months' bank account statements; and at least 2 years' income tax returns. We will cover financing your home in detail later in the chapter.

prequalification
The process of arranging with a mortgage lender, in advance of buying a home, to obtain the amount of mortgage financing the lender deems affordable to the home buyer.

THE REAL ESTATE SALES CONTRACT

Once you select a home to buy, you must enter into a sales contract. State laws generally specify that to be enforceable in court, real estate buy-sell agreements must be in writing and contain certain information, including (1) names of buyers and sellers, (2) a description of the property sufficient to provide positive identification, (3) specific price and other terms, and (4) usually the signatures of the buyers and sellers. Real estate sales transactions often take weeks and sometimes months to complete. They involve a fair amount of legal work and therefore require expert assistance in preparation. Contract requirements help keep the facts straight and reduce the chance for misunderstanding, misrepresentation, or fraud.

Although these requirements fulfill the minimums necessary for court enforcement, in practice real estate sales contracts usually contain several other contractual clauses relating to earnest money deposits, contingencies, personal property, and closing costs. An **earnest money deposit** is the money you pledge when you make an offer, to show good faith. If, after you sign a sales contract, you withdraw from the transaction without a valid reason, you forfeit this deposit. A valid reason for withdrawal would be one stated in the contract as a contingency clause. With a **contingency clause,** you can condition your agreement to buy on such factors as the availability of financing, a termite or other physical inspection of the property, or the advice of a lawyer or real estate expert. Generally speaking, your lawyer should review and approve all agreements before you sign them.

earnest money deposit
Money pledged by a buyer to show good faith when making an offer to buy a home.

contingency clause
A clause in a real estate sales contract that makes the agreement conditional on such factors as the availability of financing, property inspections, or obtaining expert advice.

CLOSING THE DEAL

Real Estate Settlement Procedures Act (RESPA)
A law that requires mortgage lenders to give potential borrowers a government publication that describes the closing process and to provide clear, advance disclosure of closing costs to home buyers.

After you obtain financing and your loan has been approved, the closing process begins. Although closing expenses still may climb into the thousands of dollars, home buyers can often save significant amounts if they shop for financing, insurance, and other closing items rather than merely accepting the costs quoted by any one lender or other provider of closing services.

The **Real Estate Settlement Procedures Act (RESPA)** governs closings on owner-occupied houses, condominiums, and apartment buildings of four units or fewer. This act reduced closing costs primarily by prohibiting kickbacks made to real estate agents and others from lenders or title insurance companies in conjunction with closing services and by requiring clear, advance disclosure of closing costs to home buyers. Lenders must give potential borrowers a U.S. Department of Housing and Urban Development booklet entitled *Settlement Costs and You: A HUD Guide for Homebuyers.* The booklet sets forth the specific requirements of RESPA and can take much of the mystery out of the closing process.

title check
The research of legal documents and courthouse records to verify that title to a property is free of all liens and encumbrances and the seller conveying title actually has the legal interest he or she claims.

TITLE CHECK. Numerous legal interests can exist in real estate simultaneously: for example, those of the owners, lenders, lienholders (such as an unpaid roofing contractor), and easement holders. Therefore, before you take title to a property, you should make sure the title is free of all liens and encumbrances (except those that are specifically referred to in the sales contract) and that the seller who is conveying title to you actually has the legal interest he or she claims.

Although it is up to you to question the quality of the title to the property you are buying, in most cases an attorney or title insurance company performs a **title check,** which consists of the necessary research of legal documents and courthouse records. The customary practices and procedures and the costs involved vary widely throughout the country. Regardless of the specific custom in your area, you should make some form of title check an essential part of your closing process.

closing statement
A statement provided to both buyer and seller at or before the actual closing that accounts for the monies that change hands during that procedure.

CLOSING STATEMENT. A **closing statement,** provided to both buyer and seller at or before the actual closing, accounts for the monies that change hands during that procedure. The statement reconciles the borrower's and the seller's costs and shows how much the borrower owes and the seller receives from the transaction. Before closing a home purchase transaction, you should be given an opportunity to review the closing statement and have your questions answered. Be sure to carefully and critically review the statement to make sure it is accurate and consistent with the contractual terms of the transaction; if not, have the statement corrected before closing the deal.

CONCEPT CHECK

5-14. Describe some of the steps home buyers can take to improve the home-buying process and increase their overall satisfaction with their purchases.

5-15. What role does a real estate agent play in the purchase of a house? What is the benefit of the *Multiple Listing Service?* How is the real estate agent compensated, and by whom?

5-16. Why should you investigate mortgage loans and prequalify for a mortgage early in the home-buying process?

5-17. What information is normally included in a real estate sales contract? What is an *earnest money deposit?* What is a *contingency clause?*

5-18. Describe the steps involved in closing a home-purchase transaction.

Financing the Transaction [LG6]

The success of a real estate transaction often hinges on obtaining a mortgage with favorable terms. Earlier in the chapter, we saw that mortgage terms can have a dramatic effect on the amount you can afford to spend on a home.

A **mortgage loan** is secured by the property. This means that in the event of default by the borrower the lender obtains the legal right to liquidate the property to recover the funds it is owed. To obtain such a loan, you must be familiar with the available sources and types of mortgage loans. It is also helpful to understand the economics of mortgage refinancing.

SOURCES OF MORTGAGE LOANS

The major sources of home mortgages today are commercial banks, thrift institutions, and mortgage bankers or brokers. Some *credit unions* also make mortgage loans available to their members. During the past few years, *commercial banks,* formerly viewed primarily as short-term lenders, have become a major force in the residential mortgage market. Commercial banks also are an important source of *interim construction loans* used by persons who are building or remodeling a home. These loans provide short-term financing during the construction period. After the home is completed, the homeowner obtains *permanent financing,* in the form of a standard, long-term, first mortgage loan, and uses the proceeds from it to repay the construction loan.

Thrift institutions include *savings and loan associations (S&Ls)* and *savings banks.* S&Ls may use customers' deposits to make loans or originate and sell loans to private investors. S&Ls concentrate on first mortgage loans on one- to four-family dwellings although some actively participate in the commercial real estate market as well. Although their lending policies are dictated by regulators and mortgage market conditions, their terms are often more attractive than those of other mortgage lenders. Until recently, S&Ls were the largest source of home mortgages. Due to problems in the thrift industry, many home buyers, concerned about having a long-term loan with an S&L that might not be around in a few years, have turned to other mortgage lenders.

Savings banks, 90 percent of which are located in the Northeast, direct a lot of their mortgage-lending money to their depositors. Because they are most often *mutual* organizations, and therefore depositor-owned, the terms of their mortgage loans tend to be slightly more favorable than those made by commercial banks and S&Ls.

Another way to obtain a mortgage loan is through a mortgage banker or mortgage broker. Both solicit borrowers, originate loans, and place them with mortgage lenders such as life insurance companies and pension funds. Whereas **mortgage bankers** often use their own money to initially fund mortgages they later resell, **mortgage brokers** take loan applications and then find lenders willing to grant the mortgage loans under the desired terms. Another difference is that mortgage bankers deal primarily in government-insured and government-guaranteed loans, whereas mortgage brokers concentrate on finding conventional loans for consumers.

USING A MORTGAGE BROKER. A mortgage broker can save you the time and inconvenience of talking with a large number of lenders. Brokers typically have computer programs that help you compare the effective costs of loans with different terms. Most brokers have ongoing relationships with many different types of lenders, thereby increasing your chances of finding a loan even if you would not qualify at a commercial bank or thrift institution. They can often simplify the financing process by cutting through red tape, negotiating more favorable terms, and reducing the amount of time to close the loan.

mortgage loan
A loan secured by real property; in the event of default by the borrower the lender obtains the legal right to liquidate the property to recover the funds it is owed.

mortgage banker
A firm that solicits borrowers, originates primarily government-insured and government-guaranteed loans, and places them with mortgage lenders; often uses its own money to initially fund mortgages it later resells.

mortgage broker
A firm that solicits borrowers, originates primarily conventional loans, and places them with mortgage lenders; merely takes loan applications and then finds lenders willing to grant the mortgage loans under the desired terms.

However, not all mortgage brokers are competent. Some have been known to misrepresent the services they can provide or recommend a loan that might not be best suited to their clients' needs. Before working with a particular mortgage broker, carefully investigate the firm and its reputation. Realtors, bankers, and other buyers can provide leads to good brokers. To help you get the best rate and terms, the broker should represent 10 or more lenders from around the United States. Ask potential brokers how many of their loan applications are actually funded; about 70 percent or more should result in closings. If your state licenses mortgage brokers, be sure to choose one that is licensed and has been in business for several years. Many brokers are certified by the National Association of Mortgage Brokers although this is not a requirement. You should also request a written estimate of closing costs; most competent brokers will provide this information and justify each cost.

Most mortgage brokers earn their income from commissions and origination fees paid by the lender. These lender costs are typically passed on to the borrower in the points charged on the loan. The borrower often must pay application, processing, and document preparation fees to the lender at closing. If a loan has no points, the buyer may have to pay a fee directly to the broker, which should be paid at closing. A broker who asks for up-front fees and promises to find a loan is one to avoid.

Rather than use a mortgage broker, you may wish to shop for a mortgage on your own or with the assistance of your realtor, who is usually a knowledgeable source of information about various lenders and is legally prohibited from collecting fees or kickbacks for helping to arrange financing.

ONLINE MORTGAGE RESOURCES. Shopping for the best mortgage rate has become a lot easier, thanks to the Internet. Many sites allow you to search for the best fixed-rate or adjustable-rate rate mortgage in your area. HSH Associates, a mortgage consulting firm, has a Web site at **www.hsh.com** that lists mortgages offered by banks, mortgage companies, and brokerage firms across the country, along with information on prevailing interest rates, terms, and points. Bank Rate, **www.bankrate.com**, and similar sites also offer mortgage comparisons. Shopping via the Internet gives you tremendous leverage when dealing with a lender. For example, if a local mortgage lender offers a 3-year adjustable-rate mortgage (ARM) with 1.20 points and a 6.75 percent rate, but a lender in a different state offers the same term with the same rate and only 1 point, you can negotiate with your local lender to get a better deal.

Although the Internet is still primarily a source of comparative information, online lenders hope that home buyers will also choose to apply for and close a loan online. E-LOAN, **www.eloan.com**, is a large online-only mortgage bank. Submit your information to LendingTree, **www.lendingtree.com**, and within 24 hours you'll receive bids from four lenders interested in making your loan. HomeAdvisor's Loan Direct, **www.homeadvisor.com**, provides quick information from online lenders about loans and rates available based on your finances and loan needs and preferences. You can even use its Mortgage Direct service to get pre-approved online in a matter of minutes.

 Enter your state and Mortgage Locator, **www.mortgagelocator.com**, will provide a list of online mortgage lenders in your area. The site also has a rate watch service that notifies you when a lender has the rate you want.

TYPES OF MORTGAGE LOANS

There is no single way to classify mortgages. For our purposes, we will group them in two ways: (1) terms of payment and (2) whether they are conventional, insured, or guaranteed.

As far as terms of payment are concerned, there are literally dozens of different types of home mortgages from which to choose. The most common types of mortgage loans made today are fixed-rate and adjustable-rate mortgages. We now will take a closer look at these mortgages, their features, advantages, and disadvantages.

FIXED-RATE MORTGAGE. In spite of the fact that since 1975 a number of other types of mortgages have been developed, marketed, and popularized, the **fixed-rate mortgage** still accounts for a large portion of all home mortgages written. In this mortgage both the rate of interest and the monthly mortgage payment are fixed over the full term of the loan. The most common type by far is the *30-year fixed-rate* loan. Because of the risks the lender assumes in this type of mortgage, it is usually the most expensive form of home financing.

A variation of this standard fixed-rate mortgage that is gaining in popularity is the *15-year fixed-rate* loan. Its chief appeal is that it is repaid twice as fast (15 years versus 30) and yet the monthly payments don't increase significantly. Obviously, to pay off a loan in less time, the homeowner pays more each month. But the big (pleasant) surprise is that it does not take twice as large a monthly payment to pay off the loan in half the time; rather, the monthly payment on a 15-year loan is generally only about 20 percent larger than the payment on a 30-year loan. The following table compares the basic features of 30- and 15-year fixed-rate mortgages. In both cases the purchaser borrows $80,000 at a 9 percent fixed rate of interest:

Term of Loan	Regular Payment	Total Interest Paid over Life of Loan
30 years	$643.76 per month	$151,754
15 years	$811.44 per month	$ 66,059

Perhaps the most startling feature is the substantial difference in the total amount of interest paid. In effect, you can save *about $85,000* just by financing your home with a 15-year mortgage rather than a traditional 30-year mortgage—not bad, considering it is only an $80,000 loan. Note that this amount of savings is possible even though monthly payments differ by about $168. In practice the difference in monthly payment would be even less because 15-year mortgages are usually available at interest rates that are about half a percentage point below comparable 30-year loans. Thus, if the 30-year mortgage carried a 9 percent rate, you would expect the 15-year loan to be priced at, say, 8.5 percent. The monthly payments would then amount to only $788 rather than $811—a more realistic difference in monthly payments of *$144* ($788 − $644).

Although the idea of paying off a mortgage in 15 years instead of 30 may seem like a good one, you should first consider how long you plan to stay in the house. If you plan to sell the house in a few years, paying off the loan faster may not make much sense. In addition, the tax deductibility of mortgage interest makes a mortgage one of the least expensive sources of borrowing. You should also determine whether you can earn a higher rate of return on the increase in the monthly payment for a 15-year mortgage than the rate of interest on the loan. If so, you would be better off investing the difference and taking a 30-year loan. You can also shorten the mortgage term by making extra principal payments on a regular basis or at times when you have extra funds, without committing to the shorter term.

Some lenders offer other types of fixed-rate loans. The term of a **balloon-payment mortgage** is often 5, 7, or 10 years. The interest rate is fixed, typically at .25 to .5 percent below the 30-year fixed rate. The monthly payments are the same as for a 30-year loan at the given rate. When the loan matures, the remaining principal balance comes due and must be refinanced. Although the lower rate results in lower monthly payments, these loans have some risk because it may be difficult to refinance them in the future, particularly if rates have risen.

fixed-rate mortgage
The traditional type of mortgage, in which both the rate of interest and the monthly mortgage payment are fixed over the full term of the loan.

balloon-payment mortgage
A mortgage with a single, very large mortgage principal payment due at a specified future date.

adjustable-rate mortgage (ARM)
A mortgage on which the rate of interest, and therefore the size of the monthly payment, is adjusted up and down in line with movements in market interest rates.

adjustment period
On an adjustable-rate mortgage, the period of time between rate or payment changes.

index rate
On an adjustable-rate mortgage, the baseline index rate that captures interest rate movements.

margin
On an adjustable-rate mortgage, the percentage points a lender adds to the *index rate* to determine the rate of interest.

interest rate cap
On an adjustable-rate mortgage, the limit on the amount that the interest rate can increase each adjustment period and over the life of the loan.

payment cap
On an adjustable-rate mortgage, the limit on the monthly payment increase that may result from a rate adjustment.

ADJUSTABLE-RATE MORTGAGE. Another popular form of home loan is the **adjustable-rate mortgage (ARM).** The rate of interest, and therefore the size of the monthly payment, is adjusted up and down in line with market interest rate movements. The mortgage interest rate is linked to a specific *interest rate index* and adjusted at specific intervals (usually once or twice a year) in accordance with changes in the index. When the index moves up, so does the interest rate on the mortgage and, in turn, the size of the monthly mortgage payment. The new interest rate and monthly mortgage payment will then remain fixed until the next adjustment date.

The term of an ARM is usually 30 years but can be 15 years. Because the size of the monthly payments will vary with interest rates, there is no way to tell what your future payments will be. However, because the borrower or home buyer assumes most or all of the interest rate risk in these mortgages, the *initial* rate of interest on an adjustable-rate mortgage is normally well below—2 to 3 percentage points—the rate on a standard 30-year fixed-rate loan. Of course, whether or not the borrower actually will end up paying less interest depends on the behavior of market interest rates during the term of the loan.

Basic Features. A home buyer should understand several basic ARM features:

- *Adjustment period:* The period of time between one rate or payment change and the next; typically 6 months or 1 year, although adjustment periods can range from 3 months to 3 or 5 years.
- *Index rate:* A baseline rate that captures the movement in interest rates. This can be tied to 6-month U.S. Treasury securities, 6-month CDs, or the average cost of funds—as measured by rates paid on CDs, savings accounts, and other investments— to savings institutions, commonly measured by the *11th Federal Home Loan Bank District Cost of Funds.*
- *Margin:* The percentage points a lender adds to the index to determine the rate of interest on an ARM; usually a fixed amount over the life of the loan. Thus *the rate of interest on an ARM equals the index rate plus the margin.* If the index at the time the loan is made is 5.5 percent and the lender charges a 2 percent margin, the initial loan is a 7.5 percent mortgage (5.5 percent + 2 percent = 7.5 percent). If the index rate rises to 6.5 percent at the next adjustment period, the interest rate on the loan rises to 8.5 percent (6.5 percent + 2 percent).
- *Interest rate caps:* Limits on the amount the interest rate can increase over a given period that protect the borrower from extreme increases in interest rates and monthly payments. *Periodic caps* limit the interest rate increase from one adjustment to the next, but *overall caps* limit the interest rate increase over the life of the loan. Many ARMs have both periodic and overall interest rate caps. Typically lenders cap *annual* rate adjustments at 1 to 2 percentage points and set lifetime interest rate caps at 5 to 8 percentage points.
- *Payment caps:* Limits on the monthly payment increase that may result from a rate adjustment—usually a percentage of the previous payment. If your ARM has a 5 percent payment cap, your monthly payments can increase no more than 5 percent from 1 year to the next—regardless of what happens to interest rates.

Because most ARMs are 30-year loans, you can determine the initial monthly payment in the same manner as for any other 30-year mortgage. For example, for an $80,000 loan at 7.5 percent (5.5 percent index rate + 2 percent margin), we can use Exhibit 5.9 to find the first-year monthly payment of $559.44. Assuming a 1-year adjustment period, if the index rate rises to 7 percent, the interest rate for the second year will be 9 percent (7 percent + 2 percent = 9 percent). The size of the monthly payment for the next 12 months will then be adjusted upward to about $642.34. This process repeats each year thereafter until the loan matures.

Beware of Negative Amortization. Some ARMs are subject to **negative amortization**—an increasing principal balance resulting from monthly loan payments that are lower than the amount of monthly interest being charged. In other words, with some of these loans you can wind up with a larger mortgage balance on the next anniversary of the loan than on the last. This occurs either when the initial payment is intentionally set below the interest charge or when the ARM has interest rates that adjust monthly although the actual monthly payment can be adjusted only annually. In this latter case, when rates are rising on these loans, the current monthly payment can be less than the interest being charged, and the difference is added to the principal, thereby increasing the size of the loan. ARMs with a cap on the dollar amount of monthly payments can also lead to negative amortization.

For example, assume the monthly payment on a 7.5 percent, 30-year, $80,000 loan is currently $560 and the loan's next annual adjustment is in 10 months. If, as a result of rising interest rates, the applicable interest rate increases to 9 percent (that is, .75 percent per month), the monthly interest owed would be $600 (.75 percent $\times$ $80,000). Thus negative amortization would occur in the amount of $40 per month ($600 interest − $560 monthly payment). If no other interest rate changes were to occur over the 10 months remaining until the next annual adjustment, at that time the mortgage balance would be $80,400—the increase of $400 is attributable to the $40 per month negative amortization over the 10 months.

When considering an ARM, be sure to learn whether negative amortization can occur. Generally, loans without the potential for negative amortization are available although they tend to have slightly higher initial rates and interest rate caps.

Other Types of ARMs. Some lenders offer **convertible ARMs,** loans that allow borrowers to convert from an adjustable-rate to a fixed-rate loan, usually at any time between the thirteenth and the sixtieth month. Although these loans seldom provide the lowest initial rate, they allow the borrower, for a fee, to convert to a fixed-rate loan if interest rates decline. A conversion fee of around $500 is typical, and the fixed rate is normally set at .25 to .5 percent above the going rate on fixed-rate loans at the time you convert. Borrowers who like the generally low initial ARM rates and feel that interest rates will decline during the first 60 months or so of the loan may find the convertible ARM an attractive compromise between a fixed-rate and an adjustable-rate loan.

With a **two-step ARM,** the ARM has just two interest rates The first is set for an initial period of 5 to 7 years. The rate then steps up for the remaining term of the loan.

Choosing an Index. The index on your ARM significantly affects the level and stability of your mortgage payments over the term of the loan. With the demise of the 1-year U.S. Treasury bill, formerly one of the most common indexes used by lenders, lenders have turned to other short-term indexes, including LIBOR (the *London Inter Bank Offering Rate,* a base rate similar to the prime rate but used in the international marketplace). Recently, some lenders have begun to use CD-based indexes. The 11th Federal Home Loan Bank District Cost of Funds is popular in the western United States although the use of cost of funds indexes is gaining in other parts of the country as well.

The most important difference between the indexes is their volatility. LIBOR and CD rates are quite volatile because they quickly respond to changes in the financial markets. The 11th District Cost of Funds index is much less volatile because it represents an average of the cost of funds to S&Ls in the District. It tends to lag other short-term rate movements, both up and down, and exhibits a fairly smooth pattern over time. To more fully understand how one particular index behaves relative to another, you may want to compare the index rates over the past several years.

So what does this mean for the home buyer considering an ARM? If your mortgage is tied to a LIBOR or CD index, you can expect sharper and more frequent upward and downward

negative amortization
When the principal balance on a mortgage loan increases because the monthly loan payment is lower than the amount of monthly interest being charged; some ARMs are subject to this undesirable situation.

convertible ARM
An adjustable-rate mortgage loan that allows borrowers to convert from an adjustable-rate to a fixed-rate loan, usually at any time between the 13th and the 60th month.

two-step ARM
An adjustable-rate mortgage with just two interest rates: one for the first 5 or 7 years of the loan, and another for the remaining term of the loan.

interest rate movements. On the other hand, cost of funds indexes move more slowly in both directions. To choose which is better for you, consider the annual rate cap on a particular mortgage, the relative level of interest rates, and your future interest rate expectations. If you have a low rate cap of about 1 to 2 percentage points and you think rates are going down, you may be comfortable with a more volatile index.

Some lenders offer special first-year "teaser" rates that are set below the index rate on the loan. Be wary of lenders who advertise very low rates; ask them if the first-year rate is based on the index and then verify the rate for yourself. Be sure you can comfortably make the monthly mortgage payment when the interest rate steps up to the indexed rate.

Monitoring Your Mortgage Payments. You should carefully monitor your mortgage over its life. Always verify the calculation of your loan payment when rate or payment adjustments are made. To verify your payment amount, you need to know the index rate, the margin, and the loan formula used to make the adjustment; all are found in the loan agreement. The interest rates for the most commonly used indexes are readily available in the financial press and are published weekly in the real estate section of most newspapers. The loan formula tells you when the rate is set—for example, 45 days before the adjustment date—and the margin on the loan. You can use a handheld business calculator (as described earlier) to calculate the payment once you know the new rate, the number of years until the loan is paid off, and the current principal balance.

If you suspect you are being overcharged, call your lender and ask for an explanation of the rate and payment calculations. Special mortgage checking services will review your ARM for a fee of about $70 to $100.

FIXED-RATE OR ADJUSTABLE-RATE? Fixed-rate mortgages are popular with home buyers who plan to stay in their homes for at least 5 to 7 years and want to know what their payments will be. Of course, the current level of interest rates and your expectation about future interest rates will significantly affect your choice of a fixed-rate or adjustable-rate mortgage. In 1984 when the average interest rate on a 30-year mortgage loan was a historically high 13.76 percent, many people chose adjustable-rate mortgages to avoid being locked in to the then-prevailing high rates. In early 2001 the average interest rate range on fixed-rate loans was just below 7 percent for 30 years, whereas the average ARM interest rate was 6.5 percent. Many home buyers chose fixed-rate mortgages at these attractive rates, and others with existing adjustable-rate mortgages refinanced them with fixed-rate loans to lock in the low rates. But even when interest rates are low, as they were in 2001, the choice between a fixed-rate and an adjustable-rate mortgage can be difficult. As the *Money in Action* box on page 213 shows, experts disagree.

OTHER PAYMENT OPTIONS. In addition to standard fixed-rate and adjustable-rate mortgage loans, some lenders offer variations designed to help first-time home buyers such as the following plans:

graduated-payment mortgage
A mortgage that starts with unusually low payments that rise over several years to a fixed payment.

growing-equity mortgage
Fixed-rate mortgage with payments that increase over a specific period. The extra funds are applied to the principal so the loan is paid off more quickly.

shared-appreciation mortgage
A loan that allows a lender or other party to share in the appreciated value when the home is sold.

- **Graduated-payment mortgages** are loans with unusually low payments for the first few years that gradually rise until year three or five, then remain fixed. The low initial payments appeal to people who are just starting out and expect their income to rise. If this does not occur, however, it could result in a higher debt load than the borrower can handle.
- **Growing-equity mortgages** are fixed-rate mortgages with payments that increase over a specific period. The extra funds are applied to the principal so a conventional 30-year loan would be paid off in about 20 years. However, you can accomplish the same thing without locking yourself into a set schedule by taking a fixed-rate mortgage that allows prepayments.

MONEY IN ACTION

Twist My ARM?

The low interest-rate environment of the 1990s and early 2000s created a boom time for fixed-rate mortgages. And no wonder. Borrowers like the idea of locking in 7 percent interest rates for 15 or 30 years. Anyone who is old enough to remember the 1970s, when interest rates were more than double current levels, knows that low interest rates don't last forever. But ARMs can still be attractive even with a narrow gap between fixed-rate and adjustable-rate home financing. The savings, even if just a percent or two, may offset the risk that interest rates will rise sharply over the next several years.

In today's interest rate environment, however, the ARM has not offered a risk worth taking. From mid-2000 to early 2001, at times the spread was only 0.125 percent in some parts of the country, and in February 2001 the average ARM was about 6.5 percent, versus the 7.0 percent fixed rate. "The current gap between fixed-rate mortgages and 1-year adjustable-rate mortgages is the narrowest it has been since at least March 1983," said Keith Gumbinger, analyst at HSH Associates, which publishes mortgage information.

If you opt for an ARM and interest rates go up, you could soon be paying well above the fixed rate. With most ARMs, banks can adjust the rate as much as 2 percent per year, and up to 6 percent over the life of the mortgage. So your 6.5 percent initial rate could jump to 8.5 percent, 10.5 percent, and so on. Will interest rates go up? No one really knows. At least with a fixed-rate mortgage, you know where you stand month in and month out. That's one of the reasons why fixed-rate mortgages are more popular than ARMs, making up 75 percent of all mortgages.

Budget stability means a lot. If you choose an ARM and inflation re-ignites, boosting interest rates, then your mortgage payment could rise beyond your ability to pay. Most people's mortgage is their biggest budget item. You don't want your largest monthly expense to go through the roof due to factors beyond your control.

So why choose an ARM? Interest rate spreads will not always be so slim. When the rate spread is larger, ideally 2 to 2.5 percent, ARMs are cheaper than fixed-rate mortgages. And even a 1.5 percent spread can save you money. That may not seem like much, but choosing a 5.5 percent ARM instead of a 7 percent fixed rate on a $100,000 loan saves about $1,500 per year. And for every year that your ARM rate stays below 7 percent, short-term rates would have to go above 7 percent to break even with your fixed-rate loan. For example, if for the first 3 years of your mortgage short-term rates are 5.5 percent, 6.0 percent, and 6.5 percent, then rates would have to be 7.5 percent, 8.0 percent, and 8.5 percent for the next three years before your ARM even approached the fixed-rate loan's 7 percent annual interest expense.

Another reason to consider an ARM is that there are more attractive options today compared with a few years ago. You can now find ARMs that don't adjust for 5 or 7 years. That's particularly good if you think you'll be trading up to a new house in the next few years.

Sources: Adapted from Nancy Boles, "Take the Fixed," *Money Matters,* December 1997, p. 4; Ira Carnahan, "Forget the Spread," *Forbes,* January 22, 2001, p. 142; Denise Fields, "Go with the Adjustable," *Money Matters,* December 1997, p. 4; and Pamela Yip, "Adjustable-Rate Loans Out for Now", *Arizona Republic,* October 13, 2000, p, D2.

- **Shared-appreciation mortgages** are loans that have a below-market interest rate because the lender or other party shares from 30 to 50 percent of the appreciated value when the home is sold. This can be a useful tool if you absolutely cannot afford the higher rates on a conventional loan, but keep in mind that with appreciation of only 2 percent per year for just 5 years, such a loan could cost you up to $5,000 in shared equity on a $100,000 property.
- **Biweekly mortgages** are loans on which payments equal to half of a regular monthly payment are made every 2 weeks rather than once a month. Because you make 26 payments (52 weeks/2), which is the equivalent of 13 monthly payments, the principal balance declines at a faster rate, and you pay less interest over the life of the

biweekly mortgage
A loan on which payments equal to half the regular monthly payment are made every 2 weeks.

loan. Once again, with most 30-year mortgages you can make extra principal payments at any time, without penalty. This may be better than committing to a biweekly mortgage, which often charges an extra processing fee.

- **Buy-downs** are a type of seller financing sometimes offered on new homes. A builder or seller arranges for mortgage financing with a financial institution at interest rates well below market rates—8 percent financing on his homes at a time when the market rate of interest is around 9 or 9.5 percent. Typically the builder or seller subsidizes the loan, giving the buyer the impression that he or she can finance a home bought from him at a special low interest rate. However, the reduced interest rate may be for only a short period or the buyer will pay for the reduced interest in the form of a higher purchase price.

buy-down
Financing made available by a builder or seller to a potential new-home buyer at well below-market interest rates, often only for a short period.

conventional mortgage
A mortgage offered by a lender who assumes all the risk of loss; typically requires a down payment of at least 20 percent of the value of the mortgaged property.

FHA mortgage insurance
A program under which the Federal Housing Administration (FHA) offers lenders mortgage insurance on loans having a high loan-to-value ratio; its intent is to encourage loans to home buyers who have very little money available for a down payment and closing costs.

VA loan guarantee
A guarantee offered by the U.S. Veterans Administration to lenders who make qualified mortgage loans to eligible veterans of the U.S. Armed Forces and their unmarried surviving spouses.

CONVENTIONAL, INSURED, AND GUARANTEED LOANS. A **conventional mortgage** is a mortgage offered by a lender who assumes all the risk of loss. To protect themselves on this type of mortgage, lenders usually require a down payment of at least 20 percent of the value of the mortgaged property. (For lower down payments, the lender usually requires *private mortgage insurance,* as described earlier in the chapter.) Experience has shown that high borrower equity greatly lessens the chance of default on a mortgage and subsequent loss to the lender. However, such a high down payment requirement makes home buying more difficult for many families and individuals.

To promote home ownership, the federal government, through the Federal Housing Administration (FHA), offers lenders mortgage insurance on high loan-to-value ratio loans. These loans usually feature low down payments, below-market interest rates, few if any points, and relaxed income or debt ratio qualifications.

The **FHA mortgage insurance** program helps people buy homes even when they have very little money available for a down payment and closing costs. In exchange for a mortgage insurance premium of 2.25 percent of the loan amount—which is paid by the borrower at closing or included in the mortgage—plus another .5 percent annual renewal fee, the FHA agrees to reimburse lenders for losses up to a specified maximum amount if the buyer defaults. The minimum required down payment on an FHA loan is 3 percent on the first $25,000 plus 5 percent on the amount over $25,000. The interest rate on an FHA loan is generally about .5 percent to 1 percent lower than the rate on conventional fixed-rate loans. The affordability ratios used to qualify applicants for these loans are typically less stringent (i.e., higher) than those used for conventional loans. The maximum mortgage amount the FHA can insure is based on the national *median* price of homes and varies depending on location.

Guaranteed loans are similar to insured loans but better—if you qualify. **VA loan guarantees** are provided by the U.S. Veterans Administration to lenders who make qualified mortgage loans to eligible veterans of the U.S. Armed Forces and their unmarried surviving spouses. This program, however, does not require lenders or veterans to pay a premium for the guarantee. In many instances an eligible veteran must pay only closing costs; in effect, under such a program, a veteran can buy a home with no down payment. (This can be done *only once* with a VA loan.) The mortgage loan—subject to a maximum of about $200,000—can amount to as much as 100 percent of a purchased property's appraised value. VA loans include a 2 percent funding fee (which is lower if the down payment is 5 percent or more). The VA sets the maximum interest rate, which, like FHA loans, is usually about .5 percent below the rate on conventional fixed-rate loans. To qualify, the veteran's maximum monthly installment loan payment ratio can be equal to 41 percent of monthly *gross* income. The VA loan guarantee is an important fringe benefit available to those who have served in the armed forces.

You should also check into the availability of other special mortgage loan programs sponsored by state and local public agencies. Like FHA and VA mortgage programs, these typically offer below-market interest rates and reduced down payment requirements.

REFINANCING YOUR MORTGAGE

Sometimes, after you've purchased a home and closed the transaction, interest rates on similar loans drop. If rates drop by 1 to 2 percent or more, you should consider the economics of refinancing. Many people who obtained mortgage loans during periods of high interest rates found refinancing attractive when rates dropped in 1991–1993, 1996–1998, and again in 2001. Loans with fixed rates as high as 13 percent could be refinanced for fixed rates as low as 6.75 percent.

The decision to refinance should be made after carefully considering the terms of the old and new mortgages, the anticipated number of years you expect to remain in the home, any prepayment penalty on the old mortgage, and the closing costs associated with the new mortgage.

Worksheet 5.4 presents a form that can be used to analyze the impact of refinancing. The data for the Philipatos family's analysis is shown. Their existing 10 year-old, 12 percent mortgage, with original principal of $80,000, has a current balance of $74,250 and monthly payments of $823 per month for 20 more years. If they refinance the $74,250 balance at the prevailing rate of 9 percent over the remaining 20-year life of the current mortgage, the monthly payment would drop to $668. The Philipatoses are very happy with their house and plan to live there for at least 5 more years. They will not have to pay any penalty for prepaying

WORKSHEET 5.4

MORTGAGE REFINANCING ANALYSIS FOR THE PHILIPATOS FAMILY

Using the form below, the Philipatoses find that by refinancing the $74,250 balance on their 10-year-old, $80,000, 12-percent, 30-year mortgage (which has no prepayment penalty and requires payments of $823 per month) with a 9-percent, 20-year mortgage requiring $668 montly payments and $2,400 in total after-tax closing costs, it will take 22 months to break even. Because the Philipatoses plan to stay in their home for at least 60 more months, the refinancing is easily justified.

MORTGAGE REFINANCING ANALYSIS

Name _Demi and Nicholas Philipatos_   Dated _September 6, 2002_

Item	Description		Amount
1	Current monthly payment (Terms: _$80,000, 12%, 30 years_)		$ 823
2	New monthly payment (Terms: _$74,250, 9%, 20 years_)		668
3	Monthly savings, pretax (Item 1 − Item 2)		$ 155
4	Tax on monthly savings [Item 3 × tax rate (_28_ %)]		43
5	Monthly savings, after-tax (Item 3 − Item 4)		$ 112
6	Costs to refinance:		
	a. Prepayment penalty	$ 0	
	b. Total closing costs (after-tax)	2,400	
	c. Total refinancing costs (Item 6a + Item 6b)		$ 2,400
7	Months to break even (Item 6c ÷ Item 5)		22

their current mortgage, and closing and other costs associated with the new mortgage are $2,400 after taxes. Substituting these values into Worksheet 5.4 reveals (in Item 7) that it will take the Philipatoses 22 months to break even with the new mortgage. Because 22 months is considerably less than their anticipated minimum 5 years (60 months) in the home, the economics easily support refinancing their mortgage under the specified terms.

There are two basic reasons to refinance—to reduce the monthly payment or to reduce the total cost over the term of the loan. If a lower monthly payment is the objective, the analysis is relatively simple: Determine how long it will take for the monthly savings to equal your closing costs (see Worksheet 5.4).

If your objective is instead to reduce the total costs over the life of the loan, the analysis is more complex. The term of the new loan versus the existing loan is a critical input. If you refinance a 30-year loan that has been outstanding 10 years with another 30-year loan, you are actually extending the total maturity to 40 years; even with a lower interest rate, you may pay more interest. Therefore you should refinance with a shorter-term loan, one that matures no later than the original loan. (The preceding example is prepared on this basis.)

Many homeowners want to pay off their loans more quickly to free up funds to pay for their children's college education or for their retirement. By refinancing at a lower rate but continuing to make the same monthly payment, a larger portion of each payment will go toward the principal, and the loan will be paid off more quickly. Alternatively, the borrower can make extra principal payments whenever possible. Paying only an additional $25 per month on a 30-year, 9 percent, $80,000 mortgage reduces the term to about 25 years and saves about $30,000 in interest.

Some people consider the reduced tax deduction associated with a smaller mortgage interest deduction as a disadvantage of refinancing. Although the interest deduction may indeed be reduced as a result of refinancing, the important concern is the actual after-tax cash payments that must be made. In this regard, refinancing with a lower-interest-rate mortgage (with all other terms assumed unchanged) will always result in lower after-tax cash outflows, and is therefore economically appealing. Of course, as demonstrated in Worksheet 5.4, the reduction in after-tax cash outflows (that is, monthly savings) needs to be compared with the refinancing costs to make the final refinancing decision.

Because new mortgage products are offered regularly, you should carefully check all your options before refinancing. Remember that when you refinance, most lenders require that you have at least 20 percent equity in your home, based on a current market appraisal. Be sure to check with your existing lender because many financial institutions are willing to refinance their existing loans, often charging fewer points and lower closing costs than a new lender would charge.

CONCEPT CHECK

5-19. Describe the various sources of mortgage loans. What role might a *mortgage broker* play in obtaining mortgage financing?

5-20. Briefly describe the two basic types of mortgage loans. Which has the lowest initial rate of interest? What is *negative amortization,* and which type of mortgage can experience it? Discuss the advantages and disadvantages of each mortgage type.

5-21. Differentiate between conventional, insured, and guaranteed mortgage loans.

5-22. What factors should you take into account when deciding whether to refinance your mortgage to reduce the monthly payment? How can the refinancing decision be made?

SUMMARY

LG1. Implement a plan to choose and buy or lease an automobile. The purchase of an automobile, usually the second largest expenditure a person will make, should be based on thorough market research and comparison shopping. Important purchase considerations include affordability, operating costs, new versus used or nearly new car, type of car and its features, and reliability and warranties. Knowing the dealer's cost is the key to negotiating a good price, and the economics of leasing versus purchasing the car with an installment loan should be considered once the price is set. The four components of the lease payment are the capitalized cost, residual value, money factor, and lease term. It's important to consider the other terms of the lease, such as annual mileage allowance and early termination penalties, before signing a lease contract.

LG2. Identify housing alternatives that meet your needs. A family can meet its housing needs in many different ways. In addition to single-family homes, there are condominiums, cooperative apartments, and numerous types of rental units. You should evaluate the advantages and disadvantages of each to choose the best one for your current lifestyle.

LG3. Evaluate the benefits and costs of home ownership and estimate how much you can pay for a home. In addition to the emotional rewards, other benefits of home ownership are the tax shelter and inflation hedge it provides. Home ownership costs include the down payment, points and closing costs, monthly mortgage payments, property taxes and insurance, and normal home maintenance and operating expenses. Any of these can amount to a considerable sum of money. All of them should be carefully considered to estimate how much you can afford to spend on a home.

LG4. Assess the rental option and perform a rent-or-buy analysis. Many people rent because they cannot afford to buy a home; others choose to rent because renting is less costly or more convenient for their lifestyle and economic situation. The rental contract, or lease agreement, describes the terms under which you can rent the property: rent payment, term, restrictions, and so forth. Rent-or-buy analysis can help you choose the least costly alternative. You should also consider qualitative factors, such as how long you plan to stay in an area, and perform the analysis over a several-year time horizon.

LG5. Describe the home-buying process. Normally, people shopping for a home seek the help of a real estate agent to obtain needed information, access to properties, and advice; the agents involved split a 5 to 7 percent commission, paid by the seller, when the transaction is closed. It's a good idea to prequalify for a mortgage before starting to look for a house. A real estate sales contract is used to confirm in writing all terms of the transaction between the buyer and seller. After a mortgage loan is approved, the loan is closed. A closing statement shows how much the borrower owes and the seller receives from the transaction.

LG6. Choose mortgage financing that meets your needs. Mortgage loans can be obtained from commercial banks, S&Ls, and savings banks, and through a mortgage banker or mortgage broker. Although there are many types of mortgage loans available, the most widely used are 30- and 15-year fixed-rate mortgages and adjustable-rate mortgages (ARMs). Sometimes interest rates will drop a number of years after closing, and mortgage refinancing will become attractive. The refinancing analysis takes into account the difference in terms between the old and new mortgages, any prepayment penalty on the old mortgage, closing costs, and the number of years you plan to stay in the home.

QUESTIONS AND PROBLEMS

1. Janet Forrester just graduated from college and needs to buy a car to commute to work. She estimates that she can afford to pay about $300 per month for a loan or lease and has about $1500 in savings to use for a down payment. Develop a plan to guide her through her first car buying experience, including researching car type, deciding whether to buy new or used, negotiating price and terms, and financing the transaction.

2. *Use Worksheet 5.1.* Chris Svenson is trying to decide whether to lease or purchase a new car costing $12,000. If he leases, he will have to make a $400 security deposit and agree to make monthly payments of $285 over the 36-month term of the closed-end lease. If, on the other hand, he purchases the car, he will have to make an $1,800 down payment and will finance the balance with a 36-month loan requiring monthly payments of $340; in addition, he will have to pay a 6 percent sales tax ($720) on the purchase price, and he expects the car to have a residual value of $4,300 at the end of 3 years. Chris can earn 4 percent interest on his savings. Use the automobile lease versus purchase analysis (Worksheet 5.1) to find the total cost of both the lease and the purchase and recommend the best strategy to Chris.

3. How much would you have to put down on a house costing $100,000 if the house had an appraised value of $105,000 and the lender required an 80 percent loan-to-value ratio?

4. Using the maximum ratios for a conventional mortgage, how big a monthly payment could the Bacon family afford if their gross (before-tax) monthly income amounted to $4,000? Would it make any difference if they were already making monthly installment loan payments totaling $750 on two car loans?

5. How much might a home buyer expect to pay in closing costs on a $95,000 house with a 10 percent down payment? How much in total would the home buyer have to pay at the time of closing in the above transaction, taking into account closing costs, down payment, and a loan fee of 3 points?

6. Find the *monthly* mortgage payments on the following mortgage loans using the table in Exhibit 5.9:
    a. $80,000/6.5 percent/30 years
    b. $105,000/8 percent/20 years
    c. $95,000/10.5 percent/15 years

7. *Use Worksheet 5.2.* Selena and Rodney Jackson wish to estimate the amount they can afford to spend to purchase their first home. They have a combined annual income of $47,500 and have $27,000 available to make a down payment and pay closing costs. The Jacksons estimate that homeowner's insurance and property taxes will be $125 per month. They expect the mortgage lender to use a 30 percent (of monthly gross income) mortgage-payment affordability ratio, to lend at an interest rate of 8 percent on a 30-year mortgage, and to require a 15 percent down payment. Based on this information, use the home affordability analysis form in Worksheet 5.2 to determine the maximum-priced home the Jacksons can afford.

8. *Use Worksheet 5.3.* Rebecca Serra is currently renting an apartment for $625 per month and pays $275 annually for renter's insurance. She just found a townhouse she can buy for $85,000. She has enough cash for a $10,000 down payment and $4,000 in closing costs. Her bank is offering 30-year mortgages at 9 percent per year. Rebecca estimated the following costs as a percentage of the home's price: property taxes, 2.5 percent; homeowner's insurance, .5 percent; and maintenance, .7 percent. She is in the 28 percent tax bracket. Using Worksheet 5.3, calculate the cost of each alternative and recommend the less costly option—rent or buy—to Rebecca.

9. What would the monthly payments be on a $75,000 loan if the mortgage were set up as:

    a. A 15-year, 10 percent fixed-rate loan?

    b. A 30-year adjustable-rate mortgage in which the lender added a margin of 2.5 to the index rate (which presently stands at 6.5 percent)?

    Find the monthly mortgage payments for the first year only.

10. *Use Worksheet 5.4.* Latha Yang purchased a condominium 4 years ago for $70,000. She has been paying $630 per month on her $60,000, 12 percent, 25-year mortgage. The current loan balance is $58,165. Recently, interest rates have dropped sharply, causing Latha to consider refinancing the condo at the prevailing 9 percent rate. She expects to remain in the condo for at least 4 more years and has found a lender that will make a 9 percent, 21-year, $58,165 loan requiring $515 monthly payments. Although there is no prepayment penalty on her current mortgage, Latha will have to pay $1,500 in closing costs on the new mortgage. She is in the 15 percent tax bracket. Based on this information, use the mortgage refinancing analysis form (Worksheet 5.4) to determine whether Latha should refinance her mortgage under the specified terms.

APPLYING PERSONAL FINANCE

Getting in Touch with Your Local Housing Market

What is the best source of information about available housing in your community? The answer is a well-informed professional real estate agent whose business is helping buyers find and negotiate the purchase of the most suitable property at the best price. But there is another source of information about available housing that is less personal and easy to examine: the local newspaper. Almost anything you want to know about the local housing scene is summarized in the real estate classified ads section of the paper. In many larger cities, at least one edition each week (typically the Sunday edition) includes feature articles and statistics on the local, as well as national, housing market.

Review recent issues of your local newspaper and describe the market for purchased homes and rental housing. Use information such as location, size of property, price or rent, lease requirements, etc. You should observe that the housing market is very fragmented, making it more difficult to make good purchase and rent decisions. See if you can answer questions like: What is the average size of a house or apartment in your community? What is the typical sale price or monthly rent per square foot? Is the purchase market competitive? How about the rental market? How great a difference exists in prices and rents between the most and least desirable areas of the community? From your study of the local market, summarize its conditions and be prepared to participate in class discussion of the local real estate market.

CONTEMPORARY CASE APPLICATIONS

5.1   The McNeils' New Car Decision: Lease versus Purchase

Jim and Margaret McNeil, a dual-income couple in their late 20s, want to replace their 7-year-old car, which has 80,000 miles on it and needs some expensive repairs. After reviewing their budget, the McNeils conclude that they can afford auto payments of not more than $350 per month and a down payment of $2,000. They enthusiastically decide to visit a local dealer after reading its newspaper ad offering a closed-end lease on a new car for a monthly payment of $245. After visiting with the dealer, test driving the car, and discussing the lease terms with the salesperson, they remain excited about leasing the car, but decide to wait until the following day to finalize the deal. Later that day the McNeils begin to question their approach to the new-car acquisition process, and decide to carefully reevaluate their decision.

Questions

1. What are some of the basic purchase considerations the McNeils should take into account when choosing which new car to buy or lease? How can they get the information they need?
2. How would you advise the McNeils to research the lease versus purchase decision before visiting the dealer? What are the advantages and disadvantages of each alternative?
3. Assume the McNeils can get the following terms on a lease or a bank loan for the car, which they could buy for $15,000:

   Lease: 48 months, $245 monthly payment, 1 month's payment required as a security deposit, $350 end-of-lease charges; residual value of $6,775 is the purchase option price at the end of the lease.

   Loan: $2,000 down payment, $13,000, 48-month loan at 10 percent interest requiring a monthly payment of $330. They assume the car's value at the end of 48 months will be the same as the residual value. Sales tax is 6 percent.

   They can currently earn interest of 4 percent annually on their savings. They expect to drive about the same number of miles per year as they do now.

   a. Use the format given in Worksheet 5.1 to determine which deal is better for the McNeils.
   b. What other costs and terms of the lease option might affect their decision?
   c. Based on the available information, should the McNeils lease or purchase the car, and why?

5.2   Evaluating a Mortgage Loan for the Newtons

Farrah and Sam Newton, both in their mid 20s, have been married for 4 years. Sam has an accounting degree and is presently employed as a cost accountant at an annual salary of $42,000. The Newtons have two children, ages 6 months and 3 years. At present, they are renting a duplex but wish to buy a home in the suburbs of their rapidly developing city. They have decided they can afford a $105,000 house and hope to find one with the features they desire in a good neighborhood.

The insurance costs on such a home are expected to be $500 per year, taxes are expected to be $1,000 per year, and annual utility bills are estimated at $1,200—an increase of $500 over those they pay in the duplex. The Newtons are considering financing their home with a fixed-rate, 30-year, 9 percent mortgage. The lender charges 2 points on mortgages with 20 percent down and 3 points if less than 20 percent is put down (the commercial bank with which the Newtons will deal requires a minimum of 10 percent down). Other closing costs are estimated at 5 percent of the purchase price of the home. Because of their excellent credit record, the bank will probably be willing to let the Newtons' monthly mortgage payments equal as much as 28 percent of their monthly gross income. Since getting married, the Newtons have been saving for the purchase of a home and now have $24,000 in their savings account.

Questions

1. How much would the Newtons have to put down if the lender required a minimum 20 percent down payment? Could they afford it?

2. Given the Newtons want to put only $15,000 down, how much would closing costs be? Considering only principal and interest, how much would their monthly mortgage payments be? Would they qualify for a loan using a 28 percent affordability ratio?

3. Using a $15,000 down payment on a $105,000 home, what would the Newton's loan-to-value ratio be? Calculate the monthly mortgage payments on a PITI basis.

4. What recommendations would you make to the Newtons? Explain.

5.3   Julie's Rent-or-Buy Decision

Julie Brown is a single woman in her late 20s. She currently rents an apartment in the fashionable part of town for $900 a month. After considerable deliberation, she is seriously considering the purchase of a luxury condominium for $125,000. She intends to put 20 percent down and expects that closing costs will amount to another $5,000; a commercial bank has agreed to lend her money at the fixed rate of 9 percent on a 15-year mortgage. Julie would have to pay an annual condominium owner's insurance premium of $600 and property taxes of $1,200 a year (she is presently paying renter's insurance of $550 per year). In addition, she estimates that annual maintenance and upkeep expenses will be about .5 percent of the price of the condo (which includes a $30 monthly fee to the property owners' association). Julie's income puts her in the 28 percent tax bracket (she itemizes her deductions on her tax returns), and she earns an after-tax rate of return on her investments of around 4 percent.

Questions

1. Given the information provided above, evaluate and compare Julie's alternatives of remaining in the apartment or purchasing the condo, using Worksheet 5.3.

2. Working with a friend who is a realtor, Julie has learned that luxury condos like the one she is thinking of buying are appreciating in value at the rate of 3.5 percent a year and are expected to continue doing so. Would such information affect the rent-or-buy decision made in Question 1? Explain.

3. Discuss any nonquantitative factors that should be considered when making a rent-or-buy decision.

4. Which alternative would you recommend for Julie in light of your analysis?

MONEY ONLINE

DRIVING HOME, SWEET HOME!

Note: Web addresses change frequently, so you may need to determine the home page and do a site search to find the page or topic that's referenced.

1. **www.nhtsa.dot.gov**
   Has there been a recall on your vehicle? Search at "Recalls" on the Web site of the National Highway Traffic Safety Administration to check not only on your vehicle but also on child safety seats and school buses. While you're there, be sure to examine the crash test results for your vehicle as well.

2. **www.edmunds.com/roadtests/comparisontests**
   How do the new cars stack up against one another? Edmunds has done the comparison tests for you on the most popular new vehicles. Read through the results of their road tests, view pictures of the vehicles, and learn the different features of your dream car.

3. **www.kbb.com**
   What's your car worth? Consult the Kelly Blue Book to help you with the pricing of both new and used vehicles. KBB also has a section for valuing used motorcycles, street and dirt bikes, ATVs, scooters, mopeds, sidecars, watercraft, and snowmobiles.
4. **www.autosite.com/new/loanlse/calc.asp**
   Thinking of leasing a car instead of buying? Use AutoSite's handy "Loan Lease Calculator" to help you make your decision. Scroll down to the bottom of the page and find Leasing Tips such as "Do's and Don'ts of Leasing," "Types of Leases," "Advantages of Leasing," "Disadvantages of Leasing," and "What is a Lease and How Does It Work?"
5. **www.bluecollardollar.com/loan.html**
   Want to pay off your loan early? Use BlueCollarDollar's handy calculator "How Long Will it Take?" to determine how rapidly you can pay off your loan by paying extra each month. While you're at their Web site, read through their common sense approach to finance and debt.
6. **www.homeloans-credit-personalloans.com**
   Need help obtaining a home mortgage? Use American Mortgage and Home Loan's free service designed to help match borrowers with the best financing programs nationwide. Learn the mortgage lingo, use their calculators, or find out the current mortgage rates.
7. **www.interest.com/calculators/discount.shtml**
   Should you pay points and buy down the interest rate on your home mortgage? Use Moneyadvisor's handy calculator to see how long it would take you to recoup the cost of paying discount points. Enter a rate of 7.5 percent with no points and 7.25 percent with 1 discount point on a 30-year loan for $100,000 to see that you would need to own the home at least 59 months before it would be worthwhile to pay the extra discount point.
8. **www.relibrary.com**
   Do you have questions concerning buying a home? This Real Estate Library has the answers! For starters, click on "Buyer and Seller Tools" for help with every aspect of the home buying or selling process. Consult "Legal" for legal forms and information. Attend "Mortgage 101" classes or click on "Lenders by State" to find a mortgage lender in your state.

Just for Fun!
9. **www.creonline.com**
   Interested in investing in real estate? Visit the Web site of Creative Real Estate Online for plenty of articles and information on handing the financing, getting started, and generating cash flow.
10. **www.xmission.com/~realtor1/index.html**
    Shop for real estate around the world! Realty Guide International contains links to real estate resources and professionals worldwide. Click on "Geographic Realty Links" to locate property or on "Finance" to find banking and mortgage information. Consult their "Business Directory" to find everything from appraisers to relocation services and roofing contractors.

PART III

Managing Credit

CHAPTER 6
Borrowing on Open
Account

CHAPTER 7
Using Consumer
Loans

Chapter 6

Borrowing on Open Account

LEARNING GOALS

LG1.   Describe the reasons for using consumer credit and identify its benefits and problems.

LG2.   Develop a plan to establish a strong credit history.

LG3.   Distinguish among the different forms of open account credit: bank credit cards, other credit cards and charge accounts, and revolving credit lines.

LG4.   Apply for, obtain, and manage open account credit.

LG5.   Choose the right credit cards and recognize their advantages and disadvantages.

LG6.   Avoid credit problems, protect yourself against credit card fraud, and understand the personal bankruptcy process.

The House of Credit Cards Falls

"It's amazing how many banks will extend a $10,000 credit line to you when you buy a house," notes Randy Walker. "When a new furnace, air conditioning unit, and roof ate up our available credit, we just added more credit cards and kept on buying." Jan decided to stay home when their first daughter was born, and then Randy was unemployed for eight weeks. "That really put us in a tail-spin," he recalls. "I had been earning $50,000 a year with a monthly mortgage payment of $1,150, a car payment, and hardly any savings."

Soon the Walkers, who live in central Illinois, could barely cover the credit card monthly interest charges. "Our budget was so tight that even buying groceries was hard," Jan says. "We ignored the warning signs and continued using credit to get by. We were by no means disciplined in our spending." After weighing their options, they consulted an attorney and filed for bankruptcy in October 1999. Because Randy didn't expect much salary growth, they filed Chapter 7 (liquidation) instead of Chapter 13 (debt restructuring). "Knowing what we do now, we should have tried everything possible—like low interest loans from relatives or credit counseling—to resolve our situation before filing," Randy says. "If someone had asked, 'Do you really know what you're getting into?' we might have taken another route." Although the bankruptcy court permitted them to keep their house, car, and other personal effects, the stigma attached to bankruptcy caused them emotional scars. For one thing, they must answer "yes" when forms ranging from credit to employment ask: Have you ever declared bankruptcy?

When they were discharged from bankruptcy in June 2000, the Walkers took firm control of their personal finances. With almost no credit available for three years, they had to manage their cash better; Randy even worked a second job for a while. They used their few retail credit cards to reestablish their credit, charging small amounts that they paid off religiously. "But that black cloud of bankruptcy hung over us for what seemed like forever," Randy says. By studying the following chapter, you will learn how to manage your credit wisely and not get into trouble like the Walkers did.

▇ The Basic Concepts of Credit [LG1, LG2]

Just say "Charge it." With those two little words and a piece of plastic, you can buy gas for your car, have a gourmet meal at an expensive restaurant, or furnish an apartment. It happens *several hundred million times a day* across the United States. Credit, in fact, has become an entrenched part of our everyday lives, and we as consumers use it in one form or another to purchase just about every type of good or service imaginable. Indeed, because of the ready availability and widespread use of credit, our economy is often called a "credit economy." And for good reason: by mid-year 2000, individuals in this country had run up almost *$1.5 trillion dollars* in consumer debt—and that *excludes* home mortgages.

Consumer credit is important in the personal financial planning process because of the impact it can have on (1) the attainment of financial goals, and (2) cash budgets. For one thing, various forms of consumer credit can help you reach your financial objectives by enabling you to acquire some of the more expensive items in a systematic fashion without throwing your whole budget into disarray. But there's another side to consumer credit: It has to be paid back! Unless credit is used intelligently, the "buy-now-pay-later" attitude can quickly turn an otherwise orderly budget into a budgetary nightmare and lead to some serious problems—even bankruptcy! So, really, the issue is one of moderation and affordability.

In today's economy, consumers, businesses, and governments alike use credit to make transactions. Credit helps businesses supply the goods and services needed to satisfy consumer demand. In addition, business credit provides higher levels of employment and helps raise our overall standard of living. Local, state, and federal governments borrow for various projects and programs that also increase our standard of living and create additional employment opportunities. Clearly, borrowing helps fuel our economy and enhance the overall quality of our lives. Consequently, consumers in a credit economy need to know how to establish credit and how to avoid the dangers of using it improperly.

WHY BORROW?

People typically use credit as a way to pay for goods and services that cost more than they can afford to take from their current income. This is particularly true for those in the 25 to 44 age group, who simply have not had time to accumulate the liquid assets required to pay cash outright for major purchases and expenditures. As people begin to approach their mid-40s, however, their savings and investments start to build up, and their debt loads tend to decline, which is really not too surprising when you consider that the median household net worth for those in the 45 to 54 age group is *80 percent more* than those aged 35 to 44.

Whatever their age group, people tend to borrow for several major reasons:

- **To avoid paying cash for large outlays.** Rather than pay cash for large purchases, such as houses and cars, most people borrow a portion of the purchase price and then repay the loan on some scheduled basis. Spreading payments over time makes big-ticket items more affordable, and consumers get the use of an expensive asset right away. Most people consider the cost of such borrowing a small price to pay for the immediate satisfaction they get from owning the house, car, or whatever it happens to be. In their minds, at least, the benefits of current consumption outweigh the interest costs on the loan. Unfortunately, while the initial euphoria of the purchase may wear off over time, the loan payments remain—and perhaps for many more years to come.
- **To meet a financial emergency.** For example, people may need to borrow to cover living expenses during a period of unemployment, or to purchase plane tickets to visit a sick relative. As indicated in Chapter 4, however, use of savings (not credit) is a more preferred way to provide for financial emergencies.
- **For convenience.** Merchants as well as banks offer a variety of charge accounts and credit cards that allow consumers to charge just about anything—from gas and oil or clothes and stereos to doctor and dental bills and even college tuition. Further, in many places—restaurants, for instance—using a credit card is far easier than writing a check. A credit card purchase provides a permanent, itemized record of the transaction that simplifies the budgeting process. Although such transactions usually incur no interest (at least initially), these credit card purchases are still a form of borrowing, because payment is not made at the time of the transaction.
- **For investment purposes.** As we'll see in Chapter 11, it's relatively easy for an investor to partially finance the purchase of many different kinds of investment vehicles with borrowed funds. In fact, *margin loans,* as they're called, have reached an all-time high in this country, amounting to over $275 billion in early 2000.

EXHIBIT 6.1

MINIMUM PAYMENTS MEAN MAXIMUM YEARS

Paying off credit card balances at the minimum monthly amount required by the card issuer will take a long time and cost you a great deal of interest, as the following table demonstrates. The calculations here are based on a minimum 3 percent payment and 17.5 percent annual interest rate.

Original Balance	Years to Repay	Interest Paid	Total Interest Paid as Percent of Original Balance
$5,000	18.4	$4,541	90.8%
4,000	17.2	3,595	89.9
3,000	15.7	2,649	88.3
2,000	13.5	1,703	85.2
1,500	11.9	1,230	82.0
1,000	9.8	757	75.7
500	6.1	284	56.8

IMPROPER USES OF CREDIT

Many people use consumer credit to live beyond their means. Overspending is the biggest danger in borrowing, especially because it's so easy to do. Once hooked on "plastic," people may use their credit cards to make even routine purchases and don't realize they have overextended themselves until it's too late. Overspenders simply won't admit that they're spending too much. As far as they're concerned, they can afford to buy all those things because, after all, they still have their credit cards and can still afford to pay the minimum amount each month.

Unfortunately, such spending eventually leads to mounting bills. And by making only the minimum payment, borrowers pay a huge price in the long run. Look at Exhibit 6.1, which shows the amount of time and interest charges required to repay credit card balances if you make only a minimum payment of 3 percent of the outstanding balance. For example, if you carry a $3,000 balance—which is about *half* the national average—on a card that charges 17.5 percent annually, it would take you nearly 16 years to retire the debt, and your interest charges would total *almost $2,650—or more than 88 percent of the original balance!* And some cards offer even lower minimum payments of 2 to 2.5 percent. While such small payments may seem like a good deal, clearly they do not work to your advantage and only increase the time and amount of interest required to repay the debt!

To avoid the possibility of future repayment shock, you should keep in mind the following types of transactions for which you should *not* (routinely, at least) use credit: (1) to meet basic living expenses; (2) to make impulse purchases, especially expensive ones; and (3) to purchase nondurable (short-lived) goods and services. Except in situations where credit cards are used occasionally for the sake of convenience (such as for gasoline and entertainment) or payments on recurring credit purchases are built into the monthly budget, a good rule to remember when considering the use of credit is that *the product purchased on credit should outlive the payments.*

Unfortunately, people who overspend eventually arrive at the point where they must choose to either become delinquent in their payments or sacrifice necessities, such as food and clothing. If payment obligations are not met, the consequences are likely to be a damaged credit rating, lawsuits, or even personal bankruptcy. Exhibit 6.2 lists some common

EXHIBIT 6.2

SOME CREDIT DANGER SIGNS

If one or more of these signs exist, you should take them as an indication that it is time to proceed with caution in your credit spending. Be prepared to revise and update your spending patterns, cut back on the use of credit, and be alert for other signs of overspending.

You may be headed for serious trouble if:

- You regularly use credit cards to buy on impulse.
- You postdate checks to keep them from bouncing.
- You regularly exceed the borrowing limit on your credit cards.
- You never add up all your bills, to avoid facing grim realities.
- You now take 60 or 90 days to pay bills you once paid in 30.
- You have to borrow just to meet normal living expenses.
- You often use one form of credit—such as a cash advance from a credit card—to make payments on other debt.
- You can barely make the minimum required payments on bills.
- You are using more than 20 percent of your take-home income to pay credit card bills and personal loans (excluding mortgage payments).
- You have no savings.
- You are so far behind on credit payments that collection agencies are after you.

---

signals that indicate it may be time to stop buying on credit. *Ignoring the telltale signs that you are overspending can only lead to more serious problems.*

ESTABLISHING CREDIT

The willingness of lenders to extend credit depends on their assessment of your creditworthiness—that is, your ability to repay the debt on a timely basis. They look at a number of factors in making this decision, such as your present earnings and net worth. Equally important, they look at your current debt position and your credit history. Thus it's worth your while to do what you can to build a strong credit rating.

FIRST STEPS IN ESTABLISHING CREDIT. First, open checking and savings accounts. They signal stability to lenders and also indicate that you handle your financial affairs in a businesslike fashion. Second, use credit—open one or two charge accounts and use them periodically, even if you prefer paying cash. For example, get a Visa card and make a few credit purchases each month (don't overdo it, of course). You might pay an annual fee or interest on some (or all) of your account balances, but in the process, you'll become identified as a reliable credit customer. Third, obtain a small loan, even if you don't need one. If you don't actually need the money, put it in a liquid investment, such as a money market account or certificate of deposit. The interest you earn should offset some of the interest expense on the loan; you can view the difference as a cost of building good credit. (It goes without saying that you should repay the loan promptly, perhaps even a little ahead of schedule, to minimize the difference in interest rates—don't pay off the loan too quickly, though, as lenders like to see how you perform over an extended period of time.) Keep in mind, your ability to obtain a large loan in the future will depend in part on how you managed smaller ones in the past.

BUILD A STRONG CREDIT HISTORY. From a financial perspective, maintaining a strong credit history is just as important as developing a solid employment record! Don't take credit lightly, and don't assume that getting the loan or the credit card is the toughest part. It's not. That's just the first step; servicing it (i.e., making payments) in a prompt and timely fashion—month in and month out—is the really tough part of the consumer credit process. And in many respects, it's the most important element of consumer credit, as it determines your creditworthiness. By using credit wisely and repaying it on time, you're establishing a *credit history* that tells lenders you're a dependable, reliable, and responsible borrower.

The consumer credit industry keeps very close tabs on your credit and your past payment performance (more on this when we discuss *credit bureaus* later in the chapter). So the better job you do in being a responsible borrower, the easier it will be to get credit when and where you want it. The best way to build up a strong credit history and maintain your creditworthiness is to *consistently* make payments *on time,* month after month. Being late occasionally—say, two or three times a year—might label you a "late payer." When you take on credit, you have an *obligation* to live up to the terms of the loan, including how and when the credit will be repaid.

If you foresee difficulty in meeting a monthly payment, let the lender know and usually some sort of arrangements can be made to help you through the situation. This is especially true with installment loans that require fixed monthly payments. If you have one or two of these loans and, for some reason or another, you encounter a month that's going to be really tight, the first thing you should try to do (other than trying to borrow some money from a member of the family) is get an extension on your loan. Don't just skip a payment, because that's going to put your account into a *late status until you make up the missed payment*—in other words, until you make a *double* payment, your account/loan will remain in a late status, subject to a monthly late penalty. The alternative of trying to work out an extension with your lender obviously makes a lot more sense.

Here's what you do. Explain the situation to the loan officer and ask for an extension of one (or two) months on your loan. In most cases, so long as this hasn't occurred before, the extension is almost automatically granted. The maturity of the loan is formally extended for a month (or two), and the extra interest of carrying the loan for another month (or two) is either added to the loan balance or, more commonly, paid at the time the extension is granted (such an extension fee generally amounts to a fraction of the normal monthly payment). Then, in a month (or two), you pick up where you left off and resume your normal monthly payments on the loan. This is the most sensible way of making it through those rough times because it doesn't harm your credit record. Just don't do it too often.

To summarize, here are some ways to build a strong credit history:

- Use credit only when you can afford it and only when the repayment schedule fits comfortably into the family budget—in short, don't overextend yourself.
- Fulfill all the terms of the credit.
- Be *consistent* in making payments *promptly.*
- Consult creditors immediately if you cannot meet payments as agreed.
- Be truthful when applying for credit. Lies are not likely to go undetected.

 The American Banker's Association provides helpful information about shopping for credit and managing debt at its consumer education site, **www.aba.com/Consumer+Connection/default.htm**.

HOW MUCH CREDIT CAN YOU STAND? Sound financial planning dictates that if you are going to use credit, you should have a good idea of how much you can comfortably tolerate. The easiest way to avoid repayment problems and ensure that your borrowing will not place an undue strain on your monthly budget is to *limit the use of credit to your ability*

EXHIBIT 6.3

ALTERNATIVE CONSUMER CREDIT GUIDELINES BASED ON ABILITY TO REPAY

Using this credit guideline, the amount of consumer credit you should have outstanding depends on the montly payment you can afford to make.

Monthly Take-Home Pay	Monthly Consumer Credit Payments		
	Low Debt Safety Ratio (10%)	*Manageable* Debt Safety Ratio (15%)	*Maximum* Debt Safety Ratio (20%)
$1,000	$100	$150	$ 200
1,250	125	188	250
1,500	150	225	300
2,000	200	300	400
2,500	250	375	500
3,000	300	450	600
3,500	350	525	700
4,000	400	600	800
5,000	500	750	1,000

debt safety ratio
The proportion of total monthly consumer credit obligations to monthly take-home pay.

to repay the debt! A useful *credit guideline* (and one widely used by lenders) is to make sure your monthly repayment burden does not exceed 20 percent of your monthly *take-home pay.* Most experts, however, regard the 20 percent figure as the *maximum* debt burden and strongly recommend **debt safety ratios** closer to 10 to 15 percent—perhaps even lower if you plan on applying for a new mortgage in the near future. Note that the monthly repayment burden here is *exclusive* of your monthly mortgage obligation.

To illustrate, consider someone who takes home $2,500 a month. Using a 20 percent ratio, she should have monthly consumer credit payments of no more than $500—that is, $2,500 × .20 = $500. This is the maximum amount of her monthly disposable income she should have to use to pay off both personal loans and other forms of consumer credit (such as credit cards and education loans). This, of course, is not the maximum amount of consumer credit she can have outstanding—in fact, her total consumer indebtedness can, and likely would, be considerably larger. The key factor is that with her income level, her *payments* on this type of debt should not exceed $500 a month. (*Caution:* This is not to say that credit terms should be lengthened just to accommodate this guideline; rather, in all cases, it is assumed that standard credit terms apply.)

Exhibit 6.3 provides a summary of low (10 percent), manageable (15 percent), and maximum (20 percent) monthly credit payments for a number of income levels. Obviously, the closer your total monthly payments are to your desired debt safety ratio, the less future borrowing you can undertake. Conversely, *the lower the debt safety ratio, the better shape you're in, creditwise, and the easier it should be for you to service your outstanding consumer debt.*

To find your own debt safety ratio, simply use the following formula:

$$\text{Debt safety ratio} = \frac{\text{Total monthly consumer credit payments}}{\text{Monthly take-home pay}}$$

Thus, if you take home $1,360 a month and make total payments of $180 a month on outstanding consumer credit, you will have a debt safety ratio of $180/$1,360 = 13 percent, well within the manageable range.

THE SPECIAL CREDIT PROBLEMS OF WOMEN. At one time, a woman stood very little chance of getting credit on her own. In most lenders' minds, she was too much of a risk; even if she was gainfully employed, she might become pregnant and lose her job. Today, the Equal Credit Opportunity Act (ECOA), discussed more fully later in the chapter, has removed most of these credit obstacles. Creditors cannot check into a woman's marital status or childbearing plans and, with two-income families, must consider the woman's income on the same basis as the man's, even if it's part-time employment.

Even with these and other protections, however, some women—especially those who are divorced or widowed—still have difficulty getting credit if they do not have their own credit history. The following steps can help overcome this problem:

* **Use your own name when filing a credit application.** Use your legal name, not a social title, such as Mrs. Thomas Watkins. A married woman can choose from several legal names; for example, if your maiden name is Joan Brown and you take your husband's name of Watkins, you can choose Joan Watkins or Joan Brown Watkins. Use your legal name consistently to build your own credit history.
* **Make sure any information reported to the credit bureau is in your name as well as your husband's.**
* **Consider retaining a credit file separate from your husband's** when you marry, particularly if you have already established a good credit rating. You should notify creditors of your name change and intention to maintain your own file.

A FINAL WORD OF CAUTION. One of the real dangers of credit cards and other forms of open account credit is that they are so easy to use. Too many people tend to overlook the fact that they must eventually pay for the merchandise that's been charged with their cards; yet each time they make a transaction this way, they are incurring a liability to the issuer. Indeed, as the following *Money in Action* box illustrates, a growing number of people are learning this lesson the hard way! The bottom line is, if credit is used properly, it can go a long way in helping you manage your personal finances; misuse it and you're just asking for trouble.

Once you do obtain credit, be prepared for the onslaught of unsolicited credit card offers that will be mailed to you. In the year 2000 alone, credit card issuers mailed out *more than 3 billion* pieces of mail, each one promoting some offer for a credit card. One consumer, in fact, collected all the offers and, after totaling them up, found she was eligible for $1 million in credit. Of course, there is no way she could service the debt had she accepted all the offers, but even so, they kept coming and coming. *What's the best thing to do with these unsolicited offers?* Tear them up and toss them in the garbage!

CONCEPT CHECK

6-1. Why do people borrow? What are some of the improper uses of credit? Are there any dangers associated with borrowing? Explain.

6-2. Describe the general guidelines lenders use to calculate an applicant's maximum debt burden. How can you use the *debt safety ratio* to determine whether your debt obligations are within reasonable limits?

6-3. What steps can you take to establish a good credit rating? What extra steps might be necessary for a woman?

MONEY IN ACTION

Beware the Credit Card Trap!

Daniel Pena graduated from college with more than a degree—he also left school with almost $10,000 in credit card debt. Over four years of school, he'd used his six credit cards to ring up bills for a computer, video and stereo gear, restaurant meals, concert tickets, and clothing. Although Pena had planned to go on to medical school, those plans are now on hold while he works to pay off his credit cards. "It's going to take me a few years of living frugally before it's all paid off," he says.

Pena isn't alone. The typical U.S. family carried a monthly credit card balance of $7,942 in 2000, compared with $2,985 in 1990. Nearly half of consumers say they sometimes have trouble paying the minimum monthly payments on their cards. Problems with credit cards often begin in college when 60 percent of students get their first cards. Seventy percent of those students carry balances over $2,000, with 20 percent *owing $10,000 or more when they graduate.* Although credit cards are convenient, without proper management, they can become a permanent drain on your financial future.

How can you avoid the credit card trap? First, shop wisely for a card. Choose a card with low interest rates and little or no annual fees. Watch out for cards with variable interest rates that adjust with market rate changes—when rates go up, you may find yourself with considerably more debt than you originally anticipated due to the higher interest costs. Also, limit the number of cards you own. It can be tempting to take advantage of mailings or special marketing offers that offer you additional cards, but in reality most people need only one or two credit cards.

A surefire way to avoid problems is to pay your outstanding balances in full each month. Consider this: if you charge $4,000 worth of merchandise, but pay only the 2 percent minimum balance required by many card companies each month, you'll need 38 years to pay off the debt!

Be careful of what you charge. A good rule of thumb is to charge no more than you can comfortably repay within three months. Use cash, not credit, for routine purchases like food, toiletries, entertainment, and other discretionary items.

If you do find yourself with a huge credit card debt, develop a plan to systematically pay down the debt as soon as possible and consider transferring balances to a lower-rate card. Most importantly, change your spending habits. Try not to use your charge cards while paying down your balance, and when you emerge (triumphantly) from debt, don't ever again allow yourself to charge more than you can afford to pay.

Sources: Hank Ezell, "College Students and Credits: Freshmen Testing Independence Need to Be Taught the Dangers," *Atlanta Journal and Constitution,* August 20, 2000, p. G3; Mary C. Hickey, "Credit Cards: Working Toward a Major in Debt," *Business Week,* September 25, 2000, p. 192E10; "Reminder: Don't Take Too Much Credit," *Christian Science Monitor,* January 22, 2001, p. 14; Russ Wiles, "The 12 Days of Christmas Are a Fine Time to Review Credit-Card Tips," *Arizona Republic,* December 10, 2000, p. D1; and Carolyn Wood, "Credit Cards May Get Cut from College Campuses," *University Wire,* April 13, 2000.

■ Types of Open Account Credit [LG3]

open account credit
A form of credit extended to a consumer in advance of any transaction; type of credit that accompanies charge accounts and credit cards.

Open account credit is a form of credit extended to a consumer in advance of any transactions. Typically, a retail outlet or bank agrees to allow the consumer to buy or borrow up to a specified amount on open account. Credit is extended as long as the consumer does not exceed the established **credit limit,** and makes payments in accordance with the specified terms. Open account credit issued by a retail outlet, such as a department store or oil company, is usually applicable only in that establishment or one of its locations. In contrast, open account credit issued by banks, such as *MasterCard* and *Visa* accounts, can be used to make purchases at a wide variety of businesses. In the remainder of this chapter, we will direct our attention to the various types and characteristics of open account credit; in Chapter 7, we will look at various forms of single-payment and installment loans.

Having open account credit is a lot like having your own personal line of credit—it's there when you need it. But unlike most other forms of debt, consumers who use open account credit can often avoid paying interest charges *if they promptly pay the full amount of their account balance.* For example, assume that in a given month you charge $75.58 on an open account at a department store. Sometime within the next month or so, you will receive a **credit statement** from the store that summarizes recent transactions on your account. Now, if there are no other charges and the total account balance is $75.58, you can (usually) avoid any finance charges by paying the account in full before the next billing date.

Open account credit generally is available from two broadly defined sources: (1) financial institutions and (2) retail stores/merchants. *Financial institutions* issue general-purpose credit cards as well as secured and unsecured revolving lines of credit and overdraft protection lines. Commercial banks have long been a major provider of consumer credit; and since deregulation, so have S&Ls and credit unions. Deregulation has also brought other financial institutions into this market—most notably, major stock-brokerage firms, consumer finance companies, and a growing list of commercial banks that have gone *interstate* to market their credit cards and other consumer credit products. *Retail stores and merchants* make up the other major source of open account credit. They provide credit to promote the sales of their products. Their principal forms of credit include open charge accounts and credit cards.

Of the various types of open account credit, the two biggest are *bank credit cards* and *retail charge cards.* Together, there are nearly 2 billion of these cards outstanding today. Let's now take a closer look at the many forms of open account credit: bank credit cards, retail charge cards, 30-day charge accounts, travel and entertainment cards, prestige cards, affinity cards, secured credit cards, *debit cards,* and several kinds of *revolving lines of credit,* including overdraft protection lines, unsecured lines of credit, and home equity credit lines—all of which are available from banks and other financial services institutions.

BANK CREDIT CARDS

Probably the most popular form of open account credit is the **bank credit card** issued by commercial banks and other financial institutions—Visa and MasterCard are the two dominant types. These cards allow their holders to charge purchases worldwide at literally millions of stores, restaurants, shops, and gas stations, as well as at state and municipal governments, colleges and universities, medical groups, and mail-order houses—not to mention the Internet, where they have become the currency of choice. They can be used to pay for almost anything—groceries, doctor bills, college tuition, airline tickets, and car rentals. Thousands of banks, S&Ls, credit unions, brokerage houses, and other financial services institutions issue Visa and MasterCard, and each issuer, within reasonable limits, can set its own credit terms and conditions. In recent years, several more big-league players have entered the field. Sears, for example, introduced the *Discover Card* (now a part of Morgan Stanley Dean Witter), American Express its *Blue Card,* and AT&T its *Universal Card* (which is actually just a special Visa or Mastercard).

FEATURES OF BANK CREDIT CARDS

Bank credit cards can be used to borrow money as well as buy goods and services on credit. Because of their potential for use in thousands of businesses and banks, they can be of great convenience and value to consumers. Individuals who use them, however, should be thoroughly familiar with their basic features.

credit limit
A specified amount beyond which a customer may not borrow or purchase on credit.

credit statement
A monthly statement that summarizes the transactions in a consumer credit account; includes a record of new charges, credits and payments, any interest charges, and the minimum monthly payment required on the account.

bank credit card
A credit card issued by a bank or other financial institution that allows the holder to charge purchases at any establishment that accepts it; can also be used to obtain cash advances.

line of credit
The maximum amount of credit a customer is allowed to have outstanding at any point in time.

LINE OF CREDIT. The **line of credit** provided to the holder of a bank credit card is set by the issuer for each card. It is the maximum amount that the cardholder can owe at any point in time. The size of the credit line depends on both the applicant's request and the results of the issuer's investigation of the applicant's credit and financial status. Lines of credit offered by issuers of bank cards can reach $50,000 or more, but for the most part they range from about $500 to $2,500. Although card issuers fully expect you to keep your credit within the specified limits, most won't take any real action unless you extend your account balance a certain percentage beyond the account's stated maximum. For example, if you had a $1000 credit limit, you probably wouldn't hear a thing from the card issuer until your outstanding account balance exceeded, say, $1,200; that is, 20 percent above the $1000 line of credit. On the other hand, don't count on getting off scot-free, because most card issuers assess *over-the-limit* fees whenever you go over your credit limit (more on this later).

cash advance
A loan that can be obtained by a bank credit cardholder at any participating bank or financial institution; it begins to accrue interest immediately and requires no formal application.

CASH ADVANCES. In addition to purchasing merchandise and services, the holder of a bank credit card can also obtain a **cash advance** from any participating bank. Cash advances are loans on which interest begins to accrue immediately. They are transacted in the same fashion as merchandise purchases except that they take place at a commercial bank or some other financial institution and involve the receipt of cash (or a check) instead of goods and services. Another way to get a cash advance is to use the "convenience checks" you receive from the card issuer to pay for purchases. You can even use your credit card to draw cash from an ATM, any time of the day or night. Usually, the size of the cash advance from an ATM is limited to some nominal amount (perhaps $300), though the amount you can obtain from the teller window at a bank is limited only by the unused credit in your account. Thus, if you've used only $1,000 of a $5,000 credit limit, you can take out a cash advance of up to $4,000.

OTHER FEATURES. Bank credit cards sure aren't what they used to be! The fact is, credit cards today offer a lot more than just a convenient way of getting credit. Because the market has become so competitive, card issuers have had to offer all sorts of services and features (some would call them "gimmicks") in an attempt to get you to use their cards. One popular feature is the so-called *buyer protection plan,* which automatically protects most items of merchandise purchased with your credit card against loss, theft, or damage for up to 90 days. For example, if the purchased item breaks during the 90-day period, the card issuer will see that the item is replaced for free.

Here's a list of some of the other services offered:

- High-value travel accident insurance
- Full-value auto rental insurance coverage
- 24-hour toll-free travelers' emergency message service
- Lost card registration
- Discounts on long-distance phone calls
- Price protection plans
- 24-hour toll-free customer service lines
- Extended warranties on products purchased with the card
- 100% reimbursement protection against fraud or theft of card
- Year-end summaries breaking down purchases by groups (e.g., airline tickets, entertainment, transactions at gas stations, etc.)

Although it is not clear just how valuable the above mentioned services really are, one thing is sure: they do act to keep interest costs on credit cards high. For make no mistake about it, one way or another, cardholders will end up paying for all these services!

REBATE (CO-BRANDED) CREDIT CARDS. One of the fastest growing segments of the bank card market is the **rebate (co-branded) credit card**, which combines features of a traditional bank credit card with an incentive: either cash, merchandise rebates, airline tickets, or even investments. Over 50 million cardholders carry Visa or MasterCard rebate cards, and new types are introduced regularly. Among the many incentive programs are:

- **Frequent flyer programs.** In this program, the cardholder earns free frequent flyer miles for each dollar charged on his or her credit card. These frequent flyer miles can then be used with airline-affiliated programs for free tickets, first-class upgrades, and other travel-related benefits. Examples include Delta Sky Miles, American Airlines Visa or MasterCard, United Airlines Mileage Plus Visa or MasterCard, and American Express and Diners Club programs, with miles that can be used on one of several airlines.

- **Automobile rebate programs.** General Motors offers a bank credit card that allows the cardholder to earn annual rebates of 5 percent for new car purchases or leases, up to specified limits. While the amount of the GM rebate depends on the model of car purchased (or leased), Citibank's Drivers Edge rebates 1% of your charges, up to $500 annually, for almost any new car bought.

- **Other merchandise rebates.** An increasing number of companies are participating in bank card rebate programs, including, for example, Carnival Cruise Lines (4 percent, up to $500 per cruise). Some major oil companies also offer rebate cards, where the cardholder earns credit that can be applied to the purchase of the company's gasoline. Several regional phone companies even offer rebates on phone calls. (A good site for finding information about these and other rebate card offers is **www.cardtrak.com**.)

Are rebate cards a good deal? Well, yes and no. You should evaluate these cards carefully by looking at your usage patterns and working out the annual cost of the cards before and after the rebate, to see if they make sense for you. Don't get so carried away with the gimmick that you lose sight of the total costs. Most incentive cards carry higher interest rates than regular bank cards. These cards work best for those who can use the rebates, charge a lot, and who don't carry high monthly balances. For example, suppose you charge $2,200 a year on a GM rebate card and carry a monthly balance of $1,100. If the interest rate is 18 percent, the annual cost is about $198, and you earn a $110 rebate ($2,200 × .05) that reduces the cost to $88 if you use the rebate.

Frequent flier cards, in contrast, are best for high-volume chargers who do not carry balances. For example, with $25,000 in charges on an American Airlines card you earn one domestic coach ticket. If you pay in full each month and assume the ticket is worth $500, the net benefit after the $50 annual fee is $450. But if you charge only $2,200 and carry a $1,100 balance, the card costs $248 per year (assuming interest at 18 percent and a $50 annual fee) and earns less than 10 percent of a ticket. In that case, you would be better off with a low-rate card.

INTEREST RATES ON BANK CARD CHARGES. With few exceptions, the *annual* rate of interest charged on bank credit cards ranges from about 14 to 20 or 22 percent; in fact, in early 2000, the national average was nearly 17½ percent (17.33% to be exact). However, some states have **usury laws** that limit these rates to something more like 12 to 15 percent. The interest rate on merchandise purchases may differ from that on cash advances.

 Which credit cards are best? The Citizens for Fair Credit Card Terms, a nonprofit consumer organization, offers free independent ratings at **www.cardratings.com** that evaluate interest rates, fees, and benefits of leading cards.

rebate (co-branded) credit card
A bank credit card that combines features of a traditional bank credit card with an additional incentive, such as rebates and airline mileage.

usury laws
State laws governing interest rates on consumer and other types of credit.

prime (base) rate
The rate of interest a
bank uses as a base
for loans to indi-
viduals and small to
midsize businesses.

Most of these cards have variable interest rates that are tied to an index that moves with market rates. The most popular is the **prime (or base) rate**, the rate a bank uses as a base for loans to individuals and small or midsize businesses. These cards adjust their interest rate monthly or quarterly, and have a minimum and maximum rate. If the issuing bank's terms are prime +9.4 percent, with a minimum of 12.9 percent and a maximum of 19.8 percent, and the prime rate is 7.5 percent, the interest on balances would be 16.9 percent. Some cards have rates as low as prime +2.5 percent, although they tend to adjust rates monthly. Bank cardholders should be aware that *general interest rate hikes will increase the interest they pay on outstanding balances* (as was the case in late 1999 and early 2000, when the Federal Reserve initiated a series of rate hikes).

Generally speaking, *the interest rates on credit cards are higher than any other form of consumer credit.* But more and more banks—even the bigger ones—now offer more competitive rates, *especially to their better customers.* Many offer a special low introductory rate (called a *teaser rate*) for the first six months or a year. Moreover, a growing number of banks are willing to negotiate their fees as a way to retain their customers. Whether this trend will have any significant impact on reducing interest rates and fees remains to be seen, but at least most consumers would agree it is a step in the right direction.

grace period
A short period of
time, usually 20 to
30 days, during
which you can pay
your credit card bill
in full and not incur
any interest charges.

Bank credit card issuers must disclose interest costs and related information to consumers *before* extending credit. In the case of purchases of merchandise and services, the specified interest rate may not apply to charges until after the **grace period**. During this short period, usually 20 to 30 days, you can pay your credit card bill in full and avoid any interest charges. Once you carry a balance—i.e., when you don't pay your card in full during the grace period—the interest rate is usually applied to any unpaid balances carried from previous periods, as well as any new purchases made. Interest on cash advances, however, *begins the day the advance is taken out.*

OTHER FEES. In addition to the interest charged on bank credit cards, there are a few other fees you should be aware of. To begin with, many—though not all—bank cards levy *annual fees* just for the "privilege" of being able to use the card. In most cases, the fee is around $25 to $40 a year, though it can amount to much more for prestige cards. Sometimes, this annual fee will be waived in the first year, but you'll be stuck with it for the second and every other year you hold the card. As a rule, the larger the bank or S&L, the more likely it is to charge an annual fee for its credit cards. What's more, many issuers also charge a *transaction fee* for each cash advance; this fee usually amounts to about $5 per cash advance *or* 3 percent of the amount obtained in the transaction, whichever is more.

And now, more and more card issuers are coming up with new ways to sock it to you. These include: late-payment fees, over-the-limit charges, foreign transaction fees, and balance transfer fees. For example, if you're a bit late in making your payment, at some banks you'll be hit with a late-payment fee—which is really a redundant charge because you're already paying interest on the unpaid balance. In a similar fashion, if you happen to go over your credit limit, you'll get hit with a charge for that, too (again, this is on top of the interest you're already paying). Critics really dislike this fee because they maintain it's very difficult for cardholders to know when they've hit their credit ceilings. Some card issuers today are even going so far as to slap you with a fee for *not using your credit card*—Mellon Bank, for example, charges a $15 fee to customers (cardholders) who don't use their credit cards in a 6-month period. The card issuers justify these charges by saying it costs money to issue and administer these cards, so they have a right to charge these fees if you don't use their cards. Of course, you have the right to let the issuer know what you think of these charges by canceling your card! Regardless of when or why any of these fees are levied, the net effect is that *they add to the true cost of using bank credit cards.*

OTHER CREDIT CARDS AND CHARGE ACCOUNTS

In addition to bank cards, credit cards are also issued by most large retailers. You should be aware of these and several other kinds of credit cards and charge accounts, including 30-day charge accounts, travel and entertainment cards, prestige cards, affinity cards, and secured credit cards.

RETAIL CHARGE CARDS. **Retail charge cards** are the second largest category of credit card and are issued by department stores, oil companies, airlines, car rental agencies, and so on. These cards are popular with merchants because they build consumer loyalty and enhance sales; consumers like them because they are a convenient way to shop. These cards carry a pre-set credit limit—a line of credit—that varies with the creditworthiness of the cardholder.

This form of credit is most common in department and clothing stores and other high-volume outlets, where customers are likely to make several purchases each month. Most large oil companies offer charge cards that allow customers to buy gas and oil products, but they're expected to pay for such purchases in full upon receipt of the monthly bill. To promote the sale of their more expensive products, oil companies frequently offer revolving credit for use in purchasing items such as tires, batteries, and accessories. Many families have—and regularly use—five or six different retail charge cards. Interest on most retail charge cards is fixed at 1.5 to 1.85 percent monthly, or 18 to 22 percent per year. These cards are generally more expensive than bank credit cards, as the rate of interest on them is about *2 percent higher* than that charged on a bank-issued credit card.

30-DAY CHARGE ACCOUNT. Commonly offered by certain types of businesses for the general convenience of their customers, the **30-day**, or **regular**, **charge account** requires the customer to pay the full amount billed within 10 to 20 days after the billing date. If payment is made within the specified period, no interest is charged; if received after the due date, however, an interest penalty is usually tacked on to the account balance. These accounts generally do not involve the use of a charge card. They are offered by various types of public utilities (such as gas and electric companies, telephone companies, and so on), as well as some doctors and dentists, drugstores, and repair services.

TRAVEL AND ENTERTAINMENT CARDS. **Travel and entertainment (T&E) cards** are similar to bank credit cards in that they enable holders to charge purchases at a variety of locations. Although these cards used to be accepted primarily at travel- and entertainment-related businesses—like hotels, airlines, and restaurants—they have now found their way into all sorts of establishments, from upscale department and clothing stores to gas stations and drugstores. Like most bank cards, T&E cards today offer a full array of services, including frequent flyer miles, collision coverage (for car rentals), and luggage insurance. T&E cards have annual fees of up to $1,000 just for the privilege of using them. In sharp contrast to retail and bank credit cards, however, most T&E cards do *not* carry an extended line of credit. Instead, the outstanding balances must be *paid in full* within either one or two billing periods for the account to remain current. *American Express* is, by far, the biggest issuer of this type of card (with over 30 million cardholders worldwide), followed by *Diners Club* (almost 7 million). However, these numbers are minute compared with the number of bank credit cards outstanding—in 1999, there were over 250 million Visa cards and another 200 million or so MasterCards in circulation (and that's just in the U.S.; worldwide, the numbers are much higher).

In 1994, American Express added a new twist to this segment of the market by introducing the *Optima card.* Like the regular American Express card, the Optima card is aimed

retail charge card
A type of credit card issued by retailers, airlines, and so on, that allows customers to charge goods and services up to a pre-established amount.

30-day (regular) charge account
A charge account that requires customers to pay the full amount billed within 10 to 20 days after the billing date.

travel and entertainment (T&E) card
A credit card, such as American Express or Diners Club, accepted by travel and entertainment-related establishments, as well as a growing number of other businesses and stores; these cards require the holder to pay current balances *in full.*

at affluent cardholders who want not only convenience, but also a regular revolving charge account that carries with it a line of credit. Because the Optima card's outstanding balance does not have to be paid in full each month, it is, for all practical purposes, just another type of *bank credit card!* Its special feature is a 25-day interest-free grace period for all new purchases, *whether or not you carry a balance.* Most credit cards immediately charge interest on new purchases if the cardholder has an outstanding balance. However, this feature comes at a cost: The card's interest rate is higher than that of many other credit cards. Then, in 1999, American Express launched its *Blue card,* aimed at Generation Xers. This product allows the holder to carry balances, with their own line of credit. But what makes this card so unusual is that it's a *total internet-functional product,* from start (applications are taken on line) to finish (payments are also made on line). In addition, it is the first major card issued in the United States with a smart chip built in.

prestige card
A type of bank or T&E card that offers higher credit limits, has stricter requirements for qualification, and generally offers more features than its "regular" counterpart.

PRESTIGE CARDS. Not all credit cards are created alike. Some offer many more advantages and features than others. That's precisely what **prestige cards** are; they offer higher credit limits (up to $100,000 or more), worldwide travel services, and other features meant to attract the upscale cardholder. Such cards impose higher credit standards for qualification, and sometimes charge higher annual fees. MasterCard, Visa, American Express, and Optima all offer prestige cards—in either gold or silver or platinum, or in the color of some other precious metal. Indeed, platinum (generally considered to be the "ultimate" in credit cards) and other prestige cards now make up the fastest growing segment of the credit card market. The color of the "ultimate" prestige card changed a bit in 2000, when American Express introduced its special, invitation only, *Black charge card,* with a $1,000 annual fee that gives the cardholder access to an almost unlimited line of credit as well as a whole menu of high-end customer services.

Exhibit 6.4, on pages 240–241, compares some of the major features of different bank and T&E cards. Most of these cards are fully interchangeable, because they perform many of the same functions. Together these cards account for about 80 to 85 percent of all credit card activity, the balance of the transactions being made with retail charge cards.

affinity cards
A standard bank credit card issued in conjunction with some charitable, political, or other sponsoring non-profit organization; these cards are a source of revenue to the sponsoring group since they normally earn a small percentage of all retail transactions.

AFFINITY CARDS. Credit cards with a cause—that's the way to describe **affinity cards.** These cards are nothing more than standard bank Visa or MasterCards that are issued in conjunction with a sponsoring group—most commonly, some type of charitable, political, or professional organization. So named because of the bond between the sponsoring group and its members, affinity cards are sponsored by such nonprofit organizations as MADD, the American Association of Individual Investors, the American Wildlife Fund, AARP, and Special Olympics. In addition, they are issued by college and university alumni groups, labor organizations, religious and fraternal groups, and professional societies. In many cases, all you have to do is support the cause to obtain one of these cards (as in the case of MADD). In other cases, you'll have to belong to a certain group in order to get one of their cards (for example, be a graduate of the school or member of a particular professional group to qualify).

Why even bother to carry one of these cards? Unlike traditional bank cards, affinity cards make money for the group backing the card, as well as for the bank, because the sponsoring groups receive a share of the profits (usually one-half to one percent of retail purchases made with the card). So, for the credit cardholder, it's a form of "painless philanthropy." But to cover the money that goes to the sponsoring organization, the cardholder usually pays higher fees or higher interest costs. In spite of this, some may view these cards as a great way to contribute to a worthy cause. Others, however, may feel it makes more sense to use a traditional credit card and then write a check to their favorite charity. (For the latest affinity card offers, visit **www.cardtrak.com** and go to the affinity card folder.)

SECURED CREDIT CARDS. You may have seen the ad on TV where the announcer says that no matter how bad your credit, you can still qualify for one of their credit cards. The pitch may sound too good to be true; and in some respects it is because there's a catch. Namely, the credit is "secured"—meaning you have to put up *collateral* in order to get the card! These are so-called **secured**, or **collateralized, credit cards** where the amount of credit is determined by the amount of liquid collateral you're able to put up. These cards are targeted at people with no credit or bad credit histories, who don't qualify for conventional credit cards. Issued as Visa or MasterCard, except for the collateral, they're like any other credit card. To qualify, a customer must deposit a certain amount (usually $500 or more) into a 12 to18 month certificate of deposit that the issuing bank holds as collateral. The cardholder then gets a credit line equal to the deposit. If the customer defaults, the bank has the CD to cover its losses. By making payments on time, it's hoped that these cardholders will establish (or reestablish) a credit history that may qualify them for a conventional (unsecured) credit card. Even though fully secured, these cards still carry annual fees and finance charges that are equal to, or greater than, those of regular credit cards. (Credit can also be established, of course, by using a single-payment loan [discussed in Chapter 7] that's secured with a CD.)

secured (collateralized) credit cards
A type of credit card that's secured with some form of collateral, like a bank CD; with these cards, the amount of credit you get depends on how much collateral you can put up.

 Looking for the best rates on credit cards? CardWeb.com (**www.cardweb.com**) lets you compare credit card offers from major providers.

DEBIT CARDS

It looks like a credit card, it spends like a credit card, it even has the familiar MasterCard and Visa credit card markings. But it's not a *credit* card—rather, it is a *debit* card. Simply put, a **debit card** provides direct access to your checking account and, as such, *works like writing a check*. For example, when you use a debit card to make a purchase, the amount of the transaction is charged directly to your checking account. Thus, using a debit card is not the same thing as buying on credit; it may appear that you are charging it, but actually you are paying with cash. Accordingly, there are no finance charges to pay.

Debit cards are becoming very popular, especially with consumers who want the convenience of a credit card but not the high cost of interest that comes with them. There are over 115 million debit cards in the U.S. today, which together account for about 20 percent of all credit/debit card transactions. They are accepted at most establishments displaying the Visa or MasterCard logo but function as an alternative to writing checks. If you use a debit card to make a purchase at a department store or restaurant, the transaction will show up on your next monthly *checking account* statement. Needless to say, to keep your records straight, you should enter debit card transactions directly into your checkbook ledger as they occur and treat them as withdrawals, or checks, by subtracting them from your checking account balance. Debit cards can also be used to gain access to your account through 24-hour teller machines or ATMs—which is the closest thing to a cash advance that these cards have to offer.

The big disadvantage of a debit card, of course, is that it does not provide a line of credit. In addition, it can cause overdraft problems if you fail to make the proper entries to your checking account or inadvertently use it when you think you are using a credit card. Also, some debit card issuers charge a transaction fee or a flat annual fee; and even some *merchants* may charge you for using your debit card. On the plus side, a debit card does not carry with it the potential credit problems and high costs that credit cards do. Further, it is every bit as convenient to use as a credit card—in fact, if convenience is the major reason you use a credit card, you might want to consider switching to a debit card for at least some transactions, especially at outlets such as gas stations that give discounts for cash purchases and consider a debit card to be as good as cash.

debit card
A card used to make transactions for *cash* rather than credit; replaces the need for cash or checks by initiating charges against one's *checking* account.

EXHIBIT 6.4

MAJOR CREDIT CARD FEATURES

There are some important differences among the major credit cards, including the annual fee, maximum amount of credit available, required minimum monthly payment, and the credit criteria used.

BANK CARDS	MasterCard*	Gold MasterCard*	Platinum MasterCard*	VISA*
Annual fee	$0–$50, as set by issuing bank	$0–$75, as set by issuing bank	$0–$100 or more, as set by issuing bank	$0–$75, as set by issuing bank
Criteria	Set by issuing bank	Set by issuing bank	Set by issuing bank	Set by issuing bank
Minimum credit	$200	$5,000	$10,000	$200
Maximum credit	$10,000	$25,000	$100,000	$10,000
Minimum payment	Bank sets according to state regulations; expressed as a percentage of amount owed.			
Individual receipts returned	No	No	No	No
Cash machine link	Yes	Yes	Yes	Yes
Cash advances available	Yes	Yes	Yes	Yes

T&E CARDS	American Express (Green/Gold)
Annual fee	$55/$75
Criteria	Minimum income of $15,000/$20,000
Minimum credit	None/$10,000
Maximum credit	None
Minimum payment	Balance
Individual receipts returned	Yes (photocopies)
Cash machine link	Yes (bank checking)
Cash advances available	No/Yes

*Data for MasterCard and Visa are meant to reflect the features typically found on the vast majority of these cards; unfortunately, more exact information is not available because the cards are issued by thousands of financial institutions worldwide, and these institutions are mostly free to set their own standards.

prepaid card
A plastic card with a magnetic strip or microchip that stores the amount of money the purchaser has to spend and deducts the value of each purchase; eliminates the need to use cash.

PREPAID CARDS. Tired of fumbling for change to buy a candy bar from a vending machine or to use a pay phone? Buy a **prepaid card** and your pockets won't jingle with coins anymore. These "smart cards" can now be used to purchase a variety of items—phone calls, meals in some employee cafeterias, vending machine snacks—and their use is increasing. You pay a fixed amount, which is then stored on either a magnetic strip or rechargeable microchip on the card. Each time you make a purchase, the amount is electronically deducted from the card. First used for public transportation fares in large cities, prepaid cards are now used by many companies. In fact, you might be carrying one yourself, as they have become very popular on college campuses, where they're used to purchase meals, books, long distance

EXHIBIT 6.4 *continued*

Premier VISA[a]	Platinum VISA[a]	Discover Card	American Express Optima	Amex Blue
$0–$75, as set by issuing bank	$0–$100 or more, as set by issuing bank	$0	$25 (waived first year and if used three times per year thereafter)	$0
Set by issuing bank	Set by issuing bank	Varies by state	Minimum income of $20,000	Determined by credit department
$5,000	$10,000	$1,000	Determined by credit department	Determined by credit department
$25,000	$100,000	None	Determined by credit department	Determined by credit department
Bank sets according to state regulations; expressed as a percentage of amount owed.		Percentage of amount owed	Set by state law; expressed as percentage of amount owed	Determined by credit department
No	No	No	Yes (photocopies)	No
Yes	Yes	Yes	Yes	Yes
Yes	Yes	Yes	Yes	Yes

American Express (Platinum/Black)	Citicorp Diners Club
$300/$1,000	$80
Minimum charged by holder must be $10,000 annually/Invitation Only	Minimum income of $25,000
$10,000	None
None	None
Balance	Balance
Yes (photocopies)	Only upon request
Yes	Yes
Yes	Yes

phone calls, and other items. The popularity of these "electronic purses" is increasing, as consumers and merchants alike find them convenient. And they're likely to become even more popular as the microchips that are being embedded in these smart cards today can be used to not only execute transactions, but also store such things as electronic plane tickets or theater tickets. In addition, it is easier to control Internet fraud with them, as they have electronic readers which plug easily into your computer for authenticity verification.

REVOLVING CREDIT LINES

Revolving lines of credit are offered by banks, brokerage houses, and other financial institutions. These credit lines normally do not involve the use of credit cards. Rather, they are accessed by simply writing checks on regular checking accounts or specially designed credit

revolving line of credit A type of open account credit offered by banks and other financial institutions that can be accessed by writing checks against demand deposit or specially designated credit line accounts.

line accounts. They are a form of open account credit and often represent a far better deal than credit cards, not only because they offer more credit but also because they can be a lot less expensive. Also, according to the latest tax laws, there may even be a tax advantage to using one of these other kinds of credit!

These lines basically provide their users with ready access to borrowed money (that is, cash advances) through revolving lines of credit. They are every bit as convenient as credit cards, since access is gained by simply writing a check. The three major forms of open (non–credit card) credit are: overdraft protection lines, unsecured personal lines of credit, and home equity credit lines.

overdraft protection line
A line of credit linked to a checking account that allows a depositor to overdraw the account up to a specified amount.

OVERDRAFT PROTECTION. An **overdraft protection line** is simply a line of credit linked to a checking account that enables a depositor to overdraw his or her checking account up to a predetermined limit. These lines are usually set up with credit limits of $500 or $1,000, but they can be for as much as $10,000 or more. The consumer taps this line of credit by simply writing a check. If that particular check happens to overdraw the account, the overdraft protection line will automatically advance funds in an amount necessary to put the account back in the black. In some cases, overdraft protection is provided by *linking the bank's credit card to your checking account.* These arrangements act like regular overdraft lines, except when the account is overdrawn, the bank automatically taps your credit card line and transfers the money into your checking account. It's treated as a cash advance from your credit card, but the result is the same as a regular overdraft protection line; it automatically covers overdrawn checks.

Unfortunately, you never know for sure just how much a given check will overdraw your account (if in fact it does). The reason is that unless you write very few checks, the balance shown on your checkbook ledger will seldom be the same as the amount shown by the bank. The way to handle this is to simply record the check in your checkbook ledger as you normally would, including the new balance after the check is written. If this overdraws your account—at least as far as your checkbook ledger is concerned—this will not be a problem, because you have an overdraft protection line to cover it. If it does, in fact, overdraw your account, the bank will notify you of this in a matter of days and inform you that it has advanced funds to your checking account. The amount of the advance will be shown on the notice and should immediately be entered into your checkbook ledger as a *deposit.*

Funds advanced from an overdraft protection line usually carry an interest rate of 12 to 15 percent, though rates as high as 16 to 18 percent are not all that uncommon. Once an advance is made, a monthly repayment schedule is set up for systematically repaying the loan, along with all interest charges—generally with monthly payments being spread out over a period of 18 to 36 months. A statement is sent out each month, along with the monthly check statement, summarizing any activity in the overdraft protection line (new advances, repayments, new balance, and amount of credit still available) and indicating the required monthly payment. Note that because there ordinarily is no limit on the number of times you can overdraw your account, the amount of the monthly payment will change every time the bank advances money to your account.

It should be clear that if you are not careful, you can quickly exhaust this line of credit by writing a lot of overdraft checks. As with any line of credit, there is a limit to how much you can obtain. You should be extremely careful with such a credit line and *under no circumstances take it as a license to routinely overdraw your account!* Doing so on a regular basis is a signal that you are probably mismanaging your cash and/or living beyond your budget. It is best to view an overdraft protection line strictly as an *emergency* source of credit—and any funds advanced should be repaid as quickly as possible.

unsecured personal credit line
A line of credit made available to an individual on an as-needed basis in the form of check-writing privileges against it.

UNSECURED PERSONAL LINES. Another form of revolving credit is the **unsecured personal credit line**, which basically makes a line of credit available to an individual on an as-needed basis. In essence, it is a way of borrowing money from a bank, S&L, credit union, savings bank, or brokerage firm any time you wish, without going through all the hassle of setting up a new loan.

Here is how it works. Suppose you submit a loan application for a personal line of credit at your bank. Once you have been approved and the credit line established, you will be issued *checks* that you can write against it. Thus, if you need a cash advance, all you need to do is write a check (against your credit line account) and deposit it into your checking account. Alternatively, if you need the money to buy some high-ticket item—say, an expensive stereo system—you can just make the credit line check out to the dealer and, when it clears, it will be charged against your unsecured personal credit line as an advance. (These credit line checks look and "spend" just like regular checks and as such do not have to be channeled through your normal checking account.)

Personal lines of credit are usually set up for minimums of $2,000 to $5,000 and often amount to $25,000 or more. As with an overdraft protection line, once an advance is made, repayment is set up on a monthly installment basis. Depending on the amount outstanding, repayment is normally structured over a period of two to five years; to keep the monthly payments low, larger amounts of debt are usually given longer repayment periods. As a rule, these credit lines are set up with adjustable rates of interest so that the interest charged on advances varies with some benchmark rate, such as the prime rate—normally floating 2 to 4 percentage points above the prime/benchmark rate. Thus, if the prime rate goes up (or down) by, say, 1 percent, the cost of the credit line will also go up (or down) by the same 1 percent. Monthly statements summarize the activity in the credit line and stipulate the required minimum monthly payment.

Although these credit lines do offer attractive terms to the consumer, they do not come without their share of problems, perhaps the biggest of which is the ease with which cash advances can be obtained. In addition, these lines normally involve *substantial* credit limits and are about as easy to use as credit cards. This combination can have devastating effects on a family's budget if it leads to overspending or excessive reliance on credit. To be safe, these lines should be used only for emergency purposes or to make *planned credit expenditures*. In addition, systematic repayment of the debt should be built into the budget, and every effort should be made to ensure that the use of this kind of credit will not place an undue strain on the family finances.

HOME EQUITY CREDIT LINES.   Here is a familiar situation. A couple buys a home for $85,000; some 10 years later, it is worth $165,000. The couple now has an asset worth $165,000 on which all they owe is the original mortgage, which may now have a balance of, say, $45,000. The couple clearly has built up a substantial amount of equity in their home: $165,000 − $45,000 = $120,000. But how can they tap that equity without having to sell their home? The answer is to obtain a **home equity credit line**. Such lines are much like unsecured personal credit lines except that they are *secured* with a second mortgage on the home. Offered by most banks, S&Ls, major brokerage firms, and a growing number of credit unions, these lines of credit allow you to tap up to 100 percent (or more) of the equity in your home by merely writing a check. For a variety of reasons, including attractive tax features (which we'll examine below), the popularity of home equity credit lines has grown almost exponentially. Indeed, the amount of home equity loans outstanding today actually *exceeds* the amount of credit card debt outstanding!

While there are banks and financial institutions that do allow their customers to borrow up to 100 percent of the *equity* in their homes—or, in some cases, even more—the majority of the lenders set their maximum credit lines at 75 to 80 percent of the *market value* of the home, which reduces the amount of money they'll lend. The typical home equity credit line has a minimum of $10,000 in available credit and an advance period of 5 to 20 years, during which you can tap into the line by writing checks or using a special

home equity credit line
A line of credit issued against the existing equity in a home.

credit card. At the end of the advance period, you must stop borrowing and begin to repay the principal and interest over a 10- to 20-year period. Of course, you can always pay these lines off earlier, and many consumers have the self-discipline to pay down the line quickly. (A word of caution about high-value home equity lines: Some banks and finance companies are willing to lend up to 125 percent of the current market value of your home so long as the excess borrowed amount is used to either pay down credit cards or pay for home improvements—which is why these things are sometimes called *home improvement loans*. These loans may appear tempting, but watch out, for their interest rates are often much higher than average—sometimes as much as 5 or 6 percentage points higher—and you won't be able to treat all the interest paid as a tax deductible expense.)

Here's how these lines work. The couple in the earlier example has built up an equity of $120,000 in their home—equity against which they can borrow through a home equity credit line. Assuming they have a good credit record and using a 75 percent loan-to-market-value ratio, a bank would be willing to lend up to $123,750; that is, 75 percent of the value of the house is .75 × $165,000 = $123,750. Subtracting the $45,000 still due on the first mortgage, we see that our couple could qualify for a home equity credit line of a whopping $78,750. Note, in this case, that if the bank had been willing to lend the couple *100 percent of the equity* in their home, it would have given them a (much higher) credit line of $120,000, which is the difference between what the house is worth and what they still owe on it. Most lenders don't like to do this because it results in very large credit lines and, perhaps more important, it doesn't provide the lender with any cushion should the borrower default.

 If you need a home equity line of credit but your credit is not the best, Bankrate.com can point you to the best rates in your own state or suggest a more distant bank with a good deal: **www.bankrate.com/brm/bcd/creditpage.asp**.

Home equity lines also have an interesting tax feature that you should be aware of—that is, the annual interest charges on such lines may be fully deductible for those who itemize. This is the only type of consumer loan that still qualifies for such tax treatment. According to the latest provisions of the tax code, a homeowner is allowed to *fully deduct the interest charges on home equity loans of up to $100,000*, regardless of the original cost of the house or use of the proceeds. Indeed, the only restriction is that *the amount of total indebtedness on the house cannot exceed its fair market value*—which is highly unlikely, because homeowners usually cannot borrow more than 75 to 80 percent of the market value of the house anyway. (Effectively, the interest on that portion of the loan that exceeds $100,000, or 100 percent of the market value of the house—whichever is lower—*cannot* be treated as a tax-deductible expense.) In our preceding example, the home owners could take out the full amount of their credit line ($78,750), and every dime they paid in interest would be tax deductible. If they paid, say, $7,400 in interest, and if they were in the 28 percent tax bracket, this feature would reduce their tax liability by some $2,070—(i.e., $7,400 × .28)—given, of course, that they itemize their deductions.

Not only do home equity credit lines offer shelter from taxes, they're also among *the cheapest forms of consumer credit*. While other types of consumer credit may cost 15 to 18 percent or more, home equity lines can be had for about 9.5 to 12 percent (representative rates in 2000). To see what that can mean to you as a borrower, assume you have $10,000 in consumer debt outstanding. If you had borrowed that money through a standard consumer loan at, say, 16.5 percent, you'd pay interest of $1,650 per year—none of which would be tax deductible. But borrow the same amount through a home equity credit line at, say, 11 percent, and you'll pay only $1,100 in interest. That's all tax deductible though, so if you're in the 28 percent tax bracket, the after-tax cost to you would be $1,100 × (1 − .28) = $792. This is less than half the cost of the other loan! So, which would you rather pay for a $10,000 loan,

$1,650 or $792? That's really not a tough decision; but it does explain, in large part, why these lines have become so popular and are today one of the fastest growing forms of consumer credit.

Home equity credit lines are offered by a variety of financial institutions, from banks and S&Ls to major brokerage houses. All sorts of credit terms and credit lines are available; most of these lines carry repayment periods of 10 to 15 years, or longer. What is perhaps most startling, however, is the maximum amount of credit available under these lines—indeed, $100,000 figures are not at all unusual. And it's precisely because of the enormous amount of money available that this form of credit should be used with caution. *The fact that you have equity in your home does not mean that you have the cash flow necessary to service the debt that such a credit line imposes.* Remember that your house is the collateral. If you can't repay the loan, you could lose it! At the minimum, paying for major expenditures through a home equity credit line should be done only after you have determined that you can afford the purchase and the required monthly payments will fit comfortably within your budget.

Perhaps the biggest problem with this type of credit is the temptation to use the long-term repayment schedules available on home equity loans to keep payments *artificially* low and, in so doing, purchase items whose lives will be nowhere near as long as that of the associated debt. For example, to use a 15-year second mortgage to buy a car with a 5-year life makes absolutely no sense! You will still be paying for the car 10 years after you have sold it. The fact is that if the only way you can afford the car is to buy it with 15 years of payments, you cannot afford it in the first place. Home equity credit lines can be an effective way of tapping the built-up equity in a home, but you should avoid using them to buy items you could not otherwise afford.

CONCEPT CHECK

6-4. What is *open account credit?* Who are the main providers and what are the main categories of this form of credit?

6-5. What is a *line of credit?* Does a line of credit come with all types of credit cards?

6-6. How do bank credit cards and *travel and entertainment* cards differ? Comment on the following statement: "If used intelligently, bank credit cards can be quite useful."

6-7. What is the attraction of *rebate cards?* List and briefly describe some of the more popular services and features that are now being offered on bank credit cards.

6-8. Explain how you could use your credit card to obtain a *cash advance.* Does it make any difference whether you obtain the cash advance from an ATM or the bank's teller window?

6-9. How is the interest rate typically set on bank credit cards? In terms of interest rate, does it matter if you use your credit card to purchase merchandise or obtain a cash advance?

6-10. Many bank card issuers impose different types of fees; briefly describe three of these fees. Do these fees have any impact on the true (effective) cost of using credit cards? Explain.

6-11. Explain the difference between a *retail charge card* account and a *30-day charge account.* What's a *secured credit card* and how does it differ from a *prestige card?*

6-12. What is a *debit card?* How is it similar to a credit card? How does it differ?

6-13. Describe how *revolving credit lines* provide open account credit. How would you obtain an advance from an *overdraft protection line?* What are the basic features of a *home equity credit line?*

■ Obtaining and Managing Open Account Credit [LG4]

Americans love to use their charge cards. In the year 2000 alone, they bought around *$1 trillion* in goods and services on credit. And this figure is rising as more places accept "plastic," consumers find credit and debit cards more convenient than cash or checks, and the number of other benefits, like rebates and frequent flyer miles, continues to grow.

For the sake of convenience, people often maintain a variety of open accounts. Nearly every household, for example, uses 30-day charge accounts to pay their utility bills, phone bills, and so on. In addition, most families have one or more retail charge cards, a couple of bank cards, and possibly a T&E card; some people, in fact, may have as many as 15 to 20 cards, or more. And that's not all—Families can also have one or more revolving credit lines in the form of overdraft protection, an unsecured personal line, or a home equity line. When all these cards and lines are totaled together, a family conceivably can have tens of thousands of dollars of readily available credit. It is easy to see why consumer credit has become such a popular way of making relatively routine purchases. Although open account credit can increase the risk of budgetary overload, these accounts can serve as a useful way of keeping track of expenditures.

OPENING AN ACCOUNT

Unlike many 30-day charge accounts, retail charge cards, bank credit cards, T&E cards, and revolving lines of credit all require *formal application procedures*. Let's look now at how you'd go about obtaining open account credit, including the normal credit application, investigation, and decision process. We'll couch our discussion in terms of credit cards, but keep in mind that similar procedures apply to other revolving lines of credit as well.

THE CREDIT APPLICATION. With nearly a billion credit cards in the hands of American consumers, one would think that consumer credit is readily available. And it is— but you have to apply for it. Applications are usually available at the store or bank involved. Sometimes they can be found at the businesses that accept these cards or obtained on request from the issuing companies. Exhibit 6.5 provides an example of a bank credit card application. In this case, it is for a Yahoo! Platinum Visa Card. The information requested in this online credit application concerns personal/family matters, housing, employment and income, existing charge accounts, and credit references. Such information is intended to provide the lender with insight about the applicant's creditworthiness. In essence, the lender is trying to determine whether the applicant has the *character* and *capacity* to handle the debt in a prompt and timely manner. (As mentioned earlier, credit card issuers are continually blitzing America's mailboxes with preapproved offers for their cards. But even these come-ons require a credit application, though they tend to be shorter than if you had requested the application on your own.)

credit investigation
An investigation that involves contacting credit references or corresponding with a credit bureau to verify information on a credit application.

THE CREDIT INVESTIGATION. Once the credit application has been completed and returned to the establishment issuing the card, it is subject to a **credit investigation**. The purpose is to evaluate the kind of credit risk you pose to the lender (the party issuing the credit or charge card). So be sure to fill out your credit application carefully. Believe it or not, they really do look at those things. The key items lenders look at are how much money you make, how much debt you presently have outstanding and how well you handle it, and how stable you are (for example, your age, employment history, whether you own or rent a home, and so on). Obviously, the higher your income and the better your credit history, the greater the chances of having your credit application approved.

EXHIBIT 6.5

AN ONLINE CREDIT CARD APPLICATION

You can apply for many credit cards today right on the Internet, which is the case with the *Yahoo! Visa Card* application shown here. This credit application, like most, seeks information about the applicant's place of employment, monthly income, place of residence, credit history, and other financial matters that are intended to help the lender decide whether or not to extend credit.

Yahoo! Platinum Visa Card

Apply Online Today! It's Secure, It's Fast, It's Easy!

Please Tell Us About Yourself

| First Name: [   ] | M.I.: [ ] | Last Name: [   ] |

(You must be a U.S. resident to apply. No P.O. Boxes please.)

Address Line 1: [   ]

Address Line 2: [   ]

City: [   ]   **State:** [ ]   **Zip Code:** [   ] - [ ]

Lived There: [0 ▼] years [0 ▼] months   **Home Phone:** [ ] - [ ] - [ ]

(You must be 18 or older to be considered for a credit card)

Date of Birth: [ ] / [ ] / [ ] (MM-DD-YYYY)   **SSN:** [ ] - [ ] - [ ]

Mother's Maiden Name: [   ]   **Dependents:** [0 ▼] *(Excluding yourself)*

E-mail Address: [   ]

If you provide us with your email address, when you become a First USA Cardmember, we'll keep you informed about upcoming special values via email.

Please Tell Us About Your Job

(If retired, note previous employer. If self-employed, note nature of business.)

Employer: [   ]   **Position:** [   ]

Worked There: [0 ▼] years [0 ▼] months   **Work Phone:** [ ] - [ ] - [ ]

Please Provide Some Financial Information

**Alimony, child support, or separate maintenance income need not be revealed if you do not wish it to be considered as a basis for repaying this obligation.

Annual Household Income: $ [   ] .00

Please select the type(s) of bank account(s) you have: [▼]

Monthly Rent or Mortgage: $ [   ] .00   **Select Residence:** [▼]

2nd Cardholder

Yes, please send a second card at no extra cost for:

First Name: [   ]   **M.I.:** [ ]   **Last Name:** [   ]

As a part of the investigation process, the lender will attempt to verify much of the information provided by you on the credit application—for obvious reasons, false or misleading information will almost certainly result in outright rejection of your application. For example, the lender may verify your place of employment, level of income, current debt load and debt service history, and so forth. Often, this can be done through one or two quick phone calls. If you've lived in the area for a number of years and have established relations with a local bank, a call to your banker may be all it takes to confirm your credit-worthiness. If you haven't established such bank relations—and most young people have not—the lender is likely to turn to the local credit bureau for a *credit report* on you.

credit bureau
An organization, typically established by local banks and merchants, that collects and stores credit information about individual borrowers and, for a specified fee, supplies it to financial institutions that request it.

THE CREDIT BUREAU. Basically a **credit bureau** is a type of reporting agency that gathers and sells information about individual borrowers. If, as is often the case, the lender does not know you personally, it must rely on a cost-effective way of verifying your employment and credit history. It would be far too expensive and time consuming for individual creditors to confirm your credit application on their own, so they turn to credit bureaus that maintain fairly detailed credit files about you. Information in your file comes from one of three sources: creditors who subscribe to the bureau, other creditors who supply information at your request, and publicly recorded court documents (such as tax liens or bankruptcy records).

Contrary to popular opinion, your credit file does *not* contain everything anyone would ever want to know about you—there's nothing on your lifestyle, friends, habits, or religious or political affiliations. Instead, most of the information is pretty dull stuff, and covers such things as:

- Your name, social security number, age, number of dependents, and current and previous addresses
- Your employment record, including current and past employers and salary data, if available
- Your credit history, including the number of loans and credit lines you have, number of credit cards issued in your name, your payment record, and account balances
- Public records data involving bankruptcies, tax liens, foreclosures, civil suits, and criminal convictions
- The names of firms and financial institutions that have recently requested copies of your file.

While one late MasterCard payment probably won't make much of a difference on an otherwise clean credit file, a definite pattern of delinquencies (consistently being 30 to 60 days late with your payments) or a personal bankruptcy certainly will. Unfortunately, poor credit traits will stick with you for a long time, because delinquencies will remain on your credit file for as long as 7 years and bankruptcies for 10 years. An example of an actual credit bureau report (or at least a part of one) is provided in Exhibit 6.6. It demonstrates the kind of information you can expect to find in one of these reports.

Local credit bureaus (there are about a thousand of them) are established and mutually owned by local merchants and banks. They collect and store credit information on people living within the community and make it available, for a fee, to members who request it. If the information requested can be transmitted over the phone, by fax, or by e-mail, the cost of the inquiry is typically about $5 or $10. On the other hand, if the credit bureau must obtain, either through its own investigation or from another credit bureau, additional information to update the applicant's file, the cost of the report will be much higher.

Local bureaus are linked together nationally through one of the "big three" national bureaus—Trans-Union, Equifax Credit Information Services, and Experian (formerly TRW Credit Data)—each of which provides the mechanism for obtaining credit information from almost any place in the United States. It's important to understand that credit bureaus merely collect and provide credit information. They do not analyze it, they do not rate it (or at least they're not supposed to), and they certainly do not make the final credit decision.

Credit bureaus have been heavily criticized because of the large numbers of reporting errors and their poor record in correcting these errors on a timely and efficient basis. And consumers have been frustrated by the time-consuming process and credit bureaus' apparent "care less" attitude about their mistakes—as far as they are concerned, you are guilty

EXHIBIT 6.6

AN EXAMPLE OF A CREDIT BUREAU REPORT

Displayed here is an actual credit report from a major credit reporting bureau. These reports have been revised and are easier to understand. Notice that in addition to some basic information, the report deals strictly with credit information—including payment records, past due status, and types of credit; also reported is a summary of any relevant public records (see item 1).

This is your consumer identification number. Please refer to this number when you call or write.

ID # XXXXXXXXXXXXX

```
MARY R. CONSUMER
1500 RAINBOW LANE
ANYTOWN, CA 90000-0000
```

ITEM	ACCOUNT NAME	DESCRIPTION	STATUS/PAYMENTS
1	*KEARNEY MESA MUN CT 8950 CLAIRMONT MESA BLVD SAN DIEGO, CA 92101 REFERENCE # 00	THE ORIGINAL AMOUNT OF THIS COURT ITEM IS $300. THE PARTY THAT BROUGHT THIS ACTION AGAINST YOU OR THE COURT REFERENCE NUMBER IS	THIS JUDGMENT WAS FILED IN 04/01/90 AND PAID IN FULL ON 06/20/90.
2	AMERICAN EXPRESS CO P O BOX 7871 SROC FORT LAUDERDALE, FL 33329 NATL CREDIT CARDS ACCT #	THIS CREDIT CARD ACCOUNT WAS OPENED 04/75 AND HAS 1 MONTH REPAYMENT TERMS. YOU HAVE CONTRACTUAL RESPONSIBILITY FOR THIS ACCOUNT AND ARE PRIMARILY RESPONSIBLE FOR ITS PAYMENT. THE HIGH BALANCE OF THIS ACCOUNT IS $72.	AS OF 06/98 THIS ACCOUNT IS PAID IN FULL AND ALL PAYMENTS HAVE BEEN PAID ON TIME.

***CREDIT LINE CLOSED - CONSUMER'S REQUEST - REPORTED BY SUBSCRIBER

ITEM	ACCOUNT NAME	DESCRIPTION	STATUS/PAYMENTS
3	BANK OF BOSTON NA 15 WESTMINSTER STREET PROVIDENCE, RI 02903 BANKING ACCT #	THIS CREDIT CARD ACCOUNT WAS OPENED OVER 10 YEARS AGO AND HAS REVOLVING REPAYMENT TERMS. YOU ARE OBLIGATED TO REPAY THIS JOINT ACCOUNT. THE CREDIT LIMIT OF THIS ACCOUNT IS $2,100.	AS OF 02/94 THIS ACCOUNT IS PAID IN FULL AND ALL PAYMENTS HAVE BEEN PAID ON TIME.
4	COUNTRYWIDE FUND CORP 400 COUNTRYWIDE WAY SIMI VALLEY, CA 93065 UNDEFINED FIRM TYPE ACCT #	THIS CONVENTIONAL REAL ESTATE LOAN WAS OPENED 1993 AND HAS 30 YEAR REPAYMENT TERMS. YOU ARE OBLIGATED TO REPAY THIS JOINT ACCOUNT. THE ORIGINAL AMOUNT OF THIS ACCOUNT IS $370,000.	AS OF 01/98 THIS ACCOUNT IS CURRENT AND ALL PAYMENTS HAVE BEEN PAID ON TIME. YOUR BALANCE AS OF 12/31/98 IS $345,067. YOUR SCHEDULED MONTHLY PAYMENT IS $2,447. THE LAST PAYMENT REPORTED TO TRW WAS MADE ON DATE UNAVAILABLE. PAYMENT HISTORY: CCCCCCCCCCCC/CCCCCC

YOUR CREDIT HISTORY WAS REVIEWED BY:

THE FOLLOWING INQUIRIES ARE REPORTED TO THOSE WHO ASK TO REVIEW YOUR CREDIT HISTORY.

ITEM	ACCOUNT NAME	DATE	REMARKS
5	MOSSY DATSUN INC. 2700 NATIONAL CITY BLVD NATIONAL CITY, CA 91950 AUTOMOTIVE	11/26/00	INQUIRY MADE FOR CREDIT EXTENSION, REVIEW OR OTHER PERMISSIBLE PURPOSE FOR UNSPECIFIED REPAYMENT TERMS. THE AMOUNT IS UNSPECIFIED.
6	FIRESTONE TIRE 6275 EASTLAND ROAD BROOK PARK, OH 44142 UNDEFINED FIRM TYPE	09/04/99	INQUIRY MADE FOR CREDIT EXTENSION, REVIEW OR OTHER PERMISSIBLE PURPOSE FOR UNSPECIFIED REPAYMENT TERMS. THE AMOUNT IS UNSPECIFIED.

![Financial Road Sign icon] **Financial Road Sign**

What to Look for in Your Credit Report
1. Verify your name, address, social security number, driver's license number, spouse's name, and address.
2. Review your credit history. Note errors such as late payments you believe were made on time or disputed bill amounts.
3. Some credit reports use payment codes ranging from 1 to 9. An R1 or I1 indicates a good payment history.
4. Check the public records section for inaccuracies about bankruptcies, judgments, and tax liens.
5. If you find a mistake, follow the report's instructions. It may take as long as 30 days to have disputed information removed from your credit report.

Source: Pat Curry, "How to Read and Understand Your Credit Report," *Bankrate.com*, November 27, 2000, **www.bankrate.com**.

until proven innocent. Fortunately, things have changed in recent years as the major credit bureaus have taken a more consumer-oriented approach, greatly improving their customer service and dispute resolution procedures and making reports easier to read. Many of these changes were formalized by a 1995 amendment to the Fair Credit Reporting Act (described later in the chapter) that established industry guidelines for credit reporting procedures. According to this legislation, credit bureaus must provide you with low-cost copies of your own credit report, and they must have toll-free phone numbers. Disputes must be resolved in 30 days and take the consumer's documentation into account, not just the creditor's. Better procedures are required to ensure that reports are corrected properly and errors do not reappear; and creditors are now liable—and can be sued by consumers—if they do not correct credit reporting errors.

Even with these changes, credit bureaus still make mistakes. Unfortunately, when they do, it can mean *big* problems for you, because a credit report can affect whether or not you get credit (or maybe even a job, as some employers look at potential employees' credit reports as a type of character reference—these employers do, however, have to ask you to sign a waiver allowing them to check your credit report!). Millions of Americans have learned the hard way that their credit records are riddled with errors. You should ensure that your credit report accurately reflects your credit history. Here are some things you can do.

If you plan to take out a big loan—to finance, say, a new car—it might pay to get a copy of your credit report before you do anything. Knowing what kind of information credit agencies have collected on you—and whether it's correct—can save you a lot of time later. *It's especially important for young adults and married women to make sure that all accounts for which they are individually or jointly liable are listed in their credit files, as lenders are normally reluctant to consider applicants with little or no credit history.* As for errors, most people don't know there are any in their reports until it's too late. Particularly troubling is *adverse* information about you (i.e., that you're a deadbeat or don't pay your bills on time) that simply isn't true. Common inaccuracies include bad debts of another person with a similar name, tax liens or judgments that have been satisfied, and disputes with merchants that have been resolved.

It's not hard to get a copy of your credit report, and *most consumer advisors recommend you review your files at the major bureaus annually.* You can obtain a copy of your credit report by submitting a written request that includes your name, spouse's name, current and prior (five years') addresses, date of birth, social security number, verification of this information (such as a copy of a driver's license), current employer, and your signature. Fees for reports vary by state and range from about $3 to $8 for an individual report. If you've been denied credit within 60 days of your request, you are entitled to a *free copy* of your credit report. Most local credit bureaus are listed in the Yellow Pages of the phone book. The addresses, Web sites, and toll-free phone numbers for the three national credit bureaus are provided below:

- Equifax Credit Information Services
  P.O. Box 105873
  Atlanta, GA 30348
  www.equifax.com or phone 1-800-997-2493

- Trans-Union Corporation
  Consumer Disclosure Center
  P.O. Box 1000
  Chester, PA 19022
  www.transunion.com or phone 1-800-888-4213

- Experian (formerly TRW)
  www.experian.com or phone 1-888-397-3742

Once you receive your credit report, review it carefully. If you find any errors, send a letter immediately, describing the situation. Include the name of the creditor, the account number, the reason the information is wrong, and any available proof, such as a cancelled check showing payment was made. Request a copy of the corrected file to be sure the mistake is indeed corrected. If the creditor still disagrees with your claim, you can submit a 100-word statement that is included in your file as an explanation for the dispute.

THE CREDIT DECISION. Using the data provided by the credit applicant, along with any information obtained from the credit bureau, the store or bank must decide whether or not to grant credit. Very likely, some type of **credit scoring** scheme will be used to make the credit decision. By assigning values to such factors as your age, annual income, number of years on your present job, whether you rent or own your home and how long you have lived there, age of your cars, number and type of credit cards you hold, level of your existing debts, whether you have savings accounts, whether you have a phone, and general credit references, an overall credit score for you can be developed. There may be 10 or 15 different factors or characteristics that are considered, and each characteristic will receive a score based on some predetermined standard. For example, if you're 26 years old, single, earn $32,500 a year (on a job that you've had for only two years), and rent an apartment, you might receive the following scores:

credit scoring
A method of evaluating an applicant's creditworthiness by assigning values to such factors as income, existing debts, and credit references.

1. Age (under 25)	5 points
2. Marital status (single)	−2 points
3. Annual income ($30–35 thousand)	12 points
4. Length of employment (2 yrs. or less)	4 points
5. Rent or own a home (rent)	0 points
	19 points

Based on information obtained from your credit application, similar scores would be assigned to another seven to ten factors.

In all cases, the stronger your personal traits or characteristics, the higher the score you'll receive. For instance, if you had been 46 years old (rather than 26), you might have received 18 points for your age factor, being married rather than single would have given you 9 points, and earning $75,000 a year would obviously have been worth a lot more than earning $32,500! The idea is that the more stable you are *perceived* to be, the more income you make, the better your credit record, and so on, the higher the score you should receive. In essence, statistical studies have shown that certain personal and financial traits can be used to determine your credit worthiness. Indeed, the whole credit scoring system is based on extensive statistical studies, which identify the characteristics to look at and the scores to assign. It's all very mechanical: assign a score to each characteristic, add up the scores, and, based on that total score, determine the creditworthiness of the applicant. While it may sound simple, credit scoring has, in fact, come under sharp criticism of late because very few people really know the specifics of what determines credit scores. To alleviate some of the mystery, Congress has been working on the *Fair Credit Disclosure Act;* and two of the three major credit bureaus, Trans-Union and Experian, are developing ways to more fully describe their credit-risk ratings. In addition, Fair, Isaac—the firm that produces the widely used *FICO Scores*—has shed some light on the matter by revealing the five major components (along with their respective weights) that go into their credit scores. They are as follows: payment history (35%), outstanding debt (30%), credit history (15%), number of new credit inquiries (10%), and types of credit (10%).

Generally, if your score equals or exceeds a predetermined minimum, you will be given credit; if not, credit will be refused. Sometimes borderline cases are granted credit on a limited basis. For example, a large department store that normally limits the outstanding balance on its revolving charge accounts to $500 might give a customer with a marginal credit score a revolving charge account with a $200 credit limit. Even when a formal credit scoring scheme is used, the credit manager or loan officer is normally empowered to offer credit if such action seems appropriate. Applicants who are granted credit are notified and sent a charge card and/or checks, along with material describing the credit terms and procedures.

COMPUTING FINANCE CHARGES

annual percentage rate (APR)
The actual or true rate of interest paid over the life of a loan.

average daily balance (ADB) method
A method of computing finance charges by applying interest charges to the average daily balance of the account over the billing period.

Because card issuers do not know in advance how much you will charge on your account, they cannot specify the dollar amount of interest you will be charged. But they can—and must, according to the Truth in Lending Act (defined later in this chapter)—disclose the *rate of interest* they charge and their method of computing finance charges. This is the **annual percentage rate (APR)**, the true rate of interest paid over the life of the loan, and must be calculated in the manner outlined by law. Remember, it is your right as a consumer to know—and the obligation of the lender to tell you—the dollar amount of charges (where applicable) and the APR on any financing you consider.

The amount of interest you pay for open account credit depends in part on the method the lender uses to calculate the balances on which they apply finance charges. Most bank and retail charge card issuers use one of four variations of the **average daily balance (ADB) method**, which applies the interest rate to the average daily balance of the account over the billing period. According to Bankcard Holders of America, a nonprofit consumer education organization, the most common method (used by an estimated 95 percent of bank card issuers) is the *average daily balance including new purchases*. The other techniques are average daily balance excluding new purchases, two-cycle average daily balance including new purchases, and two-cycle average daily balance excluding new purchases. Balance calculations under each method are as follows:

- **ADB including new purchases.** For each day in the billing cycle, add the outstanding balance, including new purchases, and subtract payments and credits, then divide by the number of days in the billing cycle.
- **ADB excluding new purchases.** Same as first method, *excluding* new purchases.
- **Two-cycle ADB including new purchases.** Calculated like the first method, but using the average daily balance for both the current and previous billing cycles.
- **Two-cycle ADB excluding new purchases.** Same as the above two-cycle method, but *excluding* new purchases.

These different balance calculations can have a significant impact on finance charges, and you should be aware that the finance charges of two cards with the same APR but different methods of calculating balances may differ dramatically. It's very important to know the method your card issuer uses. Most banks compute finance charges for a 1-month period, though some issuers (among them Discover Card) still use the *two-cycle average daily balance method*. As we can see from the comparisons in Exhibit 6.7, carrying a balance on a credit card can turn out to be very expensive.

Let's look at an example of how to calculate balances and finance charges under the most popular method, *the average daily balance including new purchases*. Assume you have a LastBank Visa card with a monthly interest rate of 1.5 percent. Your statement for the billing period extending from October 10, 2001, through November 10, 2001—a total of 31 days—shows that your beginning balance was $582, you made purchases of $350 on October 15 and $54 on October 22, and you made a $25 payment on November 6. Therefore, the outstanding balance for the first 5 days of the period (October 11 through 15) was $582; for the next 7 (October 16 through 22), it was $932 ($582 + $350); for the next 15 days (October 23 through November 6) it was $986 ($932 + $54); and the last 4 days, it was $961

EXHIBIT 6.7

FINANCE CHARGES FOR DIFFERENT BALANCE CALCULATION METHODS

The way a credit card issuer calculates the average daily balance on which the consumer pays finance charges has a big effect on the amount of interest you actually pay, as the following table demonstrates.

Example: A consumer starts the first month with a zero balance and charges $1,000, of which he pays off only the minimum amount due ($\frac{1}{36}$th of balance due). The next month, he charges another $1,000. He then pays off the entire balance due. This same pattern is repeated three more times during the year. The interest rate is 19.8%.

	Finance Charges
Average Daily balance (including new purchases):	$132.00
Average Daily Balance (excluding new purchases):	$ 66.00
Two-cycle Average Daily Balance (including new purchases):	$196.20
Two-cycle Average Daily Balance (excluding new purchases):	$131.20

Source: Courtesy of Bankcard Holders of America, Salem, Virginia.

EXHIBIT 6.8

FINDING THE AVERAGE DAILY BALANCE AND FINANCE CHARGE

The average daily balance including new purchases is the method most widely used by credit card issuers to determine the monthly finance charge on an account:

	Number of Days **(1)**	**Balance** **(2)**	**(1) × (2)** **(3)**
	5	$582	$2,910
	7	$932	6,524
	15	$986	14,790
	4	$961	3,844
Total	31		$28,068

Average daily balance $= \dfrac{\$28,068}{31} = \$905.42$

Finance Charge: $\$905.42 \times .015 = \$13.58$

($986 less the $25 payment). We can now calculate the average daily balance using the procedure shown in Exhibit 6.8; the outstanding balances are weighted by the number of days that the balance existed and then averaged (divided) by the number of days in the billing period. By multiplying the average daily balance of $905.42 by the 1.5 percent interest rate, we get a finance charge of $13.58.

MANAGING CREDIT CARD ACCOUNTS

Congratulations! You have applied for and been granted a bank credit card, and a retail charge card from your favorite department store. You carefully reviewed the terms of the credit agreement and understand how finance charges are computed for each account. Now you must manage your accounts efficiently, using the monthly statement to help you make the required payments on time, and to track purchases and returned items.

THE STATEMENT. If you use a credit card, you will receive monthly statements similar to the sample bank card statement in Exhibit 6.9, showing billing cycle and payment due dates, interest rate, minimum payment, and all account activity during the current period. Retail charge cards have similar monthly statements, but without a section for cash advances. (Revolving line of credit lenders will also send you a monthly statement showing the amount borrowed, payments, and finance charges.) The statement summarizes your account activity: the previous balance (the amount of credit outstanding at the beginning of the month, not to be confused with past-due, or late, payments); new charges made during the past month (four in this case); any finance charges (interest) on the unpaid balance; the preceding period's payment; any other credits (such as those for returns); and the new balance (previous balance plus new purchases and finance charges, less any payments and credits).

Although merchandise and cash transactions are separated on the statement, the finance charge in each case is calculated at the rate of 1.5 percent per month (18 percent annually). Many card issuers charge a higher rate for cash advances than for purchases. Note that the average daily balance method is used to compute the finance charge in this statement.

You should review your statements promptly each month. Save your receipts and use them to verify statement entries for purchases and returns *before* paying. If you find any errors or suspect fraudulent use of your card, first use the issuer's toll-free number to report any problems. Then always follow up *in writing* within 60 days of the postmark on the bill.

minimum monthly payment
In open account credit, a minimum specified percentage of the new account balance that must be paid in order to remain current.

PAYMENTS. Credit card users can avoid *future* finance charges by paying the total new balance shown on their statement each month. For example, if the $534.08 total new balance shown in Exhibit 6.9 is paid by the September 21, 2000 due date, no additional finance charges will be incurred. (The cardholder, however, will still be liable for the $4.40 in finance charges incurred to date.) If cardholders cannot pay the total new balance, they can pay any amount that is equal to or greater than the **minimum monthly payment** specified on the statement. If they do that, however, they will incur additional finance charges in the following month. Note that the account in Exhibit 6.9 has a minimum payment of 5 percent of the new balance, rounded to the nearest full dollar. As shown at the bottom of the statement, this month's minimum payment is $27: $534.08 × .05 = $26.70 = $27.00. If the new balance had been less than $200, the bank would have required a payment of $10 (which is the absolute minimum dollar payment), or of the total new balance, if less than $10. Cardholders who fail to make the minimum payment are considered in default on their account, and the bank issuing the card can take whatever action it deems necessary.

RETURNING MERCHANDISE. When you return merchandise purchased with a credit card, the merchant will issue a *credit* to your account. The credit is transacted in the same fashion as a purchase and will appear on your statement as a *deduction* from the balance. If you purchase an item and have problems with it, you may not have to pay that part of your credit card bill if you have attempted in good faith to resolve the problem with the merchant. This protection is provided by the Fair Credit Billing Act, discussed later in the chapter. Of course, if the problem is resolved in the merchant's favor, you will ultimately have to pay.

EXHIBIT 6.9

A BANK CREDIT CARD MONTHLY STATEMENT

Each month, a bank credit cardholder receives a statement that provides an itemized list of charges and credits, as well as a summary of previous activity and finance charges.

Please detach the above portion and return it with your payment to insure proper credit.

Bank Card Statement
Retain this statement for your records.

Account Number 123-XYZ-45678	Name(s) Mr. Bill A. Bitshort Mrs. Bonnie R. Bitshort	8-24-00 Statement Date	09-21-00 Payment Due Date

ACCOUNT ACTIVITY

Previous Balance	203.64
Payments −	119.89
Credits −	.00
Subtotal	83.75
New Transaction +	445.93
Finance Charge +	4.40
Late Charge +	.00
NEW BALANCE	534.08

Credit Status
Your Credit Limit is:

2000.00
Your Available Credit is:

1465.92

FINANCE CHARGE CALCULATION

Amounts Subject to Finance Charge		This Month's Charge	
A. *Average Daily Balance	293.25 =	4.40	ENTIRE BAL. 1.5% 18.00%
B. *Cash Advance	.00 =	.00	Monthly Periodic Rate / Nominal Annual Rate
C. *Loan Advance	.00 =	.00	
		4.40	18.00%
*Finance Charges explained on reverse side		Finance Charge	Annual Percentage Rate

---

Mail Billing Inquiries to: Post Office Box 7760, Van Nuys, California, 85258, or call 800/000-0000
For Inquiries on Past Due Accounts, Overlimits or Credit Line Increase, call 800/000-0000

Posted Mo./Day	Transaction Description or Merchant Name and Location		Purchase Mo./Day	Bank Reference Number	Purchases/ Advances/Debits	Payments Credits
8-08	AMERICA WEST AIRLINES	LOS ANGELES	07-25	850000008823395192	42.00	
8-13	HACIENDA MOTORS	COSTA MESA	08-05	015400018537022316	166.86	
8-15	RICOS RESTAURANT	PALM SPRG	08-10	114500018856161722	132.47	
8-12	PAYMENT—THANK YOU		08-11	4501000182MD02139		119.89
8-24	RENEES RESTAURANT	NEWPORT	08-13	114500068201632483	104.60	

Notice See reverse side for important information

					Total Debits 445.93	Total Credits 119.89
MIN. PAYMENT: 27.00		**NEW BALANCE:** 534.08				

Use Financenter's Credit Card Calculators,
www.financenter.com/calculate/cards_calculate.fcs, to find
out how interest rate changes affect your balance, if debt
consolidation makes sense, and answers to similar questions.

CONCEPT CHECK

6-14. Briefly describe the basic steps involved in opening a charge account; provide your answer from the customer's point of view. Describe *credit scoring* and explain how it's used (by lenders) in making a credit decision.

6-15. Describe the basic operations and functions of a *credit bureau*. What kind of information do they gather about you? Is there anything you can do if the information they have on file is wrong?

6-16. What is the *annual percentage rate (APR)?* Describe the most common method used to compute finance charges. What are the legal requirements with respect to disclosure of interest rates and charges?

6-17. The monthly statement is a key feature of bank and retail credit cards. What does this statement typically disclose? Why are merchandise and cash-advance transactions often separated on bank card statements?

▇ Using Credit Wisely [LG5, LG6]

Does it seem that every week there's at least one new credit card application in your mailbox? Well, there's a very good reason for that, because each year, the 20,000 or so institutions and organizations that issue these cards mail out *over 3 billion* credit card applications! Every one of these unsolicited pieces of junk mail tries to give the impression that their offer is better than all the rest. It's very easy to be overwhelmed by all these choices. And although we've discussed how credit cards and revolving lines of credit can simplify your life financially, you can get into trouble unless you use them wisely. That's why you should carefully shop around to choose the right credit cards for your personal situation, understand the advantages and disadvantages that credit cards present, know how to resolve credit problems, and how to avoid the ultimate cost of credit abuse—bankruptcy.

SHOP AROUND FOR THE BEST DEAL

They say it pays to shop around, and when it comes to credit cards, that adage certainly applies. With all the fees and high interest costs, it pays to get the best deal possible. So, where do you start? Most credit experts suggest the first thing you should do is step back and take a look at yourself. What kind of "spender" are you, and how do you pay your bills? The fact is, no single credit card is right for everyone. If you pay off your card balance each month, you'll want a card that's different from the one that's right for someone who carries a credit balance from month to month and may only pay the minimum due.

Regardless of which category you fall into, there are basically four card features to look for:

• Annual fees
• Rate of interest charged on account balance
• Length of the grace period
• Method of calculating balances

Now, if you normally pay your account balance in full each month, get a card with *no annual fees and a long grace period*. The rate of interest on the card is really irrelevant, since you don't carry account balances from month to month anyway.

In sharp contrast, if you don't pay your account in full, then look for cards that charge *a low rate of interest on unpaid balances*. The length of the grace period isn't all that important here, but obviously, other things being equal, you're better off with low (or no) annual fees. Sometimes, however, "other things aren't equal," in which case you have to decide between

EXHIBIT 6.10

PUBLISHED INFORMATION ABOUT BANK CREDIT CARD TERMS

Information about low-cost credit cards is readily available in the financial media. Here's an example of what you can find in *Money* magazine. Notice the report lists the *cards with the lowest rates* (which are probably best for people who regularly carry an account balance), and *no-fee cards with the lowest rates* (which are probably best for people who pay their accounts in full each month). The rates and fees shown here are for standard cards, but almost identical rates and fees apply to the card issuer's premium (silver and gold) cards.

Money Monitor			
Credit Cards	Rate	Annual fee	Telephone
CARDS WITH THE LOWEST RATES			
Pulaski Bank & Trust (Ark.)[1]	8.75%	$35	800-980-2265
Wachovia Bank (Del.)	9.50	88	800-241-7990
USAA Savings Bank (Nev.)	10.50	45	800-922-9092
NO-FEE CARDS WITH THE LOWEST RATES			
Capital One Bank (Va.)[1,2]	9.90	0	800-822-3397
Wachovia Bank (Del.)	10.90	0	800-241-7990
First Internet Bank of Indiana	12.00	0	888-873-3424
Average all cards	17.36		

Notes: All rates are subject to change. Rates are for standard cards as of Oct. 17 from Bankrate.com and are variable unless otherwise indicated. Survey does not include Internet-only cards or American Express Blue.

[1]Fixed rate. [2]Visa only.

Source: *Money,* Dec. 2000, p. 216.

interest rates and annual fees. If you're not a big spender and don't build up big balances on your credit card (i.e., the card balance rarely goes above $400 or $500), then *avoid* cards with annual fees and get one with as *low* a rate of interest as possible. (*Note*: The above situation would probably apply to most college students—or at least it should.) On the other hand, if you do carry big balances (say, $1,000 or more), then you'll probably be better off *paying an annual fee* (even a relatively high one) *to keep the rate of interest on the card as low as possible.* For example, with a $2,000 average balance, your total yearly finance charges (including annual fees) will be *less* with a card that has, say, a $50 annual fee and an interest rate of 15 percent than one which has no annual fee but charges a higher (19 percent) rate of interest.

The bottom line is—don't take the first credit card that comes along. Instead, get the one that's right for you. To do that, learn as much as you can about the credit cards you've been offered or are considering. Be sure to read the credit agreement carefully and look for information about annual fees, grace periods, interest rates, and how finance charges are calculated. And don't overlook all those other charges and fees you may get socked with if you're ever late with a payment or go over your credit limit; not that you're going to make it a habit of doing these things, but just in case. Also, if the local deals aren't all that great, you might want to consider cards that are offered nationally. Many banks market their cards throughout the United States, and it may pay to check them out. To help you do that, look to publications like *Money* magazine and *Kiplinger's Personal Finance* magazine. They have Internet sites located at **www.money.com** and **www.kiplinger.com**, respectively. *Money* and *Kiplinger's* regularly publish information about banks and other financial institutions that offer low-cost credit cards nationally, an example of which is provided in Exhibit 6.10.

Or you can order a report of the best credit card deals around the country from Cardweb ($5; CardTrak Newsletter, Box 1700, Frederick, MD 21702; 800-344-7714), or the *Bank Rate Monitor*—located on the Internet at **www.bankrate.com**—which has detailed rate information for credit cards (as well as for home equity lines of credit, mortgages, and CDs).

ADVANTAGES AND DISADVANTAGES OF CREDIT CARDS

Bank credit cards and retail charge cards can simplify your life, financially, if they are used properly. Their most significant advantage is that by charging purchases, customers can delay payment until the end of the billing period. Of course, because of the high finance charges levied on balances carried from period to period, there is no real advantage to delaying payment beyond this point. Some of the basic advantages and disadvantages of using these cards follow.

ADVANTAGES. The major reasons to use credit cards include interest-free loans, simplified record keeping, returns and resolution of unsatisfactory purchase disputes, convenience and security, and use in emergencies.

- **Interest-free loans**. Most credit and charge cards provide short-term, interest-free loans on the purchase of goods or services. As discussed earlier, these *grace periods* generally cover a 20- to 30-day period of time during which you can pay your bill in full and not incur any interest charges (note that such grace periods do not apply to cash advances). Unfortunately, while most banks still offer grace periods, the trend is definitely to shorten the length of this period. As a rule, you should use credit cards primarily to charge merchandise and services, and then pay the monthly statements in full to avoid any finance charges. If the card issuer does not offer a grace period, or includes current purchases in the average daily balance, the card should be used only in financial emergencies, because interest would be charged from the time of the transaction.
- **Simplified record keeping**. Both bank and retail credit cards provide detailed records of transactions in the form of monthly statements that consolidate records of purchases. No matter how many and varied the purchases made at a department store or the number of places where bank credit card transactions occur, the consumer receives only one statement from each card. This greatly simplifies the record-keeping process and makes bill paying a lot easier. Indeed, businesses are increasingly turning to plastic, as they too view the use of credit cards as an easy way to keep track of expenses and provide their clients with detailed accounts of spending.
- **Returns and resolution of unsatisfactory purchase disputes**. When you purchase an item on credit and later wish to return it, you need only have the store credit your retail or bank card account. Some stores issue only store credit, which can be used only at that retailer, to compensate customers who return items purchased for cash. Also, resolving any disagreement over goods or services purchased is easier if you charged them and have not yet paid for them. In that case, you have about 30 days to ensure that they are satisfactory; if not, you can refuse to pay that amount.
- **Convenience and security**. Many people use charge cards because they are convenient and eliminate the need to write a check each time a purchase is made. By charging all transactions during the month, the customer need write only one check to pay each card issuer's monthly bill. This can be a real time-saver for people who use their bank cards to make a large number of transactions at a variety of places or who purchase

many items at a given store during the month. Using a charge card can also allow for more security. If you lose your wallet or purse, you lose the amount of cash you had at the time. On the other hand, if your credit card is stolen, your loss is limited by law (we'll discuss this later). Also, when traveling to a foreign country, you can use your credit card *without having to worry about currency exchange rate hassles.*

- **Use in emergencies**. Finally, credit cards allow the holder to purchase needed items when sufficient cash is not available. With proper planning and budgeting, the consumer should be able to avoid running short of cash; however, charging a needed item because of a cash shortage may be justifiable in some situations. A tendency to run short of cash on a regular basis, however, signals the need to reevaluate one's budget.

DISADVANTAGES. Bank credit cards and retail charge cards have two major disadvantages: (1) They enable the user to overspend, and (2) their high interest costs add to the price of the purchase.

- **Tendency to overspend**. People who don't use budgets tend to forget that what they charge must eventually be paid for. The credit card gives them a sense of buying power that may not be supported by their actual income; as a result, they often avoid paying the full amount of the bill. Because they can't cover their ever-increasing bills, they make only the minimum payments and thus incur costly finance charges.
- **High interest costs on unpaid balances**. The rate of interest charged on unpaid credit card balances is usually quite high. The typical 1.4 percent per month represents an annual rate of around 17 percent, and in a number of states, the APR can go as high as 21 percent (1.75 percent per month) or more. With rates like that, the purchase of a $1,000 stereo system can quickly turn into credit card payments of $2,000 or $3,000. To make matters even worse, the interest paid on most forms of consumer loans—including all types of credit cards—is no longer tax deductible.

AVOIDING CREDIT PROBLEMS

As more places accept credit cards, and as shopping online becomes more widely accepted, the volume of credit card purchases has grown tremendously—and so has the level of credit card debt. It's not unusual to find people using credit cards to solve cash flow problems; even the most careful consumers can occasionally find themselves with mounting credit card debt, especially after the year-end holiday buying season. The real problems occur when the situation is no longer temporary and the debt continues to increase. If overspending is not curtailed, the size of the unpaid balance may place a real strain on the budget. Essentially, individuals who let their credit balances build up are *mortgaging their future*. By using credit, they are actually committing a part of their future income to make payments on the debt. Unfortunately, the more income that has to go just to make payments on charge cards (and other forms of consumer credit), the less there is available for other purposes.

The best way to avoid credit problems is to be disciplined when using credit. Reduce the number of cards you carry, and don't rush to accept all of the tempting preapproved credit card offers that fill your mailbox. A wallet full of cards can work against you in two ways. Obviously, the ready availability of credit could tempt you to overspend and incur too much credit card debt. But there's another, less obvious, danger: when you apply for a loan, lenders look at the *total amount* of credit you have available as well as at the outstanding balances on your credit cards. If you have a lot of unused credit capacity, it may be harder to get a major loan because of lender concerns that you could become overextended. So think twice before accepting a new credit card. You really don't need three or four bank cards. Two is

MONEY IN ACTION

Protect Yourself from Identity Theft

When Shon Boulden, 22, applied for his first credit card, he received a nasty shock: his credit report showed there were already dozens of credit card accounts open in his name with thousands of dollars of delinquent bills. Boulden was a victim of identity theft.

According to the federal government, over 500,000 people have their financial identities stolen each year, and the problem is growing. Identity thieves obtain personal data such as social security, driver's license, and credit card numbers and then use the information to open credit and bank accounts in the victim's name. Once the accounts are set up, the thieves spend freely—and the delinquent payments go on the victim's credit report. Most victims don't discover the theft until their checks bounce or their real credit cards are rejected.

It can take months, even years, to untangle the mess. Although victims usually aren't held responsible for more than $50 in fraudulent credit card charges, the damage to their good names and credit history can be long-lasting. They can have trouble getting mortgages, car loans, and even jobs. Experts say the best defense is a good offense. Protect your personal information. *Don't throw out credit card receipts, cancelled checks, pre-approved offers of credit or any other papers that contain identifying information without shredding them first.* If you have a roommate, keep your personal records in a safe place. Many victims of identity theft find out the culprit was someone they knew.

Next, be careful about giving out personal identification to businesses, Web sites, and others whom you do not know. Do not give credit card numbers, account passwords, or other sensitive data in response to unsolicited e-mails or phone calls, even if they claim to be from a business you know. Although giving your social security number to an employer is unavoidable, you can ask your employer what they will do to protect the information.

If your bills don't arrive on time, it could be a sign that someone has changed your address on the account or has stolen the bill from your mailbox. Review your bank, telephone, and credit card statements carefully every month to see if there are any charges or transactions listed that you don't recognize. It's also a good idea to request a credit report from one of the major credit bureaus once a year to look for suspicious activity conducted under your name.

If you are a victim of identity theft, take action immediately. Report the crime to the Federal Trade Commission's Identity Theft Hotline at 877-438-4338. Next, contact all creditors listed on your credit report to inform them of the problem. Let your local police know about the crime and, if you suspect the mail was used, notify your local postmaster.

Sources: Sandra Block, "Don't Fall Prey to Identity Thieves," *USA Today*, September 12, 2000, p. 3B; Mike Madden, "Congress Considers Making Financial Companies More Responsible for ID Theft," *Gannett News Service*, September 14, 2000, p. ARC; "FTC Finds Sharp Rise in ID Theft," *Dallas Morning News*, July 13, 2000, p. 3D.

---

the most financial advisors suggest you carry: perhaps one rebate card, if you charge enough to make the benefit worthwhile, and a low-rate card for purchases you want to repay over time. And should you decide to start using a new card (because their offer was just too good to pass up), then *get rid of one of your old cards*—physically cut up the old card and inform the issuer in writing that you're canceling your account.

Suppose that, despite all your efforts, you find that your credit card balances are higher than you'd like and you anticipate having problems reducing them to a more manageable level. The first step is to stop making any new charges until you pay off (or pay down) the existing balances. Then commit to a repayment plan. One good strategy is to pay off the highest-interest cards first, keeping the original payment rather than reducing it as your balance drops, or, even better, pay more than the minimum—even if it's just $10 more. You'd be surprised how much difference this makes.

You may also want to consider transferring your balances to a card with a low introductory rate and paying off as much as possible before the rate increases. Another option is to consolidate all your credit card debt and pay it off as quickly as possible using a lower-rate loan, such as a home equity line of credit. This can be a risky strategy, however. If you continue to be undisciplined about repaying your debts, you could lose your home. And clearing up your credit card balances may tempt you to start the credit card borrowing cycle all over again.

IMPORTANT CONSUMER CREDIT LEGISLATION

Just as you have an obligation to repay your debt in a prompt and timely fashion, lenders also have certain legal obligations they're expected to fulfill when they extend credit. Accordingly, when you apply for credit, it's in your best interest to be aware of the legal obligations of the issuing establishment.

A number of important consumer protection laws pertain to the extension of credit. The major concerns of credit legislation have been *credit discrimination* (Equal Credit Opportunity Act); *disclosure of credit information* (Consumer Credit Reporting Reform Act); *billing procedures, errors, complaints, and recourse on unsatisfactory purchases* (Fair Credit Billing Act); *disclosure of finance charges, other fees, credit terms, and loss of credit card* (Consumer Credit Protection [Truth in Lending] Act); and *protection against collector harassment* (Fair Debt Collection Practices Act). The key provisions of these acts are summarized in Exhibit 6.11.

CREDIT CARD FRAUD

Despite all the legislation, there are still people out there who are doing their very best to rip you off! In fact, plastic has become the vehicle of choice among crooks as a way of defrauding and stealing from both you and the merchants that honor credit cards. No doubt about it—credit card crime is big business, with estimated losses of between $4 billion and $8 billion a year! Stolen account numbers (obtained by dishonest employees or even by thieves going through the trash to find discarded receipts) are the biggest source of credit card fraud. Not surprisingly, the latest methods of credit card fraud revolves around the Internet. Be especially careful where you use your credit card in cyberspace. Most, if not all, of the major, big-name sites are about as secure as they can get, but when you go to one of the less-reputable sites, you may well be asking for trouble by giving them your credit card number! Remember, all the bad guys need to order merchandise or services over the phone or on the Internet is your account number. Even worse, a crook who also has your bank account number or home address may be able to get a credit card or open other types of charge accounts—*all in your name!* Unfortunately, as the accompanying *Money in Action* box explains, when that happens, you've just become another victim of *identity theft.*

Basically, "it's us against them," and the first thing you have to understand is that the credit card you're carrying around is a very powerful piece of plastic. Be careful with it. And don't count on retail merchants to protect you—for example, in a test conducted by *Money* magazine, only 5 percent of merchants checked signatures against the card and most accepted purchases made with borrowed cards. To reduce your chances of being defrauded, here are some suggestions you should follow:

- Never, ever, give your account number to people or organizations *who call you*—no matter how legitimate it sounds, if you didn't initiate the call, don't give out the information!
- It's okay to give your account number over the phone (if you initiated the call) when ordering or purchasing something from a major catalog house, airline, hotel, and so on, but don't do it for any other reason.

 **EXHIBIT 6.11**

MAJOR CONSUMER CREDIT LEGISLATION

The following exhibit summarizes the provisions of the most important federal consumer credit protection laws.

Equal Credit Opportunity Act (ECOA) (1975, amended 1977)
- Credit discrimination on the basis of sex or marital status is illegal.
- Lenders may not ask questions about an applicant's sex, marital status, and childbearing plans.
- Lenders must view women's income the same as men's and include alimony and child support as part of a woman's income.
- Credit discrimination based on race, national origin, religion, age, or the receipt of public assistance is illegal.
- If a husband and wife open a joint account or cosign a loan, the credit grantor must report the information to the credit bureau in the name of both parties.

Consumer Credit Reporting Reform Act (1996) (an update of the Fair Credit Reporting Act [1971, amended 1994])
- Credit bureau reports must contain accurate, relevant, and recent information about the personal and financial situation of credit applicants.
- Only bona fide users of financial information may review credit files.
- Consumers who are refused credit or whose borrowing costs increase as the result of a credit investigation must be told why and given the name and address of the reporting credit agency.
- Consumers have the right to review their credit files personally and correct any inaccurate information.
- Credit bureaus must have toll-free phone numbers and provide consumers one low-cost report every two years.
- Disputes must be resolved in 30 days and consider the consumer's documentation.
- Credit bureaus must have formal procedures to correct reports.
- Creditors can be sued by consumers for not correcting credit reporting errors.
- Employers must get written permission to review prospective or current employees' credit files.

Fair Credit Billing Act (1975)
- At least 14 days prior to the payment-due date, creditors must mail bills that include all credits and refunds for the period in which they occurred.
- Customers must notify the creditor in writing of any billing errors within 60 days of the date they receive the statement.
- Credit issuers have 30 days to respond to customer inquiries about billing errors and 90 days to resolve the complaint, during which time creditors may not collect the bill or issue an unfavorable credit report.
- Credit cardholders may withhold payment for unsatisfactory goods or services charged to their accounts if, after good-faith attempts, they cannot satisfactorily work out their disagreement with the seller.
- Merchants may give cash discounts of any size to customers who pay cash instead of using credit.

Consumer Credit Protection Act (Truth in Lending) (1969, amended 1971 and 1982)
- Prior to extending credit, all lenders must disclose both the dollar amount of finance charges and the annual percentage rate charged (accurate to the nearest 0.25 percent), as well as other loan terms and conditions.
- Every credit card must contain some form of user identification—generally a picture or signature.
- The credit card owner's liability for a lost or stolen card is limited to a maximum of $50 per card.
- Companies may not send out unrequested credit cards (unsolicited credit card applications are allowed).

Fair Debt Collection Practices Act (1978, amended 1996)
- Credit customers must be informed in writing within five days of first contact by collector of the amount owed, to whom, and how to dispute the claim (written notice sent within 30 days).
- The collector must cease collection efforts until he sends the customer written verification of the debt. The customer can prevent a collector from communicating with him or her by notifying the collector in writing.
- Collectors may not (1) use abusive language, threaten the customer, or call at inconvenient times or at the place of work; (2) misrepresent themselves; (3) use unfair tactics in an effort to collect the debt; (4) contact anyone else about the customer's debt unless they are trying to locate him or her; and (5) collect an amount greater than the debt or apply payments to another disputed debt.

Fair Credit and Charge Card Disclosure Act (1988)
- Card issuers must provide full disclosure of all fees, grace periods, and other financial terms in unsolicited application invitations.
- Card issuers must notify you in advance when your account is about to be renewed.

- Now, the same precautions should be exercised *when purchasing something over the Internet* with your credit card—don't do it *unless* you're dealing at the site of a major retailer who uses state-of-the-art protection against fraud and thievery. (Credit card companies are fighting back on Internet fraud by introducing smart-chip technology and developing other methods of thwarting fraud. For example, American Express recently announced a new program (called "Private Payments") where a cardholder who wants to purchase something online is given a unique, one-time number to use when making the online purchase—once used, the number can never be used again, and, best of all, the cardholder's actual credit card number is never part of the transaction and therefore cannot be stolen.)

- When paying for something *by check*, don't put your credit card account number on the check and don't let the store clerk do it—show the clerk a check guarantee card (if you have one), a driver's license, or some other form of identification—but *not* your social security number.

- Don't put your phone number or address (and certainly not your social security number) on credit/charge slips, even if the merchant asks for it—they're *not* entitled to it anyway; but if the clerk insists, just scribble down any number you want.

- When using your card to make a purchase, *always keep your eye on it* (so the clerk can't make an extra imprint); and if the clerk makes a mistake and wants to make another imprint, ask for the first imprint, and tear it up on the spot.

- Always draw a line on the credit slip through any blank spaces above the total, so the amount can't be altered.

- *Destroy* all carbons and old credit slips; and when you receive your monthly statement, be sure to *go over it promptly* to make sure there are no errors (if you find a mistake, call or send a letter immediately, detailing the error).

- If you lose a card or it's stolen, *report it to the card issuer immediately*—the most you're ever liable for with a lost or stolen card is $50 (per card), but if you report the loss *before* the card can be used, you won't be liable for any unauthorized charges (the phone number to call is listed on the back of your statement).

- Destroy old cards or those you no longer use.

BANKRUPTCY: PAYING THE ULTIMATE PRICE FOR CREDIT ABUSE

It certainly wouldn't be an overstatement to say that during the 1980s and 1990s, *debt was in!* In fact, the explosion of debt that has occurred since 1980 is almost incomprehensible. The national debt more than quintupled, from less than a trillion dollars when the 1980s began to about $5.7 trillion by late 2000. Businesses also took on debt at a rapid pace. And, not to be outdone, consumers were using credit like there was no tomorrow. So it shouldn't be too surprising that when you couple this heavy debt load with a serious economic recession (like the one we had in 1990 to 1991) and a very slow economic recovery (from 1992 to 1993), you have all the ingredients of a real financial crisis. And that's just what happened, because personal bankruptcies soared—indeed, nearly a million people a year filed for **personal bankruptcy** during that period. Even during the strong economic expansion from 1994 to 1997, the number of bankruptcies continued to climb; since 1997, although the number of bankruptcies has declined a bit, they still number over one million a year.

When too many people are too heavily in debt, a recession (or some other economic reversal) can come along and push many of them over the edge. But let's face it, the recession is not the main culprit here, because the only way a recession can push you over the edge is if you're already sitting on it! The real culprit is excess debt. Some people simply

personal bankruptcy A form of legal recourse open to insolvent debtors in which they may petition a court for protection from creditors and arrange for the orderly liquidation and distribution of their assets.

abuse credit by taking on more than they can afford. Maybe they're pursuing a lifestyle beyond their means, or an unfortunate event—like the loss of a job—takes place.

Whatever the cause, sooner or later, they start missing payments and their credit rating begins to deteriorate. Unless some corrective actions are taken, this is followed by repossession of property and, eventually, even bankruptcy. These people basically have reached the end of a long line of deteriorating financial affairs. Households that cannot resolve serious credit problems on their own need help from the courts. Two legal remedies that are widely used under such circumstances include (1) the Wage Earner Plan and (2) straight bankruptcy.

Wage Earner Plan
An arrangement for scheduled debt repayment over future years that is an alternative to straight bankruptcy; used when a person has a steady source of income and there is a reasonable chance of repayment within 3 to 5 years.

WAGE EARNER PLAN. The **Wage Earner Plan** (as defined in *Chapter 13* of the U.S. Bankruptcy Code) is a workout procedure that involves some type of debt restructuring—usually by establishing a debt repayment schedule that's more compatible to the person's income. It may be a viable alternative for someone who has a steady source of income, not more than $750,000 in secured debt and $250,000 in unsecured debt, and a reasonably good chance of being able to repay the debts in 3 to 5 years. A majority of creditors must agree to the plan, and interest charges, along with late-payment penalties, are waived for the repayment period. Creditors usually will go along with this plan because they stand to lose more in a straight bankruptcy. After the plan is approved, the individual makes periodic payments to the court, which then pays off the creditors. Throughout the process, the individual retains the use of, and keeps title to, all of his or her assets.

straight bankruptcy
A legal proceeding that results in "wiping the slate clean and starting anew"; most of a debtor's obligations are eliminated in an attempt to put the debtor's financial affairs in order.

STRAIGHT BANKRUPTCY. **Straight bankruptcy**, which is allowed under *Chapter 7* of the bankruptcy code, can be viewed as a legal procedure that results in "wiping the slate clean and starting anew." About 70 percent of those filing personal bankruptcy choose this route. However, straight bankruptcy does not eliminate all the debtor's obligations, nor does the debtor necessarily lose all his or her assets. For example, the debtor must make certain tax payments and keep up alimony and child-support payments but is allowed to retain certain payments from social security, retirement, veterans', and disability benefits. In addition, the debtor may retain equity in a home (up to $15,000), a car (up to $2,400), and other personal assets, such as clothing, books, and tools of his or her trade. These are minimums as established by federal regulations; generally, state laws are much more generous with regard to the amount the debtor is allowed to keep. The choice of federal or state regulations would depend on the debtor's assets.

OTHER BANKRUPTCY OPTIONS. Although most individual bankruptcies involve either straight liquidations or Wage Earner Plans, several other options have been added recently. To begin with, the U.S. Supreme Court ruled that individuals can now file for reorganization under *Chapter 11* of the bankruptcy code—a type of bankruptcy that had previously been reserved mostly for businesses. Chapter 11 bankruptcy is for individuals who don't qualify for Chapter 13 reorganization—either because they exceed the debt limitations or do not have a regular source of income—but who want to try to restructure their debt. For these people, Chapter 11 is really the only alternative to straight bankruptcy. Like the Wage Earner Plan discussed above, Chapter 11 filers can restructure their debts, or a portion of them, to be repaid over time. The big difference is that in Chapter 11 bankruptcy, the creditors vote on—and can possibly block—the restructuring plan. This, of course, means the reorganization process can drag on for years and involve hefty legal fees.

The second alternative now available is a so-called *Chapter 20* bankruptcy—it's labeled as such because it combines parts of both Chapters 7 and 13. Although not actually a part of the bankruptcy code, this procedure allows individuals to wipe out their unsecured debt, as per Chapter 7, *and* then use Chapter 13 to restructure their secured debt, including mortgages and home equity loans and nondischargeable debts, such as certain tax and child support payments.

In the last several years, Congress has been discussing several potential reforms to bankruptcy legislation. At this time, nothing has been signed into law, but the impetus on Capital Hill is to accomplish something soon. Both side of the debate are represented: the consumers by various consumer groups, and the creditors by their lobbyists. The overall goal seems to be to tighten the bankruptcy laws because filings are so high and many filers evade creditors through the bankruptcy process, even though they have the means to pay. Generally speaking, the overall goals of the proposed legislation are to allow fewer Chapter 7 filings and instead force petitioners to file under a Chapter 13 plan. Currently, a sticking point is a new measure, which would allow credit card companies to insert waivers into cardholder agreements lifting protection of pension plans not covered by the Employee Retirement Income Security Act (ERISA). Thus a cardholder could be signing away a pension should illness, etc. befall him or her—an issue, not surprisingly, that has become a cause for great concern.

USING THE SERVICES OF A CREDIT COUNSELOR

Filing for bankruptcy is a serious matter and should only be taken as a last resort. For one thing, it's going to stick with you for a long time (it will remain in your credit file for up to 10 years) and certainly won't help your chances of getting credit in the future. It often makes a lot more sense to try to work problems out before they get so bad that bankruptcy is the only workable alternative. Some people can do that on their own but, in many cases, it may be a good idea to seek the help of a *credit counselor*.

Credit counselors work with a family to set up a budget and may even negotiate with creditors to establish workable schedules for repaying outstanding debts. The counseling service will often go so far as to collect money from the debtor and distribute it to creditors. There are private firms that, for a fee, will act as intermediaries between borrowers and creditors and provide counseling services. These counselors generally attempt to reduce the size of payments, the size of outstanding debt, or both. However, their fees can run as much as 20 percent of the amount owed.

credit counselor A professional financial advisor who assists overextended consumers in repairing budgets for both spending and debt repayment.

Another option is a nonprofit agency, such as those affiliated with the nationwide network of *Consumer Credit Counseling Services* (CCCS) (800-388-2227). You'll get many of the services that private agencies provide, at a lower cost. Of course, as with any financial advisor, you should check out a credit counselor's credentials, fees, services provided, and track record *before* using his or her services. Be cautious; sometimes these organizations aren't all they appear to be. For example, nonprofit groups like CCCS often advertise themselves as charitable organizations, although they are mostly funded by creditors. Unfortunately, there have been cases where these counselors were encouraging debtors to get into repayment plans they couldn't afford and ultimately couldn't pay. And these groups sometimes neglect to discuss the option of bankruptcy—even when it is in the consumer's best interest.

 In over your head with credit card debt? The National Foundation for Consumer Credit (**www.nfcc.org**) has links to credit counseling agencies, free budgeting calculators, and helpful tips on getting out of debt.

To avoid falling into such a trap, debtors should explore all their options before seeking the help of a credit counselor. First, advisors suggest, try contacting your creditors yourself; you can probably work out a deal on your own if you have few lenders and need only 2 to 3 months to catch up. If, however, you have six or more creditors, you should probably see a credit counselor. Make sure to ask your counselor for *several debt-reduction options* appropriate for your financial situation. More importantly, face up to credit and debt problems as soon as they occur, and do everything possible to avoid ruining your credit record.

CONCEPT CHECK

6-18. What are some of the key factors you should consider when choosing a credit card? Given your current spending habits, what types of cards would be best for you and why?

6-19. Describe briefly the advantages and disadvantages of using credit cards.

6-20. How does consumer credit legislation relate to (a) credit discrimination, (b) disclosure of credit information, (c) disclosure of finance charges, (d) loss of credit card, (e) errors, complaints, and recourse on unsatisfactory purchases, (f) protection against collector harassment, and (g) credit card renewal notices?

6-21. Discuss the steps you would take to avoid and/or resolve credit problems.

6-22. What's the biggest source of credit card fraud? List at least five things you can do to reduce your chances of being a victim of credit card fraud.

6-23. Explain the conditions that might make bankruptcy necessary. Distinguish between a *Wage Earner Plan* and *straight bankruptcy*. How might you use the services of a credit counselor?

SUMMARY

LG1. **Describe the reasons for using consumer credit and identify its benefits and problems.** Families and individuals use credit as a way to pay for relatively expensive purchases and, occasionally, to deal with a financial emergency. In addition, consumer credit is being used increasingly, simply because it is so convenient. Finally, it is also used to partially finance the purchase of various types of investments. Unfortunately, while there are some definite positive aspects to the use of consumer credit, there are also some negatives, the most important being that it can be misused to the point where people live beyond their means by purchasing goods and services they simply can't afford. Such overspending can get so bad that it eventually leads to bankruptcy.

LG2. **Develop a plan to establish a strong credit history.** Establishing a strong credit history is an important part of personal financial planning. Opening checking and savings accounts, obtaining one or two credit cards and using them judiciously, and taking out a small loan and repaying it on schedule are ways to show potential lenders that you can handle credit wisely. Be sure to use credit only when you are sure you can repay the obligation, make payments promptly, and notify a lender immediately if you cannot meet payments as agreed. Using the debt safety ratio, you can calculate how much of your monthly take-home pay is going to consumer credit payments. One widely used credit capacity guideline is that total monthly consumer credit payments (exclusive of your mortgage payment) should not exceed 20 percent of your monthly take-home pay.

LG3.   **Distinguish among the different forms of open account credit: bank credit cards, other credit cards and charge accounts, and revolving credit lines**. Open account credit is one of the most popular forms of consumer credit; it is available from various types of financial institutions and from all sorts of retail stores and merchants. The major types of open account credit include bank credit cards, retail charge cards, 30-day charge accounts, travel and entertainment cards, and various forms of revolving lines of credit. Many bank cards offer an incentive such as rebates or merchandise discounts. Be sure to calculate the total cost of the card, based on your spending patterns, to determine whether these special cards make sense for you. Although credit cards account for a significant portion of consumer transactions, revolving lines of credit also provide their users with ready access to borrowed money (by simply writing checks). Basically, there are three types of revolving credit lines: overdraft protection lines, unsecured personal lines of credit, and home equity credit lines.

LG4.   **Apply for, obtain, and manage open account credit**. Most types of open account credit require formal application, which generally involves an extensive investigation of your credit background and an evaluation of your creditworthiness. This usually includes checking credit bureau reports. You should verify the accuracy of these reports regularly and promptly correct any errors. The amount of finance charges, if any, due on consumer credit depends in large part on the technique used to compute the account balance; the average daily balance method is the most common today. Managing your accounts involves understanding the monthly statement and making payments on a timely basis.

LG5.   **Choose the right credit cards and recognize their advantages and disadvantages**. With so many different types of credit cards available, it pays to shop around to choose the best credit card for your needs. You should consider your spending habits and then compare the fees, interest rates, grace period, and any incentives. If you pay your balance off each month, you will want a card with low annual fees; if you carry a balance, a low interest rate is your best bet. Advantages of credit cards include interest-free loans, simplified record keeping, ease of making returns and resolving unsatisfactory purchase disputes, convenience and security, and use in emergencies. The disadvantages are the tendency to overspend and high interest costs on unpaid balances.

LG6.   **Avoid credit problems, protect yourself against credit card fraud, and understand the personal bankruptcy process**. Avoiding credit problems requires self-discipline. Keep the number of cards you use to a minimum and be sure you can repay any balances quickly. When credit card debt gets out of control, adopt a payment strategy to pay off the debt in as short a time as possible by looking for a low-rate card, paying more than the minimum payment, and not charging any additional purchases until the debt is repaid. Another option is a consolidation loan. To protect yourself against credit card fraud, don't give out your card number unnecessarily, destroy old cards and receipts, verify your credit card transactions, and report a lost card or suspicious activity immediately. A solution to credit abuse, albeit a drastic one, is personal bankruptcy. Those who file for bankruptcy work out a debt restructuring program under Chapter 13's Wage Earner Plan or Chapter 7's straight bankruptcy. If you have serious problems managing personal credit, a credit counselor may be able to help you learn to control spending and work out a repayment strategy.

QUESTIONS AND PROBLEMS

1. After graduating from college last fall, Janet Price took a job as a consumer credit analyst at a local bank. From her work reviewing credit applications, she realizes that she should begin establishing her own credit history. Describe for Janet several steps she could take to begin building a strong credit record. Does the fact that she took out a student loan for her college education help or hurt her credit record?

2. Brett Willard has a monthly take-home pay of $1,685; he makes payments of $410 a month on his outstanding consumer credit (excluding the mortgage on his home). How would you characterize Brett's debt burden? What if his take-home pay were $850 a month, and he had monthly credit payments of $150?

3. Calculate your own debt-safety ratio. What does it tell you about your current credit situation and your debt capacity? Does this information indicate a need to make any changes in your credit use patterns, and, if so, what steps should you take?

4. Mary Maffeo has an overdraft protection line. Assume that her October 2001 statement showed a latest (new) balance of $862. If the line had a minimum monthly payment requirement of 5 percent of the latest balance (rounded to the nearest $5 figure), what would be the minimum amount she would have to pay on her overdraft protection line?

5. Don and Judy Nesbit have a home with an appraised value of $180,000 and a mortgage balance of only $90,000. Given that an S&L is willing to lend money at a loan-to-value ratio of 75 percent, how big a home equity credit line can Don and Judy obtain? How much, if any, of this line would qualify as tax deductible interest if their house originally cost $100,000?

6. Sylvia Galano, a student at City Community College, has a balance of $380 on her retail charge card; if the store levies a finance charge of 21 percent per annum, how much monthly interest will be added to her account?

7. Alan Bell recently received his monthly MasterCard bill for the period June 1–30, 2001, and wants to verify the monthly finance charge calculation, which is assessed at a rate of 15 percent per year and based on average daily balances including new purchases. His outstanding balance, purchases, and payments are as follows:

Previous balance:	$386
Purchases:	
June 4	137
June 12	78
June 20	98
June 26	75
Payments:	
June 21	35

What is his average daily balance and the finance charge for the period? (Use a table like the one in Exhibit 6.8 for your calculations.)

8. Mark Strom is trying to decide whether to apply for a credit card or a debit card. He has $7,500 in a savings account at the bank and spends his money frugally. What advice would you have for Mark? Describe the benefits and drawbacks of each type of card.

9. Jean Wong was reviewing her credit card statement and noticed several charges that did not look familiar to her. Jean is unsure as to whether she should pay the bill in full and forget about the unfamiliar charges, or "make some noise." If some of these are not hers, is she still liable for the full amount of the charges? Is she liable for any part of these charges, even if they are fraudulent?

APPLYING PERSONAL FINANCE

Have You Ever Applied for Credit?

Have you ever applied for credit? Perhaps you can now. This is a very simple project designed to introduce you to the credit application process. Go to a department store, bank, or S&L and get an application for a VISA, MasterCard, American Express, Optima, Discover, or any other credit card (the department store may have a credit card of its own). Take it home and fill it out as best you can. After you fill out the application, take a close look at it and try to do a *self-evaluation of your own credit worthiness.* Based on the information you have provided, do you think you would qualify for the credit card? What do you see as your major strengths? What are your major weaknesses? Is there anything you can do about them?

CONTEMPORARY CASE APPLICATIONS

6.1   The Cullens Seek Some Credit Card Information

Michael and Roberta Cullen are a newly married couple in their mid-20s. Michael is a senior at a state university and will graduate in the summer of 2002. Roberta graduated last spring with a degree in marketing and recently started working as a sales rep for the Alhambra Corporation. She supports both of them on her monthly salary of $2,000 after taxes. At present, the Cullens pay all their expenses by cash or check. They would, however, like to use a bank credit card for some of their transactions. Because neither Michael nor Roberta is familiar with how to go about applying for a credit card, they approach you for help.

Questions
1. Advise the Cullens on how they should go about filling out a credit application.
2. Explain to them the procedure the bank will probably follow in processing their application.
3. Tell them about credit scoring, and how the bank will arrive at a credit decision.
4. What kind of advice would you offer the Cullens on the "correct" use of their card? What would you tell them about building a strong credit record?

6.2   Lisa Starts Over After Bankruptcy

A year after declaring bankruptcy and moving with her daughter back into her parents' home, Lisa Lamphere is about to get a degree in nursing. As she starts out in a new career, she also wants to begin a new life—one built on a solid financial base. Lisa will be starting out as a full-time nurse at a salary of $42,000 a year, and plans to continue working at a second (part-time) nursing job at an annual income of $10,500. She will be paying back $24,000 in bankruptcy debts and wants to be able to move into an apartment within a year, then buy a condo or house in five years.

Lisa will not have to pay rent for the time she lives with her parents. And she will have child care at no cost, which will continue after she and her daughter are able to move out on their own. While the living arrangement with her parents is great financially, the accommodations are "tight," and Lisa's work hours interfere with her parents' routines. Everyone agrees that one more year of this is about all the family feels it can take. However, before Lisa is able to make a move, even into a rented apartment, she will have to reestablish credit over and above paying off her bankruptcy debts. To rent the kind of place she'd like, she will need to have a good credit record for a year, and to buy a home she will need to sustain that credit standing for at least 3 to 5 years.

Questions

1. In addition to opening checking and savings accounts, what else might Lisa do to begin establishing credit with a bank?
2. While Lisa is unlikely to be able to obtain a major bank credit card for at least a year, how might she begin establishing credit with local merchants?
3. What's one way she might be able to obtain a bank credit card? Explain.
4. How often should Lisa monitor her credit standing with credit reporting services, like Experian?
5. What general advice would you offer with regard to getting Lisa back on track to a new life financially?

MONEY ONLINE

GIVE US CREDIT!

Note: Web addresses change frequently, so you may need to determine the home page and do a site search to find the page or topic that's referenced.

1. **www.cardweb.com**
   Learn the whole story behind those credit card offers. Pull up CardWeb's site and click on "CardOffers." Select three cards of your choice and search until you find the terms of their offers. Look for words such as *disclosure* or *terms and conditions*. Compare the cards on the following points:

   a. Annual percentage rate for purchases
   b. Variable rate information
   c. Grace period for purchases
   d. Annual fee
   e. Method of computing the balance for purchases
   f. Minimum finance charge
   g. Late-payment fee
   h. Over-the-limit fee
   i. Transaction fee for cash advances
   j. Annual percentage rate for cash advances

2. **www.powersource.com/cccs**
   Overdosed on debt? Consumer Credit Counseling Service provides budget counseling, educational programs, debt management assistance, and housing counseling. Their counseling services are available online, by telephone, or in person in either Spanish or English. Perhaps you've already dug your way out of debt using the services CCCS provides. Share your story by clicking on "Client Profile," and maybe you will inspire someone else to turn his or her life around!

3. **www.consumer.gov/sentinel**
   What's the latest trend in consumer fraud? Pull up the Consumer Sentinel's site and click on "Fraud Trends" to learn the most reported consumer complaint categories. Use this site to get the facts on consumer frauds, report your fraud complaints, and learn how U.S., Canadian, and Australian law enforcers work together with the private sector to combat fraud.

4. **www.ftc.gov**
   Have a complaint against a business? File it online with the Federal Trade Commission (FTC), the agency in charge of enforcing a variety of federal antitrust and consumer protection laws. Among its many offerings, the FTC's Web site also provides information on consumer protection, the FTC's investigative and law enforcement authority, business guidance, and economic issues.

5. **www.ftc.gov/foia/index.htm**

   Find out what's on your record! The Freedom of Information Act (FOIA) is a federal law that provides public access to federal government records by requiring that agencies automatically make public certain types of records. The law also sets up a way for the public to request copies of records that are *not* routinely placed on the FTC's public record. Learn more about the FOIA at this site and then click "Secure On-Line Request Form" to obtain access to records about you.

6. **www.bankruptcy.org**

   Are you at a high risk for bankruptcy? What are the alternatives to bankruptcy? What are the statistics on bankruptcy? Visit Bankruptcy.Org's Web site for information on personal bankruptcy to help you avoid making that Ten-Year Mistake!

Just for Fun!

7. **www.americanexpress/student**

   What effect will paying an extra $10 per month have on your credit card debt? Use American Express' Debt Reduction Calculator to find out. Under "Student Services," click on "Money Management Tools." While you're there, also click on "Managing Your Credit" to get useful information on credit management and how to maintain a good credit record.

8. **www.mastercard.com/consumer/student**

   Master your money! Attend Master Card's "Money Management 101" class to find educational material on managing your credit, budgeting your money, obtaining financial aid, and finding a job. Click on "Online Research Resources" for pages and pages of links to academic resources to help you out with your studies.

Chapter 7

Using Consumer Loans

LEARNING GOALS

LG1.   Know when to use consumer loans and differentiate between the major types.

LG2.   Identify the various sources of consumer loans.

LG3.   Choose the best loans by comparing finance charges, maturity, collateral, and other loan terms.

LG4.   Describe the features of, and calculate the finance charges on, single-payment loans.

LG5.   Evaluate the benefits of an installment loan and understand the terms of the loan purchase contract.

LG6.   Determine the costs of installment loans and analyze whether it is better to pay cash or take out a loan.

College Financing by Degrees

"Looking back on the past 10 years, I wonder how I managed it all!" exclaims Gwen Thomas, a 42-year-old psychotherapist who lives near Portland, Maine. Widowed in 1994, when sons David and Jeffrey were 13 and 10, the family was emotionally and financially devastated. "It was really touch and go for a while," she recalls. "My income was small, and my husband's life insurance was inadequate. My main concern was taking care of the kids, pulling us together as a family. She resisted taking out loans because basically she is "debt-averse," rarely carrying a balance on her credit cards—maybe for school clothes, Christmas shopping—and then repaying it in a few months.

However, she realized she'd have to borrow to send her sons to college. At the same time, her car was on its last legs and the house needed a new roof. "It was truly terrifying to think about sending two boys to college. I had no one to fall back on; I was it! But for me, education was the top priority, so I used every possible financial resource." Both boys were able to finance about half of their college expenses with federal and college-sponsored grants; the other half was split among federal, college-sponsored, and home equity loans and personal funds—part-time and summer jobs and family savings. Gwen also used a home equity loan to buy a car and fix the roof. She thought about cashing in part of her retirement fund, but realized that she had better not because it was her only source of retirement savings. Plus, the fund was invested in stocks and bonds which were performing very well. "Funding our education was a family effort. We cut expenses drastically and took no vacations; the boys had no cars or computers. My aim was to keep our loans as small as possible," Gwen explains.

Through sound personal financial planning and wise use of consumer loans, Gwen and her sons have improved their lives. Chapter 7 tells you what to look for if you, too, need to borrow to reach financial goals.

■ Basic Features of Consumer Loans [LG1, LG2]

At several points in this book, we have discussed the different types of financial goals that individuals and families can set for themselves. These goals often involve substantial sums of money and may include such things as a college education or the purchase of a new car. One way to reach these goals is to systematically save the money. Another is to use a loan to at least partially finance the transaction. Consumer loans are important to the personal financial planning process because of the help they provide in reaching certain types of financial goals. Working a major expenditure or purchase into a financial plan can be done just as easily with a consumer loan as it can by saving. The key, of course, is to successfully manage the credit by keeping the amount of debt used and debt-repayment burden *well within your budget*!

USING CONSUMER LOANS

As we saw in Chapter 6, the use of open account credit can prove helpful to those who plan and live within their personal financial budgets. More important to the long-run achievement of personal financial goals, however, are single-payment and installment consumer loans. These long-term liabilities are widely used to finance goods that are too expensive to buy from current income, to help with a college education, or to pay for certain types of nondurable items, like expensive vacations. Of course, the extent to which this type of borrowing is used must be governed by personal financial plans and budgets.

These loans differ from open account credit in a number of ways, including the formality of their lending arrangements. That is, while open account credit results from a rather informal process, **consumer loans** are *formal, negotiated contracts* that specify both the terms for borrowing and the repayment schedule. In addition, whereas an open account credit line can be used over and over again, consumer loans are one-shot transactions that are made for specific purposes. Because there is no revolving credit with a consumer loan, there is no more credit available (from that particular loan) once it is paid off. Further, there are no credit cards or checks issued with this form of credit. Finally, while open account credit is used chiefly to make repeated purchases of relatively low-cost *goods and services*, consumer loans are used mainly to *borrow money* to pay for big-ticket items.

consumer loans
One-time loans made for specific purposes using formally negotiated contracts specifying the borrowing terms and repayment.

collateral
An item of value used to secure the principal portion of a loan.

DIFFERENT TYPES OF LOANS

Although they can be used for just about any purpose imaginable, most consumer loans fall into one of the five following categories:

- **Auto loans.** Financing a new car, truck, SUV, or minivan is the single most common reason for borrowing money through a consumer loan. Indeed, auto loans account for about 35 percent of all consumer credit outstanding. Generally speaking, about 80 to 90 percent of the cost of a new vehicle (somewhat less with used cars) can be financed with credit; the buyer must provide the rest through a *down payment*. The loan is *secured* with the auto, meaning that the vehicle serves as **collateral** for the loan and can be repossessed by the lender should the buyer fail to make payments. These loans generally have maturities that run from 36 to 60 months, perhaps longer (e.g., 72-month loans are not uncommon today for luxury automobiles).
- **Loans for other durable goods**. Consumer loans can also be used to finance other kinds of *costly durable goods,* such as furniture, home appliances, TVs, stereos, home computers, recreational vehicles, and even small airplanes and mobile homes. These loans are also secured by the items purchased and generally require some down payment. Maturities vary with the type of asset purchased: 9- to 12-month loans are common for less costly items, such as TVs and stereos, whereas 10- to 15-year loans (or even longer) are normal with mobile homes.
- **Education loans**. Getting a college education is another very important reason for taking out a consumer loan. Such loans can be used to finance either undergraduate or graduate studies, and there are special government-subsidized loan programs available to students and parents; we'll discuss student loans in more detail in the following section.
- **Personal loans**. These loans are typically used for nondurable expenditures, such as an expensive European vacation or to cover temporary cash shortfalls. Many personal loans are made on an *unsecured* basis—that is, there is no collateral with the loan other than the borrower's good name.
- **Consolidation loans**. This type of credit is used to straighten out an unhealthy credit situation. When consumers overuse credit cards, credit lines, or consumer loans, and

can no longer service the debt in a prompt and timely fashion, a consolidation loan may help control this deteriorating credit situation. By borrowing money from one source to pay off other forms of credit, borrowers can replace, say, five or six monthly payments that total $400 with one payment amounting to $250. *Consolidation loans are usually expensive, and people who use them must be careful to stop using credit cards and other forms of credit until they repay the loans. Otherwise, they may end up right back where they started.*

STUDENT LOANS. Today, the annual cost of a college education ranges from about $8,000 at a state school to well over $25,000 at many private colleges—and the cost is rising at about 4 or 5 percent a year, well above the inflation rate. Many families, even those who started saving for college when their children were young, are faced with higher than expected bills. Fortunately, many different types of financial aid programs exist, including some federal programs described below, as well as state, private, and college-sponsored programs.

Certainly paying for a college education is one of the most legitimate reasons for going into debt. Although you could borrow money for college through normal channels—that is, take out a regular consumer loan from your bank and use the proceeds to finance an education—there are better ways to go about getting education loans. That's because the federal government (and some state governments) have available several different types of subsidized educational loan programs. The four federally sponsored programs are:

* Stafford loans (Direct and Federal Family Education Loans—FFEL)
* Perkins loans
* Supplemental Loans for Students (SLS)
* Parent Loans (PLUS)

The Stafford and Perkins loans have the best terms and are the foundation of the government's student loan program. SLS and PLUS are *supplemental loans* for students who demonstrate a need but, for one reason or another, do not qualify for Stafford or Perkins loans, or whose total need is not being met by the other types of aid they are receiving. Whereas Stafford, Perkins, and SLS loans are made directly to students, PLUS loans are made to the parents or legal guardians of college students. Probably the best place to look for information about these and other programs is the Internet; for example, look up FASTWEB (which stands for *Financial Aid Search Through the WEB*). This site, which is free, not only provides details on all the major, and some of the not-so-major, student loan programs, but also has a service that matches individuals with scholarships and loans, and even goes so far as to provide form letters to use in requesting more information (the address for this Web site is: **www.fastweb.com**).

To see how student loans work, let's take a look at the Stafford loan program (except where noted, the other three federally subsidized programs have much the same standards and follow the same procedures as discussed here). Stafford loans carry low, government-subsidized interest rates; most major banks as well as some of the bigger S&Ls and credit unions participate in the program. Actually, the loans are made directly by one of the participating banks or financial institutions (in the case of the Stafford FFEL loan program), although the student has no direct contact with the lending institution. Instead, the whole process—and it really is quite simple—begins with a visit to the school's financial aid office, where a financial aid counselor will help you determine your eligibility. To be eligible, you have to demonstrate a *financial need*, where the amount of your financial need is defined as the cost of attending school *LESS* the amount that can be paid by you or your family (in these programs, students are expected to contribute something to their educational expense, regardless of their income). In addition, you have to be making *satisfactory*

 Financial Road Sign

How to Get the Best Auto Loan Deal
You're ready to buy the car of your dreams. To find the best financing deal, follow these tips:
1. Don't be fooled by "low monthly payments," which may mean longer loan terms and paying more in interest.
2. Shop for a loan *before* you go to the dealer's showroom to have the most negotiation power. Dealer financing can cost more than bank and credit union auto loans. If you do finance through the dealer, ask about add-on costs or loan processing fees.
3. Consider applying a rebate to your down payment and financing a smaller amount rather than taking the low interest rate option.

Source: Lucy Lazarony, "Auto Loans Negotiations Salted with Landmines," *Bankrate.com*, February 8, 2001, **www.bankrate.com**.

progress in your academic program and you cannot be in default on any other student loans. (Each academic year, you will have to fill out a Free Application for Federal Student Aid [FAFSA] statement that shows these qualifications are being met. The financial aid office will have the forms available in hard copy, or you can complete and submit the form on the Web at **www.fafsa.ed.gov**). In effect, so long as you can demonstrate a financial need, are making satisfactory academic progress, and are not a deadbeat, you'll probably qualify for a Stafford loan.

Now all you have to do to obtain a loan is complete a simple application form, which is then submitted to *your school's financial aid office*. You do *not* have to deal with the bank (your school will submit all the necessary papers to the institution actually making the loan in the case of a FFEL loan, or directly to the federal government in the case of a Stafford Direct loan), and you will not be subject to any credit checks (although with SLS or PLUS loans, you may be subject to a credit judgment by the lender). The latest innovation in this procedure involves transmitting the application, like the one in Exhibit 7.1, electronically to the necessary parties, thus reducing paperwork and speeding up the processing. Most schools are converting to this method, if they haven't already done so.

There are specific loan limits with each of the four programs. For example, with Stafford loans, you can borrow up to $2,625 per academic year for first-year studies, $3,500 for the second year, and $5,500 per academic year thereafter, up to a maximum of $23,000 for undergraduate studies—you can obtain even more if you can show that you are no longer a dependent of your parents; i.e., that you're an *independent* undergraduate student paying for your college education on your own. Graduate students can qualify for up to $8,500 per academic year. The maximum for both undergraduate and graduate loans combined is $138,500. Should you require even more money—that is, if your financial need exceeds the maximum amount of a Stafford loan—you can also apply for an SLS loan. There's no limit on the *number* of loans you can have, only on the maximum dollar amount that you can receive annually from each program.

Each year, right on through graduate school, a student can take out a loan from one or more of these government programs. Over time, that can add up to a lot of loans and a substantial amount of debt—all of which has to be repaid. But here's another nice feature: in addition to carrying low (government-subsidized) interest rates, loan repayment does not begin until after you're out of school (for the Stafford and Perkins programs only—repayment on SLS and PLUS loans normally begins within 60 days of loan disbursement). In addition, interest does not begin accruing until you get out of school (except, of course, with SLS or PLUS loans, where interest starts accumulating with the first disbursement). Of course, while you're in school, the lenders will receive interest on their loans, but it's paid by the federal government! Once repayment begins, you start paying interest on the loans, which may be tax deductible (according to the Taxpayer Relief Act of 1997, you can deduct interest on most types of student loans for the first 60 months, though the deduction is capped at $2,500). As a rule, student loans are amortized with monthly (principal and interest) payments over a period of 5 to 10 years. To help you service the debt, if you have a number of student loans outstanding, you can *consolidate* the loans, at a single blended rate, and extend the repayment period to as far as 20 years. In addition, you can ask for either an *extended repayment* for a longer term of up to 30 years; a *graduated repayment schedule*, which will give you low payments in the early years and then higher payments later on; or an *income-contingent repayment plan*, with payments that fluctuate annually according to your income and debt levels. But no matter what you do, *take the repayment provisions seriously, because defaults will be reported to credit bureaus and become a part of your credit file*! What's more, due to recent legislation, you cannot get out of repaying your student loans by filing for bankruptcy—no matter which Chapter you file under (7 or 13), *student loans are no longer dischargeable in a bankruptcy proceeding.*

EXHIBIT 7.1

A STUDENT LOAN APPLICATION FORM FOR A STAFFORD LOAN

This is a standard application form for Stafford loans, and requests only the most basic information about the student borrower. It does not require information about a student's credit history, income level, and so on. Indeed, the student only has to fill out the top (shaded) part of the application, which includes the actual promissory note that the student is expected to sign.

Application and Promissory Note for Federal Stafford Loans (subsidized and unsubsidized)

OMB No. 1840-0717 Form Approved Exp. Date 03/31/99
WARNING: Any person who knowingly makes a false statement or misrepresentation on this form is subject to penalties which may include fines or imprisonment under the United States Criminal Code and 20 U.S.C. 1097.

Guarantor or Program Identification
UNITED STUDENT AID FUNDS, INC. 94

US

Borrower Section
Please print neatly or type. Read the instructions carefully.

1. Last Name / First Name / MI
2. Social Security Number
3. Permanent Street Address (If P.O. Box, see instructions.)
   City / State / Zip Code
4. Telephone Number ( )
5. Loan Period (Month/Year) From: To:
6. Driver's License Number (List state abbreviation first.)
7. Lender Name / City / State / Zip Code
8. Lender Code, if known
9. Date of Birth (Month/Day/Year)

10. **References:** You must provide two separate references with different U.S. addresses. The first reference should be a parent or legal guardian (if living). Both references must be completed fully.

   Name 1. _____ 2. _____
   Permanent Address
   City, State, Zip Code
   Area Code/Telephone ( ) _____ ( ) _____
   Relationship to Borrower

Loan Assistance Requested

11. I request the following loan type(s), to the extent I am eligible (see instructions):
   ☐ a. Subsidized Federal Stafford   ☐ b. Unsubsidized Federal Stafford

12. I request a total amount under these loan types not to exceed (see instructions for loan maximums): My school will certify my eligibility for each loan type for which I am applying. The amount and other details of my loan(s) will be described to me in a disclosure statement.
   $ _____ .00

13. If I check yes, I am requesting postponement (deferment) of repayment for my Stafford and prior SLS loan(s) during the in-school and grace periods. If I check no, I do not want to defer repayment.
   ☐ a. Yes, I want a deferment   ☐ b. No, I do not want a deferment

14. If I check yes, I am requesting that the lender add the interest on my unsubsidized Stafford and prior SLS loan(s) which accrues during the in-school and deferment periods, to my loan principal (capitalization). If I check no, I prefer to pay the interest.
   ☐ a. Yes, I want my interest capitalized   ☐ b. No, I prefer to pay the interest

15. If my school participates in electronic funds transfer (EFT), I authorize the school to transfer the loan proceeds received by EFT to my student account.
   ☐ a. Yes, transfer funds   ☐ b. No, do not transfer funds

Continued on the reverse side.

Promissory Note
Promise to Pay: I promise to pay to the lender, or a subsequent holder of this Promissory Note, all sums disbursed (hereafter "loan" or "loans") under the terms of this Note, plus interest and other fees which may become due as provided in this Note. If I fail to make payments on this Note when due, I will also pay reasonable collection costs, including attorney's fees, court costs, and collection fees. I understand I may cancel or reduce the size of any loan by refusing to accept any disbursement that is issued. I understand that this is a Promissory Note. I will not sign this Note before reading it, including the writing on the reverse side, even if otherwise advised. I am entitled to an exact copy of this Promissory Note and the Borrower's Rights and Responsibilities. My signature certifies I have read, understand, and agree to the terms and conditions of this Application and Promissory Note, including the Borrower Certification and Authorization printed on the reverse side and the accompanying Borrower's Rights and Responsibilities statement.

THIS IS A LOAN(S) THAT MUST BE REPAID.

16. Borrower's Signature _____   Today's Date (Month/Day/Year) _____

School Section
To be completed by an authorized school official.

17. School Name
18. Street Address
   City / State / Zip Code
19. Loan Period (Month/Day/Year) From: To:
20. Grade Level
21. Enrollment Status (Check one.) ☐ Full Time ☐ At Least Half Time
22. Anticipated Completion (Graduation) Date (Month/Day/Year)

23. School Code/Branch
24. Cost of Attendance $ .00
25. Federal Expected Family Contribution $ .00
26. Estimated Financial Aid $ .00
27. Certified Loan Amounts
   a. Subsidized $ .00
   b. Unsubsidized $ .00

28. Telephone Number ( )
29. Recommended Disbursement Date(s) (Month/Day/Year)
   1st / 2nd
   3rd / 4th
30. School Certification (See box on the reverse side.)
   Signature of Authorized School Official
   Print or Type Name and Title
   Date
   Check box if electronically transmitted to guarantor: ☐

Lender Section
To be completed by an authorized lending official.

31. Lender Name
   Street Address
   City / State / Zip Code
32. Lender Code/Branch
33. Telephone Number ( )
34. Lender Use Only
35. Amount(s) Approved
   a. Subsidized $ .00   b. Unsubsidized $ .00
36. Signature of Authorized Lending Official   Print or Type Name, Title, and Date

1/31/94   LENDER COPY

MONEY IN ACTION

College Financing 101: Best Bets for Student Loans

Worried about paying for college? You have plenty of company. Tuition costs have more than doubled in the past twenty years, forcing most students to plan carefully when it comes to paying for school. Financial aid programs based on merit and need, such as scholarships, grants, and work-study, may foot some of the bill. To start the process, fill out the Free Application for Student Aid, or FAFSA, and submit it to your school. Other sources of financial aid can be uncovered through local civic, religious, and professional groups. Commercial Internet sites, such as **www.fastweb.com**, can also help track down financial aid resources.

Unfortunately, financial aid hasn't kept pace with the spiraling growth of tuition costs. Many students and their families need to apply for education loans in order to fully finance their education. Choices include private loans and government-funded loans such as the federal PLUS, Perkins, or Stafford loan programs. Most states also offer some kind of student lending program. Plan carefully when shopping for education loans. In many cases, it may make sense for parents and students to share the burden of borrowing for college. Parents may use home equity lines of credit, which allow them to borrow 50 to 80 percent of the market value of their home, or apply for federal PLUS loans or private loans from banks or other organizations. However, there are advantages to the student taking out a federally subsidized education loan in their own name. Students are usually eligible for lower-rate loans and are more likely to be able to deduct interest payments from their taxes.

Before taking out an education loan, consider how much debt you will be able to handle after graduation. As a rule of thumb, financial planners suggest that students borrow no more than 8 to 10 percent of their expected take-home pay after graduation. Bear in mind that the average take home pay for college graduates is about $37,000, or about $2,200 a month, enough to comfortably support a maximum debt of $25,000 with a 10-year repayment schedule and an 8.25% interest rate. If you think you'll be interested in a job that pays a less-than-average starting salary, you should plan on borrowing accordingly. You can get an idea of the starting salaries for your planned career at websites like Salary.com (**www.salary.com**).

After you graduate, the repayment plan you choose can make a difference. Payment plans that call for equal monthly installments are usually least expensive in the long run. Stretching out installments may cut your monthly bill but will greatly increase the total amount of interest you pay on the loan. Prepaying your loan, however, can cut your overall costs dramatically. Paying just an extra $25 a month on a 10-year, $10,000 PLUS loan, for instance, will slash your repayment time to 7.7 years and save you over $1,000 in interest. Whatever loan option you choose, remember it's nearly impossible to walk away from repaying a student loan. Congress has tightened the rules regarding discharging loans in cases of financial hardship, even if you declare bankruptcy. So, as with any other type of debt, borrow wisely.

Sources: Brandi Lee, "Financial Aid Stress Has Cure," *University Wire*, August 29, 2000; Avery Comarow, Ted Gest, Jeannye Thorton, "Here's the Real Deal on Aid," *U.S. News and World Report*, September 18, 2000, p. 86; Penelope Wang, "Saving & Spending/Education: Now the Real Application," *Money*, January 1, 2001, p. 128.

In summary, here are some things about student loans to keep in mind:

- Check with your school's financial aid office to see what programs are available and then apply early.
- Register on FASTWEB (**www.fastweb.com**) for scholarships, grants, and loans that will be matched to your background.
- Borrow no more than you need—remember, these loans are eventually going to have to be repaid.
- Consider work-study as an alternative to borrowing.

- Become aware of loan forgiveness programs for selected occupations (military, law enforcement, Peace Corps, and so on).
- Take the loan repayment provisions seriously—defaults aren't taken lightly and can cause serious credit problems for you.
- Once you begin repaying the loans, take the interest deduction, up to the maximum allowed, on your (itemized) tax return.
- If you're having problems servicing the loans, contact the lender and see if some arrangements can be worked out (most lenders would rather work with you than have you default).

In addition to the government programs described above, other types of financial assistance are available to help you finance a college education, as described in the accompanying *Money in Action* box.

 To find advice on financing college (loans and scholarships) and helpful online calculators, check out Embark.com's financing section, **www.embark.com/college/ugrad_finance.asp**.

SINGLE PAYMENT OR INSTALLMENT PAYMENTS. Consumer loans can be broken into categories based on the type of repayment arrangement—single-payment or installment. **Single-payment loans** are made for a specified period of time, at the end of which payment in full (principal plus interest) is due. They generally have maturities ranging from 30 days to a year; rarely do these loans run for more than a year. Sometimes single-payment loans are made to finance purchases or pay bills when the cash to be used for repayment is known to be forthcoming in the near future; in this case, they serve as a form of **interim financing**. In other situations, single-payment loans are used by consumers who want to avoid being strapped with monthly installment payments and choose instead to make one large payment at the end of the loan. Often these loans are negotiated on short notice in order to meet some unexpected need.

Installment loans, in contrast, are repaid in a series of fixed, scheduled payments rather than in one lump sum. The payments are almost always set up on a monthly basis, with each installment being made up partly of principal and partly of interest. For example, out of a $75 monthly payment, $50 might be credited to principal and the balance to interest. These loans are typically made to finance the purchase of a good or service for which current resources are inadequate. The repayment period can run from 6 months to 6 years or more. Installment loans have become a way of life for many consumers. They are popular because they provide a convenient way to "buy now and pay later" in fixed monthly installments that can be readily incorporated into a family budget. The process of using installment loans to finance purchases is often referred to as "buying on time."

FIXED OR VARIABLE RATE LOANS. The majority of consumer loans are made at fixed rates of interest—that is, the interest rate charged (as well as the monthly payment) remains the same over the life of the obligation. However, variable rate loans are also being made with increasing frequency, especially on *longer-term installment loans*. As with an adjustable-rate home mortgage, the rate of interest charged on such credit changes every 6 to 12 months, in keeping with prevailing market conditions. If market interest rates go up, the rate of interest on the loan goes up accordingly, as does the monthly loan payment. These loans have periodic adjustment dates (6 to 12 months apart), at which time the interest rate and monthly payment are adjusted as necessary. Once an adjustment is made, the new rate remains in effect until the next adjustment date (sometimes the payment

single-payment loan
A loan made for a specified period of time, at the end of which payment in full is due.

interim financing
The use of a single-payment loan to finance a purchase or pay bills in situations where the funds to be used for repayment are known to be forthcoming in the near future or permanent financing is to be arranged.

installment loan
A loan that is repaid in a series of fixed, scheduled payments rather than a lump sum.

amount remains the same, but the number of payments changes). Many variable rate loans have caps on the maximum increase per adjustment period, and also over the life of the loan.

Variable rates can also be used with single-payment loans, but the mechanics are a bit different. That is, the rate charged is usually pegged to the *prime rate*, or some other "base" rate. It's meant to be reflective of the bank's cost of funds, and moves in response to fundamental credit conditions in the market. Changes in the prime rate are widely reported in the media because of the widespread impact the prime has on the cost of borrowing. Here's how the prime rate is used to set the interest rate on a single-payment loan. Instead of putting a single, specific rate on a loan, it might be quoted at, say, prime plus 3 points; under these conditions, if prime is 8 percent, the borrower starts with a rate of interest of $8 + 3 = 11$ percent. If the prime rate changes, the rate of interest on the loan changes automatically, except in this case the adjustment is made *immediately* (there are usually no adjustment dates with single-payment, variable rate loans). The loan will then carry a new rate of interest that will remain in effect until the next change. At maturity, interest charges at the different rates will be totaled and added to the principal to determine the size of the (single) loan payment. Generally speaking, variable rate loans are desirable *if interest rates are expected to fall* over the course of the loan; in contrast, fixed rate loans are preferable *if interest rates are expected to rise.*

Regardless of whether the loans are fixed or variable, their cost tends to vary with market conditions. As a rule, when interest rates move up or down in the market, so will the cost of consumer loans. Inevitably, there are going to be times when *the cost of credit simply becomes too high to justify borrowing* as a way of making major purchases. So when market rates start climbing, you should ask yourself whether the cost is really worth it. Financially, you may be far better off delaying the purchase until rates come down.

WHERE CAN YOU GET CONSUMER LOANS?

Consumer loans can be obtained from a number of sources, including commercial banks, consumer finance companies, credit unions, savings and loan associations, sales finance companies, life insurance companies, possibly even brokerage firms, pawnshops, or friends and relatives. *Commercial banks* dominate the field and provide nearly half of all consumer loans. Behind banks are *consumer finance companies* and then *credit unions*; together, about 75 percent of all consumer loans are originated by these three financial institutions! Interestingly, S&Ls are not much of a force in this market, and they're becoming even less so over time. The selection of a lender often depends on both the rate of interest being charged and the ease with which the loan can be negotiated. Exhibit 7.2 provides a summary of the types of loans, lending policies, costs, and services offered by the major providers of consumer loans. Of course, today, it's becoming easier than ever to obtain consumer loans online. Just go to **Yahoo** and search for "installment loans" and you'll end up with literally hundreds of web sites. Some of these sites will actually accept applications online, whereas others offer a brief listing of their services, along with a toll-free phone number.

COMMERCIAL BANKS. Because they offer various types of loans at attractive rates of interest, commercial banks are a popular source of consumer loans. One nice thing about commercial banks is that they typically charge lower rates than most other lenders, in large part because they take only the best credit risks and are able to obtain relatively inexpensive funds from their depositors. The demand for their loans is generally high, and they can be selective in making consumer loans. Commercial banks usually lend only to customers with good credit ratings who can readily demonstrate an ability to make repayment in accordance with the specified terms. They also give preference to loan applicants who are account holders. The fact that an applicant is already a good customer of the bank enhances his or her chances of being approved for the requested financing. Although banks prefer to make loans secured by some type of collateral, they also make unsecured loans to their better customers. The interest rate charged on a bank loan may be affected by the loan's size, terms, and whether it is secured by some type of collateral.

CONSUMER FINANCE COMPANIES. Sometimes called *small loan companies*, **consumer finance companies** make secured and unsecured (signature) loans to qualified individuals. These companies do not accept deposits but obtain funds from their stockholders and through open market borrowing. Because they do not have the inexpensive sources of funds that banks and other deposit-type institutions do, their interest rates are generally quite high. The actual rates charged by consumer finance companies are regulated by interest rate ceilings (or usury laws) set by the states in which they operate. The maximum allowable interest rate may vary with the size of the loan, and the state regulatory authorities may also limit the length of the repayment period. Loans made by consumer finance companies typically are for $5,000 or less and are secured by some type of collateral. Repayment is required on an installment basis, usually over a period of 5 years or less.

> **consumer finance company**
> A firm that makes secured and unsecured personal loans to qualified individuals; also called a *small loan company*.

Consumer finance companies specialize in small loans to high-risk borrowers. Of course, these loans are quite costly, but they may be the only alternative for people with poor credit ratings. Some people are attracted to consumer finance companies because of the ease with which they can obtain loans. Because of the high rates of interest charged, individuals should consider this source only after exhausting all others.

CREDIT UNIONS. As it now stands, only members can obtain installment and single-payment loans from credit unions (*Note*: Although you still have to be a member of a credit union to obtain loans and other services, Congress has recently passed legislation enabling credit unions, if they so choose, to offer membership to just about anybody they want, rather than just a certain group of people.) Because they are nonprofit organizations with minimal operating costs, credit unions charge relatively low rates on their loans. They make either unsecured or secured loans, depending on the size and type of loan being requested. Generally speaking, membership in a credit union provides the most attractive borrowing opportunities available, because their interest rates and borrowing requirements are usually more favorable than other sources of consumer loans. An added convenience of a credit union loan is that loan payments can often be deducted directly from payroll checks.

SAVINGS AND LOAN ASSOCIATIONS. Savings and loan associations (as well as savings banks) primarily make mortgage loans. Even so, although they are not major players in the consumer loan field, S&Ls are permitted to make loans on such consumer durables as automobiles, televisions, refrigerators, and other appliances. In addition, they can make certain types of home improvement and mobile-home loans, as well as some personal and educational loans. Among other things, financial deregulation has enabled S&Ls to enter the consumer loan market. Since 1982, federally chartered S&Ls have been allowed to invest a portion of their assets in consumer loans, although they have pulled back from these loans, as certain "S&L bailout" legislation mandated that they direct more of their lending to home mortgages. As a rule, the rates of interest on consumer loans at S&Ls are fairly close to the rates charged by commercial banks; if anything, they tend to be a bit more expensive. Like their banking counterparts, the rates charged on specific loans will, in the final analysis, depend on such factors as the type and purpose of the loan, the duration and type of repayment, and the overall creditworthiness of the borrower.

EXHIBIT 7.2

THE MAJOR SOURCES OF CONSUMER LOANS

Banks, finance companies, and other financial institutions provide a full range of consumer credit products to their customers. These institutions follow a variety of lending policies and lend money at different rates of interest.

	Commercial Banks	Consumer Finance Companies
TYPES OF LOANS	• Single-payment loans • Installment loans • Passbook loans • Check-credit plans • Credit card loans • Second mortgages • Education loans	• Installment loans • Second mortgages
LENDING POLICIES	• Seek customers with established credit history • Often require collateral or security • Prefer to deal in large loans, such as auto, home improvement, and modernization, with the exception of credit card and check-credit plans • Determine repayment schedules according to purpose of loan • Vary credit rates according to the type of credit, time period, customers' credit history, and security offered • May require several days to process a new credit application	• Often lend to consumers without established credit history • Often make unsecured loans • Often vary rates according to size of loan balance • Offer a variety of repayment schedules • Make a higher percentage of small loans than other lenders • Maximum loan size limited by law • Process applications quickly, often the same day as application is made
COSTS	• Lower than some lenders, because they: — Take fewer credit risks — Lend depositors' money, a relatively inexpensive source of funds — Deal primarily in large loans, which yield larger dollar income without raising administration costs	• Higher than most because they: — Take greater risks — Must borrow and pay interest on money to lend — Often deal in small loans, which are costly to make and yield a small income
SERVICES	• Offer several different types of consumer credit plans • May offer financial counseling • Handle credit transactions confidentially	• Provide credit promptly • Make loans to pay off accumulated debts willingly • Design repayment schedules to fit the borrower's income • Usually offer financial counseling • Handle credit transactions confidentially

EXHIBIT 7.2 *continued*

Credit Unions	Savings and Loan Associations	Life Insurance Companies
• Installment loans • Share draft credit plans • Credit card loans • Second mortgages • Education loans	• Installment loans • Home improvement loans • Education loans • Savings account loans • Second mortgages	• Single or partial payment loans
• Lend to members only • Make unsecured loans • May require collateral or cosigner for loans over a specified amount • May require payroll deductions to pay off loan • May submit large loan applications to a committee for approval • Offer a variety of repayment schedules	• Will lend to all creditworthy individuals • Often require collateral • Loan rates vary depending on size of loan, length of payment, and security involved • As a result of the "S&L bailout," are becoming less of a force in the consumer loan field	• Lend on cash value of certain types of life insurance policies • No date or penalty on repayment • Deduct amount owed from value of policy benefit if death or other maturity occurs before repayment
• Lower than most because they: — Take fewer credit risks — Lend money deposited by members, which is less expensive than borrowed money — Often receive free office space and supplies from sponsoring organization — Are managed by members whose services in most cases are donated — Enjoy federal income tax exemptions	• Lower than some lenders because they: — Lend depositors' money, a relatively inexpensive source of funds — Secure most loans by savings accounts, real estate, or some other asset	• Lower than many because they: — Take no risk — Pay no collection costs — Secure loans by cash value of policy (and are thus lending the policyholders their own money)
• Design repayment schedules to fit borrowers' income • Generally provide credit life insurance without extra charge • May offer financial counseling • Handle credit transactions confidentially	• Often offer financial counseling • Specialize in mortgages and other housing-related loans • Handle credit transactions confidentially	• Permit repayment at any time or not at all, if borrower chooses to use the cash value of the policy as a source of repayment • Handle credit transactions confidentially

sales finance company
A firm that purchases notes drawn up by sellers of certain types of merchandise, typically big-ticket items.

captive finance company
A sales finance company that is owned by a manufacturer of big-ticket merchandise. GMAC is a captive finance company.

SALES FINANCE COMPANIES. Businesses that sell relatively expensive items—such as automobiles, furniture, and appliances—often provide installment financing to purchasers of their products. Because dealers cannot afford to tie up their funds in installment contracts, they sell them to a **sales finance company** for cash. This procedure is often referred to as "selling paper," because merchants in effect sell their loans to a third party. When the sales finance company purchases these notes, customers are usually notified to make payments directly to it.

The largest sales finance organizations are the **captive finance companies** owned by manufacturers of big-ticket items—automobiles and appliances. General Motors Acceptance Corporation (GMAC) and General Electric Credit Corporation (GECC) are just two examples of captive finance companies that purchase the installment loans made by the dealers of their products. Also, most commercial banks act as sales finance companies by buying paper from auto dealers and other businesses. The cost of financing through a sales finance company is generally a little higher than the rates charged by banks and S&Ls, particularly when you let the dealer do all the work in arranging the financing (dealers normally get a cut of the finance income, so it's obviously in their best interest to secure as high a rate of interest as possible). However, since the early 1980s, automakers have also been using interest rates on new-car loans as a marketing tool. They do this by dropping the rate of interest on car loans *(for selected models)* to levels well below the market. For example, not long ago, GM was offering 1.9 percent, 5-year financing on some of their cars. Auto manufacturers use these loan rates (along with rebates) to stimulate sales by keeping the cost of buying a new car down. Clearly, cutting the cost of borrowing for a new car can result in big savings!

 Shopping for a new car? Get current auto loan rates in your state, shop for the best dealer incentives, and use the handy loan calculator at Edmund's, **www.edmunds.com**.

cash value (of life insurance)
An accumulation of savings in an insurance policy that can be used as a source of loan collateral.

LIFE INSURANCE COMPANIES. Life insurance policyholders may be able to obtain loans from their insurance companies. That's because certain types of policies not only provide death benefits but also have a savings function, in which case they can be used as collateral for loans. (*Be careful with these loans, however, as they could involve a tax penalty if certain conditions are not met.* A detailed discussion of life insurance is presented in Chapter 8.) Life insurance companies are required by law to make loans against the **cash value**—the amount of accumulated savings—of certain types of life insurance policies. The rate of interest in this type of loan is stated in the policy, and it used to be set as low as 5 or 6 percent. The newer policies, however, carry loan rates that aren't set until the loans are made; that usually means borrowing money at or near prevailing market rates. Although you will be charged interest for as long as the policy loan is outstanding, these loans do not have repayment dates—in other words, you do not have to pay them back. When you take out a loan against the cash value of your life insurance policy, you are really borrowing from yourself. Therefore, the amount of the loan outstanding, plus any accrued interest, will be deducted from the amount of coverage provided by the policy—effectively lowering your insurance coverage and endangering your beneficiaries with a lower pay-out should you die before repayment. The chief danger in life insurance loans is that they do not have a firm maturity date; consequently, borrowers may lack the motivation to repay them.

In addition to life insurance companies, many other *financial services organizations* are entering the consumer loan field. Indeed, it's now possible to get home equity lines and other consumer loan products from most of the major brokerage firms, like Merrill Lynch or Prudential Securities. In 1999, another major financial services organization—American Express—launched its *Membership Banking* product, which provides a full menu of banking services, from money market and checking accounts to CDs, electronic bill payments, and lines of credit that are linked to their credit and charge card services. While it's true that banks, credit unions, and consumer finance companies dominate the consumer loan field, other players are entering the market and, in the process, offering borrowers options and choices they never had before.

FRIENDS AND RELATIVES. Sometimes, rather than going to a bank or some other financial institution, there may be a close friend or relative who is willing to lend you money. In many cases, such loans are attractive because little or no interest is charged. The terms will, of course, vary depending on the financial needs of the borrower, but they should be specified in some type of loan agreement that states the costs, conditions, and maturity date of the loan, as well as the obligations of both borrower and lender. Not only does a written loan agreement reduce opportunities for disagreement and unhappiness, it also protects both borrower and lender should either of them die or other unexpected events occur. *Still, given the potential for disagreement and conflict inherent in this type of arrangement, borrowing from friends or relatives is not advisable*, and should be seriously considered only when there are no other viable alternatives, or perhaps if the terms of credit are so much better than those available from the more traditional sources.

If, for one reason or another, you still feel compelled to either borrow or lend money in this fashion, it is recommended that you structure the loan carefully. Here are some guidelines to follow when setting up loans to friends or family:

* *Lend only money you can afford to give away*. Accountants estimate that between 20 percent and 50 percent of these types of loans are never repaid, so plan for the worst.
* *Make the arrangement businesslike*. Draw up a formal promissory note with specific terms that have been agreed to by both parties. Most office supply stores have samples. If a default does occur, this formal note is the necessary proof for an income tax deduction for the loss.
* *Charge interest if the note won't be quickly paid back*. An interest rate just above what you could get on your savings, but lower than prevailing loan rates, is recommended.
* *Both parties must understand that this is a loan, not a gift*. Be specific about repayment terms, establishing weekly or monthly payments, or a lump-sum agreement.

And remember, a loan to or from a friend or family member is far more than a run-of-the-mill banking transaction: the interest is emotional, and the risks are the relationship itself!

As a last resort, you might even want to consider a *pawn shop*—if you have some sort of valuable asset (like a piece of jewelry, a musical instrument, or a CD player) you can leave as collateral. Such establishments tend to proliferate during economically tough times, as an increasing number of people turn to them as a source of "financing." As long as you have an asset to pawn, you may be able to obtain a short-term, single payment loan from one of these shops. But bear in mind that the amount of money you receive is likely to be only a small fraction of the perceived resale value of the asset you pawn. Moreover, the rate of interest charged on the loan can be extremely high, and the pawned asset can be sold if you do not repay the loan within the designated period of time.

CONCEPT CHECK

7-1. Discuss the difference between consumer loans and open-account credit.
7-2. List and briefly discuss the five major reasons for borrowing money through a consumer loan.
7-3. Identify several different types of federally sponsored student loan programs. Briefly note some of the basic features of these programs and how they differ from regular consumer loans. As a college student, what aspects of these student loan programs appeal to you the most?
7-4. Define and differentiate between (a) fixed and variable rate loans and (b) a *single-payment loan* and an *installment loan*.
7-5. Compare the consumer lending activities of (a) *consumer finance companies* and (b) *sales finance companies*. Describe a *captive finance company*.
7-6. Discuss the role of (a) credit unions and (b) savings and loan associations in consumer lending. Point out any similarities or differences in their lending activities. How do they compare to commercial banks?

■ Managing Your Credit [LG3]

Borrowing money to make major acquisitions—and, in general, using consumer loans—is a sound and perfectly legitimate way to conduct your financial affairs. Meeting a major financial goal by buying on credit can be worked into your network of financial plans, and servicing the debt can be factored into your monthly cash budget. Doing it this way certainly is far superior to borrowing in a haphazard manner, giving little or no consideration to debt repayment. When borrowing is well thought out in advance and *full consideration is given not only to the need for the asset or item in question but also to the repayment of the ensuing debt*, sound credit management is the result. And sound credit management underlies effective personal financial planning.

From a financial planning perspective, you should ask yourself two questions when considering the use of a consumer loan: (1) Does making this acquisition fit into your financial plans, and (2) does the required debt service on the loan fit into your monthly cash budget? If the expenditure in question will seriously jeopardize your financial plans or if the repayment of the loan is likely to place an undue strain on your cash budget, you should definitely reconsider the purchase! Perhaps it can be postponed, or you can liquidate some assets in order to come up with more down payment. You may even have to alter some other area of your financial plan in order to work the expenditure in. Whatever route you choose, the key point is to make sure that borrowing will be fully compatible with your financial plans and cash budget *before* the loan is taken out and the money spent.

SHOPPING FOR LOANS

Once you have decided to use credit, it is equally important that you shop around and evaluate the various costs and terms available. You may think the only thing you need do to make a sound credit decision is determine which source offers the lowest finance charge. But this could not be farther from the truth—for as we'll see below, finance charges are just one of the factors to consider when shopping for a loan.

FINANCE CHARGES. What's it going to cost me? For a lot of people, that's one of the first things they want to know when taking out a loan. And that's appropriate, because borrowers should know what they're going to have to pay to get the money. Lenders are required by law to clearly state all finance charges and other loan fees. Find out the effective (or true) *rate* of interest you're going to have to pay on the loan, and whether the loan carries a fixed or variable rate. Obviously, *so long as everything else is equal*, it's in your best interest to secure the least expensive loan. In this regard, ask the lender what the *annual rate of interest* on the loan will be, because it's easier (and far more relevant) to compare percentage rates on alternative borrowing arrangements than the dollar amount of the loan charges. This rate of interest is known as the *APR* (annual percentage rate) and includes not only the basic cost of money, but also any additional fees that might be required on the loan (APR will be more fully discussed later). Also, if it's a variable rate loan, find out what the interest rate is pegged to, how many "points" are added to the base rate, how often the loan rate can be changed, and if rate caps exist. Just as important, how will the lender make the periodic adjustments—will the *size* of the monthly payment change, or the *number* of monthly payments? To avoid any future shock, it's best to find these things out before the loan is made.

 To get the latest consumer loan rates, plus helpful guides on borrowing, visit Bankrate.com, **www.bankrate.com**.

LOAN MATURITY. Try to make sure that the size and number of payments will fit comfortably into your spending and savings plans. As a rule, the cost of credit increases with the length of the repayment period. Thus, to lower your cost, you should consider shortening the loan maturity—but only to the point where doing so will not place an unnecessary strain on your cash flow. For although a shorter maturity may reduce the cost of the loan, it will also increase the size of the monthly loan payment. Indeed, finding a monthly loan payment you will be comfortable with is a critical dimension of sound credit management. Fortunately, the personal computer provides an effective way of evaluating different loan configurations. Altering the loan maturity is just one way of coming up with an affordable monthly payment; with the aid of a personal computer (through either a piece of software or a site on the Internet), you can quickly run through all sorts of alternatives to find the one that will best fit your monthly budget. (The "tools" section of most major financial services sites on the Internet have "calculators" that enable you to quickly and easily figure interest rates and monthly loan payments for all sorts of different types of loans; generally, all you have to do is plug in a few key pieces of information, hit "calculate," and the computer does the rest. For example, go to **www.kiplinger.com/tools** and try out their calculators.)

TOTAL COST OF THE TRANSACTION. When comparison shopping for credit, always look at the total cost of both the price of the item purchased *and* the price of the credit. Retailers often manipulate both sticker prices and interest rates, so you really will not know what kind of deal you are getting until you look at the total cost of the transaction. Along this line, comparing *monthly payments* is a good way to get a handle on total cost. It is a simple matter to compare total costs: just add the amount put down on the purchase to the total of all the monthly loan payments; other things being equal, the one with the lowest total is the one you should pick.

COLLATERAL. Make sure you know up front what collateral (if any) you will have to pledge on the loan and what you stand to lose in case you default on your payments. Actually, if it makes no difference to you and if it is not too inconvenient, using collateral often makes sense, because it may result in *lower* finance charges—perhaps half a percentage point or so.

OTHER CREDIT CONSIDERATIONS. In addition to the preceding guidelines, other questions you should ask include the following: Can you choose a *payment date* that will be

MONEY IN ACTION

A Lender's Worst Nightmare: Borrowers Who Ask Questions

For decades, the average borrower had just three questions: How much money can I borrow? What's my monthly payment? And when can I have the money? That mind-set allowed lenders to charge 18 percent and more for credit card interest. Now, however, many consumers are wising up. They're asking questions about high interest costs and lending fees and comparing competitive offers from lenders before committing.

Why have so many borrowers become so much more sophisticated? One reason is increased media attention on financial issues. Magazines, newspapers, radio, and television are filled with personal finance advice articles and programs. The Internet is also making it easier to comparison shop for everything from credit cards to auto loans. Another factor: the huge volume of direct mail offers from competing lenders promising low interest rates and minimum fees. An increasing number of "card surfers" are switching credit cards frequently to take advantage of low introductory rates before moving on to the next deal.

Unfortunately, not all consumers are yet savvy enough about shopping for loans and credit cards. Because they don't know how to ask the right questions, they may fall victim to predatory lenders—lenders who use unfair credit practices to suck unwary consumers into higher interest rates and poor credit terms. That's what happened to Helen Ferguson, a 78-year-old widow who saw an advertisement on television for a lending company that promised to consolidate the payments on the two mortgages she had taken out for home repairs by refinancing the loans. What Ferguson didn't know when she signed the loan papers, however, was that she was giving the company the right to charge lender fees totaling more than ten percent of the loan balance. The loan also carried hefty prepayment penalties, which meant Ferguson couldn't refinance with another bank without paying the penalties first. When Ferguson had trouble meeting the payments, she was forced to refinance again and again with the same lender—taking on a larger debt each time to cover all of the extra fees—until she almost lost her house.

Congress, the Federal Trade Commission, and organizations like the American Association of Retired Persons are all pushing for legislative changes that would make it harder for predatory lenders to operate. However, smart borrowers won't wait for those changes. To protect yourself, get all the facts before you sign on the dotted line for any loan. Ask if this is the lowest priced loan you qualify for and shop around to compare rates from other lenders. Always read the loan documents carefully, paying special attention to fees, terms, and conditions. Ask for explanations of any items you don't fully understand and then find out if this is standard lending practice. Get a copy of the lender's Notice of Right to Cancel or Notice of Rescission, which spells out your rights about canceling the loan, usually within 3 days. Finally, remember the old adage: if it sounds too good to be true, it probably is.

Sources: Michael D. Larson, "Predatory Lending: One Victim's Story," *Bankrate.com*, April 14, 2000, **www.bankrate.com**; Shelly K. Schwartz, "Don't Fall Prey to Lenders," CNNfn, March 15, 2000, **cnnfn.cnn.com**, "Payday Loans Not the Answer to Financial Woes," *Regulatory Intelligence Data*, May 3, 2000.

compatible with your spending patterns? Can you obtain the loan *promptly and conveniently?* What are the charges for late payments, and are they reasonable? Will you receive a refund on credit charges if you prepay your loan? Or will you have to pay prepayment penalties? Taking the time to look around for the best credit deal will pay off, not only in reducing the cost of such debt but also in keeping the burden of credit in line with your cash budget and financial plans. In the long run, you are the one who has the most to gain (or lose). Thus *you should see to it that the consumer debt you undertake does in fact have the desired effects on your financial condition.* As suggested in the accompanying *Money in Action* box, the lenders may not like the idea, but you're paying for the loan, so you might as well make the most of it!

KEEPING TRACK OF YOUR CREDIT

To stay abreast of your financial condition, it is a good idea to periodically take inventory of the consumer debt you have outstanding. You should do this a minimum of once a year, and ideally every 3 or 4 months. To take inventory of what you owe, simply prepare a list of all your outstanding consumer debt. Include *everything except your home mortgage*—installment loans, single-payment loans, credit cards, revolving credit lines, overdraft protection lines, and home equity credit lines.

You might find Worksheet 7.1 helpful in preparing a list of your debts. To use it, simply list the current monthly payment and the latest balance due for each type of consumer credit outstanding; then, total both columns to see how much you are paying each month and how large a debt load you have built up. Hopefully, when all the numbers have been totaled up, you will not be surprised to learn just how much you really do owe.

A way to quickly assess your debt position is to compute your *debt safety ratio* (we looked at this ratio in Chapter 6) by dividing the total monthly payments (from the worksheet) by your monthly take-home pay. If 20 percent or more of your take-home pay is going to monthly credit payments, you are relying too heavily on credit; in contrast, if your debt safety ratio works out to 10 percent or less, you are in a strong credit position. *Keeping track of your credit and holding the amount of outstanding debt to a reasonable level is the surest way to maintain your creditworthiness.*

CONCEPT CHECK

> 7-7. What two questions should be answered before taking out a consumer loan? Explain.
>
> 7-8. List and briefly discuss the different factors you should consider when shopping for a loan. How would you determine the total cost of the transaction?

$ Financial Road Sign

What Do Lenders Look For?

What do lenders look for when reviewing loan applications and credit reports? Here are their top questions:

1. Do you pay your bills on time?
2. How much of your income is already committed to debt repayment?
3. How much available credit do you already have, even if it's not currently being used?
4. How stable and responsible are you? How long have you been with your employer and lived at the same address?
5. Are there many recent inquiries on your credit report? (Lenders see this as a sign that you may be applying for lots of credit.)

Source: "Your credit report: what lenders look for," *Bankrate .com*, February 11, 2000, **www.bankrate.com**.

Single-Payment Loans [LG4]

Unlike most types of consumer loans, a single-payment loan is repaid in full with a single payment on a given due date. The payment usually consists of principal and all interest charges. Sometimes, however, interim interest payments may have to be made (for example, every quarter), in which case the payment at maturity is made up of principal plus any unpaid interest. Although installment loans are far more popular, single-payment loans still have their place in the consumer loan market.

Single-payment loans can be secured or unsecured and can be taken out for just about any purpose, from buying a new car to paying for a vacation. They are perhaps most useful when the funds needed for a given purchase or transaction are temporarily unavailable but are expected to be forthcoming in the near future. By helping you cope with a temporary cash shortfall, these loans can serve as a form of interim financing until more-permanent arrangements can be made.

Single-payment loans can also be used to help establish or rebuild an individual's credit rating. Many times, a bank will agree to a single-payment loan for a higher credit risk customer if an equal amount is deposited into an account at the bank, with both the loan and deposit having the same maturity. In this manner, the bank has the principal of the

 **WORKSHEET 7.1**

TRACKING YOUR CONSUMER DEBT

A worksheet like this allows you to keep track of your outstanding credit along with your monthly debt service requirements. Such information is a major component of sound credit management.

AN INVENTORY OF CONSUMER DEBT

Name **John & Mary Jergens**   Dated **June 14, 2001**

Type of Consumer Debt	Creditor	Current Monthly Payment*	Latest Balance Due
Auto loans	1. GMAC	$ 342.27	$ 13,796
	2.		
	3.		
Education loans	1. U.S. Dept. of Education	117.00	7,986
	2.		
Personal installment loans	1. Bank One	183.00	5,727
	2. B of A	92.85	2,474
Home improvement loan			
Other installment loans	1.		
	2.		
Single-payment loans	1.		
	2.		
Credit cards (retail charge cards, bank cards, T&E cards, etc.)	1. MBNA Visa	42.00	826.
	2. Amex Blue	35.00	600
	3. Sears	40.00	1,600
	4.		
	5.		
	6.		
	7.		
Overdraft protection line	Hiland Schools Credit Union	15.00	310
Personal line of credit			
Home equity credit line	Wells Fargo	97.00	9,700
Loan on life insurance			
Margin loan from broker			
Other loans	1. Mom & Dad	—	2,500
	2.		
	3.		
	Totals	$ 964.12	$ 45,519

$$\text{Debt safety ratio} = \frac{\text{Total monthly payments}}{\text{Monthly take-home pay}} \times 100 = \frac{\$\ 964.12}{\$5,200.00} \times 100 = \underline{18.5}\ \%$$

*Leave the space blank if there is *no* monthly payment required on a loan (e.g., as with a single-payment or education loan).

loan fully secured and need only be concerned about the difference between the rate charged for the loan and the rate paid on the deposit.

IMPORTANT LOAN FEATURES

The first thing you have to do when applying for either a single-payment or installment loan is submit a **loan application**, an example of which is shown in Exhibit 7.3. Basically, the loan application provides the lending institution with information about the purpose of the loan, whether it will be secured or unsecured, and the financial condition of the borrower. The loan officer uses this document, along with other information (such as a credit report from the local credit bureau and income verification), to determine whether you should be granted the loan—here again, some type of *credit scoring* (as discussed in Chapter 6) may be used to make the decision. As part of the loan application process, you should also consider the various features of the debt, the three most important of which are loan collateral, loan maturity, and loan repayment.

LOAN COLLATERAL. Most single-payment loans are secured by certain specified assets. For *collateral*, lenders prefer items they feel are readily marketable at a price sufficiently high to cover the principal portion of the loan—for example, an automobile, jewelry, or stocks and bonds. If a loan is obtained to purchase some personal asset, that asset may be used to secure it. In most cases, lenders do not take physical possession of the collateral but instead file a **lien**, which is a legal claim that permits them to liquidate the collateral to satisfy the loan in the event the borrower defaults. The lien is filed in the county courthouse and is a matter of public record. If borrowers maintain possession or title to *movable* property—such as cars, TVs, and jewelry—the instrument that gives the lenders title to the property in event of default is called a **chattel mortgage**. If lenders hold title to the collateral—or actually take possession of it, as in the case of stocks and bonds—the agreement giving them the right to sell these items in case of default is a **collateral note**.

LOAN MATURITY. As indicated earlier, the maturity, or term, on a single-payment loan usually extends for a period of 1 year or less and very rarely goes out to 2 years or longer. When you request a single-payment loan, you should be sure the term is long enough to allow you to obtain the funds to repay the loans, but not any longer than necessary. Don't stretch the maturity out too far, since the dollar amount of the finance charges paid increases with time. Because the loan is retired in a single payment, the lender must be assured that you will be able to repay it even if certain unexpected events occur in the future. The term of your single-payment loan therefore must be reconciled with your budget, as well as your ability to pay. If the money you plan to use for repayment will be received periodically over the term of the loan, an installment-type loan may be more suitable.

LOAN REPAYMENT. The repayment of a single-payment loan is expected to take place at a single point in time: on its maturity date. Occasionally the funds needed to repay this type of loan will be received prior to maturity. Depending on the lender, the borrower might be able to repay the loan early and thereby reduce the finance charges. Credit unions often permit early repayment of these loans with *reduced* finance charges. Commercial banks and other single-payment lenders, however, may not accept early repayments; or, if they do, they may charge a **prepayment penalty** on them. This penalty normally amounts to a set percentage of the interest that would have been paid over the remaining life of the loan. The Truth in Lending Act requires lenders to disclose in the loan agreement whether, and in what amount, prepayment penalties are charged on a single-payment loan. *A borrower should understand this information before signing a loan agreement.*

loan application
An application that provides a lender with information about the purpose of the requested loan, whether it will be secured or unsecured, and the applicant's financial condition.

lien
A legal claim that permits the lender, in event the borrower defaults, to liquidate the items serving as collateral to satisfy the obligation.

chattel mortgage
A mortgage on personal property given as security for the payment of an obligation.

collateral note
A legal note that gives the lender the right to sell collateral in the event of the borrower's default on the obligation.

prepayment penalty
An additional charge you may owe if you decide to pay off your loan prior to maturity.

EXHIBIT 7.3

A CONSUMER LOAN CREDIT APPLICATION

A typical loan application, like this one, contains information about the persons applying for the loan, including source(s) of income, current debt load, and a brief record of employment.

NICHOLAS FINANCIAL, INC.
CONSUMER LOAN CREDIT APPLICATION

Source_____ ☐PB_____ Payoff_____ ☐FB_____ ☐New

LOAN INFORMATION

Amount Requested $	Purpose		Application Type ☐Individual ☐Joint

COLLATERAL INFORMATION

☐Motor Vehicle: Year____ Make_____ Model_____ Miles_____
☐Personal Property ☐Other (Describe)

APPLICANT INFORMATION

Name (Last, First, M.I.)

Social Security # - -	Date of Birth / /	☐Married ☐Unmarried ☐Separated	# of Dependents

CO-APPLICANT INFORMATION

Name (Last, First, M.I.)

Social Security # - -	Date of Birth / /	☐Married ☐Unmarried ☐Separated	# of Dependents

APPLICANT RESIDENCE INFORMATION

Address (Number, St, and Apt. or Lot # if applicable)	Telephone #
City, State, Zip Code	Time At Residence Years / Months /
Previous Address	Time At Residence Years / Months /

☐Rent ☐Live with Parents ☐Own ☐Other_____	Landlord or Mortgage Holder Name: Phone #:	Monthly Payment $

CO-APPLICANT RESIDENCE INFORMATION

Address (Number, St, and Apt. or Lot # if applicable)	Telephone #
City, State, Zip Code	Time At Residence Years / Months /
Previous Address	Time At Residence Years / Months /

☐Rent ☐Live with Parents ☐Own ☐Other_____	Landlord or Mortgage Holder Name: Phone #:	Monthly Payment $

APPLICANT EMPLOYMENT INFORMATION

Employer	Employer Telephone
Employer Address	Position

Gross Income: $ ☐Weekly ☐Bi-weekly ☐Monthly	Time At Job Years / Months /

Other Income: $ Source	Alimony, Child support, or separate maintenance income need not be revealed if you do not wish to have it considered as a basis for repaying this obligation.

Previous Employer & location	Previous Emp. Phone #
Position	Time At Job Years / Months /

CO-APPLICANT EMPLOYMENT INFORMATION

Employer	Employer Telephone
Employer Address	Position

Gross Income: $ ☐Weekly ☐Bi-weekly ☐Monthly	Time At Job Years / Months /

Other Income: $ Source	Alimony, Child support, or separate maintenance income need not be revealed if you do not wish to have it considered as a basis for repaying this obligation.

Previous Employer & location	Previous Emp. Phone #
Position	Time At Job Years / Months /

APPLICANT CREDIT REFERENCES

Creditor	Payment	Balance

☐Checking Bank Name_____ Acct#_____
☐Savings Bank Name_____ Acct#_____

CO-APPLICANT CREDIT REFERENCES

Creditor	Payment	Balance

☐Checking Bank Name_____ Acct#_____
☐Savings Bank Name_____ Acct#_____

AUTHORIZATION AND SIGNATURES

By signing this application, you promise that all information provided to Nicholas Financial, Inc. is true and complete. You also promise that you have revealed any pending lawsuits or unpaid judgements against you. You intend the seller and/or assignee to rely upon these promises in deciding whether to extend credit to you. You authorize a full investigation of your credit record and your employment history. You also authorize the seller and/or assignee to release information about your credit experience with them. You understand that Nicholas Financial, Inc. will retain this application whether or not it is approved. I understand that if the application is for a loan secured by real property that a additional information will be required.

Applicant Signature	Date

Co-Applicant Signature	Date

104111798

Occasionally an individual will borrow money using a single-payment loan, only to discover that he or she is short of money when the loan comes due—after all, making one big loan payment can cause a real strain on one's cash flow. Should this happen to you, don't just let the payment go past due; rather, *inform the lender in advance so a partial payment, loan extension, or some other arrangement can be made.* Under such circumstances, the lender will often agree to a **loan rollover**, in which case the original loan is paid off by taking out another loan. The lender will usually require that all the interest and at least part of the principal be paid at the time of the rollover. Thus, if you originally borrowed $5,000 for 12 months, the bank might be willing to lend you, say, $3,500 for another 6 to 9 months as part of a loan rollover. In this case, you'll have to "pay down" $1,500 of the original loan, along with all interest due. However, you can expect the interest rate on a rollover loan to go up a bit; that is the price you pay for falling short on the first loan. Also, you should not expect to get more than one, or at the most two, loan rollovers—a bank's patience tends to grow somewhat short after a while!

loan rollover
The process of paying off a loan by taking out another, usually with the requirement that all interest and at least some of the principal on the original loan be paid at the time of rollover.

FINANCE CHARGES AND THE ANNUAL PERCENTAGE RATE

As indicated in Chapter 6, the Consumer Credit Protection Act, or Truth in Lending Act, requires lenders to disclose both the dollar amount of finance charges and the annual percentage rate (APR) of interest. A sample **loan disclosure statement** applicable to either a single-payment or installment loan can be seen in Exhibit 7.4. Note that such a statement discloses not only interest costs, but also other fees and expenses that may be tacked on to the loan. Although disclosures like this allow you to compare the various borrowing alternatives, you still need to understand the methods used to compute finance charges, because similar loans with the same *stated* interest rates may have different finance charges and APRs. The two basic procedures used to calculate the finance charges on single-payment loans are the *simple interest method* and the *discount method*.

loan disclosure statement
A document lenders are required to supply borrowers that states both the dollar amount of finance charges and the APR applicable to a loan.

SIMPLE INTEREST METHOD. Interest is charged only on the *actual loan balance outstanding* in the **simple interest method**. This method is commonly used on revolving credit lines by commercial banks, S&Ls, and credit unions. To see how it is applied to a single-payment loan, assume that you borrow $1,000 for two years at a 12 percent annual rate of interest. On a single-payment loan, the actual loan balance outstanding for the two years will be $1,000, because no principal payments will be made until this period ends. With simple interest, the finance charge, F_s, is obtained by multiplying the *principal* outstanding by the stated annual rate of interest and then multiplying this amount by the term of the loan:

simple interest method
A method of computing finance charges in which interest is charged on the actual loan balance outstanding.

$$F_s = P \times r \times t$$

where

F_s = finance charge calculated using simple interest method
P = principal amount of loan
r = stated annual rate of interest
t = term of loan, as stated in years (for example, t would equal 0.5 for a 6-month loan, 1.25 for a 15-month loan, and 2.0 for a 2-year loan)

Substituting $1,000 for P, .12 for r, and 2 for t in the equation, we see that the finance charge, F_s, on this loan equals some $240 ($1,000 × .12 per year × 2 years). Because the size of the loan payment with this type of credit arrangement is found by adding the finance charges to the principal amount of the loan, you would have to make a loan payment of $1,000 + $240 = $1,240 at maturity to retire this debt.

EXHIBIT 7.4

A LOAN DISCLOSURE STATEMENT

The loan disclosure statement informs the borrower of all charges (finance and otherwise) associated with the loan and the annual percentage rate (APR). In addition, it specifies the payment terms as well as the existence of any balloon payments.

FEDERAL TRUTH IN LENDING ACT DISCLOSURES

You have the right to receive at this time an itemization of the Amount Financed.

☐ I want an itemization.   ☐ I do not want an itemization.

ANNUAL PERCENTAGE RATE The cost of your credit as a yearly rate. %	Your payment schedule will be:

Number of Payments	Amount of Payments	When Payments Are Due

FINANCE CHARGE The dollar amount the credit will cost you. $

Insurance: Credit life insurance and credit disability insurance are not required to obtain credit, and will not be provided unless you sign and agree to pay the additional cost.

Type	Premium	Signature
Credit Life		I want credit life insurance _____ SIGNATURE
Credit Life and Disability		I want credit life and disability insurance _____ SIGNATURE
Joint Credit Life		I want joint credit life insurance _____ SIGNATURE
Joint Credit Life and Disability		I want joint credit life and disability insurance _____ SIGNATURE

AMOUNT FINANCED The amount of credit provided to you or on your behalf. $

TOTAL OF PAYMENTS The amount you will have paid after you have made all payments scheduled. $

e means an estimate

You may obtain property insurance from anyone you want that is acceptable to Bank One, Arizona, NA. If you get the insurance through Bank One, Arizona, NA, you will pay $_____ for _____ months of coverage.

Security: You are giving a security interest in the property being purchased.

Filing Fees: $_____

Late Charge: If a payment is late, you will be charged $10 or 5% of the payment, whichever is less.

Prepayment: If you pay off early, you will not have to pay a penalty.

Assumption: Someone buying your house may, subject to conditions, be allowed to assume the remaining obligation on the original terms.

See your contract documents for any additional information about nonpayment, default, and any required repayment in full before the scheduled rate.

Each undersigned acknowledges receipt of one copy of the above fully completed Disclosure Statement prior to consummation of the proposed transaction. Each undersigned further acknowledges this disclosure statement is not a commitment to extend credit, or to provide or acquire insurance.

DATED _____, 20_____   (X) _____
                                               (DEBTOR'S SIGNATURE)

BANK ONE, ARIZONA, NA   (X) _____
                                               (DEBTOR'S SIGNATURE)

BY _____   _____

Source: Bank One, Arizona, NA.

EXHIBIT 7.5

FINANCE CHARGES AND APRs FOR A SINGLE-PAYMENT LOAN ($1,000 LOAN FOR TWO YEARS AT 12% INTEREST)

Sometimes what you see is not what you get—such as when you borrow money through a discount loan and end up paying quite a bit more than the quoted rate.

Method	Stated Rate on Loan	Finance Charges	APR
Simple interest	12%	$240	12.0%
Discount	12	240	15.8

To calculate the true, or annual, percentage rate (APR) of interest on this loan, the average annual finance charge is divided by the average loan balance outstanding, as follows:

$$APR = \frac{\text{Average annual finance charge}}{\text{Average loan balance outstanding}}$$

The figure for the average annual finance charge is found by dividing the total finance charge by the life of the loan (in years). In our example, the result is $120 ($240/2). Because the loan balance outstanding remains at $1,000 over the life of the loan, the average loan balance outstanding is $1,000. Dividing the $120 average annual finance charge by the $1,000 average loan balance outstanding, we obtain an APR of 12 percent. Thus, the APR and the stated rate of interest are equivalent: They both equal 12 percent. This is always the case when the simple interest method is used to calculate finance charges, *regardless of whether loans are single-payment or installment.*

DISCOUNT METHOD. Although it is not widely used anymore, the **discount method** calculates total finance charges on the full principal amount of the loan, which is then subtracted from the amount of the loan. The difference between the amount of the loan and the finance charge is then disbursed (paid) to the borrower—in other words, finance charges are paid in advance and represent a discount from the principal portion of the loan. The finance charge on a single-payment loan using the discount method, F_d, is calculated in exactly the same way as for a simple interest loan:

$$F_d = F_s = P \times r \times t$$

Using the above method, the finance charge, F_d on the $1,000, 12 percent, 2-year, single-payment loan is, of course, the same $240 we calculated earlier. However, in sharp contrast to simple interest loans, the loan payment with a discount loan is the original principal amount of the loan, P, because the finance charges on the loan are deducted from the loan proceeds. Thus, for the $1,000 loan above, the borrower will receive $760—which is found by subtracting the interest charges from the loan principal ($1,000 less $240)—and in 2 years will be required to pay back $1,000.

To find the APR on this discount loan, substitute the appropriate values into the APR equation cited above. For this 2-year loan, the average annual finance charge is $120 ($240/2). However, as explained above, since this is a discount loan, the borrower will receive only $760. And because this is a single-payment loan, the average amount of money outstanding is also $760. When these figures are used in the APR equation, we find the true

discount method
A method of calculating finance charges in which interest is computed, then subtracted from the principal, and the remainder is disbursed to the borrower.

rate for this 12 percent discount loan is more like 15.8 percent ($120/$760). Clearly, the discount method yields a much higher APR on single-payment loans than does the simple interest method. Exhibit 7.5 contrasts the results from both methods for the single-payment loan example discussed here.

CONCEPT CHECK

> 7-9.   What is a *lien*, and under what circumstances is it part of a consumer loan?
>
> 7-10. Briefly describe and differentiate between (a) a *chattel mortgage* and (b) a *collateral note*.
>
> 7-11. When might you request a *loan rollover*?
>
> 7-12. Describe the two methods used to calculate the finance charges on a single-payment loan. As a borrower, which method would you prefer? Explain.

 ## ▇ Installment Loans [LG5, LG6]

Installment loans (known as ILs for short) differ from single-payment loans in that they require the borrower to repay the debt in a series of installment payments (usually on a monthly basis) over the life of the loan. Installment loans have long been one of the most popular forms of consumer credit—right up there with credit cards! Much of this popularity is, of course, due to the convenient way in which the loan repayment is set up; not surprisingly, most people find it easier on their checkbooks to make a series of small payments rather than one big one.

A REAL CONSUMER CREDIT WORKHORSE!

As a financing vehicle, there are few things installment loans can't do—which explains, in large part, why this form of consumer credit is so widely used. ILs, in fact, account for nearly two-thirds of all consumer debt outstanding (excluding home mortgages). Installment loans can be used to finance just about any type of big-ticket item imaginable. New car loans are, of course, the dominant type of IL, but this form of credit is also used to finance home furnishings, appliances and entertainment centers, camper trailers and other recreational vehicles, even expensive vacations; and, of course, more and more college students are turning to this type of credit as the way to finance their education.

Not only can they be used to finance all sorts of things, installment loans can also be obtained at many locations. You'll find them at banks and other financial institutions, as well as major department stores and merchants that sell relatively expensive products. Go into a home appliance store to buy a high-priced stereo and chances are you'll be able to arrange for IL financing right there on the spot. These loans can be taken out for just a few hundred dollars, or they can involve thousands of dollars—indeed, ILs of $25,000 or more are not uncommon. What's more, they can be set up with maturities as short as six months to as long as 7 to 10 years, even 15 years!

Most installment loans are secured with some kind of collateral—for example, the car or home entertainment center you purchase with the help of an IL will usually end up serving as collateral on the loan. Even personal loans used to finance things like expensive vacations can be secured—in this case, the collateral could be securities, CDs, or some other type of financial asset. One rapidly growing segment of this market is, in fact, ILs secured by second mortgages. These so-called *home equity loans* are similar to the home equity credit lines discussed in Chapter 6, except they involve a set amount of money loaned over a set period of time (often as long as 15 years), rather than a revolving credit line from which you can borrow, repay, and reborrow. Thus, if a borrower needs, say, $25,000 to help pay for an expensive new boat, he would simply take out a loan in that amount and secure it with a second mortgage on his home. For all practical purposes, this loan would be like any other IL in the sense that it's for a set amount of money and is to be repaid over a set period of time in monthly installments. In addition to their highly competitive interest rates, a big attraction of *home equity loans* is that the interest paid on them usually can be used as a tax deduction. So, borrowers get the double benefit of *low interest rates and tax deductibility*! As with home equity credit lines, however, failure to repay could result in the loss of your home.

 Find out about federal protection laws for borrowers and get tips on financing consumer loans at the Federal Trade Commission site, **www.ftc.gov**.

THE INSTALLMENT PURCHASE CONTRACT

All the information relevant to a transaction that's being financed on an installment loan basis is included in the **installment purchase contract**. This agreement specifies the obligations of both the purchaser (borrower) and the lender. Although its form is likely to vary with the lender, it will probably contain four basic components: a sales contract, a security agreement, a note, and an insurance agreement. A sample installment purchase contract containing all four of these components is presented in Exhibit 7.6.

SECURITY AGREEMENT. The **security agreement** (or **security interest**) indicates whether the lender has control over the item being purchased. Although state laws determine whether or not the borrower retains legal title to the collateral, the lender files a lien on the collateral in order to make the security interest public. In either case, the lender retains control over the collateral. If default does occur, the lender can sell the collateral and use the proceeds to satisfy the unpaid balance on the loan and cover any costs incurred in this process. The lender must pay to the borrower any excess funds obtained from the liquidation of the collateral. However, if a *deficiency* occurs—that is, if the proceeds from liquidation are *not* sufficient to satisfy the loan—the borrower may or may not be liable for the unsatisfied portion of the debt, depending on state law (in some states, the lender cannot turn to the borrower to make up the deficiency).

THE NOTE. The formal promise on the part of the borrower to repay the lender is spelled out in the **note**. It states all the legal obligations of both the borrower and the lender, and outlines all details concerning repayment, default, and disposition of collateral. The note is normally secured by the sales contract, or security agreement, which provides the lender with a security interest in the assets being acquired. It is the document that, when signed by both borrower and lender, legally binds the two parties to the terms and conditions stated therein. Although many of the detailed provisions of the note in Exhibit 7.6 are on the reverse side of the contract (not shown), the entire document, once signed, is considered to be the note.

CREDIT LIFE INSURANCE. Sometimes, as a condition of receiving an installment loan, a borrower is required to buy **credit life insurance** and possibly **credit disability insurance**. Credit life (and disability) insurance is tied to a particular IL and basically provides

installment purchase contract
An agreement that specifies the obligations of both the purchaser (borrower) and seller (lender), drawn up when a purchase transaction is being financed on an installment basis.

security agreement (security interest)
In an installment purchase contract, a legal agreement that indicates whether the lender retains control over the item being purchased.

note
In an installment purchase contract, the formal promise on the part of the borrower to repay the lender in accordance with the terms specified in the agreement.

credit life (or disability) insurance
A type of life (or disability) insurance, sold in conjunction with installment loans, in which the coverage decreases at the same rate as the loan balance.

EXHIBIT 7.6

AN INSTALLMENT PURCHASE CONTRACT

The installment purchase contract contains all the particulars of a given installment loan, including terms of payment, type and amount of credit insurance, financing arrangement, and other pertinent information.

RETAIL INSTALLMENT CONTRACT AND SECURITY AGREEMENT (Goods)

Date _____ , 20_____

———— SELLER (CALLED "YOU") ————
NAME _____
ADDRESS _____
CITY _____ STATE ____ ZIP _____
SALESMAN _____

———— BUYER (CALLED "I") ————
NAME _____
NAME _____
ADDRESS _____
CITY _____ STATE ____ ZIP _____

ANNUAL PERCENTAGE RATE The cost of your credit as a yearly rate.	FINANCE CHARGE The dollar amount the credit will cost you.	AMOUNT FINANCED The amount of credit provided to you or on your behalf.	TOTAL OF PAYMENTS The amount you will have paid after you have made all payments scheduled.	TOTAL SALES PRICE The total cost of my purchase on credit, including my downpayment of $ _____
%	$	$	$	$

← Terms

My payment schedule will be:

Number of Payments	Amount of Payments	When Payments Are Due
		, 20— and same date of each following month

← Security Agreement

Security: I gave you a security interest in the goods or property being purchased.
Late Charge: If I don't pay any payments in 10 days after it's due, I shall also pay 5% of that payment but not over $5.00.
Prepayment: If I pay off early, I may be entitled to a refund of part of the finance charge.
See the contract document for any additional information about nonpayment default; any required repayment in full before the scheduled date, and prepayment refunds.

← Late Charges

DESCRIPTION OF GOODS	MANUFACTURER	MODEL NO.	RETAIL NO.	CASH SALE PRICE
				$
				$

← Insurance

INSURANCE DISCLOSURE

NO INSURANCE IS REQUIRED FOR THIS SALE. I may buy any insurance from anyone I choose. Only if requested and for cost stated below, you or buyer of this contract will obtain insurance. Charges will be included in the Amount Financed. I understand this is the only insurance you offer and you (or buyer of this contract) expect to profit from its sale. I consent to this. The one Buyer signing this insurance Disclosure will be insured when coverage begins, unless a different Buyer's name appears here:

(WRITE "YES" OR "NO" AS DESIRED, DATE, AND SIGN, IF NONE DESIRED, SIGN BELOW.)
___ Credit Life® .... $ ____
___ Credit Disability® .... $ ____
___ Property insurance .... $ ____

_____
DATE   SIGNATURE
NO INSURANCE DESIRED: _____
                        SIGNATURE

ITEMIZATION OF AMOUNT FINANCED

Sales Tax (if any) $ ____
1. Cash Sale Price .... $ ____
2. a. Cash Downpayment .... $ ____
   b. Trade-in .... $ ____
   DESCRIPTION _____
   Total Downpayment (a – b) .... $ ____
3. Unpaid Balance of Cash Sale Price (1 – 2) ...... $ ____
4. Insurance (for term of credit)
   Credit life .... $ ____
   Credit Disability .... $ ____
   Property .... $ ____
   Total Insurance Charges .... $ ____
5. Amount Financed (3 – 4) .... $ ____
6. Finance Charge .... $ ____
7. Total of Payments (5 – 6) .... $ ____
8. Total Sale Price (1 – 4 – 6) .... $ ____
9. Payable in ____ monthly payments of $____ each beginning _____ and continuing same day of each month until fully paid.

← Financing

PROMISE TO PAY. Instead of the Cash Price. I promise to pay the total Sale Price and I agree to pay you (or buyer of this contract) a Total of Payments in monthly payments in the amounts and on the dates stated above. I will pay at your business address, or other address given me. If more than one Buyer is named above, you may enforce this contract against all or any Buyers, but not in a combined amount greater than amount owed.

← Note

PREPAYMENT. If I fully prepay before the final due date, the amount I owe will be reduced by (a) unearned Finance charges computed at the Annual Percentage Rate shown above, the unpaid balances of Amount Financed scheduled for the time after prepayment to maturity, (b) unearned credit insurance charges determined by the "Rule of 78ths", and (c) unearned property insurance charges determined by assuming an equal part is carried each month.

← Prepayment Provision

FAILURE TO PAY. If I don't pay on time, all my payments may become due at once, and without notifying me before bringing suit, you may sue me for the total amount I owe, less the same unearned Finance Charges I would receive if I fully prepaid. You may also repossess the goods described above.
SECURITY. You waive any security interest in my home that could result if the goods are installed.

← Acceleration Clause

NOTICE
ANY HOLDER OF THIS CONSUMER CREDIT CONTRACT IS SUBJECT TO ALL CLAIMS AN DEFENSES WHICH THE DEBTOR COULD ASSERT AGAINST THE SELLER OF GOODS OR SERVICES OBTAINED PURSUANT HERETO OR WITH THE PROCEEDS HEREOF, RECOVERY HEREUNDER BY THE DEBTOR SHALL NOT EXCEED AMOUNTS PAID BY THE DEBTOR HEREUNDER.
NOTICE TO THE BUYER: 1. Do not sign this agreement before you read it or if it contains any blank spaces. 2. You are entitled to an exact copy of this contract.

I HAVE READ AND RECEIVED A COMPLETED, READABLE, SIGNED COPY OF THIS CONTRACT.
SELLER: _____ BUYER: _____
By: _____ BUYER: _____

insurance that the loan will be paid off if the borrower dies (or becomes disabled) before the loan matures. In essence, these policies insure the borrower for an amount sufficient to repay the outstanding loan balance. The seller's (or lender's) ability to dictate the terms of these insurance requirements is either banned or restricted by law in many states. If this type of insurance is required as a condition of the loan, its cost must be added in the finance charges and included as part of the APR. From the borrower's perspective, credit life and disability insurance is NOT a very good deal: *It's very costly and really does little more than provide lenders with a very lucrative source of income.* Not surprisingly, because it is so lucrative, some lenders aggressively push it on unsuspecting borrowers and, in some cases, even require it as a condition for granting a loan. The best advice is to avoid it if at all possible!

SPECIAL FEATURES. In addition to the major points discussed above, installment purchase contracts often contain several other features that should be of interest to borrowers. These special features generally are contained in clauses to the sales contract or note that pertain to default, repossession, and balloon payment.

An **acceleration clause** allows the lender to demand immediate repayment of the entire amount of the unpaid debt in the event the purchaser defaults on loan payments. Although this clause is customary in installment loans, the lender is likely to allow a late payment or levy a penalty instead of calling the loan by exercising the acceleration clause.

Most installment purchase contracts contain *recourse clauses* that stipulate the action the lender can take in case of default, such as wage garnishment and repossession. Some purchase agreements allow the lender to collect a portion of the purchaser's (borrower's) wages if he or she defaults on payments by garnishing the borrower's wages. **Garnishment** is a legal method of getting an employer to pay a portion of a borrower's wages to the lender. The borrower must, of course, be in default, and a court order must be issued enabling the employer to take such action. The Federal Garnishment Law specifically limits the amount of an employee's weekly wages that can be garnisheed to no more than the smaller of (1) 25 percent of take-home pay or (2) the amount by which weekly take-home pay exceeds 30 times the federal minimum hourly wage. Many state laws have completely prohibited garnisheeing or have placed severe restrictions on this practice.

The act of seizing collateral when the borrower defaults on a loan is termed **repossession**. In many states, the ability of the lender to repossess collateral is limited (and may even require a court order), but in others, collateral can be repossessed without notice and even "stolen," in effect, from the borrower. Quite often the lender must follow detailed procedures when selling repossessed items to satisfy unpaid debts. The repossessed item is eventually sold at auction or by some other means, and the amount due the merchant or lender, along with legal and other expenses in connection with the repossession, is taken from the sale proceeds. If this amount is not enough to cover the loan, the customer may or may not be liable for the remaining portion.

Sometimes installment purchase agreements are set up in such a fashion that the final payment is considerably larger than the others. The Truth in Lending Act requires that any **balloon payment**, which is defined as a payment more than twice the size of the normal installment payment, be clearly identified as such. For example, if a loan required payments of $200 per month for 23 months followed by a final payment of $1,000 in the 24th month, the existence of the $1,000 balloon payment would have to be clearly disclosed. Because balloon clauses have been abused by some lenders and can place borrowers in an undesirable position, some states prohibit their use in loans. It is best not to enter into an agreement that includes such a clause, because balloon payments can cause real financial strain when they fall due. Only if you had adequate savings, or were expecting a known sum of money at some future date, could the use of a balloon payment be justified.

acceleration clause A clause in an installment loan contract that allows the lender to demand immediate repayment of the entire outstanding loan balance if the purchaser defaults on loan payments.

garnishment Court-ordered payment of a portion of a defaulting borrower's wages to a lender.

repossession The act of seizing collateral when the borrower defaults on an installment loan.

balloon payment A final payment on an installment loan that is substantially larger than the normal installment payment.

 **EXHIBIT 7.7**

A TABLE OF MONTHLY INSTALLMENT LOAN PAYMENTS (TO REPAY A $1,000/SIMPLE INTEREST LOAN)

A table like this one can be used to find the monthly payments on a wide variety of simple interest installment loans. Although it's set up to reflect payments on a $1,000 loan, with a little modification it can easily be used with any size loan (the principal can be more or less than $1,000).

Rate of Interest	Loan Maturity						
	6 Months	12 Months	18 Months	24 Months	36 Months	48 Months	60 Months
7.5%	$170.33	$86.76	$58.92	$45.00	$31.11	$24.18	$20.05
8.0	170.58	86.99	59.15	45.23	31.34	24.42	20.28
8.5	170.82	87.22	59.37	45.46	31.57	24.65	20.52
9.0	171.07	87.46	59.60	45.69	31.80	24.89	20.76
9.5	171.32	87.69	59.83	45.92	32.04	25.13	21.01
10.0	171.56	87.92	60.06	46.15	32.27	25.37	21.25
10.5	171.81	88.15	60.29	46.38	32.51	25.61	21.50
11.0	172.05	88.50	60.64	46.73	32.86	25.97	21.87
11.5	173.30	88.62	60.76	46.85	32.98	26.09	22.00
12.0	172.50	88.85	60.99	47.08	33.22	26.34	22.25
12.5	172.80	89.09	61.22	47.31	33.46	26.58	22.50
13.0	173.04	89.32	61.45	47.55	33.70	26.83	22.76
14.0	173.54	89.79	61.92	48.02	34.18	27.33	23.27
15.0	174.03	90.26	62.39	48.49	34.67	27.84	23.79
16.0	174.53	90.74	62.86	48.97	35.16	28.35	24.32
17.0	175.03	91.21	63.34	49.45	35.66	28.86	24.86
18.0	175.53	91.68	63.81	49.93	36.16	29.38	25.40

FINANCE CHARGES, MONTHLY PAYMENTS, AND APR

Earlier in this chapter, we discussed finance charges and annual percentage rates (APRs), and illustrated the simple interest and discount methods of determining finance charges on single-payment loans. In this section, we look at the use of simple and add-on interest to compute finance charges and monthly payments for installment loans (technically, discount interest can also be used with ILs, but because this is rare, we ignore it here). For purposes of illustration, we will use a 12 percent, $1,000 installment loan that is to be paid off in 12 monthly payments. As in the earlier illustration for single-payment loans, interest is the only component of the finance charge; the presence of any other loan charges (such as credit life insurance, or title and notary fees) is ignored.

USING SIMPLE INTEREST. When simple interest is used with ILs—and most major banks and S&Ls use it on their installment loans—interest is charged only on the outstanding balance of the loan. Thus, as the loan principal declines with monthly payments, the amount of interest being charged decreases as well. Because finance charges change each month, the procedure used to find the interest expense is mathematically very complex. Fortunately, this is not much of a problem in practice due to the widespread use of desktop computers/computer terminals, hand-held financial calculators (which we'll illustrate below), and preprinted finance tables—an example of which is provided in Exhibit 7.7. Essentially, the tables provide the *monthly payment* that would be required to

EXHIBIT 7.8

MONTHLY PAYMENT ANALYSIS FOR A SIMPLE INTEREST INSTALLMENT LOAN (ASSUMES A $1,000, 12 PERCENT, 12-MONTH LOAN)

Part of each monthly payment on an installment loan goes to interest and part to principal. As the loan is paid down over time, less and less of each payment goes to interest, and more and more goes to principal.

Month	Outstanding Loan Balance (1)	Monthly Payment (2)	Interest Charges $[(1) \times 0.01]$ (3)	Principal $[(2) - (3)]$ (4)
1	$1,000.00	$88.85	$10.00	$78.85
2	921.15	88.85	9.21	79.64
3	841.51	88.85	8.42	80.43
4	761.08	88.85	7.61	81.24
5	679.84	88.85	6.80	82.05
6	597.79	88.85	5.98	82.87
7	514.92	88.85	5.15	83.70
8	431.22	88.85	4.31	84.54
9	346.68	88.85	3.47	85.38
10	261.30	88.85	2.61	86.24
11	175.06	88.85	1.75	87.10
12	87.96	88.85	0.89	87.96
Total		$1,066.20	$66.20	$1,000.00

Note: Column 1 values for months 2 through 12 are obtained by subtracting the principal payment shown in column 4 for the preceding month from the outstanding loan balance shown in column 1 for the preceding month; thus, $1,000 − $78.85 = $921.15, which is the outstanding loan balance in month 2.

retire an installment loan that carries a given simple rate of interest and has a given term to maturity. Because the tables have interest charges built right into them, the monthly payments shown cover both principal and interest.

Note that the loan payments shown in Exhibit 7.7 cover a variety of interest rates (from $7\frac{1}{2}$ to 18 percent) and loan maturities (from 6 to 60 months). The values in the table represent the monthly payments required to retire a $1,000 loan. Although it's assumed you're borrowing $1,000, the table can be used with any size loan. For example, if you're looking at a $5,000 loan, just multiply the monthly loan payment from the table by 5—that is, $5,000/$1,000 = 5; or, if you have, say, a $500 loan, multiply the loan payment by .5 ($500/$1,000 = .5). In many respects, this table is just like the mortgage loan payment schedule introduced in Chapter 5, except we use much shorter loan maturities here than with mortgages.

Here's how to use the table in Exhibit 7.7. Suppose we want to find the monthly payment required on our $1,000, 12 percent, 12-month loan. Looking under the 12-month column and across from the 12 percent rate of interest, we find a value of $88.85; that is the monthly payment it will take to pay off the $1,000 loan in 12 months. When the monthly payments ($88.85) are multiplied by the term of the loan in months (12), the result will be total payments of $88.85 × 12 = $1,066.20. The difference between the total payments on the loan and the principal portion represents the *finance charges on the loan*—in this case, $1,066.20 − $1,000 = interest charges of $66.20.

Instead of using a table like the one in Exhibit 7.7, you could have just as easily used a handheld financial calculator to *find the monthly payment on an IL*. Here's what you'd do: First, set the *payments per year (P/Y)* key to 12 to put the calculator in a *monthly payment* mode. Now, to find the monthly payment needed to pay off 12 percent, 12-month, $1,000 installment loan, do the following:

1. Punch 12 and press the **N** key.
2. Punch 12.0 and press the **i** key.
3. Punch 1,000 and press **PV.**
4. To calculate the size of the monthly payment, press the **CPT** key and then hit **PMT.**

A value of -88.8488 (or something very close to this) should appear in the calculator display. Rounding the numbers and ignoring the minus sign, you have the monthly payment on this IL: $88.85.

From each monthly payment a certain portion goes to interest, and the balance is used to reduce the principal. Because the principal balance declines with each payment, the amount that goes to interest also *decreases* whereas the amount that goes to principal *increases*. Exhibit 7.8 illustrates this cash flow stream. Note that because *monthly* payments are used with the loan, the interest column in Exhibit 7.8 is also based on a *monthly* rate of interest—that is, the annual rate is divided by 12 to obtain a monthly rate (12 percent per year/12 = 1 percent per month). This monthly rate is then applied to the outstanding loan balance to find the monthly interest charges in column 3. Because interest is charged only on the outstanding balance, *the annual percentage rate (APR) on a simple interest IL will always equal the stated rate*—in this case, 12 percent.

 LendingTree.com (**www.lendingtree.com**) lets you compare loan rates and fees from up to four lenders instantly.

add-on method
A method of calculating interest by computing finance charges on the original loan balance and then adding the interest to that balance.

ADD-ON METHOD. A number of installment loans, particularly those obtained directly from retail merchants or made at finance companies and the like, are made using the **add-on method.** Add-on loans are very expensive; indeed, they generally rank as one of the most costly forms of consumer credit, with APRs that are often well above rates charged even on many credit cards. With add-on interest, the finance charges are calculated using the *original* balance of the loan; this amount (the total finance charges) is then added-on to the original loan balance to determine the total amount to be repaid. Thus, the amount of finance charges on an add-on loan can be found by using the familiar simple interest formula:

$$F = P \times r \times t$$

Given the $1,000 loan we have been using for illustrative purposes, the finance charges on a 12 percent, 1-year add-on loan would be

$$F = \$1,000 \times .12 \times 1 = \$120.$$

Compared with the finance charges for the same loan on a simple interest basis ($66.20), the add-on loan is a lot more expensive, a fact that will also show up in monthly payments and APR. Keep in mind that both of these loans would be quoted as "12 percent" loans; thus, you may think you are getting a 12 percent loan, but looks can be deceiving—especially when you are dealing with add-on interest! So, when taking out an installment loan, make sure you find out whether simple or add-on interest is being used to compute finance charges. And if it's add-on you might want to consider looking elsewhere for the loan.

To find the monthly payments on an add-on loan, all you need to do is add the finance charge ($120) to the *original* principal amount of the loan ($1,000) and then divide this

EXHIBIT 7.9

COMPARATIVE FINANCE CHARGES AND APRs (ASSUMES A $1,000, 12 PERCENT, 12-MONTH INSTALLMENT LOAN)

In sharp contrast to simple interest loans, the APR with add-on installment loans is much higher than the stated rate.

	Simple Interest	Add-on Interest
Stated rate on loan	12%	12%
Finance charges	$ 66.20	$ 120.00
Monthly payments	$ 88.25	$ 93.33
Total payments made	$1,066.20	$1,120.00
APR	12%	21.4%

sum by the number of monthly payments to be made. In the case of our $1,000, one-year loan, this results in monthly payments of $93.33, found as follows:

$$\frac{\text{Monthly}}{\text{payments}} = \frac{\$1,000 + \$120}{12} = \frac{\$1,120}{12} = \$93.33$$

As expected, these monthly payments are much higher than the ones with the simple interest loan ($88.85).

Because the actual rate of interest with an add-on loan is considerably higher than the stated rate, we must determine the loan's APR. That can easily be done with a financial calculator. Here's how you *find the APR on an IL* using a financial calculator. First, set the *payments per year (P/Y)* key to 12 to put the calculator in a *monthly payment* mode. Then, to find the annual percentage rate (APR) of interest being charged on a $1,000, 12-month, 12 percent add-on installment loan, do the following:

1. Punch 12 and press **N**.
2. Punch 1,000 and press **PV**.
3. Punch −93.33 and then hit the **PMT** key (*make sure you enter the value of 93.33 as a negative*, or you'll end up with an "error"—i.e., the calculator won't be able to solve the problem).
4. To calculate the APR on this loan, press the **CPT** key and the the **i** key.

A value of 21.45 should appear in the calculator display—that's the APR on this add-on loan. (Note: The same procedure [keystrokes] shown above can also be used to find the APR on a simple interest installment loan.) Thus, when all is said and done, we find that the APR on this 12% add-on-loan ends up to be more like 21.4%. Clearly, when viewed from an APR perspective, this add-on loan turns out to be a very expensive form of financing! (A rough but reasonably accurate rule of thumb is that the APR on an add-on loan is about *twice* the stated rate—thus, if the loan is quoted at an add-on rate of 9 percent, you're probably going to end up paying a true rate that's closer to 18 percent.) This is because when add-on interest is applied to an installment loan, the interest included in each payment is charged on the initial principal even though the outstanding loan balance is reduced as installment payments are made. A summary of comparative finance charges and APRs for the simple interest and add-on interest methods is presented in Exhibit 7.9.

Under the Truth in Lending Act, the exact APR (accurate to the nearest 0.25 percent) must be disclosed to borrowers. Note that not only interest but also any other fees required to obtain a loan are considered part of the finance charges and should be included in the computation of the APR.

PREPAYMENT PENALTIES. Another type of finance charge that's often found in installment loan contracts is the *prepayment penalty,* an additional charge you may owe if you decide to pay off your loan prior to maturity. When you pay off a loan early, you may find that you owe quite a bit more than you expected, especially if the lender uses the **Rule of 78s,** (or **sum-of-the-digits method**) to calculate the amount of interest paid and the principal balance to date. You might think that paying off a $1,000, 12 percent, one-year loan at the end of six months would mean that you have paid about half of the principal and owe somewhere around $500 to the lender. Well, that's just not so with a loan that uses the rule of 78s! This method charges more interest in the early months of the loan, on the theory that the borrower has use of more money in the early stages of the IL and should pay more finance charges in the early months of the loan and progressively less later. There's nothing wrong with that, of course, as that's the way all loans operate. But what is wrong is the fact that the rule of 78s front-loads an inordinate amount of interest charges to the early months of the loan, thereby producing a much higher principle balance than you would normally expect (remember: the more of the loan payment that goes to interest, the less that goes to repayment of principle).

To see how this works, let's assume we want to pay off the $1,000, 12 percent, one-year add-on loan after six months. Using the Rule of 78s, of your $559.98 in total payments (that is, 6 payments at $93.33 each = 6 × $93.33 = $559.98), just $389.73 went to principal—all the rest went to interest. As a result, even though you have made payments for half of the life of the loan, you still owe more than 60 percent of the principal—the same loan under simple interest would have paid off $485 in principal after six months. So, before signing the loan agreement, be sure to ask how the interest will be calculated, just in case you decide to prepay the loan.

Rule of 78s (sum-of-the-digits method)
A method of calculating interest that has extra-heavy interest charges in the early months of the loan, on the theory that the borrower has use of more money in the early stages of the IL.

 Having trouble managing your debt? Find credit counselors and attorneys who can help at GotTrouble.com, **www.gottrouble.com**.

BUY ON TIME OR PAY CASH?

Often when you buy a big-ticket item, you have little choice but to take out a loan to finance the purchase—the acquisition (perhaps it's a new car) is just so expensive that you cannot afford to pay cash. And even if you do have the money, you may still be better off using something like an IL *if the cash purchase would end up severely depleting your liquid reserves.* But don't just automatically take out a loan. Rather, take the time to find out if, in fact, that's the best thing to do. Such a decision can easily be made by using Worksheet 7.2. This worksheet considers the cost of the loan relative to the after-tax earnings generated from having your money in some type of short-term investment vehicle. A basic assumption here is that the consumer has an adequate level of liquid reserves, and that these reserves are being held in some type of savings account. (Obviously, if this is not the case, there's little reason to go through the exercise, because you have no choice but to borrow the money.) Essentially, it boils down to this: *If it costs more to borrow the money than you can earn in interest, then draw the money from your savings to pay cash for the purchase; if not, consider taking out a loan.*

WORKSHEET 7.2

TO BORROW OR NOT TO BORROW

Using a worksheet like the one shown here, you can decide whether to buy on time or pay cash by comparing the (after-tax) cost of interest paid on a loan with the after-tax interest income lost by taking the money out of savings and using it to pay cash for the purchase.

BUY ON TIME OR PAY CASH

Name **John E. Jones**   Dated **February 28, 2001**

■ **Cost of Borrowing**		
1. Terms of the loan		
a. Amount of the loan	$ 12,000.00	
b. Length of the loan (in years)	3 yrs.	
c. Monthly payment	$ 387.24	
2. Total loan payments made (monthly loan payment × length of loan in months) $ **387.24** per month × **36** months		$ 13,940.64
3. Less: Principal amount of the loan		$ 12,000
4. Total interest paid over life of loan (line 2 − 3)		$ 1,940.64
5. Tax considerations:		
• Is this a home equity loan (where interest expenses can be deducted from taxes)?	☐ yes ☒ no	
• Do you itemize deductions on your federal tax returns? . . .	☒ yes ☐ no	
• If you answered yes to BOTH questions, then proceed to line 6; if you answered no to *either one* or *both* of the questions, then proceed to *line 8* and use *line 4* as the after-tax interest cost of the loan.		
6. What federal tax bracket are you in? (use either 15, 28, 31, 36, or 39.6%)	___%	
7. Taxes saved due to interest deductions (line 4 × tax rate, from line 6: $_____ × ___%)		$ —
8. Total after-tax interest cost on the loan (line 4 − line 7)		$ 1,940.64
■ **Cost of Paying Cash**		
9. Annual interest *earned* on savings (annual rate of interest earned on savings × amount of loan: **5** % × 12,000.00)		$ 600.00
10. Annual after-tax interest earnings (line 9 × [1 − tax rate] — e.g., 1 − 28% = 72%: $**600.00** × **72**%)		$ 432.00
11. Total after-tax interest earnings over life of loan (line 10 × line 1b: $ **432.00** × **3** years)		$ 1,296.00
■ **Net Cost of Borrowing**		
12. Difference in cost of borrowing vs. cost of paying cash (line 8 minus line 11)		$ 644.64

BASIC DECISION RULE: *Pay cash* if line 12 is positive; *borrow the money* if line 12 is negative.

Note: For simplicity, compounding is ignored in calculating *both* the cost of interest and interest earnings.

To see how this works, consider the following situation: You're thinking about buying a second car (a nice, low-mileage used vehicle) and after the normal down payment, you still need to come up with $12,000. This balance can be taken care of in one of two ways: (1) You can take out a 36-month, 10 percent IL (according to Exhibit 7.7, the *Table of Monthly Loan Payments*, such an IL would have a monthly payment of $32.27 × 12 = $387.24—you'd of course come up with pretty much the same monthly payment by using a financial calculator); or (2) you can pay cash for the car by drawing the money from a money fund (the fund currently pays 5 percent interest, and that's expected to hold for the foreseeable future). We can now use the worksheet to decide whether to buy on time or pay cash—the complete details of which are provided in Worksheet 7.2. In this case, we assume the loan is a standard IL, where the interest does not qualify as a tax deduction, and that you're in the 28 percent tax bracket. Note in the worksheet that by borrowing the money, you'll end up paying nearly $1,941 in interest (line 4), none of which is tax deductible. In contrast, by leaving your money on deposit in the money fund, you'll receive only $1,296 in interest, after taxes (see line 11). Taken together, we see the net cost of borrowing (line 12) is nearly $650—in essence, you'll be paying over $1,900 to earn less than $1,300, which certainly doesn't make much sense! Clearly, it's far more cost-effective in this case to pay cash for the car, for by doing so you will save nearly $650.

Although such a figure provides a pretty convincing reason for avoiding a loan, occasions might arise where the actual dollar spread between the cost of borrowing and interest earned is very small, perhaps only $100 or less (actually, if our example had involved a home equity loan, where interest is tax deductible, the net cost of borrowing [line 12] would have dropped to $101). Being able to deduct the interest on a loan can lead to a relatively small spread, but it can also occur, for example, if the amount being financed is relatively small—say, you want $1,500 or $2,000 for a ski trip to Colorado. Under these circumstances, and so long as the spread stays sufficiently small, you may decide it's still worthwhile to borrow the money in order to maintain a higher level of liquidity. Although this course of action is perfectly legitimate when very small spreads exist, it makes less sense as the gap starts to widen.

CONCEPT CHECK

7-13. Briefly describe the basic features of an installment loan. What is a home equity loan and how are these loans similar to other installment loans? What are the major advantages and disadvantages of home equity loans?

7-14. Briefly describe an *installment purchase contract*, and define the four basic components such a contract is likely to contain.

7-15. Explain the purpose and describe the general content of the *note* that is ordinarily included as part of an installment purchase agreement.

7-16. Explain why a borrower is often required to purchase *credit life and disability insurance* as a condition for receiving an installment loan. Is this a good deal for the borrower?

7-17. Discuss each of the following features that may be included in an installment purchase agreement: (a) *acceleration clause*, (b) *wage garnishment*, (c) *repossession* feature, and (d) *balloon* clause.

7-18. Define simple interest as it relates to an installment loan.

7-19. Under what conditions does it make more sense to pay cash for a big-ticket item than to borrow the money to finance the purchase? Are there ever times when borrowing the money is the best course of action?

SUMMARY

LG1. **Know when to use consumer loans and differentiate between the major types.** Single-payment and installment loans are formally negotiated consumer loan arrangements used mainly to finance big-ticket items. Most of these consumer loans are taken out as auto loans, loans for other durable goods, education loans, personal loans, and consolidation loans.

LG2. **Identify the various sources of consumer loans.** Consumer loans can be obtained from a number of sources, including commercial banks (the biggest providers of such credit), consumer finance companies, credit unions, S&Ls, sales finance (and captive finance) companies, life insurance companies (and other financial services organizations), and, finally, as a last resort, your friends and relatives.

LG3. **Choose the best loans by comparing finance charges, maturity, collateral, and other loan terms.** Before taking out a consumer loan, you should be sure the purchase is compatible with your financial plans and that you can service the debt without straining your budget. When shopping for credit, it's in your best interest to compare such loan features as finance charges (APRs), loan maturities, monthly payments, and collateral requirements and choose the loan with terms that are fully compatible with your financial plans and cash budget.

LG4. **Describe the features of, and calculate the finance charges on, single-payment loans.** In a single-payment loan, the borrower is obligated to make just one principal payment (at the maturity of the loan), though he or she may be required to make one or more interim interest payments. Such loans are usually made for a period of 1 year or less, and are normally secured by some type of collateral. A major advantage of the single-payment loan is that it doesn't require monthly payments and therefore won't tie up the borrower's cash flow. Finance charges can be calculated using either the simple interest method, which applies the interest rate to the outstanding loan balance, or the discount method, where the interest is calculated the same way as simple interest, but then deducted from the loan principal, resulting in a higher APR.

LG5. **Evaluate the benefits of an installment loan and understand the terms of the loan purchase contract.** In an installment loan, the borrower agrees to repay the loan through a series of equal installment payments (usually monthly) until the obligation is fully repaid; in this way, the borrower can come up with a loan-repayment schedule that fits neatly into his or her financial plans and cash budget. This highly popular form of consumer credit can be used to finance just about any type of big-ticket asset or expenditure, and many of them are taken out as home equity loans to capture tax advantages. The main parts of the purchase contract are the sales contract, which sets forth the terms of the arrangement; the security agreement, giving the lender control of the item being purchased; the note, or formal promise to repay; and the insurance agreement, which specifies whether the borrower has to obtain credit life insurance.

LG6. **Determine the costs of installment loans and analyze whether it is better to pay cash or take out a loan.** Most single-payment loans are made with either simple or discount interest, whereas most ILs are made with either simple or add-on interest. So long as simple interest is used, the actual finance charge will always correspond to the stated rate of interest; in contrast, when add-on or discount rates are used, the APR will always be more than the stated rate. In the final analysis, whether it makes sense to borrow rather than pay cash comes down to a matter of which is the least costly alternative.

QUESTIONS AND PROBLEMS

1. Assume you have been shopping for a new car and intend to finance it, in part, through an installment loan. The car you are looking for has a sticker price of $15,000. Big A Autos has offered to sell it to you for $2,500 down and finance the balance with a loan that will require 48 monthly payments of $329.17; Cars-Are-Us will sell you exactly the same vehicle for $3,000 down plus a 60-month loan for the balance, with monthly payments of $260.91. Which is the better deal? Explain.

2. *Use Worksheet 7.1.* Every 6 months, Neal Simone takes an inventory of the consumer debts he has outstanding. The latest tally showed the following list: he still owed $4,000 on a home improvement loan (monthly payments of $125); he was making $85 monthly payments on a personal loan that had a remaining balance of $750; he had a $2,000, secured single-payment loan that is due late next year; he had a $70,000 home mortgage on which he was making $750 monthly payments; he still owed $8,600 on a new-car loan (monthly payments of $375); he had a $960 balance on his Visa card (minimum payment of $40), a $70 balance on his Shell credit card (balance due in 30 days), and a $1,200 balance on a personal line of credit ($60 monthly payments). Use Worksheet 7.1 to prepare an inventory of Neal's consumer debt. Find his debt-safety ratio given that he has take-home pay of $2,500 per month; would you consider this ratio to be good or bad? Explain.

3. Find the finance charges on a 7½ percent, 18-month single-payment loan when interest is computed using the simple interest method. Find the finance charges on the same loan when interest is computed using the discount method. Determine the APR in each case.

4. Sally Gibbs has to borrow $4,000. First State Bank will lend her the money for 12 months through a single-payment loan at 13.5 percent discount; Home Savings and Loan will make her a $4,000 single-payment, 12-month loan at 15 percent simple. Where should Sally borrow the money? Explain.

5. Assuming that interest is the only finance charge, how much interest would be paid on a $5,000 installment loan to be repaid in 36 monthly installments of $166.10? What is the APR on this loan?

6. After careful comparison shopping, Chris Jenkins decided to buy a new Nissan Maxima. With some options added, the car had a price of $27,500—including plates and taxes. Because he could not afford to pay cash for the car, he used some savings and his old car as a trade-in to put $7,500 down and financed the rest with a $20,000, 60-month loan at a simple interest rate of 9½ percent.
   a. What will his monthly payments be?
   b. How much total interest will Chris pay in the first year of the loan? (Use a monthly payment analysis procedure similar to the one in Exhibit 7.8.)
   c. How much interest will Chris pay over the full (60-month) life of the loan?
   d. What is the APR on this loan?

7. Joan Clark plans to borrow $5,000 and repay it in 36 monthly installments. This loan is being made at an annual add-on interest rate of 11½ percent.
   a. Assuming the only component of the finance charge is interest, calculate this charge.
   b. Use your finding in part **a** to calculate the monthly payment on the loan.
   c. Using a financial calculator, determine the APR on this loan.

8. *Use Worksheet 7.2 to help Shirley make this credit decision:*
   a. Consider the following situation: Shirley Chen wants to buy a home entertainment center. Complete with a big-screen TV, VCR, and sound system, the unit would cost

$4,500. Shirley has over $15,000 in a money fund, so she can easily afford to pay cash for the whole thing (the fund is currently paying 5.5 percent interest, and Shirley expects that yield to hold for the foreseeable future). To stimulate sales, the dealer is offering to finance the full cost of the unit with a 36-month installment loan at 9 percent, simple. Shirley wants to know: Should she pay cash for this home entertainment center or buy it on time? (Note: assume Shirley is in the 28 percent tax bracket and that she itemizes deductions on her tax returns.) Briefly explain your answer.

    b. Rework the preceding problem, assuming Shirley has the option of using a 48-month, 9.5 percent home equity loan to finance the full cost of this entertainment center. Again, use Worksheet 7.2 to determine if Shirley should pay cash or buy on time. Does your answer change (from the one you came up with in part **a**)? Explain.

9. Due to a job change, Alex Rodriquez just relocated to the Pacific Northwest. He sold what furniture he had before he moved, so he's now shopping for new furnishings. He's found the perfect assortment of couches, chairs, tables, and beds at a local furniture store to fill his two-bedroom apartment; the total cost for everything is $6,400. Because of the cost of the move, Alex is a bit short of cash right now and has therefore decided to take out an installment loan in the amount of $6,400 to pay for the furniture. The furniture store has offered to lend him the money for 48 months at an add-on interest rate of $8\frac{1}{2}$ percent. The credit union at Alex's place of employment has also offered to lend him the money—they said they'd give him the loan at an interest rate of 12 percent, simple, but only for a term of 24 months.

    a. Compute the monthly payments for both of the loan offers.

    b. Determine the APR for both loans.

    c. Which is more important: low payments or a low APR? Explain.

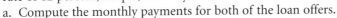

APPLYING PERSONAL FINANCE

Getting the Loan is Only Half the Battle

Owning a new car is a dream that just about everybody has. Trouble is, in most cases, that also means you have to come up with a loan to finance the purchase. And that is where this project comes in—it is aimed at helping you understand how loan payments are set up and how the loans place an obligation (burden?) on you as the borrower.

    Here's the deal. Let's say, as a graduation gift, your parents have promised to make the down payment on a new car, *but you must come up with a loan to finance the rest.* The only condition is that you have your degree in hand. *You can pick out ANY new car (or pickup, 4-wheel drive, etc.,) you want,* and your folks will provide you with 30 percent of the *total* cost of the vehicle to be used as the down payment.

    To complete this project, pick out the kind of new vehicle you want to own and go to a dealer near you to find out what your new car will cost—use *the sticker price* and be sure to add in any dealer prep and destination charges, plus the cost of plates and taxes (for simplicity, let's assume the cost of plates and taxes equals *four percent of the car's sticker price*). Tally up the *total* cost of the car (sticker price plus dealer prep, destination charges, plates, and taxes); how much of a loan will you have to take out? Assume you can get financing at the bank at 13 percent, simple; what will your car payments be if you take out a 3-year loan? What happens if you make that a 5-year loan? How do you think these car payments would fit into your budget? What kind of income do you think you would have to make to comfortably afford those payments (i.e., so the car payments do not put a strain on your budget)? If the payments are more than you thought they would be (do not be surprised if they are), what can you do to bring them down?

CONTEMPORARY CASE APPLICATIONS

7.1   Financing Marilyn's Education

At age 19, Marilyn Bronson is in the middle of her second year of studies at a community college in San Diego. She has done well in her course work; majoring in prebusiness studies, she currently has a 3.75 grade point average. Marilyn lives at home and works part-time as a filing clerk for a nearby electronics distributor. Her parents cannot afford to pay her tuition and college expenses—she is virtually on her own as far as college goes. Marilyn hopes to transfer to the University of Texas, Austin next year. She has already been accepted and feels she would get an excellent education there. After talking with her counselor, Marilyn feels she will not be able to hold down a part-time job and still manage to complete her bachelor's degree program at Texas in 2 years. Knowing that on her twenty-second birthday she will receive approximately $35,000 from a trust fund left her by her grandmother, Marilyn has decided to borrow against the trust fund to support herself during the next 2 years. She estimates she will need $25,000 to meet tuition, room and board, books and supplies, travel, personal expenditures, and so on during that period. Unable to qualify for any special loan programs, Marilyn has found two sources of single-payment loans, each requiring a security interest in the trust proceeds as collateral. The terms required by each potential lender are as follows:

a. California State Bank will lend $30,000 at 10 percent discount interest. The loan principal would be due at the end of 2 years.

b. National Bank of San Diego will lend $25,000 under a 2-year note. The note would carry a 12 percent simple interest rate and would also be due in a single payment at the end of 2 years.

Questions

1. How much would Marilyn (a) receive in initial loan proceeds and (b) be required to repay at maturity under the California State Bank loan?

2. Compute (a) the finance charges and (b) the APR on the loan offered by California State Bank.

3. Compute (a) the finance charges and (b) the APR on the loan offered by the National Bank of San Diego. How big a loan payment would be due at the end of two years?

4. Compare your findings in Questions 2 and 3, and recommend one of the loans to Marilyn. Explain your recommendation.

5. What other recommendations might you offer Marilyn relative to the disposition of the loan proceeds?

7.2   Cameron Gets His 4-Runner

Cameron Lew, a 27-year-old bachelor living in Charlotte, North Carolina, has been a high school teacher for 5 years. For the past 4 months, he has been thinking about buying a Toyota 4-Runner, but feels he is not able to afford a brand-new one. Recently, however, a friend, John McKenzie, has offered to sell him his fully loaded Toyota 4-Runner Ltd. John wants $19,500 for his SUV, which has been driven only 8,000 miles and is in very good condition. Cameron is eager to buy the vehicle but has only $7,000 in his savings account at Tar Heel Bank. He expects to net $6,000 from the sale of his Chevrolet Camero, but this will still leave him about $6,500 short. He has two alternatives for obtaining the money:

a. Borrow $6,500 from the First National Bank of Charlotte at a fixed rate of 12 percent per annum, simple interest. The loan would be repaid in equal monthly installments over a 3-year (36-month) period.

b. Obtain a $6,500 installment loan requiring 36 monthly payments from the Charlotte Teacher's Credit Union at a 6.5 percent stated rate of interest. The add-on method would be used to calculate the finance charges on this loan.

Questions

1. Using Exhibit 7.7 or a financial calculator, determine the required monthly payments if the loan is taken out at First National Bank of Charlotte.
2. Compute (a) the finance charges and (b) the APR on the loan offered by First National Bank of Charlotte.
3. Determine the size of the monthly payment required on the loan from the Charlotte Teacher's Credit Union.
4. Compute (a) the finance charges and (b) the APR on the loan offered by the Charlotte Teacher's Credit Union.
5. Compare the two loans and recommend one of them to Cameron. Explain your recommendation.

MONEY ONLINE

LOANS AND MORE LOANS!

Note: Web addresses change frequently, so you may need to determine the home page and do a site search to find the page or topic that's referenced.

1. **www.nelliemae.com**
   What are your student loan options? Whether you're an undergraduate, graduate, or professional student, learn the basics of student loans from Nellie Mae, a leading national provider of higher education loans for students and parents. Receive entrance and exit counseling, apply online, check on your loan's status, and calculate your payments at this site.

2. **nces.ed.gov/ipeds/cool**
   Find the college that best suits you. The National Center for Education Statistics in the U.S. Department of Education has prepared College Opportunities On-Line to help students and their parents compare over 9,000 colleges and the costs to attend them. Visit the Department of Education's main site at www.ed.gov for information concerning student financial aid.

3. **www.usaaedfoundation.org**
   Find useful information on obtaining loans and managing debt at the USAA Educational Foundation's Web site. Click on "Financial" and scroll down to "College Financing" to search for scholarships, explore financial aid options, and find student loan information. Under "Basic Finance," find topics on managing credit and debt, setting financial goals, personal recordkeeping, and avoiding fraud.

4. **www.teri.org**
   Don't qualify for financial aid? Find student loans based on your creditworthiness rather than your family's income. The Education Resources Institute (TERI), a private, not-for-profit institution, provides education financing and information services to students and their families. Their loan program is designed to meet the needs of students in all phases of their education—whether undergraduate, graduate, or professional. TERI also offers a series of loans for students enrolled in specialized programs of study.

5. **www.bankrate.com**

   Find the best loan rates in your area! Select the product you're interested in and your state at Bankrate's Web site to comparison shop among the loan, credit, or savings offerings in your area. Learn basic loan information, calculate your loan payment, or research your bank's financial condition at this site.

6. **www.consumer.gov**

   What three things should you do immediately if someone tries to steal your identity? Click on "Identity Theft" and "If You're a Victim" to find out from the Web site of the Federal Consumer Information Center. Learn about the federal and state laws concerning identity theft, how to file a complaint, and what you can do to minimize your risk of identity theft occurring to you. Also at this site, click "Contact" for an extensive list of links to other government agencies, or click on "About" to learn what these various agencies do.

7. **www.quicken.com/saving/debt**

   Create an action plan to reduce your debt using Quicken's interactive Debt Reduction Planner. Determine how much of your savings to contribute toward your debt and how much of your expenses to cut out in order to pay off your debt sooner. Graphically view changes in the level of your debt as you work through various debt reduction scenarios.

Just for Fun!

8. **www.publicdebt.treas.gov**

   Think you have a lot of debt? Check out the amount of the government's debt on this day. Scroll down to "Public Debt" and click on "Total Treasury Securities Outstanding" to find the amount down to the penny. Compare today's debt with that from a year ago, 5 years ago, 10 years ago, and various other times in the past. Also learn about savings bonds, Treasury securities, and the regulation of the government securities market at the Web site of the Bureau of the Public Debt.

9. **moneycentral.msn.com**

   Take the Spending Quiz! Click on "Saving and Spending" at MSN's MoneyCentral and scroll down to find this and other useful tools, such as the Debt Evaluator, Savings Calculator, and Debt Consolidator.

PART IV

Managing Insurance Needs

CHAPTER 8
Insuring Your Life

CHAPTER 9
Insuring Your Health

CHAPTER 10
Protecting Your Property

Chapter 8

Insuring Your Life

LEARNING GOALS

LG1.   Explain the role insurance planning plays in personal financial planning, and the relationship between risk and insurance.

LG2.   Discuss the primary reasons for life insurance and identify those who need coverage.

LG3.   Calculate how much life insurance you need.

LG4.   Differentiate among the various types of life insurance policies and describe their advantages and disadvantages.

LG5.   Become familiar with the key features of life insurance policies.

LG6.   Choose the best life insurance policy for your needs at the lowest cost.

Lessons in Life

Debra Gard was doubtful when her insurance agent suggested that her husband Larry needed additional life insurance. After all, unlike 56 percent of Americans, the Gards already had a life insurance policy. "I thought it was too expensive and something we didn't need at the time," says Debra. "But Larry was a stickler when it came to the family. He insisted we have the protection."

Less than a year later, Larry Gard was diagnosed with terminal cancer. Medical bills began to accumulate and Debra was forced to quit her job to stay home and care for him. She worried how she'd be able to support their two small children after Larry was gone.

Fortunately, the additional life insurance Larry had purchased provided the answer. It had an accelerated benefits provision. This gives policyholders access to their life insurance benefits *before* they die if they become terminally ill or develop serious medical problems. More than 40 million life insurance policies now contain an accelerated benefits provision. Debra and Larry used the money to pay medical bills and cover other expenses during Larry's illness.

After Larry died the following year, at age 55, Debra received the remaining portion of the policy's death benefit. This helped her pay the mortgage and other bills while she adjusted to his death and looked for another job.

"Losing Larry was very difficult and completely unexpected," says Debra today. "It's hard, but I know he wants me to go on. I'm just thankful that the insurance money enabled us to spend time together before Larry passed away."

Sources: "Expanded Offerings," *Boston Business Journal*, May 15, 2000, downloaded from **www.bizjournals.com/boston/stories/2000/05/15/focus1.html**; "Real Life Stories," the Life and Health Insurance Foundation, **www.life-line.org**, downloaded 12/28/00; Peter Keating and Mari McQueen, "Solving the Mysteries of Life Insurance," *Money* Web site, **www.money.com**, downloaded 12/14/00; Lisa Karam Middleton, "More Life Insurers Offer Accelerated Death Benefit," Insure.com, **www.insure.com**, downloaded 12/18/00.

■ Basic Insurance Concepts [LG1]

Every successful financial plan should include adequate life insurance coverage. Life insurance *protects your dependents from financial loss in event of your untimely death*. Although death benefits are a key concern of life insurance, some types of life insurance policies also possess attractive investment attributes. In essence, life insurance provides an umbrella of protection for your financial plans. *It not only protects what you already have (like providing funds to pay off the mortgage on your home) but also helps ensure the attainment of unfulfilled financial goals (such as the future education of your children).* Being informed about life insurance is clearly just as important to financial planning as being well versed about taxes and investments. As with any other aspect of financial planning, you want to get as much from your insurance dollar as possible.

Over a period of years, the difference between buying life insurance wisely and unwisely can easily add up to thousands of dollars in extra premiums and many times that amount in lost protection. Wide differences exist among the available types of life insurance policies, their costs, and the quality of the companies and agents that sell them. This chapter shows how you can intelligently determine how much life insurance protection you and your family need and explains the different types of life insurance policies available today. Although the choices may seem overwhelming, you'll see that most policies, despite their different names, are little more than variations of several basic types.

INSURANCE PLANNING

No one likes to think about the possibility of losing everything they have acquired and planned for, but unforeseen events do occur. Accidents, serious illness, or the untimely death of family members can result in substantial financial burdens and leave you or your family without adequate income. Disasters—like flood, earthquake, or fire—can destroy personal property like your home or car.

This is where insurance comes into the financial planning process. Its basic purpose is *to protect you and your dependents from losing the assets that you've already acquired, and to shield you and your family from an interruption in your expected earnings.* In short, insurance lends a degree of certainty to your financial plans.

Auto and homeowners insurance, for example, reimburse you for damage or destruction to existing assets. *Life insurance,* in contrast, is meant to replace income that would have been earned had premature death not occurred—income that can easily total millions of dollars over the course of a college graduate's career. In practical terms this means providing funds so the family can keep their home, maintain an acceptable lifestyle, and provide for children's education or other special needs. *Disability insurance* does the same should you become disabled, and *hospitalization and health insurance* covers the medical costs arising from illness or accidents. Insurance planning, therefore, involves anticipating the losses to which your assets and income could be exposed, and protecting against such losses by weaving insurance into your financial plans. To do so, you will have to make decisions about life, health, and property insurance.

THE CONCEPT OF RISK

In insurance, *risk* is defined as uncertainty with respect to economic loss. Whenever you and your family have a financial interest in something—whether it is your life, health, home, car, boat, or job—you face the risk that your budget will be upset or your net worth reduced if that item is lost or damaged. Because of the devastating effect such losses can have on your financial well being, you must devise ways to deal with risk. You can take steps to avoid a loss *before* it occurs through *risk avoidance* and *loss prevention.* If losses occur anyhow, you'll need an economical way of covering them, which is what you obtain from *risk assumption* and *insurance.*

RISK AVOIDANCE. The simplest way to deal with risk is to avoid the act that creates it. As an example, people who are afraid they might lose everything they own because of a lawsuit resulting from an automobile accident could avoid driving. With respect to life and health risks, avid skydivers or bungee jumpers might want to choose another recreational activity!

Although **risk avoidance** can be an effective way to handle some risks, such action is not without its costs. For instance, people who avoid driving suffer considerable inconvenience, and the retired skydiver may find he or she now suffers *more* stress, which can lead

risk avoidance
Avoidance of an act that would create a risk.

to different types of health risks. Risk avoidance is an attractive way to deal with risk only when the estimated cost of avoidance is less than the estimated cost of handling it in some other way.

LOSS PREVENTION AND CONTROL. In a broad sense, **loss prevention** can be defined as any activity that reduces the probability that a loss will occur (such as driving within the speed limit to lessen the chance of being in a car accident). **Loss control,** in contrast, is any activity that lessens the severity of loss once it occurs (such as wearing a safety belt or buying a car with air bags). Loss prevention and loss control should be important parts of the risk management program of every individual and family. In fact, insurance provides a reasonable means for handling risk only when people use effective loss prevention and control measures. For example, if everybody drove fast and recklessly, risk avoidance might be the only effective way to deal with the risk of an automobile accident—automobile, life, and health insurance would be too expensive to buy.

loss prevention
Any activity that reduces the probability that a loss will occur.

RISK ASSUMPTION. With **risk assumption,** you choose to accept and bear the risk of loss. Risk assumption can be an effective way to handle many types of potentially small exposures to loss when insurance would be too expensive. (For example, the risk of having your *Personal Financial Planning* text stolen probably doesn't justify buying insurance.) It is also a reasonable approach in the face of very large exposures that you cannot ordinarily prevent, or against which you cannot secure insurance (nuclear holocaust, for instance). Unfortunately, people often assume risks unknowingly. They may be unaware of various exposures to loss or think that their insurance policy offers adequate protection when, in fact, it doesn't. Therefore *one objective of these three chapters on insurance is to help you recognize the loss exposures you will face and understand when risk assumption is the preferred manner for handling certain risks.*

loss control
Any activity that reduces the severity of loss once it occurs.

risk assumption
The choice to bear or accept the risk of loss.

INSURANCE. Insurance permits society to reduce financial risks and share losses. Insurance companies combine the loss experiences of large numbers of people and, by using statistical information known as *actuarial data,* they are able to estimate the risk of loss faced by the insured population. Each person then contributes a relatively small amount (the insurance premium) in exchange for a promise from the insurance firm that he or she will be reimbursed for any covered losses. Insured individuals gain because they are able to transfer their risk to the insurer. Insurance companies, in turn, realize a gain if they have accurately estimated the number of insured losses that will occur.

An insurance policy is a contract between you (the insured) and an insurance company (the insurer) under which the insurance company promises to pay for your losses according to the specified terms. From your perspective, *you are transferring the risk of loss to the insurance company.* The insurance company is willing to accept the risk because it hopes to make a profit by collecting premiums from a large number of policyholders (commonly referred to as *insureds*), investing the money, and paying out losses and expenses that are less than the collected premiums and investment earnings. Insurers can do this because they are able to combine many insureds into a "pool," for which losses are more predictable than for any one of the insureds individually.

The premiums you pay for insurance usually come out of your current income. Thus the heart of the insurance decision is the comparison of the premiums you are willing (and able) to take from your current income relative to the need for, and the amount of, protection you will receive from the insurance you buy. The decision is difficult because, although there is a risk you might suffer losses from certain unforeseen events, you can't be certain when or even if such events will occur. This discussion of risk and the following explanation of underwriting should help you to better understand the whole concept of insurance and the role that it can play in your financial planning. Later in this chapter, we'll also provide some discussion of the factors to consider when making decisions about life insurance coverage.

UNDERWRITING

underwriting
In insurance, the process used by insurers to decide who can be insured and to determine applicable rates.

In all types of insurance the insurer must decide whom it can insure and then determine the applicable rates. This function is called **underwriting.** Through underwriting, insurance companies try to guard against *adverse selection,* which happens when only high-risk clients apply for, and get, insurance coverage. Underwriters design rate-classification schedules so that people pay premiums equal with their chance of loss. The success of any insurance company is highly dependent on the quality of its underwriting. If the underwriting standards are too high, people will be unjustly denied coverage, and insurance sales will drop. On the other hand, if standards are too low, many insureds will pay less than their fair share, and the insurance company's solvency could be jeopardized.

A basic problem facing underwriters is selecting the best criteria for classifying the people they insure. Because a perfect relationship does not exist between available criteria and loss experience, some people invariably believe they are being charged more than they should be for their insurance. For example, a life insurance company may charge higher premiums to an applicant who is slightly overweight, even if he or she has no other health problems.

Life insurance underwriting begins by asking potential insureds to complete an application designed to gather information about their risk potential. For example, does the applicant engage in hazardous activities such as piloting a plane, scuba diving, or racing motorcycles? Do they smoke or have they had their driver's license suspended? Have they been charged with driving under the influence of drugs or alcohol? These and other factors may indicate that the applicant is at a higher risk for experiencing loss. The application also asks about the potential insured's health, including height and weight, existing or previous medical problems, substance abuse problems, and family medical history. Most life insurance companies also ask for medical records and require applicants to take tests to rule out human immunodeficiency virus and drug abuse.

All these factors are then used to determine whether to accept you, and, based on your risk factors, what premium to charge. For example, someone in excellent health is usually considered "preferred" and pays the lowest premium. Other typical categories include standard, preferred smoker, and smoker. Those with special medical conditions—high cholesterol or diabetes, for example—fall into rated categories and pay considerably higher premiums if they are accepted.

All life insurance policies contain an *incontestability clause* that gives the insurance company 1 to 2 years to investigate all information provided by the insured in the application. If it discovers a material false statement during that period—for example, that you smoke when you said you didn't or you failed to disclose a medical condition—the company can rescind the contract. After the elapsed period, the insurer cannot challenge the validity of the policy, regardless of whether the insured has died or is still living.

Aside from incontestability, the insurance company can adjust the cost of a policy at any time if the insured misstated his or her age or sex in the application. Let's assume, for example, that a 35-year-old male applies for a life insurance policy by mail and says on the application that he's a 35-year-old female because he knows that females of the same age pay lower premiums. When he dies and the company discovers the error, it will award a sum equal to the amount of insurance that the premiums paid would have purchased had the insurer known the applicant was male. Note that the policy is not voided but simply *modified* to conform to the facts.

Although, historically, insurers have assigned different rates to men and women, some states now have laws requiring that the same rates and underwriting standards apply to both males and females. Such laws illustrate the conflict between underwriting standards that seem to make sense based on the insurers' actuarial tables and those that are considered fair by the general public and their elected representatives.

Underwriting is perhaps more an art than a science. Insurers are always trying to improve their underwriting capabilities in order to set rates that will provide adequate protection against insolvency and yet be reasonable for most policyholders. Underwriting standards and practices also vary from insurance company to insurance company. You can usually save money by shopping around for an insurance company that has underwriting practices most favorable to your specific characteristics and needs. For instance, some life insurers offer discounts to nonsmokers and to people in better-than-average health. Many companies also offer discounts to those in preferred low-risk occupations, such as professionals and business executives.

CONCEPT CHECK

8-1. Discuss the role insurance plays in the financial planning process. Why is it important to have enough life insurance?

8-2. Define (a) *risk avoidance,* (b) *loss prevention,* (c) *loss control,* (d) *risk assumption,* and (e) *underwriting.* Explain their interrelationships, if any.

8-3. Explain the purpose of underwriting. What are some of the factors underwriters consider when evaluating a life insurance application?

How Much Life Insurance Is Right For You? [LG2, LG3]

As we've already discussed, life insurance should be considered as part of careful financial planning. It can provide important financial protection for your loved ones in event of your unexpected death, helping them maintain a comfortable standard of living, pay debts, and reach goals like attending college. Many people, however, put off the decision to buy life insurance. A partial explanation for this tendency is that life insurance is intangible. You can't see, smell, touch, or taste its benefits. A life insurance policy is also associated with something unpleasant in many people's minds—namely, death. People don't like to talk about death, or the things closely associated with it, so they often put off considering their life insurance needs. Although most people, especially family breadwinners, recognize that they may need life insurance, many believe that purchasing it can be delayed another month—or two or three.

BENEFITS OF LIFE INSURANCE

Although the primary purpose of buying life insurance is to protect your family members financially after your death, some types of life insurance policies also offer other benefits, including: (1) protection from creditors, (2) a vehicle for savings, and (3) tax benefits. Understanding these features will help you make a better-informed decision about life insurance and how it fits into your financial plan.

PROTECTION FROM CREDITORS. When a person dies, all assets and liabilities are added up, and the heirs receive what is left after all legitimate claims against the estate have been satisfied. However, a life insurance policy can be structured so death benefits will be paid to a named beneficiary rather than the deceased's estate. This way the cash proceeds do not become a part of the estate. Even if the insured had more liabilities than assets, the proceeds of the insurance policy could not be used to liquidate them. Similarly, creditors who have successfully secured judgments against persons with substantial accumulations of life insurance cash values probably cannot levy any claim on those assets. State laws differ with respect to the rights of creditors to the death benefits or cash values of life insurance policies; in nearly all cases, however, both can be better protected than such assets as stocks, bonds, mutual funds, and investment real estate.

VEHICLE FOR SAVINGS. In addition to protection from creditors, some types of life insurance policies can serve as a vehicle for savings, particularly for those people who are looking for safety of principal. The financial returns on the savings element in life insurance policies are often contrasted with investments in stocks, bonds, mutual funds, and real estate. In particular, *variable life policies,* which we will discuss in greater detail later in this chapter, are more investment vehicles than they are life insurance products. As such, they can be legitimately compared to other investment outlets. However, be careful in assuming that all life insurance policies can be considered savings instruments. As we'll see, the comparison is often inappropriate. Certainly, any time you consider the purchase of life insurance primarily because of its tax-sheltered investment properties, you should evaluate that transaction relative to what you can earn (on an after-tax basis) from alternative investment vehicles. More often than not, you'll find that better returns are available from alternative investments, especially when you factor in load fees, steep surrender charges, and other expenses.

By far, the biggest share of life insurance is sold for the insurance protection it provides—without question, that's why most people buy life insurance policies. It's the *death protection* they're after, and the savings feature of some policies are just a pleasant byproduct. The savings feature is not something to overlook, but it's not the principal reason for purchase.

TAX BENEFITS. Life insurance proceeds, as a rule, are not subject to state or federal income taxes. Further, if certain requirements are met, policy proceeds can pass to named beneficiaries free of any *estate* taxes. Generally, though, to qualify for this estate tax exemption, the insured person must relinquish various "incidents of ownership" in his or her policy, including the right to change the beneficiary, to take the policy's cash surrender value, and to choose a settlement option. When the named beneficiary is a spouse, the sacrifice of these rights is unnecessary. In these cases the life insurance proceeds typically can be excluded from estate taxes as part of the marital deduction. (We'll cover estate planning in Chapter 15.)

The ability to financially protect your family after your death, along with some of the other potential benefits of some types of life insurance, shouldn't be overlooked in financial planning. However, this doesn't mean that everyone should rush out and stock up on as much life insurance as they can buy. Careful insurance planning means determining whether life insurance is necessary and, if so, choosing the right amount and type of coverage. In this section we'll address both issues.

WHO NEEDS LIFE INSURANCE?

The first question to ask about life insurance is if, in fact, you need it! Many people just assume they need life insurance, but this isn't always the case. Many factors, including your personal life situation and other financial resources, play a role in determining the need for life insurance. Remember, the major purpose of life insurance is to *provide financial security for dependents in the event of death.* As we've discussed, life insurance can also provide other benefits, but they are all a distant second to the primary reason for buying life insurance.

Your life insurance needs change throughout your life. When you are single, you may not need any life insurance at all, unless you are a single parent or support other relatives. Children also don't need life insurance. Some agents may argue that life insurance is a good way to save money for future needs like college or retirement, but the truth is, higher-yielding savings vehicles usually pay better returns on your investment.

Once you marry, your need for life insurance may change, depending on your spouse's earning potential and the assets, such as a house, that you want to protect. *The need for life insurance increases the most when children enter the picture* because young families would suffer the greatest financial hardship from the premature death of a parent. Even a non–wage-earning parent may need some life insurance to ensure that children will be adequately provided for if the parent died. As families build assets, their life insurance requirements continue to change, both in terms of the amount of insurance and the types of policies necessary to meet their objectives and protect their assets. Other life changes also affect insurance needs. For example, the loss of a spouse through divorce or death may require additional life insurance on the surviving spouse. In contrast, once children finish college, their parents' need for life insurance coverage may drop. In later years the amount of life insurance needed varies depending on the availability of other financial resources, such as pension plans and investments, to provide for your dependents. All of this explains why life insurance planning should occur continuously throughout your life and within your overall personal financial planning framework.

CALCULATING YOUR INSURANCE NEEDS

Two techniques are commonly used to estimate an individual's life insurance needs: the *multiple earnings approach* and the *needs approach.*

The **multiple earnings approach** gained its popularity based on its simplicity rather than its soundness. With this technique, you calculate the amount of life insurance to buy by simply multiplying your gross annual earnings by some (largely arbitrary) selected number. Multiples of 3, 5, or even 10 times earnings are often used to find the amount of life insurance coverage needed. Life insurance agents have tables with multiples based on age, family situation, and gross annual pay. For example, the table might show that a married 35-year-old male with two children earning $40,000 a year should use a multiple of 8.7 if he wants to replace 75 percent of this income. His total life insurance coverage, therefore, should amount to $40,000 × 8.7, or $348,000. This amount is then compared with the life insurance the person already has from existing individual policies or other sources. If the person has $50,000 from an employer's group life insurance policy and another $50,000 in death benefits from the company's pension plan, his remaining life insurance needs are $248,000 (that is, $348,000 − $50,000 − $50,000). At best, the multiple earnings procedure should be used only to get a very rough approximation of life insurance needs. Although simple to use, the multiple earnings method fails to fully recognize the financial obligations and resources of the individual.

Most professional life insurance agents have abandoned the multiple earnings approach in favor of the **needs approach.** This method specifically considers the financial obligations a person may have and his or her financial resources *in addition to life insurance.* Essentially, the needs approach involves three steps: (1) estimate the total economic resources needed if the individual were to die; (2) determine all financial resources that would be available after death, including existing life insurance and pension plan death

multiple earnings approach
A method of determining the amount of life insurance coverage needed by multiplying gross annual earnings by some (largely arbitrary) selected number.

needs approach
A method of determining the amount of life insurance coverage needed by considering the person's financial obligations and his or her available financial resources *in addition to life insurance.*

benefits; and (3) subtract available resources from the amount needed to calculate how much additional life insurance is required.

When assessing economic needs, you must consider your particular family situation. Premature death will create greater financial hardship for certain types of families. For example, single parents, especially those with no additional resources (such as a divorced spouse who can take over in the event of premature death), typically need larger amounts of life insurance to provide for dependents. Likewise, two-income families that depend on a second income to make ends meet must insure both spouses adequately. "Blended" families, which include children from prior marriages, require more protection for the larger family unit in event of one parent's death, and a parent may need to provide coverage for dependent children not living with him or her. Families in the "sandwich" generation must protect both children and any elderly relatives they support from the severe financial impact caused by a wage earner's death. In each of these cases adequate life insurance can provide financial security for dependents.

ASSESSING ECONOMIC NEEDS. The basic question the needs approach asks is: *What financial resources will the survivors need should the income producer die tomorrow?* Although life insurance often plays a role in retirement or estate planning, it primarily protects families from financial loss resulting from the death of an income producer. In this role, life insurance can provide money for the following financial needs: (1) family income, (2) additional expenses, (3) debt liquidation, (4) surviving spouse's income, (5) money for special requirements, such as the children's education, and (6) liquidity. Let's look more closely at the six major financial needs of a typical family.

Family Income. The principal financial need of most people who support dependents is to protect their family's income. They want to make sure their family will be able to continue to live comfortably if they die. This may involve providing for elderly relatives or nonrelated dependents and dependent children. Perhaps the best way to estimate the amount of monthly income necessary to sustain a family is to develop a budget covering all expenses likely to be incurred. As discussed in Chapter 2, major items in most family budgets are housing costs, utilities, food, clothing, and medical and dental needs. Other expenses include property taxes, insurance, recreation and travel, and savings.

One important question you must answer as you develop a post-death family budget is, "What standard of living do I want my family to have?" Although some people feel a reduced level of consumption is in order, others want their families to maintain their present standard of living. Still others would like to leave their families with the same level of consumption as if they had continued to live and work.

A final point to keep in mind concerning family income is that many families depend on two incomes. Emphasis traditionally has been placed on insuring the family against the income loss of the father. However, working mothers can also die unexpectedly. Therefore, to the extent that a family (with either one or two incomes) depends on the woman's income to make ends meet, *that income should be counted as part of the family income need.* Equally important because the death of a working mother can have devastating effects on the family structure and the family budget, *her life should also be adequately insured.* In keeping with the growing importance of women in the workforce, life insurance sales on the lives of women have increased dramatically in recent years. Whereas in 1965 only 10 percent of all policies were sold to women, by 1995 that number had risen to nearly 40 percent!

Additional Expenses. In most households adult family members are responsible for performing many family and household services. For example, a mother who does not work outside of the home still provides childcare, cooking, cleaning, and other services. If she were to die, these services would represent new expenses to be paid out of the family's income. Because such expenses could stretch the family budget to the breaking point, they should be recognized and included when estimating insurance needs.

Pay Off Debts. In the event of their deaths most breadwinners prefer to leave their families relatively debt-free. To accomplish this, it's necessary to calculate the average amount due for outstanding bills. This amount would include the balances on credit cards, department store accounts, installment loans, and other similar obligations. It would also include estimated funeral expenses. In addition, some heads of household will want to leave enough money to pay off their home mortgages and will include this amount in their debt-liquidation estimates.

Surviving Spouse's Income. Once children are on their own, the monthly household expenses should decrease substantially. Nevertheless, the surviving spouse may need monthly support for the remainder of his or her life. Therefore an estimate of the survivor's life expectancy and the amount of income they will need must be calculated.

Special Financial Needs. In addition to the economic needs already discussed, some people would like to provide for the special financial needs of their family. These needs might include a college education fund for the children, special care for a disabled or chronically ill dependent, or an emergency fund for unexpected financial burdens.

Liquidity. Often we may have assets but no cash. Real estate investors, for example, are notorious for owning several million dollars' worth of properties but bouncing checks for $100. Similarly, many farmers are land rich and cash poor. People who keep a very high percentage of their wealth in nonliquid assets often need life insurance to provide enough cash to avoid estate shrinkage. Life insurance proceeds keep the mortgages paid and assets maintained until they can be sold in an orderly fashion at their fair market value.

AVAILABLE RESOURCES. After estimating the lifetime financial needs of dependents, the next step is to list all current resources that will be available for meeting those needs. For most families, money from savings, investments, and social security survivor's benefits make up the largest non–life insurance financial resources. Additional resources include proceeds from employer-sponsored group life insurance policies and the death benefits payable from accumulated pension plans and profit-sharing programs. Another important source is income that can be earned by the surviving spouse or children. If the surviving spouse is skilled and readily employable, his or her earnings could be a family's largest available resource. In addition, many families have real estate (in addition to their homes), jewelry, stocks, bonds, and other assets that can be liquidated to meet financial needs. After developing a complete list of available resources, you should make some reasonable estimate of their value. Although this step can be difficult due to the changing values of many of the assets, coming up with a set of reasonably accurate estimates is certainly within reach.

NEEDS LESS RESOURCES. The last step in the needs approach to life insurance planning is to subtract the total available resources from the total needed to satisfy all of the family's financial objectives. If available resources exceed needs, the family requires no additional life insurance. If the resources are less than the needs—as is the case in most families with children—the difference is the amount of additional life insurance necessary to provide the family with its desired standard of living.

Generally, insurance proceeds can be invested until the money is actually needed, at an after-tax rate of return that exceeds inflation. This after-tax, after-inflation return may be 1 to 2 percent for reasonably conservative investments, and even higher for more risky investments.

By now, you can see that insurance planning based on the needs concept can become quite complex. A competent financial planner or life insurance agent who understands the process can guide you through the planning stage. Virtually all life insurance companies today have computer programs set up to determine the life insurance requirements of families using the needs approach. In addition, there are plenty of Internet and computer software programs that enable you to run your own analysis.

 Estimate the amount of life insurance your family needs for financial security with the Life Insurance Coverage Needs Analyzer in the Tools section of InsWeb, **www.insweb.com**.

Regardless of which procedure you use, remember that *life insurance needs are not static.* The amount and type of life insurance you need today will probably differ from the amount and type suitable for you 10 or 20 years from now. As with other areas of your personal financial plan, you should review and adjust life insurance programs (as necessary) at least every 5 years, or after any major changes in the family (for example, the birth of a child, the purchase of a home, or a job change).

THE NEEDS APPROACH IN ACTION: THE BENSON FAMILY

To illustrate how to use the needs approach in insurance planning, consider the hypothetical case of Bill and Joan Benson. The Bensons' primary desire is to have enough insurance on Bill's life to take care of Joan (age 35) and their two children (ages 6 and 8) should Bill die. Their priorities are to (1) leave the family debt free, (2) ensure an income for Joan and their children until the youngest child is age 18, (3) provide funds for Joan to make the transition from homemaking to gainful employment, and (4) establish a fund that will permit the children to obtain college education or begin careers. Because the Bensons know that insurance needs change, they believe a 5-year planning horizon is appropriate. At the end of that period, Bill and Joan will reevaluate the family's needs and resources to see if their life insurance program warrants modification. We'll use Worksheet 8.1 to calculate the current life insurance needs of the Benson family.

FAMILY ECONOMIC NEEDS. Because the Bensons use credit sparingly, their outstanding debts are limited to a mortgage (with a current balance of $135,000), an automobile loan ($4,000), and miscellaneous charge accounts ($1,000). The balances on these debts currently total $140,000. The mortgage is in its early years and will not decrease significantly during the 5-year planning period. Although the existing auto loan will be amortized (paid off) within their 5-year planning period, the Bensons expect to have a new loan for a replacement vehicle. Bill therefore believes that $140,000 will be adequate to pay off all their existing debts. In addition, the Bensons would like to have $15,000 available to pay estate administration expenses, taxes, and funeral costs. (These items are listed on lines 1 and 2 of part A of Worksheet 8.1.)

Bill and Joan have reviewed their budget and feel that monthly living expenses for Joan and the two children would be $3,000 while the children are still living at home (12 years). During the period after both children leave home and until Joan retires at age 65 (18 years), the Bensons estimate Joan's monthly living expenses will be $2,500 in current dollars. After Joan's retirement, they anticipate her living expenses to fall to $2,200 a month. The life

social security survivor's benefits Benefits included under provision of social security that are intended to provide basic, minimum support to families faced with the loss of their principal wage earners.

WORKSHEET 8.1

DETERMINING THE NEED FOR LIFE INSURANCE

A worksheet like this one can be used to determine life insurance requirements according to the needs approach.

Insured's Name ___Bill and Joan Benson___   Date ___January 2002___

A. Family Income Needs				Totals
1. Debt Liquidation				
a. House mortgage	$135,000			
b. Other loans	$ 5,000			
c. Total debt (a + b)				$140,000
2. Final expenses				$ 15,000
3. Annual income needs:	Period 1	Period 2	Period 3	
a. Monthly living expenses	$ 3,000	$ 2,500	$ 2,200	
b. Less: Social security survivor's benefits	2,741	0	1,100	
c. Less: Surviving spouse's income	0	2,250	0	
d. Less: Other pension benefits and income	0	0	700	
e. Net monthly income needed (a − b − c − d)	259	250	400	
f. Net yearly income needed (12 × e)	3,108	3,000	4,800	
g. Number of years in period	12	18	22	
h. Funding needed each period (f × g)	$ 37,296	$54,000	$105,600	
i. Total living needs (add line h for each period)				$ 196,896
4. Spouse reeducation fund				$ 25,000
5. Children's opportunity fund				$ 50,000
6. Other needs				$ 0
7. TOTAL INCOME NEEDS (add right column)				$426,896
B. Financial Resources Available				
1. Savings and investments	$ 65,000			
2. Group life insurance	$ 65,000			
3. Other life insurance	$ —			
4. Other resources	$ —			
TOTAL RESOURCES AVAILABLE (1 + 2 + 3 + 4)				$130,000
C. Additional Life Insurance Needed (A − B)				
(Note: no additional insurance is needed if number is negative.)				$ 296,896

expectancy of a woman Joan's age is 87 years, so the Bensons calculate that Joan will spend about 22 years in retirement.

    Bill and Joan begin by considering the amount of **social security survivor's benefits** Joan and the children may be eligible to receive if Bill dies. Survivor benefits are intended

EXHIBIT 8.1

APPROXIMATE MONTHLY SOCIAL SECURITY SURVIVOR'S BENEFITS

These benefits apply to the families of qualified wage earners who died in 2001; like other aspects of social security, the amount of monthly benefits depends in large part on the covered worker's level of income.

Approximate Monthly Survivors Benefits if the Worker Dies in 2001 and Had Steady Earnings

Age and Family	Deceased Worker's Earnings in 2000				
	$20,000	$30,000	$40,000	$50,000	$60,000
Age: 35					
Each child	$ 610	$ 794	$ 978	$1,105	$1,191
Spouse caring for child	609	794	978	1,105	1,191
Spouse at full retirement	814	1,059	1,304	1,473	1,588
Family maximum	1,341	1,972	2,300	2,578	2,779
Age: 45					
Each child	609	792	975	1,103	1,189
Spouse caring for child	609	792	975	1,103	1,189
Spouse at full retirement	812	1,056	1,300	1,471	1,588
Family maximum	1,334	1,968	2,294	2,574	2,774
Age: 55					
Each child	609	791	974	1,101	1,172
Spouse caring for child	609	791	974	1,101	1,172
Spouse at full retirement	812	1,055	1,298	1,585	1,563
Family maximum	1,334	1,967	2,291	2,569	2,735

Source: Social Security Administration.

to provide basic, minimum support to families faced with the loss of their principal wage earners. In addition to the elderly and disabled, the principal recipients of social security survivor's benefits are (1) unmarried children under age 18 (or 19 if still in high school), (2) nonworking spouses with children under age 16, and (3) surviving spouses age 60 and over. There are limits placed on the total amount of survivor's benefits that can be paid to a household, and if the surviving spouse returns to work, the amount of benefits will be reduced if earnings exceed certain limits. In 2001, for example, benefits would be reduced if the surviving spouse earns more than $10,680 a year.

Exhibit 8.1 shows the approximate monthly social security survivor benefits available to the surviving dependents of qualified wage earners who died in 2001. Note that the level of benefits depends on the wage earner's age at death, earnings history, and the number of survivors. These benefits used to be difficult to predict. Now, however, you can get a fairly accurate estimate of the benefits your survivors would be entitled to receive on your death at the Social Security Administration's Web site at **www.ssa.gov**. You can also obtain a *Personal Earnings and Benefits Estimate Statement* by calling the Social Security Administration's toll-free number, 1-800-772-1213. (This statement is discussed in Chapter 14, and an actual sample is reproduced in Exhibit 14.4.)

According to the Social Security Administration's estimate based on Bill's current earnings, Joan and the children will receive a maximum of $2,741 per month in social security survivor's benefits initially, assuming she does not work or remarry. When their youngest child reaches age 16, Joan's benefits will stop, and each child's benefits will also stop when they graduate from high school. Even so, because the worksheet we are using is an estimate, we will assume they receive $2,741 a month for the full 12 years (Period 1 of the worksheet). As each child reaches age 18, the family's benefits will be reduced and when the youngest child reaches that age, all survivor benefits will stop. When Joan reaches retirement age, she will receive $1,100 per month from Bill's survivor's benefits, in addition to her own social security benefits.

Knowing what they'd receive from social security, the Bensons subtracted that amount from their target income (of $3,000 a month) to arrive at a *net monthly income* (line 3e on the worksheet) for Period 1. This is the amount of income they'll have to make up from some source other than social security to preserve their present standard of living. This is the basic income level they want to maintain until the youngest child has reached 18 years of age, 12 years from now. Thus they estimate that it should take about $37,296 to provide the family with $3,108 a year for 12 years. (See the Period 1 column of the worksheet.) Actually, given that money has a time value, it would take something *less* than the $37,296 to provide the needed income, but this complication can be ignored so long as we also disregard future inflation, which in fact would add to the amount needed. *In essence, because one element (inflation) will have at least a partially offsetting effect on the other (present value), we will ignore both of them in our calculation.* Because we're *estimating* future needs, there is little to be gained by trying to fine-tune these projections with even more estimates of future inflation rates and potential rates of return on invested capital.

A similar procedure is used to estimate available income for Period 2, the years after the children leave home and until Joan retires, and then Period 3, the years after Joan retires. Note that Period 2 is called the "Blackout Period," so-named because it is a time during which the surviving spouse receives no social security benefits. However, Joan expects to work during this period, and feels she should be able to make a net monthly income of around $2,250 (in current dollars). That leaves her short about $250 a month, for a total need of $54,000 during the Blackout Period.

As mentioned earlier, the Bensons estimate that Joan's living expenses after retirement should drop even more (to around $2,200 a month). Because Joan will have worked for nearly 20 years, they think it is reasonable to assume she will earn retirement benefits of her own. However, to be on the safe side, they estimate Joan's retirement benefits as only $700 a month. In addition, once Joan reaches retirement age, she will once again be eligible for monthly social security benefits—which they estimate at about $1,100 a month. Based on this information, Joan will need a total of $105,600 to preserve her standard of living during retirement. Therefore the Benson's total income needs over Joan's lifetime (Periods 1 through 3) are $196,896, shown as the total income needs (line 3i) on the worksheet.

Although Joan is trained as a stockbroker, because she will not work until both children are raised, they are concerned that her previous education may be somewhat out of date. Thus they would like to have enough money to allow Joan to return to college for several years. They believe $25,000 should be sufficient for this purpose. Finally, both Bill and Joan want to guarantee that their children will have the money necessary for educational or other opportunities that may be available when they reach age 18. To do this, they want to establish an opportunity fund of $50,000. The Bensons feel that should complete the family's economic needs, all of which are summarized in the top part (Section A) of Worksheet 8.1. Note that the total amount necessary to meet their financial goals, should Bill die within the next 5 years, would be $426,896.

AVAILABLE FINANCIAL RESOURCES. Bill is employed as an assistant professor at a state university. Although the university has a retirement program, it does not provide any pre-retirement survivor's benefits. However, Bill is covered by an employer-sponsored group life insurance policy in the amount of 1 year's gross salary ($65,000). The Bensons also have roughly $65,000 in several mutual funds and a money market deposit account. These investments were obtained in part from an inheritance and from a $20,000 advance against Bill's textbook royalties.

Other potential resources, such as a promised gift of $20,000 from Joan's Aunt Sarah, a travel accident life insurance policy with a $10,000 face value, and assorted personal property, are ignored in the planning process because of uncertainty as to either their amount or their availability. For example, Aunt Sarah may decide to donate the money to charity, or Bill may die from a cause unrelated to his travel insurance. Overall, then, the resources the Bensons can count on to help achieve their economic objectives total $130,000, as summarized in the lower part (Section B) of Worksheet 8.1.

ADDITIONAL LIFE INSURANCE NEEDED. As shown in the bottom line of Worksheet 8.1, the difference between the monies available and the amount required is $296,896. This sum equals the amount of additional life insurance the Bensons will need on Bill's life to provide the family's desired standard of living. The amount of the life insurance a family needs to meet desired expenses often exceeds the family's willingness or ability to pay for it. Even after a careful search for the right type of policy at the best price, a family might decide they just cannot afford all the insurance they would like. In these cases the family must rank needs by priority and reassess available resources. For example, the family may have included a college education fund in the preliminary plans, but not considered income from employment of the surviving spouse or children. The family could decide, however, to let the children work their way through college and have the surviving spouse seek employment. Thus the family can adjust the ability and willingness to pay for life insurance to meet economic needs and limitations.

CONCEPT CHECK

8-4. Discuss some of the benefits of life insurance in addition to protecting family members financially after the primary wage-earner's death

8-5. Explain the circumstances under which a single college graduate would or would not need life insurance. What life-cycle events would change this initial evaluation, and how might they affect his or her life insurance needs?

8-6. Discuss the two most commonly used ways to determine a person's life insurance needs.

8-7. Name and explain the most common economic needs that must be satisfied after the death of a family breadwinner.

■ What Kind of Policy Is Right For You? [LG4]

After you determine the amount of life insurance necessary to meet your family's financial requirements, you must decide on the type of insurance policy that will best fit your needs. Generally speaking, most families can effectively satisfy their insurance needs through the use of one of the three basic types of life insurance: term life, whole life, or universal life. These three products account for 90 to 95 percent of all life insurance sales—with term life being the biggest seller, followed by whole life policies and then universal life. There are, of course, other types of policies available to consumers, but, as we will see, most are simply modifications of these three types.

At **www.life-line.org**, the site for the nonprofit Life and Health Insurance Foundation, an insurance education organization, you'll find information to help you sort out your life insurance options.

TERM LIFE INSURANCE

Under the provisions of a **term life insurance** policy, the insurance company agrees to pay a stipulated amount of money if the insured dies during the policy period. The period of coverage most often used is 5 years, with premiums payable annually, semiannually, or quarterly. However, many other periods of coverage and payment plans are available. Term insurance is the purest form of life insurance in that it provides a stipulated amount of life insurance (that is, death benefits) and nothing more. There are *no* investment or savings features associated with it. Term insurance can be an economical way to purchase life insurance, on a temporary basis, for protection against financial loss resulting from death, *especially in the early years of family formation when affordability is so important.*

Nearly all life insurance companies sell some form of term insurance. In addition, employer-sponsored group life insurance plans and companies that sell directly to the public through mail, newspaper, or magazine advertisements often offer term insurance at very low rates. Unfortunately, in the past, many families, because of either lack of knowledge or poor advice, did not properly incorporate term life insurance into their insurance programs. As consumers have become more knowledgeable, however, term life insurance sales have increased accordingly.

TYPES OF TERM INSURANCE. The most common types of term insurance are straight (or level) term and decreasing term. With regard to term policies, there are two important provisions that you should always be aware of: the renewability of the policy and its convertibility to a whole life policy.

Straight Term. Policies written for a given number of years—for example, 1, 5, 10, 20, or now even 30 years —are called **straight-term** (or level-term) **policies.** In such policies the *amount* of life insurance coverage remains unchanged throughout the effective period of the policy. In contrast, the *annual premium* on a straight-term policy may increase each year, as with *annual renewable term policies,* or remain level throughout the policy period, as with *level-premium term policies.*

Exhibits 8.2 and 8.3 list representative annual premiums for annual renewable term and level-premium term life policies, respectively. Note that annual renewable term policies start out with relatively low annual premiums, but they increase rapidly over time; in contrast, level-premium policies start out with higher annual premiums, but because they do not change over time, their total cost is considerably less than the cost of a renewable term policy.

Decreasing Term. Because the death rate increases with each year of life, the premiums on straight-term policies for each successive period of coverage will also increase. As an alternative, some term policies *maintain a level premium* throughout all periods of coverage, but *the amount of protection decreases.* Such a policy is called a **decreasing-term policy** because the amount of protection decreases over its life. Decreasing term is used when the amount of needed coverage declines over time. For example, decreasing-term policies are popular with homeowners who want a level of life insurance coverage that will decline at about the same rate as the balances on their home mortgages. Families with young children use these policies to ensure a sufficient level of family income while the kids are growing up. As they grow older, the amount of coverage needed decreases until the last child becomes independent and the need expires.

term life insurance
Insurance that provides only death benefits, for a specified period, and does not provide for the accumulation of cash value.

straight-term policy
A term insurance policy that is written for a given number of years, with coverage remaining unchanged throughout the effective period.

decreasing-term policy
A term insurance policy that *maintains a level premium* throughout all periods of coverage, but *the amount of protection decreases.*

EXHIBIT 8.2

REPRESENTATIVE ANNUAL RENEWABLE TERM LIFE INSURANCE PREMIUMS; $100,000 POLICY, PREFERRED NONSMOKER RATES

When you buy term life insurance, you are basically buying a product that provides life insurance coverage and nothing more. The following table shows representative rates for several age categories and selected policy years; actual premiums increase every year. As you can see, females pay less than males for coverage, and premiums increase sharply with age.

Policy Year	Age 25		Age 40		Age 60	
	Male	Female	Male	Female	Male	Female
1	$ 130	$ 119	$ 148	$ 139	$ 366	$ 252
5	169	147	252	219	927	562
10	218	187	426	368	1,702	1,080
15	196	176	647	507	2,666	1,313
20	279	259	1,258	1,054	4,574	2,989
Total Cost, 20 years	$3,777	$3,381	$9,871	$8,287	$38,457	$22,346

EXHIBIT 8.3

REPRESENTATIVE LEVEL-PREMIUM TERM LIFE RATES; $100,000 PREFERRED NONSMOKER POLICY

This table shows annual, representative rates for $100,000 of level-premium term life insurance. Although level premium costs less than annual renewable term for the same period, you must requalify at the end of each term to retain the low premium.

Age	5 Year		10 Year		15 Year		20 Year	
	Male	Female	Male	Female	Male	Female	Male	Female
25	$140	$132	$140	$132	$155	$140	$ 170	$162
30	143	132	143	132	155	141	176	164
35	149	134	150	136	172	152	202	181
40	185	159	196	166	216	187	267	230
50	344	271	380	298	450	344	565	419
60	599	365	650	404	N/A	N/A	1,075	645

Again, remember that the choice between decreasing and level term policies, and between the length of level term policies, will affect the amount of premiums you'll pay over time. Exhibit 8.4 shows the differences in total premiums that would be paid over a 20-year period for $250,000 in life insurance using a 20-year level term policy, a decreasing term policy, or a level term policy that is renewed annually. Note that in the 20th year, the death benefit from the decreasing term policy has dropped to $12,500.

EXHIBIT 8.4

COMPARISON OF TERM LIFE PREMIUMS OVER 20 YEARS

The total premiums for a 20-year, $250,000 term life insurance policy differ considerably, depending on whether you buy a level term policy, decreasing term policy, or a level term policy that is renewed annually. Note that in the 20th year, the death benefit from the decreasing term policy has dropped to $12,500.

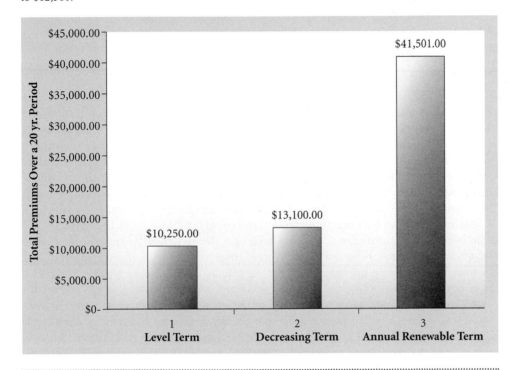

Source: Quickquote.com, **www.quickquote.com/pix/litvswl_big.gif** (accessed July 23, 2001).

RENEWABILITY AND CONVERTIBILITY PROVISIONS. A **renewability** provision allows the insured to renew his or her policy for another term of equal length, without having to show evidence of insurability. Renewal is at the option of the insured, but the premium increases to offset the greater chance of death at older ages. Generally, term policies may be renewed at the end of each term until the insured reaches age 65 or 70. If you buy term insurance, it's a good idea to obtain a *guaranteed renewable provision* in your policy. Otherwise, if you become uninsurable due to accident or illness during the policy period, you will lose your chance to renew your protection. Today, this valuable provision is standard in most term policies at no extra cost. Certainly, you should *never* buy a term policy that does not have guaranteed renewability.

You should also be aware that with a level-premium term policy, you typically must requalify medically at the end of the guaranteed rate period to renew the policy at favorable rates. If you are in poor health, the guaranteed renewable provision simply allows you to continue the existing policy, but at much higher annual renewable term rates.

A **convertibility** provision allows the insured to convert coverage to a comparable whole life policy (discussed below) without evidence of insurability. The convertibility feature

renewability
A term life policy provision that allows the insured to renew his or her policy for another term of equal length, without having to show evidence of insurability.

convertibility
A term life policy provision that allows the insured to convert the policy to a comparable whole life policy without evidence of insurability.

guarantees insureds that (1) they will not lose their insurance protection at the end of the period, and (2) on conversion, they will have lifelong protection (as long as they pay their premiums, of course). The convertibility provision can be useful to persons who need a large amount of death protection at a relatively low cost, but who also want to continue their insurance coverage throughout their lives. This way, term coverage can be purchased to provide for a large amount of immediate death protection, and then later, when the insured has more income (and saving for retirement and liquidity for estate taxes become the more dominant issues), the policy can be converted to whole life. A convertibility option is standard with most of today's term policies.

Many convertible policies place some limitations on when the conversion can take place. For example, a 10-year term policy may stipulate that the conversion has to be made before the end of the eighth year, or a term policy to age 65 may require conversion prior to age 61.

ADVANTAGES AND DISADVANTAGES OF TERM LIFE. Because term insurance offers an economical way to purchase a large amount of life insurance protection over a given (relatively short) period, it is particularly advantageous during the child-rearing years. With the guaranteed renewable and convertible options, coverage can be continued throughout the insured's life although the cost will continually grow due to the increased chance of death. Indeed, increasing cost is the main disadvantage of term insurance and is a principal reason why people discontinue needed coverage. Recently, however, the insurance industry has started to offer a new 30-year straight-term policy. For example, a 35-year-old man who qualifies for preferred rates could have recently locked in a $250,000 death benefit for 30 years for as low as $360 a year. These newer, longer policies tend to negate one of the major disadvantages of term insurance. As with all insurance policies, however, before signing up, make sure that the rate is fully locked in for the duration of the policy.

Criticizing term insurance on the basis of increasing cost, however, is similar to finding fault with homeowner's insurance for not paying for a loss caused by an automobile accident. Clearly, the purpose of homeowner's insurance is not to provide automobile coverage, just as the purpose of a term policy is *not* to provide lifelong coverage. Instead, the objective of term insurance is *to provide a large amount of protection, at a reasonable cost, for a limited period*—something it accomplishes very well!

WHOLE LIFE INSURANCE

whole life insurance
Life insurance designed to offer financial protection for the entire life of the insured; it provides stipulated death benefits and allows for the accumulation of *cash values.*

cash value
The accumulated refundable value of an insurance policy; results from the investment earnings on paid-in insurance premiums.

Few people ever outlive the need for some type of life insurance. Accordingly, **whole life insurance,** as the name implies, is designed to offer financial protection for the entire life of an individual. In addition to death protection, whole life insurance has a *savings* feature, called **cash value,** which results from the investment earnings on paid-in insurance premiums. Thus, *whole life provides not only insurance coverage but also a modest return on your investment.* The idea behind cash value is to provide the insurance buyer with a tangible return while he or she also receives insurance coverage—the savings rates on whole life policies are normally *fixed* and *guaranteed* to be more than a certain rate (say, 4 to 6 percent). Exhibit 8.5 illustrates how the cash value in a whole life policy builds up over time. Obviously, the longer the insured keeps the policy in force, the greater the cash value. Whole life is available through several different payment plans, including continuous-premium, limited-payment, and single-premium, all providing for accumulation of cash values.

Life insurance companies set aside assets (that is, they "accumulate reserves") to pay the claims expected from the policies they issue. As time goes by, the cash value of a policy—the amount of assets allocated for each person insured—increases to reflect the greater chance

EXHIBIT 8.5

ILLUSTRATION OF THE CASH VALUE AND PURE DEATH PROTECTION IN A WHOLE LIFE POLICY

Here is an example of the projected cash value for an actual $200,000 whole life policy issued by a major life insurer to a male, age 30. For each year of the illustration, the difference between the $200,000 death benefit and the projected cash value represents the *death protection* offered by the insurer.

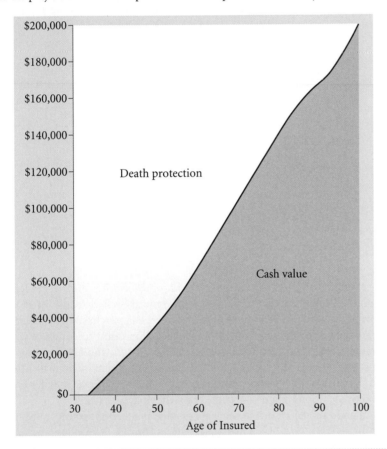

of death that comes with age. If policyholders decide to cancel their contracts prior to death, that portion of the assets set aside to provide payment for the death claim is available to them. This right to a cash value is termed the policyholder's **nonforfeiture right.** Policyholders, by terminating their insurance contracts, forfeit their rights to death benefits. Likewise, the company must forfeit its right to keep all the monies paid by these policyholders for the future death benefit it is no longer required to pay.

TYPES OF WHOLE LIFE POLICIES. Although a wide variety of whole life policies exists, we'll describe only the major ones—continuous-premium, limited-payment, and single-premium—here. To get a feel for the cost of these policies, look at the representative rates shown in Exhibit 8.6. By contrasting the premiums in this exhibit with those in Exhibits 8.2 and 8.3, you can readily see how much more expensive whole life is relative to term life. That is the price you pay for the savings/investment feature included with whole life.

nonforfeiture right
A life insurance feature that gives the policyholder, on policy cancellation, the portion of those assets that had been set aside to provide payment for future death claims.

EXHIBIT 8.6

REPRESENTATIVE WHOLE LIFE INSURANCE ANNUAL PREMIUMS; $100,000 POLICY, PREFERRED NONSMOKER RATES

As with any life insurance product, the older you are, the more expensive it is to buy whole life. Also, whole life is more costly than term because you are getting an investment/savings account, represented by the cash value column, in addition to life insurance coverage. Of course, the actual amount of cash value will depend on the actual dividend rate, which is subject to change (up or down) in keeping with current market conditions.

Age	Annual Premium		Premiums Paid through Year 20		Total Cash Value at Year 20*
	Male	Female	Male	Female	Male/Female
25	$ 988	$ 941	$19,760	$18,820	$ 30,894
30	1,233	1,188	24,460	23,760	38,971
35	1,473	1,438	29,460	28,760	46,223
40	1,833	1,788	36,660	35,760	55,980
50	2,816	2,666	55,425	52,425	76,225
60	4,291	3,899	85,820	77,980	112,765

*Guaranteed cash value plus annual dividends at the assumed annual rate of 6.8 percent.

Continuous Premium. Under a *continuous-premium whole life* policy, or *straight life,* as it's more commonly called, individuals pay a level premium each year until they die or exercise a nonforfeiture right. The earlier in life the coverage is purchased, the lower the annual premium. Life insurance agents often use this as a selling point to convince younger people to buy now. Their argument is that the sooner you buy, the less you pay. What they mean by this is what you pay *annually* rather than the total payments over the life of the policy. Of course, the sooner people purchase whole life, the longer they have coverage in force, but (all other things being equal) the *more* they pay in total.

Although good reasons (such as securing needed protection, savings, and insurability) do exist for many young people to buy whole life, it should seldom be purchased by anyone simply because the annual premium will be less than if it is purchased later.

Of the various whole life policies available, continuous-premium/straight life offers the greatest amount of permanent death protection and the least amount of savings per dollar of premium paid. Because the emphasis of whole life insurance for most families is *death protection* rather than savings, the continuous-premium policy is usually the wisest choice when filling a permanent life insurance need.

Limited Payment. The *limited-payment whole life* policy offers coverage for the entire life of the insured but schedules the payments to end after a certain period. For example, 20-pay life, 30-pay life, paid-up at age 55, and paid-up at age 65 are types of commonly sold limited-pay whole life policies. Under the 20-pay and 30-pay life contracts, the policyholder makes level premium payments for a period of 20 or 30 years, respectively. Under the premium schedule of paid-up at age 55, 65, or other stipulated-age policies, the policyholder makes premium payments until he or she attains the stated age. Of course, for any individual, the shorter the period over which premiums are payable, the larger the amount of the annual premium. In all of these cases, on completion of the scheduled payments, *the insurance remains in force at its face value for the remainder of the insured's life.*

Some insurance companies try to convince consumers to buy limited-payment policies by stressing the "large" savings element that will develop and the fact that the policyholder won't have to pay premiums for his or her entire life. This logic fails on two points. First, for most people the primary purpose of whole life insurance is permanent protection against financial loss resulting from death, not the accumulation of savings. Second, even if people buy continuous-premium whole life (straight life) policies, they need to pay the premium only as long as they wish to keep the policies in force for their full face value. Straight life policyholders may stop payment of premiums at any time after the policy accumulates some nonforfeiture value. Then, rather than take this benefit in cash, they can convert the policy to one that is paid up for some amount less than the original face value of the policy. We'll discuss this further in subsequent sections.

The preceding discussion is not intended to imply that limited-payment policies are undesirable. If lifelong death protection is the primary aim of the life insurance policy, the insured should purchase continuous-premium whole life instead of a limited-payment policy. Because more continuous-premium whole life insurance can be purchased with the same number of dollars as limited-payment whole life, people who need whole life insurance are probably better off using continuous-premium (straight) life insurance to get the most from their life insurance dollars. Then, once their insurance needs are reduced, they can convert the policy to a smaller amount of paid-up life insurance. On the other hand, if people have life insurance already in force that is sufficient to protect against income loss, they can use limited-payment policies as part of their savings or retirement plans.

Single Premium. Continuous-premium and limited-payment whole life policies represent methods of acquiring life insurance on an installment basis. In contrast, a *single-premium whole life* policy is purchased with one cash premium payment at the inception of the contract, thus buying life insurance coverage for the rest of your life. The single-premium policy has only limited usefulness in the life insurance programs of most families. However, because of its investment attributes, single-premium life insurance, or *SPLI* for short, appeals to those looking for a *tax-sheltered investment vehicle.*

From an investment perspective, SPLI is attractive because, like any whole life insurance policy, interest/investment earnings within the policy are tax-deferred. It also provides some life insurance coverage—usually just enough to qualify under IRS rules—but this is basically an added bonus. (Of course, the death benefits from an SPLI policy are treated like those from any other life insurance policy and pass tax-free to the beneficiaries.) Minimum premiums usually run around $5,000, though most buyers today put in much more. Once the purchase is made, investment earnings start to build up tax-free.

There is a catch, however: Any cash withdrawals or loans taken against the SPLI cash value before you reach age $59\frac{1}{2}$ will receive a double whammy from the IRS. First, they are likely to be treated as a gain, rather than a return of your premium payment, so they will be subject to income taxes. Second, the IRS will assess an additional 10 percent penalty against the withdrawal or loan. Because of these severe tax limitations, SPLI is ill-suited for young families with moderate incomes. The SPLI product is most appropriate for middle-aged, high-income individuals who want to supplement their retirement plans or cover potential estate planning needs, and who also need some additional life insurance protection.

ADVANTAGES AND DISADVANTAGES OF WHOLE LIFE. The most noteworthy feature of whole life insurance is that premium payments contribute toward building an estate, regardless of how long the insured lives. This feature results because the face value of the policy is paid on death, or alternatively because the insured can borrow against or withdraw cash value—which can be significant, as the final column of Exhibit 8.6 shows—when the need for insurance protection has expired. A corresponding benefit of whole life (except single-premium) is that individuals who need insurance for an entire lifetime can budget their premium payments over a relatively long period, thus eliminating the problems of affordability and uninsurability often encountered with term insurance in later years.

Some people like whole life because the periodic payments force them to save regularly. There is also the favorable tax treatment afforded to accumulated earnings—as your earnings build up on a tax-sheltered basis, the underlying cash value of the policy also increases at a much faster rate than it otherwise would. Insurance experts also point out that the whole life policy offers other potentially valuable options in addition to death protection and cash value. Some of these options include the continuation of coverage after allowing the policy to lapse because premiums were not paid (nonforfeiture option) and the ability to revive an older, favorably priced policy that has lapsed (policy reinstatement). These and other options will be discussed in a later section on insurance contract features.

The most frequently cited disadvantages of whole life insurance are that (1) it provides less death protection per premium dollar than term insurance, and (2) it provides lower yields than many investment vehicles. Returns on most whole life insurance policies are just not all that competitive. As with term insurance, the negative aspects of whole life often arise from misuse of the policy. In other words, a *whole life policy should not be used to obtain maximum return on investment.* However, if a person wishes to combine a given amount of death protection for the entire life of the insured (or until the policy is terminated) with a savings plan that provides a *moderate* tax-sheltered rate of return, whole life insurance may be a wise purchase.

One way to keep the cost of whole life down is to consider the purchase of *low-load* whole life insurance. Low-load products are sold directly by insurers to consumers, sometimes via a toll-free number or over the Internet, thereby eliminating sales agents from the transaction. With traditional whole life policies sold by an agent, sales commissions and marketing expenses account for between 100 and 150 percent of the first year's premium, and between 20 and 25 percent of total premiums paid over the life of the policy. In comparison, only about 5 to 10 percent of low-load policy premiums go to cover selling and marketing expenses. As a result, cash values grow much more quickly. In one case a 50-year-old male was able to purchase a low-load policy with a $500,000 death benefit for an annual premium of $7,500. Within 5 years his cash surrender value was projected to be more than $36,000, although a comparable, fully loaded policy was projected to produce only a $24,000 cash value.

UNIVERSAL LIFE INSURANCE

universal life insurance
A form of cash value insurance that combines term insurance (death benefits) with a tax-deferred savings/investment account that pays interest at competitive money market rates.

Universal life insurance is a form of cash value insurance that combines term insurance, which provides the death benefits of the policy, with a tax-sheltered savings/investment account that pays interest, usually at competitive money market rates. Exhibit 8.7 shows representative premiums and cash values for a $100,000 universal life policy.

The special feature of a universal life policy is that the death protection (or pure insurance) portion and the savings portion are identified separately in its price. This is referred to as *unbundling.* Traditionally, for whole life insurance, you pay a premium to purchase a stated face amount of coverage in a policy with a *fixed cash-value schedule.* Not so with universal life. When you make a premium payment on a universal life policy, part pays administrative fees and the remainder is put into the cash value, or savings portion of the policy, where it earns a certain rate of return. This rate of earnings varies with market yields, but is guaranteed to be more than some stipulated minimum rate (say, 4 percent). Then, each month the cost of 1 month's term insurance is withdrawn from the cash value to purchase the required death protection. As long as there's enough in the savings portion to buy death protection, the policy will stay in force. Should the cash value grow to an unusually large amount, the amount of insurance coverage has to be increased in order for the policy to

EXHIBIT 8.7

REPRESENTATIVE UNIVERSAL LIFE INSURANCE ANNUAL OUTLAYS; $100,000 POLICY, PREFERRED NONSMOKER RATES

Universal life premiums are lower than whole life and can vay over the policy's life. After deducting the cost of the death benefit and any administrative fees from your annual contribution, the rest goes into an accumulation account and builds at a variable rate—in this example, the current rate is 7.4 percent. The guaranteed rate, however, is only 4 percent, so your actual cash value may be less.

	Annual Outlay		Premiums Paid through Year 20		Cash Surrender Value at Year 20*	
Age	Male	Female	Male	Female	Male	Female
25	$2,419	$2,358	$$8,380	$$7,160	$$6,091	$$5,048
30	$2,505	$2,425	$10,100	$$8,500	$$8,137	$$6,176
35	$2,644	$2,534	$12,880	$10,680	$11,235	$$8,453
40	$2,841	$2,682	$16,820	$13,640	$15,107	$11,399
50	$1,469	$1,146	$29,380	$22,920	$25,168	$20,074
60	$2,598	$1,992	$51,960	$39,840	$36,638	$32,633

*Based on an assumed annual rate of 7.4%.

retain its favorable tax treatment (tax laws require that the death benefits in a universal life policy *must always exceed the cash value* by a stipulated amount).

The clear separation of the protection and savings elements in the universal policy has raised the question of whether or not this type of insurance is in fact whole life insurance. This question is important because the accumulation of cash values in whole life policies arises partly from interest credited to them. Under present tax laws, *this accumulation occurs tax-free as long as the cash value does not exceed the total premiums paid to the insurer.* However, if a whole life policy is surrendered for its cash value, and that cash value exceeds the premiums paid, then *the gain* is taxed. As a result of an Internal Revenue Service ruling and federal legislation, universal life policies enjoy the same favorable tax treatment as do other forms of whole life insurance—that is, death benefits are tax-free and, prior to the death of the insured, amounts credited to the cash value, including investment earnings, accumulate on a tax-deferred basis.

BASIC STRUCTURE. Insurance companies sell a variety of policies under the heading of universal life. In spite of the different names, the basic structure of these policies is pretty much the same. The premium you pay for the policy, called the *annual contribution or annual outlay,* is deposited in an *accumulation account.* The insurer credits interest to the account at a current rate and deducts from it the cost of the death benefits (and other expenses). The size of the deduction for the death protection depends on the amount of term insurance to be purchased and the age of the insured. The crediting of interest and the deducting of expenses and insurance coverage costs usually occur monthly. The insurance company sends the insured an annual statement summarizing the monthly credits and deductions.

Within the basic structure of a universal life insurance policy, there are two types of death protection. The first type, known as Option A, provides a level death benefit. As the cash value increases, the amount of pure insurance protection *decreases*. The second type, Option B, provides a stated amount of insurance plus the accumulated cash value. Thus the death benefit at any time varies with the rate of earnings on the savings plan and will increase along with the accumulated cash value.

THE FLEXIBILITY FEATURE. An important characteristic of universal life insurance is its flexible nature. The annual premium you pay can be increased or decreased from year to year. This feature exists because the cost of the death protection *may be covered from either the annual premium or the accumulation account* (that is, cash value). Thus as long as the accumulation account is adequate, you can choose to skip an annual premium and cover the cost of the death protection from the accumulation account. In addition, the death benefit can be increased or decreased, and you can change from the level benefit type of policy to the cash value plus a stated amount of insurance. Note, however, that evidence of insurability is usually required if the death benefit is to be increased.

This flexibility allows you to adapt the levels of death protection to your life-cycle needs. For example, you'll probably want to increase the death benefit when you have another child and, conversely, decrease it when your children are grown. If you get a divorce or your spouse dies, you can adjust the components of a universal life policy to better meet your current financial needs—say, decrease the death benefit and increase the tax-deferred savings portion—whereas with whole life, your policy is fixed.

SOME PRECAUTIONS. One of the attractions of a universal life insurance policy is the promise of the cash value being credited at the "current" rate of interest. For example, the *current* rate of interest may be 5.5 percent, compared with a *guaranteed* minimum rate of 4 percent. Make it a point to find out just what current rate of interest is used to credit earnings to your accumulation account. A common rate is that on 90-day U.S. Treasury bills. Other rates, however, may be used. Another precaution regarding universal life is that you may be attracted to the policy because of the relatively low interest charge on loans that you can take from your cash value. However, cash value equal to the size of the loan is usually then credited with only the *guaranteed interest rate* of 4 to 4.5 percent—thus some or all of what you gain on one hand will be lost on the other, so the net advantage is usually not all that big a deal.

Universal life's flexibility in making premium payments, although an attractive feature, is also one of its major drawbacks. A policyholder who economizes on premium payments in early years may find that he or she must pay higher premiums than originally planned in later policy years to keep the policy in force. Indeed, some policyholders buy universal life expecting their premiums to vanish once cash value builds to a certain level. All too often, however, the premiums never disappear altogether, or, if they do, they reappear when interest rates fall below the rate in effect at the time the policy was purchased.

You should also evaluate the charges or fees that the insurance company levies on its universal life policies. Ask the insurance agent about the front-end load or commission you'll have to pay on the first premium, the expense charge on each annual premium, investment expense charged by the insurer in determining the "current" rate of return, and any other charges you may be assessed. Most states require that the insurance company issue an annual disclosure statement that spells out premiums paid, expenses and mortality costs, interest earned, and beginning and ending cash values.

OTHER TYPES OF LIFE INSURANCE

In addition to term, whole life, and universal life, you can buy several other types of life insurance policies, including variable life insurance, insurance on multiple lives, group life, credit

EXHIBIT 8.8

REPRESENTATIVE VARIABLE LIFE INSURANCE VALUES, $100,000 POLICY, PREFERRED NONSMOKER, MALE, AGE 45

Variable life insurance pays a death benefit related to the policy's investment returns. The cash value created over the life of the policy is also related to investment return. The illustration below shows the effects of 6 percent and 12 percent annual returns over a 20-year period. Lower returns will result in lower cash value and death benefits; higher returns will result in higher cash value and death benefits.

Policy Year	Total Premiums Paid	6% return		12% return	
		Cash value	Death benefit	Cash value	Death benefit
1	$ 1,575	$ 995	$100,995	$ 1,064	$101,064
5	8,705	5,244	105,244	5,705	104,869
10	19,810	10,592	110,592	15,365	115,365
15	33,986	15,093	115,093	27,688	127,688
20	52,079	17,080	117,080	43,912	143,913

life, mortgage life, industrial life insurance, special-purpose policies, and deferred-premium life insurance. These policies serve very diverse needs. Some may help you meet specific needs, although others are simply more expensive alternatives to traditional types of life insurance.

VARIABLE LIFE INSURANCE. A basic feature of *whole* life insurance is that it combines insurance coverage and a savings account into one package. *Universal* life extends this concept by being a bit more aggressive with the savings component, and thereby offering the potential for slightly higher returns and a quicker build-up of cash value. A **variable life insurance** policy goes even further; it allows the policyholder to decide how to invest the money in the savings (cash value) component, thus offering the highest and most attractive level of investment returns. Unlike whole or universal life policies, however, *no minimum return is guaranteed.* In addition, as the name implies, the amount of insurance coverage provided will vary with the profits (and losses) generated in the investment account. Thus, in variable life insurance policies, the amount of death benefits payable are, for the most part, related to the policies' investment returns. Exhibit 8.8 demonstrates how two possible investment return scenarios would effect the cash value and death benefits of a variable life insurance policy for a 45-year-old, nonsmoking male over a 20-year period.

A variable life policy, in short, combines insurance protection with the ability to spread your money over a variety of different investment accounts, all in one convenient, tax-favored package. The investment accounts are set up just like *mutual funds,* and most firms that offer variable life policies let you choose from a full menu of different funds, ranging from money market accounts and bond funds to international investments or aggressively managed stock funds. As a policyholder, you can put your money in any one or more of the funds offered under the policy. You can also freely move your money from one fund to another as market conditions dictate. Furthermore, like all life insurance products, variable policies offer attractive tax benefits: investment earnings can grow within the policy, free of any current taxation; you can switch between funds with no tax consequences; and the policy's death benefit passes tax-free to your beneficiaries.

variable life insurance
Life insurance in which the benefits are related to the returns being generated on the investments selected by the policy holder.

Although all these features may sound great, it's important to keep in mind that variable life puts more emphasis on investments than any other life insurance product. Indeed, many observers view variable life more as an investment vehicle than a life insurance policy—that is, in many respects, they are similar to variable annuities to the extent that they have essentially wrapped an investment product around just enough life insurance coverage to make it legal. Thus, if you want the benefits of higher investment returns, you must also be willing to assume the risks of reduced insurance coverage. Bigger investment profits do, indeed, lead to more death benefits and an accelerated build-up in cash value, but investments can also end up losing money (sometimes in a big way), and that can lead to lower cash values and reduced insurance coverage although it can never fall below the minimum death benefit stated in the policy. Clearly, *you should use extreme care when buying variable life insurance.*

 Find out how well Prudential Insurance variable life policies are performing at **www.prudential.com/insurance**, where you will also find a variety of interactive tools to educate yourself about the company's products.

INSURANCE ON MULTIPLE LIVES. Reflecting the rapid growth of two-income families, knowledgeable planners and agents are recommending **joint life insurance,** or "first-to-die" insurance, as it's frequently called. Joint life pays the full death benefit when the *first* spouse dies, and is appropriate where the death of either spouse would result in a loss of income that would jeopardize the family's lifestyle. This policy usually is about 10 to 25 percent cheaper than buying two policies with the same death benefit—one on each income provider. What happens if both earners are killed in a common disaster, such as a car accident? This should not be a problem because most joint life policies have a *double indemnity* clause whereby twice the normal death benefit is paid to the beneficiaries.

> **joint life insurance**
> Life insurance on two lives that pays the full death benefit when the *first* insured person dies; also known as "first-to-die" insurance.

Companies have developed a variety of joint policies tailored to different needs. Some policies allow the surviving party to convert the policy to one providing a death benefit to his or her beneficiary. Others insure unrelated persons. These policies are ideal for business partners. If one dies, the insurance provides the funds for the remaining partner(s) to buy his or her share of the business.

In contrast, **survivorship life insurance**, also known as "last-to-die" insurance, covers two parties (who are usually married), but pay benefits only when the second insured person dies. This type of policy is normally used to help pay estate taxes. In the United States estate taxes are minimal when one married partner dies and leaves his or her estate to the surviving spouse. When the surviving spouse dies, however, his or her estate may be subject to federal estate tax rates as high as 55 percent (a rate that will drop to 50 percent in 2002 and 43 percent in 2007). Survivorship insurance immediately generates the dollars to pay such a tax. Because of certain exclusions allowed by the government, a family generally should not be concerned about estate taxes unless the total estate, including life insurance death benefits, exceeds $700,000 (a ceiling that will rise to $1 million in 2002 and to $3.5 million in 2009). (*Note:* The 2001 Tax Act introduced other estate tax revisions that are described in greater detail in Chapter 15.)

> **survivorship life insurance**
> Life insurance that covers two lives, but pays only when the *second* insured person dies; also known as "last-to-die" insurance.

GROUP LIFE INSURANCE. Under **group life insurance,** one master policy is issued, and each eligible member of the group receives a certificate of insurance. Group life is nearly always term insurance, and the premium is based on the characteristics of the group as a whole, rather than related to any specific individual. Employers often provide group life insurance as a fringe benefit for their employees. However, just about any type of group (be it a labor union, a professional association, or an alumni organization) can secure a group life policy, as long as the insurance is only incidental to the reason for the group.

> **group life insurance**
> A type of life insurance that provides a master policy for a group and a certificate of insurance for each eligible group member.

Accounting for about one-third of all life insurance in the United States, group life insurance is one of the fastest-growing areas of insurance. Many group life policies now offer coverage for dependents in addition to the group members. In addition, group life policies generally provide that if individual members leave the group, they may continue the coverage by converting their protection to individually issued whole life policies—such conversion normally does not require evidence of insurability so long as it occurs within a specified period. Of course, after conversion, the individual pays all premiums. Before buying additional coverage purchased through a group plan or converting a group policy to an individual one, it's important to compare rates. Often the premiums are more expensive than other readily available sources of term insurance.

As noted in Chapters 1 and 2, the availability of group coverage through employee benefit programs should be considered when developing a life insurance program. However, because of its potentially temporary nature and relatively low benefit amount (often equal to about 1 year's salary), it should fulfill only low-priority insurance needs. Only in rare cases should a family rely solely on group life insurance to fulfill its primary income-protection requirements.

CREDIT LIFE INSURANCE. Banks, finance companies, and other lenders generally sell **credit life insurance** in conjunction with installment loans. Usually credit life is a term policy of less than 5 years, with a face value that decreases at the same rate as the outstanding balance on the loan. Although liquidating debts on the death of a family breadwinner is often desirable, it's usually preferable to do so through an individual's term or whole life insurance rather than buying a separate credit life insurance policy. This is because credit life is one of the most expensive forms of life insurance—and one you should therefore avoid. Contrary to popular belief, a lender cannot legally reject a loan just because the potential borrower chooses not to buy credit life insurance.

credit life insurance
A type of life insurance sold in conjunction with installment loans; the coverage decreases at the same rate as the outstanding loan balance.

MORTGAGE LIFE INSURANCE. **Mortgage life insurance** is a form of term life insurance designed to pay off the mortgage balance on a home in event of the death of the borrower. As in the case of credit life, this need can usually be met less expensively by shopping the market for a suitable decreasing-term policy. Credit life and mortgage life are relatively expensive because lenders, when selecting insurers to represent, are often highly motivated by the amount of sales commission they will receive. As might be expected, an insurer who pays high commissions is often one who charges a high premium.

mortgage life insurance
A term life insurance policy on the borrower's life that names the lender as beneficiary, allowing the mortgage balance to be automatically paid off in event of the borrower's death.

INDUSTRIAL LIFE INSURANCE. **Industrial life insurance,** now called **home service life,** is a type of whole life insurance issued in policies with small face amounts, often $1,000 or less. Agents call on policyholders weekly or monthly to collect the premiums. The term *industrial* arose because when these policies first became popular they were sold primarily to low-paid industrial wage earners. Industrial life insurance costs a good deal more per $1,000 of coverage than regular whole life policies, primarily because of its high marketing costs. Even so, some insurance authorities believe that industrial life insurance offers the only practical way to deliver coverage to low-income families. Although many of the largest life insurance providers started out in this business, industrial/home service life now accounts for less than 1 percent of the total amount of life insurance in force in the United States.

industrial life insurance (home service life)
A type of whole life insurance issued in policies with relatively small face amounts (usually $1,000 or less); policyholders pay weekly or monthly premiums to purchase these policies.

SPECIAL-PURPOSE POLICIES. Certain types of policies combine some form of term and whole life insurance for coverage on one or more family members. Before buying one of these policies, try to determine whether such a policy truly meets your needs or is primarily a marketing gimmick. Although many of the special-purpose policies are sold under various company trade names, general designations are as follows: family plan policies, family income policies, family maintenance policies, and jumping juveniles.

One appealing feature of certain "family plans" is that they offer the guaranteed insurability of children. For instance, the policy might specify that when the children reach a certain age (say, 21 or 25), they can convert to a specified type of life insurance at a predetermined price regardless of their physical condition. Although special-purpose policies can fill some family needs, more than likely you'll find that these needs can be satisfied at less cost if you simply buy convertible term life or continuous-premium whole life as separate policies.

deferred-premium life insurance
Life insurance that allows for the deferral of premium payments as evidenced by a signed legally binding installment loan contract.

DEFERRED-PREMIUM LIFE INSURANCE. Several life insurance companies actively market their products to college students. However, these companies know that most college students have little money to spend on life insurance. Their answer is to sign students up for **deferred-premium life insurance,** whereby a modest amount of life insurance is actually *purchased with an interest-bearing debt obligation* that is later paid off through a series of deferred-premium payments. Apart from the fact that most college students simply do not have enough significant financial responsibilities to justify life insurance, these deferred-premium plans are generally undesirable because they place students in debt. Students who accept this type of payment plan generally are required to sign a legally binding installment loan contract (as defined in Chapter 7). Although deferred-premium plans have some legitimate business and tax-planning uses, for the majority of college students, their purchase makes no sense at all!

CONCEPT CHECK

8-8. What is *term life insurance?* Describe some of the common types of term life insurance policies.

8-9. What are the advantages and disadvantages of term life insurance?

8-10. Explain how *whole life insurance* offers financial protection to an individual throughout his or her life.

8-11. Describe the different types of whole life policies. What are the advantages and disadvantages of whole life insurance?

8-12. What is *universal life insurance?* Explain how it differs from whole life and variable life insurance.

8-13. Explain how *group life insurance* differs from standard term life insurance. What do employees stand to gain from group life?

8-14. Why should the following types of life insurance contracts be avoided? (a) *credit life insurance,* (b) *mortgage life insurance,* (c) *industrial life insurance (home service life),* and (d) *deferred-premium life insurance.*

■ Key Features of Life Insurance Policies [LG5]

When you buy a life insurance policy, you will enter into a contract with your insurance firm. The provisions in this contract spell out the policyholder's and the insurer's rights and obligations, and the features of the policy being purchased. Unfortunately, there's no such thing as a standard life insurance policy. Each insurance company uses its own wording. Policies can also vary from state to state, depending on the law of the state where the policy is sold. Nevertheless, certain elements are common in most life insurance contracts: (1) life insurance contract features and (2) other policy features.

LIFE INSURANCE CONTRACT FEATURES

The key features found in most life insurance contracts are (1) the beneficiary clause, (2) settlement options, (3) policy loans, (4) payment of premiums, (5) grace period, (6) nonforfeiture options, (7) policy reinstatement, and (8) change of policy.

BENEFICIARY CLAUSE. All life insurance policies should have one or more beneficiaries. The **beneficiary** is the person who will receive the death benefits of the policy on the insured's death. Otherwise, death benefits are paid to the estate of the deceased and are subject to the often lengthy and expensive legal procedure of going through probate. An insured person is able to name both a *primary beneficiary* and various *contingent beneficiaries*. The primary beneficiary will receive the entire death benefit if he or she is surviving when the insured dies. If the primary beneficiary does not survive the insured, the insurer will distribute the death benefits to the contingent beneficiary or beneficiaries. If neither primary nor contingent beneficiaries are living at the death of the insured, the death benefits pass to the estate of the insured and are distributed by the probate court according to the insured's will or, if no will exists, according to state law.

> **beneficiary**
> A person who receives the death benefits of a life insurance policy on the insured's death.

When naming the beneficiary, the policyholder should make sure the identification is clear. For example, a man could buy a policy and simply designate the beneficiary as "my wife." However, if he later divorces and remarries, there could be a controversy as to which "wife" was entitled to the benefits. Similarly, if children are the intended beneficiaries, problems can arise when other children become part of the insured's family. For instance, if a man named "my children" as beneficiaries, would proceeds be payable only to his natural and legitimate children, or would his adopted, illegitimate, or stepchildren also share in the proceeds? Obviously, you should consider changing your named beneficiary if circumstances, such as marital status, change.

What if *both* the insured and the primary beneficiary, such as a husband and wife, were to lose their lives in a common disaster, such as an auto accident? According to state laws, the contingent beneficiaries normally would receive the death benefits if the deaths were determined to be simultaneous. However, if the primary beneficiary were determined to have survived the insured, even by a matter of minutes, instead of going to the named contingent beneficiaries, the death benefits may instead go to the primary beneficiary's estate. This means that the death benefit would ultimately end up in the hands of the primary beneficiary's selected heirs. Imagine what could happen in a common disaster for a married couple, where both spouses have children by a previous marriage. The $500,000 death benefit from a deceased wife's insurance policy could wind up in the hands of her husband's children, with her own children receiving nothing, just because her husband survived her by a few minutes! Even for couples with no previous marriages, carefully laid plans to avoid estate taxes could be upset by a common disaster where their deaths were not quite simultaneous. (These so-called common disaster problems have been somewhat mitigated in states that have adopted the latest version of the Uniform Probate Code, which holds that a surviving spouse who expires within *120 hours (5 days)* of the insured's death will still be considered to have died simultaneously.)

To combat the common disaster problem, the insured should use a *survival clause* on the beneficiary form. For instance, a woman could specify her primary beneficiary as "My husband, Alfred, if he survives me by 60 days." As contingent beneficiaries, she could then name, "My children, Betty and Carl, in equal shares." This simple survival clause should ensure that death benefits go to her children if both she and her husband are fatally injured in a common disaster, even though he might survive her by a short time.

In summary, make sure you have named both a primary and a contingent beneficiary in any life insurance policies you buy and that no mistake can be made in determining whom the beneficiaries are. Also, be sure to use survival clauses where appropriate. Note, too, that the person you name as a beneficiary can be changed at any time as long as you did not indicate an *irrevocable beneficiary* when you took out the policy. Thus, if your wishes change, all you need to do is notify the insurance company—easy to do but also easy to forget. Therefore, when you write the premium check each year, verify that your policy's named beneficiary is still your desired beneficiary. (Similarly, you should update any prescribed settlement options—discussed next—with desired changes.)

SETTLEMENT OPTIONS. Insurance companies generally offer several ways of paying life insurance policy death proceeds. How the insurance funds will be allocated can be permanently established by the policyholder before his or her death, or left up to the beneficiary when the policy matures on the insured's death.

- **Lump sum.** This is the most common settlement option, chosen by more than 95 percent of policyholders. The entire death benefit is paid in a single amount, allowing beneficiaries to use or invest the proceeds soon after death occurs.
- **Interest only.** The insurance company keeps policy proceeds for a specified time; the beneficiary receives interest payments, usually at some guaranteed rate. This option can be useful when there is no current need for the principal—for example, proceeds could be left on deposit until children go to college, with interest supplementing family income. Typically, however, interest rates paid by insurers are lower than other savings vehicles.
- **Fixed-period.** The face amount of the policy, along with interest earned, is paid to the beneficiary over a fixed time. For example, a 55-year-old beneficiary may need additional income until social security benefits start.
- **Fixed-amount.** The beneficiary receives policy proceeds in regular payments of a fixed amount until the proceeds run out.
- **Life income.** The insurer guarantees to pay the beneficiary a certain payment for the rest of his or her life, based on the beneficiary's sex, age when benefits start, life expectancy, the policy face value, and interest rate assumptions. This option appeals to beneficiaries who don't want to outlive the income from policy proceeds and be dependent on others for support. An interesting variation of this settlement option is the *life-income-with-period-certain option,* whereby the company guarantees a specified number of payments that pass to a secondary beneficiary if the original recipient dies before the period ends.

The *Money in Action* box on page 345 provides useful advice with regard to filing a life insurance claim when the insured dies.

policy loan
An advance, secured by the cash value of a whole life insurance policy, made by an insurer to the policyholder.

POLICY LOANS. An advance made by a life insurance company to a policyholder is called a **policy loan.** These loans are available on *whole life policies* (nearly all whole life policies provide for such loans), and are secured by the cash value of the life insurance policy. Although these loans do *not* have to be repaid, any balance plus interest on the loan remaining at the death of the insured is *subtracted from the proceeds of the policy.* The rate of interest charged on older policies is customarily 5 to 8 percent per annum, and it is stated in the policy. Newer policies, in contrast, offer either a fixed-rate loan, with an interest rate normally set at about 7 or 8 percent, or a rate that varies with market interest rates on high-quality bonds. Some policies let the insured choose whether the loans will be at fixed or variable rates.

Policy loans should be taken out only in unusual circumstances because they can reduce death proceeds. One long-time advocate of whole life insurance has decried policy loans as "stealing from your widow." Although not all would agree with this emotional

MONEY IN ACTION

Filing A Life Insurance Claim

Although no one likes to think about the death of a loved one, it's important to know how to file a life insurance claim before the situation arises. This will expedite the process and provide surviving family members with access to cash quickly so they can meet pressing needs.

The first step when a family member dies is to identify the existence of all life insurance policies. Ideally, every person should leave clear instructions to their heirs concerning their existing life insurance policies. These instructions should include the policy itself, and contact information for the insurance agent or insurance company. It's unwise to keep insurance policies in bank safe-deposit boxes. In most cases these boxes are sealed temporarily when the owner dies and the heirs may have difficulty obtaining the policy paperwork.

If a policy or other information isn't readily found, don't assume that the deceased didn't have life insurance. Contact past employers to see if they had group life insurance. Some banks and credit unions also offer free life insurance to deposit customers, so it's a good idea to check with your relative's banks. If you believe the individual did buy a life insurance policy but can't find the policy or the name of the insurance company, try going through their old checkbooks or credit card receipts. If they paid for the policy by check or credit card, you may be able to find the name of the insurance company this way. In some cases the deceased's lawyer, banker, or accountant may know where the insured had his or her life insurance policy. If all else fails, there are search firms, called "heir finders," who will contact major insurance companies to see if your relative had an insurance policy. However, these firms typically charge up to 10 to 20 percent of the life insurance proceeds and should only be used as a last resort.

Once the insurance policy has been identified, contact the insurance company or agent for the necessary forms to file a claim. Every insurance company will require you to provide at least one certified copy of the insured's death certificate, so be sure to ask the funeral director for several copies.

If the insured didn't specify a payment option when the policy was purchased, the beneficiaries will decide how they wish to receive payments. As we've already discussed, each option has pluses and minuses. After the paperwork has been completed, insurance companies generally issue a settlement quickly. However, if the insured lets the policy lapse before his or her death, beneficiaries will usually receive nothing.

Sources: Mark Cybulski, "What Happens to Old Life Insurance Policies?" Insure.com, **www.insure.com**, downloaded December 21, 2000; "Filing a Claim," the American Council of Life Insurance, downloaded from **www.acli.com**; and Charles K. Plotnick and Stephan R. Leimberg, *How to Settle an Estate*, Penguin Putnam Inc. (New York), 1998, pp. 100–104.

assessment, life insurance is intended to provide basic financial protection for your dependents, and spending those proceeds prematurely definitely defeats the purpose of life insurance. On the other hand, because these loans are less expensive than borrowing from other financial institutions, they may appeal to those who wish to keep their borrowing costs low and are not bothered by the accompanying loss of death proceeds if the loans are not repaid. A word of caution: *Be very careful with these loans because unless certain conditions are met, the IRS may treat them as withdrawals, meaning they could be subject to tax penalties.* If you're in any way unsure, consult your insurance agent or a tax advisor.

PAYMENT OF PREMIUMS. All life insurance contracts have a provision that specifies when premiums, which are normally paid in advance, are due. With most insurers, the policyholder may elect to pay premiums annually, semiannually, quarterly, or monthly. In most cases insurance companies charge a fee if you decide to pay more often than annually. Some premium checks are mailed directly to the company; in other instances, a sales agent collects premiums from the policyholder. Another method of payment allows policyholders to pay premiums through automatic deduction from a bank account. In the case of the death of a policyholder who has paid premiums more than 1 month in advance, many companies refund those premiums along with the policy death proceeds.

GRACE PERIOD. The *grace period* permits the policyholder to retain full death protection for a short period (usually 31 days) after missing a premium payment date. In other words, you won't lose your insurance protection just because you're a little late in making the premium payment. If the insured dies during the grace period, the face amount of the policy less the unpaid premium is paid to the beneficiary.

NONFORFEITURE OPTIONS. As discussed earlier, a *nonforfeiture option* provides a cash value life insurance policyholder with some benefits even when a policy is terminated prior to its maturity. State laws require that all permanent whole, universal, or variable life policies (and term contracts that cover an extended period) contain a nonforfeiture provision. Instead of just taking a check in the amount of the cash value of the policy, companies usually offer the two options—*paid-up insurance* and *extended-term insurance*—described below.

- **Paid-up insurance.** The policyholder receives a policy exactly like the terminated one, except with a lower face value. In effect, the policyholder uses the cash value to buy a new, single-premium policy. For example, a policy canceled after 10 years might have a cash value of $90.84 per $1,000 of face value, which will buy $236 of paid-up whole life insurance. The cash value continues to grow because of future interest earnings, even though the policyholder makes no further premium payments. This option is useful when a person's income and need for death protection declines—when they reach age 60 or 65, for example—yet they still want some coverage.
- **Extended-term insurance.** The insured uses the accumulated cash value to buy a term life policy for the same face value as the lapsed policy. The coverage period is based on the amount of term protection a single-premium payment (equal to the total cash value) buys at the insured's present age. This option usually goes into effect automatically if the policyholder quits paying premiums and gives no instructions to the insurer.

POLICY REINSTATEMENT. As long as a whole life policy is under the reduced paid-up option or the extended-term option, the policyholder may reinstate the original policy by paying all back premiums plus interest at a stated rate, and providing evidence that he or she can pass a physical examination and meet any other insurability requirements. *Reinstatement* basically revives the original contractual relationship between the company and the policyholder. Most often, the policyholder must reinstate the policy within a specified period (3 to 5 years) after the policy has lapsed. However, before exercising a reinstatement option, a policyholder should determine whether buying a new policy (from the same or a different company) might be less costly.

CHANGE OF POLICY. Many life insurance contracts contain a provision that permits the insured to switch from one policy form to another. For instance, policyholders may decide that they would rather have paid-up at age 65 policies as opposed to their current continuous-premium whole life policies. A change of policy provision would allow this change without penalty. When policyholders change from high- to lower-premium policies, they may need to prove insurability. This requirement reduces the possibility of adverse selection against the company.

OTHER POLICY FEATURES

In addition to the key contractual features described in the preceding section, some other policy features you should be aware of are (1) multiple indemnity clause, (2) disability clause, (3) guaranteed purchase option, (4) suicide clause, (5) exclusions, (6) participation, and (7) living benefits.

MULTIPLE INDEMNITY CLAUSE. **Multiple** (most often double or triple) **indemnity clauses** double or triple the face amount of the policy if the insured dies as a result of an accident. This benefit is usually offered to the policyholder at a small additional cost. Many insurance authorities dismiss the use of a multiple indemnity benefit as irrational. This coverage should be ignored as a source of funds when programming insurance needs because it provides no protection in the event of death due to illness.

multiple indemnity clause
A clause in a life insurance policy that typically doubles or triples the policy's face amount in the event of the insured's accidental death.

DISABILITY CLAUSE. A **disability clause** in a life insurance contract may contain a waiver-of-premium benefit alone or coupled with disability income. A *waiver-of-premium benefit* excuses the payment of premiums on the life insurance policy if the insured becomes totally and permanently disabled prior to age 60 (or sometimes age 65). Under the *disability income portion,* the insured is granted not only a waiver of premium, but also receives a monthly income equal to $5 or $10 per $1,000 of policy face value. Some insurers will continue these payments for the life of the insured, whereas others terminate them at age 65. Disability riders for waiver-of-premium and disability income protection are relatively inexpensive and can be added to most whole life policies, but generally not to term policies.

disability clause
A clause in a life insurance contract containing a waiver-of-premium benefit alone or coupled with disability income.

GUARANTEED PURCHASE OPTION. The policyholder who has a **guaranteed purchase option** may purchase additional coverage at stipulated intervals without providing evidence of insurability. This option is frequently offered to buyers of a whole life policy who are under age 40. The increases in coverage usually can be purchased every 3, 4, or 5 years in amounts equal to the amount of the original policy or $10,000, whichever is lower. This option should be quite attractive to individuals whose life insurance needs and ability to pay are expected to increase over a 5- to 15-year period.

guaranteed purchase option
An option in a life insurance contract giving the policyholder the right to purchase additional coverage at stipulated intervals without providing evidence of insurability.

SUICIDE CLAUSE. Nearly all life insurance policies have a *suicide clause* that voids the contract if an insured commits suicide within a certain period, normally 2 years after the policy's inception. In these cases the company simply returns the premiums that have been paid. If an insured takes his or her own life after this initial period has elapsed, the policy proceeds are paid without question.

EXCLUSIONS. Although all private insurance policies exclude some types of losses, life policies offer very broad protection. In addition to the suicide clause, the only other common exclusions are aviation and war. In *aviation exclusions,* the primary types of losses not covered are those occurring when the insured is a relatively inexperienced private pilot or is flying in military aircraft. No restrictions apply to fare-paying passengers of commercial airlines. (Most life insurers accept without premium surcharge the pilots and crews of scheduled airliners.)

War exclusions are often inserted in policies in anticipation of or during periods of combat. They typically provide that should the insured die as a result of war, a return of premiums with interest will be made. War exclusions are intended to guard against adverse selection, which could materially disrupt the mortality experience of the company and consequently its solvency.

Should the potential insured have a hazardous occupation or hobby, the company will either exclude coverage for that activity or charge an additional premium to cover the added risk exposure. However, seldom, if ever, would a company be able to modify the premium charged or coverage offered should the insured take up, say, Formula One racing or hang gliding *after* a policy is issued.

participating policy
A life insurance policy that pays dividends reflecting the difference between the premiums that are charged and the amount of premium necessary to fund the actual mortality experience of the company.

PARTICIPATION. In a **participating policy** the policyholder is entitled to receive *policy dividends* that reflect the difference between the premiums that are charged and the amount of premium necessary to fund the actual mortality experience of the company. When the base premium schedule for participating policies is established, a company estimates what it believes its mortality and investment experience will be, and then adds a generous margin of safety to these figures. The premiums charged the policyholder are based on these overly conservative estimates.

When a company's loss experience is more favorable than estimated, a return of the overcharge is made to policyholders in the form of policy dividends. These policy dividends may be received as cash payments (which, because they are viewed as a return of premium, are not subject to taxation), left with the company to earn interest, used to buy additional paid-up coverage, or applied toward the next premium payment. The dividend option selected is purely a matter of the individual policyholder's preference. Note that it is advantageous to use the dividends to buy paid-up options when more insurance coverage is desired because these additions are available at their *net* rates, meaning they contain no load for sales expenses and consequently provide an economical way to increase coverage.

LIVING BENEFITS. A number of major life insurers, including Aetna, John Hancock, and Prudential, offer, or have offered in the past, so-called *living benefits options* with whole and universal life policies. Living benefits (or *accelerated benefits*) allow the insured to receive a percentage of his or her death benefits prior to death. Some insurers offer this option free of charge to established policyholders if the insured suffers a terminal illness expected to result in death within a specified period, such as 6 months to a year; or needs an expensive treatment, such as an organ transplant, to survive. For example, an insured dying of cancer received more than $44,000 of a $45,000 whole life policy and used the money to retire mortgage and car loans. In this case, the insured died within 2 months. If the insured had been expected to live longer, he would have received a lower living benefit. In another case, a woman needing a liver transplant to survive used living benefits from her life insurance to cover the almost $200,000 not covered by health insurance. Doing so preserved her other financial resources and prevented even greater hardships later.

Some insurers are marketing a *living benefit rider,* which allows advances of a policy's death benefit, usually about 2 percent per month, to pay for long-term health care, such as nursing home expenses. This rider can cost an extra 5 to 15 percent of the normal life insurance premium, and benefits are capped as a percentage of the death benefit. For example, a living benefit rider may cap benefits at 50 percent of the death benefit, so an insured with a $100,000 policy could receive a maximum of $2,000 per month for 25 months. The remaining $50,000 death benefit would pass to the beneficiaries on the death of the insured. Although human interest stories have been written about dying persons who receive "peace of mind" because of living benefits, critics say that these options subvert the primary purpose of life insurance, which is to provide adequate cash payments to beneficiaries to cover expenses incurred and income lost because of an insured's death.

CONCEPT CHECK

8-15. What is a *beneficiary?* A contingent beneficiary? Explain why it is essential to designate a beneficiary.

8-16. Explain the basic settlement options available for the payment of life insurance proceeds on a person's death.

8-17. What do nonforfeiture options accomplish? Differentiate between *paid-up insurance* and *extended-term insurance.*

8-18. Explain the following clauses often found in life insurance policies: (a) *multiple indemnity clause,* (b) *disability clause,* and (c) *suicide clause.* Give some examples of common exclusions.

8-19. Describe what is meant by a *participating life insurance policy,* and explain the role of policy dividends in these policies.

■ Buying Life Insurance [LG6]

Selecting a life insurance policy is a complex process. Before you begin looking for a policy, it's important to understand the competitive features of different life insurance policies. Then you can estimate how much life insurance you need to cover your dependents' financial requirements. Next, you should evaluate the different types of policies available to meet your needs, and familiarize yourself with the various provisions that life insurance contracts typically include. With this basic understanding in hand, you can then shop the market for the insurance protection best suited for you.

In the next section we'll briefly review the *needs* concept, and the types of coverages you might want to consider. To help you shop wisely, we'll then explain how to compare costs and features of policies, and provide criteria for selecting life insurance companies and agents.

REVIEW NEEDS AND COVERAGES

As discussed earlier, life insurance is used in a person's financial program to fill the gap between the resources that will be available after death and those that will be needed. In addition, some life insurance policies can effectively be used as savings vehicles.

For most young families on limited budgets, the need for death protection greatly exceeds their need to save. If you fall into this category, guaranteed renewable and convertible term insurance should account for the largest portion of your insurance protection. They provide the most life insurance coverage for the least cost, thereby preserving financial resources for meeting immediate and future consumption and savings goals. Healthy older people with many other financial resources may also prefer to use term policies to meet specific coverage needs.

Most families also need some amount of permanent insurance and savings, which a continuous-premium whole life policy can satisfy. Some financial advisors recommend that you use cash value insurance to cover your *permanent need for insurance*—the amount your dependents will need regardless of the age at which you die. (Although term insurance is less expensive, you may not be able to buy term insurance as you get older, or it may be too expensive.) Such needs may include final expenses—funeral costs and estate taxes—and either the survivor's retirement need (Period 3 in Worksheet 8.1) or additional insurance coverage, whichever is less. This amount is different for every person. Using these guidelines, the Bensons in our earlier example would need about $121,000 in permanent (whole life) insurance [in Worksheet 8.1: $15,000 final expenses (Section A, line 2) plus about $106,000 Period 3 living expenses (Section A, line 3h)] and another $176,000 in term life [in Worksheet 8.1: about $297,000 (Section C) minus about $121,000 permanent insurance]. Limited-payment whole life, variable life, and single-premium whole life policies should be purchased only when the primary goal is savings or additional tax-deferred investments and not protection against financial loss resulting from death.

Whole life or other cash value policies may make sense in several other situations as well. For example, a family history of heart disease, cancer, or similar conditions may increase your risk of developing health problems and make it hard to qualify for term insurance at a later date. If you are already over 50, term life insurance may be too expensive. Or, perhaps you've "maxed" out your other tax-deferred savings options and want to buy cash value insurance to accumulate additional retirement funds. But before buying a cash value policy, remember that many of these policies don't build up any cash value at all for the first 3 to 5 years and, on top of that, may have surrender penalties for about 10 to 15 years. Dropping a cash value policy too soon means losing the heavy up-front fees and any long-term tax benefits. So analyze all the consequences if someone suggests replacing an existing cash value policy; it may be preferable to keep it and supplement your coverage with a new policy.

COMPARE COSTS AND FEATURES

The cost of a life insurance policy can vary considerably from company to company, even for the same amount and type of coverage. Comparison shopping, therefore, can save you thousands of dollars over the life of your policy, as the comparison of term life rates for four different insurers shown in Exhibit 8.9 clearly demonstrates.

Term life quote services, available over the phone or on the Internet, can streamline the selection process by providing you, free of charge, with the names of several companies offering the lowest-cost policies based on your specifications. For example, *Quotesmith* (800-431-1147), *Life Quote* (800-521-7873), *TermQuote* (800-444-8376), and *SelectQuote* (800-343-1985) maintain databases of life insurance companies and will also act as your agent to buy the policy if you wish. In addition, Quotesmith and TermQuote provide quotes for both whole life and term insurance. Also, don't overlook companies who sell directly to the public or offer low-load policies, such as John Alden, Ameritas, Lincoln Benefit, and USAA.

Probably the fastest growing source of life insurance quotes and policies in recent years is the Internet. Indeed, it's now easier than ever to not only obtain quick, real-time quotes, but also buy insurance electronically! Buying on the Internet allows you to avoid dealing with pesky insurance salespeople, plus you can purchase the policies (usually term insurance only) on very cost-effective terms. For example, one major life insurer offers discounts of up to 20 percent for term life policies purchased online. Of course, you'll still need a physical exam, but often the insurance company will send a qualified technician/nurse to your house or office to take a blood sample and other basic readings. The *Money in Action* box on page 352 will help you make the best use of the Internet when you are ready to buy life insurance.

 Discover how easy it is to get quotes on term and whole life policies at QuickQuote's life insurance center, **www.quickquote.com/lihome.html**.

If you smoke or have a health problem, such as high cholesterol or high blood pressure, spending time to check out several companies can really pay off. Some companies are more willing to accept these risks than others and may even give you preferred rates if, within a certain period, you correct the problem. However, until you do your homework, you won't know which policy offers you the coverage you need at the lowest cost. Keep in mind, if you do have an unusual health problem or some other type of complication, an agent-sold policy may actually be cheaper than the low-cost alternatives.

 **EXHIBIT 8.9**

10-YEAR TERM LIFE PREMIUM COST COMPARISONS; $250,000 POLICY, PREFERRED RATES

The price of a 10-year level term life policy varies considerably among companies. The following table shows the extremes a male in excellent health might find when comparing the cost of a $250,000 10-year level term life policy.

Age	Company	10-Year Cost
25	A	$ 2,000
	B	1,500
	C	5,875
	D	2,580
35	A	2,000
	B	1,530
	C	6,015
	D	3,300
45	A	2,600
	B	2,700
	C	12,515
	D	6,550
55	A	5,900
	B	5,850
	C	28,815
	D	14,630

It's not enough, however, to look at current rates. You'll also need to ask how long the rates are locked in and about guaranteed rates—the maximum you can be charged when you renew. Although a guaranteed policy may cost another $20 a year, you won't be hit with unexpected rate increases later. Know how long you need the coverage and find the best rates for the total period; low premiums for a 5-year policy may jump when you renew for additional coverage. In addition, be sure you are getting the features you need, like convertibility of term policies.

Finally, be sure the policies you are comparing *are similar in terms of provisions and amounts.* In other words, you should not compare a $100,000 term life policy from one company with a $150,000 universal life policy from another. Instead, *you should first decide how much and what kind of policy you want and then compare costs.* For similar cash value policies, you may find it useful to compare interest-adjusted cost indexes that are often shown on policy illustrations. The *surrender cost index* measures the policy's cost if you surrender it at a certain point, typically 10 or 20 years, assuming premiums and dividends earn 5 percent interest. The *net payment cost index* is calculated in a similar manner but assumes that the policy is kept in force.

SELECT A COMPANY

Choosing a life insurance company is an important part of shopping for life insurance. In addition to looking for a firm that provides reasonably priced products, attractive contract features, and good customer service, it is vital to consider the financial health of any insurance firm before buying a life insurance policy. You want to be certain that the company will be around and have the assets to pay your beneficiaries should you die. Even before you die,

MONEY IN ACTION

Surfing the Internet for a Life Insurance Policy

Consumers are buying everything from books to food on the Internet, but when it comes to buying life insurance, electronic commerce is still in its infancy. Although hundreds of life insurance–related Web sites now exist, only about 2 percent of all policies are currently sold via the Internet. Industry experts expect that figure to rise as Web-based shopping services become more sophisticated and consumers gain confidence.

The Internet is already the place to turn for additional information on the various types of life insurance policies available. Industry groups like the American Council of Life Insurance, **www.acli.com**, and the Life and Health Insurance Foundation, **www.life-line.org**, operate sites that compare the features of term, whole, universal, and variable life insurance policies in great detail. These sites also provide useful calculators to help you determine the amount of life insurance your family needs.

Once you've determined the type and amount of life insurance you need, online shopping sites can help you educate yourself about the costs of various policies. Although initially most online shopping sites provided quotes only for term insurance, some now offer quotes on other options, such as whole and variable life policies. QuickQuote, **www.quickquote.com**, for example, gives you a fast list of instant quotes from higher-rated insurance carriers. The side-by-side comparison makes it easy to compare insurance carriers and their different policies. Other large shopping sites include Quotesmith,

www.quotesmith.com, and AccuQuote, **www.accuquote.com**. Insure.com, **www.insure.com**, offers instant quotes and also gives useful rating information for insurance companies.

Insurance companies themselves are also taking to the Internet. Nearly all large insurance companies now have their own Web sites. The best of these sites, like Prudential, **www.prudential.com**, and Nationwide, **www.bestofAmerica.com**, give online quotes, display policy prospectuses, and let existing policyholders check on the status of their policies.

Keep in mind, however, that just because you can get an online quote doesn't mean you'll be able to buy the policy at that price. The main reason: your final price will depend on the results of your physical examination and other factors. And online shopping doesn't provide personal service to help you sort through various options. For that, you'll still need an insurance broker or agent. Getting the basic data from the Internet will help make you an intelligent consumer, but using a human being may still be the best way to find a policy most suited to your needs.

Sources: Carrie Coolidge, "Life Insurance," *Forbes Best of the Web*, September 11, 2000, p. 166; Tracey Drury, "Insurance Industry Opening the 'Net," *Business First of Buffalo*, May 1, 2000, downloaded from **www.bizjournals.com/buffalo/stories/2000/05/01/focus1.html**; Vanessa Richardson, "Solving the Mysteries of Life Insurance: Where to Go on the Web," *Money* Magazine Web site, **www.money.com**, downloaded December 8, 2000; "Expanded Offerings," *Boston Business Journal*, May 15, 2000, downloaded from **www.bizjournals.com/boston/stories/2000/05/15/focus1.html**.

however, the financial stability of your insurance company is important. If the company fails, you may be forced to buy a new policy at less-favorable rates.

To narrow your choices, age and size are useful indicators. Unless a good reason exists to do otherwise, you should probably limit the companies you consider to those that have been doing business for 25 years or more and that have annual premium volume in excess of $50 million. Although these criteria will rule out a lot of smaller firms, there will still be plenty of companies left from which to choose. You may also find that one company is preferable for your term protection and another for your whole life needs.

Factors to consider before making the final choice include the firm's reputation, financial history, commissions and other fees, and the specifics of their policy provisions. If you're choosing a company for a cash value life insurance policy, the company's investment performance and dividend history is also an important consideration.

EXHIBIT 8.10

MAJOR INSURANCE RATING AGENCIES

The three biggest insurance rating agencies are A.M. Best Company, Moody's Investor Services, and Standard & Poor's Corporation; Duff & Phelps and Weiss Ratings, Inc. are smaller but growing rating agencies. Contact information for each of these agencies is given here.

A.M. Best Company
Address: Ambest Road, Oldwick, NJ 08858
Phone: 800-424-BEST
Internet address: **www.ambest.com**
Top three grades: A++, A+, and A

Duff & Phelps
Address: 55 E. Monroe Street, Suite 3500,
  Chicago, IL 60601
Phone: 312-368-3198
Internet address: **www.insure.com**
Top three grades: AAA, AA+, and AA

Moody's Investor Services
Address: 99 Church Street,
  New York, NY 10007
Phone: 212-553-0377
Internet address: **www.moodys.com**
Top three grades: Aaa, Aa1, and Aa2

Standard & Poor's Corporation
Address: 25 Broadway, New York, NY 10004
Phone: 212-208-1527
Internet address: **www.standardpoors.com**
Top three grades: AAA, AA+, and AA

Weiss Ratings, Inc.
Address: 4176 Burns Road, Palm Beach
  Gardens, FL 33410
Phone: 800-289-9222
Internet address: **www.weissratings.com**
Top three grades: A, A−, B

How do you find all of this information? Luckily, private rating agencies have done much of the work for you. These agencies use publicly available financial data from insurance firms to analyze their debt structure, pricing practices, and management strategies in an effort to determine financial stability. The purpose is to assess the insurance company's ability to pay future claims made by policyholders, known as their *claims paying ability*. In most cases insurance firms pay ratings agencies a fee for this rating service. The ratings agencies then give each insurance firm a "grade" based on their analysis of the firm's financial data.

The three biggest rating agencies include A.M. Best Company, Moody's Investor Service, and Standard & Poor's Corporation (S&P). Two smaller, but growing, rating agencies are Duff & Phelps and Weiss Ratings, Inc. Weiss does not charge a fee to the insurance firms it examines. Exhibit 8.10 provides detailed contact information for each of the major rating agencies, including their Internet address. Basic rating information is usually free of charge at these sites. You can also usually find these ratings on the insurance company's Web site, or you can ask your agent how the company is rated by Best's, Moody's, and S&P.

A.M. Best's site, **www.ambest.com**, offers more than insurance company ratings. The site also has the latest insurance industry news and trends, an insurance products guide, and links to state insurance regulatory agencies.

Each rating agency uses its own grading system. When looking at these ratings, however, keep several things in mind. With the exception of Moody's and Weiss, the ratings agencies will not publish a firm's rating if the insurer requests that it be withheld. Obviously, an insurance firm receiving a low rating is more likely to suppress publication, something that should be

EXHIBIT 8.11

LIFE INSURERS WITH TOP RATINGS FOR FINANCIAL STRENGTH

These life insurers are among those that are regularly rated at or near the top by at least two of the three leading rating agencies. These grades reflect each insurer's long-term ability to pay promised benefits to holders of insurance policies and annuities.

| | Assigned Rating | | |
Company	A.M. Best	Moody's	Standard & Poor's
AIG Life Insurance	A++	Aaa	AAA
Massachusetts Mutual Life	A++	Aa1	AAA
Northwestern Mutual Life	A++	Aaa	AAA
State Farm Life Insurance	A++	Aaa	AAA
USAA Life Insurance	A++	Aa1	AAA

viewed as a clear signal that it is an insurance company to avoid. Also, remember that a high rating doesn't ensure lasting financial stability. Even highly rated insurance firms can quickly encounter financial difficulties. In fact, in a recent report, A.M. Best noted that fewer life insurers are receiving top ratings. In 1990 there were 290 life insurers in A.M. Best's "Superior" ratings class; today, there are only 216, a 25 percent drop. It's not a bad idea, therefore, to check the ratings of your insurance carrier periodically even after you have purchased a policy.

Most experts agree that it's wise to purchase life insurance only from insurance firms that are assigned ratings by at least two of the major rating agencies and are consistently rated in the top two or three categories (say, Aaa, Aa1, or Aa2 by Moody's) by each of the major agencies from which they received ratings. Exhibit 8.11 provides a list of some highly rated life insurance companies.

SELECT AN AGENT

There's an old axiom in the life insurance business that life insurance is sold, not bought. Life insurance agents play a major role in most people's decision to buy life insurance. Unless you plan to buy all of your life insurance via the Internet, the selection of a good life insurance agent is important because you will be relying on him or her for guidance with respect to some very important financial decisions. Don't assume that just because agents are licensed they are competent and will serve your best interests. Consider an agent's formal and professional level of educational attainment. Does the agent have a college degree with a major in business or insurance? Does the agent have a professional designation, such as Chartered Life Underwriter (CLU), Chartered Financial Consultant (ChFC), or Certified Financial Planner (CFP)? These designations are awarded only to those who meet certain experience requirements and pass comprehensive examinations in such fields as life and health insurance, estate and pension planning, investments, and federal income tax law.

In addition, observe how an agent reacts to your questions. Does he or she use fancy buzzwords and stock answers or instead listen attentively and, after a period of thought, logically answer your questions? These and other personal characteristics should be considered. In most instances you should talk with several agents and discuss the pros and cons of each agent with your spouse before committing yourself. Then, when you have decided, call and ask that agent to return for another visit.

When seeking a good life insurance agent, try to obtain recommendations from other professionals who work with agents. For example, bankers in trust departments, attorneys, and accountants who are specialists in estate planning are usually good sources. In contrast, be a bit wary of selecting an agent simply because of the agent's aggressiveness in soliciting your patronage.

 Looking for an insurance agent? Try **www.iiaa.org**, a site sponsored by the Independent Insurance Agents of America, Inc.

CONCEPT CHECK

8-20. Briefly describe the steps to take when you shop for and buy life insurance.

8-21. Briefly describe the insurance company ratings assigned by A.M. Best, Moody's, and S&P's. Why is it important to know how a company is rated? What ratings would you look for in a life insurance company? Explain.

SUMMARY

LG1. **Explain the role insurance planning plays in personal financial planning, and the relationship between risk and insurance.** Adequate life insurance coverage is vital to sound personal financial planning because it not only protects that which you have already acquired, but also helps ensure the attainment of unfulfilled financial goals. The whole notion of insurance is based on the concept of risk and the different methods of handling it, including risk avoidance, loss prevention and control, risk assumption, and insurance (a cost-effective procedure that allows families to reduce financial risks by sharing losses). Through the underwriting process, insurance companies decide whom they consider an acceptable risk and the premiums to charge for coverage.

LG2. **Discuss the primary reasons for life insurance and identify those who need coverage.** Life insurance fills the gap between the financial resources available to your dependents if you should die prematurely and what they need to maintain a given lifestyle. Some policies provide only a death benefit, whereas others also have a savings component. If you have children or elderly relatives who count on your income to support them, you should include life insurance as one of several financial resources to meet their requirements. If you have no dependents, however, you probably don't need life insurance. Your life insurance needs change over your life cycle and should be reviewed regularly.

LG3. **Calculate how much life insurance you need.** There are a number of ways to determine the amount of life insurance a family should have. Although the multiple earnings approach is simple to use, most experts agree that the needs approach is the best procedure. It systematically considers such variables as family income, household and other expenses, debt liquidation, liquidity needs, and special requirements, which are then compared with the financial resources available to meet these needs.

LG4. **Differentiate among the various types of life insurance policies and describe their advantages and disadvantages.** The three basic types of life insurance policies are term life, whole life, and universal life. Term life insurance basically provides a stipulated amount of death benefits, whereas whole life combines death benefits with a modest savings program, and universal life packages term insurance with a tax-deferred investment account that pays competitive money market returns. Other types of life insurance include variable life, joint life, survivorship life, group life, credit life, mortgage life, industrial life, and deferred-premium life.

LG5. Become familiar with the key features of life insurance policies. Some important features of life insurance policies you should become familiar with are the beneficiary clause, settlement options, policy loans, payment of premiums, grace period, nonforfeiture options, policy reinstatement, and change of policy. Other policy features include multiple indemnity and disability clauses, guaranteed purchase options, suicide clause, exclusions, participation, and living benefits.

LG6. Choose the best life insurance policy for your needs at the lowest cost. To get as much coverage as possible from your insurance dollar, it is important that you not only compare costs but also buy the proper amount of life insurance and pick the right type of insurance policy. Beyond the provisions and cost of the insurance policy, you should also carefully consider the financial stability of the insurer offering the policy, paying special attention to the ratings assigned by major rating agencies. The Internet has become an excellent resource for comparison shopping. In addition to selecting a company, you must also select an agent that understands your needs.

QUESTIONS AND PROBLEMS

1. *Use Worksheet 8.1.* Janna Meyers' 65-year-old mother, who was recently widowed, now lives with her. Janna is 40, single, and earns $45,000 a year as a human resources officer for a bank, which provides life insurance coverage equal to her annual salary. She owns a condo with a market value of $100,000 and has a $70,000 mortgage on it. Other debts include a $5,000 auto loan and $3,500 in various credit card balances. Her 401(k) plan has a current balance of $24,500, and she keeps $7,500 in a money market account for emergencies. Janna is concerned that her existing insurance coverage (all of which is provided by her employer) may not be adequate to provide for her mother, who is in good health, if Janna should die. She estimates that her mother would need about $1,500 a month for living expenses, and her only income is $800 a month in social security survivor's benefits. Janna estimates that her final expenses would be about $5,000, that her mother would live another 20 years, and that she wants to provide a $15,000 contingency fund as well. Use Worksheet 8.1 to calculate Janna's total life insurance requirements and recommend the type of policy she should buy.

2. *Use Worksheet 8.1.* Given your current personal financial situation, do you feel you need life insurance coverage? Why or why not? Use Worksheet 8.1 to confirm your answer and calculate how much additional insurance (if any) you might need to purchase.

3. Using the premium schedules provided in Exhibits 8.2, 8.3, and 8.6, how much in *annual* premiums would a 25-year-old male have to pay for $100,000 of annual renewable term, level-premium term, and whole life insurance (assume a 5-year term or period of coverage)? How much would a 25-year-old woman have to pay for the same coverage? Consider a 40-year-old male (or female): Using annual premiums, compare the cost of 10 years of coverage under annual renewable and level-premium term options and whole life insurance coverage. Compare the pluses and minuses of each type of policy in relation to their price differences

4. Monica and Manuel Juarez are a dual-career couple who just had their first child. Manuel, age 29, already has a group life insurance policy, but Monica's employer does not offer life insurance. A financial planner is recommending that the 25-year-old Monica buy a $250,000 whole life policy with an annual premium of $1,670—the policy has an assumed rate of earnings of 8 percent a year. Help Monica evaluate this advice and decide on an appropriate course of action.

5. While at lunch with a group of coworkers, one of your friends mentions that he plans to buy a variable life insurance policy because it provides a good annual return and is a good way to build savings for his 5-year-old's college education. Another colleague says that she is adding coverage through the group plan's additional insurance option. What advice would you give them?

APPLYING PERSONAL FINANCE

Do-it-Yourself Life Insurance

Because the thought of death is not a particularly pleasant one, life insurance is a topic many people choose *not* to consider, even though it is very important to their overall financial well-being. This project will ask you to use your imagination to define your life insurance needs.

To complete this project, try to look ahead to when you are 35 years old. You may be married, have children, own a home and one or two cars, have a mortgage and other types of consumer debt, etc. You and/or your spouse, if you are married, will hold a job that pays fairly well (what do you think you will be making when you are 35?), and you will probably be covered by a group life insurance policy where you work (for purposes of this project, assume the amount of such coverage is equal to one year's salary). (*Note:* If you are already 35 or over, try to look ahead another five or ten years.) Now, use the *Needs Approach* and *Worksheet 8.1* to estimate your life insurance needs. Are you going to need any additional life insurance coverage? If so, how much? What kind of life insurance would you want to buy: term life, whole life, universal life, or variable life? Explain. Do not forget the cost of the coverage; use the premium schedules in Exhibits 8.2, 8.3, and 8.6, 8.7, and 8.8 to estimate the annual cost of alternative insurance policies (*Note:* All data applies to you at age 35). Carefully consider several different types (or combinations) of insurance policies on the basis of both coverage and cost. Will you be able to afford all the life insurance you need?

CONTEMPORARY CASE APPLICATIONS

8.1   Lee Hsiah's Insurance Decision: Whole Life, Variable Life, or Term Life?

Lee Hsiah, a 38-year-old widowed mother of three children, ages 12, 10, and 4, works as a product analyst for Ralston Purina. Although she is covered by a group life insurance policy at work, she feels, based on some rough calculations, that she needs additional protection. David Dustimer, an insurance agent from Siegfried Insurance, has been trying to persuade Lee to buy a $150,000, 25-year, limited-payment whole life policy. However, Lee favors a variable life policy. To further complicate matters, Lee's father feels that term life insurance is more suitable to the needs of her young family. To resolve the issue, Lee has decided to consult Terry Patrick, a childhood friend who is now a professor of insurance at a nearby university.

Questions
1. Explain to Lee the differences between a (a) whole life policy, (b) variable life policy, and (c) term life policy.
2. What are the major advantages and disadvantages of each type of policy?
3. In what way is a whole life policy superior to either a variable life or term life policy? In what way is a variable life policy superior? How about term life insurance?
4. Given the limited information in the case, which type of policy would you recommend for Ms. Hsiah? Defend and explain your recommendations.

8.2   The Kings Want to Know When Enough Is Enough

Dave and Karen King are a two-income couple in their early 30s. They have two children, ages 6 and 3. Dave's monthly take-home pay is $1,800 and Karen's is $2,100. The Kings feel that because they are a two-income family, they both should have adequate life insurance coverage. Accordingly, they are presently trying to decide how much life insurance *each one of them* needs.

To begin with, they would like to set up an education fund for their children in the amount of $80,000 to provide college funds of $10,000 a year—in today's dollars—for 4 years for each child. Moreover, in the event of either's death, they want the surviving spouse to have the funds to pay off all outstanding debts, including the $140,000 mortgage on their house. They estimate that they have $15,000 in consumer installment loans and credit cards. They also project that if either of them dies, the other probably will be left with about $10,000 in final estate and burial expenses.

As far as their annual income needs are concerned, Dave and Karen both feel very strongly that each should have enough insurance to replace their respective current income levels until the youngest child turns 18 (a period of 15 years). Though neither Dave nor Karen would be eligible for social security survivor's benefits because they both intend to continue working, both children would qualify, in the (combined) amount of around $1,400 a month. The Kings have amassed about $75,000 in investments, and they have a decreasing-term life policy *on each other* in the amount of $85,000, which would be used to partially pay off the mortgage. Further, Dave has a $60,000 group policy at work and Karen a $90,000 group policy.

Questions

1. Assume that Dave's gross annual income is $30,000 and Karen's is $40,000. Their insurance agent has given them a multiple earnings table showing that the earnings multiple to replace 75 percent of their lost earnings is 8.7 for Dave and 7.4 for Karen. Use this approach to find the amount of life insurance each should have if they wanted to replace 75 percent of their lost earnings.

2. *Use Worksheet 8.1* to find the additional insurance needed on both Dave's and Karen's lives. (Because Dave and Karen hold secure, well-paying jobs, both agree they won't need any additional help once the kids are grown; each also agrees that he/she will have plenty of income from their social security and company pension benefits to take care of themselves in retirement. Thus, when preparing the worksheet, assume "funding needs" of zero in Periods 2 and 3.)

3. Is there a difference in your answers to Questions 1 and 2? If so, why? Which number do you think is more indicative of the King's life insurance needs? Using the amounts computed in Question 2 (employing the needs approach), what kind of life insurance policy would you recommend for Dave? For Karen? Briefly explain your answers.

MONEY ONLINE

INSURE YOUR LIFE!

Note: Web addresses change frequently, so you may need to determine the home page and do a site search to find the page or topic that's referenced.

1. **www.usaaedfoundation.org**
   Who needs life insurance? Click on "Insurance" at the USAA Educational Foundation's Web site and scroll down to "Life Insurance" to find out. Other topics to explore

include "How Insurable Are You?" "Should You Replace an Existing Policy?" and "Military Insurance Options."

2. **www.northwesternmutual.com**

   How much life insurance do you need? Click on "Calculators" and work through Northwestern Mutual's interactive "Life Insurance" calculator to determine the amount of protection you may need to provide for your loved ones.

3. **www.financenter.com**

   Learn all about term life insurance. Click on "Insurance" and then on "Learn" at the FinanCenter's Web site to find the basics of term life insurance, learn the advantages and disadvantages of term life insurance, and compare the features of term insurance to those of universal life and whole life insurance.

4. **www.usaaedfoundation.org**

   How do you compare life insurance policies? Click on "Insurance" and then on "Comparing Life Insurance Policies" at USAA Educational Foundation's Web site for a guide to help you comparison shop. Discover the two cost indexes adopted by the National Association of Insurance Commissioners that can help you compare similar policies and determine the better value.

5. **www.actuary.com**

   Need to find your life insurance company's Web site? Click on "Life Insurance Companies" at the Actuary.com site for an extensive listing of links to various life insurance companies.

6. **www.insure.com/ratings/sandp.cfm**

   Find the top-rated life insurance companies that sell policies in your state. Select "Individual Life" for the "Type of Insurance," your state, and "AAA (extremely strong)" under "Rated" to pull up the list for your state. To learn more about a particular company, click on "Insurer Profile" for background information and a financial report.

7. **www.standardandpoors.com/ResourceCenter/InsurerFinStren.html**

   What do the Standard and Poor's ratings mean? Find a detailed explanation of the financial strength ratings assigned to insurance companies at Standard and Poor's Web site.

8. **www.financenter.com/learn/insurance_learn.fcs**

   What should you look for in a life insurance agent? Click on "Finding a Good Agent" at the FinanCenter's Web site for a guide in selecting an agent. Learn what questions a good agent should ask you and discover the difference between a captive and an independent agent.

9. **www.actuary.com/careerinfo.htm**

   Are you interested in a career as an actuary? Consult the Web site of Actuary.com to learn about an actuary's role in assessing risk for insurance companies, the different types of actuaries, the actuarial exams, and the employment prospects for actuaries.

10. **www.insure.com/life**

    What happens when life insurance policies are lost? Can you dispute a beneficiary on a life insurance policy? How does divorce affect your life insurance needs? Consult Insure.com's Web site to find these topics addressed or browse through their many other life-insurance-related articles.

Just for Fun!

11. **www.northwesternmutual.com**

    Play the Longevity Game! Click on "Calculators" at Northwestern Mutual's Web site, scroll down to "The Longevity Game," and work your way through this interactive quiz to get a general idea of how long you may live past retirement. While you're there, read through the secrets of long life offered by centenarians.

Chapter 9

Insuring Your Health

LEARNING GOALS

LG1. Discuss how the health care industry is changing and why you should have adequate health care insurance.

LG2. Differentiate among the major types of health care plans and identify the major private and public providers of health insurance and their programs.

LG3. Explain the basic types of medical expense coverage and policy provisions for medical expense plans.

LG4. Assess the need for and features of long-term care insurance.

LG5. Evaluate your need for and provisions of disability income insurance.

LG6. Analyze your own health care insurance needs and shop for appropriate coverage.

Solving the Health Care Puzzle

It's easy to take your health insurance plan for granted—until it isn't there anymore. In 1999 Jim Moss, an executive for a large financial institution, was laid off after his company merged with another one. Instead of moving to another large corporation, he and his wife Barbara started a small, personal-finance software company.

"We didn't realize how lucky we were," Jim says. "My company paid a large portion of our health insurance premiums and we only had to cover an annual deductible of $250 per family member. We didn't think twice about seeing a doctor for even minor complaints." For the next 18 months the Mosses (both in their early 40s) and their three children (ages 12, 10, and 7), continued with the group plan under federal COBRA legislation. But the premiums were $650 a month ($7,800 a year), and the costs were expected to rise even further.

Because their small company couldn't afford the comprehensive coverage Jim's former employer provided, the Mosses evaluated their health care priorities and looked for ways to reduce costs and solve the health care puzzle. What they needed most was coverage for catastrophic illness, surgical procedures, and outpatient testing. After exploring individual policies and group plans offered by trade associations, they switched in 2001 to an insurance plan offered by an association of small businesses. Their monthly premiums fell to about $400, but they had to make trade-offs. "We opted to 'self-insure' for routine care by choosing a high deductible, $1,000, and a 50 percent copayment. We have coverage for serious illness so we won't be ruined financially. And we've invested the money saved on premiums so it's available to help with medical expenses."

In this chapter you will learn about the different kinds of health care plans, who provides them, and various coverage options, so you can evaluate and choose the right health care insurance for your needs.

■ The Need for Health Care Insurance Coverage [LG1]

Assume you have done everything possible to establish and implement fully operational personal financial plans. You have an effective budget, keep track of expenditures, have several ongoing investment and retirement plans, and so forth. Imagine what would happen to all of this if you or a member of your family became seriously ill. Without adequate health care insurance, all your financial accomplishments and goals could be destroyed.

Consider the case of Paul Murphy, who fell off a ladder while painting his house, breaking his leg and badly spraining his back. His 5 days in the hospital were followed by 4 weeks of recuperation and physical therapy treatments before Paul could return to work. In all, his medical and hospitalization costs—ambulance, x-rays, setting the fracture, traction for his back, hospital room, physical therapy, etc.—were more than $13,000, in addition to $5,000 in lost pay.

Such expenses certainly would devastate most family budgets. That is why the next best thing to good health is probably a good health care insurance plan. If you ever have a serious illness or accident, you may discover that the road to recovery can involve not only

 **EXHIBIT 9.1**

THE RISING COST OF HEALTH CARE

Since 1960, when personal spending for health care was $23.6 billion, health care costs have risen sharply, at a rate faster than inflation, to more than $1 trillion in 2000.

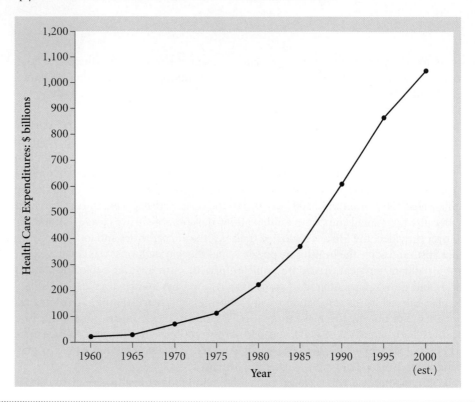

Source: *Health, United States, 2000* (Hyattsville, Maryland: National Center for Health Statistics, 2000), p. 327.

the physical pain from sickness and injury, but also economic pain. The cost can easily run into the tens of thousands of dollars once you add up hospitalization and medical expenses and the loss of income while you recover. Clearly, without adequate health care insurance to pay expenses and disability income insurance to replace lost income, a person's economic health can suffer long after he or she has recovered physically.

AN INDUSTRY IN CHANGE

The health care field is undergoing rapid changes today as rising health care costs have prompted new ways of delivering health services. Not long ago, a consumer's basic choices were the doctor's office, hospital, or health maintenance organization (HMO). Today, you may also visit a *neighborhood emergency center* for minor emergencies (on a walk-in, often 24-hour-a-day basis) or an *ambulatory outpatient surgical center* for minor surgery (both of these options are usually less costly than comparable in-hospital treatment), or a *preferred provider organization (PPO)* for hospital and medical services. These and other new ways of providing health care are discussed later in this chapter.

Another ongoing change is the rising cost of health care and the percentage of personal expenditures devoted to it. Health care represents about 13.5 percent of the U.S. GDP,

EXHIBIT 9.2

WHERE YOUR HEALTH CARE DOLLAR GOES

More than half of your health care expenditures goes toward hospitalization and physicians' costs.

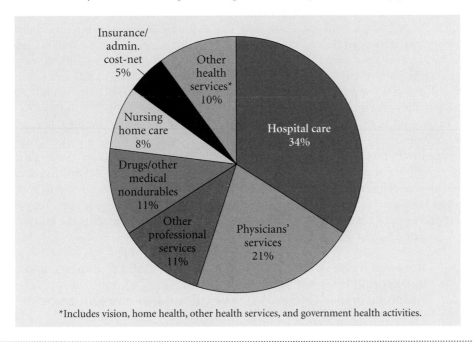

Insurance/ admin. cost-net 5%
Other health services* 10%
Nursing home care 8%
Drugs/other medical nondurables 11%
Other professional services 11%
Hospital care 34%
Physicians' services 21%

*Includes vision, home health, other health services, and government health activities.

Source: *Health Care Financing Review,* Winter 1999, cited in Table 153, *Statistical Abstract of the United States: 2000* (Washington, D.C.: U.S. Census Bureau, 2000), p. 109.

higher than any other country. As Exhibit 9.1 shows, personal health care expenditures have risen sharply since 1960, to more than *$1 trillion,* and per capita health care expenditures are now more than $4,100. Hospital costs accounted for more than one-third of those expenditures, followed by physicians' services, as Exhibit 9.2 illustrates. Health care costs continue to rise faster than prices in general. In 2000, for example, medical care costs increased by more than 5 percent, whereas the consumer price index (CPI) rose at an annual rate of 3.4 percent. Health insurance premiums are also on the rise, with projected increases as high as 10 percent a year.

Several major factors account for this phenomenon, chief among them probably being the aging U.S. population (which needs more health care), the government's Medicare and Medicaid programs, and the rapid growth in the broad base of private health care plans. About 84 out of every 100 noninstitutionalized Americans are now eligible for at least some cost reimbursement for losses resulting from illness or accident. In addition, technological advances in diagnostic and treatment techniques, new drug therapies, and major acquisitions of expensive new health care equipment and facilities by hospitals and clinics have pushed costs upward. A poor demand-and-supply distribution of health care facilities and services may be yet another factor. Administrative costs, excessive paperwork, increased regulation, and insurance fraud also contribute to rising costs.

The implementation of managed care and cost containment programs (discussed later in this chapter) has slowed the rate of growth in health care costs somewhat. Critics of managed care say the tradeoff has been lower quality of care. Meanwhile, about 42 million Americans have no health care insurance and probably another 20 million are underinsured.

MAKING SENSE OF IT ALL

If we ranked consumer insurance programs on a complexity scale, term life insurance would be at the "simple" end and health insurance at the other end. In all but rare instances life insurance pays regardless of the cause of loss. What's more, the loss itself is seldom arguable, and the amount of the loss is the face amount of the policy. In addition, each life insurance policy you own will pay regardless of any other policies you have; there are no deductibles, waiting periods, participation clauses, or chances of cancellation; and differences in policy provisions among leading insurers are relatively slight.

In contrast, each of these issues is pertinent to health insurance coverage. Because of these complicating factors, you'll need a systematic approach to design the best program for your health care needs. The wide disparity in the quality of policies makes caution imperative when shopping among them. You need to learn the different types and sources of health care plans, the types of medical expense coverage and policy provisions, and the types of long-term care and disability income coverage. Next, you need to inventory your needs and existing coverage. With that task completed, you can then shop the market for the right protection at the best price.

 How much will health care insurance cost? Get a free quote and background information, including a glossary of policy terms, at Health Insurance Quotes Wiz, **www.healthinsurancewiz.com**.

CONCEPT CHECK

> 9-1.   Why should health care insurance planning be included in your personal financial plan?
>
> 9-2.   What factors have contributed to today's high costs of health care?

■ Types and Sources of Health Care Plans [LG2]

You can obtain health care coverage in the form of an indemnity plan or a managed care plan—the fastest-growing segment of the health-care delivery industry. Both types of plans provide financial aid for losses arising from illness or accidents. Your may have a group plan through your employer or some other group or an individual plan purchased directly from the provider or a government agency. Let's now look more closely at the types of plans from which you can choose and who provides them.

TYPES OF HEALTH CARE PLANS

Most health care plans fall into one of two categories: traditional *indemnity (fee-for-service) plans* and *managed care plans,* which include health maintenance organizations (HMOs), preferred provider organizations (PPOs), and similar groups. Of Americans covered by health care insurance, about 40 percent use HMOs and 60 percent have other forms of health insurance.

TRADITIONAL INDEMNITY (FEE-FOR-SERVICE) PLANS. Traditional **indemnity (fee-for-service) plans** were the dominant form of health care insurance as recently as 1988, when they accounted for 71 percent of all private health insurance plans. By 2000, this figure had dropped to about 35 percent. (Many individual plans fall into this category; only 8 percent of those who obtain group health insurance from their employer choose indemnity plans.) With these plans, the person or organization from which you obtain health care services is separate from the insurer. The insurer pays the provider or reimburses you for expenses. You usually have unlimited choice of doctors and hospitals. To receive payment, you submit claims for medical treatment. Reimbursement is typically 80 percent of eligible costs incurred after payment of a deductible, which can range from $100 to $2,000 or more. The lower your deductible, the higher your premium payment.

The amount you receive may be based on 80 percent of the *usual, customary, and reasonable (UCR) charges*—what the insurer considers the prevailing fees within your area, *not* what your doctor or hospital actually charges. If your doctor charges more than the UCR, you may be responsible for the full amount of the excess. UCR charges vary significantly among insurers, so you may wish to compare your doctor's fees with what a plan pays. Some carriers offer indemnity plans wherein physicians who accept the insurance agree to accept the UCR payments set by the insurer.

MANAGED CARE PLANS. **Managed care plans** make up the fastest growing segment of the health care industry; the various types of these plans enroll about 65 percent of all Americans covered by health care insurance, and this percentage is increasing at a rapid pace. In a managed care plan subscribers/users contract with and make monthly payments *directly to the organization that provides the health care service.* Insurance companies may not even be involved—although today most major insurance companies offer both indemnity and managed care plans. Although managed care plans take different forms, they share certain features:

- Members receive comprehensive health care services from a designated group of doctors, hospitals, and other providers, who must meet the managed care provider's specific selection standards.
- These plans use various strategies to provide cost-efficient medical care, such as controlling the amount of care provided and emphasizing prevention of illness.

The insured pays no deductibles and only a small fee, or copayment, for office visits; most medical services—including preventive and routine care that indemnity plans may not cover—are fully covered when obtained from plan providers. HMOs, both group HMOs and individual practice associations (IPAs), and PPOs are examples of managed care plans. The *Money in Action* box on page 366 explains how you can get the most from your managed care health plan.

Health Maintenance Organization. Today more than 80 million people in the United States (about 30 percent of the total population) belong to one of more than 640 **health maintenance organizations (HMOs).** An HMO is an organization consisting of hospitals, physicians, and other health care personnel who have joined together to provide comprehensive health care services to its members. The plan includes outpatient care, such as minor surgery, doctors' office visits, and x-ray and laboratory services; hospital inpatient care; surgery; maternity care; mental health care; and prescriptions. As a member of an HMO, you pay a monthly fee that varies according to the number of persons in your family. You may also pay a flat fee of $5 to $15 each time you use an outpatient service or need a prescribed drug. However, there are no other charges to worry about—there are no doctors' fees, x-ray charges, or other expenses to HMO members who use the facilities for their health care needs.

---

indemnity (fee-for-service) plan Health care insurance plan in which the person or organization from which you get the health care services is separate from the insurer, who pays the provider or reimburses you for a specified percentage of eligible costs after payment of a deductible. These plans usually provide unlimited choice of doctors and hospitals.

managed care plan A health care plan in which subscribers/users contract directly with the provider organization, which uses a designated group of providers meeting specific selection criteria to furnish comprehensive health care services for a fixed fee. These plans emphasize cost control and preventive treatment.

health maintenance organization (HMO) An organization consisting of hospitals, physicians, and other health care personnel who have joined together to provide comprehensive health care services to its members.

MONEY IN ACTION

Choosing the Right Managed Care Plan

Over the past decade, managed care has literally taken over the health care industry. This form of health care delivery has done a good job of containing costs and emphasizing preventive care. Instead of the old fee-for-service system, in which health care providers are paid for the specific services they provide, managed care companies collect a monthly fee and provide whatever care is necessary for that fee.

Critics contend that managed care companies are managing costs but not providing quality care. Everyone represented in the managed care business, from employers to insurers to doctors, is trying to deliver care at the lowest possible cost. Often, quality suffers when an organization cuts overhead. You might wait weeks for an appointment with a doctor, for example. If you go outside your plan's health care network to find special expertise, you're likely to pay extra fees. It's not surprising that a Harris poll showed that Americans rated managed care firms second to last—just ahead of tobacco companies—when asked what industries were doing a good job serving the consumer. Even if unpopular, however, managed care is a fact of life, particularly for employees of large companies. To be an intelligent consumer, you must be your own best advocate.

Once you've joined a plan, the first step is to select a primary care physician (PCP) from the many listed. Besides taking care of your general medical needs, your PCP acts as the "gatekeeper" who decides if you need to undergo lab tests, see a specialist, or check into a hospital. Narrow your search by deciding which type of PCP you're likely to need on a regular basis. For example, if you have heart problems, look for an internist with a subspecialty in cardiology. Once you've winnowed your choice down to two or three doctors, check their credentials—where they went to medical school, whether they're board certified in a specialty, and where they have hospital admitting privileges. Finally, ask to meet each doctor and during the interview ask how much time is available for consultations. Your PCP is your health care partner, so make sure you are comfortable with his or her bedside manner.

The second step is to learn the ropes. Every managed care plan has a different set of rules. Even doctors, many of whom participate in several plans, have trouble keeping the rules straight. Let's say you're referred to a specialist and wind up visiting that specialist several times. However, your managed care rules say you're allowed only three visits. You may have to pay the difference out of your pocket, unless you know the rules up front. Or let's say a non-network surgeon is going to perform an operation on you. Even if the surgery is performed in a network hospital, you may have to pay the hospital bill because the doctor is not in the plan. Knowing ahead of time will help you decide if the extra expense is worth it.

The third step is to know how to cope with a managed care plan that refuses to authorize care because they deem it medically unnecessary. Remember that the plan's financial incentive is to do fewer procedures, not more. The best solution is to be prepared to go to a doctor outside the system for a second opinion if you think your managed care plan is wrong. If you're convinced that you need the care, you may have to pay for it outside your plan and then fight your case—either through the appropriate channels within the plan or, if necessary, in court. Despite some highly publicized cases, this scenario is relatively rare, but it illustrates a weakness in a managed care system that attempts to standardize care in order to provide cost efficiencies.

Sources: Karen Cheney, "How to Be a Managed Care Winner," *Money,* July 1997, p. 122; *Guide to Managed Care: Choosing and Using a Health Plan,* Health Insurance Association of America, **www.hiaa.org/cons/choosing.html**.

The primary purpose of HMOs is to reduce the costs of health care by using resources more efficiently and by practicing "preventive medicine"—most HMOs provide physical exams and sponsor pro-health activities such as smoking-cessation clinics, exercise programs, and so on. The advantage to members is that they are not faced with exclusions, deductibles, coinsurance, or filing insurance claims. The primary disadvantage is that members are not always able to choose their physicians. Also, members of HMOs should be sure to ask about the benefits provided should they need care outside the geographic area of their HMO.

About 20 percent of all HMO enrollees belong to a **group HMO.** In this traditional form the HMO employs a group of doctors to provide health care services *from a central facility.* These HMOs have developed primarily in larger cities. Usually the doctors and the hospital are in the same complex. Of the remaining 80 percent, half belong to *individual practice associations (IPAs)* and half to a mixed HMO that combines the features of a group HMO and IPA.

Individual Practice Association. An **individual practice association (IPA),** the most popular type of HMO, differs from a group HMO in that its services are *not provided from a central facility.* IPA physicians (who practice out of their own offices) and community hospitals provide services to IPA members and non-members alike. The financial and service arrangements of an IPA are similar to a group HMO, with only the physical facility being different. As a member of an IPA, you prepay monthly and are entitled to a wide range of health care services. IPAs appeal to people who would like some choice of physician. They also extend the advantages of an HMO into less-populated regions where central facilities are not feasible.

Preferred Provider Organization. A **preferred provider organization (PPO)** is a managed care plan that has characteristics of both the IPA form of HMO and an insurance plan. A PPO provides greater flexibility than traditional HMOs, offering comprehensive health care services to its subscribers within a network of physicians and hospitals. In addition, it provides insurance coverage for medical services not provided by the PPO network. A PPO, which can be administered by an insurance company or a provider group, contracts for services from designated physicians and hospitals who agree to accept a negotiated fee schedule. You will benefit from the lower price if you use those physicians and hospitals. Like other forms of managed care, PPOs use certain techniques, such as reviewing proposed treatment, to assure the efficient and cost-effective delivery of health care.

Other Managed Care Plans. In addition to the plans described above, you may encounter two other managed care plans. The **exclusive provider organization (EPO)** is a variation of a PPO. Like a PPO, it contracts with providers to offer services to members at reduced cost, but reimburses only when affiliated providers are used. Plan members who use a nonaffiliated provider must bear the entire cost. The **point-of-service (POS) plan** is a hybrid form of HMO that allows members to go outside the HMO network for care. Payment for non-affiliated physician services is similar to indemnity plan payments: The plan pays a specified percentage of the cost after satisfaction of an annual deductible. This plan is becoming more popular because it combines the features of the HMO with freedom of choice.

WHO PROVIDES HEALTH CARE INSURANCE?

Third-party providers of health care insurance cover about 80 percent of personal health care expenditures. The major sources of health care insurance include private companies—health care insurance companies, managed care organizations, and Blue Cross/Blue Shield plans, which may be purchased through a group or on an individual basis—and government agencies. Private health care insurance plans cover more than 72 percent of the people in the United States, with about 67 percent receiving all or part of their coverage from employer-sponsored health plans. Until recently, there were clear distinctions among the private providers and the health care plans they offered. Today, however, these differences have blurred, and there are many organizations from which to choose the right plan for

group HMO
An HMO that provides health care services *from a central facility;* most prevalent in larger citites.

individual practice association (IPA)
A form of HMO in which subscribers receive services from physicians operating out of their own offices and from community hospitals rather than from a central facility.

preferred provider organization (PPO)
Health care provider that combines the characteristics of the IPA form of HMO with an insurance plan to provide comprehensive health care services to its subscribers within a network of physicians and hospitals.

exclusive provider organization (EPO)
A managed care plan that is similar to a PPO, but reimburses members only when affiliated providers are used.

point-of-service (POS) plan
A hybrid form of HMO that allows members to go outside the HMO network for care; the plan reimburses members for non-affiliated services at a specified percentage of the cost after satisfaction of an annual deductible.

EXHIBIT 9.3

WHO PAYS FOR PERSONAL HEALTH CARE EXPENDITURES?

Consumers pay for about 20 percent of health care costs, with the remaining 80 percent covered by third-party payers like federal, state, and local government and private insurance companies.

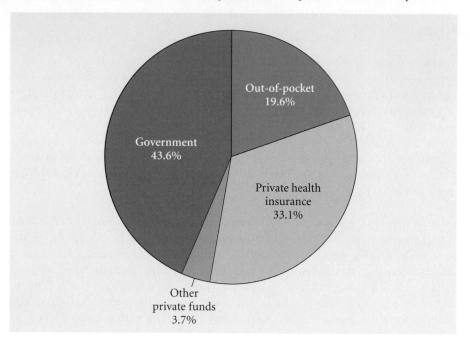

Source: *Health, United States, 2000* (Hyattsville, Maryland: National Center for Health Statistics, 2000), p. 327.

your particular needs. About 14 percent are covered by public sources, including Medicaid. Government programs— federal, state, and local—pay the largest share (almost 44 percent) of health care costs, as Exhibit 9.3 demonstrates.

As the costs of health care continue to rise, so do the premiums we must pay for health insurance. In 1960 only 2 percent of disposable personal income went toward health care premiums; by 1985 this figure reached almost 5 percent; and by 1995 it had risen to and leveled off at about 6.0 percent. From 1990 to 2000 insurance premiums doubled, whereas consumer prices in general rose by about one-third. The average annual cost for companies to cover workers is $2,426 for a single person and $6,351 for a family. Of those amounts the average employee contribution is $624 for a single person and $1,656 for family coverage.

group health care insurance
A type of health care insurance consisting of contracts written between a group (e.g., employer, union, or association) and a private insurance company, Blue Cross/ Blue Shield plan, or managed care organization.

GROUP VERSUS INDIVIDUAL HEALTH CARE INSURANCE. You can purchase health care insurance from group plans, usually obtained through your employer but also available through trade or professional associations, or directly from the provider in the open market as individual health care insurance.

Group health care insurance refers to health care contracts written between a group (usually an employer, union, credit union, college or university, or other organization) and the health care provider: a private insurance company, Blue Cross/Blue Shield plan, or managed care organization. Typically, group plans provide comprehensive medical expense

EXHIBIT 9.4

EMPLOYEE HEALTH CARE PLAN CHOICES

Many people prefer to pay more for a flexible health care plan such as a preferred provider organization (PPO), which is the most popular type of group plan.

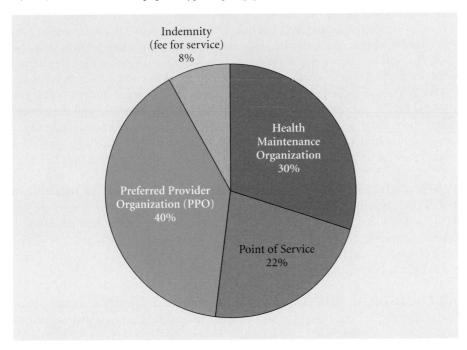

Source: Ann Perry, "Health Plans Move toward the Realm of More Choices," *San Diego Union-Tribune*, November 5, 2000, pp. H1, H4.

Financial Road Sign

Key Questions for Choosing a Health Care Plan:
1. How much will it cost on a monthly basis?
2. Are there deductibles I must pay before the insurance begins to help cover my costs?
3. What doctors, hospitals, and other medical providers are part of the plan?
4. Are there enough of the kinds of doctors I want to see?
5. If I use doctors outside a plan's network, how much more will I pay to get care?
6. Are there any limits to how much I must pay in case of major illness?

coverage, and many also offer prescription drug, dental, and vision care services. The coverage provided by any given plan is subject to negotiation between the group and the insurer, and the group may offer several types of plans.

If you work for an organization of more than just a few employees, you will probably be covered by some type of group health care plan. With the high cost of health insurance, most employers now require employees to pay a portion of the cost. Some groups choose to *self-insure,* which means the employer or other group takes responsibility for full or partial payment of claims. Trade associations and professional groups may offer group insurance to their members at attractive rates.

Because managed care programs help control costs, fewer large employers are offering indemnity plans in their benefit packages. About 60 percent allow employees to choose between indemnity and managed care plans. Typically, an employee can choose between several deductible levels for indemnity plan coverage and one or more managed care options. Most employees selected PPOs for their insurance needs, as Exhibit 9.4 shows.

When a person leaves the group, existing group plan coverage can be continued for 18 months if the employee pays the full premiums plus an administrative fee. The employee can, within the 18 months, elect to convert to an individual plan although the cost may be quite high. (Continuation of group coverage is discussed in more detail later in this chapter.)

At one time, group health care coverage was far superior to individual coverage, especially in terms of availability and cost to the employee. Today, however, the differences between group and individual coverage have narrowed, and many of the advantages of group coverage have disappeared. To control rising medical costs, many employers no longer guarantee universal coverage but underwrite employee applications much the way insurers do. Employers are also shifting a larger percentage of the cost to employees, in the form of larger premium contributions, copayments, and deductible amounts.

You may want to compare group and individual policies before deciding which coverage to buy. With the rise in corporate downsizings, many employees may lose group benefits; many opt for individual coverage to prevent coverage lapses and avoid the difficulty of getting coverage later if health problems develop. Another advantage of individual coverage is the ability to tailor the coverage to the person's needs. In contrast, an individual under a group plan is entitled only to the benefits available in the master group plan. And although the protection afforded under many group plans is excellent, some families still need to supplement this coverage with an individual health care plan. They let group health care insurance serve as the foundation on which they build their individual health care insurance programs.

PRIVATE INSURERS. Private insurance companies sell a variety of indemnity and managed care plans to groups and individuals. Some of the well-known carriers are Aetna, CIGNA, and Prudential. As noted earlier, managed care plans are offered by a variety of providers, including dedicated organizations that provide only managed care (such as Kaiser-Permanente), and other firms (such as private insurers and Blue Cross/Blue Shield) that also offer indemnity plans.

Blue Cross/Blue Shield plans
Prepaid hospital and medical expense plans under which health care services are provided to plan participants by member hospitals and physicians.

BLUE CROSS/BLUE SHIELD. In a technical sense **Blue Cross/Blue Shield plans** are not insurance policies but rather prepaid hospital and medical expense plans. Until 1994, these plans were nonprofit health care service organizations. Since then, the 47 independent, local, member companies have been for-profit corporations. This move was designed to make it easier for plans to obtain funding and compete more effectively in the health care field.

Blue Cross contracts with hospitals, who in exchange for a fee or payment agree to provide specified hospital services to members of groups covered by Blue Cross. Similarly, Blue Shield plans are contracts for surgical and medical services. These plans serve as intermediaries between the groups that want these services and the physicians who contractually agree to provide them. Today, most Blue Cross and Blue Shield plans have combined to form one provider. Blue Cross/Blue Shield organizations compete for business with private insurance companies (many of which are nonprofit mutual insurance companies) and attempt to retain a portion of their income to finance growth.

Currently, about 77 million people are covered by some type of Blue Cross/Blue Shield protection, including about 55 million in its own managed care programs. Because they are producer cooperatives, benefit payments are seldom made to the subscriber but rather directly to the participating hospitals and physicians.

GOVERNMENT-SPONSORED HEALTH CARE. Federal and state agencies also provide health care coverage. Social Security Administration programs provide a considerable amount of coverage for losses arising from illness, accidents, and disability. *Workers' compensation* is a state program that covers medical expenses, rehabilitation, and disability income for job-related medical conditions. Let's take a closer look at Social Security and workers' compensation programs.

Social Security's Medicare Program. Many people think of Social Security as primarily concerned with retirement benefits. But as its official name—*Old-Age, Survivor's, Disability,* *and Health Insurance (OASDHI)* —indicates, this federal program provides other coverage as well. Health benefits are provided under two separate programs: (1) *Medicare,* discussed below, and (2) disability income, discussed later in the chapter. (The federal government also partly funds the *Medicaid* program; however, it is primarily a state-run public assistance program that provides benefits only to those unable to pay for health care.) All Social Security cash benefit programs automatically adjust payments periodically to reflect increases in the cost of living. These increased benefits depend, however, on the government's ability to raise taxes—a subject of much heated debate in recent years.

Although **Medicare** is a health care plan primarily designed to help persons 65 and over meet their health care costs, it now also covers many persons under age 65 who are recipients of monthly Social Security disability benefits. Funds for Medicare benefits come from Social Security taxes paid by covered workers and their employers. Medicare has two primary components: (1) basic hospital insurance and (2) supplementary medical insurance.

- *Basic hospital insurance.* This coverage (commonly called *Part A*) provides inpatient hospital services—room and board and other customary inpatient services—for the first 90 days of illness, after applying a deductible ($792 in 2001) for the first 60 days of illness. Coinsurance provisions, applicable to days 61 through 90 of the hospital stay, can reduce benefits further. Medicare also covers all or part of the cost of up to 100 days in post-hospital extended-care facilities, such as nursing homes providing *skilled care.* (However, it does not cover the most common types of nursing home care—*intermediate and custodial care.*) It also covers some post-hospital health services, such as intermittent nursing care, therapy, rehabilitation, and home health care. Deductible and coinsurance amounts are revised annually to reflect changing medical costs.

- *Supplementary medical insurance.* The **supplementary medical insurance (SMI)** program (commonly called *Part B*) covers: (1) physicians' and surgeons' services; (2) home health service (visitation by a registered nurse); (3) medical and health services, such as x-rays, diagnostics, laboratory tests, rental of necessary durable medical equipment, prosthetic devices, and ambulance trips; and (4) limited psychiatric care. Unlike the basic hospital plan, *SMI is a voluntary program for which participants pay premiums,* which are then matched with government funds. SMI is open to nearly anyone age 65 or over who enrolls and pays the required monthly premiums ($50 in 2001), which are the same regardless of age, health status, or sex. With SMI, the insured pays 20 percent of costs after a $100 deductible and SMI pays 80 percent of *approved charges*—not 80 percent of whatever the physician bills—so actual payment may be substantially less than 80 percent of the total bill. In addition, neither Part A nor Part B of Medicare pays for prescription drugs taken outside of the hospital.

Although Medicare pays for many health care expenses for those over 65, there are still gaps in coverage. About 70 percent of Medicare enrollees supplement their benefits with private "Medigap" insurance policies.

Workers' Compensation Insurance. **Workers' compensation insurance** programs are mandated by every state and also the federal government to compensate workers for job-related illness or injury. Although workers' compensation legislation, benefit amounts, and payment periods differ in each state, benefits often include medical and rehabilitation expenses, disability income, and scheduled lump-sum amounts for death and certain injuries, such as dismemberment. These laws are designed to lighten the burden of job-related illness or injury to the worker. Employers bear nearly the entire cost of worker's compensation plans in most states. Premiums are based on merit; employers who file the most claims pay the highest rates. Consequently, employers try to reduce accidents and

Medicare
A health care plan administered by the federal government to help persons age 65 and over, and others receiving monthly Social Security disability benefits, meet their health care costs.

supplementary medical insurance (SMI)
A *voluntary program* under Medicare (commonly called *Part B*) that provides payments for services not covered under *basic hospital insurance (Part A)*, such as physicians' and surgeons' services, home health service, and x-ray and laboratory services, and *requires participants to pay premiums.*

workers' compensation insurance
A type of health care insurance, required by state and federal governments and nearly paid in full by employers in most states, that compensates workers for job-related illness or injury.

injuries to keep premiums low. Self-employed persons who are covered under the law must make contributions for themselves and their employees.

Workers' compensation insurance covers four basic areas:

- *Medical and rehabilitation expenses.* Hospital, surgical, and other related expenses, including prosthetic devices, to help employees recover and reenter the workforce as quickly as possible. Some jurisdictions provide retraining services to help seriously injured victims find new employment.
- *Disability income.* Pays a specified percentage of the covered person's predisability earned wages, up to some maximum amount, usually limited to one-and-a-half times the average weekly wage of workers within that state, for a specified period.
- *Lump-sum payments.* Paid to employees who suffer dismemberment in work-related accidents, or to their beneficiaries in event of death.
- *Second-injury funds.* Relieve employers of the additional worker's compensation premium they might incur if they employ an already handicapped worker who is further injured on the job.

OTHER SOURCES OF HEALTH CARE COVERAGE. Supplementing traditional health care plans are several other sources of funds or services. As we'll discuss in Chapter 10, homeowner's and automobile insurance policies contain limited amounts of medical expense protection. Homeowner's policies cover accidents to visitors (although not to members of the insured household). Automobile policies may cover you if you are involved in an automobile accident regardless of whether you are in a car, on foot, or on a bicycle. Further, if someone negligently injures you, you have legal grounds on which to collect from that person or his or her liability insurer.

In addition to Social Security, various other government programs help pay medical expenses. Medical care is provided for people who have served in the armed services and were honorably discharged, and for military personnel and their dependents. Public health programs exist to treat communicable diseases, handicapped children, and mental health disorders. Federal, state, and local government combined now spend well more than $500 billion a year on health care expenses. When people—especially elderly and low-income persons—suffer illness or accident, a government program is often available to help out.

CONCEPT CHECK

9-3.   Describe the features of traditional *indemnity (fee-for-service) plans* and explain the key differences between them and *managed care plans.*

9-4.   "HMOs attempt to reduce the cost of health care to individuals and families through more efficient utilization of health care personnel and facilities, and by practicing preventive medicine." Briefly explain how these organizations work. Contrast group HMOs, IPAs, and PPOs.

9-5.   What is *group health care insurance?* Differentiate between group and individual health care insurance.

9-6.   Who are the primary providers of health care insurance? Discuss the basics of the *Blue Cross/Blue Shield plans.*

9-7.   What is the formal name used for Social Security? Briefly describe eligibility for and benefits of Social Security's *Medicare* program.

9-8.   What is the objective of workers' compensation insurance statutes? Explain (a) lump-sum payments and (b) second-injury funds as they relate to workers' compensation.

Medical Expense Coverage and Policy Provisions [LG3]

Thus far, we have discussed the major types of health care insurance plans and their providers. Now we will examine the various types of medical expense coverage and some special insurance plans you *don't* need. In addition, we will review the policy provisions you will typically find in your medical expense plan, and take a brief look at common cost containment provisions.

TYPES OF MEDICAL EXPENSE COVERAGE

The primary forms of medical expense coverage are designed to pay for hospital, surgical, prescription drug, laboratory and x-ray, physicians' office, and dental expenses. To save money, narrowly defined plans may be purchased to cover what you consider the most important segments of health care, such as hospitalization or surgery, for example. Or, if you can afford it and want the comfort of broader coverage, you can purchase major medical or comprehensive major medical coverage to help you pay for most or all health care costs.

HOSPITALIZATION INSURANCE. *Hospitalization insurance* policies reimburse you for the costs of hospital room (semiprivate) and board and other expenses incidental to hospitalization. In the United States more people are covered by some type of hospitalization insurance than any other kind of private health care insurance. Basically, hospitalization insurance pays for a portion of: (1) the hospital's daily semiprivate room rate, which typically includes meals, floor nursing, and other routine services; and (2) ancillary expenses, such as use of an operating room, laboratory tests, x-ray examinations, and medicine received while hospitalized. Some hospitalization plans simply pay a flat daily amount for each day the insured is in the hospital, regardless of actual charges. Numerous hospitalization plans now also offer reimbursement for some outpatient and out-of-hospital services, such as in-home rehabilitation, services provided at an ambulatory care center, diagnostic and preventive treatment, and preadmission testing.

In most policies hospitalization insurance is written to cover daily, semiprivate room and board charges for up to a specified number of days, such as 90, 120, or 360. The maximum reimbursement for ancillary expenses, in contrast, may be a stated dollar amount or sometimes a multiple of the daily room rate. Thus, if the room and board rate were $250 per day, applying a multiple of 15 would result in an ancillary expense limit of $3,750.

SURGICAL EXPENSE INSURANCE. *Surgical expense insurance* provides coverage for the cost of surgery in or out of the hospital. Most plans reimburse *reasonable and customary* surgical expenses based on a survey of surgical costs during the previous year. Some plans still pay according to a *schedule of benefits*, reimbursing up to a fixed maximum for a particular surgical procedure. For example, the policy might state that you would receive no more than $1,000 for an appendectomy or $900 for diagnostic arthroscopic surgery on a knee. Scheduled benefits are often inadequate when compared with typical surgical costs.

Surgical expense coverage will usually pay for almost any type of surgery required to maintain the health of the insured. Most surgical expense policies cover the cost of anesthetics and their administration, although these benefits may also be covered in an "additional benefits" provision of a hospitalization insurance policy. Surgical expense policies may also include payment for nonemergency treatment using x-rays or radium and a limited diagnostic allowance for x-rays and lab fees. Surgical expense coverage is usually provided as an integral part of a hospitalization policy or as a rider to such a policy.

Most elective cosmetic surgeries, such as the proverbial "nose job" or "tummy tuck," are typically excluded from reimbursement. Cosmetic surgery following a deforming accident is often reimbursed, however. A more controversial area is exclusion of experimental surgery, especially certain types of organ transplants and experimental treatments for cancer or other diseases. If a high mortality rate or unproven benefit is associated with such procedures, insurers normally will seek to exclude them.

PHYSICIANS EXPENSE INSURANCE. *Physicians expense insurance,* previously called *regular medical expense,* covers the cost of physician fees for nonsurgical care in a hospital, including consultation with a specialist. Also covered are x-rays and laboratory tests performed outside of a hospital. Home, clinic, or doctor's office visits normally are not covered except through special provisions. Plans are offered on either a reasonable and customary or scheduled benefit basis. Often, the first few visits with the physician for any single cause will be excluded. This exclusion serves the same purpose as the deductible and waiting period features found in other types of insurance.

major medical plan
An insurance plan designed to supplement the basic coverage of hospitalization, surgical, and physicians expenses; used to finance medical costs of a more catastrophic nature.

MAJOR MEDICAL INSURANCE. **Major medical plans** provide broad coverage for nearly all types of medical expenses resulting from either illnesses or accidents. As the name implies, the amounts that can be collected under this coverage are relatively large. Lifetime limits of $500,000, $1,000,000, or higher are common, and some policies have no limits at all. The trend in recent years has been toward higher benefit levels.

Because hospitalization, surgical, and physicians expense coverage meets the smaller health care costs, major medical is used to finance medical costs of a more catastrophic nature. Approximately 84 percent of all Americans are covered by some type of major medical health plan. Many people use major medical with a high deductible to protect against catastrophic illness. To give insureds an incentive to avoid unnecessary medical costs, major medical plans typically are written with provisions that limit payments to less than full reimbursement. These policy provisions are discussed in a subsequent section.

comprehensive major medical insurance
A health care insurance plan that combines, into a single policy, basic hospitalization, surgical, and physicians expense coverage with major medical protection.

COMPREHENSIVE MAJOR MEDICAL INSURANCE. A **comprehensive major medical insurance** plan combines basic hospitalization, surgical, and physicians expense coverage with major medical protection to form a single policy, usually with a low deductible. Comprehensive major medical insurance is often written under a group contract. However, some efforts have been made to make this type of coverage available on an individual basis.

DENTAL INSURANCE. *Dental insurance* covers necessary dental health care and some dental injuries sustained through accidents. (Expenses for accidental damage to natural teeth are normally covered under standard surgical expense and major medical policies.) Dental coverage may provide for oral examinations, including x-rays, cleanings, fillings, extractions, inlays, bridgework, dentures, oral surgery, root canal therapy, and orthodontics. Of course, dental policies vary with respect to the number of these items included within the coverage.

Some dental plans contain provisions limiting reimbursement (particularly with regard to orthodontics) to a portion—often 50 percent on many procedures—of the expenses incurred, and others have "first dollar protection"—they pay for all claims. But the maximum limit on many dental policies often is low—say $1,000 to $2,500 per patient—so these plans do not fully protect against unusually high costs for dental work. Most dental coverage is written through group insurance plans, although some companies do offer individual and family policies.

SPECIAL INSURANCE PLANS YOU *DON'T* NEED. An examination of every type of health care insurance coverage available would fill a book twice the size of this one. However, the types of health care plans already discussed are sufficient to meet the protection needs of most individuals and families. Other popular plans often are simply frills and gimmicks. These plans may be classified as accident, sickness, or hospital income policies.

Sound insurance programming seldom dictates the purchase of these types of policies. Nevertheless, large-scale marketing efforts by some insurers, coupled with public misunderstanding, has brought about their proliferation. Hopefully, the following discussion will help you guard against a potentially unwise purchase.

Accident policies pay a specified sum to an insured who is injured in a certain type of accident. The most common types of accident policies are those relating to travel accidents. These policies are often sold in conjunction with oil company and travel and entertainment credit cards or at airports. Their primary shortcoming is that the fixed amount of the payment is not directly related to the actual amount of the loss. Also, as noted earlier, because only certain types of accidents are covered, it becomes impossible to structure a systematic insurance program using these plans.

Sickness policies are similar in design and shortcomings to accident policies except that a named disease, as opposed to an accident, conditions the payment. Sickness policies may be written separately or in conjunction with accident policies. *Dread disease policies* are a popular version of sickness insurance. Cancer policies appear to be the most common, with some organ transplant policies also being offered. Some states, such as New York, prohibit the sale of single dread disease policies; that is, such coverage can be sold only as part of other hospitalization, surgical, or accident policies.

Hospital income policies typically guarantee the insured a specific daily, weekly, or monthly amount as long as the insured remains hospitalized. However, they generally exclude illnesses that could result in extended hospitalization (for example, mental illness) and health conditions that existed at the time the policies were purchased. Several of these plans have been accused of returning in benefits only 10 to 20 cents of each $1 of premiums collected.

The basic problem with buying policies that cover only a certain type of accident, illness, or financial need is that major gaps in coverage will occur. Clearly, the financial loss can be just as great regardless of whether the insured falls down a flight of stairs or contracts cancer, lung disease, or heart disease. Most limited-peril policies should be used only to supplement a comprehensive insurance program if the coverage is not overlapping. Dread disease and hospital income policies are often offered directly through television and newspaper advertisements.

POLICY PROVISIONS OF MEDICAL EXPENSE PLANS

To compare the health care plans offered by different insurers, you need to evaluate whether they contain liberal or restrictive provisions. Generally, policy provisions can be divided into two groups: terms of payment and terms of coverage.

TERMS OF PAYMENT. Four provisions govern how much your health care plan will pay: (1) deductibles, (2) the participation (coinsurance) clause, (3) the policy's internal limits, and (4) the coordination of benefits clause, if any.

Deductibles. Because major medical insurance plans are designed to supplement basic hospitalization, surgical, and physicians expense plans, those offered under an indemnity (fee-for-service) plan often have a relatively large *deductible,* typically $500 or $1,000. The **deductible** represents the initial amount *not* covered by the policy and therefore the responsibility of the insured. Comprehensive major medical plans tend to offer lower deductibles, sometimes $100 or less. Most plans offer a calendar-year, all-inclusive deductible. In effect, this allows a person to accumulate the deductible from more than one incident of use. Some plans also include a *carryover provision* where any part of the deductible that occurs during the final 3 months of the year (October, November, and December) can be applied to the current year's deductible and can *also* be applied to the following calendar year's deductible. In a few plans the deductible is on a per-illness or per-accident basis. If you were covered by this type of policy with a $1,000 deductible and suffered three separate accidents in the

deductible
The initial amount *not* covered by an insurance policy and therefore the responsibility of the insured; it is usually determined on a calendar-year or on a per-illness or per-accident basis.

course of a year, each requiring $1,000 of medical expenses, you would not be eligible to collect any benefits from the major medical plan.

participation (coinsurance) clause
A provision in many health insurance policies stipulating that the insurer will pay some portion—say, 80 or 90 percent—of the amount of the covered loss in excess of the deductible.

Participation (Coinsurance). Another feature of most major medical insurance policies is some type of **participation,** or **coinsurance, clause.** This provision stipulates that the company will pay some portion—say, 80 or 90 percent—of the amount of the covered loss in excess of the deductible rather than the entire amount. Coinsurance helps reduce the possibility that policyholders will fake illness and discourages them from incurring unnecessary medical expenses. Although comprehensive major medical plans normally have a participation clause, too, this clause often does not apply to expenses related to basic hospitalization, surgical, and physicians expense coverage.

Because major medical limits now go up to $1 million or more, many plans have a *stop-loss provision* that places a cap on the amount of participation required. Without a stop-loss provision, a $1 million medical bill could leave the insured with, say, $200,000 of costs. Often such provisions limit the insured's participation to less than $10,000, and sometimes as little as $2,000.

internal limits
A feature commonly found in health insurance policies that places a constraint on the amounts that will be paid for certain specified expenses—even if the overall policy limits are *not* exceeded by the claim.

Internal Limits. Most major medical plans are written with **internal limits** that place constraints on the amounts paid for certain specified expenses—even if the overall policy limits are *not* exceeded by the claim. Charges that are commonly subject to internal limits are hospital room and board, surgical fees, mental and nervous conditions, and nursing services. Like with participation, or coinsurance, clauses, the insurer wants to give the insured an incentive to control costs by avoiding unreasonably high medical expenses, thereby keeping premiums down. Therefore, if an insured elects a highly expensive physician or medical facility, he or she will be responsible for paying the portion of the charges that are above a "reasonable and customary" level or beyond a specified maximum amount. The example in the following section illustrates how deductibles, coinsurance, and internal limits constrain the amount a company is obligated to pay under a major medical plan.

Major Medical Policy: An Example. Assume that Frank Payne, a graduate student, has coverage under a major medical insurance policy that specifies a $500,000 lifetime limit of protection, a $1,000 deductible, an 80 percent coinsurance clause, internal limits of $350 per day on hospital room and board, and $2,000 as the maximum payable surgical fee. Recently he was hospitalized for 5 days to remove a small tumor. He incurred the following costs:

Hospitalization: 5 days at $500 a day	$2,500
Surgical expense	1,800
Other covered medical expenses	1,800
Total medical expenses	$6,100

Because of the coinsurance clause in the policy, however, the maximum the company has to pay is 80 percent of the covered loss in excess of the deductible. In the absence of internal limits the company would pay $4,080 (.80 × [$6,100 – $1,000]). The internal limits further restrict the payment. Even though 80 percent of the $500-per-day hospitalization charge is $400, the most the company would have to pay is $350 per day. Therefore the insured becomes liable for $50 per day for 5 days, or $250. The surgical expense is below the $2,000 internal limit, so the 80 percent coinsurance clause applies and the insurer will pay $1,440 (.80 × $1,800). The company's total obligation is reduced to $3,830 ($4,080 – $250), whereas the insured must pay a total of $2,270 ($1,000 deductible + .20[$6,100 – $1,000] coinsurance + $250 excess hospital charges). The lesson here is that although major medical insurance can offer very large amounts of reimbursement, you may still be left responsible for substantial payments.

EXHIBIT 9.5

HOW TO GET YOUR HEALTH CARE INSURANCE CLAIMS PAID

The following guidelines will help you cut through red tape to get your health care insurance claims paid:

1. *Treat your insurance claims almost like tax records.* Keep them, along with any supporting documentation, and keep them up-to-date. Set up a good filing system.
2. *List every claim, including the doctor's name, the date of the treatment, the type of treatment, the charge, and the date the claim was filed.* Photocopy it along with the bills or other supporting documents you submit and keep the copies in your file folder.
3. *Double check your claim form for accuracy before filing.* Make sure all the information is complete and correct; with computer processing, a typographic error or missing item could delay your claim or even cause it to be rejected.
4. *File all claims promptly, even if you don't think you are covered.* You need to file claims, usually within 6 to 12 months of the date of service, to meet your annual deductible.
5. *If 30 days pass and you haven't heard from the carrier, call or write.* Keep a record of all correspondence and telephone calls.
6. *If a claim is rejected, don't take "no" for an answer.* Find out why the claim is denied and provide additional information if required. The reason may be a misspelled name or transposed numbers or an incorrect diagnostic code. Properly documented appeals for covered services have a high likelihood of success.
7. *If your claim is not handled to your satisfaction, go directly to the company's claims supervisor or home office.* Sometimes a letter to the company president breaks the logjam. As a last resort, tell the company that you will file a complaint with the state insurance department—and do it if necessary.
8. *Keep good records of utilization review approvals for hospital admissions or medical procedures.* You are ultimately responsible for getting these approvals, so be sure to allow enough time before your hospitalization and request written confirmation.

Sources: Adapted from Jane Bennett Clark, "Insurance Fumbles—and How to Recover," *Kiplinger's Personal Finance Magazine*, January 1995, pp. 124–125; and Albert B. Crenshaw, "Persistence Pays Health Claims," *Washington Post*, January 7, 2001, p. H2.

Coordination of Benefits. In contrast to most property and liability insurance plans, which we'll discuss in Chapter 10, health care insurance policies are not contracts of *indemnity.* This means that insureds can collect multiple payments for the same illness or accident unless health care insurance policies include a **coordination of benefits provision.** This clause prevents you from collecting more than 100 percent of covered charges by collecting benefits from more than one policy. For example, many private health care insurance policies coordinate benefits provisions with medical benefits paid under workers' compensation. In contrast, some companies widely advertise that their policies will pay claims regardless of other coverage the policyholder has. Of course, these latter types of insurance policies often cost more per dollar of protection. From the standpoint of insurance planning, the use of policies with coordination of benefits clauses can help you prevent coverage overlaps and, ideally, reduce your premiums.

Considering the complexity of medical expense contracts, the various clauses limiting payments, and coordination of benefits with other plans, one might expect that insurers often pay only partial claims and sometimes completely deny claims. If you make a claim and do not receive the payment you expected, do not give up. Exhibit 9.5 provides some guidelines on how you might go about getting your health care insurance claims paid.

coordination of benefits provision
A provision often included in health care insurance policies to prevent the insured from collecting more than 100 percent of covered charges; it requires that benefit payments be coordinated in event the insured is eligible for benefits under more than one policy.

TERMS OF COVERAGE. A number of contract provisions affect the value of a health care insurance plan to you. Some of the more important provisions address (1) the persons and places covered, (2) cancellation, (3) preexisting conditions, (4) pregnancy and abortion, (5) mental illness (6) rehabilitation coverage, and (7) continuation of group coverage.

Persons and Places Covered. Some health care insurance policies cover only the named insured, whereas others offer protection to all family members. Of those that offer family coverage, some terminate benefits payable on behalf of children at age 18 and others continue them to age 24 as long as the child remains in school or is single. *If you are in this age group, you or your parents should check to see if you are covered under your parents' policy.* If not, sometimes by paying an additional premium, you can add such coverage. Some policies protect you only while you are in the United States or Canada; others offer worldwide coverage but exclude certain named countries.

Cancellation. Many health care insurance policies are written to permit *cancellation* at any time at the option of the insurer. Some policies explicitly state this; others do not. To protect yourself against premature cancellation, you should buy policies that specifically state that the insurer will not cancel coverage as long as premiums are paid.

preexisting condition clause
A clause included in most individual health care insurance policies that permits permanent or temporary exclusion of coverage for any physical or mental problems the insured had at the time the policy was purchased; this clause, if included at all, is much less restrictive in group policies.

Preexisting Conditions. Most health care insurance policies sold to individuals (as opposed to group/employer-sponsored plans) contain a **preexisting condition clause.** This means the policy might exclude coverage for any physical or mental problems you had at the time you bought it. In some policies the exclusion is permanent; in others, it lasts only for the first year or two the coverage is in force. Group insurance plans may also have preexisting condition clauses, but these tend to be less restrictive than those in individually written policies.

Pregnancy and Abortion. Many individual and group health care insurance plans include special clauses for medical expenses incurred through pregnancy or abortion. Some liberal policies pay for all related expenses, including sick-leave pay during the final months of pregnancy, whereas others pay for medical expenses that result from pregnancy or abortion complications but not for routine procedure expenses. In the most restrictive cases the policy offers no coverage for any costs of pregnancy or abortion.

Mental Illness. Mental illness and emotional disorders are perhaps America's most prevalent but least talked about health problems. The high-pressure "get ahead" lives that many people lead often give rise to drug and alcohol abuse, stress-related physical disability, and various forms of psychosis or neurosis. In addition, family problems, economic setbacks, and chemical imbalances within the body can contribute to poor mental health. Yet although a mental illness or emotional disorder at some time strikes one out of three families, many of those affected will not admit they need help.

Compounding this problem, many health care insurance plans omit or offer reduced benefits for treatment of mental disorders. For example, a health insurance policy may offer hospitalization benefits that continue to pay as long as you remain hospitalized—except for mental illness. It may restrict payment for mental illness to one-half the normally provided payment amounts and for a period not to exceed 30 days. Unfortunately, mental illness is the number one sickness requiring long-term hospital care. Because coverage for mental illness is an important insurance protection, check your policies to learn how liberal—or how restrictive—they are with respect to this feature.

Rehabilitation Coverage. In the past, health care insurance plans focused almost exclusively on reasonable and necessary medical expenses. If an illness or accident left an insured partially or totally disabled, no funds normally would be available to help the person retrain for employment and a more productive life. Now, though, many policies include *rehabilitation coverage* for counseling, occupational therapy, and even some educational or job-training programs. This is a good feature to look for in major medical and disability income policies.

Continuation of Group Coverage. Under the *Consolidated Omnibus Budget Reconciliation Act (COBRA)*, passed by Congress in 1986, an employee who leaves the group voluntarily or involuntarily (except in the case of "gross misconduct") may elect to continue coverage for up to 18 months by paying premiums to his or her former employer on time (up to 102 percent of the company cost). The employee retains all benefits previously available, except for disability income coverage.

Similar continuation coverage is available for retirees and their families for up to 18 months or until they become eligible for Medicare, whichever occurs first. The dependents of an employee may be covered for up to 36 months under COBRA under special circumstances, such as divorce or death of the employee. After the continuation coverage required by COBRA expires, most states provide for conversion of the group coverage to an individual policy regardless of the current health of the insured and without evidence of insurability. These state provisions also apply to employees in firms with less than 20 employees (these small firms are not bound by COBRA requirements). Premium charges and benefits of the converted policy are determined at the time of conversion.

COST CONTAINMENT PROVISIONS FOR MEDICAL EXPENSE PLANS

Considering the continued inflation in medical costs, it's hardly surprising that insurers, along with employers that sponsor medical expense plans, are looking for ways to limit the costs incurred. During the past decade, various cost containment provisions have been added to almost all medical expense plans, both indemnity and managed care policies. Although the success of such provisions has been limited, you are likely to find them in your own health care insurance plan. Among these cost containment provisions are:

- *Pre-Admission Certification:* Requires you to receive approval from your insurer before entering the hospital for a scheduled stay. Such approval is not normally required for emergency stays.
- *Continued Stay Review:* To receive normal reimbursement, the insured must secure approval from the insurer for any stay that exceeds the originally approved limits.
- *Second Surgical Opinions:* Many plans *require* second opinions on specific, nonemergency procedures and, in their absence, may reduce the surgical benefits paid. Most surgical expense plans now provide for full reimbursement of the cost of second opinions.
- *Waiver of Coinsurance.* Because insurers can save money on hospital room and board charges by encouraging outpatient surgery, many now agree to waive the coinsurance clause and pay 100 percent of surgical costs for outpatient procedures. A similar waiver is sometimes applied to generic pharmaceuticals. For example, the patient may choose between an 80 percent payment for a brand-name pharmaceutical that cost $35 or a 100 percent reimbursement for its $15 generic equivalent.

CONCEPT CHECK

9-9. Differentiate between *hospitalization insurance* and *surgical expense insurance.* Define and compare reasonable and customary surgical expenses to a schedule of benefits under surgical expense insurance.

9-10. What is a *major medical plan*? What are its common features? What is *comprehensive major medical insurance*?

9-11. Describe a hospital income policy. How does it differ from medical expense coverages that offer hospitalization insurance?

9-12. Briefly describe the following policy provisions commonly found in medical expense plans: (a) deductibles, (b) coinsurance, (c) coordination of benefits, and (d) preexisting conditions.

9-13. Briefly describe the key provisions of the *Consolidated Omnibus Budget Reconciliation Act (COBRA)* as they relate to continuation of group coverage when an employee voluntarily or involuntarily leaves the group.

9-14. Explain the cost containment provisions commonly found in medical expense plans. How might the provision for *second surgical opinions* help an insurer contain its costs?

■ Long-Term Care Insurance [LG4]

Thanks to ever-improving health care and better knowledge about health risks, such as smoking and poor diet, our population is living longer and will probably continue to do so. In fact, those age 85 and above are expected to constitute about 5 percent of the population by the year 2050, up from about 1 percent in 1990. People reaching advanced ages often become too frail to perform basic activities of everyday life, such as eating, bathing, and dressing. You probably know some elderly persons who needed to enter a nursing home or hire special care in their own home because they simply could not adequately care for themselves.

Although no one likes to think about spending years in a nursing home, this possibility is more likely than ever with today's longer life expectancies. About 50 percent of all men and 67 percent of all women (women live longer) will require nursing home care at some point in their lives. Even if you are still young, someone in your family may need long-term care. So it is important to understand how this coverage works, whether it makes sense given your family situation, and how to choose an insurance policy.

long-term care
The delivery of medical and personal care, other than hospital care, to persons with chronic medical conditions resulting from either illness or frailty.

Long-term care is the term often used to describe the delivery of medical and personal care, other than hospital care, to persons with chronic medical conditions resulting from either illness or frailty. The cost of such care can be very expensive. For instance, the cost of nursing home care averages almost $56,000 per year—$153 per day—but can exceed $90,000 per year in some major cities. By the year 2060, the cost could be $250,000 a year! Home health care can cost $1,000 a month or more for three weekly visits. Considering the likelihood of living to an advanced age in the United States and the costs of adequate long-term care, we must ask ourselves, "Who will pay the price?"

FINANCING LONG-TERM CARE

Although two-thirds of Americans worry about the cost of long-term care and its impact on their standard of living, a survey by the National Council on the Aging shows that only 35 percent have done any planning for it and only six million have purchased long-term

EXHIBIT 9.6

PAYING THE BILL FOR NURSING HOME CARE

Consumers pay almost one-third of nursing home care costs out of their own pockets, with Medicare paying for almost half of these costs. Although private insurance currently pays for only about 5 percent of nursing home costs, this portion is expected to grow as more people become aware of the need for long-term care insurance.

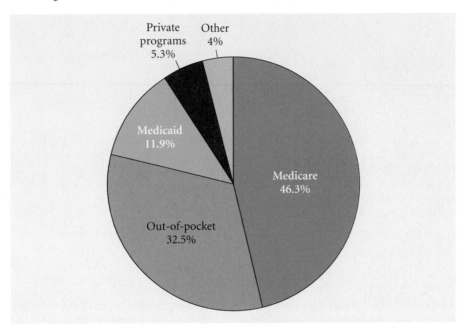

Source: *Health, United States, 2000* (Hyattsville, Maryland: National Center for Health Statistics, 2000), p. 327.

care insurance. Yet this is not an area of financial planning to neglect. Exhibit 9.6 shows that consumers pay almost one-third of nursing home care costs out of their own pockets, with primary third-party financing coming from Medicare and government programs such as Medicaid (which pays benefits only to the indigent, as defined by strict state-specific eligibility laws).

Often the persons receiving nursing home care cannot afford to cover such a large personal expense, so the younger generation ends up footing the bill. Although Exhibit 9.6 shows that private insurance has not been much of a factor in the past, the market for it is developing and expanding rapidly as more people become aware of the reality and cost of long-term care. Major medical insurance plans exclude most of the costs related to long-term care, so a special policy is required. Fortunately, more than 100 private insurers offer long-term care policies. Most are indemnity policies that pay a fixed dollar amount for each day you receive specified care either in a nursing home or at home.

LONG-TERM CARE INSURANCE PROVISIONS AND COSTS

Because the market for long-term care insurance is evolving, few experts are surprised at the wide range of policy provisions and premiums currently being offered. Because of substantial variation in product offerings, you must be especially careful to evaluate the important policy provisions. They include: (1) type of care, (2) eligibility requirements, (3) services

EXHIBIT 9.7

TYPICAL PROVISIONS IN LONG-TERM CARE INSURANCE POLICIES

Long-term care insurers offer a wide range of provisions in their policies. A typical policy includes the following:

Services covered	Skilled, intermediate, and custodial care
	Home health care
	Adult day care (often)
Benefit eligibility	Physician certification/medically necessary
Daily benefit	$50–$300/day, nursing home
	$25–$150/day, home health care
Benefit period	3–4 years
Maximum benefit period	5 years; unlimited
Waiting period	0–100 days
Renewability	Guaranteed
Preexisting condition	Conditions existing 6 months prior to policy coverage
Inflation protection	Yes, for an additional premium
Deductibility periods	0, 20, 30, 90, 100 days
Alzheimer's disease coverage	Yes
Age limits for purchasing	40–84

covered, (4) daily benefits, (5) benefit duration, (6) waiting period, (7) renewability, (8) pre-existing conditions, (9) inflation protection, and (10) premium levels. Exhibit 9.7 summarizes the typical provisions of policies offered by leading insurers. Of course, policy provisions are important factors in determining the premium for each policy.

TYPE OF CARE. Some long-term care policies offer benefits only for nursing home care, whereas others pay only for services in the insured's home, such as skilled or nonskilled nursing care, physical therapy, homemakers, and home health aides. Because you cannot easily predict whether a person might need to be in a nursing home, most financial planners recommend policies that cover both. Many of these policies focus on nursing home care, and any expenses for health care in the insured's home are covered in a rider to the basic policy. Many policies also cover assisted living, adult daycare and other community care programs, alternative care, and respite care for the caregiver.

ELIGIBILITY REQUIREMENTS. Some very important provisions determine whether the insured will receive payment for claims. These are known as *gatekeeper* provisions. The most liberal policies state that the insured will qualify for benefits as long as his or her physician orders the care. A common and much more restrictive provision pays only for long-term care that is medically necessary for sickness or injury.

One common gatekeeper provision requires the insured's inability to perform a given number of *activities of daily living* (ADLs) such as bathing, dressing, or eating. Some policies also provide care for cognitive impairment or when medically necessary and prescribed by the patient's physician. In the case of an Alzheimer's patient who remains physically healthy, inclusion of cognitive abilities as ADLs would be extremely important. Newer policies no longer require a certain period of nursing home care before covering home health care services.

SERVICES COVERED. Most policies today cover several levels of service in state-licensed nursing homes; specifically skilled, intermediate, and custodial care. *Skilled care* is needed when a patient requires constant attention from a medical professional, such as a physician or registered nurse. *Intermediate care* is provided when the patient needs medical attention or supervision but not the constant attention of a medical professional. *Custodial care* provides assistance in the normal activities of daily living, but no medical attention or supervision; a physician or nurse may be on call, however. Most long-term care policies also cover home care services, such as skilled or nonskilled nursing care, physical therapy, homemakers, and home health aides provided by state-licensed or Medicare-certified home health agencies. Newer policies no longer require a certain period of nursing home care before covering home health care services.

DAILY BENEFITS. Long-term care policies reimburse the insured for services incurred up to a daily maximum. For nursing home care policies, the daily maximums generally range from $50 to $300 depending on the amount of premium the insured is willing to pay. For combination nursing home and home care policies, the maximum home care benefit is normally half the nursing home maximum.

BENEFIT DURATION. The maximum duration of benefits ranges from 1 year to the insured's lifetime. Lifetime coverage is very expensive, however. The consumer should realize that the average stay in a nursing home is now about $2\frac{1}{2}$ years. Most financial planners recommend the purchase of a policy with a duration of 3 to 6 years to provide the insured with protection for a longer-than-average period of care.

WAITING PERIOD. Even if the insured meets the eligibility requirements of his or her policy, he or she must pay long-term care expenses during the **waiting,** or **elimination, period.** Typical waiting periods are 90 to 100 days. Although premiums are much lower for policies with longer waiting periods, the insured must have liquid assets to cover his or her expenses during that period. If the insured is still receiving care after the waiting period expires, he or she will begin to receive benefits for the duration of the policy as long as its eligibility requirements continue to be met.

RENEWABILITY. Most long-term care insurance policies now include a **guaranteed renewability** provision to ensure continued coverage for your lifetime as long as you continue to pay the premiums. This clause does not ensure a level premium over time, however. Nearly all policies allow the insurer to raise premiums if the claims experience for your peer group of policyholders is unfavorable. Watch out for policies with an **optional renewability** clause. These policies are renewable *only at the option of the insurer.*

PREEXISTING CONDITIONS. Many policies include a *preexisting conditions clause,* similar to those explained earlier, ranging from 6 to 12 months. On the other hand, many policies have no such clause, which effectively eliminates one important source of possible claim disputes.

INFLATION PROTECTION. Many policies offer riders that, for an additional premium, allow you to increase your benefits over time so that benefits roughly match the rising cost of nursing home and home health care. Most inflation protection riders allow you to increase benefits by a flat amount, often 5 percent, per year. Others offer benefits linked to the rise in the CPI. Most policies discontinue inflation adjustments after either 10 or 20 years. Inflation protection riders can add between 25 and 40 percent to the basic premium for a long-term care insurance policy.

waiting (elimination) period
The period, after the insured meets the policy's eligibility requirements, during which he or she must pay long-term care expenses; after the waiting period expires, the insured will begin to receive benefits for the duration of the policy as long as its eligibility requirements continue to be met.

guaranteed renewability
Policy provision ensuring continued insurance coverage for the insured's lifetime as long as he or she continues to pay the premiums. The insurer may raise premiums in the future, however, if the claims experience for the insured's peer group of policyholders is unfavorable.

optional renewability
Contractual clause allowing the insured to continue insurance *only at the option of the insurer.*

Financial Road Sign

Standards for a Good Long-Term Care Policy:

1. At least 1 year of nursing home or home health care coverage, including intermediate and custodial care, and coverage for Alzheimer's disease.
2. Inflation protection.
3. A detailed "outline of coverage" describing the policy's benefits, limitations, and exclusions.
4. A long-term care insurance shopper's guide that helps you decide whether long-term care insurance is appropriate for you.
5. A guarantee against cancellation or non-renewal because of age or deteriorating physical or mental health.
6. The right to return the policy for a refund within 30 days of purchase.
7. No requirement that policyholders first be hospitalized to receive nursing home or home health care benefits, or first receive a higher level of care before receiving lower care levels.

Source: The National Association of Insurance Commissioners, cited in *HIAA Guide to Long-Term Care Insurance*, **www.hiaa.org/cons/ guideltc.html#cover**.

PREMIUM LEVELS. Long-term care insurance is not inexpensive, and premiums vary widely among insurance companies. For example, a healthy 65-year-old may pay about $2,000 per year for a policy that pays for 4 years' care at $100 per day for nursing home care and $50 per day for home care, with a 100-day waiting period and a 5 percent inflation rider. The same coverage may cost a 50-year-old $850 per year, and a 79-year-old, $5,900 per year. Because of this marked rise in premium with age, some financial planners recommend buying long-term care insurance when you are fairly young.

smart.sites Confused about long-term care insurance coverage? The Guide to Long-Term Health Care at the Health Insurance Association of America site, **www.hiaa.org/cons/guideltc.html**, will provide the answers.

WHO NEEDS LONG-TERM CARE INSURANCE?

Although long-term care policies have improved in recent years and now offer broader coverage and more options, they are still expensive. And the odds of needing more than 1 year of nursing home care before you reach age 65 are 1 in 33. On the other hand, the expense of a prolonged nursing home stay could cause severe financial hardship to your family. As a result, some children are either buying or sharing the cost of policies for their parents. Before buying one for yourself or a relative, you should ask the following questions:

- *Do you have a lot of assets to preserve for your dependents?* Because you must deplete most of your assets before Medicaid will pay for nursing home care, some financial advisors recommend that people over 65 whose net worth is more than $100,000 and income exceeds $50,000 a year consider long-term care insurance—*if* they can afford the premiums. The very wealthy, however, may prefer to self-insure.
- *Can you afford the premiums?* Premiums of many good-quality policies can be 5 to 7 percent of annual income or more. Such high premiums may cause more financial hardship than the cost of the nursing home stay. You may be better off investing the amount you would spend in premiums; it would then be available for *any* future need, including long-term health care.
- *Is there a family history of disabling disease?* This factor increases your odds of needing long-term care. In addition, because women live longer, they are more likely to become disabled.
- *Do you have family who can care for you?* The availability of relatives or home health services to provide care can reduce the cost of long-term care.

Women in particular should consider the benefits of long-term care insurance for themselves and their loved ones. Not only do women live longer, and thus are more likely to require long-term care, but they are also the primary caregivers for other family members. As with any insurance policy, the consumer must carefully compare the key provisions and the premiums quoted on long-term care insurance policies offered by different insurers.

If you decide that you or a relative should have long-term care insurance, be sure to buy from a financially sound company (based on ratings from the major ratings agencies) that has experience in this market segment. Here are some additional guidelines to help you choose the right policy.

- *Buy the policy while you're healthy.* Once you have a disease, such as Alzheimer's or multiple sclerosis, or have a stroke, you become uninsurable. The best time to buy is when you're in your mid-50s or 60s.
- *Buy the right types of coverage—but don't buy more coverage than you need.* Your policy should cover skilled, intermediate, and custodial care, and also adult day care centers and assisted living facilities. If you have access to family caregivers or home

health services, select a policy with generous home health benefits; if not, opt for only nursing home coverage. To reduce costs, increase the waiting period before benefits start; the longer you can cover the costs yourself, the lower your premiums. You may also choose a shorter benefit payment period; 3 years is a popular choice, but the average nursing home stay is about 2½ years. Lifetime coverage increases the premium for a 65-year-old by as much as 40 percent.

* *Understand what the policy covers and when it pays benefits.* The amounts paid, benefit periods, and services covered vary among insurers. One rule of thumb is to buy a policy that covers 80 to 100 percent of current nursing home costs in your area. Some policies pay only for licensed health care providers, whereas others include assistance with household chores. Know how the policy defines benefit eligibility.

CONCEPT CHECK

9-15. Why should a consumer consider purchasing a long-term care insurance policy?

9-16. Describe the differences among long-term care policies with respect to (a) type of care, (b) eligibility requirements, and (c) services covered. List and discuss some other important policy provisions.

9-17. Discuss some of the questions one should ask before buying long-term care insurance. What guidelines can be used to choose the right policy?

■ Disability Income Insurance [LG5]

When a family member becomes sick for an extended period, the effect on the family goes beyond medical bills. The Health Insurance Association of America estimates that a 35-year-old worker has a 12 percent chance of becoming disabled for 3 months; this chance increases to 70 percent by age 55. These percentages are the same as the chance of dying, but although most Americans have life insurance, few have taken steps to protect their family should a serious illness or accident prevent them from working for an extended period.

The best way to protect against the potentially devastating financial consequences of a health-related disability is with disability income insurance. **Disability income insurance** provides families with weekly or monthly payments to replace income when the insured is unable to work as a result of a covered illness, injury, or disease. Some companies also offer disability income protection for a homemaker-spouse; such coverage helps pay for the services that the spouse would normally provide.

Almost all employers offer disability income insurance at advantageous rates. However, coverage is often voluntary, and you may have to pay the entire premium yourself. Group coverage is usually a good buy, however: Premiums for employer-sponsored group coverage average $175 to $300 a year—about one-third the cost of comparable private coverage. A disadvantage is that if you change jobs, you may lose the coverage. The benefits from a group plan in which you pay the premiums are tax-free (unless paid through a flexible spending account). Be sure to run a needs analysis, as described in the instructions for Worksheet 9.1, to ensure that you have enough coverage for your needs.

Social Security offers disability income benefits, but you must be unable to do *any* job whatever to receive benefits. Benefits are payable only if your disability is expected to last at least 1 year (or to be fatal), and do not begin until you have been disabled for at least 5 months. The actual amount paid is a percentage of your previous monthly earnings, with

disability income insurance
Insurance that provides families with weekly or monthly payments to replace income when the insured is unable to work as a result of a covered illness, injury, or disease.

some statistical adjustments. The percentage is higher for people with low earnings. A 35-year-old who earns $20,000 and has dependents would receive $1,261 per month (about 76 percent of earnings); if he or she earned $50,000, the amount rises to $2,215 per month (53 percent of earnings).

The need for disability income coverage is great, yet generally ignored by the public. Although most workers receive some disability insurance benefits from their employer, in many cases the group plan falls short and pays only about 60 percent of salary for a limited period. The first step in considering disability income insurance is to determine the dollar amount your family would need (typically monthly) in the event an earner becomes disabled. Then you can buy the coverage you need or supplement existing coverage if necessary.

ESTIMATING YOUR DISABILITY INSURANCE NEEDS

The overriding purpose of disability income insurance is to replace all (or most) of the income—that is, earnings—that would be lost if you became disabled and physically unable to hold a job. In essence, it should enable you to maintain a standard of living at or near your present level. To help decide how much disability income insurance is right for you, use Worksheet 9.1 to estimate your monthly disability benefit needs (this is a procedure developed and recommended by the Consumer's Union of the United States, publishers of *Consumer Reports*). Here is all you have to do:

1. *Calculate take-home pay.* Disability benefits are generally, but not always, tax-free, so you typically need to replace only your *take-home* (after-tax) pay. Benefits from employer-paid policies are fully or partially taxable. To estimate take-home pay, subtract income and Social Security taxes paid from your gross earned income (salary only). Divide this total by 12 to get your monthly take-home pay.
2. *Estimate the monthly amounts of disability benefits from government or employer programs:*
   a. *Social Security benefits.* Get an estimate of your benefits by calling 1-800-772-1213 for a *Personal Earnings and Benefit Estimate Statement.* An insurance agent may also have a computer program that can easily calculate it. As of 2000, the average Social Security disability benefit ranged from $1,261 to $2,600 per month for a wage earner with dependents, depending on age and income.
   b. *Other government programs* with disability benefits for which you qualify (armed services, Veterans Administration, civil service, the Federal Employees Compensation Act, state workers' compensation systems). There are also special programs for railroad workers, longshoremen, and people with black-lung disease.
   c. *Company disability benefits.* Ask your company benefits supervisor to help you calculate company-provided benefits, including sick pay or wage continuation plans (for all practical purposes, these are short-term disability income insurance) and plans formally designated as disability insurance. For each benefit your employer offers, check on its tax treatment.
   d. *Group disability policy benefits.* A private insurer provides the coverage, and you pay for it, often through payroll deduction.
3. *Add up your existing monthly disability benefits.*
4. *Subtract your existing monthly disability benefits from your current monthly take-home pay.* The result will show the estimated monthly disability benefits you will need to maintain your present after-tax income. Note that investment income and spousal income (if he or she is presently employed) are ignored because it is assumed this income will continue and is necessary to maintain your current standard of living. If your spouse is presently unemployed but would enter the workforce in the event you ever became disabled, his or her estimated monthly income (take-home pay) could be subtracted from item 4 of Worksheet 9.1 to determine your net monthly disability benefit needs.

 **WORKSHEET 9.1**

ESTIMATING DISABILITY INCOME INSURANCE NEEDS

Using a worksheet like this makes the job of estimating disability benefit needs a lot easier.

DISABILITY BENEFIT NEEDS

Name(s) _____ Date _____

1. Estimate current monthly *take-home* pay $ _____
2. Estimate existing monthly disability benefits:
   a. Social Security benefits $ _____
   b. Other government benefits   _____
   c. Company benefits   _____
   d. Group disability policy benefits   _____
3. Total existing monthly disability benefits (2a + 2b + 2c + 2d) $ _____
4. **Estimated monthly disability benefits needed ([1] − [3])** $ _____

 smart.sites   MoneyCentral's Quick Reference section on disability income insurance includes a good discussion on taxability of group insurance benefits: **moneycentral.msn.com/quickref/quickref.asp?Cat=2&Topic=2#h**.

DISABILITY INCOME INSURANCE PROVISIONS AND COSTS

The scope and cost of your disability income coverage depends on its contractual provisions. Although disability income insurance policies can be very complex, certain features are important, including (1) definition of disability, (2) benefit amount and duration, (3) probationary period, (4) waiting period, (5) renewability, and (6) other provisions.

DEFINITION OF DISABILITY. Disability policies vary in the standards you must meet to receive benefits. Some pay benefits if you are unable to perform the duties of your customary occupation—the *own occupation* (or "Own Occ") definition—whereas others pay only if you can engage in no gainful employment at all—the *any occupation* (or "Any Occ") definition. Under the "Own Occ" definition, a professor who lost his voice, but still could get paid to write or do research, would receive full benefits because he could not lecture, a primary function of his occupation. With a *residual benefit option,* you would be paid partial benefits if you can only work part time or at a lower salary. The "Any Occ" definition is considerably less expensive because it gives the insurer more leeway in determining whether the insured should receive benefits.

Individual disability policies may contain a *presumptive disability* clause that supersedes the previously discussed definition of disability when certain types of losses occur. Loss of both hands, sight in both eyes, and hearing in both ears are examples where the insured may be *presumed* totally disabled and may receive full benefits even though he or she still can be employed in some capacity.

BENEFIT AMOUNT AND DURATION. Most individual disability income policies pay a flat monthly benefit, which is stated in the policy, whereas group plans pay a fixed percentage of gross income. In either case, insurers normally will not agree to amounts in excess of 60 to 70 percent of the insured's gross income. Insurers will not issue policies for the full amount of gross income because this would give some people an incentive to fake a disability (for example, "bad back") and collect more in insurance benefits than they normally would receive as take-home pay.

Monthly benefits can be paid for a few months or for a lifetime. If you are ensured substantial pension, Social Security, or other benefits at retirement, a policy that pays benefits until age 65 is adequate. Most people, however, will need to continue their occupations for many more years and should consider a policy offering lifetime benefits. Many policies offer benefits for periods as short as 2 or 5 years. Although these policies may be better than nothing, they do not protect against the major financial losses associated with long-term disabilities.

PROBATIONARY PERIOD. Both group and individual disability income policies are likely to include a probationary period, usually 7 to 30 days, which is a time delay from the date the policy is issued until benefit privileges are available. Any disability stemming from an illness, injury, or disease that occurs during the probationary period is *not* covered—even if it continues beyond this period. This feature keeps costs down.

WAITING PERIOD. The waiting, or elimination, period provisions in a disability income policy are similar to those discussed for long-term care insurance. Typical waiting periods range from 30 days to 1 year. If you have an adequate emergency fund to provide family income during the early months of disability, you can choose a longer waiting period and substantially reduce your premiums, as shown in Exhibit 9.8.

With most insurers, you effectively can trade off an increase in the waiting period from, say, 30 days to 90 days for an increase in the duration of benefits from 5 years to age 65. In fact, as Exhibit 9.8 shows, the premium charged by this insurer for a policy covering a 35-year-old male with a 30-day waiting period and 2-year benefit period ($698) is about the same as one charged for benefits payable to age 65 with a 6-month waiting period ($692). Accepting this type of trade-off usually makes sense because the primary purpose of insurance is to protect against a catastrophic loss, rather than smaller losses that are better handled through proper budgeting and saving.

RENEWABILITY. Most individual disability income insurance is either *guaranteed renewable* or *noncancelable*. As with long-term care policies, guaranteed renewability ensures that you can renew the policy until you reach the age stated in the clause, usually age 65. Premiums can be raised over time if justified by the loss experience of all those in the same class (usually based on age, sex, and occupational category). Noncancelable policies offer guaranteed renewability, but also guarantee that future premiums will remain the same as those stated in the policy at issuance. Because of this stable premium guarantee, noncancelable policies generally are more expensive than those with only a guaranteed renewability provision.

OTHER PROVISIONS. The purchasing power of income from a long-term disability policy that pays, say, $2,000 per month could be severely affected by inflation. In fact, a 3 percent inflation rate would reduce the purchasing power of this $2,000 benefit to less than $1,500 in 10 years. To counteract such a reduction, many insurers offer a *cost-of-living adjustment (COLA)*. With a COLA provision, the monthly benefit is adjusted upward each year, often in line with the CPI, although these annual adjustments are often capped at a given rate, say 8 percent. Although some financial advisors suggest buying COLA riders, others feel the 10 to 25 percent additional premium is not worth it with today's low inflation rate.

Although the COLA provision applies only once the insured is disabled, the *guaranteed insurability option (GIO)* can allow you to purchase additional disability income insurance in line with inflation increases while you are still healthy. Under the GIO, the price of

 EXHIBIT 9.8

DISABILITY INCOME INSURANCE PREMIUM COSTS

The cost of disability income insurance varies with the terms of payment as well as the length of the waiting period. Because they have longer life expectancies, women pay substantially higher rates than men. This table shows premiums for basic disability income coverage for a 35-year-old that pays $2,000 per month in benefits, with guaranteed premiums to age 65. Any additional features, such as inflation riders cost more.

Benefit Period	2 Years		5 Years		To Age 65		Lifetime	
Waiting Period	Male	Female	Male	Female	Male	Female	Male	Female
30 days	$698	$1,192	$922	$1,601	$1,284	$2,327	$1,402	$2,508
60 days	539	983	715	1,145	986	1,674	1,086	1,821
90 days	427	587	559	809	746	1,163	829	1,281
6 months	386	514	514	728	692	1,067	774	1,183
One year	358	464	475	660	638	972	718	1,086

 EXHIBIT 9.9

10 SUGGESTIONS FOR BUYING DISABILITY INCOME INSURANCE

1. *Start with your employee benefits;* you may be able to supplement a basic policy at group rates 15–35 percent below individual rates. Also, women may get unisex rates. Understand what your group policy covers and how it defines disability. Group plans generally pay 60 percent of base salary and may be limited in both maximum payment and benefit period; you may need to fill in gaps with individual insurance.
2. *Buy an individual policy if you think you won't qualify later.* You can buy a small policy with a rider that allows you to buy more later.
3. *Get several price quotes;* rates vary considerably.
4. *Make sure the insurance company is financially strong.*
5. *To reduce premiums and still get adequate coverage, lengthen waiting periods.* Going from 30 to 90 days can save 20 percent; to 1 year, 30 percent. Stretch the period for as long as possible based on your financial resources.
6. *A policy with benefits to age 65, not lifetime, saves 25 percent on a 40-year-old male's premium.* Once you reach retirement, you should be able to use other resources. (That's why it's important to consider disability coverage just one part of your overall personal financial plan.)
7. *Consider including a residual benefit option.* This makes up the income shortfall if you work only part-time or in a lower-paying job.
8. *Decide if you want to pay more for "own occupation" coverage.* The premium increases about 10 percent; you'll have to decide if it's worth it, depending on your current occupation.
9. *Ask about discounted premiums.* Some companies offer 10 percent off if you provide copies of tax returns or prepay premiums.
10. *Include an exclusion for a recurring medical problem.* You can reduce your premium if you exclude problems like a bad back or knee.

Sources: Adapted from "Disability Coverage Offers Safety Net," *Newsday*, July 25, 1999, p. F8; Toddi Gutner, "Keeping Covered While You're Convalescing," *Business Week Online*, November 16, 2000, **www.businessweek.com**; and Mari McQueen, "Back on Your Feet," *Money*, April 2000, p. 159.

this additional insurance is fixed at the inception of the contract and you do not have to prove insurability.

A *waiver of premium* is standard in disability income policies. If you are disabled for a minimum period, normally 60 or 90 days, the insurer will waive any future premiums that come due while you remain disabled. In essence, the waiver of premium provides you with additional disability income insurance in the amount of your regular premium payment.

Remember that disability income insurance is just one part of your overall personal financial plan. You'll need to find your own balance between cost and coverage. Exhibit 9.9 provides some suggestions for buying the right policy.

CONCEPT CHECK

9-18. What is *disability income insurance?* Explain the waiting period provisions found in such policies.

9-19. Describe both the liberal and strict definitions used to establish whether an insured is disabled. Why is benefit duration an important consideration when shopping for disability income coverage?

■ A Guide to Buying Health Care Insurance [LG6]

Let's now discuss how to systematically plan purchases of health care insurance. In many ways the approach here is similar to that proposed for life insurance in Chapter 8. With health care insurance, however, you generally must consider a variety of plans and sources for your protection.

Start by listing your potential areas of loss; determine what types of coverage and other resources are available to you; and, to spot gaps in your present protection, subtract your total coverage and resources from the amount of your potential losses. Once you have identified gaps in protection, you can structure a health care insurance plan that is best for you.

MATCHING NEEDS AND RESOURCES

Most people need protection against two types of losses that can result from illness or accident: (1) expenses for medical bills, rehabilitation counseling, and training and education; and (2) loss of income or household services caused by an inability to work. The amount for medical expenses cannot be easily estimated, but in cases of long-term, serious illness, medical bills and related expenses can run into the hundreds of thousands of dollars. Thus you should probably figure you face potential hospitalization, surgical, pharmaceutical, and other charges of at least $250,000 and, with a protracted disability, as high as $1 million. In contrast, the income need is relatively easy to calculate: it is simply a percentage of your (or your spouse's) current monthly earnings—most people believe that 60 to 75 percent is sufficient.

Money's Health Care Navigator, an interactive worksheet you'll find at **www.money.com/money/depts/insurance**, lets you select treatment preferences to develop a personal worksheet comparing the benefit level of three health care plans.

In the next step of your health care insurance purchase planning, you should match your present resources against your needs. Exhibit 9.10 should help you perform this task. It sets forth a checklist for the sources and types of health care coverage you might already have. Among these resources you should rely most on Social Security, present group coverage, Blue Cross/Blue Shield, individual coverage, savings, and employer wage continuation plans. The remaining sources of recovery are less significant for planning purposes because they typically restrict payments to specified types of illnesses or accidents.

After you have identified your present sources of coverage, you should examine the plan provisions to learn their terms of payment and the extent of coverage they provide. The key policy provisions that should most concern you will vary with the type of coverage—that is, medical expense, long-term care, or disability income plans. Use the previous discussions of provisions for each type of policy to evaluate your current coverage. If you find gaps for

EXHIBIT 9.10

A CHECKLIST OF SOURCES AND TYPES OF HEALTH CARE COVERAGE

Health care insurance can be obtained from a variety of providers, each offering various types of coverage.

SOCIAL SECURITY
Disability income
Medicare (medical expenses)
Medicaid (medical expenses)

EXISTING INDIVIDUAL RESOURCES
Present individual coverage
Family resources
Savings

WORKERS' COMPENSATION
Disability income
Medical expenses
Rehabilitation
Lump sum

WAGE CONTINUATION PLAN (EMPLOYER)
Sick leave
Short-term disability
Long-term disability

GROUP HEALTH PLANS
Hospitalization expenses
Surgical expenses
Physicians' expenses
Major medical
Comprehensive major medical
Pharmaceuticals
Chiropractic, optometry, etc.
Dental
Mental illness
Rehabilitation
Long-term care

OTHER PLANS
Homeowner's medical expenses
Auto medical expenses
Negligence claim
Veterans' medical benefits
Indian health services
Public health clinics (for example, communicable
    diseases, maternal and child health,
        migrant health expense)

BLUE CROSS/BLUE SHIELD
Hospitalization expenses
Surgical expenses
Physicians' expenses
Other expenses

which you do not have adequate coverage or savings, you need to arrange ways in which to meet potential losses.

COMPONENTS OF YOUR HEALTH CARE PLAN

Throughout this chapter, we have emphasized the need for good health insurance protection to cover the costs of illness or accident. However, a good health care plan encompasses much more than a means of financing medical expenses, lost income, and replacement services. It should also incorporate other means of risk reduction. Accordingly, recall from Chapter 8 that you can deal with risk in four ways: risk avoidance, loss prevention and control, risk assumption, and insurance. Although these four methods apply to all types of risk, each is especially useful in developing health care plans.

RISK AVOIDANCE. Looking for ways to avoid exposure to loss is a good starting point for a health care plan. For example, people who do not stand on the backs of chairs to reach into high places seldom fall off chairs; people who do not take illegal drugs never have to worry about disability from overdose; people who refuse to ride on motorcycles avoid the risk of injury from this relatively dangerous means of transportation; and people who do not smoke in bed will never doze off and start a fire in their house.

LOSS PREVENTION AND CONTROL. Encouraging people to accept responsibility for their own well-being and to live healthier lifestyles can prevent illness and reduce high health care costs. Smoking, alcohol and drug dependency, improper diet, inadequate sleep, and lack of regular exercise contribute to more than 60 percent of all diagnosed illnesses, including heart disease, cancer, tuberculosis, and mental disorders. In contrast, the odds are overwhelming that if you maintain a basic program for fitness, you will miss fewer days of work, spend less on medical bills, and live a healthier and happier life.

The National Safety Council reports that more than one-half of all automobile accidents could be prevented if motorists followed highway safety laws. Driving under the influence of alcohol and drugs accounts for about half of all automobile fatalities; alcohol abuse is a leading cause of injury and death among college students and other young persons. (This toll on youth has prompted most states to raise the minimum legal drinking age.) Further, accident data overwhelmingly document the loss prevention effectiveness of safety belts, shoulder straps, and child passenger seats. Smoke alarms, bathtub safety mats, and proper storage of chemicals, pesticides, cleaning fluids, and prescription drugs are easy and effective measures for reducing loss frequency and severity. In summary, regardless of whether you are at home, school, work, or play—or traveling in between—you should integrate accident prevention measures into your health care plans.

RISK ASSUMPTION. The next essential step in preparing a health care plan involves considering the risks you are willing to retain. Some risks pose relatively small loss potential; you can budget for them rather than insure against them. Choosing insurance plans with deductibles and waiting periods is a form of risk assumption. It is more economical to pay small losses from savings than to pay higher premiums to insure them. Similarly, although you are wise to buy policies with high limits, few people are willing to pay the premium for 100 percent reimbursement of all losses above the deductible. To increase insurance affordability, most people assume part of the risk of large losses through participation or coinsurance, internal limits, and maximum aggregate limits. It is impossible to live in a world in which you avoid, prevent, or insure all your risks. That's why you should explicitly identify the types and amounts of risk that you are willing and able to bear before you buy health care coverage—or, for that matter, any type of insurance coverage.

SHOPPING FOR HEALTH CARE INSURANCE

Our goal throughout this chapter has been to give you a systematic way to decide what health insurance (or other health care financing plan—HMO, PPO, Blue Cross/Blue Shield, and so on) you should buy. Now that you have a plan that incorporates risk avoidance, loss prevention and control, and risk assumption, you can shop for health care insurance. As you do, you should focus on three areas: (1) cost of coverage, (2) selecting health care insurance as an employee benefit, and (3) quality of agent and company.

COST OF COVERAGE. In some ways shopping for health care insurance is like shopping for a car. Both are major purchases. It is likely that a family would spend as much or more each month for their medical insurance as they do on an auto loan payment. Today an individual can expect to pay $150 to $300 per month for a health care plan; a family, $350 to $600 per month or more. In addition, you would not simply compare, say, major medical coverage from Blue Cross/Blue Shield with that of Prudential any more than you would blindly choose between a Chevrolet and a Toyota. In each instance you need to compare competitive offerings feature for feature. What provisions do available health care insurance policies contain? What are their definitions of an accident? What exclusions apply? What persons and places are covered? What are the applicable deductibles, methods of payment, duration of benefits, and participation percentages? Big cost differences exist among health care insurance plans just as they do among different models of Chevrolets and Fords, but you can judge which is the best buy only after you have compared the costs of various plans to the features they offer.

SELECTING HEALTH CARE INSURANCE AS AN EMPLOYEE BENEFIT. As noted earlier, many people obtain health insurance coverage through their employer group. In some cases the employer offers only one plan and pays for it entirely or partially. When this is the case the employee should evaluate the plan's benefits and costs and decide whether to be part of the plan and whether additional individual coverage is required.

The trend now, however, among medium and large employers is to offer employees a choice of fringe benefits (a *flexible-benefit ["cafeteria"] plan* as discussed in Chapter 2). Often the menu of benefits includes more than one health care insurance option, so the employee can choose among a major medical plan, a group HMO, and perhaps an IPA in addition to choosing the amount of life insurance, disability income insurance, and other benefits he or she might like. In a typical example, you might receive $400 a month to "spend" on any of the following benefits for you and your family:

- Health care coverage: major medical: $200 deductible, $425; $500 deductible, $345; group HMO, $422; IPA, $480; dental insurance, $55
- Disability income coverage, $28
- Life insurance options for employee only: term life: $75,000, $11; $150,000, $21
- Accidental death coverage of $500,000, $15

After reviewing the menu, you see that your employer has given you enough ($400) to purchase the least expensive health care insurance policy for your family and one or more other coverages, depending on which you select. If you want more comprehensive "first-dollar" health care coverage and any of the other plans (dental, disability income, and life insurance), the company will deduct the additional cost from your paycheck. Before making this decision, compare the cost of coverage through your employer with that available through individual policies.

Generally, life and disability income coverage, like health care coverage, is much more reasonably priced through group plans than through an individual policy. Most group plans establish rates based on age bands (20–24, 25–29, 30–34, etc.) to ensure the group plan is always a good bargain compared with individual plans. This ensures that younger, healthier people will sign up for the group plan and helps the group (usually the employer) meet the minimum enrollment requirements of the insurer.

If your spouse is employed, then you should also evaluate his or her benefit package before making any decisions. Also, *remember that the purpose of insurance is to protect against very large possible losses rather than to pay relatively small expenses.* Therefore, if your family depends on your income to live, don't select dental insurance *instead of* life and disability income coverage.

Another important area of group coverage is retiree benefits. Because the number of companies providing health care benefits to retirees has decreased sharply, you may no longer be able to count on receiving employer-paid benefits once you retire. So it is important to know what your options are to ensure you and your family have continued health care coverage. At some companies, retirees can pay a portion of the premium cost; other companies have dropped it altogether. You will need to consider COBRA coverage and look for group coverage through an HMO or professional organization, which is cheaper than individual plans. Once you turn 65, Medicare will cover basic medical expenses, but you will probably want to supplement this coverage with one of the 10 standard Medigap plans, which will cost from $600 to $2,500 per year for a 65-year-old, depending on coverage.

QUALITY OF AGENT AND COMPANY. As with all types of insurance, you should buy health care plans from an agent who will listen to your needs and answer your questions with well thought out responses—not sales jargon and pressure—and from a company that is rated highly for financial soundness by at least two of the major rating agencies, as discussed in Chapter 8. Also, look for a health care insurer that settles claims fairly and promptly, avoiding companies with narrow and unusual, legalistic claims practices. Friends with claims-settlement experience and the consumer division of your state's department of insurance regulation can help you learn about an insurer's record for service after a loss. You should be just as concerned about the financial soundness and claims service of your group insurance underwriters as you would be when purchasing an individual health care policy.

CHOOSING A HEALTH CARE PLAN

Once you have familiarized yourself with the different health care plans and providers and reviewed your needs, you must choose one or more plans to provide coverage for you and your dependents. We've already discussed how to do this for long-term care and disability income insurance, so here we will focus on health care insurance.

If you are employed, first review the various health care plans your company offers. If you can't get coverage from an employer, get plan descriptions and policy costs from several providers, including a group plan from a professional or trade organization, if available, for both indemnity and managed care plans. Then take your time and carefully read the plan materials to understand exactly what is covered, and at what cost. Next, add up what you have spent on medical costs over the past few years and what you might expect in the future, so you can see what your costs would be under various plans. Worksheet 9.2 provides a convenient checklist to help you compare plan costs and benefits.

How do you find health care insurance if you have just graduated from college, don't yet have a job, and can no longer be covered by your parents' policy? Or maybe you are between jobs or need time to search out the best policy but don't want to be without protection. The *Money in Action* box on page 396 will help you with these situations.

You'll have to ask yourself some difficult questions to decide whether you want an indemnity or a managed care plan, and then to choose the particular plan:

- **How important is cost compared with having freedom of choice?** You may have to pay more to stay with your current doctor if he or she is not part of a managed care plan you are considering. Also, you have to decide if you can live with the managed care plan's approach to health care.
- **Will you be reimbursed if you choose a managed care plan and want to see an out-of-network provider?** For most people, the managed care route is cheaper, even if you visit a doctor only once a year, because of indemnity plan "reasonable charge" provisions.
- **What types of coverage do you need?** Everyone has different needs; one person may want a plan with good maternity and pediatric care, whereas another wants outpatient mental health benefits. Make sure the plans you consider offer what you want.

HEALTH CARE PLAN CHECKLIST

This worksheet provides a convenient checklist that can be used to compare the costs and benefits of competing health care plans:

	Company 1	Company 2	Company 3
PLAN TYPE (HMO, PPO, ETC.)			
COSTS			
Premium per month			
Annual deductible: Per person/ Per family			
Copayment percent after deductible			
Copay or % coinsurance per office visit			
Copay or % coinsurance for "wellness" care			
COVERED MEDICAL SERVICES WITHIN NETWORK			
Inpatient hospital services			
Outpatient surgery			
Physician visits (in the hospital)			
Office visits (provider)			
Skilled nursing care			
Medical tests and x-rays			
Prescription drugs			
Mental health care			
Drug and alcohol abuse treatment			
Home health care visits			
Rehabilitation facility care			
Physical therapy			
Speech therapy			
Hospice care			
Maternity care			
Chiropractic treatment			
Preventive care and checkups			
Well-baby care			
Dental care			
Other covered services			
OTHER PROVISIONS			
Out-of-network coverage			
Medical service limits, exclusions, or preexisting conditions			
Requirements for utilization review, pre-authorization, or certification procedures			

Source: Developed from information in *HIAA Guide To Health Insurance*, **www.hiaa.org/cons/guidehi.html**.

MONEY IN ACTION

Health Care Insurance: Don't Leave School Without It!

Jessica Cullen was thrilled to find a job in fund-raising soon after graduating from college. However, the position was at a nonprofit organization that offered no health insurance benefits. She was able to continue her coverage on her parents' policy for 6 months, but was then without coverage. Jessica has plenty of company because young adults age 18 to 24 and 25 to 34 are the two largest groups of uninsured persons in this country.

If you, like Jessica, find yourself at a company without a group plan or at a company that requires a waiting period for plan eligibility, you have several options. Health care insurance providers offer short-term policies specifically designed to act as a bridge for college graduates seeking employment or people between jobs who hope to find work soon. The plans, from such companies as Golden Rule and Fortis Health, typically provide up to 6 months of major medical coverage. Premiums for a plan with a $250 deductible run about $40 to $60 a month depending on age, sex, and health. These plans are easy to obtain, and no physical or waiting period is required; it is usually just a matter of filling out a brief form and mailing a check.

These policies are best viewed as stop-gap measures. Although they are better than no insurance, they have limitations. For instance, Golden Rule applies a deductible to each injury or illness. Typical plans cover hospitalization expenses and doctor visits but not dentistry, pregnancy, cosmetic surgery, or mental disorders. They exclude pregnant women, people with health conditions that would make them ineligible for a fully underwritten plan of insurance, and people seeking coverage while traveling outside the United States.

There are several issues besides price to consider when looking for a short-term policy. Many insurance companies will not write a second short-term policy if you don't find work by the time your policy expires. In addition, most companies require that you pay the premium for the entire coverage period at the outset. Seek out a plan that offers pro-rated refunds if you cancel your policy prematurely, or one that lets you pay monthly rather than all at once.

Recent graduates who fear their job search may last a year or more may want to investigate standard, long-term, individual coverage that they can maintain indefinitely. Individual plans usually require a physical or "evidence of insurability," and the premiums cost a minimum of $100 to $200 per month. Choose the highest deductible you can reasonably handle to reduce premiums. Group plans, which are often available through college alumni groups, religious and social organizations, local chambers of commerce or state business associations, are nearly as expensive but tend to offer more benefits for the cost.

A more expensive way for recent grads, especially those with preexisting conditions, to get insurance is to extend their coverage under a parent's group plan. The federal government's COBRA legislation requires companies to extend coverage for former dependents up to 36 months if they pay the full premium, which can run $150 to $300 a month, plus a 2 percent administrative fee. However, to qualify you must act fast; the deadline for signing up is 60 days from the existing policy's expiration date.

Sources: Sandra Block, "Job Hoppers Shouldn't Let Health Insurance Trip Them Up," *USA Today*, September 7, 1999, p. 3B; Catherine Siskos, "Don't Get Sick," *Kiplinger's Personal Finance*, July 2000, pp. 80–83.

- **How good is the managed care network?** Look at the participating doctors and hospitals to see how many of your providers are part of the plan. Check out the credentials of participating providers; a good sign is accreditation from the National Committee for Quality Assurance (NCQA). Are the providers' locations convenient for you? What preventive medical programs does it provide? Has membership grown? Talk to friends and associates to see what their experiences have been with the plan.
- **How old are you and how is your health?** Many financial advisors recommend buying the lowest-cost plan—which may be an indemnity plan with a high deductible— if you're young and healthy.

 You're between jobs and need a temporary major medical health insurance policy. What type of policy can you get? How much would you have to pay? Check out Golden Rule at **www.goldenrule.com**.

CONCEPT CHECK

9-20. Briefly discuss the procedures for (a) determining health care insurance needs, (b) matching needs and resources, and (c) preparing a health care plan.

9-21. Describe the role of (a) risk avoidance, (b) loss prevention and control, and (c) risk assumption in the process of preparing a health care plan.

9-22. Describe the procedures used to evaluate and select health care insurance as an employee benefit.

9-23. Describe the following considerations that must be addressed when shopping for health care insurance: (a) cost of coverage and (b) quality of agent and insurance company.

SUMMARY

LG1. **Discuss how the health care industry is changing and why you should have adequate health care insurance.** The health care field is undergoing rapid changes today as rising health care costs have prompted new ways of delivering health services. The emphasis is on cost containment through managed care programs and preventive medicine. Because of the high cost of health care, the potential for economic loss from illness or accident is large. Adequate health care insurance coverage can protect you and your family.

LG2. **Differentiate among the major types of health care plans and identify the major private and public providers of health insurance and their programs.** In addition to the traditional indemnity health care insurance programs, individuals and families can obtain health care services directly from specific provider groups under managed care plans. With these plans the subscribers/users contract with and make monthly payments to the organization that provides the health care services. The most common examples of these plans are HMOs—both group HMOs and IPAs— and PPOs.

Important private providers of health care coverage include insurance companies, managed care organizations, and Blue Cross/Blue Shield. Today insurance companies and Blue Cross/Blue Shield also offer managed care programs. Health care insurance can be acquired through a group policy from an employer or other group and individual health insurance policies. Two government programs that provide health benefits are Social Security, which provides medical insurance and long-term disability insurance, and workers' compensation for job-related illness or injury.

LG3.   **Explain the basic types of medical expense coverage and policy provisions for medical expense plans.** The basic types of medical expense coverage are hospitalization insurance, surgical expense insurance, physicians expense insurance (which covers nonsurgical care), and major medical insurance (which covers all types of medical expenses). Some health insurers offer comprehensive major medical policies that combine basic hospitalization, surgical, and physicians expense coverage with a major medical plan to form a single policy. Other types of coverage include dental insurance, long-term care insurance (which covers out-of-hospital care for those with chronic illnesses or frailty), and disability income insurance (designed to replace wages lost as a result of illness or accident).

The most important provisions in medical expense insurance policies pertain to terms of payment, terms of coverage, and cost containment. How much your medical expense plan will pay depends on deductibles, participation (coinsurance), internal limits, and coordination of benefits. The terms of coverage encompass the persons and places covered, cancellation, preexisting conditions, pregnancy and abortion, mental illness, rehabilitation, and continuation of group coverage. Some of the more common cost containment provisions are pre-admission certification, continued stay review, second surgical opinions, and waiver of coinsurance.

LG4.   **Assess the need for and features of long-term care insurance.** Long-term care insurance covers nonhospital expenses, such as nursing home care or home health care, caused by chronic illness or frailty. The availability of coverage depends on provisions addressing type of care, eligibility requirements, services covered, renewability, and preexisting conditions. Terms-of-payment provisions include daily benefits, benefit duration, waiting period, and inflation protection. Premium levels result from differences in coverage and payment provisions, and vary widely among insurance companies.

LG5.   **Evaluate your need for and provisions of disability income insurance.** The loss of family income caused by the disability of a principal earner can be at least partially replaced by disability income insurance. Disability insurance needs can be estimated by subtracting the amount of existing monthly disability benefits from current monthly take-home pay. Important coverage terms include the definition of disability, probationary period, renewability, guaranteed insurability, and waiver of premium. Provisions pertaining to benefit amount and duration, waiting period, and cost-of-living adjustments define the terms of payment. Because these policies are expensive, you should choose as long a waiting period as possible given your other available financial resources.

LG6.   **Analyze your own health care insurance needs and shop for appropriate coverage.** From a health care insurance perspective, most people need protection from two types of losses: (1) the cost of medical bills and other associated expenses and (2) loss of income or household services caused by an inability to work. A good health care plan should use risk avoidance, loss prevention and control, and risk assumption strategies to reduce risk and the associated need and cost of insurance.

The best way to buy health care insurance is to match your insurance needs with the various types of coverage available. When shopping for health care insurance, consider the cost of coverage, the cost of health care insurance as an employee benefit, the quality of both the agent and the insurer or managed care provider, and your own medical needs and care preferences.

QUESTIONS AND PROBLEMS

1. Susana Chang was seriously injured in a skiing accident and broke both her legs and an arm. Her medical expense bills were 5 days hospitalization at $800 per day, including room and other services; $4,300 in physician's fees (including the time she was in the hospital and 5 follow-up office visits); $320 in prescription medicines; and $1,200 for physical therapy treatments.
   a. If she has an indemnity plan with a $500 deductible that pays 80 percent of her charges and has a $5,000 stop-loss provision, how much will she have to pay out of pocket? (Assume that charges fall within the customary and reasonable payment amounts.)
   b. What would you estimate to be her out-of-pocket costs if she belonged to an HMO and used its providers? (The copayment for office visits is $12.)
   c. Monthly premiums are $155 for the indemnity plan and $250 for the HMO. If she had no other medical expenses for the year, which plan provides more cost-effective coverage for Susana?

2. Discuss the pros and cons of long-term care insurance. Does it make sense for anyone in your family at the present time? Why or why not? What factors might change this decision in the future?

3. *Use Worksheet 9.1.* John Fitzmorris, a 35-year-old computer programmer, earns $72,000 a year; his monthly take-home pay is $3,750. His wife, Linda, works part-time at their children's elementary school but receives no benefits. John's employee benefit plan includes group disability income insurance with coverage for a total of $2\frac{1}{2}$ years at $2,250 per month. The Fitzmorris family is concerned about their financial well-being if John were to be disabled for an extended period.
   a. Use Worksheet 9.1 to calculate John's disability benefit needs assuming he will not qualify for Social Security.
   b. Based on your answer in part **a**, make some recommendations to John about the type and size of disability income policy he should buy, including a discussion of possible provisions he might want to include. Would you advise him to buy own occupation coverage? Why or why not? What other factors should he take into account when choosing a policy?

4. *Use Worksheet 9.1.* Calculate your own disability income insurance need using Worksheet 9.1. Discuss how you would go about purchasing this coverage.

5. *Use Worksheet 9.2.* Search the Internet or use other resources to gather information about two or three health care insurance policies, including one HMO. With Worksheet 9.2 as a guide, compare the policies' features. Select the one best for you, and explain your reasoning.

6. Given your current situation, discuss the factors that would be important to you in choosing a health care plan. What type of plan would you select, and why? What steps can you take to keep your health care costs down?

APPLYING PERSONAL FINANCE

What Is Your Health Care Coverage?

Are you covered by a health insurance plan through your parents, your job, or some other source? What are its provisions? The purpose of this project is to answer these and other questions about health care insurance.

Everyone should have some form of health care coverage. Make a list of the possible health care needs you are likely to have during the year. Be sure to include potential accident risks, such as a sprained ankle playing softball, etc., to which you are typically exposed as a result of your lifestyle activities. Once the list is complete, obtain a copy of the health care insurance policy under which you are covered and evaluate it in light of your needs. (*Note:* Because it's likely you're covered under a group policy, if you don't have a copy of the policy, you should be able to obtain it directly from the group administrator at the company through which your insurance is provided. If you cannot obtain your own policy, get a typical policy from a friend or directly from a health insurer. Read the policy and note its major provisions. Is there a deductible? Is there coinsurance? What are the policy limits? Can you go to any doctor? Are there limits to the amounts paid for some procedures? Answers to these and other questions should be easy to find in the descriptive information about the policy. If you belong to a health maintenance organization (HMO), your responses may differ significantly from someone with a traditional health care insurance policy. Does the policy adequately meet your health care insurance needs?

CONTEMPORARY CASE APPLICATIONS

9.1   Evaluating Rick's Health Care Coverage

Rick Lannefeld was a self-employed window washer earning approximately $500 per week. One day, while cleaning windows on the eighth floor of the First National Bank Building, he tripped and fell from the scaffolding to the pavement below. He sustained severe multiple injuries but miraculously survived the accident. He was immediately rushed to Mt. Sinai Hospital for surgery. He remained there for 60 days of treatment, after which he was allowed to go home for further recuperation. During his hospital stay, he incurred the following expenses: surgeon, $2,500; physician, $1,000; hospital bill, room and board, $250 per day; nursing services, $1,200; anesthetics, $300; wheelchair rental, $70; ambulance, $60; and drugs, $350. Rick has a major medical policy with LIC Corporation that has a $3,000 deductible clause, an 80 percent coinsurance clause, internal limits of $180 per day on hospital room and board, and $1,500 as a maximum surgical fee. The policy provides no disability income benefits.

Questions

1. Explain the policy provisions as they relate to deductibles, coinsurance, and internal limits.
2. How much should Rick recover from the insurance company? How much must he pay out of his pocket?
3. Would any other policies have offered Rick additional protection? What about his inability to work while recovering from his injury?
4. Based on the information presented, how would you assess Rick's health care insurance coverage? Explain.

9.2   Benito and Teresa Get a Handle on Their Disability Income Needs

Benito Fernandez and his wife, Teresa, have been married for 2 years and have a 1-year-old son. They live in Detroit, where Benito is a supervisor for Ford Motor Company. He earns $3,200 per month, of which he takes home $2,300. As an employee of Ford, he and his family are entitled to receive the benefits provided by the company's group health insurance policy. In addition to major medical coverage, the policy provides a monthly disability income benefit amounting to 20 percent of the employee's average monthly take-home pay for the most recent 12 months prior to incurring the disability. (*Note:* Benito's average monthly take-home pay for the most recent year is equal to his current monthly take-home pay.) In the instance of complete disability, Benito would also be eligible for Social Security payments of $700 per month.

Teresa is also employed. She earns $700 per month after taxes working part-time at a nearby grocery store. The store provides her with no benefits other than Social Security. Should Benito become disabled, Teresa would continue to work at her part-time job. If she became disabled, Social Security would provide monthly income of $300. Benito and Teresa spend 90 percent of their combined take-home pay to meet their bills and provide for a variety of necessary items. They use the remaining 10 percent to fulfill their entertainment and savings goals.

Questions

1. How much, if any, additional disability income insurance does Benito require to ensure adequate protection against his becoming completely disabled? Use Worksheet 9.1 to assess his needs.
2. Does Teresa need any disability income coverage? Explain.
3. What specific recommendations with respect to disability income insurance would you give Benito and Teresa to provide adequate protection for themselves and their child?

MONEY ONLINE

INSURE YOUR HEALTH!

Note: Web addresses change frequently, so you may need to determine the home page and do a site search to find the page or topic that's referenced.

1. **www.quicken.com/insurance**
   How can consumers evaluate their health care plan? Look under "Health Insurance" and click on "Is This Plan Any Good?" at Quicken's Insurance Center for information on finding insurance company financial-health ratings, researching the plan, dealing with grievances and appeals, and what to expect from emergency services and specialists. Scroll down to "Materials and Resources" for a list of publications and organizations to further assist you in determining the quality of your health care plan.

2. **www.insure.com/health**
   What benefits must health plans issued in your state include? Click on "The Insure.com's Health Insurance Laws and Benefits Tool" to find out. While you're at Insure.com's Web site, browse through their many articles on health insurance, which cover topics such as how to judge the quality of a health plan, medical savings accounts, and health insurance for college students.

3. **hprc.ncqa.org**
   How does your health plan rate? Look at your company's Health Plan Report Card prepared by the National Committee for Quality Assurance (NCQA). Click on "Create Report Card" to pull up the specifics on your company or to view a list of all NCQA-Accredited Plans.

4. **www.actuary.com**
   Need to find your health insurance company's Web site? Click on "Health Insurance Companies" at the Actuary.com site for an extensive listing of links to various health insurance companies.

5. **www.medicare.gov/Nursing/Overview.asp**
   Need information on a nursing home? Visit Medicare's Web site for a "Checklist" for selecting a nursing home or to find a Medicare- and Medicaid-certified nursing home in your area at "Nursing Home Compare." Learn the "Alternatives to Nursing Home Care" and read "Resident Rights."

6. **www.northwesternmutual.com**
   How likely are you to be affected by a long-term disability? At Northwestern Mutual's Web site, click on "Calculators" and then on "Is There a Gap in Your Plan?" to calculate the odds that you will become disabled for 90 or more days before you reach age 65. Other useful calculators include "Disability Insurance Gap" and "Disability Insur-ance Needs" to help you determine whether you have enough disability insurance.

7. **www.ssa.gov/disability**
   Learn about Social Security's two disability programs at the Web site of the Social Security Administration. Consult "How to Apply" to find the eligibility requirements or click on "Disability Planner" and "Supplemental Security Income" to read up on the services and benefits provided.

8. **www.medicare.gov**
   Learn all about Medicare at the official U.S. government site for Medicare information. Find information on coverage, eligibility, and enrollment under "Medicare Basics."

Compare health plans at "Medicare Health Plan Compare" or locate a supplemental policy at "Medigap Compare."

9. **www.pueblo.gsa.gov/crh/insurance.htm**

Find your state's insurance regulator. Scroll through the list at the Web site of the Federal Consumer Information Center to find the office responsible for enforcing your state's insurance laws. Find information to help you choose an insurance policy or learn how to file an insurance-related complaint.

Just for Fun!

10. **www.nih.gov/nia**

What are the latest developments in health and aging research? Search the Web site of the National Institute on Aging to keep up with the exciting discoveries being made that will ultimately work to improve the health and longevity of all people.

Chapter 10

Protecting Your Property

LEARNING GOALS

LG1.   Discuss the importance and basic principles of property insurance, including types of exposure, indemnity, and coinsurance.

LG2.   Identify the different coverages provided by a homeowner's insurance policy.

LG3.   Select the right homeowners' insurance policy for your needs.

LG4.   Analyze the different coverages in a personal automobile policy (PAP) and choose the most cost-effective policy.

LG5.   Describe other forms of property and liability insurance.

LG6.   Choose a property and liability insurance agent and company, and settle claims.

FIRE!

Standing outside on a cold winter night, Bill and Marsha Stanley watched 12 years of their lives go up in flames as their 18th century Colonial home in a Boston suburb burned almost to the ground. They were thankful that no one was injured, except for a neighbor bitten by their German Shepherd, who got loose during the fire.

As they later discovered, their tragedy went beyond losing years of family memorabilia. They had insured the house for $250,000 with replacement-cost coverage. However, their homeowner's insurance policy capped coverage at 125 percent of the policy value, or $312,500—and contractors estimated it would cost at least $350,000 to rebuild the house. In addition, the policy wouldn't pay to duplicate certain historic features.

The Stanleys could either use savings to pay the excess amount or downsize the new house to stay within the reimbursed amount. They decided to build a slightly smaller house but to keep the special touches that made the home unique, even if it meant paying for it themselves. Having a videotape of the contents of the house in their bank safe-deposit box helped them document their claims more fully and receive the full reimbursement allowed.

The dog bite might have posed another problem. Because the dog got loose in an emergency situation, the neighbor decided not to sue and settled for an agreed-on amount. Dog bites account for one-third of all homeowners' claims every year, so the Stanleys realized they needed to review their liability coverage as well.

When the Stanleys reevaluated their new homeowner's policy, they made sure to get unlimited replacement-cost coverage and an automatic annual inflation adjustment. They also read the fine print more carefully to ensure there were no big gaps in coverage. They decided to increase their liability coverage because the standard $100,000 in their homeowner's policy was not adequate. They were able to purchase $1 million of liability coverage for a small premium increase—well worth the price for their peace of mind. With the Stanleys' experiences in mind, let's begin our study of property and liability insurance.

Some Basic Principles of Property Insurance [LG1]

Suppose a severe storm destroyed your home. Could you afford to replace it? Most people could not. To protect yourself from this and similar types of property loss, you need property insurance. In addition, not a day goes by that you don't face some type of risk of negligence. For example, you might be distraught over a personal problem and unintentionally run a red light, seriously injuring a pedestrian. Because the consequences of this and other potentially negligent acts can cause financial ruin, appropriate liability insurance is essential.

Accordingly, property and liability insurance should be as much a part of your personal financial plans as life and health insurance. Such coverage protects the assets you have already acquired and safeguards your progress toward achieving your financial goals. In particular, **property insurance** guards against catastrophic losses of real and personal property caused by such perils as fire, theft, vandalism, windstorms, and many other calamities. **Liability insurance,** in contrast, offers protection against the financial

property insurance
Insurance coverage that protects real and personal property from catastrophic losses caused by a variety of perils, such as fire, theft, vandalism, and windstorms.

liability insurance
Insurance that protects against the financial consequences that may arise from the insured's responsibility for property losses of or injuries to others.

consequences that may arise from the insured's responsibility for property losses of or injuries to others.

Although people spend a lot of money for insurance coverage, few really know what they are getting for their premium dollars. Even worse, the vast majority of people are totally unaware of any gaps, overinsurance, or underinsurance in their property and liability insurance programs. Because such inefficient and inadequate insurance protection is completely at odds with the objectives of personal financial planning, you should become familiar with the principles of property and liability insurance.

The basic principles of property and liability insurance pertain to types of exposure, the principle of indemnity, and coinsurance. Each of these principles is discussed in the following sections.

TYPES OF EXPOSURE

Most individuals face two basic types of exposure: physical loss of property and loss through liability.

peril
A cause of loss.

EXPOSURE TO PROPERTY LOSS. The vast majority of property insurance contracts define the property covered and name the **perils**—the causes of loss—for which insurance proceeds will be available. Some property contracts offer protection on a more comprehensive basis, however, and limit coverage by excluding certain types of property and perils. As a rule, most property insurance contracts impose two obligations on the property owner: (1) developing a complete inventory of the property being insured and (2) identifying the perils against which protection is desired.

Property Inventory. Do you know the value of all the property you own? If you are like most people, you don't, nor do you have an itemized property list for insurance purposes. A complete property inventory will not only help you select the most appropriate coverages but will also help you settle a claim if a loss occurs. All property insurance companies require you to show proof of loss when making a claim, and your personal property inventory, along with corresponding values at the time of inventory, can serve as evidence to satisfy the company.

Ordinarily, a family has a home, household furnishings, clothing and personal accessories, lawn and garden equipment, and motor vehicles (intended for road use), all of which need to be insured. Fortunately, most homeowners' and automobile insurance policies provide coverage for these types of belongings. But many families also own such items as motorboats and trailers, various types of off-road vehicles, business property and inventories, jewelry, stamp or coin collections, furs, musical instruments, antiques, paintings, bonds and other securities, and items of special value, such as expensive cameras, golf clubs, electronic recording and playing equipment, or personal computers. Coverage for these belongings often requires special arrangements with the insurer.

To help policyholders prepare inventories, many insurance companies have easy-to-complete personal property inventory forms available. A partial sample of one such form is shown in Exhibit 10.1. In addition, people can supplement these inventory forms with photographs or videotapes of their belongings. For insurance purposes, a picture may truly be worth a thousand words. Regardless of whether the completed inventory forms are supplemented with photographs or videotapes, *every effort should be made to keep these documents in a safe place,* where they can't be destroyed—like a safe-deposit box. As an added protection, you might even consider keeping a *duplicate copy* somewhere; for example, with a parent or trusted relative. Remember, you may need these photographs and inventories if something serious does happen and you have to come up with an authenticated list of property losses.

EXHIBIT 10.1

A PERSONAL PROPERTY INVENTORY FORM

Using a form like this will help you keep track of your personal property, including date of purchase, original price, and replacement cost. Note that this exhibit is only part of a 19-page homeowner's inventory record; this particular inventory record is put out by the *Personal Insurance Division of the Chubb Insurance Companies*, and includes not only household furnishings, but also clothing, electrical appliances, books and tools, electronic equipment, and various items of exceptional value, like china, antiques, fine art, jewelry, and so forth.

Living Room

Article	Qty.	Date Purchase	Purchase Price	Replacement Cost
Air conditioners (window)				
Blinds/shades				
Bookcases				
Books				
Cabinets				
Carpets/rugs				
Chairs				
Chests				
Clocks				
Couches/sofas				
Curtains/draperies				
Decks				
Fireplace fixtures				
Hassocks				
Lamps/lighting fixtures				
Mirrors				
Musical instruments				
Pictures/paintings				
Records/tapes				
Planters				
Stereo equipment				
Tables				
Television sets				
Wall units				
Other				
Other				
Other				

Living Room

Stereo System

Brand	
Model	
Serial #	Date purchased
Purchase price $	Replacement cost $

Stereo Receiver/Tuner

Brand	
Model	
Serial #	Date purchased
Purchase price $	Replacement cost $

Turntable

Brand	
Model	
Serial #	Date purchased
Purchase price $	Replacement cost $

Cassette Deck

Brand	
Model	
Serial #	Date purchased
Purchase price $	Replacement cost $

Compact Disc Player

Brand	
Model	
Serial #	Date purchased
Purchase price $	Replacement cost $

Source: *Homeowner's Inventory,* Chubb Insurance Companies, Personal Insurance Division, Warren, NJ, 1998.

Identifying Perils. Many people feel a false sense of security after buying insurance because they believe they are safeguarded against all contingencies. The fact is, however, that certain *perils* cannot be reasonably insured. For example, most homeowners' or automobile insurance policies limit or exclude damage or loss caused by flood, earthquake, mud slides, mysterious disappearance, war, nuclear radiation, and wear and tear. In addition, property insurance contracts routinely limit coverage on the basis of location of the property, time of loss, persons involved, and the types of hazards to which the property is exposed. (These limitations are explained further in subsequent sections of this chapter.)

LIABILITY EXPOSURES. We all encounter a variety of liability exposures every day. Driving a car, entertaining guests at home, or being careless in performing professional duties are some of the more common liability risks. Loss exposures that result from these activities are examples of **negligence**—the failure to act in a reasonable manner or to take necessary steps to protect others from harm. However, even if you are never negligent and always prudent, someone might *think* you are the cause of a loss and bring a costly lawsuit against you. Losing the judgment could cost you thousands—or even millions—of dollars. A debt that size could force many families into financial ruin and even bankruptcy.

Fortunately, you can buy *liability insurance* coverage to protect against losses resulting from each of these risks, *including the high legal fees* required to defend yourself against suits that may or may not have merit. It's important to include adequate liability insurance in your overall insurance program, either through your homeowner's and automobile policies or through a separate umbrella policy.

PRINCIPLE OF INDEMNITY

The **principle of indemnity** states that the insured may not be compensated by the insurance company in an amount exceeding the insured's economic loss. Most property and liability insurance contracts are based on this principle—although, as noted in Chapters 8 and 9, this principle does not apply to life and health insurance. Several important concepts related to the principle of indemnity include actual cash value, subrogation, and other insurance.

ACTUAL CASH VALUE VERSUS REPLACEMENT COST. The principle of indemnity also limits the amount an insured may collect to the **actual cash value** of the property: the replacement cost less the amount of physical depreciation. Some insurers guarantee replacement cost without taking depreciation into account—for example, most homeowners' policies will settle building losses on a replacement cost basis if the proper type and amount of insurance is purchased. Without a replacement-cost provision, however, it is common practice to deduct the amount of depreciation to obtain the actual cash value. If an insured property is damaged, the insurer is obligated to pay no more than what the property would cost new today (its replacement cost) less the amount of depreciation from wear and tear.

For example, assume that fire destroys two rooms of furniture and it would cost $5,000 to replace the furniture. The actual age of the furniture was 6 years, and it was estimated to have a useful life of 10 years. Therefore, at the time of loss the furniture was subject to an assumed physical depreciation of 60 percent (6 years ÷ 10 years)—in this case, $3,000. Because the actual cash value is estimated at $2,000 ($5,000 replacement cost minus $3,000 depreciation), the maximum the insurer would have to pay is $2,000. Note that the original cost of the property has no bearing on the settlement.

SUBROGATION. After an insurance company pays a claim, its **right of subrogation** allows it to request reimbursement from the person who caused the loss or from that

negligence
The failure to act in a reasonable manner or to take necessary steps to protect others from harm.

principle of indemnity
An insurance principle stating that an insured may not be compensated by the insurance company in an amount exceeding the insured's economic loss.

actual cash value
A value assigned to an insured property that is determined by subtracting the amount of depreciation from its replacement cost.

right of subrogation
The right of an insurer, who has paid an insured's claim, to request reimbursement from the person who caused the loss or that person's insurer.

person's insurance company. For example, assume you are in an automobile accident in which the other party damages your car. You may collect from your insurer or the at-fault party's insurer but not from both (at least not for the same loss). If you receive payment from your insurance company, you must subrogate (transfer) to it your right to sue the other person. Clearly, to collect the full amount from both parties would leave you better off after the loss than before it. Such an action would violate the principle of indemnity. Because the party who caused the accident (or loss) is ultimately responsible for paying the damages, the insurance company can go after the responsible party to collect its loss (the amount it paid out to you).

OTHER INSURANCE. Nearly all property and liability insurance contracts have an *other-insurance clause* that prohibits insured persons from insuring their property with two or more insurance companies and then collecting in full for a loss from all companies. The other-insurance clause normally states that if a person has more than one insurance policy on a property, each company is liable for only a pro-rated amount of the loss based on its proportion of the total insurance covering the property. Without this provision, insured persons could use duplicate property insurance policies to actually profit from their losses.

COINSURANCE

Coinsurance, a provision commonly found in property insurance contracts, requires policyholders to buy insurance in an amount equal to a specified percentage of the replacement value of their property. If that's not done, then the *policyholder* is required to pay for a proportional share of the losses. In essence, the coinsurance provision stipulates that if the property isn't properly covered, the property owner will become the "coinsurer" and bear part of the loss. If the policyholder has the stipulated amount of coverage (usually 80 percent of the value of the property), then the insurance company will reimburse him or her for covered losses dollar for dollar up to the amount of the policy limits. Otherwise, payment will be based on a specified percentage of loss.

Assume, for example, that John and Mary have a fire insurance policy on their $200,000 apartment building with an 80 percent coinsurance clause. The policy limits must equal or exceed 80 percent of the value of their building. Further assume that they had run short of money and decided to save by buying a single $120,000 policy instead of a minimum of $160,000 (80 percent × $200,000) as required by the coinsurance clause. If a loss occurred, the company would be obligated to pay only 75 percent ($120,000/$160,000) of the loss, up to the amount of the policy limit. Thus, on damages of $40,000, the insurer would pay only $30,000 (75 percent × $40,000). Obviously, you should closely evaluate the coinsurance clause of any property insurance policy so you will not have an unexpected additional burden in event of loss.

coinsurance
In property insurance, a provision that requires a policyholder to buy insurance in an amount equal to a specified percentage of the replacement value of their property; if not, the *policyholder* is required to pay for a proportional share of the losses.

CONCEPT CHECK

10-1. Briefly explain the fundamental concepts related to property and liability insurance.

10-2. Explain the *principle of indemnity*. Are any limits imposed on the amount an insured may collect under this principle?

10-3. Explain the *right of subrogation*. How does this feature help lower insurance costs?

10-4. Describe how the *coinsurance* feature works.

■ Homeowners' Insurance [LG2, LG3]

Although homeowners' insurance is often thought of as a single type of insurance policy, homeowners can choose from four different forms (HO-1, HO-2, HO-3, and HO-8). Two other forms (HO-4 and HO-6) meet the needs of renters and owners of condominiums (Exhibit 10.2). An HO-4 renter's policy offers essentially the same broad protection as an HO-2 homeowner's policy, except that the coverage does not apply to the rented dwelling unit because tenants usually do not have a financial interest in the real property.

All HO forms are divided into two sections. Section I applies to the dwelling, accompanying structures, and personal property of the insured. Section II deals with comprehensive coverage for personal liability and for medical payments to others. The scope of coverage under Section I is least with an HO-1 policy and greatest with an HO-3 policy. HO-8 is a modified coverage policy for older homes used to insure houses that have market values well below the cost to rebuild. The coverage in Section II is the same for all forms.

In the following paragraphs we'll explain the important features of homeowners' forms HO-2 and HO-3, the most commonly sold policies. (As Exhibit 10.2 shows, HO-1 is a very basic policy with relatively narrow coverage. Because it is seldom used, it is not covered in detail here.) The coverage offered under the HO-2 and HO-3 forms is basically the same; the differences lie only in the number of perils against which protection applies.

PERILS COVERED

named peril policy
An insurance policy that names the perils covered individually.

As mentioned previously, a peril is defined as a cause of loss. Some property and liability insurance agreements, called *comprehensive* policies, cover all perils except those specifically excluded, whereas **named peril policies** name the perils covered individually.

SECTION I PERILS. The perils against which the home and its contents are insured are shown in Exhibit 10.2. The coverage on household belongings is the same for the HO-2 and HO-3 forms, but coverage on the house and other structures (for example, a detached garage) is comprehensive under HO-3 and a named peril in HO-2. Whether homeowners should buy an HO-2 or an HO-3 form depends primarily on the amount they are willing to spend to secure additional protection. In some states the premium differential is small, making an HO-3 policy the better buy. In other states the HO-2 form has a substantially lower premium. Also, the size of the premiums for the HO-2 and HO-3 policies can differ substantially among insurance companies. Because of its more limited coverage, the purchase of an HO-1 is not recommended. (A special note on the HO-8 is presented later.)

Note in Exhibit 10.2 that the types of Section I perils covered include just about everything from fire and explosions to lightning and wind damage, to theft and vandalism; unfortunately, these are all perils to which any homeowner is exposed. Although the list of perils is quite extensive, a couple of types are specifically excluded from most homeowners' contracts—in particular, *most policies (even HO-2 and HO-3 forms) exclude earthquakes and floods.* The catastrophic nature of such events causes widespread and very costly damage. In addition, many areas of the country simply are not susceptible to earthquakes and floods, and, as a result, homeowners in those areas shouldn't have to pay for coverage they don't need. But even if you live in an area where the risk of an earthquake or a flood is relatively high, you'll find that *standard homeowners' policies do not provide protection against these perils.* Fortunately, as we'll see later in this chapter, you can obtain coverage for earthquakes and floods under a separate policy or a rider.

SECTION II PERILS. The perils insured against under Section II of the homeowner's contract are the (alleged) negligence of an insured. The coverage is called *comprehensive personal liability coverage* because it offers protection against nearly any source of liability (major exclusions are noted later) resulting from negligence. It does not insure against other losses for which one may become liable, such as libel, slander, defamation of character, and contractual or intentional wrongdoings. For example, coverage would apply if you carelessly, but unintentionally, knocked someone down your stairs. If you purposely struck and injured another person, however, or harmed someone's reputation either orally or in writing, homeowners' liability coverage would not protect you.

Section II also provides a limited amount of medical coverage of persons other than the homeowner's family in certain types of minor accidents on or off the insured's premises. The basic purpose of this coverage is to help homeowners meet their moral obligations and also to help deter possible lawsuits. The limited medical payment coverage pays irrespective of negligence or fault.

PROPERTY COVERED

The homeowner's policy offers property protection under Section I for the dwelling unit, accompanying structures, and personal property of homeowners and their families. Coverage for certain types of loss also applies to lawns, trees, plants, and shrubs. However, the policy excludes structures on the premises used for business purposes (except incidentally), animals (pets or otherwise), and motorized vehicles not used in the maintenance of the premises (such as autos, motorcycles, golf carts, or snowmobiles). Further, *business inventory* (for example, goods held by an insured who is a traveling salesperson or other goods held for sale) is not covered. Although the policy does not cover business inventory, it does cover *business property* (such as books, typewriters, working materials, and microcomputers), up to a maximum of $2,500, while it is on the insured premises.

If you work at home, either full- or part-time, you may need to increase your policy's limits to protect your home office. This insurance is critical because damage to your home affects not only where you live but your source of income as well. In many cases adding a rider to your homeowner's policy can increase your home-business limits to adequate levels for your computer and office equipment and also provide some additional limited liability coverage. The cost for these riders is low, about $50 per year, depending on how many coverages you include. If you need greater protection, you should investigate a separate business owner's policy that offers broader coverage for business liability, all-risk protection for equipment, and business income protection if damage to your home results in lost income.

PERSONAL PROPERTY FLOATER

As we will see later in this chapter, policies limit the types and amounts of coverage provided. Your homeowner's policy may offer less protection than you need for many expensive items of personal property. To overcome this deficiency, you can add the **personal property floater** (**PPF**) as an endorsement to your homeowner's policy or take out a separate floater policy. *The PPF provides either blanket or scheduled coverage of items not adequately covered in a standard homeowner's policy*—which covers only an amount equal to 50 percent of the dwelling value.

A *blanket, or unscheduled, PPF* provides the maximum protection available for virtually all the insured's personal property. *Scheduled PPFs* list the items to be covered and supplement coverage under a homeowner's contract. These coverages are especially useful for property valued at more than the Schedule C limits on amounts payable and perils insured, and they include loss, damage, and theft. Some of the more popular uses of PPFs are for furs, jewelry, personal computers and peripheral equipment, photographic equipment, silverware, fine art and antiques, musical instruments, and stamp and coin collections. For example, you should itemize a diamond ring valued at $7,500 because it is worth more than the standard $1,000 Schedule C allowance for jewelry theft. Generally, insurance companies require appraisals to determine value before scheduling items.

personal property floater (PPF)
An insurance endorsement or policy that provides either blanket or scheduled coverage of expensive personal property not otherwise covered in a standard homeowner's policy.

EXHIBIT 10.2

A GUIDE TO HOMEOWNER'S POLICIES

The amount of insurance coverage you receive depends on the type of homeowner's (HO) policy you select. And, as seen here, insurance coverage can also be obtained for those who live in *rental units* (HO-4) or who own units in a *condominium* (HO-6).

Coverage	HO-1 (Basic Form)	HO-2 (Broad Form)	HO-3 (Special Form)
		Section I Coverages	
A. Dwelling	$15,000 minimum	Minimum varies by company	Minimum varies by company
B. Other structures	10% of A	105 of A	10% of A
C. Personal property	50% of A	50% of A	50% of A
D. Loss of use	10% of A	20% of A	20% of A
Covered perils	Fire or lightning	Fire or lightning	Dwelling and other structures covered against risks of direct physical loss to property except losses specifically excluded
	Windstorms (including tornadoes) or hail	Windstorms (including tornadoes) or hail	
	Explosion	Explosion	Personal property covered by same perils as HO-2 plus damage by glass or safety glazing material, which is part of a building, storm door, or storm window
	Riot or civil commotion	Riot or civil commotion	
	Aircraft	Aircraft	
	Vehicles	Vehicles	
	Smoke	Smoke	
	Vandalism or malicious mischief	Vandalism or malicious mischief	
	Theft	Theft	
	Breakage of glass (limit of $100)	Breakage of glass	
	Volcanic eruption	Volcanic eruption	
		Falling objects	
		Weight of ice, snow, or sleet	
		Accidental discharge of water or steam	
		Accidental tearing, cracking, or burning of a heating, air conditioning, fire sprinkler, or water heating system	
		Freezing	
		Sudden and accidental damage from electrical current	
		Section II Coverages (Minimums)	
E. Personal liability	$100,000	$100,000	$100,00
F. Medical payments to others	$1,000 per person	$1,000 per person	$1,000 per person

RENTERS' INSURANCE: DON'T MOVE IN WITHOUT IT

If you live in an apartment (or some other type of rental unit), you should be aware that although the building you live in is very likely fully insured, *your furnishings and other personal belongings are not.* Rather, as a renter (or even as the owner of a condominium unit), you need a special type of HO policy to obtain insurance coverage on your possessions.

Consider, for example, the predicament of Lois Weaver. She never got around to insuring her personal possessions in the apartment she rented in Denver. One wintry night, a water pipe ruptured, and escaping water damaged her furniture, rugs, and other belongings. When the building owner refused to pay for the loss, Ms. Weaver hauled him into court—and lost. How could she have lost? Simple: *Unless a landlord can be proven negligent—and this one wasn't—*

EXHIBIT 10.2 *continued*

HO-4 (Renters'—Contents, Broad Form)	HO-6 (Condominium Unit Owner's)	HO-8 (Older House Form)
Section I Coverages		
Not applicable Not applicable Minimum varies by company 20% of C	$1,000 minimum Not applicable Minimum varies by company 40% of C	Same as HO-1, except losses are paid based on the amount required to repair or replace the property using common construction materials and methods.
Same perils as HO-2 for personal property	Same perils as HO-2 for personal property	Same perils as HO-1, except theft coverage applies only to losses on the residence premises up to a maximum of $1,000; certain other coverage restrictions also apply.
Section II Coverages (Minimums)		
$100,000 $1,000 per person	$100,000 $1,000 per person	$100,000 $1,000 per person

he or she isn't responsible for a tenant's property. The moral of this story is clear—once you've accumulated a good deal of personal belongings (from clothing and home furnishings to stereo equipment, TVs, computers, and VCRs), you'd better make sure they are covered by insurance, even if you're only renting a place to live! Otherwise you risk losing everything you own.

Apparently many tenants don't realize that, as surveys show most of them are without insurance. That's unfortunate because renters' insurance is available at very reasonable rates. The policy, which is called Renters' Form HO-4, is a scaled-down version of homeowners' insurance; it covers the contents of a house, apartment, or cooperative unit, but not the structure itself. Owners of condominium units need Form HO-6; it's similar but includes a minimum of $1,000 in protection for any building alterations, additions, and decorations paid for by the policyholder. Like regular homeowners' insurance, HO-4 and HO-6 policies include liability coverage and protect you at home and away. For example, if somebody is injured and sues you, the policy would pay for damages up to a specified limit, generally $100,000, although some insurers go as high as $500,000.

A standard renter's insurance policy covers furniture, carpets, appliances, clothing, and most other personal items for their cash value at the time of loss. The cost of renters' insurance isn't high: Expect to pay around $200 to $250 a year for about $15,000 in coverage, depending on where you live. For maximum protection, you can buy *replacement-cost insurance* (discussed again later in this chapter), which pays the actual cost of replacing articles with comparable ones—though some policies limit the payout to four times the cash value. You'll pay more for this, naturally—perhaps as little as another 10 percent, or perhaps much more, depending on the insurer. Also, the standard renter's policy provides only limited coverage of such valuables as jewelry, furs, and silverware. Coverage varies, although some insurers now pay up to $1,000 for the loss of watches, gems, and furs, and up to $2,500 for silverware. For larger amounts, you need an endorsement or a separate policy, called a PPF, as discussed earlier.

Renters' insurance pays for losses caused by fire or lightning, explosion, windstorms, hail, theft, civil commotion, aircraft, vehicles, smoke, vandalism and malicious mischief, falling objects, building collapse, and the weight of ice and snow. Certain damages caused by water, steam, electricity, appliances, and frozen pipes are covered as well. Plus, if your residence can't be occupied because of damage from any of those perils, the insurer will pay for any increase in living expenses resulting from, say, staying at a hotel and eating in restaurants. The liability coverage also pays for damages and legal costs arising from injuries or damage caused by you, a member of your family, or a pet, on or off your premises.

 Not sure how to value your personal property? Yahoo Finance's home insurance section, **insurance.yahoo.com/hr/home.html**, has a quick quote calculator that helps you estimate a value.

COVERAGE: WHAT, WHO, AND WHERE?

Homeowners' policies define not only what losses they cover—they also set forth the persons and locations covered.

TYPES OF LOSSES COVERED. A person can suffer three different types of property-related losses when misfortune occurs: (1) the direct loss of property, (2) indirect loss that occurs due to the loss of the damaged property, and (3) extra expenses resulting from direct and indirect losses. Homeowners' insurance contracts offer compensation for each type of loss.

Section I Coverage. When a house is damaged by an insured peril, the insurance company will pay reasonable living expenses a family might incur while the home is being repaired. Also, in many instances the insurer will pay for damages caused by perils other than those mentioned in the policy if a named peril is determined to be the underlying cause of the loss. Assume, for instance, that lightning (a covered peril) strikes a house while a family is away and knocks out all the power, which causes $400 worth of food in the freezer and refrigerator to spoil. The company will pay for the loss even though temperature change (the direct cause) is not mentioned in the policy.

Section II Coverage. In addition to paying successfully pursued liability claims against an insured, the homeowner's policy includes coverage for (1) the cost of defending the insured, (2) any reasonable expenses incurred by an insured in helping the company's defense, and (3) the payment of court costs. Because these three types of costs apply even in cases in which the liability suit is without merit, coverage in these areas is an added benefit that can save you thousands of dollars in attorney fees.

PERSONS COVERED. The homeowner's policy covers the persons named in the policy and the members of their families who are residents of the household. A person can be a resident of the household even while temporarily living away from home. For example, college students who live at school part of the year and at home during vacations are normally classified as household residents. Therefore their parents' homeowner's policy usually covers their belongings at school—things like stereo equipment, TVs, personal computers, and microwave ovens. But there could be limits and exceptions to the coverage, so check the policy to make sure what is and is not covered (for example, some companies may consider a student living off-campus to be independent and therefore ineligible for coverage under his or her parents' insurance). The standard homeowner's contract also extends limited coverage to guests of the insured.

LOCATIONS COVERED. Although some insurance contracts have territorial exclusions, most homeowners' policies offer coverage worldwide. Consequently, an insured's personal property is fully covered even if it is loaned to the next-door neighbor or kept in a hotel room in Outer Mongolia. The only exception is property left at a second home, such as a beach house or resort condominium—in which case coverage is reduced to 10 percent of the policy limit on personal property, except while the insured is actually residing there.

Homeowners and their families have liability protection for their negligent acts wherever they occur. This liability protection, however, does not include negligent acts involving certain types of motorized vehicles (like large boats and aircraft), or arising in the course of employment or professional practice. It does include golf carts (when used for golfing purposes) and recreational vehicles, such as snowmobiles and minibikes, provided they are used on the insured premises.

LIMITATION ON PAYMENT

The principle of indemnity, actual cash value, subrogation, and other insurance features that restrict the amount paid under a property and liability insurance contract have already been described. In addition to these features, replacement-cost provisions, policy limits, and deductibles also influence the amount an insurance company will pay for a loss.

REPLACEMENT COST. The amount necessary to repair, rebuild, or replace an asset at today's prices is the **replacement cost.** When replacement-cost coverage is in effect, a homeowner's reimbursement for damage to a house or the accompanying structures is based on the cost of repairing or replacing the structure. This means the insurer will repair or replace damaged items without taking any deductions for depreciation. Here is an illustration of a replacement-cost calculation for a 2,400-square-foot home with a two-car garage:

replacement cost
The amount necessary to repair, rebuild, or replace an asset at today's prices.

Dwelling: 2,400 sq. ft. at $72 per sq. ft.	$172,800
Extra features: built-in appliances, mahogany cabinets, 3 ceiling fans	8,600
Porches, patios: back screened and trellised patio	2,700
Two-car garage: 900 sq. ft. at $24 per sq. ft.	21,600
Other site improvements: driveway, storage, landscaping	4,700
Total replacement cost	$210,400

The $210,400 represents the amount of money it would take today to fully replace the home in question. Keep in mind, however, that *for homeowners to be eligible for reimbursement on a full replacement-cost basis, they must keep their homes insured for at least 80 percent of the amount it would cost to build them today, exclusive of the value of the land.* In periods of inflation homeowners must either increase their coverage limits on the dwelling unit every year or take a chance on falling below the 80 percent requirement. Alternatively, for a nominal cost homeowners can purchase an *inflation protection rider* that automatically adjusts the amount of coverage in keeping with prevailing inflation rates.

The inflation protection rider basically eliminates the chance of a coinsurance penalty. Without the rider, if the 80 percent condition is not met, the coinsurance penalty kicks in; the maximum compensation for total or partial losses will therefore be based on a specified percentage of loss. With the inflation protection rider, this would not happen.

Contrary to popular opinion, replacement cost and actual cash value may not bear any relationship to a home's market value. Because replacement cost and actual cash value relate only to the physical structure and do not consider the influence of location, a home's market value can be in excess of its replacement cost or below its actual cash value. Also, even if a home is in an excellent state of repair, its market value may be lessened because of functional obsolescence within the structure. In fact, the HO-8 homeowners' form (older houses) was adopted in partial response to this problem. In many older neighborhoods a 2,200-square-foot home might have a market value, excluding land, of, say, $95,000; the replacement cost, though, might be $160,000. The HO-8 policy solves this problem so homeowners don't have to buy more expensive coverage based on replacement value. This policy covers property in full up to the amount of the loss or up to the property's market value, whichever is less.

Although coverage on a house is often on a *replacement-cost basis,* standard coverage on the contents may be on an *actual cash-value basis,* which deducts depreciation from the *current replacement cost* for claims involving furniture, clothing, and other belongings. Some policies offer, for a slight increase in premium, replacement-cost coverage on contents. Because the additional premium required to buy replacement-cost coverage is generally only about 5 to 15 percent more, you should seriously consider this option—and an inflation protection rider on the dwelling—when buying homeowners' insurance.

POLICY LIMITS. In Section I of the homeowner's policy the amount of coverage on the dwelling unit (coverage A) establishes the amounts applicable to the accompanying structures (coverage B), the unscheduled personal property (coverage C), and the temporary living expenses (coverage D). Generally, the limits under coverages B, C, and D are 10, 50, and 10 to 20 percent, respectively, of the amount of coverage under A (see Exhibit 10.2).

For example, if the house were insured for $150,000, the limits for coverages B, C, and D would be $15,000, $75,000, and $30,000, respectively (that is, 10 percent × $150,000; 50 percent × $150,000; and 20 percent × $150,000). Each of these limits can be increased if insufficient to cover the exposure. Also, for a small reduction in premium, some companies will permit a homeowner to reduce coverage on unscheduled personal property to 40 percent of the amount on the dwelling unit.

Remember that homeowners' policies usually specify internal limits for certain types of personal property included under the coverage C category. These coverage limits are within the total dollar amount of coverage C, and in no way act to increase that total. For example, the dollar limit for losses for money, bank notes, bullion, and related items is $200, and securities, accounts, deeds, evidences of debt, manuscripts, passports, tickets, and stamps have a $1,000 limit. As mentioned earlier, loss from jewelry theft is limited to $1,000, and payment for theft of silverware, goldware, and pewterware has a $2,500 limit.

Some policies also offer $5,000 coverage for home computer equipment. You can increase these limits by purchasing higher Schedule C coverages.

In Section II the personal liability coverage (in part E) often tops out at $100,000, and the medical payments portion (part F) normally has a limit of $1,000 per person. Additional coverages included in Section II consist of claim expenses, such as court costs and attorney fees, first aid and medical expenses, including ambulance costs, and damage to others' property of up to $500 per occurrence.

Although these are the most common limits, most homeowners need additional protection, especially liability coverage. In these days of high damage awards by juries, a $100,000 liability limit may not be adequate. The cost to increase the liability limit with most companies is nominal. For example, the annual premium difference between a $100,000 personal liability limit and a $300,000 limit is likely to be only $40 to $50! You can also increase personal liability coverage with a personal liability umbrella policy, discussed later in the chapter.

DEDUCTIBLES. Each of the preceding limits on recovery constrains the maximum amount payable under the policy. In contrast, *deductibles* limit what a company must pay for small losses. Deductibles help reduce insurance premiums because they do away with the frequent small loss claims that are proportionately more expensive to administer. The standard deductible in most states is $250 on the physical damage protection provided in Section I. However, choosing higher deductible amounts of $500 or $1,000 results in considerable premium savings—as much as 10 percent in some states. Deductibles do not apply to liability and medical payments coverage because insurers want to be notified of all claims, no matter how trivial. Otherwise, they could be notified too late to properly investigate and prepare adequate defenses for resulting lawsuits.

HOMEOWNERS' PREMIUMS

It might be useful at this point to bring together the previous comments concerning the premiums on homeowners' insurance policies. Generally speaking, the insured selects a homeowner's contract form to provide physical damage coverage on the dwelling, up to at least 80 percent of the cost to rebuild at today's prices. Basic amounts of coverage are then set as a percentage of the amount of protection placed on the dwelling unit and apply to the other structures on the site, personal property, and loss of use. Each of these property damage coverages is subject to a deductible of $250 or more. The homeowner's policy also includes basic amounts of protection for liability losses ($100,000), medical payments to others ($1,000 per person), and additional coverages, such as damage to property of others ($500).

For this basic package of protection, an insurer will quote a premium. As you might expect, the size of these insurance premiums will vary widely, depending on the insurance provider (company) and the location (neighborhood/city/state) of the property. Bottom line: It pays to shop around! When you're shopping, a check sheet like the one in Exhibit 10.3 will help you compare policies and policy coverages.

Most people need to modify the basic package of coverage to add an inflation rider and increase the coverage on their homes to 100 percent of the replacement cost. Also, changing the contents protection from actual cash value to replacement cost and scheduling some items of expensive personal property may be desirable. Most insurance professionals also advise homeowners to increase their liability and medical payments limits. Each of these changes will result in an additional premium charge.

At the same time, you can reduce your total premium by increasing the amount of your deductible. Because it is better to budget for rather than insure small losses, larger deductibles

EXHIBIT 10.3

WHAT EVERY BUYER NEEDS TO KNOW ABOUT HOMEOWNER'S INSURANCE

Here's a convenient checksheet to use when shopping for homeowner's insurance; notice that this checksheet lists not only information that you should give to your insurance agent (key items about your dwelling, types of coverage you're looking for, etc.), but also the cost of the insurance, net of any discounts. In effect, this checksheet enables you to clearly spell out the type of insurance you're looking for and for the agent to tell you how much that's going to cost.

INFORMATION TO GIVE AGENTS OR INSURANCE COMPANIES

Address of property to be insured: _____

Number of losses in the past three years if covered by homeowner's or fire insurance: _____

Description of dwelling:
    Number of apartments or households in building _____
    Construction (frame, brick, etc.) _____
    Number of stories _____
    Number of rooms _____
    Total square feet _____
    Age of dwelling _____
    Age of roof _____
    Age/type of furnace _____
    Number of smoke detectors _____
    Security devices _____
    Owner occupant? _____
    Inside city limits? _____
    Name of fire department _____
    Distance from fire hydrant/fire station _____
    Business in the home? _____

Current dwelling replacement cost $_____
Current market value of dwelling and land $_____
Purchase price of dwelling $_____

Property coverage:
    Dwelling (100% of replacement cost) _____
    Other structures (detached garages, sheds, fences) _____
    Unscheduled personal property (contents of home) _____
    Additional living expense (usually 20% of dwelling coverage)

Deductible for property coverage ($500 or $1,000 recommended): $_____

Liability coverage:
    Personal liability (bodily injury and property damage) $_____
    Medical payments to others $_____

Riders:
    Business activities _____
    Earthquake _____
    Flood _____
    Scheduled personal property (antiques, computer equipment, jewelry, silverware, etc.) _____
    Secondary residence (vacation home) _____
    Windstorm (not included in basic coverage in some coastal areas) _____

INFORMATION TO GET FROM AGENTS OR INSURANCE COMPANIES

	Insurer *(current)* _____	(#2) _____	(#3) _____
Policy forms (perils included)	_____	_____	_____
Coverage exclusions	_____	_____	_____
Inflation guard included?	_____	_____	_____
Discounts available:			
Auto policy with same insurer	_____	_____	_____
New home/renovation	_____	_____	_____
Nonsmoker	_____	_____	_____
Renewal/longtime policyholder	_____	_____	_____
Security devices	_____	_____	_____
Senior citizen	_____	_____	_____
Smoke detectors/fire extinguishers/fire-retardant roof	_____	_____	_____
Storm shutters	_____	_____	_____
Other	_____	_____	_____
Annual premium:	_____	_____	_____
Installment charges (if applicable):	_____	_____	_____

Source: *Kiplinger's Smart Ways to Save on Insurance*, Winter 1997, p. 19.

MONEY IN ACTION

Keep Your Insurance Premiums from Going through the Roof

Anyone who pays monthly premiums for homeowners' insurance can tell you that it's not cheap. But homeowners' insurance is also an absolute necessity because most people can't afford to bear the risk of a catastrophic loss to a home. Fortunately, the industry is competitive and prices vary. So the first step to keeping premiums down is to shop around. The major national companies are easily accessible by telephone and the Internet, and those sources will give you an idea of price ranges. Ask if a company offers a 5 percent to 15 percent discount on your homeowner's policy if you use the same company for auto insurance.

But cost shouldn't be the only factor in selecting a policy. Ask a friend or colleague who has done business with the company whether it has a reputation for good service. If a claim is filed, do they pay right away, or do they make life difficult? Do they have a local office and an agent with whom you can meet personally, or does the insurance company operate out of a distant city?

Once you've chosen a company, you can reduce your premiums even more by making certain decisions. If you've got a choice between buying a new home and an older home, be aware that the older home, although quaint, may cost more because of the antiquated heating and plumbing systems. Statistically, newer homes are less susceptible to fire and other hazards, and are therefore less costly to insure. The closer your home is to a fire station, the lower your premium will be. A house near a fault line in California is going to cost more to insure than the same home in Montana. Frame and brick homes, because of their resistance to earthquake and wind damage, respectively, also reduce your premium. Avoiding areas that are prone to floods can save several hundred dollars in flood insurance—a risk homeowners' insurance doesn't cover.

Some companies offer discounts if you install a sprinkler system or a burglar alarm. Other ways to reduce the risk of loss include installing multiple smoke detectors and fire extinguishers and using deadbolt locks to increase your security. Some insurers offer lower premiums if none of the residents in the house smoke, because smoking accounts for more than 23,000 residential fires per year.

One way *not* to save money is to underinsure. It's imperative to get "guaranteed replacement-cost" coverage, not just actual cash value. Your insurance agent should be able to help you come up with the right figure. Make sure a company representative visits your home to measure and photograph it. Otherwise it will be difficult to set appropriate replacement-cost amounts. You could find yourself overinsured or underinsured, and either pay too much in premiums or be underprotected.

It's likely that replacement cost will be higher than actual cash value because the cost to build is usually higher than the cost to buy. Don't scrimp on liability coverage, either; it's important to be covered for damages if someone who's injured on your property sues you.

It's a good idea to review your homeowner's insurance coverage every other year; a review can establish that your premium is still competitive and ensure that your coverage is still adequate to completely rebuild your home in the event of a catastrophe.

Sources: Robert J. Bruss, "Don't Waste Money by Overinsuring," *San Diego Union-Tribune,* July 9, 2000, p. H11; Matthew Heimer, "Property Assessment," *Smart Money,* November 2000, pp. 154-166; Elizabeth Razzi, "Protecting Your Home—And Your Wallet," *Kiplinger's Smart Ways to Save on Insurance,* Winter 1997, p. 15; "Twelve Ways to Save on Homeowner's Insurance," **insurance.yahoo.com/hr/savings.in.html**; and **www.insure market.com**.

are becoming more popular. Also, you may qualify for discounts for deadbolt locks, monitored security systems, and other safety features, such as smoke alarms and sprinkler systems. Indeed, as explained in the *Money in Action* box above, there are a lot of other things you can do to help keep your homeowner's insurance premiums in check.

CONCEPT CHECK

10-5. What are the perils against which most properties are insured under various types of homeowners' policies?

10-6. What types of property are covered under a homeowner's policy? When should you consider adding a *PPF* to your policy? Are the following included in the coverage of a standard policy: (a) an African parrot, (b) a motorbike, (c) Avon cosmetics held for sale, and (d) Tupperware for home use?

10-7. Describe (a) types of losses, (b) persons, and (c) locations that are covered under a homeowner's policy.

10-8. Describe *replacement-cost coverage* and compare this coverage to *actual cash value.* Which is preferable?

10-9. What are *deductibles?* Do they apply to either liability or medical payments coverage under the homeowner's policy?

Automobile Insurance [LG4]

Another asset that involves major exposure to loss is the automobile. Damage to this asset or negligence in its use can result in significant losses. Each year in the United States more than 6 million motor vehicle accidents account for more than 41,000 deaths, 3 million disabling injuries, and economic loss of $150 billion. In addition, indirect monetary losses to society result from police and legal costs and from the lost productive capacity of capital and human resources. Fortunately, insurance can protect individuals against a big part of these costs.

Automobile insurance is actually a group of several coverages packaged together. You can adjust any coverage to suit your needs. The next sections of this chapter describe the major features of automobile insurance, starting with typical coverages of a private passenger automobile policy. We'll also explain how no-fault laws, in force in many states, typically affect reimbursement for losses caused by automobile accidents. Finally, we will discuss auto insurance premiums and financial responsibility laws.

INSURANCE COVERAGE

personal automobile policy (PAP)
A comprehensive automobile insurance policy developed to be easily understood by the "typical" insurance purchaser; it is made up of six parts.

The **personal automobile policy (PAP)** is a comprehensive automobile insurance policy developed to be easily understood by the "typical" insurance purchaser; it is made up of six parts. The first four parts identify the coverages provided in the policy:

- Part A: Liability coverage
- Part B: Medical payments coverage
- Part C: Uninsured motorists coverage
- Part D: Coverage for damage to your vehicle

Part E pertains to your duties and responsibilities should you ever be involved in an accident, and Part F defines some general or basic provisions of the policy, including policy coverage period and the right of termination. We'll focus mostly on the types of coverage in Parts A through D of the policy.

You are almost sure to purchase liability, medical payments, and uninsured motorists protection. You may, however, choose *not* to buy protection against damage to your automobile if it is "worn" and of relatively little value. On the other hand, if you have a loan against your car, you will probably be required to have physical damage coverage—part D—at least equal to the amount of the loan. Let's take a closer look at the coverage provided by parts A through D.

PART A: LIABILITY COVERAGE. Most states require that you buy at least a minimum amount of liability insurance. As part of the liability provisions of a PAP, the insurer agrees to (1) pay damages for bodily injury and property damage for which you become legally obligated due to an automobile accident, and (2) settle or defend any claim or suit asking for such damages. This provision for legal defense is quite important. It can mean a savings of thousands of dollars because even a person who is not at fault in an automobile accident may be compelled to prove his or her innocence in court. Note, though, that the coverage is for a defense in civil cases only. It provides no defense against any criminal charges against the insured as a result of an accident (such as a drunk driver who's involved in an accident).

In addition to providing reimbursement for bodily injury and property damage, the automobile liability portion of your insurance policy includes certain supplemental payments for items such as expenses incurred in settling the claim, reimbursement of premiums for appeal bonds, bonds to release attachments of the insured's property, and bail bonds required as a result of an accident. These supplemental payments are not restricted by the applicable policy limits.

Policy Limits. Although the insurance company provides both bodily injury and property damage liability insurance under part A, it typically sets *a single dollar limit up to which it will pay for damages from any one accident.* Typical limits are $50,000, $100,000, $300,000, and $500,000. You'd probably be well advised to consider nothing less than $300,000 coverage in today's legal liability environment. Damage awards are increasing, and the insurer's duty to defend you *ends when the coverage limit has been exhausted.* It is very easy to "exhaust" $50,000 or $100,000, leaving you to pay any additional costs above the policy limit. So be sure to purchase adequate coverage—*regardless of the minimum requirements in your state.* Otherwise, you place your assets at risk.

Some insurers make so-called *split limits* of liability coverage available, with the first amount in each combination the per-individual limit and the second the per-accident limit. Some policy limit combinations for protecting individuals against claims made for **bodily injury liability losses** are $10,000/$20,000; $25,000/$50,000; $50,000/$100,000; $100,000/$300,000; and $500,000/$1,000,000. Thus, if you purchased the $50,000/$100,000 policy limits, the maximum amount any one person negligently injured in an accident could receive from the insurance company would be $50,000. Further, the total amount that the insurer would pay to all injured victims in one accident would not exceed $100,000. If a jury awarded a claimant $80,000, the defendant whose insurance policy limits were $50,000/$100,000 could be required to pay $30,000 out of his or her pocket ($80,000 award–$50,000 paid by insurance). For the defendant, this could mean loss of home, cars, bank accounts, and other assets. In many states, if the value of these assets is too little to satisfy a claim, the defendant's wages may be garnished (taken by the court and used to satisfy the outstanding debt).

The policy limits available to cover **property damage liability losses** are typically $10,000, $25,000, and $50,000. In contrast to bodily injury liability insurance limits, property damage policy limits are stated as a per-accident limit without specifying any limits applicable on a per-item or per-person basis.

Persons Insured. Two basic definitions in the PAP determine who is covered under the liability coverage: insured person and covered auto. Essentially, an *insured person* includes you

bodily injury liability losses
A provision in a PAP that protects the insured against claims made for bodily injury; may specify coverage as a combination of per-individual and per-accident limits.

property damage liability losses
A provision in a PAP that protects the insured against claims made for damage to property; specified on a per-accident basis.

(the named insured) and any family member, any person using a covered auto, and any person or organization that may be held responsible for your actions. The *named insured* is the person named in the declarations page of the policy. The spouse of the person named is considered a named insured if he or she resides in the same household. Family members are persons related by blood, marriage, or adoption who reside in the same household. An unmarried college student living away from home usually would be considered a family member. *Covered autos* are the vehicles shown in the declarations page of your PAP, autos acquired during the policy period, any trailer owned, and any auto or trailer used as a temporary substitute while your auto or trailer is being repaired or serviced. An automobile that you lease for an extended time can be included as a covered automobile.

The named insured and family members have part A liability coverage regardless of the automobile they are driving. However, for persons other than the named insured and family members to have liability coverage, they must be driving a covered auto and there must be reasonable belief that they are entitled to do so.

When a motorist who is involved in an automobile accident is covered under two or more liability insurance contracts, the coverage *on the automobile* is primary and the other coverage is secondary. For example, if Dan Slater, a named insured in his own right, was involved in an accident while driving Diana Bauer's automobile (with permission), a claim settlement in excess of the limits of Diana's liability policy would be necessary before Dan's liability insurance would apply. If Diana's insurance had lapsed, Dan's policy would then offer primary protection (but it would apply to Dan only and not to Diana).

PART B: MEDICAL PAYMENTS COVERAGE. Medical payments coverage provides for payment to a covered person of an amount no greater than the policy limits for all reasonable and necessary medical expenses incurred within 3 years of an automobile accident. It provides for reimbursement even if other sources of recovery, such as health or accident insurance, also make payments. In addition, in most states the insurer reimburses the insured for medical payments even if the insured proves that another person was negligent in the accident and receives compensation from that party's liability insurer.

As with liability insurance, discussed in the previous section, and uninsured motorists insurance, detailed in the following section, a person need not be occupying an automobile when the accidental injury occurs to be eligible for benefits. Injuries sustained as a pedestrian or on a bicycle in a traffic accident are covered, too. (Motorcycle accidents normally are not covered.) This insurance also pays on an excess basis. For instance, if you are a passenger in a friend's automobile during an accident and suffer $8,000 in medical expenses, you can collect under your friend's medical payments insurance up to his or her policy limits. Further, you can collect (up to the amount of your policy limits) from your insurer the amount in excess of what the other medical payments provide. Of course, you may also collect from the liability insurance of another person involved in the accident if that person can be shown to have been at fault. In addition, you may also be able to collect from your health care insurance policy.

Policy Limits. Medical payments insurance usually has per-person limits of $1,000, $2,000, $3,000, $5,000, or $10,000. Thus an insurer conceivably could pay $60,000 or more in medical payments benefits for one accident involving a named insured and five passengers. Most families are advised to buy the $5,000 or $10,000 limit because although they may have an ample amount of other health care insurance available, they cannot be certain that their passengers are equally well protected. Having automobile medical payments insurance also reduces the probability that a passenger in your auto will sue you and attempt to collect under your liability insurance coverage (in those states that permit it).

Persons Insured. Coverage under an automobile medical payments insurance policy applies to the named insured and family members who are injured while occupying an automobile (whether owned by the named insured or not) or when struck by an automobile or trailer of any type. It also applies to any other person occupying a covered automobile.

PART C: UNINSURED MOTORISTS COVERAGE. **Uninsured motorists coverage** is available to meet the needs of "innocent" victims of accidents who are negligently injured by uninsured, underinsured, or hit-and-run motorists. Nearly all states require uninsured motorists insurance to be included in each liability insurance policy issued. The insured is allowed, however, to reject this coverage in most of these states. Rejecting uninsured motorists coverage is not a good idea, however, because there are about 25 million uninsured drivers, and many others who have insurance carry only the minimum requirements. In many states a person also may collect if the negligent motorist's insurance company is insolvent. Under uninsured motorists insurance, an insured is legally entitled to collect an amount equal to the sum that could have been collected from the negligent motorist's liability insurance had such coverage been available, up to a maximum amount equal to the policy's stated *uninsured motorists limit.*

uninsured motorists coverage
Automobile insurance designed to meet the needs of "innocent" victims of accidents who are negligently injured by uninsured, underinsured, or hit-and-run motorists.

Three points must be proven to receive payment through uninsured motorists insurance: (1) another motorist must be at fault; (2) this motorist had no available insurance or was underinsured; and (3) damages were incurred. Property damage is not included in this coverage in most states. Therefore, under uninsured motorists coverage, you generally can collect only for losses arising from bodily injury. If the motorist and insurer cannot agree on the terms of the settlement of a claim under uninsured motorists coverage, the motorist can seek an attorney to negotiate the claim. If a mutually agreeable settlement still cannot be worked out, the insured has the right to have the case arbitrated by a neutral third party. In most cases the accident victim and the insurer are then bound to accept the decision of the arbitrator. In addition to *uninsured* motorists, for a nominal premium you can also obtain protection for *underinsured* motorists—that is, for coverage when you're involved in an accident where the driver at fault has a liability limit much lower than your claim. Under such coverage, your insurance company makes up the difference and then goes after the negligent driver for any deficiency.

Policy Limits. Uninsured motorists insurance is available at fairly low cost (usually around $50 to $75 per year). It is often sold with basic limits of $10,000 to $20,000, with additional amounts available for a small premium increase. Because the cost of this coverage is very small compared to the amount of protection it provides, drivers should purchase at least the minimum available limits of uninsured motorists insurance.

Persons Insured. Uninsured motorists protection covers the named insured, family members, and any other person occupying a covered auto.

PART D: COVERAGE FOR PHYSICAL DAMAGE TO A VEHICLE. This part of the PAP provides coverage for damage to your auto. There are two basic types of coverage provided: collision and comprehensive (or "other than collision").

Collision Insurance. **Collision insurance** is automobile insurance that pays for collision damage to an insured automobile *regardless of who is at fault.* The amount of insurance payable is the actual cash value of the loss in excess of a stated deductible. Remember that actual cash value is defined as replacement cost less depreciation. Therefore, if a car is demolished, an insured will be paid an amount equal to the car's depreciated value minus any deductible.

collision insurance
Automobile insurance that pays for collision damage to an insured automobile *regardless of who is at fault.*

comprehensive automobile insurance
Coverage that protects against loss to an insured automobile caused by any peril (with a few exceptions) *other than collision.*

Lenders typically require the purchase of collision insurance on cars they finance. In some cases—especially when the auto dealer is handling the financing—the lender will attempt to sell this insurance. Generally, you should *avoid buying any type of automobile insurance from car dealers or finance companies.* Rather, buy such insurance from your regular insurance agent and include it (collision insurance) as part of your full auto insurance policy (PAP). A full-time insurance agent is better trained to properly assess and meet a motorist's insurance needs. Moreover, often the collision provisions of your insurance policy will fully protect you, even in a rental car. Thus you may not need to purchase the expensive supplemental collision insurance when you rent a car. But be sure to check your PAP to see what coverage it provides for rental cars. In addition, many credit cards offer collision insurance when you charge a car rental on that card.

Purchasers of collision insurance may select from one of several deductibles available— $50, $100, $250, or even $1,000. As with homeowners' insurance, selecting higher deductibles reduces collision premiums. For example, one large automobile insurance company reports that collision coverage with a $50 deductible on a relatively new car costs $177 per year, whereas the $100 deductible costs $150 per year. Thus a motorist who buys the $50 deductible is paying $27 annually for an additional $50 of collision protection.

 No one wants to think about car accidents, but it's important to know what to do when you have one. At eHow (**www.ehow.com**), click on "Automotive Center," then "Driving and Safety" to find "eHow to Take Action After a Car Accident."

Comprehensive Automobile Insurance. **Comprehensive automobile insurance** protects against loss to an insured automobile caused by any peril (with a few exceptions) *other than collision.* This broad coverage includes, but is not limited to, damage caused by fire, theft, glass breakage, falling objects, malicious mischief, vandalism, riot, and earthquake. Contrary to popular belief, the automobile insurance policy normally does *not* cover theft of personal property left in the insured automobile. (The off-premises coverage of the homeowner's policy may cover the loss if the auto was locked at the time the theft occurred.) The maximum compensation provided under this coverage is the actual cash value of the automobile.

Exhibit 10.4 illustrates how the four basic parts of a PAP (part A: Liability coverage; part B: Medical payments coverage; part C: Uninsured motorists coverage; and part D: Collision and comprehensive coverage) might be displayed in a typical automobile insurance policy.

NO-FAULT AUTOMOBILE INSURANCE

The concept of **no-fault automobile insurance** is based on a system that reimburses the parties involved in an accident without regard to negligence. The principle is, "My insurance policy should pay the cost of my injuries, and your insurance policy should pay the cost of yours," regardless of who is at fault in an accident. Under the concept of *pure* no-fault insurance, the driver, passengers, and injured pedestrians are reimbursed by the insurer of the car for economic losses stemming from bodily injury. The insurer thus does not have to provide coverage for claims made for losses caused to other motorists. Each insured party is compensated by his or her own company, regardless of which party caused the accident. In return, legal remedies and payments for pain and suffering are restricted.

Unfortunately, the advocates of no-fault forgot that liability insurance was never intended to serve as the primary system for compensating injured parties. Its sole purpose is to protect the assets of the insured, not to pay losses, *per se.* This same concept applies to all liability insurance. The medical payments, collision, and comprehensive insurance

EXHIBIT 10.4

THE FOUR PARTS OF AN AUTOMOBILE INSURANCE POLICY

This automobile insurance statement for 6 months of coverage illustrates how the four major parts (A through D) of a personal auto policy (PAP) might be incorporated into a typical auto policy. Note in this case that the premium for comprehensive/collision damage is relatively low due to the age of the car (a 1995 Chevrolet Cavalier); also note that this driver enjoyed a premium reduction of more than $130 for the 6 months due to a good driving record, plus having other insurance with the same provider.

ANYSTATE MUTUAL INSURANCE COMPANIES   **AUTO RENEWAL**

Anystate Mutual Automobile Insurance Company
1665 West Anywhere Drive
Yourtown, AZ 95380   1995 CHEVROLET CAVALIER

POLICY NUMBER	PERIOD COVERED	DATE DUE	PLEASE PAY THIS AMOUNT
ABC-123-XYZ-456	MAY 26 2001 to NOV 26 2001	MAY 26 2001	$403.01

1 H -1582   A

Jones, Drew E. & Linda S.
240 E. Hazelwood St. # 50
Yourtown, AZ 95815-4045

Coverages and Limits				Premiums
Part A	A	Liability		
		Bodily Injury 50,000/100,000		
		Property Damage 50,000		$224.40
Part B	M	Medical 5,000		35.03
Part C	U	Uninsured Motor Vehicle		
		Bodily Injury 15,000/30,000		26.10
	W	Underinsured Motor Vehicle		
		Bodily Injury 15,000/30,000		12.40
Part D	D-WG	100 Deductible Comprehensive		44.00
	G	250 Deductible Collision		58.08
	H	Emergency Road Service		3.00

Amount Due $403.01

Your premium is based on the following ... If not correct, contact your agent.

1995 CHEVROLET CAVALIER
Class   1F30502

Drivers of vehicle in your household...
There are no male or unmarried female drivers under age 25.

Younger drivers included if rated on another car insured with us.

Ordinary use of vehicle...
To and from work or school, more than 100 miles weekly. Driven more than 7,500 miles annually. (National average is 10,000 miles annually.)

Your premium has already been adjusted by the following:

Premium Reductions

Multiple Line	$17.16
Multicar	44.52
Accident Free	70.84

Source: Adapted from a State Farm Insurance Company quote.

coverages discussed earlier serve this compensation purpose to a certain extent. In addition, families can and should purchase widely available life, health care, and disability protection, which will protect them not only for losses resulting from automobile accidents but also for nearly all other types of economic loss resulting from accident or illness. In fact, the numerous cries that no-fault automobile insurance is needed to compensate people for losses incurred in automobile accidents have probably had a harmful effect on overall

no-fault automobile insurance
A concept of automobile insurance that favors reimbursement without regard to negligence. Under *pure* no-fault, each insured party is compensated by his or her own insurance, regardless of which party caused the accident.

insurance planning; they have detracted from public understanding of the need for full life and health care insurance programs. After all, there is no reason to be more concerned about the person who is injured in an automobile accident than about the homeowner who sustains injury while repairing his or her house.

Nevertheless, some valid arguments have been put forth by proponents of no-fault insurance. Many states have passed laws to modify the coverages offered by family automobile policies. However, *no state has yet adopted a pure no-fault insurance plan.*

Basically, the various state laws governing no-fault insurance can be differentiated according to whether: (1) no-fault and liability insurance is compulsory and (2) there are any restrictions on lawsuits. The laws of the separate states vary substantially as to both the amount of no-fault benefits provided and the degree to which the restrictions for legal actions apply. Most states provide from $2,000 to $10,000 in personal injury protection and restrict legal recovery for pain and suffering to cases in which medical or economic losses exceed some threshold level, such as $500 or $1,000. In all states recovery based on negligence is permitted for economic loss in excess of the amount payable by no-fault insurance.

Overall, most of the no-fault laws that have been passed fall short of accomplishing the two objectives fundamental to no-fault insurance—that is, elimination of liability as a basis for recovery, and provision of adequate compensation for all accident victims. Further, the no-fault concept gained its largest public support because its advocates promised it would contribute to lower insurance premiums. As might be expected, based on the laws now on the books, that has not always been achieved. In those states with substantive laws, though, some efficiencies have been gained. Still, because only a few states have required substantial amounts of personal injury protection, most seriously injured accident victims will continue to turn to the liability system or their own life and health care insurance coverages for large amounts of compensation.

AUTOMOBILE INSURANCE PREMIUMS

What you pay for car insurance depends on many things, including where you live, what kind of car you drive, what kind of coverage you have, the amount of your deductibles, and so forth. One thing is sure, the size of the typical car insurance premium is anything but uniform. The fact is, average auto insurance premiums—for basically the same coverage—vary all over the map, as shown in Exhibit 10.5. If you're fortunate enough to live in one of the low-premium states (such as North Dakota, Iowa, Maine, or Wyoming), you're probably *relatively* satisfied with the cost of your car insurance; on the other hand, if you're in one of the more expensive states (like New Jersey, California, Rhode Island, or Massachusetts), you may well be feeling the pinch of these high and, in many cases, rapidly increasing auto insurance rates.

After 2 years of declining rates, auto insurance premiums began to climb again in 2001 in many states, including New York, Florida, and Texas. Insurers cite higher health care and vehicle repair costs and larger liability payouts as justification for the rate increases. Unhappy residents in many of the high-premium states are protesting against these rates and are demanding—through their state legislators and the ballot box—a return to what they see as more-reasonable premiums.

FACTORS AFFECTING PREMIUMS

With this in mind, let's look at how auto insurance premiums are set. Among the factors that influence automobile insurance rates are (1) rating territory, (2) the amount of use the automobile receives, (3) the personal characteristics of the drivers, (4) the type of automobile, and (5) the insured's driving record.

EXHIBIT 10.5

COMPARATIVE AUTO INSURANCE PREMIUMS

Average annual auto insurance premiums vary all over the map. The annual premium in the most expensive state (New Jersey) is more than twice the cost for the same coverage in the least expensive state (North Dakota). There is also considerable variation within states; urban drivers typically pay more than rural ones.

State	Average Annual Premium	State	Average Annual Premium
Alabama	$ 632	Montana	$ 471
Alaska	771	Nebraska	518
Arizona	818	Nevada	843
Arkansas	589	New Hampshire	622
California	718	New Jersey	1,138
Colorado	764	New Mexico	676
Connecticut	901	New York	960
Delaware	845	North Carolina	564
District of Columbia	1,033	North Dakota	452
Florida	771	Ohio	581
Georgia	672	Oklahoma	575
Hawaii	797	Oregon	630
Idaho	494	Pennsylvania	722
Illinois	607	Rhode Island	852
Indiana	583	South Carolina	655
Iowa	459	South Dakota	479
Kansas	532	Tennessee	587
Kentucky	617	Texas	731
Louisiana	830	Utah	619
Maine	492	Vermont	534
Maryland	769	Virginia	564
Massachusetts	816	Washington	710
Michigan	737	West Virginia	725
Minnesota	680	Wisconsin	552
Mississippi	653	Wyoming	492
Missouri	611	U.S. AVERAGE	$ 699

Source: The National Association of Insurance Commissioners, cited in Table 850, *Statistical Abstract of the United States: 2000* (Washington, DC: U.S. Census Bureau, 2000), p. 531.

- **Rating territory.** Rates are higher in geographic areas where the accident rates, number of claims filed, and average cost of claims paid are higher. Rates reflect auto repair costs, hospital and medical expenses, jury awards, and rates of theft and vandalism in the locale. Even someone with a perfect driving record will be charged the rates in effect for the area where the automobile is principally garaged. (Some jurisdictions prohibit the use of rating territories, age, and sex factors because they believe these factors unfairly discriminate against the urban, the young, and the male.)
- **Use of the automobile.** Drive less and you pay less! The lower your total annual miles, the lower your rates, because you have a lower probability of being in an accident. Rates are also lower if the insured automobile is not usually driven to work or driven fewer than 3 miles one way to work. Premiums rise slightly if you drive more than 3 but fewer than 15 miles to work, and rise more if your commute exceeds 15 miles each way.

- **Drivers' personal characteristics.** Such things as the age, sex, and marital status of the insured affect automobile insurance premiums. Insurance companies base the premium differentials on the number of accidents involving certain age groups. For example, drivers age 25 and under make up only about 15 percent of the total driving population but are involved in nearly 30 percent of the auto accidents and 26 percent of all fatal accidents. Male drivers are involved in a larger percentage of fatal crashes, so unmarried males age 29 or under and married males under age 25 pay higher premiums than older individuals. Females over age 24 and married females of any age are exempt from the youthful operator classification and pay lower premiums.
- **Type of automobile.** Insurance companies charge higher rates for automobiles classified as intermediate-performance, high-performance, and sports vehicles, and for rear-engine models. Some states even rate four-door cars differently from two-door models. If you are thinking of buying, say, a Corvette or a Porsche Boxster, you'd better be prepared to handle some pretty hefty insurance rates.
- **Driving record.** The driving records—traffic violations and accidents—of insureds and those who live with them affect premium levels. The more severe types of traffic convictions—driving under the influence of alcohol or drugs, leaving the scene of an accident, homicide or assault arising out of the operation of a motor vehicle, and driving with a revoked or suspended driver's license—result in higher insurance premiums. In addition, any conviction for a traffic violation that results in the accumulation of points under a state point system may result in a premium surcharge. Included in this category are such moving violations as speeding, running a red light, failure to yield the right of way, and illegal passing, but not parking violations, improper registration, lack of an operator's license, or lack of a valid safety sticker. In most states, accidents determined to be the fault of the insured also incur points and a premium surcharge.

automobile insurance plan
An arrangement that provides automobile insurance to drivers who have been refused regular coverage under normal procedures; formerly called an *assigned-risk plan.*

In many states a driver with lots of traffic violations is placed in an **automobile insurance plan** (formerly called an *assigned-risk plan*) that provides automobile insurance for those refused regular coverage under normal procedures. The automobile insurance plan generally offers less coverage for higher premiums. Even with the high premiums, however, insurers lost $2.3 billion on this type of business in a recent 5-year period.

 Can you save money on homeowners' or auto insurance by using a direct underwriter? Get a quote from Geico Direct, **www.geico.com**, and compare it with your current policies and premiums.

DRIVING DOWN THE COST OF CAR INSURANCE

Comparison shopping for car insurance really pays off. According to a recent study from Progressive Insurance Company, the national average spread between the highest and lowest 6-month rates available for new policies was $481. In Kentucky and Texas the average variance topped $700! Yet only one-third of car owners shop around for auto coverage.

One of the best ways to reduce the cost of car insurance is to take advantage of the variety of discounts most auto insurers offer. Taken together, such discounts can knock 5 to 50 percent off your annual premium. Exhibit 10.6 summarizes some of the discounts given by top auto insurance companies. Some give overall *safe-driving* (accident-free) discounts, and most give youthful operators lower rates if they have had *driver's training*—some states, in fact, have laws that require insurers to offer lower premiums to any driver, young or old, who has taken driver's training. High school and college students may also receive *good-student* discounts for maintaining a B average or by being on the dean's list at their school.

EXHIBIT 10.6

TYPES OF DISCOUNTS OFFERED BY LEADING AUTO INSURERS

Listed here are 10 of the most common types of discounts offered by some of the leading auto insurers. Although most of these discounts apply to the total cost of the insurance, some apply to only a certain portion of the coverage (for example, the antitheft discount applies only to the cost of the comprehensive portion of the policy).

Type of Discount	Savings Offered
• Driver's training	Range 5–40%; most commonly 10–15%; not available in all states
• Good student	Range 5–30%; commonly 25%
• Student away at school	Some companies put policyholders in a lower-price bracket; others offer discounts, usually 10–40%
• Carpool	Some companies put policyowners in a lower-price bracket; others offer discounts of 5–25%
• Multicar	Range 10–25%; usually about 15%
• Passive restraints	Range 20–60%; full front airbag discounts range from 40–60%
• Antitheft devices	Range 5–50%; state laws in MI, RI, IL, MA, NY, and KY mandate such discounts; however, some companies offer these discounts in other states, too
• Mature driver	Range 5–15%; discounts may start at age 50; driving habits, employment, and retirement affect discount; some companies put policyholder into lower price bracket
• Farmer	Range 10–30%; most commonly 10%; some companies put policyholder into a lower-price bracket
• Defensive-driving course	Range 5–15%; not available in all states; some state laws mandate such a discount

Source: Adapted from George E. Rejda, *Principles of Risk Management and Insurance,* 7th ed. (Boston, Mass.: Addison-Wesley, 2001).

Nearly all insurance companies provide discounts to families with two or more automobiles insured by the same company (the *multicar* discount). Most insurers also offer discounts to owners who install *antitheft devices* in their cars. Likewise, a number of insurers offer *nonsmoker* and *nondrinker* discounts. There are even companies that specialize in insuring only certain portions of the population. For example, certain insurers accept only persons who are educators or executives and others accept only government employees. Although not offering discounts in the normal sense, these companies often have lower premiums because, through more selective underwriting, they are able to reduce losses and operating expenses.

Clearly, it's to your advantage to look for and use as many of these discounts as you can. Take another look at the auto insurance statement in Exhibit 10.4, and you'll see that the insured was able to reduce his overall cost of coverage by nearly 25 percent by qualifying for just three of the discounts. Another very effective way to drive down the cost of car insurance is to *raise your deductibles* (as discussed earlier in this chapter). This often overlooked tactic can have a dramatic effect on the amount of insurance premium you pay. For example, the difference between a $100 deductible and a $500 deductible may be as much as 30 percent on comprehensive coverage and 25 percent on collision insurance; request a $1,000 deductible and you may save as much as 45 to 50 percent on both comprehensive and collision insurance.

Fill out an online questionnaire with Progressive Insurance Company (www.progressive.com) and you get not only quotes on its insurance, but also prices for up to three of its competitors.

EXHIBIT 10.7

FINANCIAL RESPONSIBILITY REQUIREMENTS FOR SELECTED STATES

Most states have financial responsibility laws that require motorists involved in auto accidents to furnish proof of financial accountability up to certain minimum dollar amounts; as seen here, those financial liability limits vary by state.

State	Liability Limits, $000	State	Liability Limits, $000
Alaska	50/110/25	New Jersey	15/30/5
California	15/30/5	Ohio	12.5/25/7.5
Florida	10/20/20	Oregon	25/50/10
Illinois	20/40/15	South Carolina	15/30/5
Minnesota	30/60/10	Texas	20/40/15

FINANCIAL RESPONSIBILITY LAWS

financial responsibility laws Laws that *require motorists to buy a specified minimum amount of automobile liability insurance.* They attempt to force motorists to be financially responsible for the damage they cause, and are legally obligated to pay, as a result of automobile accidents.

The annual losses from automobile accidents in the United States run into billions of dollars. For this reason, **financial responsibility laws** have been enacted in most states, whereby motorists *must buy a specified minimum amount of automobile liability insurance,* or provide other proof of comparable financial responsibility. These laws attempt to force motorists to be financially responsible for the damage they cause as a result of automobile accidents. For example, Exhibit 10.7 lists the requirements for 10 states. The first number refers to bodily injury limits per person; the second, per accident; and the third is for property damage. Note that the required limits are very low in most states—well below what you should carry. Even New Jersey, with the highest rates in the country, requires only 15/30/5 coverage.

Financial responsibility laws fall into two categories. *Compulsory auto insurance laws* require motorists to show evidence of insurance coverage *before* they can receive their license plates. Penalties for not having liability insurance include fines and suspension of driver's license. The second type requires motorists to show evidence of their insurance coverage only *after* they are involved in an accident. If they then fail to demonstrate compliance with the law, their registrations and driver's licenses are suspended. This law has been criticized on the grounds that it allows negligent motorists to have one "free" accident. Although motorists who are not able to fulfill their financially responsibility lose their driving privileges, victims may never recover their losses.

CONCEPT CHECK

10-10. Briefly explain the major coverages available under the personal auto policy (PAP). Which persons are insured under (a) automobile medical payments coverage and (b) uninsured motorists coverage?

10-11. Explain the nature of (a) automobile collision insurance and (b) automobile comprehensive insurance.

10-12. Define *no-fault insurance* and discuss its pros and cons.

10-13. Describe the important factors that influence the availability and cost of auto insurance.

10-14. Discuss the role of *financial responsibility laws* and describe the two basic types currently employed.

Other Property and Liability Insurance [LG5]

Although homeowners' and automobile insurance policies represent the basic protection needed by most families, other property and liability insurance contracts may be appropriate for some people. Among those discussed here are popular forms of supplemental property insurance coverage—earthquake insurance, flood insurance, and other forms of transportation insurance— and the personal liability umbrella policy.

SUPPLEMENTAL PROPERTY INSURANCE COVERAGE

Because homeowners' policies exclude certain types of damage, you may want to consider some of the following supplemental coverages.

EARTHQUAKE INSURANCE. Although most people think of California when earthquakes are mentioned, areas in other states are also subject to this type of loss. Very few homeowners buy this coverage even though the premiums are relatively inexpensive. These policies typically carry a 15 percent deductible on the replacement cost of a home damaged or destroyed by earthquake. You have to pay a lot out of pocket before you can collect on the policy.

FLOOD INSURANCE. Before 1968, floods were regarded by most private insurers as an uninsurable peril because the risk could not be spread among people who were not located in flood-prone areas. But in 1968, the federal government established a subsidized flood insurance program in cooperation with private insurance agents, who can now sell this low-cost coverage to homeowners and tenants living in designated communities. In addition, the flood insurance program encourages communities to initiate land-use controls to reduce future flood losses.

OTHER FORMS OF TRANSPORTATION INSURANCE. In addition to automobile insurance, you may wish to insure other types of vehicles, such as mobile homes, recreational vehicles, or boats.

- **Mobile-home insurance.** Special insurance policies for mobile-home owners offer blanket protection against the same perils covered in an HO-2 form, plus personal property and personal liability coverage. Rates are typically higher for mobile homes because losses on mobile homes from wind or fire damage occur much more often than for wood or brick houses.
- **Recreational vehicle insurance.** Recreational vehicles may include all-terrain vehicles, antique automobiles, dune buggies, go-carts, minibikes, trail motorcycles, camping vehicles (motorized and trailer type), snowmobiles, and customized vans. Complete coverage generally is available for these vehicles, including bodily injury and property damage liability, medical payments, physical damage, and theft. Not all insurance companies write recreational vehicle coverage. Shop carefully because more restrictions apply and rates will vary substantially depending on driver's age, vehicle use, and policy owner's location. Pay particular attention to who and what are covered and to where and when coverage applies. You may be able to insure some types of recreational vehicles—including motorcycles and mopeds— through a Miscellaneous Type Vehicle Endorsement to your personal auto policy.
- **Boat insurance.** Homeowners' policies offer limited protection for boats less than 26 feet in length (or some other stipulated maximum) or those with motors under 25 horsepower. To get proper liability, medical payments, and physical damage

and theft coverage, you need either a boat and motor endorsement on your homeowner's policy or a specially designed boat-owner's policy. Because physical damage and theft provisions of boat policies are not standardized, make certain that you know which coverage applies and which losses are not covered.

PERSONAL LIABILITY UMBRELLA POLICY

personal liability umbrella policy
An insurance policy that provides excess liability coverage for both homeowners' and automobile insurance and additional coverage not provided by either of those policies.

Persons with moderate to high levels of income and net worth may want to take out a **personal liability umbrella policy.** It provides added liability coverage for both homeowners' and automobile insurance and additional coverage not provided by either of those policies. Umbrella policies often include limits of $1 million or more. In addition, some provide added amounts of coverage for a family's major medical insurance.

Because middle- and upper-income individuals are logical targets for liability claims, umbrella protection provides a desirable, added layer of coverage. The premiums are usually quite reasonable for the broad coverage afforded ($150 to $300 a year for as much as $1 million in coverage). Although the protection is comprehensive, it does contain a number of exclusions. As a rule, to purchase a personal liability umbrella policy, the insured party must already have relatively high liability limits ($100,000 to $300,000) on their auto and homeowner's coverage.

Do you need the extra protection a personal liability umbrella policy provides? Clearly, as discussed in the *Money in Action* box on page 433, the answer is yes if you have sizable assets that could be seized to pay a judgment against you and for which your homeowner's and automobile policies don't fully cover the value. But you may also need this coverage if you rent your home to others or have house sitters or unbonded hired help, such as gardeners or babysitters, because you're responsible for any injuries they incur or may cause. And you may need this coverage if you work from home and clients visit you at your home office.

CONCEPT CHECK

> 10-15. Briefly describe the following supplemental property insurance coverages: (a) earthquake insurance (b) flood insurance, and (c) other forms of transportation insurance.
>
> 10-16. What is a *personal liability umbrella policy?* Under what circumstances might it be a wise purchase?

■ Buying Insurance and Settling Claims [LG6]

If you're thinking about buying property and liability insurance, the first step is to develop an inventory of exposures to loss and arrange them from highest to lowest priority. Losses that lend themselves to insurance protection are those that seldom occur but have the potential for being substantial—for example, damage to a home and its contents or liability arising out of a negligence claim. Less important, but nevertheless desirable, is insurance to cover losses that could be disruptive to the financial plans of a family, even though they would not result in insolvency. Such risks include physical damage to automobiles, boats, and other personal property of moderate value. Lowest priority exposures can easily be covered by savings or from current income. Low-dollar deductibles, for instance, usually serve only to increase premiums. Likewise, personal property of minor value, such as an old auto (one that is not a collectible), may not merit coverage—at least as far as collision insurance is concerned. In addition to inventorying exposures and

MONEY IN ACTION

Don't Wait Until It's Too Late to Get an Umbrella

At a swimming party, a 16-year-old dove into a pool and hit his head on the bottom. He was paralyzed from the neck down, and the case resulted in a $1.5 million settlement against the homeowner. A 22-year-old suffered permanent eye damage when he was struck by a golf ball. He sued the golfer, and won a judgment of $160,000. Had the golfer and the homeowner had an umbrella policy that picks up excess liability, they would have been spared great financial distress. In today's litigious society a $1 million judgment for such accidents is, unfortunately, all too common. True, the odds are small that you'll be involved in such an accident. But it takes only one brush with tragedy to ruin you financially.

The vast majority of claims under umbrella liability policies arise from car accidents, but they also arise from a myriad of other causes: a visitor who slips on your stairs, a babysitter who's poked in the eye by your kids, a neighbor bitten by your dog, a bicyclist with whom you collide, a so-called friend who sues you for slander—the situations are endless. That's why an umbrella policy that costs $150 to $300 per year, depending on your geographical location (big cities tend to cost more), could be very desirable, particularly for people with homes, swimming pools, boats, golf clubs, dogs, and other sources of potential liability.

Umbrella policies supplement homeowners', auto, and boat policies and typically cover liability beyond $300,000. The smallest policies pay $1 million per incident beyond what's covered by the underlying policy, although many companies, such as Nationwide Insurance, offer up to $2 million in coverage. So if you have $300,000 of personal liability protection on your auto policy and a $2 million umbrella, you would have a total of $2.3 million worth of insurance.

The easiest way to buy an umbrella policy is through the same company that sold you your basic coverage. Note that most umbrella policies do not cover business liability or your liability as a board member of a nonprofit organization. Small businesses and home-based businesses need separate liability insurance to cover suits against the business. These business people are risking huge financial losses because a standard homeowner's policy does not cover losses to a business located inside a home. If the UPS person trips over your children's toys while delivering a business package, your liability insurance won't apply. Director's and officer's insurance will cover board members. Professionals such as doctors, dentists, lawyers, architects, engineers, and anyone else who could be sued as a result of their work should consider having professional liability insurance to cover malpractice suits.

Some excess liability policies cover the cost of legal defense and others do not. You should determine whether your coverage includes this feature and whether there are any limits on legal costs in the policy. Some policies will exclude swimming pools, or pools that have diving boards. Others won't insure young drivers. As with any insurance policy, you can't simply compare the price of one umbrella to another unless you're comparing apples with apples.

If paying the premium for an umbrella policy is a hardship, then consider boosting the deductibles on your basic policies from $100 to $500, or from $500 to $1,000. The reduction in premiums will likely pay for the umbrella policies, thus protecting you against financial calamity.

Sources: Brad Burg, "When Umbrella Coverage Won't Keep You Dry," *Medical Economics*, April 12, 1999, downloaded from FindArticles.com, **www.findarticles.com**; Ronaleen R. Roha, "Do You Need This Umbrella," *Kiplinger's Personal Finance Magazine*, July 1995, p. 81; Nationwide Insurance, **www.nationwide.com**; "Small Business Owners: Don't Forget Insurance," *The Arlington Morning News*, May 21, 2000, p. 13A.

deciding on appropriate coverage and deductibles, you should exercise care in selecting the property insurance agent and the insurer. Also, a knowledge of the procedures involved in settling property and liability claims can help you obtain maximum benefits from policies when claims do arise.

PROPERTY AND LIABILITY INSURANCE AGENTS

captive agent
An insurance agent who represents only one insurance company and is more or less an employee of that company.

independent agent
An insurance agent who may place coverage with any company with which he or she has an agency relationship, as long as the insured meets that company's underwriting standards.

Most property insurance agents fall into the captive or independent category. A **captive agent** is one who represents only one insurance company and is more or less an employee of that company. Allstate, Nationwide, and State Farm are major insurance companies that market their products through captive agents. **Independent agents,** in contrast, typically represent between two and ten different insurance companies. These agents may place your coverage with any of the companies with which they have an agency relationship as long as you meet the underwriting standards of that company. Well-know companies that operate through independent agents include Hartford, Kemper, Chubb, and Travelers. It is difficult to generalize with respect to the superiority of agents. In some cases an independent agent will provide the best combination of low-cost insurance and good service, whereas in others the captive agent might be the better choice. Because of wide differences in premiums and services, it usually pays to comparison shop.

Property insurance agents should be willing to take the time to go over your total property and liability insurance exposures. As you should know by now, there is much more to the purchase of property insurance than simply signing applications for homeowners' and automobile insurance. You must inventory property; identify exposures; choose the covered perils, limits, deductibles, and floater policies; and consider other items we've discussed throughout this chapter. In the property insurance industry, agents who meet various experiential and educational requirements, including passing a series of written examinations, qualify for the *Chartered Property and Casualty Underwriter (CPCU)* or *Certified Insurance Counselor (CIC)* designation.

Another alternative to consider is companies that sell directly to the consumer through an 800 number or online. Generally, their premiums are lower. Examples of direct sellers are Amica Mutual (800-242-6422), Erie (800-458-0811), Geico (800-841-3000), and USAA (800-531-8111).

PROPERTY AND LIABILITY INSURANCE COMPANIES

Although selecting an agent is probably the most important step when purchasing property and liability insurance, you should also ask questions about the company, including its financial soundness, claims-settlement practices, and the geographic extent of its operations (this could be important if you are involved in an accident 1,000 miles from home). As with any form of insurance, you should check the company's ratings (see Chapter 8) and stick with those rated in the top categories, such as the companies listed in Exhibit 10.8. The agent should be a good source of information about the technical aspects of a company's operations, whereas friends and acquaintances often can provide insight into its claims-settlement policy. And of course, there's also the Internet, which offers a wealth of information about various property and liability insurance products. Indeed, many insurance companies now have elaborate home pages on the Web that provide basic information about the provider and its product, direct you to local agents, or let you crunch numbers to generate sample premiums.

 What is your insurance carrier's financial strength rating? Go to Moody's Web site (**www.moodys.com**), click "Insurance," then "Insurance Financial Strength Ratings," and select either the life/health or property/casualty category.

SETTLING PROPERTY AND LIABILITY CLAIMS

Generally speaking, insurance companies settle claims promptly and fairly, especially life and health care insurance claims. In settling property and liability claims, though, some

EXHIBIT 10.8

TOP-RATED PROPERTY AND LIABILITY INSURERS

These property and liability insurers are among those that regularly receive the top grade from at least two leading rating agencies.

Company	Assigned Rating		
	A.M. Best	Standard & Poor's	Moody's
American Home Assurance	A++	AAA	Aaa
Employers Reinsurance	A++	AAA	Aaa
Federal Insurance	A++	AAA	Aa1
General Reinsurance	A++	AAA	—
Government Employees Insurance Co. (GEICO)	A++	AAA	Aaa
National Union Fire Insurance	A++	AAA	Aaa
State Farm Mutual Automobile	A++	AAA	Aaa
United Services Automobile Association	A++	AAA	Aaa
USAA Casualty Insurance	A++	AAA	—

Sources: **www.ambest.com**, **www.standardandpoors.com**, **www. moodys.com**.

chance for claimant–insurer disagreement does exist. The following discussion reviews the claims-settlement process and the people who participate in it. First, however, let's consider what you should do immediately following an accident.

FIRST STEPS FOLLOWING AN ACCIDENT. After an accident, obtain and record the names and addresses of all witnesses, drivers, occupants, and injured parties, along with the license numbers of the automobiles involved. Immediately notify law enforcement officers and your insurance agent of the accident. You should never admit liability at the scene of an accident or discuss it with anyone other than the police and your insurer. Remember, before it can be determined who, if anyone, is legally liable for an accident, the requisites of liability must be established. Also, the duties of the police are to assess the probability of a law violation and maintain order at the scene of an accident—not to make judgments with respect to liability.

STEPS IN CLAIMS SETTLEMENT. If you're involved in an accident, one of the first things you're going to have to decide is whether or not you even want to file a claim. Should you opt to file a claim—and most experts agree, unless it's a very minor or insignificant accident, the best course of action is to file a claim—it'll probably involve the following steps.

1. *Notice to your insurance company.* You must notify your insurance company that a loss (or potential for loss) has occurred. Timely notice is extremely important.
2. *Investigation.* Insurance company personnel may talk to witnesses or law enforcement officers, gather physical evidence to determine whether the claimed loss is covered by the policy, and check to make sure that the date of the loss falls within the policy period. If you delay filing your claim, you hinder the insurer's ability to check the facts. All policies specify the time period within which you must give notice. Failure to report can result in your loss of the right to collect.
3. *Proof of loss.* This step usually requires you to give a sworn statement. When applicable, you must also show medical bills, an inventory and certified value of lost property (for example, a written inventory, photographs, and purchase receipts), an employer statement of lost wages, and, if possible, physical evidence of damage (x-rays if you claim a back injury, a broken window or pried door if you claim a break-in and theft at your house).

Financial Road Sign

What to Do When a Claim Is Denied
Fight back if your homeowners' or automobile insurance company refuses to pay all or part of a claim.
1. *Document everything.* Get written copies of police or fire department reports and outside appraisals, and take photos.
2. *Don't accept "no" for an answer.* Complain to your insurer and ask for another review.
3. *File and follow up on your appeal promptly.* Some companies have a 1-year limit on challenges, starting with the date of the first decision.
4. *Go to your state's insurance department.* Insurers then have about 6 weeks to resolve a dispute.
5. *Don't bother filing a lawsuit for small claims.* State regulators can't force a solution, but most lawyers won't handle lawsuits for relatively small amounts.

Source: Matthew Heimer, "Staking Claims," *Smart Money*, November 2000, p. 164.

claims adjustor
An insurance specialist who works for the insurance company as an independent adjustor, or for an adjustment bureau. He or she investigates claims, looking out for the interests of the company.

After you submit proof of loss, the insurer may (1) pay you the amount you asked for; (2) offer you a lesser amount; or (3) deny that the company has any legal responsibility under the terms of your policy. If the amount is disputed, most policies provide for some form of claims arbitration. You hire a third party, the company hires a third party, and these two arbitrators together select one more person. When any two of the three arbitrators reach agreement, their decision binds you and the company to their solution.

When a company denies responsibility, you do not get the right of arbitration. In such an instance the company is saying the loss does not fall under the policy coverage. You must then either forget the claim or bring in an attorney or, perhaps, a public adjustor (discussed next).

CLAIMS ADJUSTMENT. Usually the first person to call when you need to file a claim is your insurance agent. If your loss is relatively minor, the agent can quickly process it and, in fact, will often give you a check right on the spot. If your loss is more complex, your company will probably assign a claims adjustor to the case.

Adjustors. The **claims adjustor** is an insurance specialist who work for the insurance company, as an independent adjustor, or for an adjustment bureau. The adjustor investigates claims, looking out for the interests of the company—which might very well be to keep you, its customer, satisfied. However, many claimants think insurance companies have more money than they know what to do with and are out to collect all that is possible. Thus the adjustor walks a fine line: he or she must diligently question and investigate, while at the same time offering service to minimize settlement delays and financial hardship. To promote your own interest in the claim, you should cooperate with the adjustor and answer inquiries honestly—keeping in mind that the company writes the adjustor's paycheck.

Public Adjustors and Attorneys. Thus far we have been discussing claims submitted to your own insurance company. In accidents in which a question of fault arises, you may have to file a claim against a negligent party's insurer. In these instances the insurer will still use an adjustor, but this person will be looking out for the insurer's (and its policyholders') economic interests without any regard to keeping you satisfied. If you are not happy with the offered settlement, you might have to hire an attorney to negotiate the claim for you. Because the attorney will have a better understanding of the law and the legal provisions of your policy than you do, hiring one greatly improves your chances of collecting the amount you're entitled to. Keep in mind, however, that attorneys will often charge 25 to 50 percent of any amount they get for you (the exact amount of the fee is negotiable). The use of a costly attorney is nonetheless often worthwhile if you are not being treated fairly by the insurance company's adjustor.

CONCEPT CHECK

10-17. Differentiate between *captive* and *independent insurance agents.* What characteristics should you look for when choosing both an insurance agent and an insurance company for purposes of buying property or liability insurance?

10-18. Briefly describe the key aspects of the claims-settlement process, explaining what to do after an accident, the steps in claim settlement, and the role and types of *claims adjustors.*

SUMMARY

LG1. **Discuss the importance and basic principles of property insurance, including types of exposure, indemnity, and coinsurance.** Property and liability insurance protects against the loss of real and personal property that can occur from exposure to various types of perils. In addition, such insurance protects against loss from lawsuits based on your alleged negligence. The principle of indemnity limits the insured's compensation to the amount of economic loss. The coinsurance provision requires that the policyholder buy insurance coverage that equals a set percentage of the property's value to receive full compensation under the policy's terms.

LG2. **Identify the different coverages provided by a homeowner's insurance policy.** Most homeowners' insurance policies are divided into two major sections. Section I covers the dwelling unit, accompanying structures, and personal property of the insured. Section II pertains mainly to comprehensive coverage for personal liability and medical payments to others. The most commonly sold homeowners' policies (Forms HO-2 and HO-3) cover a broad range of perils, including damage from such occurrences as fire or lightning, windstorms, explosions, aircraft, vehicles, smoke, vandalism, theft, freezing, and so on. Personal property coverage is typically set at 50 percent of the coverage on the dwelling.

LG3. **Select the right homeowners' insurance policy for your needs.** Everyone should have some form of homeowners' insurance, whether you own a single-family house or a condominium, or rent an apartment. Renters' insurance covers your personal possessions. Except for the house and garage, which are covered on a replacement-cost basis, homeowners' or renters' insurance normally reimburses all losses on an actual cash-value basis, subject to applicable deductibles and policy limits. However, for an additional premium, you can usually obtain replacement-cost coverage on personal belongings. Within Section I, internal limits are set for various classes of property. You may wish to increase these limits if you have valuable property. One way to do so is with a personal property floater (PPF). Because the standard Section II liability limit is only $100,000, it's a good idea to buy additional liability coverage, generally available at minimal cost. To reduce premiums, choose a policy with a higher deductible.

LG4. **Analyze the different coverages in a personal automobile policy (PAP) and choose the most cost-effective policy.** Automobile insurance policies usually contain provisions that protect the insured from loss due to personal liability, medical payments, uninsured motorists, collision (property damage to the vehicle), and comprehensive coverage (which applies to nearly any other type of noncollision damage your car might suffer, such as theft or vandalism). The factors that influence the policy premium include where you live, how much you drive, and your personal characteristics, type of car, and driving record. Most automobile insurers offer discounts for good driving records, safety and antitheft devices, driver's training courses, and similar factors. Other ways to reduce premiums are through higher deductibles and eliminating collision coverage if your car is old.

LG5. **Describe other forms of property and liability insurance.** In addition to the major forms of homeowners' and automobile insurance, a variety of other property and liability coverages is available, including supplemental property insurance coverage—earthquake insurance, flood insurance, and other forms of transportation insurance (mobile-home, recreational vehicle, and boat insurance)—and personal liability umbrella policies.

LG6. **Choose a property and liability insurance agent and company, and settle claims.** Before buying property and liability coverage, you should evaluate your exposure to loss and determine the coverage needed. You should also carefully select the insurance agent and insurance company to obtain appropriate coverage at a reasonable price. Equally important—make sure the agent and company you deal with have reputations for fair claims-settlement practices. Before filing a claim, you should decide whether the amount of damage warrants a claim. Document all claims properly and file promptly. In the event of a complex loss claim, expect your insurer to assign a claims adjustor to the case.

QUESTIONS AND PROBLEMS

1. Assume Marcus Browning had a property insurance policy of $100,000 on his home. Would a 90 percent coinsurance clause be better than an 80 percent clause in such a policy? Give reasons to support your answer.

2. Last year Steve and Jessica Morgan bought a home with a dwelling replacement value of $250,000 and insured it (via an HO-3 policy) for $210,000. The policy reimburses for actual cash value and has a $500 deductible, standard limits for Schedule C items, and no scheduled property. Recently, burglars broke into the house and stole a 2-year-old television set with a current replacement value of $600 and an estimated life of 8 years. They also took jewelry valued at $1,850 and silver flatware valued at $3,000.
   a. If the Morgans' policy has an 80 percent coinsurance clause, do they have enough insurance?
   b. Using the Schedule C limits listed in the text on page 412, calculate how much the Morgans would receive if they filed a claim for the stolen items.
   c. What advice would you give the Morgans about their homeowner's coverage?

3. Vickie Korte's luxurious home in the suburb of Broken Arrow, Oklahoma, was recently gutted in a fire. Her living and dining rooms were completely destroyed, and the damaged personal property had a replacement price of $27,000. The average age of the damaged personal property was 5 years, and its useful life was estimated to be 15 years. What is the maximum amount the insurance company would pay Vickie, assuming it reimburses on an actual cash-value basis?

4. Doris and Ed Barnow, both graduate students, moved into an apartment near the university. Doris wants to buy renters' insurance, but Ed thinks they don't need it because their furniture isn't worth much. Doris points out that, among other things, they do have some expensive computer and stereo equipment. To help the Barnows resolve their dilemma, suggest a plan for deciding how much insurance to buy, and give them some ideas for finding a policy.

5. Robert Taylor has a PAP with coverages of $25,000/$50,000 for bodily injury liability, $25,000 for property damage liability, $5,000 for medical payments, and a $500 deductible for collision insurance. How much will his insurance cover in each of the following situations? Will he have any out-of-pocket costs?
   a. He loses control and skids on ice, running into a parked car and causing $3,785 damage to the unoccupied vehicle and $2,350 to his own car.
   b. He runs a stop sign and causes a serious auto accident, badly injuring two people. The injured parties win lawsuits against him for $30,000 each.
   c. Taylor's wife borrows his car while hers is being repaired. She backs into a telephone pole and causes $450 damage to the car.

APPLYING PERSONAL FINANCE

Taking a Look at Your Homeowner's (or Renter's) Policy

If you own your own home (or even if you rent), you need property and liability insurance to protect you from loss. But what does your policy really cover? You may be surprised at the breadth of coverage, or lack of it, depending on your policy. The purpose of this project is to help you become familiar with your insurance.

Find your homeowner's (or renter's) insurance policy. Look at the depth of coverage. Note if there are any discounts on the premium because you have a smoke detector, because no one in the house smokes, or for any other reason. What are the policy limits? Do they seem high enough? How does inflation affect the policy limits? Are there any exclusions? Compare policies. Do others seem to be more complete? What about cost? There are so many ways that policies differ. Perhaps this exercise will help you find better protection.

CONTEMPORARY CASE APPLICATIONS

10.1   The Salvatis' Homeowners' Insurance Decision

Rodrigo and Anita Salvati, ages 30 and 28, respectively, were recently married in Chicago. Rodrigo is an electrical engineer with Geophysical Century, an oil exploration company. Anita has a master's degree in special education and teaches at a local junior high school. After living in an apartment for 6 months, the Salvatis have negotiated the purchase of a new home in a rapidly growing Chicago suburb. Republic Savings and Loan Association has approved their loan request for $108,000, which represents 90 percent of the $120,000 purchase price. Prior to closing the loan, the Salvatis must obtain homeowners' insurance for the home. The Salvatis currently have an HO-4 renter's insurance policy, which they purchased from Rodrigo's tennis partner, Kelly Duvall, who is an agent with Kramer's Insurance Company. To learn about the types of available homeowners' insurance, Rodrigo has discussed their situation with Kelly, who has offered a variety of homeowners' policies for Rodrigo's and Anita's consideration. He has recommended that the Salvatis purchase an HO-3 policy because it would provide them with comprehensive coverage.

Questions
1. What forms of homeowners' insurance are available? Which forms should the Salvatis consider?
2. What are the perils against which the home and its contents should be insured?
3. Discuss the types of loss protection provided by the homeowners' policies under consideration.
4. What advice would you give the Salvatis regarding Kelly's suggestion? What coverage should they buy?

10.2   Auto Insurance for Heather Weisbach

Heather Weisbach of Phoenix, Arizona, is a divorced 40-year-old loan officer at the Frontier National Bank of Arizona; Heather has a 16-year-old son. She has decided to use her annual bonus as a down payment on a new car. One Saturday afternoon in late December, she visited Chuck Thomas's Auto Mall and purchased a new, fully equipped Pontiac for $23,000. To obtain insurance on the car, Heather called her agent, Jane Cunningham, who represents Farmers Insurance Company, and explained her auto insurance needs. Jane said she would investigate the various options for her. Three days later, Heather and Jane got together to review her coverage options. Jane offered several proposals, including various combinations of the following coverages: (a) basic automobile liability insurance, (b) uninsured motorists coverage, (c) automobile medical payments insurance, (d) automobile collision insurance, and (e) comprehensive automobile insurance.

Questions

1. Describe the key features of these insurance coverages.
2. Are there any limitations on these coverages? Explain.
3. Indicate the persons who would be protected under each coverage.
4. What kind of insurance coverages would you recommend Ms. Weisbach purchase? Explain your recommendation.

MONEY ONLINE

PROTECT YOUR PROPERTY!

Note: Web addresses change frequently, so you may need to determine the home page and do a site search to find the page or topic that's referenced.

1. **www.usaaedfoundation.org**
   Buying a home? Read up on homeowners' insurance at the USAA Educational Foundation's Web site. Click on "Insurance" and then on "Homeowners Insurance" for an extensive primer on the subject. Interested in building a home or remodeling? Pull up "Builder's Risk Insurance" to learn what insurance concerns you will encounter during the process.

2. **www.partners2.financenter.com/consumer/learn/guides/rentinsure/rins inventory.fcs**
   Take an inventory of your property. Use the FinanCenter's handy Property Inventory Worksheet included at "Taking Inventory" at their Insurance Guide to Renter's Insurance.

3. **www.quicken.com/insurance**
   Should you buy renters' insurance? How does a renter's policy protect your personal property? Find answers to these and other "Common Renters Questions" in Quicken's Insurance Center under "Home/Renters Insurance."

4. **www.fema.gov/nfip**
   Do you need flood insurance? Visit the Web site of the Federal Emergency Management Association to learn about the National Flood Insurance Program. At "Select a Quick Link" choose from topics such as "Cost of Flood Insurance," "How to Purchase and Pay for Flood Insurance," and "Ways to Reduce Flood Damage to Your Home or Business," or read through a "Standard Flood Insurance Policy."

5. **www.redcross.org**
   What disaster services does the Red Cross provide? How can you prepare for a disaster? Learn the answers to these questions and how to deal with children and animals before, during, and after a disaster at the Web site of the American Red Cross.

6. **www.quicken.com/insurance**
   Are you doing all you can to save money on your auto insurance? Take Quicken's "Auto Savings Quiz" to learn how savvy you are and to find tips on how to save even more on your premiums. Then click on "Homeowners Savings Quiz" to discover new ways to save on your homeowner's insurance.

7. **www.insure.com**

   What options do you have when your insurance company totals your car? What should you do in event of an auto accident? Should you buy a salvaged vehicle? Browse through Insure.com's offerings at "Auto" to find the answers to these and many, many other frequently asked questions concerning autos and auto insurance.

8. **quicken.com/insurance**

   Burglarproof your car! Visit Quicken's Insurance Center and learn how to thwart thieves with the many vehicle theft-prevention devices now available. Not only will you be more likely to hang on to your car, but you may be able to lower your insurance premiums as well!

9. **www.nicb.org/services/top_stolen_cars.html**

   What are the most commonly stolen vehicles? Visit the National Insurance Crime Bureau's Web site to view the hottest top ten. Then pull up **www.nicb.org/services/top_theft_areas.html** to see the areas recording the greatest number of vehicle thefts.

10. **biz.wellsfargo.com/products/insurance/insurance.jhtml**

    Do you have a business of your own? Visit Wells Fargo's "Small Business Insurance" center for information and quotes on insuring your business from property damage, theft, and the liability you may face as a business owner. Click on "FAQ" to learn more about professional liability insurance, umbrella insurance, commercial auto insurance, workers' compensation, and the insurance needed when you have a home-based business.

Just for Fun!

11. **wellsfargo.insurezone.com/account.view/glossary_public.html**

    Learn the lingo! Consult Wells Fargo's handy list of "Insurance Terms" for help deciphering the language of insurance. Scroll through the list or click on the letter of the alphabet at the top of the page to find a particular term.

PART V

Managing Investments

CHAPTER 11
Investment Planning

CHAPTER 12
Investing in Stocks
and Bonds

CHAPTER 13
Investing in Mutual
Funds

Chapter 11

Investment Planning

LEARNING GOALS

LG1. Discuss the role that investing plays in the personal financial planning process and identify several different investment objectives.

LG2. Distinguish between primary and secondary markets, as well as listed exchanges and the over-the-counter market.

LG3. Explain the process of buying and selling securities and recognize the different types of orders.

LG4. Develop an appreciation of how various forms of investment information can lead to better investing skills and returns.

LG5. Gain a basic understanding of the growing impact that the computer and the Internet are having on the field of investments.

LG6. Describe an investment portfolio and how you'd go about developing and managing a portfolio of securities.

Riding the Market's Roller Coaster

Starting in the spring of 2000, Michael Janson began to panic as tech stocks tumbled, and the value of his small portfolio fell. He and his wife Karen, an elementary school teacher, had started investing in 1997, as soon as Michael finished medical school. They were able to catch the end of the phenomenal stock market surge in the late 1990s. Because Michael loves technology and follows the latest trends, he decided to allocate a sizable percentage of their investment funds to the tech sector, especially to new, fast-growing dot.com companies that were making their stockholders very wealthy.

Karen was more conservative and decided to invest her 401(k) plan in a mutual fund that covered a wider range of growth stocks and one that focused on blue chip, well-known companies. She, too, was uneasy as the broader markets also took a dive. As novice investors they didn't know what to do: should they sell their stocks before they incurred greater losses, or was the market going through one of its periodic corrections?

Michael searched various financial Web sites to gain some insight into what more experienced investors were doing. Because he and Karen were investing for the long term—their goals include buying a home and starting a college fund for baby Sarah and any future children—Michael realized that panic selling was a bad move. Markets go through many up and down cycles over time and therefore, he feels the most important thing is to stay invested so that he can earn a fully compounded return on his funds. Karen's more balanced portfolio was more successful in riding out the market dips. So Michael redistributed his portfolio among more market sectors and has seen his portfolio grow once again.

In this chapter, you'll learn about investment planning, securities markets, brokers, securities transactions, information sources, and portfolio strategies so, like the Jansons, you too can build your own portfolio.

■ The Objectives and Rewards of Investing [LG1]

People invest their money for all sorts of reasons. Some do it as a way to accumulate the down payment on a new home; others do it as a way to supplement their income; still others invest to build up a nest egg for retirement. Actually, the term *investment* means different things to different people. That is, while millions of people *invest* regularly in securities like stocks, bonds, and mutual funds, others *speculate* in commodities or options. **Investing** is generally considered to take more of a long-term perspective and is viewed as a process of purchasing securities wherein stability of value and level of return are somewhat predictable. **Speculating**, on the other hand, is viewed as a short-term activity that involves the buying and selling of securities in which future value and expected return are highly uncertain. Obviously, speculation is far more risky than investing.

If you're like most investors, at first you'll probably keep your funds in some form of savings vehicle (as described in Chapter 4). Once you have *sufficient savings*—for emergencies and other purposes—you can begin to build up a *pool of investable capital*. This

investing
The process of placing money in some medium such as stocks or bonds in the expectation of receiving some future benefit.

speculating
A form of investing in which future value and expected returns are highly uncertain.

often means making sacrifices and doing what you can to *live within your budget*. Granted, it's far easier to spend money than to save it, but if you're really serious about getting into investments, you're going to have to accumulate the necessary capital! In addition to a savings and capital accumulation program, it's also important to have adequate *insurance coverage* to provide protection against the unexpected (we discussed different kinds of insurance in Chapters 8, 9, and 10). For our purposes here, we will assume you are adequately insured and that the cost of insurance coverage is built into your family's monthly cash budget. Ample insurance and liquidity (cash and savings) with which to meet life's emergencies are two *investment prerequisites* that are absolutely essential for the development of a successful investment program. Once these conditions are met, you are ready to start investing.

BUT HOW DO I GET STARTED?

Contrary to what you may believe, there is really nothing magical about the topic of investments—in fact, so long as you have the capital to do so, it's really quite easy to get started in investing. The terminology may seem baffling at times and some of the procedures and techniques quite complicated. But don't let that mislead you into thinking there is no room for the small, individual investor. Nothing could be farther from the truth! For as we will see in this and the next two chapters, individual investors have a wide array of securities and investment vehicles to choose from. Further, opening an investment account is no more difficult than opening a checking account.

How, then, do you get started? To begin with, you need some money—not a lot; $500 to $1,000 will do, although $4,000 or $5,000 would be better (and remember, this is *investment capital* we're talking about here—money you've accumulated above and beyond any basic emergency savings). In addition to money, you need knowledge and know-how. You should never invest in something you are not sure about—that is the quickest way to lose money. Learn as much as you can about the market, different types of securities, and various trading strategies. This course you're taking on personal finance is a good start, but you may want to do more. For one thing, you can become a regular reader of publications such as *Money*, *The Wall Street Journal*, *Barron's*, and *Forbes* (these and other sources of information are reviewed later in this chapter). Also, try to stay up with major developments as they occur in the market; start following the stock market, interest rates, and developments in the bond market.

We strongly suggest that, after you've learned a few things about stocks and bonds, you set up a portfolio of securities on paper and make *paper trades* in and out of your portfolio, for six months to a year to get a feel for what it is like to make (and lose) money in the market. Start out with an imaginary sum of, say, $50,000 (as long as you are going to dream, you might as well make it worthwhile). Then keep track of the stocks and bonds you hold, record the number of shares bought and sold, dividends received, and so on. Throughout this exercise, be sure to use actual prices (as obtained from *The Wall Street Journal* or your local newspaper) and keep it as realistic as possible. If you have access to a computer, you might want to use one of the *portfolio tracking* programs offered at such sites as **Quicken.com** or **MSN MoneyCentral**; there are some powerful Internet sites out there that make it very easy to track the behavior of a portfolio of securities. The advantage to creating a paper portfolio is clear: if you're going to make mistakes in the market, you're much better off doing so on paper. Also, if your parents, relatives, or friends have done a lot of investing, talk to them! Find out what they have to say about investing, pick up some pointers and possibly even learn from their mistakes. Eventually, you will gain a familiarity with the market and become comfortable with the way things are done there. When that happens, you will be ready to take the plunge.

At that point, you will also need a way to invest—more specifically, a broker and some investment vehicle in which to invest. As we will see later in this chapter, the stockbroker is the party through whom you will be buying and selling stocks, bonds, and other securities. If your relatives or friends have a broker they like and trust, have them introduce you to him or her. Alternatively, visit several of the brokerage firms in your community; talk to one of their brokers about your available investment funds and your investment objectives.

As a beginning investor with limited funds, it is probably best to confine your investment activity to the basics. Stick to stocks, bonds, and mutual funds. Avoid getting fancy, and certainly don't try to make a killing each and every time you invest—that will only lead to frustration, disappointment, and very possibly, heavy losses. Further, *be patient*! Don't expect the price of the stock to double overnight, and don't panic when things fail to work out as expected in the short run (after all, security prices do occasionally go down). Finally, remember that you do not need spectacular returns in order to make a lot of money in the market. Instead, be consistent and let the concept of compound interest work for you. Do that and you'll find that just $2,000 a year invested at the fairly conservative rate of 10 percent will grow to well over $100,000 in 20 years! While the type of security in which you invest is a highly personal decision, you might want to give serious consideration to some sort of mutual fund as your first investment (see Chapter 13). Mutual funds provide professional management and diversification that individual investors—especially those with limited resources—can rarely obtain on their own.

 Zacks Investment Research (**www.zacks.com**) offers a comprehensive "Investing 101" tutorial and a glossary of financial terms.

THE ROLE OF INVESTING IN PERSONAL FINANCIAL PLANNING

Buy a car, build a house, enjoy a comfortable retirement—these are goals we would all like to attain some day and are, in many cases, the centerpieces of well-developed financial plans. As a rule, a financial goal such as building a house is not something we pay for out of our cash reserves; the cost (in most cases, even the down payment) is simply too great to allow for that. Instead, we must accumulate the funds over time, which is where investment planning and the act of investing enter into the personal financial planning process. By investing our money, we are letting it work for us.

It all starts with an objective—a particular financial goal we would like to achieve within a certain period of time. Take the case of the Thompsons. Shortly after the birth of their first child, they decided to start building a college education fund. After performing some rough calculations, they concluded they'd need to accumulate about $60,000 over the next 18 years to have the kind of money they feel they'll need for their daughter's education. Simply by setting that objective, the Thompsons created a well-defined, specific financial goal. The purpose is to meet the educational needs of their child, and the amount of money involved is $60,000 in 18 years. But how do they reach their goal? The first thing they must decide is where the money will come from. While part of it will come from the return (profit) on their investments, they still have to come up with the *investment capital*.

COMING UP WITH THE CAPITAL. So far, the Thompsons know how much money they want to accumulate, and how long they have to accumulate it. The only other thing they need to determine at this point is the *rate of return* they feel they can earn on their money. Having taken a financial planning course in college, the Thompsons know that the amount of money they'll have to put into their investment program depends in large part on *how much they can earn from their investments*—the higher their rate of return, the less they'll have to put up. Let's say they feel comfortable using a 9 percent rate of return. That's a fairly conservative number—one that won't require them to put all or most of their money into a bunch of high-risk investments—and they're reasonably certain they can reach that level of return, on average, over the long haul. It's important to use some care in coming up with a projected rate of return. Don't saddle yourself with an unreasonably high rate, as that will simply reduce the chance of reaching your targeted financial goal.

Probably the best way of arriving at a reasonable projection is to look at what the market has done over the past 5 to 10 years, and then use the average return performance over that period as your estimate—or, if you want to be a bit more conservative, knock a point or two off the market's return. (This is especially true today due, in large part, to the *phenomenal returns the stock market turned in during the last half of the decade of the '90s.* Fully compounded returns of over 25% are just not common; thus, instead of knocking off just a point or two, you might want to reduce the long-term (10–15 year) returns on stocks by 5 or 6 points—just to be on the safe side.) To help you in this regard, take a look at the statistics that appear at the bottom of this page; they show the average annual returns on stocks, bonds, and U.S. Treasury bills over various holding periods of from 5 to 25 years.

Notice that, over all five of the holding periods (unless you had put just about everything into short-term U.S. Treasury bills), generating an average return of around 10 to 12 percent (or even more) was well within the reach of most investors. Of course, there's no guarantee these returns will happen again in the next 10 to 20 years, but at least the past does provide us with a basis—or "handle"—for making projections into the future.

Now, returning to our problem at hand, there are two ways of coming up with the capital needed to reach a targeted sum of money: (1) you can make a lump-sum investment right up front and let that amount grow over time; or (2) you can set up a systematic savings plan and put away a certain amount of money each year. Worksheet 11.1 is designed to help you find the amount of investment capital you'll need to reach a given financial goal. It employs the *compound value* concept discussed in Chapter 2, and is based on a given financial target (line 1), and a projected average rate of return on your investments (line 2). Note that you can use the worksheet to find either a required lump-sum investment (part A), or an amount that will have to be put away each year in a savings plan (part B). For our purposes here, we'll assume the Thompsons have $7,500 to start with (this comes mostly from gifts their daughter received from her grandparents). Since they know they'll need a lot more than that to reach their target, the Thompsons decide to use part B of the worksheet to find out how much they'll have to save annually.

Holding Periods	Stocks (as measured by the DJIA)	High-grade Corp. Bond Returns	Stocks and Bonds Together (50/50)	Returns on Short-Term U.S. Treasury Bills	Stocks, Bonds, and T-Bills Combined ($\frac{1}{3}$-$\frac{1}{3}$-$\frac{1}{3}$)
5 years: 1995–99	26.4%	8.8%	17.6%	4.9%	13.4%
10 years: 1990–99	18.1	8.7	13.4	4.8	10.5
15 years: 1985–99	19.1	10.6	14.8	5.5	11.7
20 years: 1980–99	17.6	10.7	14.1	6.8	11.7
25 years: 1975–99	16.3	9.8	13.1	6.8	11.0

WORKSHEET 11.1

FINDING THE AMOUNT OF INVESTMENT CAPITAL

A worksheet like this one can be used to find out how much money you must come up with to reach a given financial goal. Note that this worksheet is based on the same future value concept we first introduced in Chapter 2.

DETERMINING AMOUNT OF INVESTMENT CAPITAL

Financial goal: _To accumulate $60,000 in 18 years for the purpose of meeting the cost of daughter's college education._

1. Targeted Financial Goal (see Note 1)	$ 60,000
2. Projected Average Return on Investments	9.0%
A. Finding a Lump Sum Investment:	
3. Future Value Factor, from Appendix A	
■ based on _____ years to target date and a projected average return on investment of _____	
4. Required Lump Sum Investment	
■ line 1 ÷ line 3	$
B. Making a Series of Investments over Time:	
5. Amount of Initial Investment, if any (see Note 2)	$ 7,500
6. Future Value Factor, from Appendix A	
■ based on __18__ years of target date and a projected average return on investment of __9%__	4.72
7. Terminal Value of Initial Investment	
■ line 5 × line 6	$ 35,400
8. Balance to Come from Savings Plan	
■ line 1 − line 7	$ 24,600
9. Future Value Annuity Factor, from Appendix B	
■ based on __18__ years to target date and a projected average return on investment of __9%__	41.3
10. Series of Annual Investments Required over Time	
■ line 8 ÷ line 9	$ 596

Note 1: The "targeted financial goal" is the amount of money you want to accumulate by some target date in the future.

Note 2: If you're starting from scratch—i.e., there is *no* initial investment—enter zero on line 5, *skip* lines 6 and 7, and then use the total targeted financial goal (from line 1) as the amount to be funded from a savings plan; now proceed with the rest of the worksheet.

The first thing to do is find the future value of the $7,500 initial investment—the question here is: How much will that initial lump-sum investment grow to over an 18-year period of time? Using the compound value concept and the appropriate "future value factor" (from Appendix A), we see, in line 7, that this deposit will grow to some $35,400. That's nearly 60 percent of the targeted $60,000 that we already have covered. Thus, by subtracting the terminal value of the initial investment (line 7) from our target (line 1), we come up with the amount that must be generated from some sort of annual savings plan— see line 8. (*Note*: If you were starting from scratch, you'd enter a zero in line 5, and the amount in line 8 would be equal to the amount in line 1.) Again, using the appropriate future value factor (this time from Appendix B), we find the Thompsons will have to put away/invest just $600 a year (actually $596) to reach their target of $60,000 in 18 years. That is, the $596 a year will grow to $24,600, which, when added to the $35,400 that the initial $7,500 will grow to, equals the Thompson's targeted financial goal of $60,000. (By the way, they can also reach their target by making a lump-sum investment right up front of $12,712—try working out part A of the worksheet on your own, and see if you can come up with that number.) As you might have suspected, the last few steps in the worksheet can just as easily be done on a good hand-held calculator. That is, once the size of the nest egg has been determined (as in Step 8, for example), a financial calculator can be used to find the amount of money that must be put away each year to fund the nest egg—see below for the specific calculator key strokes.

You can use a financial calculator to *find the annual payments necessary to fund a target amount* by first putting the calculator in the *annual compounding* mode. Then, to determine the amount of money that must be put away *each year*, at a 9% rate of return, to accumulate $24,600 in 18 years, do the following:

1. Punch 18 and then press **N**.
2. Punch 9.0 and then press **i**.
3. Punch −24,600 (make sure you enter this value as a negative) and then press **FV**.
4. Now, to calculate the amount of money that must be put away annually, press the **CPT** key and then the **PMT** key.

A value of 595.62 should appear in the calculator display, which is the amount of money that must be put away each year to reach the targeted amount of $24,600 in 18 years. (*Note:* The calculator keystrokes shown above basically takes you from steps 8 to 10 in Worksheet 11.1. You can also do steps 5 to 7 on the calculator by letting **N** = 18; **i** = 9.0; **PV** = −7,500; and then solve for (**CPT**)**FV**. Try it—you should come up with a number pretty close to the amount shown on line 7 of Worksheet 11.1.)

AN INVESTMENT PLAN PROVIDES DIRECTION. Now that the Thompsons know how much they have to save each year, their next step is to decide how they will save it. Probably the best thing to do in this regard is to follow some type of *systematic routine*— for example, build a set amount of savings each month or quarter into the household budget, and then stick with it. But whatever procedure is followed, keep in mind that all we are doing here is accumulating the required investment capital. That money still has to be put to work in some kind of investment program, and that's where an investment plan comes into the picture. Basically, an **investment plan** is nothing more than a simple, preferably written, statement that explains how the accumulated investment capital will be invested for the purpose of reaching the targeted goal. In the example we've been using, the Thompsons' capital accumulation plan calls for a 9 percent rate of return as a target they feel they can achieve. Now they have to come up with a way of obtaining that 9 percent return on their money—meaning they have to specify, in general terms at least, the kinds of investment vehicles they intend to use. *When completed, an investment plan is a way of*

investment plan
A statement, preferably written, that specifies how investment capital will be invested for the purpose of achieving a specified goal.

translating an abstract investment target (in this case, a 9 percent return) *into a specific investment program.*

WHAT ARE YOUR INVESTMENT OBJECTIVES?

Some people buy securities for the protection they provide from taxes (that's what tax shelters are all about). Others want to have money put aside for that proverbial rainy day or, perhaps, to build up a nice retirement nest egg. *Your goals tend to set the tone for your investment program, and they play a major role in determining how conservative (or aggressive) you're likely to be in making investment decisions.* In a very real way, they provide a purpose for your investments. Given that you have adequate savings and insurance to cover any emergencies, the most frequent investment objectives are to (1) enhance current income, (2) save for a major purchase, (3) accumulate funds for retirement, and (4) seek shelter from taxes.

CURRENT INCOME. The idea here is to put your money into investments that will enable you to supplement your income. In other words, it's for people who want to live off their investment income. A secure source of high current income, from dividends or interest, is the principal concern of such investors. Retired people, for example, often choose investments offering high current income—at low risk. Another common reason for seeking supplemental income is that a family member requires extended costly medical care. Even after insurance, such recurring costs can heavily burden a family budget without this vital income supplement.

MAJOR EXPENDITURES. People often put money aside, sometimes for years, to save up enough to make just one major expenditure, the most common ones being:

- The down payment on a home
- Money for a child's college education
- Some capital for going into business
- An expensive (perhaps once-in-a-lifetime) vacation
- The purchase of a very special, expensive item
- Funds for retirement (discussed in the following section)

Whatever your goal, the idea is to set your sights on something and then go about building your capital with that objective in mind. It sure makes the act of investing more pleasurable. Once you have a handle on how much money you're going to need to attain one of these goals (following a procedure like the one illustrated with Worksheet 11.1), you can specify the types of investment vehicles you intend to use. For example, you might follow a low-risk approach by making a single lump-sum investment in a bond that matures in the year in which you need the funds; or you could follow a more risky investment plan that calls for investing a set amount of money over time in something like a growth-oriented mutual fund (where there is little or no assurance of what the terminal value of the investment will be). Of course, for some purposes—such as the down payment on a home or a child's education—you will probably want to accept a lot less risk than for others, as the attainment of these goals should not be jeopardized by the types of investment vehicles you choose to employ.

RETIREMENT. Accumulating funds for retirement is *the single most important reason for investing.* Too often, though, retirement planning occupies only a small amount of our time, because we tend to rely very heavily on employers and social security for our retirement needs. As many people learn too late in life, that can be a serious mistake. A much better approach is to review the amounts of income you can realistically expect to receive from social security and your employee pension plan, and then decide, based on your retirement goals, *whether or not they will be adequate to meet your needs*. You'll probably find that you'll have to supplement them through personal investing. Obviously, the earlier in life you make this assessment, the greater your opportunity to accumulate the needed funds. (Retirement plans are discussed in Chapter 14.)

SHELTER FROM TAXES. As Chapter 3 explained, federal income tax law does not treat all sources of income equally. For example, if you own real estate—either directly or through some pooling arrangement—you may be able to take depreciation deductions against certain other sources of income, thereby reducing the amount of your final taxable income. This tax write-off feature can make real estate an attractive investment vehicle for some investors, even though its pretax rate of return may not appear very high. The goal of sheltering income from taxes is a legitimate one and, for some investors, often goes hand in hand with the goals of saving for a major outlay or for retirement. Clearly, if you can avoid paying taxes on the income from an investment, you will, all other things considered, have more funds available for reinvestment during the period.

DIFFERENT WAYS TO INVEST

Once you've established your investment objectives, there are a variety of investment vehicles you can use to fulfill those goals. Various types of investment vehicles are briefly described in the following paragraphs; most of these securities will be more fully explained in the next two chapters.

COMMON STOCK. *Common stocks* are basically a form of *equity*—meaning that, as an investment, they represent an ownership interest in a corporation. Each share of stock symbolizes a fractional ownership position in a firm; for example, one share of common stock in a corporation that has 10,000 shares outstanding would denote a 1/10,000 ownership interest in the firm. A share of stock entitles the holder to equal participation in the corporation's earnings and dividends, an equal vote, and an equal voice in management. From the investor's perspective, the return to stockholders comes from dividends and/or appreciation in share price. Common stock has no maturity date and, as a result, remains outstanding indefinitely. (Discussed in Chapter 12.)

BONDS. In contrast to stocks, *bonds* are *liabilities*—they're IOUs of the issuer. The bondholder actually loans money to the issuer. Governments and corporations issue bonds that pay a stated return, called *interest*. When an individual invests in a bond, he or she receives a stipulated interest return, typically paid every 6 months, plus the return of the principal (face) value of the bond at maturity. For example, if you purchased a $1,000 bond that paid 10 percent interest in semiannual installments, you could expect to receive $50 every 6 months (that is, 10% × $1,000 × .5 years) and at maturity recover the $1,000 face value of the bond. Of course, a bond can be bought or sold prior to maturity at a price that can differ from its face value because bond prices, like common stock prices, do fluctuate in the marketplace. (Discussed in Chapter 12.)

PREFERREDS AND CONVERTIBLES. These are forms of hybrid securities in that each has the characteristics of both stocks and bonds; in essence, they are a cross between the two. *Preferred securities* are issued as stock and, as such, represent an equity position in a corporation. Unlike common stock, however, preferreds have a stated (fixed) dividend rate, payment of which is given preference over dividends to holders of common stock. Like bonds, preferred stocks are usually purchased for the current income (dividends) they pay.

A *convertible security*, in contrast, is a special type of fixed-income obligation (usually a bond, but sometimes a preferred stock) that carries a conversion feature permitting the investor to convert it into a specified number of shares of common stock. Convertible securities, therefore, provide the fixed-income benefits of a bond (interest) while offering the price appreciation (capital gains) potential of common stock. (Discussed in Chapter 12.)

MUTUAL FUNDS. An organization that invests in and professionally manages a diversified portfolio of securities is called a *mutual fund*. A mutual fund sells shares to investors, who then become part-owners of the fund's securities portfolio. Most mutual funds issue and repurchase shares at a price that reflects the underlying value of the portfolio at the time the transaction is made. Mutual funds have become very popular with individual investors because they offer not only a wide variety of investment opportunities but also a full array of services that many investors find particularly appealing. (Discussed in Chapter 13.)

REAL ESTATE. Investments in *real estate* can take many forms, ranging from raw land speculation to limited-partnership shares in commercial property. The returns on real estate can come from rents, capital gains, and certain tax benefits. Unfortunately, estimating both the risk and the return in a real estate venture can be difficult and usually requires expert advice, particularly with respect to income tax implications. (A type of publicly traded real estate investment—known as a real estate investment trust, or REIT for short—is discussed in Chapter 13.)

COMMODITIES, FINANCIAL FUTURES, AND OPTIONS. *Commodities* are contracts to buy/sell such things as cotton, corn, wheat, coffee, and cocoa, as well as raw materials (like copper, silver, and oil), at some future date. *Financial futures* are just like commodities, except they apply to certain types of financial instruments, like stock prices, bond interest rates, even foreign currencies. Commodities and financial futures are actively traded in what is known as the *futures markets*. Because they do not pay interest or dividends, the returns on commodities and financial futures contracts are derived solely from the change in the price of the underlying commodity or financial instrument. These are very risky investments, because losses can mount up quickly and, in a short period of time, far exceed the amount invested.

In a similar fashion, *options* give the holder the right to buy or sell common stocks (and other financial instruments) at a set price, over a specified period of time. Again, to earn a positive return one must correctly anticipate future price movements in the underlying financial asset. In contrast to futures contracts, the price paid for an option is the maximum amount that can be lost; however, options have very short maturities, and consistent losses can quickly exhaust one's investment capital. Futures and options are often referred to as **derivative securities** to the extent that they derive their value from the price behavior of some underlying real or financial asset.

derivative securities
Securities such as futures and options, whose value is derived from (or linked to) the price behavior of an underlying real or financial asset.

CONCEPT CHECK

11-1. Briefly discuss the relationship between *investing* and personal financial planning. Do these two activities complement each other?

11-2. What's the difference between an *investment plan* and a capital accumulation plan? Are they in any way related?

11-3. Identify four major investment objectives. Why is it important to have one or more investment objective(s) when embarking on an investment program? Of the various investment objectives, which two would *you* consider most important? Explain.

Securities Markets [LG2]

It takes more than money to be a successful investor. Indeed, as anyone who's found success in the market will tell you, *there is no substitute for being an informed investor!* Among other things, that means you must understand the institutions, mechanisms, and procedures involved in making security transactions. We looked at some investment fundamentals above; in the balance of this chapter, we will examine different securities markets and market transactions, sources of investment information, online investing, and ways to manage your investment holdings.

securities markets
The marketplace in which stocks, bonds, and other financial instruments are traded.

The term **securities markets** is generally used to describe the place where stocks, bonds, and other financial instruments are traded. The securities markets can be broken into two parts: capital markets and money markets. The *capital market* is where long-term securities (those with maturities of more than a year) are traded, while the *money market* is the marketplace for short-term, low-risk credit instruments with maturities of one year or less, like U.S. Treasury bills, commercial paper, negotiable certificates of deposit, and so on. Both types of markets provide a vital mechanism for bringing the buyers and sellers of securities together. Some of the more popular money market securities were discussed in Chapter 4, where we looked at short-term investment vehicles. This chapter considers the capital markets.

PRIMARY OR SECONDARY MARKETS

The securities markets can also be divided into primary and secondary segments. The *primary market* is the market where new securities are sold to the public—where one party to the transaction is always the issuer. The *secondary market*, in contrast, is where old (outstanding) securities are bought and sold—here the securities are "traded" between investors. A security is sold in the primary market just once, when it is originally issued by the corporation or some governmental body, like a state or municipality. Subsequent transactions, in which securities are sold by one investor to another, take place in the secondary market. As a rule, when people speak of the securities markets, they are referring to the secondary market, because that is where the vast majority of security transactions take place.

PRIMARY MARKETS. When a corporation sells a new issue to the public, several financial institutions participate in the transaction. To begin with, the corporation will probably use an *investment banking firm*, which specializes in *underwriting* (selling) new security issues. The investment banker will give the corporation advice on pricing and other aspects of the issue and will either sell the new security itself or arrange for a *selling group* to do so. The selling group is normally made up of a number of brokerage firms, each of which accepts the responsibility for selling a certain portion of the new issue. On very large issues, the originating investment banker will bring in other underwriting firms as partners and form an *underwriting syndicate* in an attempt to spread the risks associated with underwriting and selling the new securities.

prospectus
A document made available to prospective security buyers that describes the firm and a new security issue.

A potential investor in a new issue must be provided with a **prospectus**, which is a document describing the firm and the issue. Certain federal agencies have the responsibility of ensuring that all the information included in a prospectus is an accurate representation of the facts. Many times investors have trouble purchasing new security issues because all shares have been sold—often before the official sale date. Also, if the new shares are sold using rights or warrants, the ability to purchase the new securities will be somewhat restricted, because only the holders of these rights or warrants can buy the stock.

SECONDARY MARKETS. The secondary markets permit investors to execute transactions among themselves—it's the marketplace where an investor can easily sell his or her holdings to someone else. Included among the secondary markets are the various *securities exchanges*, in which the buyers and sellers of securities are brought together for the purpose of executing trades. In addition, there is the **over-the-counter (OTC) market**, made up of a nationwide network of brokers and dealers who execute transactions in securities that are not listed on one of the exchanges. The **organized securities exchanges** typically handle securities of larger, better-known companies, and the over-the-counter market handles mostly the smaller, lesser-known firms—though, as we'll see later, there are a lot of big, well-known firms that trade in the OTC market. The organized exchanges are well-structured institutions that bring together the market forces of supply and demand; the over-the-counter market is basically a mass telecommunications network linking buyers and sellers. Most of the transactions of small investors are made in the secondary market; as such, we will focus on it throughout this chapter.

ORGANIZED SECURITIES EXCHANGES

The market forces of supply and demand are brought together in organized securities exchanges. So-called **listed securities** are traded on organized exchanges and account for about half of the total dollar volume of all shares traded in the U.S. stock market—the Nasdaq/OTC market accounts for the rest. All trading in listed securities is carried out in one place (such as the New York Stock Exchange on Wall Street) and under a broad set of rules by people who are *members* of the exchange. Members are said to "own a seat" on the exchange, a privilege obtained by meeting certain financial requirements. Only the securities of companies that have met established listing requirements are traded on the exchange, and those firms must comply with various regulations to ensure they will not make financial or legal misrepresentations to their stockholders. Firms must not only comply with the rules of the specific exchange, but also must fulfill certain requirements as established by the Securities and Exchange Commission (SEC), which will be discussed later.

NEW YORK STOCK EXCHANGE. The *New York Stock Exchange (NYSE)* is the largest and most prestigious organized securities exchange in the world. Known as "the big board," it lists over *275 billion* shares of stock that, at year-end 1999, had a market value of some *$12.2 trillion*. Membership on the NYSE is limited to 1,366 seats. Most seats are owned by brokerage firms, the largest of which—Merrill Lynch—owns more than 20.

The NYSE has the most stringent listing requirements of all the organized exchanges. For example, in order to be listed, a firm must have at least 2,000 stockholders, each owning 100 shares or more. It must also have a minimum of 1.1 million shares of publicly held stock outstanding; demonstrated pretax earning power of $2.5 million (or $25 million in cash flow) at the time of listing; a market value (of publicly held shares) of $60 million for new stocks, or $100 million for stocks that transfer from another market or stock exchange; and pay a listing fee. Firms that fail to continue to meet listing requirements can be *delisted*. More than 3,000 firms from around the world list their shares on the NYSE.

AMERICAN STOCK EXCHANGE. The *American Stock Exchange (AMEX)* is the second largest organized stock exchange in terms of the number of listed companies; when it comes to the dollar volume of trading, however, the AMEX is actually smaller than the two largest *regional* exchanges (the Midwest and Pacific). Its organization and procedures are similar to those of the NYSE, though its membership costs and listing requirements are not as stringent. There are approximately 660 seats on the AMEX, and it is home to around 1,000 listed stocks and a handful of listed corporate bonds. The AMEX handles only about

over-the-counter (OTC) market
The market in which securities not listed on one of the organized exchanges are traded, usually those of smaller, lesser-known firms.

organized securities exchanges
Exchanges where various types of securities are traded by exchange members for their own accounts and the accounts of their customers.

listed security
A security that has met the prerequisites for, and thus is traded on, one of the organized securities exchanges.

2 percent of the total annual dollar volume of shares traded on *organized* security exchanges. In contrast, the NYSE handles around 90 percent of all common shares traded on organized exchanges, so the AMEX is nowhere near the New York exchange in terms of size or stature. Further, whereas the NYSE is home for many of the biggest and best-known companies in the world, firms traded on the AMEX are much smaller and, with few exceptions, would hardly qualify as "household names." All this is changing, however, as the stock market landscape was altered dramatically in 1998, when *Nasdaq* (see below)—a major market force in the U.S. market—took over the American Stock Exchange and shortly thereafter, the Philadelphia Stock Exchange (a major regional exchange). Thus, the AMEX today functions as a subsidiary of the Nasdaq—the principle market maker in the OTC market. A number of major changes have been made to enable the AMEX to create its own market niche and, in so doing, become more competitive with the NYSE. One area where the AMEX has really become the dominant player is in so-called *index shares*, or *exchange traded funds (ETFs)*, which we'll examine in Chapter 13 when we discuss mutual funds.

REGIONAL STOCK EXCHANGES. In addition to the NYSE and AMEX, there are a handful of so-called **regional exchanges**. The number of securities listed on each of these exchanges is typically in the range of 100 to 500 companies. As a group they handle around 8 percent of all shares traded on organized exchanges. The best-known of these are the Midwest, Pacific, Philadelphia, Boston, and Cincinnati exchanges. These exchanges deal primarily in securities with local and regional appeal. Most are modeled after the NYSE, but their membership and listing requirements are considerably more lenient. To enhance their trading activity, regional exchanges will often list securities that are also listed on the NYSE or AMEX.

>
> What are the stock markets doing today? Get the latest market summary and other statistics at the New York Stock Exchange site, **www.nyse.com/marektinfo/marketinfo.html**.

THE OVER-THE-COUNTER MARKET

Unlike an organized exchange, the over-the-counter (OTC) market is not a specific institution but, instead, exists as an intangible relationship between the buyers and sellers of securities. Securities traded in this market are sometimes called **unlisted securities**. It is the fastest-growing segment of the stock market, accounting for about 50 to 55 percent of the total dollar volume of domestic shares traded, and today trades close to *35,000* issues. The market is linked by a mass telecommunications network. Unlike those in the organized securities exchanges, trades in the OTC market represent *direct* transactions between investors and securities dealers—that is, the investors buy from and sell to the securities dealers, whereas on the listed securities exchanges the broker acts as a middleman between buyers and sellers. All municipal bonds, along with most government and corporate bonds and a numerical majority of common stocks, are traded in the OTC market. Dealers make markets in certain OTC securities by offering to either buy or sell them at stated prices.

NASDAQ. A part of the OTC market is made up of a select list of stocks that trade on the *National Association of Securities Dealers Automated Quotation System (Nasdaq)*, which provides up-to-the-minute quotes and bid/ask prices on several thousand securities. (The **bid** and **ask prices** represent, respectively, the highest price offered to purchase a given security and the lowest price at which the security is offered for sale. In effect, an investor pays the ask price when *buying* securities and receives the bid price when *selling* them.)

There are about 5,000 actively traded issues in the Nasdaq portion of the OTC market, and, of these, about 3,800 or so are part of the so-called *National Market System (NMS)*. The

---

regional exchanges
Organized securities exchanges (other than the NYSE and AMEX) that deal primarily in securities having a local or regional appeal.

unlisted security
A security that is traded in the over-the-counter market; such a trade is made directly between the investor and the security dealer.

bid price
The price at which one can sell a security.

ask price
The price at which one can purchase a security.

National Market System is reserved for the biggest and most actively traded stocks, and, in general, for those stocks that have a *national following*. These securities are widely quoted, and the trades are executed about as efficiently here as they are on the floor of the NYSE. A number of large and well-known firms are found on the Nasdaq National Market System, including companies like Intel, Oracle, Dell Computers, Microsoft, Starbucks, Northwest Airlines, Worldcom, Cisco Systems, Herman Miller, and Hollywood Entertainment. Generally speaking, the big-name stocks traded on the Nasdaq/NMS receive about as much national visibility and are about as liquid as those traded on the NYSE, and new ways of more efficiently executing trades are constantly being brought to the market. Indeed, as discussed in the accompanying *Money in Action* box, one of the newest, fastest, and least costly ways of executing trades not only on the Nasdaq, but also the NYSE (and other organized exchanges), is by using Electronic Communications Networks (ECNs).

The situation is considerably different, however, for OTC stocks that are not part of Nasdaq—which applies to the vast majority of the firms traded in the OTC market. These include the very small firms that may not even have much of a regional following, let alone a national constituency. These stocks are *thinly traded*, meaning there's not much of a market for them, and they often lack any measurable degree of liquidity. Many of these stocks appear in the so-called *pink sheets*. So named because of the color of paper used, the pink sheets are published daily and are available from brokers.

The companies who use pink-sheet listings are either unable or unwilling to meet the financial reporting requirements of the SEC. They cover the full spectrum of securities, including new, rapidly growing firms, obscure but well-established firms that are closely held, companies on the verge of bankruptcy, and penny stocks peddled by shady brokers. Although quotes on pink-sheet companies today are available electronically, prices are updated only when there's significant trading or when requested by traders making markets in pink-sheet stocks, so quotes may not be current. The quotes for these thinly traded securities reflect the value set by the market maker, not market forces. Because dealers mark up prices, often by large amounts, your final price may be much higher than the actual selling price, making it harder to earn a profit when you sell the stock. If you decide to buy a pink-sheet stock, make sure your broker is prepared to negotiate long and hard on your behalf.

FOREIGN SECURITIES MARKETS

In addition to those in the United States, there are organized securities exchanges in more than 100 other countries worldwide. Indeed, actively traded markets can be found not only in the major industrialized nations like Japan, Great Britain, Germany, and Canada, but also in emerging economies as well. In terms of market capitalization (total market value of all shares traded), the New York Stock Exchange is the biggest stock market in the world, followed by the Nasdaq market. After these two U.S. markets comes the Tokyo stock market, followed by the London market, then Paris, Frankfurt, and Toronto. Other major exchanges are located in Sydney, Zurich, Hong Kong, Singapore, Rome, and Amsterdam. In addition to these markets, you'll also find developing markets all over the globe—from Argentina and Armenia to Egypt and Fiji, from Iceland, Israel, and Malaysia to New Zealand, Russia, and Zimbabwe. Surely, as these and other markets begin to develop, they'll open up opportunities not only for investors in those countries, but also for U.S. investors willing to go off-shore in search of returns.

REGULATING THE SECURITIES MARKETS

A number of laws have been enacted to regulate the activities of various participants in the securities markets and provide for adequate and accurate disclosure of information to potential and existing investors. State laws, which regulate the sale of securities within state

MONEY IN ACTION

ECNs Lead the Way to 21st-Century Investing

Some new players have arrived on Wall Street, shaking up not only the traditional organized exchanges like the New York Stock Exchange (NYSE), but also giving Nasdaq—which as the world's first electronic stock market always prided itself on being at the forefront of technological innovation—a run for its money. *Electronic communications networks (ECNs)* are privately owned electronic trading networks that make transactions directly between buyers and sellers of securities. The ECNs' trading volume already accounts for about one third of all Nasdaq transactions, as well as an increasing share of NYSE volume.

Unlike the auction setting of the organized exchanges, ECNs bypass the dealer and provide a more open, less centralized system. These new electronic middlemen automatically match customer's electronic buy and sell orders in less than a second, without human intervention. Online investors prefer this speed to the slower competitive bid system at the NYSE. If there is no immediate match, the ECN acts like a broker and posts the request on the Nasdaq under its own name. The trade will be executed if another trader is interested in making the transaction at the posted price. ECNs also allow investors to execute trades outside of normal trading hours for the organized exchanges and Nasdaq.

ECNs can save customers money because they take a transaction fee of less than 1 percent, either per share or based on order size. Customers get the best price quickly, and at narrower spreads (the difference between the highest price to buy and the lowest price to sell). The electronic order handling system is less prone to errors, too. "A market maker has the ability to manipulate the quote, delay the

trade until the most [advantageous] time, and widen the spread," said John Wheeler, manager of trading for American Century Investments, an investment company that owns part of the Archipelago ECN.

Archipelago, Datek's Island, Reuter's Instinet, Bloomberg Tradebook, MarketXT, BRUT, ARCA and Redibook are some of the major ECNs now in operation. While most ECNs are registered as broker-dealers, some have applied to the SEC to become full-fledged exchanges, a status that would allow them to post quotes on the NYSE system.

In response to the ECNs' challenge, the NYSE is developing an electronic trading process of its own, although limited initially to small orders. The Nasdaq market, meanwhile, is building a centralized trading system to compete with ECNs.

There's likely to be an ECN in your investing future. In December 2000, Datek Online Brokerage Services became the first major online brokerage firm to allow its customers to direct Nasdaq trades to the ECN or market maker of their choice. Through Datek Direct, investors have several options, including routing orders to Datek's Island ECN, through Nasdaq SelectNet to an ECN of their choice, or Nasdaq SelectNet to a market maker.

Sources: "Datek Online Enables Customers to Route Orders to ECNs and Market Makers," *PRNewswire*, December 4, 2000, downloaded from **www.morningstar.com/news**; Tom Lauricella, "You Say You Want a Revolution," *Smart Money*, January 2000, pp. 32–34; Odyll Santos, "Automated Trading Systems Muscling In," *Morningstar.com*, June 30, 2000, downloaded from **www.morningstar.com/news**; and Tom Walker, "Breaking Down the Wall," *Atlanta Journal and Constitution*, January 3, 2000, p. S1.

borders, typically establish procedures that apply to the sellers of securities doing business within the state. The most important and far-reaching securities laws, however, are those enacted by the federal government:

- **Securities Act of 1933.** This act was passed by Congress to ensure full disclosure of information with respect to new security issues and to prevent a stock market collapse similar to the one that occurred during 1929–1932. It requires the issuer of a new security to file a registration statement containing information about the new issue with the **Securities and Exchange Commission (SEC),** an agency of the U.S. government established to enforce federal securities laws.

- **Securities Exchange Act of 1934.** One of the most important pieces of securities legislation ever passed, it expanded the scope of federal regulation and formally established the SEC as the agency in charge of the administration of federal securities laws. The act gives the SEC power to regulate organized securities exchanges and the over-the-counter market by extending disclosure requirements to outstanding securities. It requires the stock exchanges and the stocks traded on them to be registered with the SEC. In essence, the Securities acts of 1933 and 1934 regulated not only securities exchanges and securities markets, but also the disclosure of information on new and outstanding securities.

- **Investment Company Act of 1940.** This act protects those purchasing investment company (mutual fund) shares. It established rules and regulations for investment companies and formally authorized the SEC to regulate their practices and procedures. It requires the investment companies to register with the SEC and to fulfill certain disclosure requirements. The act was amended in 1970 to prohibit investment companies from paying excessive fees to their advisors as well as charging excessive commissions to purchasers of company shares. From the point of view of the individual investor, this act provides protection against inadequate or inaccurate disclosure of information, and against being charged excessive fees indirectly by the fund's advisors, and directly through the commissions paid to purchase fund shares.

- **Other Significant Federal Legislation.** The *Maloney Act of 1938* provides for the establishment of trade associations for the purpose of self-regulation within the securities industry; this act led to the creation of the **National Association of Securities Dealers (NASD),** which is made up of all brokers and dealers who participate in the OTC market. The NASD is a self-regulatory organization that polices the activities of brokers and dealers to ensure that its standards are upheld. The SEC supervises the activities of NASD, thus providing investors with further protection from fraudulent activities. The *Investment Advisors Act of 1940* was passed to protect investors against potential abuses by investment advisors who sell their services to the investing public. The *Securities Investor Protection Act of 1970* created the SIPC (Securities Investor Protection Corp.), an organization that protects investors against the financial failure of brokerage firms, much like the FDIC protects depositors against bank failures (we'll examine the SIPC later in this chapter). The *Insider Trading and Securities Fraud Enforcement Act of 1988* toughened penalties for securities fraud and required brokerage firms to establish written policies to prevent trading abuses by their employees; it also made it easier for investors to bring legal action against brokers.

In addition to securities legislation, the *stock exchanges* themselves play important roles in monitoring and regulating the companies, brokerage firms, traders, and other parties that deal in listed securities. Likewise, most *brokerage firms* go to great lengths to prevent trading abuses by aggressively policing their own employees.

BULL MARKET OR BEAR?

The general condition of the market is termed *bullish* or *bearish*, depending on whether security prices are rising or falling over extended periods of time. Changing market conditions generally stem from changing investor attitudes, changes in economic activity, and certain governmental actions aimed at stimulating or slowing down the economy. Prices go *up* in **bull markets;** these favorable markets are normally associated with investor

Securities and Exchange Commission (SEC) An agency of the federal government that regulates the disclosure of information about securities and generally oversees the operation of the securities exchanges and markets.

National Association of Securities Dealers (NASD) An agency made up of brokers and dealers in over-the-counter securities that regulates the operations of the OTC market.

bull market A condition of the market normally associated with investor optimism, economic recovery and expansion; characterized by generally rising securities prices.

EXHIBIT 11.1

THE FIVE BIGGEST BULL MARKETS SINCE THE SECOND WORLD WAR (AS MEASURED BY CHANGES IN THE DJIA)

The prices of most stocks will go up in a bull market. Thus it is hard to lose money—though not impossible, because not all stocks will appreciate in value during such markets. The most recent bull market started in November 1990, but by late 2000 was beginning to run out of steam.

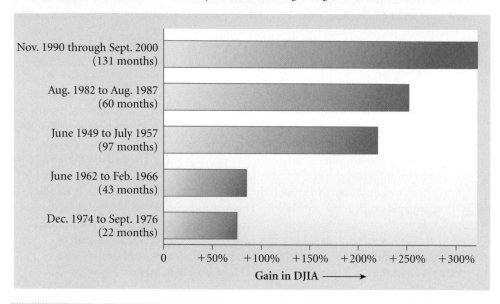

optimism, economic recovery, and growth. In contrast, prices go *down* in **bear markets,** which are normally associated with investor pessimism and economic slowdowns. These terms are used to describe conditions in the bond and other securities markets as well as the stock market. For example, the bond market is considered bullish when interest rates fall, causing bond prices to rise; on the other hand, a bear market in bonds exists when bond prices fall (which occurs when rates rise). As a rule, investors are able to earn attractive rates of return during bull markets and only low (or negative) returns during bear markets. Market conditions are difficult to predict and usually cannot be identified until after they exist.

Over the past 50 or so years, the behavior of the stock market has been generally bullish, reflecting the growth and prosperity of the economy. Exhibit 11.1 shows the five biggest bull markets since the Second World War, the longest of which lasted 131 months—from November 1990 through September 2000. The most notorious of the five was surely the one that started in August 1982 and peaked in August 1987. This is the one that's associated with the big market crash of October 19, 1987, when in a *single day*, the market, as measured by the Dow Jones Industrial Average, dropped by a whopping 508 points! Actually, the market had started dropping in late August and by mid-October had already fallen some 400 points. Then came "Black Monday," when the market experienced its biggest and hardest crash in history, not only in absolute numerical terms (508 points), but also in percentage and dollar terms: In one day, the market fell nearly 23 percent and lost roughly a half *trillion* dollars in value.

bear market
A condition of the market typically associated with investor pessimism and economic slowdown; characterized by generally falling securities prices.

Ten years later, almost to the day, it happened again. On October 27, 1997, the DJIA dropped 554 points (a new record) on volume of 685 million shares (also a record). In percentage terms, however, the market ended the day down just over 7 percent, which wasn't even close to the record. (The 7 percent decline was only the twelfth largest in percentage terms.) But, unlike the 1987 crash, this one didn't last long; the market recovered all its losses within two weeks, and within two months the October decline was little more than a distant memory. In stark contrast, it took over two and a half years for the market to recover from the 1987 crash. Then, as the market entered a new century, an even bigger drop occurred, on April 14, 2000, when the DJIA plunged an eye-popping 617 points. That decline, however, amounted to a fall of "only" 5.5% and hardly compares with the crash of 1987, which in percentage terms was about 4 times as bad! Fortunately, days such as October 19, 1987, and October 27, 1997, are the exceptions rather than the rule. More often than not, the stock market offers attractive returns, rather than just wild price volatility.

CONCEPT CHECK

11-4. Explain what is meant by the *securities markets* and briefly describe the difference between the money market and the capital market. Give some examples of the types of securities found in the money market; in the capital market.

11-5. How does a primary market differ from a secondary market? Where are most securities traded—in the primary or secondary market?

11-6. What are *organized securities exchanges?* What is the difference between the New York Stock Exchange and the American Stock Exchange? What are *regional exchanges,* and what role do they play?

11-7. Describe the operations of the *over-the-counter market;* compare and contrast it with organized securities exchanges. What are Nasdaq and the National Market System?

11-8. Explain the difference between a *bull market* and a *bear market.* How would you characterize the current state of the stock market? Are we in a bull market or a bear market?

11-9. Briefly summarize the key provisions of major securities legislation.

Making Transactions in the Securities Markets [LG3]

In many respects, dealing in the securities markets almost seems like you are operating in another world—one with all kinds of unusual orders and strange-sounding transactions. Actually, making securities transactions is relatively simple once you understand the basics—in fact, you will probably find it is no more difficult than using a checking account! Indeed, while making money in the market isn't all that easy, making transactions is.

STOCKBROKERS

Stockbrokers, or **account executives** and **financial consultants,** as they're also called, purchase and sell securities for their customers. Although deeply ingrained in our language, the term *stockbroker* is really somewhat of a misnomer, because such an individual assists you in the purchase and sale of not only stocks but also bonds, convertibles, mutual funds, options, and many other types of securities. Brokers must be licensed by the exchanges on

stockbroker (account executive, financial consultant) A person who buys and sells securities on behalf of clients and provides them with investment advice and information.

which they place orders and must abide by the strict ethical guidelines of the exchanges and the SEC. They work for brokerage firms and in essence are there to execute the orders placed. The largest stockbrokerage firm, Merrill Lynch, has brokerage offices in virtually every major U.S. city (and many foreign countries). Orders from these offices are transmitted by brokers to the main office of Merrill Lynch and then to the floor of one of the stock exchanges, or to the OTC market, where they are executed. Although the procedure for executing orders on organized exchanges differs a bit from that in the OTC market, you as an investor would never know the difference, because you would place your order with the broker in exactly the same fashion.

SELECTING A BROKER.   If you decide to start investing with a so-called *full-service broker*, it's important to select someone *who understands your investment objectives, and who can effectively help you pursue them.* If you choose a broker whose own disposition toward investing is similar to yours, you should be able to avoid conflict and establish a solid working relationship. A good place to start the search is to ask friends, relatives, or business associates to recommend a broker. It is not important—and often not even advisable—to know your stockbroker socially because most, if not all, of your transactions/ orders will probably be placed by phone. In addition, a strict business relationship eliminates the possibility of social concerns interfering with the achievement of your investment objectives. This does not mean, of course, that your broker's sole interest should be commissions. Indeed, a broker should be far more than just a salesperson; *a good broker is someone who's more interested in your investments than his or her commissions.* Should you find you're dealing with someone who's always trying to get you to trade your stocks, or who's pushing new investments on you, then by all means, dump that broker and find a new one!

full-service broker
A broker who, in addition to executing clients' transactions, provides them with a full array of brokerage services.

discount broker
A broker with low overhead who charges low commissions and offers little or no services to investors.

online broker
Typically a discount broker through which investors can execute trades electronically/online through a commercial service or on the Internet. (Also called Internet broker or electronic broker.)

FULL-SERVICE, DISCOUNT, AND ONLINE BROKERS.   Just a few years ago, there were three distinct types of brokers—full-service, discount, and online—and each occupied a well-defined market niche. Today, the lines between these three types of brokers are no longer clear cut. Most brokerage firms, even the most traditional ones, now offer online services to compete with the increasingly popular online firms. And many discount brokers now offer services once available only from a full-service broker, like research reports for clients. The traditional **full-service broker** offers investors a full array of brokerage services, including investment advice and information, execution of securities transactions, holding securities in safe keeping, online brokerage services, and margin loans. Such services are fine for those investors who want such help—and are willing to pay for them! In contrast, those investors who simply want to execute trades and aren't interested in obtaining the full array of brokerage services should consider either a *discount broker* or *online broker*. **Discount brokers** tend to have low overhead operations and offer fewer customer services than full-service brokers. Those with the very lowest commissions and who offer hardly any of the normal broker services, other than executing trades, are called *deep discounters*. Many discount brokers, however, do provide research and other services, but charge higher commissions. Transactions are initiated by calling a toll-free number—or visiting the broker's Web site—and placing the desired buy or sell order. The brokerage firm then executes the order at the best possible price and confirms the details of the transaction by phone, e-mail, or regular mail. Depending on the size of the transaction, *discount brokers can save investors from 30 to 80 percent of the commissions charged by full-service brokers*. The investor who does not need the research and advisory help available from full-service brokers may find discount brokers especially attractive.

With the technology that's available to almost anyone today, it's not surprising that investors can just as easily trade securities online as on the phone. All you need is an **online**

broker (also called *Internet* or *electronic brokers*) and you, too, can execute trades electronically online. The investor merely accesses the online broker's Web site to open an account, review the commission schedule, or see a demonstration of the available transactional services and procedures. Confirmation of electronic trades can take as little as 10 seconds and most occur within one minute. Online investing is becoming increasingly popular, particularly among affluent, young investors who enjoy surfing the Web—so much so, in fact, that it has prompted virtually every traditional full service broker (and many discount brokers) to offer online trading to their clients. The rapidly growing volume of business done by discount and online brokers attests to their success. Today, many banks and savings institutions are making discount and online brokerage services available to depositors who wish to buy stocks, bonds, mutual funds, and other investment vehicles. Some of the major full-service, discount, and online brokers are listed across the bottom of this page.

BROKERAGE SERVICES. While discount or online brokers offer little more than execution of trades, that's certainly not the case with full-service brokers. Indeed, these brokers offer their clients a wide variety of brokerage services. For that reason, selecting a good *brokerage firm* is often just as important as choosing a good broker, because not all brokerage firms provide the same services. Try to select a broker with whom you can work and who is affiliated with a firm that provides the types of services you are looking for. Many brokerage firms, for example, provide a wide array of free information, ranging from stock and bond guides to research reports on specific securities or industries. Some have a research staff that periodically issues analyses of economic, market, industry, or company behavior and events, and relates them to its recommendations for buying or selling certain securities. As a brokerage firm client, you can expect to receive monthly bulletins discussing market activity and possibly even a recommended investment list. You will also receive an *account statement* describing all your transactions for the period, commission charges, interest charges, dividends and interest received, the securities you currently hold, and your account balances.

Most brokerage offices provide up-to-the-minute stock price quotations and world news. Stock price information can be obtained either from the quotation board (a large screen that electronically displays security transactions within minutes of their occurrence) or from the computerized telequote system. World news, which can significantly affect the stock market, is obtained from a news wire service. Most offices also have a reference library the firm's clients can use. Another valuable service offered by most major brokerage firms is the automatic transfer of surplus cash left in a customer's account into one of the firm's money funds, thereby allowing the customer to earn a reasonable rate of return on temporarily idle funds. Brokerage houses will also hold your securities for you, as protection against their loss; the securities kept in this way are said to be held in *street name*. Some of these services are also offered by discount brokerages.

Type of Broker		
Full-Service	**Discount**	**Online**
A.G. Edwards	American Express Brokerage	AccuTrade
Morgan Stanley Dean Witter	Charles Schwab	Ameritrade
Merrill Lynch	Muriel Siebert	E*Trade
Paine Webber	Norwest Brokerage	Fidelity Brokerage Services
Prudential Securities	Olde	Net Investor
Salomon Smith Barney	Quick & Reilly	T. Rowe Price Brokerage

smart.sites Confused about which broker is right for you? Use The Motley Fool's checklist, 10 Ways to Size Up a Broker, at the Fool's Discount Brokerage section, **www.fool.com/dbc**.

Securities Investor Protection Corporation (SIPC)
A nonprofit corporation, created by Congress and subject to SEC and congressional oversight, that insures customer accounts against the financial failure of a brokerage firm.

INVESTOR PROTECTION. As a client, you are protected against the loss of securities or cash held by your broker by the **Securities Investor Protection Corporation (SIPC)**—a nonprofit corporation authorized by the Securities Investor Protection Act of 1970 to protect customer accounts against the financial failure of a brokerage firm. Although subject to SEC and congressional oversight, the SIPC is *not* an agency of the U.S. government.

SIPC insurance covers each account for up to $500,000 (of which up to $100,000 may be in cash balances held by the firm). Note, however, that SIPC insurance does not guarantee that the dollar value of the securities will be recovered. It only ensures that *the securities themselves will be returned*. So, what happens if your broker gives you bad advice, and, as a result, you lose a lot of money on an investment? SIPC won't help you, as it's not intended to insure you against bad investment advice. Instead, if you have a dispute with your broker, first discuss the situation with the managing officer at the branch where you do your business. If that doesn't do any good, then write or talk to the firm's compliance officer and contact the securities office in your home state. If you still don't get any satisfaction, you may have to take the case to **arbitration**, a process whereby you and your broker present the two sides to the argument before an arbitration panel, which then makes a decision about how the case will be resolved. If it's *binding* arbitration, and it usually is, you have no choice but to accept the decision—you cannot go to court to appeal your case. Many brokerage firms, in fact, require you to resolve disputes by going to binding arbitration. Thus, before you open an account, check the brokerage agreement to see if it contains a binding arbitration clause.

arbitration
A procedure used to settle disputes between a brokerage firm and its clients; both sides of the "story" are presented to a board of arbitration, which makes a final and often binding decision on the matter.

Binding arbitration wouldn't be so bad if the track record were more evenly balanced, but, until recently, most brokerage firms not only required investors to submit to binding arbitration, but also specified which arbitration panels could be used. Not surprisingly, 90 percent of those panels were sponsored by the NASD or the NYSE. There was considerable controversy as to whether the panels, which prior to 1989 were often composed entirely of people with strong ties to the securities industry, were fair to investors. As a result of pressure from the SEC and a July 1990 court decision in New York State, *many investors now have the option of using either securities industry panels or independent arbitration panels, such as those sponsored by the American Arbitration Association (AAA)*—which is considered more sympathetic toward investors. In addition, only one of the three arbitrators on a panel can be connected to the securities industry. Recently, the NASD and other securities organizations began encouraging investors to *mediate* disputes and voluntarily negotiate a settlement rather than immediately going into arbitration. Although mediation is not binding, it can further reduce costs and time for both investors and brokers. Although these remedies may help resolve disputes, the fact remains that the best way to avoid either mediation or arbitration is to *use care when selecting a broker in the first place, and then carefully evaluate the advice he or she offers*.

odd lot
A quantity of fewer than 100 shares of a stock.

round lot
A quantity of 100 shares of stock, or multiples thereof.

ODD OR ROUND LOTS. Security transactions can be made in either odd or round lots. An **odd lot** consists of fewer than 100 shares of stock, while a **round lot** represents a 100-share unit or multiples thereof. The sale of 400 shares of stock would be considered a round-lot transaction, but the purchase of 75 shares would be an odd-lot transaction; trading 250 shares of stock would involve two round lots and an odd lot. Because the purchase or sale of odd lots requires additional processing and the assistance of a specialist (an *odd-lot dealer*), an added fee—known as an *odd-lot differential*—is often tacked on to the normal commission charge, driving up the costs of these small trades. Indeed, the relatively high cost of an odd-lot trade is why it's best to deal in round lots whenever possible.

EXHIBIT 11.2

REPRESENTATIVE BROKER COMMISSIONS ON COMMON STOCK TRANSACTIONS

The amount of broker commissions paid on a common stock transaction obviously will vary with the market value of the transaction. You will pay a commission when you buy stocks and again when you sell them.

Value of Transaction	Fees for an Odd or Round Lot
Up to $2,500	$30 + 1.7% of the value of the transaction
$2,500 to $6,250	$56 + .66% of the value of the transaction
$6,250 to $20,000	$76 + .34% of the value of the transaction

BROKERAGE FEES. Brokerage firms receive commissions for executing buy and sell orders for their clients. Brokerage commissions are said to be *negotiated*, which means that they are not fixed. In practice, however, most firms have *established* fee schedules that they use with small transactions (on larger, mostly institutional trades, negotiation of commissions actually does take place). Although these fees are not really negotiated, they do differ from one brokerage firm to another; thus it pays to shop around. Also if you're an "active trader," generating a couple thousand dollars (or more) in annual commissions, then by all means try to negotiate a reduced commission schedule with your broker. Chances are, they'll probably cut a deal with you—the fact is, brokers much prefer traders to buy-and-hold investors, because traders generate a lot more commissions.

The suggested fee schedule used by one large brokerage firm to set commissions on *common stock* transactions is given in Exhibit 11.2. Although this schedule does not specifically levy a premium on odd-lot transactions, the fixed-cost fee component does tend to raise their per-share cost. (In addition to the fees shown in the schedule, some brokerage firms charge a differential of 5 to 10 cents per share on odd-lot transactions.) If the fee schedule in Exhibit 11.2 were used to calculate brokerage fees on the purchase of 80 shares of XYZ stock at $30 per share, the total value of the transaction would be $2,400 (80 shares × $30/share) and the brokerage fee would therefore be $30 + 1.7% (2,400) = $30 + $40.80 = $70.80; that amounts to about 3 percent of the value of the transaction. Generally speaking, brokerage fees on a round lot of common stock will amount to approximately 2 to 4 percent of the transaction value. (As a rule, at full-service brokerage firms, the broker gets to keep about 40 percent of the commission and the brokerage firm gets the rest.)

As the number of discount brokerage firms grows, there is greater variation in fees charged and services offered. The way commissions are calculated also varies; some firms base them on the dollar value of the transaction, some on the number of shares, and some use both. Exhibit 11.3 provides a list of representative commissions at eight discount and online brokerage firms. (*Note:* Many *discount* brokers, especially the larger ones, also offer online brokerage services, so there is a good deal of overlap here.) The firms with higher commissions generally offer more services; moreover many discounters charge clients extra for research services.

Brokerage commissions on bond transactions differ from those on stock transactions. Brokerage firms typically charge a minimum fee of $25 to $30, regardless of the number of bonds involved. For multiple bond transactions, the brokerage cost per $1,000 corporate bond typically amounts to around $10 (which is decidedly lower than that on a stock transaction). The commission schedules for other securities, such as mutual funds and

EXHIBIT 11.3

COMPARISON OF DISCOUNT AND ONLINE BROKERS' COMMISSIONS

They say it pays to shop around, and that advice certainly applies when it comes to selecting a broker. Just look at the different commissions these brokers charge to execute essentially the same trade—to trade 500 shares of a $50 stock, for example, the commission ranges from $5 to $155 at the listed discount and online brokers, and as high as $399 at one of the major full-service brokers.

Firm	**Commission**		
	100 shares at $50/share ($5,000)	500 shares at $50/share ($25,000)	1,000 shares at $5/share ($5,000)
AccuTrade (DB)*	$30.00	$ 38.00	$ 48.00
Brown & Co. (OLB)*	5.00	5.00	5.00
Charles Schwab (DB)	55.00	155.00	90.00
Fidelity Brokerage Services (OLB)	25.00	25.00	25.00
Muriel Siebert (DB)	45.00	113.00	57.00
National Discount Brokers (OLB)	14.75	14.75	14.75
Olde Discount (DB)	40.00	100.00	52.50
Quick & Reilly (OLB)	14.95	14.95	14.95
Average of 65 discount brokerage firms (DB)	40.63	89.88	66.37
Highest discount broker (DB)	65.00	195.00	120.00
Lowest discount broker (DB)	15.00	15.00	15.00
Average of 76 online brokerage firms (OLB)	18.81	21.07	20.16
Highest Online brokers (OLB)	45.60	156.00	77.00
Lowest Online brokers (OLB)	5.00	4.95	4.95
Major full-service firm	$99.90	$399.00	$200.00

*Note: **DB** indicates fees & commissions as a "Discount Broker"; **OLB** indicates fees & commissions as an "Online Broker."

Source: Adapted from Jean Henrich, "The 2000 Discount Broker Survey: A Guide to Commissions and Services," *AAII Journal*, January 2000; and a major full-service stock brokerage firm.

options, differ from those used with stocks and bonds (we will look at some of these in the next chapter).

The magnitude of brokerage commissions is obviously an important consideration when making security transactions, because these fees tend to raise the overall cost of purchasing securities and lower the overall proceeds from their sale.

EXECUTING TRADES

For most individual investors, a securities transaction involves placing a buy or sell order, usually by phone or on the Net, and later getting a confirmation that it has been completed. They have no idea what happens to their orders. In fact, a lot goes on—and very quickly—once the order is placed. It has to, because on a typical day, the NYSE alone executes for more than 100,000 trades, and many thousands more occur on the Nasdaq, the AMEX, and the other exchanges. In most cases, if the investor places a market order (which we will explain below), it should take *less than two minutes* to place, execute, and confirm a trade.

The process starts with a phone call to the broker, who then transmits the order via sophisticated telecommunications equipment to the stock exchange floor, or to the OTC market, where it is promptly executed. Confirmation that the order has been executed is transmitted back to the original broker and then to the customer. Once the trade takes place, the investor has three (business) days to "settle" his or her account with the broker—that is, to pay for the securities.

As we noted earlier, investors can also use their PCs to execute online securities trades. There are more than 75 online brokers, including AccuTrade, Net Investor, Trading Direct, and Charles Schwab, all of whom are there to execute investor trades in a prompt, efficient, and low-cost manner. In an online trade, your order goes by modem from your computer to the brokerage computer, which checks the type of order and confirms that it is in compliance with regulations. It is then transmitted to the exchange floor or an OTC dealer for execution. The time for the whole process, including a confirmation that is sent back to your computer, is usually one minute or less.

TYPES OF ORDERS

Investors may choose from several different kinds of orders when buying or selling securities. The type of order chosen normally depends on the investor's goals and expectations with respect to the given transaction. The three basic types of orders are the market order, limit order, and stop-loss order.

MARKET ORDER. An order to buy or sell a security at the best price available at the time it is placed is a **market order**. It is usually the quickest way to have orders filled, because market orders are executed as soon as they reach the trading floor. In fact, on small trades of less than a few thousand shares, it takes only about 15 to 20 seconds to fill a market order once it hits the trading floor! These orders are executed through a process that attempts to allow *buy orders* to be filled at the lowest price and *sell orders* at the highest, thereby providing the best possible deal to both the buyers and sellers of a security. Because of the speed with which market orders are transacted, the investor can be sure that the price at which the order is completed will be very close to the market price that existed at the time it was placed.

LIMIT ORDER. An order to buy at a specified price (or lower), or sell at a specified price (or higher) is known as a **limit order**. The broker transmits a limit order to a *specialist* dealing in the given security on the floor of the exchange. The specialist makes a notation in his or her "book" indicating the limit order and limit price. The order is executed as soon as the specified market price is reached and all other such orders with precedence have been filled. The order can be placed to remain in effect until a certain date or until canceled; such an instruction is called a **good 'til canceled (GTC) order**. For example, assume you place a limit order to buy 100 shares of a stock at a price of 20, even though the stock is currently selling at 20.50. Once the specialist has cleared all similar orders received before yours, and the market price of the stock is still at $20 or less, he or she will execute the order. Although a limit order can be quite effective, it can also cost you money! If, for instance, you wish to buy at 20 or less and the stock price moves from its current $20.50 to $32 while you are waiting, your limit order will have caused you to forgo an opportunity to make a profit of $11.50 ($32.00 − $20.50) per share. Had you placed a market order, this profit would have been yours.

STOP-LOSS ORDER. An order to *sell a stock* when the market price reaches or drops below a specified level is called a **stop-loss**, or **stop order**. Used to protect the investor against rapid declines in stock prices, the stop order is placed on the specialist's book and activated when the stop price is reached. At that point, the stop order becomes a *market order*

market order
An order to buy or sell a security at the best price available at the time it is placed.

limit order
An order to either buy a security at a specified or lower price or to sell a security at or above a specified price.

good 'til canceled (GTC) order
A limit order placed with instructions that it remain in effect indefinitely or until canceled.

stop-loss (stop) order
An order to sell a stock when the market price reaches or drops below a specified level.

to sell. This means that the stock is offered for sale at the prevailing market price, which could be less than the price at which the order was initiated by the stop. For example, imagine that you own 100 shares of DEF, which is currently selling for $25. Because of the high uncertainty associated with the price movements of the stock, you decide to place a stop order to sell at $21. If the stock price drops to $21, your stop order is activated and the specialist will sell all your DEF stock at the best price available, which may be $18 or $19 a share. Of course, if the market price increases, or stays at or about $25 a share, nothing will have been lost by placing the stop-loss order.

MARGIN TRADES: BUYING SECURITIES ON CREDIT

When you're ready to buy securities, you can do so by putting up your own money, or by borrowing some of the money. *Buying on margin*, as it is called, is a common practice that allows investors to use borrowed money to make security transactions. Margin trading is closely regulated and is carried out under strict *margin requirements* set by the Federal Reserve Board. These requirements specify the amount of *equity* an investor must put up when buying stocks, bonds, and other securities. The most recent requirement is 50 percent for common stock, which means that at least 50 percent of each dollar invested must be the investor's own; the remaining 50 percent may be borrowed. For example, with a 50 percent margin requirement, you could purchase $5,000 worth of stock by putting up only $2,500 of your own money and borrowing the remaining $2,500. Other securities besides stocks can be margined, and these have their own margin requirements; Treasury bonds, for example, can be purchased with a margin as low as 10 percent.

margin purchase
The purchase of securities with borrowed funds, the allowable amount of which is limited by the Federal Reserve Board.

To make **margin purchases**, you must open a *margin account* and have a minimum of $2,000 in cash (or *equity* in securities) on deposit with your broker. Once you meet these requirements, the brokerage firm will loan you the needed funds (at competitive interest rates) and retain the securities purchased as collateral. You can also obtain loans to purchase securities from your commercial bank, but the Fed's margin requirements still apply. To see how margin trading works, assume the margin requirement is 50 percent and that your brokerage firm charges 9 percent interest on margin loans (brokerage firms usually set the rate on margin loans at 1 to 3 points above prime, or at the prime rate for large accounts). If you want to purchase a round lot (100 shares) of Engulf & Devour, which is currently trading at $50 per share, you can either make the purchase entirely with your own money or borrow a portion of the purchase price. The cost of the transaction will be $5,000 ($50/ share × 100 shares). If you margin, you will put up only $2,500 of your own money (50 percent × $5,000) and borrow the $2,500 balance. Exhibit 11.4 compares the rates of return you would receive with and without the 50 percent margin. This is done for two cases: (1) a $20 per share increase in the stock price, to $70 per share, and (2) a $20 per share decrease in the stock price, to $30 per share. It is assumed the stock will be held for one year and all broker commissions are ignored.

As indicated in Exhibit 11.4, the use of margin allows you to increase the return on your investment when stock prices increase. Indeed, one of the major attributes of margin trading is that it allows you to *magnify your returns*—that is, you can use margin to reduce your equity in an investment and thereby magnify the returns from invested capital when security prices go up. As seen in Exhibit 11.4, the return on your investment when the stock price increases from $50 to $70 a share is 40 percent *without* margin and 71 percent *with* margin. However, when the stock price declines from $50 to $30 per share, the return on your investment will be a *negative* 40 percent without margin and a whopping *89 percent loss* with margin. Clearly, the use of margin magnifies losses as well as profits! If the price of the stock in our example continues to drop, you will eventually reach the point at which your equity in the investment will be so low that the brokerage house will require you to

 **EXHIBIT 11.4**

THE IMPACT OF MARGIN TRADING ON INVESTMENT RETURNS

The rate of return an individual earns on his or her investment is affected, among other things, by the amount of margin being used; unfortunately, although margin trading can magnify profits, it will also magnify losses.

Transaction	Without Margin	With Margin
THE INITIAL INVESTMENT		
Amount invested	$5,000	$2,500
Amount borrowed	0	2,500
Total purchase (100 shares @ $50)	$5,000	$5,000
PRICE *INCREASES*: SELL STOCK FOR $70/SHARE ONE YEAR LATER		
Gross proceeds (100 shares @ $70)	$7,000	$7,000
Less: Interest @ 9% of amount borrowed	0	225
Net proceeds	$7,000	$6,775
Less: Total investment	5,000	5,000
Net profit (loss)	$2,000	$1,775
Return on your investment (net profit ÷ amount invested)	$\dfrac{\$2,000}{\$5,000} = 40\%$	$\dfrac{\$1,775}{\$2,500} = 71\%$
PRICE *DECREASES*: SELL STOCK FOR $30/SHARE ONE YEAR LATER		
Gross proceeds (100 shares @ $30)	$3,000	$3,000
Less: Interest @ 9% of amount borrowed	0	225
Net proceeds	$3,000	$2,775
Less: Total investment	5,000	5,000
Net profit (loss)	($2,000)	($2,225)
Return on your investment (net profit ÷ amount invested)	$\dfrac{(\$2,000)}{\$5,000} = (40\%)$	$\dfrac{(\$2,225)}{\$2,500} = (89\%)$

either provide more collateral or liquidate the investment. The risks inherent in buying on margin make it imperative that you thoroughly acquaint yourself with the risk-return tradeoffs involved *before* using margin in your investment program.

SHORT SELLING: THE PRACTICE OF SELLING BORROWED SECURITIES

Most security transactions are *long transactions;* they are made in anticipation of increasing security prices in order to profit by buying low and selling high. A **short sale** transaction, in contrast, is made in anticipation of a decline in the price of a security. Although not nearly as common as long transactions, short selling is often done by the more sophisticated investor as a way to profit during a period of declining prices. When used by individual investors, most short sales are made with common stocks. When an investor sells a security short, the broker borrows the security and then sells it on behalf of the short seller's account—short sellers actually *sell securities they don't own.* The borrowed shares must, of course, be replaced in the future. If the investor can repurchase the shares at a lower price, a profit will result. In effect, the objective of a short sale is to take advantage of a drop in price by first selling high and then buying low (which, of course, is nothing more than the old "buy low, sell high" adage in reverse).

short sale
A transaction that involves selling borrowed securities with the expectation that they can be replaced at a lower price at some future date; generally made in anticipation of a decline in the security's price.

Short selling is perfectly legitimate; there's nothing illegal or unethical about it. Indeed, because the shares sold are *borrowed securities*, numerous rules and regulations protect the party that lends the securities and govern the short-sale process. One regulation, for example, permits stocks to be sold short only when the last change in the market price of the stock has been upward. Another safeguard is the requirement that all proceeds from the short sale of the borrowed securities be held by the brokerage firm—the short seller never sees any of this money! In addition, the short seller must deposit with the broker a certain amount of money (equivalent to the prevailing initial margin requirement) when the transaction is executed—so even a short-sale transaction involves an investment of capital.

A short-sale transaction can be illustrated with a simple example (one that ignores brokerage fees). Assume that Patrick O'Sullivan wishes to sell short 100 shares of Advanced Buggy-Whips, Inc. at $52.50 per share. After Pat has met the necessary requirements (including making a margin deposit of $52.50 × 100 × 50% = $2,625), his broker borrows the shares and sells them, obtaining proceeds of $5,250 (100 shares × $52.50/share). If the stock price goes down as Pat expects, he will be able to repurchase the shares at the lower price. Now suppose the price drops to $40 per share, and he repurchases the 100 shares. Pat will make a profit, because he will have been able to replace the shares for $4,000 (100 shares × $40/share), which is below the $5,250 received when he sold the stock. His profit will be $1,250 ($5,250 − $4,000). If, on the other hand, the stock price rose to, say, $60 per share, and Pat repurchased the stocks at that price, he would sustain a loss of $750 ($52.50 − $60.00 = −$7.50 × 100 = −$750.00). Because of the high risk involved in short sales, you should thoroughly familiarize yourself with this technique and all its pitfalls *before* attempting to short sell any security.

CONCEPT CHECK

11-10. What is a *stockbroker*? Why does the selection of a broker play such an important role in the purchase of securities?

11-11. "Stockbrokers not only execute buy and sell orders for their clients, they also offer a variety of additional services." Explain what some of these services are.

11-12. Describe the role that *discount brokers* play in carrying out security transactions. To whom are their services especially appealing? What are *online brokers* and what kind of investors are most likely to use them?

11-13. What is the SIPC, and how does it protect investors? Does the SIPC protect investors against loss? Explain.

11-14. What is *arbitration*? Is that the same thing as mediation? Explain.

11-15. Name and describe three basic types of orders.

11-16. What are *margin* requirements? Why might an investor buy securities on margin?

11-17. What is a *short sale*? Explain the logic behind it.

Becoming an Informed Investor [LG4]

Face it: Some people are more knowledgeable about investing than others. As a result, they may use certain investment vehicles or tactics that are not even in the vocabulary of others. Investor know-how, in short, defines the playing field. It helps determine how well you'll meet your investment objectives. Being knowledgeable about investments is important, because one of the key elements in successful investing is *knowing how to achieve decent rates of return without taking unnecessary risks.*

Basing investment decisions on sound information lies at the very heart of any successful investment program. Indeed, there is simply no substitute for being informed when it comes to making investment decisions. While it can't guarantee success, it can help you avoid unnecessary losses—like the ones that happen all too often when people put their money into investment vehicles they don't fully understand. Such results aren't too surprising, because these investors violate the first rule of investing: *Never start an investment program, or buy an investment vehicle, unless you're thoroughly familiar with what you're getting into!* Before making any major investment decision, you should thoroughly investigate the security and its merits. Formulate some basic expectations about its future performance, and gain an understanding of the sources of risk and return. This can usually be done by reading the popular financial press and referring to other print or Internet sources of investment information.

There are four basic types of investment information you should try to follow; they are:

- **Economic developments and current events**. To help you evaluate the underlying investment environment.
- **Alternative investment vehicles**. To keep you abreast of market developments.
- **Current interest rates and price quotations**. To monitor your investments and also stay alert for developing investment opportunities.
- **Personal investment strategies**. To help you hone your skills and stay alert for new techniques as they develop.

In the final analysis, the payoff of an informed approach to investing is both an improved chance of gain and a reduced chance of loss. While there are many sources of investment information, you, as a beginning investor, should concentrate on the more common ones, such as annual stockholders' reports, the financial press, brokerage reports, advisory services, investment advisors, and of course, as we'll see, the Internet.

ANNUAL STOCKHOLDERS' REPORTS

Every publicly traded corporation is required to provide its stockholders and other interested parties with **annual stockholders' reports**. These documents provide a wealth of information about the companies, including balance sheets, income statements, and other summarized statements for the latest fiscal year, plus a number of prior years. Annual reports usually describe the firm's business activities, recent developments, and future plans and outlook. Financial ratios describing past performance are also included, along with other relevant statistics. In fact, annual reports provide a great deal of insight into the company's past, present, and future operations. You can obtain them for free directly from the companies, through a brokerage firm, or at most large libraries; and with today's technology, most companies are also posting their annual reports on the Internet, so now you can obtain them online.

Here are some suggestions to help you get the most information when reading an annual report:

- **Start with the Highlights or Selected Financial Data sections**. These provide a quick overview of performance by summarizing key information, such as the past two years' revenues, net income, assets, earnings per share (EPS), and dividends. EPS have the most effect on the stock's price, so watch them closely.

annual stockholders' report
A report made available to stockholders and other interested parties that includes a variety of financial and descriptive information about a firm's operations during the past several years.

- **Read the chief executive's letter**. But read it with a careful eye, looking for euphemisms like "a slowing of growth" for drop in earnings.
- **Move on to the discussion of operations in Management's Discussion and Analysis**. This section provides information on sales, earnings, debt, inventory levels, litigation, taxes, and so on.
- **Review the financial statements, including the notes**. These will tell you about the company's financial condition and performance. Look for trends in sales, costs, profit, cash position, inventory, and net working capital.
- **Read the auditor's report**. This statement from the independent accountants who review the numbers has two paragraphs when everything is fine; a third paragraph or terms like "except for" or "subject to" means there may be problems you need to understand.

 If annual reports confuse you, the *Guide to Understanding Financial Reports* at the IBM Investor site, **www.ibm.com/investor/financialguide**, will help you understand these valuable information sources.

THE FINANCIAL PRESS

The most common source of financial news is the local newspaper. The newspapers in many larger cities often devote several pages to business and financial information and, of course, big-city papers, like the *New York Times* and the *Los Angeles Times*, provide investors with even more financial information. Other, more specific sources of financial news include *The Wall Street Journal*, *Barron's*, *Investor's Business Daily*, and the "Money" section of *USA Today*. These are all national publications that include articles on the behavior of the economy, the market, various industries, and individual companies. But the most comprehensive and up-to-date coverage of financial news is provided Monday through Friday by *The Wall Street Journal*, whereas *Barron's* concentrates on the week's activities as they relate to the financial markets and individual security prices. Other excellent sources of investment information include magazine-type publications, such as *Money*, *Forbes*, *Fortune*, *Business Week*, *Bloomberg Personal Finance*, *Smart Money*, *Worth*, and *Kiplinger's Personal Finance*. (Today, of course, the Internet is rapidly becoming a major source of information for investors; we will discuss this source in more detail later in this chapter.)

ECONOMIC DATA. Summaries and analyses of economic events can be found in all the above sources. Economic data include news items related to government actions and their effects on the economy; political and international events as they pertain to the economy; and statistics related to price levels, interest rates, the federal budget, and taxes.

MARKET DATA. Usually presented in the form of averages, or indexes, *market data* describe the general behavior of the securities markets. The averages and indexes are based on the price movements of a select group of securities over an extended period of time. They are used to capture the overall performance of the market as a whole. You would want to follow one or more of these measures *to get a feel for how the market is doing over time* and, perhaps, an indication of what lies ahead. The absolute level of the index at a given point in time (or on a given day) is far less important than *what's been happening to that index over a given period of time*. The most commonly cited market measures are those calculated by Dow Jones, Standard & Poor's, the New York Stock Exchange, the American Stock Exchange, and Nasdaq (for the OTC market). These measures are all intended to keep track of the behavior in the stock market, particularly stocks on the NYSE (the Dow, S&P, and NYSE averages all follow stocks on the big board). In addition, several averages and indexes follow the action in other markets, including the bond, commodities, and options markets, and even the markets for mutual funds, real estate, and collectibles. However, because all these other averages and indexes are not followed nearly as much as those of stocks, we will concentrate here on stock market performance measures.

Dow Jones Averages. The granddaddy of them all and probably the most widely followed measure of stock market performance is the **Dow Jones Industrial Average (DJIA)**. Actually, the Dow Jones averages, which began in 1896, are made up of four parts: (1) an industrial average based on 30 stocks; (2) a transportation average based on 20 stocks; (3) a utility average based on 15 stocks; and (4) a composite average based on all 65 industrial, transportation, and utility stocks. (Dow Jones has recently added a couple more market indexes to their line up: the DJ U.S. Total Market index and the DJ World index, which excludes the U.S.) The makeup of the 30 stocks in the DJIA does change a bit over time as companies go private, are acquired by other firms, or become less of a force in the marketplace. For example, in the past few years, Allied Signal, Chevron, Goodyear, Sears, Travelers, and Union Carbide were dropped from the DJIA and replaced with Citigroup, Home Depot, Honeywell, Intel, Microsoft, and SBC Communications. Most of the stocks are picked from the NYSE, but there are a few Nasdaq shares in there, like Intel and Microsoft. Although these stocks are intended to represent a cross section of companies, there is a strong bias toward blue chips, which is one of the major criticisms of the Dow Jones Industrial Average. Critics also claim that an average made up of only 30 blue-chip stocks—out of some 5 or 6 thousand issues—is hardly representative of the market. However, the facts show that as a rule, the behavior of the DJIA closely reflects that of other broadly based stock market measures—with the possible exception of the Nasdaq. Exhibit 11.5 lists the 30 stocks in the DJIA, along with some important dates in its life.

Dow Jones Industrial Average (DJIA) The most widely followed measure of stock market performance; consists of 30 blue-chip stocks listed mostly on the NYSE.

Standard & Poor's Indexes. The **Standard & Poor's (S&P) indexes** are similar to the Dow Jones averages to the extent that they both are used to capture the overall performance of the market. However, some important differences exist between the two measures. For one thing, the S&P uses a lot more stocks; the popular S&P 500 composite index is based on 500 different stocks, whereas the DJIA uses only 30 stocks. What's more, the S&P index is made up of all large NYSE stocks, as well as some major AMEX and OTC stocks, so there's not only more issues in the S&P sample, but also a greater breadth of representation. And, finally, there are some technical differences in the mathematical procedures used to compute the two measures; the Dow Jones is an *average*, whereas the S&P is an *index*. In spite of these technical differences, however, the two measures behave pretty much the same and are used in much the same way.

Standard & Poor's (S&P) indexes Indexes compiled by Standard & Poor's Corporation; similar to the DJIA but employ different computational methods and consist of far more stocks.

There are eight basic S&P indexes: (1) an industrial index based on 400 stocks; (2) a transportation index of 20 stocks; (3) a public utility index of 40 stocks; (4) a financial index of 40 stocks; (5) a composite index for all 500 of the stocks used in the first four indexes; (6) the *MidCap 400*; (7) the *SmallCap 600*; and (8) the composite *S&P 1500* made up of the S&P 500, 400, and 600 indexes. The MidCap index is made up of 400 medium-sized companies—those with market values that, for the most part, range from about $500 million to $3 billion, or more, while the SmallCap index consists of small companies, with market caps of around $500 million or less.

 **EXHIBIT 11.5**

THE DOW JONES INDUSTRIAL AVERAGE

The DJIA is made up of 30 of the bluest of blue-chip stocks and has been closely followed by investors for the past 100 years or so.

THE 30 STOCKS IN THE DJIA:

Aluminum Co. of Amer.	General Electric	McDonald's
American Express	General Motors	Merck
AT&T	Hewlett-Packard	Minnesota M&M
Boeing	Home Depot	Microsoft
Caterpillar	Honeywell	Philip Morris
Citigroup	IBM	Procter & Gamble
Coca-Cola	Intel	SBC Communications
DuPont	International Paper	United Technologies
Eastman Kodak	J.P. Morgan	Wal-Mart
Exxon Mobil	Johnson & Johnson	Walt Disney

SOME IMPORTANT DATES FOR THE DOW:

May 26, 1896	The Dow Jones Industrial Average makes its debut; originally made up of just 12 stocks (of the 12 stocks that originally made up the DJIA, only GE is still on the list).
January 12, 1906	Closes above 100 for the first time.
October 28, 1929	The infamous "1929 crash"; Dow drops 38.33 points in one day.
October 29, 1929	The Dow drops another 30.57 points—in just *two* days, the market value of stocks drops an incredible 25%; these two days are considered the start of the Great Depression.
March 12, 1956	Closes above 500 for the first time.
November 14, 1972	Closes above 1000 for the first time.
December 6, 1974	Closes at 577.60 to end the worst bear market since the 1930s.
April 27, 1981	Closes at 8-year high of 1,024.0.
August 12, 1982	Closes at 776.92, as the market bottoms out and the Great Bull Market of the 1980s and 1990s is born.
October 19, 1987	The market crashes; the DJIA closes at 1,738.74, for a record 1-day drop of 508 points (23%).
December 31, 1987	Closes *the year* at 1,938.83, up 2% for the year, even after the crash.
December 31, 1988	Closes at 2,168.57, up 12% for the year; the first time the market has ended the year above 2,000.
April 27, 1989	Market moves to a post-crash high of 2,433.10, which totally wipes out the loss of October 19, with about 200 points to spare.
July 16, 1990	Closes just short of 3,000, at 2,999.75; two weeks later, Iraq invades Kuwait and the market goes into a free-fall, tumbling to 2,365.10 by October 11.
April 17, 1991	Closes above 3,000 for the first time.
February 23, 1995	Closes above 4,000 for the first time.
November 21, 1995	Closes above 5,000 for the first time.
October 14, 1996	Closes above 6,000 for the first time.
February 13, 1997	Closes above 7,000 for the first time.
July 16, 1997	Closes above 8,000 for the first time.
October 27, 1997	Stocks plunge as the market falls 554 points (a new record) to 7,161.15.
April 6, 1998	Closes above 9,000 for the first time.
March 29, 1999	Closes above 10,000 for the first time.
May 3, 1999	Closes above 11,000 for the first time.
March 16, 2000	Market goes up a record 499.19 points to 10,630 as the DJIA gains 4.93% in a single day.
April 14, 2000	A month later, stocks plunge more than 617 points (a new 1-day record) to 10,305; the drop, however, amounts to "only" 5.5% and doesn't even rank in the top ten.

The S&P 500, like the DJIA, is widely followed by the financial media, and is reported not only in publications like *The Wall Street Journal* and *Barron's*, but also in most of the major newspapers around the country and other market outlets. The S&P has a much lower value than the DJIA—for example, in November 2000, the Dow stood at over 10,600, whereas the S&P index of 500 stocks was just under 1,400. Now this does not mean that the S&P consists of less valuable stocks; rather, the disparity is due solely to the different methods used to compute the measures.

The NYSE, AMEX, and Nasdaq Indexes. The most widely followed exchange-based indexes are those of the New York Stock Exchange (NYSE), the American Stock Exchange (AMEX), and the Nasdaq (for the OTC market). The **NYSE index** includes all the stocks listed on the "big board." In addition to the composite index, the NYSE publishes indexes for industrials, utilities, transportation, and finance subgroups. The behavior of the NYSE Industrial index closely mimics that of the DJIA and the S&P 500.

The **AMEX index** reflects share prices on the American Stock Exchange. Made up of all stocks on the AMEX, it is set up in such a way that it directly captures the actual *percentage change* in share prices. For example, if the price change in AMEX stocks from one day to the next were +3 percent, the AMEX index would likewise increase by 3 percent over the previous day's value. Like the NYSE indexes, the AMEX index is often cited in the financial news.

Activity in the OTC market is captured by the **Nasdaq indexes**, which are calculated like the S&P and NYSE indexes. The most comprehensive of these indexes is the *Nasdaq composite index*, which is calculated using virtually all the stocks traded on the Nasdaq system. The other Nasdaq indexes are the industrial, insurance, bank, computers, and telecommunications indexes. In addition, there is the *Nasdaq 100 Index*, which tracks the price behavior of the biggest 100 (nonfinancial) firms traded on the Nasdaq—companies like Microsoft, Intel, Oracle, Cisco, Staples, and Dell Computers. The Nasdaq Composite is often used today as a benchmark in assessing the price behavior of *high tech* stocks. This index is far more volatile than either the Dow or the S&P and way out-performed other market measures from 1995 to 1999—before taking a big dive in 2000 and 2001.

In addition to the major indexes described above, another measure of market performance is the **Wilshire 5000 Index**, which is also known as the *Wilshire Total Market Index*. Published by Wilshire Associates, Inc., the Wilshire 5000 is reported daily in *The Wall Street Journal* and many other major publications. Although this index originally covered some 5,000 stocks, today that number is up to more like 6,000 or 7,000 stocks (clearly, the number of stocks covered has changed but the name hasn't). Whatever the number, it's estimated that the Wilshire index reflects the *total market value* of 98–99% of all publicly-traded stocks in this country. In essence, it shows what's happening in the stock market as a whole—the dollar amount of market value added or lost as the market moves up and down. In this index, one point is worth $1 *billion* (vs. about 1 cent in the DJIA). Thus, the Wilshire can be used to not only track the behavior of the U.S. stock market, but also give you a pretty accurate reading as to the size of our market on any given day. For example, in November 2000, the Wilshire index stood at nearly 13,000. Because this index is in billions of dollars, a measure of 13,000 translates into a total market value of some $13 *trillion!!* In addition, the Frank Russell Co., a pension advisory firm, produces three indexes that are also widely followed by market participants. Probably the most popular is the *Russell 2000*, which tracks the behavior of 2,000 relatively small companies and is widely felt to provide a fairly accurate measure of the small-cap segment of the market. There is also the *Russell 1000*, which follows the price behavior of the 1,000 largest companies in this country, and the *Russell 3000*, which is a combination of the two previously mentioned indexes.

NYSE index
An index of the performance of all stocks listed on the New York Stock Exchange.

AMEX index
An index of the performance of all stocks listed on the American Stock Exchange.

Nasdaq index
An index, supplied by the National Association of Securities Dealers, that tracks the performance of stocks traded in the OTC market.

Wilshire 5000 index
An index of the total market value of the 6,000 to 7,000 (originally 5,000) or so most actively traded stocks in this country.

INDUSTRY DATA. Local newspapers, *The Wall Street Journal*, *Barron's*, and various financial publications regularly contain articles and data about different industries. For example, Standard & Poor's *Industry Surveys* provides detailed descriptions and statistics for all the major industries; on a smaller scale, *Business Week* and other magazines regularly include indexes of industry performance and price levels. Other industry-related data can be obtained from industry trade associations, one example of which is the American Petroleum Institute.

COMPANY DATA. Articles about the performance and new developments of companies are included in local newspapers, *The Wall Street Journal*, *Barron's*, and most investment magazines. The prices of the securities of all listed companies and the most active over-the-counter stocks are quoted daily in *The Wall Street Journal*, *Investor's Business Daily*, and *USA Today*, and weekly in *Barron's*. Many daily newspapers also contain stock price quotations, though in the smaller ones the listing may be selective; in some cases, only stocks of local interest are included.

STOCK QUOTES. To see how price quotations work and what they mean, consider the quotes that appear daily (M–F) in *The Wall Street Journal*. As we'll see, the quotations provide not only current prices, but a great deal of additional information as well. A portion of the NYSE stock quotations from *The Wall Street Journal* is presented in Exhibit 11.6. (Here we look at *stock quotes*; in chapter 12, we'll look at *bond quotes*.) Let's use the **Disney** quotations for purposes of illustration. These quotes were published on May 24, 2001, and are for trades that occurred the day before, on May 23. A glance at the quotations shows that stocks, like most other securities, are quoted in dollars and cents. That may not sound like a big deal, but it is, for up until the year 2000, stocks had been quoted in fractions, mostly in eighths of a dollar, where each $\frac{1}{8}$ of a point was worth $12\frac{1}{2}$ cents. That all changed in 2000, when stock quotes were switched over to decimals (i.e., dollars and cents).

    Looking at the Disney quotes, the first column (YTD % CHG) gives the stock's year-to-date change in price; note that Disney's stock has gone up 14.4 percent since the first of the year. The two columns labeled "HI" and "LO" show the highest and lowest prices at which the stock sold during the past 52 weeks. You can see that Disney has traded between $43 and $26 per share during the preceding 52-week period. Listed to the right of the company's name is its *stock symbol* (Disney goes by the three-letter initial "DIS"). These stock symbols are the abbreviations used on the *market tapes* seen in brokerage offices and on television, as well as on Internet sites such as Quicken to identify specific securities. The figure listed right after the stock symbol is the annual cash dividend paid on each share of stock. This is followed by the dividend yield. (Note: Because Disney paid a cash dividend of $.21 per share, its dividend yield is just 0.6 percent, which is found by dividing the 21 cents in dividends by the closing price of $33.11.) The next entry is the P/E ratio, which is the current market price divided by the per share earnings for the most recent 12-month period. Because it is believed to reflect investor expectations concerning the firm's future prospects, the P/E ratio is closely followed by investors as part of the stock valuation process. Note that the "cc" in the P/E column indicates that Disney was trading at more than 100 times its earnings.

    The daily volume follows the P/E ratio. Here, the sales numbers are listed in round lots (of 100 shares), so a figure of 59521 for Disney indicates that 5,952,100 *shares* of Disney stock were traded on May 23. The next entry, labeled "LAST," shows the closing (final) price of $33.11, at which the stock sold on the day in question. Finally, as the final column (NET CHG) shows, Disney closed down $1.39. This means that the stock closed $1.39 lower than the day before (May 22), when it closed at $34.50.

EXHIBIT 11.6

LISTED STOCK QUOTES

This list summarizes 1 day's trading activity and price quotes for a group of stocks traded on the New York Stock Exchange. Note that in addition to the latest stock prices, a typical stock quote conveys an array of other information.

YTD % CHG	52 WEEKS HI	LO	STOCK (SYM)	DIV	YLD %	PE	VOL 100s	LAST	NET CHG	
+ 14.1	29	19.44	Delta&Pine **DLP**	.16	.7	20	1488	23.88	− 0.27	Year-to-date change in price, in percentages
− 11.1	1.88	0.93	DeltaWdsde **DLW** s		—	1	111	1	—	High and low prices for previous 52 weeks
▲+ 5.8	24.71	16.56	DelticTimber **DEL**	.25	1.0	17	341	25.25	+ 0.55	
+ 34.2	28.25	15.99	DeluxeCp **DLX** s	1.48	5.4	—	3196	27.62	− 0.22	Company name and stock symbol
− 1.7	12.30	4.31	♣ DnbryRes **DNR**		—	3	2216	10.81	− 0.71	
− 23.6	15.88	7.95	Dept56 **DFS**		—	5	106	8.79	—	Annual dividends per share for past 12 months
+ 24.7	14.38	6.19	DescSA ADR **DES**	e	—	—	308	7.95	+ 0.15	
− 22.4	69	20.76	♣ DtscheTel ADR **DT**	.56e	2.5	—	31872	22.69	− 0.65	Dividend yield (dividends as percent of share price)
▲+ 30.7	17.30	11.63	DevDivRlty **DDR**	1.48	8.5	16	2256	17.40	+ 0.25	
− 9.6	41.50	25.94	DeVry **DV**		—	43	937	34.13	− 0.64	
− 3.8	45.49	32.13	Diageo ADS **DEO**	1.38e	3.2	—	2233	42.70	+ 0.34	Price/earnings ratio: $\left(\dfrac{\text{market price}}{\text{earnings per share}}\right)$
+ 38.3	78.55	29.69	DiagnstPdt **DP**	.48	.6	35	354	75.52	− 0.80	
+ 25.9	15.75	9.88	DialCp **DL**	.16	1.2	dd	1194	13.85	− 0.15	
+ 2.6	47.94	29.56	BmndOffshr **DO**	.50	1.2	71	11071	41.03	− 1.72	Share volume, in hundreds
− 5.0	36.38	22.94	Diebold **DBD**	.64	2.0	20	1644	31.71	− 0.50	
+ 52.4	21.50	11.50	DillrdCapTr **DDT**	1.88	9.4	—	142	20	+ 0.04	
+ 43.7	22.50	9.44	Dillards **DDS**	.16	.9	15	15661	16.98	− 2.54	Closing (final) price for the day—this is also the price used to compute dividend yield and the P/E ratio
+ 22.8	36.30	14.87	DimeBcp **DME**	.48f	1.3	24	4467	35.99	− 0.19	
▲+100.0	11.09	2	♣ Dimon **DMN**	.20	1.8	18	2660	11	− 0.05	
+134.7	12.98	4.88	DiscntAuto **DAP**		—	14	135	12.91	− 0.04	
+ 14.4	43	26	Disney **DIS**	.21	.6	cc	59521	33.11	− 1.39	
− 18.1	19.75	11.90	Dist&Srv ADR **DYS**	.25e	1.8	—	510	14.29	− 0.66	
− 7.1	18.80	11.75	DoleFood **DOL**	.40	2.6	13	1429	15.22	− 0.06	
− 1.7	24.05	12.80	DirGenl **DG**	.13	.7	30	21797	18.55	+ 0.05	Net change in price from previous day
+ 27.5	24.80	13.63	♣ DirThrfty **DTG**		—	8	416	23.90	− 0.15	
▲+ 57.8	25	12.31	DominResVA **DOM**	3.02e	12.4	—	874	24.38	− 0.61	
+ 0.6	69.99	42.44	♣ DominRes **D**	2.58	3.8	28	8229	67.38	+ 0.79	
+ 0.3	66.56	53	♣ DominRes PIES n	2.81e	4.5	—	744	62.70	+ 0.40	
+ 9.1	11.38	6.63	♣ Dorntar g **DTC**	.14g	—	—	114	10.02	+ 0.01	
+ 11.5	31.80	18.81	♣ Donaldson **DCI**	.30	1.0	20	1383	31.02	− 0.61	

Source: *The Wall Street Journal,* May 24, 2001.

The same quotation system is used for Nasdaq *National Market* stocks. However, a slightly different procedure is used with AMEX and OTC securities that are not part of the National Market system—that is, for many AMEX and OTC stocks, only the stock name, symbol, volume, closing price, and change in price are included in the quotes.

Quotes for preferred stocks can also be found in many major newspapers, or in publications like *The Wall Street Journal.* In most newspapers, the quotes for preferred stocks are commingled with those of common stock, although they're easy to pick out—just look for the letters "pf" or "pr" right after the company's name. *The Wall Street Journal,* however, has a separate listing for preferred stock quotes, which includes the name of the stock, the annual dividend, the dividend yield, closing prices, and change in price. A single company can have any number of preferred stock issues outstanding, in which case each issue is identified alphabetically, such as "pfA," "pfB," etc. Normally each issue will also have its own annual dividend—for example, the pfA may have a $5.00 dividend, while the pfB may have annual dividends of $3.81. Finally, note that although a company may have any number of preferred issues outstanding, a quote will appear in the paper only if the stock actually traded on the day in question. (We will examine preferred stocks in more detail in the next chapter; however, suffice it to say at this point that the key attraction of most preferred stock is the *substantial level of the dividends that they pay*—an amount, by the way, that is usually fixed for the life of the issue.)

BROKERAGE REPORTS

The reports produced by the research staffs of the major (full-service) brokerage firms provide still another important source of investor information. These reports cover a wide variety of topics, from economic and market analyses to industry and company reports, news of special situations, and reports on interest rates and the bond market. Reports on certain industries or securities prepared by the house's backoffice research staff may be issued on a regular basis and contain lists of securities within certain industries classified as to the type of market behavior they are expected to exhibit. Brokerage houses will also regularly issue analytical reports on specific securities, along with recommendations as to the type of investment returns expected and whether to buy, hold, or sell the securities in question.

ADVISORY SERVICES

A number of subscription advisory services—available both in print and online—provide information and recommendations on various industries and specific securities. The services normally cost from $50 to several hundred dollars a year. Although these costs may be tax deductible, only the most active investors will find them worthwhile, because you can usually review such materials (for free) at your broker's office, at university and public libraries, or online. Probably the best known financial services are those provided by Standard & Poor's, Moody's Investors Service, and Value Line Investment Survey. Each offers an array of services. Both Standard & Poor's and Moody's publish manuals containing historical facts and financial data on thousands of corporations, broken down by industry groups. Standard & Poor's publishes a monthly stock guide and bond guide, each of which summarizes the financial conditions of a few thousand issues; Moody's also publishes stock and bond guides. And a number of reports are also prepared weekly, like Standard & Poor's *Outlook.*

Separate reports on specific companies are another valuable type of subscription service. An example of one such stock report is given in Exhibit 11.7. This report, prepared by Standard & Poor's, presents a concise summary of a company's financial history, current finances, and future prospects; a similar type of report, with even more emphasis given to the security's investment merits and future prospects, is also available from *Value Line*. Recommended lists of securities, broken down into groups on the basis of investment objectives, constitute still another type of service. In addition to these popular subscription services, numerous *investment letters*, which periodically advise subscribers on the purchase and sale of securities, are available. Finally, by subscribing to weekly chart books, investors may also obtain graphs showing stock prices and volume over extended periods of time. (We'll discuss online services a little later in this chapter.)

INVESTMENT ADVISORS

Successful investors often establish themselves as professional investment advisors. In this capacity, they attempt to develop investment plans consistent with the financial objectives of their clients. Many of the better-known investment advisors limit their practice to a select group of wealthy individuals who have similar investment objectives, whereas others accept clients with diverse goals. Professional advisors generally do not accept clients with investment assets of less than $50,000, and the more "elite" ones are likely to require considerably larger holdings. Annual fees for advisory services, which may involve the complete management of the client's money, are likely to range from about 1 percent to as much as 2 or 3 percent of assets under management.

You can obtain the services of a professional money manager in several ways: (1) you can hire an *independent investment advisor* (but they're usually pretty expensive and prefer to deal with well-heeled clients); (2) you can go to the *trust department of a major bank* (many offer their investment services to the general public at very reasonable costs, and you don't have to die or have a trust account to obtain such services—all you have to do is enter into a simple *agency agreement*); (3) if you deal with a full-service brokerage firm, you can check with your broker to see if they offer fee-based *wrap accounts* (in these portfolio management accounts, your brokerage firm takes over the full-time management of your investments, in return for a flat annual fee—but watch out, that annual fee can get pretty hefty); or (4) you might consider the services of a *financial planner* (preferably a *fee-based* planner who has a strong track record in the field of *investments*). If you're thinking of using a professional money manager, the best thing to do is shop around—look at the kind of returns he or she has been able to generate (in good markets and bad), and don't overlook the matter of cost—find out up front how much you'll have to pay and what the fee is based on. Equally important, find out if the advisor has a specialty and, if so, make sure it's compatible with your investment objectives; for example, don't go to a financial planner who specializes in high-risk limited partnerships or high-cost variable annuities if you're not interested in those kinds of investment.

CONCEPT CHECK

11-18. Identify and briefly discuss the four basic types of information that you, as an investor, should try to follow.

11-19. Describe some of the major sources of investment information.

11-20. What role do market averages and indexes play in the investment process?

11-21. Briefly describe the *DJIA, S&P 500, S&P 600, Nasdaq Composite, Nasdaq 100, Russell 2000,* and *Wilshire 5000* indexes; which segments of the market does each track?

EXHIBIT 11.7

AN S&P STOCK REPORT

An S&P report like this one provides a wealth of information about the operating results and financial condition of the company and is an invaluable source of information to investors.

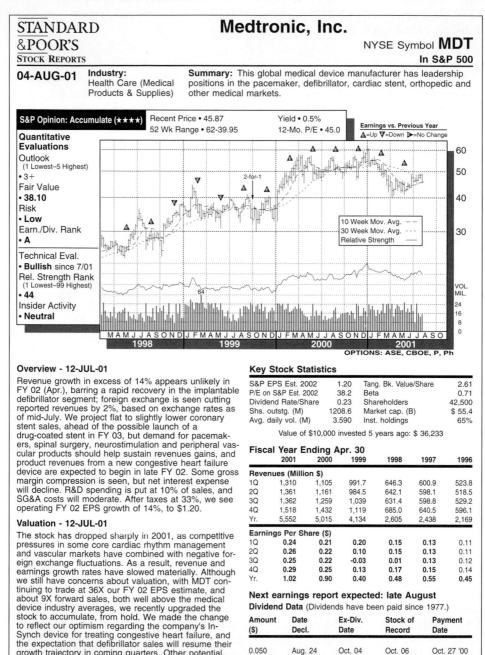

STANDARD &POOR'S
STOCK REPORTS

Medtronic, Inc.

NYSE Symbol **MDT**

In S&P 500

04-AUG-01

Industry: Health Care (Medical Products & Supplies)

Summary: This global medical device manufacturer has leadership positions in the pacemaker, defibrillator, cardiac stent, orthopedic and other medical markets.

S&P Opinion: Accumulate (★★★★)

Recent Price • 45.87
52 Wk Range • 62-39.95

Yield • 0.5%
12-Mo. P/E • 45.0

Quantitative Evaluations

Outlook
(1 Lowest–5 Highest)
• 3+

Fair Value
• **38.10**

Risk
• **Low**

Earn./Div. Rank
• **A**

Technical Eval.
• **Bullish** since 7/01

Rel. Strength Rank
(1 Lowest–99 Highest)
• **44**

Insider Activity
• **Neutral**

Earnings vs. Previous Year
▲=Up ▼=Down ►=No Change

10 Week Mov. Avg. — –
30 Week Mov. Avg. - - -
Relative Strength —

2-for-1

64

VOL. MIL.

MAMJJASOND JFMAMJJASOND JFMAMJJASOND JFMAMJJASO
1998   1999   2000   2001

OPTIONS: ASE, CBOE, P, Ph

Overview - 12-JUL-01

Revenue growth in excess of 14% appears unlikely in FY 02 (Apr.), barring a rapid recovery in the implantable defibrillator segment; foreign exchange is seen cutting reported revenues by 2%, based on exchange rates as of mid-July. We project flat to slightly lower coronary stent sales, ahead of the possible launch of a drug-coated stent in FY 03, but demand for pacemakers, spinal surgery, neurostimulation and peripheral vascular products should help sustain revenues gains, and product revenues from a new congestive heart failure device are expected to begin in late FY 02. Some gross margin compression is seen, but net interest expense will decline. R&D spending is put at 10% of sales, and SG&A costs will moderate. After taxes at 33%, we see operating FY 02 EPS growth of 14%, to $1.20.

Valuation - 12-JUL-01

The stock has dropped sharply in 2001, as competitive pressures in some core cardiac rhythm management and vascular markets have combined with negative foreign exchange fluctuations. As a result, revenue and earnings growth rates have slowed materially. Although we still have concerns about valuation, with MDT continuing to trade at 36X our FY 02 EPS estimate, and about 9X forward sales, both well above the medical device industry averages, we recently upgraded the stock to accumulate, from hold. We made the change to reflect our optimism regarding the company's In-Synch device for treating congestive heart failure, and the expectation that defibrillator sales will resume their growth trajectory in coming quarters. Other potential catalysts for the stock include progress in the development of drug coated coronary stents, and increased penetration for the Gem III AT defibrillator.

Key Stock Statistics

S&P EPS Est. 2002	1.20	Tang. Bk. Value/Share	2.61
P/E on S&P Est. 2002	38.2	Beta	0.71
Dividend Rate/Share	0.23	Shareholders	42,500
Shs. outstg. (M)	1208.6	Market cap. (B)	$ 55.4
Avg. daily vol. (M)	3.590	Inst. holdings	65%

Value of $10,000 invested 5 years ago: $ 36,233

Fiscal Year Ending Apr. 30

	2001	2000	1999	1998	1997	1996
Revenues (Million $)						
1Q	1,310	1,105	991.7	646.3	600.9	523.8
2Q	1,361	1,161	984.5	642.1	598.1	518.5
3Q	1,362	1,259	1,039	631.4	598.8	529.2
4Q	1,518	1,432	1,119	685.0	640.5	596.1
Yr.	5,552	5,015	4,134	2,605	2,438	2,169
Earnings Per Share ($)						
1Q	0.24	0.21	0.20	0.15	0.13	0.11
2Q	0.26	0.22	0.10	0.15	0.13	0.11
3Q	0.25	0.22	-0.03	0.01	0.13	0.12
4Q	0.29	0.25	0.13	0.17	0.15	0.14
Yr.	1.02	0.90	0.40	0.48	0.55	0.45

Next earnings report expected: late August

Dividend Data (Dividends have been paid since 1977.)

Amount ($)	Date Decl.	Ex-Div. Date	Stock of Record	Payment Date
0.050	Aug. 24	Oct. 04	Oct. 06	Oct. 27 '00
0.050	Oct. 26	Jan. 03	Jan. 05	Jan. 26 '01
0.050	Mar. 08	Apr. 04	Apr. 06	Apr. 27 '01
0.058	Jun. 28	Jul. 03	Jul. 06	Jul. 27 '01

A Division of The **McGraw·Hill** *Companies*

EXHIBIT 11.7 *continued*

STANDARD
&POOR'S
STOCK REPORTS

Medtronic, Inc.

04-AUG-01

Business Summary - 12-JUL-01

Medtronic, formed in 1949 by E. Bakken (who invented the first battery-powered cardiac pacemaker) and P. Hermundslie, this medical device maker has leading positions in cardiac rhythm management, neurological/spinal, vascular, and cardiac surgery markets.

Cardiac rhythm management products (50% of FY 00 (Apr.) revenues) include implantable pacemakers to treat bradycardia (slow or irregular heartbeats). Bradycardia pacing systems, sold under the Thera, Elite and Kappa names, include pacemakers, leads and accessories. Some models are noninvasively programmed by a physician to adjust sensing, electrical pulse intensity, duration, rate and other factors, as well as pacers that can sense in both upper and lower heart chambers and produce appropriate impulses.

Implantable cardioverter defibrillators (ICDs), sold under the Jewel and Gem names, treat tachyarrhythmia (abnormally fast heart beats) by monitoring the heart; when very rapid heart rhythm is detected, they send either a series of electrical impulses or an electrical shock to restore normal heart rhythm. In June 2000, MDT gained FDA approval to market the Jewel AF, the first ICD that allows for detection and treatment of arrhythmias of both the upper and lower heart chambers.

Neurological and spinal products (25%) include implantable devices that provide spinal cord and brain stimulation to treat pain and tremor; devices, instruments, computer-assisted visualization products and biomaterials to treat disorders of the cranium and spine; implantable programmable drug delivery systems to treat chronic intractable pain, tremor and spasticity; and items such as shunt assemblies to treat hydrocephalus, other vascular access devices and trauma products.

Vascular products (16%) support treatment of diseased and damaged coronary and peripheral blood vessels. Products include both modular and laser-cut stent systems. In coronary stent markets, MDT's principal product is the S670 in both over-the-wire and rapid exchange perfusion platforms. The unit also sells peripheral vascular products, including the AneuRx and Talent stent grafts for minimally invasive abdominal aortic aneurysm repair therapy.

Cardiac surgery products (9%) include heart valves, perfusion systems, cannulae, surgical accessories and blood-handling products used to maintain and monitor vital signs during open-heart surgery. In August 2000, MDT gained FDA approval for its Mosaic pig tissue heart valve, a product that incorporates a flexible stent.

FY 00 R&D spending totaled $480 million (9.6% of sales). Projects cover areas such as cardiovascular disorders, heart valves, implantable drug delivery systems, spinal fusion products, catheters, stents and stented grafts, and heart failure.

Per Share Data ($)

(Year Ended Apr. 30)	2001	2000	1999	1998	1997	1996	1995	1994	1993	1992
Tangible Bk. Val.	NA	2.61	1.99	1.68	1.34	1.41	1.45	1.13	0.91	0.84
Cash Flow	NA	1.10	0.57	0.63	0.68	0.59	0.43	0.32	0.28	0.23
Earnings	1.02	0.90	0.40	0.48	0.56	0.47	0.32	0.25	0.22	0.17
Dividends	0.12	0.14	0.12	0.11	0.10	0.08	0.05	0.04	0.04	0.03
Payout Ratio	12%	16%	30%	23%	17%	17%	16%	17%	15%	18%
Cal. Yrs.	2000	1999	1998	1997	1996	1995	1994	1993	1992	1991
Prices - High	62.00	44.62	38.37	26.37	17.46	15.00	6.98	5.96	6.53	5.89
- Low	32.75	29.93	22.71	14.40	11.12	6.54	4.32	3.22	3.95	2.40
P/E Ratio - High	61	50	97	55	31	32	22	24	29	35
- Low	32	33	58	30	20	14	14	13	18	14

Income Statement Analysis (Million $)

	2001	2000	1999	1998	1997	1996	1995	1994	1993	1992
Revs.	NA	5,015	4,134	2,605	2,438	2,169	1,742	1,391	1,328	1,177
Oper. Inc.	NA	1,871	1,535	1,017	901	759	543	396	332	305
Depr.	NA	243	213	138	117	112	107	63.0	54.7	59.4
Int. Exp.	NA	13.0	28.8	8.2	9.4	8.0	9.0	8.2	10.4	13.4
Pretax Inc.	NA	1,630	822	702	809	668	442	347	313	243
Eff. Tax Rate	NA	33%	43%	35%	35%	34%	34%	33%	33%	34%
Net Inc.	NA	1,099	468	457	530	438	294	232	212	162

Balance Sheet & Other Fin. Data (Million $)

	2001	2000	1999	1998	1997	1996	1995	1994	1993	1992
Cash	NA	448	376	383	251	461	324	181	156	110
Curr. Assets	NA	3,013	2,395	1,552	1,238	1,343	1,104	846	775	696
Total Assets	NA	5,669	4,870	2,775	2,409	2,503	1,947	1,623	1,286	1,163
Curr. Liab.	NA	992	990	572	519	525	456	439	348	309
LT Debt	NA	14.0	17.6	16.2	13.9	15.3	14.2	20.2	10.9	8.6
Common Eqty.	NA	4,491	3,655	2,044	1,746	1,789	1,335	1,053	841	796
Total Cap.	NA	4,520	3,703	2,074	1,762	1,850	1,385	1,090	857	823
Cap. Exp.	NA	342	226	148	171	164	96.9	86.0	87.4	77.2
Cash Flow	NA	1,342	681	595	647	549	401	295	266	221
Curr. Ratio	NA	3.0	2.4	2.7	2.4	2.6	2.4	1.9	2.2	2.3
% LT Debt of Cap.	NA	0.3	0.5	0.8	0.7	1.0	1.0	1.9	1.3	1.0
% Net Inc.of Revs.	NA	21.9	11.3	17.6	21.7	20.1	16.9	16.7	15.9	13.7
% Ret. on Assets	NA	20.6	11.0	17.6	21.3	19.7	16.5	15.9	17.5	14.8
% Ret. on Equity	NA	26.6	14.8	24.1	29.5	28.0	24.7	24.5	26.2	21.9

Data as orig reptd.; bef. results of disc opers/spec. items. Per share data adj. for stk. divs. Bold denotes diluted EPS (FASB 128)-prior periods restated. E-Estimated. NA-Not Available. NM-Not Meaningful. NR-Not Ranked.

Office– 710 Medtronic Pkwy., N.E., Minneapolis, MN 55432-5604. **Tel–** (763) 514-4000. **Website–** http://www.medtronic.com **Chrmn & CEO–** W. W. George. **Vice Chrmn–** G. D. Nelson. **Pres & COO–** A. D. Collins Jr. **SVP & Secy–** R. E. Lund. **SVP & CFO–** R. L. Ryan. **Investor Contact–** Tracy Burns (763-505-2692). **Dirs–** M. R. Bonsignore, W. R. Brody, P. W. Chellgren, A. D. Collins Jr., W. W. George, A. M. Gotto Jr., B. P. Healy, T. E. Holloran, G. D. Nelson, J.-P. Rosso, R. L. Schall, J. W. Schuler, G. W. Simonson, G. M. Sprenger, R. A. Swailin. **Transfer Agent & Registrar–** Wells Fargo Minnesota, N.A., St. Paul. **Incorporated–** in Minnesota in 1957. **Empl–** 21,490. **S&P Analyst:** Robert M. Gold

Online Investing [LG5]

Just a few years ago, online investing focused on finding the lowest transaction cost at one of the few discount brokers offering cheap electronic trades. It seemed more like a fad than a lasting trend. Today, the Internet is a major force in the investing environment. It has opened the world of investing to individual investors, creating a more level playing field and providing access to tools formerly restricted to professionals. Not only can you trade many types of securities online, you can also find a wealth of information, from real-time stock quotes to securities analysts' research reports. The savings from online investing in terms of time and money are huge. Instead of weeding through mounds of paper, investors can quickly sort through vast databases to find appropriate investments, monitor their current investments, and make securities transactions—all without leaving their computers.

THE GROWTH OF ONLINE INVESTING

Online investing's popularity has grown almost as fast as stock market valuations. In just one year, from 1998 to 1999, the percentage of online securities trades jumped from 27% to more than 50%. Indeed, by mid-year 2000, investors had opened over 16 million online accounts at the scores of brokerage firms offering online services! Why does online investing attract thousands of new investors daily? Because the Internet makes buying and selling securities convenient, simple, inexpensive, and fast. In today's rapidly changing stock market, it provides the most current information, updated continuously. Even if you prefer to use a human broker, the Internet provides an abundance of resources to help you become a more informed investor.

How can you successfully navigate through the cyber-investing universe? You probably already have the technology you need: a computer, modem, and an Internet service provider (or ISP, as they are more commonly known) to connect you to the Internet. Open your Web browser and you are ready to explore the multitude of investing sites. Typically one site includes a combination of resources for novice and sophisticated investors alike. For example, take a look at Exhibit 11.8, which shows the home page for *E*Trade*, a major online brokerage firm (**www.etrade.com**). With a few clicks of the mouse, you can learn about E*Trade's services, open an account, or place an order to trade securities. In addition, you can get a quick overview of recent market activity, obtain price quotes and research reports, or use their services to track a whole portfolio of securities. You can use their site to select stocks, bonds, and mutual funds, get advice on retirement planning and saving for college, go to their Knowledge Center to learn about the markets, even do your banking at their *E*Trade Bank*.

ONLINE INVESTOR SERVICES

As the E*Trade Web site (above) reveals, the Internet offers a full array of online investor services, from up-to-the-minute stock quotes and research reports to charting services and portfolio tracking. When it comes to investing, you name it and you can probably find it online! Unfortunately, although many of these are truly high-quality sites that offer valuable information, many others are pure garbage, so you have to use care when entering the world of online investing. But even if you confine yourself to the quality sites, the fact is all this information can be overwhelming and even intimidating. It takes time and effort to use the net wisely. Let's take some time here to review the kinds of investor services you can find online, starting with investor education sites.

EXHIBIT 11.8

INVESTOR RESOURCES AVAILABLE ONLINE

There's a wealth of investor information and services available online. Here, for example, we see the home page for *E*Trade*. By going to this one Web site, you can check the day's market news, get research reports, look up stock quotes, obtain information about specific mutual funds, and more.

http://www.etrade.com

INVESTOR EDUCATION. The Internet offers a wide array of tutorials, online classes, and articles to educate the novice investor. Even experienced investors will find sites that expand their investing knowledge. Although most good investment-oriented Web sites include many educational resources, here are a few good sites that feature *investment fundamentals:*

- *The Motley Fool* (**fool.com**) *Fool's School* has sections on fundamentals of investing, mutual fund investing, choosing a broker, investment strategies and styles, lively discussion boards and more.
- America Online's (AOL) *Money Basics* (developed with *Smart Money* magazine and for subscribers only) offers Investing 101, which covers basic investment theory, risk management, asset categories, and taxes. Other departments include building and managing your portfolio, investment strategies, and personal finance topics.
- Zacks Investment Research (**www.zacks.com**), a free site from *The Wall Street Journal,* is an excellent starting place to learn what the Internet can offer investors.
- Nasdaq (**nasdaq.com**) has an Investor Resource section that helps with financial planning and choosing a broker.

Other good educational sites include leading personal finance magazines like *Money* (**www.money.com**), *Kiplinger's Personal Finance Magazine* (**www.kiplinger.com**), and *Smart Money* (**www.smartmoney.com**).

INVESTMENT TOOLS. Once you are familiar with the basics of investing, you can use the Internet to develop financial plans and set investment goals, find securities that meet your investment objectives, analyze potential investments, and organize your portfolio. Many of these tools, once used only by professional money managers, are free to anyone who wants to go online. You'll find financial calculators and worksheets, screening and charting tools, and portfolio trackers at the Web sites of large brokerage firms, as well as other financial sites. You can even set up a personal calendar that notifies you of forthcoming earnings announcements and receive alerts when one of your stocks has hit a predetermined price target.

Investment Planning. Online calculators and worksheets can help you find answers to your financial planning and investing questions. With them, you can figure out how much to save each month for a particular goal, such as the down payment for your first home, a college education for your children, or to be able to retire by the time you reach 55. For example, Fidelity (**Fidelity.com**) has a wide selection of planning tools that deal with such topics as investment growth, college planning, and retirement planning—even a "spend or save" calculator. One of the best sites for financial calculators is FinanCenter.com (**www.finan center.com**). It includes over 100 calculators for financial planning, insurance, auto and home buying, and investing. Exhibit 11.9 illustrates a calculator that will help you determine the stock price you'll need to achieve to generate a given rate of return. Other investment-related calculators show the tax and return difference between selling a stock before or after one year, your current yield from dividends, how currency exchange rates affect foreign stock transactions, how fees and costs affect your mutual fund purchases, bond yield to maturity, whether a taxable or tax-exempt bond provides a better return, and more.

Investment Research and Screening. One of the best investor services offered online is the ability to conduct in-depth research on stocks, bonds, mutual funds, and other types of investment vehicles. Go to a site like **Quicken.com** or **Kiplinger.com**, click on the "investments" tab, and you can obtain literally dozens of pages of financial and market information about a specific stock or mutual fund—an example of which is seen in Exhibit 11.10.

EXHIBIT 11.9

ONLINE FINANCIAL CALCULATORS

At sites like *FinanCenter.com,* you'll find calculators, similar to the one shown here, to help you with your investment planning. In this particular case, just input the variables for your situation and the calculator will show you the selling price at which you will earn your desired rate of return.

http://www.calcbuilder.com

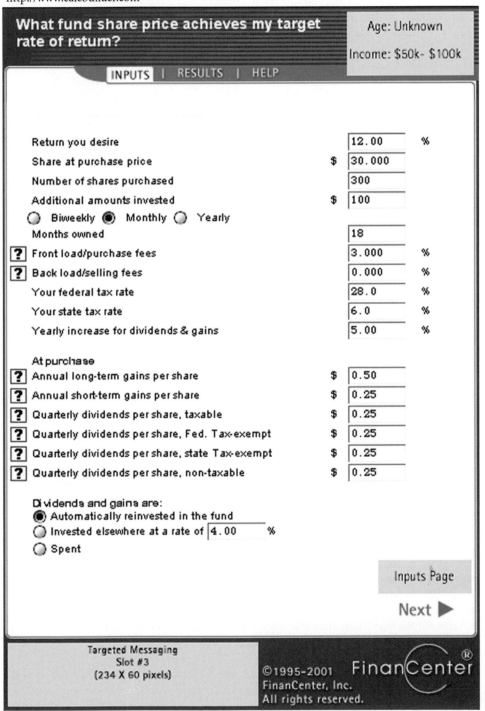

What fund share price achieves my target rate of return?		Age: Unknown
		Income: $50k– $100k

INPUTS | RESULTS | HELP

Return you desire	12.00	%
Share at purchase price	$ 30.000	
Number of shares purchased	300	
Additional amounts invested	$ 100	
○ Biweekly ● Monthly ○ Yearly		
Months owned	18	
[?] Front load/purchase fees	3.000	%
[?] Back load/selling fees	0.000	%
Your federal tax rate	28.0	%
Your state tax rate	6.0	%
Yearly increase for dividends & gains	5.00	%

At purchase

[?] Annual long-term gains per share	$ 0.50	
[?] Annual short-term gains per share	$ 0.25	
[?] Quarterly dividends per share, taxable	$ 0.25	
[?] Quarterly dividends per share, Fed. Tax-exempt	$ 0.25	
[?] Quarterly dividends per share, state Tax-exempt	$ 0.25	
[?] Quarterly dividends per share, non-taxable	$ 0.25	

Dividends and gains are:
● Automatically reinvested in the fund
○ Invested elsewhere at a rate of 4.00 %
○ Spent

Inputs Page

Next ►

Targeted Messaging
Slot #3
(234 X 60 pixels)

Source: FinanCenter.com; **www.calcbuilder.com** (accessed June 12, 2001).

For example, you can find historical and forecasted information about a firm's earnings, earnings per share, dividend yields, growth rates, and more in both tabular and graphic formats; you can also track the behavior of a specific stock relative to a market index, or to one or more of its major competitors. And many of these sites have links back to the company itself, so with a couple clicks of the mouse, you can obtain the company's annual report, detailed financial statements, and historical summaries of a full array of financial and market ratios. Moreover, you'll find sites that offer detailed reports produced by major brokerage firms (some of which require a nominal charge).

In addition to the types of research information described above, investors can also use various *online screening tools* to identify attractive and potentially rewarding investment vehicles. Most major sites, like Quicken, Morningstar, or MSN Money Central, offer screening tools. Basically, these tools enable you to quickly sort through huge databases of stocks and mutual funds to find those that meet specific characteristics, such as stocks with low or high P/E multiples, small market capitalizations, high dividend yields, specific revenue growth, and low debt to equity ratios. For mutual funds you might specify a certain type of fund, a particular industry or geographical sector, and low fees. Each screening tool uses a different method to sort. You answer a series of questions to specify the type of stock or fund you're looking for, performance criteria you desire, cost parameters, and so on. The screen then provides a list of stocks (or funds) that have met the standards you've set. You can then do more research (as described above) on the listed stocks (or mutual funds) to decide which ones you want to further pursue.

Portfolio Tracking   Almost every investment-oriented Web site includes *portfolio-tracking tools*. Simply enter the number of shares held and the symbol for those stocks or mutual funds you wish to follow and the tracker automatically updates the value of your portfolio every time you check. You can usually link to more detailed information about each stock or mutual fund. The features, quality, and ease of use of stock trackers varies, so check several to find the one that meets your needs. Quicken.com, MSN MoneyCentral Investor (**investor.msn.com**) and E*Trade (**www.etrade.com**) all have portfolio trackers that are easy to set up and use. Quicken's tracker, also available on Excite and AOL, alerts you whenever an analyst changes the rating on one of your stocks or funds and tells you how well you are diversified among the major asset classes or sectors you hold.

 For a one-stop financial portal, head to MSN MoneyCentral Investor (**moneycentral.msn.com**). You'll find good educational articles, research, interactive tools like Research Wizard, and a portfolio tracker. (Many tools don't run on Macintosh.)

DAY TRADING.   As we saw previously, trading stocks (and other securities) online has become very popular among investors—if for no other reason than the rock-bottom cost of executing such trades. Face it, it's an easy, convenient, and low-cost way of trading securities. But for some investors, trading stocks online is so compelling that they become day traders. The opposite of buy-and-hold investors with a long-term perspective, **day traders** buy and sell stocks quickly throughout the day. They hope their stocks will continue to rise in value for the very short time they own them—sometimes just seconds or minutes—so they can make quick profits. Some short sell as well, looking for small price decreases. True day traders do not own any stocks overnight—hence the term *day trader*—because they believe the chance of prices changing radically overnight (from the close on one day to the open on the next) can lead to large losses. While day trading is not illegal or unethical, *it is highly risky*. To compound their risk, day traders usually buy on margin to earn even higher returns. But as we've seen, margin trading also increases the risk of larger losses.

day trader
An investor who buys and sells stocks (and other securities) rapidly throughout the day in the hopes of making quick profits.

EXHIBIT 11.10

AN EXAMPLE OF ONLINE INVESTMENT RESEARCH

Here's just a small sample of the type of investment research available online; this Quicken report provides information about the price, valuation, growth, and financial strength of Oracle Corp. At this site, you can also obtain stock price and return charts, analysts ratings, comparative performance, insider trading activity, complete financial statements, SEC filings, and more.

Quicken.com - Fundamentals

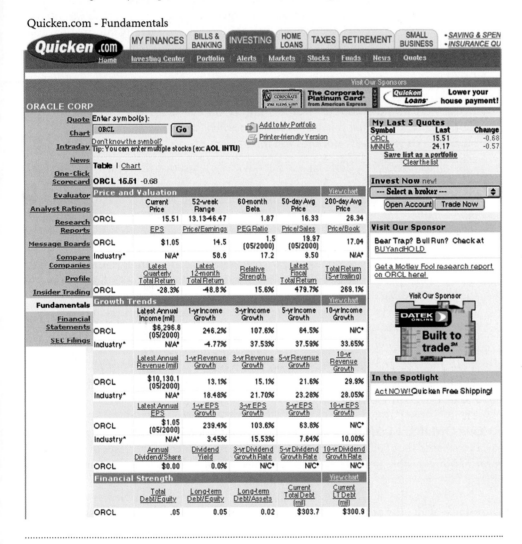

Source: Quicken; **www.Quicken.com/investments** (accessed June 12, 2001).

Until recently, day trading was a little-known activity. Now that the Internet makes investment information and transactions accessible to the masses, it is a dangerously popular one. Day traders watch their computer screens continuously, trying to track numerous ticker quotes and price data to identify market trends. It's a very difficult task, essentially a very stressful full-time job—yet pitches for day trading make it seem like an easy route to quick riches. Quite the reverse is true. Day traders typically incur major financial losses when they start trading. Some never reach profitability. Day traders also have high expenses for brokerage commissions, training, and computer equipment. By some estimates, they must make a 50 to 60 percent profit just to break even on fees and commissions.

USING THE INTERNET WISELY

The power of the Internet as an investing tool is alluring. Do-it-yourself investing is now possible for the average investor, even novices who have never before bought stock. However, online investing also carries risks. The Internet requires investors to exercise the same—and possibly more—caution than they would if they were getting information from and placing orders with a human broker. You don't have the safety net of a live broker suggesting that you rethink your trade. The ease of point-and-click investing can be the financial downfall of inexperienced investors. Drawn by stories of others who have made lots of money, many novice investors take the plunge before they acquire the necessary skills and knowledge—often with disastrous results. Online or off, the basic rules for smart investing are still the same: *know what you are buying, from whom, and at what level of risk.*

Here are a couple other guidelines you might want to consider when investing online:

- *Do your own research*—don't take somebody else's word that the security's a good one.
- *Don't let the speed and ease of making online transactions blind you to the realities of online trading.* More frequent trades mean high transaction costs. Although some brokers advertise per-trade costs as low as $8, the average online transaction fee is higher (about $23 in March 2000). If you trade often, it will take longer to recoup your costs. Studies reveal that the more often you trade, the harder it is to beat the market. Plus, on short-term trades of less than a year, you'll pay taxes on profits at the higher ordinary income tax rates, not the lower capital gains rate.
- *Don't believe everything you read on the Internet.* It's easy to be impressed with a screen full of data touting a stock's prospects or to act on a hot tip you find on a discussion board or online chat room. Stick to the sites of major brokerage firms, mutual funds, academic sites, and well-known business and finance publications.

The bottom line is just be careful and exercise due care. Be skeptical—if it sounds too good to be true, it probably is!

AVOID ONLINE SCAMS. Before leaving our discussion of online investing, we should say a few words about *online scams*. The fact is, just as the Internet increases the amount of information available to all investors, it also makes it easier for scam artists and others to spread false news and manipulate information. Anyone can sound like an investment expert online, posting stock tips with no underlying substance. The problem is you may not know the real identity of the person touting or panning a hot stock on the message boards. The person panning a stock could be a disgruntled former employee or a short seller. In the fast-paced online environment, two types of scams seem to turn up the most: *pump-and-dump* schemes—where promoters hype stocks, quickly send the prices sky-high, and then dump them at inflated prices, and *get-rich-quick scams*—where promoters sell worthless investments to naïve buyers. One well-publicized pump-and-dump scheme demonstrates how easy it is to use the Internet to promote stocks. In September 2000, the SEC caught a 15-year-old boy who made more than $270,000 by promoting small company stocks. The self-taught young investor would buy a block of a company's shares and then send out a barrage of false and misleading e-mail messages and message board posts singing the praises of that stock and the company's prospects. Once this misinformation pushed up the stock price, he sold and moved on to a new target company.

To crack down on cyber-fraud, the SEC created the Office of Internet Enforcement. The agency now has 15 staff members and several regional offices that quickly take action against reports of suspected hoaxes and prosecute the offenders. Former SEC chairman Arthur Levitt cautions investors to remember that the Internet is basically another way to send and receive information, one which has no controls for accuracy or truthfulness. The SEC Web site (**www.sec.gov/consumer/offertip.htm**) includes some valuable tips on how to avoid investment scams. Here are three questions every investor should ask:

- *Is the stock registered?* Check the SEC's EDGAR database and with your state securities regulator (**www.nasaa.org**).
- *Who is making the sales pitch?* Make sure the seller is licensed in your state. Check with the NASD to see if they have a record of complaints or fraud.
- *Is it too good to be true?* Then it probably is. Just because it's on the Web doesn't mean it's legitimate.

Another place to check on possible frauds is Stock Detective, a section of the Financial Web portal site (**www.financialweb.com/skdindex.asp**) that investigates suspicious stocks and reports on SEC activities against investment fraud.

CONCEPT CHECK

11.22. Describe the impact the Internet has had on the world of investing. What are some of the products and services that you, as an individual investor, can now obtain online?

11.23. Briefly describe several different types of online investment tools and note how they can help you become a better investor.

11.24. What is *day trading* and how does it differ from the more traditional approach to investing?

11.25. What are some common types of online investment scams and hoaxes? How can you protect yourself from them?

▓ Managing Your Investment Holdings [LG6]

As noted previously, buying and selling securities is not difficult; the hard part is finding securities that will provide the kind of return you're looking for. Like most individual investors, in time you too will be buying, selling, and trading securities with ease. Eventually, your investment holdings will increase to the point where you are managing a whole portfolio of securities. In essence, a **portfolio** is a collection of investment vehicles assembled to meet a common investment goal. For instance, Bill Hansen's investment portfolio is made up of 150 shares of Cisco Systems, 200 shares of Home Depot, 100 shares of General Electric, 100 shares of America Online, and 10 Verizon Communications convertible bonds. But a portfolio is far more than a collection of investments! For a portfolio breathes life into your investment program; *it's an investment philosophy that provides guidelines for carrying out your investment program.* A portfolio, in effect, combines your personal and financial traits with your investment objectives to give some structure to your investments.

Seasoned investors often devote a good deal of attention to constructing diversified portfolios of securities. Such portfolios consist of stocks and bonds selected not only for their returns but also for their combined risk-return behavior. The idea behind **diversification** is that by combining securities with dissimilar risk-return characteristics, you can

portfolio
A collection of securities assembled for the purpose of meeting common investment goals.

diversification
The process of choosing securities having dissimilar risk-return characteristics in order to create a portfolio that will provide an acceptable level of return and an acceptable exposure to risk.

produce a portfolio of reduced risk and more predictable levels of return. In recent years, investment researchers have shown that you can achieve a noticeable reduction in risk simply by diversifying your investment holdings. For the small investor with a moderate amount of money to invest, this means that *investing in a number of securities rather than a single one should be beneficial.* The payoff from diversification comes in the form of reduced risk without a significant impact on return. For example, Joan Rainer, who has all of her $30,000 portfolio invested in just one stock (Stock A), might find that by selling two-thirds of her holdings and using the proceeds to buy equal amounts of Stocks B and C, she will continue to earn the same level of return—say, 15 percent—while greatly decreasing the associated risk. Professional money managers emphasize the point that investors should not put all their eggs in one basket but instead should hold portfolios that are diversified across a broad segment of businesses.

BUILDING A PORTFOLIO OF SECURITIES

Developing a portfolio of investment holdings is predicated on the assumption that diversification is a desirable investment attribute that leads to improved return and/or reduced risk. Again, as emphasized previously, holding a variety of investments is far more desirable than concentrating all your investments in a single security or industry (for example, a portfolio made up of nothing but auto stocks, such as GM, Ford, and Daimler Chrysler, would hardly be well diversified). Of course, when you first start investing, you probably will not be able to do much, if any, diversifying because of insufficient investment capital. However, as you build up your investment funds, your opportunities (and need) for diversification will increase dramatically. Certainly, by the time you have $10,000 to $15,000 to invest, you should start to diversify your holdings. To give you an idea of the kind of portfolio diversification employed by investors, take a look at the following numbers; they show the types of investments held by *average individual investors:*

Type of Investment Product	Percent of Portfolio (August 2001)
Stocks and stock funds	62.0%
Bonds and bond funds	21.0
Short-term investments (CDs, money mkt. dep. accts., etc.)	17.0
Total	100.0%

This portfolio reflects the results of a monthly asset allocation survey conducted by the *American Association of Individual Investors,* and shows the portfolio holdings of a typical individual investor. Whether this is what your portfolio should look like depends on a number of factors, including your own needs and objectives.

INVESTOR CHARACTERISTICS. To formulate an effective portfolio strategy, begin with an honest evaluation of your own financial condition and family situation. Pay particular attention to such variables as:

- Level and stability of income
- Family factors
- Investment horizon
- Net worth
- Investment experience and age
- Disposition toward risk

These are the variables that set the tone for your investments. They determine the kinds of investments you should consider and how long you can tie up your money. For your portfolio to work, it must be tailored to meet your personal financial needs. Your income, family responsibilities, relative financial security, experience, and age all enter into the delicate equation that yields a sound portfolio strategy. For example, a married investor with young children probably would not be interested in high-risk investments until some measure of financial security has been provided for the family. Once that investor has ample savings and insurance protection for the family, he or she may be ready to undertake more risky ventures. On the other hand, a single investor with no family responsibilities would probably be better able to handle risk than one who has such concerns. Simply stated, an *investor's risk exposure should not exceed his or her ability to bear risk.*

The size and certainty of an investor's employment income also has a significant bearing on portfolio strategy. An investor with a secure job is more likely to embark on a more risk-oriented investment program than one with a less secure position. Income taxes bear on the investment decision as well. The higher an investor's income, the more important the tax ramifications of an investment program become. For example, municipal bonds normally yield about 25 to 30 percent less in annual interest than corporate bonds, because the interest income on municipal bonds is tax-free. On an after-tax basis, however, municipal bonds may provide a superior return if an investor is in a tax bracket of 28 percent or higher.

An individual's investment experience also influences the appropriateness of an investment strategy. Normally, investors assume higher levels of investment risk gradually over time. It is best to "get one's feet wet" in the investment market by slipping into it slowly rather than leaping in head first. Investors who make risky initial investments very often suffer heavy losses, damaging the long-run potential of the entire investment program. A cautiously developed investment program will likely provide more favorable long-run results than an impulsive, risky one. Finally, investors should carefully consider risk. High-risk investments not only have high return potential but also a high risk of loss. Remember, by going for the home run (via a high-risk, high-return investment), the odds of striking out are much higher than by going for a base hit (a more conservative investment posture).

INVESTOR OBJECTIVES. Once an investor has developed a personal financial profile, the next question is: "What do I want from my portfolio?" This seems like an easy question to answer. Ideally, we would all like to double our money every year by making low-risk investments. However, the realities of the highly competitive investment environment make this outcome unlikely, so the question must be answered more realistically. There generally is a tradeoff between earning a high current income from an investment and obtaining significant capital appreciation from it. An investor must choose one or the other; it is difficult to obtain both from a single investment vehicle. It is possible, of course, in a *portfolio*, to have a *balance* of both income and growth (capital gains), but more often than not, that involves "tilting" the portfolio one direction (e.g., toward income) or the other (toward growth). The price of having high appreciation potential in the portfolio is low current income potential. One must balance the certainty of high current income and limited price appreciation with the uncertainty of high future price appreciation.

The investor's needs may determine which avenue to choose. For instance, a retired investor whose income depends in part on his or her portfolio will probably choose a lower-risk, current income–oriented approach out of the need for financial survival. In contrast, a high-income, financially secure investor (a doctor, for instance) may be much more willing to take on risky investments in the hope of improving his or her net worth. Likewise, a young investor with a secure job may be less concerned about current income and more able to bear risk. This type of investor will likely be more capital-gains oriented

 Financial Road Sign

Top Portfolio Pitfalls
Avoiding these *common mistakes* will make you a better and more successful investor:

- Not defining objectives and priorities for each investment and reviewing them regularly
- Not rebalancing your portfolio every few years to keep asset allocation percentages current
- Owning too many different stocks, bonds, and mutual funds
- Inefficient use of tax strategies
- Paying too much in mutual fund fees
- Excessive stock overlap in various 401(k) and mutual fund holdings.

Source: Sue Stevens, "Top 10 Portfolio Pitfalls," *Morningstar* *.com*, June 15, 2000, downloaded from **www.morningstar.com**.

and may choose speculative investments. As an investor approaches age 60, the desired level of income likely rises as retirement approaches. The more senior investor will be less willing to bear risk and will want to keep what he or she has, because these investments will soon be needed as a source of retirement income.

ASSET ALLOCATION AND PORTFOLIO MANAGEMENT

asset allocation
A plan for dividing a portfolio among different classes of securities in order to preserve capital by protecting the portfolio against negative market development.

A portfolio must be built around an individual's needs, which, in turn, depend on income, family responsibilities, financial resources, age, retirement plans, and ability to bear risk. These needs shape one's financial goals. But to create a portfolio geared to those goals, you need to develop an **asset allocation** strategy. Basically, all that asset allocation involves is a decision on how to divide your portfolio among different types of securities. For example, what portion of your portfolio is going to be devoted to short-term securities, longer bonds and bond funds, and common stocks and equity funds? In asset allocation, emphasis is placed on *preservation of capital*. The idea is to position your assets in such a way that you can protect your portfolio from potential negative developments in the market, while still taking advantage of potential positive developments. Asset allocation is one of the most overlooked yet most important aspects of investing. Indeed, there's overwhelming evidence that, over the long run, *the total return on a portfolio is influenced far more by its asset allocation plan than by specific security selections.*

Asset allocation deals in broad categories and *does not tell you which individual securities to buy or sell.* It might look something like this:

Type of Investment	Asset Mix
Short-term securities	5%
Longer bonds (7- to 10-year maturities)	20%
Equity funds	75%
Total portfolio	100%

As you can see, all you're really doing here is deciding how to cut up the pie. You still have to decide which particular securities to invest in. Once you've decided that you want to put, say, 20 percent of your money into intermediate-term (7- to 10-year) bonds, your next step is to select those specific securities. For ideas on how to start your own portfolio, even if you don't have a lot of money, see the *Money in Action* box on page 493.

Once you establish your asset allocation strategy, you should check it regularly for two reasons: first, to make sure that your portfolio is in fact in line with your desired asset mix, and, second, to see if that mix is still appropriate for your investment objectives. Here are some reasons to reevaluate your asset allocation:

- A major change in personal circumstances—marriage, birth of a child, loss of a spouse from divorce or death, child graduating from college, loss of job, or family illness, for example—that changes your investment goals.
- The proportion of an asset rises or falls considerably, changing your target allocation for that class more than, say, 5 percent.
- You're close to reaching a certain goal (such as saving for your child's college or for your retirement).

You may find that your portfolio requires *rebalancing* to bring it back into line or to reallocate assets. For example, suppose your asset allocation plan calls for 75 percent equities and the stock market falls so that stocks represent only 65 percent of your total portfolio. If you are still bullish on the market and stocks are still appropriate for

MONEY IN ACTION

How to Build a Portfolio When You're Just Starting Out

You've set aside funds for emergencies, developed long-term goals and an investment strategy including an asset allocation plan to reach them, and are ready to start investing. But where do you go from here? The following framework will help you invest wisely so you don't end up with an assortment of investments that do not meet your needs. If your funds are limited at first, start with your largest asset category and add the others as more money becomes available. No matter what asset allocation strategy you choose, you have several ways to make your portfolio grow. You can use mutual funds, individual stocks, or both.

A balanced or asset allocation mutual fund with an asset mix of stock and bonds matching your plan is a conservative approach. It appeals to many novice investors and provides instant diversification among asset classes with just one investment. You can add to this fund regularly until you have enough money—and investment experience—to move into specific fund categories or individual stocks. The main disadvantage to this approach is that you don't control the asset mix.

If you are more daring, you can use a stock index fund which invests in the Standard and Poor 500 as the core of your portfolio. This requires more risk tolerance, because you're starting with just common stocks, but the core fund itself is fairly conservative. Over time, you should be able to ride the market's ups and downs, particularly if you have a longtime horizon.

With either strategy, you then diversify into other investment categories to meet allocation goals. If you want to stay with funds, you'd increase your equity percent with a stock fund. Or you may decide to branch out to individual stocks to emphasize a certain sector in your portfolio, although you can also select a sector fund. With the core (index) approach, adding an intermediate bond fund creates your own balanced fund. Or you might buy small-cap or international funds. Don't agonize if you are a few percentage points from your plan; use the target percents as a general guide.

Building a portfolio of individual stocks takes more time and discipline than the fund route. Dividend reinvestment plans (DRPs), offered by 1,000 companies, are a way for an investor with limited funds to buy stocks and also keep expenses down. After you own at least one share of stock, you can reinvest dividends in more shares and buy stock directly from the company, usually without a fee. Be sure to study the shareholder information packages and DRP prospectuses from companies that interest you.

Diversify with shares in a variety of industries and economic sectors, and include growth, value, and income stocks. Your goal should be about 10 to 15 companies, but focus on quality, not quantity; 4 good stocks are better than 10 bad ones. Know whether you can buy more shares monthly or quarterly.

Remember to invest regularly in your funds or stocks, every month or pay period if possible. You'll be surprised how quickly your investments grow. Review your holdings regularly and rebalance your portfolio as needed. And be patient; unless you hold your investments for a while, transaction costs and taxes will wipe out profits.

Sources: Adapted from Karen Hube et al., "Time to Check Your Investment Strategy," *Wall Street Journal*, January 6, 2000, pp. C1, C18; Maria Crawford Scott, "How to Implement Your Strategy If You Are Starting from Scratch," AAII Journal, February 1995, pp. 18–20; Sue Stevens, Adding Stocks to Your Mutual-Fund Portfolio," *Morningstar.com*, June 22, 2000, downloaded from **www.morningstar.com/news**.

your portfolio, you may view this as a good time to buy stocks and, in so doing, bring your portfolio back up to 75 percent equities. If your personal goals change, or if you think the market may not recover in the near future, you may decide to change your percentages so as to hold fewer stocks. However, don't be too quick to rebalance; you must allow for some variation in the percentages, as market fluctuations may make it impossible to constantly

EXHIBIT 11.11

FOUR MODEL PORTFOLIOS

The type of portfolio you put together will depend on your financial and family situation as well as on your investment objectives. Clearly, what is right for one family may be totally inappropriate for another.

Family Situation	Portfolio
Newlywed couple:	80 to 90% in common stocks, with three-quarters of that in mutual funds aiming for maximum capital gains and the rest in growth-and-income or equity-income funds 10 to 20% in a money market fund or other short-term money market securities
Two-income couple:	60 to 70% in common stocks, with three-quarters of that in blue chips or growth mutual funds and the remainder in more aggressive issues or mutual funds aiming for maximum capital gains 25 to 30% in discount Treasury notes whose maturities correspond with the bills for college tuition 5 to 10% in money market funds or other short-term money market securities
Divorced mother:	40 to 50% in money market funds or other short-term money market securities 50 to 60% in growth and income mutual funds
Older couple:	60 to 70% in blue-chip common stocks or growth mutual funds 25 to 30% in municipal bonds or short- and intermediate-term discount bonds that will mature as they start to need the money to live on 5 to 10% in CDs and money market funds

maintain exact percentages. And don't forget the costs from commissions or sales charges and tax considerations.

Security selection and portfolio management are recurring activities that become an almost routine part of your investment program. You receive an interest or dividend check, and you have to find a place to put it; you add new capital to your investment program, or one of the Treasury notes you're holding matures, and you have to decide what to do with the money. These events occur with considerable regularity, so you're likely to be faced with a series of little (and sometimes not so little) investment decisions over time. This, in short, is portfolio management: the initial construction and ongoing administration of a collection of securities and investments.

Portfolio management involves the buying, selling, and holding of various securities for the purpose of meeting a set of predetermined investment needs and objectives. To give you an idea of portfolio management in action, Exhibit 11.11 provides examples of four different portfolios, each developed with a particular financial situation in mind. Note in each case that the asset allocation strategies and portfolio structures change with the different financial objectives. The first one is the *newlywed couple;* in their late 20s, they earn $58,000 a year and spend just about every cent. They have managed to put away some money, however, and are quickly beginning to appreciate the need to develop a savings program. Next there is the *two-income couple;* in their early 40s, they earn $115,000 a year and are concerned about college costs for their children, ages 17 and 12. Next is the *divorced mother;* she is 34, has custody of her children, ages 7 and 4, and receives $40,000 a year in salary and child support. Finally, we have the *older couple;* in their mid-50s, they are planning for retirement in 10 years, when the husband will retire from his $95,000-a-year job.

KEEPING TRACK OF YOUR INVESTMENTS

Keeping track of your investment holdings is essential to a well-managed securities portfolio. Just as you need investment objectives to provide direction for your portfolio, so too do you need to *monitor* it by keeping informed about what your investment holdings consist of, how they have performed over time, and whether they have lived up to your expectations. Sometimes investments fail to perform the way you thought they would. Their return may be well below what you would like, or perhaps you may even have suffered a loss. In either case, it may be time to sell the investments and put the money elsewhere. A monitoring system for keeping track of your investments should allow you to identify such securities in your portfolio. In addition, it should enable you to stay on top of the holdings that are performing to your satisfaction. Knowing when to sell and when to hold can have a significant impact on the amount of return you are able to generate from your investments—certainly it will help you keep your money fully invested.

You can use something like Worksheet 11.2 to keep an inventory of your investment holdings. All types of investments can be included on this worksheet—from stocks, bonds, and mutual funds to real estate and savings accounts. To see how it works, consider the investment portfolio that has been built up over the last 15 years or so by John and Mary Maffeo, a two-income couple in their early 50s. As the figures in Worksheet 11.2 reveal, John and Mary hold common and preferred stock in five companies, three bond issues, two mutual funds, some real estate, and two savings accounts. In addition to the type and description of the investment vehicles, the worksheet contains the dates the investments were made (the purchase date is needed for tax purposes), the original amount of the investment, the amount of annual income currently being earned from it, and its latest market value. (Using such a worksheet in conjunction with an online portfolio tracker would provide an investor with plenty of information about the performance of his or her portfolio—the *worksheet* providing long-term information from the date of purchase of an asset, and the *online portfolio trackers* providing year-to-date or annual returns.)

Worksheet 11.2 lists all the investments John and Mary held as of December 2001, regardless of when they were purchased. In contrast, any securities/investments sold during the year (2001) would not be included. A report like this should be prepared at least once a year, and preferably every three to six months. When completed, it will provide a quick overview of your investment holdings and let you know where you stand at a given point in time. Note that the Maffeos earn almost $5,000 a year from their investments and that—thanks, in large part, to their investments in a couple of stocks and stock funds—their holdings have grown from around $100,000 to more than $435,000! In fact, they have only one security that is not doing too well—Pall Corp. All the rest are quite profitable.

CONCEPT CHECK

> 11-26. Explain why it might be preferable for a person to invest in a *portfolio* of securities rather than in a single security. Be sure to mention risk and return in your response.
>
> 11-27. Briefly describe the concept of *asset allocation* and note how it works. Give an example of an asset allocation scheme. Discuss the role that asset allocation plays in the management of a portfolio.
>
> 11-28. What, if anything, can be gained from keeping track of your investment holdings?

KEEPING TABS ON YOUR INVESTMENT HOLDINGS

A worksheet like this one will enable you to keep track of your investment holdings and identify investments that are not performing up to expectations.

AN INVENTORY OF INVESTMENT HOLDINGS

Name(s): John & Mary Maffeo   Date: December 2001

Type of Investment	Description of Investment Vehicle	Date Purchased	Amount of Investment (Quote—$ Amount)	Amount of Annual Income from Dividends, Interest, etc.	Latest Market Value (Quote—$ Amount)	Comments/Planned Actions
Common stock	250 shares—McDonald's	12/8/90	8.25-$2,062	$860	30.50 (now 1,000 shs.)-$30,500	A keeper
Common stock	300 shares—Disney	10/20/92	15-$4,500	0	35 (now 900 shs.)-$31,500	Another keeper
Common stock	400 shares—Pall Corp.	4/10/93	23.50-$9,400	$264	18.50 (now 400 shs.)-$7,400	DUMP IT!
Common stock	150 shares—Intel	8/11/95	8.50-$1,275	$84	45 (now 1,200 shs.)-$54,000	Doing great...
Preferred stock	100 shares—Dupont pf 4.50	1/26/89	50.75-$5,075	$450	62.25-$6,225	
Corporate bond	$5,000—Pacific Telephone 7 1/4-08	8/19/92	75½-$3,775	$363	94 3/4-$4,738	
Corporate bond	$7,000—Texaco 5 3/4-07	2/27/87	39¼-$2,748	$402	94½-$6,615	
Treasury bond	$6,000—U.S. Treasury 7 1/2-05	10/4/95	62-$3,720	$450	102-$6,120	
Mutual fund	750 shares—Fidelity Growth Company	6/16/89	15.75-$11,812	$120	88.75-$66,562	A good fund...
Mutual fund	500 shares—Vanguard 500 Index	1/17/88	25.70-$12,850	$994	132.60-$66,300	Stay with it!
Real estate	Four-plex at 1802 N. 75 Ave.	9/16/87	$140,000-$28,000	N/A	(est.) $250,000-$158,000	Time to sell?
Savings	1-year/6.5% CD at First National Bank	6/10/00	N/A-$10,000	$650	N/A-$10,000	
Savings	Money Fund at Paine Webber	3/13/95	N/A-$7,200	$340	N/A-$7,200	
Totals			$102,417	$4,977	$435,160	

Instructions: List number of shares of common and preferred stock purchased as part of the description of securities held; then put the price paid per share under the "Quote" column and total amount invested (number of shares × price per share) under the "$ Amount" column. Enter the principal (par) value of all bonds held in place of number of shares; "$ Amount" column for bonds = principal value of bonds purchased × quote (for example, $5,000 × .755 = $3,775). List mutual funds as you did for stock. For real estate, enter total market value of property under "Quote" column and amount actually invested (down payment and closing costs) under "$ Amount." Ignore the "Quote" column for savings vehicles. For "Amount of Income" column, list total amount received from dividends, interest, and so on (for example, dividends per share × number of shares held). Under "Latest Market Value," enter market price as of the date of this report (for instance, in December 2001, Pall Corp. was trading at 18.50). The latest market value for real estate is entered as an estimate of what the property would likely sell for (under "Quote") and the estimated amount of equity the investor has in the property (under "$ Amount").

SUMMARY

LG1. **Discuss the role that investing plays in the personal financial planning process and identify several different investment objectives.** Investing plays an important part in personal financial planning, as it is the vehicle through which many of your financial goals can be reached. Your investment activities should be based on a sound investment plan that is linked to an ongoing savings plan. Most people invest their money to enhance their current income, accumulate funds for a major expenditure, save for retirement, or shelter some of their income from taxes.

LG2. **Distinguish between primary and secondary markets, as well as listed exchanges and the over-the-counter market.** Stocks, bonds, and other long-term securities are traded in the capital, or long-term, markets. Newly issued securities are sold in the primary markets, whereas transactions between investors occur in the secondary markets. Listed securities are traded on organized exchanges, like the New York and American stock exchanges, as well as on a number of smaller regional exchanges. In contrast, the over-the-counter (OTC) market handles thousands of unlisted securities.

LG3. **Explain the process of buying and selling securities and recognize the different types of orders.** The securities transaction process starts when you call and place an order with your broker, who then transmits it via sophisticated telecommunications equipment to the floor of the stock exchange or the OTC market, where it is promptly executed and confirmed. Investors can buy or sell securities in odd or round lots by simply placing one of the three basic types of orders: a market order, limit order, or stop-loss order.

LG4. **Develop an appreciation of how various forms of investment information can lead to better investing skills and returns.** Becoming an informed investor is essential to developing a sound investment program. Vital information about specific companies and industries, the securities markets, the economy, and different investment vehicles and strategies can be obtained from such sources as annual stockholders' reports, brokerage and advisory service reports, and the financial press. In addition, the personal computer is rapidly becoming a popular source of investment information.

Various averages and indexes, such as the Dow Jones Industrial Average, the Standard & Poor's Indexes, the NYSE, AMEX, and Nasdaq indexes, provide information about daily market performance. These averages and indexes not only measure performance in the overall market, they also provide standards of performance for specific types of stocks, such as transportation issues, banks, insurance companies, and public utilities.

LG5. **Gain a basic understanding of the growing impact that the computer and the Internet are having on the field of investments.** The computer and the Internet have empowered individual investors by providing information and tools formerly available only to investing professionals, thereby greatly simplifying the investing process. The savings they provide in terms of time and money are huge. Investors get the most current information, including real-time stock price quotes, market activity data, research reports, educational articles, and discussion forums. Tools such as financial planning calculators, stock screening programs, and portfolio tracking are free at many sites. Buying and selling securities online is convenient, simple, inexpensive, and fast.

LG6. **Describe an investment portfolio and how you'd go about developing and managing a portfolio of securities.** While an investment portfolio represents a collection of the securities/investments you hold, it also provides a focus and purpose to your investing activities. Developing a well-diversified portfolio of investment holdings enables an investor to not only achieve given investment objectives, but also enjoy reduced exposure to risk and a more predictable level of return. To develop such a portfolio, the investor must carefully consider his or her level and stability of income, family factors, financial condition, experience and age, and disposition toward risk. Designing an asset allocation strategy, or mix of securities, that's based on these personal needs and objectives is also an important part of portfolio management. You should monitor your investment portfolio regularly to measure its performance and make changes as required by return data and lifecycle factors.

QUESTIONS AND PROBLEMS

1. *Use Worksheet 11.1*   Ashley Jobst is a young career woman who's presently employed as the managing editor of a well-known business journal. While she thoroughly enjoys her job and the people she works with, what she would really like to do is open a bookstore of her own. In particular, she would like to open her store in about 8 years, and she figures she'll need about $50,000 in capital to do so. Given she thinks she can make about 10 percent on her money, use Worksheet 11.1 to find the following:
   a. How much would Ashley have to invest today, in one lump sum, to end up with $50,000 in 8 years?
   b. If she's starting from scratch, how much would she have to put away annually to accumulate the needed capital in 8 years?
   c. How about if she already has $10,000 socked away; how much would she have to put away annually to accumulate the required capital in 8 years?
   d. Given Ashley now has an idea of how much she has to save, briefly explain how she could use an *investment plan* to help her reach her objective.

2. Jim Jefferies has just purchased two different stocks. His first transaction involved 100 shares of CZ Corp. at $49.50 per share, and the second was 60 shares of Big Blue Computers at $15 per share. For each transaction, calculate the amount of brokerage commissions Jim will have to pay, and express them as a percentage of the total cost of each stock. Use the brokerage fee schedule in Exhibit 11.2.

3. Assume Cecile Higgins places an order to buy 100 shares of Kodak; explain how the order will be processed if it is a market order. Would it have made any difference if it had been a limit order? Explain.

4. Sarah Jordan wants to buy 300 shares of PepsiCo, which is currently selling in the market for $45 a share. Rather than liquidate all her savings, she decides to borrow through her broker. Assume the margin requirement on common stock is 50 percent and the brokerage firm charges 9 percent interest on margin loans. What would be the interest cost on the transaction if Sarah sold the stocks at the end of one year? If the stock rises to $60 a share by the end of the year, show the kind of profit (in dollars) and return (in percentages) Sarah would earn if she makes the investment with 50 percent margin; contrast this to what she would make if she uses no margin.

5. Which of the following would offer the best return on investment? Assume you buy $5,000 in stock in all three cases; also, ignore interest costs in all your calculations.
   a. Buy a stock at $80 without margin, and sell it at $120 one year later.
   b. Buy a stock at $32 with 50 percent margin, and sell it one year later at $41.
   c. Buy a stock at $50 with 75 percent margin, and sell it in one year at $65.

6. How much profit (if any) would Buster Summers make if he short sold 300 shares of stock at $75 a share and the price of the stock suddenly tumbled to $60?

7. Using a resource like *The Wall Street Journal* or *Barron's* (either in print or online), find the latest values for each of the following market averages and indexes, and indicate how each has performed over the past six months:
   a. DJIA
   b. Dow Jones U.S. Total Market
   c. S&P 500
   d. NYSE Composite
   e. AMEX index
   f. Nasdaq Composite
   g. MidCap 400
   h. Wilshire 5000
   i. Russell 2000

8. Using the stock quotations in Exhibit 11.6, find the 52-week high and low for *Dillards Department Stores* common stock (stock symbol: DDS). How much does the stock pay annually in dividends, and what is its latest dividend yield? How many shares of Dillards changed hands (were traded), what was the closing price, and at what P/E ratio was the stock trading? There are 30 stocks listed in Exhibit 11.6; which one has had the largest year-to-date increase in price? The largest drop in price? Which three stocks had the highest dividend yields, and which three had the highest closing prices?

9. Using the S&P report in Exhibit 11.7, find the following information as it pertains to Medtronic:
   a. Amount of revenues (that is, sales) the company generated in 2001.
   b. Latest annual dividends per share and dividend yield.
   c. Earnings (per share) projections for 2002.
   d. Number of common shares outstanding.
   e. Book value per share and earnings per share in 2000.
   f. Where is the stock traded?
   g. How much long-term debt did the company have in 2000?
   h. When was the company formed and who were its founders?
   i. What was the company's effective tax rate in 2000?

10. The following is an *Online Investing* question and requires access to the Internet. First, go to the Quicken web site at **www.quicken.com**, click on the "INVESTING" tab from the menu along the top, then enter the stock symbol MDT (for Medtronic) in the "Quotes & Research" box and hit "Go". Now, from the menu on the left, click on "Compare Companies"; this site will enable you to compare the performance of Medtronic, Inc. to some of its close competitors. Select any three companies from the list provided (e.g., St. Jude Medical), then choose "Fundamentals" and hit the "Compare" key. Briefly review the comparative information provided and answer the following questions:
    a. Of the four stocks shown (Medtronic and the three firms you selected), which one has the best 12-month return? Which one has the poorest?
    b. Which stock has the best total 5-year return?
    c. Rank the four stocks (from best to worst) in terms of their 1-year income growth rates (%).
    d. Which stock has the highest annual EPS (earnings per share)?
    e. Which stock pays the most in annual dividends?
    f. Which stock has the highest market cap? Which has the lowest?
    g. Which stock is currently trading at the highest market price; which is trading at the lowest price?
    h. Based on the information shown, if you had to select ONE of these four stocks, which would it be? Briefly explain why.

11. **Use Worksheet 11.2** to help Rebecca and Andrew Cook, a married couple in their early 30s, evaluate their securities portfolio, which includes the following holdings:

1. *Adams Express* (NYSE—stock symbol: ADX): 100 shares bought in December 1994 for $18 per share (stock had a 3 for 2 split in 2000, so the Cooks now own 150 shares of ADX).

2. *Fannie Mae* (NYSE—stock symbol: FNM): 250 shares purchased in December 1995 for $24.25 per share (stock had a 4 for 1 stock split in 1996, so the Cooks now own 1000 shares of FNM).

3. *Bed Bath and Beyond* (Nasdaq—stock symbol: BBBY): 150 shares purchased in 1997 at $8.75 per share (stock has since had *two* 2 for 1 stock splits, so the Cooks now own 600 shares of BBBY).

4. *Starbucks* (Nasdaq—stock symbol: SBUX): 200 shares purchased in 1998 at $15.25 per share (stock split 2 for 1 in 1999, so the Cooks now own 400 shares of SBUX).

5. The Cooks also have $8,000 in a 3-year *bank CD* that pays 6.15% annual interest.

   a. Based on the latest quotes obtained from *The Wall Street Journal*, or elsewhere, complete Worksheet 11.2.

   b. What's the total amount the Cooks invested in these securities, the annual income they now receive, and the latest market value of their investments?

APPLYING PERSONAL FINANCE

The Annual Report to Stockholders

The investments business is one where information is used to make the best decision. One excellent source of information about companies is the companies themselves—in particular, the annual reports they issue to their stockholders. The purpose of this project is for you *to familiarize yourself with a company's annual stockholders' report.*

The annual report is a document that provides financial and operating information about a company to its owners, the stockholders. What you have to do in this project is obtain a copy of the latest annual report for an NYSE, AMEX, or Nasdaq stock—perhaps a stock you would like to own. (Copies can be found in many public and college libraries, local brokerage offices, or on the Internet.) Carefully study the annual report and prepare a *Corporate Profile* of the firm you selected using the following categories:

a. Name of company
b. Current market price of the stock
c. Location of corporate headquarters
d. Brief description of the company
e. Brief history of the company
f. Major products
g. Sales and profit summaries
h. Other relevant financial ratios and measures
i. Recent developments and future plans

Note: Confine your Corporate Profile report to *two pages or less*; use the above category headings directly in your report—that is, start each element of the report with the specific heading.

Based on the annual report and your Corporate Profile, what do you like or dislike about the company and, all things considered, do you think the stock would make a good investment candidate? Explain.

CONTEMPORARY CASE APPLICATIONS

11.1   The Thomsons Struggle with Two Investment Goals

Like a lot of married couples, Steve and Barbara Thomson are trying their best to deal with not one, but two very important investment objectives: (1) building up an *education fund* to put their two children through college; and (2) building up a *retirement nest egg* for themselves. Their children are now 10 and 12 years old, and the oldest will be starting college in 6 years. Steve and Barbara want to have $40,000 set aside *for each child* by the time each one starts college (so they have 6 years remaining for one child and 8 with the other). As far as their retirement plans are concerned, the Thomsons both hope to retire at age 65, in 20 years. Both Steve and Barbara work and together they currently earn about $90,000 a year.

Six years ago, the Thomsons started a college fund by investing $6,000 a year in short-term CDs. That fund is now worth $45,000—enough to put one of the kids through any one of the in-state colleges. In addition, they have $50,000, which they received from an inheritance, invested in several mutual funds, and another $20,000 in a tax-sheltered retirement account. Steve and Barbara feel they'll easily be able to continue to put away $6,000 a year for the next 20 years—in fact, Barbara thinks they'll be able to put away even more, particularly after the children are out of school. The Thomsons are pretty conservative investors and feel they can probably earn about 8 percent on their money. (You can ignore taxes in this exercise.)

Questions

1. Using **Worksheet 11.1,** determine whether the Thomsons have enough money *right now* to meet the educational needs of their children. That is, will the $45,000 they've accumulated so far be enough to put their children through school, given they can invest their money at 8 percent? Remember, they want to have $40,000 set aside for *each* child by the time each one starts college.
2. Regarding their retirement nest egg, assuming *no additions* are made to either the $50,000 they now have in mutual funds or the $20,000 in the retirement account, how much would these investments be worth in 20 years, given they can earn 8 percent?
3. Now, if they can invest $6,000 a year for the next 20 years and apply all that to their retirement nest egg, how much would they be able to accumulate given their 8 percent rate of return?
4. How do you think the Thomsons are doing with regard to meeting their twin investment objectives? Explain.

11.2   Col Takes Stock of His Securities

Col Thomas is 32 years old, single, and works as a designer for a major architectural firm. He is well paid and over time has built up a sizable portfolio of investments. He considers himself an aggressive investor and, because he has no dependents to worry about, likes to invest in high-risk–high-return securities. His records show the following:

1. In 1997, Col bought 100 shares of *America Online* (NYSE; symbol: AOL) at $75 a share—the stock has since split 2 for 1 *four times*, so he now owns 1,600 shares of the stock.
2. In 1998 he bought 250 shares of *WD-40 Co.* (Nasdaq; symbol: WDFC) at $30 a share.
3. In 1997, Col bought 200 shares of *Franklin Resources* (NYSE; symbol: BEN) at $52 a share—Col now owns 400 shares, as the stock has since split 2 for 1.
4. In early 1999, he bought 450 shares of *Fisher Scientific* (NYSE; symbol: FSH) at $17.50 a share.

5. Also in 1999, Col bought 200 shares of *Emulex Corp.* (Nasdaq; symbol: EMLX) at $32 a share—he now owns 800 shares of the stock, as it has had *two* 2 for 1 stock splits.
6. He has $8,000 in a 4-percent money market mutual fund.

Every three months or so, Col prepares a complete, up-to-date inventory of his investment holdings.

Questions

1. Use a form like **Worksheet 11.2** to prepare a complete inventory of Col's Investment holdings. (*Note:* Look in the latest issue of *The Wall Street Journal* to find the most recent market value of the five *stocks* in Col's portfolio.)
2. What is your overall assessment of Col's investment portfolio? Does it appear that his personal net worth is improving as a result of his investments?
3. Based on the worksheet you prepared in Question 1, do you see any securities that you think Col should consider selling?

MASTER THE MARKETS!

Note: Web addresses change frequently, so you may need to determine the home page and do a site search to find the page or topic that's referenced.

1. **www.ftc.gov/bcp/conline/edcams/investment/index.html**
   Does that investment offer sound too good to be true? Then it probably is! Search the Federal Trade Commission's site for investment alerts, scams, and frauds. Then click the links to other Investment Information Resources. While you're there, scroll down to Online Quiz and click on "Test Your Investment I.Q."
2. **smartmoney.com/maps**
   What color is the market today? Pull up SmartMoney's fantastic Map of the Market to view the performance of over 600 companies at once! Click on the map's Control Panel to see the top 5 market gainers or losers for various time periods. Use this wonderful tool to create a map of your own portfolio.
3. **www.nyse.com/about/education/curriculum.html**
   Educate yourself about the markets and investments. The New York Stock Exchange presents seven chapters of material in their curriculum entitled "You and the Investment Word." Work your way through such topics as *How the NYSE Operates, Why Stock Prices Go Up and Down,* and *Protecting the Markets.* Worksheets follow each chapter to help you test your knowledge.
4. **www.gomez.com**
   Find the broker who's right for you. Click on "Expert Rankings" and at "Choose an Industry," select "Broker." Sort the list according to your needs, read the reviews on the brokers which interest you, and let Gomez help you find the broker who best suits your investing style.
5. **www.investorguide.com**
   Take charge of your own investing! The InvestorGuide Web site was designed specifically to provide a one-stop site for the needs of Internet investors. Find the latest news, research your investments, or link to the homepages of over 6000 companies. Connect with other investors at Investorville or consult the Answer Center for answers to hundreds of commonly asked questions.

6. **schwabwomen.com**

   Visit the site designed with women in mind. Schwab addresses the hurdles and pitfalls some women investors face. Consult their Life Event Series to find such topics as "Changing Jobs," "Before and After a Divorce," and "Raising Money-Wise Children."

7. **www.ino.com**

   Interested in options? Visit INO.com, the largest, all-encompassing Web site for futures, options, equities, and foreign exchange traders. Read up on the latest news or join in the discussion forum.

8. **www.fool.com**

   Learn investing wisdom from the Fool. Go to Fool's School and work your way through the 13 Steps to Investing Foolishly. Tap into the Fool's stock research information or learn more about investing strategies, retirement, or personal finance.

9. **wps.fidelity.com/publicsector/participants/rp/keythings.htm**

   Learn from the master! Let Peter Lynch advise you on *Key Things Every Investor Should Know*. Polish off your learning session by taking the quiz at the end and reading through his informative answers.

Just for Fun!

10. **fantasystockmarket.com**

    Trade for free with $100,000 Fantasy Dollars! Let Fantasy Stock Market track your portfolio and rank you against the other players. Even better, create a league for your class. See how your returns compare with the others in your league, and then see how your league stacks up against the other leagues.

11. **nyse.com/floor/floor.html**

    Visit the trading floor of the New York Stock Exchange, the largest equities marketplace in the world! Click on "Anatomy of a Trade" for a step-by-step account of how trades are executed or "On the Floor" for a panorama of the trading floor. Which NYSE company has been listed the longest? Find out at "Listed Company FAQs."

Chapter 12

Investing in Stocks and Bonds

LEARNING GOALS

LG1.   Describe the various types of risks to which investors are exposed, as well as the sources of return.

LG2.   Know how to search for an acceptable investment, based on risk, return, and yield.

LG3.   Discuss the merits of investing in common stock and be able to distinguish among the different types of stocks.

LG4.   Become familiar with the various measures of performance and how to use them in putting a value on stocks.

LG5.   Describe different types of bonds and note how these securities are used as investment vehicles.

LG6.   Distinguish between preferred stocks and convertible securities, and note the investment merits of each.

Internet Surfer Wipes Out

Jill Kessler, a 23-year-old Midwestern grad student majoring in finance, started investing when her dad gave her some stock when she was 11. She loved watching her portfolio grow, adding to it from summer job earnings.

After playing it safe with blue chip stocks and mutual finds, Jill decided that she had learned enough to take more risk. She loved surfing online technology stock discussion groups and jumped at a tip to buy into a 2-year-old wireless technology company. It sounded so good that she sold some of her mutual funds and put 25 percent of her portfolio into the stock. Afraid she would miss out if she didn't buy quickly, Jill skipped her usual in-depth research. Although her dad cautioned her to be very wary of this speculative type of investment, she felt she was ready to take on more risk. While he agreed she could indeed handle more risk in her portfolio at this point in her life, he was not happy with the way she planned to do it.

To Jill's dismay, this company was a loser. In fact, the poster who first brought the stock to the message boards was an employee. He hyped the stock, painting a very optimistic picture about the future for the company's main product. He failed to mention that the patent hadn't been issued, and soon after Jill bought the stock another company with a similar product patented the technology first.

Jill learned her lesson the hard way, losing a big chunk of the portfolio that she'd been building for over 10 years. It would take a while to recoup her losses. She vowed *never* to invest without doing her homework first, especially when the stock tips come from anonymous investors. In Chapter 12 you'll learn how to evaluate stocks and bonds so that you too can be an informed investor.

The Risks and Rewards of Investing [LG1, LG2]

Most rational investors are motivated to buy or sell securities based on the security's expected (or anticipated) return—buy if the return looks good, sell if it doesn't. Of course, it's a lot more complex than that, but this statement pretty much describes the role that *return* plays in the investment decision-making process. A security's return, however, is just part of the story, for you cannot consider the return on an investment without also looking at its *risk*—the chance that the actual return from an investment may differ from (fall short of) what was expected. Generally speaking, you'd expect riskier investments to provide higher levels of return. Otherwise, what incentive is there for an investor to risk his or her capital? These two concepts of risk and return are of vital concern to investors and as such, before we take up the issue of investing in stocks and bonds, we'll look more closely at the risks of investing and the various components of return. Equally important, we'll see how these two components (risk and return) can be used together to find potentially attractive investment vehicles.

THE RISKS OF INVESTING

business risk
The degree of uncertainty associated with a firm's earnings and consequent ability to pay interest and dividends.

As noted previously, when selecting investments, you should look at potential returns and the level of perceived risk to which the investment is exposed. The fact is, just about any type of investment is subject to one type of risk or another—some more than others. The basic types of investment risk are business risk, financial risk, market risk, purchasing power risk, interest rate risk, liquidity risk, and event risk. Obviously, other things being equal, you'd like to reduce your exposure to these risks as much as possible.

BUSINESS RISK. When you invest in a company, you may have to face up to the possibility that the firm will fail to maintain sales and profits, or even stay in business. Such failure is due either to economic or industry factors or, as is more often the case, to poor decisions on the part of management. In a general sense, this is **business risk**; it may be thought of as the degree of uncertainty surrounding the firm's earnings and subsequent ability to meet principal and interest payments on time. Companies that are subject to high degrees of business risk generally experience wide fluctuations in sales, have widely erratic earnings, and can, in fact, experience substantial operating losses every now and then.

financial risk
A type of investment risk associated with the mix of debt and equity financing used by the issuing firm.

FINANCIAL RISK. **Financial risk** relates to the amount of debt used to finance the firm. Look to the company's balance sheet to get a handle on a firm's financial risk. As a rule, companies that have little or no long-term debt are fairly low in financial risk. This is particularly so if a company has a healthy earnings picture as well. The problem with debt financing is that it creates principal and interest obligations that have to be met regardless of how much profit the company is generating. As with business risk, financial risk can lead to failure (as in the case of bankruptcy), or a rate of return that is sharply below your expectations.

market risk
A type of investment risk associated with factors such as changes in political, economic, and social conditions and investor tastes and preferences that may cause the market price of a security to change.

MARKET RISK. **Market risk** results from the behavior of investors in the securities markets. The fact is, prices of stocks and bonds will sometimes change even though business and financial risks, and other intrinsic factors, stay about the same. Such changes may have little to do with the securities themselves but instead are due to changes in political, economic, and social conditions or in investor tastes and preferences. Essentially, market risk is reflected in the *price volatility* of a security—the more volatile the price of a security, the greater its perceived market risk.

purchasing power risk
A type of risk, resulting from possible changes in price levels, that can have a significant effect on investment returns.

PURCHASING POWER RISK. Possible changes in price levels within the economy also result in risk. In periods of rising prices (inflation), the purchasing power of the dollar declines. This means that a smaller quantity of goods and services can be purchased with a given number of dollars. An awareness of **purchasing power risk** and changes in purchasing power allows investors to select investments that are best suited for a given price level environment. In general, investments whose values tend to move with general price levels (like stocks or real estate) are most profitable during periods of rising prices, whereas those providing fixed returns (like bonds) are preferred during periods of declining price levels/inflation.

fixed-income securities
Securities such as preferred stocks and bonds that offer purchasers fixed periodic returns.

INTEREST RATE RISK. **Fixed-income securities**, which include preferred stocks and bonds, offer investors a fixed periodic return and, as such, are most affected by **interest rate risk**. As interest rates change, the prices of these securities fluctuate, decreasing with rising interest rates and increasing with falling rates. For example, the prices of fixed-income securities drop when interest rates increase, in order to provide investors with rates of return competitive with those of securities offering higher levels of interest income.

interest rate risk
A type of risk, resulting from changing market interest rates, that mainly affects fixed-income securities.

Changes in interest rates are the result of fluctuations in the supply of or demand for money. These fluctuations are caused by various economic actions of the government or the interactions of business firms, consumers, and financial institutions.

LIQUIDITY RISK. The risk of not being able to liquidate an investment conveniently and at a reasonable price is called **liquidity** (or **marketability**) **risk**. The liquidity of a given investment vehicle is important because it provides investors with a safety valve in case they ever have to get out. In general, investment vehicles traded in *thin markets*, in which supply and demand are small, tend to be less liquid than those traded in *broad markets*. However, to be liquid, an investment must be easily salable at a reasonable price. One can generally enhance the liquidity of an investment merely by cutting its price. For example, a security recently purchased for $1,000 would not be viewed as highly liquid if it could be sold only at a significantly reduced price, such as $500. Vehicles such as mutual funds, or the stocks and bonds of major companies listed on the New York Stock Exchange, are generally highly liquid; others, such as an isolated parcel of raw land in rural Georgia, are not.

liquidity risk
A type of risk associated with the inability to liquidate an investment conveniently and at a reasonable price.

EVENT RISK. More than just a buzz word used by the financial media, **event risk** is real, and it can have a direct and dramatic impact on investment return. Basically, it occurs when something substantial happens to a company and that event, in itself, has a sudden impact on the company's financial condition. Event risk goes beyond business and financial risk, and it doesn't necessarily mean the company or market is doing poorly. Instead, it involves an event that is largely (or totally) unexpected, and which has a significant and usually immediate effect on the underlying value of an investment. A good example of event risk was the action by the Food and Drug Administration several years ago to halt the use of silicone breast implants. The share price of Dow Chemical—the dominant producer of this product—was quickly affected (in a negative fashion) as a result of this single event! Event risk can take many forms, although fortunately its impact tends to be confined to certain companies, securities, or segments of the market.

event risk
The risk that some major, unexpected event will occur, leading to a sudden, substantial change in the financial condition of a firm; for example, a company could go through a leveraged buy-out.

 At RiskGrades (**www.riskgrades.com**) you can compare the risk of a particular stock or your portfolio with the overall market.

THE RETURNS FROM INVESTING

Any investment vehicle—be it a share of stock, a bond, a piece of real estate, or a stock option—has just two basic sources of return: *current income* and *capital gains*. Some investments offer only one source of return (for example, options provide only capital gains), but many offer both income and capital gains, which together make up what is known as the *total return* from an investment. Of course, where both elements of return are present, the relative importance of each will vary among investments. Whereas current income is more important with bonds, capital gains usually make up a larger portion of total return in the case of common stocks.

CURRENT INCOME. Current income is generally received with some degree of regularity over the course of a year, and may take the form of dividends on stock, interest from bonds, or rents from real estate. People who invest to obtain income look for investment vehicles that will provide regular and predictable patterns of income. Preferred stocks and bonds, which are expected to pay known amounts at specified times (quarterly or semiannually, for example), are usually viewed as good income investments.

CAPITAL GAINS. The other type of return available from investments is capital appreciation (or growth), which is reflected in an increase in the market value of the investment vehicle. Capital gains occur when you're able to sell a security for more than you paid for it, or when your security holdings go up in value. Investments that provide greater growth potential through capital appreciation normally have lower levels of current income, because the firm achieves its growth by reinvesting its earnings instead of paying dividends out to the owners. Many common stocks, for example, are acquired for their capital gains potential.

INTEREST-ON-INTEREST: AN IMPORTANT ELEMENT OF RETURN

Question: When does an 8 percent investment end up yielding only 5 percent? Answer: Probably more often than you think! Of course, it can happen when investment performance fails to live up to expectations. But it can also happen even when everything goes right. That is, so long as at least part of the return from an investment involves the periodic receipt of current income (such as dividends or interest payments), that income has to be *reinvested* at a given rate of return in order to achieve the yield you thought you had going into the investment. To see why that's so, consider an investor who buys an 8 percent U.S. Treasury bond and holds it to maturity, a period of 20 years. Each year the bondholder receives $80 in interest, and at maturity, the $1,000 in principal is repaid. There is no loss in capital, no default; everything is paid right on time. Yet this sure-fire investment ends up yielding only 5 percent. Why? Because the investor failed to reinvest the annual interest payments he was receiving. By not plowing back all the investment earnings, the bondholder failed to earn any *interest-on-interest*.

Now take a look at Exhibit 12.1. It shows the three elements of return for our 8 percent, 20-year bond: (1) the recovery of principal, or capital gain, if any is earned; (2) periodic interest income; and (3) the interest-on-interest earned from reinvesting the periodic interest payments. Observe that because the bond was originally bought at par ($1,000), you start off with an 8 percent investment. Where you end up depends on what you do with the profits (interest earnings) from this investment. If you don't reinvest the interest income, you'll end up on the 5 percent line.

To move to the 8 percent line, you have to earn interest-on-interest from your investments. Specifically, because you started out with an 8 percent investment, that's the rate of return you have to earn when reinvesting your income. The rate of return you start with, in effect, is the required, or minimum, reinvestment rate. Put your investment profits to work at that rate and you'll earn the rate of return you set out to; fail to do so and your return will decline accordingly. And keep in mind that even though we used a bond in our illustration, so long as current income is part of an investment's return, *this same principle applies to any type of long-term investment vehicle*. It's just as relevant to common stocks and mutual funds as it is to long-term bond instruments. This notion of earning interest-on-interest is what the market refers to as a *fully compounded rate of return*. It's an important concept because you can't start reaping the full potential from your investments until you start earning a fully compounded return on your money.

Thus, if periodic investment income is a part of your investment return, the reinvestment of that income and interest-on-interest are matters you're going to have to deal with. In fact, *interest-on-interest is a particularly important element of return for investment programs that involve a lot of current income*. This is so because, in contrast to capital gains, current income has to be reinvested by the individual investor. (With capital gains, the investment vehicle itself is doing the reinvesting, all automatically.) It follows, therefore, that if your investment program tends to lean toward income-oriented securities, then interest-on-interest—and the continued reinvestment of income—will play an important role in defining the amount of investment success you have. However, as explained in the accompanying *Money in Action* box, there are other factors that also affect investment success—like whether it's a man or woman doing the investing.

THE RISK-RETURN TRADE-OFF

Generally speaking, the amount of risk associated with a given investment vehicle is directly related to its expected return. This universal rule of investing means that if you want a higher level of return, you will probably have to accept a greater exposure to risk. Thus investors should expect to be compensated for taking higher levels of risk by earning higher rates of return. But while higher risk generally is associated with higher levels of return, this relationship doesn't necessarily work in the opposite direction. That is, you can't just invest in a high-risk security and expect to automatically earn a high rate of return. Unfortunately, it doesn't work that way—risk simply isn't that predictable!

 EXHIBIT 12.1

THREE ELEMENTS OF RETURN FOR AN 8 PERCENT, 20-YEAR BOND

As seen here, the long-term return from an investment (in this case, a bond) is made up of three parts: recovery of capital, current income, and interest-on-interest; of the three components, interest-on-interest is particularly important, especially for long-term investments.

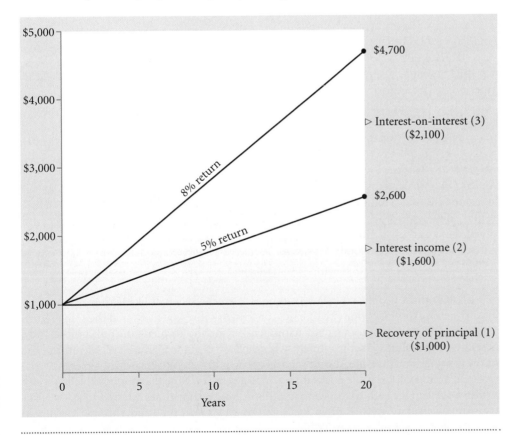

MONEY IN ACTION

Learn from the Ladies

For years men were thought to have an edge when it came to investing. Of course, until fairly recently women were not as likely to take charge of their own investments. But look at the results of two recent studies:

- The National Association of Investors Corporation surveyed returns of all-male and all-female investment clubs in 1999. The women's groups annual returns averaged 32.1 percent—almost 10 points higher than their male counterparts.
- University of California at Davis finance professors Terrance Odean and Brad Barber studied the investment results of 35,000 households over a 6-year period. Portfolios managed by women earned returns 1.4 percent higher than male-managed portfolios, after adjustments for risk differences.

Why do women earn better returns? Lisa Kraynak, executive vice president of iVillage Money Life, an investment site for women investors, believes that women do more research. "Women like to get a lot of information, a lot of people's opinions," she says.

Women invest for the long term, whereas men are looking to make a quick buck. The Odean/Barber study considers male investor overconfidence a major fault. Men tend to trade stocks more often than women as they chase profits—their buy-and-sell rate is 45 percent higher per year than women's. Single men are even more active, trading 67 percent more than single women. The more you trade, the more your commissions erode any gains.

But commissions alone don't necessarily lower returns. Going in and out of the market isn't good for anyone, male or female. A discount brokerage firm's research showed that the most active traders averaged 11.4 percent annual returns, compared with the 16.4 percent average return for all households surveyed.

Active traders may be out of the market when their stocks post good returns. For example, an Ibbotson Associates study shows if you invested $1 in stocks at the end of 1979 and left it alone until year-end 1999, you'd have $26.82. If during that time period you took the dollar out of the market during the 15 months when stocks performed best, you'd have only $6.81. "It's like changing lanes all the time and finding out at the end you had to pay a price for each time," explains Mr. Odean.

Women take a long-term view for a good reason: they live longer than men. They also have a higher chance of becoming a single parent. As a result, they have a greater incentive to manage their money wisely to achieve financial security during retirement.

"Some guys I know are always telling me to buy this one and sell that one. I've learned not to pay attention to them," says Bette Moore, a 56-year-old Florida investor. Doing it her way has paid off: Her portfolio has doubled in just 2 years to over six figures.

Sources: adapted from Harriet Johnson Brackey, "Study: Female Investors Better: Women Don't Seem to Buy, Sell as Often as Men Do," *Dallas Morning News*, July 31, 2000, p. 4D; Mark Ingebretsen, "Stock Tip: Women's Ways Work," *Access*, July 16, 2000, p. 6; and R. Douglas Van Eaton, "The Psychology Behind Common Investor Mistakes," *AAII Journal*, April 2000, pp. 2–5.

---

risk-free rate of return
The rate of return on short-term government securities, such as Treasury bills, that have no default risk or maturity premiums.

Because most people are believed to be risk averse—they dislike taking risks—some incentive for taking risks must be offered. If a low-risk investment offered the same return as a high-risk one, investors would naturally opt for the former—or, put another way, investors would choose the investment with the least risk for a given level of return. The direct relationship between risk and return is shown in Exhibit 12.2, which generalizes the risk-return tradeoff for some popular investment vehicles. Note that it is possible to receive a positive return for zero risk, such as at point A; this is sometimes referred to as the **risk-free rate of return**, which is often measured by the return on a short-term government security, such as a 90-day Treasury bill.

EXHIBIT 12.2

THE RISK-RETURN RELATIONSHIP

In the field of investments, there generally is a direct relationship between risk and return: the more risk you face, the greater the return you should expect to generate from the investment.

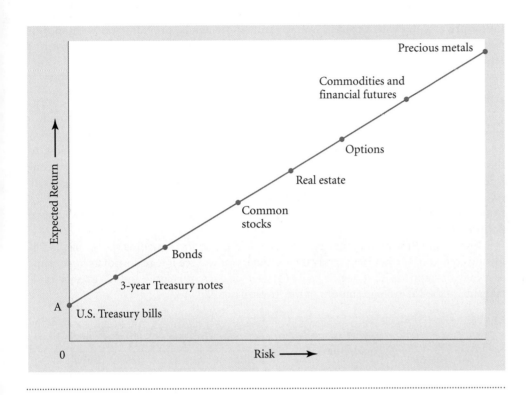

WHAT MAKES A GOOD INVESTMENT?

In keeping with the preceding risk-return discussion, it follows that the value of any investment depends on the amount of return it is expected to provide relative to the amount of perceived risk involved. This basic rule applies to any type of investment vehicle, be it stocks, bonds, convertibles, options, real estate, or commodities. In this respect, they should all be treated the same.

FUTURE RETURN. In the field of investments, the only return that matters is *the expected future return*. Aside from the help they can provide in getting a handle on future income, past returns are of little value to investors—after all, it is not what the security did last year that matters, but, rather, what it is expected to do next year.

Earlier, we defined returns as being made up of current income and capital gains. To get an idea of the future return on an investment, we must formulate expectations of its future current income and future capital appreciation. To illustrate, assume you are thinking of buying some stock in Rose Colored Glasses, Inc. (RCG). By reviewing several financial reports, you have come up with an estimate of the future dividends and price behavior of RCG as follows:

Expected average annual dividends,
2001–03 $2.15 a share
Expected market price of the stock,
2003 $95.00 a share

Because the stock is now selling for $60 a share, the difference between its current and expected future market price ($95 − $60) represents the amount of *capital gains* you can expect to receive over the next three years—in this case, $35 a share. The projected future price, along with expected average annual dividends, provides you with an estimate of the *stock's future income stream;* what you need now is a way to measure *expected return.*

APPROXIMATE YIELD. Finding the exact rate of return on this (or any) investment involves a highly complex mathematical procedure. However, you can obtain a reasonably close estimation of expected return by computing the investment's *approximate yield*. This measure provides a rate of return (yield) that is remarkably close to the exact figure; and it is relatively easy to use. Best of all, this barometer of return considers not only current income and capital gains, but interest-on-interest as well. As such, *approximate yield provides a measure of the fully compounded rate of return* from an investment and, in so doing, represents a viable measure of expected return performance.

The method for finding the approximate yield on an investment is shown in the following equation. If you briefly study the formula, you will see it is really not as formidable as it may first appear. All it does is relate (1) average current income and (2) average capital gains to the (3) average amount of the investment.

$$\text{Approximate yield} = \frac{\text{Average annual current income} + \left[\dfrac{\text{Future price of investment} - \text{Current price of investment}}{\text{Number of years in investment period}}\right]}{\left[\dfrac{\text{Current price of investment} + \text{Future price of investment}}{2}\right]}$$

$$= \frac{CI + \left[\dfrac{FP - CP}{N}\right]}{\left[\dfrac{CP + FP}{2}\right]}$$

where

CI = *average* annual current income (amount you expect to receive annually from dividends, interest, or rent)
FP = expected future price of investment
CP = current market price of investment
N = investment period (length of time, in years, that you expect to hold the investment)

To illustrate, let's use the Rose Colored Glasses example again. Given the average annual dividends (CI) of $2.15, current stock price (CP) of $60, future stock price (FP) of $95, and an investment period (N) of 3 years (you expect to hold the stock from 2001 through 2003), you can use this equation to find the expected approximate yield on RCG as follows:

$$\text{Approximate yield} = \frac{\$2.15 + \left[\dfrac{\$95 - \$60}{3}\right]}{\left[\dfrac{\$60 + \$95}{2}\right]}$$

$$= \frac{\$2.15 + \left[\dfrac{\$35}{3}\right]}{\left[\dfrac{\$155}{2}\right]}$$

$$= \frac{\$2.15 + \$11.67}{\$77.50} = \frac{\$13.82}{\$77.50}$$

$$= \underline{\underline{17.8\%}}$$

In this case, if your forecasts of annual dividends and capital gains hold up, an investment in Rose Colored Glasses should provide a return of around 17.8 percent per year.

Whether you should consider RCG a viable investment candidate depends on how this level of expected return stacks up to the amount of risk you must assume. Suppose you have decided the stock is moderately risky. To determine whether the expected rate of return on this investment will be satisfactory, you can compare it to some benchmark. One of the best is the rate of return you can expect from a *risk-free* security, such as a *U.S. Treasury bill*. The idea is that the return on a *risky* security should be greater than that available on a risk-free security (this is the concept underlying the graph in Exhibit 12.2). If, for example, U.S. T-bills are yielding, say, 5 or 6 percent, then you'd want to receive considerably more—perhaps 12 to 15 percent—to justify your investment in a moderately risky security like RCG. In essence, the 12 to 15 percent is your **desired rate of return**—it is the minimum rate of return you feel you should receive in compensation for the amount of risk you must assume. *An investment should be considered acceptable only if it's expected to generate a rate of return that meets (or exceeds) your desired rate of return.* In the case of RCG, the stock *should* be considered a viable investment candidate, because it more than provides the minimum or desired rate of return. In short, even after factoring in the perceived exposure to risk, the stock still generates a sufficiently attractive expected return—one that *exceeds* the amount you deserve, based on the risks involved.

desired rate of return
The minimum rate of return an investor feels should be earned in compensation for the amount of risk assumed.

CONCEPT CHECK

12-1. Describe the various types of risk to which investors are exposed. What is meant by the risk-return tradeoff? What is the *risk-free rate of return*?

12-2. Briefly describe the two basic sources of return to investors. What is interest-on-interest, and why is it such an important element of return?

12-3. What is the *approximate yield* measure and how would it be used to make an investment decision? What is the *desired rate of return* and how would it be used to make an investment decision?

Investing in Common Stock [LG3, LG4]

Common stocks appeal to investors for a variety of reasons. To some, investing in stocks is a way to hit it big if the issue shoots up in price; to others, it is the level of current income they offer. In fact, given the size and diversity of the stock market, it is safe to say that no matter what the investment objective, there are common stocks available to fit the bill. Not surprisingly, common stocks are a popular form of investing, used by literally millions of individuals and a variety of financial institutions.

The basic investment attribute of a share of common stock is that it enables the investor to participate in the profits of the firm, which is how it derives its value. Every shareholder is, in effect, a part-owner of the firm and, as such, is entitled to a piece of its profit. However, this claim on income is not without its limitations, for common stockholders are really the **residual owners** of the company, meaning they are entitled to dividend income and a prorated share of the company's earnings only after all the other obligations of the firm have been met. Equally important, as residual owners, *holders of common stock have no guarantee that they will ever receive any return on their investment.*

residual owners
Shareholders of the company, they are entitled to dividend income and a share of the company's profits only after all of the firm's other obligations have been met.

COMMON STOCK AS A FORM OF INVESTMENT

Given the underlying nature of common stocks, when the market is strong, investors can generally expect to benefit from steady price appreciation. A good example is the performance in 1999, when the market, as measured by the Dow Jones Industrial Average (DJIA) went up more than 25%. But 1999 was even better for tech stocks and the Nasdaq market, which was up an incredible 85% for the year. Unfortunately, when markets falter, so do investor returns. A recent example of such behavior was the 48% drop that occurred in the Nasdaq market from March through early December of 2000. But perhaps the most dramatic example of a market gone bad is the hair-raising experience of 1987. In that year, stock prices had shot up almost 30 percent in the first six months, only to experience a terrible crash on October 19. That day was not just another bad day in the market—it was the *worst* day in the market's history. Stock prices, as measured by the DJIA, fell 508 points on volume of over 600 million shares. The day set a number of records, including the largest point drop, the largest 1-day volume of shares traded, and the largest percentage decline (23 percent), almost twice the previous single-day record.

Ten years later, almost to the day, it happened again. On October 27, 1997, the Dow Jones Industrials dropped 554 points (a new record) on volume of 685 million shares (also a record). In percentage terms, however, the market ended the day down just over 7 percent, which wasn't even close to the record. But unlike the 1987 crash, this one didn't last long: The market recovered all its losses *within two weeks*, and within two months the October decline was little more than a memory. In stark contrast, it took more than $2\frac{1}{2}$ years for the market to recover from the 1987 crash. Then, as the market entered a new century, *an even bigger drop* occurred, on April 14, 2000, when the DJIA plunged an eye-popping 617 points. That decline, however, amounted to a fall of "only" 5.5 percent and hardly compares with the crash of '87, which in percentage terms was about four times as bad!

Fortunately, days such as October 19, 1987, and April 14, 2000, are the exceptions rather than the rule. More often than not, the stock market offers attractive returns, rather than just risk and wild price volatility. Take a look at Exhibit 12.3. It shows the behavior of the market from 1982 through mid-year 2000—a period that marks one of the greataest bull markets on record. This market run, which began in August 1982, has seen the Dow soar more than 1,400 percent. Among its many achievements, this market stands out because of the extent to which it has moved in a relatively short period of time. That is, the Dow has gone from less than 1,000 points to over 11,000—and most of that advance occurred in the five-year period from 1995 to 1999. Clearly, it's this kind of resiliency and overall market performance that explains the appeal of common stocks.

ISSUERS OF COMMON STOCK. Shares of common stock can be issued by any corporation in any line of business. Even so, although all corporations have stockholders, not

 EXHIBIT 12.3

THE GREAT BULL MARKET OF 1982–2000

One of the greatest bull markets ever began on August 12, 1982, with the Dow at 777, and has continued for more than 18 years. It was strong enough to survive three market crashes (one in 1987, another in 1997, and a third in April, 2000) and one mild recession/ bear market (in 1990); indeed, this bull market had only two down years (one in 1990, and again in 2000), as it marched to a high of more than 11,000.

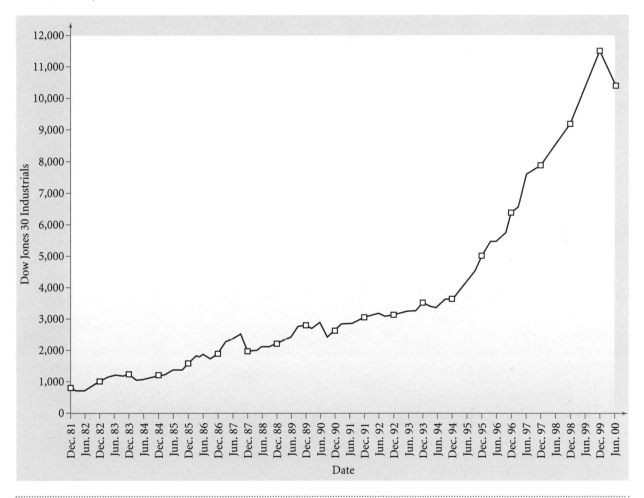

all of them have publicly traded shares. The stocks of interest to us in this book are the so-called *publicly traded issues*—the shares that are readily available to the general public and that are bought and sold in the open market. Just about every facet of American industry is represented in the stock market. You can buy shares in public utilities, airlines, mining concerns, manufacturing firms, online companies and retail organizations, or in financial institutions like banks and insurance companies.

Aside from the initial distribution of common stock when the corporation is formed, subsequent sales of additional shares may be made through a procedure known as a *public offering*. In a public offering, the corporation, working with its underwriter, simply offers the investing public a certain number of shares of its stock at a certain price. Exhibit 12.4 depicts the announcement for such an offering. Note in this case that *Community Health*

 **EXHIBIT 12.4**

AN ANNOUNCEMENT OF A NEW COMMON STOCK ISSUE

Here the company is issuing 18 million shares of stock at a price of just over $28 per share. For Community Health Systems, that will mean some $500 million in new capital. Note that in addition to selling stock in the United States, 3.6 million shares were sold offshore (outside the U.S.) to foreign investors—a tactic that's become fairly common today as companies go global in their search for capital.

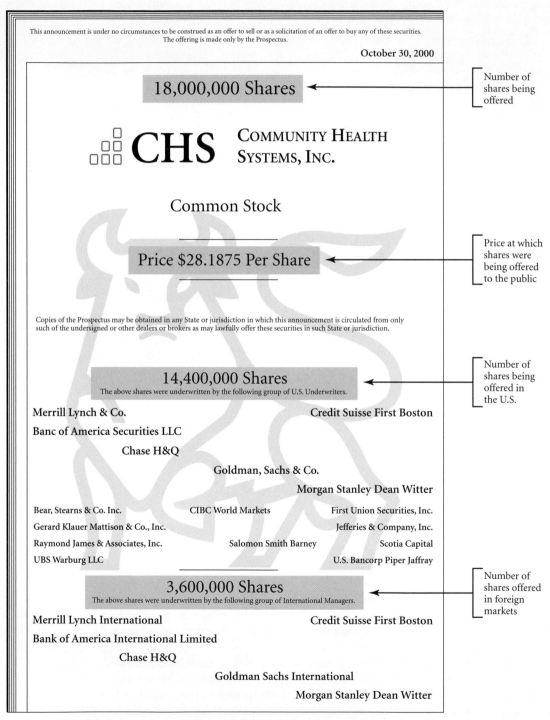

This announcement is under no circumstances to be construed as an offer to sell or as a solicitation of an offer to buy any of these securities. The offering is made only by the Prospectus.

October 30, 2000

18,000,000 Shares — Number of shares being offered

CHS COMMUNITY HEALTH SYSTEMS, INC.

Common Stock

Price $28.1875 Per Share — Price at which shares were being offered to the public

Copies of the Prospectus may be obtained in any State or jurisdiction in which this announcement is circulated from only such of the undersigned or other dealers or brokers as may lawfully offer these securities in such State or jurisdiction.

14,400,000 Shares — Number of shares being offered in the U.S.
The above shares were underwritten by the following group of U.S. Underwriters.

Merrill Lynch & Co.   Credit Suisse First Boston
Banc of America Securities LLC
Chase H&Q

Goldman, Sachs & Co.
Morgan Stanley Dean Witter

Bear, Stearns & Co. Inc.   CIBC World Markets   First Union Securities, Inc.
Gerard Klauer Mattison & Co., Inc.   Jefferies & Company, Inc.
Raymond James & Associates, Inc.   Salomon Smith Barney   Scotia Capital
UBS Warburg LLC   U.S. Bancorp Piper Jaffray

3,600,000 Shares — Number of shares offered in foreign markets
The above shares were underwritten by the following group of International Managers.

Merrill Lynch International   Credit Suisse First Boston
Bank of America International Limited
Chase H&Q

Goldman Sachs International
Morgan Stanley Dean Witter

Systems, Inc. is offering 18,000,000 shares of stock at a price of $28.1875 per share. When issued, the new shares will be commingled with the outstanding shares (they are all the same class of stock), and the net result will be an increase in the number of shares outstanding.

VOTING RIGHTS. The holders of common stock normally receive *voting rights*, which means that for each share of stock held, they receive one vote. In certain instances, common stock may be designated as nonvoting at the time of issue, but this is the exception rather than the rule. Although different voting systems exist, the small stockholders need not concern themselves with them because, regardless of the system used, the chance they will be able to affect corporate control with their votes is quite slim.

Corporations have annual stockholders' meetings, at which time new directors are elected and special issues are voted on. Because most small stockholders are unable to attend these meetings, they can use a proxy to assign their votes to another person, who will vote their stock for them. A **proxy** is merely a written statement assigning voting rights to another party.

proxy
A written statement used to assign a stockholder's voting rights to another person, typically one of the directors.

BASIC TAX CONSIDERATIONS

Common stocks provide income in the form of dividends, usually paid quarterly, and/or capital gains, which occurs when the price of the stock goes up over time. As indicated in Chapter 3, from a tax perspective, it does make a difference how the investment income is earned. That is, whereas dividends are fully taxable at regular tax rates (up to 39.6 percent), capital gains are subject to a maximum tax of 20 percent, for securities held more than 12 months—or, if you're in the 15 percent tax bracket, the long-term capital gains tax rate falls to 10 percent. Thus, no matter what your "normal" tax bracket (from 15 to 39.6 percent), long-term capital gains are subject to less tax than are dividends; see Chapter 3 for details on the new capital gains tax rates.

Of course, there is no tax liability on any capital gains until the stock is actually sold (*paper gains*—that is, any price appreciation that occurs on stock that you still own—accumulate tax-free). Taxes are due on any dividends and capital gains in the year in which the dividends are received or the stock is actually sold. Thus, if you received, say, $125 in dividends in 2000, you would have to include that income on your 2000 tax return.

Here is how it all works: Assume, for example, that you just sold 100 shares of common stock for $30 per share. Also assume the stock was originally purchased two years ago for $20 per share and that during the current year you received $1.25 per share in cash dividends. For tax purposes, you would have a capital gain of $1,000—($30/share − $20/share) × 100 shares—and $125 in dividend income—$1.25/share × 100 shares. If you were in the 31 percent tax bracket, your dividends would be subject to a 31 percent tax rate (that is, $125 × .31 = $38.75 in taxes), but the capital gains you earned would be subject to a tax rate of only 20 percent, because you held the stock for more than 12 months—that is, $1000 × .20 = $200 in taxes. Thus, you'd end up paying $238.75 ($38.75 + $200.00) in taxes. Whatever you are left with would represent your after-tax income—in this case, it would be $1,125 − $238.75 = $886.25.

TYPES OF DIVIDENDS

Corporations pay dividends to their common stockholders in the form of cash and/or additional stock. *Cash dividends* are the most common. Because firms can pay dividends from earnings accumulated from previous periods, stockholders may receive dividends *even in periods when the firm shows a loss*. Cash dividends are normally distributed quarterly in an amount determined by the firm's board of directors. For example, if the directors declared a quarterly cash dividend of 50 cents a share, and you owned 200 shares of stock, you would receive a check for $100.

A popular way of assessing the amount of dividends received is to measure the stock's dividend yield. Basically, **dividend yield** is a measure of common stock dividends on a relative (percent), rather than absolute (dollar), basis—that is, the dollar amount of dividends received is related to the market price of the stock. As such, dividend yield is an indication of the rate of current income being earned on the investment. It is computed as follows:

dividend yield
The percentage return provided by the dividends paid on common stock; calculated by dividing the cash dividends paid during the year by the stock's market price.

$$\text{Dividend yield} = \frac{\text{Annual dividends received per share}}{\text{Market price per share of stock}}$$

Thus, a company that annually pays $2 per share in dividends and whose stock is trading at $50 a share will have a dividend yield of 4 percent ($2/$50 = .04). Dividend yield is widely used by income-oriented investors looking for (reasonably priced) stocks that have a long and sustained record of regularly paying higher-than-average dividends.

Occasionally the directors may declare a stock dividend as a supplement to or in place of cash dividends. **Stock dividends** represent new shares of stock being issued to existing stockholders. Although they often satisfy the needs of some investors, stock dividends really have no value, because they represent the receipt of something already owned. For example, when a firm declares a 10 percent stock dividend, each shareholder receives one-tenth of a share of stock for each share owned—in other words, a stockholder with 100 shares of stock will receive 10 new shares. Because all stockholders receive a 10 percent increase in the number of shares they own, their proportion of ownership in the firm remains unchanged.

stock dividends
New shares of stock distributed to existing stockholders as a supplement to or substitute for cash dividends.

Moreover, the total market value of the shares owned is (roughly) the same after the stock dividend as before. Why is that so? Because the price of the stock will usually fall in direct proportion to the size of a stock dividend. Thus, in our example above, a drop in price will bring the total market value of 110 shares (after the stock dividend) to about the same as the total market value of the 100 shares that existed before the dividend. Clearly, under such circumstances, the investor is right back where he started from: He's received nothing of value. The shareholder who has received a stock dividend can, of course, sell the new shares to cash out the dividend. But then the value of the stocks owned by that shareholder will be reduced—granted, he'll then own the same number of shares as before the stock dividend, but they'll be worth less.

SOME KEY MEASURES OF PERFORMANCE

Professional money managers and seasoned investors tend to use a variety of financial ratios and measures when making investment decisions, particularly when common stock is involved. They look at such things as dividend yield (mentioned earlier), book value, return on equity, earnings per share, and price/earning multiples to get a feel for the investment merits of a particular stock. In short, they use these and other ratios to help them decide whether to invest in a particular stock. Fortunately, most of the widely followed ratios can be found in published reports (like *Value Line*—an example of which is shown in Exhibit 12.5), so you don't have to compute them yourself. Even so, if you're thinking about buying a stock, or already have a position in common stock, there are a few measures of performance you'll want to keep track of. These would include book value (or book value per share), net profit margin, return on equity, earnings per share, price/earnings ratio, and beta. (Note in Exhibit 12.5 that all these ratios are reported by *Value Line*, in this case for Medtronic, Inc.)

EXHIBIT 12.5

A VALUE LINE REPORT FOR MEDTRONIC, INC.

A variety of information about a company's performance and financial condition is widely available in published reports, like the *Value Line* Report shown here for Medtronic, Inc. Note that the highlighted data (covering everything from a stock's dividend yield to its beta) represent just a small sample of what's available in these reports.

Price/earnings ratio   Dividend yield

MEDTRONIC, INC NYSE-MDT

RECENT PRICE	P/E RATIO	(Trailing: 55.8, Median: 26.0)	RELATIVE P/E RATIO	DIV'D YLD	VALUE LINE
53	49.1		3.53	0.4%	222

TIMELINESS 2 Raised 9/4/98
SAFETY 3 Lowered 3/19/93
TECHNICAL 2 Raised 3/17/00
BETA 1.15 (1.00 = Market)

Beta

2003-05 PROJECTIONS
Ann'l Total
Price Gain Return
High 65 (+25%) 6%
Low 45 (-15%) -3%

Insider Decisions
Institutional Decisions

Earnings per share (EPS)
Dividends per share
Book value per share
Net Profits ($)
Net Profit Margin (%)
Return on Equity (ROE)

BUSINESS: Medtronic, Inc. is the world's largest manufacturer of implantable biomedical devices, with sales to over 120 countries. Cardiac Rhythm Management products (bradycardia & tachycardia) accounted for 49.9% of '99 sales; Neurological and Spinal, 25.0%; Vascular products (stents), 15.8%; and Cardiac Surgery (heart valves, perfusion systems), 9.3%. Int'l business: 34.6% of '99 sales (33.6% of profits). Acq. five companies in '98. '99 depr. rate: 14.5%; R&D, 9.6% of sales. Est'd plant age: 8 years. Has 24,899 emps. 42,500 stkhldrs. Off. & dir. control .9% of common (7/00 proxy). Chmn. & CEO: William W. George. Pres. & COO: Arthur D. Collins, Jr. Inc.: MN. Addr.: 7000 Central Ave. N.E., Minneapolis, MN 55432. Tel.: 612-514-4000. Internet: www.medtronic.com

Medtronic is off to a slightly slower-than-expected start in the fiscal year that began on May 1st. Worldwide revenues were up 15.6% in the first quarter, on a year-over-year basis. Although quite respectable by almost any standard, the gain was well below those achieved in recent quarters, and $70 million shy of our target. Sales of implantable defibrillators were likely hurt by a competitor's price cuts, while a reduction in capital spending slowed the hospital market for external defibrillators. Meantime, Vascular sales were depressed by a mid-quarter production stoppage of AneuRx abdominal aortic aneurysm stent grafts, due to the discovery of a manufacturing defect. Last, foreign exchange dynamics had a $20 million negative impact on the top line. Share net was only a penny below our estimate, however, as gross margins surpassed our expectations.

Per-share profits should still expand at a high-teens rate in both fiscal 2000 and 2001. The aforementioned shortfall, notwithstanding, Medtronic's overall business remains fundamentally strong. Neurological, Spinal, and ENT revenues advanced by 23% (to $340 million) in the July period. Top-line contributions from the Vascular segment were up 45% (to $225 million), lifted by the S660 and S670 stents. Looking forward, the company has a well-stocked pipeline that ought to keep revenues and earnings ascending at a healthy clip. The BeStent II should be launched in the United States shortly, followed soon thereafter by the S7X, a follow-up platform to the highly successful S670. Other prospects that Medtronic will soon be filing regulatory submissions for include the InSync and InSync ICD devices (for congestive heart failure), and the Chronicle, hemodynamic monitor, and the AT-500 atrial pacer. Also in the pipeline are the Activa (for Parkinson's disease), and the Gem III tachy family, which ought to help the company compete against Guidant's recently approved Prism offerings.

These shares are timely for the year ahead. They aren't inexpensive, however, even after their modest retreat following the release of first-quarter results. Accordingly, we think conservative investors should wait for better entry points.

George Rho   September 8, 2000

Company's Financial Strength A+
Stock's Price Stability 60
Price Growth Persistence 90
Earnings Predictability 90

book value
The amount of stock-holders' equity in a firm; determined by subtracting the company's liabilities and preferred stock value from the value of its assets.

BOOK VALUE. The amount of stockholders' equity in a firm is measured by **book value**. This accounting measure is determined by subtracting the firm's liabilities and preferred stocks from the value of its assets. Book value indicates the amount of stockholder funds used to finance the firm. For example, assume Rose Colored Glasses (RCG) had assets of $5 million, liabilities of $2 million, and preferred stock valued at $1 million. The book value of the firm's common stock would be $2 million ($5 million − $2 million − $1 million). If the book value is divided by the number of shares outstanding, the result is *book value per share*. If RCG had 100,000 shares of common stock outstanding, its book value per share would be $20 ($2,000,000/100,000 shares). Because of the positive impact it can have on the growth of the firm, you'd like to see book value per share steadily increasing over time; also, look for stocks whose market prices are comfortably above their book values.

net profit margin
A key measure of corporate profitability that relates the net profits of a firm to its sales; it shows the rate of return the company is earning on its sales.

NET PROFIT MARGIN. As a yardstick of profitability, **net profit margin** is one of the most widely followed measures of corporate performance. Basically, this ratio relates the net profits of the firm to its sales, providing an indication of how well the company is controlling its cost structure. The higher the net profit margin, the more money the company earns. Look for a relatively stable—or even better, an increasing—net profit margin.

return on equity (ROE)
ROE captures the overall profitability of the firm, as it provides a measure of the returns to stockholders; it is important because of its impact on the growth, profits, and dividends of the firm.

RETURN ON EQUITY. Another very important and widely followed measure, **return on equity** (or ROE, for short) reflects the overall profitability of the firm. It captures, in a single ratio, the amount of success the firm is having in managing its assets, operations, and capital structure. Return on equity is important because it has a direct and significant impact on the profits, growth, and dividends of the firm. The better the ROE, the better the financial condition and competitive position of the company. Look for a stable or increasing ROE, and watch out for a falling ROE, as that could spell trouble.

earnings per share (EPS)
The return earned on behalf of each share of common stock during a given 12-month period; calculated by dividing all earnings remaining after paying preferred dividends by the number of common shares outstanding.

EARNINGS PER SHARE. With stocks, the firm's annual earnings are usually measured and reported in terms of **earnings per share (EPS)**. Basically, EPS translates total corporate profits into profits on a per-share basis and provides a convenient measure of the amount of earnings available to stockholders. Earnings per share is found by using the following simple formula:

$$\text{EPS} = \frac{\text{Net profit after taxes} - \text{Preferred dividends paid}}{\text{Number of shares of common stock outstanding}}$$

For example, if RCG reported a net profit of $350,000, paid $100,000 in dividends to preferred stockholders, and had 100,000 shares of common outstanding, it would have an EPS of $2.50 [($350,000 − $100,000)/100,000]. Note that preferred dividends are *subtracted* from profits because they have to be paid before any monies can be made available to common stockholders. The magnitude of earnings per share is closely followed by stockholders because it represents the amount the firm has earned on behalf of each outstanding share of common stock. Here, too, look for a steady rate of growth in EPS.

PRICE/EARNINGS RATIO. When the prevailing market price of a share of common stock is divided by the annual earnings per share, the result is the **price/earnings (P/E) ratio**, which is viewed as an indication of investor confidence and expectations. The higher the price/earnings multiple, the more confidence investors are presumed to have in a given security. In the case of RCG, whose shares are currently selling for $30, the price/earnings ratio is 12 ($30 per share/$2.50 per share). This means that RCG stock is selling for 12 times its earnings. P/E ratios are important to investors because they reveal how aggressively the stock is being priced in the market. Watch out for very high P/Es—i.e., P/Es that are way out of line with the market—because that could indicate the stock is being overpriced (and thus might be headed for a big drop in price). P/E ratios are not static, but tend to move with the market: When the market's soft, a stock's P/E will be low, and when things heat up in the market, so will the stock's P/E.

BETA. A stock's **beta** is an indication of its *price volatility*; it shows how responsive the stock is to the market. In recent years, the use of betas to measure the *market risk* of common stock has become a widely accepted practice, and as a result, published betas are now available from most brokerage firms and investment services. The beta for a given stock is determined by a statistical technique that relates the stock's historical returns to the market. The market (as measured by something like the S&P index of 500 stocks) is used as a benchmark of performance, and it always has a beta of 1.0. From there, everything is relative: low-beta stocks—those with betas of less than 1.0—have low price volatility (they're relatively price-stable), while high-beta stocks—those with betas of more than 1.0—are considered to be highly volatile. In short, the higher a stock's beta, the more risky it is considered to be. Stock betas can be either positive or negative, though the vast majority are positive, meaning the stocks move in the same general direction as the market (that is, if the market is going up, so will the price of the stock).

Actually, beta is an *index* of price performance and is interpreted as a percentage response to the market. Thus, if RCG has a beta of, say, 0.8, it should rise (or fall) only 80 percent as fast as the market—if the market goes up by 10 percent, RCG should go up only 8 percent (10 percent $\times$ .8). In contrast, if the stock had a beta of 1.8, it would go up or down 1.8 times as fast—the price of the stock would rise higher and fall lower than the market. Clearly, other things being equal, if you're looking for a relatively conservative investment, you should stick with low-beta stocks; on the other hand, if it's capital gains and price volatility you're after, then go with high-beta securities.

 Enter a stock's ticker symbol or the company name and 411 Stocks, **www.411stocks.com**, pulls together a complete page of stock data: price, news, discussion groups, charts, and fundamentals.

 Analyze the analysts at BulldogResearch (**www.bulldogresearch .com**). You'll find evaluations of the performance of more than 3000 securities analysts based on the accuracy and consistency of their earning predictions.

PUTTING A VALUE ON STOCK

No matter what kind of investor you are or what your investment objectives happen to be, sooner or later you will have to face one of the most difficult questions in the field of investments: *How much are you willing to pay for the stock?* To answer this question, you have to put a value on the stock. Such measures as book value, earnings per share, P/E multiples, and betas are a part of the *fundamental analysis* used to determine the underlying value of a share of stock.

Basically, the notion of fundamental analysis is that the value of a stock depends on its expected stream of future earnings. Once you have a handle on the expected stream of future earnings, you can use that information in the *approximate yield* formula (Equation 12.1) to find the *expected rate of return on the investment*. If the expected return from the investment exceeds your desired or minimum rate of return, you should make the investment—in effect,

price/earnings (P/E) ratio
A measure of investors' confidence in and expectations for a given security; calculated by dividing the prevailing market price per share by the annual earnings per share.

beta
An index of the price volatility imbedded in a share of common stock; provides a reflection of how the price of a share of stock responds to market forces.

$ **Financial Road Sign**

Investing Myths
As appealing as these well-known "rules" may be, don't accept them as the absolute truth:
1. *Stocks outperform bonds over the long term.* The historical annualized return on stocks may be 10 to 12 percent, but over rolling 10-year periods you may earn less than 10 percent about half the time. Over 30 years, you have a 77 percent chance of topping 10 percent.
2. *Small-cap stocks beat large-cap stocks.* While small-cap stocks tend to outperform large-caps over the long run, since the mid-'80s, the Russell 2000 index has lagged the S&P 500.
3. *Value stocks outperform growth stock.* Not always. In one study of large-cap companies, the difference between growth and value stocks was insignificant.
4. *Asset allocation accounts for 90 percent of your returns.* Although asset allocation is indeed important, don't overlook *security selection*; it also plays a key role.

Source:
Walter Updegrave, "Everything You Think You Know about Investing is Wrong," *Money*, May 1999, pp. 127–136.

you should be willing to pay the current or prevailing market price. Put another way, with fundamental analysis you are trying to determine whether or not you should pay the current or prevailing market price for the stock. If the return you expect from the investment (via the approximate yield equation) is less than your desired rate of return, you should not buy the stock (at its current market price), because it is currently "over-priced" and, as such, you will not be able to earn your desired rate of return.

TYPES OF COMMON STOCK

Common stocks are often classified on the basis of their dividends or their rate of growth in EPS. Among the more popular types of common stock are blue-chip, growth, tech stocks, income, speculative, cyclical, defensive, mid-cap, and small cap stocks.

BLUE-CHIP STOCKS. These are the cream of the common stock crop; **blue chips** are stocks that are unsurpassed in quality and have a long and stable record of earnings and dividends. They are issued by large, well-established firms that have impeccable financial credentials—firms like GE, Merck, Wal-Mart, Citigroup, and Home Depot. These companies hold important, if not leading, positions in their industries and often determine the standards by which other firms are measured. Blue chips are particularly attractive to investors who seek quality investment outlets that offer decent dividend yields and respectable growth potential. Many use them for long-term investment purposes, and, because of their relatively low-risk exposure, as a way of obtaining modest but dependable rates of return on their investment dollars. They are popular with a large segment of the investing public and, as a result, are often relatively high priced, especially when the market is unsettled and investors become more quality-conscious.

GROWTH STOCKS. Stocks that have experienced, and are expected to continue experiencing, consistently high rates of growth in operations and earnings are known as **growth stocks.** A good growth stock might exhibit a *sustained* rate of growth in earnings of 15 to 20 percent (or more) over a period during which common stocks are averaging only 6 to 8 percent. American International Group, Enron Corp., Starbucks, Lowe's, Medtronic, and Intel are all prime examples of growth stocks. These stocks normally pay little or nothing in dividends, because the firm's rapid growth potential requires that its earnings be retained and reinvested. The high growth expectations for these stocks usually cause them to sell at relatively high P/E ratios, and they typically have betas in excess of 1.0. Because of their potential for dramatic price appreciation, they appeal mostly to investors who are seeking capital gains rather than dividend income.

TECH STOCKS. Over the past 10 to 15 years, *tech stocks* have become such a dominant force in the market that they deserve to be put in a class all their own. **Tech stocks** basically represent the technology sector of the market, and include all those companies that produce or provide technology-based products and services such as computers, semiconductors, data storage devices, computer software and hardware, peripherals, Internet services, content providers, networking, and wireless communications. These are the so-called *new economy* stocks issued by the companies that are changing the way things are being done in this country and around the world. They provide high-tech equipment, networking systems, and online services to all lines of businesses, schools, healthcare facilities, communication firms, governmental agencies, and home users. Although some of these stocks are listed on the NYSE and AMEX, the vast majority are traded on the Nasdaq. There are literally thousands of companies that fall into the tech stock category, including everything from very small firms providing some service on the Internet to huge multinational companies. Certainly, this is a category where it's safe to say that not all stocks are equal—here you'll find companies that generate lots of revenues and profits, companies that have lots of revenues but little or no profits, even companies that don't have much in the way of sales and even less in the way of profits (but supposedly lots of potential). These stocks would likely fall into either the *growth stock* category (see above) or the *speculative stock* class (see below), though some of them are legitimate *blue chips*. Although tech stocks may offer the potential for attractive (and in some cases, phenomenal) returns, they also involve considerable risk, and (for the most part anyway) are probably most suitable for the more risk-tolerant investor. Included in the tech stock category you'll find some big names, like Yahoo, Microsoft, Cisco Systems, and Amazon.com, as well as many not-so-big names like Intergraph Corp., Synopsys, Abgenix, Exodus, and Avid Technology.

INCOME STOCKS VERSUS SPECULATIVE STOCKS. Stocks whose appeal is based primarily on the dividends they pay out are known as **income stocks**. They have a fairly stable stream of earnings, a large portion of which is distributed in the form of dividends. Income shares have relatively high dividend yields and, as such, are ideally suited for investors who are seeking a relatively safe and high level of current income from their investment capital. An added (and often overlooked) feature of these stocks is that, unlike bonds and preferred stock, holders of income stock can expect *the amount of dividends paid to increase over time*. Examples of income stock include Duke Power, American Electric Power, Consolidated Edison, Bell Atlantic, Ford, H.J. Heinz, and Bank One. Because of their low risk, these stocks commonly have betas of less than 1.0.

Rather than basing their investment decisions on a proven record of earnings, investors in **speculative stocks** gamble that some new information, discovery, or production technique will favorably affect the growth of the firm and inflate the price of its stock. For example, a company whose stock is considered speculative may have recently discovered a new drug or located a valuable resource, such as oil. The value of speculative stocks and their P/E ratios tend to fluctuate widely as additional information with respect to the firm's future is received. The betas for speculative stocks are nearly always well in excess of 1.0. Investors in speculative stocks should be prepared to experience losses as well as gains, since *these are high-risk securities*. They include companies like Cytyc Corp., Krispy Kreme, JAKKS Pacific, Siebel Systems, and Zomax, Inc.

CYCLICAL STOCKS OR DEFENSIVE STOCKS. Stocks whose price movements tend to follow the business cycle are called **cyclical stocks**. This means that when the economy is in an expansionary stage (recovery or expansion), the prices of cyclical stocks increase, and during a contractionary stage (recession or depression), they decline. Most cyclical stocks are found in the basic industries—automobiles, steel, and lumber, for example; these industries are sensitive to changes in economic activity. Investors try to purchase cyclical stocks just prior to an expansionary phase and sell just before the contraction occurs. Because they tend to move with the market, these stocks always have positive betas. Caterpillar, Genuine Parts, Maytag Corp., Harnischfeger, and Timken are examples of cyclical stocks.

The prices and returns from **defensive stocks**, unlike those of cyclical stocks, are expected to remain stable during periods of contraction in business activity. For this reason, they are often called *countercyclical*. The shares of consumer goods companies, certain public utilities, and gold mining companies are good examples of defensive stocks. Because they are basically income stocks, their earnings and dividends tend to hold their market prices up during periods of economic decline. Betas on these stocks are quite low and occasionally even negative. Bandag, Checkpoint Systems, Union Corp., and WD-40 are all examples of defensive stocks.

blue-chip stock A stock known to provide a safe and stable return; generally issued by companies expected to provide an uninterrupted stream of dividends and good long-term growth prospects.

growth stock A stock whose earnings and market price have increased over time at a rate well above average.

tech stock A stock that represents the technology sector of the market and includes companies that provide technology-based products and services.

income stock A stock whose chief appeal is the dividends it pays out; typically offers dividend payments that can be expected to increase over time.

speculative stock Stock that is purchased on little more than the hope that its price per share will increase.

cyclical stock Stock whose price movements tend to parallel the various stages of the business cycle.

MID-CAPS AND SMALL CAPS. In the stock market, a stock's size is based on its market value—or, more commonly, on what is known as its *market capitalization* or *market cap*. A stock's market cap is found by multiplying its market price by the number of shares outstanding. Generally speaking, the market can be broken into three major components, or segments, as measured by a stock's market "cap":

Small cap . . . . Stocks with market caps of less than $1 billion
Mid-cap . . . . . Market caps of $1 billion to $4 or $5 billion
Large cap . . . . Market caps of more than $4 or $5 billion

In addition to these three segments, another is reserved for the *really small* stocks, known as *micro-caps*. Many of these stocks have market caps well below $100 million (some as low as $10–$15 million), and should only be used by investors who fully understand the risks involved and can tolerate such risk exposure.

Of the three major categories above, the large cap stocks are the real biggies—the AT&Ts, GEs, and Microsofts of the world. Many of these are considered to be blue-chip stocks, and, although there are far fewer large cap stocks than any of the other market cap categories, these companies account for about 80 to 90 percent of the total value of all U.S. equity markets. Just because they're big, however, doesn't mean they're better. Indeed, both the small and mid-cap segments of the market tend to hold their own with, or even outperform, large stocks over time.

Mid-cap stocks are a special breed unto themselves and offer investors some very attractive return opportunities. They provide much of the sizzle of small-stock returns, but without all the price volatility. At the same time, because these are fairly good-sized companies, and many of them have been around for a long time, they offer some of the safety of the big, established stocks. Among the ranks of the mid-caps are such well-known companies as Tootsie Roll, Wendy's International, Barnes & Noble, Cox Radio, Hertz, and Liz Claiborne, in addition to some not-so-well-known names. For the most part, although these securities offer a nice alternative to large stocks without all the drawbacks and uncertainties of small caps, they probably are most appropriate for investors who are willing to tolerate a bit more risk and price volatility.

Some investors consider small companies to be in a class by themselves. They believe these firms' stocks hold especially attractive return opportunities, which in many cases, has turned out to be true. Known as **small cap stocks**, these companies generally have *annual revenues* of less than $250 million, and, because of their size, spurts of growth can have dramatic effects on their earnings and stock prices. Anchor Financial, Sonic Corp., Papa John's, Sky West, and Dreyers Ice Cream are just some of the better-known small cap stocks. Now although some small caps (like Dreyers Ice Cream, for example) are solid companies with equally solid financials, that's definitely not the case with most of them! Indeed, because many of these companies are so small, they don't have a lot of stock outstanding, and their shares are not widely traded. In addition, small company stocks have a tendency to be "here today and gone tomorrow." Although some of these stocks may hold the potential for high returns, investors should also be aware of the very high risk exposure that comes with many of them.

MARKET GLOBALIZATION AND THE ALLURE OF FOREIGN STOCKS

In addition to all the different types of stocks mentioned previously, a growing number of American investors are turning to foreign markets as a way to earn attractive returns. Such securities became increasingly popular during the 80s and 90s, and many investment advisors

defensive stock
Stock that tends to exhibit price movements contrary to movements in the business cycle; often called counter-cyclical stock.

mid-cap stock
A stock whose total market value—that is, number of shares outstanding × market price per share—falls somewhere between $1 billion and $3 to $4 billion; these mid-sized companies offer attractive return potential without lots of price volatility.

small cap stock
A stock with a total market value of less than $1 billion that offers high growth and above average returns but at a cost of high risk.

today recommend that investors put at least part of their capital into foreign stocks. A good deal of this interest has come about as advances in technology and communications, together with the gradual elimination of political and regulatory barriers, have allowed investors to make cross-border securities transactions with relative ease. Because of these changes, not only are more and more Americans beginning to invest in foreign securities, but foreign investors are becoming major players in U.S. markets as well. The net result is a rapidly growing trend toward market globalization, whereby investing is practiced on an international scale rather than confined to a single (domestic) market.

Ironically, as our world is becoming smaller, our universe of investment opportunities is growing by leaps and bounds! Consider, for example, that in 1970 the U.S. stock market accounted for fully *two-thirds of the world market*. In essence, our stock market was twice as big as all the rest of the world's stock markets *combined*. That's no longer true, for in 1999 the U.S. share of the world equity market had dropped to less than 50 percent. Today, the world equity markets are dominated by just six countries that together account for about 80 percent of the total market; these six countries are:

	Market Value (Mid-year, 2000)
United States	$17.0 trillion
Japan	$ 4.4 trillion
United Kingdom	$ 2.8 trillion
Germany	$ 1.5 trillion
France	$ 1.4 trillion
Canada	$ 820 billion

Clearly, the United States is still the biggest player, but as these numbers show, there are some very big markets that exist beyond our borders. And keep in mind, these are just the six biggest markets. In addition to these six, another dozen or so markets, like Switzerland, Australia, Italy, Singapore, and Hong Kong, are also regarded as major world players—not to mention a number of relatively small, emerging markets, like Mexico, South Korea, Thailand, and Russia. Thus, investors who confine all their investing to the U.S. markets are missing out on a big chunk of the worldwide investment opportunities. Not only that, they're missing out on some very attractive returns as well! Over the 20-year period from 1980 through 1999, the U.S. stock market provided the highest annual return just *once*—in 1982. And that statistic pertains to just the 8 or 10 largest (major) markets of the world—it doesn't include some of the smaller (emerging) markets that, in recent years, have provided some spectacular returns. Of course, it also ignores some spectacular crashes that have occurred recently in these same emerging markets—like the major meltdowns that took place in 1997–98 in Thailand, Indonesia, Malasia, Korea, and the Philippines.

So, if you're looking for better returns, you might want to give some thought to investing in foreign stocks. There are several different ways of doing that. Without a doubt, from the perspective of an individual investor, the best and easiest way is through *international mutual funds* (we'll discuss such funds in Chapter 13). Mutual funds aside, you could, of course, buy securities directly in the foreign markets. *Investing directly* is not for the uninitiated, however. For although most major U.S. brokerage houses are set up to accommodate investors interested in buying foreign shares, many *logistical* problems still have to be faced. Fortunately, there is an easier way, and that is to buy *foreign securities that are denominated in dollars and traded directly on U.S. exchanges*. One such investment vehicle is the American Depository Receipt (ADR). ADRs are just like common stock, except that each ADR represents a specific number of shares in a specific foreign company. Indeed, the shares of more than 1,000 companies from some 50 foreign countries are traded on U.S. exchanges as ADRs—companies like Sony, Nestlé, Ericsson Telephone, Nokia, Vadafone Airtouch, Shanghai Petro-chemicals, and Grupo Televisa, to mention just a few. ADRs are a great way to invest in foreign stocks because they are bought and sold, on American markets, just like stocks in U.S. companies—and their prices are quoted in dollars, not British pounds or German marks. Furthermore, all dividends are paid in dollars.

 Everything you ever wanted to know about ADRs is at J.P. Morgan's ADR Site, www.adr.com, where you'll find general information about the ADR market and can search by company, region, or industry.

Whereas the temptation to go after higher returns may be compelling, keep one thing in mind when investing in foreign stocks—that is, whether investing in foreign securities directly or through something like ADRs, the whole process of investing involves a lot more risk. That's because *the behavior of foreign currency exchange rates plays a vital role in defining returns to U.S. investors.* As the U.S. dollar becomes weaker (or stronger) relative to the currency in which the foreign security is denominated, the returns to U.S. investors, from investing in foreign securities, will increase (or decrease) accordingly. Currency exchange rates can, in fact, have a dramatic impact on investor returns and quite often can convert mediocre returns, or even losses, into very attractive returns—and vice versa. Only one thing really determines whether the impact is going to be positive or negative, and that's the behavior of the U.S. dollar relative to the currency in which the foreign security is denominated. In effect, *a stronger dollar has a negative impact on total returns to U.S. investors, and a weaker dollar has a positive impact.* Thus, other things being equal, the best time to be in foreign securities is when the dollar is *falling,* because that increases returns to U.S. investors.

 If investing in U.S. companies isn't enough for you, head for WorldlyInvestor (www.worldlyinvestor.com), a comprehensive portal just for international investing.

INVESTING IN COMMON STOCK

The first step in investing is to know *where* to put your money; the second is to know *when* to make your moves. The first question basically involves matching your risk and return objectives with the available investment vehicles. As noted earlier, *a stock (or any investment vehicle for that matter) should be considered a viable investment candidate only so long as it promises to generate a sufficiently attractive rate of return* and, in particular, one that fully compensates you for any risks you have to take. Thus, if you're considering the purchase of a stock, you should expect to earn more than what you can get from T-bills or high-grade corporate bonds. The reason: Stocks are riskier than bills or bonds, so you deserve more return. Indeed, if you can't get enough return from the security to offset the risk, then you shouldn't invest in the stock!

SELECTING A STOCK. Granted, you want an investment that provides an attractive rate of return—one that meets or exceeds your required return. So, how do you go about selecting such a stock? The answer is by doing a little digging and crunching a few numbers. Here's what you'd want to do: To begin with, find a company you like and then take a look at how it has performed over the past 3 to 5 years. Find out what kind of growth rate (in sales) it has experienced, if it has a strong ROE and has been able to maintain or improve its profit margin, how much it has been paying out to stockholders in the form of dividends, and so forth. This kind of information is readily available in publications like *Value Line* and *S&P Stock Reports* (which we discussed in Chapter 11), or online, at a number of sites. The idea is to find stocks that are financially strong, have done well in the past, and continue to be market leaders or hold prominent positions in a given industry or market segment. Looking at the past is only the beginning, however; what's really important to stock valuation is the *FUTURE!* That is, as we discussed earlier in this chapter (see the section "What Makes a Good Investment?"), *the value of a share of stock at any point in time is a function of future returns, not past performance.*

So, let's turn our attention to the expected future performance of the stock. The idea is to assess the *outlook* for the stock, thereby *gaining some insight about the benefits to be derived from investing in it.* Of particular concern are future dividends and share price behavior. As a rule, it doesn't make much sense to go out more than 2 or 3 years because the accuracy of most forecasts begins to deteriorate rapidly after that point. Thus, using a 3-year investment horizon, you'd want to forecast annual dividends per share for each of the next 3 years, *plus* the future price of the stock at the end of the 3-year holding period (obviously, if the price of the stock is projected to go up over time, you'll have some capital gains). You can try to generate these forecasts yourself, or you can look to a publication like *Value Line* to obtain projections (*Value Line* projects dividends and share prices 3 to 5 years into the future). Once you have projected dividends and share price, you can use the approximate yield equation to determine the expected return from the investment.

To see how that can be done, consider the common shares of Medtronic, Inc., the world's largest manufacturer of implantable biomedical devices. According to *Value Line* (refer back to Exhibit 12.5), the company has very strong financials; its sales have been growing at around 17 percent per year for the past 5 years, it has a net profit margin of more than 20 percent, and an ROE of around 23 percent. Thus, historically, the company has performed very well and is definitely a market leader in its field. Late in the year 2000, the stock was trading at around $53 a share, and was paying annual dividends at the rate of about 19 cents a share. *Value Line* was projecting dividends to go up to about 35 or 36 cents a share within the next 3 to 5 years; they were also estimating the price of the stock could rise to as high as $65 or $70 a share within 3 years.

Using these *Value Line* projections and given current dividends (in 2000) of 19 cents a share, we could expect dividends of, say, 23 cents a share next year, 28 cents a share the year after (in year 2), and 35 cents a share in year 3—that is, if dividends do, in fact, grow as estimated by *Value Line.* Now, because the approximate yield equation uses "average annual current income" as one of the inputs, let's use the midpoint of our projected dividends (28 cents a share) as a proxy for average annual dividends. In addition, given this stock is currently trading at around $53 a share, has a projected future price of $67.50 a share (the midpoint between the estimated price of $65 to $70 a share), and we have a 3-year investment horizon, we can find our expected return as follows:

$$\frac{\text{Approximate Yield}}{(\text{Expected Return})} = \frac{\$0.28 + \left[\dfrac{\$67.50 - \$53.00}{3} \right]}{\left[\dfrac{\$67.50 + \$53.00}{2} \right]}$$

$$= \frac{\$0.28 + \$4.83}{\$60.25} = \underline{\underline{\mathbf{8.48\%}}}$$

Thus, if Medtronic stock performs as expected, it should provide us with a return of around 8.5 to 9 percent. (And by the way, using a hand-held calculator and the same input as above—i.e., N = 3, PV = −53.00, PMT = .28, and FV = 67.50, then computing (CPT) I— you'll end up with an expected return of 8.88 percent; try it on your own.) Very likely, this return will *fall short* of our required rate of return (which probably should be more like 12 to 15 percent), in which case the stock should *NOT* be considered a viable investment candidate. According to our standards, the stock is currently over-valued. But don't just

$ Financial Road Sign

"For Sale" Signs
When should you sell a stock? The following questions will help you decide:

1. *Have you found a significantly better place to put your money?* Don't forget to include brokerage commissions and capital gains taxes when making this calculation.

2. *Is the reason you originally bought the stock still valid?* Check the fundamentals. The company may have changed direction or management.

3. *Will you need the money soon?* If you need the money in a few years, it probably should not have been in stocks in the first place.

Source: "Ask the Fool," *San Diego Union-Tribune,* March 4, 2001, p. H5.

disregard the stock; Medtronic is a very good company and bears watching—who knows, the market may hit a little turbulence and the price of the stock could come down enough to make it a very attractive buy?

TIMING YOUR INVESTMENTS. Once you find a stock you think will give you the kind of return you're looking for, you're ready to deal with the matter of timing your investment. So long as the prospects for the market and the economy are positive, the time may be right to invest in stocks. On the other hand, there are a couple of conditions when investing in stocks doesn't make any sense at all. In particular, *don't* invest in stocks if:

- You feel *very strongly* that the market is headed down in the short run. If you're absolutely certain the market's in for a big fall (or will continue to fall, if it's already doing so), then wait until the market drops, and buy the stock when it's cheaper.
- You feel uncomfortable with the general tone of the market—it lacks direction, or there's way too much price volatility to suit you. For example, this became a problem prior to and after the October 1987 crash, when computer-assisted trading started taking over the market. The result was a stock market that behaved more like a commodities market, with an intolerable amount of price volatility. When this happens, fundamentals go out the window, and the market simply becomes too risky. Do what the pros do, and wait it out on the sidelines.

WHY INVEST IN STOCKS? There are three basic reasons for investing in common stock: (1) to use the stock as a warehouse of value, (2) to accumulate capital, and (3) to provide a source of income. Storage of value is important to all investors, because nobody likes to lose money. However, some investors are more concerned about it than others and therefore put safety of principal first in their stock selection process. These investors are more quality-conscious and tend to gravitate toward blue chips and other nonspeculative shares. Accumulation of capital generally is an important goal to individuals with long-term investment horizons. These investors use the capital gains and dividends that stocks provide to build up their wealth. Some use growth stocks for such purposes; others do it with income shares; still others use a little of both. Finally, some people use stocks as a source of income; to them, a dependable flow of dividends is essential. High-yielding, good-quality income shares are usually their preferred investment vehicle.

ADVANTAGES AND DISADVANTAGES OF STOCK OWNERSHIP. Ownership of common stock has both advantages and disadvantages. Its advantages are threefold. First, the potential returns, in the form of both dividend income and price appreciation, can be quite substantial. The return performance of common stocks over the recent past, as well as over extended periods of time, has been impressive, to say the least! Second, many stocks are actively traded (there are literally thousands of such actively traded stocks) and as such they are a highly liquid form of investment—meaning they can be quickly bought and sold. Finally, they don't involve any direct management (or unusual management problems) and market/company information is usually widely published and readily available.

Risk, the problem of timing purchases and sales, and the uncertainty of dividends are all disadvantages of common stock ownership. Although potential common stock returns may be high, the risk and uncertainty associated with the actual receipt of that return is also great. Even though careful selection of stocks may reduce the amount of risk to which the investor is exposed, the risk-return tradeoff cannot be completely eliminated. In other words, high returns on common stock are not guaranteed; they may or may not occur depending on numerous economic, industry, and company factors. The timing of purchases and sales is closely related to risk. Many investors purchase a stock, hold it for a period of time during which the price drops, and then sell it below the original purchase price—that is, at a loss. The proper strategy, of course, is to buy low and sell high, but the problem of predicting price movements makes it difficult to implement such a plan.

BE SURE TO PLOW BACK YOUR EARNINGS. Unless you're living off the income, the basic investment objective with stocks is the same as it is with any other security: to earn an attractive, fully compounded rate of return. This requires regular reinvestment of dividend income. And there's no better way to accomplish such reinvestment than through a **dividend reinvestment plan (DRP)**. The basic investment philosophy at work here is that if the company is good enough to invest in, it's good enough to reinvest in. In a dividend reinvestment plan, shareholders can sign up to have their cash dividends automatically reinvested in additional shares of the company's common stock—in essence, it's like taking your cash dividends in the form of more shares of common stock. The idea is to put your money to work by building up your investment in the stock. Such an approach can have a tremendous impact on your investment position over time, as seen in Exhibit 12.6.

Today, over 1,000 companies (including most major corporations) have DRPs, and each one provides investors with a convenient and inexpensive way to accumulate capital. Stocks in most DRPs are acquired free of any brokerage commissions, and most plans allow *partial participation.* That is, rather than committing all their cash dividends to these plans, participants may specify a portion of their shares for dividend reinvestment and receive cash dividends on the rest. Some plans even sell stocks to their DRP investors at below-market prices—often at discounts of 3 to 5 percent. In addition, most plans credit fractional shares to the investors' accounts. Shareholders can join these plans simply by sending in a completed authorization form to the company. Once in the plan, the

dividend reinvestment plan (DRP)
A program offered by over 1,000 major corporations whereby stockholders can choose to take their dividends in the form of more shares of the company's stock, rather than cash; it provides a relatively painless way of earning a fully compounded rate of return.

EXHIBIT 12.6

CASH OR REINVESTED DIVIDENDS

Participating in a dividend reinvestment plan is a simple yet highly effective way of building up capital over time. Over the long haul, it can prove to be a great way of earning a fully compounded rate of return on your money.

> *Situation:* Buy 100 shares of stock at $25 a share (total investment $2,500); stock currently pays $1 a share in annual dividends. Price of the stock increases at 8 percent per year; dividends grow at 5 percent per year.

Investment Period	Number of Shares Held	Market Value of Stock Holdings	Total Cash Dividends Received
TAKE DIVIDENDS IN CASH			
5 years	100	$ 3,672	$ 552
10 years	100	$ 5,397	$1,258
15 years	100	$ 7,930	$2,158
20 years	100	$11,652	$3,307
PARTICIPATE IN A DRP			
5 years	115.59	$ 4,245	$0
10 years	135.66	$ 7,322	$0
15 years	155.92	$12,364	$0
20 years	176.00	$20,508	$0

number of shares you hold will begin to accumulate with each dividend date. There is a catch, however—even though these dividends take the form of additional shares of stock, *reinvested dividends are taxable, in the year they're received*, just as if they had been received in cash.

CONCEPT CHECK

12.4.   From a tax perspective, would it make any difference to an investor whether the return on a stock took the form of dividends or capital gains? Explain.

12.5.   What's the difference between a cash dividend and a *stock dividend?* Which would you rather receive?

12.6.   Define and briefly discuss each of the following common stock measures: (a) *book value*, (b) ROE, (c) *earnings per share* (EPS), (d) *price/earnings (P/E) ratio*, and (e) *beta*.

12.7.   Briefly discuss some of the different types of common stock. Which types would be most appealing to you, and why?

12.8.   With so many different types of stocks to choose from in the United States, why would an American investor even want to consider investing in foreign markets? Identify two or three different ways of investing in foreign stock markets. As an individual investor, which approach would you find most appealing? Why are currency exchange rates so important to investors in foreign markets.

12.9.   Under what conditions would a stock be considered a viable investment candidate? What are *dividend reinvestment plans*, and how do they fit into a stock investment program?

Investing in Bonds [LG5]

In contrast to stocks, *bonds are liabilities*—they're nothing more than publicly traded IOUs where the bondholders are actually *lending money* to the issuer. They represent borrowed funds and as such are a form of *debt capital*. Bonds are often referred to as *fixed-income securities* because the debt service obligations of the issuer are fixed—that is, the issuing organization agrees to pay a *fixed amount of interest periodically and to repay a fixed amount of principal* at or before maturity. Bonds normally have face values of $1,000 or $5,000, and maturities of 10 to 30 years or more.

WHY INVEST IN BONDS?

Like many other types of investment vehicles, bonds provide investors with two kinds of income: (1) They provide a generous amount of current income, and (2) they can often be used to generate substantial amounts of capital gains. The current income, of course, is derived from the interest payments received periodically over the life of the issue. Indeed, this regular and highly predictable source of income is today one of the most important reasons for buying bonds. But these securities can also produce capital gains, which occurs whenever market interest rates fall. A basic trading rule in the bond market is that *interest rates and bond prices move in opposite directions*: When interest rates rise, bond prices fall; and when they drop, bond prices rise. Thus, it is possible to buy bonds at one price and, if interest rate conditions are right, to sell them some time later at a higher price. Of course, it is also possible to incur a capital loss should market rates move against the investor.

Taken together, the current income and capital gains earned from bonds can lead to attractive and highly competitive investor returns.

Bonds are also a highly versatile investment outlet. They can be used conservatively by those who seek high current income, or aggressively by those who actively go after capital gains. Bonds have long been considered an excellent way of getting high current income, but only since the advent of volatile interest rates have they also become recognized as trading vehicles—that is, as a way to earn fat returns from capital gains. Investors found that the number of profitable trading opportunities increased substantially as wider and more frequent swings in interest rates began to occur.

Finally, bond issues, being of generally high quality, can be used for the preservation and long-term accumulation of capital. In fact, some individuals, regularly and over the long haul, commit all or a good deal of their investment funds to bonds because of this single attribute.

BONDS VS. STOCKS

Although bonds definitely do have their good points—low risk and high levels of current income, along with *desirable diversification properties*—they also have a significant downside: their *comparative* returns. The fact is, *relative to stocks*, the long-run returns on bonds don't hold up very well. For example, during the decade of the '90s (from January 1990 through December 1999), long-term corporate bonds produced average annual returns of 8.7 percent, whereas stocks (as measured by the S&P 500) turned in average returns of 18.2 percent. That difference meant that a $10,000 investment in bonds would have led to a terminal value of some $23,000, versus more than $53,000 for stocks.

That's a high opportunity cost to pay for holding bonds, and it prompted some market observers to question whether bonds should have *any place at all* in an investment portfolio. They reasoned that since market interest rates have dropped so low, bonds really don't have much to offer, other than relatively low returns. But that view ignores one of the key roles of bonds: *the element of stability they add to a portfolio!* The fact is, bonds possess excellent portfolio diversification properties and, except for the most aggressive of investors, have a lot to contribute from a portfolio perspective. Indeed, as a general rule, adding bonds to a portfolio will—*up to a point*—have a much bigger impact on (lowering) risk than it will on return! Face it: you don't buy bonds for their high returns (except when you think interest rates are heading down); rather, you buy them for their current income and the stability they bring to a portfolio. And that's still true, even today. What's more, it's imperative to keep in mind that most of the comparative return performance over the decade of the '90s was due to a *phenomenal 5-year run (from 1995 through 1999) for stocks*. Thus, should stock returns come back down to earth and return to more normal levels (which has to happen, sooner or later), then bond returns will once again become more competitive!

BASIC ISSUE CHARACTERISTICS

A bond is a negotiable, long-term debt instrument that carries certain obligations on the part of the issuer. Unlike the holders of common stock, bondholders have no ownership or equity position in the issuing firm or organization. This is so because bonds are debt, and the bondholders, in a roundabout way, are only lending money to the issuer.

As a rule, bonds pay interest every 6 months. The amount of interest paid is a function of the **coupon**, which defines the annual interest that will be paid by the issuer to the bondholder. For instance, a $1,000 bond with an 8 percent coupon would pay $80 in interest every year—generally in the form of two $40 semiannual payments. The principal amount

coupon
That feature on a bond that defines the annual interest income the issuer will pay the bondholder.

of a bond, also known as *par value*, specifies the amount of capital that must be repaid at maturity—thus there is $1,000 of principal in a $1,000 bond.

Of course, debt securities regularly trade at market prices that differ from their principal (or par) values. This occurs whenever an issue's coupon differs from the prevailing market rate of interest; in essence, the price of an issue will change until its yield is compatible with prevailing market yields. Such behavior explains why a 7 percent issue will carry a market price of only $825 when the market yield is 9 percent; the drop in price is necessary to raise the yield on this bond from 7 percent to 9 percent. Issues with market values lower than par are known as *discount bonds* and carry coupons that are less than those on new issues. In contrast, issues with market value in excess of par are called *premium bonds* and have coupons greater than those currently being offered on new issues.

mortgage bond
A bond secured by a claim on real assets, such as a manufacturing plant.

equipment trust certificate
A bond secured by certain types of transportation equipment, like railroad cars and airplanes.

debenture
An unsecured bond issued on the general credit of the firm.

sinking fund
A provision in a bond that specifies the annual repayment schedule that will be used to pay off the issue, and the amount of principal that will be retired each year.

call feature
A feature often included in bond (or preferred stock) issues that allows the issuer to retire the security prior to maturity at some specified, predetermined price.

TYPES OF ISSUES. A single issuer may have any number of bonds outstanding at a given point in time. In addition to their coupons and maturities, bonds can be differentiated from one another by the type of collateral behind them. In this regard, the issues can be viewed as having either junior or senior standing. *Senior bonds* are *secured* obligations, because they are backed by a legal claim on some specific property of the issuer that acts as *collateral* for the bonds. Such issues include **mortgage bonds**, which are secured by real estate, and **equipment trust certificates**, which are backed by certain types of equipment and are popular with railroads and airlines. *Junior bonds*, on the other hand, are backed only with a promise by the issuer to pay interest and principal on a timely basis. There are several classes of *unsecured* bonds, the most popular of which is known as a **debenture**. Exhibit 12.7 shows the announcement for a very large new issue that came out in June 2000. This particular issue happens to be a *note*, but, just like a debenture, it too is unsecured (essentially, this note is nothing more than a short-term debenture). Even though there was no collateral backing this obligation, the issuer—in this case, Hewlett Packard—was able to sell $1.5 *billion* worth of these securities at an interest rate of just 7.15 percent.

SINKING FUND. Another provision that's important to investors is the **sinking fund**, which stipulates how a bond will be paid off over time. Not all bonds have these requirements, but for those that do, a sinking fund specifies the annual repayment schedule that will be used to pay off the issue and indicates how much principal will be retired each year. Sinking fund requirements generally begin one to five years after the date of issue and continue annually thereafter until all or most of the issue has been paid off. Any amount not repaid by maturity (which might equal 10 to 25 percent of the issue) is then retired with a single balloon payment.

CALL FEATURE. Every bond has a **call feature**, which stipulates whether a bond can be called (that is, retired) prior to its regularly scheduled maturity date, and, if so, under what conditions. Usually, a bond cannot be called until it has been outstanding for 5 years or more. Call features are used most often to replace an issue with one that carries a lower coupon; in this way, the issuer benefits by being able to realize a reduction in annual interest cost. In an attempt to compensate investors who have their bonds called out from under them, a *call premium* (usually equal to about a half to one year's interest) is tacked on to the par value of the bond and paid to investors, along with the issue's par value, at the time the bond is called. For example, if a company decides to call its 12 percent bonds some 15 years before they mature, it might have to pay $1,090 for every $1,000 bond outstanding (a call premium equal to 9 months' interest—$120 × .75 = $90—would be added to the par value of $1,000).

Although this might sound like a good deal, it's really not. Indeed, the only party that benefits from a bond refunding is the issuer. The bondholder loses a source of high current

EXHIBIT 12.7

AN ANNOUNCEMENT OF A NEW CORPORATE DEBT ISSUE

This $1.5 *billion* Global Note was issued by Hewlett Packard in 2000 and is secured by nothing more than the good name of the company. Raising this kind of money without having to put up any collateral may be hard to imagine, but for big, financially secure companies like HP, it's done all the time! And note that the price was right: the coupon on this unsecured debt is only 7.15 percent. Even so, over the short, 5-year life of this note, HP will be paying more than $100,000,000 in interest!

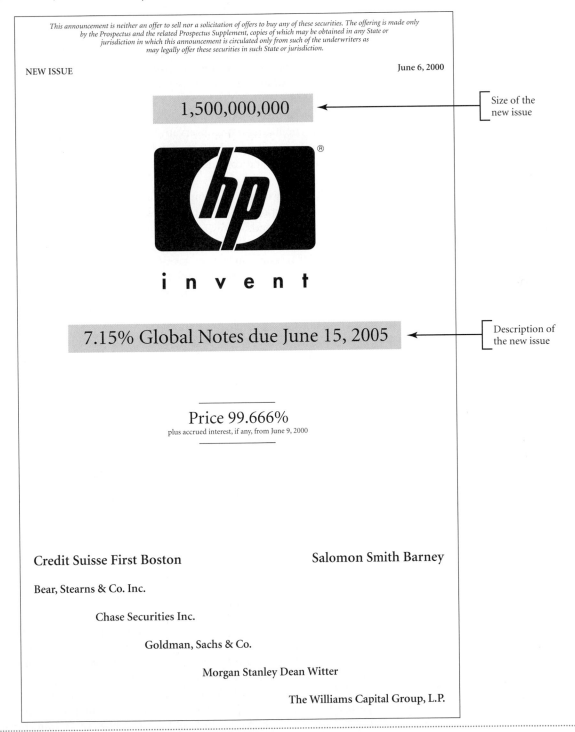

This announcement is neither an offer to sell nor a solicitation of offers to buy any of these securities. The offering is made only by the Prospectus and the related Prospectus Supplement, copies of which may be obtained in any State or jurisdiction in which this announcement is circulated only from such of the underwriters as may legally offer these securities in such State or jurisdiction.

NEW ISSUE   June 6, 2000

1,500,000,000 ← Size of the new issue

7.15% Global Notes due June 15, 2005 ← Description of the new issue

Price 99.666%
plus accrued interest, if any, from June 9, 2000

Credit Suisse First Boston   Salomon Smith Barney

Bear, Stearns & Co. Inc.

Chase Securities Inc.

Goldman, Sachs & Co.

Morgan Stanley Dean Witter

The Williams Capital Group, L.P.

Source: *The Wall Street Journal*, July 12, 2000.

income—for example, the investor may have a 12 percent bond called away at a time when the best he or she can do in the market is maybe 7 or 8 percent. To avoid this, stick with bonds that are either *noncallable* (these issues cannot be called or retired prior to maturity, for any reason), or that have long *call-deferment periods*, meaning they can't be called for refunding (or any other purpose) until the call-deferment period ends.

THE BOND MARKET

One thing that really stands out about the bond market is its size—the U.S. bond market is huge and getting bigger almost every day. Indeed, from a $250 billion dollar market in 1950, it has grown to the point where, in early 2000, the amount of bonds outstanding in this country reached nearly $15 *trillion!* Given such size, it's not surprising that today's bond market offers securities to meet just about any type of investment objective and suit virtually any type of investor, no matter how conservative or aggressive. As a matter of convenience, the bond market is usually divided into four segments, according to type of issuer: Treasury, agency, municipal, and corporate.

Treasury bond
A federal government obligation that has a maturity of more than ten years and pays interest semiannually; also called a government bond.

TREASURY BONDS. **Treasury bonds** (sometimes called *Treasuries* or *governments*) are a dominant force in the bond market and, if not the most popular, certainly are the best known. The U.S. Treasury issues bonds, notes, and other types of debt securities (such as the Treasury bills discussed in Chapter 4) as a means of meeting the ever increasing needs of the federal government. All Treasury obligations are of the highest quality (backed by the full faith and credit of the U.S. government), a feature that, along with their liquidity, makes them extremely popular with individual and institutional investors, both here and abroad. Indeed, Treasury securities are traded in all the major markets of the world, from New York to London to Tokyo.

Treasury notes are issued with maturities of 2, 5, and 10 years, whereas *Treasury bonds* carry 30-year maturities. The Treasury issues its notes and bonds at regularly scheduled auctions, the results of which are widely reported by the financial media. It's through this auction process that the Treasury establishes the initial yields and coupons on the securities it issues. Actually, because of the ever-widening federal budget *surplus*, the Treasury has announced that it will be sharply reducing the issuance of new notes and bonds. Indeed, the supply of these securities is to be reduced across the board as the Treasury eliminates the auctions of some maturities all together, and reduces the size or frequency of others. Even so, a full array of Treasury notes and bonds is still available in the after-market, but many of those may soon become extinct as well, as the Treasury uses big chunks of the budget surplus to pay down the national debt by *buying back outstanding Treasury securities.* All Treasury notes and bonds are sold in minimum denominations of $1,000, and although interest income is subject to normal federal income tax, *it is exempt from state and local taxes.* Also, the Treasury today issues only *noncallable* securities—the last time the U.S. Treasury issued callable debt was in 1984.

Treasury inflation-indexed bond (TIPS)
A type of Treasury security that provides protection against inflation by adjusting investor returns for the annual rate of inflation.

In 1997, the Treasury began issuing its newest security, the **Treasury inflation-indexed bond—or TIPS** as they're also known, which stands for "Treasury Inflation-Protection Securities." Basically, these securities—which are issued as notes with 10-year maturities, and bonds with 30-year maturities—provide investors with the opportunity to stay ahead of inflation by periodically adjusting their returns for any inflation that has occurred. That is, if inflation is running at an annual rate of, say, 3 percent, then at the end of the year the par (or maturity) value of your bond will increase by 3 percent (actually, the adjustments to par value are done every 6 months). Thus, the $1000 par value will grow to $1,030 at the end of the first year and, if the 3 percent inflation rate continues for the second year, the par value will once again move up, this time from $1,030 to $1,061 (or $1,030 × 1.03). Unfortunately,

MONEY IN ACTION

TIPS: What's In It For You?

Some people have the mistaken impression that they can't lose money in U.S. Treasury bonds. But they can—not because the government can't pay, but because bond prices fall in a rising inflationary environment (the higher inflation, of course, leads to higher interest rates, which ultimately lead to the lower bond prices). Now, the U.S. government wants investors to buy its bonds without fearing inflation. So, in 1997, Uncle Sam created TIPS, Treasury Inflation-Protection Securities.

Here's how TIPS work: Suppose in early 2000 the government issues a 10-year bond with a $1,000 face value that pays, say, 4 percent interest, or $40 per year. That rate stays fixed for the life of the issue, but interest is paid on the inflation-adjusted principal amount—that is, if the Consumer Price Index rises, *so does the face amount of the bond*. For example, because the CPI rose 3.4 percent in 2000, the new face amount was adjusted up to $1,000 × 1.034 = $1,034. Therefore, the annual interest payment was $41.36 (4 percent of $1,034). When the TIPS mature in ten years, the investor gets the inflation-adjusted face value at that time, which could be as much as $2,000 if inflation takes off. TIPS also protect you if *deflation* occurs. The bond's value will *not* fall below face value.

Unfortunately, the IRS considers the increase in par value as taxable income, so the investor is going to have to pay taxes on it (just like he or she would have to pay taxes on the interest income). Thus, the IRS collects taxes on the increased value of the bond (the tax has to be paid in the year in which the increase in par value occurs), even though the increased par value isn't collected until the bond matures.

Take a look at what happens to a conventional bond if inflation is rekindled. Investors get 6 percent per year, or $60, no matter what happens to the level of prices. In 10 years, that $1,000 principal will certainly have less purchasing power than it does today. It might be able to buy just $700 worth of goods. In addition, rising inflation generally means rising interest rates. In the marketplace, conventional bond prices fall when interest rates rise. Therefore, an investor who wishes to sell a conventional bond prior to maturity will probably take a loss if interest rates are higher than when the bond was purchased.

TIPS protect investors from such bond price erosion. TIPS are not so great, however, if inflation stays dormant, because the investor is getting only 3 or 4 percent on his or her money. You could get that kind of interest at your local bank, and you don't need to lock up your money nearly as long as you do with a TIP. Of course, inflation looks pretty tame these days. So, as one professional investor puts it, buying TIPS today is like buying flood insurance during a drought.

Sources: Burton Malkiel, "Hot Tips?" *Bloomberg Personal*. September 1997, p. 39; "When Does a 3.5 Percent Bond Yield Beat 6.5 Percent? *Kiplinger's Personal Finance Magazine*, April 1997, p. 16; Robert Barker, "A Bond Anybody Can Love," *Business Week*, June 19, 2000, p. 260; Jonathan Clements, "Need a Lift? Inflation Bonds Are Handy," *The Wall Street Journal*, December 12, 2000, p. C1; James Grant, "An Inflation Tip," *Forbes*, October 30, 2000, p. 402.

the coupons on these securities are set very low, as they're meant to provide investors with so-called *real (inflation-adjusted) returns*. Thus, one of these bonds might carry a coupon of only 3½ percent (at a time when regular T-bonds are paying, say, 6½ or 7 percent). But there's an upside even to this: The actual size of *the coupon payment will increase over time as the par value on the bond goes up*. For investors who are concerned about inflation protection, these securities may be just the ticket. But as the accompanying *Money in Action* box suggests, these securities are a lot more complex than your normal Treasury bond.

AGENCY BONDS. **Agency bonds** are an important segment of the U.S. bond market. Though issued by political subdivisions of the U.S. government, *these securities are not obligations of the U.S. Treasury*. An important feature of these securities is that they customarily

agency bond
An obligation of a political subdivision of the U.S. government; typically provides yields above the market rates for Treasury bonds.

provide yields comfortably above the market rates for Treasuries and, therefore, offer investors a way to increase returns with little or no real difference in risk. Some of the more actively traded and widely quoted agency issues include those sold by the Federal Farm Credit Bank, the Federal National Mortgage Association (or "Fannie Maes," as they are more commonly known), the Federal Land Bank, the Student Loan Marketing Association, and the Federal Home Loan Bank. Although these issues are not the direct obligations of the U.S. government, a number of them actually do carry government guarantees and thus effectively represent the full faith and credit of the U.S. Treasury. Moreover, some have unusual interest-payment provisions (interest is paid monthly in a few instances and yearly in one case), and, in some cases, the interest is exempt from state and local taxes.

smart.sites If bonds are still a mystery to you, the Bond Market Association's "Investing in Bonds" site (**www.investinginbonds.com**) has a wealth of practical and educational tools and useful links.

municipal bond
A bond issued by state and local governments for the purpose of financing certain projects; interest income is usually exempt from federal taxes.

serial obligation
An issue, usually a municipal bond, that is broken down into a series of smaller bonds, each with its own maturity date and coupon rate.

revenue bond
A municipal bond serviced from the income generated from a specific project.

general obligation bond
A municipal bond backed by the full faith and credit of the issuing municipality rather than by the revenue generated from a given project.

MUNICIPAL BONDS. **Municipal bonds** are the issues of states, counties, cities, and other political subdivisions, such as school districts and water and sewer districts. They are unlike other bonds in that their interest income is usually free from federal income tax (which is why these issues are known as *tax-free bonds*). Note, however, that the same tax-free status does not apply to any capital gains that may be earned on these securities—that is, such gains are subject to the usual federal taxes. A tax-free yield is probably the most important feature of municipal bonds and is certainly a major reason why individuals invest in them. Exhibit 12.8 shows what a taxable bond (like a Treasury issue) would have to yield to equal the take-home yield of a tax-free municipal bond. It demonstrates how the yield attractiveness of municipal bonds varies with an investor's income level; clearly, the higher the individual's tax bracket, the more attractive municipal bonds become.

As a rule, the yields on municipal bonds are substantially lower than the returns available from fully taxable issues. Thus, unless the tax effect is sufficient to raise the yield on a municipal to a level that equals or exceeds the yields on taxable issues, it obviously doesn't make sense to buy municipal bonds. You can determine the return a fully taxable bond would have to provide in order to match the after-tax return on a lower-yielding tax-free issue by computing what is known as a municipal's *fully taxable equivalent yield:*

$$\text{Fully taxable equivalent yield} = \frac{\text{Yield of Municipal bond}}{1 - \text{Tax rate}}$$

For example, if a certain municipal bond offered a yield of 6 percent, an individual in the maximum 39.6 percent federal tax bracket would have to find a fully taxable bond with a yield of nearly 10 percent to reap the same after-tax return: that is, $6\% \div (1 - .396) = 6\% \div .604 = 9.93\%$.

Municipal bonds are generally issued as **serial obligations**, meaning that the issue is broken into a series of smaller bonds, each with its own maturity date and coupon rate. Thus, instead of the bond having just one maturity date 20 years from now, it will have a series of, say, 20 maturity dates over the 20-year time frame. Because such a diversity of municipal bonds is available, investors must also be careful to assess their quality to ensure that the issuer will not default. Although it may not seem that municipal issuers would default on either interest or principal payments, it does occur! Investors should be especially cautious when investing in **revenue bonds**, which are municipal bonds serviced from the income generated from specific income-producing projects, such as toll roads. Unlike issuers of so-called **general obligation bonds**—which are backed by the full faith and

EXHIBIT 12.8

TABLE OF TAXABLE EQUIVALENT YIELDS

Tax-exempt securities generally yield less than fully taxable obligations, and, because of that, you have to be in a sufficiently high tax bracket (28 percent or more) to make up for the yield shortfall.

| | To Match a Tax-Free Yield of: | | | | | |
	5%	6%	7%	8%	9%	10%
Tax Bracket*	You Must Earn This Yield on a Taxable Investment:					
15 %	5.88	7.06	8.24	9.41	10.59	11.76
28	6.94	8.33	9.72	11.11	12.50	13.89
31	7.25	8.70	10.15	11.59	13.04	14.49
36	7.81	9.38	10.94	12.50	14.06	15.63
39.6	8.28	9.93	11.59	13.25	14.90	16.56

*Federal tax rates in effect on Jan. 1, 2001.

credit of the municipality—the issuer of a revenue bond is obligated to pay principal and interest *only if a sufficient level of revenue* is generated. General obligation municipal bonds, in contrast, are required to be serviced in a prompt and timely fashion regardless of the level of tax income generated by the municipality.

Caution should be used when buying municipal bonds because *some of these issues are tax-exempt and others are not.* One effect of the far-reaching Tax Reform Act of 1986 was to change the status of municipal bonds used to finance nonessential projects so their interest income is no longer exempt from federal taxes. Such bonds are known as *taxable munies,* and they offer yields considerably higher than normal tax-exempt securities. Buy one of these issues and you'll end up holding a bond whose interest income is *fully taxable* by the IRS.

CORPORATE BONDS. The major nongovernmental issuers of bonds are corporations. The market for **corporate bonds** is customarily subdivided into several segments, which include *industrials* (the most diverse of the group), *public utilities* (the dominant group in terms of volume of new issues), *rail and transportation bonds,* and *financial issues* (banks, finance companies, and so forth). The corporate bond market offers the widest range of issue types. There are *first mortgage bonds, convertible bonds* (discussed in the next section), *debentures, subordinated debentures,* and *income bonds,* to mention just a few. Interest on corporate bonds is paid semiannually, and sinking funds are common. The bonds usually come in $1,000 denominations and are issued on a term basis with a single maturity date. Maturities usually range from 5 to 10 years, to 30 years or more. Many of the issues—particularly the longer-term bonds—carry call provisions that prohibit prepayment of the issue during the first 5 to 10 years. Corporate issues are popular with individuals because of their relatively high yields.

corporate bond
A bond issued by a corporation; categories include industrials, public utilities, railroad and transportation bonds, and financial issues.

THE SPECIAL APPEAL OF ZERO COUPON BONDS. In addition to the standard bond vehicles described above, investors can also choose from several types of *specialty issues*—bonds that, for the most part, have unusual coupon or repayment provisions. That's certainly the case with **zero coupon bonds,** which, as the name implies, are bonds issued without coupons. To compensate for their lack of coupons, these bonds are sold at

zero coupon bond
A bond that pays no annual interest but sells at a deep discount to par value.

a deep discount from their par values and then increase in value over time, at a compound rate of return, so at maturity they are worth much more than their initial investment. Other things being equal, the cheaper the bond, the greater the return one can earn (for example, whereas a 10 percent bond might sell for $239, an issue with a 6 percent yield will cost a lot more—$417).

Because they have no coupons, these bonds pay nothing to the investor until they mature. In this regard, zero coupon bonds are like the Series EE savings bonds we discussed in Chapter 4. Strange as it may seem, this is the main attraction of zero coupon bonds. Because there are no interest payments, investors need not worry about reinvesting coupon income twice a year; instead, the fully compounded rate of return on a zero coupon bond is virtually guaranteed at the rate that existed when the issue was purchased. For example, in mid-2000, good-grade (corporate) zero coupon bonds with 20-year maturities were available at yields of around 8 percent; thus, for just a little over $200, investors could buy a bond that would be worth 5 times that amount, or $1,000, when it matures in 20 years. Best of all, they would be *locking in* an 8 percent compound rate of return on their investment capital for the full 20-year life of the issue.

Because of their unusual tax exposure (even though the bonds do not pay regular yearly interest, the IRS treats the annually accrued interest as taxable income), zeros should be used only in tax-sheltered investments, such as individual retirement accounts (IRAs), or be held by minor children who are likely to be taxed at low rates, if at all.

Zeros are issued by corporations, municipalities, and federal agencies; you can even buy U.S. Treasury notes and bonds in the form of zero coupon securities. Until about 10 or 12 years ago, major brokerage houses used to package U.S. Treasury securities as zeros and sell them to the investing public in the form of investment trusts. These unit trusts were marketed under such names as *TIGRS*, *CATS*, and *LIONS* and became enormously popular with investors. Seeing this, the Treasury decided to eliminate the middleman and "issue" their own form of zero coupon bond, known as *Treasury STRIPS*, or *STRIP-Ts*, for short. When that happened, the market for CATS and other felines pretty much dried up. (Some old issues are still out there, but the new issue market for these securities has virtually disappeared.) Actually, the Treasury does not issue zero coupon bonds, but instead, *they allow government securities dealers to take regular coupon-bearing notes and bonds in stripped form*, which can then be sold to the public as zero coupon securities. Essentially, the coupons are stripped from the bond, repackaged, and then sold separately as zero coupon bonds. For example, a 20-year Treasury bond has 40 semiannual coupon payments, plus one principal payment—each of these 41 cash flows can be repackaged and sold as 41 different zero coupon securities, with maturities that range from 6 months to 20 years.

BOND RATINGS

Bond ratings are like grades: A letter grade is assigned to a bond, which designates its investment quality. Ratings are widely used and are an important part of the municipal and corporate bond markets. The two largest and best known rating agencies are Moody's and Standard & Poor's. Every time a large, new corporate or municipal issue comes to the market, it is analyzed by a staff of professional bond analysts to determine its default risk exposure and investment quality. The financial records of the issuing organization are thoroughly examined and its future prospects assessed. The result of all this is the assignment of a bond rating at the time of issue that indicates the ability of the issuing organization to service its debt in a prompt and timely manner. Exhibit 12.9 lists the various ratings assigned to bonds by each of the two major agencies. Except for slight variations in designations (Aaa versus AAA, for example), the meanings and interpretations are basically the

EXHIBIT 12.9

MOODY'S AND STANDARD & POOR'S BOND RATINGS

Agencies like Moody's and Standard & Poor's rate corporate and municipal bonds; the ratings provide an indication of the bonds' investment quality (particularly with respect to an issue's default risk exposure).

Bond Ratings*

Moody's	S&P	Description
Aaa	AAA	*Prime-Quality Investment Bonds*—This is the highest rating assigned, denoting extremely strong capacity to pay.
AaA A	AA A	*High-Grade Investment Bonds*—These are also considered very safe bonds, though they're not quite as safe as Aaa/AAA issues; double-A-rated bonds (Aa/AA) are safer (have less risk of default) than single-Λ-rated issues.
Baa	BBB	*Medium-Grade Investment Bonds*—These are the lowest of the investment-grade issues; they're felt to lack certain protective elements against adverse economic conditions.
Ba B	BB B	*Junk Bonds*—With little protection against default, these are viewed as highly speculative securities.
Caa Ca C	CCC CC C D	*Poor-Quality Bonds*—These are either in default or very close to it; these are often referred to as Zombie Bonds.

*Some ratings may be modified to show relative standing within a major rating category; for example, Moody's uses numerical modifiers (1, 2, 3), whereas S&P uses plus (+) or minus (−) signs.

same. Note that the top four ratings (Aaa through Baa; or AAA through BBB) designate *investment-grade bonds*—such ratings are highly coveted by issuers because they indicate financially strong, well-run companies or municipalities. The next two ratings (Ba/B; or BB/B) are where you'll find most **junk bonds**; these ratings mean that although the principal and interest payments on the bonds are still being met, the risk of default is relatively high, as the issuers generally lack the financial strength found with investment-grade issues. While junk bonds—or *high yield bonds*, as they're also known—are popular with some investors, it should be understood that these are highly speculative securities. They may offer high rates of return, but they also involve substantial amounts of risks; in particular, there's a very real likelihood that the issue may encounter some difficulties.

Once a new issue is rated, the process doesn't stop there. Older, outstanding bonds are also regularly reviewed to ensure that their assigned ratings are still valid. Most issues will carry a single rating to maturity, but it is not uncommon for some to undergo revision. Finally, although it may appear that the issuing firm or municipality is receiving the rating, it is actually the individual issue that is being rated. As a result, a firm (or municipality) can have different ratings assigned to its issues; the senior securities, for example, might carry one rating and the junior issues a slightly lower rating. Most bond investors pay careful attention to ratings, because they can affect comparative market yields—specifically, the higher the rating, the lower the yield of an obligation, other things being equal. Thus, whereas an A-rated bond might offer an 8 percent yield, a comparable AAA issue would probably yield something like 7.25 or 7.50 percent.

junk bond
Also known as *high-yield bonds*, these are highly speculative securities that have received low ratings from Moody's or Standard & Poor's; the low ratings mean the issuers could have difficulty meeting interest and principal payments as they come due.

BOND QUOTES. Exhibit 12.10 contains examples of both corporate and Treasury bond quotes; these quotes were for trades that occurred on December 7, 2000. To understand the system used with corporate bonds, look at the Duke Energy (DukeEn) issue. The row of numbers immediately following the company name gives the coupon and the year in which the bond matures; the "$7\frac{1}{2}25$" means that this particular bond carries a $7\frac{1}{2}$ percent annual coupon and will mature sometime in the year 2025. Such information is important, because it lets investors differentiate among the various bonds issued by the same corporation. The next column, labeled "Cur Yld," provides the *current yield* being offered by the issue at its *current market price*. Current yield is found by dividing the bond's annual coupon (here, 7.50%, or $75.00) by the issue's closing price ($98\frac{1}{8}$ or $981.25), which in this case amounts to 7.6 percent. The "Vol" column represents the actual number of bonds traded; there were 10 of these bonds traded on this day. Price information is contained in the last two columns. Like stocks, bond quotes also show just the closing price, along with the net change in the closing price from the day before. *All bonds are quoted as a percent of par*, meaning that a quote of, say, 85 translates into a price of 85 percent of the bond's par value. Because corporate bonds typically have par values of $1,000, a bond quote of 85 means the price is really $850 (85% $\times$ $1,000). Corporate bonds are traded in fractions of $\frac{1}{8}$, but each fraction is worth 1.25 *dollars*. Thus, Duke Energy's closing price for the day was $981.25, found by multiplying the quoted price by $1,000; that is, $98\frac{1}{8}$ = 98.125% of par = .98125 $\times$ $1,000 = $981.25.

Convertibles are also listed along with other corporate bonds. They are easy to find—just look for the letters "cv" in the current yield column, such as in the case of the Kerr McGee $5\frac{1}{4}$-10 convertibles in Exhibit 12.10. Except for the "cv" in the current yield column, all other aspects of the quote are exactly like that for any other listed corporate bond. Also listed in Exhibit 12.10 are some zero coupon bonds issued by Honeywell (Honywll). Such bonds have the letters "zr" in place of their coupons; for example, with the Honeywell bonds, the "zr07" means the issue is a zero coupon bond that matures in 2007. Note that on December 7th, this particular zero coupon bond traded at 66 per cent of par—in dollars, that means the bond was trading at $660. That's what investors were paying for this issue in late 2000; in return, they will receive about $1\frac{1}{2}$ times that amount ($1,000) sometime in the year 2007.

U.S. Treasury (and agency) bond quotes are listed in thirty-seconds of a point. With government bonds, the figures to the right of the colon (:) show the number of thirty-seconds in the fractional bid or ask price. For example, look at the bid price of the $9\frac{3}{8}$ percent U.S. Treasury issue. It's quoted at 117:24 (bid), which translates to $117\frac{24}{32}$, or 117.75 percent of par. Note the "ask" price is 117:28, or 117.875 percent of par; this is the price you'd pay to buy the bonds. Thus, if you want to buy 15 of these bonds (with a par value of $15,000), you will end up paying $17,681.25 (that is, $15,000 $\times$ 1.17875). Indeed, with just $15,000 to invest, you could buy only 12 of these bonds—with each bond trading at $1,178.75, the number of bonds you can buy is: $15,000 $\div$ 1,178.75 = 12.73 bonds. Because you can only deal in whole bonds (you cannot buy fractional issues), you'll either have to settle for 12 bonds, or come up with some more money. Government bond listings include not only the coupon (see the "rate" column of the Treasury quotes in Exhibit 12.10) but also the year and *month* of maturity. When there is more than one date in the maturity column (see the $11\frac{3}{4}$ Treasury bond, with a maturity of 05–10), the second figure is the maturity date and the first indicates when the bond becomes freely callable. This bond matures in February 2010, and carries a call deferment provision through February 2005. If there is only one date, the bond is *non-callable*.

Treasuries are quoted in bid/ask terms; *bid* means what bond dealers are willing to pay (and how much you can sell them for) and *ask* is what they will sell the bonds for (or what it will cost you to buy). The "Yld" column is *not* the issue's current yield but the bond's *yield to maturity* (which we will discuss in the next section).

EXHIBIT 12.10

CORPORATE AND TREASURY BOND PRICE QUOTES

Corporate and U.S. Treasury bonds are quoted as a precent of their par value. However, corporate bonds are quoted in eighths of a point, whereas Treasuries are quoted in thirty-seconds. Par for these bonds is normally $1,000, so each point in a bond quote is worth $10 (and each $\frac{1}{8}$ of a point, $1.25). Thus, a quote of $89\frac{1}{4}$ is *not* $89.25, but $892.50 ($1,000 × .8925); likewise, a quote of 115 translates to $1,150 ($1,000 × 1.15).

Corporate Bonds

BONDS	CUR YLD.	VOL.	CLOSE	NET CHG.
Conseco 10½04	.11.5	114	91½	...
Conseco 10¼02	.13.6	73	75½	+ 1½
CrownC 7⅛02	..11.3	40	63¼	+ 2¼
CypSemi 4s05	...cv	5	88	...
Deere 8.95s19	...8.4	15	107	+ 1
Dole 7s03	......7.4	60	94½	...
Dole 7⅞13	.....9.1	12	86¼	− ½
DukeEn 7½.25	...7.6	10	98⅛	− ⅝
FeODS 8⅛02	....8.1	24	100⅞	+ 1
FnclFed 4½05	...cv	2	93	− 1
FemntGn zr13	.....	3	19	− 8½
GBCB 8⅜07	....10.6	10	79	+ 1
GEICap 7⅞06	...7.3	29	108½	+ 1½
GMA 5½01	.....5.6	3	97¾	− ¼
GMA 6⅛08	.....6.7	20	91¾	+ ⅜
GulfMo 5s56f	...9.6	27	52	− 4¾
HewlPkd zr17	......	20	51	...
Hilton 5s06	cv	20	82	+ ¼
Hollngr 8⅝05	...8.9	25	97¼	¦ 1¼
Honywll zr01	......	40	95¹⁷⁄₃₂	+ ⅓
Honywll zr07	......	50	66	+ 1⅝
Honywll zr09	......	50	55	+ 2⅞
HuntPly 11¾04	.13.4	5	88	− 2
IBM 7¼02	.....7.1	50	101⅜	+ ⅜
IBM 7½13	.....7.3	16	103⅛	− ¾
IBM 8⅜19	....	32	109⅞	+ 2⅝
KaulB 7¾04	...8.3	70	93¾	− ⅜
KaulB 9⅝06	....9.8	127	98	+ ¼
KenlE 4½04	cv	34	82	− ½
KerrM 5¼10	cv	5	119¼	...
KerrM 7½14	cv	18	95⅞	− 1⅜
Koppers 8½04	..9.9	8	86	− 3
Leucadia 7¾13	..8.9	20	87	− 2
Loews 3⅛07	cv	40	82	− ¼
LglsLt 8.2s23	...8.2	25	99½	− 1½
Lucent 7¼06	....7.5	98	97	+ ¼

Duke Energy → DukeEn 7½.25

Honeywell → Honywll zr07

Kerr McGee → KerrM 5¼10

Corporate bond quote

Zero coupon bond quote

Convertible bond quote

Treasury Bonds

RATE	MATURITY MO/YR	BID	ASKED	CHG.	ASKED YLD.
6¾	May 05n	105:16	105:17	+ 1	5.33
12	May 05	125:17	125:23	...	5.40
6½	Aug 05n	104:20	104:22	+ 1	5.35
10¾	Aug 05	121:21	121:27	...	5.41
5¾	**Nov 05n**	**102:03**	**102:04**		**5.25**
5⅞	Nov 05n	102:07	102:09	...	5.34
5⅝	Feb 06n	101:05	101:07	1	5.35
9⅜	Feb 06	117:24	117:28	+ 1	5.38
6⅞	May 06n	106:31	107:01	...	5.37
7	Jul 06n	107:22	107:24	+ 1	5.38
6½	Oct 06n	105:17	105:19	+ 1	5.37
3⅜	Jan 07i	97:21	97:22	− 1	3.80
6¼	Feb 07n	104:18	104:20	+ 1	5.36
7⅝	Feb 02-07	101:31	102:01	− 1	5.82
6⅝	May 07n	106:24	106:26	+ 2	5.36
6⅓	Aug 07n	104:07	104:09	+ 2	5.35
7⅞	Nov 02-07	104:00	104:02	+ 1	5.63
3⅝	Jan 08i	98:29	98:30	+ 3	3.80
5 ½	Feb 08n	100:27	100:29	+ 3	5.35
5⅝	May 08n	101:19	101:21	+ 2	5.35
8⅜	Aug 03-08	106:23	106:25	...	5.62
4¾	Nov 08n	96:04	96:06	+ 3	5.35
8¾	Nov 03-08	108:12	108:14	+ 1	5.59
3⅞	Jan 09i	100:16	100:17	+ 4	3.80
5½	May 09n	100:30	101:00	+ 2	5.35
9⅛	May 04-09	110:27	110:31	+ 2	5.57
6	Aug 09n	104:10	104:12	+ 4	5.36
10⅛	Nov 04-09	116:21	116:25	+ 1	5.57
4¼	Jan 10i	103:15	103:16	+ 2	3.79
6½	Feb 10n	108:04	108:05	+ 4	5.36
11¾	Feb 05-10	122:26	123:00	+ 1	5.52
10	May 05-10	117.00	117:10	+ 2	5.54
5¾	**Aug 10n**	**103:10**	**103:11**	**+ 4**	**5.30**
12¾	Nov 05-10	130:23	130.29	+ 2	5.51
13⅞	May 06-11	138:21	138:27	+ 2	5.51
14	Nov 06-11	142:13	142:19	+ 3	5.49
10⅜	Nov 07-12	127:19	127:25	+ 4	5.50

Treasury bond quote → 9⅜ Feb 06

Callable Treasury bond quote → 11¾ Feb 05-10

Source: *The Wall Street Journal*, Dec. 8, 2000.

BOND PRICES AND YIELDS

The price of a bond is a function of its coupon, maturity, and the movement of market interest rates. *When interest rates go down, bond prices go up, and vice versa.* The relationship of bond prices to market rates is captured in Exhibit 12.11. Basically, the graph serves to reinforce the *inverse* relationship between bond prices and market interest rates; note that *lower* rates lead to *higher* bond prices. The exhibit also shows the difference between premium and discount bonds. A **premium bond** is one that sells for more than its par value, which occurs whenever market interest rates drop below the coupon rate on the bond; a **discount bond**, in contrast, sells for less than par, and is the result of market rates being greater than the issue's coupon rate. Thus the 10 percent bond in our illustration traded as a premium bond when market rates were at 8 percent, but as a discount bond when rates stood at 12 percent.

premium bond
A bond that has a market value in excess of par; occurs when interest rates drop below the coupon rate.

discount bond
A bond with a market value lower than par; occurs when market rates are greater than the coupon rate.

When a bond is first issued, it is usually sold to the public at a price that equals, or is very close to, its par value. Likewise, when the bond matures—some 15, 20, or 30 years later—it will once again be priced at its par value. But what happens to the price of the bond in between is of considerable concern to most bond investors. In this regard, we know that the extent to which bond prices move depends not only on the *direction* of change in interest rates, but also on the *magnitude* of such changes; for the greater the moves in interest rates, the greater the swings in bond prices. But there's more, for bond prices will also vary according to the coupon and maturity of the issue—that is, bonds with *lower coupons* or *longer maturities* will respond more vigorously to changes in market rates and undergo *greater price swings*. It should be obvious, therefore, that if interest rates are moving up, the investor should seek high coupon bonds with short maturities, because this will cause minimal price variation and *preserve as much capital as possible.* In contrast, if rates are heading down, that's the time to be in long-term bonds—if you're a speculator looking for lots of capital gains, then go with long-term, *low coupon* bonds, whereas if you're trying to lock in a high level of coupon (interest) income, then stick with long-term, *high coupon* bonds that offer plenty of call protection (which you can get from issues that are noncallable or have extended call-deferment periods).

CURRENT YIELD AND YIELD TO MATURITY. The *yield* on a bond is the rate of return you would earn if you held the bond for a stated period of time. The two most commonly cited bond yields are current yield and yield to maturity. **Current yield** reflects the amount of annual interest income the bond provides relative to its current market price. The formula for current yield is:

current yield
The amount of current income a bond provides relative to its current market price.

$$\text{Current yield} = \frac{\text{Annual interest income}}{\text{Market price of bond}}$$

As you can see, the current yield on a bond is basically the same as the dividend yield on a stock. Assume, for example, that a 9 percent bond with a $1,000 face value is currently selling for $910. Because annual interest income would amount to $90 (i.e., .09 × $1,000) and the current market price of the bond is $910, its current yield would be 9.89 percent ($90/$910). This yield, which is commonly quoted in the financial press, would be of interest to *investors seeking current income*; other things being equal, the higher the current yield, the more attractive a bond would be to such an investor.

yield to maturity
The annual rate of return a bondholder, purchasing a bond today, would earn if he or she held it to maturity.

The annual rate of return a bondholder would receive *if he or she held the issue to its maturity* is captured in the bond's **yield to maturity**. This measure captures both the annual interest income and the recovery of principal at maturity; in addition, it includes the impact of interest-on-interest and therefore provides a fully compounded rate of return. If a bond is purchased at its face value, its yield to maturity will equal the coupon,

EXHIBIT 12.11

PRICE BEHAVIOR OF A BOND WITH A 10 PERCENT COUPON

A bond will sell at its par value so long as the prevailing market interest rate remains the same as the bond's coupon (for example, when both coupon and market rates equal 10 percent). However, when market rates drop, bond prices rise, and vice versa; moreover, as a bond approaches its maturity, the price of the issue will always move toward its par value, no matter what happens to interest rates.

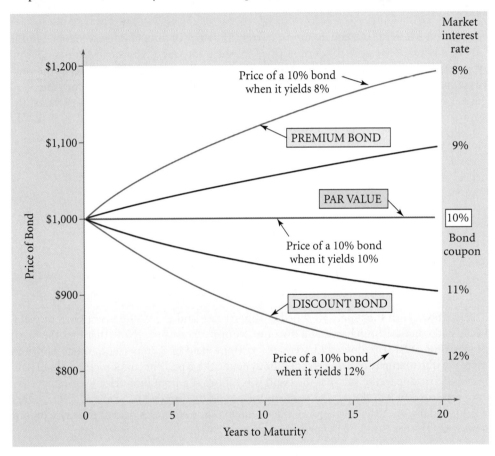

or stated, rate of interest. If it is purchased at a discount, its yield to maturity will be greater than the coupon rate because the investor will receive, in addition to annual interest income, the full face value of the bond even though he or she paid something less than par—in effect, the investor will earn some capital gains on the investment. Of course, if the bond is purchased at a premium, the opposite will be true: The yield to maturity on the issue will be less than its coupon rate because the transaction will involve a capital loss—that is, the investor will pay more for the bond than he or she will get back at maturity.

You can find the yield to maturity on a bond by using the *approximate yield* formula introduced earlier in this chapter. Actually, using a hand-held financial calculator (which we'll demonstrate in the following) results in a yield to maturity that's far more accurate, and is, in fact, very close to the measure used in the market; the only difference is that market participants normally use semi-annual compounding in their calculations, whereas we use annual compounding. Employing the formula approach for now, by setting the future price *(FP)* of the investment equal to the bond's face value ($1,000), you can use the following version of the approximate yield equation to find the *approximate yield to maturity on a bond:*

$$\text{Approximate Yield to Maturity} = \frac{\left[\dfrac{CI + \$1,000 - CP}{N}\right]}{\left[\dfrac{CP + \$1,000}{2}\right]}$$

As you will recall, CI equals annual current income (or annual interest income, in the case of a bond), CP stands for current price (of the bond), and N is the investment period (the number of years to maturity). Assume, for example, you are contemplating the purchase of a $1,000, 9 percent bond with 15 years remaining to maturity, and that the bond currently trades at a price of $910. Given CI = $90, CP = $910, and N = 15 years, the approximate yield to maturity on this bond will be:

$$\text{Approximate Yield to Maturity} = \frac{\$90 + \left[\dfrac{\$1,000 - \$910}{15}\right]}{\left[\dfrac{\$910 + \$1,000}{2}\right]}$$

$$= \frac{\$90 + \left[\dfrac{\$90}{15}\right]}{\left[\dfrac{\$1,910}{2}\right]} = \underline{\underline{10.05\%}}$$

This is above both the 9 percent stated (coupon) rate and the 9.89 percent current yield, because the bond is purchased at a discount from its face value. (Note that had the bond been selling at $1,090, it would have had a current yield of 8.26 percent and an approximate yield to maturity of 8.04 percent—both below the 9 percent coupon rate; such behavior would be due to the fact that the bond was selling at a premium price.)

You can also *find the yield to maturity on a bond* by using a financial calculator; here's what you'd do. With the calculator in the *annual mode,* to find the yield to maturity on our 9 percent, 15-year-bond that's currently trading at $910:

1. Punch 15 and then press the **N** key.
2. Punch −910 (be sure to enter this as a negative value) and then press **PV**.
3. Punch 90 and then **PMT**.
4. Punch 1,000 and then the **FV** key.
5. Now, press the **CPT** key and then the **i** key.

A value of 10.19 should appear in the calculator display—this is the yield to maturity on the bond in question (and it's a *more accurate* measure of yield than that found by using the "approximate" procedure).

Yield to maturity measures are used by investors to assess the underlying attractiveness of a bond investment. The higher the yield to maturity, the more attractive the investment, other things being equal. *If a bond provided a yield to maturity that equaled or exceeded an investor's desired rate of return, it would be considered a worthwhile investment candidate,* because it would promise a yield that would adequately compensate the investor for the level of risk involved.

12-10. What is the difference between a secured bond and an unsecured bond? Give a few examples of each. Briefly describe the following bond features: (a) *sinking funds*, (b) *call features*, and (c) *coupon*.

12-11. Are *junk bonds* and *zero coupon bonds* the same? Explain. What are the basic tax features of a tax-exempt *municipal bond*? Are there such things as *taxable* municipal bonds? Explain.

12-12. Illustrate why an investor in a high tax bracket would prefer municipal bonds to other investment vehicles.

12-13. Explain the system of bond ratings used by Moody's and Standard & Poor's.

12-14. What effects do current market interest rates have on the price behavior of outstanding bonds?

Preferreds and Convertibles [LG6]

Preferreds and *convertibles* are corporate securities that are senior to common stock. Although preferred stocks are actually a form of equity, they, along with convertibles, are considered fixed-income securities because their level of current income is fixed. Convertible securities, issued initially as either bonds or preferred stocks, are subsequently convertible into shares of the issuing firm's common stock. Preferred stocks, in contrast, are issued and remain as equity. Preferreds derive their name in part from the preferential claim on income they command—that is, all preferred dividends must be paid before any payments can be made to holders of common stock.

PREFERRED STOCKS

Preferred stocks carry a dividend, usually fixed, that is paid quarterly and stated either in dollar terms or as a percent of par (or stated) value. They are considered to be *hybrid securities* because they possess features of both common stocks and corporate bonds. That is, they are like common stocks in that they pay dividends, *which may be passed* when corporate earnings fall below certain levels. Moreover, preferreds represent equity ownership and are issued without stated maturity dates. They are, however, also a lot like bonds in that they provide investors with a prior claim on income and assets, and the level of current income is usually fixed for the life of the issue. Most important, because these securities usually trade on the basis of the yield they offer to investors, *they are viewed in the marketplace as fixed-income obligations* and, as a result, are treated much like bonds.

PREFERRED STOCK FEATURES. Preferred stocks possess features that not only distinguish them from other types of securities, but also help differentiate one preferred from another. For example, the amount of dividends that an issue pays is a common way of describing preferred stocks—thus, a company could have a "three-dollar" preferred stock outstanding (meaning the issue pays $3 per share in annual dividends) and another issue of preferred that pays $4.75 a share in yearly dividends. These are two separate issues and would trade at two different prices. Many preferred stocks today are issued with call features, which means they can be retired if the issuing company decides to do so, and some even have sinking fund provisions, indicating how they will be paid off over time (sinking fund preferreds, in effect, have implied maturity dates). In addition to these features, preferred stock investors should also determine whether the stock is "cumulative" or "noncumulative."

cumulative (preferred stock)
A preferred stock feature requiring that any passed dividends must be paid before distributing any dividends to common stockholders.

Cumulative versus Noncumulative. Most preferred stocks are **cumulative**, which means that any dividends passed in previous periods must be paid in full before any dividends can be distributed to common stockholders—in essence, if the preferred stockholders do not receive any dividends, then neither do the common shareholders. For example, assume a firm has outstanding a *$4 preferred stock* (which means the stated dividend is $4 per year, or $1 per quarter) and that the last two quarterly dividends have not been paid. Before any dividends can be paid to the common stockholders, the preferred stockholders must be paid the $2 of past dividends *plus the current quarterly dividend of $1*. Had the preferred stock been *noncumulative*, only the current $1 dividend would have to be paid before distributing any earnings to the common stockholders.

INVESTING IN PREFERREDS. Most individuals invest in preferred stocks because of the high current income they provide in the form of annual dividends. Moreover, such dividend income is highly predictable even though it lacks legal backing and can be passed. It's not surprising, therefore, that dividend yield is the key ingredient in evaluating the investment appeal of most preferred stocks. *Dividend yield*—which is found by dividing annual dividend income by the market price of the stock—is a reflection of an issue's current yield and, as such, is used to assess preferred stock investment opportunities. Other things being equal, the higher the dividend yield, the more attractive the investment vehicle. For example, suppose a certain preferred stock pays a dividend of $2 per year and is currently priced at $20; this preferred would have a dividend yield of $2/$20 = 10%. Whether a 10 percent return from this preferred stock makes for a good investment depends on (1) the amount of risk exposure involved and (2) the kinds of returns you can generate elsewhere—in other words, if you can earn better than 10 percent on other similarly risky investments, then do it!

Once you invest in a preferred, you should keep your eyes on market interest rates, because preferred stock prices are closely related to prevailing market rates; after all, you are investing in a *fixed-income security* whose value is determined chiefly by its (dividend) yield. When the general level of interest rates moves up, the yields on preferreds rise and their prices *decline* accordingly; in contrast, when rates drift down, the yields on preferreds decrease and their prices *rise*. Thus, like that of any fixed-income security, the price behavior of most good-grade preferred stocks is inversely related to market interest rates.

WATCH OUT FOR RATINGS. Like bonds, the investment quality of preferred stocks is also rated by Moody's and Standard & Poor's, the bond rating agencies. These two agencies assign ratings largely on the basis of their judgment regarding the relative safety of dividends. The greater the likelihood that the issuer will be able to service the preferred in a prompt and timely fashion, the higher the rating. Much like bonds, the top four ratings designate investment-grade (high-quality) preferreds. Although preferreds come in a full range of agency ratings, most tend to fall in the medium-grade categories (a and baa) or lower. Generally speaking, higher agency ratings reduce the market yield of an issue. A preferred's agency rating should be closely monitored by serious, long-term investors, because they not only eliminate much of the need for basic security analysis, but also help investors define an appropriate level of yield for a potential preferred stock investment.

CONVERTIBLE SECURITIES

Convertible issues, more popularly known simply as *convertibles*, represent still another type of fixed-income security. Although they possess the features and performance characteristics of both fixed-income and equity securities, *convertibles should be viewed primarily as a form of equity*. Most investors commit their capital to such obligations not because of their attractive yields, but because of the potential price performance the stock side of the issue offers. In short, convertible securities are popular with individual investors because of the *equity kicker* they provide. Not surprisingly, whenever the stock market is strong, convertibles tend to do well, and vice versa. Irrespective of whether they're issued as *convertible bonds* (the most common type of convertible) or *convertible preferreds*, these securities are closely linked to the firm's equity position and are therefore usually considered interchangeable for investment purposes. Except for a few peculiarities, such as the fact that preferreds pay dividends rather than interest and do so on a quarterly rather than semiannual basis, convertible bonds and convertible preferreds are evaluated in pretty much the same way. The following discussion on convertible bonds, therefore, applies to convertible preferreds as well.

ISSUE FEATURES. Convertible bonds are usually issued as debentures (ie, unsecured debt), but they carry the provision that, within a stipulated time period, *they may be converted into a certain number of shares of the issuing company's common stock.* (Convertible *notes* are just like convertible bonds except the debt portion of the security carries a *short-term* [5 to 10 year] maturity; other than the life of the debt, there's no real difference between the two types of issues—they're both unsecured debt obligations and they're usually subordinated to other forms of debt. Most important, they're both convertible into common stock on pretty much the same terms. Thus, for our purposes here, we'll use the terms interchangeably.)

Generally speaking, there is little or no cash involved at the time of conversion; the investor merely trades in the convertible bond (or note) for a stipulated number of shares of common stock. Exhibit 12.12 provides some specifics about a convertible note recently issued by Cypress Semiconductor Corp. Note that this obligation was originally issued as a $3\frac{3}{4}$ percent subordinated (unsecured) note. The reason the issue carries such a low coupon (compared to prevailing market rates of more like 7 or 8 percent) is, of course, the fact that it offers an attractive conversion feature—in particular, each $1,000 note can be converted into Cypress stock at roughly $62.55 a share. Thus, *regardless of what happens to the market price of the stock*, the convertible investor can redeem each note for 15.98 shares of the company's stock (i.e., $1,000 ÷ $62.55 = 15.98 shares). If at the time of conversion, Cypress stock is trading in the market at, say, $125 a share, then the investor would have just converted a $1,000 debt obligation into $1,997.50 worth of stock (15.98 × $125 = $1,997.50).

The key element of any convertible issue is its **conversion privilege**, which stipulates the conditions and specific nature of the conversion feature. First, it states exactly when the bond can be converted. Sometimes, there will be an initial waiting period, of 6 months to perhaps 2 years after the date of issue, during which time the issue cannot be converted. The *conversion period* then begins, after which the issue can be converted at any time. Technically it is the *bondholder* who has the right to convert the bond into common stock, but more commonly the issuing firm will initiate the conversion by calling the issue. From the investor's point of view, the most important item of information is the **conversion ratio**, which specifies the number of shares of common stock that the bond can be converted into. For example, a $1,000 convertible bond might stipulate a conversion ratio of 20, meaning that you can "cash in" one convertible bond for 20 shares of the company's stock. (*Note:* The Cypress convertibles in Exhibit 12.12 have an implied conversion ratio of 15.98 shares.)

CONVERSION VALUE. Given the significance of the price behavior of the underlying common stock to the value of a convertible security, one of the most important measures to a convertible bond investor is conversion value. In essence, **conversion value** is an indication of what a convertible issue would trade for *if it were priced to sell on the basis of its*

conversion privilege
The provision in a convertible issue that stipulates the conditions of the conversion feature, such as the conversion period and conversion ratio.

conversion ratio
A ratio that specifies the number of shares of common stock into which a convertible bond can be converte d.

conversion value
A measure of what a convertible issue would trade for if it were priced to sell on the basis of its stock value; found by multiplying the conversion ratio by the current market price of the underlying common stock.

EXHIBIT 12.12

A NEWLY ISSUED CONVERTIBLE BOND

Holders of this Cypress Semiconductor note can convert it into the company's common stock at the stated conversion price of $62.548 per share. As a result, they would receive 15.988 shares of stock in exchange for each $1,000 convertible bond they hold. Prior to conversion, the bondholders will receive annual interest income of $37.50 for each bond.

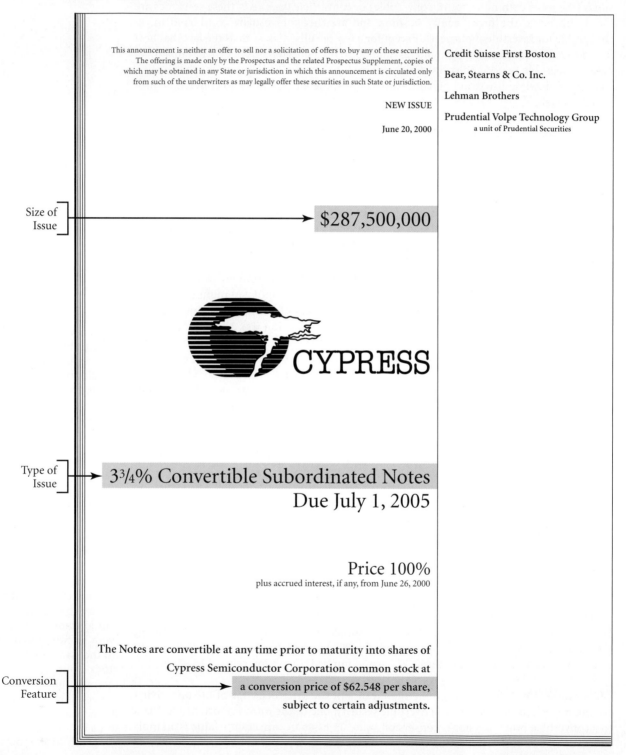

This announcement is neither an offer to sell nor a solicitation of offers to buy any of these securities. The offering is made only by the Prospectus and the related Prospectus Supplement, copies of which may be obtained in any State or jurisdiction in which this announcement is circulated only from such of the underwriters as may legally offer these securities in such State or jurisdiction.

NEW ISSUE

June 20, 2000

Credit Suisse First Boston

Bear, Stearns & Co. Inc.

Lehman Brothers

Prudential Volpe Technology Group
a unit of Prudential Securities

Size of Issue → $287,500,000

CYPRESS

Type of Issue → 3³/4% Convertible Subordinated Notes
Due July 1, 2005

Price 100%
plus accrued interest, if any, from June 26, 2000

The Notes are convertible at any time prior to maturity into shares of Cypress Semiconductor Corporation common stock at

Conversion Feature → a conversion price of $62.548 per share,

subject to certain adjustments.

stock value. Conversion value is easy to find: simply multiply the conversion ratio of the issue by the current market price of the underlying common stock. For example, a convertible that carried a conversion ratio of 20 would have a conversion value of $1,200 if the firm's stock traded at a current market price of $60 per share (20 × $60 = $1,200). Unfortunately, convertible issues seldom trade precisely at their conversion value; rather, they invariably trade at **conversion premiums**, which means the convertibles are priced in the market at more than their conversion values. For example, a convertible that traded at $1,400 and had a conversion value of $1,200 would have a conversion premium of $200 (that is, $1,400 − $1,200 = $200).

conversion premium
The difference between a convertible security's market price and its conversion value.

INVESTMENT MERITS. Convertible securities appeal to investors who want *the price potential of a common stock along with the downside risk protection of a corporate bond*. This two-sided feature is critical with convertibles and is virtually impossible to match with straight common or straight debt. As a rule, whenever a convertible trades near or above its par value ($1,000), it will exhibit price behavior that closely matches that of the underlying common stock; if the stock goes up in price, so will the convertible, and vice versa. In fact, because of the conversion ratio, the price change of the convertible will *exceed* that of the common. For example, if a convertible carries a conversion ratio of, say, 20, then for every point the common stock goes up (or down) in price, the price of the convertible will move in the *same direction by a multiple of 20*. Because of the obvious importance of the underlying common stock, investors should carefully consider this element before investing in convertibles. If the future prospects for a stock are promising, the convertible could turn out to be a good investment.

A final feature of convertible bonds is that the current income earned from interest payments normally exceeds the income from the dividends that would be received from a comparable investment in the underlying common stock. For example, a $1,000 convertible with an 8 percent coupon would yield $80 per year to the holder; if the convertible carried a conversion ratio of 20, and each share of stock paid $2.50 in dividends, an investment in 20 shares of the firm's stock would provide only $50 per year in dividend income. Thus, with convertibles it is possible to reap the advantages of common stock (in the form of potential upward price appreciation) and still generate improved current income.

CONCEPT CHECK

> 12-15. What is preferred stock? Distinguish between a *cumulative* preferred and *noncumulative* preferred stock.
>
> 12-16. What is a convertible bond? Why do investors buy convertible securities?
>
> 12-17. Describe the *conversion privilege* of a convertible security. Explain how the market price of the underlying common stock affects the market price of the convertible bond.

SUMMARY

LG1. **Describe the various types of risks to which investors are exposed, as well as the sources of return.** Although investing offers returns in the form of current income and/or capital gains, it also involves risk; the basic types of investment risk are business risk, financial risk, market risk, purchasing power risk, interest rate risk, liquidity risk, and event risk—all of which combine to affect the level of return from an investment.

LG2. **Know how to search for an acceptable investment, based on risk, return, and yield.** The value, and therefore the acceptability, of any investment is a function of the amount of return it's expected to produce relative to the amount of perceived risk involved in the investment. Investors are entitled to be compensated for the risks they must accept in an investment; therefore, the more risk there is in an investment, the more return you should expect to earn. This risk-return trade-off is generally captured in the "desired rate of return," which is that rate of return you feel you should receive in compensation for the amount of risk you must assume. So long as the expected return on an investment (the return you *think* you'll earn) is greater than the desired rate of return (the return you *should* earn), it should be considered an acceptable investment candidate—one worthy of our attention.

LG3. **Discuss the merits of investing in common stock and be able to distinguish among the different types of stocks.** Common stocks are a popular form of investing that can be used to meet just about any investment objective—from capital gains or current income to some combination of both. Investors can choose from blue chips, growth, or tech stocks; income, speculative, cyclical, or defensive stocks; and small- or mid-cap stocks. If they're so inclined, they can even buy foreign stocks by investing in ADRs (American Depositary Receipts).

LG4. **Become familiar with the various measures of performance and how to use them in putting a value on stocks.** The value of a share of stock is based in large part on various performance measures like dividend yield, book value, net profit margin, return on investment (ROE), earnings per share, price/earnings (P/E) ratio, beta, and approximate yield, which can be used to provide a measure of expected return. Investors look at these measures to gain insights about the financial condition and operating results of the company, and ultimately, to obtain input needed to measure the expected return (approimate yield) on the stock.

LG5. **Describe different types of bonds and note how these securities are used as investment vehicles.** Bonds are another popular form of investing; they are basically the publicly issued debt of corporations and various levels of government (from the U.S. Treasury and various agencies of the U.S. government to state and local—municipal—governments). Known as fixed-income securities, these obligations can be used to generate either current income or capital gains (which occurs when market rates go down).

LG6. **Distinguish between preferred stocks and convertible securities, and note the investment merits of each.** Preferred stocks and convertible bonds combine the features of both equity and debt securities, and are widely used by individual investors. Preferred stocks are like common stocks to the extent that they pay dividends, but are also like bonds in that they provide investors with a fixed claim on assets and a fixed level of income. In contrast, convertible bonds are issued as debt securities but they carry a provision that allows their holders to convert the bonds into shares of common stock.

QUESTIONS AND PROBLEMS

1. What makes for a good investment? Use the approximate yield formula to rank the following investments according to their expected returns:
   a. Buy a stock for $45 a share, hold it for 3 years, then sell it for $75 a share (the stock pays annual dividends of $3 a share).

    b. Buy a security for $25, hold it for 2 years, then sell it for $60 (current income on this security is zero).

    c. Buy a 1-year, 12 percent note for $950 (assume the note has a $1,000 par value and that it will be held to maturity).

2. Selected financial information about Engulf and Devour, Inc. is provided as follows:

Total assets	$20,000,000
Total liabilities	$ 8,000,000
Total preferred stock	$ 3,000,000
Total annual preferred stock dividends	$ 240,000
Net profits after tax	$ 2,500,000
Number of shares of common stock outstanding	500,000 shares
Current market price of common stock	$50.00 a share
Annual common stock dividends	$ 2.50 a share

    Using the above information, compute the following:

    a. The stock's dividend yield

    b. Book value per share

    c. Earnings per share

    d. P/E ratio

3. Assume you've just inherited $350,000 and have decided to invest a big chunk of it ($250,000 to be exact) in common stocks. Your objective is to build up as much capital as you can over the next 15 to 20 years, and you're willing to tolerate a "good deal" of risk.

    a. What *types* of stocks (for example, blue chips, income stocks, and so on) do you think you'd be most interested in and why? Come up with at least three different types of stocks and briefly explain the rationale for each.

    b. Would your selections change if you were dealing with a smaller amount of money— say, only $50,000? What if you were a more risk-adverse investor?

4. Using the resources available at your campus or public library, select a company from *Value Line* that would be of interest to you. (*HINT:* choose a company that's been publicly traded for at least 10 to 15 years, and *avoid* public utilities, banks, and other financial institutions.) Obtain a copy of the latest *Value Line* report on your chosen company. Using the forecasted data reported in *Value Line*, determine the following. (*Note:* Use a 3-year holding period throughout this exercise.)

    a. What's the latest price of the stock you selected and how much is the stock currently paying in annual dividends?

    b. According to *Value Line*, what are the (approximate) projected dividends per share for each of the next 3 years? Also, what's the (approximate) estimated price of the stock at the end of the 3-year holding period?

    c. Use Use the approximate yield equation to find the expected return on this stock.

    d. If you were investing in this stock, what would you want to earn as a minimum/ required rate of return? Briefly explain how you came up with that number.

    e. Would you consider this stock to be a worthwhile investment candidate? Explain.

5. An investor in the 28 percent tax bracket is trying to decide which of two bonds to select: One is a 6.5 percent U.S. Treasury bond selling at par and the other is a municipal bond with a 5.25 percent coupon, which is also selling at par. Which of these two bonds should the investor select? Why?

6. Describe and differentiate between a bond's (a) current yield and (b) yield to maturity. Why are these yield measures important to the bond investor? Find the (approximate) yield to maturity of a 20-year, 9 percent, $1,000 par value bond trading at a price of $850. What's the current yield on this bond?

7. Which of the following three bonds offers the highest current yield? Which one has the highest yield to maturity?
   a. A 9.5 percent, 20-year bond quoted at $97\frac{3}{4}$
   b. A 16 percent, 15-year bond quoted at $164\frac{5}{8}$
   c. A 5.25 percent, 18-year bond quoted at 54

8. Using the bond quotes in Exhibit 12.10, how much would you pay for the following bonds? (Assume all the bonds have $1,000 par values.)
   a. The $6\frac{1}{8}$% GMAC (GMA) bond that matures in 2008
   b. The $10\frac{1}{2}$% Conseco bond that matures in 2004
   c. The Hewlett-Packard (HewlPkd) zero-coupon bond that matures in 2017
   d. The Hilton 5% convertible bond that matures in 2006
   e. The $9\frac{1}{8}$% Treasury bond that matures in May 2009

9. Find the conversion value of a convertible bond that carries a conversion ratio of 24, given that the market price of the underlying common stock is $55 a share. Would there be any conversion premium if the convertible bond had a market price of $1,500? If so, how much?

10. A certain 6 percent convertible bond (maturing in 20 years) is convertible into 20 shares of the company's common stock. The bond has a par value of $1,000 and is currently trading at $800; the stock (which pays a dividend of 75 cents a share) is currently trading in the market at $35 a share. Use the above information to answer the following questions:
    a. What is the current yield on the convertible bond? What is the dividend yield on the company's common stock? Which provides more current income: the convertible bond or the common stock? Explain.
    b. What is the bond's conversion ratio? Its conversion price?
    c. What is the conversion value of this issue? Is there any conversion premium in this issue? How much?
    d. What is the (approximate) yield to maturity on the convertible bond?

11. Using the resources available at your campus or public library, work the following problems. (Note: Show your work for all your calculations.)
    a. Select any two *common* stocks, and determine the dividend yield, earnings per share, and P/E ratio for each.
    b. Select any two *bonds*, and determine the current yield and (approximate) yield to maturity of each.
    c. Select any two *preferred* stocks, and determine the current yield of each.
    d. Select any two *convertible debentures*, and determine the conversion ratio, conversion value, and conversion premium for each.

APPLYING PERSONAL FINANCE

The Type of Common Stock: Does It Really Matter?

Generally speaking, investors believe the kinds of stocks they own have a lot to do with the kinds of returns they are able to generate. How about you? Do you really believe it makes all that much difference? Well, there is one way to find out—let's put this belief to the test. We will conduct this test on *two pairs* of completely different types of stock. One pair will match the performance of a *blue chip* stock against a *speculative* stock; the other will involve a *growth* stock versus an *income* stock. Thus we have:

- Blue chip versus speculative
- Growth versus income

What you have to do is select four different stocks—one blue chip, one speculative issue, one growth stock, and one income stock. (You can pick from the stocks noted in this chapter, or you can come up with the four stocks from any source you want: your parents, a relative or friend, or even a broker. Of course, if you happen to own a stock that you feel falls into one of the four categories, then by all means, use it.) Now, go to your public or campus library, to a nearby brokerage office, or online and look up your stocks in something like *S&P Stock Reports* or *Value Line* (be sure to get the latest available copy), or perhaps some Internet site like **Quicken.com**. For each stock, obtain information on:

- The company's growth and earnings (EPS)
- Growth in dividends per share
- Dividend yield
- Price/earnings ratio
- The stock's beta

In addition, compute each stock's *approximate* yield for the past year, based on what the stock is trading for today versus the price it sold for a year ago, as well as the dividends (if any) paid over the past 12 months (price and dividend information can be obtained from *The Wall Street Journal* or *Barron's*). Now compare the performance of the blue chip stock against the speculative issue, and the growth stock relative to the income issue. Make a note of any differences and be prepared to discuss your findings. Does your evidence support the belief that the kind of stock you own really does make a difference?

CONTEMPORARY CASE APPLICATIONS

12.1   The Jordons' Problem: What to Do with All That Money?

A couple in their early 30s, Allen and Sandra Jordon recently inherited $90,000 from one of their relatives. Allen earns a comfortable income as a sales manager for Smith and Johnson, Inc., and Sandra does equally well as an attorney with a major law firm. Because they have no children and do not need the money, they have decided to invest all their inheritance in stocks, bonds, and perhaps even some money market instruments. However, because they are not very familiar with the market, they turn to you for help.

Questions
1. What kind of *investment approach* do you think the Jordons should adopt—that is, should they be conservative with their money or aggressive? Explain.
2. What kind of *stocks* do you think the Jordons should invest in? How important is *current income* to them (i.e., dividends or interest income)? Should they be putting any of their money into *bonds*? Explain.
3. Construct an investment portfolio that you feel would be right for the Jordons; invest the full $90,000. Put *actual* stocks, bonds, preferreds, and/or convertible securities in the portfolio; also, if you like, you may put up to *one-third* of the money into short-term securities like CDs, Treasury bills, money funds, or MMDAs. Select any securities you want, so long as you feel they would be suitable for the Jordons. Make sure the portfolio consists of *six or more different securities*; use the latest issue of *The Wall Street Journal* to determine the market prices of the securities you select. Show the amount invested in each security, along with the amount of current income (from dividends and/or interest) that will be generated from the investments. Briefly explain why you selected the particular securities for the Jordons' portfolio.

12.2   Kathy Decides to Try Her Hand at Investing

Kathy Karras is a 26-year-old management trainee at a large chemical company. She is single and has no plans for marriage. Her annual salary is $34,000 (placing her in the 28 percent tax bracket), and her monthly expenditures come to approximately $1,500. During the past year or so, Kathy has managed to save around $8,000, and she expects to continue to save at least that amount each year for the foreseeable future. Her company pays the premium on her $35,000 life insurance policy. Because Kathy's entire education was financed by scholarships, she was able to save money from the summer and part-time jobs she held as a student. Altogether, she has a nest egg of nearly $18,000, out of which she would like to invest about $15,000. She will keep the remaining $3,000 in a money market account that pays 4.5 percent interest; she will use this money only in the event of an emergency. Although Kathy can afford to take more risks than someone with family obligations, she does not wish to be a speculator; rather, she simply wants to earn an attractive rate of return on her investments.

Questions

1. What investment options are open to Kathy?
2. What chance does she have of earning a satisfactory return on her investments if she invests her $15,000 in (a) blue-chip stocks, (b) growth stocks, (c) speculative stocks, (d) corporate bonds, or (e) municipal bonds?
3. Discuss the factors you would consider when analyzing these alternative investment vehicles.
4. What recommendation would you make to Kathy with respect to her available investment alternatives? Explain.

MONEY ONLINE

SOAR WITH STOCKS!

Note: Web addresses change frequently, so you may need to determine the home page and do a site search to find the page or topic that's referenced.

1. **quote.yahoo.com**
   Find the ticker symbol for not only stocks and mutual funds, but also for market indexes and corporate bonds at Yahoo's Lookup site. Enter any part of the name of the security and click on "Lookup" to bring up a listing of all the securities with those letters in their names. Type in "papa" for Papa John's Pizza and find that this company's ticker is PZZA and it is listed as Papa Johns International, Inc.

2. **my.zacks.com**
   Screen your stocks at Zacks. Click on "Screening," then on "Predefined Screening," and select "Top Value" and "Large Cap" to view a list of the current top-value, large-cap stocks. Select other screens, follow the markets, track your portfolio, or find the latest market news at this comprehensive investing Web site.

3. **quote.yahoo.com**
   Find a profile of your company or mutual fund at Yahoo. Type in the ticker, and under "Other Info," find a Profile of your company along with Research, News, Charts, and other useful information. For starters, look up the profiles for T, PG, IBM, and AOL. Then build a portfolio of your favorite securities and track their performance.

4. **www.aaii.com**

   Select your securities using information prepared specifically with the individual investor in mind. The American Association of Individual Investors specializes in providing education in the areas of stock investing, mutual funds, portfolio management, and retirement planning. Sample their trial membership or read their promotional articles while at their site.

5. **www.nasdaq.com**

   Use asset allocation techniques to develop a diversified portfolio. Look under Personal Finance and attend Nasdaq's "University" to determine the combination appropriate for you. Use their worksheet to tailor your asset mix to fit your needs and investment style.

6. **www.bondsonline.com**

   Interested in bonds? Bonds Online furnishes extensive information on all types of bonds. Their "Bond Search/Quote Center" allows you to search for bonds with certain characteristics. Find a list of corporate bonds that mature in 2010 by clicking on "Corporate Bonds" and typing in 2010 for both the Minimum and Maximum Maturity Ranges. Set Display Properties to "Coupon" and then click "Find Bonds" to bring up the list displayed in order of their coupon rates.

7. **www.bankofny.com/adr**

   Invest internationally the convenient way with American Despositary Receipts. Visit the Web site of the Bank of New York, the world's largest depositary for American Depositary Receipts (ADRs) and Global Depositary Receipts (GDRs). Find up-to-date information about depositary receipts as well as site links to many companies that issue DRs. While you're there, you can also access news, pricing, analytical tools, and historical financial data for depositary receipts.

8. **quote.yahoo.com**

   Need historical quotes? Yahoo provides quite an extensive database. Type in "T" for AT&T and then click on "Chart." You want a big chart, so if a small chart comes up, click on one of the "Big" offerings underneath the chart. Once you pull up a big chart, look underneath for "Historical Quotes." You can set the quotes for various time periods and to include daily, weekly, or monthly quotes and the dividends. If you need a copy of this information to work with on your computer, simply click on "Download Spreadsheet Format."

Just for Fun!

9. **www.better-investing.org**

   Join the National Association of Investment Clubs. This non-profit organization is dedicated to providing a program of sound investment information, education and support to help create successful, lifetime investors. While you're at their Web site, view the NAIC Top 100 Index compiled from the stocks most widely held by NAIC investors. This index racked up returns greater than both the Dow Jones Industrials and S&P 500 for the five and ten year periods ending December 2000!

Chapter 13

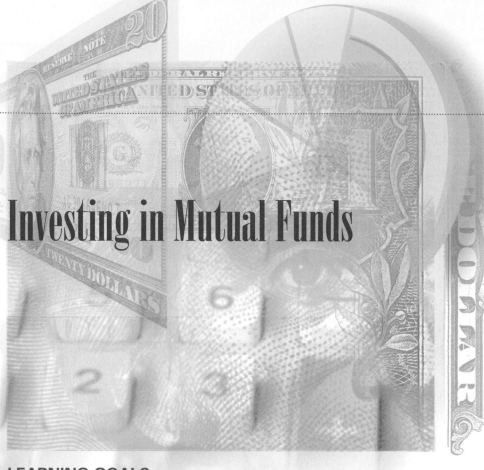

Investing in Mutual Funds

LEARNING GOALS

LG1.   Describe the basic features and operating characteristics of a mutual fund.

LG2.   Differentiate between open- and closed-end funds, as well as other types of professionally managed investment companies, and discuss the various types of fund loads and charges.

LG3.   Discuss the types of funds available to investors, and the variety of investment objectives these funds seek to fulfill.

LG4.   Identify and discuss the different kinds of investor services offered by mutual funds.

LG5.   Gain an understanding of the variables that should be considered when selecting funds for investment purposes.

LG6.   Identify the sources of return and calculate the rate of return earned on an investment in a mutual fund.

Not to Their Mutual Benefit...

When John Townsend left his job, he and his wife Jamie knew they had a 60-day time period to roll over his 401(k) retirement account into another investment. They knew they wanted to stay with mutual funds to get diversification and professional money management and decided to invest the entire proceeds in various funds in the American Express AXP Fund family. After all, they reasoned, American Express is a prestigious financial services company and should have high quality funds.

Unfortunately, looks aren't everything. During a period when the Russell 1000 gained 31 percent, their investment in AXP Progressive, a midcap fund, lost 24 percent. "It couldn't even make a profit in one of the greatest bull markets, even though it was 97 percent invested in stocks!" John said. Looking more closely at the AXP funds they held, John discovered mistakes aplenty. The AXP Mutual fund held large cash positions in a strong bull market. AXP Diversified Equity-Income belied its name, with an overly heavy concentration in bank stocks. Other funds had too much exposure to the falling Japanese yen or mortgage-backed debt. Over a 5-year period 21 of the 26 AXP funds lagged the average performance of their peer group, and many were at the bottom of their groups.

In addition, any profits the Townsends might have earned would have been eroded by high front-end loads of 5 percent, recently raised to 5.75 percent on fund investments below $50,000. "We should have done our own research instead of letting the American Express salesperson paint a rosy picture for us," comments Jamie. After sustaining heavy losses, the Townsends transferred their funds into an account at Charles Schwab, where they could choose from a variety of no-load fund families. As you read the following chapter, you'll learn how to select mutual funds to meet your own financial goals.

Source: Adapted from Richard Ten Wolde, "Dysfunctional Families," *Smart Money,* July 2000, pp. 139–143.

■ Mutual Funds: Some Basics [LG1, LG2]

For individual investors today, mutual funds are, without a doubt, the investment vehicle of choice. The fact is, more people invest in mutual funds than any other type of investment product. The reason they are so popular is that they offer not only a variety of interesting investment opportunities, but also a wide array of services that many investors find appealing. They provide an easy and convenient way to invest, and are especially suited to beginning investors and those with limited investment capital. A mutual fund is basically a financial services organization that receives money from its shareholders and invests those funds on their behalf in a diversified portfolio of securities. Thus, when investors buy shares in a mutual fund, they actually become *part owners of a widely diversified portfolio of securities.* In an abstract sense, a mutual fund can be thought of as the *financial product* that's sold to the public by an investment company. That is, the investment company builds and manages a portfolio of securities and sells ownership interests—shares of stock—in that portfolio through a vehicle known as a mutual fund. This concept underlies the whole mutual fund structure and is depicted in Exhibit 13.1.

EXHIBIT 13.1

THE BASIC MUTUAL FUND STRUCTURE

A mutual fund brings together the funds from numerous individual investors and uses this pool of money to acquire a diversified portfolio of stocks, bonds, and other securities.

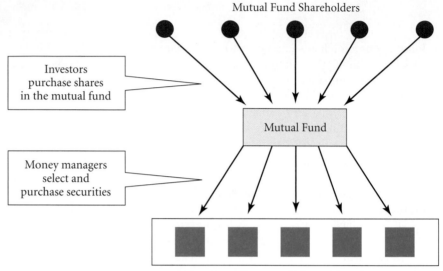

THE MUTUAL FUND CONCEPT

The first mutual fund in this country was started in Boston in 1924; by 1940, there were 68 mutual funds in operation, and by 1980 there were 564. But that was only the beginning, for the next 20 years saw unprecedented growth in the mutual fund industry, as assets under management grew to over $7 trillion in 2000. Indeed, by 2000, *there were nearly 8,000 publicly traded mutual funds.* (Actually, counting duplicate or multiple fund offerings from the same portfolio, there were more like *12,000 funds available*—such duplication occurs because sometimes two or three versions of the same fund will be offered, with each "fund" having a different type of load charge or fee structure.) To put that number in perspective, *there are more mutual funds in existence today than there are stocks listed on the New York and American exchanges combined!* The fund industry has grown so much, in fact, that it is now *the largest financial intermediary* in this country—ahead of even banks.

Mutual funds are big business in the United States and, indeed, all over the world. As the year 2000 began, an estimated 83 million individuals in 48 million U.S. households owned mutual funds. That's nearly half of U.S. households! Clearly, mutual funds appeal to a lot of investors—investors who come from all walks of life and all income levels. And they all share one common view: they've decided, for one reason or another, to turn the problems of security selection and portfolio management over to professional money managers. Questions of which stock or bond to select, when to buy, and when to sell have plagued investors for about as long as there have been organized securities markets. Such concerns lie at the very heart of the mutual fund concept and, in large part, are behind the growth in funds. The fact is, a lot of people simply lack the time, the know-how, or the commitment to manage their own securities. As a result, they turn to others. And more often than not, that means mutual funds.

Want to know more about the mutual fund industry, from the funds themselves to fund investors and legislation affecting funds? The Investment Company Institute Web site (**www.ici.org**) has all the answers.

POOLED DIVERSIFICATION. The mutual fund concept is based on the simple idea of turning the problems of security selection and portfolio management over to professional money managers. In essence, a mutual fund combines the investment capital of many people with similar investment goals, and invests the funds in a wide variety of securities. Investors receive shares of stock in the mutual fund and, through the fund, are able to enjoy much wider investment diversification than they could otherwise achieve. To appreciate the extent of such diversification, you need only look at Exhibit 13.2. It provides a partial list of the securities held in the portfolio of a major mutual fund (actually, just two pages out of a 28-page list of security holdings). Observe that in January 2000, this fund owned anywhere from 1,200 shares of Turnstone Systems to 2 *million* shares of Viad Corp. Furthermore, note that within each industry segment, the fund diversified its holdings across a number of different stocks. Clearly, except for all but the super-rich, this is far more diversification than most investors could ever hope to attain. Yet each investor who owns shares in this fund is, in effect, a part owner of this diversified portfolio of securities.

Of course, not all funds are as big or as diversified as the one depicted in Exhibit 13.2. Even so, no matter what the size of the fund, as the securities held by it move up and down in price, the market value of the mutual fund shares moves accordingly. And when dividend and interest payments are received by the fund, they too are passed on to the mutual fund shareholders and distributed on the basis of prorated ownership. For example, if you own 1,000 shares of stock in a mutual fund and that represents, say, 1 percent of all shares outstanding, you would receive 1 percent of the dividends paid by the fund. When a security held by the fund is sold for a profit, the capital gain is also passed on to fund shareholders. The whole mutual fund idea, in fact, rests on the concept of **pooled diversification**, and works very much like insurance, whereby individuals pool their resources for the collective benefit of all the contributors.

pooled diversification
A process whereby investors buy into a diversified portfolio of securities for the collective benefit of the individual investors.

WHY INVEST IN MUTUAL FUNDS?

Mutual funds can be used by individual investors in a variety of ways. Thus, whereas one investor may buy a fund because of the substantial capital gains opportunities it provides, another may buy a totally different fund not for its capital gains, but for its current income. Regardless of the kind of income a fund provides, individuals tend to use these investment vehicles for one or more of the following reasons: (1) to achieve diversification in their investment holdings; (2) to obtain the services of professional money managers; (3) to generate an attractive rate of return on their investment capital; and (4) for the convenience they offer.

DIVERSIFICATION. Certainly, as we saw above, diversification is a primary motive for investing in mutual funds. This ability to diversify, in effect, allows investors to sharply reduce their exposure to risk by indirectly investing in a number of different types of securities and companies, rather than just one or two. If you have only $500 or $1,000 to invest, you obviously will not achieve much diversification on your own. However, if you invest that money in a mutual fund, you will end up owning part of a diversified portfolio made up perhaps of several hundred securities, or even more.

PROFESSIONAL MANAGEMENT. Another major appeal of a mutual fund is the professional management it offers. Of course, management is paid a fee from the fund's earnings, but the contributions of a full-time expert manager should be well worth the cost.

EXHIBIT 13.2

A PARTIAL LIST OF PORTFOLIO HOLDINGS

This list represents just *two pages* of security holdings for this particular fund; the total list of holdings goes on for another 26 pages and includes stocks in hundreds of different companies. Certainly, this is far more diversification than most individual investors could ever hope to achieve.

Common Stocks – continued	Shares	Value (Note 1) (000s)
SERVICES – continued		
Services – continued		
The Go-Ahead Group PLC	225,000	$ 2,170
Thomas Group (a)	170,900	1,987
Velcro Industries NV	114,500	1,489
Viad Corp.	2,000,000	52,625
Wesco, Inc.	200,000	745
		202,600
TOTAL SERVICES		408,763
TECHNOLOGY – 17.9%		
Communications Equipment – 0.6%		
Champion Technology Holdings Ltd. .	100,000	7
KTK Telecommunications Engineering Co. Ltd.	100,000	493
Kyosan Electric Manufacturing Co. Ltd.	500,000	1,173
LoJack Corp. (a)	110,500	856
Perceptron, Inc. (a)	233,500	934
Tallgrade Communications, Inc. (a)(d)	509,000	29,586
Turnstone Systems, Inc.	1,200	35
		3,084
Computer Services & Software – 5.4%		
Affiliated Computer Services, Inc. Class A (a)	1,000,000	39,750
Aladdin Knowledge Systems Ltd. (a)	315,000	5,906
Analysts International Corp.	100,000	1,256
Avantl Corp. (a)	1,227,600	21,867
Black Box Corp. (a)(d)	1,400,000	82,775
Computer Learning Centers, Inc. (a)(d)	1,161,200	2,177
Condor Technology Solutions, Inc. (a)	134,000	184
Cotelligent, Inc. (a)	352,800	1,852
Daitec Co. Ltd.	425,200	6,215
Directrix, Inc. (a)	90,000	529
Fair, Isaac & Co., Inc.	520,000	23,790

	Shares	Value
GSE Systems, Inc. (a)(d)	353,800	1,548
Infinium Software, Inc. (a)	152,500	867
Informa Group PLC	875,000	8,312
JDA Software Group, Inc. (a)	1,000,000	20,000
Mapics, Inc. (a)	676,000	10,140
Meta Group, Inc. (a)	75,000	1,697
National Data Corp.	5,000	160

Source: *Fidelity Low-Priced Stock Fund*, January 2000.

These pros know where to look for return, and how to avoid unnecessary risk; at the minimum, their decisions should result in better returns than the average investor can achieve.

FINANCIAL RETURNS. Although professional managers *may* be able to achieve returns that are better than what small investors can generate, the relatively high purchase fees, coupled with the management and operating costs, tend to reduce the returns actually earned on mutual fund investments. However, the mutual fund industry has not attracted millions of investors because of the substandard returns they generate! Quite the contrary; over the long haul, mutual funds have been able to provide relatively attractive returns. Look at Exhibit 13.3.

EXHIBIT 13.3

THE COMPARATIVE PERFORMANCE OF MUTUAL FUNDS FOR THE 10½-YEAR PERIOD THROUGH JUNE 2000

The type of fund you invest in has a lot to do with the kind of return you can expect. For example, had you put $10,000 in a typical technology fund in January 1990, that investment would have grown to over $180,000 by mid-year 2000; in contrast, had you invested the same $10,000 in a typical foreign stock fund, it would have grown to only $26,000!

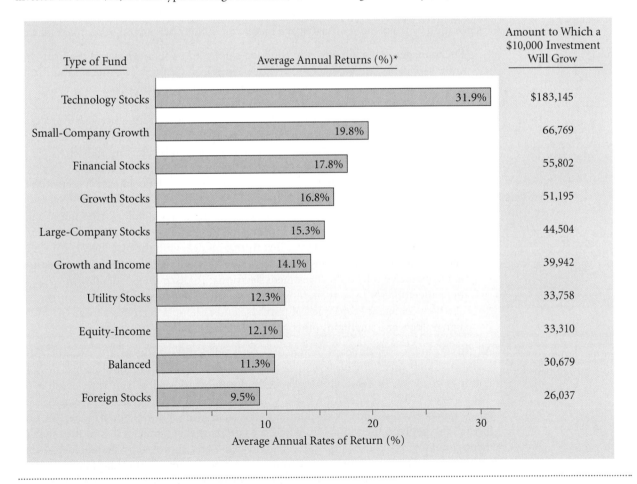

*Assumes reinvestment of all dividends and capital gains distributions.

Source: *Morningstar*, June 2000.

It shows the average return performance on a variety of different types of mutual funds and is indicative of the kind of returns investors were able to achieve over the $10\frac{1}{2}$-year period from January 1990 through mid-year 2000. With such return potential, it's easy to see why investors are so anxious to put their money into mutual funds—in many cases, it's probably safe to say that these returns are considerably better than what individual investors could have done on their own.

CONVENIENCE. The fact that mutual fund shares can be purchased through a variety of sources is still another reason for their appeal. Mutual funds make it easy to invest, and most do not require a great deal of capital to get started. They are relatively easy to acquire, they handle all the paperwork and record keeping, their prices are widely quoted, and it is usually possible to deal in fractional shares. Opening a mutual fund account is about as easy as opening a checking account. Just fill in a few blank spaces, send in the minimum amount of money, and you're in business!

HOW MUTUAL FUNDS ARE ORGANIZED AND RUN

Although it's tempting to think of a mutual fund as a monolithic entity, that's really not accurate. Various functions—investing, record keeping, safekeeping, and others—are split among two or more companies. Besides the fund itself, which is organized as a separate corporation or trust and *is owned by the shareholders*, there are several other main players:

- The **management company** runs the fund's daily operations. These are the firms we know as Fidelity, Vanguard, T. Rowe Price, American Century, Dreyfus, and so forth; they are the ones that create the funds in the first place. Usually, the management firm also serves as investment advisor.
- The **investment advisor** buys and sells the stocks or bonds and otherwise oversees the portfolio. Usually, three parties participate in this phase of the operation: the *money manager*, who actually runs the portfolio and makes the buy and sell decisions; *securities analysts*, who analyze securities and look for attractive investment candidates; and *traders*, who try to buy and sell big blocks of securities at the best possible price.
- The **distributor** sells the fund shares, either directly to the public or through certain authorized dealers (such as major brokerage houses and commercial banks). When you request a prospectus and sales literature, you deal with the distributor.
- The **custodian** physically safeguards the securities and other assets of a fund, without taking an active role in the investment decisions. To discourage foul play, an independent party (a bank, in most cases) serves in this capacity.
- The **transfer agent** keeps track of purchase and redemption requests from shareholders and maintains other shareholder records.

All this separation of duties is designed for just one thing—to protect the mutual fund investor/shareholder. Obviously, you can always lose money if your fund's stock or bond holdings go down in value. But that's really the only risk of loss you face, because the chance of ever losing money from fraud, scandal, or a mutual fund collapse is actually quite low—almost nonexistent. For in addition to the separation of duties noted earlier, the only formal link between the mutual fund and the company that manages it (i.e., the management company) is a contract that must be renewed—and approved by shareholders—on a regular basis. One provision of this contractual arrangement is that the fund's assets—stocks, bonds, cash, or other securities in the portfolio—*can never be in the hands of the management company*. As still another safeguard, each fund must have a board of directors, or trustees, elected by shareholders and charged with keeping tabs on the management company and renewing its contract. The bottom line is that in more than 75 years, there has never been a major crisis or scandal in the mutual fund industry, nor, with all the tight regulations and structural firewalls in place, is there ever likely to be one.

 Who's managing your fund? Brill's Mutual Fund Interactive interviews a top mutual find portfolio manager each week and has archives of past profiles (**www.fundsinteractive.com/profiles.html**).

OPEN-END VERSUS CLOSED-END

Although all mutual funds may appear to be organized in pretty much the same way, investors should be aware of some major differences. One way that funds differ is with respect to how they are structured. That is, funds can be set up either as *open-end companies*, which can sell an unlimited number of ownership shares, or as *closed-end companies*, which can issue only a limited number of shares.

OPEN-END INVESTMENT COMPANIES. The term *mutual fund* is commonly used to denote an open-end investment company. Such organizations are the dominant type of investment company and account for well over 95 percent of assets under management. In an **open-end investment company**, investors actually buy their shares from, and sell them back to, the mutual fund itself. When they buy shares in the fund, the fund issues new shares of stock and fills the purchase order with these new shares. There is no limit to the number of shares the fund can issue, other than investor demand. Further, all open-end mutual funds stand behind their shares and buy them back when investors decide to sell. Thus, there is never any trading among individuals. Many of these funds are very large and hold billions of dollars' worth of securities. Indeed, in mid-2000 the average stock or bond fund had about $750 million in assets under management, and there were more than 800 billion-dollar funds in existence.

Buy and sell transactions in an open-end mutual fund are carried out at prices based on the current value of all the securities held in the fund's portfolio. This is known as the fund's **net asset value (NAV)**; it is calculated at least once a day and represents the underlying value of a share of stock in a particular fund. NAV is found by taking the total market value of all securities held by the fund, subtracting any liabilities, and dividing the result by the number of shares outstanding. For example, if on a given day, the market value of all the securities held by the XYZ mutual fund equaled some $10 million, and if XYZ on that day had 500,000 shares outstanding, the fund's net asset value per share would amount to $20 ($10,000,000/500,000 = $20). This figure would then be used to derive the price at which the fund shares could be bought and sold. (As we'll see later, NAV is generally included in the fund's quoted price, and indicates the price at which an investor can *sell* shares—or, the price an investor would pay to *buy no-load funds*.)

CLOSED-END INVESTMENT COMPANIES. Although the term *mutual fund* is supposed to be used only with open-end funds, it is, as a practical matter, regularly used with closed-end investment companies as well. Basically, **closed-end investment companies** operate with a fixed number of shares outstanding and do *not* regularly issue new shares of stock. In effect, they have a capital structure like that of any other corporation, except that the corporation's business happens to be investing in marketable securities. Like open-end funds, closed-end investment companies have enjoyed remarkable growth in the past decade or so. For while there were only 34 of these funds in existence in 1980, by mid-year 2000, there were more than 500 closed-end funds, with total net assets of nearly $160

open-end investment company
A company that can issue an unlimited number of shares that it buys and sells at a price based on the current market value of the securities it owns; also called a mutual fund.

net asset value (NAV)
The price at which a mutual fund will buy back its own shares; NAV represents the current market value of all the securities the fund owns, less any liabilities.

closed-end investment company
An investment company that issues a fixed number of shares, which are themselves listed and traded on an organized securities exchange or in the OTC market.

billion—still just a tiny fraction of the more than $7 trillion invested in open-end funds. Shares in closed-end investment companies are actively traded in the secondary market, just like any other common stock, but, unlike open-end funds, *all trading is done between investors in the open market.* The fund itself plays no role in either buy or sell transactions; once the shares are issued, the fund is out of the picture. By far, most closed-end investment companies are traded on the New York Stock Exchange, a few are on the American Exchange, and, occasionally, some are traded in the OTC market or on some other exchange.

Many of the investment advisors that run closed-end funds (like Putnam, Kemper, Nuveen, MFS, and Franklin-Templeton) also manage open-end funds, often with similar investment objectives. So, why would they do that? The answer is, because these are two different animals. While it may not appear so, some major differences exist between open- and closed-end funds. To begin with, because closed-end funds have a fixed amount of capital to work with, they don't have to worry about stock redemptions or new money coming into the fund. As such, they don't have to be concerned about keeping cash on hand to meet redemptions.

Equally important, closed-end funds can be more aggressive in their investment styles and invest in obscure yet attractive securities, even if they are not actively traded (because there'll be no pressure on the portfolio manager to cash in these securities at inopportune times). And, because they don't have new money flowing in all the time, they don't have to worry about finding new investments. Instead, they can concentrate on a set portfolio of securities and do the best job they can in managing them. But that also puts added pressures on the money managers, because their investment styles and fund portfolios are closely monitored and judged by the market. That is, the share prices of closed-end companies are determined not only by their net asset values, but also by general supply and demand conditions in the market. As a result, depending on the market outlook and investor expectations, closed-end companies generally trade at a discount or premium to NAV. For example, a fund with a net asset value of $10 per share would be selling at a *discount* of $1 if it were trading at $9 and at a *premium* of $1 if it were quoted at a price of $11. Share price discounts can become quite large at times—for example, it is not unusual for discounts to amount to as much as 25 to 30 percent of net asset value. In contrast, price premiums occur less often and seldom exceed 10 to 15 percent.

EXCHANGE-TRADED FUNDS

exchange-traded fund (ETF)
An open-end mutual fund that trades as a listed security (principally on the AMEX); usually structured as an index fund that's set up to match the performance of a certain segment of the market.

Combine some of the operating characteristics of an open-end fund with some of the trading characteristics of a closed-end fund and what you'll end up with is something called an *exchange-traded fund.* While these securities are being promoted as the newest product to hit the fund world, they're really a re-creation of an old product that's been around since the early 90s. Technically, an **exchange-traded fund** (ETF) is a type of open-end mutual fund that trades as a listed security on one of the stock exchanges (mostly the AMEX). Actually, all ETFs thus far (through mid-year 2000) have been structured as *index funds,* set up to match the performance of a certain segment of the market; they do this by owning all or a representative sample of the stocks in a targeted market segment or index (we'll examine traditional index funds in more detail later in this chapter). Thus, ETFs offer the professional money management of traditional mutual funds and the liquidity of an exchange-traded stock.

Even though ETFs are like closed-end funds (in that they are traded on listed exchanges), *they are in reality open-end mutual funds,* where the number of shares outstanding can be increased or decreased in response to market demand. That is, while ETFs can be bought or sold like any stock on a listed exchange, *the ETF distributor can also create new shares or redeem old shares.* This is done to prevent the fund from trading at (much of) a premium or discount, thereby avoiding one of the big pitfalls of closed-end funds. By mid-year 2000, there were more than 60 ETFs listed on the American Stock Exchange, and every one of them was based on some domestic or international stock market index. The biggest and oldest (started in 1993) are based on the S&P 500, and are known as *Spiders*. In addition to spiders, there are *Diamonds* (which are based on the DJIA), *Qubes* (based on the NASDAQ 100 and so-named because of their QQQ ticker symbol), and ETFs based on 19 international markets (from Australia and Canada to Germany, Japan, and the UK). Just about every major U.S. Index, in fact, has its own ETF, along with a lot of minor indexes that cover very specialized segments of the market. The net asset values of ETFs are set at a fraction of the underlying index value at any given point in time. For example, if the S&P 500 index stands at, say, 1464.46, the ETF on that index will trade at around $146.50 (or about $\frac{1}{10}$ of the index); likewise, the ETF on the Dow is set at $\frac{1}{100}$ of the DJIA (thus, when it is at say, 10449.30, the ETF will trade at around 104.50).

ETFs combine many of the advantages of closed-end funds with those of traditional (open-end) index funds. That is, like closed-end funds, you can buy and sell ETFs at *any time of the day* by placing an order through your broker (and paying a standard commission just like you would with any other stock); in contrast, you *cannot* trade a traditional open-end fund on an intraday basis, as all buy and sell orders for these funds are filled at the end of the trading day, at closing prices. What's more, because ETFs are passively managed, they offer all the advantages of any index fund: low costs, low portfolio turnover, and low taxes. The fund's tax liability is kept low because ETFs rarely distribute any capital gains to shareholders; you could hold one of these things for decades and never pay a dime in capital-gains taxes (at least not until you sell the shares).

TWO OTHER TYPES OF INVESTMENT COMPANIES

In addition to open-end, closed-end, and exchange-traded funds, there are two other types of investment companies that should be discussed at this point. They are: (1) unit investment trusts, and (2) real estate investment trusts. The first type, a unit investment trust, is similar to a mutual fund to the extent that it, too, invests primarily in marketable securities, like stocks and bonds; real estate investment trusts, in contrast, invest primarily in various types of real estate or real estate–related types of investments, like mortgages.

UNIT INVESTMENT TRUST. A **unit investment trust (UIT)** represents little more than an interest in an *unmanaged* pool of investments. UITs are like mutual funds to the extent that both involve portfolios of securities. But that's where the similarity ends, because once a portfolio of securities is put together for a UIT, it is simply held in safekeeping for investors under conditions set down in a trust agreement. Traditionally, these portfolios were made up of various types of fixed-income securities, with long-term municipal bonds being, by far, the most popular type of investment vehicle. Because there is no trading in the portfolios, the returns, or yields, are fixed and fairly predictable—at least for the short term. Not surprisingly, these unit investment trusts appeal mainly to income-oriented investors looking for a safe, steady stream of income.

In the early 1990s, brokerage firms began aggressively marketing a new type of investment product—the *stock-oriented UIT*. These new equity trusts caught on quickly with investors seeking capital gains and attractive returns, and by year-end 1999, accounted for nearly 70 percent of this $95 billion market. A popular theme among equity trusts is the "dogs of the Dow" strategy of selecting (and holding) the five or ten companies in the DJIA paying the highest dividend yields—although growth stock, high yield, and market index trusts also do well. Stock trusts are normally offered with terms that range from

unit investment trust (UIT)
A type of investment vehicle whereby the trust sponsors put together a largely fixed/unmanaged portfolio of securities and then sell ownership units in the portfolio to individual investors.

1 year (typical of the Dow Dogs products) to 5 years (found on many stock index trusts). Except for the shorter terms (1 to 5 years for equity trusts versus 15 to 30 years for fixed-income products), these trusts are really no different from the traditional bond-oriented UITs: Once the portfolios are put together, they usually remain untouched for the life of the trust.

Various sponsoring brokerage houses put together these diversified pools of securities and then sell units in the pool to investors (each *unit* being like a share in a mutual fund). For example, a brokerage house might put together a diversified pool of corporate bonds that amounts to, say, $100 million. The sponsoring firm would then sell units in this pool to the investing public at anywhere from $250 (for many equity trusts) to $1,000 per unit (common for fixed-income products). The sponsoring organization does little more than routine record keeping, and it services the investments by collecting coupons or dividends and distributing the income (often monthly) to the holders of the trust units. There is a dark side to UITs, however—*they tend to be very costly*. These products can have not only substantial up-front transaction costs, but hefty annual fees as well. For example, many equity UITs carry load charges of 1 to 3 percent and then another 1.5 to 2.5 percent in annual fees—both of which are well above what you'd pay for a typical equity mutual fund. Brokers argue that they earn those fat fees by removing fear and greed from the investment process, and by enabling investors to build a well-diversified portfolio at a reasonable cost.

real estate investment trust (REIT)
A business that accumulates money for investment in real estate ventures by selling shares to investors; like a mutual fund, except REITs confine their investments to real estate and/or mortgages.

REAL ESTATE INVESTMENT TRUSTS. A **real estate investment trust** (**REIT**) is a type of closed-end investment company that invests money in mortgages and various types of real estate investments. A REIT is like a mutual fund in that it sells shares of stock to the investing public and uses the proceeds, along with borrowed funds, to invest in a portfolio of real estate investments. The investor, therefore, owns a part of the real estate portfolio held by the real estate investment trust. The basic appeal of REITs is that they enable investors to receive both the capital appreciation and the current income from real estate ownership without all the headaches of property management. *REITs are also popular with income-oriented investors because of the very attractive dividend yields they provide.*

There are three basic types of REITs: those that invest in *properties*, such as shopping centers, hotels, apartments, and office buildings (the so-called *property*, or *equity*, REITs); mortgage REITs—those that invest in mortgages; and *hybrid* REITs, which invest in both properties and mortgages. Mortgage REITs tend to be more income-oriented—they emphasize their high current yields (which is to be expected from a security that basically invests in debt). In contrast, while equity REITs may promote their attractive current yields, most of them also offer the potential for earning varying amounts of capital gains (as their property holdings appreciate in value). In mid-2000, there were nearly 200 publicly traded REITs, which together held over $125 billion in various real estate assets. Equity REITs dominate, accounting for about 85-90 percent of the market.

REITs must abide by the Real Estate Investment Trust Act of 1960, which established requirements for forming a REIT as well as rules and procedures for making investments and distributing income. Because they are required to pay out nearly all their earnings to the owners, they do quite a bit of borrowing to obtain funds for their investments (although, in today's market environment, they do try to keep the amount of leverage they employ to reasonable levels). A number of insurance companies, mortgage bankers, commercial banks, and real estate investment companies have formed REITs, many of which are traded on the major securities exchanges. Like mutual funds, the income earned by a REIT is not taxed, but *the income distributed to the owners is designated and taxed as ordinary income.* Although the poor performance of REITs during the 1973 to 1975 recession caused them to fall into disfavor among investors, subsequent restructuring of their portfolios has rekindled a good deal of interest in this form of investing.

SOME IMPORTANT COST CONSIDERATIONS

When you buy or sell shares in a *closed-end* investment company, or in *EFTs* for that matter, you pay a commission just as you would with any other listed or OTC common stock transaction. This is not so with *open-end* funds, however. In particular, the cost of investing in an open-end mutual fund depends on the types of fees and load charges that a fund levies on its investors.

LOAD FUNDS. Most open-end mutual funds are so-called **load funds**, because they charge a commission *when the shares are purchased* (such charges are often referred to as *front-end loads*). Front-end loads can be fairly substantial and amount to as much as $8\frac{1}{2}$ percent of the *purchase price* of the shares. The fact is, however, very few funds today charge the maximum; instead, many funds charge commissions of only 2 or 3 per cent—such funds are known as **low-load funds**. There is a commission to pay on low-load funds, but it's relatively small. The good news on front-end load funds is that there's normally no charge or commission to pay when you *sell* your shares! Occasionally, however, you will run into funds that charge a commission—or a so-called *redemption fee*—when you sell your shares. Known as **back-end load funds**, they may charge as much as $7\frac{1}{4}$ percent of the value of the shares sold, although back-end loads tend to decline over time and usually disappear altogether after 5 or 6 years. The purpose of such charges is to discourage investors from trading in and out of the funds over short periods of time.

NO-LOAD FUNDS. Some open-end investment companies charge you nothing at all to buy their funds; these are known as **no-load funds**. Actually, relatively few pure no-loads are left today, charging nothing to buy, sell, or hold their funds. Probably less than 40 percent of the funds sold today are true no-loads; all the rest charge some type of load or fee. Indeed, even funds that don't have front-end loads (and, thus, may appear as no-loads) can have back-end load charges that you have to pay when you sell your fund shares, or something called a 12(b)-1 fee, which you would pay for as long as you hold your shares.

12(b)-1 FEES. Also known as *hidden loads*, **12(b)-1 fees** have been allowed by the SEC since 1980, and were originally designed to help no-load funds cover their distribution and marketing expenses. Not surprisingly, their popularity spread rapidly among fund distributors, so that they are now used by many open-end mutual funds. The fees are assessed annually and can amount to as much as 1 percent of assets under management. In good markets and bad, they're paid right off the top. And that can take its toll. Consider, for instance, $10,000 in a fund that charges a 1 percent 12(b)-1 fee. That translates into an annual charge of *$100 a year*, certainly not an insignificant amount of money.

The latest trend in mutual fund fees is the so-called *multiple class sales charge*. You'll find such arrangements at firms like American Express IDS, Dreyfus, Merrill Lynch, MFS, Kemper, Smith Barney, Prudential, and others. The way it works is that the mutual fund will issue different classes of stocks on the same fund or portfolio of securities. Thus, rather than having just one class of stock outstanding, there might be three of them: Class A shares might have normal (relatively high) front-end loads; Class B stock might have no front-end loads, but substantial back-end loads along with a modest annual 12(b)-1 fee; and finally, Class C shares might carry maximum 12(b)-1 fees and nothing else. In other words, you choose your own poison.

To try and bring some semblance of order to fund charges and fees, in 1992 the SEC instituted a series of caps on mutual fund fees. Under the 1992 regulations, a mutual fund cannot charge more than 8.5 percent in *total sales charges and fees*, and that includes front- and back-end loads as well as 12(b)-1 fees. Thus, if a fund charges a 5 percent front-end

load fund
A mutual fund on which a transaction cost (associated with the purchase of shares) is levied.

low-load fund
A mutual fund in which commissions charged on purchases of shares range between only 1 and 3 percent of the purchase price.

back-end load
A commission charged for redeeming mutual fund shares.

no-load fund
A mutual fund on which no transaction fees are charged.

12(b)-1 fee
A type of fee that's charged annually and which is supposed to be used to offset the promotion and selling expenses of a mutual fund; known as a hidden load because it's often used by funds as an indirect way of charging commissions.

load and a 1 percent 12(b)-1 fee, it can charge a maximum of only 2.5 percent in back-end load charges—otherwise, it will violate the 8.5 percent cap. In addition, the SEC set a 1 percent cap on annual 12(b)-1 fees and, perhaps more significantly, stated that true "no-load" funds cannot charge more than 0.25 percent in annual 12(b)-1 fees (if they do, they have to drop the no-load label in their sales and promotional material).

management fee
A fee paid to the professional money managers who administer a mutual fund's portfolio.

MANAGEMENT FEES. The **management fee** is the cost you incur to hire the professional money managers to run the fund's portfolio of investments. These fees are also assessed annually and usually range from less than .5 percent to as much as 3 or 4 percent of assets under management. All funds—whether they are load or no-load, open- or closed-end—have these fees; and, like 12(b)-1 fees, they bear watching, because high management fees will take their toll on performance. As a rule, the size of the management fee is totally unrelated to the fund's performance—you'll pay the same amount whether it's been a winning year or a real loser.

KEEPING TRACK OF FUND FEES AND LOADS. Critics of the mutual fund industry have come down hard on the proliferation of fund fees and charges. Indeed, some would argue that all the different kinds of charges and fees are really meant to do one thing: confuse the investor. The fact is that a lot of funds were going to great lengths—lower a cost here, tack on a fee there, hide a charge somewhere else—to make themselves look like something they weren't. The funds were following the letter of the law, and, indeed, were fully disclosing all their expenses and fees. The trouble was that the funds were able to neatly hide all but the most conspicuous charges in a bunch of legalese. Fortunately, steps have been taken to bring fund fees and loads out into the open.

For one thing, fund charges are more widely reported now than they were in the past. Most notably, today you can find detailed information about the types and amounts of fees and charges on just about any mutual fund by accessing a variety of web sites, such as **www.quicken.com/investments/mutualfunds/**; **www.kiplinger.com/investing/funds/**; or **www.morningstar.com/Funds/Nutsbolts/**. Alternatively, you can use the mutual fund quotes that appear daily in (most) major newspapers and in *The Wall Street Journal*. For example, take a look at the *Wall Street Journal* quotations in Exhibit 13.4; note the use of the letters "r," "p," and "t." If you see an "r" behind a fund's name, it means the fund charges some type of *redemption fee*, or back-end load, when you sell your shares; this is the case, for example, with the Dreyfus Aggressive Value Fund. The use of a "p," in contrast, means the fund levies a *12(b)-1 fee*, which you'll have to pay, for example, if you invest in the Dreyfus Global Growth Fund. Finally, a "t" indicates funds that charge *both* redemption fees and 12(b)-1 fees; notice that's what you get with the FBR Financial Services Fund. The point is, don't be surprised to find load funds that also charge redemption and/or 12(b)-1 fees; and the same goes for no-load funds, as they're allowed to charge annual 12(b)-1 fees of 0.25 percent and still call themselves "no-load" funds. The quotations, of course, tell you only the *kinds* of fees charged by the funds; they don't tell you how much is charged. To get the specifics on the amount charged, you'll have to turn to other sources. Furthermore, these quotes (which are fairly representative of what you'd find in other major newspapers) *tell you nothing about the front-end loads*, if any, charged by the funds. Refer once again to the quotes in Exhibit 13.4 and compare the Dodge & Cox Balanced and FPA Paramount funds. They look alike, don't they? But they're not. For even though neither of them charges redemption or 12(b)-1 fees, one of them is a no-load fund, the other is not: Dodge & Cox does not charge a front-end load, whereas the FPA fund comes with a hefty 6½ percent front-end load. As a point of interest, the three other funds highlighted in Exhibit 13.4—Dreyfus Aggressive Value, Global Growth, and FBR Financial Services—don't charge front-end loads either, but you'd never know that from the quotes. (It should be noted that *The Wall Street Journal* also

EXHIBIT 13.4

MUTUAL FUND QUOTES

Open-end mutual funds are listed separately from other securities, and have their own quotation system, an example of which is shown here in quotes from *The Wall Street Journal*. Note that these securities are also quoted in dollars and cents and that the quotes include not only the fund's NAV, but year-to-date (YTD) returns as well. Also included as part of the quotes is an indication of whether the fund charges redemption and/or 12(b)-1 fees.

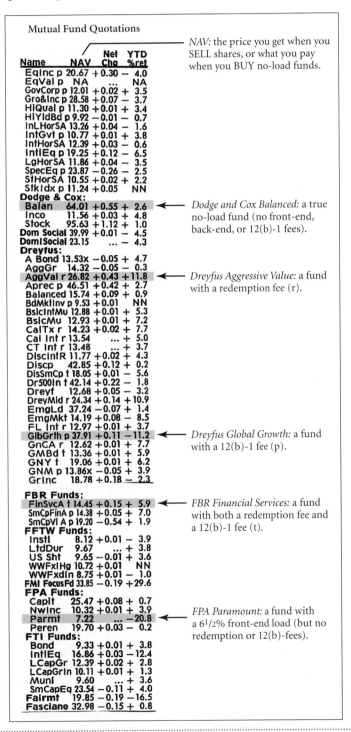

Mutual Fund Quotations

NAV: the price you get when you SELL shares, or what you pay when you BUY no-load funds.

Name	NAV	Net Chg	YTD %ret
EqInc p	20.67	+0.30	− 4.0
EqVal p	NA	...	NA
GovCorp p	12.01	+0.02	+ 3.5
Gro&Inc p	28.58	+0.07	− 3.7
HiQual p	11.30	+0.01	+ 3.4
HiYldBd p	9.92	−0.01	− 0.7
InLHorSA	13.26	+0.04	− 1.6
IntGvt p	10.77	+0.01	+ 3.8
IntHorSA	12.39	+0.03	− 0.6
IntlEq p	19.25	+0.12	− 6.5
LgHorSA	11.86	+0.04	− 3.5
SpecEq p	23.87	−0.26	− 2.5
StHorSA	10.55	+0.02	− 2.2
StkIdx p	11.24	+0.05	NN
Dodge & Cox:			
Balan	**64.01**	**+0.55**	**+ 2.6**
Inco	11.56	+0.03	+ 4.8
Stock	95.63	+1.12	+ 1.0
Dom Social	39.99	+0.01	− 4.5
DomISocial	23.15	...	− 4.3
Dreyfus:			
A Bond	13.53x	−0.05	+ 4.7
AggGr	14.32	−0.05	− 0.3
AggVal r	**26.82**	**+0.43**	**+11.8**
Aprec p	46.51	+0.42	+ 2.7
Balanced	15.74	+0.09	+ 0.9
BdMktInv p	9.53	+0.01	NN
BsicIntMu	12.88	+0.01	+ 5.3
BsicMu	12.93	+0.01	+ 7.2
CalTx r	14.23	+0.02	+ 7.7
Cal Int r	13.54	...	+ 5.0
CT Int r	13.48	...	+ 3.7
DiscIntR	11.77	+0.02	+ 4.3
Discp	42.85	+0.12	+ 0.2
DisSmCp t	18.05	+0.01	− 5.6
Dr500In t	42.14	+0.22	− 1.8
Dreyf	12.68	+0.05	− 3.2
DreyMid r	24.34	+0.14	+10.9
EmgLd	37.24	−0.07	+ 1.4
EmgMkt	14.19	+0.08	− 8.5
FL Int r	12.97	+0.01	+ 3.7
GlbGrth p	**37.91**	**+0.11**	**−11.2**
GnGA r	12.62	+0.01	+ 7.7
GMBd t	13.36	+0.01	+ 5.9
GNY t	19.06	+0.01	+ 6.2
GNM p	13.86x	−0.05	+ 3.9
GrInc	18.78	+0.18	− 2.3
FBR Funds:			
FinSvcA t	**14.45**	**+0.15**	**+ 5.9**
SmCpFinA p	14.38	+0.05	+ 7.0
SmCpVl A p	19.20	−0.54	+ 1.9
FFTW Funds:			
Instl	8.12	+0.01	− 3.9
LtdDur	9.67	...	+ 3.8
US Sht	9.65	−0.01	+ 3.6
WWFxlHg	10.72	+0.01	NN
WWFxdIn	8.75	+0.01	− 1.0
FMI FocusFd	33.85	−0.19	+29.6
FPA Funds:			
Capit	25.47	+0.08	+ 0.7
NwInc	10.32	+0.01	+ 3.9
Parmt	**7.22**	**...**	**−20.8**
Peren	19.70	+0.03	− 0.2
FTI Funds:			
Bond	9.33	+0.01	+ 3.8
IntlEq	16.86	+0.03	−12.4
LCapGr	12.39	+0.02	+ 2.8
LCapGrIn	10.11	+0.01	+ 1.3
Muni	9.60	...	+ 3.6
SmCapEq	23.54	−0.11	+ 4.0
Fairmt	19.85	−0.19	−16.5
Fasciano	32.98	−0.15	+ 0.8

Dodge and Cox Balanced: a true no-load fund (no front-end, back-end, or 12(b)-1 fees).

Dreyfus Aggressive Value: a fund with a redemption fee (r).

Dreyfus Global Growth: a fund with a 12(b)-1 fee (p).

FBR Financial Services: a fund with both a redemption fee and a 12(b)-1 fee (t).

FPA Paramount: a fund with a 6¹/2% front-end load (but no redemption or 12(b)-fees).

Source: *The Wall Street Journal*, August 2, 2000.

publishes a *Monthly Mutual Fund Review* [on the first or second Monday of each month] which, among other things, does provide some specifics on front-end loads and annual expense charges, including 12(b)-1 fees.)

In addition to the public sources noted above, the mutual funds themselves are required by the SEC to *fully disclose* all of their fees and expenses in a standardized, easy-to-understand format. Every fund prospectus must contain, right up front, a fairly detailed *fee table*, much like the one illustrated in Exhibit 13.5. Notice that this table has three parts. The first specifies all *shareholder transaction costs*. In effect, this tells you what it's going to cost to buy and sell shares in the mutual fund. The next section lists all the *annual operating expenses* of the fund. Showing these expenses as a percentage of average net assets, the fund must break out management fees, those elusive 12(b)-1 fees, and any other expenses. The third section provides a rundown of the *total cost over time* of buying, selling, and owning the fund. This part of the table contains both transaction and operating expenses and shows what the total costs would be over hypothetical 1-, 3-, 5-, and 10-year holding periods. To ensure consistency and comparability, the funds must follow a rigid set of guidelines when constructing the illustrative costs.

BUYING AND SELLING FUNDS

Buying and selling shares of *closed-end investment companies*, or *ETF's*, is no different from buying shares of common stock. The transactions are executed on listed exchanges or in the OTC market through brokers or dealers who handle the orders in the usual way. They are subject to the normal transaction costs; and because they are treated like any other listed or OTC stock, their shares can even be margined or sold short.

The situation is considerably different, however, with *open-end funds*. There are several ways of acquiring such shares, depending on whether the fund is load or no-load. Regardless of type, however, the fund is required to provide you with basic information about its operations. According to rules recently adopted by the SEC, investors now have the choice of buying into a mutual fund on the basis of a brief (two- to six-page), concise, readable document called a *fund profile*, or requesting a more detailed *prospectus* from the fund company. The fund profile is designed to tell you (in plain English and a standardized format) the most important things you need to know about a fund (e.g., its investment objectives, principle risks, fees and expenses, etc.) without overwhelming you with a bunch of unnecessary legalese. Likewise, the fund prospectuses are now far more user-friendly, as they, too, must be simplified and downsized (by removing all the irrelevant "boilerplates"); they must be written in plain English, as well.

Should you want more information than provided in either the profile or prospectus, you can always request a copy of the fund's *Statement of Additional Information*, which provides detailed information on the fund's investment objectives, portfolio composition, management, and past performance. Whether it's the fund profile (which should be good enough for most investors), the fund's prospectus, or its Statement of Additional Information, the bottom line is these publications should be required reading for anybody who's thinking about investing in a mutual fund.

In the case of load funds, investors buy the stocks from a broker or through salespeople employed by the funds—not surprisingly, many of these funds carry substantial load charges. Most brokerage firms are authorized to sell shares in a variety of load funds, and this is the easiest and most convenient way of buying funds for investors who have established brokerage accounts. Sometimes, however, the fund may not be sold through brokerage houses, in which case the investor would deal directly with the fund's commissioned salespeople—individuals who are employed by the mutual fund for the sole purpose of selling its shares.

EXHIBIT 13.5

A MUTUAL FUND FEE TABLE

Mutual funds are required by the SEC to make full disclosure of load charges, redemption fees, and annual expenses in a three-part table like the one shown here. The table must be conspicuously placed in the front part of the prospectus, not hidden somewhere in the back.

Fee Table

The following table describes the fees and expenses that are incurred when you buy, hold, or sell shares of the fund.

Shareholder Fees (paid by the investor directly)

Maximum sales charge (load) on purchases (as a % of offering price)	3.00%
Sales charge (load) on reinvested distributions	None
Deferred sales charge (load) on redemptions	None
Exchange Fees	None
Annual account maintenance fee (for accounts under $2,500)	$12.00

Annual fund operating expenses (paid from fund assets)

Management fee	0.45%
Distribution and Service (12b-1) fee	None
Other expenses	0.20%
Total annual fund operating expenses	0.65%

Example:

This example is intended to help an investor compare the cost of investing in different funds. The example assumes a $10,000 investment in the fund for one, three, five, and ten years and then a redemption of all fund shares at the end of those periods. The example also assumes that an investment returns 5 percent each year and that the fund's operating expenses remain the same. Although actual costs may be higher or lower, based on these assumptions an investor's costs would be:

1 year	$364
3 years	$502
5 years	$651
10 years	$1,086

If you happen to be interested in a no-load, or perhaps even a low-load fund, you may be pretty much on your own. You'll have to write or call the mutual fund directly (most have toll-free numbers) to obtain information. You will then receive an order form and instructions on how to buy shares; no salesperson will ever call on you. To complete the transaction, you simply mail your check, along with the completed order form, to the mutual fund or its designated agent. Before you go through all that, however, check with your bank; if it's a major (good-sized) commercial bank, it may be authorized to sell a wide variety of mutual funds. Indeed, during the past 5 to 10 years, a lot of big mutual funds have made arrangements to sell their products through major banking and other financial institutions around the country—and at no added cost to you. Thus you may be able to find just the fund you're looking for right in your local bank.

 Unlike many mutual fund Web sites, Fund Alarm (**www.fund alarm.com**) focuses not on what funds to buy but when to sell the funds you own. Its "3-Alarm Fund" lists highlight funds that have underperformed based on 3- or 5-year returns within each benchmark.

Selling shares in a fund is also a do-it-yourself affair, whether the fund is load or no-load. Because brokers and salespeople usually don't make anything on fund *sales*, they have little motivation to execute sell orders. As a result, you may find you'll have to redeem your fund shares by directly notifying the mutual fund (by mail) of your intention to sell. The fund then buys the shares back and mails you a check. But before selling your fund shares this way, check to see if the fund offers *phone switching*. This service is available from a number of investment companies, and it enables you to simply pick up the phone to move money from one fund to another—the only constraint is that the funds must be managed by the same family of funds. Most companies charge little or nothing for these shifts, although funds that offer free exchange privileges often place a limit on the number of times you can switch each year. (We'll discuss this service in more detail later in the chapter when we cover *conversion privileges*.)

CONCEPT CHECK

13-1. What is a mutual fund? Discuss the mutual fund concept; why are diversification and professional management so important?

13-2. Briefly describe how a mutual fund is organized. Who are the key players in a typical mutual fund organization?

13-3. Briefly define each of the following:
   a. *Closed-end investment company.*
   b. *Open-end investment company.*
   c. *Exchange-traded funds*
   d. *Unit investment trust.*
   e. *Real estate investment trust.*

13-4. What is the difference between a load fund and a no-load fund? Are there some advantages to either type? What is a *12(b)-1* fund? Can such a fund operate as a no-load fund?

13-5. Briefly describe a *back-end load*; a *low load*; a *hidden load*. How can you tell what kind of fees and charges a fund has?

Types of Funds and Fund Services [LG3, LG4]

Some mutual funds specialize in stocks and others in bonds; some funds have maximum capital gains as their investment objective, and some seek high current income. Some funds will appeal to speculators, and others primarily to income-oriented investors. Every fund has a particular investment objective, some of the more common ones being capital appreciation, income, tax-exempt income, preservation of investment capital, or some combination thereof. Disclosure of a fund's investment objective is required by the SEC, and each fund is expected to do its best to conform to its stated investment policy and objective.

Categorizing funds according to their investment policies and objectives is widely practiced in the mutual fund industry, as it tends to reflect similarities not only in how the funds manage their money, but also in their risk and return characteristics. Some of the more popular types of mutual funds include growth, aggressive growth, value, equity-income, balanced, growth-and-income, bond, money market, index, sector, socially responsible, international, and asset allocation funds. Let's now take a look at the various types of mutual funds to see what they are and how they operate. After we do that, we'll look at the kinds of investor services these funds offer.

TYPES OF FUNDS

GROWTH FUNDS. The objective of a *growth fund* is simple—capital appreciation. Long-term growth and capital gains are the primary goals of such funds, and as a result they invest principally in common stocks that have above-average growth potential. Because of the uncertain nature of their investment income, growth funds involve a fair amount of risk exposure. They are usually viewed as long-term investment vehicles that are most suitable for the more aggressive investor who wants to build capital and has little interest in current income.

AGGRESSIVE GROWTH FUNDS. These are the so-called performance funds that tend to increase in popularity when the markets heat up. *Aggressive growth funds* are highly speculative investment vehicles that seek large profits from capital gains; in many respects, they are really an extension of the growth fund concept. Many are fairly small, with portfolios consisting mainly of high-flying common stocks. Also known as "capital appreciation" or "small cap" funds, they often buy stocks of small, unseasoned companies, stocks with relatively high price/earnings multiples, and stocks whose prices are highly volatile. Some of these funds even go so far as to use leverage in their portfolios (that is, they buy stocks on margin by borrowing part of the purchase price). All this is designed, of course, to yield big returns. However, aggressive growth funds are also highly speculative and are perhaps the most volatile of all the fund types. When the markets are good, these funds do well; when the markets are bad, they typically experience substantial losses.

VALUE FUNDS. *Value funds* confine their investing to stocks considered to be *undervalued* by the market; that is, the funds look for stocks that are fundamentally sound but have yet to be discovered, and as such, remain undervalued by the market. These funds, in effect, hold stocks as much for their underlying intrinsic values as their *growth potential*. In stark contrast to growth funds, value funds look for stocks with relatively low P/Es, high dividend yields, and moderate amounts of financial leverage. They prefer undiscovered companies that offer the potential for growth, rather than those that are already experiencing rapid growth. Value investing is not easy! It involves extensive evaluation of corporate financial statements and any other documents that will help fund managers *uncover* *value (i.e., investment opportunities) before the rest of the market does* (that's the key to getting the low P/Es). And the approach seems to work. For even though value investing is generally regarded as being *less risky* than growth investing (lower P/Es, higher dividend yields, fundamentally stronger companies all translate into reduced risk exposure), the long-term returns to investors in value funds is quite competitive with that earned from growth or even aggressive growth funds. Thus, value funds are often viewed as a viable investment alternative for relatively conservative investors who are looking for the attractive returns that common stocks have to offer, yet want to keep share price volatility and investment risk in check.

EQUITY-INCOME FUNDS. *Equity-income funds* emphasize current income, which they provide by investing primarily in high-yielding common stocks. Capital preservation is also a goal of these funds, and so is capital gains, although capital appreciation is not their primary objective. They invest heavily in high-grade common stocks, some convertible securities and preferred stocks, and occasionally even junk bonds or certain types of high-grade foreign bonds. They like securities that generate hefty dividend yields, but also consider potential price appreciation over the longer haul. In general, because of their emphasis on dividends and current income, these funds tend to hold higher-quality securities that are subject to less price volatility than the market as a whole. They're generally viewed as a fairly low-risk way of investing in stocks.

BALANCED FUNDS. *Balanced funds* are so named because they tend to hold a balanced portfolio of both stocks and bonds, and they do so for the purpose of generating a well-balanced return of current income and long-term capital gains. In many respects, they're a lot like equity-income funds, except that balanced funds usually put much more into fixed-income securities; generally they keep at least 25 to 50 percent of their portfolios in bonds, and sometimes more. The bonds are used principally to provide current income, and stocks are selected mainly for their long-term growth potential. The funds can, of course, tilt the emphasis in their security holdings one way or the other. Clearly, the more the fund leans toward fixed-income securities, the more income oriented it will be. For the most part, balanced funds tend to confine their investing to high-grade securities, and are therefore usually considered a relatively safe form of investing, one where you can earn a competitive rate of return without having to endure a lot of price volatility.

GROWTH-AND-INCOME FUNDS. Like balanced funds, *growth-and-income funds* also seek a balanced return made up of current income and long-term capital gains, but they place a greater emphasis on growth of capital. Moreover, unlike balanced funds, growth-and-income funds put most of their money into equities—indeed, it's not unusual for these funds to have 80 to 90 percent of their capital in common stocks. They tend to confine most of their investing to high-quality issues, so you can expect to find a lot of growth-oriented blue-chip stocks in their portfolios, along with a fair amount of high-quality income stocks. One big appeal of these funds is the fairly substantial returns many of them have been able to generate over the long haul. But then, these funds do involve a fair amount of risk, if for no other reason than the emphasis they place on stocks and capital gains. Consequently, growth-and-income funds are most suitable for those investors who can tolerate their risk and price volatility.

BOND FUNDS. As their name implies, *bond funds* invest in various kinds of fixed-income securities. Income is their primary investment objective, although they do not ignore capital gains. There are three important advantages to buying shares in bond funds rather than investing directly in bonds. First, bond funds generally are more liquid; second, they offer a cost-effective way of achieving a high degree of diversification in an otherwise expensive investment vehicle (most bonds carry minimum denominations of $1,000 to $5,000, or more); and third, bond funds will automatically reinvest interest and other income, thereby allowing the investor to earn fully compounded rates of return. There are more than 4,000 publicly traded bond funds which, together, have about $1 *trillion* worth of bonds under management.

Although bond funds are usually considered a fairly conservative form of investment, they are not totally without risk, because the prices of the bonds held in the funds' portfolios will fluctuate with changing interest rates. Although many of the funds are basically conservative, a growing number are becoming increasingly aggressive—in fact, much of the growth that bond funds have experienced in the recent past can be attributed to this new investment attitude. No matter what your tastes, you'll find a full menu of bond funds available, including:

- *Government bond funds*, which invest in U.S. Treasury and agency securities.
- *Mortgage-backed bond funds*, which put their money into various types of mortgage-backed securities issued by agencies of the U.S. government (like GNMA issues). These funds appeal to investors not only because they provide diversification and a more affordable way to get into these securities, but also because they have a provision that allows investors (if they so choose) to reinvest the *principal* portion of the monthly cash flow, thereby enabling them to preserve, rather than consume, their capital.
- *High-grade corporate bond funds*, which invest chiefly in investment-grade securities rated triple-B or better.
- *High-yield corporate bond funds*, which are risky investments that buy *junk bonds* for the yields they offer.
- *Convertible bond funds*, which invest primarily in (domestic and possibly foreign) securities that can be converted or exchanged into common stocks; by investing in convertible bonds and preferreds, the funds offer investors some of the price stability of bonds, along with the capital appreciation potential of stocks.
- *Municipal bond funds*, which invest in tax-exempt securities and are suitable for investors looking for tax-free income. Like their corporate counterparts, municipals can also come out as either high-grade or high-yield funds. A special type of municipal bond fund is the so-called *single-state* fund, which invests in the municipal issues of only one state, thus producing (for residents of that state) interest income that is *fully* exempt from not only federal taxes, but state (and possibly even local/city) taxes as well.
- *Intermediate-term bond funds*, which invest in bonds with maturities of 7 to 10 years, or less, and offer not only attractive yields but relatively low price volatility as well; shorter (2- to 5-year) funds are also available and can be used as substitutes for money market investments by investors looking for higher returns on their money, especially when short-term rates are way down.

MONEY MARKET MUTUAL FUNDS. With the introduction of the very first *money fund* in 1972, the concept of investing in a portfolio of short-term money market instruments caught on like wildfire. The reason for their popularity is really quite simple: Money funds gave investors with modest amounts of capital access to the higher-yielding end of the money market, where many instruments require minimum investments of $100,000 or more. Today, there are about 1,200 money funds that, together, hold about $1.7 *trillion* in assets.

Actually, there are several different kinds of money market mutual funds. **General-purpose money funds** essentially invest in any and all types of money market investment vehicles, from Treasury bills to corporate commercial paper and bank certificates of deposit. They invest their money wherever they can find attractive short-term returns. The

general-purpose money fund
A money market mutual fund that invests in virtually any type of short-term investment vehicle, so long as it offers an attractive rate of return.

tax-exempt money fund
A money market mutual fund that limits its investments to tax-exempt municipal securities with short maturities.

government securities money fund
A money market mutual fund that limits its investments to short-term securities of the U.S. government and its agencies, thus eliminating any default risk.

vast majority of money funds are of this type. The **tax-exempt money fund** limits its investments to tax-exempt municipal securities with very short (30- to 90-day) maturities. Because their income is free from federal income tax, they appeal predominantly to investors in high tax brackets. **Government securities money funds** were established as a way of meeting investors' concern for safety. In essence, these funds eliminate any risk of default by confining their investments to Treasury bills and other short-term securities of the U.S. government or its agencies (such as the Federal National Mortgage Association).

Money funds are highly liquid investment vehicles, and are very low in risk because they are virtually immune to capital loss. However, the interest income they produce tends to follow interest rate conditions, and as such, the returns to shareholders are subject to the ups and downs of market interest rates. (Money funds were discussed more fully in Chapter 4, along with other short-term investment vehicles.)

INDEX FUNDS. "If you can't beat 'em, join 'em." That saying pretty much describes the idea behind *index funds*. Essentially, an index fund is a type of mutual fund that buys and holds a portfolio of stocks (or bonds) equivalent to those in a market index like the S&P 500. An index fund that's trying to match the S&P 500, for example, would hold the same 500 stocks that are held in that index, in exactly (or very nearly) the same proportion. Rather than trying to beat the market, as most actively managed funds do, *index funds simply try to match the market*—that is, to match the performance of the index on which the fund is based. They do this through low-cost investment management; in fact, in most cases, the whole portfolio is run almost entirely by a computer that matches the fund's holdings with those of the targeted index. Besides the S&P 500, a number of other market indexes are used, including the S&P Midcap 400, Russell 2000, and Wilshire 5000, as well as value-stock indexes, growth-stock indexes, international-stock indexes, and even bond indexes.

The approach of index funds is strictly buy-and-hold. Indeed, about the only time there's a change to the portfolio of an index fund is when the targeted market index alters its "market basket" of securities. (Occasionally an index will drop a few securities and replace them with new ones.) A pleasant by product of this buy-and-hold approach is that the funds have extremely low portfolio turnover rates and, therefore, very little in *realized* capital gains. As a result, aside from a modest amount of dividend income, these funds produce very little taxable income from year to year, which leads many high-income investors to view them as a type of tax-sheltered investment.

In addition to their tax shelter, however, these funds provide something else; as boring as the whole idea may sound, by simply trying to match the market, index funds actually produce *highly competitive returns* to investors! The fact is that it's very tough to outperform the market, whether you are a professional money manager or a seasoned individual investor. Index funds readily acknowledge this fact and, as such, don't even try to outperform the market; instead, all they try to do is match the returns. Surprisingly, the net result of this strategy, along with a *very low cost structure*, is that most index funds readily outperform the vast majority of all other types of stock funds. Indeed, historical data show that only abut 20 to 25 percent of stock funds outperform the market. Because a (true) index fund will pretty much match the market, these funds tend to produce better returns than 75 to 80 percent of competing stock funds. Granted, every now and then the fully managed stock funds will have a year when they outperform index funds, but those are the exception rather than the rule! Especially when you look at multi-year returns (covering periods of 3 to 5 years, or more), where you'll find that most fully managed stock funds just can't keep up with index funds.

SECTOR FUNDS. As the name implies, a *sector fund* restricts its investments to a particular sector of the market. In effect, these funds concentrate their investment holdings in the one or more industries that make up the targeted sector. For example, a *health care* sector fund would confine its investments to those industries that make up this segment of the market: drug companies, hospital management firms, medical suppliers, and biotech concerns. Its portfolio would then consist of promising growth stocks from those industries. The underlying investment objective of sector funds is *capital gains*. In many respects, they are similar to growth funds and thus should be considered speculative in nature.

The idea behind the sector fund concept is that the really attractive returns come from small segments of the market. Thus, rather than diversifying the portfolio across wide segments of the market, you should put your money where the action is. This notion may warrant consideration by the more aggressive investor who is willing to take on the added risks that often accompany these funds. Among the more popular sector funds are those that concentrate their investments in real estate (REITs), technology, energy, financial services, leisure and entertainment, natural resources, electronics, chemicals, computers, telecommunications, utilities, and, of course, health care.

SOCIALLY RESPONSIBLE FUNDS. For some, investing is far more than just cranking out some financial ratios. To these investors, the security selection process doesn't end with bottom lines, P/E ratios, growth rates, and betas; rather, it also includes the *active, explicit consideration of moral, ethical, and environmental issues*. The idea is that social concerns should play just as big a role in the investment decision as profits and other financial matters. Not surprisingly, there are a number of funds today that cater to such investors; known as **socially responsible funds**, they actively and directly incorporate morality and ethics into the investment decision.

These funds will consider only what they view as socially responsible companies for inclusion in their portfolios—if a company doesn't meet certain moral, ethical, or environmental tests, they simply won't consider buying the stock, no matter how good the bottom line looks. Generally speaking, these funds abstain from investing in companies that derive revenues from tobacco, alcohol, or gambling; are weapons contractors; or operate nuclear power plants. In addition, the funds tend to favor firms that produce "responsible" products and services, have strong employee relations, have positive environmental records, and are socially responsive to the communities in which they operate. Although these screens may seem to eliminate a lot of stocks from consideration, these funds (most of which are fairly small) still have plenty of securities to choose from, so it's not all that difficult for them to keep their portfolios fully invested.

As far as performance is concerned, the general perception is that there's a price to pay for socially responsible investing in the form of lower average returns. That's not too surprising, however, for as you add more investment hurdles or screens, you're likely to reduce return potential. But for those who truly believe in socially responsible investing, perhaps they are willing to put their money where their mouths are!

socially responsible fund
A type of mutual fund that puts social concerns on the same level of importance as financial returns, investing only in companies that meet certain moral, ethical, and/or environmental tests.

 If socially-responsible funds appeal to you, the Social Investment Forum (**www.socialinvest.org**) is a good first stop. You'll find information, contacts, resources, and performance records on funds with a conscience.

INTERNATIONAL FUNDS. In their search for higher yields and better returns, American investors have shown a growing interest in foreign securities. Sensing an opportunity, the mutual fund industry was quick to respond with a proliferation of so-called **international funds**—a type of mutual fund that does all or most of its investing in foreign securities. Just look at the number of international funds around today versus a few years ago. In 1985, there were only about 40 of these funds; by 2000, that number had grown to nearly 1,900. The fact is, a lot of people would like to invest in foreign securities but simply

international fund
A mutual fund that does all or most of its investing in foreign securities; also includes global funds, a special type of international fund that invests in both international and domestic securities.

don't have the experience or know-how to do so. International funds may be just the ticket for such investors, *provided they have at least a basic appreciation of international economics.* Because these funds deal with the international economy, balance of trade positions, and currency valuations, investors should have at least a fundamental understanding of what these issues are and how they can affect fund returns.

Technically, the term *international fund* is used to describe a type of fund that *invests exclusively in foreign securities*, often confining the fund's activities to specific geographical regions (like Mexico, Australia, Europe, or the Pacific Rim). In contrast, there is also another class of international funds, known as *global funds*, which invest not only in foreign securities, *but also in U.S. companies*—usually multinational firms. As a rule, global funds provide more diversity and, with access to both foreign and domestic markets, can go wherever the action is.

Regardless of whether they're global or international (from here on, we'll use the term "international" to apply to both), you'll find just about any type of fund you could possibly want in the international sector. There are international *stock* funds, international *bond* funds, even international *money market* funds; in addition, there are aggressive growth funds, balanced funds, long-term growth funds, high-grade bond funds, and so forth. Thus, no matter what your investment philosophy or objective, you're likely to find what you're looking for in the international area.

Basically, these funds attempt to take advantage of international economic developments in two ways: (1) by capitalizing on changing foreign market conditions, and (2) by positioning themselves to benefit from devaluation of the dollar. They do so because they can make money not only from rising share prices in a foreign market, but, perhaps just as important, from a falling dollar (which, in itself, produces capital gains to American investors in foreign securities and international funds). Many of these funds, however, will attempt to protect their investors from currency exchange risks by using various types of *hedging strategies.* That is, by using foreign currency options and futures (or some other type of derivative product), the fund will try to eliminate (or reduce) the effects of currency exchange rates. Some funds, in fact, do this on a permanent basis—in essence, these funds hedge away exchange risk so they can concentrate on the higher returns that foreign securities offer. Most others are only occasional users of currency hedges and will employ them only if they feel there's a real chance of a substantial swing in currency values. But even with currency hedging, international funds are still considered fairly high-risk investments and should be used only by investors who understand and are able to tolerate such risks.

ASSET ALLOCATION FUNDS. Studies have shown that the most important decision an investor can make is to decide where to allocate his or her investment assets. This is known as *asset allocation*, and, as we saw in Chapter 11, basically involves deciding how you're going to divide your investments among different types of securities. For example, what portion of your money is going to be devoted to money market securities, what portion to stocks, what portion to bonds? Asset allocation deals in broad terms and does not address individual security selection. Even so, as strange as it may sound, asset allocation has been found to be a far more important determinant of total returns on a well-diversified portfolio than individual security selection.

Because a lot of individual investors have a tough time making asset allocation decisions, the mutual fund industry has, not surprisingly, created a product to do the job for them. Known as *asset allocation funds*, these funds spread investors' money across all different types of markets. That is, while most mutual funds concentrate on one type of investment—whether stocks, bonds, or money market securities—asset allocation funds put money into all these markets. Many of them also include foreign securities in their asset allocation scheme, and some may even include inflation-resistant investments like gold or real estate.

These funds are designed for people who want to hire fund managers not only to select individual securities for them, but also to make the strategic decision of how to allocate money among the various markets. Here's how many asset allocation funds work. The money manager will establish a desired allocation mix—it might look something like this: 50 percent of the portfolio goes to U.S. stocks, 10 percent to foreign securities, 30 percent to bonds, and 10 percent to money market securities. Securities are then purchased for the fund in this proportion, and the overall portfolio maintains the desired mix. Actually, each segment of the fund is managed almost as a separate portfolio, so securities within, say, the stock portion are bought, sold, and held as the market dictates. Now, here's what really separates asset allocation funds from the rest of the pack: *As market conditions change over time, the asset allocation mix will change as well*. Thus, if the U.S. stock market starts to soften, funds will be moved out of stocks to some other area; as a result, the stock portion of the portfolio may drop to, say, 35 percent and the foreign securities portion may increase to 25 percent. Of course, there's no assurance that the money manager will make the right moves at the right time, but that's the idea behind these funds.

Asset allocation funds are supposed to provide investors with one-stop shopping; that is, just find an asset allocation fund or two that fits your needs and invest in it (or them), rather than going out and buying a couple stock funds, a couple bond funds, and so on. The success of these funds rests not only on how good a security picker the money manager is, but also on how good a job he or she does in timing the market and moving funds among different segments of the market. Of course, you don't have to use the services of a professional money manager to develop a portfolio of mutual funds. But if you do want to develop a portfolio on your own, you might want to pay attention to the suggestions contained in the accompanying *Money in Action* box.

SERVICES OFFERED BY MUTUAL FUNDS

Ask most investors why they buy a particular mutual fund and they'll probably tell you that the fund provides the kind of income and return they're looking for. Now, no one would question the importance of return in the investment decision, but there are other reasons for investing in mutual funds, not the least of which are the valuable services they provide. Some of the most sought-after *mutual fund services* are automatic investment and reinvestment plans, regular income programs, conversion and phone-switching privileges, and retirement programs.

AUTOMATIC INVESTMENT PLANS. It takes money to make money, and for an investor that means being able to accumulate the capital to put into the market. Unfortunately, that's not always the easiest thing in the world to do. Enter mutual funds, which have come up with a program that makes savings and capital accumulation as painless as possible. The program is the **automatic investment plan** and it allows fund shareholders to automatically funnel fixed amounts of money *from their paychecks or bank accounts* into a mutual fund. It's very much like a payroll deduction plan that treats savings a lot like insurance coverage—that is, just as insurance premiums are automatically deducted from your paycheck (or bank account), so too are investments to your mutual fund.

This fund service has become very popular, as it allows shareholders to invest without having to think about it. Just about every major fund group offers some kind of automatic investment plan. To enroll, a shareholder simply fills out a form authorizing the fund to siphon a set amount (usually it has to be a minimum of $25 to $100 per period) from your bank account or paycheck at regular intervals—typically monthly or quarterly. Once enrolled, you'll be buying shares in the funds of your choice every month or quarter (most funds deal in fractional shares); of course, if it's a load fund, you'll still have to pay normal sales charges on your periodic investments.

automatic investment plan
A type of automatic savings program that enables an investor to systematically channel a set amount of money into a given mutual fund; it provides investors with a convenient way to accumulate capital.

MONEY IN ACTION

Advice for Successful Mutual Fund Investing

For many investors, mutual funds represent an easy route to a diversified, professionally managed portfolio. But it's not enough to pick a few funds and then ignore them. Here are some common-sense rules to help you be a savvy mutual fund investor.

Use "top performance" lists carefully—if at all! It's tempting to put your money in one of the current "hot" funds on the "best funds" lists in personal finance magazines. Funds reach the top of the list because they are different. They may be riskier, holding more volatile stocks, or may concentrate on an industry that is hot right now. Very often sector funds are top performers in a given year. But who knows if the same sector will do well next year? In fact, most top funds do well in the short run. What is perhaps more useful, however, is to recognize that funds that consistently lag their peers usually continue to post below-average returns.

Don't over-diversify. You don't need lots of funds for a solid asset allocation strategy. A recent Ibbotson Associates study revealed that for investors with a $100,000 portfolio, the optimal number of funds is 10. This allows you to cover the main asset bases— large U.S. stocks, corporate and government bonds, small U.S. stocks, cash, and foreign stocks. Even if your portfolio is larger, you don't need more funds. If your portfolio is considerably smaller, start with fewer funds and add others over time. Adding funds won't penalize your performance, but it may increase the effort and time to monitor your portfolio. In addition, more funds means higher expenses (more on this follows).

Size counts. A fund's size should be appropriate for its investment objective. Certain fund categories— large stock index, government bonds, money market—need size to operate efficiently in their liquid market sectors. Expenses will be a smaller percentage of fund assets, too. For funds in less-liquid market segments, such as small stocks and emerging markets, being too big is a disadvantage. Actively managed funds that perform well and experience a large inflow of new money may have problems investing all that money effectively.

Expenses and fees add up. Many fund investors neglect to factor in expenses and other fees when choosing funds on the basis of performance. Compare a fund's expense ratio with its category average. Bond funds are less expensive than stock funds to manage, international funds are more costly than domestic ones, large funds are cheaper than small ones, and index funds cost less to run than actively managed funds. Know what is included in fund performance statistics. Sales charges (loads) and transaction fees are not included in performance figures, so they will reduce returns dollar for dollar. In sharp contrast, ongoing fees like 12(b)-1, management, and administrative fees are part of the expense ratio and already accounted for in performance statistics.

Wait for a new manager or fund to prove itself. Choose funds with at least a 3-year history so that you have some indication of its track record. The same is true for new fund managers. Avoid new funds; there are plenty of seasoned funds. You can then compare performance with the peer group over time.

Sources: Adapted from Charles Jaffe, "Cool It! That's Advice for Fickle Investors Who Chase Hot Funds," *San Diego Union-Tribune*, July 16, 2000, p. I-4; Russ Wiles, "Some Advice for Collectors: 10 Funds Is Enough, New Study Says, *Arizona Republic*, June 1, 2000, p. D1.

To remain diversified, you can divide your money among as many funds (within a given fund family) as you like; and you can get out of the program anytime you like, without penalty, by simply contacting the fund. Although convenience is perhaps the plans' chief advantage, they also make solid investment sense, because one of the best ways of building up a sizable amount of capital is to systematically add *funds to your investment program over time.* The importance of making regular contributions to your

◨ EXHIBIT 13.6

THE EFFECTS OF REINVESTING INCOME

Reinvesting dividends and/or capital gains can have tremendous effects on one's investment position. This graph shows the results of a hypothetical investor who initially invested $10,000 and, for a period of 15 years, reinvested all dividends and capital gains distributions in additional fund shares. (No adjustment has been made for any income taxes payable by the shareholder—which would be appropriate so long as the fund was held in, say, an IRA or Keogh account.)

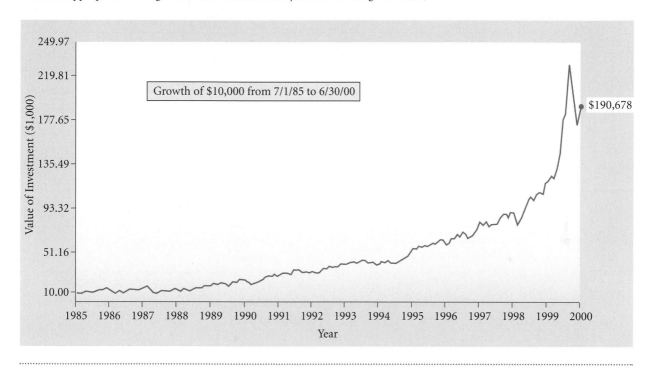

Growth of $10,000 from 7/1/85 to 6/30/00

$190,678

Source: *Morningstar Principia Pro,* June 30, 2000.

investment program cannot be overstated—it ranks right up there with compound interest!

AUTOMATIC REINVESTMENT PLANS. *This is one of the real draws of mutual funds,* and it's a service that's offered by just about every open-ended mutual fund. Whereas automatic investment plans deal with money shareholders put into a fund, automatic *reinvestment* plans deal with the disposition of dividends and other distributions the funds pay to their shareholders. Much like the dividend reinvestment plans we looked at with stocks, the **automatic reinvestment plans** of mutual funds enable you keep all your capital fully employed. Through this service, dividend and capital gains income is *automatically used to buy additional shares in the fund*. Keep in mind, however, that even though you reinvest your dividends and capital gains, the IRS still treats them as cash receipts and taxes them in the year in which they are paid.

The important point is that by plowing back profits (reinvested dividends and capital gains distributions), the investor can essentially put his or her profits to work in generating even more earnings. Indeed, the effects of these plans on total accumulated capital over the long haul can be substantial. Exhibit 13.6 shows the long-term impact of

automatic reinvestment plan A plan often offered by mutual funds that allows share owners to elect to have dividends and capital gains distributions reinvested in additional fund shares.

EXHIBIT 13.7

ALL IN THE FAMILY

Here are 15 of the largest fund families, each one of which offers investors a full range of stock, bond, and money funds; these companies do everything they can to keep your money in the family.

Fund Families	Total Number of Funds Available	Total Amount of Assets Under Mgmt. ($ Billions)
Fidelity	326	$628.8
Vanguard	90	508.4
Putnam	201	237.4
Franklin-Templeton	207	156.8
T. Rowe Price	81	154.7
American Century	95	93.2
MFS	168	92.8
American Express	108	91.4
Morgan Stanley Dean Witter	263	83.9
Oppenheimer	151	75.5
Merrill Lynch	284	67.2
Van Kampen	135	59.6
Dreyfus	261	54.4
Evergreen	204	37.6
Prudential	200	36.3

Note: Number of funds in existence at mid-year 2000; assets under management for stock and bond funds only.

Source: *Morningstar Principia Pro*, Release Date: June 30, 2000.

one such plan. (These are the actual performance numbers for a *real* mutual fund—Fidelity Growth Company.) In the illustration, we assume the investor starts with $10,000 and, except for the reinvestment of dividends and capital gains, *adds no new capital over time*. Even so, note that the initial investment of $10,000 grew to nearly $191,000 over a 15-year period (which, by the way, amounts to a compound rate of return of almost 21¾ percent). Clearly, so long as care is taken in selecting an appropriate fund, *attractive benefits can be derived from the systematic accumulation of capital offered by automatic reinvestment plans.*

REGULAR INCOME. Although automatic reinvestment plans are great for the long-term investor, how about the investor who's looking for a steady stream of income? Once again, mutual funds have a service to meet this kind of need. It's called a **systematic withdrawal plan**, and it's offered by most open-ended funds. Once enrolled in one of these plans, you will automatically receive a predetermined amount of money every month or quarter.

To participate, shareholders are usually required to have a minimum investment of $5,000 to $10,000, and the size of the withdrawal must usually be $50 or more per month. Depending on how well the fund is doing, the income derived from the fund may actually be greater than the withdrawals, thus allowing the investor not only to receive regular

systematic withdrawal plan
A plan offered by mutual funds that allows shareholders to be paid specified amounts of money each period.

income but also enjoy an automatic accumulation of *additional* shares in the plan. On the other hand, if the fund is not performing well, the withdrawals could eventually deplete the original investment.

CONVERSION PRIVILEGES. Sometimes investors find it necessary to switch out of one fund and into another; for example, their investment objectives may change, or the investment environment itself may have changed. **Conversion** (or **exchange**) **privileges** meet the needs of these investors in a convenient and economical manner. Investment companies that offer a number of different funds to the investing public—known as *fund families*—usually provide conversion privileges that enable shareholders to move easily from one fund to another; and, as we saw earlier, this is usually done by phone (as in *phone switching*). The only limitation is that the investor must confine the switches within the same *family* of funds. For example, an investor can switch from a Dreyfus growth fund to a Dreyfus money fund, or to its income fund, or to any other fund managed by Dreyfus.

> **conversion (exchange) privileges** A feature offered by many investment companies that allows investors to switch from one mutual fund to another within a family of funds.

With some fund families, the alternatives open to investors seem almost without limit; indeed, some of the larger families offer literally hundreds of funds. One investment company (Fidelity) has over 300 different funds in its family, and provides everything from high-performance stock funds to bond funds, tax-exempt funds, a couple dozen sector funds, and several dozen money funds.

Most fund families, especially the bigger ones, offer investors a full range of investment products, as they all try to provide one-stop mutual fund shopping. Whether you want an equity fund, a bond fund, or a money fund, these fund families have something for you. More than four hundred fund families are in operation today, every one of which has some type of conversion privilege. Fifteen of the largest of these fund families are listed in Exhibit 13.7; note that, together, these 15 families have nearly $2.4 trillion in assets under management, and offer more than 2,700 different stock and bond funds to the investing public. (Note that many of these funds are actually duplicates of the same portfolio, as fund distributors will often use multiple distribution channels or have multiple load/commission structures; as a result, several "different" mutual funds will be sold on the same portfolio of securities.)

Conversion privileges are attractive because they permit investors to manage their holdings more aggressively by allowing them to move in and out of funds as the investment environment changes. Unfortunately, there is one major drawback; although you never see the cash, the exchange of shares from one fund to another is regarded, for tax purposes, as a sale followed by a subsequent purchase of a new security. As a result, if any capital gains exist at the time of the exchange, the investor is liable for the taxes on that profit.

RETIREMENT PLANS. As a result of government legislation, self-employed individuals are permitted to divert a portion of their pretax income into self-directed *retirement plans*. And all working Americans, whether they are self-employed or not, are allowed to establish individual retirement accounts —either in the form of a standard tax-deductible IRA, or the newest type of retirement account, the Roth IRA (all of which we'll look at in the next chapter). Today all mutual funds provide a special service that allows individuals to quickly and easily set up tax-deferred retirement programs as either IRA or Keogh accounts—or, through their place of employment, to participate in a qualified tax-sheltered retirement plan, like a 401(k), for example. The funds set up the plans and handle all the administrative details in such a way that the shareholders can take full advantage of available tax savings.

CONCEPT CHECK

13-6.   Briefly describe each of the following types of mutual funds:
   a. Aggressive growth funds
   b. Equity-income funds
   c. Growth-and-income funds
   d. Bond funds
   e. Sector funds
   f. Socially responsible funds
   g. International funds
   h. Index funds
13-7.   What is an asset allocation fund and how do these funds differ from other types of mutual funds?
13-8.   If growth, income, and capital preservation are the primary objectives of mutual funds, why do we bother to categorize them by type? Do you think such classifications are helpful in the fund selection process? Explain.
13-9.   What are fund families? What advantages do these families offer investors? Are there any disadvantages?
13-10. Briefly describe some of the investor services provided by mutual funds. What are automatic reinvestment plans and how do they differ from automatic investment plans? What is phone switching, and why would an investor want to use this type of service?

◼ Making Mutual Fund Investments [LG5, LG6]

Suppose you are confronted with the following situation. You have money to invest and are trying to select the right place to put it. You obviously want to pick a security that meets your idea of acceptable risk, but also one that will generate an attractive rate of return. The problem is you have to make the selection from a list of nearly 8,000 securities. Sound like a "mission impossible"? Well, that's basically what a typical investor is up against when trying to select a suitable mutual fund. But perhaps if the problem is approached systematically, it may not be so formidable a task after all. For as we will see, it is possible to whittle down the list of alternatives by matching one's investment needs with the investment objectives of the funds.

THE SELECTION PROCESS

When it comes to mutual funds, one question that every investor has to answer is: Why invest in a mutual fund to begin with; why not just go it alone (that is, buy individual stocks and bonds directly)? For beginning investors, or investors with little capital, the answer is pretty simple—mutual funds provide far more diversification than they could ever get on their own, plus they get the help of professional money managers, and at a very reasonable cost to boot.

For more seasoned, better-heeled investors, the answers are probably a bit more involved. Certainly, the diversification and professional money management come into play, but there are other reasons as well. The competitive returns that mutual funds offer have to be a factor with many investors, and so do the services they provide. A lot of well-to-do investors have simply decided that they can get better returns over the long haul by carefully selecting mutual funds than by trying to invest on their own. As a result, they put all or a big chunk of their money into funds. Many of these investors will use part of their capital to buy and sell individual securities on their own, and the rest will be used *to buy mutual funds that invest in areas they don't fully understand or don't feel well-informed about*—for example, they will use mutual funds to get into foreign markets or as the way to buy mortgage-backed securities. For more on the question of which way to go—mutual funds or individual securities—see the accompanying *Money in Action* box.

Once a decision to use mutual funds has been made, the investor will then have to decide which funds to buy. The selection process itself (especially with regard to the *types* of funds to purchase) obviously plays an important role in defining the amount of success you will have with mutual funds. It means putting into action all you know about investing to gain as much return as possible from an acceptable level of risk. Given that you have an asset allocation strategy in place and you are trying to select funds compatible to your targeted mix, the selection process begins with an assessment of your own investment needs; this sets the tone for your investment program. Obviously, what you want to do is select from those 8,000 or so funds the one or two (or three or four) that will best meet your investment needs.

OBJECTIVES AND MOTIVES FOR USING FUNDS. Selecting the right investment means finding those funds that are most suitable to your investment needs. *The place to start is with your own investment objectives.* In other words, why do you want to invest in a mutual fund, and what are you looking for in a fund? Obviously, an attractive rate of return would be desirable, but there is also the matter of ensuring a tolerable amount of risk exposure. Face it, some investors are more willing to take risks than others, and this is certainly an important ingredient in the selection process. More than likely, when you look at your own risk temperament in relation to the various types of mutual funds available, you will discover that certain types of funds are more appealing to you than others. For instance, aggressive growth or sector funds will probably *not* be attractive to individuals who wish to avoid high exposure to risk.

Another important factor in the selection process is the intended use of the mutual fund. That is, do you want to invest in mutual funds as a way of *accumulating capital* over an extended period of time, to *speculate* with your money in the hopes of generating high rates of return, or to *conserve your capital* by investing in low-risk securities where preservation of capital is as important, or more so, than return on capital. This is helpful information, because it puts into clearer focus the question of exactly what you are trying to do with your investment dollars. Finally, there is the matter of the types of services provided by the fund. If there are services you are particularly interested in, you should be sure to look for them in the funds you select. Having assessed what you are looking for in a fund, you now want to look at what the funds have to offer.

WHAT FUNDS HAVE TO OFFER. The ideal mutual fund would achieve maximum capital growth when security prices rise, provide complete protection against capital loss when prices decline, and achieve high levels of current income at all times. Unfortunately, such funds do not exist. Instead, just as each individual has a set of investment needs, each fund has its own *investment objective*, its own *manner of operation*, and its own *range of services*. These three parameters are useful in helping you assess investment alternatives. But where does the investor look for such information? One obvious place is the fund's *profile* (or its prospectus), where information on investment objectives, portfolio composition, management, and past performance can be obtained. In addition, publications such as *The Wall Street Journal, Barron's, Money, Fortune,* and *Forbes* provide all sorts of useful data and information about mutual funds. These sources publish a wealth of operating and performance statistics in a convenient and easy-to-read format. What's more, services are

MONEY IN ACTION

Stocks and Bonds or Mutual Funds—Which Will It Be?

If you've got a certificate of deposit maturing at a bank and you've decided to invest in the markets, then you've got a choice to make: individual securities or mutual funds.

Stocks give you a shot at big-time gains, but you can also lose your shirt unless you're properly diversified. Mutual funds spread the risk and provide a smoother return, although you're probably not going to get rich. From 1995 to mid-2000, only about 25 percent of all U.S. diversified mutual funds beat the S&P 500. In many years buying big blue-chip stocks like General Electric and Microsoft would have been a better investment. Of course, that's easy to say in hindsight. You also could have been a proud investor in eToys, and watched as the stock price soared to 86, and then lost everything when the company went out of business.

Individual bonds are probably less volatile than most bond mutual funds. If interest rates go up, then the net asset value of your bond mutual fund will almost certainly go down. Your individual bond will go down in price, too, but you may not care if you're holding the bond until maturity, content to collect income every 6 months.

Which is right for you: stocks and bonds or mutual funds? Be honest. Do you have time to study the markets? If not, then mutual funds with their professional money managers may be a better bet. On the other hand, if your goal is to buy the ten largest stocks in the Dow or a handful of high-grade corporate bonds and sit tight, then you probably don't need a mutual fund.

If you're interested in something a bit more exotic—say international investing or junk bonds—then a mutual fund's professional management is a big selling point. After all, do you really have the time or expertise to research that Russian oil company's prospects or that high-flying cable-TV company's balance sheet?

The biggest plus of a mutual fund is that you don't have to decide what securities to buy or sell. Because the typical fund holds 50 to 100 securities or more, you are automatically diversified. Mutual funds are also good for systematic investing. You can easily put 10 percent of your paycheck into the market every month by sending a check or having your friendly mutual fund transfer the funds from your checking account. It's not so easy to buy individual securities with a fixed amount of cash.

But the advantages of mutual funds do not come without costs. Even if you stick with no-load mutual funds, you'll pay 1 to 2 percent of your fund's value to cover expenses. That really hurts in the bond arena, because bond returns are typically in the single digits. In this era of discount brokerage firms, you can buy and hold stocks and bonds for a fraction of the cost of a mutual fund management fee.

The last consideration, although not the least important, is your tax status. Mutual funds have a major disadvantage because every year they pay out capital gains that represent the fund manager's net realized profits for the year. You must report these gains on your taxes—whether or not you actually redeemed shares. You can avoid this problem by putting mutual funds in your tax-deferred retirement accounts. You may want to look for funds that limit distributions. Individual stocks and bonds may generate dividends and interest, but they do not generate capital gains until you actually sell them.

Sources: Sarah C. Bush, "Five Tips for Choosing a Bond Fund," *Morningstar.com*, June 8, 2000, downloaded from **news.morning star.com/news**; Jonathan Clements, "Individual Stocks' Allure: Lower Taxes," *Wall Street Journal*, June 13, 2000, p. C1; Peter Di Teresa, "Should You Buy Bonds or Bond Funds?" *Morningstar.com*, August 24, 2000, downloaded from **news.morningstar.com/news**; Jason Zweig, "Stocks or Funds," *Money Magazine*, April 1998, p. 93.

available that provide background information and assessments on a wide variety of different kinds of funds. Among the best in this category are *Morningstar's Mutual Funds* (an excerpt of which is shown in Exhibit 13.8), Wiesenberger's *Investment Companies* (an annual publication with quarterly updates), Standard & Poor's/Lipper Analytical's *Mutual Fund Profiles* (a publication that comes out in four quarterly editions), and *Value Line*

EXHIBIT 13.8

MUTUAL FUND INFORMATION

Investors who want in-depth information about the operating characteristics, investment holdings, and market performance of mutual funds can usually find what they're looking for in publications like *Morningstar Mutual Funds*, or, as shown here, from computer-based information sources like *Morningstar's Principia*.

Source: *Morningstar Principia Pro*, Release Date: September 30, 2000.

Mutual Fund Survey (which produces reports similar to their stock reports, except they apply to mutual funds). In addition, all sorts of performance statistics are available on disks or on the Internet for easy use on home computers—for example, quarterly or annually updated software is available, at very low cost, from *Morningstar* or the American Association of Individual Investors (AAII). Using sources like these, investors can obtain information on such things as investment objectives, load charges and annual expense rates, summary portfolio analyses, services offered, historical statistics, and reviews of past performance.

WHITTLING DOWN THE ALTERNATIVES. At this point, fund selection becomes a process of elimination as investor needs are weighed against the types of funds available. A large number of funds can be eliminated from consideration simply because they fail to meet these needs. Some may be too risky; others may be unsuitable as a storehouse of value. Thus, rather than trying to evaluate 8,000 different funds, you can use a process of elimination to narrow the list down to two or three *types* of funds that best match your investment (and asset allocation) needs.

From here, you can whittle the list down a bit more by introducing other constraints. For example, because of cost considerations, you may want to deal only in no-load or low-load funds (more on this below); or you may be seeking certain services that are important to your investment goals. Now we're ready to introduce the final (but certainly not the least important) element in the selection process: *the fund's investment performance.* Useful information includes (1) how the fund has performed over the past five to seven years; (2) the type of return it has generated in good markets as well as bad; (3) the level of dividend and capital gains distributions, which is an important indication not only of how much current income the fund distributes annually, but also the fund's *tax-efficiency* (as a rule, funds that have low dividends and low asset turnover expose their shareholders to less taxes and therefore have higher tax-efficiency ratings); and (4) the type of investment stability the fund has enjoyed over time (or, put another way, the amount of volatility/risk in the fund's return). By evaluating such information, it is possible to identify some of the more successful mutual funds—the ones that not only offer the investment objectives and services you seek but also provide the best payoffs. And while you're doing this, you might want to keep in mind some of the fund facts noted in Exhibit 13.9.

STICK WITH NO-LOADS OR LOW-LOADS. There's a longstanding "debate" in the mutual fund industry regarding load funds and no-load funds. The question is: do load funds add value? And if not, why pay the load charges? As it turns out, the results generally don't support load funds. Indeed, rather than producing superior returns, load fund returns, in general, don't seem to be any better than the returns from no-load funds and, in fact, in many cases, the funds with abnormally high loads and 12(b)-1 charges often produce returns that are far *less* than what you can get from no-loads! And, because of compounding, the differential returns tend to widen with longer holding periods.

That should come as no surprise, however, because big load charges and/or 12(b)-1 fees do nothing more than *reduce your investable capital* and, therefore, reduce the amount of money you have working for you. In fact, the only way a load fund can overcome this handicap is to *produce superior returns*—which is no easy thing to do, year in and year out. Granted there are a handful of load funds that have produced very attractive returns over extended periods of time, but they are the exception rather than the rule.

Obviously, it's in your best interest to pay close attention to load charges (and other fees) whenever you're considering an investment in a mutual fund. As a rule, to maximize returns, *you should seriously consider sticking to no-load funds, or low-loads* (funds that have total load charges, including 12(b)-1 fees, of 3 percent or less). Or at the very minimum,

EXHIBIT 13.9

SOME MUTUAL FUND FACTS EVERY INVESTOR SHOULD KNOW

Mutual funds are meant to provide investors with a simple, yet effective, way of buying into the stock and bond markets. Unfortunately, fund investing isn't always as simple as it looks. So, here are a few fund facts every investor should keep in mind when making mutual fund investments.

- Stock funds that get hit hard in market crashes aren't necessarily bad investments.
- Even great funds have bad years now and then.
- Most stock (and bond) funds fail to beat the market.
- You don't need a broker to buy mutual funds.
- A fund that doesn't charge a sales commission isn't necessarily a no-load fund.
- If you own more than a dozen different funds, you probably own too many.
- Mutual fund names are often misleading.
- Bond funds with high yields don't necessarily produce high returns.
- Money-market funds are not risk-free (you never know what kind of return you're going to earn with these things).
- If the market crashes, it will probably be too late to sell your fund shares (the damage will probably already have been done).
- Most mutual fund investors are wimps (because they put way too much into low-risk debt funds).
- Even bad funds sometimes rank as top performers.

you should consider a more expensive load fund *only* if it has a much better performance record (and offers more return potential) than a less expensive fund. There may well be times when the higher costs are justified, but far more often than not, you're better off trying to minimize load charges. That shouldn't be all that hard to do, however, as there are literally thousands of no-load and low-load funds to choose from; and they come in all different types and sizes.

 MAXfunds (**www.maxfunds.com**) offers investors an entertaining and educational site to help make better investing decisions. It also covers lesser-known and smaller funds. Much of its research is unique to the site, and the data is easy to understand.

GETTING A HANDLE ON MUTUAL FUND PERFORMANCE

If you were to believe all the sales literature, you'd think there was no way you could go wrong by investing in mutual funds. Just put your money into one of these funds and let the good times roll! Unfortunately, the hard facts of life are that *when it comes to investing, performance is never guaranteed.* And that applies just as much to mutual funds as it does to any other form of investing. Perhaps even more so, because with mutual funds, the single variable that drives a fund's market price and return behavior is the performance of the fund's portfolio of securities.

MEASURING FUND PERFORMANCE. Basically, any (open- or closed-end) mutual fund has three potential sources of return: (1) dividend income, (2) capital gains distribution, and (3) change in the fund's share price. Depending on the type of fund, some will derive more income from one source than another; for example, we would normally expect

EXHIBIT 13.10

A SUMMARY OF INCOME AND CAPITAL CHANGES

The return on a mutual fund is made up of (1) the (net) investment income the fund earns from dividends and interest, and (2) the realized and unrealized capital gains the fund earns on its security transaction. Mutual funds provide such information to their shareholders in a standardized format (like the statement here), which highlights, among other things, key income, expense, and capital gains information.

	2001	2000	1999
1. **Net asset value, beginning of period:**	$24.47	$27.03	$24.26
2. **Income from investment operations:**			
3. Net investment income	$ .60	$ .66	$ .50
4. Net gains on securities (realized and unrealized)	6.37	(1.74)	3.79
5. Total from investment operations	6.97	(1.08)	4.29
6. **Less distributions:**			
7. Dividends from net investment income	($ .55)	($ .64)	($ .50)
8. Distributions from realized gains	(1.75)	(.84)	(1.02)
9. Total distributions	(2.30)	(1.48)	(1.52)
10. **Net asset value, end of period:**	$29.14	$24.47	$27.03
11. **Total return:**	28.48%	(4.00%)	17.68%
12. **Ratios/supplemental data:**			
13. Net assets, end of period ($000)	$307,951	$153,378	$108,904
14. Ratio of expenses to average net assets	1.04%	0.85%	0.94%
15. Ratio of net investment income to average net assets	1.47%	2.56%	2.39%
16. Portfolio turnover rate*	85%	144%	74%

Portfolio turnover rate measures the number of shares bought and sold by the fund against the total number of shares held in the fund's portfolio; a high turnover rate (for example, in excess of 100 percent) would mean the fund has been doing a lot of trading.

income-oriented funds to have higher dividend income than capital gains distributions. Mutual funds regularly publish reports that recap investment performance. One such report is *The Summary of Income and Capital Changes,* an example of which is provided in Exhibit 13.10. This statement gives a brief overview of the fund's investment activities, including expense ratios and portfolio turnover rates. Of interest to us here is the top part of the report (which runs from "Net asset value, beginning of period" to "Net asset value, end of period"—lines 1 to 10). This is the part that reveals the amount of dividend income and capital gains distributed to the shareholders, along with any change in the fund's net asset value.

Dividend income (see line 7 of Exhibit 13.10) is the amount derived from the dividend and interest income earned on the security holdings of the mutual fund. When the fund receives dividends or interest payments, it passes these on to shareholders in the form of dividend payments. The fund accumulates all the current income it has received for the period and then pays it out on a prorated basis. Capital gains distributions (see line 8) work on the same principle, except they are derived from the capital gains actually earned by the fund. This capital gains distribution applies only to *realized* capital gains—that is, where the securities holdings were actually sold and capital gains actually earned. *Unrealized* capital gains (or paper profits) are what make up the third and final element in a mutual fund's return, *for when the fund's securities holdings go up or down in price, its net asset value moves accordingly*. This change (or movement) in the NAV is what makes up the unrealized capital gains of the fund. It represents the profit shareholders would receive (and are entitled to) if the fund were to sell its holdings.

A simple but effective way of measuring performance is to describe mutual fund returns in terms of the three major sources of return noted above—dividends earned, capital gains distributions received, and change in share price. These payoffs can be converted to a convenient return figure by using the standard *approximate yield* formula that was first introduced in Chapter 12. The calculations necessary for finding such a return measure can be shown by using the 2001 figures from Exhibit 13.10. Referring to the exhibit, we can see that this hypothetical no-load fund paid $.55 per share in dividends and another $1.75 in capital gains distributions; also, its price (NAV) at the beginning of the year (that is, at year-end 2000) of $24.47 rose to $29.14 by the end of the year (see lines 1 and 10, respectively). Putting this data into the familiar approximate yield formula, we see that the hypothetical mutual fund provided an annual rate of return of 26.0 percent. (Note that the computed return of 26.0 percent differs a bit from the 28.48 percent "Total return" shown on the table in Exhibit 13.10—see line 11. That's due to a *slight variation in computational procedures;* i.e., whereas the approximate yield measure uses the average price or NAV in the denominator, the total return measure in the table uses the price at NAV at the *beginning of the period only.*)

$$\text{Approximate yield} = \frac{\text{Dividends and capital gains distributions} + \left[\dfrac{\text{Ending price} - \text{Beginning price}}{\text{1-year time period}}\right]}{\left[\dfrac{\text{Ending price} + \text{Beginning price}}{2}\right]}$$

$$= \frac{(\$.55 + \$1.75) + \left[\dfrac{\$29.14 - \$24.47}{1}\right]}{\left[\dfrac{\$29.14 + \$24.47}{2}\right]}$$

$$= \frac{\$2.30 + \$4.67}{\$26.80} = \frac{\$6.97}{26.80} = \underline{\underline{26.0\%}}$$

WHAT ABOUT FUTURE PERFORMANCE?   There's no question that approximate yield is a simple, yet highly effective measure that captures all the important elements of mutual fund return. Unfortunately, looking at past performance is one thing, but how about the future? Ideally, we would want to evaluate the same three elements of return over the future much like we did for the past. The trouble is, when it comes to the future performance of a mutual fund, it's extremely difficult—if not impossible—to get a handle on what the future holds as far as dividends, capital gains, and NAV are concerned. The reason: a mutual fund's future investment performance is directly linked to the future makeup of its securities portfolio—which is impossible to predict. It's not like evaluating the expected performance of a share of stock, where you're keying in on one company. With mutual funds, investment performance depends on the behavior of many different stocks and bonds.

So, where do you look for insight into the future? Most market observers suggest you do two things. First, give careful consideration to the *future direction of the market as a whole.* This is important, because the behavior of a well-diversified mutual fund tends to reflect the general tone of the market. Thus, if the feeling is that the market is going to be generally drifting up, that should bode well for the investment performance of mutual funds.

Second, take a good hard look at the past performance of the mutual fund itself, as that's a good way to get an indication of how successful the fund's investment managers have been. In essence, the success of a mutual fund rests in large part *on the investment skills of the fund managers.* So, when investing in a mutual fund, look for consistently good performance, in up as well as down markets, over extended periods of time (5 to 7 years, or more). Most important, check to see if the same key people are still running the fund. Although past success is certainly no guarantee of future performance, a strong team of money managers can have a significant bearing on the level of fund returns. Put another way, when you buy a mutual fund, you're buying a formula (investment policy + money management team) that has worked in the past, in the expectation that it will work again in the future.

CONCEPT CHECK

13-11. What are the most common reasons for buying mutual funds? Is financial return important to mutual fund investors? Explain.

13-12. Briefly describe the steps in the mutual fund selection process. Why is it important to have a clear understanding of what your own investment objectives and motives are?

13-13. Why does it pay to invest in no-load funds rather than load funds? Under what conditions might it make sense to invest in a load fund?

13-14. Identify three potential sources of return to mutual fund investors, and briefly discuss how each could affect total return to shareholders. Which would you rather have: $100 in dividend income or $100 in capital gains distribution? $100 in realized capital gains or $100 in unrealized capital gains? Explain.

13-15. How important is the general behavior of the market in affecting the price performance of mutual funds? Why is a fund's past performance so important to the mutual fund selection process? Does the future behavior of the market matter any in the selection process? Explain.

SUMMARY

LG1. **Describe the basic features and operating characteristics of a mutual fund.** Mutual fund shares represent ownership in a diversified, professionally managed portfolio of securities; many investors who lack the time, know-how, or commitment to manage their own money turn to mutual funds as an investment outlet. By investing in mutual funds, shareholders benefit from a level of diversification and investment performance they might otherwise find difficult to achieve.

LG2. **Differentiate between open- and closed-end funds, as well as other types of professionally managed investment companies, and discuss the various types of fund loads and charges.** Investors can buy either open-end funds, which have no limit on the number of shares they can issue, or closed-end funds, which have a fixed number of shares outstanding and which trade in the secondary markets like any other share of common stock. In addition, they can invest in exchange-traded funds, or ETFs, which possess characteristics of both open- and closed-end funds, REITs (which invest primarily in various types of real estate products), or unit investment trusts. There is a cost, however, to investing in mutual funds (and other types of professionally managed investment products). The fact is, mutual fund investors face a full array of loads, fees, and charges, including front-end loads, back-end loads, annual 12(b)-1 charges, annual management fees, and so forth. Some of these costs are one-time charges (like front-end loads), but others (like 12(b)-1 and management fees) are paid annually.

LG3. **Discuss the types of funds available to investors, and the variety of investment objectives these funds seek to fulfill.** Each fund has an established investment objective that determines its investment policy and identifies it as a certain type of fund. Some of the more popular types of funds are growth, aggressive growth, value, equity-income, balanced, growth-and-income, bond, money, index, sector, socially responsible, asset allocation, and international funds. The different categories of funds have different risk-return characteristics and are important variables in the fund selection process.

LG4. **Identify and discuss the different kinds of investor services offered by mutual funds.** In addition to their investment returns, many investors buy mutual funds to take advantage of the various investor services they offer, such as automatic investment and reinvestment plans, systematic withdrawal programs, low-cost conversion and phone-switching privileges, and retirement programs.

LG5. **Gain an understanding of the variables that should be considered when selecting funds for investment purposes.** The fund selection process generally starts by assessing your own needs and wants; this sets the tone for your investment program and helps you decide on the types of funds to look at. Next, take a look at what the funds have to offer, particularly with regard to the fund's investment objectives and investor services—here, narrow down the alternatives by aligning your needs with the types of funds available. From this list of funds, introduce the final selection tests: fund performance and cost—other things being equal, look for high performance and low costs.

LG6. **Identify the sources of return and calculate the rate of return earned on an investment in a mutual fund.** The investment performance of mutual funds is largely a function of the returns the money managers are able to generate from their securities portfolios; generally speaking, strong markets translate into attractive returns for mutual fund investors. Mutual funds have three basic sources of return: (1) dividends; (2) capital gains distributions; and (3) changes in the fund's NAV (as accruing from unrealized capital gains). The approximate yield measure recognizes these three elements and provides a simple yet effective way of measuring the annual rate of return from a mutual fund.

QUESTIONS AND PROBLEMS

1. Contrast *mutual fund ownership* with the *direct investment in stocks and bonds*. Assume your class is going to debate the merits of investing through mutual funds versus investing directly in stocks and bonds. Develop some pro and con arguments on each side of this debate and be prepared to discuss them in class. If you had to choose one side to be on, which would it be? Explain.

2. Using the mutual fund quotes in Exhibit 13.4, and assuming you can buy these funds at their quoted net asset values, how much would you have to pay to buy each of the following funds?
   a. Fairmont Fund (Fairmt)
   b. FPA Capital Fund (Capit)
   c. Dreyfus Aggressive Growth Fund (AggGr)
   d. Dreyfus GNMA Bond Fund (GMBd)
   e. FMI Focus Fund (FMI FocusFd)
   Which of these five funds have 12(b)-1 fees? Which ones have redemption fees? Are any of them no-loads? Which fund has the highest year-to-date return ? Which has the lowest?

3. Let's imagine that you've just inherited $20,000 from a rich uncle. Now you're faced with the problem of trying to decide how to spend it. You could make a down payment on a condo, or, better yet, on that Corvette that you've always wanted. Or, you could spend your windfall more profitably by building a mutual fund portfolio. Let's say that after a lot of soul searching, you decide to do the latter: build a mutual fund portfolio. Your task at hand is to develop a $20,000 mutual fund portfolio—use actual funds and actual quoted prices, invest as much of the $20,000 as you possibly can, and be specific! Briefly describe the portfolio you ended up with, including the investment objectives you are trying to achieve.

4. For *each pair* of funds listed below, select the fund that would be the *least* risky; briefly explain your answer:
   a. Growth versus growth-and-income
   b. Equity-income versus high-grade corporate bonds
   c. Intermediate-term bonds versus high-yield municipals
   d. International versus balanced

5. What investor service is most closely linked to the notion of a fund family? If a fund is not part of a family of mutual funds, can it still offer a full range of investor services? Explain. Using something like *The Wall Street Journal*, or perhaps your local newspaper, find two examples of fund families; list some of the mutual funds they offer.

6. Using a source like *Barron's, Forbes, Money*, or perhaps even *Morningstar* (if it's readily available to you), select five mutual funds—(a) a growth fund, (b) an index fund, (c) a sector fund, (d) an international fund, and (e) a high-yield corporate bond fund—that you feel would make good investments. Briefly explain why you selected each of the funds.

7. About a year ago, Dave Kidwell bought some shares in the Hi-Flyer Mutual Fund. He bought the stock at $24.50 a share, and it now trades at $26.00. Last year the fund paid dividends of 40 cents a share and had capital gains distributions of $1.83 a share. Using the approximate yield formula, what rate of return did Dave earn on his investment? Would he have made a 20 percent rate of return if the stock had risen to $30 a share?

8. Describe an ETF and explain how these funds combine the characteristics of open- and closed-end funds. Looking in the Vanguard family of funds, which one of their funds would most closely resemble a "Spider" (SPDR). In what respects are the Vanguard fund (that you selected) and Spiders the same; how are they different? If you could invest in only one of them, which would it be? Explain.

9. A year ago, the Full-Bore Growth Fund was being quoted at an NAV of $21.50 and an offer price of $23.35; today it's being quoted at $23.04 (NAV) and $25.04 (offer). Use the approximate yield formula to find the rate of return on this load fund, given it was purchased a year ago and its dividends and capital gains distributions over the year totaled $1.05 a share. (*Hint:* You, as an investor, buy fund shares at the offer price and sell at the NAV.)

10. Listed below is the per-share performance record of the East Coast Growth-and-Income fund for 2001 and 2000:

	2001	2000
1. **Net asset value, beginning of period:**	$58.60	$52.92
2. **Income from investment operations:**		
3. Net investment income	$1.39	$1.35
4. Net gains on securities (realized and unrealized)	8.10	9.39
5. Total from investment operations	9.49	10.74
6. **Less distributions:**		
7. Dividends from net investment income	($ .83)	($1.24)
8. Distributions from realized gains	(2.42)	(3.82)
9. Total distributions	(3.25)	(5.06)
10. **Net asset value, end of period:**	$64.84	$58.60

Use this information to find the rate of return earned on the East Coast G-&-I fund in 2000 and in 2001. What is your assessment of the investment performance of this fund for the 2000-2001 period?

APPLYING PERSONAL FINANCE

Mutual Funds—A Great Way to Start!

More and more investors are turning to mutual funds as a way to invest. And there's good reason for that; for as we saw in this chapter, mutual funds offer convenience, diversification, and the services of professional money managers. Indeed, it is generally recommended that the best way to start off an investment program is by investing in mutual funds. In this project, you will show how you'd use mutual funds as a beginning investor. Assume you have inherited or been awarded a small sum of money ($15,000), the full amount of which you have decided to invest. Using one or two of the information sources noted in this chapter (like *Morningstar, Barron's, Forbes*, or an online site), select two mutual funds from the following fund categories:

1. Growth
2. Equity-income
3. Balanced
4. Growth and income
5. Bond
6. Socially-responsible

(**Note:** You can select *any two funds you want*, the only constraint is that they have to come from *two different fund categories*.) First, you are going to have to decide which two fund *categories* you feel will best meet your financial needs and risk tolerance, and then which *fund* (from within each of the two categories) you find most attractive. After you have made your selections, provide the following information for each of the two funds selected:

a. Name of fund
b. Type of fund (i.e., growth, equity-income, etc.)
c. Size of fund
d. Load charges (if any)
e. Other fees and charges (if any—e.g., does it have a 12(b)-1 fee?)
f. How has the fund performed over the past 3 and 5 years?
g. How much did the fund pay out last year in dividends? In capital gains distributions?
h. What was the *approximate yield* on the fund last year? (You will probably have to compute this yourself.)

    i.   Does the fund offer automatic reinvestment plans? Phone switching? What other services?

    j.   Briefly explain why you selected this fund.

CONTEMPORARY CASE APPLICATIONS

13.1   Dave's Dilemma: Common Stocks or Mutual Funds?

Dave Brubaker has worked in the management services division of Ace Consultants for the past 5 years. He currently earns an annual salary of about $65,000. At 33, he is still a bachelor and has accumulated about $60,000 in savings over the past few years. He keeps his savings in a money market account, where it earns about 4.5 percent interest. Dave wants to earn "a bigger bang from the buck" and as such, is contemplating withdrawing $50,000 from his money market account and investing it in the stock market. He feels that such an investment can easily earn more than 4.5 percent. Marlene Bellamy, a close friend, suggests that he invest in mutual fund shares. Dave has approached you, his broker, for advice.

Questions

1. Explain to Dave the key reasons for purchasing mutual fund shares.
2. What special fund features might help Dave achieve his investment objectives?
3. What types of mutual funds would you recommend to Dave?
4. What recommendations would you make with respect to Dave's dilemma about whether to go into stocks or mutual funds? Explain.

13.2   Marge Ponders Mutual Funds

Marge Simmons is the director of a major charitable organization in Springfield, Ohio. A single mother of one young child, she earns what could best be described as a "modest income." Because charitable organizations are not notorious for their generous retirement programs, Marge has decided it would be best for her to do a little investing on her own. She would like to set up a program that enables her to supplement her employer's retirement program and, at the same time, provide some funds for her child's college education (which is still some 12 years away). Although her income is modest, Marge feels that with careful planning, she could probably invest about $250 a quarter (and, with luck, maybe increase this amount over time). She presently has about $15,000 in a bank savings account, which she would be willing to use to kick off this program. In view of her investment objectives, she is not interested in taking a lot of risk. Because her knowledge of investments extends to savings accounts, series EE bonds, and a little bit about mutual funds, she approaches you for some investment advice.

Questions

1. In view of Marge's long-term investment goals, do you think mutual funds are an appropriate investment vehicle for her?
2. Do you think she should use her $15,000 savings to start off a mutual fund investment program?
3. What type of mutual fund investment program would you set up for Marge? Include in your answer some discussion of the types of funds you would consider, the investment objectives you would set, and any investment services (like withdrawal plans) you would seek. Would taxes be an important consideration in your investment advice? Explain.

MONEY ONLINE

PROSPER WITH MUTUALS!

Note: Web addresses change frequently, so you may need to determine the home page and do a site search to find the page or topic that's referenced.

1. **www.quicken.com/investments/mutualfunds/finder**
   Find your fund! Work through Quicken's Popular Searches, EasyStep Search, or Full Search to find the mutual funds that best suit your investing goals. While you're there, click on "Top 25 Funds" to view the top 25 performing mutual finds in 50 different categories.

2. **www.quicken.com**
   Once you've found your funds, let Quicken help you evaluate them. Type in FBGRX and VFINX (separate the symbols with a space between them) to compare Fidelity's Blue Chip Growth Fund with Vanguard's 500 Index Fund. Click on "Evaluator" and then work through the numbered steps—Return vs. Risk, Fund Holdings, Cost of Ownership, and Summary—to analyze the two funds in detail.

3. **www.morningstar.com**
   Attend Morningstar's "University" to learn how to analyze your funds, stocks and portfolios like a Morningstar analyst. Sample their Primers, attend the Investing Classroom or Ask the Professor your investment questions. Then click on "Portfolio" to enter your personal portfolio and use Morningstar's sophisticated tracking system to help you determine not only your gain or loss but also the cost basis of your investment when you're ready to sell.

4. **www.nasdaq.com**
   Spiders, Diamonds, and Qubes! Now you can hold all the stocks of your favorite industry in one fund! Click on "Exchange Traded Funds" at Nasdaq's Web site to learn more about these funds, the different ETFs available, and if they are right for you and your investment objectives.

5. **nareit.com**
   Interested in real estate but don't want to own property directly? Consider the greater liquidity and portfolio diversification that generally can be had with Real Estate Investment Trusts versus owning property outright. Explore the Web site of the National Association of Real Estate Investment Trusts to learn more about REITs.

6. **www.sec.gov/info/advisers.shtml**
   What are the laws in regard to mutual fund companies? Read through the various laws, rules and regulations concerning both mutual funds and investment advisors at the Securities and Exchange Commission's Web site.

7. **www.nasaa.org**
   Need to make a complaint concerning an investment? You may do so electronically at the Web site of the North American Securities Administration by scrolling down the side bar and clicking on "Investment-Related Complaint." You may also click on "Find Regulator" to find the name, address, phone number and Web site of your state's securities regulator.

8. **www.fabian.com**
   Is your fund a lemon? First view the Lipper Benchmark Chart and then see how your fund stacks up by clicking on Fabian's "Lemon List." Read the "Fabian Lemon Laws" to see how he evaluates these overcharging, underachieving funds.

Just for Fun!

9. **smartmoney.com/maps**

 View the mutual fund market in color! Click on SmartMoney's "Mutual Fund Map" for a revealing view of the 1,000 most important funds. Track and compare performance, expenses, *Morningstar* rankings, and more at this information-packed Web site.

10. **smartmoney.com/maps**

 Color code your own portfolio! Scroll down to "Map Your Portfolio" to use SmartMoney's revolutionary color-coding tool to track your own portfolio and instantly see how your investments are performing in relation to one another!

11. **brill.com**

 Keep current with the mutual fund market. Subscribe to MFI's Mutual Fund Alert and receive their free weekly newsletter by e-mail!

PART VI

Retirement and Estate Planning

CHAPTER 14
Planning for
Retirement

CHAPTER 15
Preserving Your Estate

Chapter 14

Planning for Retirement

LEARNING GOALS

LG1.   Recognize the importance of retirement planning and identify the three biggest pitfalls to good planning.

LG2.   Establish retirement goals and estimate your future income needs.

LG3.   Explain the eligibility requirements and benefits of the social security program.

LG4.   Differentiate among the different types of basic and supplemental employer-sponsored pension plans.

LG5.   Describe the various types of self-directed retirement plans.

LG6.   Choose the right type of annuity for your retirement plan.

His Stocks Retired Before He Did

Doug Williams was feeling very pleased with himself. The 45-year-old computer engineer had consistently contributed to his retirement funds, both through his company's 401(k) plan and a Roth IRA. He reviewed his portfolios regularly and made changes when necessary, but basically had invested for the long term. With a balance of mutual funds, stocks, and bonds, he thought his assets were well balanced and would see him through any sort of market condition until his planned retirement at age 60.

As the stock market took off in the 1990s, Doug began to shift a higher percentage of his portfolio to stocks, and because he had more than 15 years to go, decided to be more aggressive in his choices. Unfortunately, his taste ran to tech stocks, and like many others he rode them up to new heights—then watched with dismay as his portfolio dropped 65 percent in 2000.

Doug had lived through other market dips, but none were as severe as this one. He vowed to change his strategy by factoring in the possibility of a long market downturn. He prepared a new income plan to figure out what he would need to invest, given his reduced portfolio. He planned to monitor his retirement holdings carefully, and to diversify into bonds, cash equivalents, and international mutual funds to ride out any future market volatility. He also decided to investigate annuities to see if they could help him rebuild his nest egg.

Today it is more important than ever to take control of your retirement funds and choose your investments wisely. This chapter explains how to assess your own needs and develop your own plan, so that you, too, will be ready for retirement.

■ An Overview of Retirement Planning [LG1, LG2]

Do you know your life expectancy? Well, if you're in your late teens or early 20s, you'll probably live another 60 or 70 years. While this prospect may sound delightful, it also brings into focus the need for careful retirement planning. After all, you may only work for about 40 of those years—perhaps less—and spend 20 or more years in retirement. The challenge, of course, is to do it in style—and that is where retirement planning comes into play! But to enjoy a comfortable retirement, you must start *now*—for one of the biggest mistakes people make in retirement planning is waiting too long to begin. Yet the longer you wait, the harder it will be to reach the kind of retirement income you would like.

Make no mistake about it, accumulating adequate retirement funds is a daunting task that takes careful planning. Like budgets, taxes, and investments, retirement planning is vital to your financial well-being and is a critical link in your personal financial plans. Even so, it's difficult for most people under the age of 30 to develop a well-defined set of retirement plans. There are just too many years to go until retirement and too many uncertainties to deal with: inflation, social security, family size, the type of pension you'll receive—if any—and how much money you will have when you're ready to retire. However, it's just this kind of uncertainty that makes retirement planning so important. To cope with uncertainty, you must plan for a variety of outcomes, and monitor and modify your plans as your hopes, abilities, and personal finances change.

ROLE OF RETIREMENT PLANNING IN PERSONAL FINANCIAL PLANNING

The financial planning process would be incomplete without *retirement planning*. Certainly there is no financial goal more important than achieving a comfortable standard of living in retirement. In many respects, retirement planning captures the very essence of financial planning. It is forward looking (perhaps more so than any other aspect of financial planning), has an impact on both your current and future standard of living, and, if successful, can be highly rewarding and make a significant contribution to your net worth.

Okay, it's important; so where do you start? Well, like most aspects of financial planning, you need a goal or an objective—that is, the first step in retirement planning is to set *retirement goals* for yourself. Take some time to define the things you want to do in retirement, the standard of living you hope to maintain, the level of income you would like to receive, and any special retirement goals you may have (like buying a retirement home in Arizona, or taking an around-the-world cruise). Such goals are important because *they give direction to your retirement planning*. Of course, like all goals, they are subject to change over time as the situations and conditions in your life change.

Once you know what you want out of retirement, the next step is to establish the *size of the nest egg* you're going to have to build to achieve your retirement goals. In essence, how much money will you need to retire the way you would like?

The final step is to formulate an *investment program* that will enable you to build up your required nest egg. This usually involves creating some type of systematic savings plan (putting away a certain amount of money each year) and identifying the types of investment vehicles that will best meet your retirement needs. This phase of your retirement program is closely related to two other aspects of financial planning—investment and tax planning.

Investments and investment planning (see Chapters 11 through 13) are the vehicles through which you build up your retirement funds. They constitute the active, ongoing part of retirement planning in which you manage and invest the funds you have set aside for retirement. It is no coincidence that a major portion of most individual investor portfolios is devoted to building up a pool of funds for retirement. Taxes and tax planning (see Chapter 3) are also important, because one of the major objectives of sound retirement planning is to legitimately shield as much income as possible from taxes and, in so doing, maximize the accumulation of retirement funds.

THE THREE BIGGEST PITFALLS TO SOUND RETIREMENT PLANNING

Human nature being what it is, people often get a little carried away with the amount of money they want to build up for retirement. Face it, having a nest egg of $3 million or $4 million would be great, but it's beyond the reach of all but a tiny fraction of the population. Besides, you don't need that much to live comfortably in retirement. So set a more realistic goal. But when you set that goal, remember: it's not going to happen by itself; you have to do something to bring it about. And this is precisely where things start to fall apart. Why? Because when it comes to retirement planning, people tend to make three big mistakes:

- They start too late.
- They put away too little.
- They invest too conservatively.

Many people in their 20s, or even 30s, find it hard to put money away for retirement. More often than not, that's because they have other, more pressing financial concerns to worry about—like buying a house, retiring a student loan, or paying for child care. The net result is that they *put off retirement planning until later in life*—in many cases, until they're in their late 30s or 40s. Unfortunately, the longer people put it off, the less they're going to have in retirement. Or, it means they're not going to be able to retire as early as they'd hoped. Even worse, once people start a retirement program, *they tend to be too skimpy and put away too little*. Although this, too, may be due to pressing family needs, all too often it boils down to lifestyle choices. They'd rather spend for today than save for tomorrow. As a result, they end up putting maybe $1,000 a year into a retirement plan when, with a little more effective financial planning and family budgeting, they could easily afford to save two or three times that amount.

On top of all this, many *people tend to be far too conservative* in the way they invest their retirement money. Too often, people fail to achieve the full potential of their retirement programs because they treat them more like savings accounts than investment vehicles! The fact is, they place way too much of their retirement money into *low-yielding*, fixed-income securities like CDs and treasury notes. While you should *never speculate* with something as important as your retirement plan, you do not have to totally avoid risk. There's nothing wrong with following an investment program that involves a reasonable amount of risk, so long as it results in a correspondingly higher level of return. Caution is fine, but being overly cautious can be very costly in the long run. Indeed, a low rate of return can have an enormous effect on the long-term accumulation of capital and, in many cases, may mean the difference between just getting by or enjoying a comfortable retirement.

All three of these pitfalls become even more important when we introduce *compound interest*. Why is that so? Because *compounding essentially magnifies the impact of these mistakes*. To illustrate, consider the first variable—starting too late. If you were to start a retirement program at age 35 by putting away $2,000 a year, it would grow to more than $150,000 by the time you're 65 when invested at an average rate of return of 6 percent. Not a bad deal, considering your total out-of-pocket investment over this 30-year period is only $60,000. But look at what you end up with if you start this investment program 10 years earlier, at age 25: That same $2,000 a year will grow to over $300,000 by the time you're 65. Think of it—for another $20,000 ($2,000 a year for an extra 10 years), you can double the terminal value of your investment! Of course, it's not the extra $20,000 that's doubling your money; rather, it's *compound interest* that's doing most of the work!

And the same holds true for the rate of return you earn on the investments in your retirement account. Take the second situation above—starting a retirement program at 25. Earning 6 percent means a retirement nest egg of over $300,000; increase that rate of return to 10 percent (a reasonable investment objective), and your retirement nest egg will be worth nearly $900,000! *You're still putting in the same amount of money,* but because your money is working harder, you end up with a much bigger nest egg. Of course, when you seek higher returns (as you would when you go from 6 percent to 10 percent), that generally means you also have to take on more risks. But that may not be as much of a problem as it appears, because in retirement planning, *the one thing you have on your side is time* (unless you start your plan very late in life). And the more time you have, the less of a burden risk becomes. That is, the more time you have, the easier it is to recover from those temporary market setbacks.

On the other hand, if you simply cannot tolerate the higher risks that accompany higher returns (and, certainly, some people cannot), then stay away from the higher-risk

 **EXHIBIT 14.1**

BUILDING UP YOUR RETIREMENT NEST EGG

The size of your retirement nest egg will depend on when you start your program (period of accumulation), how much you contribute each year, and the rate of return you earn on your investments. As seen in this table, you can combine these variables in a number of different ways to end up with a given amount at retirement.

	Amount of Accumulated Capital from							
	Contribution of $2,000/yr. at These Average Rates of Return				Contribution of $5,000/yr. at These Average Rates of Return			
Accumulation Period*	4%	6%	8%	10%	4%	6%	8%	10%
10 yrs. (55 yrs. old)	$ 24,010	$ 26,360	$ 28,970	$ 31,870	$ 60,030	$ 65,900	$ 72,440	$ 79,690
20 yrs. (45 yrs. old)	59,560	73,570	91,520	114,550	148,890	183,930	228,810	286,370
25 yrs. (40 yrs. old)	83,290	109,720	146,210	196,690	208,230	274,300	365,530	491,730
30 yrs. (35 yrs. old)	112,170	158,110	226,560	328,980	280,420	395,290	566,410	822,460
35 yrs. (30 yrs. old)	147,300	222,860	344,630	542,040	368,260	557,160	861,570	1,355,090
40 yrs. (25 yrs. old)	190,050	309,520	518,100	885,160	475,120	773,790	1,295,260	2,212,900

*Assumes retirement at age 65; parenthetical figure, therefore, is the age at which the person would start his or her retirement program.

investments! Rather, stick to safer, lower-yielding securities and find some other ways to build up your nest egg. For instance, contribute more each year to your plan or extend the length of your investment period. The only other option—and not a particularly appealing one—is to accept the fact that you will not be able to build up as big a nest egg as you had thought and, therefore, will have to accept a lower standard of living in retirement. All else being the same, it should be clear that the more you sock away each year, the more you're going to have at retirement. That is, put away $4,000 a year, rather than $2,000, and you are going to end up with twice as much money at retirement.

The combined impact of these three variables is seen in Exhibit 14.1. Note that it's really the combination of these three factors that determines the amount you will have at retirement. Thus, you can offset the effects of earning a lower rate of return on your money by increasing the amount you put in each year or by lengthening the period over which you build up your retirement account—meaning you start your program earlier in life (or work longer and retire later in life). The table shows that *there are several different ways of getting to roughly the same result;* that is, knowing the kind of nest egg you'd like to end up with, you can pick the combination of variables (period of accumulation, annual contribution, and rate of return) that you're most comfortable with.

RETIREMENT GOALS

People have all sorts of retirement goals. Playing more golf, fishing, traveling, or pursuing a favorite hobby are just a few examples. In order to have the income to realize these goals, people should consider the age at which they will retire and what their financial position is likely to be at that time.

AGE AT RETIREMENT. Estimating when you are likely to retire is important, because it lets you know how much time you have to save for retirement. Although it's not uncommon for workers to retire at age 60, or even 55, more and more people today remain in the workforce until age 70 or longer. If you think that a *shorter* working career is for you, then you must take the steps to put more money aside each year for retirement than others who plan to work for as long as they are physically and mentally capable.

FINANCIAL POSITION AND GOALS. Your financial position at retirement depends not only on your retirement plans but—perhaps even more so—on your choice of career and lifestyle. Remember that the quality of your life and lifestyle goals must be chosen on the basis of projected income and expenditures. Devoting some income toward retirement is essential to economic security in old age. You must be careful, therefore, not to satisfy low-priority, short-run desires at the expense of high-priority, long-run objectives.

ESTIMATING INCOME NEEDS

Retirement planning would be much simpler if we lived in a static economy. Unfortunately (or perhaps fortunately), we don't, and as a result, both your personal budget and the general economy are subject to considerable change over time. All of which make accurate forecasting of retirement needs difficult at best. Even so, it is a necessary task, and one you can handle in one of two ways. One strategy is to plan for retirement over *a series of short-run time frames*. A good way to do this is to state your retirement income objectives as a percentage of your present earnings. For example, if you desire a retirement income equal to 80 percent of your final take-home pay, you can determine the amount necessary to fund this need. Then, every 3 to 5 years, you can revise and update your plan.

Alternatively, you can follow *a long-term approach* in which you actually formulate the level of income you would like to receive in retirement, along with the amount of funds you must amass to achieve that desired standard of living. Rather than addressing the problem in a series of short-run plans, this approach goes 20 or 30 years into the future—to the time when you will retire—to determine how much saving and investing you must do today to achieve your long-run retirement goals. Of course, if conditions or expectations should happen to change dramatically in the future (as they very well could), it may be necessary to make corresponding alterations to your long-run retirement goals and strategies.

 Cnnfn's comprehensive retirement planning site (**cnnfn.cnn.com/retirement**) includes the latest news affecting retirement plans and educational articles on key topics.

DETERMINING FUTURE RETIREMENT NEEDS. To illustrate how future retirement needs and income requirements can be formulated, let's consider the case of Jack and Lois Spellman. In their mid-30s, they have two children and an annual income of about $60,000 before taxes. Up to now, Jack and Lois have given only passing thought to their retirement. But even though it's still some 30 years away, they recognize it's now time to give some serious consideration to their situation to see if they will be able to pursue a retirement lifestyle that appeals to them. Worksheet 14.1 provides the basic steps to follow in determining retirement needs. This worksheet shows how the Spellmans have estimated their retirement income and determined the amount of investment assets they must accumulate to meet their retirement objectives.

Jack and Lois began their calculation by determining what their *household expenditures* will likely be in retirement. Their estimate is based on maintaining a "comfortable" standard of living—one that will not be extravagant yet will allow them to do the things they would like in retirement. A simple yet highly effective way to derive an estimate of expected household expenditures is to base it on the current level of such expenses. Assume the Spellmans' annual household expenditures (excluding savings) currently run about $42,000 a year—

Beat the Retirement Clock
These tips will help you take a hard look at your lifestyle, your resources, and many other things you may take for granted while you are still employed.

1. Know how much you will need to retire in comfort.
2. Think about where you want to live and the cost of living in those locations.
3. Find out about your Social Security benefits.
4. Learn about your employer's pension or profit sharing plan.
5. Contribute to a tax-sheltered savings plan.
6. Put money into an IRA.
7. Don't cash out your retirement plan every time you change jobs—instead roll it over to an IRA or some other tax-sheltered program.
8. Start now, set goals, and stick to them.
9. Understand basic investment principles.
10. Don't neglect insurance planning.

WORKSHEET 14.1

ESTIMATING FUTURE RETIREMENT NEEDS

This worksheet will help you define your income requirements in retirement, the size of your retirement nest egg, and the amount you must save annually to achieve your given retirement goals.

PROJECTING RETIREMENT INCOME AND INVESTMENT NEEDS

Name(s) _Jack & Lois Spellman_   Date _June 2002_

I. Estimated Household Expenditures in Retirement:

A. Approximate number of years to retirement	30
B. *Current* level of annual household expenditures, excluding savings	$ 42,000
C. Estimated household expenses in retirement as a *percent* of current expenses	70%
D. Estimated annual household expenditures in retirement (B × C)	$ 29,400

II. Estimated Income in Retirement:

E. Social security, annual income	$ 13,000
F. Company/employer pension plans, annual amounts	$ 9,000
G. Other sources, annual amounts	$ 0
H. Total annual income (E + F + G)	$ 22,000
I. Additional required income, or annual shortfall (D − H)	$ 7,400

III. Inflation Factor:

J. Expected average annual rate of inflation over the period to retirement	5%
K. Inflation factor (in Appendix A): Based on _30_ years to retirement (A) and an expected average annual rate of inflation (J) of _5%_	4.32
L. Size of inflation-adjusted annual shortfall (I × K)	$ 32,000

IV. Funding the Shortfall:

M. Anticipated return on assets held *after* retirement	10%
N. Amount of retirement funds required—size of nest egg (L ÷ M)	$ 320,000
O. Expected rate of return on investments *prior* to retirement	8%
P. Compound interest factor (in Appendix B): Based on _30_ years to retirement (A) and an expected rate of return on investments of _8%_	113.3
Q. Annual savings required to fund retirement nest egg (N ÷ P)	$ 2,824

Note: Parts I and II are prepared in terms of current (today's) dollars.

---

this information can be readily obtained by referring to their most recent income and expenditures statement. Making some obvious adjustments for the different lifestyle they will have in retirement—their children will no longer be living at home, their home will be paid for, and so on—the Spellmans estimate that they will be able to achieve the standard of living they'd like in retirement at an annual level of household expenses equal to about 70 percent of the current amount. Thus, *in terms of today's dollars,* their estimated household expenditures in retirement will be $42,000 \times .70 = $29,400$. (This process is summarized in steps A through D in Worksheet 14.1.)

ESTIMATING RETIREMENT INCOME. The next question is: Where will they get the money to meet their projected household expenses of $29,400 a year? They have addressed this problem by estimating what their *income* will be in retirement—again *in terms of today's dollars*. Their two basic sources of retirement income are social security and employer-sponsored pension plans. Based on today's retirement tables they estimate that they will receive about $13,000 a year from social security (as we'll see later in this chapter, you can receive an estimate directly from the Social Security Administration of what your future social security benefits are likely to be when you retire) and another $9,000 from their employer pension plans, for a total projected annual income of $22,000. When this is compared to their projected household expenditures, it is clear the Spellmans will be facing an annual shortfall of $7,400 (see steps E through I in Worksheet 14.1). This is the amount of retirement income they must come up with; otherwise, they will have to reduce the standard of living they hope to enjoy in retirement.

At this point, we need to introduce the *inflation factor* to our projections in order to put the annual shortfall of $7,400 in terms of retirement dollars. Here we make the assumption that both income and expenditures will undergo approximately the same average rate of inflation, causing the shortfall to grow by that rate over time. In essence, 30 years from now, the annual shortfall is going to amount to a lot more than $7,400. How large it will grow to will, of course, be a function of what happens to inflation. Assume the Spellmans think inflation, on average, over the next 30 years will amount to 5 percent—while that's a bit on the high side by today's standards, the Spellmans decide to use it anyway as they would rather overestimate the effects of inflation than underestimate them. Using the compound value table from Appendix A, we find that the *inflation factor* for 5 percent and 30 years is 4.32; multiplying this inflation factor by the annual shortfall of $7,400 gives the Spellmans an idea of what that figure will be by the time they retire: $7,400 \times 4.32 = $31,970$, or nearly $32,000 a year (see steps J to L in Worksheet 14.1). Thus, based on their projections, the shortfall will amount to $32,000 a year when they retire 30 years from now. *This is the amount they will have to come up with through their own supplemental retirement program.*

FUNDING THE SHORTFALL. The final two steps in this estimation process are to determine (1) *how big the retirement nest egg must be* to cover the projected annual income shortfall, and (2) *how much to save each year* to accumulate the required amount by the time the Spellmans retire. To find out how much money they are going to have to accumulate by retirement, they must estimate the rate of return they think they will be able to earn on their investments *after* they retire. This will tell them how big their nest egg will have to be by retirement in order to eliminate the expected annual shortfall of $32,000. Let's assume this rate of return is estimated at 10 percent, in which case the Spellmans must accumulate $320,000 by retirement. This figure is found by *capitalizing* the estimated shortfall of $32,000 at a 10 percent rate of return: $32,000 \div .10 = $320,000$ (see steps M and N). Given a 10 percent rate of return, such a nest egg will yield $32,000 a year: $320,000 \times .10 = $32,000$. And so long as the capital ($320,000) remains untouched, it will generate the same amount of annual income for as long as the Spellmans live and can eventually become a part of their estate.

smart.sites   Want an online approach to determine how much you'll need to retire? Visit T. Rowe Price Associates's site **www.trowprice.com/retirement/troweretireIRAHome.html** and use their Retirement Planning Worksheet.

Now that the Spellmans know how big their nest egg has to be, the final question is: How are they going to accumulate such an amount by the time they retire? For most people, that means setting up a *systematic savings plan* and putting away a certain amount *each* year. To find out how much must be saved each year to achieve a targeted sum in the future, we can use the table of annuity factors in Appendix B. The appropriate interest factor is a function of the rate of return one can (or expects to) generate and the length of the investment period. In the Spellmans' case, there are 30 years to go until retirement, meaning the length of their investment period is 30 years. If they feel they will be able to earn an average rate of return of 8 percent on their investments over this 30-year period, they will want to use an 8-percent, 30-year interest factor; from Appendix B, we see that this equals 113.3. Because the Spellmans must accumulate $320,000 by the time they retire, *the amount they will have to save each year* (over the next 30 years) can be found by *dividing* the amount they need to accumulate by the appropriate interest factor; that is, $320,000 ÷ 113.3 = $2,824 (see steps O to Q in Worksheet 14.1).

As you might have suspected, the last few steps in the worksheet can just as easily be done on a good handheld calculator. That is, with the calculator in the *annual mode,* to find the amount that must be put away annually to fund a $32,000 retirement nest egg in 30 years, given an expected annual return of 8 percent, do the following.

1. Punch 30 and then press **N.**
2. Punch 320,000 and press the **FV** key.
3. Punch 8.0 and the **i** key.
4. Now, press the **CPT** key and then the **PMT** key.

A value of −2,824.78 should appear in the calculator display; ignoring the minus sign, you have the amount that must be put away annually to reach a target of $320,000 in 30 years. (*Note:* The size of the *inflation-adjusted annual shortfall* [step L in Worksheet 14.1] can also be computed using a hand-held calculator by letting **PV** = 7,400; **i** = 5.0; **N** = 30; and then solve for/compute **(CPT)FV.** Try it. You should end up with an answer **(FV)** equal (or close) to $31,982.37.

The Spellmans now know what they must do to achieve the kind of retirement they want: Put away $2,824 a year and invest it at an average annual rate of 8 percent over the next 30 years. If they can do that, they will have their $320,000 retirement nest egg in 30 years. Of course, they could have been more aggressive in their investing and assumed an average annual rate of 10 percent, in which case, either they'd end up with a bigger nest egg at retirement, or they could get away with saving less than $2,824 a year. Now, how they actually invest their money so as to achieve the desired 8 (or 10) percent rate of return will, of course, be a function of the investment vehicles and strategies they use. All the worksheet tells them is how much money they will need, not how they will get there; it is at this point that investment management enters the picture.

The procedure outlined here admittedly is a bit simplified and does take a few short-cuts, but considering the amount of uncertainty imbedded in the long-range projections being made, it does provide a viable estimate of retirement income and investment needs. The procedure certainly is far superior to the alternative of doing nothing! One important simplifying assumption in the procedure, though, is that it ignores the income that can be derived from the *sale of a house.* The sale of a house not only offers some special tax features (see Chapter 3) but can generate a substantial amount of cash flow as well. Certainly, if inflation does occur in the future (and it will!), it will very likely drive up home prices right along with the cost of everything else. A lot of people sell their homes around the time they retire and either move into smaller houses (often in Sun Belt retirement communities) or decide to rent in order to avoid all the problems of homeownership. Of course, the cash flow from the sale of a house can have a substantial effect on the size of the retirement nest egg. However, rather than trying to factor it into the forecast of retirement income and needs, we suggest that you *recognize* the existence of this cash flow source in your retirement planning, and consider it as a cushion against all the uncertainty inherent in retirement planning projections.

COMPUTER-BASED RETIREMENT PLANNING

Like many other areas of our life, retirement planning has become a lot easier as a result of the computer. Most fully integrated financial planning software—like *Quicken* or *WealthBuilder*, for example—contain retirement planning programs that perform many of the same forecasting functions found in Worksheet 14.1. In addition, there are so-called "dedicated" software packages that focus almost entirely on retirement planning. But it's the *Internet* that really brings retirement planning right to our doorsteps, as there are literally hundreds of websites that offer online retirement planning. For example, *Smartmoney.com* has its "Retirement Worksheets," *Quicken.com* offers a "Retirement Planner," and *Bloomberg.com* has its "Retirement Calculator." In essence, with most of these programs and Web sites, all you do is answer a few key questions about expected inflation, desired rate of return on investments, and current levels of income and expenditures, and the computer determines the size of any income shortfall, the amount of retirement funds that must be accumulated over time, and different ways to achieve the desired retirement nest egg.

As with any Web site or software, you should consider the features of each to find the one that works best for you. *An attractive feature of most of these programs is the ability to easily run through a series of "what-if" exercises.* By just punching a few buttons, you can change one or more key variables to see how they impact the size of your retirement nest egg and the amount of money you must put away annually. For example, you can find out what would happen if you failed to achieve the desired rate of return on your investments. In addition to this important retirement planning function, such software often allows you to track various retirement accounts to readily see how your performance is stacking up to your retirement goals—whether you are ahead of schedule, and, if not, what you can do to get back on track. Thus, modern, computer-based retirement planning assists you not only in establishing retirement goals and plans, but also in keeping track of your progress toward those objectives. Of course, as with other areas of financial planning, you should reevaluate your retirement needs whenever the underlying assumptions change—for example, if your personal circumstances change (job loss, divorce, and so on) or inflation rises.

SOURCES OF RETIREMENT INCOME

As Exhibit 14.2 reveals, the three principal sources of income for retired people are social security, assets (income-producing types, such as savings, stocks, and bonds), and pension plans. For the average retiree, these categories will account for about 90 percent of total retirement income. Just about every retired worker receives social security income, about 65 to 85 percent obtain at least some of their income from savings or investment assets, and, surprisingly, only about half (40 to 55 percent) receive benefits from some type of employer-provided pension plan. However, keep in mind these are *sources* of retirement income and not dollar amounts. The *amount* of income retired individuals will receive will, of course, vary from amounts that are barely above the poverty line to six-figure incomes. The amount received in retirement depends on a number of variables, the most important of which is the level of preretirement earnings. Obviously, the more individuals make before they retire, the more they will receive in social security benefits and from company-sponsored pension plans—and, very likely, the greater the amount of income-producing

EXHIBIT 14.2

SOURCES OF INCOME FOR THE AVERAGE RETIREE

Note that *government assistance* (which is made up mostly of social security benefits) is the single largest source of income for the average U.S. retiree. This source alone is almost as much as the average retiree receives from company pension plans *and* personal wealth/investment assets *combined*.

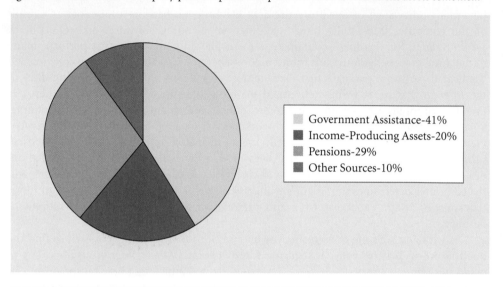

- Government Assistance–41%
- Income-Producing Assets–20%
- Pensions–29%
- Other Sources–10%

Source: The 10th Annual Retirement Confidence Survey, cosponsored by the Employee Benefit Research Institute and the American Savings Education Council, 2000.

assets they will hold. In this chapter, we will examine social security and various types of pension plans and retirement programs. In addition, we will look briefly at an investment vehicle designed especially for retirement income: the *annuity*.

CONCEPT CHECK

14-1. Discuss the relationship of retirement planning to financial planning; do investment and tax planning have a role in retirement planning? Identify and briefly discuss each of the steps in the retirement planning process.

14-2. Identify and briefly discuss the three biggest mistakes people tend to make when setting up retirement programs. Which of these three do you think is most important? Explain. What role does compound interest play in all this?

14-3. How do retirement goals and income needs fit in the retirement planning process? Discuss briefly the advantages of using PC programs or the Internet for retirement planning.

14-4. What are the most important sources of retirement income for most people?

Social Security [LG3]

The Social Security Act of 1935 was landmark legislation. Not only did it create a basic retirement program for working Americans at all income levels, it also established a number of other social programs, all of which are administered under the auspices of the *Old Age, Survivor's, Disability, and Health Insurance (OASDHI) program*. Some of the other services include supplementary security income (SSI), Medicare, unemployment insurance, public assistance, welfare services, and provision for black lung benefits. This chapter gives primary attention to the old age and survivor's portion of the act, because it has a direct bearing on retirement planning. The disability and health/Medicare benefits of social security are discussed in Chapter 9.

BASIC CONCEPTS

To fully appreciate the underlying merits of social security as a retirement program, you need to understand its (1) financing and (2) solvency.

FINANCING. The cash benefits provided by social security are derived from the payroll taxes (FICA) paid by covered employees and their employers. The tax rate in 2001 was 7.65 percent—this is the amount paid by employees, and an equal amount was paid by employers. Self-employed people are also covered by social security, and in 2001 they had to pay the total rate of 15.3 percent (that is, 7.65% × 2); because there are no employers to share the burden, self-employed people have to pay the full amount themselves.

Regardless of whether the individual is an employee or self-employed, the indicated tax rate stays in effect only until the employee reaches a maximum *wage base*, which increases each year. For 2001, basic social security taxes were paid on the first $80,400 of wages earned or self-employed income. Thus, the maximum social security tax paid by an *employee* in 2001 was $6,150 ($80,400 × .0765), and by the *self-employed* was $12,301 ($80,400 × .153). Note that starting in 1991, a second tax was added to cover the rising costs of Medicare. Now, once the social security wage base is passed, the new, higher Medicare wage base kicks in and employees are subject to a tax rate of 1.45 percent *on all earnings* over $80,400, whereas the added earnings of the self-employed are taxed at the rate of 2.9 percent.

SOLVENCY. A lot of people fear that social security will run out of money by the time they are ready to collect their benefits. This is because a larger percentage of our population will be elderly in future years than has been the case in the past. For instance, as shown in Exhibit 14.3, the percentage of persons age 65 or over is expected to increase to 20.1 percent of the population by the year 2030, up from just 5.4 percent in 1930 and 12.5 percent in 1990. This trend means that *retirement benefits will be mushrooming at the very same time that proportionately fewer people will be available in the work force to support those collecting social security*. For example, in 1955, there were seven workers supporting each person on social security, but by the year 2000, that number had fallen to roughly two workers for each social security beneficiary.

Congress has long been aware of the existence of this problem, and recently took action to slowly raise the retirement age from 65 to 67, beginning in 2000. As the current legislation stands, by the year 2027, a person will have to wait until age 67 to collect full social security benefits. At the same time, the penalty for early retirement (age 62) is being increased substantially. Whereas today an individual can retire at age 62 and collect 80 percent of the full benefits, in the future that person will collect only *70 percent* of the full benefits upon early retirement. This revised penalty structure will also be fully phased in by the year 2027. (*Note:* These rules are subject to change and, in fact, it seems that Congress and the administration are always discussing ways to "fix social security." These include raising the social security tax rate, sharply raising the amount of income subject to the tax, raising the retirement age, and partly "privatizing" social security.) Whether past or future changes

EXHIBIT 14.3

THE GROWING PRESENCE OF THE SENIOR CITIZEN

As the population grows older, the demands and pressures on the integrity of the social security system will increase accordingly.

Year	Percent of Population 65 and Over	Year	Percent of Population 65 and Over
1930	5.4	1990	12.5
1940	6.8	2000	12.8
1950	8.1	2010	13.4
1960	9.2	2020	16.3
1970	9.8	2030	20.1
1975	10.3	2040	20.7
1980	11.3	2050	20.4

Source: Adapted from U.S. Bureau of the Census, *Statistical Abstract of the United States,* 114th edition, Washington, D.C., Table No. 16, p. 16.

to the social security system will be sufficient to save it remains to be seen. But in response to the question, "will there be any money left by the time I get to retirement age?" all we can say is that the probability that social security will have funds to pay out benefits is as close to 100 percent as any future economic plan can be—at least for the next 30 years or so.

WHO IS COVERED?

As mandated by Congress, social security coverage today extends to just about all gainfully employed workers. There are currently only two major classes of employees exempt from *mandatory* participation in the social security system: (1) federal *civilian* employees who were hired before 1984 and are covered under the Civil Service Retirement System; and (2) employees of state and local governments who have chosen not to be covered (although the vast majority of these employees are covered through *voluntary participation* in social security). In addition, certain marginal employment positions, such as newspaper carriers under age 18 and full-time college students working in fraternity and sorority houses, are also exempt. But by far, the largest number of workers in these excluded classes are employees of state and local governments. These groups are not forced to participate because the federal government is not empowered to impose a tax on state and local governments—although once in the program, these employees have to stay in, as they no longer have the option of voting to leave.

WHEN ARE YOU ELIGIBLE FOR BENEFITS?

Social security payments are not paid automatically to eligible individuals (or their dependents). An application for benefits must be filed with the Social Security Administration, which then determines the applicant's eligibility for benefits based on whether he or she has had enough quarters (3-month periods) of participation in the system. To qualify for full retirement benefits, nearly all workers today must be employed in a job covered by social security for at least 40 quarters, or 10 years. These quarters need not be consecutive. Once this 40-quarter requirement is met, the worker becomes fully insured and remains eligible for retirement payments even if he or she never works again in covered employment. Note, however, that when yearly covered wages are computed, zeros are inserted for years in which no social security taxes were paid—which substantially reduces the size of future monthly benefit payments.

The surviving spouse and dependent children of a *deceased worker* are also eligible for monthly benefits if the worker was fully insured at the time of death or, in some special cases, if certain other requirements are met. Workers may be considered fully insured if they had six quarters of coverage during the 3-year period preceding the time of death.

SOCIAL SECURITY RETIREMENT BENEFITS

Basic social security benefits that are important to retired people and their dependents include (1) old-age benefits and (2) survivor's benefits. Both programs provide extended benefits to covered workers and their spouses; the major provisions of each program are briefly described in the material that follows.

OLD-AGE BENEFITS. Workers who are fully covered (that is, who have worked the required 40 quarters under social security) may receive old-age benefits for life once they reach the age of 65 (or higher age after 2000, as stated earlier). In addition, workers who elect to retire early—at age 62—will receive *reduced benefits*, currently 80 percent of the full benefits; this amount is scheduled to gradually decline by the year 2027 to only 70 percent of the full amount. If the retiree has a spouse 65 or older, the spouse may be entitled to benefits equal to one-half of the amount received by the retired worker. The spouse may also elect early receipt of reduced benefits at age 62.

In the case of two-income families, both the husband and wife may be eligible for full social security benefits. When they retire, they can choose to receive their benefits in one of two ways: each can (1) take the full benefits to which each is entitled from his or her account, or (2) take the husband and wife benefits of the higher-paid spouse. If each takes his or her own full share, there are no spousal benefits; if they take the husband and wife benefits of the higher-paid spouse, they effectively receive 1.5 shares. Obviously, two-income couples should select the option that provides the greatest amount of benefits (the amount of social security benefits will be described later).

SURVIVOR'S BENEFITS. If a covered worker dies, the spouse can receive survivor's benefits from social security. These benefits include a small lump-sum payment of several hundred dollars, followed by monthly benefit checks. The lump-sum amount is paid automatically upon application. To be eligible for monthly payments, the surviving spouse generally must be at least 60 years of age, or have a dependent and unmarried child of the deceased worker in his or her care. (To qualify for *full* benefits, the surviving spouse must be at least 65 years of age; reduced benefits are payable between ages 60 and 65.) If the children of a deceased worker reach age 16 before the spouse reaches age 60, the monthly benefits cease and do not resume until the spouse turns 60. This period during which survivor's benefits are not paid is sometimes called the *widow's gap*. (As we saw in Chapter 8, social security survivor's benefits play a key role in life insurance planning.)

HOW MUCH ARE MONTHLY SOCIAL SECURITY BENEFITS?

The amount of social security benefits to which an eligible person is entitled is set by law and defined according to a fairly complex formula. Until recently, it was difficult to predict

EXHIBIT 14.4

YOUR SOCIAL SECURITY STATEMENT

The Social Security Administration keeps a lifetime record of your earnings; thus, when you apply for benefits, it checks your earnings record to see if you've worked long enough to qualify, and then determines the amount of your monthly benefits. The statement shown on this and the facing page, prepared by the Social Security Administration, is intended to provide an estimate of what one's future benefits are likely to be (*Note:* Statement *excludes* record of Medicare credit.)

FACTS ABOUT YOUR SOCIAL SECURITY

We based your benefit estimates on these facts:

Your name	I.M. Somebody
Your date of birth	February 31, 1943
Your estimated taxable earnings per year after 2000	$72,600.00
Your Social Security number	000-00-0000

YOUR EARNINGS RECORD AT A GLANCE

Years You Worked	Maximum Yearly Earnings Subject to Social Security Tax*	Your Taxed Social Security Earnings
1956	$ 4,200	18
1957	4,200	369
1958	4,200	45
1959	4,800	1,645
1960	4,800	889
1961	4,800	259
1962	4,800	566
1963	4,800	1,840
1964	4,800	4,800
1965	4,800	4,800
1966	6,600	6,600
1967	6,600	6,600
1968	7,800	0
1969	7,800	0
1970	7,800	7,053
1971	7,800	7,800
1972	9,000	9,000
1973	10,800	10,800
1974	13,200	13,200
1975	14,100	14,100
1976	15,300	15,300
1977	16,500	16,500
1978	17,700	17,700
1979	22,900	22,900
1980	25,900	25,900
1981	29,700	29,700
1982	32,400	32,400
1983	35,700	35,700
1984	37,800	37,800
1985	39,600	39,600
1986	42,000	42,000
1987	43,800	43,800

EXHIBIT 14.4 *continued*

Years You Worked	Maximum Yearly Earnings Subject to Social Security Tax*	Your Taxed Social Security Earnings
1988	45,000	45,000
1989	48,000	48,000
1990	51,300	51,300
1991	53,400	53,400
1992	55,500	55,500
1993	57,600	57,600
1994	60,600	60,600
1995	61,200	61,200
1996	62,700	62,700
1997	65,400	65,400
1998	68,400	68,400
1999	72,600	72,600
2000	76,200	76,200

Totals over your working career:
Estimated taxes for Social Security:
    You Paid: $71,250   Your Employers Paid: $68,100

Retirement   You have earned enough credits to qualify for benefits. At your current earnings rate, if you stop working . . .
At age 62, your payment would be about .... $1,239 a month
If you continue working until . . .
    your full retirement age (65 and 4 months), your payment would be about ..... $1,618 a month
    age 70, your payment would be about .... $2,230 a month
Note: When you continue working beyond your full retirement age, your benefit amount increases because of your additional earnings and the special credits you will receive for delaying your retirement. This increased benefit can be important to you later in your life. It also can increase the future benefit amounts your family and survivors could receive.

Disability   You have earned enough credits to qualify for benefits. If you become severely disabled right now . . .
Your payment would be about .... $1,568 a month

Family   If you get retirement or disability benefits, your spouse and children may also qualify for benefits.

Survivors   You have earned enough credits for your family to receive the following benefits if you die this year.
Total family benefits cannot be more than .... $2,773 a month
Your child .... $1,188 a month
Your spouse who is caring for your child .... $1,188 a month
Your spouse who reaches full retirement age .... $1,584 a month

Your spouse or minor child may be eligible for a special one–time death benefit of $255.

Medicare   You have earned enough credits to qualify for Medicare at age 65. Even if you do not retire at age 65, be sure to contact Social Security three months before your 65th birthday to enroll in Medicare.

*Information added for this Exhibit only; it is **NOT** part of the Social Security statement.

EXHIBIT 14.5

SELECTED MONTHLY SOCIAL SECURITY RETIREMENT BENEFITS

The social security benefits listed here are initial, *first-year benefits*. As time passes, the beneficiary will receive correspondingly higher benefits as the cost of living goes up. For example, the maximum benefit payable to someone who retired in 1980 was $572 a month; by 2000 those benefits had grown to $1,433 a month.

Latest Benefits (2000)	Career Earnings Level		
	Low	Medium	High
Retired worker, age 65	$769	$1,224	$1,433
Retired worker, age 62	615	979	1,146
Family benefits:			
Retired worker and spouse, both 65	$1,153	$1,836	$2,149
Retired worker and spouse, both 62	922	1,468	1,719
Two-income couple[a]			
Both retire at 65	$1,538	$2,448	$2,866
Both retire at 62	1,230	1,958	2,292

[a]*Both* in the same career income category and *both* eligible for normal benefits at their career income levels.

Source: *Understanding Social Security Benefits, Social Security Administration,* **www.ssa.gov**, Dec. 14, 2000.

your future benefits. In 1988, however, the Social Security Administration introduced a computerized benefits estimation service. Under this program, the Social Security Administration is required by law to provide all covered workers with a *Social Security Statement* containing information similar to that shown in Exhibit 14.4. This statement is sent out annually and is supposed to arrive about three months before the covered worker's birthday. (You can also request a statement by going to the Social Security Administration Web site: **www.ssa.gov**.) "Your Social Security Statement" lists the year-by-year social security earnings you've been credited with, and shows (in today's dollars) what benefits you can expect under three scenarios: (1) if you retire at age 62 and receive 80 percent of the full benefit (or less, depending on your age); (2) the full benefit at age 65 to 67 (depending on your year of birth); and (3) the increased benefit (of up to 8 percent per year) that's available if you delay retirement until age 70. The statement also estimates what your children and surviving spouse would get if you die, and how much you'd receive monthly if you became disabled.

Using information provided by the Social Security Administration, we can describe the *current level of benefits* (for someone who retired in 2000); this is done in Exhibit 14.5. The benefits, *as of 2000*, are for a retired worker, a retired worker and nonworking spouse, and a two-income couple for low, medium, and high career income levels (a *high* income worker is one whose annual earnings equaled or exceeded the maximum social security tax base). Bear in mind the figures listed in the exhibit represent amounts that the beneficiaries will receive in the *first year* of their retirement. Those amounts will, of course, be adjusted upward each year with subsequent increases in the cost of living. But be careful! Don't just automatically assume that social security will provide you with an additional source of income during retirement. For as the accompanying *Money in Action* box reveals, with some pension plans your social security benefits may actually lead to *lower* pension benefits.

MONEY IN ACTION

Social Security and Pension Benefits: When More of One Means Less of Another

One reason that people approaching retirement have been willing to stick with one company through thick and thin was the promise of a pension. But some companies are using a loophole to reduce those pension payments. The companies are *projecting what the retiree is going to collect in social security benefits, and reducing their pensions dollar for dollar*. Naturally, this comes as quite a surprise to retirees.

How can they justify such an act? Because employers today contribute 7.65 percent of workers' pay, up to a maximum of $80,400 (in 2001) to fund social security benefits, many companies try to recover the costs of those benefits by reducing benefits paid. Such "integration" formulas affect more than half of the 30 million or so Americans covered by pensions in the private sector. Employees also contribute 7.65 percent of their wages toward social security benefits.

The Tax Reform Act of 1986 made it legal for employers to subtract social security from a pension plan, although they cannot reduce a benefit by more than half. Employees don't have a right to prohibit a company from using social security integration, although trade groups have tried to stop the practice. For example, the Pensions Committee of the Institute of Electrical and Electronics Engineers issued a formal statement opposing the integration of pension benefits with social security benefits. The reasons: it reduced benefits, harming lower paid workers disproportionately, and it has not resulted in the expansion of private pension plan coverage of U.S. workers, which was the original intent of the legislation.

The problem is most widespread for companies that offer defined benefit plans, which promise a fixed payment for life. It doesn't directly affect people with defined contribution plans, such as 401(k)s, in which the employee is primarily responsible for building his or her nest-egg. However, for companies with both defined benefit and defined contribution plans, the 401(k) balance is often used by employers to reduce the combined social security and defined benefit target they think a person should receive in retirement.

Some employers figure it's fair to subtract half the social security benefit, because the company paid half the tax. If a retiree gets $600 per month from social security, then the company would reduce its pension benefit by $300. Needless to say, most employees fail to see that logic.

Sources: Ellen E. Schultz, "The Pension Eraser: Integrating Social Security Can Cut Benefits," *The Wall Street Journal*, March 12, 1997, p. C1; Melanie D. Goldman, "Integration: When the Check Isn't in the Mail," *Atlanta Business Chronicle*, June 30, 1997. **http://www.amcity.com/atlanta/stories/063097/focus2.html**; Institute of Electrical Engineers, 1995, **http://www.ieee.org/usah/DOCUMENTS/FORUM/LIBRARY/POSITIONS/benefits.html**.

Note also that the benefits shown in Exhibit 14.5 *may be reduced* if the social security recipient is *under age 65 and is still gainfully employed*—perhaps in a part-time job. In particular, retirees aged 62 through 64 are subject to a so-called "earnings test," which effectively limits the amount of income they can earn before they start losing some (or all) of their social security benefits. In 2001, that limit was $10,680 per year (this earnings limit rises annually with wage inflation). The rule states that if you're a social security recipient aged 62 through 64, you'll lose $1 in benefits for every $2 you earn above the earnings test amount ($10,680 in 2001). Thus if you earned, say, $15,000 a year at a part-time job, you'd lose $2,160 in annual social security benefits—i.e., $15,000 − $10,680 = $4,320 ÷ 2 = $2,160. That's $180 a month you'd lose simply because you hold a job that pays you more than the stipulated maximum. Not a very fair deal! But at least it applies only to early retirees. Once you reach age 65 (or older), the retirement earnings test no longer applies. The Senior Citizens' Freedom to Work Act of 2000 removed all earnings restrictions for anyone aged 65 or older. Thus, effective January 2000, anyone aged 65 or older can earn any amount they want, and not lose one penny in social security benefits. In contrast to earned income, there never have been any limits on so-called "unearned income" derived from such sources as interest, dividends, rents, or profits on securities transactions—a retiree can receive an unlimited amount of such income without any benefits reduction.

TAXES ON BENEFITS. No longer are social security benefits a source of tax-free income. In 1984, Congress passed legislation to tax the benefits paid to "upper-income beneficiaries." Specifically, as the law presently stands, *social security retirement benefits are subject to federal income taxes if the beneficiary's annual income exceeds one of the following base amounts:* $25,000 for a single taxpayer, $32,000 for married taxpayers filing jointly, and zero for married taxpayers filing separately. In determining the amount of income that must be counted, the taxpayer starts with his or her *adjusted gross income* as defined by the present tax law (see Chapter 3) and then adds all nontaxable interest income (such as income from municipal bonds) plus a stipulated portion of the social security benefits received. Thus, if for single taxpayers the resulting amount is between $25,000 and $34,000, 50 percent of social security benefits are taxable. If income exceeds $34,000, 85 percent of social security benefits is subject to income tax. If the combined income of married taxpayers filing joint returns is between $32,000 and $44,000, 50 percent of the social security benefits is taxable. The percentage of benefits taxed increases to 85 percent when their combined income exceeds $44,000.

SOCIAL SECURITY AND RETIREMENT PLANNING

No one can accurately predict the amount of social security benefits that will be paid 30 or 40 years from now. For retirement planning purposes, however, it seems reasonable to expect social security to provide the average retired wage earner (who is married) with perhaps 40 to 60 percent of the wages that he or she was earning in the year before retirement—assuming, of course, that the retiree has had a full career working in covered employment. Social security therefore should be viewed as *a foundation for your retirement income.* By itself, *it is insufficient to allow a worker and spouse to maintain their preretirement standard of living.* For people who earn in excess of the wage base, a lower percentage of total preretirement wages will be replaced by social security. Consequently, it's essential that average and upper-middle-income families plan to supplement their social security retirement benefits with income from other sources. Two popular sources are pensions (and retirement programs) and annuities. These topics are discussed in the next two sections.

CONCEPT CHECK

14-5. What benefits are provided under the Social Security Act, and who is covered? Describe the basic operations of the social security system.
14-6. Discuss the old-age and survivor's benefits provided to retirees and their dependents under the social security program.
14-7. Does social security coverage relieve you of the need to do some retirement planning on your own? Explain. What is a *Social Security Statement,* and how would such a statement help you in your retirement planning?

Pension Plans and Retirement Programs [LG4, LG5]

Accompanying the expansion of the social security system has been a corresponding growth in employer-sponsored pension and retirement plans. In 1940, when the social security program was in its infancy, fewer than 25 percent of the workforce had the benefit of an employer-sponsored plan. Today, better than 50 percent of all wage earners and salaried workers (in both the private and public sectors) are covered by some type of employer-sponsored retirement or profit-sharing plan.

In 1948, the National Labor Relations Board (NLRB) ruled that pensions and other types of insurance programs are legitimate subjects for collective bargaining. In response, many employers established new pension plans or liberalized the provisions of existing ones to meet or anticipate union demands. Qualified pension plans (discussed later) allow firms to deduct for tax purposes their contributions to employee retirement programs. Even better, the employees can also deduct these contributions from their taxable income; as a result, the participants are able to build up their own retirement funds on a tax-deferred basis. Eventually, of course, when the funds are paid out as benefits, the employees will have to pay taxes on this income.

Government red tape, however, has taken a toll on pension plans. In particular, the **Employee Retirement Income Security Act of 1974** (sometimes referred to as **ERISA** or the *Pension Reform Act*), established to protect employees participating in private employer retirement plans, has actually led to a reduction in the number of new retirement plans started among firms, especially the smaller ones. Indeed, the percentage of workers covered by company-sponsored plans has fallen dramatically since the late 1970s. It's estimated that today, *in the private sector*, only about 40 percent of all full-time workers are covered by company-financed plans—even worse, only about one-third (or less) of the part-time labor force is covered. In contrast, there has been a significant increase in salary-reduction forms of retirement plans (discussed later). In addition to ERISA, the widespread availability of Keogh plans, individual retirement arrangements (IRAs), and other programs has lessened the urgency of small firms (and bigger ones as well) to offer their own company-financed pension plans.

Employee Retirement Income Security Act (ERISA) A law passed in 1974 to ensure that workers eligible for pensions actually receive such benefits; also permits uncovered workers to establish individual tax-sheltered retirement plans.

EMPLOYER-SPONSORED PROGRAMS: BASIC PLANS

Employers can sponsor two types of retirement programs—*basic plans*, in which employees automatically participate after a certain period of employment, and *supplemental plans*, which are mostly voluntary programs and which enable employees to increase the amount of funds being set aside for retirement. We will look first at some of the key characteristics of basic plans. Apart from financing, there are certain features of employer-sponsored pension plans that you should become familiar with, including participation requirements, contributory obligations, benefit rights, retirement age, and methods of computing benefits.

PARTICIPATION REQUIREMENTS. In most pension plans, employees must meet certain criteria before they become eligible for participation. Most common are requirements relating to years of service, minimum age, level of earnings, and employment classification. Years of service and minimum-age requirements are often incorporated into retirement plans in the belief that a much higher labor turnover rate applies to both newly hired and younger employees. Therefore, to reduce the administrative costs of the plans, employees in these categories are often excluded—at least, initially—from participation. Once these (or any other) participation requirements are met, the employee automatically becomes eligible to participate in the program.

noncontributory pension plan
A pension plan in which the employer pays the total cost of the benefits.

contributory pension plan
A pension plan in which the employee bears a portion of the cost of the benefits.

vested rights
Employees' nonforfeitable rights to receive benefits in a pension plan based on their own and their employer's contributions.

WHAT'S YOUR CONTRIBUTION? Whether you, as an employee, have to make payments toward your own pension depends on the type of plan you're in. If you belong to a **noncontributory pension plan**, the employer pays the total cost of the benefits—you don't have to pay a thing. Under a **contributory pension plan**, the cost is shared by both the employer and the employee. Today the trend is toward contributory plans. In addition, nearly all plans for employees of federal, state, and local governments require a contribution from the employee. In contributory plans, the employee's share of the costs is often between 3 and 10 percent of annual wages and is typically paid through a payroll deduction. Probably the most common arrangement is for the employer to match the employee's contribution such that the employee puts up half the annual contribution and the employer puts up the other half. When employees who have participated in a contributory retirement plan terminate employment prior to retirement, they are legally entitled to some benefit, based on the amount of their own contributions. Usually this benefit is a cash lump sum, but in some cases it can be taken as a monthly payment at retirement. Whether departing employees receive any benefit from the *employer's* contributions depends on the plan's benefit rights.

VESTED INTEREST: A RIGHT TO THE BENEFITS. Not everyone who participates in a pension plan will earn the right to receive retirement benefits. Pension plans impose certain criteria that must be met before the employee can obtain a nonforfeitable right to a pension, known as **vested rights**. Prior to 1974, employers often required workers to be employed for 25 years or more before vesting would occur. An employee who left before completing this period of employment (and plenty did) would lose all the previously earned pension benefits. Because of the high mobility of labor and capital, many workers at retirement faced the prospect of having no pension. One of the principal purposes of ERISA was to eliminate this unfair practice (which indirectly contributed to the social problem of low incomes among the aged). ERISA required covered employers to grant employees vested rights after no more than 10 years of employment (when there was no partial vesting prior to 10 years of service), or alternatively, 15 years, where partial vesting began after 5 years.

Although ERISA was certainly a step in the right direction, even better vesting requirements came along in 1986 with the Tax Reform Act. A provision of that act accelerated the vesting period so that, as it now stands, *full vesting* rights are required after only 5 to 7 years of employment. More specifically, companies must now choose between two vesting schedules. One, the so-called *cliff vesting*, requires full vesting after no more than 5 years of service—but you obtain no vesting privileges until then. It's sort of a "zero-one" proposition; there are no vesting privileges at all for the first 5 years, and then all of a sudden you're fully vested. Once vested, you're entitled to everything that's been paid in so far (your contributions *plus* your employer's) and everything that will be contributed in the future. Under the alternative procedure, the so-called *graded schedule*, vesting takes place gradually over the first 7 years of employment. At the minimum, after 3 years you would have a nonforfeiture right to at least 20 percent of the benefits, with an additional 20 percent each year thereafter until you're 100 percent vested after 7 years. Note, however, that these are minimum standards, and employers can grant more favorable vesting terms.

To illustrate the vesting process, assume that a medium-sized firm offers a plan in which full vesting of benefits occurs after 5 years. The plan is contributory, with employees paying 3 percent of their salaries and the employer paying an amount equal to 6 percent of the salaries. Under this plan, employees cannot withdraw the contributions made by the employer until they reach retirement. The plan provides annual benefits in the amount of $11 per year of service for each $100 of an employee's final monthly earnings—the amount earned during the final month in the employ of the firm. Therefore, an employee who worked a minimum of 5 years for the firm would be eligible for a retirement benefit from that company even if he or she left the company at, say, age 30.

However, because of inflation, the value of the benefit for a worker who left the firm long before retirement age would be very small. Consequently, the employee might be better off simply withdrawing his or her own contributions (which always vest immediately) and terminating participation in the plan at the same time he or she leaves the employer. Of course, any worker who leaves the firm prior to accumulating 5 years of service would be entitled only to a return of his or her own contributions to the plan (plus nominal investment earnings). *And whenever you terminate employment, resist the urge to spend the money you have built up in your retirement account! Over time, that can have a devastating effect on your ability to accumulate retirement capital. Instead, when you take money out of one retirement account, roll it over into another one.*

RETIREMENT AGE. Nearly all retirement plans specify when an eligible employee is entitled to benefits—in most cases, at age 65. Often pension plans also provide an early retirement age. In these cases, employees may begin receiving reduced benefits prior to the normal retirement age. Many retirement plans for public employees give workers the option of retiring after a stated number of years of service (say, 30 or 35) at full benefits, regardless of their age at the time. In the past, the trend in pension plans was toward earlier permissible retirement ages. However, now that many have begun to argue in favor of increasing the age for mandatory retirement (that is, letting people work longer), it is expected that there will be little motivation to further reduce the normal retirement age.

DEFINED CONTRIBUTIONS OR DEFINED BENEFITS. The method used to compute benefits at retirement is spelled out in detail in every retirement plan. The two most commonly used methods are the defined contribution plan and the defined benefits plan. A **defined contribution plan** specifies the amount of contribution that the employer and employee must make. At retirement, the worker is awarded whatever level of monthly benefits those contributions will purchase. Although such factors as age, income level, and the amount of contributions made to the plan have a great deal to do with the amount of monthly benefits received at retirement, probably no variable is more important than the level of *investment performance* generated on the contributed funds.

A defined contribution plan promises nothing at retirement except the returns the fund managers have been able to obtain. The only thing that's defined is the amount of contribution that the employee and/or employer have to make (generally stated as a percent of the employee's income). The benefits at retirement depend totally on investment results. Of course, there's a certain standard of care that's followed by the investment managers, so there is some protection provided to the plan participants (indeed, most of the investing is confined to high-quality investment vehicles). But even so, that still leaves a lot of room for variability in returns. There'll be a big difference in retirement benefits for someone who's in a fund that's earned 6 percent versus someone who's in a fund that's earned 12 percent.

Under a **defined benefits plan**, the formula for computing benefits, not contributions, is stipulated in the plan provisions. These benefits are paid out regardless of how well (or poorly) the retirement funds are invested. If investment performance falls short, the employer has to make up the difference to come up with the benefits agreed to in the plan. This type of plan allows employees to determine before retirement how much their monthly retirement income will be. Often the number of years of service and amount of earnings are prime factors in the formula. For example, a worker might be paid 2.5 percent of his or her final 3-year average annual salary for each year of service. Thus, the *annual* benefit to an employee whose final 3-year average annual salary was $65,000 and who was with the company for 20 years would be $32,500 (2.5% × $65,000 × 20 years).

defined contribution plan
A pension plan that specifies the amount of contributions that both employer and employee must make; it makes no promises concerning the size of the benefits at retirement.

defined benefits plan
A pension plan in which the formula for computing benefits is stipulated in its provisions, thus allowing the employee to determine prior to retirement how much his or her retirement income will be.

Other types of defined benefits plans may simply pay benefits based on (1) a consideration of earnings excluding years of service, (2) a consideration of years of service excluding earnings, or (3) a flat amount with no consideration given to either earnings or years of service. Many defined benefits plans also increase retirement benefits periodically to help retirees keep up with the cost of living. In periods of high inflation, these increases are essential to maintain retirees' standards of living. Today, there are more than 40 million people (workers and retirees) covered by defined benefits plans. However, while the number of *people covered* by such plans continues to rise, the number of (private sector) defined benefit *plans in existence* has steadily declined, from about 115,000 plans in 1985 to less than 40,000 today. Not surprisingly, most of that decline has been among the smaller plans with 100 or fewer participants.

Regardless of the method used to calculate benefit amounts, the employee's basic concern should be with the percent of final take-home pay the plan is likely to produce at retirement. A pension is usually thought to be good if, when combined with social security, it will result in a monthly income equal to about 70 to 80 percent of preretirement net earnings. To reach this goal, however, today's employees must take some responsibility, because there's a growing trend for *companies to switch from defined benefits plans to defined contribution programs.* Whereas in 1975, about 85 percent of all plans were defined benefits plans, today fewer than half are. Companies don't like the idea of being faced with undefined future pension liabilities—after all, the pension/retirement payments that don't come from investment earnings have to be made up from company earnings, and that means lower profits. So more and more companies are avoiding these problems by changing over to defined contribution plans—indeed, there are far more defined contribution plans today than there are defined benefits plans. And in cases where the firms are sticking with their defined benefits plans, the benefits are often so meager that they don't come close to the desired 70 to 80 percent income target. (Some of the defined contribution plans don't either.)

In either case, *the employee is being forced to assume more responsibility for ensuring the desired level of postretirement income.* The logic from the company's perspective is that if obtaining a comfortable standard of living in retirement is a worthwhile objective, the employee should be willing to help achieve it. That might mean participating in a company-sponsored supplemental retirement plan or possibly even setting up your own self-directed program (we'll look at both supplemental and self-directed plans later). All this means that where you end up in retirement will depend, more than ever, on what *you've* done, rather than on what your employers have done. *Very likely, you're the one who is going to control not only how much goes into the company's retirement programs, but where it goes as well.*

qualified pension plan
A pension plan that meets specified criteria established by the Internal Revenue Code.

QUALIFIED PENSION PLANS. The Internal Revenue Code permits a corporate employer making contributions to a **qualified pension plan** to deduct from taxable income its contributions to the plan. As a result, the employees on whose behalf the contributions are made do not have to include these payments as part of their taxable income until the benefits are actually received. Further, in contributory plans, *the employee can also shelter his or her contributions from taxes.* In other words, such contributions are not counted as part of taxable income in the year in which they are made, but instead act to reduce the amount of taxable income reported to the IRS, and therefore lead to lower taxes for the employee.

Still another tax advantage of these plans is that any and all investment income is allowed to accumulate tax free; as a result, investment capital can build up quicker. Yet, in spite of all these tax benefits, a lot of firms still believe that the costs of regulation exceed any benefits that might result and therefore choose to forgo the procedures required for having a plan qualified. Probably the biggest disadvantage of nonqualified pension plans from the employee's perspective is that any contributions made to *contributory* plans are fully taxable and, as such, are treated just like any other type of income—in other words, the contributions are made on an after-tax basis and are therefore *not* sheltered from taxes.

EMPLOYER-SPONSORED PROGRAMS: SUPPLEMENTAL PLANS

In addition to basic retirement programs, many employers offer supplemental plans. These plans are often *voluntary* and enable employees to not only increase the amount of funds being held for retirement but also enjoy attractive tax benefits. Essentially, there are three types of supplemental plans: profit-sharing, thrift and savings, and salary reduction plans.

PROFIT-SHARING PLANS. Profit-sharing plans permit employees to participate in the earnings of their employer. A **profit-sharing plan** may be qualified under the IRS and become eligible for essentially the same tax treatment as other types of pension plans. An argument in support of the use of profit-sharing plans is that they encourage employees to work harder because the employees benefit when the firm prospers. Whether these types of plans accomplish this goal is debatable. One advantage of profit-sharing plans from the firm's viewpoint, however, is that they do not impose any specific levels of contribution or benefits on the part of the employer. When profits are low, the employer makes smaller contributions to the plan; and when profits are high, the firm pays more.

To provide reasonable returns, many employers establish minimum and maximum amounts to be paid as contributions to profit-sharing plans, regardless of how low or high corporate earnings are. Contributions to profit-sharing plans can be invested in certain types of fixed-interest products, stocks and bonds, or, in many cases, securities issued by the employing firm itself. Employees who receive the firm's securities may actually benefit twice. When profits are good, larger contributions are made to the profit-sharing plan *plus* the price of the shares already owned is likely to increase.

A number of big-time, major firms offer *voluntary profit-sharing plans* that invest heavily in their own stock. It's not unusual in many of these cases for long-term career employees to accumulate several hundred thousand dollars worth of the company's stocks. And we're not talking about highly paid corporate executives here; rather, these are just average employees who had the discipline to consistently divert a portion of their salary to the company's profit-sharing plan. *There is a very real and important downside to this practice, however*—that is, if the company should hit hard times, not only could you face salary cuts (or even worse, the loss of a job), but the value of your profit-sharing account very likely will take a big tumble as well. Just look what happened to employees in the tech sector in 2000 and 2001!

profit-sharing plan
An arrangement in which the employees of a firm participate in the company's earnings.

THRIFT AND SAVINGS PLAN. **Thrift and savings plans** were established to supplement pension and other fringe benefits. Most plans require the employer to make contributions to the savings plan in an amount equal to a set proportion of the amount contributed by the employee. For example, an employer might match an employee's contributions at the rate of 50 cents on the dollar up to, say, 6 percent of salary. Thus, an employee making $40,000 a year could pay $2,400 into the plan annually, and the employer would kick in another $1,200. These contributions are then deposited with a trustee, who invests the money in various types of securities, including stocks and bonds of the employing firm. With IRS-qualified thrift and savings plans, the *employer's* contributions and earnings on the savings are not included in the *employee's* taxable income until he or she withdraws these sums. Unfortunately, this attractive tax feature does not extend to the employee's contributions, and, as a result, any money put into one of these savings plans is still considered part of the employee's taxable income—subject to regular income taxes.

thrift and savings plan
A plan established by an employer to supplement pension and other fringe benefits, in which the firm makes contributions in an amount equal to a set proportion of the employee's contribution.

Thrift and savings plans usually have more-liberal vesting and withdrawal privileges than pension and retirement programs. Often the employee's right to the contributions of the employer becomes nonforfeitable immediately upon payment, and the total savings in the plan can be withdrawn by giving proper notice. Employees who terminate participation in such a plan, however, are frequently prohibited from rejoining it for a specified period, such as 1 year. An employee who has the option should seriously consider participation in a thrift plan, because the returns are usually pretty favorable—especially when you factor in the added kicker provided by the *employer's* contributions.

SALARY REDUCTION PLANS. Another type of supplemental retirement program—and certainly the most popular judging by employee response—is the **salary reduction plan**, or the so-called **401(k) plan** as it's more popularly known. Although our discussion here will center on 401(k) plans, similar programs are available for employees of public, nonprofit organizations. Known as *403(b) plans* or *457 plans*, they offer many of the same features and tax shelter provisions as 401(k) plans. (Workers at public schools, colleges, universities, nonprofit hospitals, and similar organizations have 403(b) plans, whereas those who work for a state or local government probably have a 457 plan, as do employees at some tax-exempt organizations.)

Today, more and more companies are cutting back on their contributions to traditional (defined benefits) retirement plans and are turning, instead, to 401(k) plans, a type of defined contribution plan. More than 80 percent of all companies with more than 200 employees now offer 401(k) plans. In 2000, the amount of assets held in 401(k) plans exceeded $1.7 trillion, up from just $300 billion in 1990 (in addition, another $800 billion or so was held in 403(b) and 457 plans).

A 401(k) plan basically gives the employee the option to divert a portion of his or her salary to a company-sponsored, tax-sheltered savings account. In this way, the earnings diverted to the savings plan accumulate tax free. Taxes must be paid eventually, but not until the employee starts drawing down the account at retirement, presumably when he or she is in a lower tax bracket. In 2001, an individual employee could put as much as $10,500 (up to 25 percent of salary, to this maximum) into a tax-deferred 401(k) plan—this annual dollar cap will increase to $11,000 in 2002, and then go up another $1,000 per year before topping out at $15,000 in 2006. (The contribution limits for 403(b) and 457 plans will be the same as those for 401(k) plans.)

To see how such tax-deferred plans work, consider an individual who earned, say, $75,000 in 2001, and would like to contribute the maximum allowable—$10,500—to the 401(k) plan where she works. Doing so reduces her taxable income to $64,500 and, assuming she's in the 28 percent tax bracket, lowers her federal tax bill by some $2,940 (ie, $10,500 × .28). Such tax savings will offset a good portion—28 percent—of her contribution to the 401(k) savings plan. In effect, she will add $10,500 to her retirement program with only $7,560 of her own money; the rest will come from the IRS via a reduced tax bill! Further, all the *earnings* on her savings account will accumulate tax free as well.

These plans are generally viewed as highly attractive *tax shelters* that offer not only substantial tax savings but also a way to save for retirement. As a rule, so long as you can afford to put the money aside, *you should seriously consider joining a 401(k)/403(b)/457 plan if offered at your place of employment.* This is especially true considering the matching features that many of these plans offer. That is, a special attraction of 401(k) plans is that the firms offering them can sweeten the pot by matching all or a part of the employee's contributions. The vast majority of companies that offer 401(k) plans have some type of matching contributions program, often putting up 50 cents (or more) for every dollar contributed by the employee. Such matching plans provide both tax and savings incentives to individuals and clearly enhance the appeal of 401(k) plans. (Matching contributions by employers are far less common with 403(b) plans and virtually nonexistent with 457 plans.)

salary reduction, or 401(k), plan
An agreement under which a portion of a covered employee's pay is withheld and invested in some qualified form of investment; the taxes on both the contributions and the account earnings are deferred until the funds are withdrawn.

Smart.Site: mPower Cafe, (www.mpower.com) is dedicated to helping investors manage their retirement investments—401(k), 403(b), and 457 plans and individual retirement arrangements.

401(k) plans offer participants several investment options, such as equity and fixed-income mutual funds, company stock, and other interest-bearing vehicles, such as bank CDs or similar insurance company products. The typical 401(k) has about 10 choices, and some plans have as many as 20 or more. Today the trend is toward giving plan participants more options and providing seminars and other educational tools to help employees make informed retirement plan decisions. Along that line, you might want to take a look at the accompanying *Money in Action* box—it provides some helpful hints to a better 401(k).

EVALUATING EMPLOYER-SPONSORED PENSION PLANS

When you participate in a company-sponsored pension plan, you're entitled to certain benefits in return for meeting certain conditions of membership—which may or may not include making contributions to the plan. Whether your participation is limited to the firm's basic plan or includes one or more of the supplemental programs, *it's vital that you take the time to acquaint yourself with the various benefits and provisions* of these retirement plans. And be sure to familiarize yourself not only with the basic plans (even though participation is mandatory, you ought to know what you're getting for your money), but also with any (voluntary) supplemental plans you may be eligible to join.

So, how should you evaluate these plans? Most experts agree that although there are many aspects that go into a typical company-sponsored pension plan (some of which are a bit complex and difficult to evaluate), you can get a pretty good handle on essential plan provisions and retirement benefits by taking a close look at these features:

- **Eligibility requirements**—precisely what are they, and if you're not already in the plan, when will you be able to participate?
- **Defined benefits or contributions**—which one is defined? If it's the benefits, exactly what formula is used to define them? Pay particular attention to how social security benefits are treated in the formula. If it's a defined contribution program, do you have any control over how the money is invested? If so, what are your options? *What you would like to have*: a lot of attractive stock/equity mutual funds to choose from; *what you don't need*: a bunch of low-yielding investment options, like bank CDs, money market mutual funds, or fixed annuities.
- **Vesting procedures**—does the company use a cliff or graded procedure, and precisely when do you become fully vested?
- **Contributory or noncontributory**—if the plan is contributory, how much comes from you and how much from the company; and what is the total of this contribution, as a percentage of your salary? If it is noncontributory, what is the company's contribution, as a percentage of your salary?
- **Retirement age**—what is the normal retirement age, and what provisions are there for *early retirement*? What happens if you leave the company before retirement? Are the pension benefits *portable*—that is, can you take them with you if you change jobs?
- **Voluntary supplemental programs**—how much of your salary can you put into one or more of these plans, and what, if anything, is *matched* by the company? Remember, these are like defined contribution plans, so there's nothing guaranteed as far as benefits are concerned.

Getting answers to these questions will help you determine where you stand and what, if any, improvements need to be made in your retirement plans. As part of this evaluation

MONEY IN ACTION

One Hour (or so) to a Better 401(k)

Choices, choices: many employers now let you design your retirement fund portfolio to meet your particular needs and investment style. The number of investment options available in 401(k) plans has increased, too. For example, the Time Warner 401(k) recently went from 10 choices to more than 100! More companies now allow their employees to pick individual stocks as well.

All those options can be overwhelming, though, and your first reaction may be to run away from the task. You aren't alone; about half of 401(k) participants don't even know one investment their company plan offers, and 75 percent spend less than 10 hours a year evaluating and tracking their investments. When you consider that retirement savings may be your most sizable assets, spending the time to build a solid portfolio makes good financial sense. If you are uncomfortable picking individual stocks, focus on mutual funds. The following 9 steps can help narrow your investment choices to a manageable number.

1. **Max out:** Make sure you contribute as much as your plan allows. How much you save now is more important than which fund you chose. Save more, sooner. If you change jobs, don't assume that you are automatically enrolled to contribute the maximum allowed. And invest enough to receive the full employer match.

2. **Allocate your assets:** Before selecting funds, know what asset categories you need. You can use an asset-allocation worksheet like the one at Fidelity's 401(k) site, **www.401k.com**. It quickly shows a suggested investing style and the allocation that matches. If you want to invest in individual stocks, factor in the costs of activating a brokerage account plus transaction costs.

3. **Cut, cut, cut:** Review your plan's offerings and delete funds that don't match your asset allocation. Consider your other holdings as well. You can shelter bond income outside your 401(k) with tax-exempt municipal bond funds. Don't end up with too much of your company's stock

if your employer uses it to match your contributions. Eliminate any others that don't seem to fit.

4. **Hunt for bargains:** The past is no guarantee of future performance! But funds with low expense ratios are likely to outperform their peers. Personal Fund, **www.personal fund.com**, lists fund expenses so you can eliminate those above your benchmarks for the category.

5. **Use index funds:** Index funds, with their low fees, generally do better than actively managed funds in the long run. Over time, matching the market gives solid returns.

6. **Check master lists:** Use lists of mutual funds in personal finance periodicals and analyst picks from Morningstar.com (**www.morningstar.com**) to narrow the list further.

7. **Trust the old standbys:** Funds from well-regarded families like Fidelity, Vanguard, and American are usually good bets. One survey showed that these families have three times as many funds with above-average category ratings as below-average funds, and they also are likely to have below-average expenses. If a problem arises, they have the resources to correct the situation.

8. **Checks and balances:** You should now have about 10 or so funds on your list. Investigate these more carefully to be sure the fund is in the right style category; don't rely on fund names. (Fidelity's Web site is one that provides this information.)

9. **Teamwork:** If you have a partner, look at his or her holdings as well when you do your asset allocation. Otherwise you could end up with too much in one stock or industry.

Sources: Adapted from Laura Lallos, "The 60 Minute 401(k), *Money*, November 2000, pp. 85–96; Paul J. Lim, "Stocks Add Some Spice to Plain Vanilla 401(K) Plans, *U.S. News & World Report*, August 21, 2000 p. 64.

process, you should try to work up, as best as you can, *a rough estimation of what your benefits are likely to be at retirement*—you're going to have to make some projections about future income levels, investment returns, and so on, but it's an exercise well worth taking (before you start cranking out the numbers, however, check with the people who handle employee benefits at your place of work; they'll often give you the help you need). Then, using a procedure similar to what we did with Worksheet 14.1, you can estimate what portion of your retirement needs will be met from your company's basic pension plan. If there's a shortfall—*and there likely will be*—it will indicate the extent to which you need to participate in some type of company-sponsored supplemental program, such as a 401(k) plan, or (alternatively) how much you're going to have to rely on your own savings and investments to come up with the kind of standard of living you're looking for in retirement. *Such insights will enable you to more effectively dovetail the investment characteristics and retirement benefits of any company-sponsored retirement plans you're entitled to with the savings and investing that you do on your own.*

 Paying too much in 401(k) fees? Head over to Tim Younkin's top-rated consumer advocacy and education site (**www.tim younkin.com**) which helps plan participants evaluate their retirement plans.

SELF-DIRECTED RETIREMENT PROGRAMS

In addition to participating in company-sponsored retirement programs, individuals can also set up their own tax-sheltered retirement plans. There are two basic types of self-directed retirement programs: *Keogh* and *SEP plans*, which are for self-employed individuals, and *individual retirement arrangements (IRAs)*, which can be set up by just about anybody.

KEOGH AND SEP PLANS. **Keogh plans** were introduced in 1962 as part of the Self-Employed Individuals Retirement Act, or simply the Keogh Act. Keogh plans allow self-employed individuals to set up tax-deferred retirement plans for themselves and their employees. Like contributions to 401(k) plans, payments to Keogh accounts may be taken as deductions from taxable income. As a result, they reduce the tax bills of self-employed individuals. The maximum contribution to this tax-deferred retirement plan in 2001 was $35,000 per year or 20 percent of earned income, whichever is less. But as with most other tax-advantaged retirement accounts, the Tax Relief Act of 2001 will also mean higher maximum annual contributions here, too—in particular the annual contribution limit goes up to $40,000 (or 25 percent of earned income) in 2002.

Any individual who is self-employed, either full- or part-time, is eligible to set up a Keogh account. They can also be used by individuals who hold full-time jobs and "moonlight" on a part-time basis—for instance, the engineer who has a small consulting business on the side or the accountant who does tax returns in the evenings and on weekends. If the engineer, for example, earns $10,000 a year from his part-time consulting business, he can contribute 20 percent of that income ($2,000) to his Keogh account and, in so doing, reduce both his taxable income and the amount he pays in taxes. Further, he is still eligible to receive full retirement benefits from his full-time job, and to have his own IRA (though, as we'll see below, contributions to his IRA may not qualify for tax shelter).

Keogh accounts can be opened at banks, insurance companies, brokerage houses, mutual funds, and other financial institutions. Annual contributions must be made at the time the respective tax return is filed or by April 15 of the following calendar year (for example, you have until April 15, 2002, to make the contribution to your Keogh for 2001). Although a designated financial institution acts as custodian of all the funds held in a Keogh account, *the actual investments held in the account are under the complete direction of the individual contributor.* These are self-directed retirement programs where the *individual* decides which investments to buy and sell (subject to a few basic restrictions).

The income earned from the investments must be reinvested in the account and it, too, accrues tax free. All Keogh contributions and investment earnings must remain in the

Keogh plan
An account to which self-employed persons may make payments, up to the lesser of $30,000 or 20 percent of earned income per year, that may be taken as deductions from taxable income; the earnings on such accounts also accrue on a tax-deferred basis.

account until the individual turns 59½, unless he or she becomes seriously ill or disabled—early withdrawals for any other reason are subject to 10 percent tax penalties. However, the individual is *not required* to start withdrawing the funds at age 59½; the funds can stay in the account (and continue to earn tax-free income) until the individual is 70½, at which time the individual *must* begin withdrawing funds from the account—unless he or she continues to be gainfully employed past the age of 70½ (technically, a participant in a Keogh plan must begin to receive distributions from the plan by April 1 of the year that follows the *latter of:* (1) the year in which the participant turns 70½, or (2) the year in which the participant retires). Of course, once an individual starts withdrawing funds (upon or after turning 59½), all such withdrawals are treated as ordinary income and subject to normal income taxes. Thus, the taxes on all contributions to and earnings from a Keogh account will eventually have to be paid, a characteristic of any tax-*deferred* (as opposed to tax-*free*) program.

A program that's similar in many respects to the Keogh account is something called a *Simplified Employee Pension Plan*—or SEP-IRA for short. It's aimed at small-business owners, particularly those with *no employees*, who want a plan that is simple to set up and administer. SEP-IRAs *can be used in place of Keoghs*, and although they are simpler to administer and have the same dollar annual contribution cap ($35,000), their contribution rate is less generous; that is, in 2001 you could put only 15 percent of earned income into a SEP-IRA, versus 20 percent into a Keogh. However, that is also slated to change in 2002 as the annual contribution amount (and rate) will increase to $40,000 (or 25 percent of earned income)—the same as a Keogh account.

INDIVIDUAL RETIREMENT ARRANGEMENTS (IRAs). Some people mistakenly believe that an IRA is a specialized type of investment. It is not. Actually, an **individual retirement arrangement (IRA)**, or individual retirement *account*, as it's more commonly known, is virtually the same as any other investment account you open with a bank, credit union, stockbroker, mutual fund, or insurance company, except it's clearly designated as an IRA. That is, the form you complete designates the account as an IRA and makes the institution its trustee. That is all there is to it. Basically, anybody can have an IRA account, though the type of accounts that a person can have and the tax status of those accounts depend on a number of variables. All IRAs, however, have one thing in common: they're designed to encourage retirement savings on the part of individuals, which they do by sheltering the investment income earned in these accounts from income taxes.

Actually, the whole IRA landscape was altered dramatically in 1997–98, with the introduction of *Roth IRAs*. As it now stands, the individual has a full menu of different types of IRAs to choose from, including the following:

- **Traditional (Deductible) IRA**, which can be opened by anyone without a retirement plan at his or her place of employment, regardless of income level; or by couples filing jointly who, even if they are covered by retirement plans at their places of employment, have adjusted gross incomes of less than $52,000 (or single tax payers with AGIs of less than $32,000). Those individuals who qualify may make tax deductible contributions of up to $2,000 a year to their accounts (an equal tax deductible amount can be contributed by a nonworking spouse). This maximum annual contribution increases to $3,000 in 2002, $4,000 in 2005, and $5,000 in 2008 and beyond (and there's a catch-up contribution of an additional $500 to $1,000 per year that can be made by individuals age 50 or older). All earnings in the accounts grow tax free until withdrawn, when ordinary tax rates apply (though a 10 percent penalty normally applies to withdrawals made before age 59½).
- **Nondeductible (After-Tax) IRA**, which is open to anyone, regardless of their income level or whether they are covered by a retirement plan at their place of employment;

individual retirement arrangement (IRA)
A retirement plan, open to any working American, to which a person may contribute a specified amount each year (up to $2,000 per person); although annual contributions to IRAs may or may not be tax deductible (depending on the type of IRA it is), the earnings from all IRAs accrue on a tax-deferred basis. Also known, more popularly, as an *individual retirement account*.

EXHIBIT 14.6

QUALIFYING FOR AN IRA

In 1998, the ground rules for opening an IRA changed dramatically with the introduction of the new Roth IRAs. Individuals can now select from three different types of individual retirement accounts.

■ DEDUCTIBLE IRA

- For 2001, annual contributions of up to $2,000 by a working taxpayer and $2,000 by a nonworking spouse are fully deductible if the taxpayer is not covered by an employer's pension plan or has adjusted gross income of less than $32,000 a year on a single taxpayer return or $52,000 on a joint return. The maximum annual contribution will increase to $3,000 in 2002, $4,000 in 2005, and $5,000 in 2008, and there is an additional $500 to $1,000 per year catch-up contribution that can be made by those age 50 or older.
- Partial tax deductible contributions are available to joint filers with AGIs (in 2000) of $52,000 to $62,000, and to single filers with AGIs (in 2000) of $32,000 to $42,000—essentially, the deductible contribution is reduced at higher levels of AGI and phases out completely at AGI of $42,000 for single taxpayers and $62,000 for joint returns.
- The AGI ranges noted above are scheduled to rise annually through 2005/2007 so that the phase out range will rise to $50,000–$60,000 for single filers by 2005, and $80,000–$100,000 for joint filers by 2007.
- The nonworking spouse of a taxpayer covered by a deductible IRA can also contribute from $2,000 (in 2001) to $5,000 (in 2008) per year to a fully deductible IRA, provided the couple's AGI is $150,000 or less.

■ AFTER-TAX IRA

- Working taxpayers who fail to qualify for deductible IRAs, and their nonworking spouses, can make annual nondeductible IRA contributions of up to $2,000 each in 2001, rising (as outlined previously) to $5,000 in 2008.

■ ROTH IRA

- A working taxpayer with AGI of up to $95,000 on a single return or $150,000 on a joint return can make nondeductible contributions of up to $2,000 (in 2001) to $5,000 (in 2008).
- The contribution phases out at $110,000 single and $160,000 joint; partial contributions are available to single filers with AGIs of $95,000–$110,000, and joint filers with AGIs of $150,000–$160,000.
- A nonworking spouse can make after-tax contributions of up to $2,000 per year (in 2001) to $5,000 per year (in 2008) to a Roth IRA with AGI of less than $150,000 on a joint return.

---

contributions of up to $2,000 a year in 2001, rising (as with the traditional IRA) to $5,000 in 2008, can be made to this account, but they are made with after-tax dollars (i.e., the contributions are not tax deductible). However, the earnings do accrue tax free and are not subject to tax until they are withdrawn, after the individual reaches age $59\frac{1}{2}$ (funds withdrawn before age $59\frac{1}{2}$ may be subject to the 10% penalty).

- **Roth IRA**, the newest kid on the block (available only since 1998), can be opened by couples filing jointly with adjusted gross incomes of up to $150,000 (singles up to $95,000), regardless of whether they have other retirement or pension plans. But the neatest part of the Roth account is its tax features—although the annual contributions of up to $2,000 a person in 2001, rising (as with the traditional IRA) to $5,000 in 2008, are made with nondeductible/after-tax dollars, all earnings in the account grow tax free and *all withdrawals from the account are also tax free, so long as the account has been open for at least five years and the individual is past the age of $59\frac{1}{2}$*. In other words, so long as these conditions are met, you won't have to pay taxes on any withdrawals you make from your Roth IRA!

The key features and provisions of all three of these IRAs are outlined in Exhibit 14.6.

Regardless of the type, and not withstanding the conditions set out above, penalty-free withdrawals (of up to $10,000) are generally allowed from an IRA as long as the funds are being used for first-time home purchases, qualifying education costs, certain major medical expenses, or other qualified emergencies. Also, with both the traditional/deductible and nondeductible IRAs, you must start making withdrawals from your account once you reach age 70½—though this requirement does not apply to Roth IRAs. Finally, in addition to the three retirement-based IRAs, 1998 also brought us the so-called *Education IRA*, which can be set up and used to meet the future education (college) cost of a child or grandchild. Specifically, these IRAs can be opened by couples with AGIs of up to $150,000 (or singles with AGIs up to $95,000) for the benefit of a child under the age of 18. Nondeductible annual contributions of up to $500 per child are allowed in 2001, but jump to $2,000 per year beginning in 2002. As with Roth IRAs the earnings grow tax-free as long as they remain in the account, and all withdrawals (which must be made by the time the beneficiary reaches age 30) are also made tax free and penalty free, so long as the funds are used for qualifying education expenses.

IRAs are like Keogh and SEP plans in that they are *self-directed accounts*—meaning you are free to make just about whatever investment decisions you want. Actually, as with any investment, an individual can be conservative or aggressive in choosing securities for an IRA (or Keogh), though the nature of these retirement programs generally favors a more conservative approach. In fact, conventional wisdom favors funding your IRA (and Keogh) with *income-producing assets*; this would also suggest that if you are looking for capital gains, it is best to do so *outside* your retirement account. The reasons are two-fold: (1) Growth-oriented securities are by nature *more risky*, and (2) you *cannot write off losses* from the sale of securities held in an IRA (or Keogh) account. This does not mean, however, that it would be altogether inappropriate to place a good-quality growth stock or mutual fund in a Keogh or IRA—in fact, many advisors contend that growth investments should always have a place in your retirement account due to their often impressive performance and ability to counteract inflation. Such investments may pay off handsomely, because they can appreciate totally free of taxes.

In the end, of course, *it is how much you have in your retirement account that matters rather than how your earnings were made along the way*. Also, regardless of what type of investment vehicle you use, keep in mind that once you place money in an IRA, it's meant to stay there for the long haul. For like most tax-sheltered retirement programs, there are restrictions on when you can withdraw the funds from an IRA. Specifically, as noted earlier, any funds withdrawn from an IRA prior to age 59½ are subject to a 10 percent tax penalty, on top of the regular tax paid on the withdrawal. (Note, however, that you can avoid the 10 percent tax penalty and still start withdrawals before age 59½ by setting up a systematic withdrawal program that essentially pays you equal amounts over the rest of your life expectancy; obviously, unless you have a substantial amount of money in your IRA, the annual payments under this program are likely to be pretty small.) In addition, when you move your IRA account to a new firm (this is known as a "roll-over"), the transfer is subject to a *20 percent withholding tax* if the proceeds from the transfer are paid to you directly—the rule is very clear on this: If you take possession of the funds (even for just a few days), you will be hit with the withholding tax. Thus, the best way to handle IRA roll-overs is to *arrange for the transfer of funds from one firm to another*.

So, should you contribute to an IRA or not? Obviously, so long as you qualify for either a traditional/tax-deductible IRA or a Roth IRA (as per the provisions spelled out above), you should seriously consider making the maximum payments allowable. There are no special record-keeping requirements or forms to file, and the IRA continues to be an excellent vehicle for sheltering income from taxes. Indeed, probably the biggest decision you're going to have to make is which IRA is right for you—the traditional or the Roth? *Hint*: the Roth is probably most appropriate for people in their 30s or 40s.

GOVERNMENT INFLUENCE ON PENSION PLANS

The two major areas of government influence on pension plans are the Internal Revenue Code (IRC) requirements for plan qualification, and the regulations established by the Employee Retirement Income Security Act of 1974 (ERISA). The major stipulations of the IRC were discussed earlier in the chapter. At this point, we will look at the most important features of ERISA.

As the name implies, the act's primary objective is to increase the probability that eligible employees who are covered by a retirement plan will in fact receive benefits upon retirement. ERISA covers nearly all the pension and retirement plans created by private employers engaged in interstate commerce. It does not cover plans sponsored by government, charitable organizations, or firms exclusively involved in intrastate commerce. The law regulates only plans that are in existence. It does not require firms to begin a retirement plan for their employees, nor does it prohibit them from discontinuing an existing plan (as many have done to avoid the myriad ERISA regulations). Similarly, ERISA does not force companies to pay any minimum amounts to employees, other than those specified in the plans.

ERISA basically prescribes minimum standards with which covered plans must comply. These standards apply to plan provisions, funding, and administration. Among the major items treated are vesting, eligibility for participation, definition of service, minimum funding requirements, disclosure to participants, and employer fiduciary responsibility. Another important provision establishes the **Pension Benefit Guarantee Corporation (PBGC)**. The purpose of this organization is to guarantee eligible workers that certain benefits will be paid to them even if their employer's plan has insufficient assets to fulfill its commitments. Funding for the PBGC comes from charges levied against all employers regulated by ERISA. In essence, the PBGC provides plan termination insurance to covered employees. Although the implementation of ERISA has not been free of problems, most observers agree that this law is a good start in ensuring that employees who have earned pensions will, in fact, receive them.

Pension Benefit Guarantee Corporation (PBGC) An organization established under ERISA that guarantees the payment of certain pension benefits, regardless of the employer's ability to fulfill its commitments.

CONCEPT CHECK

14-8. Which basic features of employer-sponsored pension plans should you be familiar with? Explain.

14-9. Discuss the distinguishing features of (a) *basic*, (b) *qualified*, (c) *defined benefit*, and (d) *contributory pension plans*. Under which procedure will you become fully vested most quickly—cliff or graded vesting? Explain.

14-10. What is the difference between a *profit-sharing plan* and a *salary reduction*, or *401(k), plan*? Are these basic or supplemental plans?

14-11. Why is it important to evaluate and become familiar with the pension plans and retirement benefits offered by your employer? Identify and briefly discuss at least six different plan provisions that you feel would be important in such an evaluation.

14-12. Briefly describe the tax provisions of *401(k) plans* and *Keogh plans*. Would you describe these plans as tax-deferred or tax-free programs? Explain. Describe and differentiate between Keogh plans and *individual retirement arrangements*; what's the difference between a *nondeductible IRA* and an *education IRA*?

14-13. Describe ERISA, and discuss its influence on pension plans. What does *PBGC* stand for, and what function does this organization serve?

Annuities [LG6]

The number of annuity contracts in force with U.S. life insurance companies has grown tremendously in the past 15 years or so. This growth has resulted primarily from greater public awareness of annuities, due to the increased marketing efforts of life insurance companies. In addition, the surge in retirement programs has contributed to the growth of annuities, and so have the tax laws, which treat annuities as tax-sheltered investment vehicles—indeed, annuities are one of the few tax shelters left to investors today. Stripped down, annuities represent little more than an agreement to make contributions now (or in installments) in return for a series of payments later—for a fixed number of years, or for life.

THE ANNUITY PRINCIPLE

An annuity is just the opposite of life insurance. As we pointed out in Chapter 8, life insurance is the systematic accumulation of an estate that is used for protection against financial loss resulting from premature death. In contrast, an **annuity** is the systematic *liquidation* of an estate in such a way that it provides protection against the economic difficulties that could result from outliving personal financial resources. The period during which premiums are paid toward the purchase of an annuity is called the **accumulation period**; correspondingly, the period during which annuity payments are made is called the **distribution period**.

Under a pure life annuity contract, a life insurance company will guarantee regular monthly payments to an individual for as long as he or she lives. These benefits are composed of three parts: principal, interest, and survivorship benefits. The *principal* consists of the premium amounts paid in by the *annuitant* (person buying the annuity) during the accumulation period. *Interest* is the amount earned on these funds between the time they are paid and distributed. The interest earnings on an annuity accrue (that is, accumulate) tax free—note, however, while the earnings in an annuity accumulate on a tax-sheltered basis, the amounts paid into an annuity are all made with *after-tax dollars* (i.e., there is no special tax treatment given to the capital contributions). The portion of the principal and interest that has not been returned to the annuitant prior to death is the **survivorship benefit**. These funds are available to those members of the annuity group who survive in each subsequent period. By using mortality tables and estimated investment returns, life insurance companies can calculate for a group of annuitants of a given age the amount of monthly payment they can guarantee to each individual without prematurely depleting the total amount accumulated. Consequently, the risk of outliving one's income is eliminated.

CLASSIFICATION OF ANNUITIES

Annuities may be classified according to several key characteristics, including the way the premiums are paid, the disposition of proceeds, inception date of benefits, and the method used in calculating benefits. Exhibit 14.7 presents a chart of this classification system.

SINGLE PREMIUM OR INSTALLMENTS. There are two ways to pay the premiums when you purchase an annuity contract: you can make a large single (lump-sum) payment right up front, or pay the premium in installments. The **single-premium annuity contract** usually requires a *minimum investment* of anywhere from $2,500 to $10,000, with $5,000 the most common figure. These annuities have become very popular, primarily because of the attractive tax features they offer. They are often purchased just before retirement as a way of creating a future stream of income. Sometimes the cash value of a life insurance policy will be used at retirement to acquire a single-premium annuity. This is a highly effective

annuity
An investment product, created by life insurance companies that provides a series of payments over time.

accumulation period
The period during which premiums are paid for the purchase of an annuity.

distribution period
The period during which annuity payments are made to an annuitant.

survivorship benefit
On an annuity, the portion of premiums and interest that has not been returned to the annuitant prior to his or her death.

single-premium annuity contract
An annuity contract purchased with a lump-sum payment.

![EXHIBIT 14.7]

DIFFERENT TYPES OF ANNUITY CONTRACTS

The different types of annuity contracts vary according to how you pay for the annuity, how the proceeds will be disbursed, how earnings accrue, and when you will receive the benefits.

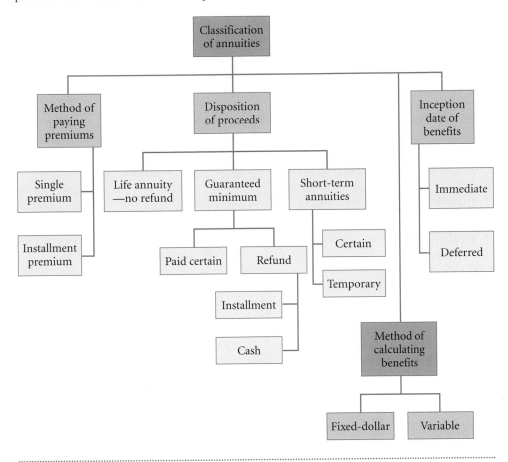

Source: Adapted from Robert I. Mehr, *Life Insurance:Theory and Practice*, rev. ed. (Dallas: Business Publications, 1977), p. 85.

use of a life insurance policy: you get the insurance coverage when you *need* it the most (while you're raising and educating your family) and then a regular stream of income when you can probably *use* it the most (after you've retired).

Although the majority of *group* annuity policies are funded with single premiums, many *individuals* still buy annuities by paying for them in installments. With these so-called **installment-premium annuity contracts**, set payments, starting as low as $100, are made at regular intervals (monthly, quarterly, or annually) over an extended period of time. Sometimes, these annuities are set up with a fairly large initial payment (of perhaps several thousand dollars), followed by a series of much smaller installment payments (of, say, $250 a quarter). There are even plans that combine the features of both single-premium and installment-premium annuities. Known as *flexible plans*, they start out with a sizable initial investment, very much like single-premium annuities, except that the investor can put more money in later, *as desired*. In this type of contract, which is common

installment-premium annuity contract
An annuity contract purchased through periodic payments made over a given period of time.

life annuity with no refund (straight life)
An option under which an annuitant receives a specified amount of income for life, regardless of the length of the distribution period; in turn, no payments or refunds are made to the person's family or estate upon his or her death.

guaranteed-minimum annuity
An annuity that provides a guaranteed minimum distribution of benefits.

life annuity, period certain
A type of guaranteed-minimum annuity in which the annuitant is guaranteed a stated amount of monthly income for life and the insurer agrees to pay that amount for a minimum number of years, regardless of whether the annuitant survives.

refund annuity
A type of guaranteed-minimum annuity that, upon the annuitant's death, makes monthly payments to the designated beneficiary until the total purchase price of the annuity has been refunded.

with variable annuities, the individual is under no obligation to make future set payments at set intervals.

 For everything you always wanted to know about annuities, Annuities Online, www.annuities.com, is the place to go.

Installment-premium contracts also carry an important *life insurance provision*, which stipulates that if an annuitant dies before the distribution period begins, the annuitant's beneficiaries will receive the market value of the contract or the amount invested, whichever is greater (note that single-premium annuities contain similar life insurance provisions, so long as the payout of benefits is deferred to some future date). In addition, the annuitant can terminate an installment-premium contract at any time, or simply stop paying the periodic installments and take a paid-up annuity for a reduced amount. One potential advantage of purchasing an installment-type annuity relatively early in life is that scheduled benefits are based on mortality rates in effect when the contract was purchased. Even if the mortality rate increases, as it normally does with the passage of time, the annuitant will not be required to pay the higher premium stipulated in contracts issued later on.

DISPOSITION OF PROCEEDS. All annuities revolve around the basic pay-now, receive-later concept, and therefore allow individuals to prepare for future cash needs, like planning for retirement, while obtaining significant tax benefits. When it comes to the distribution of an annuity, you can take a lump-sum payment, or, as is more often the case, you can *annuitize* the distribution by systematically parceling out the money into regular payments over a defined or open-ended period. Because most people choose to annuitize their proceeds (which is conceptually the way an annuity should be used), let's look at the most common annuity disbursement options:

- **Life annuity with no refund (straight life).** The annuitant receives a specified amount of income for life, whether the disbursement period turns out to be one year or 50 years. The estate or family receives no refunds when the annuitant dies. This results in the largest monthly payments of any distribution methods, because the issuer (a life insurance company) does not have to distribute the principal, if any, to the annuitant's heirs. This option is not widely used by individuals but may be found in group annuity contracts.

- **Guaranteed-minimum annuity.** In this type of contract, the benefits (future cash flows) are not limited to the annuitant only, but may also extend to named beneficiaries. There are two forms of this annuity. With a **life annuity, period certain**, the annuitant gets a guaranteed monthly income for life, with the added provision that the insurance company will pay the monthly benefits for at least a minimum number of years (five or ten, for example). If the annuitant dies soon after the distribution begins, his or her beneficiaries receive the monthly benefits for the balance of the "period certain." With a **refund annuity**, if the annuitant dies, the designated beneficiary receives monthly payments (or in some cases, a lump-sum cash refund) until the total purchase price of the annuity has been refunded.

- **Annuity certain.** This type of annuity pays a set amount of monthly income for a specified number of years, thereby filling a need for monthly income that will expire after a certain length of time. An annuitant selecting a 10-year annuity certain receives payments for 10 years after retirement, regardless of whether he or she lives for 2 or 20 more years. For example, a widow, age 52, could use a 10-year annuity certain contract to provide income until she reaches age 62 and can apply for social security benefits.

- **Temporary life annuity**. This annuity continues benefits for a specified period *only if the annuitant survives*; it therefore provides a larger monthly income than the annuity certain. If the widow mentioned above had chosen a 10-year temporary life annuity but died at age 60, no further payments would be made under the contract. This type of annuity is most appropriate for those who have no beneficiaries or who need the added income.

IMMEDIATE VERSUS DEFERRED ANNUITY. An annuitant usually has the choice of receiving monthly benefits immediately upon buying an annuity or of deferring receipt for a number of years. Logically, the first type is called an immediate annuity and the latter a deferred annuity. An **immediate annuity**, purchased with a single premium, is most often used in conjunction with the cash value or death proceeds of a life insurance policy to create a stream of cash receipts needed for retirement or to support a survivor or dependent children.

A **deferred annuity**, in contrast, can be bought with either a single payment or through an installment plan. This contract is quite flexible and can be issued with numerous options for paying the premiums and receiving the proceeds. The big advantage of a deferred annuity is that your savings can build up over time, free of taxes. With no taxes to pay, you have more money working for you and, as such, can build up a bigger retirement nest egg (of course, you'll have to pay taxes on your earnings eventually, but not until you start receiving payments from your annuity). Most annuities purchased under group contracts are immediate annuities, whereas those purchased by individuals are usually of the *deferred* type. In fact, because of their attractive tax features, a lot of people buy deferred annuities—and especially single-premium deferred annuities—more as a tax-sheltered *investment vehicle* than anything else.

FIXED VERSUS VARIABLE ANNUITY. When you put your money into an annuity, the premium is invested on your behalf by the insurance company, much like a mutual fund invests the money you put into it. From the time you pay the annuity premium until it is paid back to you as a lump sum or as an annuitized monthly benefit, you'll earn a rate of return on your investment. How that rate of return is figured determines whether you own a fixed or variable annuity. In a **fixed rate annuity** the insurance company safeguards your principal and agrees to pay a guaranteed minimum rate of interest over the life of the contract—which often amounts to little more than prevailing money market rates that existed at the time you bought the contract. These are conservative, very low risk annuity products that essentially promise to return *the original investment plus interest* when the money is paid out to the annuitant (or any designated beneficiaries).

Unlike bond mutual funds, fixed annuities do not fluctuate in value when interest rates rise or fall; your principal is therefore secure at all times. However, contrary to what many people think, these annuities are *not* backed by a specific, dedicated portfolio of securities (like mutual funds are). Rather, they are backed by the insurance company's "general account," which often consists of a wide variety of investment vehicles; and when it comes to the rate of interest paid on the annuity, *the insurance company can pay whatever they want*, as they are in no way required to pay the rate they earn on their general account! With fixed annuities, once a distribution, or pay-out, schedule has been selected, the annuitant knows right up front what the (minimum) monthly benefit will be, because it's guaranteed by the annuity contract. These *interest-earning annuities*, as they're also called, are ideally suited for the cautious investor who likes the secure feeling of knowing what his or her monthly cash flow will be.

Imagine an investment vehicle that lets you move between stocks, bonds, and money funds and, at the same time, accumulate profits tax free. That, in a nutshell, is a variable annuity. With a **variable annuity** contract, the amount that's ultimately paid out to the annuitant

annuity certain
An annuity that provides a specified monthly income for a stated number of years, without consideration of any life contingency.

temporary life annuity
An annuity in which benefits continue for a specified period, but only as long as the annuitant survives.

immediate annuity
An annuity in which the annuitant begins receiving monthly benefits immediately; often purchased with a single premium.

deferred annuity
An annuity in which benefit payments are deferred for a certain number of years; purchased with either a lump-sum payment or in installments.

fixed rate annuity
An annuity in which the insurance company safeguards your principal and agrees to pay a guaranteed rate of interest on your money; in addition, the (minimum) monthly benefit is set by the contract.

variable annuity
An annuity in which the monthly income provided by the policy varies according to the actual investment experience of the insurer.

varies with the investment results obtained by the insurance company—*nothing* is guaranteed, not even the principal! When you buy a variable annuity, *you decide* where your money will be invested, based on your investment objectives and tolerance for risk; you can usually choose from stocks, bonds, money market securities, or some combination thereof. Insurance companies typically offer five or six stock and bond funds, as well as money market investments for short-term safety; some companies even offer a relatively exotic fleet of alternatives, ranging from zero coupon bonds to real estate and foreign securities. As an annuity holder, you can stay put with a single investment for the long haul, or, as with most variable annuities, you can aggressively play the market by switching from one fund to another. Obviously, when the market goes up, investors in variable annuities do well; but, when the market falters, the returns on these policies can go down as well.

Because the payoff from a variable annuity depends to such an extent on the fate of the markets, *the annuitants take a chance that their monthly income will be less than anticipated*. Of course, most people who participate in variable annuity plans fully expect to be able to outperform fixed annuities. But that doesn't always happen, as we saw in the 1970s when a sluggish stock market led to variable annuity payments that were well below the amounts paid on corresponding fixed rate plans. Annuitants, however, do have some control over this type of risk exposure, because they can choose to go with high- or low-risk investment vehicles and, in so doing, influence the certainty of return. In effect, if you go with an account that stresses high-risk securities, you should expect a good deal of uncertainty in return—the potential for high return might be there, but so is the chance for loss. If you're uncomfortable with that, stick to annuities that offer safer investment choices (like zero coupon bonds or Treasury securities).

Also, although there's nothing to prohibit you from staying with market-sensitive variable annuities during both the accumulation and distribution periods, in most cases you can convert to a fixed annuity at distribution. What you do, in effect, is use the cash value in your variable annuity to buy a paid-up fixed annuity. In this way, you use a *variable annuity during the accumulation period* to build up your capital as much as possible, and then switch to a *fixed annuity for the distribution period* to obtain a certain, well-defined stream of future income.

SOURCES AND COSTS OF ANNUITIES

Annuities are administered by life insurance companies, and, for that reason, it should come as no surprise that they're also the leading sellers of these financial products. Annuities can also be purchased from stock brokers, mutual fund organizations, banks, and financial planners. When you buy an annuity, the cost will vary with the age of the annuitant at issue, the age of the annuitant when payments begin, the method used to distribute benefits, the number of lives covered, and the sex of the annuitant. Exhibit 14.8 provides some real-life examples of the lump-sum costs of two types of immediate annuities. Note the substantial differences that exist among the companies' premiums. These differences confirm the need to shop around before making an annuity purchase. Note, too, that in every category the cost to females is higher than the cost to males, because of the lower mortality rates among women. The differences in life expectancy for males and females can be seen in Exhibit 14.9.

In addition, as with mutual funds, there are some annual fees you should be aware of. In particular, be prepared to pay insurance fees of 1 percent or more—and that's on top of annual management fees of perhaps 1 to 2 percent paid on variable annuities. That's a total of 2 to 3 percent—or more—taken right off the top, year after year. And then there's also a *contract charge* (or maintenance fee) that's deducted annually to cover various contract-related expenses; these fees usually run from about $30 to $60 per year. Obviously, these fees can drag down returns and reduce the advantage of tax-deferred income. Finally, as

EXHIBIT 14.8

LUMP-SUM COSTS NECESSARY FOR FUNDING PAYMENTS OF $100 A MONTH

Annuity costs vary not only by the type of annuity and the sex and age of the beneficiary, but also by the company selling the contract. Clearly, it pays to shop around. Here are some costs quoted by four life insurance companies; note that it would cost a 55-year-old male about 22 percent less to buy a $100 monthly benefit through a life annuity contract from Company 2 than from Company 3.

Life Annuity with No Refund

	Male			Female		
Company	55	65	75	55	65	75
1	$13,110	$11,170	$8,510	$13,930	$12,280	$9,700
2	11,820	10,250	8,010	12,450	11,140	8,980
3	15,020	11,970	8,420	16,510	13,440	9,580
4	12,900	10,960	8,480	13,660	11,860	9,270

Life Annuity—10 Years Certain

	Male			Female		
Company	55	65	75	55	65	75
1	$13,400	$11,840	$10,170	$14,070	$12,660	$10,770
2	12,050	10,800	9,390	12,560	11,440	9,870
3	N/A	N/A	N/A	N/A	N/A	N/A
4	13,190	11,570	9,940	13,790	12,200	10,300

we'll see later, most annuities charge hefty *penalties for early withdrawal*; meaning in order to get out of a poorly performing annuity, you'll have to forfeit a chunk of your money.

THE INVESTMENT AND INCOME PROPERTIES OF ANNUITIES

A major attribute of most types of annuities is that they provide a source of income that cannot be outlived. Although individuals might be able to create a similar arrangement by simply living off the interest or dividends from their investments, they would find it difficult to engage in the systematic liquidation of their principal in a manner that would be timed to coincide closely (or exactly) with their death. Also viewed very positively is the fact that the income earned in an annuity is allowed to accumulate tax free; thus, it provides a form of *tax-sheltered investment*. Actually, the income from an annuity is *tax deferred*, meaning that taxes on the earnings will have to be paid when the annuity is liquidated.

Although shelter from taxes is an attractive investment attribute, there is a hitch. You may be faced with a big tax penalty if you close out or withdraw money from an annuity before it's time. Specifically, the IRS treats annuity withdrawals like withdrawals from an individual retirement arrangement, meaning that except in cases of serious illness, *anybody who takes money out before reaching age 59½ will incur a 10 percent tax penalty*. Thus, if you're under age 59½ and in the 28 percent tax bracket, you'll end up paying a 38 percent tax rate on any funds withdrawn from an annuity. (The IRS views withdrawals *as taxable income* until the account balance falls to the amount of original paid-in principal—after

Financial Road Sign

Are Annuities Right for You?

You may want to consider annuities if you:

1. Have contributed the maximum to your 401(k) plans and IRAs, but want more tax–deferred investment gains.
2. Prefer investing in mutual funds over individual securities.
3. Will keep the annuity for at least 15 to 20 years.
4. Are in a 28% or higher income tax bracket today, but expect to be in a lower tax bracket in retirement.
5. Don't need the annuity proceeds prior to age 59½.
6. Are unconcerned that heirs must pay ordinary income taxes on any appreciation.
7. Desire a "guaranteed" income for life in retirement.

Source: *The Motley Fool*, **www.fool.com/ retirement/annuities**.

EXHIBIT 14.9

LIFE EXPECTANCIES OF AMERICAN MEN AND WOMEN (LATEST AVAILABLE STATISTICS, 1996)

Life expectancy measures the number of years a person has left to live—for example, on average, a 20-year-old has a little over 57 years remaining. Note, however, that life expectancy varies by age, sex, and race.

Age in 1996 (years)	Expectation of Life in Years				
		White		Black	
	Total	Male	Female	Male	Female
At birth	76.1	73.9	79.7	66.1	74.2
5	71.8	69.5	75.2	62.4	70.3
10	66.9	64.5	70.2	57.5	65.4
15	61.9	59.6	65.3	52.6	60.5
20	57.2	54.9	60.4	48.0	55.7
25	52.4	50.2	55.6	43.7	50.9
30	47.7	45.6	50.7	39.4	46.2
35	43.0	40.9	45.9	35.1	41.6
40	38.4	36.4	41.1	31.0	37.1
45	33.9	31.9	36.4	27.1	32.8
50	29.5	27.5	31.7	23.4	28.5
55	25.2	23.3	27.3	19.9	24.5
60	21.2	19.4	23.0	16.7	20.7
65	17.5	15.8	19.1	13.9	17.2
70	14.1	12.6	15.4	11.2	13.9
75	11.1	9.8	12.0	9.0	11.2
80	8.4	7.3	8.9	7.0	8.5
85 & Over	6.1	5.3	6.3	5.3	6.2

Source: U.S. Bureau of the Census, Statistical Abstract of the United States, Washington, D.C., 1999, Table No. 129, p. 94.

which any further withdrawals are tax free.) Short of some type of serious illness, about the only way to tap your account penalty-free before you're 59½ is to *annuitize.* Unfortunately, the annuity payments must be spread out over your estimated remaining life span, which means the size of each monthly payment could end up being pretty small. All of which only reinforces the notion that *an annuity should always be considered a long-term investment.* Assume it's a part of your retirement program (that's the way the IRS looks at it) and that you're getting in for the long haul, because it's not that easy to get out before you turn 59½.

From an investment perspective, the returns generated from an annuity can, in some cases, prove to be a bit disappointing. For instance, as we discussed earlier, the returns on *variable annuities* are tied to returns in the money and capital markets; even so, they are still no better than what you can get from other investment vehicles—and, as you can see in Exhibit 14.10, they are often lower, due in part to higher annuity fees. And keep in mind, these differential returns aren't due to tax features, because in both cases returns were measured on a before-tax basis. But *returns from annuities are tax-sheltered,* so that makes those lower returns look a lot more attractive. If you're considering a variable annuity, go over it much the same way you would a traditional mutual fund: look for superior past

EXHIBIT 14.10

THE COMPARATIVE RETURNS OF VARIABLE ANNUITIES VERSUS MUTUAL FUNDS

Variable annuities are structured and operate very much like mutual funds, so you'd expect their performance to be comparable. But as we see here, that's not always the case.

Variable Annuity or Mutual Fund Category	Average Annual Return (Over 5-Year Period Ending 6/30/00)	
	Variable Annuities	Mutual Funds
Aggressive Growth/Small Cap	19.72%	25.51%
Growth	21.55	22.56
Growth and Income	16.64	18.37
International Stocks	16.25	16.69
Balanced	13.00	13.05
Corporate Bonds	4.50	5.55
Government Bonds	4.44	5.09
High-Yield Bonds	5.86	6.97
International Bonds	3.36	6.56

Source: *Morningstar.*

performance, proven management talents, and the availability of attractive investment alternatives that you can switch in and out of. And *pay particular attention to an annuity's total expense rate.* For although these products have a (bad) reputation for being heavily loaded with fees and charges, it is possible to find annuities with above-average performance and relatively low fee structures! That's the combination you're looking for.

As far as *fixed-rate annuities* are concerned, although many of them advertise high rates of return, a close look at the fine print reveals that such rates are guaranteed only for the first 1 to 5 years, after which time they drop to something closer to money market yields—or less. True, there are minimum guaranteed rates that the annuities have to stand behind, but these are usually so low that they're really not much help. Investors generally have little choice but to accept the going rate or surrender the policy. Surrendering can be painful, however, not only because of IRS penalties, but also because of the hefty *surrender fees* that are found on many of these contracts (these fees often amount to 5 to 10 percent of the account balance in the first year and then gradually decline to zero, normally over a period of 5 to 7 years).

It's possible to get around a surrender fee if the annuity has a *bailout* clause. Such a provision allows you to withdraw your money, free of any surrender fees, if the rate of return on the annuity falls below a certain level (say, a point or so below the initial rate). But you have to act fairly quickly, because the bailout provision may exist for only a limited period. Of course, even if you exercise a bailout provision, you may still have to face a tax penalty for early withdrawal—unless you transfer the funds to another annuity through what is known as a *1035 exchange.*

HOW GOOD IS THE INSURANCE COMPANY? One final point: if you're seriously considering buying an annuity, make sure you carefully read the contract and see what the guaranteed rates are, how long the initial rate applies, and if a bailout provision exists. Just as important, because *the annuity is only as good as the insurance company that stands behind it*, check to see how the company is rated by Best's, Standard & Poor's, or Moody's. It's important to make sure that the insurance company itself is financially sound before buying one of its annuity products. After all, there is no FDIC or other federal agency to step in and pick up the pieces.

In Chapter 8 we provided a list of some of the stronger life insurance companies; *that same list can be used to check out the issuer of a fixed or variable annuity*. You can also do the checking yourself by referring to Best's, Standard & Poor's, or Moody's. These independent rating agencies provide quality ratings (on hundreds of insurance companies) that are much like those found in the bond market and are meant to reflect the financial strength of the firm. Letter grades are assigned on the principle that the stronger the company, the lower the risk of loss—accordingly, if security is important to you, stick with insurers that carry one of the top ratings (A++ or A+ for Best's; AAA or AA for S&P; and Aaa or Aa for Moody's); see Chapter 8 for more discussion on these insurance ratings and how they work.

CONCEPT CHECK

14-14. What is an annuity? Briefly explain how an *annuity* works, and also how it differs from a life insurance policy. Differentiate between a *single-premium annuity* and an *installment-premium annuity*.

14-15. Briefly explain the four procedures that are most widely used in the distribution of annuity proceeds. Which one results in the highest monthly payment?

14-16. Describe and differentiate among (a) an *immediate annuity*, (b) a *deferred annuity*, (c) a *straight life annuity*, and (d) a *refund annuity*.

14-17. What is a *fixed-rate annuity*, and how does it differ from a *variable annuity*? Does the type of contract (whether it's fixed or variable) have any bearing on the amount of money you'll receive at the time of distribution? Explain. Which type of contract would probably be most suitable for someone who wants a minimum amount of risk exposure? What's the purpose of a bailout provision in a fixed-rate annuity?

14-18. How do variable annuity returns compare to mutual fund returns? Can you offer any logical reasons as to why there would be any difference in comparable returns? Explain.

SUMMARY

LG1.   Recognize the importance of retirement planning and identify the three biggest pitfalls to good planning. Retirement planning plays a vital role in the personal financial planning process. It employs many of the same basic principles and concepts of effective financial planning, including the establishment of financial goals and strategies, the use of savings and investment plans, and the use of certain insurance products, like annuities. The three biggest pitfalls to sound retirement planning are starting too late, not saving enough, and investing too conservatively.

LG2.   Establish retirement goals and estimate your future income needs. Rather than address retirement planning in a series of short-run (3- to 5-year) plans, it's best to take a long-term approach and look 20 to 30 years into the future to determine how much saving and investing you must do today to achieve the retirement goals you've set for tomorrow. Implementing a long-term retirement plan involves determining future retirement needs, estimating retirement income from known sources (like social security and company pension plans), and deciding how much to save and invest each year to build up a desired nest egg.

LG3. **Explain the eligibility requirements and benefits of the social security program.** Social security forms the basic foundation for the retirement programs of most families; except for a few exempt classes (mostly government employees), almost all gainfully employed workers are covered by social security. Upon retirement, covered workers are entitled to certain monthly benefits, as determined mainly by the employee's earning history and age at retirement.

LG4. **Differentiate among the different types of basic and supplemental employer-sponsored pension plans.** Employer-sponsored pension and retirement plans provide a vital source of retirement income to many individuals. Such plans can often spell the difference between enjoying a comfortable standard of living in retirement or a bare subsistence. In *basic* retirement programs, all employees participate after a certain period of employment. These plans can be defined contribution or defined benefits plans. There are also several forms of *supplemental* employer-sponsored programs, including profit-sharing plans, thrift and savings plans, and, perhaps the most popular of all, salary reduction plans like the so-called 401(k) plans.

LG5. **Describe the various types of self-directed retirement plans.** In addition to company-sponsored retirement programs, individuals can set up their own self-directed tax-sheltered retirement plans; it is through such plans that most individuals can build up the nest eggs they will need to meet the retirement objectives they have set for themselves. The basic types of self-directed retirement programs are Keogh and SEP plans for self-employed individuals, and various forms of IRAs, which can be set up by any salary or wage earner.

LG6. **Choose the right type of annuity for your retirement plan.** Annuities are also an important source of income to retired people. Basically, an annuity is an investment vehicle that allows investment income to accumulate tax-deferred and provides for the systematic liquidation (payout) of all invested capital and earnings over an extended period of time. A wide variety of annuities exists, including single payment and installment-premium, fixed and variable, and immediate and deferred; different payout options also exist.

QUESTIONS AND PROBLEMS

1. DeShawn Thomas, a 25-year-old personal loan officer at First State Bank, understands the importance of starting early when it comes to saving for retirement. She has designated $2,000 per year for her retirement fund and assumes she will retire at age 65.
   a. How much will she have if she invests in CDs and similar money market instruments that earn 4 percent on average?
   b. How much will she have if she invests in equities instead and earns 12 percent on average?
   c. DeShawn is urging her friend, Mark Randolph, to start his plan right away, too, as he is 35. What would his nest egg amount to if he invested in the same manner as DeShawn and he, too, retires at age 65? Comment on your findings.
2. *Use Worksheet 14.1* to help Al and Linda Gonzales, who would like to retire while they are still relatively young—in about 20 years. Both have promising careers, and both make good money. As a result, they are willing to put aside whatever is necessary to achieve

a comfortable lifestyle in retirement. Their current level of household expenditures (excluding savings) is around $75,000 a year, and they expect to spend *even more* in retirement; they think they'll need about 125 percent of that amount (note: 125 percent equals a multiplier factor of 1.25). They estimate that their social security benefits will amount to $20,000 a year in today's dollars and they will receive another $35,000 annually from their company pension plans. They feel that future inflation will amount to about 3 percent a year; in addition, they think they will be able to earn about 12 percent on their investments prior to retirement and about 8 percent afterward. Use Worksheet 14.1 to find out how big their investment nest egg will have to be and how much they will have to save annually in order to accumulate the needed amount within the next 20 years.

3. Many critics of the social security program feel that participants are getting a substandard investment return on their money. Discuss why you agree or disagree with this point of view.

4. Use Exhibit 14.5 to determine the amount of social security retirement benefits that Elwood Cheeseater would receive annually if he had a high level of career earnings, is age 62, has a dependent wife (also age 62), and a part-time job that pays him $24,000 a year. If Elwood also receives another $47,500 a year from a company pension and some tax-exempt bonds that he holds, will he be liable for any tax on his social security income? Explain.

5. Diane Fein has just graduated from college and is considering job offers from two companies. Although the salary and insurance benefits are similar, the retirement programs are not. One firm offers a 401(k) plan that matches employee contributions with $.25 for every $1 contributed by the employee, up to a $10,000 limit. The other has a contributory plan that allows employees to contribute up to 10 percent of their annual salary through payroll deduction and matches it dollar for dollar. The plan vests fully after 5 years. Because Diane is unfamiliar with these plans, explain the features of each to her so she can make an informed decision.

6. John Yee is an operations manager for a large manufacturer. He earned $68,500 in 2001 and plans to contribute the maximum allowed to the firm's 401(k) plan. Assuming John is in the 28 percent tax bracket, calculate his taxable income and the amount of his tax savings. How much did it actually cost John on an after-tax basis to make this retirement plan contribution?

7. At what age would you like to retire? What type of lifestyle do you envision (for example, where do you want to live, do you want to work part-time, and so on)? Discuss the steps you think you should take to realize this goal.

8. Describe the three basic types of IRA (traditional, Roth, and nondeductible), including their respective tax features and what it takes to qualify for each. Which is most appealing to you personally? Explain.

9. Dave Jones is in his early 30s and is thinking about opening an IRA; however, he can't decide whether to open a traditional/deductible IRA or a Roth IRA, so he turns to you for help.

   a. To help you in your explanation, you decide to *run some comparative numbers on the two types of accounts*; for starters, use a 25-year period to show Dave what contributions of $2,000 per year will amount to (after 25 years), given he can earn, say, 10 percent on his money. Will the type of account he opens have any impact on this amount? Explain.

   b. Given Dave is in the 30 percent tax bracket (and will remain there for the next 25 years), determine the annual and total (over 25 years) tax savings he will enjoy from the $2,000-a-year contributions to his IRA; contrast the (annual and total) tax savings he would generate from a traditional IRA with that from a Roth IRA.

c. Now, fast-forward 25 years. Given the size of Dave's account in 25 years (as computed in part **a**), assume he takes it all out in one lump sum. If he's still in the 30 percent tax bracket, how much will he have, *after taxes*, with a traditional IRA compared with a Roth IRA? How do the taxes computed here compare with those computed in part **b**? Comment on your findings.

d. Based on the numbers you computed above, as well as any other factors, what kind of IRA would you recommend Dave set up? Explain. Would the fact that maximum contributions are scheduled to increase to $5,000 per year make any difference in your analysis? Explain.

10. Explain how the purchase of a variable annuity is much like an investment in a mutual fund. Do you, as a buyer, have any control over the amount of investment risk to which you're exposed in a variable annuity contract? Explain.

11. Briefly explain why annuities are a type of tax-sheltered investment. Is there anything you have to give up to obtain this tax-favored treatment? (Hint: age 59½)

12. Why is it important to check the financial ratings of an insurance company when buying an annuity? Why should you look at past performance when considering the purchase of a variable annuity?

APPLYING PERSONAL FINANCE

What Does Your Ideal Retirement Plan Look Like?

Wouldn't it be great if you could work at a place where your *employer* allowed you *to design your own retirement program?* Well, that is exactly what you are going to be able to do in this project. Take a few minutes to think about the types of provisions and benefits you would like to find in a *basic* employer-sponsored retirement plan. Develop an outline of your plan, being sure to give due consideration to the following issues:

1. Would the plan be contributory or noncontributory?
2. Stated as a *percent* of your base salary, how much would be put into your retirement plan each year? (Be realistic.)
3. Eligibility and vesting provisions?
4. Portability—if so, how much?
5. Retirement age; provisions for early retirement?
6. Defined contributions or benefits?
7. Would the plan be qualified?
8. Would you want a voluntary supplemental plan as part of your program? If you could have only one supplemental plan, what would it be?

Provide a brief discussion/summary of the features of your plan; note any disadvantages. (As an aside, you might want to hold on to your ideal retirement plan to see how the retirement program at the company where you now work—or at the job you land after graduation—stacks up against this wish list of yours.)

CONTEMPORARY CASE APPLICATIONS

14.1   Comparing Pension Plan Features: Which Plan Is Best?

Mary Maloney and Ellen Saperstein are neighbors in Kansas City. Mary works as a systems engineer for United Foods Corporation, Topeka Foods Division, while Ellen works as an executive assistant for U.S. Steel and Castings. Both are married, have two children, and are well paid. Before Mary and Ellen joined their respective companies, there had been some employee unrest and strikes. To counteract these problems, their firms had developed job enrichment and employee motivation programs. Of particular interest are the portions of these programs that deal with pensions and retirement.

Topeka Foods has a contributory plan under which 5 percent of the employees' annual wages is deducted to meet the cost of the benefits. An amount equal to the employee contribution is also contributed by the company. The plan uses a 7-year graded vesting procedure; it has a normal retirement age of 60 for all employees and the benefits at retirement are paid according to a defined contribution plan.

Although *U.S. Steel and Castings* has a minimum retirement age of 60, it provides an extension period of 5 to 6 years before compulsory retirement. Employees (full-time, hourly, or salaried) must meet participation requirements. Further, in contrast to the Topeka plan, the U.S. Steel and Castings program has a noncontributory feature. Annual retirement benefits are computed according to the following formula: 2 percent of the employee's final annual salary for each year of service with the company is paid upon retirement. The plan vests immediately.

Questions

1. Discuss the basic features of the retirement plans offered by Topeka Foods and U.S. Steel and Castings.
2. Which plan do you think is more desirable considering the basic features, retirement age, and benefit computations, as explained?
3. Explain how you would use each of these plans in developing your own retirement program.
4. What role, if any, could the purchase of annuities play in these retirement programs? Discuss the pros and cons of using annuities as a part of retirement planning.

14.2   Evaluating Millie Wilson's Retirement Prospects

Millie Wilson is 57 years old and has been widowed for 13 years. Never remarried, she has worked full-time since her husband died—in addition to raising her two children, the youngest of whom is now finishing college. Forced back to work in her 40s, her first job was in a fast-food restaurant. Eventually, she upgraded her skills sufficiently to obtain a supervisory position in the personnel department of a major corporation, where she is now earning $58,000 a year.

Although her financial focus for the past 13 years has, by necessity, been on meeting living expenses and getting her kids through college, she feels she can now turn her attention to her retirement needs. Actually, Millie hasn't done too badly in that area either. Due to some shrewd investing of the proceeds from her husband's life insurance policy, Millie has accumulated the following investment assets:

Money market securities, stocks, and bonds	$72,600
IRA and 401(k) plans	$47,400

Other than the mortgage on her condo, the only other debt she has is $7,000 in college loans.

Millie would like to retire in 8 years and recently hired a financial planner to help her come up with an effective retirement program. He has estimated that for her to live comfortably in retirement, she'll need about $37,500 a year (in today's dollars) in retirement income.

Questions
1. Use **Exhibit 14.5** to estimate the amount of annual income Millie can expect from social security.
2. After taking into account the income she'll receive from social security and her company-sponsored pension plan, the financial planner has estimated that Millie's investment assets will have to provide her with about $15,000 a year to meet the balance of her retirement income needs. Assuming a 6 percent *after-tax* return on her investments, how big of a nest egg will she need to earn that kind of income?
3. Given she can invest the money market securities, stocks, and bonds (the $72,600) at 5 percent after taxes, and the amount she's presently accumulated in her tax-sheltered IRA and 401(k)—the $47,400—at 9 percent, how much will her investment assets be worth in 8 years, when she retires?
4. Millie's employer matches her 401(k) contributions dollar for dollar, up to a maximum of $3,000 a year. If she continues to put $3,000 a year into that program, how much more will she have in 8 years, given a 9 percent rate of return?
5. What would you advise Millie about her ability to retire in eight years, as she hopes to?

MONEY ONLINE

RETIRE IN STYLE!

Note: Web addresses change frequently, so you may need to determine the home page and do a site search to find the page or topic that's referenced.

1. **www.quicken.com/retirement**
   How much will you need to retire? Find out by using Quicken's Retirement Tool, "Build a Retirement Plan." While you're there, look under "Retirement Basics" to learn more about a 401k, IRA, Pension Plan, 403b, or Keogh.

2. **www.financenter.com**
   Plan for your retirement. Click on "Calculate" and scroll down to Retirement Calculators to find a myriad of FinanCenter calculators to help you answer such questions as—what will my expenses be after I retire, am I saving enough, how much effect can inflation have, and which savings should be used first?

3. **www.ssa.gov**
   What are the latest issues concerning Social Security? Find out at the Web site of the Social Security Administration. While you're there, learn about the services they provide for businesses, read up on Social Security laws and regulations, or report Social Security fraud. Click on "Other Sites" for links to other government Web sites of interest.

4. **www.quicken.com/retirement**
   Do you qualify for a Roth IRA? Use Quicken's Retirement Tool, "Choose the Right IRA," to find out. Also use their planner to answer questions such as which IRA option is best for you, how much will your contributions grow by retirement, what income can you expect from an IRA during retirement or should you roll over or convert your traditional IRA to a Roth?

5. **www.money.com/money/magazine/annuities**
   Are variable annuities right for you? Understand the features and complexities of these confusing investments *before* you buy one! Read through Money Magazine's educational information and then click on "Annuity Finder" to filter through the offerings.

6. **smartmoney.com/pf**
   Should you borrow from your 401k? Scroll down to Personal Finance Worksheets, click on "Should I Borrow from my 401(k)" and work through SmartMoney's Debt Management Worksheet to determine the best solution for you.

7. **www.pbgc.gov**
   What happens when a pension plan runs out of money? Learn the role of the Pension Benefit Guaranty Corporation in protecting defined benefit plans. Click on "Pension Search" to find names of people owed unclaimed benefits from pension plans that were closed.

8. **personal100.fidelity.com/retirement**
   Set up a retirement plan of your own if you're self-employed or own a small business. Fidelity's Retirement Investing Center will help you plan for your retirement, whether you're investing on your own or through an employer-sponsored plan

9. **personal.vanguard.com**
   Tap into Vanguard's wealth of investor educational material. Click on "Education, Planning & Advice" and scroll down to the Education Center to find topics such as the Basics of Asset Allocation, Your Core Investment Options, Retirement Planning Basics, and Types of Retirement Savings Plans. Use their Site Glossary to learn definitions of investment terms or find interactive resources and financial counselors

to help you with Financial Planning Solutions. Not to be missed is their comprehensive one-stop "Retirement Resource Center" for retirement education and planning.

Just for Fun!
10. **www.lib.lsu.edu/gov/fedgov.html**

   Ever wonder how to find or contact a federal agency? Consult the U.S. Federal Government Agencies Directory compiled by the Louisiana State University Libraries and find links to federal agencies on the Internet. Pull up sites belonging to the White House, the United States Supreme Court, the U.S. Senate, or House of Representatives. Search by Keyword to find the agency of your choice.

Chapter 15

Preserving Your Estate

LEARNING GOALS

LG1. Describe the role of estate planning in personal financial planning and identify the seven steps involved in the process.

LG2. Recognize the importance of preparing a will and other documents to protect you and your estate.

LG3. Explain how trusts are used in estate planning.

LG4. Determine whether a gift will be taxable and use planned gifts to reduce estate taxes.

LG5. Calculate federal and state taxes due on an estate.

LG6. Use effective estate-planning techniques to minimize estate taxes.

The Dreaded Phone Call

When the phone rang at 4 A.M., Carolyn Robbins knew immediately that it was bad news. Her 60-year-old dad Frederick had suffered massive injuries in a traffic accident and was in a coma. The doctors did not know if he would recover. Her stepmother was devastated, as she and Carolyn's dad had been married only 1 year. Carolyn flew from Los Angeles to Chicago to be with her brother at her father's bedside and to see what steps they needed to take next.

Like so many families, Carolyn's found it very hard to discuss money matters, and talking about wills and dying was even worse. Her stepmother said that the newlyweds had been meaning to revise their wills and prepare living wills and durable powers of attorney for health care but hadn't yet gotten around to them. Now they did not know what, if any, life-sustaining measures he would want taken. Fortunately—or unfortunately as the case may be—they did not have to make educated guesses as to his wishes because he died 2 days later without regaining consciousness.

Until they contacted his lawyer and found out where Frederick kept all his important papers, they were unsure how to proceed with funeral arrangements. His will named Carolyn as his executor, but he had never discussed this with her, and her older brother was upset that he was not chosen. When they found his life insurance policy, they got another surprise. He had never changed the beneficiary of his life insurance policy when he remarried, so his ex-wife was still named and would receive the proceeds.

Her dad's poor planning made Carolyn realize that no matter what your age, you need an estate plan that includes an up-to-date will. In this chapter you will learn how to protect your assets through estate planning.

■ Principles of Estate Planning [LG1]

Like it or not, no one lives forever. Although this thought may depress you, safeguarding the future of the people you care about most is one of the most important aspects of financial planning. Unless you develop plans and take steps during your lifetime to accumulate, preserve, and distribute your wealth on your death, chances are that your heirs and beneficiaries will receive only part of your estate. The rest will go (often unnecessarily) to taxes and various administrative costs. This process, called *estate planning*, requires knowledge of wills, trusts, and taxes.

Understanding these components and their interrelationships will help you minimize estate shrinkage after your death, while still achieving your lifetime personal financial goals. Also, keep in mind that not only wealthy people but also individuals of modest or moderate means need to plan their estates. Those who start saving for retirement early are likely to have sizable retirement accounts. Without proper planning, taxes could consume much of what is left in those accounts after your death.

Estate planning is the process of developing a plan to administer and distribute your assets on death in a manner consistent with your wishes and the needs of your survivors, while minimizing taxes. This process helps people accumulate enough capital to meet

estate planning
The process of developing a plan to administer and distribute your assets on death in a manner consistent with your wishes and the needs of your survivors, while minimizing taxes

college education costs and other special needs; provide financial security for family members in event of the death of the head of household; take care of oneself and one's family during a long-term disability; and provide for a comfortable retirement. However, estate planning goes beyond financial issues. It also includes plans to manage your affairs if you become disabled and a statement of your personal wishes for medical care should you become unable to make them yourself.

As with other financial planning activities, one of the major objectives of estate planning is to eliminate or minimize tax exposure. Doing so, of course, will increase the amount of your estate that ultimately will be passed on to your heirs and beneficiaries. Estate planning is closely related to insurance and retirement planning. Certainly the most important reason for buying life insurance is to provide for your family in the event of your premature death. Likewise, one of the principal challenges of effective retirement planning is to achieve a comfortable standard of living in retirement while preserving as much of your accumulated wealth as possible. This not only reduces the chances of you (or your spouse) outliving your financial resources, but also leaves money for your estate that can be passed on to your heirs and designated beneficiaries in accordance with your wishes.

Planning occurs in every estate. The estate owner and his or her professional counselors control some planning, and federal and state governments may control other planning. Planning not under the estate owner's control occurs when the estate owner forfeits the right to arrange for the disposition of assets and the minimization of tax and other estate settlement costs. Individuals who wish to plan their estates must systematically uncover problems in a number of important areas and provide solutions for them. Exhibit 15.1 lists the major types of problems and their associated causes or indicators. Techniques to avoid or minimize these problems are discussed in later sections.

WHO NEEDS ESTATE PLANNING?

Estate planning should be part of everyone's financial plan, whether you are married or single, have five children or none. For example, married couples who own many assets jointly and have designated beneficiaries for assets such as retirement funds and life insurance policies may think they don't need wills. However, a will covers many other important details, such as naming an executor to administer your estate and a guardian for your children, clarifying how estate taxes will be paid, and distributing property that doesn't go directly to a joint owner.

Partners who are not married and single persons will discover that estate planning is especially important, particularly if they own a home or other assets they want to leave to specific individuals or to charity. Unmarried couples need to put extra effort into their estate plans. They may need to make special arrangements to be sure they can indeed leave assets to a partner.

The two main areas of estate planning are *people planning* and *asset planning*.

PEOPLE PLANNING. *People planning* means anticipating the psychological and financial needs of those people and organizations you love and providing enough income or capital or both to ensure a continuation of their way of life. People planning also means keeping Mother's cameo brooch in the family and out of the pawnshop, or preserving the business that Granddad started in the early 1900s. People planning is especially important to those individuals with children who are minors; children who are exceptionally artistic or intellectually gifted; children or other dependents who are emotionally, mentally, or physically handicapped; and spouses who cannot or do not want to handle money, securities, or a business.

EXHIBIT 15.1

POTENTIAL ESTATE-PLANNING PROBLEMS AND MAJOR CAUSES OR INDICATORS

Careful estate planning can prevent many problems that arise during the settlement of an estate. The first step toward preventing problems is an awareness and understanding of their major causes or indicators.

Problem	Major Cause or Indicator
• Excessive transfer costs	Taxes and estate administrative expenses higher than necessary.
• Lack of liquidity	Insufficient cash. Not enough assets that are quickly and inexpensively convertible to cash within a short period of time to meet tax demands and other costs.
• Improper disposition of assets	Beneficiaries receive the wrong asset or the proper asset in the wrong manner or at the wrong time.
• Inadequate income at retirement	Capital insufficient or not readily convertible to income-producing status.
• Inadequate income, if disabled	High medical costs, capital insufficient or not readily convertible to income-producing status, difficulty in reducing living standards.
• Inadequate income for family at estate owner's death	Any of the above causes.
• Insufficient capital	Excessive taxes, inflation, improper investment planning.
• Special problems	A family member with a serious illness or physical or emotional problem, children of a prior marriage, beneficiaries who have extraordinary medical or financial needs, beneficiaries who can't agree on how to handle various estate matters, business problems or opportunities.

Minor children cannot legally handle large sums of money or deal directly with real estate or securities. Custodial accounts, guardianships, or trusts will provide administration, security, financial advice, and the legal capacity to act on behalf of minors. Few children are exceptionally artistic or intellectually gifted, but those who are often need—or should have—special (and often expensive) schooling, travel opportunities, or equipment. Emotionally, mentally, or physically handicapped children (and other relatives) may need nursing, medical, or psychiatric care. Clearly, outright gifts of money or property to those who cannot care for themselves are foolishly inappropriate. These individuals may need more (or less) than other children. An individual who gives all of his or her children equal shares may not be giving them equitable shares.

How many of us have handled hundreds of thousands of dollars? Think of the burden we place on others when we expect a spouse who cannot—or does not want to—handle such large sums of money or securities to do so. This is particularly burdensome when the assets being handled are his or her only assets. Engaging in people planning demonstrates a high degree of caring. People planning also involves talking about estate planning with your loved ones, as the *Money in Action* box on page 654 explains.

ASSET PLANNING. From the standpoint of wealth alone, estate planning is essential for anyone—single, widowed, married, or divorced—with an estate exceeding the "exclusion

MONEY IN ACTION

Having "The Talk"—the Adult Version

Remember when your parents sat you down to have "The Talk?" Now you should do the same with them, talking about topics that are just as hard to discuss as sex: money, their wills, and other estate-planning matters. Even though most parents plan to leave assets to their heirs, the American Association of Retired Persons (AARP) reports that almost two-thirds have not discussed end-of-life issues with family members. "When you put money, love, and death together, it's like a triple whammy," says Olivia Mellan, a Washington psychotherapist.

It is in your parents' best interests to talk about these issues. When children have no idea of their parents' wishes, handling an estate becomes a tremendous emotional and financial burden. Not only have they lost a parent, but they have the additional tasks of paying immediate expenses and trying to guess what the parent wanted.

Your parents may be uncomfortable when you bring up money, illness, and death. You can use an article, book, or an event in your own or their life to start a discussion. "Everyone knows a horror story of someone who felt guilty because they didn't know what to do," says Jim Towey, president of Aging with Dignity in Tallahassee, Florida. That provides the opening to say, "I don't want to be like that family." You can also tell them about your own estate plans: "We're thinking of rewriting our will and would like your advice." Parents love to be consulted, and they may then share their own plans. If not, you will have to take a direct approach, as Towey suggests: "Mom, Dad, I love you, and I want to be there when you need me, and I'd like to know what you want. I don't want to have to guess."

Your discussions should cover the following areas:

1. *Where do they keep their important documents?* You need to locate birth and marriage certificates, the names of financial and legal advisers, insurance policies, lists of bank accounts and investments, and a letter of last instructions.

2. *Will they have enough money to live on?* This is especially difficult to discuss but very important now that people are living longer. They may have a retirement or assisted care facility they like, or have set aside funds for in-home care. Do they have long-term care insurance to cover nursing home or in-home care?

3. *Do they have a durable power of attorney?* This gives someone appointed by the parents access to their bank accounts to pay bills in case they become incapacitated. Keep the originals at home and put copies of these documents in the safe-deposit box.

4. *Have they each prepared a health-care proxy or living will?* This sets forth decisions on the kind of care and life-prolonging procedures the parent prefers in event of hospitalization.

5. *Have they written wills or established any trusts?* Where can you find these documents?

6. *What are their wishes with regard to funeral and burial arrangements?*

Encourage your parents to share their intentions and the facts. What may be clear to them while they are writing their wills may not be so apparent to the heirs. For example, leaving different amounts to children without explaining why often leads to anger and can destroy relationships between siblings. "Sitting down and talking openly makes a family feel like they're on the same team," says David Gage, a clinical psychologist specializing in estate-planning dispute mediation.

Sources: Kathleen Adams, "Balancing Tact and Tactics," *Time*, May 15, 2000, p. F2; "Don't Keep Your Estate Plans a Secret," *Kiplinger's Retirement Report*, January 2000, downloaded from **www.kiplinger.com/retreport**; Robert Frick, "Talking to Your Parents About Money," *Kiplinger's Personal Finance*, August 1999, downloaded from **www.kiplinger.com**; and "Take Your Estate Plan for a Test Drive," *Kiplinger's Retirement Report*, August 2000, downloaded from **www.kiplinger.com/retreport**.

amount," which is $1,000,000 in 2002 and increases in steps until it reaches $3,500,000 in 2009. Note that the 2001 Tax Act provides for the complete repeal of the estate tax in 2010. When an estate involves a closely held business, estate planning is essential to stabilize and maximize its asset and income-producing values, both during the owner's lifetime and at the owner's death or disability. Likewise, estate planning is essential to avoid the special problems that occur when an estate owner holds title to property in more than one state; these problems include incurring attorneys' fees in each state and being taxed on the same assets by more than one state.

The estate-planning process gets more complicated if you are part of a blended family or have special requests. With careful planning you can be sure that your assets go to the desired beneficiaries.

 Deloitte & Touche's *Checklist for Use When a Loved One Dies* (**www.dtonline.com/estate/checklist.htm**) is a comprehensive guide to help you get through this difficult time, from making funeral arrangements and organizing financial matters to getting emotional support.

WHY DOES AN ESTATE BREAK UP?

Quite often, when people die, their estates die with them—not because they have done anything wrong but because they have not done anything. There are numerous forces that, if unchecked, tend to shrink an estate, reduce the usefulness of its assets, and frustrate the objectives of the person who built it. These include death-related costs, inflation, lack of liquidity, improper use of vehicles of transfer, and disabilities.

1. **Death-Related Costs.** When someone dies, the estate incurs certain types of death-related costs. For example, medical bills relating to a final illness and funeral expenses are good examples of *first-level death-related costs. Second-level death-related costs* consist of the fees of attorneys, appraisers, and accountants along with probate expenses—so-called administrative costs, federal estate taxes, and state death taxes (some states have both inheritance and estate taxes). Most people also die with some current bills unpaid, outstanding long-term obligations (such as mortgages, business loans, and installment contracts), and unpaid income taxes and property taxes.

2. **Inflation.** Death-related costs are only the tip of the estate-impairment iceberg. Failure to continuously reappraise and rearrange an estate plan to counter the effects of inflation can impair the ability of assets—liquid, real, and personal property and investments—to provide steady and adequate levels of financial security.

3. **Lack of Liquidity.** Insufficient cash to cover death costs and other estate obligations has always been a major factor in estate impairment. Sale of the choicest parcel of farmland or a business that has been in the family for generations, for instance, often has undesirable psychological effects on the heirs. The outcome can be a devastating financial and emotional blow.

4. **Improper Use of Vehicles of Transfer.** Assets are often put into the hands of beneficiaries who are unwilling or unable to handle them. Improper use of vehicles of transfer may pass property to unintended beneficiaries or to the proper beneficiaries in an improper manner or at an incorrect time. For example, spendthrift spouses or minors may be left large sums of money outright in the form of life insurance, through joint ownership of a savings account, or as the beneficiaries of an employee fringe benefit plan.

5. **Disabilities.** A prolonged and expensive disability of a family wage earner is often called a *living death.* Loss of income due to disability is often coupled with a massive financial drain caused by the illness itself. The financial situation is further complicated by inadequate management of currently owned assets. This not only threatens the family's financial security but also diminishes the value of the estate at an incredible speed.

WHAT IS YOUR ESTATE?

Your estate is your property—whatever you own. Your **probate estate** consists of the real and personal property you own in your own name that can be transferred at death according

probate estate
The real and personal property owned by a person that is transferred at death according to the terms of a will, or under intestate laws in the absence of a valid will.

EXHIBIT 15.2

STEPS IN THE ESTATE-PLANNING PROCESS

The estate-planning process consists of seven important steps listed below in the sequence they would be performed.

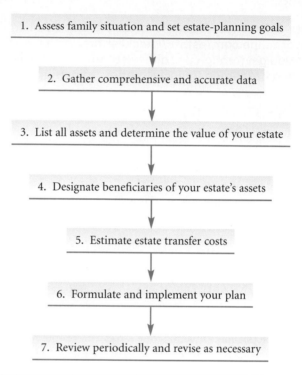

1. Assess family situation and set estate-planning goals

2. Gather comprehensive and accurate data

3. List all assets and determine the value of your estate

4. Designate beneficiaries of your estate's assets

5. Estimate estate transfer costs

6. Formulate and implement your plan

7. Review periodically and revise as necessary

gross estate
All property—both probate and non-probate—subject to federal estate taxes at a person's death.

to the terms of a will, or under intestate laws if you have no valid will. The probate estate is distinct from the gross estate (a tax law term that may encompass a considerably larger amount of property). Your **gross estate** includes all the property—both probate and nonprobate—subject to federal estate taxes at your death. Life insurance, jointly held property with rights of survivorship, and property passing under certain employee benefit plans are common examples of nonprobate assets that might be subject to federal (and state) estate taxes.

In addition, you may provide for property that is not probate property and will not be part of your estate for federal estate tax purposes yet will pass to your family and form part of their financial security program. There are two types of such assets. One is *properly arranged* life insurance. For instance, you could give assets to your daughter to allow her to purchase, pay the premiums for, and be the beneficiary of a policy on your life. At your death, the proceeds would not be included as part of your estate. The other type of financial asset that falls into this category is *Social Security*. Social Security payments to a surviving spouse and minor children generally are neither probate assets nor subject to any federal (or state) estate taxes. Because of the freedom from administrative costs and taxes, this category of assets provides unique and substantial estate-planning opportunities.

 The sample estate plan outlined at Castleman Law Firm's site, **www.castlelaw.com/samplan.htm**, provides a good overview of what an estate plan should contain.

 **EXHIBIT 15.3**

FACTUAL DATA REQUIRED IN ESTATE PLANNING

The second step in developing an effective estate plan is to gather comprehensive and accurate data on all aspects of the family. The types of factual data required by professionals are listed below.

Personal data:	Names, addresses, phone numbers, family consultants Family birth dates, occupations, health problems, support needs Citizenship, marital status, marital agreements, wills, trusts, custodianships, trust beneficiary, gifts or inheritances, Social Security numbers, education, and military service
Property (except life insurance or business):	Classification, title, indebtedness, basis, date and or manner of acquisition, value of marketable securities, and location
Life insurance:	Name of the insured, kind of policies, amounts, insurance company, agents' names and addresses
Health insurance:	Medical expense insurance: insurance company, policy benefits Disability income
Business interest:	Name, address, ownership Valuation factors: desired survivorship control; name, address, and phone number of business attorney and accountant
Employee benefits:	Group insurance plans, pension benefits
Family income:	Income of client, spouse, dependent children, income tax information
Family finances:	Budget information, investment preferences Ranking of economic objectives, capital needs, other objectives
Income and capital needs:	Retirement: planned retirement age, required amount, potential sources Disability: required amount, sources Death: expected sources of income
Liabilities:	Classification of liabilities, creditors, amounts, whether insured or secured
Factors affecting plan:	Gift propensity, charitable inclinations, emotional maturity of children, basic desires for estate distribution
Authorization for information:	Life insurance
Receipt for documents:	Personal and business

Source: Copyright © 1995 by The American College, Bryn Mawr, PA. Adapted from Confidential Personal and Financial Data form, Advanced Estate Planning Course. All rights reserved.

THE ESTATE-PLANNING PROCESS

The estate-planning process consists of seven important steps, as summarized in Exhibit 15.2. First, you must assess your family situation, evaluating its strengths and weaknesses, and set estate-planning goals. Next, gather comprehensive and accurate data on all aspects of the family. Exhibit 15.3 summarizes the data professionals require to prepare detailed estate plans. Most professional estate planners provide forms to help their clients compile this information. Then you should take inventory and determine the value of your estate. Then you must designate beneficiaries of your estate's assets, estimate estate transfer costs, and formulate and implement your plan. The final step is ongoing: review your estate plan every 3 years and revise it as circumstances dictate. Key events that should also trigger a review include the death or disability of a spouse or family member, moving to another state, changing jobs, getting married or divorced, having children, or acquiring new assets.

The objective of estate plans, of course, is to maximize the usefulness of people's assets during their lives and to achieve their personal objectives after their deaths. Once the plan has been implemented, however, you must reevaluate it on a regular basis. An estate plan is good only as long as it fits the needs, desires, and circumstances of the parties involved. As these elements change, you must modify your estate plan. Marriage or remarriage, divorce, the birth of a child, a change of job or location, and substantial changes in income, health, or living standards are the types of events that indicate a need for a review. Even if none of these occur, you should automatically review life insurance needs at least once every 2 years and perform a full estate audit at least once every 3 to 5 years (or whenever there has been a major change in the federal or state death-tax laws). Because of the general complexity of the laws relating to estate transfer, the assistance of estate planners, life insurance professionals, Certified Financial Planners (CFPs), Chartered Financial Consultants (ChFCs), accountants, and attorneys is often necessary in the planning and evaluation process. Due to the individual nature of estate planning, we cannot include more-specific guidelines in this chapter.

CONCEPT CHECK

> 15-1. Discuss the importance and goals of estate planning. Explain why estates often break up. Distinguish between the *probate estate* and the *gross estate*.
> 15-2. Briefly describe the steps involved in the estate-planning process.

◼ Wills [LG2]

will
A written and legally enforceable document that expresses how a person's property should be distributed on his or her death. It is also used to nominate an executor to manage the estate and guardians to care for minor children.

A **will** is a written, legally enforceable expression or declaration of a person's wishes concerning the disposition of his or her property on death. Unfortunately, about half of all Americans do not have wills. The importance of a valid will can be illustrated by looking at what happens when a person dies without one.

ABSENCE OF A VALID WILL: INTESTACY

intestacy
The situation that exists when a person dies without a valid will.

Intestacy describes the situation that exists when a person dies without a valid will. State intestacy laws "draw the will the decedent failed to make" to determine the disposition of the probate property of persons who have died intestate. These statutes enumerate certain preferred classes of survivors. Generally, the decedent's spouse is favored, followed by the children and then other offspring. If the spouse and children or other offspring, such as grandchildren or great-grandchildren, survive, they will divide the estate, and other relatives will receive nothing. If no spouse, children, or other offspring survive, the deceased's parents, brothers, and sisters will receive a share of the estate.

Let's use a simple example to illustrate the disposition of a typical intestate estate. Assume an individual died without a valid will. After paying debts and taxes and deducting state-defined family exemptions, that individual's separately owned property would be distributed as shown in Exhibit 15.4. If the deceased left no spouse, child, parent, sibling, grandparent, uncle, aunt, or offspring of any of the above, the state normally would take all of the property. Where property goes to the state due to the absence of a will, the property is said to *escheat to the state*. If a person without relatives dies with a valid will, his or her property will probably go to friends or to charity, rather than to the state.

EXHIBIT 15.4

DISTRIBUTION OF A TYPICAL INTESTATE ESTATE

If a person dies intestate (without a valid will), the estate will be distributed according to established state laws of intestate succession. The summary that follows is based on Utah's probate code.

Survivors	Distribution*
Spouse and offspring—children, grandchildren, etc.—not of the surviving spouse	50% to surviving spouse and other 50% to decedent's offspring by right of representation
Spouse and no offspring or decedent's offspring all by the surviving spouse	100% to surviving spouse
No spouse but offspring	Offspring by right of representation
No spouse and no offspring, but parent(s)	To parent or parents equally
No spouse, no offspring, no parents, but offspring of parents	To parents' offspring by right of representation
No spouse, no offspring, no parents, and no offspring of parents, but grandparents or offspring of grandparents	Divided half to maternal grandparents (or their offspring, if neither survive) and half to the paternal grandparents (or their offspring, if neither survive). If one side predeceased and there are no offspring, the other side takes all.
None of the above	Closest kin in equal degree; if none, reverts to the state (i.e., decedent's state is the last in line to inherit).

*Because intestate laws vary from state to state, the actual distribution of assets may differ from what is shown here.

Aside from having lost control of the disposition of the property, the person who dies intestate also forfeits the privileges of naming a personal representative to guide the disposition of the estate, naming a guardian for persons and property, and specifying which beneficiaries would bear certain tax burdens. In addition, estate planning and a valid will may minimize the amount of estate shrinkage through transfer taxes. Having a valid will—regardless of the size of an estate—is a critical element in the personal financial planning process.

LifeNet's (**www.lifenet.com**) estate-planning section explains the differences among various types of wills. It also has a calculator to help you estimate estate size, taxes, and probate costs.

PREPARING THE WILL

A will allows a person, called a **testator,** to direct the disposition of property at his or her death. The testator can change or revoke a will at any time prior to his or her death. On the death of the testator, the will becomes operative.

Will preparation, or drafting, varies with respect to difficulty and cost depending on individual circumstances. In some cases a two-page will costing $150 may be adequate although in others a complex document costing $1,500 or more may be necessary. A will must not only effectively accomplish the objectives specified for distributing assets, but it must also take into consideration income, gift, and estate tax laws. Will preparation also requires a knowledge of corporate, trust, real estate, and securities laws. Note that a will, important as it is, may be ineffective or misstate the testator's estate plan if it does not consider and coordinate assets passing outside its limits.

testator
A person whose will directs the disposition of property at his or her death.

INFORMATION REQUIREMENTS. A properly prepared will should meet three important requirements. It should:

- provide a plan for distributing the testator's assets in accordance with his or her wishes, the beneficiaries' needs, and federal and state dispositive and tax laws,
- consider the changes in family circumstances that might occur after its execution, and
- be unambiguous and complete in describing the testator's desires.

By following these general guidelines, the testator generally can develop a satisfactory will.

USE OF AN ATTORNEY. *Will drafting, no matter how modest the size of the estate, should not be attempted by a layperson.* The complexity and interrelationships of tax, property, domestic relations, and other laws make the homemade will a potentially dangerous document. Nowhere is the old adage, "He who has himself for his attorney has a fool for a client," more true, and few things may turn out more disastrous in the long run than the do-it-yourself will.

 For a "Crash Course in Wills and Trusts" and general estate-planning advice, visit the award-winning site of Michael T. Palermo, an attorney and CFP, at **www.mtpalermo.com**.

COMMON FEATURES OF THE WILL

Although there is no absolute format that must be followed when preparing a will, most wills contain eight distinct sections: (1) introductory clause, (2) direction of payments, (3) disposition of property, (4) appointment clause, (5) tax clause, (6) simultaneous death clause, (7) execution and attestation clause, and (8) witness clause. Exhibit 15.5, which presents the will of John Steven Fabian, includes generalized examples of each of these clauses. Refer to the exhibit as you read the following descriptions of the clauses. *These clauses must be tailored to individual needs and circumstances by an attorney familiar with the testator's situation.*

- **Introductory Clause.** An introductory clause, or preamble, normally states the testator's name and residence; this determines the county that will have legal jurisdiction and be considered the testator's domicile for tax purposes. The revocation statement nullifies old and forgotten wills and *codicils*—legally binding modifications of an existing will.
- **Direction of Payments.** This clause directs the estate to make certain payments of expenses. As a general rule, however, the rights of creditors are protected by law and such a clause is largely useless.
- **Disposition of Property.** Fabian's will has three examples of clauses dealing with disposition of property. The first disposes of personal effects. A testator may make a separate detailed and specific list of personal property and carefully identify each item, and to whom it is given, as an informal guide to help the executor divide the property. This list generally should not appear in the will itself because it is likely to change often. The second type of clause passes money to a specifically named party. (Be sure to use the correct legal title of a charity.) The third clause describes the distribution of residual assets after specific gifts have been made. Bequests to close relatives (as defined in the statute) who die before the testator will go to the relative's heirs unless the will includes other directions. Bequests to nonrelatives who predecease the testator will go to the other residual beneficiaries.

EXHIBIT 15.5

A REPRESENTATIVE WILL FOR JOHN STEVEN FABIAN

John Steven Fabian's will illustrates the eight distinct sections of most wills.

The Last Will and Testament of John Steven Fabian

Section 1 — Introductory Clause

I, John Steven Fabian, of the city of Chicago, state of Illinois, do, hereby make my last will and revoke all wills and codicils made prior to this will.

Section 2 — Direction of Payments

Article 1: Payment of Debts and Expenses

I direct payment out of my estate of all just debts and the expenses of my last illness and funeral.

Section 3 — Disposition of Property

Article 2: Disposition of Property

I give and bequeath to my wife, Sally Warren Fabian, all my jewelry, automobiles, books, and photography equipment, as well as all other articles of personal and household use.

I give to the Chicago Historical Society the sum of $100,000.

All the rest, residue, and remainder of my estate, real and personal, wherever located, I give in equal one-half shares to my children, Charles Elliot and Lara Sue, their heirs and assigns forever.

Section 4 — Appointment Clause

Article 3: Nomination of Executor and Guardian

I hereby nominate as the Executor of this Will my beloved wife, Sally Warren Fabian, but if she is unable or unwilling to serve then I nominate my brother, Winston James Fabian. In the event both persons named predecease me, or shall cease or fail to act, then I nominate as Executor in the place of said persons, the Northern Trust Bank of Chicago, Illinois.

If my wife does not survive me, I appoint my brother, Eugene Lawrence Fabian, Guardian of the person and property of my son, Charles Elliot, during his minority.

Section 5 — Tax Clause

Article 4: Payment of Taxes

I direct that there shall be paid out of my residuary estate (from that portion which does not qualify for the marital deduction) all estate, inheritance, and similar taxes imposed by a government in respect to property includable in my estate for tax purposes, whether the property passes under this will or otherwise.

Section 6 — Simultaneous Death Clause

Article 5: Simultaneous Death

If my wife and I shall die under such circumstances that there is not sufficient evidence to determine the order of our deaths, then it shall be presumed that she survived me. My estate shall be administered and distributed in all respects in accordance with such assumption.

Section 7 — Execution and Attestation Clause

In witness thereof, I have affixed my signature to this, my last will and testament, which consists of five (5) pages, each of which I have initialed, this 15th day of September, 2002.

John Steven Fabian

Section 8 — Witness Clause

Signed, sealed, and published by John Steven Fabian, the testator, as his last will, in the presence of us, who, at his request, and in the presence of each other, all being present at the same time, have written our names as witnesses.

(*Note:* Normally the witness signatures and addresses would follow this clause.)

- **Appointment Clause.** Appointment clauses name the *executors* (the decedent's personal representatives who administer the estate), guardians for minor children, and trustees and their successors:
- **Tax Clause.** In the absence of a specified provision in the will, so-called *apportionment statutes* of the testator's state will allocate the burden of taxes among the beneficiaries. The result may be an inappropriate and unintended reduction of certain beneficiaries' shares or adverse estate tax effects. Earlier statutes tended to charge death taxes on the residual of the estate, but today the trend is toward statutes that charge each beneficiary based on his or her share of the taxable estate. Because the spouse's share and the portion going to a charity are deducted from the gross estate before arriving at the taxable estate, neither is charged with taxes.
- **Simultaneous Death Clause.** This clause describes what happens in event of simultaneous death. The assumption that the spouse survives is used mainly to permit the marital deduction, which offers a tax advantage. Other types of clauses are similarly designed to avoid double probate of the same assets—duplication of administrative and probate costs. Such clauses require that the survivor live for a certain period, such as 30 or 60 days, to be a beneficiary under the will.
- **Execution and Attestation Clause.** Every will should be in writing and signed by the testator at its end as a precaution against fraud. Many attorneys suggest that the testator also initial each page after the last line or sign in a corner of each page.
- **Witness Clause.** The final clause helps to affirm that the will in question is really that of the deceased. All states require two witnesses to the testator's signing of the will, with the exception of Vermont, which requires three. Most states require witnesses to sign in the presence of one another, after they witness the signing by the testator. Their addresses should be noted on the will. If the testator is unable to sign his or her name for any reason, most states allow the testator to make a mark and to have another person (properly witnessed) sign for him or her.

REQUIREMENTS OF A VALID WILL

To be valid, a will must be the product of a person with a sound mind; there must have been no *undue influence* (influence that would remove the testator's freedom of choice); the will itself must have been properly executed; and its execution must be free from fraud.

1. **Mental Capacity:** You must be of "sound mind" to make a valid will. This means that you:
   (1) know what a will is and are aware that you are making and signing one,
   (2) understand your relationship with persons whom you would normally provide for, such as a spouse or children,
   (3) understand what you own, and
   (4) are able to decide how to distribute your property and have knowledge of the persons who would generally be expected to receive the estate (even though the testator is not required to leave anything to them). Generally, such capacity is presumed.
   Setting aside a will requires clear and convincing proof of mental incapacity, and the burden of proof is on the person contesting the will.
2. **Freedom of Choice:** When you prepare and execute your will, you must not be under the undue influence of another person. Threats, misrepresentations, inordinate flattery, or some physical or mental coercion employed to destroy the testator's freedom of choice are all types of undue influence.

3. **Proper Execution:** To be considered properly executed, a will must meet the requirements of the state's wills act or its equivalent. It must also be demonstrable that it is in fact the will of the testator. Most states have statutes that spell out who may make a will (generally any person of sound mind, age 18 or older [14 in Georgia and 16 in Louisiana]), the form and execution a will must have (most states require a will to be in writing and signed by the testator at the logical end, preferably in black ink), and requirements for witnesses. Generally, it is not a good idea to let a beneficiary serve as a witness. Although the will is otherwise valid, about 60 percent of the states penalize the beneficiary-witness in some way. The most common penalty is limiting the beneficiary-witness' bequest to the intestate share that he or she would receive although it could be as severe as the complete loss of any bequest to the witness or his or her spouse and offspring.

Most states now provide for a *self-proving will*. This is a will that recites in the attestation clause that the correct formalities for will execution were observed. It might read as follows:

On this date, September 15, 2002, we, the witnesses, by signing our names to this will, do hereby declare that the testator signed and executed this his last will in our presence, and that he signed it willingly, and that at his request and in the presence and hearing of one another, we signed as witnesses. We declare further that to the best of our knowledge the testator is 18 years of age or older, appears to be of sound mind, and was under no constraint or undue influence.

The witnesses' signatures then appear, generally followed by the name and address of each printed next to (or below) their respective signatures. Using a self-proving will dispenses with the need to have the witnesses sign, after the testator's death, a declaration verifying their signatures and that of the testator. Unless someone connected to the probate process raises an issue concerning the validity of one or more of the signatures, the probate court will accept the correctness of the execution. This saves time, money, and often a great deal of inconvenience to the executor.

CHANGING OR REVOKING THE WILL: CODICILS

A will is inoperative until the testator's death and therefore can be changed at any time as long as the testator has mental capacity. In fact, the testator should revise the will periodically if there is a significant change in his or her (or the beneficiaries') health or financial circumstances; if births, deaths, marriages, or divorces alter the operative circumstances; if the testator moves to a state other than where the will was executed; if an executor, trustee, or guardian can no longer serve; or if substantial changes occur in the tax law. A will can be either changed or revoked although in certain states a so-called *right of election* (explained later) exists. By reviewing your will regularly, you can be sure that it accurately reflects your current wishes.

CHANGING THE WILL. To make minor changes to an existing will, the testator draws up a **codicil.** This simple and convenient legal means of modifying a will is often a single-page document that reaffirms all the existing provisions in the will except the one to be changed. The codicil should be executed and witnessed in the same formal manner as a will.

When a will requires substantial changes, a new will is usually preferable to a codicil. In addition, if a gift in the original will is removed, it may be best to draw a new will and destroy the old, even if substantial changes are not required. This avoids offending the

Choosing Your Children's Guardian
The personal guardian you choose for your children should:
1. Be old enough (18 years old in most states).
2. Have the confidence of you and your children.
3. Have a genuine concern for your children's welfare.
4. Have the time and physical capability to handle the job.
5. Have kids close in age to your children.
6. Share your moral beliefs.

Also consider:
7. Can you provide enough assets to raise the children? If not, can your prospective guardian afford to bring them up?
8. Would your kids have to move?

Source: Adapted from "Choosing a Guardian for Your Children," *Nolo's Legal Encyclopedia,* **www.nolo.com/encyclopedia**.

codicil
A document that legally modifies a will without revoking it.

omitted beneficiary. Sometimes, however, the prior will should not be destroyed even after the new will has been made and signed. If the new will fails for some reason (because of the testator's mental incapacity, for example), the prior will may qualify. Also, a prior will could help to prove a "continuity of testamentary purpose"—in other words, that the latest will (which may have provided a substantial gift to charity) continued an earlier intent and was not an afterthought or the result of an unduly influenced mind.

REVOKING THE WILL. A will may be revoked either by the testator or automatically by the law. A testator can revoke a will in one of four ways:

1. Making a later will that expressly revokes prior wills
2. Making a codicil that expressly revokes all wills earlier than the one being modified
3. Making a later will that is inconsistent with a former will
4. Physically mutilating, burning, tearing, or defacing the will with the intention of revoking it

The law automatically modifies a will under certain circumstances, which vary from state to state but generally revolve around divorce, marriage, birth or adoption, and murder. In many states, if a testator becomes divorced after making a will, all provisions in the will relating to the spouse become ineffective. If a testator marries after making a will, the spouse receives that portion of the estate that would have been received had the testator died without a valid will—unless the will gives the spouse a larger share. If a testator did not provide for a child born or adopted after the will was made (unless it appears that such lack of provision was intentional), the child receives that share of the estate not passing to the testator's spouse that would have been given to him or her had the deceased not had a will. Finally, almost all states have some type of slayer's statute forbidding a person who commits murder from acquiring property as the result of the deed.

RIGHT OF ELECTION. Many states provide still another way to change a will: Through the **right of election,** the survivor has a right to "take against the will"—to take a specified portion of the probate estate regardless of what the will provides. Most states give this right only to the surviving spouse. One state, for example, allows a surviving spouse to take at least that share that would have been allowed had the deceased died without a valid will. This right is generally forfeited by a spouse who deserted the testator.

right of election
The right of a survivor, typically a spouse, to take a specified portion of the probate estate regardless of what the will provides.

SAFEGUARDING THE WILL

In most cases you should keep your original will in a safe-deposit box, with copies in a safe and accessible place at home and with the attorney who drafted it. Although some authorities and many attorneys recommend leaving the original will with the attorney who drafted it, this may make it awkward for the executor to choose his or her own attorney, a right the executor has regardless of who drew the will or what the will states about who should be the estate's counsel. Further, it may discourage the estate owner from changing the will or engaging a new attorney even if he or she moves out of the state in which the will is drawn.

Worksheet 15.1 contains an executor's checklist of documents and information that should be kept in a safe-deposit box. If each spouse has a separate safe-deposit box, the couple may want to keep their wills in each other's boxes. Some states provide for *lodging* of the will, a mechanism for filing and safekeeping it in the office of the probate court (also called *orphan's* or *surrogate's court*). In those states this procedure satisfies the need to safeguard the will.

WORKSHEET 15.1

A CHECKLIST OF ITEMS TO KEEP IN A SAFE-DEPOSIT BOX

This checklist itemizes the various documents and information that the executor may need to effectively carry out the terms of the will. These items should be kept in a safe-deposit box.

EXECUTOR'S CHECKLIST

Name (Testator) _____ Date _____

_____ 1. Birth certificates
_____ 2. Marriage certificates (including any prior marriages)
_____ 3. Your will (and spouse's will) and trust agreements
_____ 4. Listing of life insurance policies or certificates
_____ 5. Your Social Security numbers
_____ 6. Military discharge papers

_____ 7. Bonds, stocks, and securities
_____ 8. Real estate deeds
_____ 9. Business (buy-sell) agreements
_____ 10. Automobile titles and insurance policies
_____ 11. Property insurance policies
_____ 12. Letter of last instructions
_____ 13. Additional documents

List all checking and savings account numbers, including bank addresses and location of safe-deposit boxes:

_____   _____   _____
_____   _____   _____

List name, address, and phone number of property and life insurance agents:

_____   _____   _____
_____   _____   _____

List name, address, and phone number of attorney and accountant:

_____   _____   _____
_____   _____   _____

List name, address, and phone number of (current or past) employer. State date when you retired if applicable. Include employee benefits booklets:

_____   _____   _____
_____   _____   _____

List all debts owed to *and* owed by you:

_____   _____   _____
_____   _____   _____

List the names, addresses, telephone numbers, and birth dates of your children and other beneficiaries (including charitable beneficiaries):

_____   _____   _____
_____   _____   _____

Source: Stephen R. Leimberg, Herbert Levy, Stephen N. Kandell, Morey S. Rosenbloom, and Ralph Gano Miller, *The Tools and Techniques of Estate Planning,* 11th ed. (Cincinnati: National Underwriter Company, 1998). Reprinted with permission of the publisher.

LETTER OF LAST INSTRUCTIONS

letter of last instructions
An informal memorandum separate from the will and containing suggestions or recommendations for carrying out the decedent's wishes.

People often have thoughts they want to convey and instructions they wish others to carry out that aren't appropriate to include in their wills. A **letter of last instructions** is the best way to communicate these suggestions or recommendations. It typically takes the form of an informal memorandum separate from the will. (This letter of last instructions should not contain any bequests because it has no legal standing.) Usually it is best to make several copies of the letter, keeping one at home and the others with the estate's executor or attorney, who can deliver it to beneficiaries at the appropriate time.

A letter of last instructions might provide directions with respect to such items as:

1. Location of the will and other documents
2. Funeral and burial instructions (often a will is not opened until after the funeral)
3. Suggestions or recommendations as to the continuation, sale, or liquidation of a business (it is easier to freely suggest a course of action in such a letter than in a will)
4. Personal matters that the testator might prefer not to be made public in the will, such as statements that might sound unkind or inconsiderate but would prove of great value to the executor (for example, comments about a spendthrift spouse or a reckless son)
5. Legal and accounting services (executors are free, however, to choose their own counsel—not even testators can bind them in that selection)
6. An explanation of the actions taken in the will, which may help avoid litigation (for instance, "I left only $1,000 to my son, Ramon, because . . ." or "I made no provisions for my oldest daughter, Melissa, because . . .")
7. Suggestions on how to divide the personal property

probate process
The court-supervised process of liquidation that occurs when a person dies; it consists of collecting money owed the decedent, paying his or her debts, and distributing the remaining assets to the appropriate individuals and organizations.

ADMINISTRATION OF AN ESTATE

executor
The personal representative of an estate designated in the decedent's will.

When people die, they usually own property and owe debts. Often they will have claims (accounts receivable) against other persons. A process of liquidation, called the **probate process,** similar to that which occurs when a corporation is dissolved, might be required. In this process money owed the decedent is collected, creditors (including the tax authorities) are satisfied, and what remains is distributed to the appropriate individuals and organizations. A local court generally supervises the probate process through a person designated as an **executor** in the decedent's will, or, if the decedent died intestate (without a valid will), through a court-appointed **administrator.**

administrator
The personal representative of the estate appointed by the court if the decedent died intestate (without a valid will).

An executor or administrator, who is sometimes also referred to as the *decedent's personal representative,* must collect the assets of the decedent, pay debts or provide for the payment of debts that are not currently due, and distribute any remaining assets to the persons entitled to them by will or by the intestate law of the appropriate state. Estate administration is important for many reasons. The executor or administrator becomes the decedent's legal representative, taking care of such matters as collecting bank accounts and other contracts, releasing liability, and creating clear title to make real estate marketable. Due to the importance of the estate administration process, you should select executors who are not only familiar with the testator's affairs but also can effectively handle the responsibilities of being an executor.

power of attorney
Legal document that authorizes another person to take over one's financial affairs and act on his or her behalf.

OTHER IMPORTANT ESTATE-PLANNING DOCUMENTS

living will
A document that states, in very precise terms, the treatments that a person wants and to what degree he or she wishes them continued if he or she becomes terminally ill.

In addition to your will and the letter of last instructions, you should have several other documents to protect yourself and your family: a power of attorney, a living will, and a durable power of attorney for health care.

POWER OF ATTORNEY. If you were incapacitated by a serious illness, a **power of attorney** allows you to name as your agent the person you consider best suited to take over your financial affairs—perhaps a spouse or other relative. Although this is a simple document, it transfers enormous power to your designated appointee, so be sure you can rely on the person you choose to manage your finances responsibly. If you have investments, your power of attorney should include language that covers powers of investment on your behalf. You may want to clear your power of attorney with the brokerage firms and mutual funds where you have accounts.

LIVING WILL AND DURABLE POWER OF ATTORNEY FOR HEALTH CARE. Another important aspect of estate planning involves determining the medical care you wish to receive, or *not* receive, if you become seriously ill and unable to give informed consent. Two documents to achieve this are the *living will* and the *durable power of attorney for health care.* The **living will** states, in very precise terms, the treatments that you want and to what degree you wish them continued. You must be as specific as possible so that your wishes are clear; otherwise, a living will might be put aside because it is too vague. For example, you should define what you mean by "terminal illness." Each state has its own form for a living will, and you can usually complete them yourself.

Many experts prefer the **durable power of attorney for health care** instead of the living will; some advise having both to reinforce each other. Through the durable power of attorney for health care, you authorize an individual (your *agent*) to make health care decisions for you if you are unable to do so, either temporarily or permanently. Unlike the living will, it applies in any case where you cannot communicate your wishes, not just when you are terminally ill. You can limit the scope of the durable power of attorney and include specific instructions as to the desired level of medical treatment. You should spend some time making these decisions and then review your ideas and philosophy concerning these matters with your family and the person you designate as your agent. These documents, copies of which should be held by your designated agent and your doctor, can make it easier for your family to deal with these difficult issues.

 Aging with Dignity offers a document called *5 Wishes* that helps you express how you want to be treated if you are seriously ill and unable to speak for yourself. Download a sample at **www.agingwithdignity.org/5wishes.html**.

WHAT ABOUT JOINT OWNERSHIP?

Many people take title to property jointly either through a *joint tenancy* or as *tenants by the entirety.* These two forms of joint ownership have the following characteristics:

1. The interest of a decedent passes directly to the surviving joint tenant(s) [that is, to the other joint owner(s)] by operation of the law and is free from the claims of the decedent's creditors, heirs, or personal representatives. This is called the **right of survivorship.**
2. A **joint tenancy** may consist of any number of persons. The joint owners do not have to be related. A **tenancy by the entirety,** on the other hand, can exist only between husband and wife.
3. In the case of joint tenancy each joint tenant can unilaterally sever the tenancy. This is not the case with a tenancy by the entirety, which can be severed only by mutual agreement, divorce, or conveyance by both spouses to a third party. In some states a tenancy by the entirety can exist only with respect to real property, whereas others do not recognize such tenancies at all.
4. The co-owners have equal interests.

durable power of attorney for health care
A written power of attorney authorizing an individual (an *agent*) to make health care decisions on behalf of the principal during such times, either temporarily or permanently, when the principal is unable to make such decisions.

right of survivorship
The right of surviving joint owners of property to receive title to the deceased joint owner's interest in the property.

joint tenancy
A type of ownership by two or more parties, with the survivor(s) continuing to hold all such property on the death of one or more of the tenants. Each joint tenant can unilaterally sever the tenancy.

tenancy by the entirety
A form of ownership by husband and wife, recognized in certain states, in which the property automatically passes to the surviving spouse. Tenancy can be severed only by mutual agreement, divorce, or conveyance by both spouses to a third party.

Joint tenancy, the more common form of joint ownership, offers a sense of family security, quick and easy transfer to the spouse at death, exemption of jointly owned property from the claims of the deceased's creditors, and avoidance of delays and publicity in the estate-settlement process. The key disadvantage of joint tenancy is the inability to control jointly-owned property by a will so that the first joint owner to die cannot control the property's disposition and management on his or her death. Another disadvantage is the potential for higher tax costs often incurred in creating and severing a joint tenancy.

For example, a father who purchases and pays for property and places it in his own and his daughter's name is making a gift to her of one half of the value. On the termination of the tenancy, if the daughter receives the entire proceeds (for example, on the sale of a jointly owned home), the father is making a *second* gift to her—of *his* half interest in the property. In both situations he will have gratuitously transferred an interest to her that she did not have before. Fortunately, because federal gift tax law does not tax most interspousal transfers, the problem will not arise on a federal level between a married couple (although some states may tax such gifts). Although the property passes to the surviving spouse tax free, larger estate taxes could be due when the second spouse dies—if the estate is worth more than $1,000,000 (in 2002). Because most people believe the advantages of joint ownership of major assets, such as a home or automobile, far outweigh the potential disadvantages, it is commonly used by married couples.

You should also be familiar with two other forms of ownership: *tenancy in common* and *community property.*

tenancy in common
A form of joint ownership under which there is *no right of survivorship,* and each co-owner can leave his or her share to whomever he or she desires.

TENANCY IN COMMON. A third common form of co-ownership is called **tenancy in common.** There is *no right of survivorship,* and each co-owner can leave his or her share to whomever he or she desires. Thus the decedent owner's will controls the disposition of the decedent's partial interest in the asset. If the decedent dies without a will, the intestate succession laws of the state where the property is located will determine who inherits the decedent's interest. Tenancy in common interests can be unequal; a property owned by three co-owners could be apportioned such that their respective shares are 50 percent, 30 percent, and 20 percent of the property.

community property
A form of marital property co-ownership wherein all wages and commissions earned and property acquired by either spouse while living in a community property state are automatically owned equally by both spouses.

COMMUNITY PROPERTY. Just as tenancy by the entirety is a special form of marital property co-ownership found only in common law states (that is, states that trace their property law to England), community property is a form of marital property co-ownership based on Roman law and found primarily in the southwestern states, which had a Spanish or French influence.

Community property is all property acquired by the effort of either or both spouses during marriage while they are domiciled in a community property state. For example, wages and commissions earned and property acquired by either spouse while living in a community property state are automatically owned equally by both spouses, even if only one was directly involved in acquiring the additional wealth. Property acquired before marriage or by gift or inheritance can be maintained as the acquiring spouse's separate property.

By agreement, which typically must be in writing to be enforceable, the couple can change community property into separate property, and vice versa. Each spouse can leave his or her half of the community property to whomever he or she chooses, thus there is *no right of survivorship* inherent in this form of ownership.

CONCEPT CHECK

15-3. What is a *will?* Why is it important? Describe the consequences of dying intestate.

15-4. Describe the basic clauses that are normally included as part of a will and the requirements with respect to who may make a valid will.

15-5. How can changes in the provisions of a will be made legally? In what four ways can a will be revoked?

15-6. Indicate what is meant by each of the following: (a) *intestacy,* (b) *testator,* (c) *codicil,* (d) *right of election,* and (e) *letter of last instructions.*

15-7. What is meant by the *probate process?* Who is an *executor,* and what role does the executor play in estate settlement?

15-8. Describe briefly the importance of the following documents for estate planning: (a) *power of attorney,* (b) *living will,* and (c) *durable power of attorney for health care.*

15-9. Define and differentiate between *joint tenancy* and *tenancy by the entirety.* Discuss the advantages and disadvantages of joint ownership. How does *tenancy in common* differ from joint tenancy?

15-10. What is the *right of suvivorship?* What is *community property* and how does it differ from joint tenancy with regard to this right?

■ Trusts [LG3]

Trusts, another important tool for estate planning, facilitate the transfer of property and the income from that property to another party. Although trusts were once considered estate-planning techniques only for the wealthy, today even those of more modest means use trusts to their advantage in estate planning. This change is attributed to rising real estate values, the bull markets of the 1980s and 1990s, and marketing by estate-planning attorneys. Also, as people live longer and are more likely to marry more than once, they need ways to protect and manage assets.

A **trust** is a legal relationship created when one party, the **grantor** (also called the *settlor, trustor,* or *creator*), transfers property to a second party, the **trustee** (an organization or individual), for the benefit of third parties, the **beneficiaries,** who may or may not include the grantor. The property placed in the trust is called *trust principal* or *res* (pronounced "race"). The trustee holds the legal title to the property in the trust and must use the property and any income it produces solely for the benefit of trust beneficiaries. The trust generally is created by a written document.

The grantor spells out the substantive provisions (such as how to allocate the property in the trust and how to distribute income) and certain administrative provisions. A trust may be *living* (funded during the grantor's life) or *testamentary* (created in a will and funded by the probate process). It may be *revocable* or *irrevocable.* The grantor can regain property placed into a revocable trust and alter or amend the terms of the trust. The grantor cannot recover property placed into an irrevocable trust during its term.

Let's now look at how trusts solve various estate-planning problems.

PURPOSES OF TRUSTS

Trusts are designed for a variety of purposes. The most common motives are to attain income and estate tax savings and manage and conserve property over a long period.

trust
A legal relationship created when one party, the *grantor,* transfers property to a second party, the *trustee,* for the benefit of third parties, the *beneficiaries,* who may or may not include the grantor.

grantor
A person who creates a trust and whose property is transferred into it. Also called *settlor, trustor,* or *creator.*

trustee
An organization or individual selected by the *grantor* to manage and conserve property placed in trust for the benefit of the *beneficiaries.*

beneficiaries
Those who receive benefits—property or income—from a trust or from the estate of a decedent; may or may not include the *grantor.*

INCOME AND ESTATE TAX SAVINGS. Under certain circumstances, a grantor who is a high-bracket taxpayer can shift the burden of paying taxes on the income produced by securities, real estate, and other investments to a trust itself or to its beneficiary, both of whom are typically subject to lower income tax rates than the grantor. However, the Tax Reform Act of 1986 severely limited the ability of a person to shift income in this manner. Specifically, with certain types of trusts, the beneficiary must be more than 14 years of age; otherwise the income from the trust will be taxed at the same rate as the beneficiary's parents. In addition to possible income tax benefits, impressive *estate tax* savings are also possible because the appreciation in the value of property placed into such a trust can be entirely removed from the grantor's estate and possibly benefit several generations of family members without incurring adverse federal estate tax consequences.

MANAGEMENT AND CONSERVATION OF PROPERTY. Minors, spendthrifts, and those who are mentally incompetent need asset management for obvious reasons. However, busy executives and others who cannot or do not want to spend the countless hours necessary to handle large sums of money and other property often use trusts to relieve themselves of those burdens. The trustee assumes the responsibility for managing and conserving the property on behalf of the beneficiaries. In some cases management by the trustee is held in reserve in case a healthy and vigorous individual is unexpectedly incapacitated and becomes unable or unwilling to manage his or her assets.

SELECTING A TRUSTEE

Five qualities are essential in a trustee. He or she must:

1. possess sound business knowledge and judgment,
2. have an intimate knowledge of the beneficiary's needs and financial situation,
3. be skilled in investment and trust management,
4. be available to beneficiaries (specifically, this means the trustee should be young enough to survive the trust term), and
5. be able to make decisions impartially.

A corporate trustee, such as a trust company or bank that has been authorized to perform trust duties, may be best able to meet these requirements. A corporate trustee is likely to have investment experience and will not impose the problems created by death, disability, or absence. Unlike a family member, a corporate trustee is impartial and obedient to the directions of the trust instrument. Such objectivity adds value if there are several beneficiaries. On the other hand, a corporate trustee may charge high fees or be overly conservative in investments, impersonal, or lacking familiarity with and understanding of family problems and needs. Often a compromise involves the appointment of one or more individuals and a corporate trustee as co-trustees.

COMMON TYPES AND CHARACTERISTICS OF TRUSTS

Although there are various types of trusts, the most common are the *living trust*, the *testamentary trust*, and the *irrevocable life insurance trust*, each of which is described below. Exhibit 15.6 describes seven popular trusts.

living (inter vivos) trust
A trust created and funded during the grantor's lifetime.

LIVING TRUST. A **living (inter vivos) trust** is one created and funded during the grantor's lifetime. It can be either revocable or irrevocable and can last for a limited period or continue long after the grantor's death.

EXHIBIT 15.6

SEVEN POPULAR TRUSTS

Trusts shift assets (and thus appreciation) out of one's estate while retaining some say in the future use of the assets. The drawback is that trusts can be cumbersome and expensive to arrange and administer. Here are brief descriptions of seven popular trusts:

- **Credit Shelter Trust:** Most common trust for estate planning; couples with combined assets worth more than the "applicable exclusion amount" can gain full use of each partner's exclusion by having that amount placed in a bypass trust, that is, one that bypasses the surviving spouse's taxable estate. It is called a *credit shelter trust* because of the way the taxes are calculated using a method called the *unified credit.* The surviving spouse is usually given the right to all the trust income and, in an emergency, even has access to the principal. Thus, if the first death occurred in the year 2002, the trust would be funded with assets worth $1,000,000.

- **Qualified Terminable Interest Property (QTIP) Trust:** Usually set up in addition to a *credit shelter trust* to ensure that money stays in the family; it receives some or all of the assets in the estate over the applicable exclusion amount ($1,000,000 in 2002). (Assets left to a spouse who remarries could be claimed by the new spouse.) The survivor receives all income from the property until death, at which point the assets go to the persons chosen by the first spouse to die. Estate taxes on QTIP trust assets can be delayed until the second spouse dies. Also useful for couples with children from prior marriages.

- **Special Needs Trust:** An irrevocable trust established for the benefit of a person with disabilities. It is designed to provide extra help and life enrichment without reducing state and federal government help to the beneficiary.

- **Minor's Section 2503(c) Trust:** Set up for a minor, often to receive tax-free gifts. However, assets must be distributed by the time he or she turns 21.

- **Crummey Trust:** Used to make $10,000 tax-free gifts to children; unlike a *minor's section 2503(c) trust,* these funds do not have to be distributed at age 21. However, the beneficiary can withdraw the funds placed into the trust for a limited time (e.g., for up to 30 days), after which the right to make a withdrawal ceases.

- **Charitable Lead (or Income) Trust:** Pays some or all of its income to a charity for a period of time (either 20 years or less or someone's lifetime). Then the property is distributed to noncharitable beneficiaries. Grantor gets immediate income tax deduction based on expected future pay-out to charity.

- **Charitable Remainder Trust:** Similar to a *charitable lead trust,* except that income goes to taxable beneficiaries (e.g., the grantor or the grantor's children) and principal to a charity when the trust ends.

Revocable Living Trust. The grantor reserves the right to revoke the trust and regain trust property in a **revocable living trust.** For federal income tax purposes, grantors of these trusts are treated as owners of the property in the trust—in other words, just as if they held the property in their own names—and are therefore taxed on any income produced by the trust.

Revocable living trusts have three basic advantages:

1. Management continuity and income flow are ensured even after the death of the grantor. No probate is necessary because the trust continues to operate after the death of the grantor just as it did while he or she was alive.

revocable living trust
A trust in which the grantor reserves the right to revoke the trust and regain trust property.

2. The trustee assumes burdens of investment decisions and management responsibility. For example, an individual may want to control investment decisions and management policy as long as he or she is alive and healthy but sets up a trust to provide backup help in case he or she becomes unable or unwilling to continue managing their assets.
3. Unlike the probate process, the terms and the amount of assets placed into the trust do not become public knowledge.

The principal disadvantages of these trusts include the fees charged by the trustee for managing the property placed into the trust and the legal fees charged for drafting the trust instruments.

irrevocable living trust
A trust in which the grantor relinquishes the title to the property placed in it and the right to revoke or terminate the trust.

Irrevocable Living Trust. Grantors who establish an **irrevocable living trust** relinquish title to the property they place in it and the right to revoke or terminate the trust. (The grantor may retain the income from certain types of irrevocable trusts.) Such trusts have all the advantages of revocable trusts plus the potential for reducing taxes. Disadvantages of such a trust relate to the fees charged by trustees for managing assets placed in it; possible gift taxes on assets placed into it; in some cases the grantor's complete loss of the trust property and any income it may produce; and the grantor's forfeiture of the right to alter the terms of the trust as circumstances change.

pour-over will
A provision in a will that provides for the passing of the estate —after debts, expenses, taxes, and specific bequests—to an existing living trust.

Living Trusts and Pour-Over Wills. A will can be written so that it "pours over" designated assets into a previously established revocable or irrevocable living trust. The trust may also be named beneficiary of the grantor's insurance policies. The **pour-over will** generally contains a provision passing the estate—after debts, expenses, taxes, and specific bequests—to an existing living trust. The pour-over will ensures that the property left out of the living trust, either inadvertently or deliberately, will make its way into the trust (i.e., "pour over" into it). The trust contains provisions as to how those assets (together with insurance proceeds payable to it) will be administered and distributed. Such an arrangement provides for easily coordinated and well-administered management of estate assets.

testamentary trust
A trust created by a decedent's will and funded through the probate process.

TESTAMENTARY TRUST. A trust created by a decedent's will is called a **testamentary trust.** Such a trust comes into existence only after the will is probated. A court order directs the executor to transfer the property to the trustee to fund the trust. This type of trust does not provide any tax savings for the grantor because he or she continues to own the property until after his or her death.

irrevocable life insurance trust
An irrevocable trust, typically established by a wealthy individual, where the major asset of the trust is life insurance on the grantor's life

IRREVOCABLE LIFE INSURANCE TRUST. A wealthy individual can establish an **irrevocable life insurance trust** where the major asset of the trust is life insurance on the grantor's life. To avoid having the proceeds of the policy included in the grantor's estate, the independent trustee usually acquires the policy. The terms of the trust make it possible for the trustee to use the proceeds to pay the grantor's estate taxes and to take care of the grantor's spouse and children.

CONCEPT CHECK

15-11. Describe the basic trust arrangement, and discuss purposes for which trusts are typically established. What essential qualities should a trustee possess?
15-12. What is a *living (inter vivos) trust*? Distinguish between a *revocable living trust* and *irrevocable living trust*.
15-13. Explain what is meant by each of the following: (a) *grantor*, (b) *trustee*, (c) *beneficiary*, (d) *pour-over will*, (e) *testamentary trust*, and (f) *irrevocable life insurance trust*.

EXHIBIT 15.7

FEDERAL UNIFIED TRANSFER TAX RATES

The *unified rate schedule* below defines the amount of federal gift and estate taxes that estates of various sizes would have to pay; it incorporates the rates passed in the *Economic Growth and Tax Relief Reconciliation Act of 2001*. The rates and amounts remain the same through 2009 for estates worth up to $2,000,000. Estates under the exclusion amount pay no federal tax; anything over that amount is currently taxed at 45 to 50 percent. The exclusion amount increases annually from $1,000,000 in 2002 to $3,500,000 in 2009 (see Exhibit 15.8). From 2002 to 2009, the top tax rates for estates worth more than $2,000,000 decrease as shown below.

Taxable Estate Value		Tentative Tax		
More Than	But Not More Than	Base Amount	+Percent	On Excess Over
$ 0	$ 10,000	$ 0		
10,000	20,000	1,800	20%	$ 10,000
20,000	40,000	3,800	22	20,000
40,000	60,000	8,200	24	40,000
60,000	80,000	13,000	26	60,000
80,000	100,000	18,200	28	80,000
100,000	150,000	23,800	30	100,000
150,000	250,000	38,800	32	150,000
250,000	500,000	70,800	34	250,000
500,000	750,000	155,800	37	500,000
750,000	1,000,000	248,300	39	750,000
1,000,000	1,250,000	345,800	41	1,000,000
1,250,000	1,500,000	448,300	43	1,250,000
1,500,000	2,000,000	555,800	45	1,500,000
Top Rates, 2002				
2,000,000	2,500,000	780,800	49	2,000,000
2,500,000		1,025,800	50	2,500,000
Top rate, 2003				
2,000,000		780,800	49	2,000,000
Top rate, 2004				
2,000,000		780,800	48	2,000,000
Top rate, 2005				
2,000,000		780,800	47	2,000,000
Top rate, 2006				
2,000,000		780,800	46	2,000,000
Top rate, 2007–2009				
2,000,000		780,800	45	2,000,000
2010 and beyond:	Repealed for Estates. The maximum rate for gifts is 35% starting at $500,000.			

Source: Adapted from material in John C. Bost, *Estate Planning and Taxation, 2001–2002 Edition* (Dubuque, Iowa: Kendall Hunt, 2002).

 Gift Taxes [LG4]

Federal tax law establishes a **gift tax** on the value of certain gifts made during one's lifetime and an **estate tax** on "deathtime" gifts. Both lifetime and deathtime gifts are considered cumulatively and are subjected to the integrated progressive tax rate schedule shown in Exhibit 15.7.

The tax on gifts applies to the right to transfer property and is measured by the value of the property transferred. The *donor* is primarily liable for the tax and must file a gift tax

gift tax
A tax levied on the value of certain types of gifts made during the giver's lifetime.

estate tax
A tax levied on the value of property transferred at the owner's death.

return when his or her income tax return is filed. The graduated table of rates in Exhibit 15.7 is used for *both* gift and estate tax purposes and is known as the **unified rate schedule.** These rates apply to *all* taxable gifts—whether made during the donor's life or after his or her death—after making a number of adjustments. Assuming the applicable exclusion amount for gifts is $1,000,000, transfers take place in 2002, and death occurs in 2006, the following situations result in different total transfer taxes—that is, gift taxes plus estate taxes:

1. Fred gives his daughter a $4,000,000 taxable gift in 2002 and dies in poverty in 2006. Gift taxes equal $1,620,250.
2. Mary dies in 2006 and leaves her son a $4,000,000 estate. The estate tax equals $920,000.

Prior to passage of the 2001 Tax Act, the total tax in both of the above situations would have been the same. Today, because the gift tax exclusion amount stays at $1,000,000 and the estate tax exclusion amount is scheduled to rise from $1,000,000 in 2002 to $3,500,000 in 2009 (and the estate tax will be completely repealed in 2010), there is an advantage to incurring estate tax rather than gift tax liabilities. This advantage should be clear from the fact that the $4,000,000 estate in example 2 resulted in a much lower tax ($920,000) than the $4,000,000 gift in example 1 ($1,620,250). Therefore, as a result of the 2001 Tax Act, today many estate planners recommend against giving sizable lifetime gifts. Of course, should the 2001 Tax Act be revised or recinded, all of this may again change.

TRANSFERS SUBJECT TO GIFT TAX

Almost all property can be the subject of a transfer on which the gift tax must be paid. There is no gift tax on services that one person performs for another, nor is the rent-free use of property a taxable transfer. A tax may be payable on cash gifts, gifts of personal or real property, and both direct and indirect gifts. For example, if a father makes the mortgage payments on his adult son's home, the payment is an indirect gift from father to son. In fact, almost any shifting of financial advantage in which the recipient does not provide full consideration in money or money's worth may be considered a gift. For example, suppose your father gave you a summer home valued at $175,000 in exchange for $125,000. This type of transaction is called a *bargain sale.* The $50,000 excess value received over the consideration paid is treated as a gift. Of course, if you gave no consideration for the property, its market value ($175,000) would represent the amount of the gift.

WHEN IS A GIFT MADE?

The question of when a gift is made is important because it determines when the gift must be reported, when the gift tax, if any, must be paid, and the date at which the value of the gift is measured. Usually a gift is considered to be made *when the donor relinquishes dominion and control over the property or property interest transferred.* For example, if a mother places cash in a bank account held jointly with her son, no gift is made until the son makes a withdrawal. Until that time, the mother can completely recover the entire amount placed in the account. Therefore, when parents place property into a revocable trust for their children, no gift occurs because they have not relinquished control over the assets placed in it. However, if they later make the trust irrevocable and thereby relinquish their right to control the gift, the transfer will be considered a completed gift.

DETERMINING THE AMOUNT OF A TAXABLE GIFT

All that is transferred by an individual is not necessarily subject to a gift tax. Annual exclusions, gift splitting, charitable deductions, and marital deductions are all means of reducing the total amount for tax purposes.

ANNUAL EXCLUSIONS. Almost all gifts are subject to the gift tax, but for the reason of administrative convenience, certain transfers, or gift equivalents, are not counted. The gift tax law eliminates from the computation of taxable gifts transfers by a donor of amounts up to $10,000 per calendar year to each of any number of donees. For example, a person could give gifts of $10,000 each to 30 donees for a total of $300,000 without paying any gift tax. Further, the ability to give tax-free gifts of $10,000 per donee regenerates annually and since 1998 the $10,000 amount has been indexed for inflation. (By the time you are reading this, the annual exclusion may have reached $11,000.) This **annual exclusion** is available only for gifts of a "present interest," which means that the donee has the *immediate and unrestricted right* to use, possess, or enjoy it on receipt.

GIFT SPLITTING. **Gift splitting** equates the tax treatment of married taxpayers residing in common law states with the tax treatment of married taxpayers in community property states. When a spouse earns a dollar in a community property state, such as California or Texas, half of that dollar is deemed owned by the other spouse immediately and automatically. If a gift is made of that dollar, each spouse is considered to have given 50 cents. Similarly, in common law states, such as Colorado, New York, and Pennsylvania, federal law provides that a married donor, with the consent of his or her spouse, can elect to treat gifts as if they were made one-half by each spouse.

Because of this gift-splitting option, if a wife transfers $20,000 to her son and the required consent is given by her husband, for tax computation purposes her gift will be viewed as $10,000 and her husband will be considered to have given the other $10,000. As a result of the split, the total amount will be entirely gift-tax free because each spouse has a $10,000 annual exclusion. The wife could give $20,000 to any number of donees and, by splitting the gift with her husband, avoid the tax on the entire gift. This tax reduction technique is available even if one spouse makes all the gifts and the other spouse gives nothing. It is also available to spouses in community property states who make gifts of their separately owned property. Gift splitting is allowed, however, only for gifts from married couples to third parties.

CHARITABLE DEDUCTIONS. There is no limit on the amount that can be given gift-tax free to a qualified charity (one to which deductible gifts can be made for income tax purposes). Therefore people could give their entire estates to charity and receive gift tax deductions for the total amount. There would be no federal gift taxes regardless of the type or amount of assets transferred.

MARITAL DEDUCTIONS. Federal law permits an unlimited deduction for gift tax and estate tax purposes on property given or left to a spouse who is a U.S. citizen. Spouses who are not U.S. citizens are allowed a $100,000 per year marital deduction for gifts and no marital deduction for estates unless the property is left in a special trust, the *Qualified Domestic Trust (QDOT)*. This provision is designed to prevent tax-avoidance if the noncitizen spouse returns to his or her native country, where the bequest would then escape taxation in the United States. To receive the marital deduction, the QDOT must have at least one U.S. citizen trustee. Distributions of trust assets (but not income) to the surviving spouse result in estate tax; any trust assets remaining at the surviving spouse's death will be taxed.

REASONS FOR MAKING LIFETIME GIFTS

There are several tax-oriented reasons why estate planners recommend gift giving.

- *Gift exclusion:* A single individual can give any number of donees up to $10,000 (as adjusted for inflation after 1998) each year entirely gift-tax free, with no tax costs to either the donee or the donor. If the donor is married and the donor's spouse consents, the gift tax-free limit will be increased to $20,000 even if the entire gift is made from the donor's assets.

- *Gift tax exclusion escapes estate tax:* Fortunately, property that qualifies for the annual exclusion is not taxable and is therefore free from gift and estate taxes. Estate tax savings from this exclusion can be significant. Regardless of a gift's size— and even if it is made within 3 years of the donor's death—it typically will not be treated as part of the donor's gross estate. However, the taxable portion of lifetime gifts (technically called *adjusted taxable gifts*) pushes up the rate at which the donor's estate will be taxed.

- *Appreciation in value:* Generally, the appreciation on a gift, from the time it is made, is excluded from the donor's estate. Suppose Larry gives his son Steve a gift of stock worth $25,000. At the time of Larry's death 2 years later, the stock is worth $60,000. The amount subject to transfer taxes will be $15,000, the amount of the gift that exceeded the $10,000 annual exclusion at the time the gift was made. None of the appreciation would be subject to gift or estate taxes.

- *Credit limit:* Because of the credit that can be used to offset otherwise taxable gifts, gift taxes do not have to be paid on cumulative lifetime gifts up to the exclusion amount (e.g., up to $1,000,000 through 2003 and increasing through 2009, per Exhibit 15.8). To the extent that the credit is used against lifetime gift taxes, it is not available to offset estate taxes.

- *Impact of marital deduction:* The transfer tax marital deduction allows one spouse to give the other spouse an unlimited amount of money or other property entirely tax free without reducing the exclusion amount that can be transferred to others tax free.

CONCEPT CHECK

15-14. Answer or describe the following as they relate to federal gift taxes: (a) What is a gift? (b) When is a gift made? (c) Annual exclusion, (d) Gift splitting, (e) Charitable deduction, and (f) Marital deduction.

15-15. Discuss the reasons estate planners cite for making lifetime gifts. How and in what ways might gift giving help reduce estate shrinkage?

■ Estate Taxes and Planning [LG5, LG6]

Estate taxes may be generated when property is transferred at time of death, so one of the goals of effective estate planning is to minimize the amount of estate taxes paid. The federal estate tax is levied on the transfer of property at death. The tax is measured by the value of the property that the deceased transfers (or is deemed to transfer) to others. The parenthetical phrase "deemed to transfer" is important because the estate tax applies not only to transfers that a deceased actually makes at death but also to certain transfers made during the person's lifetime. In other words, to thwart tax-avoidance schemes, the estate tax is imposed on certain lifetime gifts that in essence are the same as dispositions of property made at death.

Although most gifts made during one's life are not part of the decedent's gross estate, there are some exceptions. A major exception pertains to life insurance given away within 3 years of the owner's death. It will be included in the owner's gross estate at its value as of

EXHIBIT 15.8

APPLICABLE EXCLUSION AMOUNT AND THE UNIFIED TAX CREDIT

The *Economic Growth and Tax Relief Act of 2001* increased the exclusion amount on a scheduled basis over the period from 2009 to 2009, with a complete repeal of the estate tax in 2010. This table shows the step-ups in the exclusion amount from 2002 through repeal in 2010. Also shown are the unified tax credit amounts over the 2002 to 2010 period.

Year	Exclusion Amount	Unified Tax Credit
2002	$1,000,000	$345,800
2003	1,000,000	345,800
2004	1,500,000	345,800
2005	1,500,000	345,800
2006	2,000,000	345,800
2007	2,000,000	345,800
2008	2,000,000	345,800
2009	3,500,000	345,800
2010	complete repeal of estate tax	330,800

Source: Adapted from material in John C. Bost, *Estate Planning and Taxation, 2001–2002 Edition* (Dubuque, Iowa; Kendall-Hunt, 2002).

the date of death. Thus, if the former owner is also the insured, the gross estate will include the proceeds (paid out amount) of the policy.

For example, 2½ years before his death, Max gives his son Eric a $1 million term insurance policy on Max's life. At the time of the gift, Max was in good health and the cash value of the term insurance policy was $0—clearly less than the $10,000 annual exclusion amount for gifts. Therefore Max did not have to file a gift tax return. Because Max died within 3 years of gifting the life insurance policy, the $1 million proceeds amount is included in his gross estate for estate tax purposes. Had Max outlived the transfer by more than 3 years, the proceeds would not have been included in his gross estate.

COMPUTATION OF THE FEDERAL ESTATE TAX

The computation of federal estate taxes involves six steps:

1. Determine the *gross estate,* the total of all property in which the decedent had an interest and that is required to be included in the estate.
2. Find the *adjusted gross estate* by subtracting from the gross estate any allowable funeral and administrative expenses, debts, and other expenses incurred during administration.
3. Calculate the *taxable estate* by subtracting any allowable marital deduction or charitable deduction from the adjusted gross estate.
4. Compute the *estate tax base.* After determining the value of the taxable estate, any "adjusted taxable gifts"—which are the taxable gifts (gifts above the annual exclusion) made after 1976—are added to the taxable estate. The unified rate schedule—the one applicable to gift taxes shown in Exhibit 15.7—is then applied to determine a *tentative tax-on-estate tax base.*

5. After the tentative tax is found, subtract any gift taxes the decedent paid on certain gifts and the *unified tax credit* (described below). The result is the *total death taxes.*
6. Determine the *federal estate tax due.* Certain credits are allowed against the total death taxes, which result in a dollar-for-dollar reduction of the tax. The dominant credit is the state death-tax credit. After reducing the total death taxes by any eligible credits, the federal estate tax due is payable by the decedent's executor, generally within 9 months of the decedent's death.

You can use Worksheet 15.2 to estimate federal estate taxes. The Worksheet shown here depicts the computations for a hypothetical situation involving the death in 2002 (when the $1,000,000 exclusion applies) of a widow who left a gross estate of $3,500,000. This worksheet is useful in following the flow of dollars from the gross estate to the federal estate tax due.

Over the period from 1997 to 2009, the Taxpayer Relief Act of 1997 and Economic Growth and Tax Relief Reconciliation Act of 2001 increased the amount that can pass free of transfer taxes. Exhibit 15.8 shows the increasing applicable exclusion amount and the **unified tax credit**—the credit that can be applied against the tentative tax-on-estate tax base—in effect from 2002 through 2009. Using Exhibit 15.7, you can determine the tentative tax on an estate. For a taxable estate of $1,000,000 in the year 2002, no tax is owed because the unified tax credit for that year is $345,800, which exactly matches the tentative tax on $1,000,000 (calculated using Exhibit 15.7). If the taxable estate in 2003 is $1,200,000, the tentative tax is $427,800 (calculated using Exhibit 15.7), and the estate tax is $82,000 ($427,800 tentative tax − $345,800 unified tax credit). Notice that a taxable estate of $1,200,000 is $200,000 above the applicable exclusion amount, so the excess is taxed at the marginal rate of 41 percent. Hence the tax owed is $82,000 ($200,000 × .41).

Worksheet 15.2 factors the unified credit for the year 2002 into the calculation at line 9b. The $345,800 shown is equal to the tentative tax on an estate tax base of $1,000,000. If the tentative tax shown on line 8 is less than the unified credit available for the decedent's year of death, there will be no federal estate tax due.

unified tax credit
The credit that can be applied against the tentative tax-on-estate tax base; the unified credit amount for any year absorbs all of the tentative tax on taxable transfers up to the exclusion amount.

STATE DEATH TAXES

Some individual's estates are also subject to state death taxes. In about 40% of the states there is an inheritance tax that is separate from the federal estate tax. Most states have switched to the pickup estate tax, described later in this section. Those states would collect the amount of the federal credit for state death taxes. Taxable estates just above the applicable exemption amount may pay more to the state than to the federal government. When the federal credit for state death taxes is phased out in 2005, only those states with separate inheritance taxes will collect any taxes.

For example, in the year 2002, a taxable estate of $1,090,000 would owe $36,900: [($1,090,000 − $1,000,000) × .41] in total federal estate taxes. A taxable estate of $1,090,000 would be eligible for a state death-tax credit of $28,680, calculated as follows using Exhibit 15.9: $20,700 + [4.2% × ($1,090,000 − $900,000)] = $20,700 + (4.2% × $190,000) = $20,700 + $7,980 = $28,680. Because the state death-tax credit is less than the $36,900 calculated for the total federal estate taxes, the estate would owe federal estate taxes of $8,220 ($36,900 − $28,680). The state would collect the $28,680 as a *pickup estate tax,* discussed later in this section.

The four basic types of state death taxes are the state inheritance tax, state estate tax, sponge tax, and pickup estate tax.

inheritance tax
A state death tax on the right to receive a decedent's property; the amount of the tax is based on the value of the property received and the beneficiary's relationship to the deceased.

INHERITANCE TAX. An **inheritance tax,** a common type of state death tax, is a tax on the right to receive a decedent's property. Fourteen states currently have inheritance taxes. The amount of the tax is based on the value of the property received and the beneficiary's

WORKSHEET 15.2

COMPUTING FEDERAL ESTATE TAX DUE

This worksheet is useful in determining federal estate tax due. Note that taxes are payable at the marginal tax rate applicable to the estate tax base (line 7), which is the amount that exists before the tax-free exclusion is factored in.

COMPUTING FEDERAL ESTATE TAX DUE

Name _____Mary Widow_____ Date _____June 10, 2002_____

Line	Computation	Item	Amount	Total Amount
1		*Gross estate*		$3,500,000
2	Substract sum of:	(a) Funeral expenses	$ 6,000	
		(b) Administrative expenses	25,000	
		(c) Debts	130,000	
		(d) Other expenses	0	
		Total		(161,000)
3	Result:	*Adjusted gross estate*		$ 3,339,000
4	Subtract sum of:	(a) Marital deduction	—	
		(b) Charitable deduction	—	
		Total		(0)
5	Result:	*Taxable estate*		$ 3,339,000
6	Add:	*Adjusted taxable gifts (post-1976)*		$ 0
7	Result:	*Estate tax base*		$ 3,339,000
8	Compute:	*Tentative tax-on-estate tax base*[a]		$ 1,477,250
9	Subtract sum of:	(a) Gift tax payable on post-1976 gifts	$ —	
		(b) Unified tax credit[b]	345,800	
		Total		($ 345,800)
10	Result:	*Total death taxes*[c]		$ 1,131,450
11	Subtract:	State death-tax credit[d]		($ 155,988)
12	Result:	*Federal estate tax due*		$ 975,462

[a]Use Exhibit 15.7 to calculate the tentative tax: $1,290,800 + [55\% \times (\$3,339,000 - \$3,000,000)] = \$1,290,800 + (55\% \times \$339,000) = \$1,477,250.$

[b]Use Exhibit 15.8 to determine the appropriate unified credit.

[c]Note that the tax amount shown on line 10 is the significant number, because most states are "pickup tax" states, meaning that the state simply collects the state death tax credit, a dollar-for-dollar credit.

[d]Use Exhibit 15.9 to calculate the state death tax credit (remember to subtract $60,000 from the taxable estate before entering the table): $\$3,339,000 - \$60,000 = \$3,279,000; \$143,100 + [7.2\% \times (\$3,279,000 - \$3,100,000)] = \$143,100 + (7.2\% \times \$179,000) = \$155,988.$

---

relationship to the deceased. In most states beneficiaries are divided into categories. The lowest rates and largest exemptions are allocated to lineal descendants—that is, those beneficiaries most closely related to the deceased. Property left to a surviving spouse is likely to be completely exempt. For example, in Pennsylvania, property left to a child of the deceased is taxed at 6 percent although the same property left to a cousin is subject to a 15 percent tax rate.

ESTATE TAX. A *state estate tax,* like the federal estate tax, is imposed on the deceased's right to transfer property and is measured by the net value of the entire property transferred. Three states currently impose an estate tax.

sponge (credit [gap] estate tax)
A tax designed to bridge the gap between a state's inheritance and estate taxes and the maximum state death-tax credit allowed against the federal estate tax.

SPONGE TAX. The **sponge tax,** also called the **credit (gap) estate tax,** bridges the gap between the state's inheritance and estate taxes and the maximum state death-tax credit allowed against the federal estate tax (see line 11 of the form for computing the federal estate tax due in Worksheet 15.2). The credit tax is best illustrated by a simple example. If a deceased's estate tax base for federal estate tax purposes is $1,500,000, a credit of up to $45,420 against the federal tax is allowed for taxes paid to the state as death taxes. Exhibit 15.9 shows how to calculate the maximum state death-tax credit allowed against federal estate taxes. The amount of any state death taxes paid may be subtracted from the federal tax, provided, however, that the maximum to be subtracted does not exceed the maximum credit (calculated using Exhibit 15.9). If the state's inheritance taxes amount to only $40,000, an additional tax—a $5,420 sponge tax—is imposed such that the total state death tax is increased to $45,420, the maximum amount of credit allowed by the federal government for state death taxes.

PICKUP ESTATE TAX. Thirty-three states have no separate inheritance tax but simply collect the amount that is allowed as the state death-tax credit against the federal estate tax (line 11). This is sometimes referred to as the *pickup estate tax* because the state collects only the state death-tax credit amount allowed against the federal estate tax (Exhibit 15.9), which in turn reduces dollar for dollar the federal estate taxes. This type of estate tax costs the decedent's estate nothing; it simply shifts money from the federal to the state treasury.

OTHER FACTORS AFFECTING THE AMOUNT OF STATE DEATH TAXES. Other factors that affect the amount of state death taxes include state exemptions and deductions, multiple-state taxation, and tax rates.

Exemptions and Deductions. Not all property is subject to taxation. Generally, states exempt property transferred to the United States, to the state itself, and to certain charitable organizations. All but a few states exempt property passing to a surviving spouse. Some states either totally or partially exempt life insurance proceeds unless payable to or for the benefit of the estate or its creditors. All states allow deductions for administrative costs, debts, funeral and last-illness expenses, and certain property taxes that are unpaid at the time of the deceased's death.

Multiple Taxation. Many individuals have summer and winter homes or land and other property in states other than where they live. Although most estates are taxed by only one state, in certain situations an estate or its beneficiaries may be liable for the taxes of more than one state. The right of a state to impose a death tax depends on the type of property involved. The general treatment of the major types of property is as follows:

- *Real estate.* Land and permanent buildings can be taxed only by the state in which the property is located.
- *Tangible personal property.* Cars, boats, and household goods can be taxed only in the state in which they are situated. A boat, for example, is taxed where it is permanently

EXHIBIT 15.9

FEDERAL ESTATE TAX CREDIT FOR STATE DEATH TAXES, 2002–2004

Credit is given on federal estate tax returns for state death taxes paid up to certain maximum amounts, as specified in the table below. *The Economic Growth and Tax Relief Reconciliation Act of 2001* reduces the state death-tax credit from present levels in three annual steps (25% in 2002, 50% in 2003, and 75% in 2004), as shown in the following table. After 2005, the state death-tax credit is repealed and replaced by a deduction for death taxes actually paid to any State or the District of Columbia.

Adjusted Taxable Estate*		Tax Year					
		2002		2003		2004	
At Least	But Not More Than	Base Amount	Rate on Excess Over Base	Base Amount	Rate on Excess Over Base	Base Amount	Rate on Excess Over Base
$100,000	$150,000	$0	0.6%	$0	0.4%	$0	0.2%
$150,000	$200,000	$300	1.2%	$200	0.8%	$100	0.4%
$200,000	$300,000	$900	1.8%	$600	1.2%	$300	0.6%
$300,000	$500,000	$2,700	2.4%	$1,800	1.6%	$900	0.8%
$500,000	$700,000	$7,500	3.0%	$5,000	2.0%	$2,500	1.0%
$700,000	$900,000	$13,500	3.6%	$9,000	2.4%	$4,500	1.2%
$900,000	$1,100,000	$20,700	4.2%	$13,800	2.8%	$6,900	1.4%
$1,100,000	$1,600,000	$29,100	4.8%	$19,400	3.2%	$9,700	1.6%
$1,600,000	$2,100,000	$53,100	5.4%	$35,400	3.6%	$17,700	1.8%
$2,100,000	$2,600,000	$80,100	6.0%	$53,400	4.0%	$26,700	2.0%
$2,600,000	$3,100,000	$110,100	6.6%	$73,400	4.4%	$36,700	2.2%
$3,100,000	$3,600,000	$143,100	7.2%	$95,400	4.8%	$47,700	2.4%
$3,600,000	$4,100,000	$179,100	7.8%	$119,400	5.2%	$59,700	2.6%
$4,100,000	$5,100,000	$218,100	8.4%	$145,400	5.6%	$72,700	2.8%
$5,100,000	$6,100,000	$302,100	9.0%	$201,400	6.0%	$100,700	3.0%
$6,100,000	$7,100,000	$392,100	9.6%	$261,400	6.4%	$130,700	3.2%
$7,100,000	$8,100,000	$488,100	10.2%	$325,400	6.8%	$162,700	3.4%
$8,100,000	$9,100,000	$590,100	10.8%	$393,400	7.2%	$196,700	3.6%
$9,100,000	$10,100,000	$698,100	11.4%	$465,400	7.6%	$232,700	3.8%
$10,100,000		$812,100	12.0%	$541,400	8.0%	$270,700	4.0%

*The *adjusted taxable estate* shown here is the estate tax base reduced by $60,000.

Source: Adapted from material in John C. Bost, *Estate Planning and Taxation, 2001–2002 Edition* (Dubuque, Iowa: Kendall-Hunt, 2002).

docked. Its registry and location for insurance purposes are examined to determine its legal location.

- *Intangible personal property.* Securities such as stocks, bonds, notes, and mortgages may, in the absence of interstate agreements, be taxed by several states. Generally, intangible personal property is taxed only by the state of the deceased's domicile. Unfortunately, if a deceased has residences in more than one state or does not clearly establish his or her state of domicile, two or more states can impose death taxes on the same intangible personal property.

Tax Rates. The rates at which transfers or receipts of property are taxed vary widely from state to state. For the 17 states that do not use the *pickup estate tax* as their method of setting death taxes, the rates vary widely from state to state. Only Pennsylvania has a flat rate; the others have graduated rates that increase as the beneficiary's share increases.

ESTATE-PLANNING TECHNIQUES

The federal and state tax laws described in the preceding paragraphs provide both problems and opportunities for the estate planner. Judicious use of certain tax-oriented strategies will minimize estate shrinkage and maximize financial security. Techniques of estate planning can be summarized by the *three Ds:* divide, defer, and discount.

DIVIDING. Each time a new tax-paying entity is created, income taxes will be saved and estate accumulation stimulated. Some of the more popular techniques are:

1. *Giving income-producing property to children, either outright or in trust.* Because each child can receive a specified amount of unearned income each year, some income tax savings may be realized each year even by persons who are not in high tax brackets.
2. *Establishing a corporation.* Incorporation may permit individuals in high tax brackets, such as doctors or other professionals, to save taxes by accumulating income in a manner subject to relatively lower income tax rates.
3. *Properly qualifying for the federal estate tax marital deduction.* This marital deduction allows an individual to pass—estate tax free—unlimited amounts to a spouse, taking full advantage of both spouses' unified credits. Properly qualifying in some estates may mean something less than fully qualifying. In other words, there are circumstances in which an advisor will properly recommend passing less than an individual's entire estate to the surviving spouse.

DEFERRING. Progressive tax rates (rates that increase as the amount of income or size of the estate increases) penalize taxpayers whose maximum earnings (or estates) reach high peaks. This makes it more difficult to gain and retain financial security. There are techniques to minimize the total tax burden by spreading income over more than 1 tax year or deferring the tax to a later period so the taxpayer can invest the tax money for a longer period of time. Examples include:

1. *Nonqualified deferred-compensation plans* for selected individuals in corporate businesses and private contractors.
2. *Making installment sales* instead of cash sales to spread the taxable gain over several years.
3. *Private annuities,* which are arrangements whereby one person transfers property to another, usually a younger family member. This recipient promises in return to pay an annuity to the original owner for as long as he or she lives. The income tax attributable to such an annuity can thereby be spread over a number of years. Furthermore, when the original owner dies, the property transferred is not part of the transferrer's estate and the annuity value drops to zero.
4. *Qualified pension and profit-sharing plans* that allow tax deferral on the income and gains from investments.
5. *Government Series EE bonds* because their earnings can be treated as taxable income at maturity rather than yearly as earned.
6. *Stocks that pay no or low dividends* but provide high price appreciation because they invest retained earnings in profitable projects.
7. *Life insurance policies* in which lifetime growth is not taxed and death values are income-tax free. If the insured survives, earnings inherent in policy values become taxable only as received, thus the tax on any gain can be deferred over a lifetime.
8. *Depreciable real estate* that yields high write-offs in years when the estate owner is earning high levels of taxable passive income.
9. *Installment payment of federal estate taxes* applicable to a business interest that equals or exceeds 35 percent of the adjusted gross estate. Payments can be spread over as

many as 14 years with only the interest being paid on the unpaid tax during the first 4 years.

10. *Possible elimination of the estate tax* in the near future, or at least additional significant increases in the applicable exclusion amount. (This is discussed in greater detail in a following section.)

Because of the popularity of tax-deferred retirement programs, these assets may comprise the bulk of a person's estate. The *Money in Action* box on page 682 discusses how to protect those accounts and make sure that your heirs get the maximum benefit.

DISCOUNTING. Even after everything has been done to accumulate an estate and reduce the income and estate tax burdens on it, there may still be a tax due. But life insurance can be used to, in effect, pay estate taxes at a discount.

Life insurance is one of the primary tools of estate planners. A person other than the insured or the insured's spouse, or a trust, can purchase a policy for an annual premium of from 3 to 6 percent of the face (death) value of the policy. If someone other than the insured owns the policy, the proceeds of such insurance will pass to the decedent's beneficiaries free of income tax, estate tax, inheritance tax, and probate costs. The beneficiaries may use such proceeds to pay death taxes, debts, and other probate and administrative costs. Life insurance proceeds can also be used to pay family expenses, special needs (such as college costs), mortgage balances, and other major expenditures. What's more, whole life and universal life insurance policies are an attractive form of loan collateral. As pointed out in Chapters 7 and 8, some lending institutions and other creditors require borrowers to obtain life insurance in an amount sufficient to repay them in the event borrowers die before fully repaying their loans.

FUTURE OF THE ESTATE TAX

The new estate tax regulations passed in 2001 raise the applicable exclusion amounts and the transfer tax rates, with a complete repeal of the estate tax in 2010. However, you should not ignore estate planning because Congress may at some future date decide to reestablish estate taxes.

As we've learned in this chapter, estate planning goes beyond minimizing taxes. It is the best way to take care of the people you love, help charitable organizations, transfer property, and spell out your wishes if you die or become disabled. Regardless of what happens to the estate tax in the future, estate planning will continue to be a key component of personal financial planning.

CONCEPT CHECK

15-16. Explain the following as they relate to federal and state estate taxes: (a) general nature of the estate tax, (b) computation of the *federal estate tax due*, (c) state inheritance tax, (d) state estate tax, (e) sponge tax, (f) pickup estate tax, (g) amount of exemptions and deductions, (h) multiple taxation, and (i) state death-tax rates.

15-17. The techniques of estate planning can be summarized by the three Ds: divide, defer, and discount. Describe and discuss each of the three Ds and their associated strategies.

MONEY IN ACTION

Making Your IRA a Survivor

For many people, their IRA will account for most of their estates—in some cases, as much as 80 percent of total assets. If you start your retirement savings early and maximize your contributions to employer-sponsored 401(k) plans or other tax-deferred programs like Keogh and 403(b), your savings will compound over your career to reach a sizable sum. Each time you change jobs and also when you retire, you must roll the proceeds from your plans into an IRA.

However, retirement accounts often get short shrift in the estate-planning process. The same people who agonize over who will get Mom's jewelry and whether to leave $5,000 or $10,000 to Cousin Joe typically neglect this important area of estate planning. They mistakenly assume that their wills also cover their retirement accounts. In fact, the disposition of these funds is governed by the beneficiary designation on each account and the custodial agreement with the bank or mutual fund company.

"The key is to pass IRA savings on to heirs intact so the money keeps growing long after you are gone," says Ed Slott, editor of *Ed Slott's IRA Advisor*. Good IRA estate planning avoids paying taxes from the IRA itself and allows an heir to stretch mandatory distributions over his or her remaining lifetime, so the savings continue to grow tax free.

Some financial planners recommend drafting a separate document called a *retirement asset will (RAW)* with details of beneficiaries and distribution arrangements. The RAW is especially useful when it comes to control of retirement assets. Without instructions from you to the contrary, the custodial agreement might allow a beneficiary to change heirs or prevent the beneficiary from changing to another money manager.

To make sure that your IRA is handled according to your wishes, follow these guidelines:

- *Designate a beneficiary on every IRA account and keep copies of the beneficiary forms with your will.* Without proof that you named a beneficiary, your IRA could be liquidated, taxed, rolled into your estate, and taxed again.
- *Provide assets to pay estate taxes without taking an IRA distribution that generates hefty taxes.* A life-insurance policy that pays when the second spouse dies is one option. The policy should be put in the heir's name and funded through annual tax-free gifts.
- *Make sure beneficiaries can move the account to another bank or fund custodian.* Some custodians may balk at this; be sure before you open an account that the custodian will honor your detailed instructions.
- *Do not name your estate as beneficiary of your IRA.* The estate must liquidate the account within a specified time and pay taxes on it.
- *Leave an IRA to younger beneficiaries to take advantage of the new stretch IRAs.* Stretch IRAs allow you to pass on your wealth for two generations and reduce the amount you must withdraw during your lifetime. For example, if a mother names her son as beneficiary, at age $70\frac{1}{2}$ she can choose to stretch benefits out over her life and her son's life. On her death, her son gets the IRA, can spread withdrawals over his remaining life expectancy, and pays only income taxes on the amount he withdraws every year. If the son names his own beneficiary, the proceeds can be spread to a third generation (but no further). Be sure your account is with a firm that permits stretch IRAs; not all do.

Sources: Sharon Epperson, "Stretch That IRA," *Time*, October 30, 2000, p. 102; Dan Kadlec, "Of Man's Estate," *Time*, May 15, 2000, p. F1; Mike McNamee, "Passing on Your IRA," *Business Week*, April 9, 2001, p. 104; and "Why You Need a Will," *Kiplinger's Retirement Report*, March 2000, downloaded from **www.kiplinger.com/retreport/archives/2000/March/estate.htm**.

SUMMARY

LG1. Describe the role of estate planning in personal financial planning and identify the seven steps involved in the process. Estate planning involves the accumulation, preservation, and distribution of an estate in a manner that will most effectively achieve an estate owner's personal goals. The seven major steps to estate planning are: (1) assess family situation and set estate-planning goals, (2) gather comprehensive and accurate data, (3) list assets and determine estate value, (4) designate beneficiaries of estate, (5) estimate estate transfer costs, (6) formulate and implement a plan, and (7) review plan periodically and revise as necessary.

LG2. Recognize the importance of preparing a will and other documents to protect you and your estate. A person who dies without a valid will forfeits important privileges, including the right to decide how property will be distributed at death and the opportunity to select who will administer the estate and bear the burden of estate taxes and administrative expenses. The will should provide a clear and unambiguous expression of the testator's wishes, be flexible enough to encompass possible changes in family circumstances, and give proper regard to minimizing income, gift, and estate taxes. A will is valid only if properly executed by a person of sound mind. Once drawn up, wills can be changed by codicil or fully revoked. The executor, named in the will, is responsible for collecting the decedent's assets, paying his or her debts and taxes, and distributing any remaining assets to the beneficiaries in the prescribed fashion.

Other important estate-planning documents include the letter of last instructions, power of attorney, living will, and durable power of attorney for health care.

LG3. Explain how trusts are used in estate planning. The trust relationship arises when one party, the grantor, transfers property to a second party, the trustee, for the benefit of a third party, the beneficiary. Although there are a variety of different types of trusts, each is designed primarily for one or both of the following reasons: to save income and estate taxes and to manage and conserve property over a long period.

LG4. Determine whether a gift will be taxable and use planned gifts to reduce estate taxes. Gifts of cash, financial assets, and personal or real property made during the donor's lifetime are subject to federal taxes. A gift of $10,000 per year (indexed for inflation since 1998) to each recipient is excluded from the donor's gift tax calculation. Generally, donations to qualified charities and gifts between spouses are also excluded from the gift tax.

LG5. Calculate federal and state taxes due on an estate. Federal estate taxes are essentially a levy on the transfer of assets at death. They are unified (coordinated) with the gift tax—which imposes a graduated tax on the transfer of property during one's lifetime—so that the rates and credits are the same for both. Today, as a result of the 2001 Tax Act, the gift tax exclusion amount stays at $1,000,000, and the estate tax exclusion amount is scheduled to rise from $1,000,000 in 2002 to $3,500,000 in 2009 (and the estate tax will be completely repealed in 2010), thereby making it advantageous to incur estate tax rather than gift tax liabilities. Once federal estate taxes are computed, certain credits are allowed, and the resulting amount is payable in full generally within 9 months of the decedent's death. States also impose taxes on estates. The four basic types of state death taxes are the state inheritance tax, state estate tax, sponge tax, and pickup estate tax.

LG6. Use effective estate-planning techniques to minimize estate taxes. Most well-defined estate plans use the three Ds of estate planning—divide, defer, and discount. Dividing involves the creation of new tax entities; deferring gives an individual the use of money that would otherwise have been paid in taxes; and discounting typically involves using life insurance to pay estate taxes with "discounted" dollars.

QUESTIONS AND PROBLEMS

1. Generate a list of estate-planning objectives that apply to your personal family situation. Be sure to consider the size of your potential estate and both people planning and asset planning.

2. Renée and Steve Burrows are in their mid-30s and have two children, ages 8 and 5. They have combined annual income of $95,000 and own a house in joint tenancy with a market value of $310,000, on which they have a mortgage of $250,000. Steve has $100,000 in group term life insurance and an individual universal life policy for $150,000. However, the Burrowses have not yet prepared their wills. Steve plans to do one soon, but they think that Renée doesn't need one because the house is jointly owned. As their financial planner, explain why it is important for both Steve and Renée to draft wills as soon as possible.

3. Prepare a basic will for yourself, using the guidelines presented in the text; also prepare your brief letter of last instructions.

4. Your best friend has asked you to be executor of his estate. What qualifications do you need, and would you accept the responsibility?

5. Joe Phillips, 48 and a widower, and Amy Parsons, 44 and divorced, were married 5 years ago. Joe has two children and Amy has one from their prior marriages. Their estate totals $1.4 million, including a house valued at $475,000, a vacation home in the mountains, investments, antique furniture that has been in Amy's family for many years, and jewelry belonging to Joe's first wife. Discuss how they could use trusts as part of their estate planning, and suggest some other ideas for them to consider when preparing their wills and related documents.

6. *Use Worksheet 15.2.* When Jim Levitt died in 2002, he left an estate valued at $2,650,000, as follows: $10,000 to the local hospital, $60,000 to his alma mater, and the remainder to his three adult children. Death-related costs and expenses were: $6,800 for funeral expenses, $40,000 paid to attorneys, $5,000 paid to accountants, and $30,000 paid to the trustee of his living trust. In addition, there were debts of $115,000. Use Worksheet 15.2 and Exhibits 15.7, 15.8, and 15.9 to calculate the state death-tax credit and the federal estate tax due on his estate.

7. Summarize any recent legislation affecting estate taxes and briefly describe its impact on estate planning. Explain why getting rid of the estate tax won't eliminate the need for estate planning.

APPLYING PERSONAL FINANCE

Preparing Your Will

Having a will is important to your heirs, even if there is not a lot of money or property currently in your estate. If you do not have a will, your state's laws will draw the will you failed to make and thereby dictate the disposition of your estate and the guardian of your children, if any, which may not be in accordance with your wishes.

For this project, think about your will and write one for your property, real or imagined, based on the paragraph forms given in the text. Be sure to specify each beneficiary and the desired disposition of your estate to each of them. Also, don't forget to name your personal representative and charge him or her with disposing of your estate in accordance with your wishes. If you wish to convey any personal thoughts or instructions that you feel cannot be properly included in your will, prepare a letter of instructions that includes these suggestions or recommendations. Remember, this exercise should help you think about the orderly disposition of your estate—the final act in the implementation of your personal financial plans.

CONTEMPORARY CASE APPLICATIONS

15.1   A Long Overdue Will for Kris

Kris Pappadopolus, a Greek national, migrated to the United States during the late 1960s. A man of many talents and deep foresight, he has during his stay in the United States built a large fleet of ocean-going oil tankers. Now a wealthy man in his 60s, he resides in Palm Springs, Florida, with his second wife, Veronica, age 35. He has two sons, who are both high school seniors. For quite a while, Kris has considered preparing a will to ensure that his estate will be aptly distributed if some unforeseen tragedy or natural cause takes his life. A survey of his estate—all legally owned by him—reveals the following:

Ranch in Amarillo, Texas	$ 500,000
Condominium in San Francisco	200,000
House in Palm Springs	600,000
Franchise in ice cream stores	2,500,000
Stock in Seven Seas International	5,000,000
Shares in Fourth National Bank	1,000,000
Corporate bonds	3,000,000
Other assets	200,000
Total assets	$13,000,000

In addition to $1 million for their education and welfare, he would like to leave each of his sons 20 percent of his estate. He wishes to leave 40 percent of the estate to his wife. The rest of the estate is to be divided among relatives, friends, and charitable institutions. He has scheduled an appointment for drafting his will with his attorney and close friend, Leonard Wiseman. Kris would like to appoint Leonard and his cousin, Plato Jones, as coexecutors of his estate. If one of them predeceases Kris, he would like his bank, Fourth National Bank, to act as coexecutor.

Questions

1. Does Kris really need a will? Explain why or why not? What would happen to his estate if he were to die without a will?
2. Explain to Kris the common features that need to be incorporated into a will.
3. Is a living trust an appropriate part of his estate plan? How would a living trust change the nature of Kris's will?
4. What are the options available to Kris if he decides to change or revoke the will at a later date? Is it more difficult to change a living trust?
5. What duties will Leonard Wiseman and Plato Jones have to perform as coexecutors of Kris's estate?

15.2   Estate Taxes on Philip Colburn's Estate

Philip Colburn of Arlington Heights, Delaware, was 65 when he retired in 1994. His wife of 35 years passed away in 1999. Her will left everything to Philip. Although her estate was valued at $750,000, there was no estate tax due because of the 100 percent marital deduction.

Their only child, Mark Colburn, is married to Alice, and they have four children, two in college and two in high school. When Philip died in 2002, his home was valued at $650,000, his vacation cabin on the lake was valued at $85,000, his investments in stocks and bonds at $890,000, and his pension funds at $345,000 (Mark was named beneficiary). Philip also owned a life insurance policy that paid proceeds of $250,000 to Mark. He left $60,000 to his church and $25,000 to his high school to start a scholarship fund in his wife's name. The rest of the estate was left to Mark. Funeral costs were $5,000. Debts and expenses totaled $90,000. Four years prior to his death, he made a gift of XYZ stock worth $170,000 jointly to Mark and Alice. Because of the two annual exclusions and the unified credit, no gift taxes were due. Use Worksheet 15.2 to guide your calculations as you answer the following questions.

Questions

1. Compute the value of Philip's *probate estate.*
2. Compute the value of Philip's *gross estate* at the time of his death.
3. Determine the total allowable deductions.
4. Calculate the *estate tax base,* taking into account the gifts given to Mark and Alice (remember the annual exclusions).
5. Use **Exhibit 15.7** to determine the *tentative tax-on-estate tax base.*
6. Subtract the appropriate *unified tax credit* (Exhibit 15.8) for 2002 from the tentative tax-on-estate tax base to arrive at the *total death taxes.* Note that there is no credit for gift tax payable on post-1976 gifts because no gift taxes had to be paid.
7. Determine the *state death-tax credit.*
8. Subtract the state death-tax credit from the total death taxes to arrive at the *federal estate tax due.*
9. Comment on the estate shrinkage experienced on Philip's estate. What might have been done to reduce this shrinkage? Explain.

MONEY ONLINE

MY WILL BE DONE!

Note: Web addresses change frequently, so you may need to determine the home page and do a site search to find the page or topic that's referenced.

1. **www.northwesternmutual.com**
   Maximize the wealth you pass on to your loved ones. Click on "Personal Planning" and then on "Estate Planning" at Northwestern Mutual's Web site for information on the entire estate-planning process. Learn the basic concepts involved and techniques used in estate planning.
2. **www.usaaedfoundation.org**
   What documents are essential in a comprehensive estate plan? Click on "Financial" and then on "Estate Planning" to find an explanation of these necessary legal documents. Read through the article to learn how trusts and life insurance are used as estate-planning tools, how to plan for probate, and how to use property ownership laws in estate planning.

3. **lifenet.com**

   Why do you need estate planning? Why do you need a will? What are the different types of wills and trusts? Tap into "Estate Planning" at LifeNET's Web site for a comprehensive overview of the entire estate-planning process.

4. **www.nolo.com/encyclopedia**

   What can you NOT do in your will? Click on "Wills & Estate Planning" and look under "Wills" for the answer to this and other estate-planning questions. Access Nolo's extensive and comprehensive encyclopedia to find topics such as "Special Property Rules for Married People," "Using Roth IRAs to Avoid Probate," and "You May Not Need a Living Trust."

5. **www.netplanning.com/consumer**

   Want to avoid common estate planning mistakes? The National Network of Estate Planning Attorneys' Estate Planning and You section offers plenty of good advice.

6. **www.nysba.org/sections/elder/elderlinks.html**

   What legal resources are available on the Internet for the elderly? Visit the Elder Law Section of the New York Bar Association's site for an extensive listing. Find a well-organized collection of links to general legal resources, federal agencies, and estate-planning sites.

7. **www.danbrady.com/articles.htm**

   Are you fiscally fit? Take a self-test by clicking on "Estate Planning Checklist" at this legal Web site. Be sure to examine "Estate Planning Concepts" for a thorough discussion of estate and gift tax provisions. Then read through "Talking with Adult Children," a discussion on the importance of involving one's children in the estate-planning process.

8. **www.nafep.com**

   What legal risks do your assets face? What steps can you take to protect your assets for your loved ones? Find out by clicking on "Protection of Your Assets from Lawsuits and Judgments" at the Web site of the National Association of Financial and Estate Planning.

9. **www.prusec.com/financial_concerns/charit.htm**

   Benefit yourself, your family, and your favorite charity as well with a charitable remainder trust. Learn what charitable remainder trusts are, how they work, and the tax benefits they can provide to you and your family at the Web site of Prudential Securities.

10. **www.estateplanninglinks.com**

    Links and more links! The Estate Planning Links Web site has links for virtually every estate planning need! Find links to legal resources, definitions, calculators, tax information, and much more.

Just for Fun!

11. **www.ca-probate.com/wills.htm**

    Read the wills of famous people and common folk alike! The Web site of California Estate Planning, Probate & Trust Law presents Wills on the Web, some of which date back to the 1400s! Find the wills of Princess Diana, John Lennon, Walt Disney, and "Shoeless" Joe Jackson. Go back in time and read the 1789 will of Benjamin Franklin or the 1493 will of Thomas Sherman of England.

Appendixes

APPENDIX A
Table of Future Value
Factors

APPENDIX B
Table of Future Value
of Annuity Factors

APPENDIX C
Table of Present Value
Factors

APPENDIX D
Table of Present Value
of Annuity Factors

APPENDIX A

Table of Future Value Factors

Instructions: To use this table, find the future value factor that corresponds to both a given time period (year) and an interest rate. To illustrate, if you want the future value factor for 6 years and 10 percent, move across from year 6 and down from 10 percent to the point at which the row and column intersect: 1.772. Other illustrations: For 3 years and 15 percent, the proper future value factor is 1.521; for 30 years and 8 percent, it is 10.062.

							Interest Rate					
Year	**2%**	**3%**	**5%**	**6%**	**8%**	**9%**	**10%**	**12%**	**15%**	**20%**	**25%**	**30%**
1	1.020	1.030	1.050	1.060	1.080	1.090	1.100	1.120	1.150	1.120	1.250	1.300
2	1.040	1.060	1.102	1.120	1.166	1.190	1.210	1.254	1.322	1.440	1.562	1.690
3	1.061	1.090	1.158	1.190	1.260	1.290	1.331	1.405	1.521	1.728	1.953	2.197
4	1.082	1.130	1.216	1.260	1.360	1.410	1.464	1.574	1.749	2.074	2.441	2.856
5	1.104	1.160	1.276	1.340	1.469	1.540	1.611	1.762	2.011	2.488	3.052	3.713
6	1.126	1.190	1.340	1.420	1.587	1.670	1.772	1.974	2.313	2.986	3.815	4.827
8	1.172	1.260	1.477	1.590	1.851	1.990	2.144	2.476	3.059	4.300	5.960	8.157
10	1.219	1.340	1.629	1.790	2.159	2.360	2.594	3.106	4.046	6.192	9.313	13.786
12	1.268	1.420	1.796	2.010	2.518	2.810	3.138	3.896	5.350	8.916	14.552	23.298
15	1.346	1.560	2.079	2.390	3.172	3.640	4.177	5.474	8.137	15.407	28.422	51.185
20	1.486	1.810	2.653	3.210	4.661	5.600	6.727	9.646	16.366	38.337	86.736	190.047
25	1.641	2.090	3.386	4.290	6.848	8.620	10.834	17.000	32.918	95.395	264.698	705.627
30	1.811	2.420	4.322	5.740	10.062	13.260	17.449	29.960	66.210	237.373	807.793	2619.936
35	2.000	2.810	5.516	7.690	14.785	20.410	28.102	52.799	133.172	590.657	2465.189	9727.598
40	2.208	3.260	7.040	10.280	21.724	31.410	45.258	93.049	267.856	1469.740	7523.156	36117.754

Note: All factors to nearest 1/1000 as shown to agree with values used in the text.

APPENDIX B

Table of Future Value of Annuity Factors

Instructions: To use this table, find the future value of annuity factor that corresponds to both a given time period (year) and an interest rate. To illustrate, if you want the future value of annuity factor for 6 years and 10 percent, move across from year 6 and down from 10 percent to the point at which the row and column intersect: 7.716. Other illustrations: For 3 years and 15 percent, the proper future value of annuity factor is 3.472; for 30 years and 8 percent, it is 113.282.

Interest Rate

Year	2%	3%	5%	6%	8%	9%	10%	12%	15%	20%	25%	30%
1	1.000	1.000	1.000	1.000	1.000	1.000	1.000	1.000	1.000	1.000	1.000	1.000
2	2.020	2.030	2.050	2.060	2.080	2.090	2.100	2.120	2.150	2.200	2.250	2.300
3	3.060	3.090	3.152	3.180	3.246	3.270	3.310	3.374	3.472	3.640	3.813	3.990
4	4.122	4.180	4.310	4.380	4.506	4.570	4.641	4.779	7.993	5.368	5.766	6.187
5	5.204	5.310	5.526	5.630	5.867	5.980	6.105	6.353	6.742	7.442	8.207	9.043
6	6.308	6.460	6.802	6.970	7.336	7.520	7.716	8.115	8.754	9.930	11.259	12.756
8	8.583	8.890	9.549	9.890	10.637	11.030	11.436	12.300	13.727	16.499	19.842	23.858
10	10.950	11.460	12.578	13.180	14.487	15.190	15.937	17.549	20.304	25.959	33.253	42.619
12	13.412	14.190	15.917	16.870	18.977	20.140	21.384	24.133	29.001	39.580	54.208	74.326
15	17.293	18.600	21.578	23.270	27.152	29.360	31.772	37.280	47.580	72.035	109.687	167.285
20	24.297	26.870	33.066	36.780	45.762	51.160	57.274	72.052	102.443	186.687	342.945	630.157
25	32.030	36.460	47.726	54.860	73.105	84.700	98.346	133.333	212.790	471.976	1054.791	2348.765
30	40.567	47.570	66.438	79.060	113.282	136.300	164.491	241.330	434.738	1181.865	3227.172	8729.805
35	49.994	60.460	90.318	111.430	172.314	215.700	271.018	431.658	881.152	2948.294	9856.746	32422.090
40	60.401	75.400	120.797	154.760	259.052	337.870	442.580	767.080	1779.048	7343.715	30088.621	120389.375

Note: All factors to nearest 1/1000 as shown to agree with values used in the text.

APPENDIX C

Table of Present Value Factors

Instructions: To use this table, find the present value factor that corresponds to both a given time period (year) and an interest rate. To illustrate, if you want the present value factor for 25 years and 7 percent, move across from year 25 and down from 7 percent to the point at which the row and column intersect: .184. Other illustrations: For 3 years and 15 percent, the proper present value factor is .658; for 30 years and 8 percent, it is .099.

					Interest Rate							
Year	2%	3%	5%	7%	8%	9%	10%	12%	15%	20%	25%	30%
1	.980	.971	.952	.935	.926	.917	.909	.833	.870	.893	.800	.769
2	.961	.943	.907	.873	.857	.842	.826	.797	.756	.694	.640	.592
3	.942	.915	.864	.816	.794	.772	.751	.712	.658	.579	.512	.455
4	.924	.888	.823	.763	.735	.708	.683	.636	.572	.482	.410	.350
5	.906	.863	.784	.713	.681	.650	.621	.567	.497	.402	.328	.269
6	.888	.837	.746	.666	.630	.596	.564	.507	.432	.335	.262	.207
8	.853	.789	.677	.582	.540	.502	.467	.404	.327	.233	.168	.123
10	.820	.744	.614	.508	.463	.422	.386	.322	.247	.162	.107	.073
12	.789	.701	.557	.444	.397	.356	.319	.257	.187	.112	.069	.043
15	.743	.642	.481	.362	.315	.275	.239	.183	.123	.065	.035	.020
20	.673	.554	.377	.258	.215	.178	.149	.104	.061	.026	.012	.005
25	.610	.478	.295	.184	.146	.116	.092	.059	.030	.010	.004	.001
30	.552	.412	.231	.131	.099	.075	.057	.033	.015	.004	.001	*
35	.500	.355	.181	.094	.068	.049	.036	.019	.008	.002	*	*
40	.453	.307	.142	.067	.046	.032	.022	.011	.004	.001	*	*

*Present value factor is zero to three decimal places.

Note: All factors to nearest 1/1000 as shown to agree with values used in the text.

APPENDIX D

Table of Present Value of Annuity Factors

Instructions: To use this table, find the present value of annuity factor that corresponds to both a given time period (year) and an interest rate. To illustrate, if you want the present value of annuity factor for 30 years and 7 percent, move across from year 30 and down from 7 percent to the point at which the row and column intersect: 12.409. Other illustrations: For 3 years and 15 percent, the proper present value of annuity factor is 2.283; for 5 years and 8 percent, it is 3.993; for 30 years and 8 percent, it is 11.258.

Interest Rate

Year	2%	3%	5%	7%	8%	9%	10%	12%	15%	20%	25%	30%
1	.980	.971	.952	.935	.926	.917	.909	.893	.870	.833	.800	.769
2	1.942	1.913	1.859	1.808	1.783	1.759	1.736	1.690	1.626	1.528	1.440	1.361
3	2.884	2.829	2.723	2.624	2.577	2.531	2.487	2.402	2.283	2.106	1.952	1.816
4	3.808	3.717	3.546	3.387	3.312	3.240	3.170	3.037	2.855	2.589	2.362	2.166
5	4.713	4.580	4.329	4.100	3.993	3.890	3.791	3.605	3.352	2.991	2.689	2.436
6	5.601	5.417	5.076	4.767	4.623	4.486	4.355	4.111	3.784	3.326	2.951	2.643
8	7.326	7.020	6.463	5.971	5.747	5.535	5.335	4.968	4.487	3.837	3.329	2.925
10	8.983	8.530	7.722	7.024	6.710	6.418	6.145	5,650	5.019	4.192	3.570	3.092
12	10.575	9.954	8.863	7.943	7.536	7.161	6.814	6.194	5.421	4.439	3.725	3.190
15	12.849	11.938	10.380	9.108	8.560	8.061	7.606	6.811	5.847	4.675	3.859	3.268
20	16.352	14.878	12.462	10.594	9.818	9.129	8.514	7.469	6.259	4.870	3.954	3.316
25	19.524	17.413	14.094	11.654	10.675	9.823	9.077	7.843	6.464	4.948	3.985	3.329
30	22.396	19.601	15.373	12.409	11.258	10.274	9.427	8.055	6.566	4.979	3.995	3.332
35	24.999	21.487	16.378	12.948	11.655	10.567	9.844	8.176	6.617	4.992	3.998	3.333
40	27.356	23.115	17.159	13.332	11.925	10.757	9.779	8.244	6.642	4.997	3.999	3.333

Note: All factors to nearest 1/1000 as shown to agree with values used in the text.

Index

Boldface = glossary term

A

abortion, health insurance and, 378
accelerated benefits, 348
    insurance, 314
acceleration clause, 299
accident, automobile, 435
accident insurance, 375
account
    accumulation, 337
    checking, 141–143
    open, borrowing on. *See* Credit
    retirement, 583. *See also* Retirement
        planning
    savings, 142–143
    share draft, 139
    wrap, 479
account executive, 461–463
account reconciliation, 161–163
accumulated period, 632
accumulated wealth, 17–18
accumulation account, 337
acquisition, asset, 17
active income, 94
actual cash value, 408
ADB. *See* Average daily balance
add-on method, 302–303
adjustable rate mortgage (ARM)
    convertible, 211
    defined, **210**
    fixed rate vs, 212
adjusted gross income, 98
adjustment
    claims, 436
    to gross income, 108
adjustments to gross income, 98
administrator of estate, **664**
ADR. *See* American Depository Report
advance, cash, 234
adverse selection, 318
advisor, investment, 479
advisory services, investment, 478–479
affinity card, 238
affordability analysis, 196–199
affordability ratio, mortgage, 195–196

after-tax IRA, 628, 629
age
    income related to, 26
    medial net worth and income
        by, 57
    retirement, 604–605, 621
agency, insurance rating, 353
agency bond, 535–536
agent
    health insurance, 394
    life insurance, 354–355
    mutual fund transfer, 562
    real estate, 203–204
agreement, security, 297
allocation, asset, 492–494
allocation fund, asset, 578–579
A.M. Best Company, 353
AMA. *See* Asset management account
amended return, 114
American Depository Report (ADR),
    525–526
American Express, 240
American Express Optima, 241
American Stock Exchange (AMEX),
    455–456, **475**
    quotation system of, 478
Amex Blue, 241
amortization, negative, 211
annual contribution, insurance, 337
annual exclusion, 672
annual percentage rate (APR)
    credit card, 252, 253
    installment loan, 303
annual stockholders' report, 471–472
annuity
    classification of, 632–636
    cost of, 636–637
    defined, **49, 632**
    investment and income properties
        of, 637–640
    principle of, 632
    private, 680
    sources of, 636
annuity certain, 634–**635**
annuity factors, 691, 693
apartment, cooperative, 187–188
application
    credit, 246

    loan, 291, 292
    online credit card, 247
    student loan, 277
approximate yield, 512–513, 521–522
APR. *See* Annual percentage rate
    credit card, **252**, 253
    installment loan, 303
arbitration, 464
ARM. *See* Adjustable rate mortgage
ask price, 456
asset allocation, 492–494
asset allocation fund, 578–579
asset management account (AMA),
    144
assets
    accumulating, 6
        for retirement, 19
    acquisition of, 17
    defined, **54**
    in estate planning, 651–652
    liquid, 54, 136
association, individual practice, 367
ATM. *See* Automated teller machine
attorney
    insurance, 436
    for will preparation, 658
audit, tax, 114–115
auto loan, 274
automated teller machine (ATM), 144
automatic investment plan, 579–581
automatic reinvestment plan, 581–582
automobile, 173–185
    buying, 7, 178–182
    buying vs leasing, 173–174, 183–185
    choosing, 174–178
    leasing, 182–185
automobile insurance plan, 420–430
    cost of, 428–429
    coverage by, 420–424
    defined, **428**
    financial responsibility laws and,
        430
    no-fault, 424–426
    premiums, 426–428
automobile loan, 61, 63
automobile rebate program, 235
average daily balance (ADB), 252, 253
average propensity to consume, 5

average tax rate, 90
aviation exclusion, 347
avoidance, risk
 health insurance and, 391–392
 life insurance and, 316–317

B

back-end load, 567
bailout clause, 639
balance, unpaid credit card, 259
balance sheet, 53–59
 assets on, 54–55
 defined, **40**
 liabilities on, 55–56
 net worth and, 56
 preparation of, 56–59
balance sheet ratio, 67–68
balanced fund, 574
balloon-payment mortgage, 209
balloon payment on consumer
  loan, **299**
bank
 commercial, **138**
 loans from, 280
 trust department of, 479
bank account record, 66
bank-by-phone account, 145–146
bank card statement, 254, 255
bank credit card, 233
 features of, 234–236
bank services, electronic, 144–149
bank statement, monthly, 161–163
banker
 investment, 454
 mortgage, 207
bankruptcy, 263–265
Barron's, 476
basic hospital insurance, Medicare, 371
bear market, 460
beneficiary, 343
 trust, **667**
benefit option, residual, 387
benefits
 accelerated, 348
 accelerated insurance, 314
 coordination of, 377–378
 disability income, 387–388
 employee, 18–19, 43–44
 life insurance, 318–320
 living, 348
 long-term care, 383
 pension plan, 621–622
 retiree health, 393–394

 social security retirement, 613–618
 social security survivor's, 325–327,
  613
beta, 521
bid price, 456
bill payment services, online, 146–148
biweekly mortgage, 213
Black Monday, 460
blue-chip stock, 522, **523**
Blue Cross/Blue Shield, 391
Blue Cross/Blue Shield plans, 370–371
Blue Cross-sponsored health care,
  370–371
boat insurance, 431, 433
bodily injury liability losses, 421
bond, mutual fund vs, 586
bond fund, 574–575
bonds, 530–545
 brokerage fee on, 465–466
 definition of, 452
 issue characteristics of, 531–534
 prices and yields of, 542–545
 ratings of, 538–541
 reason to invest in, 530–531
 series EE, 156
 stocks vs, 531
 types of, 534–538
book value, 520
borrowed securities, selling of,
  469–470
borrowing. *See* credit; loan
bracket creep, 90
broker
 car, 180
 mortgage, 207–208
 stock, 461–463
brokerage fee, 465–466
brokerage report, 478
brokerage services, 463
budget, 40
budget, cash, 69–76
 actual results compared to, 74–76
 deficits in, 72
 example of, 72–74
 process of, 70–72
budget control schedule, 75
bull market
 of 1982–2000, 515
 defined, **459**–461
business in financial planning
  environment, 23
business risk, 506
buy-down, 214
buying guide, automobile, 178
buying service, automobile, 180

C

cafeteria plan, 44
calculator, financial, 52–53
 for auto loan amount, 175
 for bond yield, 543–544
 for compound interest, 153–154
 how to use, 52–53
 online, 485
 for retirement income, 608
call-deferment period, 534
call feature, 532, 534
cap, interest rate, 210
capital
 investment, 447–451
 preservation of, 492
capital gains, 96–97, 508
 from common stock sale, 517
captive agent, 434
captive finance company, 284
car. *See* Automobile
card
 affinity, 238, 239
 credit. *See* Credit card
 debit, 144, 239
 prepaid, 240–241
 prestige, 238, 239
 retail charge, 233, 237
 travel and entertainment, 237–238
career
 changing, 16
 income related to, 29
 planning of, 29–30
 Web sites about, 35–36
cash
 dividend reinvestment vs, 529–530
 on income and expense statement,
  60–63
 in portfolio, 155
 time payment vs, 304–306
cash advance, 234
cash basis, 60
cash budget, 69–76
 defined, **70**
cash deficit, 63
cash dividend, 517–518
cash management, 135–137
cash management products,
  141–149
 checking account, 141–142
 savings account, 142
cash surplus, 63
cash value (of life insurance), 284,
  332–333
cashier's check, 163

certificate of deposit (CD), 154–155
as index for adjustable rate mortgage, 211
certification
of insurance agent, 354
pre-admission, 379
certified check, 165
certified financial planner, 47
Chapter 11 bankruptcy, 264–265
Chapter 13 bankruptcy, 264–265
charge card, retail, 233, 237
charitable deduction, 673
chartered financial consultant, 47
chattel mortgage, 291
check
title, 206
types of, 163, 165
checkbook ledger, 159
checking account
interest-paying, 142–143
maintaining of, 158–165
types of, 141–142
checklist, executor's, 662–663
child
allowance for, 14
in estate plan, 651
life insurance needs and, 321
Citicorp Diners Club, 241
claim
life insurance, 345
property insurance, 434–436
claims adjustor, 436
clause
acceleration, 299
bailout, 639
beneficiary, 343–344
contingency, 205
disability, 347
multiple indemnity, 347
other-insurance, 409
participation (coinsurance), 376
preexisting condition, 378
suicide, 347
closed-end investment company, 563
buying shares of, 570
closed-end lease, 181
closing cost, 191–**192**
closing of real estate deal, 206
closing statement, 206
co-branded credit card, 235
COBRA. *See* Consolidated Omnibus Budget Reconciliation Act
code, tax, 88
codicil, 661–662
coinsurance

property, 409
waiver of, for health care, 379
coinsurance clause, 376
COLA. *See* cost-of-living adjustment
collateral, 274, 287, 291
collateral note, 291
collateralized credit card, 239
college financing, 275–279
collision insurance, 423–424
commercial bank, 138
loans from, 280, 282
commission, 48
brokerage, 465–466
commodities, 453
common stock, 452, 513–530
brokerage fee on, 465
investing in, 526–530
issuers of, 514–517
putting value on, 521–522
tax considerations about, 517
Community Health Systems, Inc., 515–517
community property, 666
company data, 476
compound interest, 152–154
compounding, 49
comprehensive automobile insurance, 424
comprehensive major medical insurance, 374
computer-based retirement planning, 609
computer-based tax return, 117–119
computerized benefits estimation service, 616
condominium, 187, 188
Consolidated Omnibus Budget Reconciliation Act (COBRA), 379
consolidation loan, 274–275
consultant, financial, 461–463
consumer credit legislation, 261, 262
Consumer Credit Protection Act, 262
Consumer Credit Reporting Reform Act, 262
consumer debt, tracking of, 289–290
consumer finance company, 280, **281,** 282
consumer installment loan, 56, 279, 296–307
consumer loan, 272–312. *See also* Loan defined, 274
consumer price index (CPI), 25
Consumer Reports, 178
consuming, average propensity for, 5

contingency clause, 205
continuous-premium whole life policy, 334
contract
automobile sales, 180–181
installment purchase, 297–299
life insurance, 343–346
real estate sales, 205
rental, 199–200
contract charge for annuity, 636
contribution
annual insurance, 337
to pension plan, 620–621
contributory pension plan, 620
conventional mortgage, 214
conversion premium, 549
conversion privilege
mutual fund, **583**
for securities, **547**
conversion ratio, 547
conversion value, 547
convertibility of term life insurance, **331**–332
convertible ARM, 211
convertible bond fund, 575
convertible securities, 453, 546–549
quotes of, 540
cooperative apartment, 187–188
coordination of benefits, 377–378
corporate bond, 537
quotes of, 540–541
corporate debt issue, 533
cost
annuity, 636–637
consumer loan, 282–283, 287
death-related, 653
financial planning, 46
health care, 362–364, 379
health care insurance, 392–393
of home ownership, 190–196
insurance, 350
loan, 287
of long-term health care, 381–384
of renting vs buying home, 201
replacement, 408, 415–416
shareholder transaction, 570
cost containment, health care, 379
cost-of-living adjustment (COLA), 388
cost of living index, 28
counselor, credit, 265–266
coupon, 531
zero coupon bond, 537–538
coupon rate, 542–545
coverage
health insurance, 378–379

home owner's insurance, 414–415
insurance, 17
medical payment, 422
CPI. *See* Consumer price index
health insurance costs and, 363
crash, stock market, 460–461, 515
credit, 224–271
basic concepts of, 224–226
danger signs about, 228
establishing, 228–232
improper uses of, 227–228, 263–265
line of, 234
minimum payments on, 227
open, 232–233
reasons to use, 226
tax, **104**
credit application, 246
credit bureau, 248–251
credit card
account management, 254–256
affinity, 238
bank, 233–236
features of, 240–241
finance charges on, 252–253
opening account for, 245–252
prepaid, 240
prestige, 238
retail, 236
secured, 239
thirty-day charge account, 236
travel and entertainment, 236–238
wise use of, 256–266
credit card application, online, 247
credit card fraud, 261, 263
credit counselor, 265–266
credit estate tax, 677
credit investigation, 246–248
credit life insurance, 341
credit limit, 233
credit line
home equity, 243–245
revolving, 241–245
unsecured personal, 242–243
credit scoring, 251
credit statement, 233
credit union, 139, 281, 283
cumulative preferred stock, 546
current income. *See* income
current liability, 55
current needs, 5
current yield, bond, **542**
custodial account for child, 651
custodian, mutual fund, 562
cyclical stock, 523
Cypress Semiconductor Corp., 547, 548

D

daily benefits, long-term care, 383
danger sign, credit, 228
data
company, 476
industry, 476
day trader, 486–488
deadline, tax filing, 113–114
death proceeds, 344
death-related cost, 653
death taxes, state, 676–679
debenture, 532
convertible bond as, 548
debit card, 144, 239
debt
bond as, 452, 548
deferred-premium life insurance as, 342
life insurance needs and, 323
tracking of, 289–290
debt safety ratio, 230
debt service ratio, 68
decreasing term policy, 329
deductible
health insurance, 375–376
homeowner's insurance, 417
deductible IRA, 628, 629
deduction
charitable, 673
itemized, 98–100, 108
marital, 673
standard, 100–101, 108
state death tax, 678
default, on student loan, 276
defensive stock, 523, 524
deferred annuity, 635
deferred-premium life insurance, 342
deferring of estate tax, 679–680
deficit, cash, 63, 72–73
defined benefits plan, 621–**622**
defined contribution plan, 621
demand deposit, 142
dental expenses, deductible, 99
dental insurance, 374
deposit
earnest money, 205
pre-authorized, 145
types of, 142–143
deposit insurance, 140–141
depreciable real estate, 680
depreciation, 175
depression, 24
derivative securities, 453
desired rate of return, 513

disability
definition of, 387
estate affected by, 653
disability clause, 347
disability income, 372
disability income insurance, 385–390
disability insurance, credit, 297–298
disclosure statement
about fees, 48
loan, 293, 294
discount, automobile insurance, 429
discount bond, 542
discount broker, 462, 466
discount method, 295
discounting, 51
Discover Card, 241
distribution period, 632
distributor, mutual fund, 562
diversification, 489–490
pooled, 559
dividend
common stock, 517–518
preferred stock, 545
dividend reinvestment plan (DRP), 529
dividend yield, 518
preferred stock, 546
dividing an estate, 679
Dodge and Cox Balanced fund, 568–569
Dow Jones Industrial Average (DJIA)
defined, 473
drop in, 460–461, 514
important dates for, 474
down payment, 190–191
Dreyfus Aggressive Value Fund, 568–569
Dreyfus Global Growth fund, 568, 569
DRP. *See* Dividend reinvestment plan
Duff & Phelps, 353
durable goods, loan for, 274
durable power of attorney for health care, 665

E

earnest money deposit, 205
earnings, stock, 529–530
earnings per share (EPS), 520
earthquake insurance, 431
economic cycle, 23–24
economic data, 472
economic needs, life insurance and, 322, 324–326

economics of income taxes, 88–90
economy in financial planning
    environment, 23–26
Edmund's Used Car Prices, 180
education, income related to, 27, 28
education loan, 274
effective rate of interest, 152
EFTS. *See* Electronic funds transfer
    system
electronic banking services, 144–149
electronic broker, 462–463
electronic communications networks
    (ECN), 457–458
**electronic funds transfer system
    (EFTS), 144**–146
    buying and selling using, **570**
eligibility
    for long-term care insurance, 382
    for social security, 612–613
elimination period, 383
emergency
    borrowing to meet, 226
    credit card for, 259
emergency center, neighborhood, 362
emotional disorder, insurance covering,
    378–379
emotional response to money, 9–10
employee benefits, 18–19
    health care insurance as, 393–394
    managing of, 43–44
**Employee Retirement Income Security
    Act (ERISA), 619,** 631
employer-sponsored pension plan,
    619–627
end of automobile lease, 182
EPS. *See* Earnings per share
Equal Credit Opportunity Act,
    231, 262
equipment trust certificate, 532
equity, 56
equity credit line, home, 243–245
equity-income fund, 574
equity real estate investment trust, 566
equivalent yield, taxable, 537
ERISA. *See* Employee Retirement
    Income Security Act
estate planning, 19, 648–687
    defined, **649**
    estate taxes and, 674–682
    gift taxes in, 670–674
    principles of, 649–656
    trusts in, 667–670
    wills in, 656–667. *See also* Will
estate tax
    defined, **671**

federal, 674–676
    phase-out of, 680, 682
estimated taxes, 113
E*Trade Web site, 482–483
event risk, 507
exchange privileges, 583
exchange-traded fund, 564–565
excise taxes, 124
exclusion
    life insurance, 347–348
    for unified tax credit, 675
exclusive provider organization, 367
execution and attestation clause of will,
    660
execution of will, 661
executive, account, 461–463
executor, 664
    checklist for, 662–663
exemption, 109
    state death tax, 678
exemption, 101
expansion, 24
expected rate of return, 511–512
expense, medical, 373–375
expense category, 64
expenses
    defined, **60**
    estimating, 70–72
    on income and expense statement,
        60–65
    investment objectives and, 451
    rehabilitation, 372
exposure
    liability, 408
    to property loss, 406–408
extended-term insurance, 346
extension, tax filing, 114

F

Fair Credit and Charge Card Disclosure
    Act, 262
Fair Credit Billing Act, 262
Fair Debt Collection Practices Act, 262
fair market value, 54
federal deposit insurance programs,
    140
federal estate tax, 674–676
federal income tax, 86–123. *See also*
    Income tax
**Federal insurance Contributions
    Act, 93**
federal unified transfer tax rate, 671
federal withholding taxes, 92

fee, 48
    annuity, 636
    12b-1, 567–568
    brokerage, 465–466
    credit card, 236
    mutual fund management, 568–570
    surrender, 639
fee-for-service plan, 365
fee table, mutual fund, 571
FEEL loan program, 275
**FHA mortgage insurance program,
    214**
Fidelity online planning services, 484
filing, taxes, 113–115
filing extension, 114
filing status, tax, 90–92
finance charge
    on consumer loan, 286–287, 295
    on credit card, 252
    on installment loan, 303
finance company loan, 280, 281, 282
FinanceCenter Web site, 484, 485
financial assets, 6. *See also* assets
financial calculator
    for auto loan amount, 175
    for bond yield, 543–544
    for compound interest, 153–154
    how to use, 52–53
    online, 485
    for retirement income, 608
financial consultant, 461–463
financial emergency
    borrowing to meet, 226
    credit card for, 259
financial futures, 453
financial goals
    defining, **8**–10
    target dates for, 11–14
    types of, 10–11
financial institutions, types of, 138–139
financial office, school, 276
financial planner, 479
    choosing of, 46–48
    types of, 45–46
financial planning
    achieving goals of, 17–20
    defined, **7**
    environment of, 20–26
    investments in, 447–451
    life cycle of, 15–16
    process of, 6–14
    rewards of, 3–6
financial position. *See* balance sheet
financial press, 472–478

financial responsibility laws, 430
financial risk, 506
financial services marketplace, 137–141
financial statement
    income and expenses, 60–65
    in planning, 40
    uses of, 65–69
financial strength of insurance
        company, 354
financing
    college, 275–279
    interim, 279
    of long-term health care, 380–381
    mortgage, 207–214
    of social security, 611
fixed-amount insurance settlement, 344
fixed expenses, 61
fixed-income securities, 506, 546
fixed-period insurance settlement, 344
fixed rate annuity, 635
fixed rate loan, 279–280
fixed rate mortgage, 209
    adjustable rate vs, 212
flexibility of universal life insurance,
        338
flexible-benefit plan, 44
floater, personal property, 411, 413
flood insurance, 431
Fool's School section of Motley Fool,
        484
foreign securities markets, 457
foreign stock, 524–526
form
    property inventory, 407
    tax, 105–107
401(k) plan, 624, 626
franchise car dealership, 176
fraud, online investment, 488–489
freedom of choice in execution of
        will, 660
frequent flyer program, 235
full-service broker, 462
fund, mutual. *See* Mutual fund
funds transfer system, electronic,
        144–146
future needs, 6
future performance of mutual fund,
        589–592
future retirement needs, 605–607
future return on investment,
        511–512
future value, 49, 690, 691
    compound interest as, 153–154
future value of annuity factors, 691
futures, 453

G
gains, capital, 508
gap estate tax, 677
garnishment, 299
GDP. *See* Gross domestic product
GECC, 284
General Electric Credit Corporation,
        284
General Motors Acceptance
        Corporation, 284
general obligation bond, 536–537
general-purpose money fund, 575–576
geographic factors, income related
        to, 28
get-rich-quick scheme, 488–489
gift splitting, 672–673
gift tax, 671–674
GIO. *See* Guaranteed insurability
        option
global mutual fund, 577–578
globalization, market, 524–525
GMAC, 284
goals, financial
    defining of, 8–10
    in retirement planning, 604–605
    target date for, 11–14
    target dates for, 11–14
    types of, 10–11
Gold MasterCard, features of, 240
good 'til canceled order, 467
government
    economy and, 23–24
    in financial planning environment,
        21–22
government bond fund, 575
government influence on pension
        plans, 631
government securities money fund, 576
grace period
    for credit card payment, **236**
    for life insurance premium
        payment, 346
graduate school loan, 276
graduated-payment mortgage, 211
grantor, 667
gross domestic product (GDP), 24
    health insurance costs and, 362–363
gross estate, 654
gross income
    adjustments to, 98
    in example of tax return, 108
group health care insurance, 368–370,
        391
group HMO, 367

group insurance, continuation of, 379
group life insurance, 340–341
**growing-equity -payment mortgage,
        211**
growth, economic, measurement of,
        24–25
growth-and-income fund, 574
growth mutual fund, 573
growth stock, 522, 523
guaranteed insurability option (GIO),
        388–389
guaranteed-minimum annuity, 634
guaranteed purchase option, 347
guaranteed renewability
    of disability income insurance, 388
    of long-term care insurance, **383**

H
head of household, 90
    standard deduction for, 100
health insurance, 360–403
    buying of, 390–397
    cancellation of, 378
    disability income, 385–390
    long-term, 380–385
    medical expense coverage, 373–375
    need for, 360–364
    policy provisions, 375–379
    providers of, 367–372
    types of, 364–367
**health maintenance organization
        (HMO), 364, 365**–367
high-grade corporate bond fund, 575
high-yield bonds, 539
high-yield corporate bond fund, 575
history, credit, 228–229
HMO. *See* Health maintenance
        organization
home, selling of, 97
home equity credit line, 243–245
home equity loan, 296
home ownership, 189–222
    affordability analysis for, 196–199
    buying process, 202–206
    cost of, 190–196
    financing of, 207–215
    motives for, 189–190
    refinancing of, 215–216
    renting vs, 199–202
home-related records, 66
homeowner's insurance, 410–419
    checklist for, 418
    coverage by, 414–415

homeowner's insurance—cont'd
    defined, **196**
    payment limitations of, 415–417
    perils covered, 410–411
    personal property floater, 411, 413
    premiums of, 417, 419
    property covered, 411
homeowner's insurance, buying of,
    432–435
hospital income policy, 375
hospitalization insurance, 373
housing, 186–222. *See also* Home
    ownership
hybrid real estate investment trust, 566

I

identity theft, 260
immediate annuity, 635
income
    defined, **60**
    determinants of, 26–30
    disability, 372
    dual, 41–43
    estimating, 70
    gross, 94–100
    investment objectives and, 451
    life insurance needs and, 322
    mutual fund, 582–583
    portfolio strategy and, 491
    retirement, 605–610
    return from investing as, 507
    spending, 61
    surviving spouse's, 323
    tax-exempt, 96
    taxable, 94–100, 109, 112
income and expense statement, 40,
    60–65
income insurance, disability, 385–390
income shifting, 121
income stock, 523
income tax
    audit of, 114–115
    computer-based return, 117–119
    deductions in, 98–102
    defined, **89**
    economics of, 88–90
    estimated, 113
    example of, 108–113
    filing deadline for, 113–114
    filing status for, 90–92
    forms and schedules for, 105–107
    help in preparing, 115–117
    local, 125

    principles of, 87–93
    rate of, 102–104
    take-home pay and, 92–93
    tax credits, 104–105
    tax planning and, 119–123
    taxable income, 93–98
    trust and, 668
income tax planning, 19
incontestability clause, life insurance,
    318
indemnity, principle of, 408
indemnity (fee-for-service) plan, 365
independent agent, 434
independent used car lot, 177
index
    on adjustable rate mortgage,
        211–212
    AMEX, 475
    consumer price, 25
    cost of living, 28
    Nasdaq, 475
    NYSE, 475
    Standard & Poor's, 473
    Wilshire 5000, 475
index fund, 576
individual checking account, 158–159
individual proactive association, 367
individual retirement arrangement
    (IRA), 122–123, 628–630, 681
    mutual funds in, 583
industrial life insurance, 341
industry data, 476
inflation
    estate affected by, 653
    in estimating retirement income,
        607
inflation, 25
inflation hedge, home as, 189–190
inflation protection, long-term care,
    383
information
    credit card, 257
    life insurance, 350–351
    on securities markets, 470–481
    for will preparation, 658
inheritance tax, 677
Insider Trading and Securities Fraud
    Enforcement Act, 459
insolvency, 56
installment—premium annuity
    contract, 633–634
installment loan, 56, 296–307
    cash payment vs, 304–306
    defined, **279**
    finance charges on, 300

    on income and expense statement,
        61, 63
    monthly payment of, 300–304
    prepayment penalty on, 304
    purchase contract, 297–299
installment payment of federal estate
    tax, 680
installment purchase contract, 297–299
installment sales, 679
institutions, financial, 138–139
insurance
    automobile, 420–430
    buying of, 432–436
    credit life or disability, 297–298
    dental, 374
    deposit, 140–141
    disability income, 385–390
    health care, 360–403. *See also* Health
        care insurance
    homeowner's, 196, 410–420
    liability, 405–406
    life, 314–359. *See also* Life insurance
    mortgage, 214
    property, 404–441
    record of, 67
    renters', 413–414
insurance agent, 354–355
insurance company, annuity from,
    636–638
insurance planning, 17, 316
insurance rating agency, 353
interest
    installment loan, 300–302
    mortgage, 193–196
    on savings, 152–154
    security, 297
    simple, 293
    as tax deduction, 99
    of universal life insurance, 338
interest-free loan, 258
interest-on-interest, 508–509
interest only insurance settlement,
    344
interest-paying checking account,
    142–143
interest rate
    on bank card charges, 235–236
    inflation and, 26
    on unpaid credit card balance,
        259
interest rate cap, 210
interest rate risk, 506
interim financing, 279
intermediate-term bond fund, 575
intermediate-term goals, 12–14

internal limits
of health care insurance, **376**
of homeowner's insurance, 417
Internal Revenue Service (IRS), 115–116
international fund, 577–578
international investing, 525–526
Internet
financial planning sites on, 19
life insurance information on, 350–351
mortgage services on, 208
retirement planning and, 609
stock broker on, 462–463
tracking of mutual fund fees and loads on, 568
using credit card and, 263
introductory clause of will, 658
inventory, 66
property, 406–407
investigation, credit, 246–248
investing, 444–600
in bonds, 530–545. *See also* Bond
in common stock, 513–530. *See also* Common stock
in convertible securities, 546—549
defined, **445**
getting started in, 446–447
management of, 489–496
in mutual funds, 556–598. *See also* Mutual fund
objectives of, 451–452
online, 482–489
in personal financial planning, 447–451
in preferred stocks, 545–546
returns from, 507–511
risks of, 505–507
in securities markets, 454–470. *See also* Securities markets
value of investment, 511–513
vehicles for, 452–453
investment advisor, 479
mutual fund, 562
Investment Advisors Act, 459
investment banker, 454
investment company, 563–564
Investment Company Act, 459
investment plan, 450
investment trust, unit, 565–566
investments, 511–513
borrowing for, 226
defined, **54**
planning for, 17
record of, 66
tracking of, 494–495

investor characteristics, 490–491
Investor's Business Daily, 476
IRA. *See* Individual retirement arrangement
irrevocable life insurance trust, 670
irrevocable living trust, 670
IRS. *See* Internal Revenue Service
issue
common stock, 515–517
corporate debt, 533
issues, convertible, 546–549
itemized deduction, 108
itemized deductions, 98–100

J

job, second, 41
job expenses, deductible, 99
job search, online
mistakes in, 29
Web sites for, 35–36
joint checking account, 158–159
joint life insurance, 340
joint ownership, 665–666
joint tenancy, 665
junk bond, 539

K

Kelly Blue Book, 180
Keogh plan, 627
mutual funds in, 583
Kiplinger Web site, 484
Kiplinger's, credit card information in, 257

L

lease, automobile, **181**
lease agreement, 199
leasing of automobile, 173–174, 183–185
ledger, checkbook, 159
legislation
on bankruptcy, 264–265
consumer credit, 261, 262
on electronic funds transfer system, 148–149
on loans, 288
tax, 88
lending policies for consumer loans, 282–283

letter of last instructions, 664
level-premium term life insurance, 330
liabilities, 55
liability
automobile insurance, 421
bonds as, 452
liability exposure, 408
liability insurance, 405–406
buying of, 432–435
umbrella, 432
liability losses, 421
liability planning, 17
lien, 291
life annuity, 634–635
life change, 44–45
life cycle
of financial plans, 15–16
goal changes in, 12
life expectancy, 638
life income insurance settlement, 344
life insurance
basic concepts of, 315–319
benefits of, 319–320
buying of, 348–355
credit, 297–298, 341
deferred-premium, 342
in estate planning, 680
features of, 342–347
group, 340–341
industrial, 341
mortgage, 341
multiple earnings approach to, 321–324
on multiple lives, 340
need for, 320–321
needs approach to, 324–328
special-purpose, 341–342
term, 329–332
universal, 336–338
variable, 339–340
whole, 332–336
life insurance company
annuity from, 636–638
loan for, 283, 284–285
lifetime gift, 673–674
limit
automobile policy, 421, 422, 423
credit, 233
home owner's policy, 415, 416–417
internal, 376, 416–417
limit order, 467
limited-payment whole life policy, 334–335

702 Index

line of credit, 234
    revolving, 241–242
LIONS, 538
liquid assets, 54, 136
liquidity, 323
    estate affected by, 653
liquidity ratio, 67
liquidity risk, 507
listed security, 455
listed stock quotes, 476–478
living benefits, 348
living standard, 4
living trust, 668–670
    revocable, 669–670
living will, 664, 665
load, mutual fund, 568–570
load fund, 567
    buying and selling of, 570–572
loan, 272–312
    on income and expense statement, 61, 63
    installment, 56, 279, 296–307
    interest-free, 258
    management of, 286–290
    mortgage, 193–196, 207–214
    policy, 344–345
    prequalification for, 205
    shopping for, 286–288
    single-payment, 279, 289–296
    sources of, 280–286
    tracking debt and, 289–290
    types of, 274–280
    use of, 274
loan application, 291–292
loan disclosure statement, 293, 294
loan guarantee, VA, 214
loan rollover, 293
local taxes, 125–126
location, income related to, 28
long-term care, 380
long-term goals, 11
long-term health care insurance, 380–385
long-term liability, 55
loss, liability, 421
loss control, 317
loss prevention, 317
lot
    odd, 464
    round, 464
low-load fund, 567, 588–589
lump-sum annuity cost, 636–637
lump-sum payment
    health insurance, 372
    life insurance, 344

M

major medical plan, 374, 376–377
Maloney Act, 459
managed care plan, 354, 365–367
management
    cash, 136–137
    of credit card account, 254–256
    of loan, 286–290
    trust for, 668
management company, mutual fund, 562–563
management fee, 568–570
    annuity, 636
margin purchase, 468–469
marital deduction, 673
marital status, income related to, 26
market
    bond, 534–538. See also bonds
    housing, 202–205
market data, 472–474
market globalization, 524–525
market order, 467
market risk, 506
market value, fair, 54
marketability risk, 507
marketplace, financial services, 137–141
marriage, life insurance and, 321
married taxpayer, 90
    standard deduction for, 100
MasterCard, features of, 240
maturity, loan, 287
medical expense coverage, 373–375
medical expenses, deductible, 99
medical payment coverage, 422
Medicare, 371
Medtronic, Inc., 480–481
    Value Line report for, 519, 527
mental capacity, 660
mental illness, insurance covering, 378–379
merchandise, returning of, with credit card, 254, 258
Microsoft Money, 19
mid-cap stock, 524
MidCap index, 473
minimum monthly payment, 254
MMDA. See Money market deposit account
MMMF. See Money market mutual fund
mobile-home insurance, 431
model, organizational planning, 31
monetary policy, 23
money, 9

    psychology of, 9–10
    relationships and, 10
    role of, 9
    wise spending of, 4–6
Money, credit card information in, 257
money market deposit account (MMDA), 143
money market mutual fund (MMMF), 143, 575–576
Money Online, 19
monthly bank statement, 161–163
monthly mortgage payment, 194
Monthly Mutual Fund Review, 570
monthly social security benefits, 613–618
Moody's bond ratings, 539
Moody's Investor's Services, 353
Morningstar, 486
Morningstar Principia Pro, 587
mortgage
    adjustable rate, 210–214
    biweekly, 213–214
    chattel, 291
    conventional, 214
    definition of, 56
    fixed-rate, 209
    graduated-payment, 212
    growing-equity, 212
    guaranteed, 214
    insured, 214
    prequalification for, 205
    refinancing of, 215–216
    shared appreciation, 212
    sources of, 207–208
    as tax deduction, 99
mortgage-backed bond fund, 575
mortgage banker, 207
mortgage bond, 532
mortgage broker, 207–208
mortgage insurance, FHA, 214
mortgage life insurance, 341
mortgage loan, 207–214
mortgage payment, 193–196
mortgage points, 191–192
mortgage real estate investment trust, 566
Motley Fool, 484
motorist, insured, 421–422
MSN Money Central, 20, 486
multiple earning approach, 321
multiple indemnity clause, 347
Multiple Listing Service, 203
multiple lives, insurance on, 340
multiple taxation, 678–679
municipal bond, 536

municipal bond fund, 575
mutual fund, 556–598
    annuity vs, 639
    basic structure of, 557–558
    buying and selling of, 570–572
    closed-end, 563–564
    concept of, 558–559
    cost of, 567–568
    exchange-traded, 564–565
    international, 525
    investing in, 584–592
    as investment, 453
    management of, 562–563
    money market, 143
    open-end, 563
    performance of, 589–592
    quotes of, 569
    real estate investment trust, 566
    reasons to invest in, 559–562
    services offered by, 579–584
    types of, 573–579
    unit investment trust, 565–566
mutual fund sales, 149

N

named peril policy, 410–411
Nasdaq index, 456–458, **475**
National Association of Securities
    Dealers (NASD), **459**
National Market System, 457
NAV. *See* Net asset value
necessities of life, 5
needs
    current, 5
    future, 6
    health insurance, 390–391
    life insurance, 349–350
needs approach, 321–322
negative amortization, 211
**negotiable order of withdrawal
    (NOW) account, 143**
negotiation of automobile price,
    179–180
neighborhood emergency center, 362
nest egg
    building of, 151
    retirement, 604
net asset value (NAV), 563
net profit margin, 520
net worth, 56, 57
new vs used car, 176–177
New York Stock Exchange, 455
New York Stock Exchange (NYSE), 477

newspaper, financial information in,
    472–478
no-fault insurance, 424–**426**
no-load fund, 567, 588–589
nominal rate of interest, 152
noncancelable bond issue, 534
noncancelable disability income
    insurance, 388
noncontributory pension plan, 620
noncumulative preferred stock, 546
nondeductible IRA, 628–629
nondepository financial institution, 139
nonforfeiture option, 346
nonforfeiture right, 333
nonqualified deferred-compensation
    plan, 679
nonsmoker insurance rate, 330, 339
note, collateral, 291
note, installment loan, **297**
NOW. *See* Negotiable order of
    withdrawal
nursing home care, 380–385
NYSE index, 475
NYSE. *See* New York Stock Exchange

O

objective, portfolio, 491–492
obligation, serial, 536
obligation bond, general, 536–537
occupation, disability definition
    and, 387
Occupational Outlook Handbook, 29
odd lot, 464
of mutual fund, 560
offering, common stock, 515, 517
Official Used Car Guide, 180
old-age benefits, 613
online banking, 146–148
online broker, 462–463, 466
online credit card application, 247
online financial advice, 46
online investing, 482–489
    growth of, 482
    investor education about,
        484–488
    services of, 482–483
    wise use of, 488–489
online job search, 29
online mortgage services, 208
online portfolio tracking, 446
open account credit, 232–233
    opening of, 246–252
open account credit obligations, 55

open-end investment company, 563
    buying shares of, 570
open-end lease, 181
opening checking account, 158–161
operating cost of car, 175–176
optional renewability, 383
options
    financial, 453
    settlement, for life insurance, 344
order
    good 'til canceled, 467
    limit, 467
    market, 467
    stop-loss, 467–468
organization
    of financial records, 65–66
    health maintenance, 365–367
    preferred provider, 362, 367, 369
organizational planning model, 31
organized securities exchanges, 455
OTC. *See* Over-the-counter market
other-insurance clause, 409
outlay, annual insurance, 337
over-the-counter (OTC) market, 455,
    456–458
over-the-counter stocks, quotation
    system for, 478
over-the-counter stocks, Standard &
    Poor's indexes of, 473
overall interest rate cap, 210
overdraft, 160
overdraft protection, 160
overfreight protection line, 242
overspending, 259
owners, residual, 514
ownership
    joint, 665–666
    stock, 528–529

P

paid-up insurance, 346
PAP. *See* Personal automobile policy
participating policy, 348
participation clause, 376
participation requirements for pension
    plan, 619
passive income, 94
pay-as-you-go basis, 92
payment
    balloon, 299
    from estate, 658
    health insurance, 375–377
    installment loan, 299–303

payment—cont'd
    medical, 422
    minimum monthly, 254
    mortgage, 193–196, 198
    online, 146–148
    pre-authorized, 145
    stopping of, 160–161
penalty, prepayment, 291, 304
pension plan
    employer-sponsored, 619–627
    self-directed, 619–627
performance, mutual fund, 589–592
peril, 406–407
periodic interest rate cap, 210
Perkins loan, 275
permanent financing, mortgage, 207
personal automobile policy (PAP), 420
personal bankruptcy, 263–265
personal credit line, unsecured,
    242–243
personal financial planning, 7
    achieving goals of, 17–20
    defined, **7**
    environment of, 20–26
    investments in, 447–451
    life cycle of, 15–16
    process of, 6–14
    retirement planning in, 602
    rewards of, 3–6
personal financial planning, cash
    management in, 136–137
personal income, determinants of,
    26–30
personal liability umbrella policy, 432
personal loan, 274
personal property, 55
personal property floater, 411, 413
personal property insurance, 406–441.
    See also Property insurance
personal property inventory form, 407
personality, money, 9–10
physician, primary care, 366
physicians expense insurance, 374
pickup estate tax, 677–678
pitfalls to retirement planning, 602–604
PITI, 196
plan
    automobile insurance, 428
    dividend reinvestment, 529
    investment, 450
    mutual fund automatic investment,
      579–582
planner, financial, 479
    choosing of, 46–48
    types of, 45–46

planning. *See also* financial planning
    career, 29–30
    estate, 19, 648–687. *See also* Estate
      planning
    insurance, 316
    investment, 484
    retirement, 19, 600–645. *See also*
      retirement planning
planning model, organizational, 31
Platinum MasterCard, features of, 240
Platinum VISA, features of, 241
point-of-service plan, 367
points, mortgage, 191–192
policy
    disability income, 385–390
    life insurance, 328–349
    monetary, 23
    named peril, 410–412
    renters' insurance, 413–414
policy loan, 344–345
pooled diversification, 559
portfolio
    bonds in, 531
    building of, 490–492
    defined, **489**–490
    management of, 492–494
    of money market mutual fund, 143
    of mutual fund, 560
    online tracking of, 486
    tracking of, 446
portfolio income, 94
pour-over will, 670
power, purchasing, 25
power of attorney, 664
    durable, for health care, **665**
pre-admission certification, 379
pre-authorized deposits and payments,
    145
preexisting condition clause, 378
preferred provider organization, 362,
    367, 369
preferred stocks, 452, 478, 545–546
pregnancy, health insurance and, 378
Premier VISA, features of, 241
premium
    automobile insurance, 426–428
    conversion, 549
    homeowner's insurance, 417, 419
    insurance, 350
    life insurance, 345–346
    for long-term care insurance, 384
    term life insurance, 330
    whole life insurance, 334–335
premium bond, 542
prepaid card, 240–241

preparation services, tax, 115–117
prepayment penalty, 291, 304
prequalification for home loan, **205**
present value, 51
present value factors, 693
preservation of, 492
press, financial, 472–478
prestige card, 237
presumptive disability, 387
prevention, loss, 317
price
    ask, 456
    bid, 456
    bond, 542, 543
    inflation and, 25
price/earnings ratio, 520–521
price index, consumer, 25
primary care physician, 366
primary market, 454
prime rate, 236
principle of indemnity, 408
private annuity, 680
private health insurance, 370
private sale, of car, 177
privilege, conversion, 547, 583
probate estate, 653–654
probate process, 664
probationary period for disability
    income insurance, 388
problem, credit, 259–261
profession, salary for, 29
professional financial planner, 45, 479
    choosing of, 46–48
    types of, 45–46
professional management of mutual
    fund, **559**–560
professional tax preparer, 116–117
profit-sharing plan, 623
progressive tax structure, 89
property
    community, 666
    disposition of, in will, 658
    real estate investment trusts and, 566
    trust for conservation of, 668
property damage liability losses, 421
property insurance, 405–441
    automobile, 420–430
    basic principles of, 404–409
    buying of, 432–434
    homeowner's, 410–419
    renters', 413
    settling claims, 434–436
    supplemental, 431
    umbrella policy, 432–433
property inventory, 406–407

property real estate investment trust, 566
property taxes, 125, 196
prospectus, 454
protection
    from creditor, 319–320
    overdraft, 160
proxy, 517
psychology, of money, 9–10
public adjustor, 436
public offering, 515, 517
publicly traded stock issues, 515
pump-and-dump scheme, 488–489
purchase, margin, 468–469
purchase contract, installment, 297–299
purchase of car, 178–179
purchase option, on leased car, **182**
purchasing power, 25
purchasing power risk, 506

Q

qualified pension plan, 622–623
quality of life, 5
Quicken, 19
Quicken Web site, 484, 486
Quicken.com, 20
quote
    bond, 540–541
    stock, 476–478

R

rate
    of economic growth, 24
    interest, inflation and, 26
    of return, 17–18
    tax, 90, 102–104, 671
    unemployment, 24
rating
    bond, 538–541
    preferred stock, 546
rating agency, insurance, 353
rating territory, 427
ratio
    affordability, 195–196
    balance sheet, 67–68
    conversion, 547
    debt safety, 230
    price/earnings, 520–521
ratio analysis, 67–69
real estate. *See also* Home ownership
    in estate planning, 680
    as investment, 453

real estate investment trust (REIT), 566
real estate market, 202–205
real estate mortgages, 56
real estate sales contract, 205
Real Estate Settlement Procedures Act, 206
real property, 55
rebate credit card, 235
rebate program, automobile, 235
recession, 24
reconciliation, account, 161–163
record-keeping
    organizing, 65–66
    ratio analysis with, 67–69
    types of, 66–67
record keeping, credit card and, 258
recovery, 24
recreational vehicle insurance, 431
redemption fee, 568
refinancing mortgage, 215–216
refund, tax, 112
refund annuity, 634
regional exchanges, 456
regulation
    of electronic funds transfer system, 148–149
    in financial planning environment, 22
    of securities markets, 457–459
rehabilitation, insurance covering, 379
rehabilitation expenses, 372
reinvestment, dividend, 529
reinvestment plan, automatic, 581–582
REIT. *See* Real estate investment trust
relationship, money and, 10
relative, loans from, 285
renewability
    of disability income insurance, 388
    of long-term care insurance, 383
    of term life insurance, 331
renewable term life insurance, 330
rental contract, 199–200
rental unit, 188
renters' insurance, 413–414
repayment guidelines for credit, 230
repayment of student loan, 276
replacement cost, 408, 415–416
report
    annual stockholders', 471–472
    brokerage, 478
    credit bureau, 249
    Standard & Poor's stock, 480–481
    value line, 519
repossession, 299
research, investment, 484

residual benefit option, 387
residual owner, 514
residual value of leased car, 181
resources
    life insurance needs and, 323–324, 327–328
    online investor, 482–483
    online mortgage, 208
retail charge card, 233, 237
retiree health benefits, 393–394
retirement account
    individual, 122–123
    record of, 66
retirement age, 604–605, 621
retirement as investment objective, 451–452
retirement planning, 19, 601–647
    annuities in, 632–640
    computer-based, 609
    employer sponsored plans, 619–627
    goals of, 604–605
    income needs and, 605–609
    income sources and, 609–610
    mutual funds in, 583
    in personal financial planning, 602
    pitfalls of, 602–604
    self-directed programs, 627–631
    social security in, 610–618
return
    from annuity, 638
    tax, 87–123. *See also* Income tax
return on equity (ROE), 520
return on investment
    desired rate of, 513
    expected rate of, 511–512
    future, 511–512
    of mutual fund, 561–562
    rate of, 17–18
    risk-free rate of, 510
    risk-return trade-off and, 509–511
returning merchandise with credit card, 254, 258
revenue bond, 536
revocable living trust, 669–670
revocation of will, 662
revolving line of credit, 241–242
rider, living benefit, 348
right, nonforfeiture, 333
right of election, 662
right of subrogation, 408–409
right of survivorship, 665
rights, vested, 620–621
risk
    concept of, 316–318
    of investing, 506–507

risk assumption
health insurance and, 392
life insurance and, 317
risk avoidance, 316–317
health insurance and, 391–392
life insurance and, **316**–317
risk-free rate of return, 510
risk-return trade-off, 509–511
ROE. *See* Return on equity
rollover, loan, 293
Roth IRA, 628, 629
mutual funds in, 583
round lot, 464
rule of 72, 50
rule of 78s, 304

S

S&L. *See* Savings and loan association
safe-deposit box, 149
items to keep in, 663
safety of money, 139–140
safety ratio, debt, 230
salary, by profession, 29
salary reduction plan, 624, 626
sale, short, 469–470
sales, mutual fund, 149
sales contract
for car, **180–181**
real estate, 205
sales finance company, 284
sales tax, 125
local, 125–126
savings
doubling of, 50
future value of, 49–50
interest on, 152–154
life insurance as, 320
planning for, 17
reducing expenses and, 73
for retirement, 607
starting program of, 150–152
savings account, 142
savings and loan association, 281, 283
mortgage from, 207
savings and loan association (S&L), 138
savings bank, 139
savings ratio, 68
scam, online investment, 488–489
schedule, budget control, 75–76
school financial office, 276
screening, investment, 484, 486
SEC. *See* Securities and Exchange
Commission

second income, managing of, 41–43
second-injury funds, 372
second surgical opinion, 379
secondary market, 455
sector fund, 576–577
secured credit card, 239
securities, convertible, 453, 540,
546–547
Securities Act of 1933, 458–459
**Securities and Exchange Commission
(SEC),** 455, **459**
Securities Exchange Act, 459
Securities Investor Protection Act, 459
**Securities Investor Protection
Corporation, 464**
securities markets
bear or bull, 459–461
defined, **454**
foreign, 458
information about, 470–481
organized exchanges, 455–456
over-the-counter, 456–458
primary, 454
regulation of, 458–459
secondary, 455
transactions in, 461–470
security, credit card and, 258
security agreement, 297
self-directed retirement plan, 627–631
selling
of home, 97
of mutual fund, 570–572
senior citizens, population of, 612
SEP-IRA, 628
serial obligation, 536
series EE bond, 154
in estate planning, 680
services
advisory, 479
brokerage, 463
consumer loan, 282–283
long-term care, 383
mutual fund, 579–584
online investor, 482–483
tax preparation, 115–117
settlement of claim
life insurance, 344
property insurance, 434–436
share draft account, 139
share of common stock, issuers of,
515–517
shared-appreciation mortgage, 212
shareholder
as residual owner, 515
voting rights of, 517

shareholder transaction cost, 570
shelter, tax, 121–122
home as, 189
shock, financial, 15
shopping, for loan, 286–287
short sale, 469–470
short-term goals, 12–14
short-term liability, 55
shortfall in retirement income, 607–608
sickness insurance policy, 375
simple interest, 152
installment loan, 300–302
simple interest method, 293
Simplified Employee Pension Plan, 628
simultaneous death clause of will, 660
single-family home, 187
single-payment loan, 279, 289–296
single-premium annuity contract, 632
single-premium whole life policy, 335
single taxpayer, 90
standard deduction for, 100
sinking fund, 532
small cap stock, 522, 524
small loan company, 281
SmallCap index, 473
social security, 610–618
basic concepts of, 611–612
beneficiaries of, 612
disability benefits of, 386
eligibility for, 612–613
health insurance from, 391
retirement benefits of, 613–618
statement of, 614–615
Social Security Administration, 616
**social security survivor's benefits,
325**–327, 613
social security tax, 93, 124
socially responsible fund, 577
software, tax, 117
solvency of social security, 611–612
solvency ratio, 67
special-purpose life insurance, 341–342
speculating, 445–**446**
speculative stock, 523
spending, wise, 4–6
sponge tax, 677
Stafford student loan, 275
application for, 277
Standard & Poor's bond ratings, 539
Standard & Poor's Corporation, 353
**Standard & Poor's (S&P) indexes,
473**
mutual fund, 576
Standard & Poor's stock report,
480–481

standard deduction, 100, 108
standard of living, 4
state taxes, 125
    death, 676–679
stated rate of interest, 152
statement
    closing, 206
    credit, 233
    credit card, 254, 255
    of financial position, 53–59
    loan disclosure, 293, 294
    monthly bank, 161–163
    social security, 614–615
stock. *See also* Securities markets
    bonds vs, 531
    common, 513–530. *See also*
        Common stock
    in estate planning, 680
    foreign, 524–526
    mutual fund vs, 586
    preferred, 478, 545–546
stock broker, 461–463
stock dividend, 518
stock exchange, 455–456
stock market crash
    of 1987, 460, 515
    of 1997, 461, 515
stock quotes, 476–478
stock report, Standard & Poor's,
    480–481
stockholders' annual report, 471–472
stop-loss order, 467–468
stop payment, 160
straight bankruptcy, 264
straight-term policy, 329
strategy
    portfolio, 490–491
    tax, 119–123
STRIP-Ts, 538
student loan, 275–279
subrogation, right of, 408–409
suicide clause, 347
superstore, automobile, 176
supplemental pension plan, 623–625
supplemental property insurance, 431
supplementary medical insurance,
    371
surgical expense insurance, 373–374
surplus, cash, 63
surrender fee, 639
survivor's benefits, social security,
    325–327, 613
survivorship benefit, annuity, **632**
survivorship life insurance, 340
systematic withdrawal plan, 582–583

T

T-bill. *See* U.S. Treasury bill
table, mutual fund fee, 571
take-home pay, 92
tangible assets, 6
target date for financial goals, 11–14
tax, 86–131
    annuity and, 637–638
    estate, 124
    estimated, 113
    excise, 124
    federal income, 86–123. *See also*
        Income tax
    gift, 124, 671–674
    local, 125–126
    property, 196
    sales, 125
    social security, 124
    on social security benefits, 618
    state, 125
    state death, 676–679
tax audit, 114–115
tax avoidance, 119
tax clause of will, 660
tax credit, 104–105
tax credit, unified, 675
tax-deferred income, 122–123
tax evasion, 119
tax-exempt bond, 537
tax-exempt income, 96
tax-exempt money fund, 576
tax exemption, 101
tax form, 105–107
tax-free income, 122
tax planning, 19, 119–123
    estate taxes and, 674–680
    records for, 66
tax preparation services, 115–117
tax rate, 102–104
    average, 90
    estate, 679
    federal unified transfer, 671
tax record, 66
    bank statement as, 163
Tax Reform Act, 88
tax refund, 112
tax return, 87–123. *See also* Income tax
    computer-based, 117–119
tax shelter, 121–122
    annuity as, 637–638
    home as, 189
    investment as, 452
tax write-off, 121–122
taxable equivalent yield, 537

taxable income, 94–100, 109, 112
    annuity as, 637–638
    defined, **94**
taxable munites, 537
taxation
    in financial planning environment,
        21–22
    multiple, 678–679
Taxpayer Relief Act, 88
tech stock, 522, **523**
technology, 19–20
temporary life annuity, 635
tenancy by the entirety, 665
tenancy in common, 666
term life insurance, 329
terms, bank credit card, 257
territory, rating, 427
testamentary trust, 670
testator, 657
theft, identity, 260
30–day charge account, 237
thrift and savings plan, 623–624
thrift institution, mortgage from, **207**
TIGRS, 538
time deposit, 142
time payment vs cash, 304–306
time value of money, 48–49
time value of money, 49
timing, of investment, 528
TIPS. *See* Treasury inflation-indexed
    bond
title check, 206
tools, investment, 484
tracking
    investments, 495
    of mutual fund fees and loads, 568
    portfolio, online, 486
tracking of consumer debt, 289–290
trade, securities, 461–470
trade-in of old car, 178
trader, day, 486–488
traditional IRA, 628
transaction cost, shareholder, 570
transactions in securities markets,
    461–470
    brokers of, 461–466
    executing trades, 466
    margin trades, 468–469
    orders for, 467–468
    short selling, 469–470
transfer agent, mutual fund, 562
transfer subject to gift tax, 672
transfer tax rate, federal unified, 671
travel and entertainment card,
    237–238, 240

traveler's check, 163, 165
Treasury bond, 534
    quotes of, 540–541
**Treasury inflation-indexed bond
    (TIPS), 534,** 535
Treasury STRIPS, 538
trust, 667–670
    real estate investment, 566
    record of, 67
    unit investment, 565–566
trust department, bank, 479
trust services, 149
trustee, 667
Truth in Lending, 262
12b-1 fee, 567–568
two-step ARM, 211

U

umbrella liability policy, 432
underwriting, life insurance, **318**–319
unemployment rate, 24
unified rate schedule, 671
unified tax credit, 675
unified transfer tax rate, 671
**uninsured motorists coverage,
    423**
unit investment trust, 565–566
universal life insurance, 336–338
unlisted security, 456
unpaid credit card balance, 259
**unsecured personal credit line,
    242**–243
U.S. Department of Housing and
    Urban Development, 206
U.S. Treasury bill (T-bill), 154
U.S. Veterans Administration loan
    guarantee, 214
USA Today, 476
used car, price guides for, 180
usury law, 235
utility, 9

V

VA loan guarantee, 214
value
    actual cash, 408
    of common stock, 521–522
    conversion, 547
    future, 49
Value Line report, 519, 527
value mutual fund, 573–574

value pricing, of car, 178
variable annuity, 635–636, 639
variable expenses, 61
variable life insurance, 339
variable rate loan, 279–280
vehicle of transfer, improper, 653
vested rights, 620–621
Veterans Administration loan
    guarantee, 214
VISA, 240–241
voluntary profit-sharing plan, 623
voting rights of shareholders, 517

W

Wage Earner Plan, 264
waiting period
    for disability income insurance, 388
    for long-term care insurance, **383**
waiver of coinsurance, 379
Wall Street Journal, The
    mutual fund quotes in, 568–569
    stock quotes in, 476
war exclusion, 347–348
warranty, on car, 178
wealth
    accumulated, rate of return on,
        17–18
    accumulating of, 6
    defined, 6
Web site
    E*Trade, 482–483
    financial advice, 46
    financial planning, 19, 20, 46
    portfolio tracking, 446
    retirement planning, 609
    types of, 19–20
Weiss Ratings, 353
whole life insurance, 332–336
widowed taxpayer, 90
will, 656–667
    administration of estate and, 664
    changing of, 661–662
    common features of, 658–660
    defined, **656**
    joint ownership and, 665–666
    letter of last instructions and, 664
    living, 665
    pour-over, 670
    preparation of, 657–658
    record of, 67
    revocation of, 662
    safeguarding of, 662–663
    valid, 660–661

Wilshire 5000 index, 475
withdrawal, systematic mutual fund,
    582–583
witness clause of will, 660
women
    credit problems of, 231
    Equal Credit Opportunity Act
        and, 262
    investing by, 510
    life expectancy of, 638
workers' compensation, 391
**workers' compensation insurance,
    371**–372
worth, net, 56, 57
wrap, 479
wrap account, 479
write-off, tax, 121–122

Y, Z

Yahoo! Finance, 20
yield
    approximate, 512–513
    bond, 542–545
    dividend, 518
    taxable equivalent, 537
yield to maturity, 542
zero coupon bond, 537

Credits

P. 29	Financial Road Sign from "Avoid a Comedy of E-errors," by Joellen Perry, *U.S. News & World Report,* November 6, 2000. Copyright © 2000 *U.S. News & World Report.* Used with permission.
Exhibit 2.4	From "How Are You Doing?" by Walter Updegrave, *Money,* July 1999, p. 66. © 2000 Time Inc. All rights reserved.
Exhibit 5.5	From "Metropolitan Prices, Fourth Quarter 2000," National Association of REALTORS® www.nar.onerealtorplace.com/research.nsf.
P. 250	From "How to Read and Understand Your Credit Report," by Pat Curry, *Bankrate.com,* November 27, 2000. A publication of Bankrate, Inc., N. Palm Beach, Florida. Copyright © 2000.
Exhibit 6.10	From *Money,* December 2000, p. 216. © 2000 Time, Inc. All rights reserved.
Exhibit 10.3	From *Kiplinger's Smart Ways to Save on Insurance,* Winter 1997. Copyright © 1997.
Exhibit 11.6	From *The Wall Street Journal,* November 10, 2000. Copyright © 2000 Dow Jones Co., Inc. Reprinted by permission via Copyright Clearance Center.
Exhibit 11.7	Reprinted by permission of Standard & Poor's, a division of the McGraw-Hill Companies, Inc.
Exhibit 12.5	© 2000 Value Line Publishing, Inc. All rights reserved.
Exhibit 12.10	From *The Wall Street Journal,* December 8, 2000. Copyright © 2000 Dow Jones Co., Inc. Reprinted by permission via Copyright Clearance Center.
Exhibit 13.8	From *Morningstar Principia Pro,* September 30, 2000. © 2000 Morningstar. Chicago-based Morningstar, Inc. is a leading provider of investment information, research and analysis. For more information about Morningstar, visit www.morningstar.com or call 800-735-0700.
Exhibit 15.3	Copyright © 1995 by The American College, Bryn Mawr, PA. Adapted from Confidential Personal and Financial Data form. Advanced Estate Planning Course. All rights reserved.
Worksheet 15.1	From *The Tools of and Techniques of Estate Planning,* 11th ed., by Stephen R. Leimberg, Herbert Levy, Stephen N. Kandell, Morey S. Rosenbloom, and Ralph Gano Miller. (Cincinnati: National Underwriter Company, 1998). Reprinted with permission of the publisher.